ALSO BY MELVIN I. UROFSKY

Letters of Louis D. Brandeis (with David W. Levy)

American Zionism from Herzl to the Holocaust

We Are One! American Jewry and Israel

A Voice That Spoke for Justice: The Life and Times of Stephen S. Wise

A March of Liberty: A Constitutional History of the United States

A Conflict of Rights: The Supreme Court and Affirmative Action

Letting Go: Death, Dying, and the Law

Division and Discord: The Supreme Court Under Stone and Vinson, 1941–1953

Lethal Judgments: Assisted Suicide and American Law

Money and Free Speech: Campaign Finance Reform and the Courts

LOUIS D. BRANDEIS

Louis D. Brandeis on the Mauretania, *1919*

LOUIS D. BRANDEIS

A Life

Melvin I. Urofsky

PANTHEON BOOKS

NEW YORK

Copyright © 2009 by Melvin I. Urofsky

All rights reserved. Published in the United States by Pantheon Books,
a division of Random House, Inc., New York, and in Canada
by Random House of Canada Limited, Toronto.

Pantheon Books and colophon are registered trademarks of Random House, Inc.

Library of Congress Cataloging-in-Publication Data
Urofsky, Melvin I.
Louis D. Brandeis : a life / Melvin I. Urofsky.
p. cm.
Includes bibliographical references and index.
ISBN 978-0-375-42366-6
1. Brandeis, Louis Dembitz, 1856–1941.   2. Judges—United States—Biography.
3. Lawyers—United States—Biography.   4. Practice of law—United States—History.   I. Title.
KF8745.B67U749 2009
347.73'2634—dc22
{B}   2009003992

www.pantheonbooks.com

Book design by Iris Weinstein

Printed in the United States of America

First Edition

2 4 6 8 9 7 5 3 1

FOR SUSAN—
AN EVER-FIXED MARK,
AN EVER-CHANGING DELIGHT

CONTENTS

PREFACE

THE IDEALISTIC PRAGMATIST

In 1920 the Harvard Law School professor Manley Hudson journeyed to Washington, and while there paid a visit on Justice Louis D. Brandeis and his law clerk, Dean Acheson. As he usually did, Brandeis quizzed his guest about recent events at the law school and also about Hudson's role as a legal adviser to the League of Nations. While discussing his work, Hudson alluded to international law as conditional, with principles varying depending upon the situation and the nations involved. He had barely finished when, to his great surprise and alarm, Brandeis stood up and began, as Acheson described it, to thunder like an Old Testament prophet. Principles are fixed and immutable, Brandeis declared, because without reliance on established values democratic society and individual freedom are impossible. He quoted Goethe and Euripides, and on it went, a frightening display of elemental force.

The incident is indicative of a key aspect of Louis Brandeis's nature—his idealism. He once told his niece that "ideals are everything." His attraction to the law derived in part from his belief that law provided the ideal means by which free men could impose order on their behavior and at the same time allow the greatest liberty for each person. He said many times that he had joined the Zionist movement because of its idealistic nature. For Brandeis, above all things the individual mattered, and the best society allowed each person, through hard work, to achieve all that his or her talents deserved. He did not believe in the mass salvation of "isms"; the world would be made better one person at a time. The good life rested on the dignity and independence of the individual, who could then do the hard work required to sustain freedom in a democratic society.

Idealism often conjures up the image of naïveté, of a romantic and impractical quixotism; none of these words apply to Brandeis. No one could have accomplished what he did in the legal profession, as a reformer, as a Zionist leader, and as a Supreme Court justice without being tough and realistic. He did not tilt at windmills nor see the world through rose-colored glasses. Rather, as he once told his daughter, he believed life to be hard.

What set Louis Brandeis apart, what makes his life so interesting both then and now, is how he wedded this idealism to pragmatism. He never abandoned his first principles, and some of his views, especially about economics, reflected idealism more than the reality of a changing world. Indeed, he found much in modern life ugly, impersonal, and dangerous to the goals of a democratic society. In this, however, he may have been far more prescient than some of his critics.

Brandeis lived and worked in the real world, and when he confronted a problem—either as a lawyer or as a citizen—he acted, and as he once explained, he worked on the question for as long as he could, trying to come up with an effective solution. In his reforms, it is always apparent how the idealist informed the pragmatist. He believed in an economic system of free enterprise not because one could grow rich (which he did) but because the market provided a moral proving ground. His economic reforms, as well as the advice he gave to his law clients, aimed at making business run not just more smoothly but more honestly. In one of his first public endeavors he helped the liquor lobby beat back prohibition in Massachusetts. People were going to drink, he conceded, therefore make the laws regulating liquor fair to all, so that they could be effective and keep the liquor dealers out of politics. When one of his clients complained about labor unrest at his factory, Brandeis discovered that the workers had a legitimate complaint, and he helped the manufacturer devise a system that provided his men with steady employment.

Even if some of his proposals failed to work in the long run, they remain noteworthy for his refusal to give up the belief that men of goodwill, once they knew all of the facts in a case, would be able to reach a just solution fair to all parties. To those who labored in the vineyard of democratic righteousness, as it were, Brandeis offered strong support; to those who would use their power to prey upon the weak, who would distort the values he held dear, he proved an implacable foe. While some critics have lampooned his fear of bigness and his desire to maintain a small-unit economy as out of touch with modern reality, recent abuses in the banking system as well as the size of multibillion-dollar mergers remind us that Brandeis did not fear bigness because of size, but because of the effects it could have upon society, the economy, and the individual. The scandals we have seen in the highest levels of government and the contempt some of our elected leaders have shown for the Constitution remind us of the need for moral leadership and idealistic visions.

Born a little more than four years before Fort Sumter, Louis Dembitz Brandeis died just a few weeks before Pearl Harbor. In his eighty-five years he saw the Union dissolve and rejoin, railroads span and unite the nation, entrepreneurs build great factories and then combine into gigantic companies, a war for imperialism, and a war to make the world safe for democracy. He chose to become a lawyer, helped to change the practices and business of the profession, and then demonstrated how law could be used as an instrument of reform. A nonpracticing Jew who did not believe in religion, he became head of the American Zionist movement in his sixth decade and transformed it from a moribund sideshow into a powerful component of American Jewish life. He saw the work of rebuilding Palestine into a modern Jewish homeland in its most idealistic terms, and set about trying to achieve that goal by paying attention to the most basic and mundane details. He argued that judges needed to take the facts of modern life into account in their decisions and taught them how to do so. In his more than two decades on the Supreme Court he established important bases of our modern jurisprudence, including a right to privacy and the rationale for why free speech is important in a democratic society. Even when he saw how the law could be twisted to achieve the goals of narrow-minded and selfish men, he never lost faith in the ideal of rule by law.

The biographer of such a man should have no trouble explaining his importance to the times in which he lived. Historians of the legal profession can easily identify his contribution to the development of the modern law office, the practice of counsel to the situation, and the establishment of pro bono work as an important element of a lawyer's obligation to the community. Social and political scientists see Brandeis as a key figure in the progressive movement, a man respected by such diverse reformers as Theodore Roosevelt and Jane Addams, Robert La Follette and Florence Kelley. Students of American Jewish history—even while wrestling with the question of why a man who ignored religion in general should suddenly become interested in Zionism—have no doubts about the impact his ideas made on defining the relation of American Jewry to world Zionism and to the Jewish state. For those who examine the Supreme Court, Brandeis remains one of the great justices in the nation's history, the author of important opinions that continue to shape American jurisprudence.

The problem for the biographer is not that Brandeis excelled in one area, or even that he had four successful careers. In his public life we can easily track how these strands intertwined, how he used his knowledge of law to further reform, how the ideas he developed as a critique of American society at the beginning of the twentieth century shaped his ideals for the Jewish settlement in Palestine, how the knowledge he gained of the real world influenced his decisions on the Court. He liked to remind people that he had been a practicing lawyer for thirty-nine years before he donned the judicial robes. But looking at Brandeis as a lawyer, or reformer, or Zionist, or judge, or friend, or husband and father will still not give us a sense of a man who is certainly greater than the sum of these parts.

One also has to look at the seeming contradictions in his life and try to understand them. How, for example, did a man who, throughout his life, considered himself a conservative become a liberal icon? How could the man who waxed eloquent on the limits of any one person to direct large operations (each man is a "wee thing") micromanage the American Zionist movement for several years? How could someone who felt so passionately about so many things appear to so many people as cold, austere, and indifferent? How often did his moral absolutism shade over into self-righteousness and intolerance of opposition? How does one square some of his extrajudicial activities with his own professed views on the limits of judicial office?

The biographer's job would be much simpler had Brandeis been an introspective man, had he confided his thoughts to a diary, as Felix Frankfurter did, or worn his heart on his sleeve, as did another of Brandeis's lieutenants, Stephen Wise. He wrote tens of thousands of letters in his lifetime, and although many of them survive, very few cast any light on the inner man. We know that he shared his thoughts and his views on life with his wife, Alice, but aside from the letters he wrote while courting her, this exchange of views seems to have taken place in intimate conversations between them. He wrote to her almost every day when away from home as well as to his brother, Alfred, and he spoke to them of many things—his activities, the people he met, political gossip—but not about what he felt, what disappointments he may have had, what sorrows he endured. If at times he seemed two-dimensional and unfeeling to his contemporaries, he wittingly or not fostered that view.

He told his daughter Susan that he spent more than forty years culti-
vating a "general calm attitude toward every situation." We know from
other sources that he was the object of anti-Semitic sentiment, but from
his letters we have no idea of how he felt about it or if it affected him in
any way. During the bitter fight over his confirmation to the Court, he
resented the charges hurled against him, but in only one instance did
the exterior facade crack to allow us a glimpse of the anger he felt. The
"general calm attitude" apparently protected him, but it also created a
shell that not only historians but his contemporaries could not pene-
trate. The man who invented the modern legal doctrine of privacy
would no doubt say that is as it should be.

Years ago, one of his law clerks, Professor Paul A. Freund of Harvard,
told me that Brandeis had "a mind of one piece." His life, despite its
many different aspects, had in Freund's view a unity and an internal
consistency, and in my study of Brandeis I have come to appreciate the
wisdom of that insight. In a similar analogy, Judge Learned Hand
spoke of Brandeis's life as a "tapestry" whose many strands make the
pattern; to look at one thread alone not only destroys the whole but
gives the strand itself a false value.

In this work I have tried to show how Brandeis's different careers fit
in with one another, how the lawyer, the reformer, the Zionist, the
jurist, and the man each contributed to the tapestry and how interrelated they were. Throughout his life one can find a seamlessness
between what he believed and what he did, in how he dealt with the
often gritty details of a commercial law practice or a reform or a case
involving individual liberty without ever losing sight of the first principles he held so dear, ideals that undergirded his faith in democratic
society and individual freedom. He had less-endearing characteristics,
and those are also strands of the tapestry. But to look at only his pragmatism or his idealism, or at any of his four careers separately, is to lose
sight of the whole man. In his life and his work, he was always the idealistic pragmatist, one whose faith in time remained great.

LOUIS D. BRANDEIS

CHAPTER ONE

LOUISVILLE ROOTS

I n the summer of 1925, Louis Brandeis took a walk on the country road that ran outside his summer home in Chatham on Cape Cod and came across another stroller. In the course of their conversation he learned that Charles Smith, a retired railroad manager, had been born and had lived in Louisville, Kentucky. Brandeis said that he, too, came from Kentucky, and gave him his name.

"Are you connected with the great Louisville family?" Smith asked.

When Brandeis "blushingly admitted it," the justice discovered that Smith had in mind not the well-known reformer and jurist but his father and his brother, Adolph and Alfred. "He had in mind solely the grain-dealing end," Brandeis mirthfully told his brother, "and had never heard of the Washington end."

For Louis Brandeis this seemed perfectly natural. He had been born and grew up in Louisville, would return there periodically throughout his life, helped shape the small University of Louisville into a first-rate local school, and, after his death, would have his ashes interred on the front portico of the University of Louisville Law School. Throughout his life he kept up with the doings of people he had known while growing up in Louisville, both in visits back home and in letters from his family. As much as his brother, Alfred, who lived there all his life, Louis Brandeis was a son of Kentucky.

THE EXTENDED BRANDEIS FAMILY came to Louisville in 1851 from Prague, after a short sojourn in Madison, Indiana. Although they were part of that great wave of central Europeans who immigrated to America after the failed liberal revolts of 1848, their circumstances differed greatly from the poverty-stricken eastern Europeans who arrived between 1880 and 1920, the "tired . . . poor . . . huddled masses" immortalized by Emma Lazarus. In Prague, Adolph Brandeis's father owned a cotton-print mill, which Adolph managed; nearby lived Dr. Sigmund Dembitz, whose daughter Frederika would be wooed and won by Adolph.

Although not wealthy, both families enjoyed a cultured, middle-class life, replete with books, music, and, for Frederika, private tutors. In her aunt Eleanor Wehle's house in Prague, where Frederika spent many happy hours as a child, there had been dinner parties at which she and her twelve cousins had been expected to recite in German and French and to perform on musical instruments. Although comfortable compared with the working classes, both the Brandeis and the Dembitz families confronted numerous difficulties. Jews in the Austro-Hungarian Empire faced restrictions on their economic opportunities, and even within the Jewish community the families belonged to a minor and despised sect, followers of the eighteenth-century pseudo-messiah Jacob Frank. Moreover, while a noted surgeon, Sigmund Dembitz apparently had a poor head for managing his money, and the family always seemed on the brink of ruin. As for Adolph, new machinery had been introduced that would soon make his father's hand-printing plant obsolete. He left looking for work in Hamburg, where he found employment in a grocery store. But it did not pay well, and it kept him away from Frederika.

All of these factors led the Brandeis, Wehle, and Dembitz families to consider immigrating to the United States, a decision cemented by the failed liberal revolutions of 1848. Following the defeat of Napoleon, the settlement of 1815 put conservative governments in place across Europe, and by the mid-1840s a surge of resentment had built up. Revolutions broke out all across the Continent, and as far away as Brazil. When Adolph heard that rebellion had erupted in Prague, he left for home, but before he could join the fighting fell sick with typhoid fever. By the time he recovered, the rebellion had been crushed; his illness saved him from being put on a proscribed list by the Austrian government.

The elders of the families now gathered to discuss leaving Prague and going to the United States. News of the young nation, with its economic opportunities and political freedom, as well as its lack of anti-Semitic laws, had been circulating in central Europe for several decades, fueled by the enthusiastic letters home from those who had already gone to the New World. But if they went to America, what would they do? Could they become farmers or reestablish their businesses overseas? They decided to dispatch an emissary to see what the New World

offered, and in the fall of 1848 the
twenty-six-year-old Adolph Brandeis sailed to the United States.

He arrived in New York, traveled around the East Coast, then
headed west in the company of a
representative of the Rothschild
bank he had met on the boat over,
also sent to sound out business
opportunities in the United States.
As a result, Adolph not only took
in what he saw but as he learned
English had a chance to talk to
Americans he might not otherwise
have met, and thus learned a great
deal about the country, its culture,
and its economy. He thought Frederika would be amused that in
New York housewives set out
pitchers every evening on their
doorsteps with three or four cents,
and in the morning found as much
milk as they had paid for. "Isn't
that idyllic?" Always a pragmatist,

Adolph Brandeis, ca. 1865

Adolph took care to answer his fiancée's questions about what women
wore in the New World, "their dresses and lace collars." He told her
that she should make herself "some dresses and even some silk ones. Of
course we really don't know yet whether we shall live in the country or
in the city, and as things are certainly much cheaper over there than
here, you had better provide yourself in advance. The American farmers' daughters are even extravagant. So provide yourself with as much as
is necessary to look well, and in order not to get out of fashion you had
better choose dark colors."

Not everything he saw pleased him, and the burgeoning factories
with hundreds of workers at their looms appalled him. But he also saw
a country in which diligent labor would be rewarded, and wrote home
that "the hard work of these people is a kind of patriotism. They wear
themselves out to make their country bloom, as though each of them
were commissioned to show the despots of the Old World what a free
people can do."

Adolph fell in love with America, and within two months had taken out his first citizenship papers; he formally became a citizen in July 1872. He wrote enthusiastically of the freedom he saw everywhere, the compassion shown to strangers, and told Frederika that he bought a book that contained messages of the presidents. After reading of some progress in George Washington's administration, "I felt as proud and happy about it as though it had been my own doing. . . . Afterwards I laughed at myself, but there is something in it. It is the triumph of the rights of man which emerges and in which we rejoice. I feel my patriotism growing every day, because every day I learn to know the splendid institutions of this country better."

In Ohio he hired out as a farmworker and soon realized that neither he nor any of the family would be able to succeed in farming. Aside from very hard manual labor, an experience unknown to the families, farmwork proved boring, and, as Adolph told them, "this tedium can become the most deadly poison in family life . . . a man could sink to being a mere common beast of burden." City people needed to live in cities, and now he began looking for a small one with a German community that would offer opportunities for commercial success. In January 1849 he took a job in a Cincinnati grocery and realized that this might well be a path he could tread successfully. He wrote home urging the families to come, and by the time he left to meet their boat in New York in the late spring of 1849, his employer had offered him a partnership. But Adolph had already decided that in America he would work for himself, not for others, and he told Frederika that he had "various plans."

Apparently, Adolph's suggestion that the families would do better by settling in the still semifrontier Midwest had not been received well back home. While not rich, they had led urbane and cultured lives in Prague, and had no desire to give up civilization for a wilderness. Still, the Wehles, Brandeises, and Dembitzes—twenty-six people in all—came to America on board the steamer *Washington,* leaving Hamburg on 8 April 1849. Unlike immigrants of a later generation, who often had little more than the clothes on their backs and a sack that held their meager belongings, the Brandeis clan came with twenty-seven great chests and cases that included feather beds, copper pots and pans, books, and two grand pianos! They did indeed yearn to breathe free, but huddled masses they most surely were not.

THE NEXT FEW HECTIC MONTHS saw the three families trying to adjust to their new country, and while they may not have been happy with Adolph's insistence that they would do best relocating to the Midwest, he alone of them had any sense of America or the ability to converse in English. They booked passage on a barge up the Hudson River and across the Erie Canal to Buffalo, then on a steamer across Lake Erie to Sandusky, Ohio, and from there they took a train to Cincinnati, where all three families shared a large house for a while. The men quickly came to grips with the fact they had not been cut out to be farmers; the women, deprived of servants for the first time in their lives, grappled with housework. Despite these adjustments, the abandonment of older preconceptions took far less time, in fact, than Adolph had anticipated. He had told Frederika, "Our future doesn't cause me the least worry." But he had "great anxiety [about] the older people who have grown up under conditions over there, whose habits and customs are more fixed and will probably be changed only at a sacrifice."

Adolph had already chosen what he thought would be an ideal place for the families to start rebuilding their fortunes, Madison, Indiana, on a bend of the Ohio River between Cincinnati and Louisville, Kentucky. He believed Madison would become "the first city of Indiana," a prediction that did not come to pass, but the town already hosted a rail terminus as well as a port for river traffic, was the largest pork-processing center in Indiana, and had become a "hotbed of commercial capitalism." Madison also seemed to be a healthy place to live, and had completely escaped the cholera epidemic that had recently killed hundreds of people in Cincinnati. The families agreed to move, but not before Adolph and Frederika married on 5 September 1849, in a double ceremony, with Frederika's cousin Lotti Wehle marrying Adolph's brother Semmi (Samuel), a doctor. The two couples set up housekeeping together in a small house in Madison, not far from where the other Wehles lived.

Adolph had earlier spent time in Madison, traveling on behalf of his Cincinnati employer, and while there had made the acquaintance of John Lyle King, a cultured lawyer and later a member of the state legislature. In his diary King drew an acute portrait of his "Bohemian acquaintance," as well as of other members of the family. Adolph he described as "well bred, and has good manners, [and] seems familiar with the great names if not the literature of Germany." (King understandably did not know that Adolph quoted the German poet Heinrich Heine in his letters to Frederika.) After the clan had settled in, King met them all, and became their first new friend in America. The men, because they had to do business, quickly learned to speak English well enough to converse with customers and to talk politics with King. When he met the women, all they could do was nod at him and then escape into the house; they had not had any opportunity to learn more than a smattering of English and were too diffident to use it.

The families started two businesses, a factory to make starch from corn and a grocery and general produce store. The grocery business, under Adolph's direction, prospered. He traveled throughout the Ohio valley buying stock and found nearly everywhere he went communities of German-speaking settlers. He reported that sometimes he could travel sixty to eighty miles without ever hearing a word of English. The German farmers were more than willing to give their business to a fellow migrant, especially one whose company they enjoyed and who treated them fairly.

But the starch factory failed, and the prosperity that Adolph had predicted for Madison never materialized. Within two years of their arrival many of the town's businessmen and professionals, including John King, left. Adolph's clan chose to do so as well, and in 1851, shortly after Frederika had given birth to their first child, Fannie, Adolph took them from Madison down the Ohio River to Louisville, Kentucky. There Adolph and Frederika had three more children, Amy in 1852, Alfred in 1854, and the last of their children, Louis David Brandeis, on 13 November 1856.

BY THE TIME Louis came along, the family's fortunes had changed dramatically. In Louisville, Adolph found the economic opportunity that had eluded him in Madison, and he made the most of it. Although never a wealthy man, he built up a thriving business, raised his children in comfortable surroundings, and at his death in 1906 was praised by all as one of the city's outstanding citizens.

Louisville in 1851 could not be described as a frontier outpost. It had been founded in 1788 by George Rogers Clark in what then constituted the western part of Virginia. After the Kentucky area became a separate state in 1792, Louisville would be its largest settlement and remains its largest city today. Situated on the Kentucky-Indiana border at the falls of the Ohio River, Louisville served as a major entrepôt for transshipping Ohio valley produce down the river to New Orleans, and from thence to Europe. In 1851, when the Brandeises moved there, the city had a population of 43,000; ten years later it had grown to 63,500, and by 1870 had reached 78,000.

Louis, Fannie, Amy, and Alfred Brandeis, left to right

Adolph, of course, knew the area well from his prior trips on behalf of the family business in Madison, and he decided to open a wholesale grain enterprise. It grew steadily, and in 1855 he undertook a venture that would make both his name and his business. That year the wheat crop in western New York failed, and Adolph seized the opportunity to ship Kentucky white wheat to millers on the East Coast. They found the grain to be of high quality, and for the next several years Brandeis

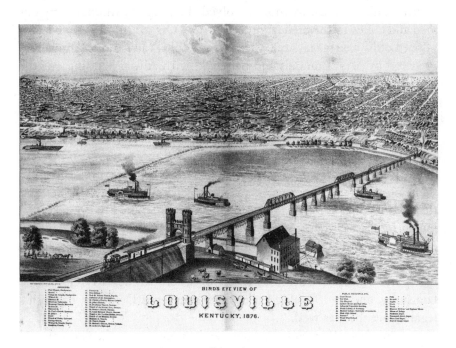

Louisville in the 1870s

and his new partner, William W. Crawford, built upon the white wheat trade to expand their holdings and branch out in other directions. At the time the Civil War broke out in April 1861, Brandeis & Crawford operated a flour mill, a tobacco factory, an eleven-hundred-acre farm, and a river steamboat, the *Fannie Brandeis.*

The growth of the firm came in the shadow of the impending war. Although a slave state, Kentucky remained loyal to the Union and sent more men to fight in the Northern armies than in the Southern. Most Kentuckians opposed abolition, but both Adolph and Frederika's brother, Lewis, held strong antislavery views; Dembitz, in fact, would be one of the delegates to the 1860 Republican convention that nominated Abraham Lincoln. The fortunes of war could easily have wiped out the firm of Brandeis & Crawford, but in fact the opposite happened.

Before the war the firm had carried on extensive trading in the South, but after Fort Sumter switched its business to the states north of the Ohio River. The Union army, needing large amounts of grain to feed its soldiers, signed several large contracts with Brandeis & Crawford, and the firm grew significantly between 1861 and 1865. Louisville also prospered, serving the Union as a supply base, a hospital, and a campground for soldiers preparing for campaigns in the upper South. Louis's earliest memory involved "helping my mother carry out food and coffee to the men from the North." On an almost daily basis in 1862, Louis, nearly six, and Alfred, then eight, carried out sandwiches prepared by Mrs. Brandeis and her cook, with Alfred handing out the food and Louis dispensing coffee from a pitcher. A few times during the war, rebel troops came so near the city the Brandeis family could hear the guns firing. On one of those occasions, Adolph took his family to safety across the river into Indiana.

Adolph and Frederika initially moved into a modest house on Center Street between Chestnut and Walnut. As the business prospered and their family grew, they moved into a larger house on First Street and then built a fashionable home on Broadway, staffed with servants, including a coachman. After the children grew up and left the house, they moved into smaller accommodations. The family took vacations and even during the Civil War went every summer for a few weeks at Newport. Adolph's success led his brother Samuel to relocate to Louisville, and in 1853 Frederika's brother, Lewis Dembitz, began his legal career there as well.

The children all attended school. Louis went first to the German and English Academy for a solid foundation in German and then to the

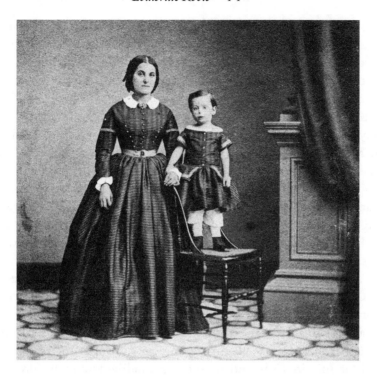

Frederika Brandeis with Louis, ca. 1859

Louisville Male High School. A surviving report card for the school year 1871–1872 shows young Louis getting nearly all 6s—the highest score—in his academic subjects, receiving all 6s in deportment with no demerits (one of his classmates later recalled that alone of all the children in Mrs. Wood's class, Louis never received a caning), and, most amazingly, never missing a day of classes. At age sixteen, he received a gold medal from the University of the Public Schools in Louisville "for pre-eminence in all his studies." The winner of the medal was expected to give a speech at graduation, but Louis, later to be renowned as a public speaker and advocate before the Supreme Court, found himself "overcome with terror at the thought of making a speech." Fortunately, he woke up that morning with laryngitis, and so was spared the ordeal.

Some of his instructors left lifelong impressions, and when he began to help in the development of the University of Louisville in the 1920s, he arranged for various collections to be named after his former teachers. The musical scores, for example, should be in honor of Louis H. Hast. "It is to this romantic German piano teacher," he declared, "that Louisville owes the beginning of its appreciation of great chamber and orchestral music." Brandeis himself studied violin with Mr. Hast, and recalled that he played second fiddle in Mr. Hast's orchestra in the overture to *Zampa*. But while he admittedly had no real talent as a musician, the experience—and Hast's example—led to his lifelong love of good music.

A private person as an adult, Brandeis rarely spoke about his youth to anyone outside the family, although he always proved willing to share memories of Louisville with correspondents who had known him or his family at that time. After his nomination to the Supreme Court in 1916, the press kept calling his secretary, Alice Harriet Grady, demanding to know more about the nominee. Finally, Brandeis gave in to Miss Grady's entreaties, and she went down to Louisville to interview his brother, Alfred, other members of the family, and acquaintances who had known him as a boy.

As the writer for the *Boston Sunday American* concluded after reading Miss Grady's report, these stories showed that "Louis D. Brandeis was just an everyday, fun-loving American BOY." The fun-loving boy, however, almost did not get out of childhood. He and his older brother, Alfred, had gathered a good-size store of fireworks to celebrate the Fourth of July in 1864 and were using small amounts of gunpowder from a large flask as fuses. They would take some powder, dampen it to reduce its volatility, connect it to a rocket, and then light the "fuse." They apparently got so immersed in what they were doing that they failed to notice they had come perilously close to the flask itself when it suddenly exploded, burning both boys on their faces.

Aware that their parents would not approve of their antics, neither one screamed, but each could see that the other's face had been blackened, and they were supposed to go for a ride with their mother the next afternoon. So they went to a pump and washed off as best they could, not realizing that the application of cold water would not only remove the soot but also lead to massive swelling. Discovery could not be evaded, and upon seeing her children, Frederika immediately sent for a doctor. It would be many weeks before their faces healed properly and the scars went away.

Like any other boy his age, Louis teased girls. He and Alfred offered to teach one of their friends how to ice-skate. They helped tie on her skates, and then each took one arm and helped her to the center of a large frozen pond. They then told her to skate back to shore, and promptly left her there. She was furious at them for weeks, but did learn to skate, and, as she recalled, Louis and Alfred always claimed that they had taught her.

At a school dance, Louis apparently got into a fight over a girl named Emma, who became the object of attention of both Louis and a class-mate, Julius Von Borries. Because of the presence of chaperones, they could not immediately slug it out, so they agreed to meet after school the follow-ing day. Word of the impending con-test leaked out (those who recalled the incident thought that Emma leaked the news, elated that the two most popular boys in school were going to fight over her), and about two hun-dred boys and girls showed up to wit-ness the fight. Julius enjoyed a slight advantage in height and weight, while Louis was quicker. No one could figure out who had won, but after fifteen minutes both had been bloodied, and their supporters carried each of them off the "field of honor" on their shoulders. Apparently, Julius and Louis became close friends afterward, while Emma seems to have been totally forgotten.

Alfred and Louis Brandeis, ca. 1863

Miss Grady also interviewed Lizzie, an African-American woman who for many years served as the cook in the Brandeis household, and who, as late as 1916, still did not warrant having her last name used in a major newspaper. Lizzie recalled how the Brandeis boys had loved hot doughnuts and waffles, and how they used to play tricks on her and the other servants. She also recalled kindness and sensitivity from both Alfred and Louis. In 1865 the Brandeises hired a former slave named Durastus as a butler at the Broadway house. It had been against the law to teach slaves to read or write, and his illiteracy appalled the two boys, so they set about teaching him his letters, either in the carriage house or in the furnace room, and these lessons continued until the family left for Europe.

In 1882 the family took Lizzie along on a vacation to the beach at Buzzards Bay, Cape Cod. By then, of course, Louis was an attorney in Boston, but he came down on the weekend to spend some time with his parents and his sister Fannie and her child. Lizzie had never been to the ocean before, and "I didn't know how white folks went in bathing." Fannie gave her a bathing suit and told her to put it on, whereupon Lizzie discovered that it did not come down below her knees. A modest woman, she did not want to be in the water in such an outfit, so she said she was afraid of the salt water. Louis, however, had figured out her problem, and thought that once she went in, she would see that the bathing dress worked well. So he took her hand, walked with her into the water, and held on to her until she was comfortable. After that, she said, she just could not get into the water often enough.

LOUIS BRANDEIS GREW UP in the arms of two families, his immediate one—parents and siblings—and an extended one of aunts, uncles, and cousins, and both had an impact on him. In addition, the Louisville of the 1850s and 1860s provided cultural and intellectual resources to augment what his parents taught at home.

Adolph and Frederika provided not only the material comforts but a warm, loving, and cultured environment for their children. Like many immigrant families they often used their native language at home. Adolph had early mastered English for business and public affairs; although Frederika learned the new language more slowly, she too came to speak it fluently. She did not, however, feel comfortable writing in English. When Adolph and Frederika went to Newport in the summer of 1865, they took the younger children with them and wrote frequently to Fannie and Amy. Most of the letters started out in German, and then the parents would remember that they had promised to write in English. Adolph's English is quite good, but Frederika made the girls promise not to show her letters to her brother, Lewis, since he would tease her. "I know I will make many mistakes, as I never wrote half a dozen of english [sic] letters." When Frederika wrote her memoirs, she did so in her mother tongue.

Like many midcentury immigrants from central Europe, Adolph and Frederika remained most comfortable with German and viewed it as a language of art and culture. They took pains so that their children would be fluent in the language, sending them to an elementary school that taught in both English and German. For years, when Brandeis would take the writings of German authors whom he liked, especially Goethe, along for vacation reading, he read them in the original. Once he rather abashedly confessed to Alfred that he had read a German author in translation, and wondered what their mother would have said about that.

Adolph set an example that would greatly influence Louis's later economic and political philosophy. In his father Louis saw a man who had bravely left his homeland and come to a new country. There Adolph had learned its language, customs, and history, and passed on his love of a free land to his children. Through hard work and perseverance he had honestly built up a thriving business that provided not only for the needs of his own family but for those of his employees as well, and which, in addition, contributed to the economic well-being of the city. Although Adolph had expanded his business as opportunities arose, he never abandoned the grain business. The mill, the farm, the riverboat, and the warehouses all served to reinforce the core business of Brandeis & Crawford—the buying and selling of grain. Adolph could and did take risks when necessary, but he did so in the field he knew; he and his partner never bought other firms for the sake of expansion or tried to monopolize a market. He left, according to one of the state's historians, "a legacy of an incorruptible name and a first class reputation for commercial sagacity and integrity."

Alfred and Louis often accompanied their father on his grain-buying trips in the Ohio valley, and in doing so came to know and respect the self-reliant farmers of the area. When Louis Brandeis the reformer spoke about an ideal society in which individuals could strive to succeed through their own merits, he spoke about the society in which his father, and later his brother, and their client farmers had worked; they provided the model of men achieving a great deal through their own efforts.

Within the household Frederika ruled. She had been reared in a cultured milieu, and as a matter of course she introduced her own children to the culture and literature she knew and loved. At an early age they read Schiller and Goethe in German and listened to her play Mozart and Beethoven on the piano. In order that they have more time to discuss music, books, and politics, she enforced a rule that the family could never talk of financial affairs or business matters at the dinner table. Moreover, neither Frederika nor Adolph would tolerate any personal criticism of other persons, even of people they did not know firsthand. According to Louis, his mother instilled in her children high moral standards. He later attributed a good part of his reformist zeal to her, and declared that in the end "the improvement of the world, reform, can only arise when mothers like you are increased thousands of times and have more children."

People described Frederika as "a woman of strong personality, well-read, a good talker, a hard worker, big-hearted, and sweet and generous to a degree." Lizzie the cook told about how she and others were trying to raise money for an orphan asylum for colored children, and each member of the committee had to raise $25, a large sum, especially for a domestic worker. Money, as Lizzie noted, "come awful hard in those days." She tentatively asked her employer if perhaps she would be willing to donate, and Frederika sat down and wrote Lizzie a check for $25.

While Frederika did not intentionally dominate a situation, people around her found her strong willed and resourceful, leading many to defer to her judgment. People categorized her as one of the "anxious" mothers, never quite content to have any of her children out of sight for too long. Louis told Miss Grady that as a boy, and until the time he left for Harvard Law School, both he and his brother, Alfred, went to see Frederika to bid her good night personally before they went to bed. When the children went out for an evening, she would lie awake until all of them had returned home.

The two girls, Fannie and Amy, doted on their youngest brother and called him "Lutz," a nickname that stuck until Fannie's death. Louis forged a particularly close relationship with both sisters, and when he went off to Harvard Law School, they wrote him teasing letters about what he did outside of class and what young women he had met. What we know about Louis's social life in Cambridge during his law school days and later in St. Louis comes almost entirely from letters he wrote to them. When Amy married a second cousin, Otto Wehle, and gave birth to a son, they named him after Louis, much to his joy. Fannie also married a second cousin, Charles Nagel, and her entreaties to Louis when he finished law school led him to take up a brief, unsatisfactory, and rather unhappy time as a young lawyer in St. Louis.

He and Alfred, his senior by nearly three years, not only were brothers but would be best friends throughout their lives. Frederika recognized the deep ties binding her two sons together, and wrote that her heart rejoiced when she saw the two of them together. "It seems to me that there were never two brothers who complemented one another so perfectly and were so completely one as you two." As boys they played together, and occasionally got into trouble, also together. Alfred would stay in Louisville, becoming one of the city's leading merchants, and after Louis settled in Boston, the two wrote to each other almost every day. When Alfred decided to move to the countryside just east of Louisville, Louis made him a house gift by buying up some additional acreage for what Alfred called "Ladless Hill" (he had four daughters).

They kept tabs on each other's health, constantly—and usually unsuccessfully—trying to get the other to slow down and rest when ill. They and their families visited often and took vacations together, and their daughters also spent much time together with their cousins. In the years when Louis traveled the country in his legal work or on political matters, if anywhere in the Midwest, he would swing down to visit Alfred in Louisville, or if that were impossible, Alfred would journey to meet him. When Louis decided to help in the development of the University of Louisville, Alfred and his family became partners in the project, believing, as did Louis, that the university would only thrive if it could foster local loyalties and support.

Whereas Louis later in life made many enemies because of his reform work and what many saw as a hard—indeed heartless—personality, Alfred, who shared nearly all of his brother's ethical and political principles, seems to have been well liked, even beloved, not only by his friends but by business competitors as well. On his death his former brother-in-law, Charles Nagel, wrote about how Alfred had "managed, midst the turmoil of modern life, to preserve his sweet and true philosophy." He had humor and wit without sting, strong convictions without intolerance, abhorrence of personal strife without fear of conflict for a good cause. Louis described Alfred's "beautiful, gladsome life . . . a joy to all who shared in his activities or with whom he came in contact."

IN ADDITION TO his immediate family, other members of the Wehle, Brandeis, and Dembitz clans played an important role in Louis's life. Uncle Samuel, Adolph's brother, and his wife, Lotti, Frederika's cousin, lived in Louisville, and Adolph and Frederika made frequent trips to visit other family members who had settled in New York and St. Louis. Outside his immediate family, however, no one influenced young Louis as much as his uncle Lewis Naphtali Dembitz, Frederika's brother.

After attending the gymnasium at Glogau University in Germany, Lewis Dembitz took one semester of law training in Prague before the family moved to America. A child prodigy, he spoke seven languages by his teens, read Latin and Greek, and could do logarithms in his head. Years later, using his own calculations, he forecast the 1869 eclipse of the sun to the minute. When Adolph first visited Madison, Indiana, he wanted John King to have his future brother-in-law read law in King's office. Louis would remember his uncle as "a living university. With him, life was an unending intellectual ferment. . . . In the diversity of

Lewis Naphtali Dembitz

his intellectual interests, in his long-ing to discover truths, in his pleasure in argumentation and the process of thinking, he reminded one of the Athenians."

He followed Adolph and Frederika to Louisville, where he established a successful law practice and also gained a reputation as a legal scholar. His highly esteemed *Kentucky Jurisprudence* (1890) and the two-volume *Treatise on Land Titles in the United States* (1895) remained standard reference volumes for Kentucky lawyers for several decades. Dembitz drafted the first Australian ballot system in the United States, contributed widely to various encyclopedias as well as law journals, and translated *Uncle Tom's Cabin* into German. He named one son after Henry Clay and the other after Abraham Lincoln.

The diminutive Dembitz (he stood only five feet tall and weighed a hundred pounds) had a way with children; he had six of his own, and his various nieces and nephews adored him. He also had a reputation for absentmindedness, and one story, perhaps apocryphal, concerns the reminders he wrote to himself, such as "Trousers on chair, shoes on floor, Dembitz in bed." Louis so admired his uncle that he changed his middle name from David to Dembitz, and there is no question that he chose law as a profession because of his uncle. From Dembitz he also received what little contact he had with Judaism.

The Brandeises never denied their Jewishness, but with the exception of Lewis Dembitz, neither did they practice it. A thriving Jewish community existed in Louisville in midcentury, but Adolph and Frederika apparently had little or nothing to do with it. They observed what one scholar has called "the secular Christianity of the United States" and sent each other Christmas gifts and cards. In her memoirs, Frederika recalled with great joy the Christmas trees and parties of her youth. As for religion itself, she wrote, "I do not believe that sins can be expiated by going to divine service and observing this or that formula; I believe that only goodness and truth and conduct that is humane and self-sacrificing towards those who need us can bring God nearer to us, and that our errors can only be atoned for by acting in a more kindly spirit." She deliberately did not impart to her children any formal religious teachings, since such doctrines, she believed, could be argued away. Rather, she wanted them to imbibe "a pure spirit and the highest ideals as to morals and love." Her parents, and this would have been true for much of the extended family, "did not associate with Jews and were different from them and so there developed in me more affection for our race as a whole than for individuals." Louis later told a newspaper reporter that his early training had been neither Jewish nor Christian. His parents "were not so narrow as to allow their religious beliefs to overshadow their interest in the broader aspects of humanity." It might well be said that Frederika, and later Louis, subscribed to the Judaism of the prophets, with its exalted moral teachings and idealism, and not to the Judaism of the priests, with its emphasis on rules and rituals.

The children had no idea of the Jewish holidays, and one Yom Kippur, the Day of Atonement, the girls had heard that the service at a nearby synagogue included some beautiful music. Fannie and Amy got permission to attend, and Frederika dispatched the boys and the carriage to pick the girls up when services concluded at dusk. The two boys drove the carriage down Broadway and waited in front of the synagogue until Fannie and Amy should appear. When the congregation started coming out, several people who recognized the Brandeis boys immediately began berating them; Jews did not ride on the Day of Atonement!

Lewis Dembitz, on the other hand, studied not only Jewish law and custom but its history and theology as well. Unlike his assimilated relatives, he lived life as an observant Jew, following the prescribed laws. Louis had no experience of the Jewish Sabbath in his parents' home, nor did he later observe it in his own. Years later he recalled vividly the Sabbath in his uncle's house, "the joy and awe with which my uncle welcomed the arrival of the day and the piety with which he observed it. I remember the extra delicacies, lighting of the candles, prayers over a cup of wine, quaint chants, and Uncle Lewis poring over books most of the day. I remember more particularly an elusive something about him which was spoken of as the 'Sabbath peace.' . . . Uncle Lewis used to say that he was enjoying a foretaste of heaven."

Nor did Dembitz restrict his Judaism to the house. He served as a member of the commission that drew up the plan of study for the Hebrew Union College, but after the Reform movement became overtly anti-Zionist, he affiliated with what became known as Conservative Judaism and helped establish the Jewish Theological Seminary in New York. A scholar of religion as well as law, Dembitz translated the books of Exodus and Leviticus for the revised English Bible of the Jewish Publication Society. A half-dozen years after his uncle's death, the comment that Lewis Naphtali Dembitz "was a noble Jew" and a Zionist piqued Louis Brandeis's interest, and started him down the road to Zionist leadership.

The sixteen years of Brandeis's childhood in Louisville left an indelible mark on him, both physically and intellectually. Although he spent the rest of his life in Boston and Washington, he never completely lost the soft accent of his native city. Malaria and the constant dosing of drugs such as quinine left him with a slight olive tone to his skin, which led many people on first impression to believe he had come from the Mediterranean. Brandeis never forgot the lessons in manners he learned at home and in southern society, and even in his old age would not sit either at the dining table or in the parlor until all the women present had been seated.

More important, the social philosophy he absorbed there manifested itself in all of his future reform activities. Louisville at the time seemed the quintessential democratic society, in which individuals, like his father and Mr. Crawford, could do well by dint of their intelligence and perseverance. There were no large factories employing thousands of people, but rather many small endeavors—farms, stores, professional offices. People knew one another, their lives entwined in a strong sense of community. Later, after he had seen the devastating effects that industrialization had on American society, Brandeis would look back to what he considered an idyllic era, one free from the curse of bigness.

More than part of this rosy recollection may have been true, but the young Brandeis, like most white southerners, ignored the large African-American population that supported much of the area's economy. Kentucky had been home to 200,000 slaves prior to the Civil War, and although the Brandeis family supported abolition, civil rights did not play a major role in the family's thinking. Although Louis left the city as a boy, it is improbable that he abandoned many of the racial attitudes that permeated it. Later, as a reformer, he never became involved in groups such as the NAACP, and while on the Supreme Court tended to go with the conservative majority in cases involving race.

BUSINESS HAD BEEN GOOD for Brandeis & Crawford, fueled first by Union demand for grain during the Civil War and then by the growth of the country in the years following Appomattox. But that same growth led to the over-construction of railroads, inflation, and speculation; the collapse of a number of eastern banks in 1873 led to a terrible depression that lasted through much of the decade. The agricultural sector had been suffering since the late 1860s, and in 1872, a harbinger of things to come, a number of southern clients went bankrupt, wiping out large sums of money owed to Brandeis & Crawford. Adolph saw that there would be greater distress in the next few years, and, unwilling to take further losses, he and Crawford chose to close the firm. They liquidated the assets and decided to await the return of better times before reopening. Adolph, prodded by Lewis Dembitz, decided to take the family to Europe, so that he and Frederika could visit relatives and friends who had not emigrated and the children could see their roots in the Old World. They left Louisville in May 1872 for a fifteen-month trip. Once in Europe, however, they kept delaying their return because of the illness of their oldest child, Fannie. It would be three years before they returned to America.

Louis, not yet sixteen, found the whole enterprise a great adventure. The family sailed from New York on 10 August 1872, aboard the SS *Adriatic.* He began a diary that went into great detail about the ship, its crew, and, its passengers. "Our ship was a large ocean steamer," he wrote, "4,000 tons, four hundred feet in length and said to be the fastest between England and America, having made one trip in 7 days and 8 hours. Our captain, a stout six-footer, is a jolly looking man and makes himself as agreeable as possible."

They arrived in Liverpool eight days later and, after a brief stay in London, made their way to the Continent. Originally Louis had planned on enrolling in the gymnasium in Vienna, but despite his gold medal from Louisville he failed the entrance examinations. He spent most of the winter in Vienna taking private lessons, attending lectures at the university, and enjoying German music and theater. In March he started off for Italy and then spent the summer in Switzerland, hiking the Alps with his father and brother. Despite the great stamina he would show in later life, especially as a canoeist, that summer found him tiring much sooner than Adolph or Alfred. On one of their excursions they sought to find the source of the Inn River. On a break, Alfred suggested that they also look for the beginnings of the Adda, to which Louis responded, "I don't see why I should have to find the source of every damned river in Europe!"

Memories of the years he traveled around Europe would remain with him his entire life, and letters to Alfred, decades after their time abroad, were full of references to places they visited and events they witnessed. "This day will remind you of Liverpool," Louis wrote on the anniversary of their arrival, and when he saw a clipping about the statue of George Washington in Lugano, he sent it to Alfred with a note, "Do you remember the thrill which we experienced when we came upon this?"

IN THE FALL OF 1873, Alfred, then nineteen, returned to Louisville to seek work. The rest of the family had intended going home then also, but Fannie's illness once again led them to defer the voyage until she had recovered. Louis decided to seek entrance to the Annen-Realschule in Dresden by having the authorities waive the entrance examination. Because of Fannie's illness, he had to make the trip to Dresden alone, and then when a family friend, who had promised to give him an introduction to the rector, proved late in arrival, Louis decided to go to the official himself. Herr Job told him straight-out that he could not be admitted without examination, and would also have to provide birth and vaccination certificates. To the latter Louis replied, "The fact that I am here is proof of my birth, and you may look at my arm for evidence that I was vaccinated." The boy who had been terrorized by the thought of giving a speech to his high-school classmates had found his tongue and the courage to argue with the rector, and he so impressed Herr Job that he was permitted to enter without the examination and the certificates.

Louis stayed at the Annen-Realschule for three terms, taking twelve courses at a time in French, Latin, German, literature, mineralogy, geography, physics, chemistry, and several branches of mathematics. He never received a grade less than 2, denoting *gut,* and in most courses he earned the top grade of 1, *sehr gut.* At the end of the third term, he won a prize, which he could choose for himself. He selected a book on Greek art by A. W. Becker, *Charakterbilder aus der Kunstgeschichte.* The German inscription on the flyleaf notes that the prize went "to the honor student, Louis Dembitz Brandeis, for industry and good behavior." Sensitive to the diminishing family fortunes, Louis earned some money by tutoring students who wanted to learn English. In Dresden, he also met Ephraim Emerton, who would become one of his best friends in Cambridge, and who suggested to Louis that he attend Harvard University.

The three terms in Dresden affected Brandeis in several ways. For the first time in his life he lived and worked outside the protective shelter of his home. Although German schooling, like that of elsewhere at the time, consisted of a great deal of memorization and rote recitation, the intellectual rigor of the school taught Brandeis a great deal. Years later he told his law clerk Paul Freund that at the Annen-Realschule he had discovered the deductive process. He said that "although he had done well in his studies theretofore," Freund recalled, "it was not until he went to Dresden that he really learned to think. He said that in preparing an essay on a subject about which he had known nothing, it dawned on him that ideas could be evolved by reflecting on your material. This was a new discovery for him." The lesson proved invaluable to Brandeis for the rest of his life, as he realized that thinking about material could lead to the resolution of a problem. He would need the facts to master, and the time to absorb and analyze them. Felix Frankfurter noted that Brandeis did not enjoy "the windfall of inspiration." Rather, "thought for him was the product of brooding. He believed in taking pains, and the corollary of taking pains is taking time."

The stay in Germany, although it reinforced the lessons of language and literature that Frederika had taught at home, also deepened Louis's love of America. A child of the frontier in many ways, he disliked the formalism and the rigid discipline that smacked more of military training than of humanistic education. Students had to tip their hats to the professors, a symbol of authoritarianism that irked him greatly. "I was a terrible little individualist in those days," he told Ernest Poole, "and the German paternalism got on my nerves." One night he found that he had forgotten his key and, standing outside his window, whistled loudly enough to wake his roommate, who came down to let him in. For this infraction of the rules he received a severe reprimand. "This made me homesick. In Kentucky you could whistle! I wanted to go back to America and I wanted to study law."

Shortly after he finished the third term of school, he joined his parents in returning to the United States. They sailed from Le Havre on 5 May 1875 under somewhat straitened circumstances compared with the trip over. Frederika and Fannie traveled second class, while Adolph, Amy, and Louis occupied third-class cabins. They reached America on 18 May, and after a visit with friends in Brookline, Massachusetts, returned home to Louisville on 1 June 1875, nearly three years after they had left. The trip allowed the adults to renew old acquaintanceships, and to see not only their homeland but also parts of Europe they had only heard about. For the children, it was a great adventure, with many of their parents' stories now made more real. But while they delighted in Europe's art and culture and physical beauties, they all returned home more devoted than ever to the United States.

While in Brookline, Louis Brandeis made arrangements to enter Harvard Law School in the fall semester of 1875.

CHAPTER TWO

HARVARD, ST. LOUIS, AND BACK

Throughout his life, Louis Brandeis had the good fortune to be in the right place at the right time, and the courage and perspicacity to grasp the opportunities before him. He achieved so much as lawyer, reformer, Zionist, and judge because the times allowed a person with his brains, courage, and imagination to seize the situation and shape it in a particular way. He began his law career at a time of great malleability in legal practice, due to the enormous social and economic changes of the late nineteenth century. He came to Harvard Law School in the fall of 1875 in the midst of the revolution in legal education. The reforms of Christopher Columbus Langdell changed the ways students learned the law, and they seemed custom-made for the young man from Louisville.

AT THE TIME, a majority of the men entering the profession did so by "reading law," a form of apprenticeship in a practicing attorney's office. After a period of five to seven years, they could be admitted to the bar by passing an oral examination administered by a local magistrate. There had been some efforts at formal instruction since the 1780s, but the few law schools that existed grew very slowly in the first two-thirds of the nineteenth century. In these schools, especially at Columbia and Harvard, the method of instruction consisted of rote memorization of assigned readings and then recitation of rules, with an occasional moot court where students could practice arguing cases.

For those with bright and inquiring minds such as Oliver Wendell Holmes Jr., attendance proved tedious at best. He described the law, as taught at Harvard in the 1860s, as "a ragbag of details" and wondered "whether the subject was worthy of the interest of an intelligent man." In an unsigned notice in the *American Law Review* in 1870, Holmes declared that "for a long time the condition of the Harvard Law School

Louis Brandeis as law student, ca. 1876

has been almost a disgrace to the Commonwealth of Massachusetts," and its degrees represent "nothing except a residence for a certain period in Cambridge or Boston." The school, he charged, had been "doing something every year to injure the profession throughout the country, and to discourage real students."

Had Brandeis turned up in Cambridge only a few years later, he might not have gained admission to Harvard. As it is, the record is rather skimpy on just why the faculty chose to let him enroll; perhaps Langdell recognized in the younger man some of the same traits that had brought himself to the attention of his law professors a generation earlier.

Langdell had studied at Harvard Law in the 1850s, staying for three years, twice the normal number of terms. The students took their meals together, and before long Langdell had been recognized as the "presiding genius." The two professors also sensed his intelligence and gave him a job as the librarian. After graduation he practiced in New York, where he won a reputation as a lawyer's lawyer, one to whom his colleagues turned when confronted with tricky questions of law. Then, in 1870, Harvard's new president, Charles William Eliot, invited Langdell to become Dane Professor of Law and to assume a new position, dean of the law school. Eliot intended to transform Harvard from a sleepy provincial college into a first-rate national university, and he wanted Langdell to effect a similar transformation in the law school.

Until 1872 matriculation required only that a young man provide some proof of "moral character," often meaning little more than membership in some prominent Boston family. Afterward applicants had to show intelligence and industry, and to convince Langdell that they would catch fire in the new learning environment he planned to build. By 1875 the faculty had begun requiring a college degree, or, lacking the bachelor of arts, candidates would have to pass examinations in

Latin (translating without a dictionary passages from Caesar's *Commentaries,* Cicero's *Orations,* or Virgil's *Aeneid*) and demonstrate proficiency in French and knowledge of Blackstone's *Commentaries.* At the time Louis Brandeis applied for entrance in the spring of 1875, he might have offered proficiency in French, but he had little Latin and knew nothing about Blackstone. He had done well at the Annen-Realschule in Dresden, but had not received any sort of degree comparable to a bachelor of arts. Just as he impressed the German headmaster, so, too, did he convince Langdell and Professor James Barr Ames that he would be the type of student they wanted in their program.

Instead of rote, Langdell and his faculty wanted students to think; instead of memorizing rules, those learning law should understand how legal rules evolved out of specific cases and factual conditions. These reforms should be seen as part of a larger movement to create a legal science that would, like the physical sciences, have means of testing theorems and arriving at the truth. "Law," Langdell declared, "considered as a science, consists of certain principles or doctrines. To have such a mastery of these as to be able to apply them with constant facility and certainty to the ever-tangled skein of human affairs, is what constitutes a true lawyer; and hence to acquire that mastery should be the business of every earnest student of law." A proper law school and its faculty would provide these sources to the students, in the form of treatises and case reporters in the library, and through a new form of textbook for the class, a book consisting of selected cases and additional materials through which a student could be led to see the development of legal principles. In the classroom, teacher and student would be colleagues in this search; rather than rote recitation, there would be a Socratic dialogue.

At first the new method antagonized some of the faculty as well as students who had been comfortable with rote recitation. Langdell and Ames would ask a man to "state a case," its facts, the route of litigation, the court's ruling, and its reasoning. This much all students could do, but then they would be asked whether they agreed with the result, whether the judge's reasoning had been correct, whether the conclusion agreed with or contradicted other cases they had read. All of this would be familiar even to first-year law students today, but the men at Harvard in the early 1870s found it confusing. Didn't the teacher know the law? If he did know it, why ask all of these questions? One day Langdell called on a student who proceeded to differ with the dean over whether a case had been correctly decided, and in the end apparently got the

Christopher Columbus Langdell

better of the argument, rousing a mixture of applause and boos from the class. Few of the students apparently realized that this exchange completely validated Langdell's teaching; the student had not blindly recited what had been written in the case, but had by reasoning figured out the rule of law it relied upon.

A dozen years after taking his degree, Brandeis lauded what he saw as the strengths of the new system. "No instructor can provide the royal road to knowledge by giving to the student the conclusions" that had to be deduced from the sources; that would defeat the whole purpose of having the student reach the right judgment through his own mental efforts. The professor's job was to show his students "how to think in a legal manner in accordance with the principles of the particular branch of the law." When one has learned the law this way, the essential legal principles are indelibly etched on the student's mind "as they never could be by mere reading or lectures; for instead of being presented as desiccated facts, they occur as an integral part of the drama of life."

BRANDEIS TOOK TO the Langdellian method like a duck to water. Blessed with a remarkable memory, Louis would have done well with any method. But his experience in Dresden had shown him that knowledge of the facts alone would not always illuminate the problem. One had to reason deductively, to see the facts and then understand how the resolution of the problem—in this case the legal principle—followed. In a letter to Otto Wehle (who had married his sister Amy), written in the spring of his first year, he could not contain his enthusiasm. You will have heard from others, he told his brother-in-law, "how well I am pleased with everything that pertains to the law." Apparently, Otto had at one time suggested that Louis read law in his office rather than going to law school, a suggestion he had declined. Louis now told Otto that his choice had been a wise one. "Law schools are splendid institutions," and aside from the large library and the high quality of the instructors he could associate with other young men "who are determined to make as great progress as possible in their studies and devote all their time to the same." The opportunities for learning at Harvard far exceeded what any law office could offer. "After one has grasped the principles which underlie the structure of the Common Law, I doubt not, that one can learn very much in an office." But not as much as one could learn that first year in law school. His enthusiasm for law schools, and his great respect for law teachers, remained with Louis for the rest of his life.

The Langdellian method encouraged instructors and students to critique the materials they studied, and Louis reveled in the variety of perspectives this produced. Charles Smith Bradley, for example, the former chief justice of Rhode Island, "never lets an opportunity escape him for lauding the English and especially American Judges." Louis recognized that Bradley's background gave him a particular slant, and went on to say that Bradley "in his deference to 'His Honor' even goes so far as to avoid offering any criticism of what has become settled by decisions, however unsupported by reason." But he also appreciated Bradley's advocacy of equity pleading, legal principles in common law that supplement strict rules of law where their application would operate harshly, so as to achieve what is sometimes referred to as "natural justice." "Whatever is 'against conscience' is to him the subject of abhorrence," Brandeis told his brother-in-law, and "he desires that there should be no distinction between what is 'legally right' and what is 'morally right.' "

On the other hand, James Barr Ames, whom Louis considered his best teacher, tried "to convince us that nine-tenths of the judges who have sat on the English Bench and about ninety-nine-hundredths of the American Judges 'did not know what they were talking about'—that the great majority of the Judges were illogical, inconsistent and unreasonable." He certainly sounded like Ames when he told Otto about a case he had argued in moot court, involving an insurance company. Louis defended the company and bemoaned the fact that the real Supreme Court had found for his opponent. Quoting an English judge in another case, he complained that the case for the plaintiff, "so far as it relies on authority, fails in precedent, and so far as it rests on principle fails in reason." I am afraid, he told Otto Wehle, that those "Supreme Court Judges will be refused admittance into paradise for the bad law they have been promulgating in this life. Many of them, surely, deserve the most dreadful punishment."

Neither then nor later did Louis hold judges in contempt, but he also never idealized them as Bradley did. He saw judges as human, and as such capable of error. Lawyers had to get judges to avoid error, by setting forth the facts and arguments they needed to determine a case properly. Time and again in his career both as a practicing attorney and as a reformer, he would say that "a judge is presumed to know the elements of law, but there is no presumption that he knows the facts." Brandeis learned and absorbed a key element of Langdell's jurisprudence; in his casebooks and lectures Langdell emphasized over and over again the necessity of the law being grounded in and related to factual conditions.

Louis belonged to the elite Pow Wow Law Club. Although debate clubs had been in existence since the establishment of the school in the 1820s, the Pow Wow had been founded when Langdell arrived. Its members attended Langdell's first-year class in Contracts, and in addition to class discussion they could argue recent cases in a more formal, courtroom-like manner against other clubs. One of the original members of the Pow Wow, Franklin Fessenden, recalled the high quality of the debates, which, "together with the mental discipline gained in Langdell's lectures, brought out the best there was in the men . . . [and] formed in them habits of industry which followed them in their later years of active work in practice at the bar and on the bench." Louis almost gushed when he called law clubs "grand institutions, a great incentive to labor." As a member of the Pow Wow, he would also have been considered one of "Kit's Freshmen," an advocate of Langdell's new method.

Brandeis excelled at Harvard and caught the attention not only of his professors but of his fellow students as well. At the time of Brandeis's appointment to the Supreme Court, one of his classmates, Philip Alexander Bruce of Virginia, recalled, "Mr. Brandeis had barely taken his seat in our class room before his remarkable talents were discovered and his claim to immediate distinction allowed." Bruce, a gifted journalist and amateur historian, went on to give a description of the young man who had "the keenest mind of [us] all." Although forty years had passed, Bruce could still recall "the pleasant voice of that youthful student, his exact and choice language, his keen intellectual face, his lithe figure, his dark yet handsome aspect, and finally the unaffected suavity of his manner, that had in it something of the polish of the Old World. Intellect, refinement, an alert and receptive spirit, were written all over his attractive personality." Another of his classmates, William E. Cushing, told his mother, "My friend Brandeis is a character in his way—

one of the most brilliant legal minds they have ever had here." Brandeis hails from Louisville, "but has spent some time in Europe, has a rather foreign look and is currently believed to have some Jew blood in him, though you would not suppose it from his appearance—tall, well-made, dark, beardless, and with the brightest eyes I ever saw. . . . The professors listen to his opinion with the greatest deference. And it is generally correct."

He finished the required two years of study with an average grade of 97 out of 100, a record that would not be duplicated in his lifetime. In those days the class chose six men to write the class oration for graduation exercises, and then the faculty selected one man to deliver it. Louis led the list his classmates chose, and both Dean Langdell and the faculty wanted him to give the oration at commencement. But university rules provided that no one could receive a degree who had not yet attained his twenty-first birthday, and clearly one could not be the class orator if one could not graduate with the class. Langdell finally sent Louis to see President Eliot, the first time Brandeis had met the man whom he then and later greatly admired.

Eliot quickly resolved the matter. "The rule," he declared, "is that the orator is to be one of those who receive a degree. The law says that you can't have a degree before you are twenty-one. You will not be twenty-one until November. Commencement is in June. I don't see, Mr. Brandeis, how you can be the orator." The meeting had taken less than three minutes, and whatever disappointment Louis may have had at the decision, he apparently admired Eliot's decisive manner in resolving the issue. Louis nonetheless planned to attend the graduation exercises to see his classmates receive their degrees. On that morning he learned that the board and the faculty, by a special vote, had passed a resolution that in light of Brandeis's academic achievement, he would not only receive a dispensation from the age rule but also receive his degree cum laude at the ceremony.

LOUIS RETURNED HOME to Louisville in the summers of 1876 and 1877 both to read law in Otto Wehle's office and to spend time with his parents. He worried about his father, who, after returning from Europe, had been unable to recoup his former financial success. Adolph had opened a cotton-factoring office, anticipating that after the ravages of war this would be a growing field. But the expectations never materialized, and Adolph had to close down. As he wrote to his son, "The act of winding up consists only in the attempt to collect bad debts, which up to now has been my only business." He did not like being unemployed, which after a lifetime of hard work and success he found "terribly distressing."

While looking forward to a relatively quiet summer in 1877 of reading law, spending time with his family, and reestablishing old friendships, Louis suddenly found himself in the middle of more excitement than he wanted. The Louisville & Nashville Railroad, following the example of eastern lines, announced a 10 percent wage reduction for all of its workers effective 1 July. Initially the L & N crews did little more than grumble, but then rail workers in eastern cities began holding protest meetings that often erupted into riots. On 21 July a meeting in Pittsburgh had exploded into violence, leaving twenty people dead. Although the railroad gave in to worker demands that their pay be restored, the tensions continued, fanned by organizers of the Workingmen's Party of the United States.

By 24 July, Louisville officials feared the worst, and violence broke out that evening. The popular mayor, Charles D. Jacob, tried to address a large group of workingmen gathered at city hall, but was shouted down. The crowd suddenly turned into a mob and headed for the L & N depot, where they threw rocks and broke windows until a contingent of police arrived and arrested some men they suspected of being the leaders. The crowd would not disperse, however, and headed back uptown, smashing windows in a number of residences, including the Brandeis house at Walnut and First streets.

Louis and Alfred immediately went to city hall, where they enrolled in a group of seven hundred citizen-volunteers, many of them veterans of the recent war, were given weapons, and set out to patrol the streets. Some nights that week Louis walked the streets with a gun; others he spent in a railroad shed. With the arrival of state militiamen, city officials dispersed the local posse, and Louis and Alfred turned in their weapons, much to the relief of their parents. Years later Brandeis recalled that the gun had probably been more dangerous to him than to anyone else. He returned to Boston that fall for a year of graduate study in the law.

LOUIS HAD COME to Harvard in somewhat straitened circumstances. His father could not afford to underwrite his younger son's legal education, so Louis borrowed money from his brother, Alfred, to pay his first year's expenses—$150 for tuition, plus room, board, and books. He lived frugally, and in the spring he applied for and received a scholarship. But Professor Bradley suggested that he turn down the award and try his hand at tutoring and signed up his own son Saunders as Louis's first pupil; before long Louis had enough pupils not only to cover his living expenses but to provide him with a small surplus.

As a graduate student, Louis continued with some tutoring, but he also received a proctorship in Harvard College, which paid fees for supervising undergraduates during exams. By the end of the year not only had Louis made enough to pay back his loan from Alfred, but he had also accrued somewhere between $1,200 and $1,500, which he sent to Alfred for investment in U.S. Treasury certificates, as well as a $600 Atchison, Topeka & Santa Fe Railroad bond, which he kept long afterward.

One would not say that Brandeis lived in poverty while at Harvard; in his first year he had borrowed enough from Alfred to cover all his expenses, but with little margin for nonessentials. In his second and third years, he earned enough that had he wanted, he could have led a very materially comfortable life. After all, he had not grown up in penury, and it would not have been unusual if he had used his tutoring money to purchase better accommodations or clothing or entertainment. But he did not. The habits of thrift that he learned at Cambridge that first year became ingrained, and even after he had become a millionaire, people commented on his austere lifestyle.

By determining to live well within his income, and conservatively investing the surplus, he could achieve a measure of financial independence. This habit would allow him, after he began his law practice, to eschew work he might find objectionable, since he would not need the income to maintain a high living style. While some people found in this pattern an echo of Puritanism, Brandeis came from an immigrant German-Jewish family in Louisville whose middle-class values demanded a certain standard of comfort. Louis did not select sacrifice or self-denial as a lifestyle; rather, he established priorities of what mattered most to him. In addition to money, he rationed his time. He had taken a violin with him to school, but stopped playing it. He recognized that he had little talent in this area and decided that his time could better be used in other activities. For Louis Brandeis, the habits he formed as a law student in the 1870s stayed with him, and in fact grew stronger, throughout his life, applied not just to the workplace but to his reform efforts, his recreation, and his domestic arrangements.

Brandeis also faced problems with his eyesight and with tiredness. It appears that in his first year at law school, he may have skimped on food and sleep, to the point where he began to feel run-down. Fortunately, he took advantage of the newly opened Hemenway Gymnasium, where the director prescribed a regimen of limited but regular exercise, a prescription that soon cured Louis of fatigue. Here again Brandeis learned a lesson that he would practice and preach to others all his life, namely, that unless one found some way to exercise the body as well as the mind, one could not do good work. As a young lawyer he belonged to a riding club, and later took up canoeing. He also took regular vacations, and all of August off. "I learned that I could do a year's worth of work in eleven months, but not in twelve." Brandeis's insistence on taking time off involved not just health; he understood that a tired person more easily made mistakes, not just of fact but of judgment as well.

The problem with his eyes could not be so easily resolved. He had been a reader since his childhood and, despite heavy course assignments, continued to read for pleasure. In his letters Brandeis mentions that he has spent "a little time every evening with English & German authors," and had come to admire the works of Ralph Waldo Emerson. He also copied out quotations from authors he liked, and these included Shakespeare, Horace Walpole, Jonathan Swift, and Matthew Arnold. But whereas at home he had read in good daylight or by the light of strong gas lamps, he now read by the less-than-ideal gas lamps in his lodgings and in the cramped law school library in Dane Hall. In 1879, Dean Langdell reported on the inadequacies of Dane Hall as a home for the law school and noted that "the library and lecture-room are each lighted from four different directions; and it would probably be safe to say that a year has never passed in which the cross-lights of these two rooms have not ruined, or seriously injured, the eyes of one or more persons."

During the summer of 1876, when he read law in Otto Wehle's office to gain some practical experience, he had severe problems focusing his eyes. He went to a well-known eye doctor in Cincinnati in August, who warned him against further reading and prescribed "total abstinence from the law" until he recovered. Louis refused to accept this prognosis and returned to Cambridge. In Boston he consulted Dr. Haskett Derby, who prescribed exercises to strengthen the eye muscles and, when Louis failed to respond to this regimen, also suggested he give up the law. Upon Adolph's advice, Louis went to New York to consult a well-known oculist. Dr. Knapp found nothing physically amiss and suggested that Louis try "to read less and think more." Given the enormous amount of reading that a law student must cover, and with important examinations on the horizon, Louis realized that he had to get help. Already blessed with a good memory, he drafted his fellow students and friends to read to him, and set up a schedule. On Mondays and Wednesdays he studied Sales with William Richards, and on Friday evening and Saturday afternoon Richards and William Keener read to him on Equity. Thursdays found his closest friend at the school, Samuel D. Warren, doing Trusts, while on Tuesday several of them met to study Property. His friend Philippe Marcou, who graduated from Harvard in 1876 and later became professor of romance languages there, read to him from German authors such as Goethe, Schiller, and Lessing.

Nonetheless, in January 1878, Louis wrote to his friend and former roommate, Walter Douglas, who had left Cambridge after taking his degree in 1877, "My eyes have been troublesome ever since last spring. The oculists agree that they are perfectly healthy, that their present useless condition is merely a freak of the nearsighted eye which will pass over. I am able to use them hardly three or four hours with most careful use but my oculists promise me a brilliant future. Hence I am not doing very much nor very satisfactory work this year." By June there had been some improvement, and he reported to Alfred, "To-day I reached one hour in my reading & shall hence forth be allowed to write one half hour each day instead of so much reading. The last week has made me more confident than ever of the efficacy of the cure and I hope by September to have my eyes strong again." Still, he could only read short letters and asked Alfred to write to him in a large and legible hand.

Brandeis would continue to have troubles with his eyes on and off throughout his life, but never again suffered the problems he endured in law school. As with his physical fatigue, he learned to pace himself, honing his memory, utilizing good lamps, and trying not to put too much strain on his eyes. As for his lament that his eyes prevented him from doing very much or doing it well, Louis exaggerated a bit. He maintained near-perfect grades, attended a variety of lectures, met people, socialized, and in general took advantage of all the resources that Harvard and Boston provided. When he told Alfred that Dr. Derby had recommended against going home to Louisville that summer to avoid the heat that might "debilitate me & thus injuriously affect the eyes," he also added, "Cambridge is beautiful now & I am becoming more & more attached to the place."

JUST AS LOUIS HAD FOUND the law so congenial a topic of study and Langdell's school the ideal place to learn the law, so he found Cambridge and Boston attractive places to live. The harsh New England winters did not faze him, and throughout his life he would revel in going for a horseback ride or a walk on a snowy, frostbitten morning. His intelligence, his handsome if slightly exotic appearance, his outgoing personality, and his friendships with classmates from Brahmin Boston opened a number of doors for him.

"I have been quite a society man for the past week," he told his sister, "out for breakfast, out for lunch, out for dinner, out for teas—almost less 'ins' than 'outs.' " William Richards, a classmate and the scion of an old Massachusetts family, invited Louis to dinner. "Of course I stayed at the Richards over night and lounged about their house the next day until half-past eleven; then made a call at the Cochrans [two sisters from Louisville visiting in Boston] and had hardly spent an hour in my room before it was time to dress for dinner at the Parkers." There he spent "a very enjoyable evening" playing a variety of games, including one called "Chumps," a type of charades, and "Yes & No," a guessing game, which led him to confide that not all Cambridge people are "intellectual giants." But, he hastened to assure his sister, this had been an "unusual rush, and seeing only comparatively little of 'Society,' I generally enjoy myself in it." Very much, however, "would surely bore me."

When his family told him about a friend back home who had become engaged, and subtly tried to find out if he had any romantic attachments, he quickly disabused them of the idea. He found the young women he met in Boston to be fun, witty, and well educated, but he thought that "Cambridge young ladies, who have had the advantages of a European education are not necessarily omniscient." None struck a spark, and on class day in 1878 he confided that he missed his childhood friend Hattie Bishop, "who is more interesting company than most girls here."

Louis was a frequent visitor at the home of Denman Ross, an architect, art collector, and occasional lecturer at Harvard. These evenings proved pleasurable, as he looked at Ross's collection of architectural prints from Europe, recognizing places he had visited only a few years earlier. At the Ross house he also met people interested in art and culture, and Louis attended several sessions of a group reading John Ruskin's *Seven Lamps of Architecture* (1849). But while he appreciated art and found architecture aesthetically interesting, the discussions showed him how little he knew about either subject. After several evenings, he told Amy that he felt he "might possibly understand architecture if I devoted a few centuries to the study of it."

Many of the cultural giants of the mid-nineteenth century still lived in Boston, and Louis met a number of them. He went to a reception at the home of John and Emily Sargent, where he "saw (literally) Longfellow & Holmes and just missed Curtis and Whittier." Professor James Bradley Thayer, whom Brandeis later described as "my best friend among the instructors," invited Brandeis to his home, where he heard Ralph Waldo Emerson lecture. At Thayer's house Louis also met a fellow Kentuckian, Nathaniel Southgate Shaler, the university's preeminent professor of geology, who took a strong interest in a bright student from

Louis and Alfred, ca. 1881

home, and with whom Brandeis would visit often. But Louis also enjoyed the ambience of everyday folk. After visiting friends in Cambridge on the Fourth of July, he went by himself into Boston to hear the concert on the common and watch the fireworks. The immense crowd and their enthusiasm for the spectacle struck him as "truly Italian," and the "naturalness with which they stretched themselves on the grass regardless of dirt & the kicks of passers & stumblers reminded me also of the descendants of the Romans."

Throughout his life, and especially at the time of the confirmation hearings in 1916, he would receive letters from men he had met while in school, each remembering some common experience, and he would respond warmly to them. James Burchard Howard wrote to wish him well in the fight and recalled when he and Louis had paid a social call on Miss Jane Smith. "I want to ask if you remember and can sing—'I am the very model of a modern Major general' as well as you did one morning just after you had heard it for the first time." He also made a lifelong friend of Walter Child, a young man then starting out in the shoe business. Louis told his brother that only a few of his friends excelled in the art of living, and he counted Child in that small group.

It is little wonder that four decades later he declared, "Those years were among the happiest of my life. I worked! For me the world's center was Cambridge."

AFTER FINISHING HIS LAW STUDIES, Brandeis spent a pleasant six weeks in Providence, Rhode Island, where he continued to tutor Professor Bradley's son. He did not make much money, but Bradley's farm was well situated, and he got plenty of outdoor exercise. He rode horseback almost every day, which he termed a "splendid exercise," and while not a first-rate rider, "I think I am improving, at least don't lose my stirrup as much as formerly and sit more firmly on my steed." He also played ball with Bradley's son, and while "my arm is nearly out of joint & hand sore, it's good exercise." Between tutoring, riding, and playing ball, Louis considered his future. He had to begin earning a living, and once he had decided where he would go, he still found himself torn over the decision.

His parents, especially his mother, wanted him to return to Louisville, where he could join his brother-in-law Otto. Louisville had the advantages of family and friends, a consideration he could not ignore. On the other hand, Louisville had still not emerged from the distress of the 1873 Panic. The ambitious Brandeis wanted to make a mark, and he doubted whether Louisville, especially in its current economic straits, would give him the opportunities he sought. He knew his choice would not please his mother, and he wrote her at length explaining his decision. After looking it over, he added, "Since writing this letter I have doubted somewhat whether I was right in the course I pursued in this matter. If after reading the letter you think I was wrong, I most humbly beg your pardon."

Boston also exerted considerable attraction. A major financial hub, it had recovered from the Panic, and both business and the city were rapidly growing. Louis had made a number of contacts while in law school, and he could have either entered an established office or opened a small partnership with one or more classmates. In addition, he would have the option, if he chose, of teaching at Harvard, and at this time Louis still contemplated the possibility of an academic career, a path encouraged by Adolph.

In the end, he decided to go to St. Louis, primarily because of the importuning of his favorite sister, Fannie, and her husband, Charles Nagel, an attorney in that city who would later be secretary of commerce in President William Howard Taft's administration, whom she had married in 1876. Fannie had visited Louis in Cambridge in September 1877 and immediately suggested that he come out to St. Louis. "Charlie and I," she wrote to her brother, "have been putting you into many things (with or without your permission)." The city had grown since the war. The latest census counted 300,000 people, and another 30,000 in the surrounding countryside. The Eads Bridge over the Mississippi had recently been completed, and one could find new construction of commercial and residential buildings all over the city. But the growth had attracted a flock of lawyers. Between 1865 and 1879 the number of attorneys in the city

Charles Nagel, Louis's brother-in-law, 1905

tripled to 428. As Nagel told him, St. Louis was overcrowded with lawyers, but because of the city's growth, opportunities did exist.

Nagel suggested that Louis start practice in the offices that he shared with Henry D'Arcy and intimated that there might be a partnership in the future. As a further inducement, Nagel wrote that his parents, friends of Adolph and Frederika's, intended to build a spacious house opposite Lafayette Park where he and Fannie would live and invited Louis to live there as well. Louis decided that he would go to St. Louis, but he declined Nagel's offer, perhaps for the same reason that he did not want to practice with his other brother-in-law in Louisville. While both Otto Wehle and Charles Nagel could smooth his road, Louis wanted to succeed on his own. Nagel accepted Louis's decision and began contacting other lawyers he knew to see if any of them had room for a new employee. The larger firms reported that they already had enough lawyers and needed no one else.

Then Nagel spoke with James Taussig, another link in Louis's extended family. Taussig enjoyed a sizable practice and occupied one office in a three-room suite at 505 Chestnut Street. His cousin George Washington Taussig occupied a second room but practiced independently. When Louis expressed interest, Taussig offered him a salary of

$50 a month with the right to develop an independent practice and retain his income from that work, as well as to do work for George and keep his fees from that source, too. Brandeis accepted and planned to leave for St. Louis at the end of the summer. But an illness kept him in Cambridge, and then he spent some additional weeks recuperating in Louisville. He arrived in St. Louis in November and took up residence in the big house at 2044 Lafayette Street along with Charles, Fannie, and the elder Nagels. On 24 October 1878, accompanied by James Taussig, who attested to his new associate's legal qualifications and moral uprightness, Louis Brandeis appeared at the circuit courthouse before Judge James J. Lindsey and was formally admitted to practice in the local bar.

The little more than seven months in St. Louis proved disappointing to the young Brandeis in many ways. He had work, as much as if not more than many young lawyers starting out at the time, mainly from James Taussig, and he described it as "interesting & instructive." But there were too many lawyers in the city, and a license to practice law there did little more than bring poor novices like himself into beggary. George Taussig also sent him some work, although in at least one instance the reason seemed clear enough. "Next week I expect to try a case for George which we both fully expect to lose," Louis told his sister Amy. "In fact, our only chance of winning rests in the possibility of total mental aberration of the judge. That, probably, is the reason why George shifts the work & responsibility onto my shoulders." Regarding another case, he told Otto Wehle that it had finally been decided—against them, "as right and justice demands," despite their best efforts to confuse the judge on the two grounds of their appeal.

In February 1879, in response to his brother-in-law's query about his legal work, Louis told him, "Most of it during the last six weeks is represent[ed] by an abstract of Record and Brief in the Case of Buford vs The Keokuk Northern Line Packet Co. et al—The brief is still in press. I must read the second proof today or tomorrow. . . . A great deal of labor, mechanical & other, was bestowed on the job and practically the whole of it is my individual & independent work, but I can't say that I am very well pleased with it." He had also written a brief for George Taussig in a case involving technical points growing out of a partnership dissolution. He had some hope for the client's chances, rising from "the entire want of preparation on the part of the opposing counsel who is here considered an 'Erudite' lawyer. If we win the case I shall have unbounded confidence in 'bad cases' hereafter."

In April he and James Taussig began working on a case of whether a creditor could sue an estate on a contract made by a trustee of that estate. The question, Louis said, "has often attracted my attention," but in his research he had found very little written about it, even in the standard works. He wrote "a little essay" on the subject, thinking perhaps of publishing it later. The conclusion he reached—that the creditor could sue—did not help their client, the trustee, and since it "might be giving weapons into the hands of the other side, I shall, of course, keep it under lock & key." After Brandeis had left St. Louis, Taussig submitted Louis's memorandum to the Missouri Court of Appeals with the aim of presenting "a view on all sides of the question." Brandeis at that point revised it and sent the piece on to Oliver Wendell Holmes Jr., who pronounced it "excellent" and published it in the *American Law Review.*

Still, despite his interest in this subject, and the fact that both Taussigs let him argue cases as well as prepare briefs, Louis found little to challenge him. "Litigation & legal business is very much depressed here," he reported. "Everybody complains & most with reason. Even in our office business is poor. A hash of old cases, dating from better times, alone serves to keep us occupied." His own practice, that is, work that he secured independent of the Taussigs, amounted to very little. "I got $5 (actually $4.75) the other day for legal advice to a woman who stumbled into my office asking for a 'Notar'—'Kennen Sie das Recht?' [Do you know the law?]." The complaint was not confined to St. Louis; Woodrow Wilson, starting out at about the same time in Atlanta, spent much of his day trying to collect on "numberless desperate claims" or merely waiting, while Sam Warren in Boston reported that many of their colleagues from law school could not make a living from their practices, but lived off family incomes.

Even if Brandeis had about the same amount of business as other young lawyers just starting out, he saw no future for himself at the local bar, in part because he heartily disliked living in St. Louis. He found the social life stultifying, especially compared with Cambridge and Boston. A lighthearted letter to his sister about efforts to put him into tableaux, or to have him play Romeo on the stage, could barely conceal his distaste. There were constant dances, "three nights out of six and one of those Sunday," and he became "heartily tired of ballroom conversation." Then, in a revealing aside, he told Amy, "I suppose the Cambridge letters may have greatly conduced to my impatience with ballroom superficiality and vapidity. There are 'lots' of nice people in that Massachusetts town." To add insult to injury, when the weather turned warm, Louis came down with repeated bouts of malaria.

No one could have been more ready to change his life than Louis Brandeis, twenty-two years old, unhappy in his work, disgusted with the society around him, and sick. The letter that came to him from Sam Warren on 5 May 1879 must have seemed like a life preserver thrown to a drowning man.

BRANDEIS AND WARREN MET at Harvard Law School and quickly became friends. The scion of an old New England family with extensive paper mill holdings, Warren had been second to Brandeis in their class standings. Upon graduation he had taken a position in the firm of Shattuck, Holmes & Munroe, but he wanted to be on his own, or better yet, in a partnership with Brandeis. During the year that Louis had weighed his options, Warren had suggested that the two open an office together; he believed that his family's paper mills and social connections would throw off enough business to keep their heads above water. Brandeis had no doubt been tempted, but the pull of family had ultimately won out. "My dear Brandeis," Warren wrote to him, "your determination to settle in St. Louis is of course absurd and indefensible in every point of view, Boston being the only locality in which a civilized man can exist."

Warren still nursed his dream, however, and maintained contact with Brandeis during the time the latter was in St. Louis. In early May 1879, he heard rumors that there might be editorial vacancies on both the *Law Reporter* and the *Law Review,* two national law journals edited out of Boston. If they could secure these part-time positions, they would earn enough to live on while they built up a practice. In their correspondence Sam also unburdened himself to his friend about his hopes. "I don't want to look forward to a life of mere routine practice." He wanted to do something worthwhile, both in his work and in his life, something that would benefit the community. "I think you would have much in common with me in this." Warren put forward two arguments that he knew would appeal to his friend, the attractiveness of Boston as a place to live and work ("life in this old city has a background, a perspective and a dignity which no other city on the continent possesses") and a call to share in his idealistic hope to do public work ("together we could make a more gallant fight").

On 30 May, Louis sat down and wrote a revealing letter to his friend, and it is worth quoting at length, because, more than any other document of this time, it captures his hopes as well as his pragmatism.

My dear Warren:

. . . The proposition to assume the editorship of one of the law-periodicals undoubtedly deserves the greatest consideration.

If, as you suggest, it would give me a living salary—that would enable me to disregard what otherwise would be a great obstacle to my going into partnership with you. On the other hand the editorship must not defeat the main purpose for which it is invoked. It seems to me essential that the position should not monopolize our time and that we should have sufficient time to devote to the law business to enable us to work up a practice. For, although I am very desirous of devoting some of my time to the literary part of the law, I wish to become known as a practicing lawyer. As a means of existing while working up a practice and as a means of becoming favorably known to the legal fraternity and also because it affords an opportunity for law-writing I regard the suggested editorship as highly desirable; but it must be in aid of and incidental to our law partnership, and not in substitution of it. Furthermore, my eyes, though quite strong again, allowing me work practically the whole day and as much as [is] ordinarily required in a lawyer's practice, must still be carefully used and would not, I fear, be able to stand much or regular night-work. Whether a legal editorship is compatible with these considerations I cannot here determine. I conceive that it might be and must beg you carefully to investigate whether it is. . . .

If you are unable to get control of the editorship for us or find it unadvisable to accept the same for the reasons stated, I wish to postpone for a little while my final answer as to starting a firm together. I wish to wait particularly for your letter giving the results of our examination of the prospects of a young law firm and more particularly your own prospects of securing business through your social and financial position.

Despite his desire to leave St. Louis, Brandeis would not act impulsively; he needed more facts. He had no problem that initially business would come because of Sam's social connections; he had enough self-confidence to believe that the two of them would soon attract clients because of their ability. But how much time would the editorship require? His eyes had certainly improved, but would they be able to stand the strain of poring over legal documents in their work and the minutiae of editorial work? Sam had been honest about the conditions facing young lawyers in Boston, but also reported that Oliver Wendell

Holmes told him that there had not been such a dearth of first-rate ability at the Boston bar in years and that he believed men of talent and energy could succeed. It would be difficult, Sam said, and even if they could pay their own way the first year, it would take time to build up a lucrative practice.

Soon afterward, Warren and Brandeis learned that the editorships would not materialize, but another option opened that had even greater appeal to Louis, a clerkship with the chief justice of Massachusetts, Horace Gray. The pay would be $500 a year for primarily part-time work, more than enough to augment even a small income from the practice. Louis sent word of the offer to his former teachers at the law school; Charles Bradley, James Thayer, and Dean Langdell all urged him to take the position, assuring him the experience would prove a valuable stepping-stone. The work he would do with Gray would be challenging, and at the same time he would have the opportunity to learn from a man whom many considered one of the finest legal minds of the time.

He made his decision and left for Boston toward the end of June, in such a hurry that he had to ask his brother-in-law to settle some accounts and to forward books and legal papers to him in Boston. The details of his new life remained somewhat hazy to him, even after arriving back in Massachusetts. To his friend Walter Douglas he wrote that he would "probably go in with Warren upon my admission to the bar. The nature of our connection is undecided. It will probably be a partnership in effect & possibly in name." He would miss some of the friends in St. Louis, but "my last year was not a contented one." He had longed for something that he had had before, and hoped that he would reclaim in Boston. "The risks I recognize as very great—but happiness & contentment are rare birds worth chasing."

Charles Nagel opposed the move, primarily because he knew that Fannie would miss her brother greatly. But on 5 July he wrote a gracious letter to Louis, telling him that he had made the right decision. In fact, from the beginning, Nagel said, "I have been divided with myself; my reason spoke for Boston, my heart was for St. Louis." But Nagel did not like the idea of a partnership with Warren, not because of Sam, whom he probably did not know, but because he feared that partnerships undertaken by men newly become lawyers had little chance of lasting. There would be discrepancies in talent, in character, and in income, all leading to tensions and jealousies. But he wished Louis well. "If Boston is a success," he conceded, "nothing in St. Louis can compare with it."

James Taussig also took Louis's departure in stride. Although he had given Louis some interesting work to do, he probably realized that the young man would not stay long. He wished Louis well and then noted, "I may say now that a longer stay would have resulted in a closer business connection between us." The mention of a future partnership surprised Louis, but as he told Nagel, "Queerly enough [it] made me feel rather good than blue. . . . The letter was surely fortifying and gave me courage & hope that I might rise here as well." Taussig also wrote a letter of commendation to Chief Justice Gray, attesting to Louis's character and work habits.

Although eager to return to Boston, Louis realized that not all of his time in St. Louis had been unhappy. He enjoyed being with his sister and her family, had been treated well by his employer, and had made some friends. Still, as he told Charles Nagel, "I do not repent of my decision although I feel how much I have lost in losing you all." In fact, had Nagel sent a telegram before Louis had left, he might well have changed his mind. On the other hand, he had great hopes for his new life, and while he would miss his family, "I find much comfort & consolation in the feeling that whatever I have achieved, or may achieve here is my own—pure and simple—unassisted by the fortuitous circumstances of family influence or social position." He wrote that knowing full well that Sam Warren's family and social position could be the fulcrum by which the two men would initially achieve success. But he also recognized that while the Warren name might initially lure in clients, how well the two lawyers served them would determine whether they came back. Somehow, Brandeis did not think that the same situation would govern in St. Louis.

The most difficult letter was to his mother. Frederika had written that if he could not be happy in St. Louis, then why had he not come home to Louisville? When he received her letter, he admitted, "It seems to me as if I were a fool to have settled here so far away, instead of staying with you and enjoying you and all your love." But he could also answer her question: "There is also ambition to be satisfied." Man is a strange animal, he mused. "He does not enjoy what he has—and he always wants what he does not yet have." Perhaps ambition was no more than a delusion, but it was one for which "one is always ready to offer a sacrifice."

CHAPTER THREE

WARREN & BRANDEIS

S hortly after arriving in Boston, Louis sat down and wrote a long letter to his brother-in-law Charles Nagel in which he talked about his new life, his work with Chief Justice Horace Gray, and his and Warren's prospects. Although he missed his friends and family in St. Louis, "I do not repent my decision. . . . I have much to hope for here." A few days later he wrote to his mother and reiterated his belief that he had made the right decision. The tensions of separation from family, knowledge that they disapproved of his move to Boston, and embarking on a new career with no resources in hand or any assurances of success worried him. "Surely I am undergoing the crucial test," he told Alfred, "and I hope I will stand it."

Brandeis, of course, did more than stand it. Within a relatively short period of time he could confidently report that the law partnership would be a success. He practiced in Boston for more than thirty-seven years, becoming one of the city's most successful attorneys. During this time the practice of law underwent a major transformation, due to the great industrial changes that occurred in the United States in the latter part of the nineteenth century, a revolution that affected all aspects of American life. Christopher Langdell's effort to transform the education of lawyers marked an early response to these forces; Louis Brandeis and his peers oversaw the transformation of the legal profession itself.

LOUIS ARRIVED IN BOSTON at the beginning of July 1879, and almost immediately began his work as secretary to Horace Gray, chief justice of the Massachusetts Supreme Judicial Court, the state's highest tribunal. In essence, he fulfilled the functions now assigned to law clerks, and his experience with Gray informed how Brandeis would work with his own clerks years later in Washington. Gray had been appointed to the Massachusetts court in 1864, after serving as its reporter for ten years, and in 1873 became chief justice. His opinions there, and on the U.S. Supreme Court, to which he would be named in 1881, evidenced clear thinking and painstaking attention to detail. Gray had something of a reputation for arrogance and impatience, and Louis had been a bit hesitant about how this might affect their working relationship. As it turned out, those aspects of his personality appeared only on the bench; in person, "he is the most affable of men, patiently listening to suggestions and objections & even contradiction."

The Massachusetts court in those days heard a number of cases in the spring term. Afterward the judges met in conference and decided the outcome, and then Gray would assign decisions to the judges, who would in turn write their opinions over the summer recess. Brandeis met with Gray each morning. They would take out a particular case, go over the record and briefs, and discuss various authorities, and, as Louis noted, Gray welcomed argument and discussion on the major points. After they sketched the outlines of the opinion, Gray would scribble a rough draft and then dictate it to his clerk for transcription in a clean hand.

Brandeis treasured these mornings, because for the first time since law school he had an opportunity to engage in serious debate about legal issues. Gray treated him, he reported, as "a person of co-ordinate position. He asks me what I think of his line of argument and I answer candidly. If I think other reasons better, I give them; if I think his language obscure, I tell him so; if I have any doubts I express them and he is very fair in acknowledging a correct suggestion or disabusing one of an erroneous idea. In these discussions & investigations I shall learn very much."

Louis did indeed learn, more, perhaps, than he realized at the time. Gray, a craftsman on the bench, reinforced in Louis the necessity of taking pains and carefully marshaling one's arguments. Although Gray listened respectfully to his young clerk's views and used them to hone his own arguments, no question existed as to where the authority resided. Years later, Mr. Justice Brandeis would encourage his own bright young men from Harvard to question him and to raise points for his consideration, but after they had done so, the final decision lay in his hands.

He also saw a fine jurist weigh matters carefully, acknowledging that while in the end one side or the other would win, merit usually existed in both parties. Brandeis recognized that in his practice he would serve the interests of his clients, but he intuitively understood that in some instances his clients might be in the wrong, and if so, it would be better for them if they acknowledged this and chose a strategy that would be in both their and the other party's better interests. Not only did this concept appeal to Brandeis's idealistic streak, but in grasping this idea, Brandeis and others would change the role of lawyer from simple advocate to counsel. Ironically, at the time of his nomination to the Supreme Court, some critics charged Brandeis with lacking a judicial temperament. In fact, Brandeis as lawyer exercised a judicial temperament throughout his career at the bar.

The work with Gray gave Louis a small income, but enough so that he could pay his own way. Sam Warren had offered to underwrite the office expenses the first year, and invited Louis to live in the Warren house on Mount Vernon Street to save rent. Brandeis stayed with the Warrens a few days upon his arrival in Boston, but then found rooms of his own with meals at Mrs. Smith's boardinghouse at 21 Joy Street, where he described himself as "very pleasantly fixed." He would, however, spend a great deal of time at the Warrens', where, according to Martin Green, Louis became "like another son to the family." Brandeis found a kindred spirit in the older Mr. Warren's belief in empirical fact, analytical clarity, and numbers. He got along well with Sam's siblings, became legal adviser to Cornelia Warren and Fiske Warren in their various undertakings, and wrote a will for Susan Warren, Sam's mother.

The connection with Warren promised well, he told his family. "There are many fine points about the man both in mind & character and it looks to me as if he would be a success. His 'push' is great—the same bulldog perseverance & obstinacy which brought me here will, I think, pave a way which he seems determined to make." The two took an office on the third floor of 60 Devonshire Street for $200 a year ("very cheap everybody says") and decided to indulge in one extravagance, a messenger boy for $3 a week. They delayed, however, deciding on just what form their affiliation would take—a simple sharing of office space or an actual partnership. Sam had always wanted the latter, but Louis wanted to hold off that decision for a little bit. After all, he would not even be able to practice law until admitted to the bar. Although Massachusetts ordinarily accepted lawyers from other states without an examination, that custom required at least a few years of actual experience, which Brandeis clearly lacked. As it turned out, Louis did not have to wait until the scheduled fall examination. Chief Justice Gray intervened, and with his sponsorship Louis was admitted to the bar on 29 July "without an examination and contrary to all principles and precedent."

Upon his admittance, he and Sam decided to form a partnership in name as well as in effect. "What I have seen of him since I am here has raised my opinion in every respect and I concluded that a closer union of our interests was desirable." Louis had apparently harbored some worries because, as he told Alfred, Sam's "seeming haughtiness [had] made him enemies at Cambridge." But Warren had recognized this as a problem and had laid aside this demeanor, adopting one more suited to impressing clients with confidence in his ability. According to custom, the initial name in a firm went to the partner first admitted

Chief Judge Horace Gray of the Massachusetts Supreme Judicial Court

to the bar. Louis, of course, had been admitted in Missouri, but Sam had earlier been admitted in Massachusetts, where they would practice. "I don't give a rap," Sam wrote to Louis about the name, "but I think it worthwhile to observe proper etiquette," and he left the matter to Louis. The firm would be known as Warren & Brandeis until 1897, although Sam left in 1888 to take over the family paper business upon the death of his father.

In the meantime, as Sam and Louis prepared to settle into their new venture, they still had time to socialize and enjoy the summer. The Warrens had a second home in Beverly, where Louis, along with various members of the Warren family, swam, rowed, sailed, and played tennis. He also renewed friendships with men he had known at Harvard and, thanks to Warren, met Oliver Wendell Holmes Jr., in whose firm Sam had worked. On the evening of Louis's admission to the bar, he, Sam, and Holmes gathered in Sam's room, where they drank a mixture of champagne and beer, "telling jokes & talking Summum bonum," or, rather, Holmes and Warren had talked, while Louis stretched out on a lounge. Six months later Louis was still enjoying the social life in Boston. He wrote to his sister Amy that he had been out to dinner several evenings in a row, including one reception at a Mrs. Macfarlane's

Sam Warren

where the conversation had been entirely in German. The good lady wanted him to play the lead in a German play she planned for her next entertainment, but Louis managed to nix the idea. "Tonight I take dinner with Marcou and hurry to a whist party at the Parker House. Have no more idea of whist than a Bauer of Gurkensalat, but that makes no difference. Played one game this week at the Fitch's and won." And a few days earlier he had gone to the Holmes residence, where his new friend read him the draft of an article he had written on trespass and negligence.

SAM AND LOUIS EXPECTED S. D. Warren & Company to be their initial client, but the ledger notes for their first case, in which the paper company sued a Martha E. Berry, show that the defendant could not be found. Despite this "failure," the Warren company would remain with Warren & Brandeis, and its successor firm, for generations. Working with the Warren company proved an important part of Louis Brandeis's education in business. While he was familiar with his father's work, he had viewed it as a boy and had not been expected to master details of finance, payroll, taxes, wholesale and retail prices, or the myriad other aspects of doing business. The Warren mills, then producing about eighteen tons of paper per day, dwarfed Brandeis & Crawford not only in size but in the complexity of its operations. Louis took seriously the idea that if he were to provide good legal advice to a corporate client, he had to know the business, and he set about doing so, going to the factories, meeting with supervisors and office staff, and asking questions. Many years later he told John Warren that he deemed his work with the company "a most important part of my education in business, and you among my tutors."

The firm soon acquired clients in New York and Rhode Island through the connections Sam and Louis had made at Harvard. Walter

Carter, a New York attorney (and in later years the father-in-law of Charles Evans Hughes), made it a point of looking out for bright Harvard Law graduates and then steering business their way. Charles Bradley, their professor at Harvard Law and former chief justice of Rhode Island, had important clients in that state, and called Brandeis in to argue a case before the Rhode Island Supreme Court. While in Providence, Brandeis stayed at Judge Bradley's house, and reported to his sister, "People have said so many kind things about my briefs and arguments that I hope something more substantial than glory may come out of it." Aside from a hefty fee, Brandeis's performance did indeed win him friends and eventual clients among Rhode Island lawyers and businessmen. The two young lawyers also began acquiring a reputation for legal acumen. Horace Gray said that he considered Brandeis "the most ingenious and most original lawyer I have ever met, and he and his partner are among the most promising law firms we have got."

A few years later Marsden Perry, a businessman in Providence, sent his lawyer, Arthur Lisle, to Boston to find the best lawyer in that city to handle a complicated matter for him. Lisle first went to see a man he knew at the General Electric Company, who promised to find out; the man contacted Lisle a few hours later and told him that the lawyer he wanted was Louis Brandeis. In the meantime, Lisle had gone over to the Westinghouse Company and talked with its chief counsel, who promptly advised him to see Brandeis. Being a thorough man, Lisle also visited two banks where his employer did business, and in each of them received the identical response—the best lawyer in Boston was Louis Brandeis. Another businessman found Brandeis in a similar manner. A Boston banker referred to Brandeis as a lawyer of unusual ability and character. "There is a man who will give you a dollar's worth for every dollar paid. He'll give you straight advice." Moreover, he's a fighter, "and he generally wins."

In the spring of 1880, Louis wrote to his brother, "Our [clients] are treating us pretty well now. We have little new business to speak of, but the cases begun before the vacation are coming to a head now and we look forward to a busy half year. Much of my time has been devoted to the Providence case." Although in the initial decision Brandeis's clients had lost, as most people assumed they would, on rehearing Louis managed to get the court to reduce the judgment against his clients by a significant amount. The firm picked up another paper manufacturer, Train, Hosford & Company, whose affairs generated a great deal of legal work, including four suits then pending in New Hampshire. In addition, William Henry Hill, an investment banker, had bought a controlling interest in the Sanford Steamship Company and asked Warren to serve as clerk of the company, which meant that Warren & Brandeis handled the company's legal business.

All told, the firm of Warren & Brandeis seems to have been a success from the start. On 2 January 1881, in sending New Year's greetings to his sister, Louis jokingly mourned, "Yesterday was a Sad Day. We buried irretrievably a half dozen of the most beautiful and lucrative lawsuits—and all for the love of our clients. Yes we settled up the complicated New Hampshire transactions by an agreement wonderfully favorable to our clients. From love of them we did it.—But I fear 'The expedition of my violent love, outran the pauser reason,' no more trips to New Hampshire—no nothing. The only consolation is that we get our opponent for a client." In their first year of business, the firm took in a little over $3,400, but of that $435 came from work for Justice Gray. For their second year Warren & Brandeis had gross earnings of $3,600, with net profits of $3,000, or nearly $59,000 in current buying power. Little wonder that Warren could confidently assert that "the success of W&B is assured."

(During this period the two young lawyers could not afford to turn away clients, and one day a woman came in with her young son complaining of a problem she was having with the local government where she lived, and asked Brandeis if he could help. It was a simple problem that Brandeis quickly resolved. A few days later the woman and her son returned. She thanked him for his service and asked what she owed him. Brandeis realized the woman did not have a great deal of money, but her pride demanded that she pay something. "Do you think a dollar would be fair?" he asked. She said that would be very fair, and gave him a dollar, which Brandeis—according to the son's later recollection—turned around and gave to him and told him to go buy candy.)

Although the firm did well with the paper companies and other large clients, it also sought business from smaller firms and individuals, many of whom were Jewish. While he did not practice his religion as did his uncle Dembitz, Brandeis never denied his origins; nor did he broadcast them. From the time he set up practice in Boston, he paid membership into the United Hebrew Benevolent Association, and he was a charter subscriber to the founding of the Federation of Jewish Charities in 1895. Louis also renewed his friendship with Jacob Hecht, a prosperous merchant whom he had met during his law school days.

The Hechts held open house on weekends, inviting an interesting mix of young artists, intellectuals, and professionals, and Louis was a regular visitor. In February 1880, Hecht retained him to sue a member of the United Hebrew Benevolent Association for back payment of annual dues, a matter that eventually led Brandeis to argue his first case before the Massachusetts Supreme Judicial Court. Brandeis acted for a number of Jewish clients and on behalf of local Jewish institutions, but contrary to one historian's arguments Jews never became the mainstay of his law practice, nor were they a majority of its clients.

While Sam worked the Brahmin side of town, Louis sought business in the German-American and Jewish communities. "I must soon go to the Turnverein, and try to be captivating," he wrote to his sister, "and get some clients." Prior to Warren & Brandeis, one man, Godfrey Morse, had handled many of the accounts of German-American Jews, but the growing prosperity of Boston's middle-class Jewish community generated far more business than a single lawyer could conduct. Now some of that business, thanks to Hecht, began to flow to 60 Devonshire Street. Jacob Hecht asked Louis to draw up his will, and at his death in 1903 the Brandeis firm acted as executor of his estate. Other prominent Boston Jewish families such as the Liebmanns, the Franks, and the Weils, along with their extensive familial contacts, joined the roster of clients. William Filene's Sons Company, later to be the Filene's department store, became clients, and the two brothers, Edward and Lincoln, would be longtime allies of Brandeis's in his reform work. That Brandeis accepted Jewish clients is not surprising, nor that, thanks to Jacob Hecht, he utilized his contacts among Boston's Jewish leaders to gain additional business. But despite his substantial income over the years, his contributions to Boston Jewish charities remained minimal, he preferred that his name not be published in the list of contributors, and he took neither an important membership role nor any leadership position in Jewish affairs until he joined the Zionist movement more than three decades later.

The historian Allon Gal claims that Brandeis suffered anti-Semitism in Boston almost from the time he set up practice there and that this experience later led him into Zionism; he bases this assumption on what Gal sees as the extensive number of Jewish clients on the firm's client list. How and why Louis Brandeis came to Zionism is the subject of another chapter, but it is far from clear that Jewish clients are evidence of anti-Semitism or that Brandeis saw himself as a victim of such prejudice, certainly not in these early years of practice.

That anti-Semitism existed in Boston is beyond doubt. Massachusetts in general and Boston in particular remained one of the most ethnically and religiously homogeneous states in the Union until the middle of the nineteenth century, when Irish immigrants began to arrive and immediately ran into a stone wall of prejudice. Bias against Jews seems to have been more abstract than particular, so that people like Brandeis, Rabbi Solomon Schindler, and his successor at Temple Israel, Charles Fleischer, moved easily among the Brahmin elite, even while the successors of the Puritans did their best to cut off immigration of Jews, Catholics, and other aliens into the United States.

There would certainly be bias against Brandeis later, when, in his reforming zeal, he attacked some of the icons of the Boston business and financial community. In these years, however, his correspondence reveals no signs of anti-Semitism, although starting around 1910 he would be quite candid in his letters to Alfred about clubs closed to Jews. Instead, his letters to his family about his social life are full of visits to different homes, meeting a variety of people, many of them members of the Brahmin elite, and few, if any, appear to have been Jewish. Much of this entrée may be credited to his being Sam Warren's partner, and some historians believe that Brandeis would have been totally excluded by the city's social elite otherwise, but he had not been excluded from gentile homes while at Harvard, and Sam did not accompany him on all his social outings.

IN HIS LETTER to Alfred detailing the firm's success in its second year, Louis warned that he did not expect the firm to enjoy as much income in its third year. "If I were Sc'ty of Treasury making out estimates I should prepare the country for a strong deficit in the budget." In fact, he really did not expect to make a great deal of money for the next fifteen years or so, "but I do expect to have a high old time for the twenty-five following." Louis appears to have been joking because only a short while later he and Sam hired their first associate, D. Blakely Hoar, who immediately took over nearly all of the firm's real estate business. Over the years, as the volume of business grew (by the time of Brandeis's nomination to the Supreme Court in January 1916, the firm's running log of cases had reached over 22,000), the office took in additional men. Charles F. Chamberlayne came to the firm as a cum laude graduate of Harvard Law School in 1884, and stayed for five years. William Harrison Dunbar, the son of the distinguished Harvard economics professor, graduated from Harvard Law in 1886 and clerked for one year for Horace Gray, by then a member of the U.S. Supreme Court, before entering the office where he would ultimately become a partner. George Read Nutter, hired in 1889, quickly proved so capable that Brandeis began referring to him as "my first lieutenant."

Louis and Sam never had a formal partnership agreement, and the firm's records indicate that at the end of the fiscal year, after deducting expenses, they divided the profits equally. In May 1888, Sam's father died, and the younger Warren left the practice to take over the family's paper interests. Apparently, Sam did not foresee this to be a permanent move, and intended at some point to return to law practice. As a result, the firm remained Warren & Brandeis, with Sam's name appearing on the letterhead, until 1897, although for all practical purposes Louis Brandeis was sole proprietor. In 1889, in order to be closer to his friend, Brandeis moved his office to 220 Devonshire Street, the same building that housed the corporate offices of S. D. Warren & Company. Although Sam never practiced law there, the office occupied by William Dunbar was known as "Mr. Warren's room."

By 1896 it was obvious that the obligations of running the family paper business would never allow Sam Warren to return to practice. In that year Dunbar, Nutter, and the other juniors made it clear that the

Louis Brandeis on horseback in Dedham, ca. 1885

office needed to be reorganized. While they had no trouble recognizing Brandeis as not only the titular but also the effective head of the practice, they chafed at what they saw as little better than hired-hand status. No matter how well they performed their work, they received little personal recognition. Dunbar, a sensitive man due, perhaps, to his partial deafness, wrote to Brandeis, "I suppose that every professional man of ordinary ambition hopes to make for himself some reputation; to have his work, if in any degree successful, count not only as a source of income but as giving his name some individual value. This result it seems to me he can reach only by having his name known and by working as a principal. Our present arrangement I think does not permit of this. My work yields to me almost literally no return except a pecuniary compensation." The problem, Dunbar went on, seems "to me the necessary consequence of an organization like ours in which there is not in fact any real partnership between the different persons associated together." He spoke, he added, not only for himself but also for George Nutter and Ezra Thayer, who had joined the firm in 1892 and would later be dean of Harvard Law School.

Brandeis initially did not respond well to Dunbar's letter, probably because he did not want to alter what was for him an ideal situation. Brandeis greatly enjoyed a particular type of case the first time he dealt with it; after that he was more than happy to delegate work to others, claiming that they needed the experience for their own professional growth. By having junior associates, Brandeis could assign to them much of the dull but necessary bread-and-butter business of any law firm, dealing himself with more interesting matters. But he recognized the justice of Dunbar's complaints, and in 1897 changed the firm's name to Brandeis, Dunbar & Nutter, giving to them the real partnership they sought.

No formal partnership agreement ever existed. Brandeis retained nearly two-thirds of the profits at this point, a figure that would diminish somewhat over the years as new partners were added and older ones received larger shares. Nonetheless, to use the modern parlance, Brandeis was the firm's "rainmaker." Older clients stayed with the firm and new ones came to it because of his reputation. While more and more of the work would be done by his partners as Brandeis took on reform efforts, he still oversaw the business and would step in when necessary. No longer did he have to go searching for new clients; they flooded through the doors. Years later he recalled that one day Samuel Clemens (Mark Twain), dressed in a shabby overcoat, showed up at his office and wanted to retain Brandeis on his behalf in a libel suit. Louis listened patiently, but advised the great author not to sue.

Once Brandeis reorganized the office, he took steps to ensure that such dissatisfaction never again occurred. He devised a personal formula that took into account each man's work and rewarded each of them generously, not only through salary, but through recognition, advancement into partnership, and greater individual authority. The rewards went not only to the lawyers but also to the growing support staff in the office. He hired E. Louise Malloch, then a girl in her teens, as a bookkeeper in 1895, and within two years had assigned her responsibility involving his personal investments. When he went on the Court in 1916, Miss Malloch took over full responsibility for his financial affairs. Alice Harriet Grady joined the firm as a secretary straight out of a business school, and she soon proved invaluable. No one in the office could type or take dictation as fast as she did, and Brandeis often used her skills as a court reporter. She bought a typewriter at her own expense and worked at nights during a trial so that Brandeis could have a record of the previous day in his hands when court resumed the next morning. She soon became Brandeis's personal secretary, and over the years he gave her increasing responsibility; according to one report, she was the highest-paid secretary in Boston. Brandeis believed so strongly that the two women contributed a great deal to the firm's success that they each received a small percentage of the profits. After her boss left the practice, Miss Grady went to work for the state bureau on savings bank insurance and rose to become deputy commissioner.

WARREN & BRANDEIS made it a rule that it would not hire anyone who had not graduated from law school (preferring men from Harvard) and was the first firm in Boston to adopt that rule. By the time Brandeis went on the Court in 1916, the firm had six partners and seven junior associates. Once in the office, the new men took part in the full spectrum of the firm's business. Adolf A. Berle Jr. recalled that despite his being junior, he had exposure to a wide range of issues and even helped draft a brief to the Massachusetts high court. The bulk of the work, as he recalled, involved numerous small matters of commercial law. Aside from Brandeis, no one in the office seems to have had any political interests. Although a number of them were involved in various civic enterprises, none of Brandeis's associates ever took on the type of reform work he did.

Brandeis in the firm's early years handled much of the trial work as well as appeals to higher courts. "I have spent much time of late before juries," he told his sister, "and am becoming quite enamored of the Common Sense of the people." He argued, successfully, his first case before the U.S. Supreme Court on 6 and 7 November 1889, and would, over the years, return to that forum a number of times. After the reorganization, however, he began to assign more court work to others, mentoring them until he believed them ready for the task. Joseph B. Eastman had not even been admitted to the bar when, working under Brandeis's supervision, he wrote the bulk of the brief submitted to the Interstate Commerce Commission in the 1913 New Haven case. When Edward McClennen joined the firm in 1895, Brandeis recognized in him the potential for a talented litigator. Brandeis assigned McClennen the Old Dominion Copper Company case in 1905, one of the largest in the firm's history, with millions of dollars in dispute. McClennen wrote the briefs, argued the case in trial court, and then took the appeal to U.S. Supreme Court. In 1914, as Brandeis attempted to juggle a half-dozen reform projects, relief arrived when McClennen came down to Washington and took over a major case involving the government-ordered dissolution of a merger between two western railroads. As Brandeis told his wife, it "will be a very interesting subject of study & he is sure to do himself credit." Brandeis later said that Ned McClennen was the best lawyer he ever knew.

By 1904 the firm had outgrown the space it had at 220 Devonshire and moved into new quarters on the top, or eleventh, floor of the Compton Building at 161 Devonshire Street. The lease had been secured during the building's construction, and as a result the floor plan differed markedly from most commercial space at the time. Each partner, as well as his secretary, had a private office, with a large area set aside for a library, along with several conference rooms. While having private offices constituted a luxury, the partners recalled the furnishings and the space as "austere." The firm stayed in those offices until 1939.

IN ORDER TO UNDERSTAND how Warren and Brandeis and their associates practiced law, one must take cognizance of the enormous changes then taking place in the United States. People living at the end of the twentieth and beginning of the twenty-first centuries can truthfully claim they are living in the midst of a major economic transformation. Globalization has altered the marketplace, and outsourcing has greatly impacted the domestic workforce. The introduction of computers both in business and in the home, and the attendant ubiquity of cell phones and of e-mail, have changed the way we communicate, do business, and even run political campaigns. With this technological revolution have come economic, political, social, and cultural dislocations that will affect how we live for decades.

The Industrial Revolution of the late nineteenth century had an even greater impact. The United States had been primarily an agrarian nation prior to the Civil War; after 1866 not only did it industrialize rapidly, but people left farming communities to move into cities, so that by 1924 more people lived in urban than in rural areas. The processes of industrialization had, of course, begun well before Fort Sumter, but they burst into full bloom after Appomattox. The gross national product in these years increased twelvefold, accompanied by the seemingly overnight creation of new industries in steel, oil, and minerals production. The value of exports from American mills and factories climbed from $434 million in 1866 to $1.5 billion in 1900, while imports more than doubled. To staff these new factories and mines, millions of immigrants came seeking better lives. Between 1815 and 1860, five million people had migrated to the United States, mostly from England, Ireland, and to a lesser extent the German states; between 1865 and 1914, twenty-five million arrived, mostly from eastern and southern Europe. The steel baron Andrew Carnegie exulted: "The old nations of the earth creep on at a snail's pace, the Republic thunders past with the rush of an express."

These cataclysmic economic changes affected every aspect of American society and would lead to the progressive movement in which Louis Brandeis played such an important role. But even earlier, they affected the American bar and how lawyers served their clients. First, the lawyer's role shifted from advocate to counsel. Advocacy did not disappear, but lawyers tried to steer their clients along paths that would avoid litigation. Second, the general practitioner, operating out of a one- or two-man office, gave way to the modern large law firm, marked by specialization and commercialization. In these two areas Brandeis took an active part, but he avoided other traits that marked so many successful lawyers of the late nineteenth century—a narrow and limited view of the legal profession and a conservatism that attempted to freeze the status quo and ignored the moral problems of industrial change.

Prior to the Civil War, the legal profession reflected the social fabric of the country. Law offices had been small, staffed by an attorney and a clerk or two, or in some instances by two or three lawyers who shared

office space and books. They dealt with fairly simple problems and conflicting interpretations of law. Lawyers did not ignore facts, but the
facts had been simpler and more easily understandable; in most legal
disputes the intelligent layperson could understand the facts, and even
the law, with as much clarity as the lawyer. Men came to lawyers, essentially, when all other recourse had failed and they stood ready to fight in
court. The attorney's duty had been to argue on his client's behalf and
make the strongest legal presentation possible. Given this situation,
the best lawyers had been the generalists; in fact, there had been few
specialists of any kind. A lawyer who hoped to earn his living in an
expanding frontier society had to know property as well as water law,
civil as well as criminal procedure.

All this began to change after the war. As society and industry grew
more complex, one-to-one relationships gave way to multilateral
undertakings; large, complex business dealings overwhelmed the older,
simpler transactions. Now it would be too expensive to go wrong, too
costly to call in a lawyer at the last minute, too damaging in both time
and money to litigate even if, in the end, one came out victorious. Businessmen, instead of charging ahead and then calling in lawyers if they
ran into trouble, began summoning their attorneys at the beginning, to
find out what the law said they could or could not do, how they could
avoid going to court. "A lawyer's chief business," said Elihu Root, a
prominent New York attorney, "is to keep his clients out of litigation."

This shift from advocate to counsel, and the adjustment to the new
requirements of practicing law, proved difficult for many.* It had been
one thing to enter a case when all of the facts had been available and
then sort out those that would be most helpful in arguing the client's
case; it was something entirely different to guess what the future would
be. New modes of business operation required a lawyer to pay close
attention to economic trends, and to evaluate conditions in which he
had little expertise. The creation of trusts and estates and corporate
organizations called for planning and analysis of a large number of variables that included matters of economics, sociology, psychology, labor,
and business, as well as law. The lawyer of the future, Holmes predicted
in 1897, would be not the law-book scholar but "the man of statistics
and the master of economics."

*Sometimes clients also had difficulty adjusting to the new strategy. One of Brandeis's long-
time clients as well as friends, Edward Filene, later wrote to him: "I recall especially of how
mystified I was at first at a great lawyer's efforts to keep his clients out of court. . . . I could not
comprehend the strategy. But you taught me the wisdom of conciliation."

The old-style generalist normally handled almost every type of case, but the new era saw the emergence of the specialist, first in commercial law as a whole and then in the various aspects of it. Soon men devoted their entire careers to real estate or trusts or receiverships or stock issues. Since big business needed all of these skills, a law firm with large industrial clients needed to have them all under one roof. Instead of small one-person offices, the new law firm would have to be big (although not even the largest firms at the end of the nineteenth century compare with modern firms that have hundreds of partners and thousands of associates and support staff in offices around the globe). In the 1890s, Paul D. Cravath in New York began hiring young lawyers who had law degrees—preferably with high marks—from elite schools. He paid them a salary as "associates," and after a five-year probationary period the brightest became partners, while the rest moved on. By the 1920s the Cravath system had become entrenched throughout the country.

While this division of labor may have provided better legal advice on particular problems, it had limitations as well. Very few lawyers could see beyond their own specialty or subspecialty to understand the larger problem. Earlier generations of lawyers had been respected as men of affairs; no one expected specialists to be anything but narrow. Businessmen might seek their skills for specific problems, but not their advice on questions of policy. Soon industrial leaders stopped asking, "What should I do?" with its moral implications, and started demanding, "Tell me the way I can get this done!" Lawyers thus abdicated their responsibility as moral instructors and confined their activity to devising the best way for corporate clients to achieve certain ends, some of them of dubious legality. "Instead of being advisers, lawyers were often collaborators in their clients' short-sightedness," Felix Frankfurter charged. "The lawyers did their clients' bidding instead of illuminating their minds to understand something about the forces with which they were dealing." The independent practitioner, admired for his good counsel, gave way to the hired hand working in a law factory. "The practice of law," claimed one critic, "has been commercialized," while another accused lawyers of having motives "as sordid and activities as mercenary as can be found in any other occupation." Brandeis's partner George Nutter clearly shared this view. Lawyers are no longer persons whose advice is followed, he declared, but people "who are hired to carry through what their employers want to have done. One purchases legal brains now in the same way as he purchases industrial labor or anything else." The close attachment of lawyers to business interests diminished their status as independent professionals and the respect from the public they had previously enjoyed.

THE BUSINESS CLIENTS who came to see Warren & Brandeis had as much need for advice and for access to specialized legal knowledge as did the large industries who patronized the big New York firms. As the firm developed and took in other lawyers, Brandeis encouraged them to develop specialties. "The organization of large offices is becoming more and more a business," he told William Dunbar, and also a professional necessity. In the new office each man must find his proper place and make that field his own. He thus serves not only the firm's clients but its members, who will look to him for guidance when dealing with matters touching on his expertise; he in turn will look to his colleagues when needing information on matters beyond his special knowledge. Whether or not one liked this type of organization, Brandeis noted, it had proved "the most effective means of doing the law work of this country," as demonstrated by the success of the great New York firms.

At the same time, Brandeis did not want an office of narrow-minded specialists, and he urged young Dunbar to seek broader intellectual horizons. "Cultivate the society of men—particularly men of affairs." This knowledge, as well as that of the law, is essential; clients would not appreciate his legal advice unless they also believed he understood their businesses. "Knowledge of the decided cases and the rules of logic cannot alone make a great lawyer. He must know, must feel 'in his bones' the facts to which they apply. . . . The man who does not know intimately human affairs is apt to make of the law a bed of Procrustes."

Brandeis did not spout generalities in his advice to his younger associate, but spoke from his own experience and belief. The modern law firm had to be well organized, and it had to have recognizable centers of expertise. But he also viewed with horror a large office that had nothing but specialists, men who were so absorbed in their narrow fields that they could not fill the new role of lawyer as counsel. In order to carry out that role, a lawyer had to be a man of experience, one who could take the information provided by the client and judge it not by some abstract formula but by the yardstick of experience. When a young man wrote to Brandeis declaring he wanted to be a lawyer and felt he was wasting his time in business, Brandeis sternly admonished him that a lawyer needs "knowledge, not only of law, but of affairs, and above all, of men and of human nature. The time you spend in business may ultimately prove to be the most profitable preparation." And he practiced what he preached.

From the time he had been in law school, Louis had understood the importance of facts, and that in dealing with clients he had to know more than they did. Years earlier he had written: "Know thoroughly each fact. Don't believe client witnesses. Examine documents. Reason; use imagination. Know bookkeeping—the universal language of business; know persons. . . . Know not only specific cases, but whole subjects. Can't otherwise know the facts. Know not only those facts which bear on direct controversy, but know all the facts and law that surround." Knowing facts not only helped him to analyze a case; it impressed clients. After all, why should people come to him unless his knowledge and perspective were greater than theirs?

ONE OF THE BEST EXAMPLES of how Brandeis served as counsel and how he used knowledge of the facts to solve a problem involved William H. McElwain, the head of a large shoe-manufacturing company in New England. As Brandeis explained, McElwain did not lack "the money-making faculty" or ambition and organizing ability. He started out with nothing and built up his firm's annual sales to more than $8.6 million in a little over a decade, when he died an untimely death at age forty-one in 1908.* McElwain came to see Brandeis in 1902, seeking his help in getting his workers to accept a wage cut without a strike. His workers had little basis for their complaint, he believed, since he paid them well and provided a safe working environment.

Brandeis promised to look into it, and began familiarizing himself with the shoe-manufacturing business by talking not only to McElwain's managers but also to the leaders of the labor unions at the plants. He learned that although the workforce did indeed enjoy high wages, they received that pay only for the weeks they worked. The shoe business ran on cycles. When salesmen sent in their orders, factories

---

*McElwain and Brandeis also became good friends, since both men shared a commitment to ideals as well as pragmatism. Upon McElwain's death after an appendicitis operation, Brandeis wrote: "I am greatly distressed at the death of my friend McElwain. He was in my opinion really the greatest man of my acquaintance—and the greatest loss to the Commonwealth—possessing the rare charm of great ability, courage, high character and personal charm. . . . I think had he lived he would have emerged from business into the field of his higher ideals and become a commanding figure in the Commonwealth."

would work on full shift to fill them. Then men would be laid off until the next batch of orders came in. Most manufacturers closed their factories completely at least twice a year for several weeks at a stretch, and often had two additional periods of slack time, when the men worked partial shifts.

McElwain's "good wages" proved to be illusory, since what a laborer would make over a year came to less than a living wage. The men understood that, and resisted the wage cut in good times knowing that there would be no money at all for the slack seasons. Brandeis also learned that this situation permeated the entire shoe-manufacturing industry; McElwain treated his workers no worse than did his competitors. As Brandeis later told a reporter, "The more I studied it the more it seemed to me absurd that men willing to work should have to be idle during ten or fifteen weeks of each year." When shoe manufacturers talked to him of seasonal conditions and averages, he exploded. "I abhor averages. I like the individual case. A man may have six meals one day and none the next, making an average of three per day, but that is not a good way to live."

When Brandeis explained this to him, McElwain agreed that something needed to be done, but what? That is how the industry had operated for as long as he knew. Brandeis suggested that McElwain reorganize the sales end of his business. Salesmen went out on the road with shoe samples for styles that would be made the following year, and they would travel until they had accumulated a fair batch of orders before filing them with the factory. However, some retailers would not put in orders until the last minute, not wanting to tie up either capital or shelf space ahead of time. Brandeis suggested that the salesmen file their orders earlier, and not accept orders from retailers unless they came in well ahead of the delivery date. Then McElwain's factory managers could plan the work for weeks, even months ahead. Set up the workforce so that the men can work regularly and so that there need be neither overtime nor enforced layoffs. Do not accept last-minute "rush" orders, since these will upset your schedule; instead, promise the customers that they will get their delivery on the date they wanted, but only if they submitted their orders in accordance with the production schedule.

McElwain agreed, and within a few years had completely revamped the shoe business. His men—and there were thousands of employees at the company's several plants—now worked more than three hundred days a year. Not only did McElwain regularize his labor force, but by imposing order on the sales force, he also rationalized the business as a whole. Brandeis liked to describe William McElwain as an enlightened businessman who recognized a problem and devised a creative and socially useful solution, without ever mentioning his own role in solving the matter. But McElwain had come to Brandeis because he respected the lawyer's knowledge both of law and of facts. He knew that Brandeis would not propose a solution until he had familiarized himself with the situation, and in doing so, Brandeis soon discovered the key piece of evidence that McElwain had overlooked. No strike occurred, no wage cuts took place, the company grew more prosperous, and its workers enjoyed high and—more important—regular wages.

The solution to McElwain's problem is perhaps the best illustration we have of how Brandeis married his idealism and his pragmatism. At his client's request he undertook to find out what each side wanted, and whether these were legitimate claims. Once he had established the facts, the pragmatist fashioned a creative solution, one that worked. To be able to do so, he needed the facts, he needed the trust of his client, and he needed knowledge of the business world to devise a plan that fit the needs of the real world.

Not all the advice that Brandeis gave involved multimillion-dollar businesses with thousands of employees. At one time one of his clients wanted to enter a partnership with another businessman who also happened to have Brandeis as his lawyer. The two men spoke at great length and worked out all of the details except the financial arrangements. They knew, however, that they wanted to be partners, and so they drew up a rough partnership agreement and took it to Brandeis. "You know our business circumstances," they told him. "Find out some more. Then take our rough agreement, put it into proper form, and you write in the dollars and cents just as you think they ought to be, and we will go ahead on that basis." Only a man whom his clients trusted would have been given such a task.

UNFORTUNATELY, NOT ALL EFFORTS at being what he called "counsel to the situation" worked out as well as the McElwain venture. During the hearings over his nomination to the Court, some of the opposition centered on cases where Brandeis had tried to be fair to all parties, but in doing so had allegedly left the clients who hired him believing he had betrayed their interests. Brandeis learned that in order for him to be effective in such a situation, all parties had to act in good faith. If not, the results could be disastrous.

One case involved P. Lennox & Company, a tanning factory in Lynn, Massachusetts, in financial difficulty. Personal notes executed by James T. Lennox, who operated the tannery with his father, as collateral for loans to the business were about to come due, and neither Lennox nor the tannery had the money to pay them. Lennox came to see Brandeis in September 1907, accompanied by his major creditor, Abe Stein, and Stein's attorney. Stein, a friend of Lennox's, wanted to see if any way could be found to help resolve the problems. Unlike Stein, Lennox's other creditors had no personal relationship to him and could not be expected to be as forgiving as Stein. One of the major creditors, the banking house of Weil, Farrell & Company, was a client of the Brandeis firm, and Stein hoped that Brandeis could use his influence to stop the creditors from forcing Lennox into bankruptcy.

In the conference among the four, which a stenographer recorded and transcribed, Brandeis made it quite clear that if he agreed to become involved, "the position I should take . . . would be to give everybody, to the very best of my ability, a square deal." The statement reflected both the notion that Brandeis would serve as counsel and his moral belief that he had a responsibility for ensuring that all sides be treated fairly. Lennox, speaking for himself and his father, assured Brandeis that they wanted to pay "a hundred cents on the dollar" to their creditors. Brandeis suggested that Lennox appoint George Nutter as trustee, to whom Lennox should assign his business assets for the benefit of the creditors. Operation of the business under an assignment might persuade the creditors to give the company more time to pay off its notes rather than pushing for bankruptcy and liquidation. It is clear from the transcript, as Stein's lawyer kept pushing Brandeis on what his role would be, that Brandeis had no interest in acting as Lennox's lawyer simply to work things out to his advantage; rather, he would be involved so that the ultimate solution would be "fair to all." When Lennox asked Brandeis point-blank if he would act as his counsel, Brandeis said, "Not altogether as your counsel, but as a trustee of your property."

Had Lennox followed Brandeis's advice, perhaps the business might have been salvaged. It is also possible that the accumulated debts had reached a point where the business could not be saved. But after signing the documents and agreeing to Nutter as trustee, James Lennox then refused to cooperate, constantly complaining to Nutter about his meager weekly draw of $100. Then evidence surfaced showing that the older Lennox had been hiding assets clearly belonging to the firm. Finally Nutter felt he had no recourse but to take the company into bankruptcy upon petition of the creditors. At this point Lennox expected Brandeis to come to his aid, and expressed anger when he learned that Brandeis and Nutter were not acting on his behalf but seemed to be serving the needs of his creditors in the bankruptcy proceedings. Lennox then retained the noted Boston attorney Sherman Whipple to represent him in court. Whipple, confused by what Lennox had told him of his transactions with Brandeis, went to see him and demanded to know the facts of his apparent abandonment of a client. As Whipple testified at the nomination hearings:

> Brandeis said, in substance, "of course, that would be a serious situation, but it is not the situation at all; I did not agree to act for Mr. Lennox when he came to me. When a man is bankrupt and can not pay his debts, . . . he finds himself with a trust, imposed upon him by law, to see that all his property is distributed honestly and fairly and equitably among all his creditors, and he has no further interest in the matter. Such was Mr. Lennox's situation when he came to me, and he consulted me merely as the trustee for his creditors, as to how best to discharge that trust, and I advised him in that way. I did not intend to act personally for Mr. Lennox, nor did I agree to." "Yes," I said, "but you advised him to make the assignment. For whom were you counsel when you advised him to do that, if not for the Lennoxes?" He said, "I should say I was counsel for the situation. . . . I was looking after the interests of everyone."

In 1916, Brandeis's opponents made the Lennox case a key part of their argument against his confirmation, claiming that this notion of "counsel to the situation" violated all proper notions of lawyerly behavior. Brandeis failed to make clear to Lennox either what his own role would be or what he expected Lennox to do vis-à-vis his creditors. Defenders of Brandeis, then as now, have argued that his stance not only flowed from the general work of the lawyer as counsel to a client but reflected creativity and a moral position that too many in the profession had abandoned.

The notion of "counsel to the situation" has seemed, even to some of Brandeis's defenders, somewhat vague, but it is a role that over the years has become part of the lawyer's practice. Geoffrey Hazard has commended the notion as "perhaps the best service a lawyer can render to anyone." The American Bar Association, on the other hand, has never quite figured out what to do about the practice. The ABA adopted its first set of aspirational standards, the Canons of Professional Ethics, in 1908, and canon 6 declared it "unprofessional to represent conflicting interests, except by express consent of all concerned given after a full disclosure of the facts." When the ABA adopted a Model Code of Professional Responsibility in 1969, it allowed lawyers to represent multiple clients if they provide full disclosure and "can adequately represent the interests of each," and may also serve as arbitrators or mediators for their clients. More recent attempts to provide guidance, such as the American Law Institute's Restatement of the Law Governing Lawyers, also failed to come up either with workable definitions or with guidance. A profession used to seeing its members primarily as advocates for their clients' interests has trouble defining a practice that seeks fairness for all parties.

There are clearly problems with acting as counsel to the situation. One, as witnessed in the Lennox case, involves poor communication. Not all lawyers are capable of determining what is in the best interests of all concerned. In addition, the interests of the different parties may not be easily amenable to a common solution, or their interests may change. This is what happened in another case brought forth in 1916 to demonstrate Brandeis's unfitness to be a judge, the matter of the Warren will.

When Samuel D. Warren Sr., the father of Brandeis's law partner, died on 11 May 1888, he left a simple will. His houses and all their artwork he left to his wife, and after some specific bequests to his brothers and sisters one-third of the remaining estate went to his widow, and two-thirds were to be divided among his five children. Because none of the children had gone into the family paper business, the older Warren suggested that it might be sold, and he named his wife, his son Sam, and Mortimer Mason, a cousin and minority partner, as executors to continue the business for eighteen months while his heirs decided on its future. At the time the Warren mills employed eight hundred workers and made annual profits of between $300,000 and $400,000. All members of the family agreed that for the sake of the workers as well as their own financial interests, the business should be continued. Sam agreed to leave his law practice to head up the enterprise and turned to Louis Brandeis to work out the details. As Moorfield Storey, the well-known Boston attorney who would later represent Sam's brother Fiske in the legal fight, noted, it was a "common practice" for a lawyer to represent an entire family in connection with a trust or business, despite potential conflicts of interest.

Warren and Brandeis created a plan whereby the three trustees leased the property to Samuel Warren, his brother Fiske, and Mortimer Mason. The Mills Trust, as it came to be known, would run for thirty-three years, or until the death of all the heirs. At least one of the operating trustees was always to be outside the family. The profits were to be distributed on a basis of five-fifteenths to Mrs. Warren, and two-fifteenths to each of the children. The trust also authorized the partners to create a reserve fund and make improvements to the mills costing up to one-third of the net income. Mrs. Warren and four of the five children lived in or around Boston, took part in the discussion, and approved the plan. Sam then sent a copy of the trust, as well as details of proposed earnings, to his brother Edward (known as Ned), a connoisseur of art then living in England. Sam explained that given a variety of factors facing the paper industry, the 1888 earnings might well be the highest they would see for a number of years. Ned signed the documents and then settled back to receive his share of the income, which he promptly invested in art.

Sam left the law practice that he loved so well, took over the business, and apparently did a good job. The mills weathered the hard times of the early 1890s, and no one in the family suffered any marked diminution of income. Although his younger brother Fiske nominally entered the business and was one of the operating partners, Fiske's true passion lay in radical politics, and he became an activist in the anti-imperialist movement of the late nineteenth and early twentieth centuries. Only Ned seemed unhappy, and felt that Sam's management of the mills did not give him the money he wanted to live abroad and indulge his passion for art. Nonetheless, peace reigned until the death of Susan Warren in 1901, leaving a vacancy on the operating board. Sam's next-youngest sibling, Henry, had also died, leaving the choice to either Ned or his sister, Cornelia. Neither Sam nor Mason believed Ned capable of serving, and each man preferred Cornelia. Ned would have none of this, and when earnings fell off, he grew angry because the company refused to advance him money. He then retained an attorney to look into the property arrangements, and in December 1909 brought suit alleging that Sam had personally profited from his dealings with the trust property and asking for a large financial settlement from Sam and the company. Thus began a protracted legal battle that ended only after Sam, bitter and depressed over Ned's attacks on him, took a gun and killed himself in February 1910.

One wonders what Brandeis—or Sam—could have done in 1888 that would have served the family's interests better. Brandeis (whom most scholars credit with coming up with the plan) made it possible for the family to continue to run the business and reap its profits, rather than having to put it on the auction block. Modern lawyers note that the trust had a number of defects, some of which reflected then-current practice, but no one at the time could have anticipated the angry dissension within the family. The terms of the arrangement could not have been clearer, and all of the Warrens, with the exception of Ned, seem to have understood that no matter how well the mills had generated profits during the older Warren's lifetime, one could not guarantee future income.

During the legal battle Ned made all sorts of accusations, primarily that Brandeis had pulled the wool over their eyes so that the family would not see that only Sam could benefit from the arrangement. Even Moorfield Storey and Sherman Whipple, both of whom opposed Brandeis's nomination, declared this nonsense, and also rebutted the claim that Brandeis had violated professional ethics by representing all of the parties. The arrangement seemed to him perfectly fair, Storey testified, and "I should have done perhaps very much as Mr. Brandeis did if I had been in his place." Whipple had looked into the matter exhaustively and declared that "the entire transaction was free from any taint of dishonest motives or intentional fraud."

Because he had been so friendly with the family and because they all seemed to trust him, Brandeis no doubt felt comfortable in drawing up the Mills Trust. He and Sam both had a highly developed, some would say overdeveloped, sense of morality, and neither would have done anything to jeopardize the interests of the other heirs. Sam had written, "I cannot think of the family and its doings without including you as a most influential part. You have encouraged our right impulses." During the suit brought by Ned, both Fiske and Cornelia made quite clear that they shared Sam's trust in Brandeis. Over the years the two men had discussed many matters relating to both the business and the trust, and if, as Ned Warren complained, there had been a breach of faith by Sam, then the same accusation could have been leveled against Louis.

But if men like Storey and Whipple defended his legal ethics, Louis still must have wrestled with charges that he had abandoned Sam in his hour of need by not representing him in the lawsuit. At the time Ned brought suit, Brandeis had been retained by *Collier's* magazine in the Pinchot-Ballinger hearings and had given up just about all other pursuits for this work. (See chapter 11.) Sam knew about it, and agreed that Edward McClennen would represent him. But it did bother Louis to hear that "Warren's death was hastened by the ingratitude of Brandeis's desertion of Warren at a critical moment because Brandeis thought his duty to public matters had priority over the claim of Warren to be defended by him against unhappy attack." Brandeis had in fact hesitated at taking on *Collier's,* and did so only with Warren's full consent.

At the time of Warren's death the trial judge had recently placed the matter in the hands of a special master to investigate the truth or falsity of the charges. Sam's death brought an end to the proceedings, and the remaining family members bought out Ned's share of the trust, the only money he received. Upon hearing of this plan, Brandeis was furious and wanted to fight the suit to an end to show the baselessness of Ned's charges. By then a grieving family wanted no further exhibition of Ned's character.

ONE SHOULD NOT THINK that all Louis Brandeis did as a lawyer involved researching different industries, giving out sage advice to businessmen, or getting himself into trouble through new legal stratagems. On many occasions litigation could not be avoided, and once involved, Brandeis would be a tireless, some said a ferocious adversary. His extraordinary range of knowledge, some from research and some from his wide reading, often made him more knowledgeable on a subject than so-called expert witnesses. Time and again he would trip up the opposition by knowing more about the business than they did. Nor did he disdain courtroom work; to the contrary, he loved it. During a quiet spell he wrote to Alfred, "I really long for the excitement of the contest—that is one covering days or weeks. There is a certain joy in the draining exhaustion and backache of a long trial, which shorter skirmishes cannot afford."

While Brandeis recognized the need for specialists, he remained a generalist throughout his career. According to his law partner Edward McClennen, the firm's business had from the start been general and unusually diverse. "It did not fall into a single class. It broadened rather than narrowed with the lapse of time." The firm counted among its clients manufacturers, merchants, investors, labor unions, and benevolent associations, as well as individuals. McClennen believed that the firm did not have any criminal practice, nor work in patents or admiralty, although he believed that Brandeis may have occasionally worked in these areas. (In fact, during the 1880s, before McClennen's time, Brandeis had gone to England to negotiate a patent license on a bleacher for S. D. Warren & Company.)

Clearly, other lawyers besides Louis Brandeis helped steer the profession away from litigation and helped create the role of lawyer as counsel. In addition, other lawyers proved fierce advocates for their clients and helped shape the modern, specialized law firm. And just as plainly, other lawyers also demonstrated great technical skill, mastery of the facts, and creativity in their practice of the law. But few of his contemporaries required the level of moral certitude that Brandeis did, either for himself or for his clients.

Time and again one heard stories of clients coming in to ask Brandeis to take on their cases. If in winter, they kept on their coats, since Brandeis deliberately kept the temperature low in his office so that people would not be tempted to chat. They would ask his help, make their case, and then be subjected to a grilling on who had the right. If Brandeis decided that his client stood in the wrong, he would tell him, and suggest reaching an accommodation as quickly as possible. If in the right, and Brandeis took the case, the client would thank him, knowing that his interests would be well protected, and then, teeth chattering, would go out into the winter's warmth. Or, if there appeared to be right on both sides, as in the McElwain case, Brandeis might seek a solution that would be in everyone's best interest.

At the nomination hearings in 1916, Brandeis's foes made much of "unethical" practices and sought to bring witnesses to testify that Brandeis did not practice law according to the established norms of the bar. The testimony of one such witness backfired on them, and tells us a great deal about this most unusual aspect of Brandeis the lawyer.

In 1907 a proxy fight broke out between E. H. Harriman and Stuyvesant Fish over control of the Illinois Central Railroad. The Harriman interests hired the New York firm of Sullivan & Cromwell to represent them and to secure proxy votes against Fish. The firm retained a young lawyer named Waddill Catchings to help manage the campaign, and he traveled to major cities to line up law firms to handle the proxy fights in their localities. Brandeis's opponents called Catchings to the stand in 1916 to show that Brandeis was a hypocrite, since at the same time that he battled the New Haven Railroad, he accepted a fee from another railroad baron, E. H. Harriman.

Brandeis, Dunbar & Nutter had been a correspondent for Sullivan & Cromwell for many years, meaning that when the New York firm had a client who needed representation in Boston, or legal work that needed to be done in Boston, they would utilize the Brandeis office. Catchings went to see George Nutter, who normally would have handled this matter. Nutter informed him that they would not be able to accept the commission unless Mr. Brandeis agreed, and explained that Brandeis was at that time heavily involved in a battle against a railroad merger. Furthermore, Nutter said, "the firm would not accept such a retainer unless Mr. Brandeis was convinced of the justness of our position; that he would not care to have his firm associated in a matter of such nature without personally passing on the merits of the contest." Catchings went into the senior partner's office, and "the hardest interview I had during the whole campaign was with Mr. Brandeis in convincing him of the justness of our cause."

Senator John D. Works asked Catchings what Brandeis wanted to know, and apparently he wanted to know everything. "I went into it from beginning to end, every argument we had and every argument Mr. Fish had, and why I believed we were entitled to the support of Mr. Brandeis." At last, after two hours of intense questioning, Brandeis agreed, and although he took no active role in the proxy fight, the firm did act for the Harriman interests. As Catchings summed up, "It was an unusual experience. I had occasion to retain other lawyers and no one ever raised that question."

WARREN & BRANDEIS MADE MONEY almost from the beginning, and after Sam left to run the family paper industry, the firm continued to flourish. Louis personally prospered and must be counted among the top-paid lawyers in the country. The range of incomes in the profession varied greatly. Young lawyers in the large firms made more than those in small offices; two-thirds of the lawyers practicing in New York at the end of the nineteenth century made about $3,000 a year; those working in the Cravath-model firms typically made thrice that amount. Of the fifteen hundred lawyers in Philadelphia in the late 1880s, fewer than one-third were thought to be self-supporting, and no more than one hundred had an income of more than $5,000 annually. In Boston of the 1890s, the best estimate is that perhaps a half-dozen men made $20,000 a year, a dozen more $10,000, and perhaps another quarter made $5,000; the remaining three-quarters earned far less. Brandeis, of course, ranked in this top echelon. In 1890, at the age of thirty-four, he earned more than $50,000 a year (well over $1 million in current value, and with no income tax), while 75 percent of the attorneys in the United States made less than $5,000. As late as 1912, when he devoted much of his time to public service, he received $105,000 from his practice. By frugal living and conservative investments, he had accumulated his first million by 1907, and another million before he went on the Court in 1916. Despite a lower income and significant gifts he made to family and to causes during the 1920s and 1930s, he died leaving an estate of more than $3 million.

The young man who told his mother that he needed to test his ambition and talents had succeeded, perhaps beyond even his expectations. He understood the legal needs of the new industrial society, and he crafted a law practice and a firm built around satisfying those needs. A generalist in an age of increasing specialization, he pioneered in the role of counsel, originating the idea of counsel to the situation, a practice that, unfortunately, most of his colleagues and even some of his clients misunderstood. At a time when lawyers as a profession appeared to be abandoning their moral compass, he held on to his.

For Louis Brandeis, law always provided the medium through which he could exercise the two great driving forces of his life, idealism and pragmatism. Once he accepted the lesson he learned from Judge Gray that both parties to a dispute might have right on their sides, the idealist in him wanted to find a solution that would be fair to all. He said he never wanted to be somebody's lawyer, a person hired to do what another desired; rather, he wanted to have clients, people who would listen to him and understand not only their position but that of the other side as well. Once that had been accomplished, the pragmatist, the legal craftsman, would step in to fashion a solution.

Louis Brandeis had indeed done well. Now the time had come to do good.

CHAPTER FOUR

FIRST STEPS

W ednesday of last week I went to see one of my friends, Rufus Coffin, play in private theatricals," Louis Brandeis wrote to his sister. The performance "was, of course, mostly poor, but that is immaterial," as Coffin had reserved a seat for him next to two "very bright girls and I was fixed for the evening." During the years that Warren & Brandeis built up its practice, Louis still found time to engage in other activities. He taught at both Harvard Law School and the Massachusetts Institute of Technology, dabbled in Democratic politics, played a key role in the law school's development, and, together with Sam Warren, wrote one of the most influential law review articles in American history. He also kept up an active social life and took the first steps toward becoming a reformer.

LOUIS'S PARTNERSHIP and, more important, his friendship with Sam Warren opened many doors to him in those early years in Boston, and in addition invitations from old law school classmates as well as from the German-Jewish community filled up the very eligible young bachelor's evening and weekend hours. His parents worried that he worked too hard and neglected his health, so he sent frequent reports of his activities outside the office to reassure them. From his boyhood he had loved the outdoors, and throughout his life would go walking in the woods whenever he could. Probably upon Warren's nomination, the Union Boat Club elected him a member, and thus gave him access to canoes on the Charles. A typical week, he related, began on Monday with a visit to "the pretty Miss Alice Smith" for a whist party; on Tuesday, his old friends Philippe Marcou and Walter Child joined him after he had attended an early evening lecture by Holmes,* and they sat up and talked till after midnight. On Wednesday he declined an invitation to a whist party at the Warrens', and instead went to visit the Cochran sisters from Louisville, then staying in Boston. The following evening he dined with Marcou and went to call on the Hechts. And this, he concluded, "is the end of Solomon Grundy."

Louis attended the theater, and saw the great Henry Irving and Ellen Terry in their touring company of Shakespeare's *Much Ado About Nothing,* and although he loved the stage, he continued to turn down invitations to take roles in local amateur productions. He found female company attractive and reported to his sister Amy about the various women he met. At a party at Professor Emerton's home, he met a Miss Page, "a lady I should say of '28 summers' and quite as many winters," whom he found extremely interesting. At dinner, instead of the trite conversation he had expected, she engaged in one of "the most remarkable variations of character, soul, and mind-painting that can be imagined." Quickly, they plunged into "the deepest conversations, such as George Eliot's characters indulge in." Knowing that Amy wanted him to marry, he then teased her, writing, "You, of course, are very much interested in this young lady because you think I am smitten with her. But Alas! It is not so. One mistress only claims me. The 'Law' has her grip on me."

"I find it interesting to meet new people," he told his brother, and at this time Louis met one young woman in whose life he would play an important part, and who would be a friend to him and to his family for the rest of her years.

---

*Although he probably did not recognize its significance at the time, the lecture he attended is considered one of the great landmarks in American legal history. Oliver Wendell Holmes Jr. had been invited to give the Lowell Institute Lectures, and he chose as his theme the common law. In a sharp break with the legal formalism of the day, Holmes opened the first of the twelve lectures with the now famous declaration that "the life of the law has not been logic; it has been experience." The publication of the lectures in 1881 marked the beginning of what is known as "sociological jurisprudence," which referred not to the academic discipline of sociology but to the call for judges to take into account nonlegal considerations, such as social and economic data, or what Holmes called the "felt necessities of the time." Holmes, and later Roscoe Pound, would be the great theorists of sociological jurisprudence, but Louis Brandeis would be its great practitioner. In 1908, when he submitted his pathbreaking brief in *Muller v. Oregon,* he put into practice the theory he had heard Holmes talk about more than a quarter century earlier. (See chapter 9.)

In 1884, Glendower and Elizabeth Evans paid a social call on Professor Barrett Wendell and his wife; Elizabeth Gardiner and Mrs. Wendell had been girlhood chums, as well as part of Boston's upper-class society. As they rang the bell, Wendell opened the door, and two young men, whom Mrs. Evans took for undergraduates, left.

"Are these some of your little charges?" she asked Wendell.

No, he replied, one of them is Louis Brandeis.

Glendower Evans turned to his wife in annoyance. "Louis Brandeis is a man I always wanted to know and here he is leaving just as we arrive." Evans had come from Philadelphia to attend Harvard Law School two years after Louis had left, and by then Brandeis's academic record and feats of memory had already become part of law school legend.

"Well," she said, "why don't we ask him to dine? We live in a nice house and he presumably lives in lodgings. He might like to come. And if he doesn't, he will say no, and no harm will be done."

They invited him to dinner and he accepted, and so Louis Brandeis became a regular visitor at 12 Otis Place. In addition to dinner, Louis quickly adopted the habit of stopping by the Evanses on Sunday mornings to see if either Glendower or Elizabeth wanted to accompany him on his walk, or to go boating on the Charles. The two men talked endlessly about anything and everything, with Elizabeth a fascinated auditor. Glen had a quick and facile mind; Holmes said that Evans's comments on *The Common Law* had been the only instructive criticisms he had received about the book.

Two years later Glendower Evans, always frail in health, died unexpectedly at age thirty, leaving Elizabeth bereft and without any idea of what to do with the rest of her life. The Sunday after the funeral, Louis showed up at 12 Otis Place, took the young widow on a walk, and continued the practice for the next several years until he married. When that happened, Elizabeth Glendower Evans (she always kept that name) became Alice Brandeis's closest friend and confidante, and Auntie B. to the Brandeis children.

But Louis did more than merely spend time with Elizabeth Evans. She was already involved in a few public activities acceptable for upper-class married women, such as serving as a trustee for the Lyman Industrial School, an institution to train delinquent girls in a trade so they could afterward earn their own living. Brandeis got her to widen her horizons. She had money, and he urged her to travel to England to find out about socialism and the Socialist Party there, and to travel in Europe as well, since the experience "will bring into your life much to

Elizabeth Glendower Evans

enrich it and give it a broader growth." At his suggestion she attended a convention of the Women's Trade Union League held at Hull House in Chicago, and from there went to Wisconsin to see La Follette progressivism first-hand. Over the years she became active in a variety of causes, from minimum-wage legislation in Massachusetts to efforts to free Sacco and Vanzetti in the 1920s. Throughout her life, she always said that she would not have known what to do after Glen's death had it not been for Louis Brandeis, whom she sometimes addressed in her letters as "Dear Elder Brother." On his seventieth birthday she wrote him a very sentimental letter, asking, "What would my life have been without you?" At her death, Brandeis could not bring himself to write a letter for her memorial service. "It's like one of my own family [died]."

LOUIS BRANDEIS BECAME the kind of alumnus that every school hopes for. From the time he left Harvard Law until his retirement from the Supreme Court, he stayed involved in the school's life and development, donating generously to particular projects that he thought would benefit the students and the school. According to James Landis, one of Justice Brandeis's clerks and later dean of Harvard Law School, Brandeis's loyalty stemmed from the gratitude he felt for what Harvard had given to him. Louis had arrived at the law school as an eighteen-year-old boy from the sticks, with relatively little in the way of formal education past high school. Harvard had not only introduced him to the rigorous study of the law but also opened other intellectual and social vistas for him. Between 1880 and 1900, Louis gave a great deal of his time to the law school. "It was," according to Landis, "his first public work; his first crusade."

Louis's work began when Professor James Bradley Thayer asked him to help collect material for a new course he planned to give in constitutional law. Then, in 1880, Thayer again came to Brandeis and sought his help. Thayer believed that Oliver Wendell Holmes would be willing to join the law school faculty, but no openings then existed, and the only way to get Holmes would be if a private donor contributed $90,000, the amount necessary to create an endowed chair. One of the students Brandeis had tutored while in law school, William Weld Jr., had just inherited $3 million. Louis arranged to meet with Weld and Thayer at his office, but a day or so before that meeting ran into Weld on the Boston Common and told him of the possibility of getting Holmes to the law school. Weld agreed to provide the entire amount. Holmes accepted the offer, but by late 1881 he knew that his name had already been proposed for a judgeship, and he made his acceptance of Harvard's offer contingent upon his remaining free to accept a judicial appointment should one arise. Holmes joined the faculty in February 1882, but left at the end of the fall term to become a judge on the Supreme Judicial Court of Massachusetts. The faculty at the law school did not view the appointment kindly; a great deal of work had gone into securing the professorship, and they believed there had been a tacit understanding that Holmes would remain at least five years. Louis made the best of the situation and wrote to his friend, "As one of the bar I rejoice. As part of the Law School I mourn. As your friend I congratulate you."

During the time Holmes taught at the law school, Louis was one of his colleagues. Thayer had been scheduled for a short leave—what would later be termed a sabbatical—in 1881, and the school lined up four instructors to take over his courses, with Louis invited to give the course on Evidence. The leave had to be postponed for a year, so Louis did not get to teach until the following year, two lectures a week for $1,000. When he received the offer from President Eliot, he sent it home to his parents, who gushed with pride. "My dearest child," his mother wrote, "how happy you make me feel! My heart is a prayer of thanksgiving." Frederika took the letter to show her brother, and Lewis Dembitz wrote to his nephew that on seeing the offer to "Louis Dembitz Brandeis," for the first time he felt glad about the name change. Were your grandfather still alive, Dembitz wrote, no one would have been prouder, "for none had a greater veneration than he for anything connected with the University."

Part of his parents' joy also reflected their worries about Louis's health. From the time he left law school, he had had intermittent bouts

Oliver Wendell Holmes Jr.

of fatigue, which Adolph and Frederika ascribed to working too hard. Life as a professor might not yield as much income as private practice, but neither would it be as physically demanding. "I am a little provoked about my health," Louis had told Alfred, "for in spite of my vacations I do not feel in real working condition as I should." Although everyone said he looked "first-rate," he did not agree, despite taking regular walks every morning, rowing on the Charles before dinner, and sleeping, "which I indulge in now extensively."

(There is some question regarding Brandeis's health during these early years in Boston, and at least two biographers have described him as "frail." There is no question that he suffered some illness in the 1880s, and complained on several occasions, as he did here, that he did not feel up to snuff. Without medical records one can only note that despite his regular exercise, he did seem to have frequent bouts of tiredness, due at least in part to the amount of work he put in building up his practice and the other activities he engaged in outside of Warren & Brandeis. None of these seemed life threatening, and may in part have been the lingering effects of the malarial bouts he had had as a child. He appears to have outgrown these symptoms after his marriage in 1891, for while there are occasional comments in his later letters about being under the weather, they are rare, and no more than even a person in quite good health would have from time to time. His ability to work at a pace that would have killed lesser men seemed to increase over the years.)

Apparently, Louis did such a good job teaching the Evidence course that Dean Langdell, upon the advice of the law school faculty, offered him an assistant professorship. Brandeis thought long and hard about this proposal, but decided against it. He had told Sam Warren when he decided to come to Boston that he wanted to make his reputation as a practicing lawyer. Nonetheless, years later when one of his clerks, James Landis, received an offer to teach at Harvard Law School, Brandeis urged him to take it. No vocation, he told Landis, afforded the challenge of teaching, and no contribution to law could more effectively be made than by men who had the leisure to learn and freedom to think. Perhaps at that point in his life he had had second thoughts about his decision, but no teacher of law in the twentieth century made as great a contribution to either the theory or the practice of law as did Louis Brandeis.

ALTHOUGH HE DID NOT TEACH again at the law school, Louis hardly reduced his commitment to it. Almost from the time the firm opened its doors, it had taken in one bright third-year student to work part-time in the office, partly as an aide for their own labors and partly as a gesture to the law school. Perhaps the most useful task he performed involved helping to organize the Harvard Law School Association in 1886.

Like Dean Langdell, Brandeis saw Harvard Law as a national institution, but in order to achieve that status, it would need financial as well as organizational support from its alumni, many of whom lived in states other than Massachusetts. Apparently, Brandeis had toyed for several years with the idea of having either prominent individuals or committees in different parts of the country assume responsibility for making known the virtues of the school, seeking out promising students, and raising money. At some point he and six other Boston-based graduates decided, with the approval and support of Langdell, to create an alumni association. In November 1886, Harvard was to celebrate the 250th anniversary of its founding, and the organizing committee decided that would be the opportunity to create a law school association.

Louis served as secretary of the committee, the mailings went out of his office, and, according to Dean Landis, it had been Brandeis's enthusiasm that "supplied the energy and the organizing ability of the group." He compiled alumni lists from the law school records to be canvassed, and identified prominent men whom he often contacted personally to draw them into the project. On 5 November 1886, the association came into being with four hundred members. It chose the distinguished James Coolidge Carter (LL.B. 1853) of New York as president and Louis Brandeis as secretary—the officer who would, in fact, lead the group.

Brandeis remained active in the Harvard Law School Association until the time he went onto the Supreme Court, although his level of involvement dropped once he began to devote more of his time and energy to reform work. The office of Warren & Brandeis on Devonshire Street doubled as the association's headquarters. He arranged the annual meetings, oversaw recruitment of new members, and set up a system of corresponding secretaries around the country. At his suggestion, the association sent out material on the law school to every American college in order to recruit applicants.

In 1889, Brandeis wrote an article that amounted to a love letter to the law school, praising the faculty, the instruction, and the atmosphere in which a great deal of learning took place. The old debate as to whether a law school or a lawyer's office provides a better opportunity for legal training, he declared, "may well be considered settled." Students live "in an atmosphere of legal thought. Their interest is at fever heat." He lauded the Langdellian revolution, and cited no less an authority than Holmes, who recalled the misgivings he had felt when he first began to teach that method. But once the discussions began, "the result was better than I even hoped it would be," and the students examined the legal questions "with an accuracy of view which they never could have learned from text-books."

While on the Court, Brandeis became the first justice to cite a law review article in an opinion, and in part that could be traced back to his enthusiastic support for the establishment of the *Harvard Law Review.* In the late 1880s a number of law schools started legal journals, edited by students with the advice and oversight of faculty, to carry the latest in legal scholarship as well as reports of important cases. Three students, John J. McKelvey, Julian W. Mack, and Joseph Beale, came up with the idea and, at James Barr Ames's suggestion, went to see Brandeis both for advice and for the means to finance it. Brandeis immediately gave a personal donation and then put them in touch with other members of the association who he thought could be of assistance. The journal began publication in 1887, and it was Brandeis who conceived the idea and raised the money to provide for the mailing of the *Review* to every member of the association.

In 1891, the *Review* reorganized and set up a separate board of trustees composed of faculty and alumni, with Brandeis as its treasurer. He continued to be a trustee right up to his appointment to the Supreme Court and took an active interest in the journal, its management, and its student editors. He assiduously attended meetings as well as the annual banquet, took every opportunity to meet with students, and freely gave of his advice regarding the management of the journal's affairs. He and Sam Warren even contributed three articles to the early issues. The importance of waterpower to the Warren paper mills made riparian law an essential part of the firm's work for the company, and the two men took what they had learned and wrote it up for the *Review.*

In recognition of his service to the law school, Harvard admitted Brandeis to Phi Beta Kappa in 1890, and the following year awarded him a Master of Arts. One final aspect of his work with the association involved the banquet to honor Christopher Columbus Langdell on his twenty-five years as dean in 1895. Brandeis helped gather the extraordinary group of distinguished jurists and scholars, including the great English legal writer Sir Frederick Pollock. Brandeis had met Pollock, through a letter of introduction from Thayer, when he went to England in 1887 to purchase the rights to an electric bleaching machine for the Warren mills. He convinced Pollock to attend, and served as his host during the festivities. (The trip to England also led Brandeis to persuade Langdell to add a course on patent law, one of the first in the country.)

Soon after this event, his growing legal practice as well as increasing reform work led Louis to resign as the association's secretary. He remained on its council, however, until 1907, after which he became the association's vice president, a position he held even after going on the Court. He served on the Visiting Committee of the law school, an oversight group of nonfaculty or administration, in 1889–1890 and then from 1891 until 1919, and participated in a number of law school functions in all those years. After he went on the bench, he took one Harvard Law School graduate as a clerk each year, and whenever the school's faculty went down to Washington, they invariably stopped in to see him. In the 1920s, when he began interesting himself in the affairs of the University of Louisville and its law school, his experience at Harvard and with the association could clearly be seen in the proposals he made.

BRANDEIS NEVER WENT LOOKING for reform work; causes seemed to find him. He did not have that inborn zeal of a crusader, for whom every perceived injustice must be fought. Moreover, for all his idealism, his practical side told him that not every wrong could be corrected. To his mother he once declared that he had only tried to fix those things that he knew could be amended, and most of the time he became involved at the behest of others. Once drawn in, he had, according to his law partner, "the true lawyer's enthusiasm to bring about what was right"; the subject of the problem did not matter, only the "lawyer's desire to bring about justice." This says both too little and too much about Brandeis.

He certainly had a refined sense of morality, but to attribute this to the legal profession ignores the many other factors that contributed to his idealism and his desire to do right, characteristics that antedated his entry into the law. While he may have taken a lawyerlike attitude in approaching these problems, the people involved, or, to be more precise, the victims of the wrong, meant a great deal to him. He did not have a disembodied idealism that ignored the humanity of others, nor did he have a practicality that ignored the real-world impact of a solution. The man who devised savings bank life insurance understood the needs of the working poor, and what an affordable insurance scheme would mean to them.

He became involved in reform little by little, initially as a lawyer to his clients. Success in one endeavor led to invitations to work on another problem. Just as he reached a point in his law practice where he no longer needed to worry about getting new business, so, too, his reputation as a successful reformer soon brought him more invitations than he could handle.

Even as his practice prospered and his work with the law school grew, Louis began to engage in community efforts and politics. He had grown up as a Republican, and in his papers is a flyer for Rutherford B. Hayes and William A. Wheeler, the Republican candidates for president and vice president in 1876, and scribbled across the top is "Louis D. Brandeis, His Ticket, Cambridge, Mass., Nov. 7, 1876," even though he could not yet vote. Four years later he told his brother that he felt "considerable interest in politics and hope[d] Garfield [would] be elected. Can't quite reconcile myself with the idea of Democratic rule yet."

But in the post–Civil War years, the GOP came increasingly under the thumb of big business, and when the party nominated James G. Blaine ("the continental liar from the state of Maine") and John A. "Black Jack" Logan in 1884, many Republicans bolted from the party, including Brandeis. Known as mugwumps, they stood for middle-class values, honesty in public affairs, and limited government. A number of Massachusetts rebels signed a "Call," declaring that "only men of high character should be elected to high office, and that the nomination just made in Chicago ought not to be supported in any contingency." The newspaper notice came to the attention of Brandeis's brother-in-law

Charles Nagel, a regular Republican. "I found your name where I expected it!" Nagel wrote. "It is not pleasant to be called a 'Tough' . . . but I cannot see my way [to go with you] this time."

Henceforth, Louis would refer to himself as a democrat with a small *d.* He refused to support William Jennings Bryan and the silverites in 1896, and seemed content with Theodore Roosevelt in the early years of the twentieth century. When his close friend Robert M. La Follette of Wisconsin ran for the Republican nomination in 1912, Brandeis took an active role in the campaign until La Follette had to withdraw following a physical breakdown. Then he met Woodrow Wilson, and he remained a "large *D*" Democrat afterward.

More than any other value, honesty in government characterized the mugwump movement, and that included not just an absence of monetary corruption but efficient and effective administration. Louis had believed in honest government even as a boy. In high school he charged the treasurer of the debating society with inaccurate accounting due to a discrepancy of forty cents. Only after the treasurer explained the mistake did Louis agree to drop the "investigation." Almost as soon as he set up his practice, Brandeis began joining various good-government organizations. In 1884 the Civil Service Reform Association of the Fifth Congressional District elected him to its executive committee. A few years later he joined the Boston Citizenship Committee (a group concerned with the assimilation of new immigrants) and then the Massachusetts Society for Promoting Good Citizenship. He subscribed to the quintessential mugwump group, the Massachusetts Civil Service Reform Association, and served on the executive committee of the Election Laws League. When he became more involved in Boston reform, he helped organize the Good Government Association, which became the most important group in the city pursuing honest municipal government.

In January 1884, he dropped a short note to Alfred. "Have had a public career of late. Lectured on 'Taxation' Sunday. Spoke against 'Woman Suffrage' before the Legislative Com'tee yesterday & appeared before the Insurance Com'tee yesterday & today. Am well & busy." Extrapolating from that brief missive, one learns that Brandeis had spoken at the South Congregational Unitarian Church to a class on the public duties of citizens. He had argued that taxation should be considered a necessary evil, the price of ordered society, and therefore a citizen's duty involved not only paying taxes but also working to make sure that burden remained as light as possible. The next day he spoke before a crowded committee in opposition to giving women the vote.

Suffrage was not a right, he claimed, but a privilege that imposed certain duties peculiar to the male sex. (He would later change his views on this matter.) At the insurance hearings, it is likely that he spoke on behalf of a client in regard to a bill proposed by the Metropolitan Life Insurance Company to impose uniform valuations on policies for the purposes of taxation.

A few years later found him extending his horizons, although he still acted on behalf of clients, to oppose the "grinding monopoly" of the Boston Disinfecting Company. The city had a health requirement that all rags imported from abroad had to be disinfected in Boston, even if they had already been disinfected overseas. Most of the rags imported by the area paper mills had, in fact, been decontaminated abroad by a cheaper but equally effective method, and the mill owners objected to having to pay to have this done a second time. Moreover, the only firm licensed by the city to do the work, the Boston Disinfecting Company, charged $5 per ton. Warren & Brandeis represented the paper companies in their petition to the Common Council to repeal the law and to substitute a measure that would achieve the same health ends without forcing the mills to pay for two disinfecting processes. The paper companies also had the backing of rail and steamship lines who feared the loss of trade to New York, which had a more lenient law regarding overseas decontamination.

According to his daughter Elizabeth, Louis in later years recollected this fight as the first time he realized the evils of monopoly. That, however, seems to be more a result of hindsight, because according to contemporary accounts he argued that the ordinance violated the due process of the paper manufacturers and that the ordinance exceeded the state's police powers. Brandeis had high hopes for winning this fight, since he believed both practical and scientific evidence to be on the paper manufacturers' side, and he thought that not even the political clout of the Boston Disinfecting Company would be able to overcome that. Unfortunately, he misgauged the power of political influence. The Common Council refused to repeal the ordinance, and one of the paper companies brought suit to force the release of a load of rags that hadn't been reprocessed. Brandeis handled the case on appeal, only to have the Supreme Judicial Court of Massachusetts decide against his client.

ABOUT THIS TIME Brandeis also began sending brief letters to the editors of Boston newspapers, commending them for editorials with which he agreed or which took his part in some dispute. As he told

Edwin Bacon, the editor of the *Boston Post,* "A reform-minded press must not only point out new evils, but remind people of old ills, so they will not be forgotten." Louis took all of the Boston newspapers, as well as those from other large cities in the state, such as Springfield. As his horizons expanded, Brandeis subscribed to a clipping service that included all of the major papers in the Northeast, and his secretary began filing the clippings—related either to him personally or to the causes that interested him—in large scrapbooks that she kept until well after he went onto the Supreme Court. His letters eventually went to papers far beyond Boston, and he built up a network of influential editors and reporters whom he used to publicize his causes. As he told Alfred, "The more the matter is canvassed & discussed (and the papers have taken up the question now), the better for us. It is only ignorance and dark dealing that we must fear." This, too, would be a theme for the rest of his career, the necessity of shedding light on public issues. Louis Brandeis had a Jeffersonian faith in the power of reason and in the ability of the common people to understand and to act wisely on even complex issues if only they had the facts at hand.

Politics interested Louis, as it did many other young men of the time. The experience with the rag case showed him, if he had not already known it, that merely having the evidence on one's side did not mean that one would automatically prevail. Just as he had concluded that mastery of the facts and knowledge of business were essential in the proper representation of clients, now he learned that knowledge of the political system would also be necessary. He could learn facts about business, and understand them based on his family background and association with the Warrens, without having to become a businessman himself—other than, of course, managing his law business. But could he also learn the ins and outs of politics while staying above the fray? Louis apparently never harbored any ideas of running for public office, although on several occasions the local Democrats sounded him out to see if he would stand for various offices. Although he dipped his toe into local politics, Louis decided he should stick with the law.

In the late nineteenth century, Boston, and indeed Massachusetts, had a reputation for clean government at a time when New York labored under the heavy hand of Boss Tweed and Tammany Hall. Ever since colonial times, officials in Massachusetts had to stand for reelection every year, giving the people an annual check on their activities. Many of the reforms that progressives in other states had to fight for during the early twentieth century had constituted part of the Massachusetts political scene for decades. This did not mean a total lack of corruption, only that in comparison with other states Massachusetts appeared honest and well governed.

Then, as now, various interests maintained agents to lobby the state legislature either in favor of legislation beneficial to their business or to oppose proposals they did not like. As one professional lobbyist told the Boston lawyer and good-government advocate Moorfield Storey, in politics as in law, "a man who pleads his own cause has a fool for a client." And the lobbyists had their clients' money to help convince legislators of the rightness of their causes.

At the suggestion of a fellow reformer, George Fred Williams, Louis began looking into the workings of the Massachusetts Protective Liquor Dealers' Association, the lobby group for liquor manufacturers and distributors. He met with William D. Ellis, the Boston agent of an Ohio distillery that was a Warren & Brandeis client, and also a member of the executive committee of the lobby. Brandeis had known Ellis for years, and the two men liked and respected each other. After discussing some general political issues, Brandeis reached into his desk and pulled out a list of Massachusetts legislators, handed it to Ellis, and asked him to check off the names of those who could be bribed. Ellis quickly did so and handed it back. "Ellis, do you realize what you are doing?" Brandeis asked, and went on to lecture him on the evils of bribery until tears supposedly rolled down the lobbyist's cheeks. What kind of example is that to set for your son? Brandeis asked. Beyond that, the tactics don't work. The legislature keeps passing laws unacceptable to your clients.

Anti-liquor interests had been agitating for some time to adopt so-called temperance measures that would then serve as a way station toward total prohibition of alcoholic beverages in the state, a policy that clearly threatened the business of liquor manufacturers and dealers, as well as local saloon owners. What could they do? Ellis wanted to know, and Brandeis outlined a plan for him. The lawyer agreed to become counsel for the Protective Association on condition that Ellis be made chair of the executive committee. No money would be spent except on Brandeis's order or approval.

Although Brandeis's unconventional brief in the Supreme Court case of *Muller v. Oregon* (1908) is well-known (see chapter 9), he submitted another unorthodox brief to the Massachusetts legislature in 1891. After carefully analyzing the existing law, he concluded it to be unworkable, and he argued that much of the crime and corruption associated with liquor grew out of the fact that such methods were the only ways these men could run their businesses. He wanted to get the liquor dealers and their money out of politics, and to do that the legislature had to ignore the demands for prohibition and adopt reasonable measures that law-abiding citizens could obey. At the front of his brief he spelled out his argument:

> Liquor drinking is not a wrong; but excessive drinking is.
> Liquor will be sold; hence the sale should be licensed.
> Liquor is dangerous; hence the business should be regulated.
> No regulation can be enforced which is not reasonable.

The current law, he told the legislative committee looking into the matter, had been unenforceable from the start, in that it banned the sale of liquor except as part of a meal. This meant that every time an honest citizen took a drink at a bar other than at mealtime, it made him a criminal. Moreover, it had been laws like this that had forced the liquor dealers into politics. You can make politicians out of any class of people, he declared, if you harass them, if you take away their livelihood, and if you deny them the means to control their own lives. The problem had a simple solution—make the liquor laws reasonable. This, of course, offended the temperance advocates, who did not want a reasonable law. The worse the law, the worse its abuses, and the better their chance of doing away with alcohol altogether. All morning, he reported in April 1891, "I was before the legislative committee fighting the errors and hypocrisies of the so-called temperance people, and carrying out my pet reform of the liquor trade by making the dealers respectable." In the end, the legislators, few of whom wanted to see alcohol banned, followed Brandeis's advice. While it may not have totally removed the liquor dealers from politics, it did do away with the corruption that had been associated with them for a number of years.

Brandeis took a great deal of satisfaction from this endeavor; he had accomplished something that benefited not only his clients the liquor dealers but also the public. He charged the Protective Association only $2,000 for his services, far less than his normal fee. One might consider this his first step on the path toward becoming the People's Attorney, and working for the public good on a pro bono basis.

A FEW YEARS LATER, his longtime friend the philanthropist Alice N. Lincoln asked Brandeis to represent her in hearings scheduled to examine conditions at the city institution for paupers on Long Island in

Boston Harbor. Brandeis later called his visit there "the most depressing & distressful experience" of his life and said that as he walked
through the syphilitic ward, he had a "sense of uncleanness." To
describe the conditions as atrocious would not do justice to this hell-
hole. The inmates subsisted on a minimal diet of watered-down gruel;
the limited toilets often did not work, so people had to urinate in the
kitchen sinks; the little clothing they had consisted of rags, and some
women stayed in bed all day because they literally had nothing to wear.
Although nominally a doctor was on call to serve the 144-bed facility,
he was rarely available. When people died—a frequent occurrence—
the staff stored their bodies in a back room until a mass grave could be
dug. At the same time, the superintendent, who lived in a house on the
grounds, ate steak every evening, attended by numerous servants.

Mrs. Lincoln had written an angry letter to the *Boston Evening Transcript,* and as a result a visiting committee had been appointed, and the
city, after much prodding, finally agreed to hold hearings before the
Board of Aldermen. Bess Evans had been named to the visiting committee, and she and Alice Lincoln soon realized that merely exposing
the terrible conditions at Long Island would not be enough. The
bureaucracy in charge of the facility resisted every suggestion for
change. They needed someone tough to challenge the officials and to
awaken the public conscience, and they asked their friend Louis Brandeis to represent them.

Brandeis agreed to do so, but he differed from them as to the strategy
to pursue. They wanted to dismiss all of the public officials involved for
corruption and violation of the poor laws that governed treatment of
institutional inmates. Brandeis believed the officials guilty of incompetence rather than corruption and thought that in some ways they had
done exactly what they had been charged to do—take care of the paupers with a minimal budget. A new set of managers would not alleviate
the conditions; the city had to change its policy from custodial care of
the paupers to trying to make them self-reliant. Above all, if they
wanted to secure change, they must not appear fanatical. "So you must
be calmer," he advised Evans, and then she would prove a more effective
advocate.

The hearings began in 1894, and the fifty-seven days of testimony
extended over nine months. One witness after another testified to the
horrid conditions on Long Island and the degrading nature of their so-
called care. At every step Brandeis hammered home his theme that no
matter how destitute, the paupers remained human beings and should
be treated as such, with compassion. They needed help, and the city

had the obligation not only to help them but also to make them independent and able to return to the community. "Men are not bad and men are not degraded because they desire to be so," he told the aldermen. "They are degraded largely through circumstances, and it is the duty of every man—and the main duty of those who are dealing with these unfortunates—to help them up and to let them feel in one way or another that there is some hope for them in life."

"They call this a Home for Paupers," he charged. "Home! With that name is associated every tender memory and feeling that one has, every attention, every kindness, and every little thing that may make one feel a little better, a little kinder toward his fellow man." Did any of the aldermen, he asked, feel any of those sentiments when they toured the facility? "Did you think for a moment when you were down there that that place is called by the city of Boston a 'home'?" There is a great deal of Brandeis the idealist talking here, despite his awareness that the city would never be able to do what he suggested.

The city did, in fact, clean up the building and improve the standards for care. But Boston had neither the knowledge nor the resources to do what Brandeis wanted done—attack the causes of pauperism so that there would be no need for institutions like Long Island. Mrs. Lincoln paid him $3,000 for his services, but by this time Louis had begun to question whether he ought to be accepting any money for public service. He gave some of it to his partners at the office to reimburse them for work the firm had done to prepare for the hearings, and the rest he gave to charity. Years later, when his son-in-law asked for advice about working pro bono, Brandeis said he had limited his gratuitous services to public causes, and he always let private individuals who hired him— even for a public service—pay something. This, he said, often allowed them to maintain their self-respect more easily than if he had served for free. And, he noted, they would also be more likely to recommend paying clients in the future. The young Brandeis wanted to work for the public good, but he also wanted to succeed in his law practice.

In 1897, Brandeis testified for the first time at a congressional hearing. He represented the New England Free Trade League in opposing the Dingley bill, which would have raised tariffs to the highest level in history, at a time when it had become clear that American manufacturing had no need of protection from foreign imports. By this time many American businesses utilized the tariff as a form of subsidy, as well as protection from less expensive foreign-made goods. Only the consumer, who had to pay more for everything from shoes to sugar to tinware, lost out.

Brandeis appeared before the House Ways and Means Committee on 11 January 1897, and while nominally appearing for his client, he also claimed to represent the public. "I desire to speak," he began, "on behalf of those who form, I believe, a far larger part of the people of the United States than any who have found representation here. I appear for those who want to be left alone, those who do not come to Congress and seek the aid of the sovereign powers of the government to bring them prosperity." When asked whom he represented, he identified the Free Trade League and "the business men and laboring men and the consumers," an answer that evoked jeers and laughter in the audience. Representative Benton McMillin (D-Tenn.) "supposed it would be in order for one man to appear who represented the consumer." John Dalzell (R-Pa.) made his displeasure clear, and said, "Oh, let him run down."

Brandeis's testimony before the committee is noteworthy in several respects. While it is not as clearly articulated as it would be within a few years, he had already come to the conclusion that high tariffs and the monopolies they fostered worked against the best interests of the country in that they choked off opportunity for small, independent businessmen, people like his father and brother, who worked hard to succeed on their own merits. A few years later he told the New England Free Trade League, of which he remained a member until after the passage of the Underwood Tariff Act in 1913:

> This asking for help from the government for everything should be deprecated. It destroys the old and worthy, sturdy principle of American life which existed in the beginning when men succeeded by their own efforts. That is what has led to the evils of the protective tariff and other laws to that end, by which men seek to protect themselves from competition. Never before did I realize the rightfulness of the movement we stand for and to which all must flock if they will save themselves and save American civilization.

Here one has a quintessential element of Louis Brandeis's progressivism—that government should not interfere with the economy to aid big business, since to do so not only violated the traditional American principle of self-reliance but also undermined the bases of democratic government.

Even while gaining attention for his work with the liquor lobby, the Long Island scandal, and the tariff hearings, Brandeis found he had less and less in common with the local Democrats and broke with the party completely in 1896 when it nominated William Jennings Bryan on a free-silver platform. Brandeis's clients such as the Filene brothers and William McElwain, as well as his own father and brother, had earned their success through brains, talent, and hard work. Like them, he valued sound monetary policies that sustained the value of the dollar, and the Democracy's adoption of a cheap money plank alienated many moderate and conservative members of the party.

In forwarding a copy of Bryan's speech, he surmised that "it must have been the voice and the manner, and above all the general temper of the audience that carried all away," for he found nothing attractive about an inflationary money policy. He asked Bess Evans to see John F. O'Sullivan, the labor reporter for the *Boston Globe,* and make sure that he did not commit himself to the silver platform. The workingmen would have the most to lose should Bryan win and Congress adopt free silver. He "hated this money question," and it would now place additional burdens on his time in the fall campaign, but he felt obligated to convince labor groups of the fallacy of free silver.

Mugwumps like Brandeis who had bolted the Republican Party a decade earlier had no intellectual difficulty in leaving the Democrats; they had acted out of principle the first time, and believed they now did so again. The hysteria that greeted Bryan's "cross of gold" speech at the convention, which he repeated over and over on the campaign trail, struck them as the mark of a populace gone mad. When Brandeis attended a Democratic ward caucus in Boston shortly after the 1896 election, defenders of the defeated Bryan challenged his right to attend a regular party meeting. The chair overruled the challenge, and Brandeis continued to see himself as a "small *d*" democrat, but in the next decade, as he embarked on a series of city and state reforms, he could count on virtually no support from Boston or Massachusetts Democratic Party leaders. In fact, he could not call on the party in any sense, since it was for all practical purposes bankrupt in both power and influence. The Boston machine survived, but with that group Brandeis had no truck. Only when he moved onto the national stage after 1910 with a reinvigorated Democracy could he exercise any power within, or draw support from, the party.

IN LATE 1889, Francis Amasa Walker, president of the Massachusetts Institute of Technology, approached Brandeis about teaching a course on business law. Walker knew that Brandeis believed that one had to understand business and its practices in order to provide good legal advice. Walker thought that MIT engineers, many of whom would work for business or become business owners themselves, ought to have a similar outlook, as well as an understanding of basic legal rules. Brandeis accepted almost immediately and agreed to offer the course during the 1891–1892 school year. He asked William Dunbar to collect cases relevant to the major points, and had others gather newspaper articles and additional materials, which he proceeded to shape into a coherent form of lectures for non–law students. Then health issues flared up, and Walker agreed to postpone the lectures for a year.

In a note to his father shortly after receiving Walker's invitation, Louis wrote that he intended in the lectures "to counteract all those monied interests." Surely anyone reading the newspapers at the time would have been aware of growing public concern over the monopolization of large sectors of industry and the behavior of millionaire robber barons. Moreover, his own experience with the Boston rag-disinfecting monopoly would have been fresh in his mind. But he did not oppose the corporate form per se, nor even large-scale enterprise by itself, and perhaps not even some combination among firms. "It is difficult to conceive how the great industrial development of the present century would have been possible," he noted. "The wealth, or at least the courage of single individuals would not have been equal to the task of constructing our railroads, of extending the systems of telegraphs over the continent, of erecting the gas and water works, of establishing banks and insurance companies, and the huge factories. In many of these enterprises great aggregations of capital were indispensable; in many they were desirable as a means of lessening the cost of the service rendered."

Brandeis had other ideas he wanted to convey to his students, among them his concern about the increasing amount of social, or protective, legislation, which Massachusetts and other states had recently begun to enact, both to protect workers and to indirectly facilitate the growth of labor unions. Brandeis did not oppose labor unions, but he believed, as he explained in a famous 1902 debate with Samuel Gompers, the president of the American Federation of Labor, they had to be subject to the same laws and constraints that applied to businesses and other organizations. Industry should not be allowed to act irresponsibly and capriciously, and neither should labor. By incorporating—an idea labor leaders like Gompers strenuously opposed—unions would both become legally respectable and gain protection from injunctions issued by courts that viewed unions as outlaw groups.

Although he would later be hailed as the People's Attorney for his defense of wages and hours legislation, at the time he prepared the MIT lectures, he opposed such laws, in part because his clients and friends had little sympathy for such regulations. If someone wanted to work long hours, as he himself did, why should the government interfere? "Working long hours in the day," he wrote in his lecture notes, "would probably be no more injurious to the health than not taking exercise, or than the eating of mince pies by people with weak digestion." The state, under its police powers, could definitely step in to protect public health, such as in sanitation rules, but at the time Brandeis saw no connection between long working hours and private health.

As for the relationship of law, the state, and the individual, the lectures showed Brandeis to be familiar and in sympathy with the writings of Thomas McIntyre Cooley and his most important work, *A Treatise on the Constitutional Limitations Which Rest upon the Legislative Power of the States of the American Union*, first published in 1868. Cooley, in many ways a Jacksonian Democrat, believed that government should not provide favors to business, and in fact equality of opportunity would best be secured by preventing government from interfering in economic affairs, including the contracting for labor. He also drew a sharp distinction between common-law and constitutional and statutory rules. Citizens wanted to know what the law required them to do and what it forbade, and so legal rules had to be clear. The common law's great strength lay in its ability to respond to changing economic and social circumstances, and here he believed that judges had not only the power but the responsibility to interpret the law so that its workings would be predictable. But, while common-law rules might be modified over time, the best way to respond to social and economic change would be through statutes or constitutional amendment, which would limit the discretion of both legislatures and courts. It seems clear from the lecture notes that at this time in his life, Brandeis subscribed to Cooley's ideas, and his views on the proper relation of the state to the economy and to the individual remained far closer to the mugwump he had been than to the progressive he would become.

Then the bloody strike at Homestead, Pennsylvania, erupted. Andrew Carnegie had recently purchased the large steel plant there and put Henry Clay Frick in charge. Both men wanted to get rid of the Amalgamated Association of Iron, Steel, and Tin Workers, which had been actively organizing steelworkers. After three months of fruitless negotiation, Frick issued an ultimatum. Either the union would accept a cut in wages, or he would lock them out of the mill and replace them with new workers. The deadline came on 30 June 1892 with no settlement. Frick erected a barbed-wire fence around the entire plant and then hired three hundred Pinkerton agents to guard the premises and to allow in only nonunion labor. The Pinkertons arrived on 6 July, and almost immediately violence began with several men on each side killed by gunfire. At Frick's request, the governor of Pennsylvania then sent in eight thousand troops to successfully crush the strike and the union. For the first two weeks of July 1892 newspapers all over the country ran the events at Homestead as their lead story on page one.

Twenty years later Brandeis told a reporter that Homestead had first set him to thinking seriously about labor relations, and how it had affected his proposed lectures at MIT:

> I had gone to some pains to prepare my lectures, tracing the evolution of the common law in its relation to industry and commerce, when one morning the newspaper carried the story of the pitched battle between the Pinkertons on the barge and barricaded steel workers on the bank. I saw at once that the common law, built up under simpler conditions of living, gave an inadequate basis for the adjustment of the complex relations of the modern factory system. I threw away my notes and approached my theme from new angles. Those talks at Tech marked an epoch in my own career.

Brandeis's later recollection, although dramatic, was not entirely accurate. While the reformer of 1911 would most certainly have sympathized with the right of labor to organize and to earn a living wage, the business lawyer of 1892, while no doubt appalled by the bloodshed, did not throw away his notes. He did write to get more information about what had happened at Homestead, but a close analysis of the lecture notes taken by one of the students indicates that instead of discarding his original plans, Brandeis simply added information on Homestead. The new material, however, did not significantly alter his view that government ought not to be involved in the economy, that while workers could organize, there had to be legal limits on union actions, and that the state ought not to use its police power to regulate working conditions. The insertions of Homestead materials show no conversion, and in fact some of the references to labor are quite negative. Brandeis at some point in his career did in fact change his mind about the role of the state and protective regulation, as well as the rights of labor to organize against superior business forces, but neither Homestead nor the MIT lectures triggered that change.

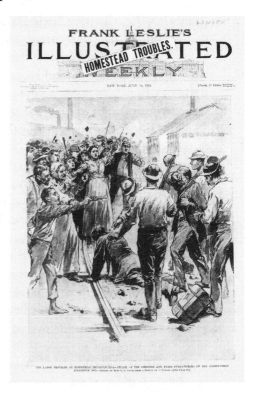

Confrontation between guards and workers at Homestead, Pennsylvania

ALTHOUGH LOUIS AND SAM Warren would remain friends until the latter's untimely death, and the firm would continue to act as legal adviser to the family and the paper business, the two men saw less of each other after 1883, when Sam married Mabel Bayard, the daughter of the Delaware senator Thomas Francis Bayard. No less a personage than Henry James considered Mabel Bayard a "happy specimen of the finished American girl—the American girl who has profited by the sort of social education that Washington gives." Unfortunately, she shared something else with many upper-class young women: a strong anti-Semitism. In those days the parents of the bride controlled the guest list to a wedding, and Mabel Bayard made sure Louis Brandeis's name was not on the list. The attractive couple soon made their home at 261 Marlborough Street in Boston's Back Bay, a major center for the city's social elite, but whenever possible Mabel Warren failed to invite her husband's friend to their gatherings.

Unfortunately, we have no mention by Brandeis of how he felt at the slight of not receiving an invitation to his best friend's wedding, and neither do we know why Sam did not insist on having him there. Nor does Mabel Warren's prejudice tell us anything about how it did, or did not, affect Brandeis. In 1883 he and Sam still shared a law practice, and Louis's letters to his sisters still talk of his socializing with the city's upper crust. Although he and Sam rarely got new clients from the

Brahmin elite, that says little about religious prejudice, since many of the Brahmins had patronized the same lawyers they had had since before the Civil War. Within the upper reaches of State Street finance, the important banking and securities houses had established relations with old-line law firms, and saw no reason to change because two bright young Harvard men had opened an office.

Naturally, the penny press of the era wanted to report on the doings of this couple and their friends, men and women who seemed to party constantly, had homes in the city and the country, rode to the hounds, sailed, and had the money to support such a lifestyle. For reasons not altogether clear, at some point Sam began to resent what he saw as press intrusion into his private life, and he turned to Louis. Brandeis did not really want to get involved (he said he would have preferred to write on the duty of publicity than on the right to privacy) but, at his friend's importuning, agreed to look into the issue. The two men then collaborated on one of the most celebrated articles in American legal history, "The Right to Privacy," published in the *Harvard Law Review* in 1890.

One needs to note immediately that the right described in the article is not the right of privacy that has been such a bone of contention among jurists and constitutional scholars ever since the Supreme Court enunciated it in 1965. Aside from the powerful and often-quoted attacks on press irresponsibility, the article in some ways is a very narrow, technical, and somewhat dry analysis of the legal rights of unpublished authors and artists. But the two men pointed the way for a much more expansive reading of what Mr. Justice Brandeis would later call "the most comprehensive of rights, and the right most valued by civilized man"—the right to be let alone.

The article begins with the following claim: that "the individual shall have full protection in person and in property is a principle as old as common law; but it has been found necessary from time to time to define anew the exact nature and extent of such protection. Political, social, and economic changes entail the recognition of new rights, and the common law, in its eternal youth, grows to meet the demands of society." They then suggested that over time, as society matured, ideas such as "the right to life" and "the right to property" also matured, to cover new notions of life and property. "Now the right to life has come to mean the right to enjoy life—the right to be let alone." In using this phrase, Warren and Brandeis essentially appealed to authority, because Judge Cooley had used the phrase "to be let alone" in his authoritative work on torts.

Being let alone meant one thing in a simpler society, where people lived in small enclaves and knew their neighbors. But now "instantaneous photographs and newspaper enterprise have invaded the sacred precincts of private and domestic life; and numerous mechanical devices threaten to make good the prediction that 'what is whispered in the closet shall be proclaimed from the house-tops.' " For years, they claimed, there had been a feeling that the law should afford some remedy for "unauthorized circulation of portraits of private persons." Here one could be forgiven for suddenly stopping and rereading the sentence—"unauthorized circulation of portraits of private persons"!

We have here a case of working with limited materials. In the nineteenth century neither federal nor state courts had expounded any jurisprudence of rights based on either the first ten amendments of the Constitution or the Fourteenth, other than a right to property and its uses, nor did invasion of privacy exist as a separate tort prior to this article. Warren and Brandeis knew that very little, if any, law existed that would protect people from snooping by an inquisitive press. They identified the evil easily enough, and in fact a good part of the article consists of moralistic attacks against an immoral press, with warnings about how the continuation of this type of journalism would belittle and pervert not just the press itself but society as well, by destroying "at once robustness of thought and delicacy of feeling. No enthusiasm can flourish, no generous impulse can survive under its blighting influence." But the two men also recognized a growing antagonism to conservative judges "making law" that would benefit conservative business interests and limit labor activity, so they did not want to appear to be asking judges to make new law in this area. Rather, by emphasizing established—if not always apposite—common-law principles, they took the position that a law creating a right to privacy already existed, and needed only to be utilized by judges when confronted by egregious violations of privacy.

Because no constitutional right to privacy existed, Warren and Brandeis seized upon a property right, the control of one's own portrait. Cases already existed where someone's picture had been used without his or her authorization, usually in connection with a product advertisement. But even if the law recognized a portrait as property, it did not mean that one could somehow equate privacy with any known form of property right. So Warren and Brandeis in essence created a tort—a civil wrong—that allowed people to recover damages for unwarranted intrusion into their private affairs. They did not equate privacy with portraiture; rather, they argued that if the law could protect a person's interest in his or her likeness, then certainly it ought to protect a more important interest, the right to be let alone. They then went on to analyze other legal principles that they believed bolstered their argument, such as copyright in one's written expression.

Over the years scholars, in analyzing and/or deconstructing the Warren and Brandeis arguments, have argued that the wrongs amounted to four separate actions, all of them trivial, or that they represented the "hypersensitivity of the patrician lawyer-merchant," or that, in effect, the two wanted to create a sense of private space. To look at the article these ways is to miss its importance. There may be some logical problems with the article's arguments, but Warren and Brandeis were the first to grapple with what would become an issue of great importance in a mechanized and regimented society: the right to be let alone. If we can get past the dry-as-dust references to English and state law cases, then we get to the heart of the matter. The two men are not really talking about physical space—although they do refer to invasions of the home—but about moral matters. Some critics have accused Warren and Brandeis of doing little more than trying to write "mugwump sensibilities" into law, that is, attempting to translate their own middle-class values into law. There is no question that the boundaries mentioned in the article are moral: the press oversteps "the obvious bounds of propriety and decency"; privacy is rooted in "the respect due to private life"; the law should penalize "the more flagrant breaches of decency and propriety." For Brandeis and for Warren, morality meant a great deal.

The intrusion into the home is not about crossing a physical boundary but about transgressing the respect that one member of a community owes to another. They are arguing not for a private space but for an "inviolate personality." They are seeking social norms that allow for what Roscoe Pound called "the mental peace and comforts of the individual." As Robert Post notes, what is most striking about the article today is the mugwump concept of community that it enunciates. To lose that privacy, according to Warren and Brandeis, would mean that the foundations of community itself would be undermined.

That community, and many of its assumptions, has largely disappeared. Legal developments in the latter part of the twentieth century have practically obliterated the laws of libel, and the constant flow of news on the private doings of the rich and famous in the press, on the Internet, and on television have led to a numbing of the senses. There is, however, a great difference in having the spotlight trained on people whose sole function in life is to be a "celebrity," and for whom there are no such things as either too much press or private matters. It is another matter completely for those who have no desire to be celebrities, who believe that at the end of the workday there should be a place of calm where the outside world can safely be shut out and none but the invited may enter.

Warren and Brandeis spoke for this latter group, but they also realized that the right to be let alone went far beyond merely being safe from the prying eyes of journalists. To be let alone meant that one could grow, could learn, could exercise his or her talents and intellects in a way that could not happen if others constantly interfered with and examined what should be essentially private. Much of the criticism of the article has tended to trivialize the insight the two men had into one of the important issues of modern times—how to protect one's personality, one's sense of self, amid the continuous pressures of a society that at times seems to recognize no individual boundaries.

Neither man naively believed that merely writing an article or even passing a law would achieve the goals they sought. "All law is a dead letter without public opinion behind it," Brandeis noted. "But law & public opinion interact, and they are both capable of being made. . . . Our hope is to make people see that invasions of privacy are not necessarily borne—and then to make them ashamed of the pleasure they take in subjecting themselves to such invasions." And in an eerily prescient aside, he noted that many people in fact want to have their private affairs made public, an attitude of which he most thoroughly disapproved. But when Sam Warren later asked Louis to draft a bill embodying the gist of their law review article, Louis ignored the request.

"The Right to Privacy" became famous overnight. An article in the 1905 *American Law Review* called it "one of the most brilliant excursions in the field of theoretical jurisprudence which the recent literature of the law discloses." Dean Roscoe Pound of Harvard Law School claimed that the article did "nothing less than add a chapter to our law." Twenty years later the *Columbia Law Review* noted that the piece "enjoys the unique distinction of having initiated and theoretically outlined a new field of jurisprudence." "The Right to Privacy" remained the most cited article in American legal scholarship until 1947, and within a few years of its appearance plaintiffs seeking damages for invasion of privacy began to win their suits, with arguments fashioned on the article's premises. Eventually, privacy of the individual as against the government or the press would become an important issue in American life and law, and in no small portion that is due to the efforts of Warren and Brandeis and later to those of Mr. Justice Brandeis.

Years later Brandeis told Alpheus Mason: "This, like so many of my public activities, I did not volunteer to do." For ever since the spring of 1890, Louis Brandeis's main interest in life had been not the writing of an article or even his law practice but the courting of his second cousin Alice Goldmark.

CHAPTER FIVE
ALICE

In the spring of 1885, Louis's brother-in-law Charles Nagel wrote to him congratulating him on the success he had enjoyed. "You are a fortunate and a deserving man," Nagel said, "and there is no one to envy you; unless it is perhaps some noble woman who thinks she might fairly be included in the halo of your happiness and herself intensify if not enlarge it." This, of course, had not been the first suggestion of this kind that Louis had heard. His sisters, both of whom had married early, constantly wanted to know if any of the young women he met in his social outings interested him in a serious way. His brother, Alfred, had married their second cousin Jennie Taussig in September 1884, and Louis took great pleasure both in Al's personal happiness and in the growing success of the firm, which Alfred had chosen to call A. Brandeis & Son. Needless to say, his parents wondered why their youngest child, as he passed his thirtieth birthday, remained unmarried.

Family mattered a great deal to Louis, and as his siblings married and had children, Uncle Louis made sure to keep up on their growth. The first of his nieces arrived the summer before he moved to St. Louis, and the young lawyer, who had probably never held a baby in his life, wrote jokingly to his sister Amy, "I hope you are bringing up little Fannie on the most approved theories of baby-training." Science had learned a great deal in the last few years, so all the old theories and practices had to be discarded. No more cradles to hold the newborn, but baskets, and "uncles are not to be made miserable by the 'Rock Me to Sleep.'" He worried that news of these new discoveries had not yet reached the shores of the Ohio River, and did not "want my niece to be behind the times." When two years later the couple named their second child Louis Brandeis Wehle, he could barely contain his pride and joy. "My *name* is in your hands," he declared, and sent little Louis a beautiful silver spoon, which elicited a "sisterly scolding" from Amy for its extravagance. He moved to St. Louis just in time to be there when his sister Fannie gave birth to a boy, Alfred Nagel. (Fannie, Amy, and Alfred, but not Louis, tended to name their children after their siblings.) Throughout his life Louis stayed in touch with his nieces and nephews, occasionally drafting them to help him on a pet cause or, in the case of his namesake, to act as his attorney at times.

BRANDEIS THOUGHT that his favorite sister, Fannie, had the best mind of any person he had ever known. Unfortunately, Fannie suffered not only from poor health but from a highly nervous temperament that led to frequent bouts of depression. "My life needs arranging," she lamented to Lutz. "Inclinations & strength clash sadly, and so much is a bore." When a few days had passed without a letter from him, she complained that she grew "so desperate in this way . . . that I make all sorts of desperate plans and resolutions." In talking about a friend whom she portrayed as depressed, she described her own feelings. "When one does not like the present and has no positive wish for the future. I know so well the mood in which the life we are leading seems 'provisional' and I know nothing more unsatisfactory." As for her son, Alfred, he was a "dear child," and Charles made a very good father, but as a parent she herself made "poor work of it."

Fannie did not live in a constant state of depression, and when she felt well, her letters reflected the fine mind that her brother later recalled. Her husband had given her a copy of Thomas Babington Macaulay's *Life and Letters* for Christmas one year, and she deemed it a book that should not be skimmed but really be read. She wrote with a marvelous dry wit of some of the people she had met, or of the beauty she had seen while walking in nearby woods and meadows. But far too often her letters to her siblings hinted at a growing depression at or just below the surface, and it seemed to take all of her effort to get through each day. Not to "think beyond the day is a good motto," she told Amy, "or perhaps not to think of the next days, but of those much further off." When she had visitors, they tired her, but if they did not come, she felt "as though the world had forsaken me."

Fannie and Charles had another child, Hildegard, born in 1886, but as the decade passed, Fannie seemed to suffer even more from exhaustion and its accompanying depression. "I have not been well these last months," she told Louis, "so often very, very tired." Then, in 1888, young Alfred, just shy of ten years, came down with typhoid fever and died, and the family chose not to tell Fannie at the time lest it aggravate her depression, a decision made possible by Fannie's own extended illness at the time. In December 1889, Louis wrote to his father urging him and Charles

to let nature take its course with Fannie—whatever that course may be. Don't force her to eat if she does not desire to do so. If there is a Providence—(& I believe there is)—he may be offering the great corrective for the suffering which she has borne. We interfered once and have had reason to regret it. I am glad she knows of Alfred's death. I cannot bear to be guilty of untruth with her anymore than I would interfere with her action as to herself in regard to eating. I have heard it said that with some patients the desire to refuse food was the one sane wish.

But Fannie did not recover, and on 5 March 1890 killed herself.

Louis immediately left for St. Louis for her funeral, stopping in Louisville to join his parents. While there, he paid a visit to his uncle Samuel, who he discovered had houseguests, his second cousins Henry Goldmark and his sister Alice.

THE GOLDMARK AND BRANDEIS CLANS knew each other well and were related through the Wehle branch of the family; Frederika Dembitz had often played with her younger cousin Regina Wehle in Prague. Whereas Adolph Brandeis had been prevented by illness from participating in the Revolution of 1848, Dr. Joseph Goldmark had been in the thick of it. A distinguished scientist at the University of Vienna, he became a deputy in the new Reichstag. Then the rebellion that his group had fomented got out of hand, and a mob killed the reactionary minister of war, Baron Latour. The conservative government indicted Goldmark for murder, even though he had had nothing to do with the assassination. Knowing that in the climate of reaction already setting in he would surely be convicted, he fled first to Switzerland and then to the United States in 1850. A few years later, the government convicted him in absentia for treason and sentenced him to death. He spent the next decade trying to clear his name, and when a new and more liberal government came to power, he returned to Vienna, stood trial, and won acquittal.

Joseph and Regina had ten children. Henry had been at Harvard at the same time that Louis had been in the law school, and they saw each

Felix Adler

other occasionally. After graduation Henry went to Germany for training as an engineer, became a well-known bridge and railroad consultant, and was most famous for the design of the Panama Canal locks. Helen married Felix Adler, the founder of the Ethical Culture movement, and she essentially ran the movement's social and educational programs. She started a visiting-nurse service for poor families and wrote one of the first manuals for mothers on the proper care of children. James went into business as a wire manufacturer and was involved in a number of good-government reforms; he also helped to set up boys' clubs affiliated with the University Settlement in New York. Josephine Clara Goldmark, known to the family as Do, became a very important part of Louis's reform work. She provided the factual research for the Brandeis brief in *Muller v. Oregon* (1908) and then, as a representative of the National Consumers League, worked with him defending other protective legislation in the courts. During the New Deal she became an influential figure in the drafting of national labor laws.

The two families had been in touch over the years, with the elder Brandeises occasionally stopping in New York to visit, or the two families vacationing near each other in the Adirondacks or New Hampshire. When Joseph Goldmark died in 1881, Louis sent a condolence note to Helen Adler, whom he knew well enough to call by her nickname, Nellie. But once he began to practice law, Louis found it harder and harder to get away to visit his own family on its summer vacations for more than a few days at a time, much less to visit relatives who might be nearby, and as a result he probably remembered Alice as a little girl, or at most a teenager. The poised, attractive, and intelligent young woman he met at Uncle Samuel and Aunt Lotti's house took his breath away.

The Goldmarks, like the Brandeis family, assumed that books, art, and music constituted an essential part of one's life. Although not formally educated, Alice had learned a great deal in her parents' house, where conversation veered from the political to the cultural with little gap in between. Like Louis, she had read widely in classic German literature and could speak German and a few other languages as well. In the 1920s she translated the memoirs of her uncle the famous composer Karl Goldmark and also translated a small book on democracy and education in Denmark. After Louis's death she translated Frederika's memoirs from German into English for the benefit of her children and grandchildren. Within a very short time, Alice and Louis discovered that they shared very similar ideas on literature and the arts, the meaning of a good life, and the duty to leave the world a better place. Their correspondence over the next few months included references to Franz Grillparzer, Shakespeare, Thomas à Kempis, Emerson, Matthew Arnold, and Voltaire, to name a few. Louis had found his soul mate, and he now set out to court her.

Alice saved nearly all of the letters that Louis wrote to her from the time they met as adults until after he went on the Court and stopped traveling. The first, dated 9 June 1890, in response to an invitation to visit her and her family at their summer vacation house in Keene Valley, in New York's Adirondack Mountains, is a fairly formal and somewhat stilted note saying that he would like to come and asking whether early July would be convenient to her family. Apparently, his efforts to get away from work proved unavailing, and at the end of July, during a weekend visit with his parents on Martha's Vineyard, he promised that he would somehow manage to get to Keene Valley before the fall. He arrived on 26 August, and as Alice noted in her diary, their conversation "picked up just where we left it in the spring." He and Alice spent the next few days walking and having "long, pleasant and thoughtful talk, never to be forgotten." They also went canoeing on the Ausable River, and Alice noted approvingly how Louis would take care of the small children, taking each of them out for a paddle. But whatever else they did, "his eyes are always upon me. We go down to the river and he tells me his story—we have found each other."

After Louis returned from the Adirondacks, his brother-in-law Charles Nagel, who had brought the four-year-old Hildegard east to visit her vacationing Brandeis grandparents, immediately saw that something was up and demanded to know what had happened. When Louis wrote again, he now employed the language of an ardent suitor. "My dear, sweet Alice," he began. Charlie Nagel had come to visit him in Boston, "and to him I could speak of you as I could speak to no one but you. Fannie's spirit surrounds us and their ideal love brings me so near to Charlie now." They had stayed up talking until one o'clock, since "there was so much to say of you and of Fannie, of Fannie and of you. How she would have rejoiced in you and felt with us!"

All of a sudden whole new vistas opened. Before their meeting "it appeared as if the only joy in life lay in the performance of duties as duties, and now there appears the happiness of living." He even began to change his habits and claimed he felt her presence when he gave up his usual after-dinner cigarette because she did not like smoking. He became impatient for the mail and exulted when the post brought him three letters. He reported on a visit to the Warrens' home shortly after the family returned from Europe with a wealth of paintings, and wished that they could have seen them together. "I am so impatient to pour out to you my thoughts and to plead for yours. I feel now that the world is so full of interest. Things which were dead to me have become instinct with life, in the thought that they will interest you." Louis's idealism struck a spark with Alice, and as she told Mrs. Evans, "He is so good and noble, every thought of him seems to purify, to elevate me. I feel myself so small, so unworthy, of the blessing which has come to me."

Sometime in early September, Louis and Alice reached an understanding that they would marry. By the second week in September he had begun telling his friends and passing on their good wishes. On the fifteenth he informed Bess, and wrote to Alice, "I wish you could have seen Mrs. Glendower Evans when I told her. She fairly bounded across the room." The legendary Charles Townsend Copeland of Harvard warned Louis, "She must like me. Tell her to—or at least to pretend to." Louis and Alice agreed that her family would make a formal announcement of the engagement on 4 October, although the prospective bridegroom could not wait and began sending letters to his close friends outside of Boston informing them of the troth. He also reported that his friends in the city were clamoring to meet her. In fact, Louis wrote, about the only person who might not be happy about the engagement would be Jim Young, with whom he had shared lodgings since 1884 and who would now have to make another arrangement.

From Sam Warren came a letter commending Louis and rejoicing that his friend had found love. Sam told Alice that he rarely spoke about Louis, lest he appear too fulsome in his praise. But to her he wanted to say so much—"his courage is high, his fidelity perfect, and his sense of honor delicate." The only part of Louis that he did not know about involved that on which he and Alice stood ready to embark, but he had no doubts that "the bravest are the tenderest, the loving are the daring." Then, in words that later seemed hollow, he expressed his hope that he and his wife would have "the *pleasure* of welcoming you to Boston, and to that important part of our lives which we have in common with Louis."

READING THE LETTERS, one cannot help but smile at the joy and happiness that they radiate, at the marking of their little anniversaries, at the impatience to be together, but there is also a glimpse at Louis's inner beliefs and hopes that he had not shared with anyone else. For seventeen years, he told Alice, "I have stood alone, rarely asking, still less frequently caring for the advice of others. I have walked my way all these years

Louis Brandeis around the time of his engagement, 1890

but little influenced by any other individual. And now, Alice, all is changed. I find myself mentally turning to you for advice and approval." Clearly, Brandeis had been influenced by others in his life; his jurisprudence came, at least in part, from Langdell, Holmes, and Thayer; he copied out lines from Emerson and William James; and he certainly cared about the views of his family. But now he had someone with whom he could share his beliefs, who could be a sounding board, whose opinion he would respect, not just on one matter but on everything they cared about. As he wrote, "I pour out my innermost thoughts to you. . . . I have longed so for the one to whom I should give all that I am, without reserve."

While he anticipated a life of happiness and love ahead of them, he also knew that they did not live in an ideal world. "People, like us, with some experience could not look into the future from this perfect present, without some apprehensions," he wrote, perhaps thinking of the death

Alice Goldmark, 1890

of his sister earlier in the year. "Only trust in me," he pleaded, and he would do everything possible to make their lives good ones.

But what constituted a good life? Not material rewards or public accolades, but service and striving counted. Louis told Alice what joy it had given him to see, on the flyleaf of her diary, paraphrasing from Matthew Arnold: "Life is not a having and a getting, but a being and becoming." Character counted above all else, and he recalled telling an acquaintance about Eliza Ward, a friend of the Brandeis family's in Louisville, who had that rare combination of beauty and mind, charm of manner and character. When he had "finished my rhapsody," one of the company asked, "What has she done?" Louis said that he answered, rather heatedly, "Done? Nothing. She is!" Character more than accomplishment mattered. "Character only is to be admired."

As for accomplishment, he told Alice that his father had recently commented on some "petty success" of his and had remarked, "You must be proud of that honor." Louis told Adolph that he could not recall "ever having been proud of anything accomplished or to have deemed any recognition an honor. Indeed, I believe the little successes I may have had were due wholly to the pressure from within, proceeding from a deep sense of obligation and in no respect to the allurement of a possible distinction." Results, of course, should not be despised, but while results sometimes attested to the drive that produced them, they could also be deceptive on that score. It is the effort, the attempt to do something worthwhile that matters. This should not be seen as hyperbole. In examining the Brandeis letters covering more than six decades, one finds very few expressing satisfaction and almost none expressing pride over the outcome of a particular reform. The only exception occurred when Woodrow Wilson named him to the Supreme Court in 1916, and that had to do as much with the vindication of his views regarding Zionism and Americanism as anything else.

Louis did not discount the idea that he might, in his lifetime, do great things, and he expected that with Alice's help and encouragement much could be accomplished. But like him, Alice valued character and right living, which they agreed meant focusing on the individual. Although it would still be several years before he began to attack the "curse of bigness," in December 1890 he told his fiancée that "we Americans particularly have been so overwhelmed with huge figures that we are apt to underestimate the value of the unit in the great mass." But he did not idealize the masses, as some reformers did. Most people, he told Alice, "lie powerless, motionless, dormant before the magnet" of leadership and example is applied, and whether they would move toward the good or the bad was a matter of chance. If it were to be for the good, then people of strong character had to show the way. He repeated this idea when telling her about the article he and Sam Warren had written on privacy. "Most of the world is in more or less a hypnotic state, and it is comparatively easy to make people believe anything, particularly the right." To this extent, Brandeis indeed shared Jefferson's faith that the people, if properly informed and led, would act wisely, but unlike the Virginian he recognized that the people could also be manipulated.

ONCE ENGAGED, Louis began commuting to New York almost every weekend, and only a pressing business matter would keep him from taking the train. He also found himself, like many a love-struck swain, having a difficult time keeping his mind on business. "I am doing many foolish things," he told Alice. "One was telling a client he could consult me tonight, and I am sure my opinion will be of little value to him." Although the engagement was not long by the standards of the time, Louis wanted to marry sooner rather than later, and while it is unlikely that Alice had second thoughts about Louis, she nonetheless seemed hesitant in setting an actual date. First it appeared that it would be 2 March, but when Louis seized upon that day, she wrote to him that it was "not quite definitely settled yet." He wisely did not push her, but appeared increasingly frustrated until she agreed to 23 March, a day that to him seemingly would never come. On 13 March, he wrote that he would happily "jump the week to come. Work attracts me no longer and I do no good here." Two days later he declared that if the date had not been immutably set, "I should feel like anticipating it, and like the Barons of old, break away and carry you off."

During these months Alice would occasionally come to Boston, chaperoned by one of her sisters and staying with Bess Evans, who became her closest friend. There was much to do in those months, not the least of which involved finding and furnishing a house. Despite his protestations in the letter that Alice should always tell him what she thought—to "exercise the prerogatives of a partner"—they quickly fell into a pattern where he would make arrangements and then check with her to see if they met her approval, which they always did.

He soon found a house for them. By the first of October he wrote that he had bought 114 Mount Vernon Street, a few blocks from the Warren residence and next door to his good friends Lorin and Margaret Deland, the latter a well-known novelist who often addressed issues of social justice in her books. Lorin, a wealthy Bostonian interested in literature and the arts, owned an advertising agency whose profits supported several local charities. Brandeis described the place to Alice as "not ideal. Only of the possible it seemed the best for us." Lorin, who apparently had plenty of time on his hands, became Louis's lieutenant in the search for a home as well as in fitting it up properly, and they both hoped that when Alice next came to Boston, she would like the building.

The letters between October 1890 and March 1891 are full of details about the house, how much it would cost to buy and install wallpaper and blinds, the gift of a large hall clock from one of Louis's clients, the offer of a dog (which they turned down), the installation of new brass and plumbing fixtures, and the like. Louis sent Alice an estimate for the shades, $25.25 for twenty-five shades, and at the bottom noted, "You & I are very economical." Workmen installed new floors and fixed broken laths, and then painters and wallpaper hangers came in to give the whole house a shiny new interior. "The yard has been cleaned out & the carpenters are finishing the coal bin today," he reported at the end of January. "The mantels are expected next week." Louis sent samples of the new wallpapers to chemists to be sure that they contained no arsenic, and he rejected any that had even a trace of the poison. Since Alice did not ride, Louis bought a small buggy, as well as lap rugs and a warm red Shaker cloak, so they could go out. He and the Delands had extended conversations about servants, since Alice clearly would direct household help and not do the work herself. Louis took over these chores in part because he was on the scene, stopping in every day to remind workmen of their promises regarding completion of different tasks. When possible, he consulted with Alice, and it is clear from the letters that she had many ideas as to color, style, and furniture that he accepted. There are no letters to the effect: "I do not like your idea on this or that."

But just as important, and as an omen of future difficulties, Alice did not, even as a girl, enjoy the robust health that one associates with a young person. Louis might complain of being tired, but one could understand that in light of the schedule of work and other activities he maintained, and as he grew older, the problem seemed to afflict him less often. But Alice lacked stamina and suffered from physical and mental exhaustion through the first three decades of their marriage, requiring frequent medical attention and stays in rest homes. This is probably the reason that while several of her sisters and brothers attended college, she did not. Louis no doubt recognized that she had a frail constitution, and so assumed the responsibility for managing their households and their lives. He dealt with the renovation of their house in Boston, arranged for the summer cottages and vacations, paid the bills, and in general took over as much of the household responsibility as he could.

There is another side to this, however, which perhaps contributed to the problem. Louis frequently told Alice that he wanted her to be his partner and his equal in the marriage. In the beginning of their courtship he would either jump right into the text of the letter without any greeting, impatient to tell her things, or address her as "My dear, dear Alice." This became "My dear, sweet girl," and then "My dear child." Granted, Louis was ten years older than Alice, but at the time of their engagement she could hardly be called a child, even metaphorically. When he wrote to her about political or cultural or idealistic matters, he spoke to her as an equal, valued her opinion, and rejoiced that they shared the same values. But in other, more practical matters, such as the work on the house or even her clothing, he adopted a tone that, if not patronizing, seemed to be more of a lesson than a love letter.

For example, during one of his visits to New York they had discussed dress, and Alice, tired from the constant fittings she had to endure from the dressmaker in preparation of her trousseau, complained that she did not care for fashion and the need to wear the latest style. Louis agreed with her and said that he "hate[d] frivolous frills and overdressing" and thought that most women had too many dresses. But "when a woman happens to be both handsome and artistic a certain obligation rests upon her. There is a call upon her thought and taste. With a woman of mind and of taste there is the same reason why her dress should be more effective as there is that her house should be more attractive or her table better." In other words, he expected her to dress in a manner appropriate to her station in life. Similarly, when she felt guilty about not taking her sister to hear a lecture because she had been tired, Louis instructed her, as one would a child, on the need to maintain her health. People who really loved her would understand, and he reported that just the other day he had come across an article in which the author had declared that "faithful maintenance of bodily health is as much a woman's duty as to speak the truth."

Louis and Alice, the products of cultured, prosperous, German-American households, reflected the attitudes of their culture and the Victorian era toward marriage. The man would be the head of the house and responsible for the economic as well as physical needs of the family. The woman would run the home, bear children, and look to the moral and emotional requirements of husband, children, and servants. In practice, Louis always treated Alice as his intellectual equal, took her advice seriously, and confided in her. He also, because of her physical infirmities, had to take over much of what would normally have been her household responsibilities.

THE DAY FIXED for the wedding, 23 March—also Alfred's birthday—finally arrived. Louis and Alice, dressed neatly but simply, took their vows in the large sunny dining room of the Goldmark house at 473 Park Avenue. Adolph and Frederika had come from Louisville, but none of the other members of the family came, not even Alfred, nor had any of Louis's close friends in Boston, such as Sam Warren, Bess Evans, or the Delands. On the bride's side, her mother, brothers, and sisters attended, as well as the redoubtable aunt Julia Wehle. Neither family believed in large weddings, and the Brandeises still mourned the loss of their oldest child only a year earlier. Apparently, no one on the Brandeis side grumbled about the small ceremony, but some of Alice's relatives, especially her uncle who had taken over the family's business and finances after the death of Joseph Goldmark, complained bitterly to Alice's mother about not being invited.

Felix Adler, Alice's brother-in-law and the head of the New York Society for Ethical Culture, officiated. Given that neither family observed Jewish ritual, Dr. Adler led a brief ceremony that emphasized the need for service to one's fellow humans. After a short reception the couple left to spend a week at the Wilder Mansion, a Massachusetts inn where they were the only guests in the off-season. Alice's sisters then mailed out what Pauline recalled as "thousands" of wedding announcements, which they "stuffed [in] the mailboxes all around our neighborhood to the disgust of the carriers."

After their honeymoon Alice and Louis moved into the house on

Mount Vernon Street. They had sent Bess Evans a key so she could unpack Alice's trunks and get everything ready for the couple on their return. Alice's younger sister Pauline, then a college freshman, recalled it as "the most wonderful house we'd ever seen, so small and so quaint and with such beautiful old furniture." From this house Louis could easily walk to his office; for recreation the Boston Common and Public Gardens were practically around the corner, with the boat club and the canoe minutes away. They lived here until they moved to larger quarters, at 6 Otis Place near Bess Evans, after their family had grown. As they had with their first house, Alice and Louis decorated it with good furniture, but little in the way of extraneous adornment. In 1916 a newspaper reporter called the Brandeis home "almost severe in its freedom from bric-à-brac and cumbersome furniture."

From all recollections of the couple by people who knew them well, Louis fulfilled the promise he made to Alice during their engagement—that she would be an equal partner in his life's work. As he became more and more involved in reform work, she became not only a sounding board for ideas but an adviser as well. As Belle La Follette wrote at the time of Louis's nomination to the Supreme Court, "It would not have been possible for him to have made the great sacrifices—to have devoted so much time, energy, and money to the public welfare, if she had been different. In all his efforts she was not only willing, but has given that whole-hearted and sustaining support which can only come from inner conviction." During his most active reform years, beginning around 1910 and ending only with his nomination, Louis was often away weeks at a time, arbitrating labor disputes in New York, advising congressional committees and cabinet officers in Washington, running the Zionist movement from wherever he might be, but he wrote to Alice every day, telling her what had transpired, whom he had met, and asking what she thought. Physically frail she may have been, but her mind proved the perfect complement to her husband's. When home, the two invariably took a long walk each day during which they discussed the issues that mattered to them most. As Felix Frankfurter noted, "Nothing petty, nothing shallow or meretricious was ever allowed to intrude into the pattern of their life together." Brandeis knew, Frankfurter declared, that the life he chose to pursue, with all its hardships and criticism, could not have been possible without Alice.

Although she did not have the physical stamina to accompany him on many of his outdoor activities, she did enjoy the canoe and became an avid bird lover. This sometimes annoyed Bess, with whom she would go walking, because in the middle of what Bess called "real conversation," Alice would suddenly espy an unusual bird and insist on pointing it out to her friend, who would respond, "Oh, yes, nice little bird," and try to get back to what they had been talking about. Whenever out in the canoe, Alice always took along a pair of field glasses so she could watch for uncommon species. Once, Louis wrote to her about a strange bird he had seen while walking to work, "chubby, about twice the size of a large fat English sparrow, with a yellow patch on top of head & somewhat yellow collar," and wondered if she could identify it for him. Alice also loved flowers and planted them in profusion at their weekend and summer homes, first in Dedham and then on the Cape. When his wife felt too tired or ill to accompany him on a walk there, Louis would always try to find a pretty flower to bring back to her.

Over the years Alice developed many interests of her own. An early advocate of votes for women, she undoubtedly helped Louis see the error of his ways, and he too came to endorse the suffrage. She served on the executive board of the Massachusetts Civic League, helped found the Women's City Club of Boston, and served as the first chair of the latter's civic affairs committee. After she met Mary Follett, she began working with her on extending the reach of public schools into the community, one of the leading ideas of progressive educational reformers at the time. This eventually led to the founding of the National Community Center Association; Alice served for many years on its executive board and became its chairperson in 1930. Prior to World War I, she joined the Massachusetts chapter of the Women's International League for Peace and Freedom, and in the 1920s became vice president of the National Council for Preservation of the Peace. During the turmoil attendant upon the Sacco and Vanzetti case in the 1920s, Alice could not participate openly, but quietly helped her friend Bess Evans, and one time, at Mrs. Evans's request, allowed members of the Sacco family to stay at one of the rental houses that Brandeis owned.

One might have expected that given Louis's wide range of acquaintances in Boston, Alice would have been welcomed into the city's society. Indeed, Mrs. Henry Lee Higginson came to call on her and welcome her to the city shortly after the couple moved into their house. Friends like Sam Warren, the Delands, and Arthur Cabot, according to Alpheus Mason, eased Alice's entrance into "cold-roast" Boston society. At least initially, Alice seemed to feel no more of the anti-Semitism growing in Boston and elsewhere than did her husband.* That, however, changed once Louis began challenging the city's financial elite in the late 1890s (see next chapter). Then many of the men who gladly called on Brandeis for his legal skills would have nothing to do with him socially, even if they belonged to the same clubs, and their wives ignored Alice completely. According to Bess Evans, when society closed its doors to the Brandeises, Alice, whatever her private feelings, publicly did not seem to care. She stood by and supported Louis's crusades. When Bess later asked Louis about this, he told her, "I could not have lived my life without Alice" in those days. "If my wife had been hurt, how could I have had the strength to go on?"

THE EARLY YEARS of their marriage may have been among the happiest in their lives. As Alice told Mrs. Evans shortly after the wedding, "I never dreamed that such happiness was possible." Louis's life also changed dramatically. Now that he had a home and no longer stayed in lodgings, Louis felt free to invite people to the house for dinner. This habit, designed to meet and learn from new and interesting people, would continue well into his years on the Court. Louis and Alice also received invitations, especially when all of his friends and many of his

---

*The only scholar to report that the Brandeises faced overt anti-Semitism in these days is Allon Gal, who claims that for all their weekend trips to Dedham, the locals ignored the family. Louis, according to Gal, had been admitted to the Dedham Polo Club at the behest of Sam Warren, but as one Brahmin wrote in 1916, "It was a club of gentlemen, and Brandeis was soon conspicuously left to 'flock by himself,' with the result that he ceased to frequent the club and his absence was not regretted." Neither Brandeis daughter recalled, other than going out to Dedham when they were children, having anything to do with the local Yankee community, which viewed the Brandeises as southern and non-Christian. Even Alice's accent (presumably not a northeastern twang) worked against her. There were a few friends there, such as the publisher Herbert Maynard, but Gal claims their families did not visit with the outsiders (*Brandeis of Boston*, 38–39). This may or may not be true, but Louis never wrote anything in his letters to Alfred about such bias at this time, though later he did. Nor did Alice ever talk about any sense of ostracism to Elizabeth Evans, her closest friend, with whom she discussed everything. Moreover, Louis and Alice were not the types of people to deliberately flaunt their "otherness," and it is curious that if, in fact, the Yankees of Dedham disliked them so much, they kept their house there for many years and spent not only weekends but sometimes even weeks there in the winter as well as the summer. The fact that they did not partake of the social activities at the Polo Club is not surprising either. Louis made it plain that he valued the facility for its stable, where he could keep his horses and have them well tended. The Brandeises never belonged to any club for socializing purposes.

clients wanted to meet the new Mrs. Brandeis, but they most enjoyed a circle of close friends that included Bess Evans and their next-door neighbors, the Delands.

Mrs. Evans recalled an annual ritual held in the Brandeis house on Louis's birthday, 13 November, every year from the time he married until he left Boston for Washington in 1916. Alice's family had brought with them a custom from Europe in which on a person's birthday they adorned his or her chair with a long strand of laurel and put flowers before the dinner plate. The festivities always began with Lorin Deland, one year older than Louis, saying, with a broad grin, "Well, Louis, poor fellow, how I pity you. The year ahead will be the most terrible of your life." Thereupon, Bess Evans, also a year older than Louis, would exclaim, "Don't you believe him, Louis, the year you are entering will be your very best!"

Their happiness grew with the births of two daughters, Susan (named after Alice's sister) on 27 February 1893 and Elizabeth (named after Mrs. Evans) on 25 April 1896. Because of Alice's frailty, there had been some concerns about her being able to have children, but a little after a year of marriage she conceived. A few days after Susan's birth Louis wrote to Bess Evans, then traveling overseas, "Susan is pronounced a very fine child. She is certainly exemplary in her behavior." The birth had been difficult for Alice and caused the doctors some alarm the first few days, but she improved steadily and then happily began to nurse the child. The proud husband described his wife as "even lovelier than before. There has been much of the time a calm madonna-like serenity and strength which seemed to lift her above things worldly." It took Alice a long time, however, before she regained her strength.

The Brandeis household soon took on a pattern that lasted for several years. Louis normally rose around 5:00 or 5:30 and, after washing, would read or do some work in preparation for the day. He came down for breakfast a little after seven, and first Susan, and then both girls, would join him. Louis enjoyed a good breakfast—oatmeal, coffee or hot chocolate, and some kind of meat, such as a pork chop or steak—while the girls had shredded wheat. Before leaving for the office at eight, he would read to them, listen to whatever stories they wanted to tell, or, after they started school, help them with their homework. If they had a question, he would not answer it directly, but send them over to the dictionary or the encyclopedia to look it up, believing that people retained what they had to learn by themselves far better than knowledge casually handed to them by another. Alice would normally rest in bed, and one of the three servants the household employed would take her breakfast upstairs to her. These morning conversations suited both Louis's interests and those of the girls. One morning he told them about Solon and the wise laws he had caused to be enacted. As he left the house, Susan ran after him crying out, "Tell me another law!" As they grew older, they became conversant with his reform work. Louis loved to tell the story that when Susan was about fourteen, he explained to her some of the issues surrounding the efforts by the New Haven Railroad to buy up all the other rail lines in New England. Susan thought for a moment and then declared, "The idea! Where would there then be any competition?" When Louis left for work, Susan would walk with him across Boston Common to his office, returning to the house with her nurse. Later, after Susan had started school, Elizabeth would join him. In the summer the stroll would be from their house in Dedham to the train station.

At the end of his workday, Louis left the office by five, walked home, changed his clothes, and, depending on weather and whim, would either go horseback riding, take out a canoe on the Charles, or even play tennis. While getting ready, he amused the children by telling them a story, such as Robert Louis Stevenson's *Kidnapped,* in serial form, always leaving them eagerly awaiting the next installment. When he traveled, he wrote every day to Alice and took pains either to add a line for the girls or, when they grew older, to write to them separately. He had to go to the Midwest on business in the spring of 1897 and, after describing to Alice the places he had been, said, "Tell Susan there is much sand in Michigan to make cakes of, and tell Elizabeth that its inhabitants are called 'suckers.' "

Louis and Alice "dressed" for dinner, although not necessarily in formal wear. But the clothes Louis wore to ride or canoe would be replaced with tie and jacket, and Alice would also change her dress. The Brandeises ate well, but not lavishly, although in later years they adopted an even simpler regimen that some of their guests considered spartan. Judge Julian W. Mack, whom Brandeis knew as one of the first editors of the *Harvard Law Review* and who later became one of his lieutenants in the American Zionist movement, enjoyed gourmet food and used to complain that when you joined Brandeis for dinner, you had to eat twice, once what they served and then a "real" meal later. But in these early years, Alice and Louis set a nice table, with meat or fish every evening, often accompanied by beer or sherry. Each of them had a sweet tooth. All his life Louis loved ice cream, while Alice enjoyed Belgian chocolates and candied fruits from S. S. Pierce.

They entertained regularly, not in large parties, but one or two people for dinner, because in small groups they could indulge in the wide-ranging and informative conversations they both loved. As the years went by, many of the guests collaborated with Louis in one or another of his reform activities, and the talk would, of course, concern politics and strategies. But history, books, music, and occasionally even gossip filled the dinner hour. According to his niece, Louis loved jokes, although, despite his reputation as one of the ablest courtroom lawyers in the nation, he could not tell a joke very well. He anticipated the punch line and would start laughing far too soon. But even if he could not tell stories well, he could listen, ask questions, and draw out from his guests information he needed to understand current public issues. This habit persisted throughout his life. Stories abound of the teas he and Mrs. Brandeis held at their Washington apartment during his tenure on the Court. He made it a point to invite young men and women who had just entered government and worked on important matters like securities regulation and social security, ask them to draw up a seat, and then proceed to grill them about their work. And many would report that problems that had confused them at the office took on a new clarity after these meetings. When they had no guests, after dinner Louis would lie down on the sofa, and Alice would read to him. On vacations he would also read to her, a pastime they both enjoyed. After a while Louis would doze off, and Alice would put the book away. In a little while he would awaken, read the *Boston Evening Transcript,* and go to bed by ten.

Alice and Louis had determined, even before their marriage, that they would live simply, and well below what his income could have afforded. Neither cared for frills, but neither did they choose shoddy. They bought clothes and furniture with an eye to quality and a style that would not go out of season in a few months. Louis had once advised Alfred to buy nothing for his house that his grandchildren could not use. He and Alice wanted the financial independence to be free to do what mattered most to them—to spend additional time with family, to engage in public works, to enjoy literature and music. Once he made enough to ensure the financial security of his family, money became not an end but a means, and he and Alice used it to support causes they believed in and to provide assistance to poorer members of the family. Financial freedom was the prerequisite to personal independence.

Brandeis also bought a small house at 194 Village Avenue in Dedham, then a rural outpost of the city frequented by many upper-class Bostonians, including Sam Warren. Later he rented summer homes on Cape Cod, finally buying one in Chatham that he kept until his death and is still in the family. Here he and Alice would indulge their passions for walking and canoeing, and here he taught these and other skills to his daughters. The family used the Dedham house not only in the summer but in milder weather in the winter as well.

One area of Louis's life Alice could not join. He had loved to travel ever since the family had gone to Europe in the 1870s, and had she had a stronger constitution, there is no doubt that the two of them would have traveled not only across the United States but to Europe as well. Brandeis often traveled on business, and as his practice expanded, these trips took him far from Boston. He and Alice planned a trip abroad for the summer of 1892 but, when they discovered she was pregnant, canceled it on the doctor's advice and rented a cottage on the beach. In 1899, before the full extent of her illness manifested itself, he had to go to Nebraska. He wrote how exciting it had been to head west from Chicago in the Portland sleeper, which made one believe one could sniff the Pacific. "Only three days from Chicago to the Pacific," he told her. "Shall we do it soon?" In 1909 he finally got to California and wrote glowing letters to Alice of the sights he saw.

Alice would accompany him on only one major trip, when he went to Europe after World War I on Zionist business. But he so loved traveling, especially into wilderness areas, that Alice encouraged him to go with his friends. He did this up to the time he went on the Court, and as the girls grew older, they became his camping companions in Maine and in Canada. Although he never owned any boat larger than a canoe, his friend Herbert White owned a yacht, the *Frolic,* and each summer Louis would spend some time at sea with White. In 1899 they sailed the *Frolic* through the wild waters of eastern Canada, stopping to fish, walk, and canoe. He wrote to Alice from Campobello, "Off the coast we had superb cod fishing. The day before we fished for flounder at Cuthie. And for several days I have been sailing much—and alone—in the Cat boat, which is a very pleasing occupation that one can spend the whole day at it. I am not a great sailor man yet, but I understand enough to know that the art can be compassed." Just as Louis needed time away from work to recharge his mental batteries, so he needed time away from Boston and its civilization to recharge himself physically.

ALTHOUGH THEIR LOVE LASTED throughout their lives, the idyllic early years of their marriage soon gave way to a lengthy period of stress and illness. As Louis became more involved in reform activities, he incurred the wrath of Boston's powerful, who objected to his attacks on their pet projects and his accusations of financial improprieties. This in turn led to increasing social exclusion, as some men and women who had once welcomed Louis and Alice into their homes closed their doors to them. Anti-Semitism, which had been growing as part of the nativist backlash against the great influx of immigrants from eastern Europe, became pronounced in a city whose ancestors had patterned themselves on the ancient Hebrews. True friends, such as Sam Warren (but not his wife), the Delands, and Bess Evans, of course, never deserted them. Under these attacks Alice bore up well. Years later, during the confirmation fight, Belle La Follette wrote in indignation at the scurrilous accusations being thrown at Louis. Recalling some of the charges made years earlier, Alice responded, "As far as mud-slinging goes—well, you and I know what such things are and it doesn't and never can trouble the spirit."

Sometime after the birth of their second child, Alice began showing symptoms not just of physical tiredness but of emotional exhaustion as well. She needed more time to rest and found it increasingly difficult to deal with the children (who had a full-time nurse) or with anything else. Eventually, she could do nothing during these "dark" days, and doctors prescribed a rest cure—she would enter a private sanitarium and be free from any responsibilities until she could regain her physical and mental strength. It is not clear exactly when Alice first took these cures, or how often she resorted to them. The first time we have clear evidence is in January 1900, and it would appear that over the next twenty or so years she entered a rest home on a dozen or more occasions.

Whenever this happened, Louis would spend more time with the children, but in the first decades of the twentieth century he faced ever-greater demands on his time from the various reforms that he joined. The family did, of course, have servants. Alice's sisters, especially Josephine, came as often as possible to help out, but Louis encouraged his daughters to be self-sufficient. At the time of the first known stay, Susan was seven and Elizabeth four, and as in most families one expected the older child to help take care of the younger. Louis wrote to Alice, "Susan says she is mistress of the house until Aunt Jo comes, and in her literalness insists upon occupying your chair. Sister [Elizabeth] is playing Susan, but poetic license permits her to keep her own seat, which she prefers." How long Alice stayed in the sanitarium that first time is impossible to tell, but she had returned home by the summer.

In September, Louis wrote to her, "I trust you and the children will have a beautiful tomorrow. It was a beautiful day ten years ago [when they agreed to marry], and you have more than fulfilled the promise to me which your 'yes' implied. You have had many hard days in these years, and we shall hope that this may come otherwise, but we shall indeed be fortunate if another ten years of such happiness is granted to us."

Unfortunately, Alice soon relapsed, and at the end of 1900 she and Louis were trying to decide what steps to take next. While she thought that going off by herself would allow her to regain her strength sooner, she also did not want to leave her family again. "You will know better than anyone else," Louis assured her, "whether you should leave the children at home, separating yourself entirely from them, or try to get the rest cure having them nearby. Think that over very carefully." Alice decided to go by herself (she told Bess Evans, "Getting away from home was such a dreadful wrench and my first days here anything but cheerful"), and Louis took as much time as he could from work and other activities to be with Susan and Elizabeth. They loved to hear him tell stories about ancient Greeks and Romans, and he proudly reported to Alice how much the girls, especially Susan, recalled from earlier stories. "Today we talked about Lucius Maulius Toruatus who sentenced his son to death for disobeying general instructions given regarding the relations of the Romans to the Capuans," Louis wrote, without commenting on what a strange choice of stories this appeared to be for an eight-year-old. He then asked Susan if she remembered what other Roman had acted similarly, and she immediately answered, "Brutus." They then moved on to the adventures of Odysseus, and Louis stretched out the story of the Greek hero's return by telling it in installments. Susan and Elizabeth apparently could barely wait for him to return each day to tell them what happened next. As he told Alice, "I think a continued story has a great advantage over short stories."

All the stories could not disguise Alice's absence, and one day when Louis returned to the house, Susan cried, "Mamma has been gone two weeks today. She said she would come back in two weeks, and I want her." Her father explained that Mamma had not yet gotten well, and "her ill-humor disappeared. She is certainly the most rational child." But while he could calm them and try to explain why their mother could not be there, the children often engaged in small arguments and temper displays. "Susan broke out Saturday in cruel protest about 'always having to read aloud to Sister.'" The next year, when Alice went away again, Susan protested against having to read to Elizabeth all the time, and in turn Elizabeth objected to running errands for her older sister. While Louis described the two as "sweet," he also told Alice that both girls reached their limits. He had to reason with them, and they soon returned to their sweet ways.

For the most part, however, the girls grew to accept their mother periodically going away, and as they got older, Louis taught them to assume some of the household duties. In 1907, the fourteen-year-old Susan went through the household papers to see if a bill from the Boston Electric Company had been paid. But they and Louis missed Alice very much. On some of her stays the family went to visit her, and sometimes Louis arranged for just Susan and Elizabeth to go. To Alice he kept up a steady stream of encouragement. "Don't lose your courage, dear, which has been so fine," he wrote. "The good times are coming." On another occasion, in tones reminiscent of his courting, he suggested that her "esteemed doctor must do a hurry-up job." He and the girls did not propose to leave her in the sanitarium much longer. "Indeed I felt quite like carrying you off with us."

One cannot be sure at the distance of so many decades exactly what afflicted Alice. Members of the family, when queried about it by scholars in later years, tended to downplay the problem, ignoring both its severity and its frequency. One historian reported that the "family described her as 'having the vapors,' which was the general nineteenth and early twentieth century description for any mild and debilitating illness of unknown cause that affected women." Philippa Strum suggests that like many other women of her generation, Alice was a victim of lack of exercise and lack of knowledge about illnesses and infections specific to women.

Recent scholarship in the field, especially by feminist historians, raises other possibilities. Great changes in society in general, and in women's roles in particular, in the late nineteenth and early twentieth centuries placed immense strain on traditional middle-class families. As more women (mostly lower-class) went into the workplace, middle-class women felt increasing pressure to adhere to the "cult of domesticity," in which women carried the role of emotional, moral, and domestic arbiters of the household. Society also viewed women as a weaker sex in every way—physical, mental, and emotional—and many women in the late nineteenth century saw themselves as ill, and society encouraged women to think of themselves that way. Society did not think badly of women who suffered physical and psychological depression, the so-called fashionable disease. It is not that women chose neurasthenia, as it is now termed, so much as that they unconsciously retreated into it in the face of the many pressures confronting them. Society, in fact, accepted neurasthenia—a condition of the genteel classes—as proof of delicacy, femininity, and sensitivity; the lower classes did not suffer from "nerves."

Alice Goldmark Brandeis had a frail constitution, but that by itself does not fully explain her illness, because much of what afflicted her seems to have been more psychological than physical. A protected child of a well-to-do family, she married a successful attorney who provided her with a house and servants. While the bearing of two children put a strain on her, as it does on most women, she did not have to take constant care of Susan and Elizabeth, clean the house, do the laundry and the cooking, or work outside the home to put food on their table. Louis cosseted her, and her exhaustion cannot be ascribed to physical demands on her. If, as many scholars suggest, neurasthenia resulted from social and psychological pressures, what might they have been? The attacks on her husband for his reform work, and the accompanying social ostracism, may also have accounted for some of the pressure later, but her initial episodes came well before these assaults began.

The experience of two other women in similar situations, Fanny Dixwell Holmes and Marion Denman Frankfurter, is informative. Like Alice, both women came from upper-middle-class homes and were very intelligent, cultured, and well-read. Both had been passionately courted by extraordinary men, Oliver Wendell Holmes Jr. and Felix Frankfurter. Although they belonged to different generations, both succumbed to neurasthenia a few years into their marriages, and it is certainly possible that marriage to high-powered men, with few outlets for their own intellectual or creative impulses, led them to retreat to their bedrooms and hide from the world. Fanny Holmes and Alice Brandeis, however, emerged from their shells when they moved to Washington and, because of their husbands' status as justices on the Supreme Court, immediately joined the highest social echelons of the nation's capital. Fanny again became the bright and clever personality she had been before her marriage, trading quips with Theodore Roosevelt as he escorted her into the White House dining room, while Alice also dined at the White House and went to the theater with Mrs. Woodrow Wilson. Marion Frankfurter, who once complained to a friend about being married to a man who was never tired, unfortunately did not recover, and in later years sank into a severe case of mental illness.

For all his love of her, which no one could deny, Louis Brandeis must at times have struck Alice as overwhelming, someone who could seemingly do everything—be a successful lawyer, a social activist, a good father to their children, a man who enjoyed strenuous physical activities, and who could run their household better than she could. The fact that Louis adored her, valued her advice, and, at least intellectually, truly did see her as his partner and equal did not relieve her anxieties that she could not live up to the high standards he set. Moreover, his treating her at times as if she were a child could not have helped. In the end, Alice would emerge as a person in her own right, with causes of her own. That, however, would take time. Between the late 1890s and the early 1920s, Alice, despite her frequent relapses, did begin to carve out this personality, with the help of Bess Evans and others. When not ill, she became an active participant in programs she cared about. Her illnesses—and the strains they put upon the family—only made the bonds between her and Louis stronger.

IN THE MIDST OF Alice's problems, Louis suddenly had to confront the mortality of his parents. At the turn of the century, Frederika had lived for seventy-one years and Adolph for nearly eighty, well above the average life spans of the time. In the summer of 1901 they came east, as they had for many years, and rented a place in Petersham, in central Massachusetts, a location convenient enough to Boston that Louis could come down to see them fairly often. He found his father had aged, but appeared to be in relatively good health, good enough for him to go horseback riding with Louis, although at a sedate pace. Frederika, however, had an advanced stage of cancer and knew that this would probably be the last time she saw her favorite child. Louis read aloud to her and to Adolph, with some of the same stories he told his daughters from Greek and Roman history. He reported that because of the morphine, his mother did not have great discomfort, "but is very tired of the whole business. She talks much of wanting to die, but also of wanting to get well." She also wanted to see Alice and her grandchildren, which Louis promised "shall be later."

Upon learning that Frederika wanted to see her and the children, Alice immediately offered to come over with them from the vacation house she and Louis had rented in Manomet Point, a few miles below Plymouth on Cape Cod Bay. Louis thanked her but immediately said no. His mother was failing rapidly, the children could not and should not be in the house, and no rooms could be found in any nearby hotel.

Louis no doubt also thought the trip might be too much for Alice, and that his mother might not live long enough to see them. In fact that is what happened; a few hours after he wrote to Alice, his mother died in the early evening of 21 August 1901. She had been unconscious all day, much to her family's relief, since they felt she had suffered enough. Adolph, as Louis noted, bore up well, as he had been expecting Frederika's death for a while. But when Louis suggested that they have her body cremated, Adolph said no; he wanted her buried in Louisville. Since Adolph wanted to stay on in Petersham rather than return to Louisville in the summer, they placed Frederika's body in a vault in a nearby larger town for eventual shipment back home.

Susan and Elizabeth Brandeis, 1900

Adolph continued to come to Petersham for the next few years. Aside from the pleasant memories he had of the years he and Frederika had vacationed there, Louis would brighten his day by taking an afternoon train over and staying overnight or even for two days from time to time, and apparently brought the girls with him occasionally. These visits gladdened Adolph enormously, and once, in 1904, when a train delay had caused Louis some problems in getting to Petersham, Adolph wrote to him that I "only hope you will not allow yourself to be discouraged from coming here by these little discouragements as your visits give charm to my life here which I could not well spare."

That would be the last summer Adolph came east. The following year he began to decline perceptibly, and in the summer of 1905 Louis spent a few weeks in Louisville with his family, visited some old friends, and rode with Al around the Kentucky countryside. He found his father just "so-so," and it appears that Adolph may also have suffered from cancer. In addition to pain medication to help him sleep, the doctors prescribed some form of stimulant that Adolph took regularly during the day, when he appeared to be more like his old self. At night, though, he grew tired and lethargic. For the most part, Louis told Alice, "he is quite his charming self and appreciative of the attentions of those about him."

Then, on 27 December 1905, Louis received an urgent telegram from his brother, reporting that Adolph had become quite ill. "Think no physical discomfort but pronounced mental confusion," Al reported. "Do not believe end can be far off." Alice and the girls had already gone to New York to spend some time with the Goldmarks, and Louis decided that as soon as he could wind up a few pending matters, he would go to Kentucky. Two days later Al sent another wire: "[Dr.] Weidner says if you want to see father so that you can talk to him better come at once." Louis immediately left Boston and arrived in time to see and talk with his father. Then the elder Brandeis rallied, and Louis returned home. A few weeks later, on 20 January 1906, Adolph Brandeis died.

The deaths of Louis's parents, while saddening, came as no surprise, since both had lived long lives. It came as a great shock, however, on his trips to Louisville to discover that his sister Amy, only three years older than he, suffered from congestive heart failure. On 17 February, only a few weeks after Adolph's death, Amy passed away. Louis did not go to her funeral, but later in the summer he took the train to Louisville to

Louis Brandeis with friends at a shelter in the Adirondacks

Louis and his daughters on a croquet field in Dedham, ca. 1899

spend some time with Alfred, his one remaining sibling, and with Amy's family.

AT THE TURN OF THE CENTURY, had Louis Brandeis been the introspective type and had he stopped to take stock of his life, he would have found little to complain about and much to be thankful for. He had succeeded in his profession and, along with other leaders of the bar, helped to transform the practice of law. In doing so, he had become one of the top earners not just in Boston but in the country, and if he had not yet achieved his goal of financial freedom, he was well on the way. He had married a woman whose political, intellectual, and cultural interests matched his own, who had given him two bright and precocious daughters, and who shared his dream of public service. His place in Boston's legal and social hierarchy seemed secure, and he had even begun to dabble in local politics and reform. For a man in his forties, he had achieved a great deal. Now he stood poised on the threshold of a second career, one that would take him from the parochial confines of Boston to the stage of national affairs, and, although he did not realize it, also cost him a great deal.

CHAPTER SIX

TRACTION AND UTILITIES

Louis Brandeis, like many of the leading progressives of this era, began his reform career locally, in his case fighting franchise corruption in Boston. He then went on to battles at the state and regional levels before moving onto the national stage. Between 1897 and 1916, Brandeis gradually developed a coherent philosophy about the nature of American society, the relation of an industrial economy to political democracy, and the need to restrain bigness both in the private sector and in the government. Brandeis, however, brought more than ideas and ideals to his reforms.

One thread that runs through all his endeavors is the need to know the facts. Elizabeth Brandeis once told the story of how, at the height of her father's fame as a reformer, a group of college students came to his office offering to help. They expected to be put to work researching great national issues, or being assigned to some senator or congressman as a liaison, and did not expect the answer they received. "Go down to City Hall," he told them, "and see what is on the agenda for the next council meeting. Pick one of those issues—garbage collection, water supply, it does not matter which one—then go and learn everything you can about it. Read past reports, talk to people, learn the topic until you know it as well as anyone. Then when you get up to speak, or to make a suggestion for change, your voice will be heard because you are knowledgeable. That is how reform works." The students did not find garbage collection or water supply on the same par as breaking up monopolies or allocating Alaska's resources, and so went back to their own studies.

The people we identify as progressives objected to the malevolent effects of industrialization on society, on politics, and on the individual. While they all recognized problems, few of them could think through the issue to propose a workable solution, and in order to do that, Brandeis believed knowledge of "all the facts that surround" to be crucial. Just as one could not argue a case for a client without knowing the details of the business, so one could not attack an evil such as municipal corruption without first learning everything one could know about it. Armed with the facts, one could then think long and hard on devising a practical solution and, with a solid proposal in hand, organize colleagues and the public in order to effect a change. Brandeis once told his daughter to take all the time necessary when figuring out a problem, but once you had all the information and had made a decision, stick to it. While some of Brandeis's views on the great questions of the early twentieth century, and his proposed solutions, may appear ill founded in hindsight, others continue to ring true a century later.

There is, however, more than a little irony in the scope and success of Brandeis's activities during this period. In later years he would talk constantly about the "smallness" of man, about the limited abilities of a single individual, and therefore a need for men and women to take on projects or businesses limited in scope and amenable to one person's judgment and direction. Yet Louis Brandeis was a whirlwind of activity in his reform years, not only involved in major campaigns of his own, but frequently serving as a resource to others in their work. At home he supported and encouraged Alice as she dealt with her health problems and guided Susan and Elizabeth as they turned into young women and then went off to college. He continued to be the lead partner in a major law firm, and after August 1914 began the transformation of the moribund American Zionist movement into a powerful political organization.

He recalled these as the happiest years of his life.

AS BOSTON AND OTHER CITIES grew in the late nineteenth century, public transportation became an increasingly important issue in municipal affairs. Cities grew because newcomers, both from the hinterlands and from overseas, came seeking work in the mills and factories that now dotted the urban landscape. In earlier times laborers lived close to their places of employment and could walk to their jobs. Cabs and horse-drawn omnibuses provided transportation for those who had to travel farther. Boston more than doubled in population between 1870 and 1900, and grew another 20 percent in the next decade. Not just factory hands had to get to work; the banks, insurance companies, and law firms that occupied the new buildings in downtown Boston also wanted transportation for their clerical workers.

Getting into downtown Boston, however, posed a problem. The city was and is relatively narrow, surrounded on three sides by water. On the fourth side stood the upper-middle-class homes of Beacon Hill, as well as the historic Boston Common, the city's famous park that dated back to the seventeenth century. The West End Street Railway Company claimed that the only way it could get a rail line downtown would be to run it across the Common and sought permission to do so in February 1893. Brandeis, in what he later called "my first important public work," opposed the plan and spoke eloquently—and successfully— against it in the legislative hearings.

The refusal to allow the West End to lay tracks across the Common reflected the fact that franchises to build and operate trolley lines on public streets had been kept pretty much under public control in Massachusetts, with charters imposing strict limits on use of streets and the amount of the fares. Large investors, however, saw the potential for great profits in these franchises, provided they could obtain charters that did not restrict how they operated, how much they could charge, and how long they could enjoy the monopoly. In 1894, Henry M. Whitney, a shady financier who had scandalized Massachusetts a few years earlier by admitting that he had spent $50,000 to secure the passage of legislation favorable to his interests, created a syndicate that included J. P. Morgan & Company to secure a charter from the state to establish a new corporation, the Boston Elevated Railway Company, which would extend Boston's public transit system by building elevated tracks into the downtown area. The charter would run for twenty-five years, a not-unusual provision, and that fall the voters of the city approved the proposal in a referendum.

Three years later, in a bill that passed with very little public notice, the legislature authorized the Boston Elevated to lease the West End Railway for ninety-nine years, subject to approval by the state Railroad Commission. The commission, however, refused to approve, and in its investigation came to the conclusion that the West End's stock had been watered, so that the 8 percent rental that the Elevated would pay to the West End would in fact amount to an 11 or 12 percent dividend on real value. Moreover, the commission declared the ninety-nine-year lease "wholly discordant with public policy," since it ran for a term of years "quadruple the length of the longest term that the legislature has [previously] consented to sanction." After agreeing to scale back the rental and the length of the lease to twenty-five years, the Elevated secured the commission's approval.

Unlike the legislative action, however, the decision of the Railroad

Commission could not be kept secret, and the machinations of the Boston Elevated became subject to public scrutiny. Conservatives—and here one must include Louis Brandeis, who strongly believed in fiscal integrity and in a tradition where the public good outweighed private interests—objected to the fact that with the lease of the West End, the Boston Elevated controlled nearly all of the street railway lines in the Boston area. Moreover, investments in the franchise, which sought a long-term charter and guaranteed fares, would be shielded from governmental interference on behalf of the public. Charles Warren, secretary of the Massachusetts Reform Club, said that although he and other members of the club believed in minimal government interference, on occasions such as this government had to step in to protect the public. In addition, the legislature's approval of a rental to West End stockholders based on watered stock made the assembly appear part of a stock manipulation for greedy speculators. On behalf of the Municipal League, a group of civic-minded business and professional men, Brandeis wrote to the board detailing the over-inflated value that the West End put on its stock, and how a rental based on that figure was unjustified.

Even while the board looked into the West End lease, the Boston Elevated went back to its friends in the legislature and secured a charter extension on its own lines as well as protection against reductions in a five-cent fare. On 30 April, hoping to prevent final passage of the measure, Brandeis wrote a lengthy letter to the *Boston Evening Transcript* protesting the provisions of House Bill No. 784 as "opposed to the established policy of the Commonwealth, and would, if enacted, sacrifice the interests of the public to that of a single corporation." In effect, the bill abandoned the oversight function that the Massachusetts legislature had exercised for many years. While streetcar fares all over America had tended to come down in the past few years, the legislature was about to saddle Boston commuters with a five-cent fare for the next thirty years. Worst of all, once this door opened, "every railroad, street railway, gas, electric light or water company might demand like privileges."

The effort came too late, and as Brandeis recognized, he had no troops to rally. The Elevated's actions had caught people off guard, and many did not comprehend how expensive the new charter would be to Boston's residents. Although Brandeis belonged to the Municipal League, and in fact chaired the Transportation Committee, he had written the letter as a private citizen. Nonetheless, the Elevated spread the rumor that the league had hired the high-priced corporate attorney to attack it. Brandeis deeply resented this charge, and he wrote to William A. Bancroft, the Elevated's president, declaring its falsity. "I have been retained by no person, association or corporation, directly or indirectly in this matter, and I have opposed it solely because I believe that the bill, if passed, would result in great injustice to the people of Massachusetts, and eventually great injustice to the capitalist classes whom you are now representing, and with whom I, as well as you, are in close connection."

This last sentence was not empty rhetoric. Throughout his life Brandeis believed in a system of private enterprise in which entrepreneurs could wager their talents to build up successful businesses in which investors could put their money in the hope of making more money. But there had to be a level playing field, and all groups—investors, businessmen, and workers—had to recognize that the interest of the public took precedence over their own. Even as he grew more hostile to big business, he did not want to tear down the system, but only ensure that all companies, no matter how big or small, played by the same set of rules and did nothing to harm the public.

Brandeis did not manufacture this philosophy out of whole cloth; rather, he had imbibed what had, until then, been the predominant ethos in Massachusetts. Brandeis and the people he worked with did not, as they saw it at the time, vie for reform; instead, they saw themselves fighting for what had been the traditional view of the proper relationship between the Commonwealth, as the defender of public interests, and private businesses and public service corporations. In this view, the state had the major responsibility for enforcing honest management and true valuation of corporate property. Stock represented a measure of the owner's interest in the enterprise as well as a guarantee fund for the corporation's creditors, and therefore strict fiscal accountability worked both for stockholders and for creditors.

By 1900, however, practically no other state in the Union shared this view of governmental responsibility. The "modern view," propagated not just by Wall Street bankers but by their allies in major financial centers such as Boston and Chicago, saw stock as a commodity that earned money and that an investor purchased at his own risk. They contended that the state had no obligation to supervise corporate management other than to prevent outright fraud, and they defined that as no more than misrepresentation. In this view, investors and not the state had the responsibility for looking after their investments, and corporate managers did whatever they had to do to make the firm profitable.

Nowhere, of course, did one find any mention of public interest or financial integrity. As Brandeis began uncovering evidence of the abandonment of fiduciary responsibility and of a "public be damned" attitude, the old-line Brahmins who bought into the modern view resented him, not just for opposing them, but for holding them up to an idealistic standard he believed they should have shared.

THE FIGHT with the Boston Elevated did not end in 1897; in some ways it had just begun. To reach the downtown without crossing the Common, one had to use either Tremont or Washington Street. Because of high real estate values, it was impracticable to widen the old narrow streets, or even to build an elevated rail line above them. The city had several years earlier constructed a subway by tunneling under Tremont Street and then ordered the surface tracks removed. The Tremont line served as a funnel by which a number of outlying lines delivered commuters downtown, and by the mid-1890s traffic had grown congested. So long as the city owned the subway, which it had leased to the Elevated on very restrictive terms, the Elevated could not gain the monopoly it sought over Boston's street railways. First the Elevated sought authority from the legislature to put back the surface tracks on Tremont Street, thus making the subway superfluous. Although the legislature agreed to the proposal, it did so with a referendum attached, and voters overwhelmingly rejected the plan. Then, in 1900, the Elevated sought the construction of a tunnel under Washington Street, which it would build at its own expense and after a thirty-year period the city would have the option of buying at cost.

This time, however, Brandeis would not stand alone in his opposition to the Elevated, but would be backed by a group of like-minded men organized in the Public Franchise League. Along with Brandeis, the roster included the retailer Edward Filene (one of Brandeis's clients); Dr. Morton Prince, a prominent physician and ex-mayor of Boston; Robert Treat Paine Jr., like his father an important philanthropist and social reformer; and Edward Warren and George Upham, whose major interest involved preserving the downtown cityscape. In the first few years, however, the driving force behind the league consisted of one man. Brandeis planned the strategy, wrote much of the publicity, marshaled the troops to lobby the legislature, and personally paid at least 20 percent of the league's operating budget. In 1905, Joseph B. Eastman became executive secretary, and for the first time Brandeis had a lieutenant who understood numbers as well as he did, believed in protecting the public interest, and who could work side by side with Brandeis

Edward A. Filene

without having to await instructions. "Joe Eastman," Brandeis later said, "has more interest in the public service and less in his own career than any man I have ever known." But even if Brandeis had to power the league, once he pointed the way, competent people like Filene and Prince could be relied on to do their jobs, especially getting the league's side of the story out to newspapers and members of the legislature.

The league managed to delay approval of the Elevated's initial bill, so the company came back with another proposal: it would build the Washington Street subway at its own expense, and on its completion the tunnel would be owned by the city, but the Elevated would have the free and sole use of it for fifty years. The proposal appealed to legislators for the simple fact that no public money would have to be expended. The Elevated, however, carried additional clout that the Public Franchise League and its ally the Board of Trade would have to work hard to overcome. The Elevated had become one of the largest employers in the city, and it carefully made sure that local political leaders, especially Democrats, had some say in who got hired. One member of the legislature privately explained that he could not vote against any measure sponsored by the Elevated, because he had three hundred constituents working for the company.

While the Elevated wanted far more than had ever been given to a municipal franchise in Boston, it only sought what its counterparts in other cities had been able to obtain—long-term favorable leases—without significant opposition. Even within Boston, members of that part of the business community associated with banks and investment houses argued for long-term franchises because the uncertainties of short, revocable leases would make it difficult to attract adequate investment capital to finance the projects. Looked at strictly in terms of business models, the fight is less a battle between the "people" and the "interests" than a contest between the newer speculative members of

Brandeis in his office

the business community who wanted to exploit modern financial methods and the traditionalists who favored conservative practices and saw the state as the protector of the public interest.

The blitz of letters and petitions to the legislature failed to stop passage, but Brandeis and the league had one more card to play. Together with other organizations that opposed the Elevated's plan, such as the Board of Trade and the Merchants' Association, they appealed to Governor Winthrop Crane, whom Brandeis had met a few months earlier in connection with another matter. Brandeis went to Crane and convinced him that signing such a bill amounted to condoning a deliberate violation of the law. Crane mirrored Brandeis's argument in his veto message. The message elated Brandeis, who told Crane that he not only had defeated a bad measure but "had done it in such a way as to teach the people what to strive for, and what to expect."

Although the league had defeated the bill, Brandeis and his colleagues understood that there would have to be a tunnel built under Washington Street to accommodate the growing need for public access into the downtown area. Rather than waiting to see what the Elevated would do, Brandeis and the league put forth a proposal in early 1902, providing for a city-owned subway to be leased to the Elevated on strict terms. The Elevated fought back with a bill of its own that in many ways copied the earlier measure that Governor Crane had vetoed, and its use of patronage and the offer to build it without public funds attracted many legislators. By late February, Brandeis had begun to wonder if the league could once again hold off the company. He urged those in the league and in the Board of Trade to step up their publicity efforts, and he personally went to see Mayor Patrick A. Collins, who appeared before a legislative committee to support the league measure.

Then, in one of those occurrences that would later become part of the Brandeis legend, the Elevated, which had appeared almost apathetic in fighting the league bill, came out in full force on the last day of hearings. Albert E. Pillsbury, the Elevated's counsel, suddenly began tossing out one set of numbers after another to show that the Elevated's income fell below expenses on many lines because of a too-liberal policy of free transfers. He asked the legislature to table the league bill, since the Elevated, in its depressed financial condition, could ill afford the high rental in the bill. No action should be taken, he urged, until the company could repair its damaged financial condition. Pillsbury deluged the committee with numbers designed to illustrate the company's poverty.

Pillsbury had deliberately waited not only until the last day of hearings but in fact until the last hour, assuming that it would take days before anyone could go through his figures to contradict him. He had not counted on Louis Brandeis and his passion to know "all the facts that surround." Brandeis had already studied the Elevated's financial reports, and even as Pillsbury reeled off his figures, Brandeis mentally analyzed them and then took the floor to rebut Pillsbury. How could the Elevated be in such bad shape when its stock had risen from 104 to 170 in less than four years? How could the situation be so desperate when, in the last year with some lines out of operation, the company still had paid $600,000 in dividends? In fact, Brandeis charged, the company had so much money on its hands that it had raised the dividend rate from 4 to 6 percent. The Elevated had the financial resources to accept the lease on the league's terms; it just did not want to do so except under arrangements that would harm the public interest. "We are here to see," he reminded the committee, "that the control rests with the community, that the Elevated Railway Company, or any company that serves us as transporters of passengers, is the servant and not the master of the public."

The committee, confused by the conflicting testimonies, decided to resume hearings a few days later, and this time Brandeis came armed with a full analysis of the Elevated's financial condition. He took the transcript of Pillsbury's statement and went over it line by line. "This statement is incorrect." "This statement is at least misleading." "This statement is grossly misleading." The analysis ran fifteen pages, and Pillsbury, when he rose to speak, could only denounce Brandeis and the league as "impractical and ignorant." While the Elevated damned Brandeis's analysis as "sophistries," the legislature agreed that the company could indeed operate the subway on the terms proposed in the league bill. There would still be some jockeying, and some last-minute attempts by the Elevated to get better terms, but the final bill authorized Boston to build and own the Washington Street subway, and to lease it to the Elevated for twenty-five years at an annual rental of 4.5 percent of the cost, the arrangement to be approved by public referendum. As Brandeis had predicted, the Elevated quickly agreed to the terms.

Brandeis and the league won the battle, and in fact over the next decade won several other skirmishes with the Elevated over the terms for new lines or extensions of existing lines into Cambridge and elsewhere. As late as 1911 the Elevated attempted to get a new long-term lease as preparation for consolidation with the West End Railway. Once again Brandeis utilized his contacts with the governor's office, then occupied by Eugene Foss, to make sure that the new franchises adhered to the Commonwealth's traditional pattern.

The Public Franchise League succeeded in its fight against the Boston Elevated and in its work on the gas schedule (see below), in large measure because of the hard work of Brandeis, Joe Eastman, and other members of the league who, if not generals in their own right, knew how to execute orders. In addition, Brandeis won over the support of influential editors and newspapers that supported the league position. They all shared a similar traditionalist philosophy about the relation of the state to private enterprise, the need to protect the public interest, and the moral necessity for fiscal integrity. They distrusted the new financial and corporate strategies, which often seemed to them little more than greedy and corrupt. In some very important ways, the battle with the Boston Elevated, indeed, much of the progressive movement itself, reflected a struggle between tradition and modernism, between older and perhaps more idealistic views of business responsibility and a concern for the public interest, on the one hand, and newer, what some might call Darwinian, ideas of the marketplace as a jungle in which only the strongest survived, with the public interest the first casualty, on the other.

In the end, market forces proved stronger than Brandeis had anticipated. Prior to 1897, investments in public utilities had been seen as practically gold plated. People needed gas, water, and transportation, and even with restrictive franchises and limited fares the stocks of these companies offered a decent and assured return on investment. After 1897, securities offered by the new industrial giants promised greater returns on investment than money put into public utility franchises with limits on the rates they could charge. Even utilities in good financial condition often had difficulty selling new stock issues because the returns could not match those of the large industrial concerns. Over the years cities and states often had to take over public utilities when they lost money and became financially untenable, or had to cut them greater slack and provide incentives to keep them operating. Here, as in many of his future battles, Brandeis spoke for the older traditions, in which morality and an idealistic concern for the public interest played a far greater role than did the realities of modern economic and financial markets.

ONE YEAR AFTER the passage of the Washington Street subway bill, Brandeis went to a conference in New York on urban reform sponsored by the National Municipal League to read a paper on the Boston Elevated fight. He played down his role and that of the Public Franchise League and instead lauded the role of the Massachusetts Board of Railroad Commissioners. In conclusion he advocated municipal ownership of the rights-of-way and a strong oversight commission to police both the conduct of the rail lines and the fares they charged. The audience response surprised him. The participants had a wider range of experience in municipal reform than he had and reflected a diverse gamut of opinions. Professor Frank Parsons in particular criticized Brandeis's paper as presenting "a too roseate account of the situation," and argued that neither of the two important commissions, those dealing with railroads and gas, had done a good job in protecting the public interest. The problem, Parsons explained, was that the commissions had very little contact with the citizenry and a great deal with the entities they supposedly regulated. As a result, the commissions soon adopted the corporation view of what constituted adequate returns on investments and the proper way to determine capitalization; in other words, the "commissions come very largely to see things from the standpoint of the corporations and not from the people's standpoint." This, of course, has become the standard—and, alas, oftentimes all too true—criticism of regulatory agencies ever since.

Brandeis listened carefully, and even though he would, throughout his life, be an advocate of public regulation of utilities rather than of public ownership, he recognized that he had limited experience in the matter. Never a "one idea man," a term he used derogatorily for those who thought that one solution would solve all problems, he understood that at different times and in different places, regulatory commissions might not be the people's protection and in fact might be, as Parsons charged, in collusion with the very interests they had been charged to oversee. This knowledge allowed him to be consistent in his overall philosophy, yet pragmatic in dealing with discrete issues. Unlike when dealing with the one-idea men, people who started out opposed to one of Brandeis's proposals could talk to him and listen to his arguments, and he in turn would listen to theirs. Just as in his law practice, he saw himself not as an advocate of any particular program but as one who sought a solution that would be fair to all of the parties.

He returned to Boston with plenty of new ideas to mull over but soon found himself confronted by numerous demands on his time. He had to be vigilant as the Boston Elevated continued its efforts to secure long-term franchises. New troubles arose over the administration of city hospitals, and his old friend and client Alice Lincoln again asked for his help. He became involved in efforts to reform the school board and in the Good Government Association, and at one time talk ran rampant over the idea of his running either for mayor or for governor, notions he considered amusing but of no practicality or even of interest to him. And as he told his father, "I occasionally have to attend to law business."

In the midst of all these activities, Brandeis received a letter from Edward Warren, chairman of the Public Franchise league, complaining that the league had failed to take an active role in combating the newly organized Boston Consolidated Gas Company, and saying that if Brandeis did not have the time or interest, a "new set of men" could be enlisted in the fight, or perhaps even a new organization might be founded.

BRANDEIS MUST HAVE BEEN aware of the problems surrounding the Consolidated, since the gas franchise had been attended by scandals of one sort or another ever since a colorful and unscrupulous financier, J. Edward O'Sullivan Addicks, had moved to Boston in 1884 and proceeded to duplicate the successful if questionable operations he had mounted in Philadelphia and Delaware. His goal, simply put, was to gain control of Boston's seven small and independent gas companies, consolidate them, water their stock by issuing certificates based on a highly inflated valuation of their assets, and then sell off the stock at a huge profit. He created the Bay State Gas Company that year and let it be known that he intended to lay down gas lines throughout the city parallel to those of the existing seven companies and then, using new technology, produce and sell gas cheaper than they could. (Gas, produced in local plants through a process of coal gasification, had become the chief means of lighting in the United States in the nineteenth century. Although natural gas had been discovered in the Southwest, it would not replace coal-based gas until the great transnational pipelines were laid down after World War I.)

Some of the local companies fought back and secured the establishment of the Board of Gas and Electric Light Commissioners, which had a great deal of power over gas companies, but before it could go into effect, four of the companies sold out to Addicks. Although their combined assets probably did not exceed $5 million, Addicks increased their capitalization to $17 million through a dazzling series of financial maneuvers. The original stockholders, at least on paper, more than doubled the value of their holdings, and Addicks boasted that he had cleared more than $7 million in profit. What makes this all the more amazing is that unlike New York and Philadelphia, Boston had long had a reputation for public financial probity. The state had some of the toughest laws on the books prohibiting stock watering and other forms of corporate fraud. This may have been one of the reasons Addicks got away with his scheme. According to Thomas Lawson, an associate of Addicks's at the time who later wrote the best-selling muckraking book *Frenzied Finance,* Boston had become far too trusting. "She had her own rules of business conduct which years of usage had consecrated into all-powerful precedent," and as a result capitalists and financiers in the city remained suspicious of quick and tricky schemes. They just did not expect someone like Addicks, and fell easily into his snares.

In the next several years other players entered the city, including the Standard Oil Company, which bought one of the remaining independents, the Brookline Company, and then used it to leverage contracts with Boston and some nearby suburbs. Moreover, Brookline sold its gas at $1.00 per thousand cubic feet, considerably less than the $1.25 charged by Bay State. While competition supposedly works to benefit the consumer, the high costs associated with laying down parallel lines as well as the purchase or building of new coal gasification plants did not lead to lower prices. Everyone recognized that the solution lay in the consolidation of all the Boston-area gas companies, the elimination of duplicate lines, and tighter control of the rates and financial practices of this new company by the Gas Commission. At the request of the competing companies, the Boston Board of Gas and Electric Light Commissioners sent a bill to the legislature to consolidate the eight area companies. Stock in the consolidated company would be limited to an amount approved by the commission and equal to the "fair value" of the combined properties. The Public Franchise League opposed the bill, but Brandeis, then occupied with other matters, did not take an active role, and the bill became law in May 1903.

The problem that so upset Edward Warren involved the capitalization of the new conglomerate. Several of the predecessor companies had been incorporated not in Massachusetts but in Delaware, which allowed just about any manipulation of stock one could envision. Under Delaware law, the company could theoretically claim a capitalization of more than $160 million, far in excess of the actual value of its assets, and more than seventeen times the amount necessary, in the opinion of the Gas Commission, to supply the needs of Boston consumers. To Warren and to others the whole issue centered on what capitalization would be established. Under Massachusetts law, publicly regulated utilities could pay a fixed dividend on their capital, and the rates charged to the public would be determined by that figure. A company that paid 7 percent on $160 million would have to charge a far higher rate to consumers than if it had a capitalization of $20 million or even $50 million. When Brandeis responded to Warren's letter, he agreed that the league should get involved, but he tried to point out that there might be other issues involved than just capitalization. And he pointedly asked, "Who are the new men you have in mind?"

The problem would be in ascertaining what constituted "fair value," and a week later Brandeis sent Warren a long letter detailing the legal precedents in the Commonwealth over how fair value should be determined. Unlike Warren and some of his colleagues in the Public Franchise League, Brandeis, while looking to protect the consumer from paying unfairly inflated rates, also had concerns about the legitimate interests of the company. Whatever Addicks and others had done, a significant investment existed in gas lines, meters, and plants for which investors should realize a fair return. When the commission began to hold hearings that winter, the Consolidated claimed that its assets had cost over $24 million, and that a fair value should be no less than $20,609,989.99. Warren and the league countered that any figure larger than $15,124,121 would be fraudulent, eventually reducing that even further to $12 million. They demanded that gas be sold at no more than eighty cents a thousand, a 20 percent reduction from the current price of a dollar. Brandeis, although he did not cut his ties with the league, left the battle over capitalization to what he termed the "one idea men," led by Warren and the league's new counsel, George W. Anderson, who as a prosecutor had brought suit against the Haverhill Gas Company the year before and secured a ruling for lower rates. Instead, Brandeis appeared as unpaid counsel for the Massachusetts Board of Trade. Both the league and the board wanted a fair value below that proposed by the Consolidated, but the board had more interest in seeing that investors secured a fair return. Brandeis agreed with this, and they allowed him to be, in effect, counsel to the situation, trying to work out a proposal that would be fair to the Consolidated, its stockholders, and the public.

The Consolidated, thanks to its deep pockets and important backers, could expect that the legislature would respond favorably to its request even if the gas commissioners did not, and introduced a bill that would have given it the figures it wanted. As with the Boston Elevated and earlier with the Boston Disinfecting Company, the fight involved far more than an academic discussion of truth and justice. Brandeis recognized the political influence of the company, and while some people then and later tended to glorify him as a fearless independent crusader, he should not be confused with Don Quixote. He utilized facts to analyze a problem and devise a solution, and then he needed political savvy to get that solution implemented. Just because he chose not to run for political office, one should not see him as apolitical. Throughout his reform career, Brandeis played the game of politics extremely well. Lacking the financial resources of his opponents, he developed potent organizations and created public opinion to counter corporate pressure on the legislature, and he utilized his extensive contacts with public officials to affect the outcome of his campaigns. In fact, in the early stages of the gas battle, while Warren and the Public Franchise League traded accusations with the Consolidated over proper capitalization, Brandeis spent his time meeting quietly with Boston's mayor and corporation counsel. On 9 March 1905, he spoke up publicly for the first time, in testifying before the Committee on Public Lighting of the state House of Representatives.

He began his testimony by stating that the Board of Trade, which he represented, "is not here to attack or defend the action" of any of the predecessor companies to the consolidation. Rather, the board's sole interest lay in ensuring that "any consolidation which may take place shall be in accordance with the wise and established policy of the Commonwealth prohibiting stock-watering of quasi-public corporations," as represented in the bill already presented by the board. He then carefully reviewed all that had happened before, the Commonwealth's historical policies on stock valuation, and the need for the legislature to act cautiously and wisely in enacting the enabling legislation. The 1903 act had provided for a consolidation that, in fact, had not yet actually occurred; that statute, however, had some serious defects that could now be corrected. No special favors should be given in special legislation; such a law would fly in the face of the Commonwealth's historic and successful traditions.

Unlike Warren's heated rhetoric (which Brandeis had unsuccessfully tried to calm), Brandeis's testimony appears cool, temperate, and seriously in search of a solution fair to all involved. There is no mention of capitalization, no tossing around of numbers, no reminders of the past duplicity of Addicks and others. It is as if Brandeis recognized that a new start had to be made, and that to do so, people had to move beyond the old issues and take a fresh approach. He would not, of course, budge on core issues such as stock watering, but that had, as he pointed out, long been the Commonwealth's policy. Moreover, he undercut the company's defense of its property rights by identifying the long-standing Massachusetts principle that companies enjoying a public franchise had to be held accountable because they also enjoyed a public trust.

In terms of accounting, Brandeis and Edward Warren differed over what items ought to be legitimately included as part of the Consolidated's fair value, and the one-idea men sharply attacked Brandeis for agreeing to any of the company's demands. Moreover, he could never get Warren to understand that the ultimate price of gas would be determined by multiple factors, not by any one of them alone. Even if, for example, capitalization were to be fixed at a low number, what would be the rate of return allowed by the law, an issue that Warren and Anderson apparently never considered? If the legislature allowed a 7 percent return on $15 million (the league's original figure), that would mean a higher charge for gas than a 5 percent return. How would future expenditures be calculated, and what would happen if new technology became available that could provide for cheaper gas? Brandeis later wrote of Warren that he had been an important member of the league, "not by reason of his ability, but mainly because of his energy and the time which he could and did give to it. He is a man essentially narrow-minded and of few ideas." Such men, whom he considered fanatics, he had written years earlier, "should be sacrificed when the end is accomplished—like animals which had borne the gods to sacrificial feasts."

As Brandeis mulled these issues over, his thoughts returned to the paper he had heard in New York two years earlier detailing the experience of the London sliding scale. In the debate between municipal ownership and regulation of private franchises, English reformers had come up with what seemed like an ideal and foolproof system. First the proper capitalization of the company's assets had to be determined, because that figure would be the basis for both profit and rates. After the company and public officials agreed on capitalization, they would also agree on the standard dividend and a normal price for gas. If, by way of technical improvements, the company could lower the cost of producing and distributing gas, it could then earn more money and increase its dividend. But it could only increase the dividend if it also reduced the price it charged for gas. If, on the other hand, the costs of production rose, the company could raise the price of gas only if it correspondingly reduced the dividend. The plan required very little interference by government other than an annual audit of the books and was, according to its advocates, self-regulating.

It seemed to Brandeis that if the sliding-scale plan could be implemented, it would provide the best means of assuring fairness to all concerned. It would also, as with the liquor lobby a decade earlier, remove the necessity of the gas company or consumer interests running to the legislature every year. He began talking to members of the legislature, the mayor, and other officials, handing out material on the sliding scale, and suggesting that this might be a way out of an otherwise very unpleasant situation. In this effort, he also made clear that he spoke for himself, and not for the Board of Trade. For them he advocated a general measure with anti-stock-watering provisions and no more, a position he made clear but that people like Warren failed to heed. He prepared a memorandum on the subject for the Public Lighting Committee, a copy of which somehow got into the hands of the *Boston Evening Transcript* and led to a very positive news story on the plan.

Up to this point, Brandeis had carefully avoided attacking the company. In his testimony on 9 March, he had not even mentioned the company or its checkered past, but had focused on the necessity of a bill that ensured fairness to all parties and fell within the Massachusetts tradition. Then the Consolidated ran a series of full-page advertisements across the state attacking the Public Franchise League and its figures, and defending its own proposed valuation. In addition, J. Harvey White, acting on behalf of the Consolidated, had sent a fake "news story" on the controversy to a number of papers. The story should be run, White insisted, "without advertising marks of any sort" and "set as news matter in news type, with a news head at the top of the column." The "news story," parading as a disinterested report, predicted that a settlement would soon be reached with all parties in essence agreeing to the Consolidated's figures. In mid-April, Samuel Bowles, the editor of the *Springfield Republican,* ran a story, but not the one White wanted. Instead, he printed the letter and charged White and the company with attempting to falsify the news and mislead the public.

The disclosures proved very embarrassing to the Consolidated and its new president, James L. Richards. The son of a farmer, Richards had amassed a fortune before he was forty, and the investment house of Kidder, Peabody & Company had chosen him to head the Consolidated. Richards, who enjoyed a reputation for personal honesty, moved quickly to distance himself from the scandal and declared that he had had nothing to do with the fake story. Moreover, he had read all of Brandeis's statements and approved of the moderate tone that he had taken in the hearings. Then a copy of the sliding-scale memorandum had come into his hands and intrigued him. Above all, he believed that Brandeis could be trusted. A mutual friend and Brandeis client, Charles Palen Hall, suggested that Richards call Brandeis, which he did on 24 April. Richards apologized for the White advertisements and said that although he had not been involved, as president of the company he would have to bear the onus for them. They then discussed nearly all of the issues outstanding, and while it would be too much to say that they resolved them in the course of the two-hour conversation, the two men recognized that they would be able to work together.

In the next few days, Brandeis met privately with Richards and with Frederick E. Snow, the Consolidated's attorney, and Snow drew up a bill incorporating their agreement. The new company would be capitalized at $15,124,600—only a few hundred dollars more than the league had originally suggested, although $3 million more than Warren now demanded—and would provide gas at the rate of ninety cents per thousand feet within a year of its implementation. The bill called for the governor to appoint a commission to consider and to report to the legislature whether the sliding scale should be adopted in Boston. The three men probably went even further, confident that they would have a say in whom the governor appointed to the commission, and that the league would support its implementation.

While Snow put the finishing touches on the legislation, Brandeis hurriedly called a meeting of the Public Franchise League and the Board of Trade at the Bellevue Hotel on 3 May, and informed them of what had occurred. Warren bitterly opposed the measure, because Brandeis had not secured the valuation that he and the league wanted, and claimed that the gas rate should have been reduced to eighty cents, not ninety. But, as Warren resentfully noted, Brandeis made such a persuasive speech that a majority of the members voted to endorse the package. The Board of Trade refused to endorse the bill, but apparently not because of the valuation. Dr. Morton Prince, who shared Warren's anger at the measure, asked whether it would be possible to reopen the question later, and in disgust and anger Brandeis replied, "Don't cry, baby!" Warren would never forget or forgive Brandeis, and began casting slurs on him for acting on a "low ethical plane." Warren resigned from the league, became a vociferous opponent of the sliding scale, and in 1916 worked feverishly to prevent Brandeis's confirmation to the Court.

Brandeis saw the agreement as a compromise, better than the 1903 act, which had serious flaws, and also as part of a larger settlement of the issue. With the backing of the league and of the Consolidated, the legislature passed it a few weeks later, and Governor William Lewis Douglas signed it into law, albeit with reservations. The legislature and the governor named a special commission, consisting of the three gas commissioners; James E. Cotter, recommended by the company; and Charles Palen Hall, a close friend of Brandeis's. In August two of the gas commissioners and Cotter went to England and Ireland to examine the sliding scale in practice. In their report all three of the gas commissioners attacked the plan (which would have essentially driven them out of business), but Cotter and Hall, with the help of Brandeis, wrote a report urging its adoption.

Opposition to the sliding scale was neither simple ignorance nor blind antagonism to progress. No one, not even Brandeis, knew if it would work. Advocates of public ownership of utilities believed there should never be private profit on gas or any other necessity of life.

Although Richards supported the sliding scale, he needed to tread carefully. While the company had responsibilities to the public, it also had to look after the interests of its investors, and a sliding scale, linking dividends to reductions in the rates, must have seemed a harebrained scheme to more than one person. And, of course, the one-idea men like Warren would never admit that the plan had any good features at all. During the fall and winter of 1905–1906, a public debate ensued in Boston about the potential for both good and bad in the proposal, and then it came time to act.

On 20 April 1906, Richards wrote to Brandeis that the Consolidated agreed to a plan including the sliding scale and setting 7 percent as the proper dividend rate, with an increase in dividends of 1 percent for every five-cent reduction in the price of gas. It seemed wiser to him, however, that the bill be introduced by the Public Franchise League, without saying specifically that the Consolidated agreed to its terms. Privately, however, he assured Brandeis that if the bill passed, the company would accept it. By then, Brandeis knew that Richards would keep his word, and it only remained for the legislature to enact the law, which it did in May. Governor Curtis Guild signed it into law on 26 May 1906.

The sliding scale went into effect with gas selling at ninety cents a thousand, the Consolidated capitalized at a little over $15 million, and the dividend rate set at 7 percent. Almost immediately the company reduced the price of gas to eighty-five cents so that it could continue paying its dividend at the old rate of 8 percent. Within a year, good management and the introduction of some new technology allowed the company to reduce the price of gas to eighty cents and to raise its dividend to 9 percent. In the short term at least, boldness and creativity seemed to produce what Brandeis had wanted, a solution fair to all concerned.

TO HIS BROTHER, Brandeis wrote, "I consider this a most important step in public economics and government—an alternative for municipal ownership—which will keep the Gas Co. out of politics." Brandeis, throughout his life, said that he wanted to keep government out of business, a sentiment that many conservatives shared; but, and perhaps more important, he also wanted to keep business out of government. Following the gas fight he made this observation a number of times. While many people had wanted a fair capitalization and cheaper gas, few of them had looked, as Brandeis did, at the interests of the company and its stockholders. And he alone seemed to understand that only a just solution would allow the company to pursue its business interests without resorting to the legislature to redress real or imagined ills. James Richards also understood this and, like Brandeis, recognized that the demand for municipal ownership could only be averted if the public believed that the utilities treated the consumer honestly.

Brandeis's victory in procuring the sliding scale drew the attention of a number of newspapers as well as many municipal reformers around the country, who wrote to him asking about details of the scheme. He provided an answer in the November 1907 issue of the *American Review of Reviews,* and how he started the article is telling: "Shall the public utilities be owned by the public?—is a question pressing for decision in nearly every American city." While it remained a matter for debate, clearly Brandeis preferred that government not get involved, other than in ensuring that privately owned franchises and utilities obeyed strict laws of financial probity and served the public interest at a reasonable price. He trumpeted the savings that Boston gas consumers had realized in the first two years of the plan, as well as the benefits to the company. "This saving was not attained by a sacrifice of the interests of the stockholder," who saw not only the dividend rise but also the value of the stock, which went from $44^1/_2$ to $57^1/_2$ in that same period and even held firm at 52 during the Panic of 1907.

As usual, Brandeis neglected to mention his own role and gave fulsome credit both to the Public Franchise League (without discussing the deep divisions in that organization) and to James L. Richards, whom he praised as the model of an enlightened business leader. For Brandeis, this combination of public-spirited citizenry and progressive entrepreneurship seemed a far better model for America's cities than public ownership. "If the demand for municipal ownership in America can be stayed, it will be by such wise legislation as the Public Franchise League has promoted and by such public service as Mr. Richards and his associates are rendering in the management of a private corporation."

THE TWO MUNICIPAL REFORMS involving street railways and the gas company are interesting less in themselves than in what they teach us about Louis Brandeis and his maturation as a reformer in a relatively short period of time. Neither problem was unique to Boston; throughout the progressive era many cities struggled with regulation of transportation and public utilities. The solution of the Boston Elevated involved no grand theories, but an insistence on traditional Massachusetts values, namely, that corporations serving the public interest had to follow rules laid down by the government. The Consolidated Gas episode started out pretty much the same way, with Brandeis and the Public Franchise League insisting on a fair capitalization in accordance with the Commonwealth's laws against stock watering.

Both fights taught Brandeis a lot. First, while he might be better informed and better organized than any of his companions, alone he could do little. One man, no matter how cogent his argument, how persuasive his facts, just could not hope to impress legislators who, for reasons both good and bad, had multiple constituencies to look after. After the first part of the Elevated fight, he would never again tackle any issue by himself. Behind him there would always be some organization, and as he went on, these groups tended to be bigger, better organized, and more persuasive.

He probably always understood that in order for reform to succeed, one had to play the political game, and between 1897 and 1916 he became a master political tactician. He made it a point to know the power brokers in state and local government, and later in Washington, so that, at appropriate times, he had access to them. One could write letters to the editor galore, but ten minutes alone with the governor could yield a veto of a bad bill.

He also understood that being too visible would make him a lightning rod for the opposition. Following the signing of the sliding-scale bill, he told his brother, "I succeeded in running this campaign mainly by putting others on the firing line: as your girls would say 'the man behind.' " Actually, for all that he tried to utilize others in writing editorials, speaking to legislators, and the like, everyone understood where the energy came from for the sliding-scale plan. Despite the split in the Public Franchise League, Brandeis managed to get a fair degree of support from those who rejected Edward Warren's blinkered approach to the problem. He had access to, and used, the editors of major area newspapers to run editorials opposing the initial valuation and then later supporting his plan. As Brandeis became a more celebrated reformer, he found it harder and harder to stay out of the limelight, no matter how many lieutenants he utilized.

Although Brandeis hoped that the sliding scale would be copied by other cities, that did not happen. Neither Brandeis, Richards, nor anyone else at the time recognized a major flaw in the system. The sliding scale was designed to improve efficiency, and it operated on the assumption that, in order to get a higher dividend rate, the company would work to increase its productivity and that the consumer would then benefit from lower prices. Everyone discounted the idea that prices would go up, because no one could conceive of a situation in which the company would not be able to control its costs. During World War I, however, the price of coal shot up dramatically, and the Consolidated proved neither able to control costs nor willing to slash dividends. The Board of Gas and Electric Light Commissioners recommended, and the legislature approved, an end to the sliding-scale experiment and returned to a system of normal utility regulation.

The sliding scale was not a gimmick, despite its failure to survive inflation and the lack of interest by others in adopting it. Aside from its creativity and its effort to forge a mutually beneficial partnership between the company and its consumers, it is of value in illustrating one aspect of what made Brandeis so successful a reformer: his willingness to look at all sides of a problem. Sometimes, as with the Boston Elevated, simple issues required straightforward solutions. But when he looked at the gas problem, he understood that the consolidation, the valuation, the setting of rates and dividends, and the need to divorce the company from politics made for a complexity that required a novel approach in order to treat all parties fairly. While he hoped that the plan might be copied, he also understood that it had solved Boston's problem because the solution fit the issues. In other places, other conditions would require different approaches. This open-minded pragmatism, while always adhering to basic traditional principles, is a hallmark of all of Brandeis's activities, a blend of the idealistic and the pragmatic.

Considering how much Brandeis attempted to protect business interests—after all, he did have a large commercial law practice—it is somewhat ironic that in these battles he began to antagonize and even alienate men who should have been standing with him in upholding the Commonwealth's traditions. Although Boston lagged behind New York in funding the new industries, the State Street banks and financial houses had become more heavily invested in the new economy. They objected to Brandeis's reminders of traditional Massachusetts practices not only because they made them uncomfortable but because they now subscribed to a new ethos that emphasized profit and downplayed public interest. Leaders of the city's financial and professional elite, men who had welcomed Brandeis into their homes and clubs, soon began to shun him. Rumors, sometimes breaking into the open, accused him of unethical or unprofessional behavior. How much of this can be attributed to anti-Semitism is impossible to determine, but whatever the reason a man who considered Boston the center of the universe now found it a much lonelier place than it had been.

FOR HIS WORK on the special committee to investigate the sliding scale, the Commonwealth paid Charles Palen Hall $2,000, and in light of how much Brandeis had helped him, especially in drafting the minority report, he wanted to share that money with him. He called Brandeis up and asked him to take part of the money. Brandeis immediately refused, and later that day wrote to Hall: "I shall take it as a personal affront if you insist upon paying to or for me in any form, shape, or manner discernible by man any part of the $2000. . . . The very best use that can be made of that fund is for you to keep it yourself, but if it will relieve your mind I shall not object if a small part of it goes to the Public Franchise League. But that is the utmost limit to which you can get my assent."

As a member of the Public Franchise League, indeed as its driving force, Brandeis clearly could not accept any fee for his services. When he represented a group such as the liquor lobby, he of course charged, but as he became more involved in public service, he developed what for the legal profession at the time many considered not only an aberrational but indeed a subversive habit—he would not accept payment. In his earliest reforms, such as working with Mrs. Lincoln on public institutions, he essentially represented her as her lawyer, and she paid him accordingly. Then he began giving his fees back, or donating them to charities, and then he stopped taking money for public work altogether.

He had said almost from the time he entered law practice that he hoped, at some point in the future, to be able to devote a portion of his time to the public good. By 1905, Brandeis was spending some days almost entirely involved in public causes. When Edward Filene tried to get a bill from Brandeis for some service Brandeis had performed during the traction fight, Brandeis kept putting him off. Finally, in exasperation, Filene went to Devonshire Street and bearded the attorney in his office. He later wrote that Brandeis "told me he never made a charge for public service of this kind; that it was his duty as it was mine to help protect the public rights; and when I remonstrated, saying that he and his family were dependent upon his income, he told me that he had resolved early in life to give at least one hour a day to public service, and later on he hoped to give fully half his time."

The idea of a lawyer doing work *pro bono publico,* for the good of the public, is now an accepted part of American legal practice, with nearly all firms paying at least lip service to the concept and many actively encouraging partners and associates to engage in such work. While it might be too much to say that Brandeis invented the practice—for surely others besides him gave of themselves to public service—he certainly focused attention on the concept and, despite the criticism he received from the established bar at the time, won public approbation as well as the title the "People's Attorney."

As he grew more famous, reporters interviewing him would ask about this odd practice, and his answer on one occasion gives us a glimpse of the man who valued his privacy and shared little knowledge about himself with the public:

> Some men buy diamonds and rare works of art; others delight in automobiles and yachts. My luxury is to invest my surplus effort, beyond that required for the proper support of my family, to the pleasure of taking up a problem and solving, or helping to solve, it for the people without receiving any compensation. Your yachtsman or automobilist would lose much of his enjoyment if he were obliged to do for pay what he is doing for the love of the thing itself. So I should lose much of my satisfaction if I were paid in connection with public services of this kind. I have only one life, and it is short enough. Why waste it on things I don't want most? I don't want money or property most. I want to be free.

Initially, Brandeis meant to give a small part of his time, not realizing that his financial success would eventually make it possible to give days, weeks, and sometimes months at a stretch to public service. While he worked to finish up the sliding-scale plan, a new problem emerged that was to require even more of his time and energy, and whose novel solution would result in what he called his most important reform.

CHAPTER SEVEN

A PERFECT REFORM

Had a person in the year 2005 suddenly received a morning paper dated 1905, the lead story on page one would have been quite familiar. Officials of a corporation with huge cash reserves had been treating the company's coffers as their own private piggy banks, using the funds for personal indulgences and illicit campaign contributions. Only the names of the firms and the officers would have been different. Instead of Tyco, Enron, and WorldCom, they would have been Equitable Life, the Prudential, and New York Life, whose executives had diverted money to risky schemes and illegal political contributions, and supported extravagant lifestyles. Magazines that until then had taken a very respectful attitude toward insurance now began examining the seamier side of the business. Thomas Lawson, the former financial pirate turned muckraker, laid bare the inner workings of the insurance industry in *Everybody's Magazine,* while Burton J. Hendrick provided "The Story of Life Insurance" for *McClure's.*

As much as any issue of the time, insurance scandals grabbed the attention of the middle classes. Average people might not understand the intricacies of vertical integration in the steel industry or the complex financial underwritings of the big banks, since they had little personal contact with either U.S. Steel or J. P. Morgan & Company. Insurance, on the other hand, hit close to home. In 1905 more than ten million people owned over twenty-one million whole or term life policies. Most of these policies insured men, with their wives and children as beneficiaries, so that usually at least four people had some form of interest in each policy. This meant that roughly half the population of the United States at that time had a real, and not an abstract, concern for the safety of the financial reserves that stood behind their policies.

Insurance official and playboy
James Hazen Hyde, 1904

The public may have recognized life insurance as a business, but they also saw it as a form of service—and a very conservative service at that—which operated in the interests of the policyholders. Policies constituted a form of bond in the company, and their owners expected the companies to take very good care of those investments.

George Perkins, an executive of the Equitable, declared that "our profession requires the same zeal, the same enthusiasm, the same earnest purpose that must be born in a man if he succeeds as a minister of the Gospel." According to the president of the Prudential, a spirit of "beneficence and ingrained love of the golden rule" infused the insurance business. Although Henry Hyde, the founder of the Equitable, had in fact been fiscally responsible, his son saw the company as a birthright to be used to support his lifestyle. James Hyde had a flashy coach-and-four, red-heeled patent leather shoes, a violet boutonniere, and nothing but disdain for those not blessed with his charm and wealth. On 31 January 1905, Hyde threw a lavish Louis XV costume party as a coming-out ball for his niece and charged it to the company. Unfortunately, others in the insurance business had the same attitude.

The scandals provoked not just legislative outcries and investigations, but demands for reform from policyholders. One such group, the New England Policy-Holders' Protective Committee, asked Louis Brandeis to represent it.

NEW ENGLAND POLICYHOLDERS had nearly $1 million in annual premiums at stake in the Equitable alone and realized that in the face of ongoing allegations, they would need a great deal more information than they had in order to protect their investments. The policyholders formed the committee on 18 April 1905 "for the purpose of advising themselves as to the condition of the Company." Many of the businessmen on the committee knew Brandeis, either as clients or because of his activities in the Boston Elevated and sliding-scale reforms. William Whitman and Edwin Abbot approached him, and he had a "stormy session" with them before they would agree to his demand that he serve without compensation. Brandeis recognized that the issues involved far more than just the protection of private policies, and while he did not yet know how the various interests fit together, he wanted to retain the freedom to serve as counsel to the situation.

As usual, he began by collecting facts. Because of the system of underwriting, that is, of smaller companies in effect insuring their risks with larger companies, the big three—the Equitable, the Mutual, and New York Life—controlled nearly half of the assets of the ninety chartered legal reserve insurance firms in the country. All told, American insurance companies had assets of more than $12 billion in 1905, and control of this wealth meant not just financial clout but political power and the ability to influence industrial policy through the financing of new corporations. Given the daily stories in the newspapers and journals of the time, it took Brandeis only a month before he delivered his first report to the committee. "The disclosures already made indicate a failure to perform fully the sacred obligation assumed by those who have managed this great trust. Neither the recovery of the profits wrongfully diverted nor mere substitution of other officers, however scrupulous and efficient, can afford an adequate remedy for the evils disclosed." Radical changes, he concluded, had to be made in the system itself.

But that would be the long-term solution. In the meantime, the committee and others like it would have to push for full disclosure of the companies' financial statements, the end to large salaries and moneys that could be diverted for private use, and the replacement of the current directors with men committed to protecting the policyholders and the public. Brandeis welcomed the news that similar protective committees had sprung up in other cities and states, because the greater the dissatisfaction expressed by the policyholders, the stronger the pressure would be on the companies to mend their ways. Because he needed "all the facts that surround," Brandeis did not look just at the abuses; the journalists and legislative investigations had already done much to uncover the misdeeds of company officials. Brandeis wanted to know how insurance worked, and what he learned outraged him.

Life insurance, as *Moody's Magazine* noted, "is a very simple business proposition, easily understood." While actuaries could not predict the length of any single life, they could predict the duration of a large number of lives. If one took, for example, one thousand people born in the same year and then looked at how long they lived, the statistician could come up with an average life expectancy and the median age at which people in this group died. For example, if that number were sixty-three, then one-half of the sample would die before their sixty-third birthday, and one-half would die after that date. Simple arithmetic would then determine how much of a premium should be charged. Theoretically, the amount paid in before that sixty-third birthday, together with money earned on those premiums, would equal the benefit paid plus enough to cover administrative expenses. While for those who died earlier the full amount of the policy might not have been paid in and earned, this would be made up by those who died later and thus paid in more.

In an age before either public or private pensions, insurance served more than one purpose. A man taking out a whole life policy on his life might want to ensure that in case he died early, there would be money for his widow to live on, or to pay off the mortgage, or to educate their children. But if he lived a full life, the cash value built up would be the money on which he could retire. For members of the middle class without large sums of capital to invest in industrial stocks, life insurance policies constituted their savings, and this explains why, more than any other scandal of the time, the abuses in the life insurance industry aroused such a public alarum. The failure of the companies would jeopardize the life savings of millions of people.

ALTHOUGH A SALARIED PERSON or a small-business man could afford to pay the premiums on a whole life policy on an annual or perhaps even quarterly basis, workingmen and workingwomen often could not. The premium on the policy would have taken too large a share of their income from factory and mill workers who could barely make ends meet. They, too, however, needed insurance, especially given the daily hazards they faced in the workplace. To meet this demand, the insurance companies created a form of term insurance, that is, policies with no accrued cash value that would remain in force only as long as the policy owner paid the weekly premiums. For many working people this seemed an ideal solution—lower coverage, to be sure, but at a much lower price, and the premium could be as little as twenty-five or fifty cents a week. In addition, the agent who sold the policy would come around to the house every week to collect the money and stamp the policy book.

Once Brandeis began digging into the facts, he learned that out of every dollar collected in industrial insurance, forty cents went to officers' salaries, agent commissions, and stockholders in the form of dividends. Moreover, out of every twelve policies written, the companies would have to pay a benefit on only one. Workers laid off could not afford to continue premiums, and the company would cancel the policy, leaving the insured with nothing. (On regular policies a cash value accrued, and if the policyholder missed a premium, it would be deducted from the cash value, and the policy would remain in force. If a policyholder for one reason or another wished to terminate the policy, the company would pay out the accrued cash value.)

The Armstrong Committee, empowered by the New York legislature to investigate the insurance abuses, began its hearings on 5 September 1905 and for the next four months laid bare the sordid practices of those who termed themselves "trustees of the most sacred trust on earth." Many insurance executives and their board members suddenly came down sick or discovered that business required them to go out of town the day before their scheduled testimony. Charles Evans Hughes, the New York attorney who served as counsel to the committee and who would later be Brandeis's colleague on the Court, forced those who did testify to reveal their high salaries, their costly perquisites paid for by the companies, their diversion of funds, their power in the financial markets, and their large and often illegal political contributions. He revealed company methods aimed at confusing small policyholders and defrauding widows and orphans out of even a minimal payout. The information Hughes elicited from the companies not only confirmed Brandeis's concerns about industrial insurance but showed that the abuses went even further than he had suspected.

Once the officials took the stand, one revelation followed another. The aging U.S. senator Thomas Collier Platt of New York acknowledged receiving cash contributions to his campaigns from the insurance companies, and in return for that money he admitted that he had "a moral obligation to defend them." John R. Hegeman, president of the Metropolitan, confirmed under oath that workingmen paid twice as much for the same amount of insurance as did regular policyholders. As for the part that industrial insurance played in a company's profit structure, Haley Fiske, the Metropolitan's vice president, candidly admitted that the companies made little or no profit off of their regular policies. When Hughes asked if that meant all of the profits came out of industrial premiums, Fiske said, "Oh, yes, sir." James Craig also confirmed that nearly forty cents out of each dollar went toward "expenses," which included profit.

In talking about the Metropolitan in its final report, the Armstrong Committee declared:

> The Industrial Department furnishes insurance at twice the normal cost to those least able to pay for it; a large proportion, if not the greater number of the insured, permitting their policies to lapse, receive no money return for their payments. Success is made possible by thorough organization on a large scale and by the employment of an army of underpaid solicitors and clerks; and from margins small in individual cases, but large in the aggregate, enormous profits have been realized upon an insignificant investment.

In short, industrial insurance amounted to little more than a legal racket to steal from the poor.

The committee, however, while identifying the evil, had no solution to propose other than a "special investigation." Moreover, the members seemed to accept that "the most serious evils"—namely, excessive premiums, enormous lapse rate, and agent hardships—"seem to be inherent in the system." Perhaps branch offices might be established to do away with agents, "but the opinion of those connected with the companies is that such a plan would be impracticable," and the committee had no information to gainsay that assertion.

BRANDEIS SPOKE TO the Commercial Club of Boston on 26 October 1905, at the height of the Armstrong Committee hearings, and the speech foreshadowed important developments in his thought over the next several years. In the audience sat many of the leading businessmen and professionals of the city, all of whom had a vested interest in the financial reliability of the insurance companies. They did not stand alone in their concern, he told them, since one-half of the total population of the country had ties to one or more insurance policies, either as the insured or as a beneficiary. Moreover, while they undoubtedly knew that insurance involved large sums of money, they may not have recognized the great size of that amount. The aggregate of all policies then in force came to nearly $13 billion, more than the entire value of all the railroads in the United States. Each year the American people paid in more than $465 million in new premiums, and the ninety reserve insurance companies in the country held assets of more than $2.5 billion, three times the total assets held by the 5,331 national banks in the country. The premiums, and the investment of these enormous assets, gave insurance companies an annual return of $613 million, more than the annual budget of the U.S. government.

While the companies occasionally wrote policies for $1 million, the average policy written by the big three averaged a little more than $2,300 on whole life policies, and less than $200 on industrial policies written for workers. Life insurance, therefore, "is in the main held by what we term 'the people'—that large class which every system of business and of government should seek to protect."

In this speech Brandeis, for the first time, began talking about what he would eventually call the "curse of bigness," although his thoughts on that subject had not yet matured. It is apparent that the very size of the insurance industry overall did not bother him; after all, people from all walks of life needed insurance, and no matter how many private companies, benevolent associations, and fraternal organizations were involved, the total amount of coverage, and the annual premiums, would add up to large numbers. What he began to complain about in this speech is the power that huge assets gave to large individual companies. The Equitable, the Mutual, and New York Life controlled assets of $1,247,331,738, and this constituted what he termed "quick capital," that is, money that could easily be applied to one project or another, or transferred about.

We have in the United States other great aggregations of assets, he told the audience, such as in the steel trust, the oil trust, the beef trust, and the transcontinental railroad systems, and in these combinations "our people recognize a menace to our welfare and our institutions." This idea, that bigness in and of itself threatened democratic society, had been in the air for many decades. Many progressives had been discussing this notion, but this is the first time that Brandeis explicitly made this connection. He did not pursue it in this talk, but over the next several years he would think about it a great deal, developing a coherent philosophy about the menace of large-scale businesses to democratic society.

Another idea first seen in this speech would later develop into his attack on those who used "other people's money." The assets of companies like U.S. Steel and the railroads resided primarily in their physical plants and facilities, but insurance companies' assets lay in free capital, and how they used this capital gave them great power over companies that needed to borrow money for plant expansion or to issue new stocks to enlarge their businesses. Prudence, and a care for the moneys invested by their policyholders, should have dictated conservative investments, such as mortgages on real estate. In fact, less than one dollar in fourteen had been invested in real estate. They had used the rest—the enormous amount of quick capital at their disposal—to support business ventures sponsored by the great banking houses, such as the Morgan firm.

People needed to know, Brandeis explained, that the important banking and investment houses had far less capital available than did the big three insurance companies, and so financiers eagerly courted the officials of the insurance companies to divert their funds to new, and occasionally risky, ventures. It had been insurance money that had made possible J. P. Morgan's effort to create a rail monopoly in the Northern Securities Trust or a shipping monopoly in the International Mercantile Marine Company, and that had financed E. H. Harriman's and Jay Gould's ambitious railroad plans. To ensure continued complicity and access to their funds, the officials of the insurance companies had been invited to sit on the boards of directors of companies into which they invested money, and these interlocking directorates— another target that Brandeis would later attack—did not serve the interests of the investors, but lined the pockets of the insurance directors. (The foppish James Hazen Hyde, for example, sat on the boards of forty-eight other companies, not because of any business acumen, but simply to ensure that money from the Equitable would continue to flow.)

If the only sin of the insurance officials had been bad judgment in choosing how to invest the policyholders' money, that would have been contemptible but not criminal. But the Armstrong investigation showed that officers of the big three had falsified the books to hide large outlays of money for personal use (such as the purchase of a $12,000 rug for the office of the president of the Mutual), that they had hidden the fact that risky stocks remained in their possession after claiming that they had been sold, that there had been fake sales—one of which involved a $600-a-year messenger in the Equitable who had given his personal note for $3.3 million in order to "purchase" a block of foreign investments—and that the companies had persistently lied about such matters. Hundreds of thousands of dollars diverted to campaign contributions wound up listed on the books as real estate expenses. The overhead expenses of the companies ran far higher than any reasonable person would allow, and inflated salaries deprived the policyholders of what should have been assets reserved for their benefit.

Brandeis objected to all of these practices not just because of their illegality but because of their immoral nature and their violation of a trust. "The degree of guilt involved in such transactions," he angrily declared, "will be appreciated only when one remembers that the life insurance business beyond all other in the world rests upon confidence—confidence that in the remote, indefinite future the present sacrifice of the policy-holder will bring protection to widow and children." It is this moral underpinning that attracted so many clergy and social workers to his side in his battle to reform industrial insurance. John Graham Brooks, one of the leading social reformers of the time, rejoiced that the moral depravity of the insurance companies had finally shocked the public into awareness. "We need a moral reawakening about this workingmen's insurance," Brooks declared, "quite as much as about our political evils."

If Brandeis had been indignant at the companies' abuse of financial trust on whole life policies, he grew livid when he turned to industrial insurance, those small policies paid for by working people on a weekly basis, and he detailed the facts of high commission rates, lapsed policies because of irregularity of employment, and the exorbitant rate that the poorest segment of the community had to pay for a necessity of life.

In contrast to the poor performance of insurance companies in managing their policyholders' money, Brandeis offered the example of the 188 savings banks in Massachusetts. Together they held about $675 million in assets, about half the aggregate of the big three insurance companies, and they took in new deposits about one-half the amount paid in by new premiums. Yet they managed this money not only wisely but at a fraction of the cost—one-thirtieth to be exact—of the insurance companies. Moreover, the "faithful treasurers of the 188 modest Massachusetts savings banks, supervised mainly by obscure but conscientious citizens," earned a higher rate on their assets than did any of the large insurance companies.

To restore confidence to policyholders, Brandeis proposed tightening state regulations over insurance companies' use of policyholders' moneys, abolishing lavish commissions, protecting policies from involuntary forfeiture, what we would now call greater transparency as to the officers and directors and the ties they had to other firms that used the reserve funds, and fuller disclosure in financial reports. At the time each state had its own insurance regulations, since an 1869 Supreme Court

Alice, Elizabeth, and Frolic, ca. 1908

decision had held insurance not to be a matter of interstate commerce. In February 1905 the Republican senator John Dryden of New Jersey, who also headed the Prudential, had introduced a bill to license insurance companies under federal authority. The insurance companies, Dryden asserted, would much prefer one set of regulations instead of forty-six, "for that would make it so much easier to shape policy."

Brandeis, however, objected to federal supervision, and here again we see the beginnings of a theme that he would enlarge upon for the rest of his life. Just as he opposed bigness in business, so he resisted bigness in government. The Dryden bill, among other things, lacked many of the features that existed in Massachusetts to protect the policyholder and did not add a single provision to safeguard the policyholder's investment. But even if the Dryden bill had been a better measure, he would still have opposed it, and he quoted from Frederick Hapgood Nash, the assistant attorney general of Massachusetts, words that would echo in his own writings for years to come: "The wisdom, discretion and honesty composite in fifty States and Territories are more to be valued than the excellence of one person appointed at Washington. State supervision is good or bad, according to the merits of the best of the commissioners. Federal supervision must be good or bad, according to the qualities of one man who is unchecked by the work of co-ordinate officials."

Brandeis did not address the issue of whether insurance companies did interstate business; he knew they did. But he always believed in putting governmental responsibility as close to home as possible. People could watch over the actions of local and state officials far better than they could someone off in Washington; the officials would know that this oversight existed and therefore act more responsibly. Later on the Court, Brandeis would be a fierce defender of federalism, but the die had been cast years earlier.

• • •

THE POLICY-HOLDERS' PROTECTIVE COMMITTEE immediately published the speech as a pamphlet, and Brandeis himself made sure it received wide circulation. Although he had told his father that there had been considerable work of late with public and private problems, including gas, railroads, and city affairs, his mind kept going back to insurance reform. He had made some specific recommendations for tightening state regulation, but even if all were adopted, the beneficiaries of those measures would be those who owned whole life policies. The workers who bought industrial insurance would not be any better off, since their problem concerned not how the company used assets but the high cost they paid for small policies and the high lapse rate resulting from their inability to make premium payments during slack seasons. While he had referred to the savings banks in his talk, Brandeis had not proposed that they become involved in insurance, a function that had never been part of their business before. It is impossible to determine at what point he began thinking about selling life insurance through savings banks, but we can tell when he began to act on it.

During his work for the Policy-Holders' Protective Committee, Brandeis had received a letter from Walter Channing Wright, an actuary and the son of Elizur Wright, who had been a leading abolitionist and an insurance reformer in the 1860s. Walter Wright had suggested that his services might be of use to the group. On 3 November, Brandeis wrote to Wright proposing that they meet soon and talk "about a matter which in the first instance is of a public nature, but which I think may ripen into a matter in which your services will be required professionally." A few weeks later they met, after which Brandeis spelled out the essential parts of what he would always consider his most successful reform effort, savings bank life insurance.

Brandeis started with a basic assumption shared by many people, that "the business of life insurance is one of extraordinary simplicity," the successful conduct of which "requires neither genius nor initiative." One did not even need unusual business judgment, just "honesty, accuracy, persistence, and economy." He also believed, as did many others, that industrial insurance had been the greatest wrong uncovered in the scandal. To provide low-cost insurance to workers, one remedy would be to have the state sell insurance in small amounts, but he immediately dismissed state intervention of this sort as "undesirable." He had, however, found a solution that would not require state action, would not need a brand-new infrastructure, and would be tied to an industry with a proven record for "honesty, accuracy, persistence, and economy"—savings banks.

Dating back to 1816, the state's savings banks were the oldest in the country, with roots deep in the community. They had no stockholders, but operated as a quasi-public trust governed by nonsalaried trustees. To create an insurance adjunct to savings banks would benefit everyone. The banks would get new customers, who would be willing to buy insurance there because of the banks' reputation for fiscal integrity. An insurance department could be introduced with minimal expense; there would be no agents, no separate buildings, no significant increase in overhead. Moreover, because one did not have to create a wholly new institution with all of the attendant costs, even if the plan did not work out, the banks themselves would not suffer the financial or moral costs of failure.

Before he could even begin to talk about this plan with bank and business leaders, Brandeis needed facts. There would, he assumed, be a relatively small cost in collecting premiums, since workers would make them by coming to the bank, just as they did now to make a deposit or withdrawal. There were, however, certain expenses unique to insurance that would be outside the purview of banking experience, such as the costs of a medical examination, expenses incident to the proof of death, and the actuarial expenses needed to set up the rate schedules. Some or all of these first two expenses might be charged to the policyholders.

Brandeis wanted a plan that would do away with the forfeiture of policies because of a single lapsed payment. Failure to make a payment should trigger some mechanism whereby the policyholder had the premium charged to a cash value, or received a reduced amount of insurance until he could make the payments. Would it be possible, he asked Wright, to have a person buy different amounts of insurance, so that if a worker had extra money, he could increase his insurance without having to take out a whole new policy? Finally, should the policyholder wish to surrender the policy, there ought to be a way that he could recover at least the amount of premiums paid in. "In other words," Brandeis told Wright, "make the investment of insurance practically convertible into a savings bank investment." He also wanted to know whether there should be a limit on how much insurance a person could buy. At present most companies would not sell more than a $150 or $200 industrial policy, while many savings banks had a maximum amount that could be deposited in an account, usually $1,000. If it would be feasible, Brandeis wanted workers to be able to buy up to $1,000 in coverage.

Clearly, a bank could not undertake such a program without a minimum number of people signing up. Wright had suggested that at least three hundred policies would have to be issued to make the program sound. If this number were correct, Brandeis thought, then it would be possible for even the smallest savings bank to undertake the plan, and the scheme could be enacted through a general law, allowing individual banks the choice to establish an insurance department; there would be no compulsion.

Brandeis had no illusion that the plan, even if successful, would drive the commercial companies out of the industrial insurance business. It would apply only to Massachusetts, although he hoped other states might emulate the experiment. More important, by giving working people a less-expensive alternative, it would force the big companies to lower their prices. Competition would force them to correct the abuses of the current system, because they would not be able to get any industrial business if they continued to pay high commissions and offered policies inferior to those of the banks.

Wright sent his first report on 1 3 December, but it failed to satisfy Brandeis. In a three-page letter Brandeis listed what he considered either missing or incomplete information, and questioned closely some of the data Wright had sent. Over the next few months Wright would supply information, and Brandeis would analyze it and then ask for additional material or further elaboration on what he had already seen. Wright also offered a variety of comments, including the observation that the greatest opposition would come from the savings banks themselves, since they "are so entirely successful in their present operations, their officers might be disinclined to accept new and more complex features in addition to their present function."

Brandeis, of course, had no need to be told what the opposition would be, nor did he expect the commercial companies to sit back quietly and give up their most lucrative source of profit. In order to win, Brandeis understood that he would have to make a compelling case for savings bank insurance, organize public support for it, gain legislative approval for the enabling legislation, and then still have the formidable task of getting the banks to agree to participate. On his side would be the outrage generated by the scandals, which at the very least would undermine the credibility of the insurance companies. He would also benefit from the fact that insurance touched almost everyone's life, making it easier to get people to understand the importance of the proposal. And last but certainly not least, Brandeis had learned a great deal from his work on the Boston Elevated and the sliding scale and his involvement with local political reformers. Savings bank insurance would call upon all that experience.

FIRST HE NEEDED to polish his proposal and make sure that he had not left an opening on which he could be attacked for making erroneous assumptions. Between January and early June 1906, Brandeis worked on the plan between numerous other demands on his time. A cursory examination of his correspondence shows that during this period he gave a speech on the need for an eight-hour workday; worked with the Public Franchise League to shepherd through the sliding-scale law and then to secure decent appointments to the Board of Gas and Electric Light Commissioners; at the governor's request proposed men to serve as Massachusetts representatives to the National Conference of Commissioners on Uniform State Laws; wrote an article on the Boston Elevated fight; began to get involved in local railroad matters; sent recommendations to the mayor regarding reforms in the city's accounting methods; fought off still another attempt by the Boston Elevated to secure a sweetheart franchise; got drawn in to the debate over how the Cambridge transit system would be connected to Boston's rail network; and maintained his law practice, including trying some cases in court. He and his family went out to Dedham regularly, and during the winter he took Susan and Elizabeth, now thirteen and ten, skating and sledding. He worried over his brother's health, and for Alfred's birthday bought him land adjacent to the farm Al was building east of Louisville. He received an invitation from his brother-in-law Felix Adler to speak before the New York Society for Ethical Culture along with Charles Evans Hughes, counsel to the Armstrong Committee, on the lessons of the investigation, "but I have all I can do to attend to home affairs this month, at office and Legislature."

To his brother Louis also began musing on political conditions, and one comment is instructive regarding the looming insurance fight. "The rising resentment at plutocratic action will make itself severely felt," he wrote. "After all, we are living in a Democracy, & some way or other, the people will get back at power unduly concentrated, and there will be plenty of injustice in the process." Unlike some of the more radical progressives, who wanted large-scale social transformation, the conservative Brandeis feared it. Like Edmund Burke, he wanted reform not for its own sake or to implement some new social vision but to forestall upheaval. Society had to change to accommodate new conditions, and if it did so gradually, then one could count on progress. If the powers that be blocked that change, pressure would build and change would still come, but at a great cost. Savings bank insurance did not aim at grand reform. Brandeis highlighted a specific but important problem, and his solution addressed it. Although an idealist, he was also a realist—he had no desire to redo the world.

Brandeis finished his draft in early June, first sent it to Wright for comment, and then mailed out dozens of copies to friends in Boston and elsewhere for their views. An encouraging response came from Charles Evans Hughes, who called the piece "a strong and unanswerable statement of the evils of industrial insurance." He, like Wright, worried

Norman Hapgood, ca. 1900

about the conservatism of the savings bank officials and urged Brandeis to expand the section showing the feasibility of the plan; but he hoped the experiment could be undertaken. Robert Herrick, an eminent Boston attorney, immediately understood the importance of a plan "whereby the poor can be helped to help themselves."

Brandeis published the piece that fall in *Collier's* magazine, and in doing so began a lifelong friendship with Norman Hapgood. Then the editor of *Collier's,* Hapgood would provide a magazine outlet for many of Brandeis's most important articles, and he would bring him in as the magazine's lawyer during the Pinchot-Ballinger hearings (see chapter 11). The article repeated much of what Brandeis had said in his Commercial Club paper, but spent far more time detailing the abuses of industrial insurance. By then, of course, he had available the hearings and report of the Armstrong Committee, and used the admissions of the insurance company officials themselves to damn the practice. He termed the entire system "vicious" and proposed that the same business could be handled more efficiently by savings banks, providing greater coverage at lesser cost to the workers and allowing a method of keeping the policies intact even if a worker missed a premium. Hapgood arranged for hundreds of reprints of the article and also allowed it to appear simultaneously in major newspapers across the country. The

Boston Evening Transcript carried the piece on 11 September, and the next day the *Boston Post* began a series of editorials endorsing the plan.

As one might expect, progressives and labor advocates immediately endorsed the plan, while the insurance industry heaped scorn on it. One industry journal denounced the project as "positively grotesque in its absurdity. It betrays the theorist and indicates an utter ignorance as to the practical workings of industrial insurance or the peculiar make-up of the wage-earning class." Frederick L. Hoffman, who worked for the Prudential as its chief statistician, declared that the article demonstrated that Brandeis lacked "the necessary knowledge and experience" required to run "so vastly important a matter as the safe and permanent conduct of a life insurance business." Another industry journal dismissed the plan outright and assured its readers that "nobody need lose any sleep over the dream of the Boston theorist."

The critics might be forgiven for not knowing much about Louis Brandeis and his passion, indeed some might call it obsession, for facts. Years earlier he had heard about a lawyer who had lost an important case because he had not checked the facts, and vowed that this would never happen to him. In his articles on insurance and other topics, no one ever caught him out with a wrong fact. Readers might disagree with the conclusions he had drawn but could not fault the accuracy of his material. Moreover, in the case of insurance, many of the facts he used came from the mouths of insurance executives themselves or from the annual financial reports companies had to file with state regulation agencies. Try as they might, they could not disprove the damning charges he leveled against industrial insurance; the insurance companies could assume, however, that with their large resources and political influence, they would be able to kill off Brandeis's plan by blocking it in the legislature.

Those who opposed the plan misunderstood what Brandeis wanted to do. They saw it as an attack on the insurance industry by a radical who wanted to dismantle the free enterprise system, a first step on the way to socializing insurance. Never a socialist, Brandeis understood, and tried to get others to see, that if left unchecked, the abuses in insurance and other big businesses would do more than anything to advance rebellion. "The talk of the agitator does not advance socialism a step," he told the Commercial Club. Rather, "the great captains of industry and of finance . . . are the chief makers of socialism." By reforming the system, Brandeis hoped to save it. Moreover, he never called for the abolition of private industrial insurance. If savings banks could offer the service at an affordable price, then the private companies, in order to compete, would have to lower their rates as well. In the *Collier's* article he returned to this theme and warned that unless workingmen could get inexpensive insurance through a private or quasi-private agency, they would soon demand that government provide it. As he told one correspondent, "true conservatism involves progress, and that unless our financial leaders are capable of progress, the institutions which they are trying to conserve will lose their foundation." In addition, the plan would, as Brandeis pointed out, allay "the rising demand for old-age pensions supported by general taxation" through some government agency. Rather, it would provide wage earners with "an opportunity of making provision for themselves for their old age," without increasing the tax burden on the rest of the community. Clearly, a conservative and not a socialist had drafted this plan.

BY THE TIME he put forth the savings bank plan, Brandeis had done a great deal of research on insurance, on savings banks, on actuarial tables, and on means of making his plan feasible. Now he had to convince the public, the state legislature, and savings bank officials that the plan should be given an opportunity to succeed; to do that he needed to educate those groups and create an organization to lobby the legislature into passage of the enabling bill. Even if he could have secured passage of the bill immediately, it would not, he believed, be the right way to do it. It was more important to get the education of "those persons who are now savings banks trustees and the wage earners as to the inequity of the present system and the necessity of developing insurance on savings banks lines, than it is to get the necessary legislation. If we should get tomorrow the necessary legislation, without having achieved that process of education, we could not make a practical working success of the plan."

Here we find one of the keys to Brandeis's success as a reformer: his belief that after one had learned the facts, after one had devised a solution, the plan could not be implemented successfully unless the people themselves grasped its essentials. Education is a key to understanding Brandeis as a lawyer, as a reformer, and as a judge. People might accuse him of being cold, haughty, and disdainful—all of which was to some extent true—but he, like Robert La Follette and a handful of other progressive leaders, truly believed in the people and their ability, once they knew the facts, to do the right thing. He described himself as a "small *d*" democrat and understood that reforms could not be devised on high and then imposed on the people. The people had to "own the reform," to use a more modern phrase, and that required education.

He also knew that he could not conduct this campaign by himself. He would, of course, write, give speeches and interviews, send out hundreds of letters, lobby bank presidents and legislators, and supervise it all. But he needed an organization, and he and his allies created the Massachusetts Savings Bank Insurance League on 26 November 1906. Within four months it had over seventy thousand members, including a number of many well-known businessmen and professionals, labor and civic leaders. To capture as many parts of the community as possible, the league had more than twenty vice presidents and an executive committee, and its brochures prominently displayed the endorsements of President Eliot of Harvard and Bishop (later Cardinal) William Henry O'Connell. As executive secretary Brandeis recruited Norman Hill White, the brother of Brandeis's sailing partner and an independently wealthy young man who responded eagerly to Brandeis's suggestion that he devote his time and energy to public service. (White, along with Brandeis, paid for the bulk of league expenses not covered

Irvin Hearst, Louis Brandeis, and Alice Grady discuss savings bank life insurance

by the modest dues; Brandeis's share, in addition to Wright's actuarial work, came to over $4,000, a substantial amount at the time.) The fact that the Republican former governor John L. Bates became one of the league's vice presidents, while another former governor, William L. Douglas, a Democrat, became its president, testified to its nonpartisanship. No doubt existed, however, as to the real leader and driving force of the league.

Brandeis brought one other person into this campaign, Alice Harriet Grady. By 1906 she headed the law firm's large secretarial staff and handled Brandeis's growing reform correspondence as his executive secretary. At one point she had considered leaving to attend the Chicago Christian Training School and devoting her life to church work. Brandeis talked her out of it. "He felt that I could do better service and enable him to do better work if I would aid him in his proposed [reform] efforts." It no doubt helped that, like him, Alice Grady could throw herself into causes and work for up to sixteen hours a day. Savings bank insurance interested her, and after Brandeis went to Washington in 1916, she went to work for the insurance plan, becoming deputy commissioner of the program in 1920. Until her death in 1934, she enjoyed Brandeis's confidence and corresponded regularly with him about savings bank insurance matters.

While Norman White handled the work of the league, arranging public meetings, mailing out literature, and recruiting new members, Miss Grady oversaw the details directly related to her boss. Brandeis started by dictating letters to her, and before long began dictating instructions: Contact X. Make sure that Y pays a call on Z. Show the list of directors to so-and-so. As he had previously delegated greater authority to her in his office, so he began giving her greater responsibility in regard to the league, and she soon became its financial secretary. Described as "originally a woman of blunt, direct manner, she schooled herself in tact. She learned to write effectively and to speak well, and developed a flair for publicity." In 1916 she even convinced Brandeis to appear in a short and now lost promotional film. The movie depicted two workers killed in an accident, one with insurance and the other without coverage, and the effects of the tragedy on their families. Brandeis himself appeared in a role, and he claimed that only Alice Grady could have induced him to become an actor. At her death, Brandeis noted that "her achievement was great. It was a grand life."

Between his first involvement with insurance reform as counsel to the New England Policy-Holders' Protective Committee on 18 April

1905 and the passage of the enabling legislation on 26 June 1907, Louis Brandeis knew little rest. He still had irons in other reform fires, led a major law firm, and continued to argue cases personally. But for most of these two years he devoted the bulk of his energy to exposing the evils of industrial insurance and working to adopt what he saw as a conservative and efficient means to provide insurance to workers. What one person called a million-to-one shot succeeded because Brandeis always kept his focus on what he wanted and adjusted his tactics as the situation demanded.

In the Massachusetts Savings Bank Insurance League, Brandeis created one of the first modern citizens' lobbies, no small accomplishment in and of itself. There had, of course, been other public-spirited groups that worked in the public interest, starting with the American Anti-slavery Society, the Woman's Christian Temperance Union, and the National Consumers League; the temperance union at one point claimed a half-million members nationally. But while some had done little more than write letters, and others had lobbied legislators, none of them had been as well organized, nor had their efforts been as well orchestrated. It is true that some groups, such as local labor unions, joined en masse, but that did not matter. The local senator or assembly-man from that district would know that a goodly number of his constituents, people he relied upon for reelection, supported this particular measure. While the insurance companies could utilize paid lobbyists and make campaign contributions, in the end politicians counted votes, and the seventy thousand members of the league far outnumbered the insurance officers and salesmen in the state. Brandeis put the numbers to good use in an educational campaign—or public relations, if you like—that proved extremely effective. On his directions hundreds of letters would go out to newspapers all over the state. He understood that in order to influence the local editor in Weymouth or Springfield, it would be more efficacious to have a local businessman or professional make the contact. Senators and assemblymen would have visitors from their hometowns—not strangers—urging them to enact the program. And Louis Brandeis seemed to be everywhere.

Brandeis often liked to quote the German poet Goethe—*"In der Beschränkung zeigt sich erst der Meister"*—that one is the master through small details, and he daily fired off letters to Norman White and others in the league about what might have seemed a small matter. After one meeting, for example, he sent Norman White a note saying that he had run into a young man who professed himself an advocate of savings bank insurance, and Norman should contact him immediately and put him to work. Also, he mentioned that he had not seen the Reverend Dole, the president of the Twentieth Century Club, at the same meeting. Dole reportedly favored the plan, and the club had some influential members. White should contact him. One will see this same attention to minute detail, what some would call micromanaging, in his leadership of the American Zionist movement after 1914 (see chapter 17).

THE CAMPAIGN MOVED FORWARD on three fronts, and Brandeis utilized the league and its members in all of them. To educate the public, the league sent out materials, organized public meetings where speakers explained the benefits of savings bank insurance and the evils of industrial insurance, and made sure that newspapers carried reports of these meetings. Its members met constantly with editors, nearly all of whom gladly supported the measure. As noted earlier, in no other reform of the time did the interests involved affect so many people so personally, and except for the most conservative newspapermen it made a good deal of sense to back a reform that would benefit their daily readers.

The second front involved convincing the legislature to enact the necessary legislation, beginning with the Joint Recess Committee appointed in 1906 to investigate the insurance scandals and to consider possible reforms. Brandeis spoke to the committee on 8 November 1906, and while he did not win the members over, he realized that he had gotten some of them thinking seriously about the plan. George L. Barnes, a Weymouth attorney and member of the committee, had first worked with Brandeis on the sliding scale, and he soon became, along with Norman White, Brandeis's eyes and ears in the legislature, alerting him to changes of mind, potential attacks, and opportunities to make a convert.

Initially, the committee voted informally to table the savings bank plan, but decided to wait until Governor Curtis Guild addressed the legislature at the beginning of 1907. Brandeis, who by now had the confidence of the governor, arranged to see him in late December, and Guild's speech fully endorsed Brandeis's plan. "I commend for your consideration," he told the legislature, "the study of plans to be submitted to you for cheaper industrial insurance that may rob death of half of its terror for the worthy poor." Five days later the Recess Committee unanimously endorsed savings bank insurance.

Although he had hoped to get the savings bank people to draft the enabling legislation, they failed to do so, and Brandeis stepped in to draw up the bill in late February. The league then sent copies to every member of the General Court, along with copies of Brandeis's *Collier's* article and other materials, and also saw that these items went to every newspaper in the state. It still proved tough sledding, as the insurance companies and their allies in the legislature used every tactic they could devise to delay matters, in the belief that the momentum the league had generated would dissipate with lack of legislative action. To counter these tactics, Brandeis asked one of his oldest friends and a classmate at Harvard Law, Judge Warren Reed, what they could do. Reed, a respected lawyer and president of the People's Savings Bank of Brockton, told Brandeis that he believed many of the legislators saw savings bank insurance as a "hobby" and not to be taken seriously. Everyone from the governor on down had said that the plan would benefit the laboring man, but until the workers took up the cause themselves, the legislators would ignore it. Brandeis immediately began contacting all the labor leaders he knew, as well as those involved in the league, to write letters to their assemblymen, supporting the plan. Brandeis had spoken to a skeptical joint committee on insurance on 21 March; he returned to continue his testimony on 2 April, and this time political leaders from both parties, labor officials, ministers, businessmen, and others crowded the committee room to voice their support. The legislators, as Reed had predicted, took note.

Brandeis kept up the pressure and suggested to Norman White that he "ought to pass the word to the Republican leaders that if the Republicans should allow the savings bank bill to be defeated or deferred they will have a very heavy burden to carry in the coming campaign." By 12 May, Representative Robert Luce, initially doubtful of the plan, had congratulated Brandeis on the effective work done by the league, and predicted the bill would win out. On 16 May the joint committee reported it favorably by a vote of 10–4. The full House of Representatives approved it by a vote of 126–46 on 5 June, and on 17 June the Senate also went along, 23–3. Curtis Guild signed the bill into law on 26 June.

The third front involved convincing the trustees of the state's savings banks first to endorse the plan and then to lead their banks into joining. Here Brandeis found that one of the characteristics he most admired about the savings bank officers, their fiscal integrity and reluctance to put the savings of their customers at risk, also led them to view the savings bank plan with reluctance. Charles Evans Hughes had warned

Brandeis about this danger, and even as he organized the league and began the work of converting the legislators, Brandeis found he could make no progress with bank officials. So he took a different tack; if he could not win over the operating officers such as the treasurers, he would try to convince the directors of the banks. He secured a list of every bank trustee in the state, and he and Norman White began planning how they could do "personal missionary work" with them. Initially, little came out of this effort. "They are a pretty tough crowd," reported Charles H. Jones, a Boston shoe manufacturer and Brandeis client who had joined the league, "and a few of them have such a strong prejudice against even listening to a proposition for anything new." (Jones fought on with Brandeis to the successful conclusion of the campaign and became the first person in Massachusetts to purchase a savings bank insurance policy.)

By the time the legislature passed the bill, Brandeis had a healthy list of bank trustees who had endorsed the plan. The day before Governor Guild signed the measure into law, Brandeis sent him a "Dear Curtis" letter, saying that in order for the plan to succeed, the men appointed as trustees of the General Insurance Guaranty Fund, the state oversight body, should all be firmly committed to its success, and he sent a list of men whom he recommended for the governor's consideration. To his brother he noted that once the appointments had been made, "another stage will pass and I shall get a step nearer vacation."

BRANDEIS RECOMMENDED Judge Reed to chair the fund, and Governor Guild agreed. It would have seemed in early July 1907 that success for the plan had been ensured. Even before passage of the measure three banks had indicated their willingness to establish insurance departments. But it took more than a year before the Whitman Bank began selling policies, and during that time Brandeis and members of the league faced a growing skepticism that the scheme would ever get off the ground. The *Boston Evening Transcript,* which had favored the plan, noted sarcastically that "the deliberation with which its preliminaries are arranged recalls the saying that when the Almighty wants to grow an oak tree he takes forty years, while a single summer suffices for a cabbage. If beginning slowly affords any test, the savings-bank insurance plan has certainly made for itself a place in the oak-tree class." Insurance companies, beaten back in the legislature, suddenly began to hope that the hated plan would die aborning.

While a number of practical details had to be worked out—after all, this was a brand-new program—the preliminaries could have gone more quickly, and even after banks began to sign on, growth was small. Brandeis never lost faith in savings bank insurance, and he watched over it until his death. He would greet every accomplishment and broadcast it to his correspondents. At the end of the first year of operation, for example, the first two banks to join announced a dividend payment to their policyholders of 8⅓ percent, meaning, as he proudly told Lincoln Steffens, that the banks are returning one monthly premium to policyholders who had paid for twelve months. Every summer after 1916, on his way from Washington to his cottage on Cape Cod, he would stop in Boston to consult with officers of the state plan. He encouraged them to contact him whenever they faced a difficulty, and he always found time to talk to them or to scribble an encouragement. In the early years of World War II, he told his brother-in-law that "in this sad world, there is one thing which is going amazingly well— savings bank life insurance."

But if initially the plan grew at a snail's pace, it had an almost immediate effect on the commercial companies. On 1 January 1907—six months before the bill became law—they cut the rate for industrial insurance by 10 percent, and two years later they cut it another 10 percent. This meant a savings to Massachusetts wage earners alone of more than $1 million a year. They also streamlined the operations and corrected some of the abuses that Brandeis and the Armstrong Committee had identified. Brandeis believed that the cut in rates came solely from the fear of competition and that the newfound social conscience professed by the Metropolitan amounted to little more than hypocrisy, although "it is to be borne in mind that imitation is the sincerest form of flattery, and hypocrisy the tribute which vice pays to virtue." The insurance companies for many years tried at each legislative session to cripple the plan through such devices as limiting the amount of insurance in any one policy or cutting the funding for the state regulatory body, only to be beaten back at each turn. Savings bank insurance did exactly what Brandeis and its backers wanted: it provided low-cost affordable insurance to those who could not afford regular policies, and it set a yardstick by which to measure the performance of private companies.

Although Brandeis hoped that other states would emulate Massachusetts, only New York adopted a similar plan, and then not until 1938. Everywhere else the conservatism of bank officials and the opposition of insurance companies easily defeated the proposal. And, of course, nowhere else did the plan have a champion as it had in Massachusetts.

Savings Bank Life Insurance celebrated its one-hundredth anniversary in 2007, and it still proudly claims Louis Brandeis as its father. The system now has over $2 billion in assets, policies with a face value of $63 billion, and the highest financial ranking possible for its administration of funds. SBLI of Massachusetts is licensed to sell insurance in fourteen other states and the District of Columbia and offers a full range of traditional banking services. Despite the savings-and-loan debacle of the 1980s, the strictly regulated and conservatively managed savings banks of Massachusetts came through the storm mostly unscathed, as did their insurance departments.

Brandeis always considered savings bank insurance his most worthwhile reform, and to some extent it undermines his claim that he never went into a reform by himself, but always at the request of another. It is true that he first got involved at the request of the Policy-Holders' Protective Committee, but they wanted him only to look into the financial condition of the Equitable so they would have sufficient information to protect their own policy investments. The men on that committee did not buy industrial insurance, and probably knew little about it. Brandeis could have fulfilled his charge by exposing the financial irregularities and suggesting ways to rectify them.

But he saw the greatest insurance evil to be the vicious system by which the companies exploited the poor, and decided to attack that wrong. He came up with the plan to sell insurance through savings banks. He organized the league, wrote articles, lobbied the legislature, gave dozens of speeches, and worked to convert the bank trustees. The solution he devised perfectly reflected his ideas, especially that when something went wrong, it should be fixed, but not by the government. The savings banks reflected his own ideas regarding public service; just as the trustees saw protection of their depositors' money as a near-sacred obligation, so he believed they would guard the integrity of the insurance plan. When the insurance executives got up before the Armstrong Committee and spoke of insurance as a public service akin to the ministry, it stank of hypocrisy. Louis Brandeis actually believed it.

In the end, the campaign for savings bank life insurance could have served as a template on which other reformers could build. Brandeis, aided by his lieutenants, identified a specific evil and then offered a unique solution that fully resolved all of the relevant issues. He created a large organization to educate the public and those who would have responsibility to implement the plan. He drafted a carefully drawn bill and shepherded it through the state legislature. He utilized both pressure by the citizens' lobby and quiet political contacts. He avoided government involvement, save for a small oversight body. Most important, savings bank insurance did exactly what its sponsors wanted and hoped. Of course, in back of all this planning stood a man with a genius for organization and the tenacious personality to carry others along with him.

All in all, a perfect reform.

CHAPTER EIGHT

TAKING ON MORGAN

Even as Louis Brandeis worked to get the savings bank insurance bill through the last obstacles in the General Court, Asa Palmer French, the U.S. attorney for Massachusetts, approached him for advice on whether the proposed merger between the New York, New Haven & Hartford Railroad and the Boston & Maine line would violate the 1890 Sherman Antitrust Act. Preoccupied with insurance, Brandeis asked his partner William Dunbar to look into it. Brandeis, despite the almost casual tone in the letter to Dunbar, already knew about the proposed merger. For the next six years he would be heavily involved in fighting the New Haven and the financial power behind it, J. P. Morgan & Company, in their effort to monopolize New England's transportation. The controversy would transform Brandeis from an important but little-known Massachusetts reformer into a national figure.

Unlike insurance reform, with its relatively straightforward moral structure, the New Haven debate pitted former allies in other reforms against each other, and while Brandeis believed the issues to be relatively clear-cut, others recognized that complex economic forces made the question anything but simple. In this fight, as in his growing opposition to monopoly and bigness, moral imperatives outweighed economic considerations, leading him to ignore important features of the debate. Moreover, where he had merely irritated some of Boston's business and financial leaders in his fight against the Elevated, in the drawn-out struggle over the New Haven he made outright enemies of many of the city's prominent citizens.

IN 1911, BRANDEIS WROTE to Norman Hapgood predicting that the New Haven Railroad, long one of the most reliable investments in the country, would soon reduce its dividend, and there would be a good story in "The Decline of New Haven and Fall of Mellen," referring to the road's president, Charles Sanger Mellen. It would be "a dramatic story of human interest with a moral—or two—including the evils of private monopoly." At the end, he suggested an epitaph or obituary notice. "Mellen was a masterful man, resourceful, courageous, broad of view. He fired the imagination of New England; but, being oblique of vision, merely distorted its judgment and silenced its conscience. For a while he trampled with impunity on laws human and divine; but as he was obsessed with the delusion that two and two make five, he fell at last the victim to the relentless rules of humble arithmetic. Remember, O Stranger: 'Arithmetic is the first of sciences and the mother of safety.' "

Mellen had indeed been arrogant and had acted, if not illegally, certainly at the margins of the law. He had been handpicked by J. P. Morgan to head the New York, New Haven & Hartford Railroad Company in 1903. Before then, he had been president of the Northern Pacific Railroad, another Morgan enterprise, and in that position had won the respect of many business leaders and public officials around the country. President Theodore Roosevelt consulted with him and termed him a "first class fellow." Although in the end the effort to consolidate New England's rail system collapsed in ignominy, at the height of the battle Mellen seemed invincible and enjoyed the support of many of Boston's leading businessmen.

For Brandeis, at all times, the fight involved moral issues, and as his thoughts on monopoly and the role of investment banking houses began to jell, he started writing on the evils of bigness and financiers who used other people's money to underwrite monopolistic schemes. At no point in the fight did he concede that there might be good reasons for New England transportation to be brought under single control, but even if there were, one still had to follow the rules. Years later he told his niece Fannie, "Lying and sneaking are always bad, no matter what the ends. I don't care about punishing crime, but I am implacable in maintaining standards."

Interestingly, for a man who prided himself on facts, Brandeis here seemed oblivious to the economic realities that led many people to support consolidation. Railroads at the time constituted the industrial arteries of the nation. Grain grown in the Midwest traveled over rail lines to ports on the East Coast for shipment overseas. Factories, wherever located, depended on railroads to bring in raw materials and then carry finished goods to markets in other parts of the country. Railroads played such an important role in the nation's economic health that following the Civil War, federal, state, and local governments had all done their best to encourage construction through tax exemptions and subsidies. In 1860 there had been 30,000 miles of track in the country; by 1916, 254,000, more than the rest of the world combined. Much of this growth had been haphazard, and as the economy matured, it no longer made sense to have multiple lines running parallel tracks to small markets. Consolidation would take place, but how, and under whose direction?

Massachusetts was one of the nation's leaders in railroading, and Boston had long enjoyed an advantage over other eastern ports because of the efficiency by which rail lines brought inland production and raw materials to the coast for shipment elsewhere and in return took imported goods to the hinterlands. Economic developments following the Civil War, however, including the construction of major trunk lines to New York and Philadelphia, undermined Massachusetts businessmen's bargaining power with the major railroad systems. In addition, the area's aging rail lines ran at high cost and needed extensive—and expensive—improvements, while the gridlike pattern in which the roads had grown required significant maintenance costs for terminals and junctions. The rise of electrified interurban street railways needed to take people to work also deprived the older lines of what had once been a profitable commuter traffic.

To many businessmen and civic leaders, consolidation made sense, since redundant facilities could be closed and a more efficient system would help the region compete against New York and Philadelphia. Instead of viewing the mergers negatively, they saw them as in the public interest. Railroading constituted the single biggest business in the state, employing over twenty thousand persons and carrying forty million passengers and twelve million tons of freight each year, and many people believed that New England in general and Massachusetts in particular could not enjoy economic prosperity without a healthy rail system. To achieve that goal, consolidation seemed essential. Moreover, combination was hardly a stranger in Massachusetts. In 1875 some sixty-two railroad companies operated in the state, and as late as 1890 there had been eight independent steam railroad lines in Massachusetts. By 1900 only two remained, the New Haven and the Boston & Maine, while the Boston & Albany tracks had been leased to the New York Central. The Massachusetts Board of Railroad Commissioners did not oppose this trend and in fact adopted policies to encourage consolidation in the name of efficiency.

So when Charles Mellen took over the New Haven line in 1903, he found a solid group of influential businessmen in Massachusetts and other parts of New England quite sympathetic to his plans, and at least in the short term he seemed to have succeeded. Within six years of his arrival, Mellen oversaw the consolidation under the New Haven of all the important interurban street railways in southern New England, the region's intercoastal steamship lines, and the Boston & Maine Railroad, which in turn owned a majority of the stock in both the Maine Central and the Boston & Albany. To accomplish this, he rode roughshod over legal obstacles as well as the growing sentiment against monopoly. He managed to get the governor of Massachusetts to push through a bill that in essence ratified illegal purchases, and he secured assurances from the president of the United States that the Justice Department would not pursue antitrust proceedings. "Paternalism must be exercised by those who have power," he told a group of businessmen, "and I think we have the power." This arrogance, as much as anything, led to his downfall and the disintegration of the empire he had built.

JUST AS MASSACHUSETTS had led the nation in building the earliest railroads, so it also pioneered in creating the first public commission to oversee rail operations in the state. In addition, over the years the legislature had passed laws restricting the sale and ownership of stock in railroads chartered in Massachusetts. In 1902, steam railroads had begun petitioning the legislature for permission to enter the electric railway business, through either purchase of existing lines or construction of new roads. Massachusetts law placed many restrictions on steam railroads, and just as it had favored railroad construction fifty years earlier, now it granted legislative favors to the interurban companies. But even with legislative aid, the electric systems did not fare well in the early twentieth century, and the Board of Railroad Commissioners urged that consolidation take place, not only among the electric lines, but with the steam roads as well. This seemed to be the way of the future, but because of competing interests in the assembly, the legislation proposed by the commission failed to advance. The growing sentiment against monopoly, fueled by the writings of Thomas Lawson and other muckrakers, also made proconsolidation legislation unpopular among many state officials.

Mellen decided to ignore the law, and in 1905, without consulting either the commission or the legislature, he began buying up interurban systems in the western part of the state through a holding company he organized in Connecticut, the Consolidated Railway Company. When called before a legislative committee the following year, Mellen admitted what he had done. "I don't want to deceive anybody," he told the committee. "I am president of the [New Haven] Railroad Company. I am president of the Consolidated Company. I am president of the boards of trustees. I am president of your street railway companies." Technically, the law had not been violated, because the New Haven did not own the interurban lines, but everyone recognized the sham involved.

Charles Sanger Mellen, 1910

The Boston & Maine, the other large system in New England, fearing that it would be put at a competitive disadvantage, immediately asked for legislative permission to buy streetcar systems, a request favored by the Railroad Commission, which drafted the enabling legislation. Another bill made such mergers legal, but gave the Railroad Commission greater authority to regulate consolidation. Robert Luce, a Republican from Somerville, objected to consolidation, and his argument anticipated how Brandeis, with whom he would be closely allied in the merger fight, approached the matter. Luce noted that the law did not allow a railroad company to sell its stock to any other corporation—foreign or domestic—without explicit permission from the General Court. The solution to the Boston & Maine's problem would be not to legalize the fraudulent purchases by the New Haven but to enforce the law and require the New Haven to divest itself of its purchases. Illegal and immoral behavior should not be rewarded, nor should it be permitted to continue. Caught between advocates of consolidation and reformers who insisted on upholding the law, the General Court passed no bill, leaving the electric rail systems Mellen had acquired under the effective control of the New Haven.

Interestingly, the public debate initially ignored the legal and moral issues Luce had raised, concentrating instead on the economic and political, and no one seemed able to reach a decision. The Board of Trade, after lengthy discussion, voted to postpone legislation until there could be further discussion. Joseph Eastman, secretary of the Public Franchise League, reported that after several debates, the members had been "unable to agree as yet whether . . . to favor a bill allowing such consolidations." The members did seem to concur that if mergers were to be permitted, then the legislature should change the law. The following year league members still could not see eye to eye on whether the proposed mergers would be in the public interest, and recommended that any legislation be put off for still another year. Although Brandeis participated in these discussions and came to oppose the purchases, he could not win over his colleagues in the league.

In June 1906, Governor Curtis Guild sent a special message to the assembly, and in it he voiced traditional Massachusetts concerns about keeping control of the state's destiny in the hands of its citizens. The New Haven, "controlled by men who are not citizens of Massachusetts," had throttled competition in the western part of the state. "Slowly, surely, the control of our railroads, the control of the passage to market of every Massachusetts product, the control of transportation to and from his work of every Massachusetts citizen, is passing from our hands to those of aliens." The legislature should act promptly to correct "this grave injustice" so that transportation within the state can "be controlled by the people of Massachusetts, and not by men beyond the reach of her law and the inspiration of her ideals."

One can smile at what we now consider an antiquated attitude, but it still thrived in the Bay State in the early twentieth century, and it meant a great deal to men like Guild and Brandeis. Perhaps consolidation made sense economically, but if it did, it had to take place within a framework of laws created by the people of Massachusetts; and those laws should protect the interests of the state's citizens and not those of private corporations, especially outside corporations.

As a central figure in the Public Franchise League, Brandeis took part in those debates and knew of the concerns raised at the meetings. But there is no mention of anything related to the New Haven in his correspondence until June 1907, when he told his brother, Alfred, "My merger position is being much attacked." (He did, however, pay attention to the financial reports of companies such as the Boston & Albany line, probably as part of the general knowledge he considered useful in his commercial law practice.) Since Brandeis had not yet issued any public statement about the New Haven's activities, one presumes that the attacks took place within the Public Franchise League discussions. By then, however, Mellen had made a great deal of progress. Despite a promise to the assembly to stop acquiring electric lines, Mellen had gone ahead in his plans. He set up another dummy corporation, the New England Investment and Security Company, and transferred to it the New Haven's holdings in interurban railways. All the directors of this company also served as directors of the New Haven, and Mellen headed both. Although technically he had broken no rules, he had once again flouted the law.

Mellen had also begun negotiating to buy a controlling interest in the Boston & Maine Railroad, and the acquisition of the street railway systems suddenly became a minor issue. If Mellen succeeded, the New Haven would in effect control all rail traffic in New England and, along with the Morgan maritime trust, control the port traffic as well. Again Mellen denied purchasing the Boston & Maine, even as he concluded negotiations to transfer nearly 110,000 shares of its stock to the New England Navigation Company, a New Haven subsidiary. Mellen even contacted President Theodore Roosevelt in April to make sure that there would be no prosecution under the Sherman Act.

If the New Haven believed the legislature would just ignore the purchase, it did not count on the fact that by now Mellen had ruffled more than a few feathers. Merger may have been the face of the new economy, but many people liked the fact that rules governing moral behavior shaped the old economy; these included the Lawrence family, which had long held a large but not controlling interest in the Boston & Maine. General Samuel Lawrence owned between fifteen thousand and sixteen thousand shares, and his son served as one of the lawyers for the line. Knowing Brandeis's views, they retained him to represent their interests and oppose the merger.

Brandeis instinctively opposed the merger for several reasons. Like Guild and others, he wanted control of Massachusetts businesses to stay in Massachusetts hands. The simple question, he wrote, is "whether the whole transportation system of Massachusetts shall be turned over to a single monopoly, and that one controlled by aliens—practically the Standard Oil and J. P. Morgan interests—parties who have great interests in other states and little in Massachusetts, and are foreign to our tradition."

In addition, although he was rapidly becoming an opponent of monopoly, he did not necessarily oppose consolidation, as was obvious in the development of the sliding-scale gas arrangement; he did, however, oppose manipulation of stocks by the large banking houses that propelled the merger mania. The bankers, in his view, did no constructive work, took no risks, used other people's money, and then grabbed up the fruits that rightfully belonged to creative and honorable entrepreneurs. One can get a sense of Brandeis's thinking by looking at what he wrote about John Murray Forbes, the founder of the Burlington line. Forbes "was a builder; not a combiner, or banker, or wizard of finance. He was a simple, hard-working business man. . . . Bold, but never reckless; scrupulously careful of other people's money, he was ready, after due weighing of the chances, to risk his own in enterprises promising success. . . . Under his wise management, and that of the men who he trained, the little Burlington became a great system." A few years after Forbes's death in 1898, the Burlington had been swallowed up by J. P. Morgan, and passed forever from its independent Boston owners.

One can dismiss Brandeis as old-fashioned, wedded to a world and an ethos that no longer existed, and blind to the realities of modern economic life, and in part that would be very true. There is a parochialism in his demand that Massachusetts railroads be owned by Massachusetts citizens. Forbes and others in the nineteenth century had built and owned many of the railroads in the western and southern parts of the country, and when these lines, like the Burlington, came under the control of Morgan or one of the other banking houses, Brandeis lamented that Bostonians no longer owned them. Yet the demand for honesty, for adherence by everyone to the same legal rules, the abhorrence of the trimmer, the faithfulness to a moral system—these qualities are not to be dismissed lightly. The very faults that Brandeis detailed in the "new economics" of the early twentieth century are akin to the practices that many modern industrial leaders claim are part of the "new economics" of the twenty-first century. They are no more admirable today than they were one hundred years ago.

Finally, Brandeis had been brought into the merger fight as a lawyer representing the Lawrences, but as in so many other battles he quickly came to the conclusion that the issues involved transcended the interests of any one party. He and the Lawrences eventually reached an agreement whereby he would not accept any fee, but they would pay for certain related expenses. Very quickly, however, Brandeis realized that he would have to devote a great deal of time to the fight, perhaps even more than he had to savings bank insurance. By now he had adopted a policy of not accepting a fee for matters that he considered in the public service, but in the merger fight he went further. His large income, simple lifestyle, and conservative investments had earned him his first million, and so he could afford to pass up lucrative legal matters when it seemed to him proper to serve the public. He recognized, however, that he generated much of the business that came to the firm; even if he did not do the actual work, clients came because of his reputation. He did not believe that his associates should suffer because of his reform proclivities, and in November 1907, six months after the Lawrences initially retained him, Brandeis dictated the following letter to E. Louise Malloch, who handled the firm's finances:

Dear Miss Malloch:

When Mr. Lawrence came in to get me to act as counsel for him in the matter of the Boston & Maine merger, he intended to retain me in the ordinary manner, and has undoubtedly supposed that I would make charges to him as in any professional matter.

I feel, however, that being a matter of great public interest in which I am undertaking to influence the opinion of others, I do not want to accept any compensation for my services.

Under the peculiar circumstances of the retainer, I do not think that my partners and others interested in the profits of the firm ought to be affected by my own feeling in this matter, and I therefore wish to substitute myself as the client of the firm in this matter so far as the charges for my own services are concerned.

So far as relates to disbursements, and charges for accountants' and stenographers' service, I will have the firm make bills to Mr. Lawrence.

I therefore enclose my personal check to the firm for $5000. for services on account.

Before the merger fight ended, Brandeis "reimbursed" his firm for more than $25,000. Edward McClennen later insisted that "his partners never sought anything of the kind or suggested it." Even had he not paid in a cent (as had been the case with the Boston Elevated, the sliding-scale, and the insurance campaigns), the firm had all of the business it could handle. Brandeis continued to practice, but gave over more and more of the work to his partners and associates and reimbursed them appropriately.

This quixotic gesture—that unlike his pro bono service, has not become a fixture of American law practice—harks back to what Louis had told Alice some fifteen years earlier, that he hoped to be successful so that he could be free. He had wanted, he told his friend and client Edward Filene, initially to give at least one hour a day to public service and then to give more later. By 1907, Brandeis had achieved his freedom, even if, because of his finely tuned morality, it meant paying for his own services so that others would not suffer even a minor loss.

Once again a reform had found him. Brandeis did not, like Cervantes's famous don, go out seeking windmills to tilt at and wrongs to right. He still saw himself as primarily a lawyer, but one who drew sharp distinctions between the private aspects of a client's complaint and those instances that involved larger public interests. Savings bank insurance seems to be the one instance in which he tackled an issue without invitation, as it were, although he came to understand the depth of the problem through his representation of the Policy-Holders' Committee. Even after he had become a nationally known reformer, Brandeis did not go out searching for battles, and in every one of his famous fights—the New Haven, Pinchot-Ballinger, protective legislation—others drew him into their causes. Although often dubbed a crusader, Brandeis never had a reform agenda. He had ideals and he had strong views on certain evils such as bigness, but he never went looking for a fight. Fights seemed to find him.

IN WRITING TO HIS BROTHER on 26 June 1907, Louis noted, "The Savings Bank bill is now in the Governor's hands. It looks as if we shall get some kind of anti-merger bill, but not as good a one as I should wish. The achievement of 80 cent gas gives me such satisfaction at this time when my merger position is being much attacked." He hoped that Curtis Guild would endorse his bill, but Brandeis found that despite his best efforts and strenuous work by his allies in the assembly, in the New Haven affair he would have little influence on the legislature and no success in getting it to adopt an antimerger measure of which he could approve.

An incident at the beginning of the fight is illustrative of the problems Brandeis confronted. He prepared a sweeping proposal that would have made it a criminal offense for the New Haven to acquire any more stock in the Boston & Maine and that required it to dispose of all the stock it held before 1 April 1908. He wanted, as he told the editor Mark Sullivan, to make the act "so clear in its terms that it would not need the interpretation of the highest court in the state to tell what it means, so that even Mr. Mellen and his counsel might not be in doubt as to what it means."

On 9 June 1907, he appeared before the legislative committee looking into the merger, and in answer to the argument that consolidation
of rail services would lead to greater efficiency in operation, he put forth
for the first time the idea that there is a limit to efficiency in consolidation, and that when an enterprise grows beyond that size, it becomes
less rather than more efficient. There is little empirical evidence or economic theory to support this assertion, but Brandeis believed it to be
true; he looked around and saw large companies that apparently operated inefficiently compared with smaller firms. He also attacked
monopoly in general, and especially the idea that regulation would protect the public from monopolistic abuse. "I do not believe it is possible
to create a power strong enough to 'properly safeguard' it."

Two days later Mellen testified and conceded that interests allied
with the New Haven had purchased the Boston & Maine stock, but he
did not want to quibble about details. How the stock had been
acquired was "immaterial. The [New Haven] stands here before the
committee, to all intents and purposes, as if it had done it itself. I do
not dodge one bit. I defy any man to show that I have not kept my
pledges to the State." When asked if he had read Brandeis's bill, Mellen
said that he had, and could only raise one objection to it: "It wasn't
strong enough. I would amend the bill by requiring the New Haven
road to sell the stock and prohibit anyone from buying it. . . . And I'd
put anybody in prison who discussed the subject." One might have
thought that Mellen's arrogance would have annoyed the committee
members, that his admission that the New Haven had bought the
stock, even though he had promised not to, would have led to some
sharp questions, but it did not.

Toward the end of the day, as Mellen finished his testimony, Brandeis
rose and asked permission to put a few questions to him. Of course, the
committee chair said, but then told Mellen that he did not have to
answer. The New Haven president accepted the offer and said he would
not give ammunition to the enemy. If Mellen will not answer questions, Brandeis suggested, "I would like to have him present while I
make certain statements." Mellen picked up his hat and immediately
headed for the door, calling back, "I will read your questions in the
newspapers in the morning, if you please."

Brandeis later said that Mellen's exit had probably been fortunate for
the antimerger side. The New Haven head had great presence and
spoke well and "had sort of mesmerized the people. I had grave doubts
as to whether I should not be the sufferer from cross-examining him."
The deprecating remark is somewhat out of character for the supremely

self-confident Brandeis, but it acknowledged the fact that at the time Mellen and his vision of a unified New England transportation system carried a great deal of popularity, especially in the legislature. While the lawmakers could not bring themselves to ratify Mellen's purchases, they rejected the Brandeis bill and passed another measure, sponsored by Speaker John Cole, allowing the New Haven to hold the Boston & Maine stock until 1 July 1908.

Brandeis continued to hammer away at the merger, both in newspaper interviews and in speeches. The New England Dry Goods Association invited him and Charles F. Choate Jr., the New Haven's counsel, to debate the issue at its meeting in February 1908. Choate declined, leaving Brandeis to pillory the company and its officials unopposed. He ticked off one reason after another why the people should fight the merger: the New Haven had defied Massachusetts law; the New Haven had not kept its promises to the legislature; the result would be a monopoly, and therefore by definition bad for the region; even worse, this would be a monopoly controlled by aliens and alien interests; large companies were not as efficient as small ones; such a combination created dangers in politics, because it could use its huge resources unscrupulously. In addition, Brandeis began claiming that the New Haven no longer enjoyed the financial strength that it had before Mellen took over, and that the acquisitions had weakened it even more.

Fairly early in the battle, Brandeis realized that the costs of the street railways, as well as the purchase of the Boston & Maine stock, must have levied a heavy drain on the railroad's resources. According to all published reports, the purchases had been paid for by the New Haven, either through its own reserves or by borrowing; there had not been any infusion of new money from J. P. Morgan & Company, the firm that controlled the New Haven. Brandeis wrote to his brother in October 1907 that he had been struggling with the New Haven reports trying to figure out the railroad's real financial condition, and if it had truthfully provided required information to the Interstate Commerce Commission and the Massachusetts Railroad Commission, there ought to be some "fun" in finding out the facts.

"I think before we get through," he told Alfred,

the estimable gentlemen who scrambled for the chance of exchanging their B & M stock for New Haven will feel that they have been served to a gold brick. At present stage of investigation it looks as if Mellen had gone ahead like other Napoleons of finance joyously as long as borrowing was easy & that he will come up against a stone wall as soon as his borrowing capacity ends. There are some indications that it has ended (with his stock at 139), and that he is resorting to all kinds of devices to get money. I have not been able to figure out yet from data available what he has done with all the money he raised & should not be at all surprised to find that some had already gone into dividends.

In the end this would prove to be the New Haven's undoing, but Brandeis's constant harping on the alleged financial weakness of the railroad brought down the wrath of Boston's financial and business establishment on his head. In the midst of the fight the Good Government Association asked Brandeis to run for mayor against John Fitzgerald, whom Brandeis and other mugwumps detested as the worst kind of machine politician. Although tempted, Brandeis declined, and as he told Alfred, "The chances of a really good fight were not the best. My course in knocking heads right and left is not exactly such as to create an 'available' candidate."

Mellen had convinced many that a unified transportation system would be the answer to Massachusetts's and especially Boston's trade problems and would put the city in a superior competitive position vis-à-vis Philadelphia, New York, and other East Coast ports. Although Brandeis did not believe that would actually happen, he conceded that people could disagree on that point. Business interests in Boston, however, had always viewed New Haven as well as Boston & Maine shares as gold-plated investments. The New Haven had paid a dividend of 8 percent or more since 1872. New England colleges, boarding schools, and church endowments all had significant investments in the New Haven; it constituted the traditional "widows-and-orphans" stock found in conservatively managed trust funds.

By attacking the New Haven's financial condition and practices, Brandeis in effect challenged not only the business sense but the financial integrity of the city's leading banking and investment houses. They had recommended New Haven stock to their customers and had invested heavily themselves. One might have thought that they would welcome information that could lead to the protection of their money, that if, as Brandeis charged, the New Haven's resources had been stretched beyond safe margins, then they ought to pull out and put their money in more secure places. Instead, they attacked not the news he brought but the messenger, blaming him for the eventual ruin of the road and losses of millions of dollars.

This attitude was personified by Major Henry Lee Higginson, a senior partner in Boston's leading investment house, Lee, Higginson & Company. Brandeis had spent the Fourth of July weekend in 1890 as a guest of Higginson's at his summer home on Lake Champlain, "communing," as he put it, "with the great and the good." Mrs. Higginson had been the first person to call on Alice after she and Louis returned from their honeymoon. At the time, Higginson and others saw Brandeis as a bright, young, and extremely capable lawyer whose interests dovetailed with their own. That identification began to erode during the fight over the Boston Elevated, since the State Street financial elite had backed one or more of the contenders for the new lines. Brandeis had initially believed that Higginson would be delighted with the outcome, since the Elevated had been financed by his archrival in the financial district, Kidder, Peabody, and wrote to him suggesting that he might wish to contribute to the costs of the Public Franchise League. Higginson never replied.

As the pace of the merger battle picked up, Brandeis's accusations involved not just Charles Sanger Mellen but lawyers and bankers closely connected to the New Haven. A subcommittee of the Massachusetts Commission on Commerce and Industry approved the Boston & Maine merger, and Brandeis pointed out that the subcommittee had been composed of three corporation lawyers all closely connected to the New Haven and therefore certainly not impartial. One of those lawyers also counted Higginson as a client, and Higginson's company had not only suggested the idea of a merger between the two lines, but then acted as an intermediary in the stock purchase. All that work, all that investment, now stood imperiled because of Brandeis's charges.

"Brandeis and his gang," Higginson wrote to Governor Eben S. Draper, "have misrepresented and used every indecent means to corrupt the public mind and deceive people." Higginson told a Treasury official in Washington that no one "should believe Brandeis on oath." In fact, no one in the Boston bar had a good word for him, and "if he had friends before, they have vanished." When Woodrow Wilson considered appointing Brandeis to his cabinet in late 1912, Higginson and his friends lobbied furiously, and, as it turned out, successfully, against it. Four years later they launched even more vitriolic attacks when the president nominated Brandeis to the Court.

The impetus for this fury came from a pamphlet Brandeis published in December 1907, the sensational *Financial Condition of the New York, New Haven & Hartford Railroad Company and of the Boston & Maine Railroad.* After working for several months, and getting no help at all in his frequent requests for information from the New Haven, Brandeis had resorted to the reports that the railroads by law had to file with the Massachusetts Board of Railroad Commissioners and with the Interstate Commerce Commission. Although anyone could get these documents, apparently no one, least of all those responsible for advising clients to buy New Haven stock, had bothered to examine them closely. From those materials Brandeis put forth two startling contentions. First, that the New Haven had so drained its resources that it now found itself in serious financial trouble, and "if the New Haven's solvency is to be maintained, A LARGE REDUCTION IN THE DIVIDEND RATE IS INEVITABLE." Second, instead of needing financial help from the New Haven, the Boston & Maine enjoyed a sounder financial condition, and those resources would in all likelihood be drained away by the New Haven. As he told a *Boston Journal* reporter, getting the facts had been very difficult, and there had been "obstacles that at times seemed to be well-nigh insurmountable." But he had gotten at what he considered the truth, and he wanted the pamphlet to be given as wide a distribution as possible among the stock- and bondholders of the two lines.

Brandeis intended that group to be aware of the problems, but not necessarily in order to protect their investment. Rather, he hoped that they would display old-fashioned New England outrage at the misuse of their money and demand change. "You are mistaken in supposing that my effort to defeat the merger is with a special desire to protect capital," he told one correspondent. "Capital must be protected in order to protect the community, but I have no special interest in the protection of capital. What I desire is to protect the community from the evils which will attend a monopoly of transportation by the New Haven, and the discussion of financial questions is only incidental." Comments such as this did not endear Brandeis to State Street.

The reaction proved even more negative than Brandeis had expected. The business press, of course, attacked him as a simpleton who had no idea of business and did not know how to read technical financial reports. Even newspapers that had supported him in other endeavors puzzled over the pamphlet. If he was right, the *Boston Traveler* asked, why had no one else found this out? The *Boston Herald* just attacked him outright, claiming that his antimerger mania had gotten him to the point that everything would now fall, "the state destroyed, the republic gasping its last breath, and humankind swept away from the starry watches of the night." Only the *Boston Evening Transcript* treated his analysis with respect and reprinted a good part of it. The pamphlet, Louis told Alfred with some understatement, "has created quite a stir. The New Haven people have supported the stock and I am told their bankers advise them not to answer it. If they don't Mellen is doomed— and I don't believe they can. Nothing but a miracle of good times could make their way smooth." And, rather candidly, he admitted, "I have made a larger camp of enemies than in all my previous fights together."

BRANDEIS TRIED TO USE the same tactics in the merger fight that he had used previously. At the same time he issued the pamphlet, he organized the Massachusetts Anti-merger League, modeled upon and with a leadership almost identical to the Savings Bank Insurance League. He bombarded newspapers with "facts," gave speeches around the state, and tried to educate the people on what he considered the evils that the merger posed. When he heard of someone opposed to the merger, he immediately tried to enlist that man in the cause. But none of these tactics worked—at least not in time. Unlike the savings bank fight, where the insurance companies had been tainted from the start because of the scandals, the New Haven enjoyed a sterling reputation and had the support of a good part of the influential business and banking community. In response to the Anti-merger League, New Haven allies created the Business Men's Merger League, which sponsored legislation, wrote letters to the newspapers, and did all those things that Brandeis had shown to be effective in the savings bank fight.

Politically, the New Haven easily outgunned the opposition, and even exposure for creating false news and making untrue statements about Brandeis's alleged private interests (such as that he was allied with the Harriman rail interests against Morgan) did little to dampen support for the merger. Unlike the antimerger people, who desperately needed state legislation to force the New Haven to divest itself of street railways and the Boston & Maine, Mellen could live, indeed thrive, on delay, and when the legislature failed to pass any measures concerning the road, it meant a victory. The longer he kept control of the Boston & Maine and the other properties, the harder it would be in the end to force them apart. To a decision by the Massachusetts Supreme Judicial Court in May 1908 that the New Haven had acquired its interurban railways illegally—and by implication the Boston & Maine as well— followed by a suggestion from the state's highest-ranking law officer that the street railways that had been sold to the New Haven should have their charters revoked, Mellen responded with a shrug. "I certainly am not disturbed by the opinion of the attorney general." Moreover, since implementing the court's decision would require legislation, Mellen and the Boston & Maine president, Lucius Tuttle, worked to block any measures introduced by opponents of the merger.

Brandeis kept writing, speaking, analyzing. He went to "a Jewish club where I talked merger last evening," he told Al, and in fact had been out every night during the week arguing against the New Haven. He pored over the line's quarterly reports, and its 31 March 1908 statement showed that in the previous nine months it ran a deficit of $2.9 million, although it continued to pay the 8 percent dividend. He believed the figures did not reflect the true extent of the deficit, since the line had to borrow $25 million to expend on equipment. He did not see how it could keep going this way without soon reducing the dividend. But in the meantime, "the merger fight goes on gaily," he claimed, and "we have made great progress with the public."

The fight went on, perhaps even "gaily," but although a few papers had begun to pay attention to the charges, few converts had been made. In March 1908, despite Brandeis's best efforts to convince it of the evils involved in the merger, a majority of the Massachusetts Commission on Commerce and Industry issued a report vindicating the New Haven on all points. Then, in June, Brandeis seemingly had a victory. The Cole Act would expire on 1 July, leaving the Boston & Maine stock still in the hands of the New Haven. In the legislative session the antimerger forces, ably led by Norman White, defeated every effort to secure a bill permitting the New Haven to keep the stock, and the House even passed a measure denouncing the purchase of the stock as against the Commonwealth's laws. Back in April, Brandeis had testified for two days before the railroad committees, trying to get them to understand the issue and enact the necessary legislation. He lobbied newspaper editors for their support, and in addition to a copy of the antimerger bill sent out a short memorandum titled "What to Do Next?" as a basis for possible editorials.

In the end, no law passed, which Brandeis saw as a complete victory, because now the New Haven, despite Mellen's bluster, would have to sell the Boston & Maine stock in order to comply with the state supreme court decision. "You must come to South Yarmouth to hear all the tale of merger killing," he crowed to his brother. "Nothing remains now but to bury the corpse. . . . I had expected two years of agony for the New Haven—& of labor for us. But death came quickly as a relief to all." He went on to predict that the New Haven, which had just declared a regular dividend of 2 percent for the quarter, would not be able to do that much longer.

As he settled in for what he thought would be a quiet summer on Cape Cod, Brandeis might be forgiven for his optimism. He had been under prolonged attack for the better part of a year, although, he claimed, "I have not suffered in mind and body, and the only effect upon my estate is to leave me more time to pound the enemy." He had seriously underestimated Charles Sanger Mellen.

EARLY IN JULY, Mellen "sold" the Boston & Maine shares held by the New Haven to a syndicate headed by John L. Billard, a wealthy Connecticut coal operator. Mellen justified the cost in legal fees and transfer taxes because "it thus leaves in friendly hands the control" of the properties. At some point, he predicted to his board, common sense would prevail in Massachusetts, and full ownership of these properties would be restored to the New Haven. On reading the news, Brandeis said that it "suits me entirely. If it is genuine it is what we want." If not genuine, then the New Haven leadership "must be even more kinds a fool than I have found the present management."

The New Haven seemed beset by attacks on other fronts as well. Attorney General Charles J. Bonaparte had filed a petition under the Sherman Antitrust Act to perpetually bar the New Haven from holding the Boston & Maine stock as well as the stock of any interstate trolley lines. In early 1909, Brandeis met with representatives of the Interstate Commerce Commission to discuss the New Haven's financial picture, and that same month Massachusetts Attorney General Dana Malone announced that he would look into whether an 1874 statute, requiring revocation of charters of railroads that broke the law, might be invoked against the street railways owned by the New Haven. Brandeis kept digging for facts, sending letters to the Board of Railroad Commissioners asking for information to explain numbers in the New Haven reports that appeared wrong to him. As late as 8 April 1909, he believed that the antimerger forces would be able to secure passage of their legislation at the current session.

Mellen, however, had a powerful ally in the new governor, Eben S. Draper, who had not said a single word about the New Haven in his campaign. On 20 April 1909, Draper urged the assembly to pass a bill that would charter an agency to purchase and hold stock in the Boston & Maine and allow any railroad incorporated under Massachusetts law to provide financing for that purchase. A few weeks later the Railroad

Committee received a bill endorsed by Draper, but drafted by the New Haven attorneys, that authorized chartering a holding company for the sole purpose of holding the stocks and bonds of the Boston & Maine. Brandeis, who had hoped the merger dead, now awoke to the new danger. They had beaten the New Haven and its business friends, but this new bill "with all the power of the gubernatorial position and party whip is very threatening." Brandeis wrote one letter after another and buttonholed as many legislators as he could, but to no avail.

The end came quickly. The governor pushed his bill through the Republican-controlled assembly. The Boston Railroad Holding Company Act, or Draper Act, of 1909 legitimized the marriage of the New Haven and the Boston & Maine and, aside from the fact that it included the word "Boston" in its title, did nothing to protect the Commonwealth against any decisions the New Haven might make in regard to its new acquisition. Technically, the New Haven would not own the Boston & Maine stock outright, but it would own the holding company that owned the stock. Despite the protests of people like Representative Charles G. Washburn that the bill was "poor business, poor law, poor politics [and] poor ethics," Governor Draper imposed party discipline, denied any opportunity for amendments, and the troops, including a number of members who had previously opposed the merger, fell into line. As Louis told his brother, "Amidst innumerable broken promises of support we got unmercifully licked but it took all the power of the Republican machine & of Bankers' money to do it, and I am well content with the fight made."

Brandeis had already suspected the Billard sale to have been a fraud, and events soon justified his apprehensions. The new holding company bought Billard's Boston & Maine stock, giving him a profit of $2 million on the transaction. Mellen, in explaining the transaction to his board of directors, assured them that the price had not been too high, because during the year or so that Billard had "owned" the stock, the New Haven effectively controlled the Boston & Maine. "For his service in securing to the New Haven immunity from attack by Massachusetts authorities," Mellen declared, "Mr. Billard's compensation was modest and moderate, and he might well exclaim, as did Warren Hastings at his celebrated trial, 'My God, when I consider my opportunities, I wonder at my moderation.' " Ironically, Henry Lee Higginson, who certainly had the opportunity to know the true circumstances of the Billard purchase, bristled when Brandeis and Norman White began charging that the sale had been a fraud. People like them, he alleged, who "do not believe that Mellen sold the Boston & Maine shares . . . probably are themselves in the habit of lying."

Given the circumstances of a business community generally in favor of consolidation and an assembly unwilling to enforce existing law, Brandeis and his allies could never work up the type of public interest and support they enjoyed in the insurance fight. Even later, after Brandeis's predictions came true, supporters of the merger never suffered any rebuke at the polls. With the state sanction for the new arrangement, the federal government dropped its antitrust charges against the New Haven, and in the summer of 1909 Mellen might well have congratulated himself that his plans for unifying all of New England's transportation had few obstacles in sight—providing, of course, that that pesky Brandeis fellow's predictions of financial ruin could be avoided.

EVEN IF HE WOULD subsequently be vindicated, Brandeis had lost the fight, and news that the Justice Department had abandoned his suit did not make him any happier. "I am rapidly becoming a Socialist," he told his brother. "What the bankers leave undone their lawyer minions supply." But Brandeis had a great deal of faith in the facts that he uncovered, and although his predictions of imminent disaster did not materialize, he did grasp what other people either failed to see or, in the case of the State Street bankers, refused to see—that the New Haven's finances had been seriously weakened because of the huge outlays required to buy the electric rail systems and the Boston & Maine, and that it could only pay the 8 percent dividend by diverting funds from areas such as equipment maintenance and replacement. He may have lost the battle, but he had no intention of abandoning the campaign.

CHAPTER NINE

AN ATTORNEY FOR THE PEOPLE

I n late 1907, Louis Brandeis had just begun to gain a national reputation because of his fight against the New Haven, and only a few
people knew of him outside of Massachusetts. During the preceding decade he had become an active progressive in the Bay State, devoting more and more time to reform work, and in doing so, he developed
some specific ideas about the legal profession and its responsibilities to
society. He also watched with growing concern how conservative
judges utilized the Due Process Clause of the Fourteenth Amendment
to erect a constitutional barrier against progressive efforts to ameliorate, through protective legislation, the harsh effects of industrialization on workers. When the National Consumers League offered him a
chance to defend a maximum-hours law before the Supreme Court,
Brandeis seized it, and his brilliant lawyering in *Muller v. Oregon* moved
him onto the national stage. From then until his appointment to the
bench in 1916, he would be counted among the preeminent progressives of the era.

THE TRANSFORMATION of the practice of law in the late nineteenth
century may have been a necessary response to the legal needs of the
new industrial society (see chapter 3), but it raised troubling questions
about the role of lawyers, their responsibilities not only to clients but
also to the public, and their status in the community. By 1900 the practice of law—the business of law—had changed. While the majority of
lawyers still operated as solo practitioners, the more lucrative work of
big banks and corporations went to larger firms whose members developed specialties designed to serve commercial clients. Where people
had previously seen lawyers as independent professionals, now, according to critics, the public saw them as hired hands, better paid to be

202 LOUIS D. BRANDEIS

sure, but with no more independence than any other employee of a large corporation. Interestingly, much of this criticism came from within the profession itself.

To take one example, George Shelton, a prominent San Francisco attorney, charged in 1900 that when a man practiced law as no more than "a means of earning his daily bread, he is prompted by no lofty ideals, stimulated by no particular enthusiasm, and seeks only pecuniary rewards as will bring him the luxuries of life before old age has deadened his powers of gratification. His motives are as sordid and his activities as mercenary as can be found in any other occupation." In 1910 the newly elected governor of New Jersey, Woodrow Wilson, called on lawyers to return to "the service of the nation as a whole, from which they have been drifting away." A few years later, former president William Howard Taft, upon joining the Yale Law School, gave a series of lectures in which he acknowledged, with great sorrow, "that the profession of law is more or less on trial."

Leaders of the bar, many of them corporate lawyers in the new large firms, heard this criticism. They believed that while they still tried to adhere to some of the older values, many of the younger and less talented lawyers indeed fit the description of hired hands and intellectual jobbers. Lawyers concerned with the loss of community leadership and moral authority explored other avenues to see if there might be some way to reclaim the high ground while recognizing the facts of modern industrial life. No one spoke as forcefully for professional reform as Louis Brandeis, and here again, as in his economics, moral fervor more than anything else characterized his views.

IN THE SPRING OF 1905, Brandeis accepted an invitation from the Harvard Ethical Society to speak on the "ethics of the legal profession" and on 4 May gave what many consider the embodiment of the reform critique of the legal profession. Brandeis certainly attacked what he considered wrong and misdirected, but his general tone was optimistic, and he titled the talk he gave that evening at Phillips Brooks House "The Opportunity in the Law."

He began by rephrasing the topic he had been asked to speak about, ethics, and declared that his listeners, "standing not far from the threshold of active life, feeling the generous impulse for service which the University fosters," wanted to know if they could lead lives that would be useful to their fellow men. One could do this in any profession, business, or trade because how people pursue their occupations is far more important than what that occupation may be. Certainly law, at least in the past, had offered plentiful opportunity for service. He then rehearsed Alexis de Tocqueville's commentary on lawyers as an American elite, because their training gives them a unique opportunity for service, and then explained how lawyers, trained to find and analyze facts, are, in a seeming paradox, judges even as they are advocates. The examination of the law and the facts shows them that there is often more than one party that has right on its side in a conflict, and so the lawyer must, as a judge, weigh the evidence and then give his client the proper advice, especially if in his judgment the client may be in the wrong.

The chairman of the ethical society had begun the session with the comment "People have the impression to-day that the lawyer has become mercenary." Brandeis tried to play this down by claiming that business had become more professionalized, and the close connection between the two gave the lawyer an important part in business affairs. There is some difficulty reconciling Brandeis's encomiums to businessmen who had created a new plane of operations that required judgment of the highest order with his later attacks on business leaders. He had, of course, William McElwain in mind, and the hope that enlightened businessmen, guided by wise, objective, and moral legal advisers, would do the right thing. It may also have been a tactical ploy, designed to show the students that he was not a rabid antibusiness populist or political radical.

But, alas, it is true, Brandeis conceded, "that at the present time the lawyer does not hold as high a position with the people as he held seventy-five or even fifty years ago." And then Brandeis, in no uncertain terms, told the Harvard undergraduates where the blame lay:

> Instead of holding a position of independence, between the wealthy and the people, prepared to curb the excesses of either, able lawyers have, to a large extent, allowed themselves to become adjuncts of great corporations and have neglected the obligation to use their powers for the protection of the people. We hear much of the "corporation lawyer," and far too little of the "people's lawyer." The great opportunity of the American Bar is and will be to stand again as it did in the past, ready to protect also the interests of the people.

He went on to attack those "leading lawyers," men who should have utilized their talent and influence for the good of the public but who perverted their abilities on behalf of corporations, "often in endeavoring to evade or nullify the extremely crude laws by which legislators sought to regulate the power or curb the excesses of corporations." He found it not only strange but disconcerting that the leaders of the bar almost unanimously ranged themselves on the side of the big corporations, and, he warned, there would be a price to pay for it. If the bar abandoned the interests of the people, then the people would rebel, through the ballot box, against the capitalists, and the results would be unhappy for all. For a generation, he charged,

> the leaders of the Bar have, with few exceptions, not only failed to take part in constructive legislation designed to solve in the public interest our great social, economic and industrial problems; but they have failed likewise to oppose legislation prompted by selfish interests. They have often gone further in disregard of the common weal. They have often advocated, as lawyers, legislative measures which as citizens they could not approve. . . . They have erroneously assumed that the rule of ethics to be applied to a lawyer's advocacy is the same where he acts for private interests against the public, as it is in litigation between private individuals.

In a private case, the lawyer's responsibility is to make the best argument for his client, knowing that the attorney for the other side will do the same and that the merits will then be weighed by a judge or jury. In cases where one side or the other is clearly in the right, the usual practice is to settle before trial. It is the lawyer's obligation to give good advice to the client and then to defend the client's interests to the best of his ability. Implicit in this argument, of course, is the assumption that a lawyer need not believe that his client is in the right; the adversarial system would resolve the issue. (Ironically, Brandeis himself, as we have seen, would later be criticized for refusing to take cases unless the client could convince him of the rightness of his complaint.) But whereas private interests could afford, and thus get, the very best legal representation, the public often did not have any attorneys looking after its interests. Lawyers of high standing had ignored the public interest, leaving its representation to less experienced, and often less capable, advocates. Moreover, those representing the private interests had refused to understand that the public did not stand in the same position vis-à-vis private corporations as did other private interests; the public good occupied— or should occupy—a higher plane of influence, and this should be recognized by those at the bar serving the great corporations.

The next generation, Brandeis warned, would, if present conditions continued, witness a growing contest between those who have and those who have not. "People are beginning to doubt whether in the long run democracy and absolutism can co-exist in the same community; beginning to doubt whether there is a justification for the great inequalities in the distribution of wealth, for the rapid creation of fortunes. . . . The people have begun to think; and they show evidence on all sides of a tendency to act." The great challenge of the coming years would be to temper this growing conflict, to mediate between the people on one side and corporate interests on the other. "Here, consequently, is the great opportunity in the law," he asserted. The country needed a new generation of lawyers who would serve as prior generations had done, looking past immediate claims toward the greater good, acting as statesmen rather than as mercenaries, recognizing the right, and acting to protect it. Nothing could better prepare his audience, he concluded, "for taking part in the solution of these problems, than the study and pre-eminently the practice of law. Those of you who feel drawn to that profession may rest assured that you will find in it an opportunity for usefulness which is probably unequalled. There is a call upon the legal profession to do a great work for this country."

(At least a few of the undergraduates present that day chose to heed Brandeis's call to enter public service. Years later, when Brandeis was about to give a campaign speech at the University of Minnesota, he told his wife that he had to take particular care in what he said to students, for one never knew what seed might be sown. "I am meeting here & there men who heard my lecture at Brooks House years ago & say it wholly changed their point of view." When Brandeis repeated the talk at the Fogg Art Museum for law school students, it made a deep and lasting impression on young Felix Frankfurter.)

One cannot miss the moralistic tone in this important talk. As a lawyer, Brandeis had attempted to serve the best interests of his clients by asking them to act in a moral manner. If in fact they did not have right on their side, then they should settle. When dealing with their workers, they should remember that they held much greater power than those who labored for them and so were obliged to treat them fairly. Similarly, his attacks on the trusts dealt less with their control of the marketplace per se than with the negative effects this control had on the nation's political life and on the opportunities of individual entrepreneurs.

In his account of what had happened to the legal profession, Brandeis spoke in the same voice as did others who lamented the loss of independence, idealism, and status. His is one of the best-known attacks, because he went further than the leaders of the bar association movement, suggesting a way that lawyers could act to regain the status they had once enjoyed in the community. Continue working blindly for the big companies, he warned, and you will make money; but you will lose not only public respect but also self-respect—you will lose your soul. Instead of being a cog in a machine that undermines the public weal, become a defender of the public good.

In invoking the notion of a people's attorney, he also made clear that dealing with the public required a different set of ethical considerations from those needed by a lawyer who spoke for one private client against another. Private clients had specific and legitimate priorities in protecting their property and investments and the return on those investments to shareholders. The public, however, had different priorities. Government is established not to make a profit but to protect its citizens and to provide services unavailable from the private sector. As such, in a conflict between private and public, a lawyer had to give greater weight to the claims of the government. This did not mean that the government would always be right, or that there might not be constitutional or statutory restrictions on the government's actions. It did mean that in the ethical universe of a lawyer, one always had to treat the public good and the private good differently, something that few lawyers at the time did.

Brandeis himself had already begun to act as a people's attorney by refusing to accept fees for work done on behalf of the public good. In 1907 he took on a case that would ever after tie that label to him.

IF WE SEE PROGRESSIVISM as a movement to mitigate the harshness of the new industrial regime, then it is easy to see why protective legislation played such an important role in the mood of the time. Men and women who worked in mines, mills, and factories of the new order often worked twelve or more hours a day in dangerous conditions for pitiful wages. Reformers wanted, among other things, to do away with child labor, establish a maximum number of hours one could work during a day and for a minimum amount of money, require effective safety precautions, and provide workmen's compensation on a broad and uniform basis. Between 1897 and 1916 they achieved nearly all of these goals on the state level, but not without opposition.

The owners of mines and factories naturally wanted to get the greatest amount of labor they could at the cheapest price, but they also objected to the very notion of government interfering with the economy—other than, of course, high tariffs to protect them against foreign competition and laws to prevent workers from organizing into labor unions. The notion of laissez-faire, that government should not be involved in the economy, had its roots in the Jacksonian opposition to government favoritism and had been enshrined as part of the Republican Party ideology after the Civil War. It had also become part of the legal system created by the Supreme Court to protect property rights, primarily through the notion of substantive due process and its companion, freedom of contract. Whatever one might claim about these ideas in the abstract, they had become powerful tools in the hands of conservative judges and lawyers to protect the sanctity of private property.

The prevailing jurisprudential philosophy of the pre–Civil War era has been labeled "instrumentalism," in which law served as a tool to promote economic growth without implicating governmental regulation. Judges used their common-law authority to create new doctrines that addressed the changing requirements of private business interests, and sought to determine what best served the public interest in a society characterized by constant change. Instrumentalism relied on the flexibility of the common law not only in adapting to new situations but also in taking the facts of those situations into account. It also allowed the states, utilizing their police powers to protect the common welfare, to step in when necessary to limit or even regulate private property. This is the jurisprudence that Louis Brandeis learned at Harvard Law School, and when he proclaimed the benefits of the common law, he meant the ability of judges to recognize facts and, applying them to the case at hand, develop a fair solution to new problems.

But in the years after the Civil War, leaders of the bench, taking their cue from Justice Stephen J. Field, moved toward more formal procedures that limited legislative power and enhanced that of the courts through judicial review. The ability of judges to void federal legislation if it ran counter to a constitutional command had, of course, been a staple of American law since John Marshall's great opinion in *Marbury v. Madison* (1803). But the Supreme Court had, before the Civil War, only exercised that power twice. After the war it began to utilize it on a regular basis to strike down efforts by Congress and then state legislatures to regulate economic activity.

The phrase "due process of law" referred to general legal rules and customs accepted as the normative base of the legal system. From its inception, it usually referred to procedural rights, some of which are statutory, some common-law, and some constitutional. For example, the right to trial by jury is a substantive right, but how jurors are chosen, how evidence may be presented, how witnesses are procured, are all procedural. The idea that due process of law could also include substantive rights to protect property appeared in only a few cases before the Civil War, but the theory began to pick up steam in the 1870s and came to be enshrined by the Court in an 1897 case, *Allgeyer v. Louisiana.* As explicated by Justice Rufus Peckham, substantive due process allowed practically no state interference with private property or with the economy other than absolutely minimal regulation to protect health and to ensure public safety. Men were not only free to choose what business or vocation they would follow but free in that vocation to succeed, to amass property, and to enjoy that property without governmental regulation.

Peckham also married into substantive due process the idea of freedom of contract, which had been developing in state courts since the war. Part of the Republican Party ideology before the war had been the notion of free labor, the right of people to work and to leave jobs, as opposed to slavery. This notion became transposed to a freedom to contract between employer and employee, with its basis in old common-law rubrics such as arm's-length negotiations—that is, the employer and the employee bargained out the labor contract on a one-to-one basis. Clearly, when a steel mill with hundreds or thousands of employees set wages, it did not do so on a personal basis, but the courts continued to act as if it did, and refused to allow the state to interfere with the labor market. To rationalize this rule, courts held that a workman's labor constituted his property, and therefore should enjoy the same protection against government interference and regulation as did private property.

These notions quickly gained adherents among conservative lawyers, who used them to defeat efforts by the state to protect workers or to regulate the workplace. At meetings of state and local bar associations, leading business lawyers reinforced the message. "We lawyers," William Guthrie told his colleagues, "are delegated not merely to defend constitutional guaranties before the courts for individual clients, but to teach people in season and out to value and respect individual liberty and the rights of property." John F. Dillon gave a lecture to the New York State Bar Association titled "Property—Its Rights and Duties," and inveighed against the viciousness of such radical measures as the income tax. William Ramsay proudly proclaimed the new dogma to his fellow attorneys: "The right to contract and to be contracted with . . . is sacred, and lies at the very foundation of the social state."

And what of the facts, especially the one thing that practically everyone recognized—that industrialization had forever changed the social, political, and economic fabric of the country, not to mention its legal foundations? Facts contradicted the new formalism, they embarrassed the assumptions of conservative advocates of substantive due process and liberty of contract, and so were ignored. Reading some of the state and federal court opinions at this time, one would think that the cases had arisen in the preindustrial age and still relied on the old common-law rules of employment and liability based on a craft shop with a master and one or two apprentices.

To Brandeis this blind refusal to take facts into account when explicating law not only made no sense but went against all of his instincts. In 1891, in one of his first public causes, reform of the liquor lobby, he had lectured the Massachusetts legislature: "No law can be effective which does not take into consideration the conditions of the community for which it is designed." Two decades later, testifying before a congressional committee, he repeated the lesson: "In all our legislation we have got to base what we do on facts and not on theories." As Paul Freund noted, Brandeis "developed his larger conception from immersion in the facts of specific cases, in the best tradition of the common law." Legal education requires "that lawyers should not merely learn rules of law" but also study the "facts, human, industrial, social, to which they are to be applied." Even after he went onto the bench, Brandeis warned his colleagues that "the logic of words should yield to the logic of realities." In an interview with a reporter, he declared, "What we must do in America is not to attack our judges, but educate them. All judges should be made to feel, as many already do, that the things needed to protect liberty are radically different from what they were fifty years back."

THE CAMPAIGN FOR protective legislation, even though it did not have any generals, nonetheless played out in a predictable and rational manner. Given the conservative opposition to any state regulation of the workplace, reformers appealed to the state's inherent police powers, the authority of any sovereign government to protect the health, safety, and welfare of its citizens. At the end of the nineteenth century, however, American jurisprudence had yet to define the boundaries between laissez-faire, with its opposition to what it saw as market interference, and the scope of the state police powers. On the one hand, an influential conservative law writer, Christopher G. Tiedeman, declared that the proper role of the government consisted of no more "than to provide for the public order and personal security by the prevention and punishment of crimes and trespasses." And by "no more" he meant just that; Tiedeman opposed any regulatory infringement on the market, even usury laws. At the other end of the spectrum, Oliver Wendell Holmes Jr. declared that the police power "may be put forth in aid of what is sanctioned by usage, or held by the prevailing morality, or strong and preponderant opinion to be greatly and immediately necessary to the public welfare."

Given this uncertainty, reformers started in an area they knew to be traditionally within the scope of the police power, protection of children. They wanted to do away with child labor, and they accomplished this by a mixture of laws mandating school attendance and banning children below a certain age from working in mines, factories, and mills. These bills met practically no resistance in state courts, and the only one to reach the Supreme Court received unanimous approval.

From there reformers moved to another group of people that the law, at that time, held to be little better than children, namely, women, and also to men working in particularly dangerous environments. One must recall that in the first decade of the twentieth century women still could not vote or serve on juries in most states and, despite the passage of married women's property laws in the mid-nineteenth century, often found themselves economically under the control of their fathers or husbands. In legal terms, women, like children and mental incompetents, were considered "persons under a disability," and therefore candidates for protection under the umbrella of state police power. Workers in perilous conditions, such as miners, also fit within traditional assumptions, and as early as 1898 the Supreme Court affirmed a Utah law that established safety standards for workers in smelters and mines where the state could reasonably find the working conditions to be hazardous to their health.

The progression, from children to women to men in hazardous occupations, would then lead to the establishment of working hours for all workers, men and women, as well as laws providing for minimum wages and employers' liability. Each step would cement the legitimacy of protective legislation for a particular group and theoretically make it easier to bring the next level of worker under the aegis of the police power. Clearly, these efforts, taking place in more than forty states, did not move in lockstep, but in general this pattern existed in most states. State courts, which had the initial review of these laws, for the most part upheld them, although a few notoriously conservative courts, such as in Illinois and New York, were among the last to go along, and then only after a Supreme Court decision had upheld the constitutionality of a particular type of statute. The entire enterprise, however, stood in danger of collapsing when the Supreme Court suddenly struck down a New York law regulating the hours of bakery workers.

The state legislature had reasoned that conditions in bakeries, with the large amount of flour dust in the air, could be hazardous to the health of the men employed there, and surely sick men (who could not afford to take a day off) should not be baking bread. There appear to have been some other considerations as well, including the effort of unionized bakeries to force nonunion shops into working shorter hours and the desire of housing reformers to eliminate bakeries from operating in tenement basements. However true these allegations may have been, a strong case could still be offered for the measure as a health and safety law. The state courts upheld the law at each level of the challenge, but the Supreme Court, by a 5–4 vote, struck it down in *Lochner v. New York* (1905).

Although the Court had upheld prior pieces of protective legislation, a majority of the justices still strongly believed in liberty of contract as the constitutional norm, and in order for the state to restrict this fundamental right, it had to show convincingly that a health or safety hazard existed. Justice Rufus Peckham brushed away the state's claims about health and safety and condemned the statute as nothing more than an effort "to regulate the hours of labor between the master and his employees (all being men, sui juris), in a private business, not dangerous to morals or in any real or substantive degree, to the health of the employees." Peckham conceded that a state could enact legislation to protect the health of workers, even bakers, but to do so it had to show that either the occupation itself or the standard working conditions related to it posed a real danger to worker health. The state had failed to do so. Peckham then posed the question: "Is this a fair, reasonable and appropriate exercise of the police power of the State, or is it an unreasonable, unnecessary and arbitrary interference with the rights of the individual?" Even more worrisome to reformers than the question itself was the tacit assumption that it would be the courts, and not the legislatures, who would answer that question.

The decision evoked powerful dissents from Justices John Marshall

Harlan and Oliver Wendell Holmes. Although Harlan accepted the basic argument of freedom of contract, he nonetheless believed the state of New York could reasonably conclude that a relation existed between working conditions in a bakery and the health of the employees. Holmes dissented in a brief statement that soon achieved classic status, for it set forward what would be called "judicial restraint," a position that would be championed by Brandeis after he took his seat on the bench. "This case is decided upon an economic theory which a large part of the country does not entertain," Holmes wrote, but "my agreement or disagreement has nothing to do with the right of a majority to embody their opinions into law." In other words, absent a specific constitutional prohibition, the state had the power to enact legislation it wanted, and the judiciary had no power to pass on its wisdom.

Predictably, conservatives applauded the decision, while the labor press denounced it. Although there have been efforts to rehabilitate the jurisprudential arguments of Peckham, reformers then and later saw the *Lochner* decision as an appalling example of judges ignoring the Constitution and, instead of deferring to the policy-making authority of elected officials, writing their own prejudices into law. And, despite the prior approval of protective legislation in both federal and state courts, progressives now worried that *Lochner,* with its harsh call for freedom of contract, would nullify laws already on the books and become a barrier to future protective legislation.

ON LABOR DAY, 4 September 1905, Joe Haselbock, an overseer at the Grand Laundry in Portland, Oregon, required one of the workers, a labor activist named Emma Gotcher, to stay overtime in violation of a 1903 law that, among other things, provided that "no female shall be employed in any mechanical establishment, or factory, or laundry in this State more than 10 hours during any one day," and which assessed punishments upon those who ignored the law. Gotcher filed a complaint, and two weeks later the state brought criminal charges against the laundry's owner, Curt Muller. Aware of the *Lochner* ruling, Muller retained William D. Fenton, an influential corporate attorney in Portland, to defend him. The trial judge, although personally opposed to the law, found Muller guilty of a misdemeanor and fined him $10. The Oregon Supreme Court, while citing *Lochner,* considered it inapposite, and upheld both the statute and the conviction. Muller appealed to the U.S. Supreme Court, claiming that the law violated the Due Process Clause of the Fourteenth Amendment by abridging the freedom of contract.

The case drew the immediate attention of both conservatives and progressives, because if the high court ruled against Oregon, then all hope of protective legislation would be lost. The ten-hour law struck a core component of the conservative creed, liberty of contract. If people wanted to work twelve, fourteen, or even eighteen hours a day and could find someone willing to hire them, then both parties could "freely" contract such an arrangement. This reasoning may have been true in an earlier and simpler economy, but industrialization had undermined the premises on which it rested—the supposed equality of both contracting parties. A village blacksmith and his assistant might have stood on roughly equal footing, but certainly no parity existed between the U.S. Steel Corporation and any of its thousands of unskilled workers, many of whom could barely speak English. Oregon, in effect, said that if all the parties of a labor contract did not stand equally, then the state under its police power could limit the right to contract in order to protect its citizens. This conservatives could not concede.

The National Consumers League, which had avidly supported the Oregon statute and protective laws in other states, now undertook to defend it and began contacting leading lawyers to see if one would take the case. When representatives of the league approached Joseph H. Choate, a pillar of the New York bar, he dismissed them out of hand, declaring that he could not understand why "a great husky Irish woman should not work in a laundry more than ten hours a day" if she wanted. Choate well understood that if the Court allowed this restriction on liberty to contract to stand, other restrictions—on hours for men, on working conditions, and even on wages—would soon follow. The laissez-faire philosophy demanded that no matter how unequal the game, no interference by the state could be permitted. Thus equality before the law was carried to its logical, yet patently unfair, extreme.

Josephine Goldmark and Florence Kelley of the league then decided to approach Louis Brandeis, whom they had wanted all along, but they had no idea how he would react. "After all," Goldmark recalled, "he had had no hand in shaping the legal record nor in presenting the defense in state courts." The decision in *Lochner* "stood menacingly in our path," and if he did agree, they only had about a month to prepare the brief. At their meeting on 14 November 1907, Brandeis agreed on two conditions. First, Oregon had to give him full control of the case; he would not serve simply as amicus curiae (friend of the court) for the league. He wanted to be in full control of the strategy, and beyond that

Josephine Goldmark, Louis's sister-in-law, and National Consumers League official

he thought it an important element of the defense that he appear as the official representative of the state. Second, the league had to provide him with massive amounts of data on the effects of long working hours on women. He wanted "facts, published by anyone with expert knowledge of industry in its relation to women's hours of labor, such as factory inspectors, physicians, trades unions, economists, social workers."

Brandeis realized that the Oregon statute would not stand a chance in the high court unless he could distinguish it from *Lochner,* and the only way to do that involved meeting the Court on its own terms. He had spotted a loophole in Peckham's opinion; the justice noted that protective legislation could be justified under the police power if the state could show proof that the measure directly addressed the health, safety, or welfare of its citizens. New York, according to Peckham, had failed to do so in regard to the bakery law. Brandeis now intended to defend the Oregon law by showing a direct connection between working hours and women's health, family life, and morals. To do that, he needed a free hand (which Oregon gladly gave him) and data to demonstrate the need for the law (which the league provided). Brandeis also had in mind an earlier Illinois decision on women's hours legislation, *Ritchie v. People* (1895), in which the state's high court had struck down an 1893 law limiting the work of women in factories to eight hours a day. That case, like *Lochner,* had been decided on the basis of freedom of contract, with the state court casually dismissing the police power argument.

Because of the limited time available to prepare the brief, Brandeis gave his sister-in-law two weeks to get "printed matter sufficiently authoritative to pass muster" and to bring it up to him in Boston. Josephine and the league swung into action, and she hired ten readers to help her. They did their research at Columbia University, the New York Public Library (then known as the Astor), and the Library of Congress. One aide, a young medical student, devoted himself completely to literature on health factors relating to occupation, and he and several of the other assistants soon discovered that the United States could furnish them with only limited data. They found plenty of articles of opinion and descriptions of working conditions, but little in the way of scientific analysis and reports of the effect of long hours on women's health. So they turned to foreign countries that had long been collecting and publishing these types of data.

Florence Kelley, director of the National Consumers League, ca. 1905

Brandeis had earlier written that "a judge is presumed to know the elements of law, but there is no presumption that he knows the facts." In the *Muller* brief he set out to make sure that the members of the nation's highest court would, at the least, have the facts before them. The traditional appellate brief, and the one that is still the norm in many cases, deals entirely with legal principles. Typically, the lawyer states a principle, then any subsidiary rules associated with it, and the cases that support them, and then does the same thing for the other rules of law on which the client is relying. In the response or reply brief, the attorney for the other side rebuts these assertions of the law. In this give-and-take, there is rarely a mention of the litigant, or of the facts surrounding the case. Normally, the trial court is where the facts are determined; appellate courts do not review questions of fact, but deal with whether the trial court made the right choices as to the law. If a case gets to the Supreme Court, the particular details are almost irrelevant, and both liberal and conservative justices agree that that is how it should be.

But what if the relevant facts had not been aired at the trial level? In most instances, a lawyer today would not be allowed to introduce new material on appeal. At the beginning of the twentieth century, however, the rules of what could be presented were somewhat different, and Brandeis gambled that given the opening he saw in *Lochner*—and the storm of criticism that had greeted that decision—the justices might be open to the type of argument he planned to present.

The brief in *Muller v. Oregon* ran 113 pages, with only two pages devoted to the law. "The legal principles applicable to this are few," it began, "and are well established." These included the right to contract for labor, and here Brandeis cited *Lochner*. This right, however, remained subject to such constraints as the state might impose on it, but if the state claimed that a restriction arose from a need to protect health or safety, then it had to have "a more direct relation, as a means to an end, and the end itself must be appropriate and legitimate," and once again he cited *Lochner*.

Therefore, the validity of the Oregon statute, which the state claimed did have a legitimate purpose—namely, to protect women workers—had to be grounded in fact, and to that end, "the facts of common knowledge will be considered under the following heads: Part I. Legislation (foreign and American) restricting the hours of labor for women. Part II. The world's experience upon which the legislation limiting the hours of labor for women is based."

The next hundred-some pages set out laws, factory reports, medical testimony, all revolving around simple facts that even the justices of the nation's highest court must have known, that women are physically different from men and that they, not men, bear children. The excerpts came from sources as varied as British House of Commons reports on bills to close shops early (1895, 1901); the Maine Bureau of Industrial and Labor Statistics report in which a doctor concluded that "woman is badly constructed for the purpose of standing eight or ten hours upon her feet" (1888); the *Journal of the Royal Sanitary Institute* (1904); medical textbooks such as *The Hygiene, Diseases, and Mortality of Occupations* (1892); a report of French district inspectors on the question of night work (1900); reports from various state bureaus charged with gathering industrial statistics; a report of the German Imperial Factory Inspectors (1895); and *La réglementation légale du travail des femmes et des enfants dans l'industrie italienne.*

Brandeis wanted to show, using what he termed "the facts of common knowledge," that not only did individual women suffer from the effects of long working hours, but because some of these women also bore the children of the next generation, society suffered; the poor health of mothers led to the poor health of their children. The sources cited included Dr. George Newman, *Infant Mortality: A Social Problem* (1906), in which the London doctor claimed that physical fatigue exerted "a decided effect in the production of premature birth, particularly if these conditions are accompanied by long hours of work." Also, by describing this material as "common knowledge," Brandeis wanted to make it easier for the justices to take judicial notice of these facts.

Brandeis then concluded that "in view of the facts above set forth and of legislative action extending over a period of more than sixty years in the leading countries of Europe, and in twenty of our States, it cannot be said that the Legislature of Oregon had no reasonable ground for believing that the public health, safety, or welfare did not require a legal limitation on women's work in manufacturing and mechanical establishments and laundries to ten hours a day."

In this brief Brandeis brought together some of the themes we have seen before: the need for facts; education of bench, bar, and public; the relationship of law to the economic, social, and political realities of the day; the need to mitigate some of the harsher aspects of industrialization; and the use of law as an instrument of social policy. In response to the formalism of classical legal thought, the new school of sociological jurisprudence called upon courts to take into account changes that occurred in the economy and society. One of the first great theorists of sociological jurisprudence, Oliver Wendell Holmes Jr., had declared that the life of the law is experience, not logic. Louis Brandeis became the great practitioner of that school of thought, and the Brandeis brief aimed to provide what Holmes deemed necessary for the growth of the law, an awareness of experience. Brandeis, like Holmes, believed that in the great common-law tradition, the exploration of an issue and the understanding of all the facts that surround would lead to the law accommodating itself to change.

While of course he played the role of advocate for Oregon, he also wanted to educate the Court and people who opposed protective legislation. Brandeis no more cared for governmental regulation than did Muller's attorneys or Joseph Choate. But as a conservative who believed that new times demand accommodation even while holding on to older values, he recognized that the greater the opposition to minimal social progress, through measures such as protective legislation, the greater would be the popular demand for more extreme measures. As counsel to a larger situation, he wanted to advise those who would freeze the status quo that it could not be done. A real need to protect workers existed, and that need would somehow be met. It would be better if men of goodwill cooperated in ameliorating the evils of industrial transition.

Fenton and Henry H. Gilfry, Muller's attorneys, chose to ignore all but the first three pages of the Brandeis brief and made absolutely no effort to respond to the more than one hundred pages of data that Brandeis claimed justified Oregon in passing its law. About the only reference is a paragraph in which they assert that "the argument based on sex ought not to prevail, because women's rights are as sacred under the Fourteenth Amendment as are men's. . . . Is there any difference between the case of a healthy, adult woman, contracting for service for more than ten hours in a laundry, and that of a man employed as a baker for more than ten hours a day? Certainly conditions are as favorable in a laundry as in a bakery."

The two sides argued the case before the Supreme Court on 15 January 1908, in the old Senate chambers in the Capitol. Some members of the National Consumers League came down from New York, aware of the revolutionary tactics their lawyer would introduce that day. Brandeis, as Ms. Goldmark described it,

> slowly, deliberately, without seeming to refer to a note, built up his case from the particular to the general. . . . It was the result of intense preparation beforehand, submerging himself first in the source material, he was determining the exclusion or inclusion of detail, the order, the selectiveness, the emphasis which marked his method. Once determined upon, it had all the spontaneity of a great address because he had so mastered the details that they fell into place, as it were, in a consummate whole.

The justices listened carefully, with few interruptions for questions.

A little over five weeks later, on 24 February, the Court unanimously upheld the Oregon statute. Justice David J. Brewer declared that the Court faced only a single question, namely the constitutionality of the Oregon statute. Before addressing that question, however, Brewer noted, "In patent cases counsel are apt to open the argument with a discussion of the state of the art. It may not be amiss, in the present case, before examining the constitutional question, to notice the course of legislation as well as expressions of opinions from other than judicial sources. In the brief filed by Mr. Louis D. Brandeis . . . is a very copious collection of all these matters." Anyone in the audience that day would surely have sat up and paid attention at this point, because the Court never referred to counsel by name, much less to any arguments put forward in their briefs.

These materials "may not be, technically speaking, authorities, and in them there is little or no discussion of the constitutional question,"

Brewer said, "yet they are significant of a widespread belief that woman's physical structure, and the functions she performs in consequence thereof, justify special legislation restricting or qualifying the conditions under which she should be permitted to toil." Although constitutional questions cannot be settled by public opinion, courts can take into account facts relating to women, and since it is clear that there is a consensus among experts that "healthy mothers are essential to vigorous offspring," the state had a legitimate reason, under its police powers, to enact this legislation. The Court's decision, Brewer concluded, did not affect the holding in *Lochner v. New York,* but in this case "rests in the inherent difference between the two sexes, and in the different functions in life which they perform." Brewer, who favored women's suffrage, admitted that the Oregon law limited a woman's contractual rights, but these limitations "are not imposed solely for her benefit, but also largely for the benefit of all." The Oregon law met the constitutional test.

PORTLAND'S *Morning Oregonian* blazoned news of the decision with a five-part headline: "STATE MAY LIMIT WOMEN'S WORK," "OREGON'S TEN-HOUR LAW SUSTAINED," "WOMEN MUST BE PROTECTED," "DIFFERENCE BETWEEN SEXES MAKES IT ESSENTIAL," and "SAFEGUARD HUMAN RACE." The *Chicago Daily Tribune* agreed with Justice Brewer that while a woman's rights, and the right to contract, could not be abridged any more than could a man's, the fact remains that the two sexes differ and that women need certain levels of protection. Florence Kelley picked up on Brandeis's theme and predicted that the way would now be open for additional protective legislation, since in any court test the state had merely to show a clear relation between the statute and health. Josephine Goldmark exalted that "a movement to extend and strengthen women's hour legislation spread over the country."

Eventually, *Muller* became a landmark decision, not only for its holding, but for the brief that Louis Brandeis filed. Known immediately as a "Brandeis brief," it altered the way that lawyers approached defense of public matters. There is always a tension between private rights, such as property and liberty to contract, and public authority, in the form of the police power. Today, when dealing with laws of economic regulation, the Court has adopted a "rational basis" test, meaning that if the legislature had a rational reason to enact the law, and if no constitutional prohibition existed, then the courts would defer, as Holmes had demanded in his *Lochner* dissent, to the wisdom of the legislature and not attempt to impose their own judgment. But when the issue is not clear, or when matters of individual rights rather than those of property are involved, lawyers have the responsibility to show the courts what the facts are surrounding the controversy and why they are important to the legal decision. For example, the brief filed by the NAACP in the original segregation cases, *Brown v. Board of Education* (1954), is very short on legal precedent—because very little existed—but replete with materials relating to the harm done by segregation to the minds and hearts of black children. The briefs filed by lawyers for retired generals, corporate executives, and others on the practical dimensions of affirmative action played a role in the Supreme Court's decision approving a race-conscious acceptance plan at the University of Michigan Law School.

One thing that often gets lost in the attention paid to the innovation of the Brandeis brief is that it, and the decision in the case, represented a victory for a lawyer. In *Muller,* indeed in all the cases in which Brandeis acted for the public interest, he saw himself not as a crusading reformer but as an attorney upholding the best practices and traditions of the American bar. While the Brandeis brief provided the tool to get facts before a court, by itself it would not have won a single case. The brief, no matter how well crafted, needed a great attorney to make it work.

Edward McClennen, Brandeis's law partner, believed that this aspect of *Muller* was often overlooked, and that if one wanted to use the case as a teaching tool, the point would be that it represented the finest example of a lawyer's work. It is true, McClennen noted, that the cause had a strong appeal to Brandeis, as did the people who invited him to be their champion. But "the impelling cause of his taking the case up was that in the state of the decisions he saw grave danger that a judicial error might be made if the case were presented in the routine manner, and that therefore he ought to do what he could to secure the right decision." Roscoe Pound, the dean of Harvard Law School, made a similar observation during the nomination fight. Brandeis's friends, Pound wrote, had made a great mistake in urging as his chief qualification his reform views. What matters, Pound averred, and "what is not generally known is that Mr. Brandeis is in very truth a very great lawyer." In looking at the brief in *Muller,* Pound claimed that beyond the advocacy of social legislation, one had to note the "breadth of perception and remarkable legal insight which enabled him to perceive the proper mode of presenting such a question."

In general, the concept of the Brandeis brief, that is, the use of non-traditional and nonlegal materials to uphold a particular view, has received widespread approval. With the exception of those judges and scholars who take an extremely narrow view of what constitutional adjudication is about, in both the courts and the academy there is agreement that in those cases where looking at prior legal rules does not really inform us about the importance of cases, courts benefit from this additional information. A court that sustains the validity of a statute, Paul Freund noted, "does so more confidently and more comfortably if some factual foundation has been established for the validity of the law."

But Brandeis himself believed that while such material might be of assistance to a judge in understanding a statute, in fact the court should not even have to consider the material, since it ought to defer to the wisdom of the legislature exercising its authority. Several years later, when Brandeis was defending an Oregon minimum-wage law, a member of the Court asked him during oral argument whether his brief, which contained all the data supporting minimum-wage legislation, also included data opposing it. Brandeis answered:

> I conceive it to be absolutely immaterial what may be said against such laws. Each one of these statements contained in the brief . . . might upon further investigation be found to be erroneous, each conclusion of fact may be found afterwards to be unsound—and yet the constitutionality of the act would not be affected thereby. This court is not burdened with the duty of passing upon the disputed question whether the legislature of Oregon was wise or unwise, or probably wise or unwise, in enacting this law. The question is merely whether you can see that the legislators had no ground on which they could, as reasonable men, deem this legislation appropriate to abolish or mitigate the evils believed to exist or apprehended. If you cannot find that, the law must stand.

In other words, except in occasional cases, there should be no need for a Brandeis brief, because courts, exercising judicial restraint, ought not to be second-guessing the legislatures.

A more serious, although somewhat ahistorical, argument is that many of the "facts" cited in the brief have, over the years, turned out to be inaccurate or misleading. A close reading of the factual portions, consisting of excerpts from contemporary authorities or public agencies, makes them "considerably less compelling than traditional accounts would have us believe." One of the leading critics of the *Muller* opinion and of the Brandeis brief, Judith A. Baer, attacked the facts Brandeis used as not being scientific. There were no controls or consideration of independent variables. Much of the evidence in the brief could have applied to overworked men, and she questioned the expertise of the authorities cited.

Brandeis constructed his argument taking from his materials only those parts that bolstered his argument, which, of course, any debater does; one does not lead with material opposed to one's argument. The problem is not so much that some allegations, such as a relationship between long workdays and alcoholism or between exhaustion and premature births, have proven more complex or less persuasive as that Brandeis and Goldmark did not have the benefit of scientific studies that would meet modern standards. The types of statistical controls that Baer alleges are missing had not yet been invented, and it flies in the face of history to attack someone for failing to use materials that did not yet exist. They worked with what they had, and when Brandeis claimed that the brief presented the "facts of common knowledge," these were indeed the facts as known at that time.

The brief in 1908 utilized what people in that year believed to be "facts," part of the progressive era's faith in scientific investigation. Moreover, whatever defects they may have had as social science, the Brandeis materials showed that the Oregon legislature had reason to act as it did, and that was all that Brandeis had to prove. The belief in how women differed from men, and how stress and work affected their reproductive roles, may be suspect now, in the light of more advanced research and better health care, but in 1908 the idea that long work by mothers could adversely affect future births seemed scientific to contemporaries, and therefore valid. As for the fact that women differed from men, if nothing else that was indeed "common knowledge." As Brandeis later told his law clerk, the brief should have been titled "What Every Fool Knows," and it did little more than tell the justices what they already knew, but in a way they could use to uphold the Oregon law.

FEMINIST SCHOLARS in the 1970s and 1980s, however, leveled a far more serious charge against Brandeis, *Muller,* and the Brandeis brief, and it is every bit as ahistorical as the attack on his materials. Their claim is that the entire argument that Brandeis put forth, and that the Court accepted, rested on the assumption that women were inferior to men and therefore needed special protection. Instead of liberating women, *Muller* carried on the legal tradition that saw women as little better than children. In this attack, Justice Brewer comes off as the chief villain, because his opinion is in fact overtly sexist. Brandeis presented a number of positions on which Brewer could have based an opinion upholding the Oregon law, and the justice chose those that emphasized the immutable differences between men and women. Brewer's talk of women as the mothers of the race harked back to the opinion of Justice Joseph P. Bradley in *Bradwell v. Illinois* (1873), in which the Court had held that states could deny women the opportunity to practice law, since they were a gentler sex and the rough brutalities of legal practice would unfit them for their proper roles as wives and mothers. Brewer may have seized on this aspect because it allowed him to uphold the law without retreating from *Lochner*.

The Court, according to Nancy Erickson, could have decided *Muller* even without the Brandeis brief, since liberty of contract had been sex-based since its inception, and by 1908 the Court could have found sufficient legal precedent to uphold women-only hours law. This, however, ignores the lingering shadow of *Lochner*. Today we know that courts in the progressive era upheld far more acts of protective legislation than they struck down, but looking at the situation in 1908, progressives could not know whether *Lochner* constituted an aberration or a predictor of the fate that all protective legislation would meet in the courts. Moreover, although the *Lochner* doctrine appeared to go into retreat, it did not die, and would come roaring back in the 1920s. Not until the New Deal would reformers be able to put through legislation that protected women and men equally from long hours and inadequate pay.

It is also important to note that at the time most women favored protective legislation. Women constituted the bulk of the National Consumers League directors and staff, and in every state that enacted such laws, women could be found in the front ranks of their advocates. Although a small minority of equal rights suffragists condemned *Muller* at the time, Alice Stone Blackwell, a leader of the fight for women's vote and editor of the *Woman's Journal,* wrote that she could not see any inconsistency between Brewer's opinion and the struggle for enfranchisement. Where, she asked, "is the inconsistency in a man's believing that women should be protected against excessive and inhuman overwork, and at the same time believing that they should be protected against taxation without representation"?

Was Louis Brandeis, despite the fact that he had become a supporter of women's suffrage, a sexist? Are the Brandeis brief and the Brewer opinion antifeminist? By today's standards they no doubt are, and as the drive for women's equality has gained strength in the last four decades, the brief's arguments and the decision appear anachronistic. One, however, has to judge Brandeis and Brewer not in the light of current conditions but in the context of the culture and economy at the start of the twentieth century. They did in fact believe that women needed to be protected, and that while some women had to work outside the home, a woman's proper sphere centered on home and hearth. Not only did they believe that, but so, too, did a majority of women at the time. In that milieu, the Brandeis argument and the Court decision did not appear discriminatory. One should also add that Brandeis and Goldmark believed just as fervently in protective legislation for men. While gathering material for the *Muller* brief, Goldmark collected a great deal of information about the effects of long hours on men's health and welfare. In 1912 the Russell Sage Foundation published a huge compendium of this material titled *Fatigue and Efficiency* that addressed not only the needs of women that had been involved in *Muller* but the far larger issue of the effect of long hours and stress on all workers.

Many years later, with the passage of Title VII of the 1964 Civil Rights Act, the implementation of Equal Employment Opportunity Commission guidelines, and other antidiscrimination laws, states found gender-based laws discriminatory and began to repeal them. State and federal courts also backed away, until finally, in *UAW v. Johnson Controls* (1991), Justice Harry Blackmun rejected the *Muller* rationale completely. Concern for women's childbearing potential, he wrote, had long been an excuse for denying women equal opportunity. Neither the courts, the legislature, nor the employer could make decisions for women between home and work, and about the type of work women could do. Such choices are for women to make.

THE SUCCESS of the Brandeis brief led the National Consumers League to defend other protective laws in the Court and encouraged more jurisdictions to enact such legislation. Between 1908 and 1917, nineteen states and the District of Columbia passed women's hours laws, while twenty states that already had them on the books extended their protection to women in additional fields and/or lowered the maximum number of hours a woman could work in a day. The league also used the decision in the case, as well as reprints of the Brandeis brief, in a publicity campaign to support protective legislation. When Illinois, whose state supreme court had struck down its first women's hour law, reenacted a less stringent version of it, the league came to its defense and working with Brandeis produced a six-hundred-page brief. Louis Brandeis argued the case in Springfield, and he believed that the league's publicity had made the Illinois court more amenable to his argument. He correctly predicted that the Illinois Supreme Court, eager to overcome some "foolish decisions" in the past, would uphold the law in *Ritchie v. Wayman* (1910). The following year, at the invitation of the state's attorney general, Brandeis successfully defended an Ohio hours law for women. This success led to a string of cases in other states, and while Brandeis did not have the time to argue each one of them personally, he continued to advise Florence Kelley and Josephine Goldmark on strategy and on the organization and content of the briefs. When a challenge rose to a New York State law banning night work for women, the New York attorney general prepared a brief in defense of the law and sent it over to the National Consumers League for comment. Brandeis and Goldmark added four hundred pages of factual material. In 1913, Oregon enacted a ten-hour limit for all industrial workers, with an additional three hours allowable at a pay rate of time and a half. Brandeis and Goldmark put together a brief that ran 1,021 pages and that utilized much of the work Goldmark had done in preparing *Fatigue and Efficiency.*

By 1914, it appeared that the progressive agenda regarding protective legislation would soon be completed. States had passed, and courts had approved, the abolishment of child labor, factory safety laws, and limitations on the hours of work for both men and women, and some states had initiated workers' compensation plans. As some conservatives had feared, *Muller* had been an "opening wedge" in the assault on liberty of contract, and they braced as reformers sought the passage of minimum-wage laws. The state dictating what an employer had to pay a worker struck at the very heart not only of freedom of contract but of the idea of a free market. Such legislation, charged Rome G. Brown, "savors of the division of property between those who have and those who have not, and the leveling of fortunes by division under government supervision." Brown aimed his remarks at a 1913 Oregon law establishing minimum wages. Although Brandeis and the league leadership had urged the state to apply the law to all workers, the legislature chose to cover only women. Once again Brandeis and his sister-in-law began putting together material, and in December 1914 the Court scheduled three days for oral argument.

We have an eyewitness account of Brandeis in oral argument in that case, and if perhaps Goldmark's recollection of his performance in *Muller* is a bit colored by distance and family affection, neither charge can be leveled against Judge William Hitz of the District of Columbia Supreme Court, a former trial lawyer himself. He had come over to the Supreme Court that day specifically to hear the Oregon case argued, and as he wrote to his friend Felix Frankfurter:

> I have just heard Mr. Brandeis make one of the greatest arguments I have ever listened to, and I have heard many great arguments. . . . The reception which he wrested from that citadel of the past was very moving and impressive to one who knows the Court. Holmes is the only one among them who has any of the light of the morning left, but even he joined in bombarding the deaf and dumb man who spoke before Brandeis. When Brandeis began to speak, the Court showed all the inertia and elemental hostility which Courts cherish for a new thought, or a new right, or even a new remedy for an old wrong, but he visibly lifted all this burden, and without orationizing or chewing of the rag he reached them all and held even [Mahlon] Pitney quiet.
>
> He not only reached the Court, but he dwarfed the Court, because it was clear that here stood a man who knew infinitely more, and who cared infinitely more, for the vital daily rights of the other people than the men who sat there sworn to protect them. It was so clear that something had happened in the Court today that even Charles Henry Butler saw it and he stopped me afterwards on the coldest corner in town to say that no man this winter had received such close attention from the Court as Brandeis got today, while one of the oldest members of the Clerk's office remarked to me that "that fellow Brandeez has got the impudence of the Devil to bring his socialism into the Supreme Court."

Another person in the courtroom that day, Charles Warren, also went away impressed. The future constitutional historian, then an assistant attorney general in the Wilson administration and a frequent observer of oral argument, told a reporter that it was one of the most effective pleas ever heard in the Court, and it was as logical and powerful as it was eloquent. The Court had extended the allotted time for each side from one hour to ninety minutes, but when Brandeis's time had expired, Chief Justice Edward Douglass White said, "Mr. Brandeis, your time is up but we will consider that the clock has stopped and you may continue." The clerk of the Court told Warren later that he could not recall that ever being done before by a chief justice.

A few weeks later Brandeis argued his last case before the Supreme Court, defending a California eight-hour workday for women, which included certain exemptions, notably for registered nurses. Opponents attacked the measure, not on the grounds of the eight-hour limit, since after *Muller* that would have been impossible, but rather on the grounds that the exemptions constituted an arbitrary and unlawful exercise of the police power. Brandeis argued that the legislature had the authority to define the public good and, in doing so, could make reasonable exceptions to general rules in order to promote the public welfare. The unique nature of nurses' work clearly made this exemption reasonable. The Court accepted the argument and unanimously upheld the law.

The decision in the California case came down five weeks after the Court heard oral argument, but the justices could not make up their minds about the Oregon law, no matter how impressed they may have been with Brandeis's persuasive powers. When he learned about the California decision, he told Al that "the Court is having some trouble with the [Oregon] Minimum Wage Case." In fact, the justices let it sit for eighteen months, then restored it to the docket shortly after Brandeis joined the Court, and heard it reargued on January 1917. With Brandeis recusing himself because of his previous involvement in the case, the Court split 4–4, thus leaving in place, at least temporarily, the Oregon court decision upholding the law.

THE DEFENSE of protective legislation constitutes an important and enduring part of Louis Brandeis's legacy as a reformer. Regardless of how contemporary feminists view the hazards of gendered protective legislation, Brandeis provided a device by which lawyers could force courts, at the very least, to be aware of the relevant facts in a case. It would not work every time, and conservative justices could, when they had the votes, brush fact-laden briefs aside. But it could also give a willing court the rationale to create new doctrine in the absence of clear legislative intent or relevant law, as in *Brown v. Board of Education.* Brandeis himself considered his fight for protective legislation an important battle; in the midst of the nomination fight, he took time to answer a college student who needed information on the eight-hour day for a school debate, referring him to the National Consumers League and the material he and Josephine Goldmark had produced.

The call to public service resonated then among idealistic lawyers, and continues to do so today. While we will occasionally refer to a public-spirited lawyer taking on big interests as a people's attorney, that sobriquet will always and uniquely belong to Louis Brandeis.

CHAPTER TEN

DEMOCRACY IN THE WORKPLACE

His championship of regularity in employment and of protective legislation clearly marked Louis Brandeis as a friend of labor. Yet despite his opposition to big business and its abuses, he should not be mistaken for an unquestioning champion of labor or of labor unions. Here as in all areas of his life and work, Brandeis sought balance, rejecting the views of both those who trumpeted the unrestricted rights of business and property and those who saw powerful labor unions as the only antidote to corporate abuses. In the years that Brandeis worked as a lawyer and reformer, he came into frequent contact with labor, learned a great deal about the workplace and labor-management relations, and had opportunities to implement novel solutions to problems between workers and employers. Workingmen and workingwomen trusted him and applauded his role in *Muller* and other cases to defend hours and wages laws, but labor leaders like Samuel Gompers differed radically from Brandeis in regard to the rights and responsibilities of labor unions, and also scientific management.

AT THE TIME Brandeis began to practice in Boston, the law tended to look on labor unions with suspicion. In many states, courts found that striking workers could be charged with the common-law crime of conspiracy. Although Chief Justice Lemuel Shaw of Massachusetts wrote one of the rare decisions holding that workers could legally strike without committing conspiracy, few judges agreed with that view. Prosecutions for conspiracy did, however, slow around the time of the Civil War; strikes themselves remained technically legal, but convincing a jury that included workingmen of conspiracy proved increasingly difficult.

Beginning with the great railroad strikes of the 1870s, however, judges gave employers a far more potent weapon—the injunction—which did not require either proof of conspiracy or a jury trial. The injunction—an order by a judge to stop a strike or other labor demonstration—could be granted quickly, and if union leaders refused to obey, they could be summarily jailed for contempt of court. The Supreme Court endorsed the use of injunctions, no matter how broadly worded, in the *Debs* case of 1895, and not only gave businessmen and their lawyers, as well as conservative judges on the federal bench, a stronger weapon to use against labor but also expanded the jurisdiction of federal courts to include local labor disputes, even if they did not involve interstate commerce.

Anticipating what the economist John Kenneth Galbraith would later call "countervailing power," progressives supported labor unions and collective bargaining as a means of giving working people parity with their employers in the bargaining process. Reformers believed that the state's police powers justified intervention in contractual disparity; most judges, however, would have none of this, believing that mere inequality in the bargaining process, without specific evidence of health or safety considerations, did not justify state interference. The potential power of large labor unions scared both industrialists and conservative judges in the same way that the power of big corporations alarmed reformers. The militant American Federation of Labor struck them as a threat to individual rights and to a market in which employer and employee could freely negotiate a labor arrangement. The fact that such a market had disappeared years earlier did not matter to the courts, any more than that the economic model of Adam Smith, which they continued to use to describe the American economy, had long since vanished as well.

While courts at both the state and the federal levels gradually accepted the need for protective legislation, as the Supreme Court did in *Muller,* they continued to oppose labor unions, and this bias endured until the end of the 1930s. Only when Congress passed the Norris–La Guardia Act of 1932 did federal courts lose their power to issue injunctions in labor disputes, and it took the National Labor Relations Act, or Wagner Act, of 1935 to secure labor's right to organize and to bargain collectively. To say that prevailing business and public sentiment in the early twentieth century looked suspiciously at labor unions would be an understatement.

•   •   •

ASIDE FROM HIS WORK with the McElwain Shoe Company, Brandeis's first direct contact with labor unions seems to have been in connection with the great anthracite coal strike of 1902 and came about at the suggestion of Henry Demarest Lloyd. An influential reformer, writer, and activist, Lloyd had written *Wealth Against Commonwealth* in 1894. Considered the first muckraking work, the book exposed the machinations of the Standard Oil Company and how it used its monopolistic power to crush competitors. Brandeis had read the book shortly after it came out and would cite it frequently.

Trouble had been building in the Pennsylvania coalfields since May 1902. Over fifty thousand anthracite coal miners in northeastern Pennsylvania had joined the United Mine Workers and walked off their jobs, demanding a 10 to 20 percent increase in pay, recognition of the union, an eight-hour day, and other benefits. Six major railroads owned four-fifths of the coalfields, and two years earlier the roads had reluctantly given in to Mark Hanna's insistence that they settle a strike and not endanger William McKinley's reelection. Hanna had since retired, and the railroad presidents, headed by the truculent George F. Baer of the Reading, adamantly opposed even talking to the unions. Assuming that the public's demand for coal would eventually force the unions to back down, the railroads closed the mines, rejected all offers at mediation, and waited for the union to collapse. But the union president, the able John Mitchell, played his cards well. Financed by contributions from other unions, the coal miners held out. Mitchell articulated a public relations campaign exposing the hardships of mine work and the abuse suffered by the workers, so that both the Hearst and the Pulitzer chains, as well as many independent newspapers, backed the union and condemned the owners. As winter approached, however, with empty coal bins in schools, hospitals, and private homes, the price of coal rose from the usual $5 a ton to $14, and the demand grew for action to settle the strike.

Baer rejected a proposal for arbitration and, in a statement that angered many people, declared that "the rights and interests of the laboring man will be protected and cared for, not by the labor agitators, but by the Christian men to whom God in His infinite wisdom has given the control of the property interests of the country, and upon the successful management of which so much depends." Even conservatives rejected this Neanderthal view, and by early fall some newspapers had begun suggesting government control of the mines or, failing that, a federal law mandating binding arbitration.

Although President Theodore Roosevelt had initially refused to intervene, the growing public demand for action led him to convene a meeting at the White House in October, where, backed by J. P. Morgan, he forced the coal operators—through a threat to send troops and have the federal government take over the mines—to agree to an impartial investigatory commission and then to accept its findings. The workers in turn agreed to go back to work on 23 October.

Lloyd, a strong supporter of labor unions, had become involved with the United Mine Workers in their strike. He had earlier met Brandeis through a common acquaintance, the Boston editor and lecturer Edwin Doak Mead, and contacted him in late November 1902. Lloyd asked for his help in putting together the miners' case that would be presented to the commission. Although Brandeis had little prior experience in labor matters, he immediately agreed and, as he usually did, demanded information. He asked Lloyd to send him a variety of materials and then put his office staff to work researching the relevant federal and state laws that bore upon the mines and up on labor.

In early December he went to Scranton, Pennsylvania, and toured the coalfields with Lloyd and Clarence Darrow, the great Chicago lawyer who served as counsel to the union. Initially, Darrow and Lloyd wanted Brandeis to prepare a brief to be submitted to the commission arguing that the companies had earnings high enough to support the workers' demands, and for this he scoured the annual reports filed by the railroads with the Interstate Commerce Commission. This required a great deal of work, and Darrow rather tentatively asked what the fee would be. Brandeis promptly replied, "I shall be glad to give such assistance as I can and shall want no compensation other than satisfaction of having aided a good cause. I will let you have a memorandum of any disbursements."

Brandeis worked quickly, but because of other commitments could

Clarence Darrow

not return to Pennsylvania to meet personally with Darrow and Mitchell. He sent them a memorandum brief outlining the major points on 12 December, and a few days later a more elaborate law memorandum that detailed what he had been able to find out about the law and the rail-owned mines, of which, he declared, little existed. But Pennsylvania, like Massachusetts, did have some laws on the books regulating what other properties railroads might own in addition to their rights-of-way and rolling stock, and these did not include coal mines. Quite possibly, therefore, the railroads' very ownership of the mines might be illegal.

Although he doubted that either the unions or the railroads would act on his suggestion, Brandeis found a familiar evil present in the coalfields, irregularity of employment. His investigation into the coalfields found that the miners averaged only 181 days of work a year. "I feel very strongly," he told Darrow, "that one of the great evils from which the employees suffer is the lack of continuous occupation, and that it would be possible for the railroads, by some change in their method of doing business . . . to run their mines continuously, and with a practically average output each day." Coal mining, he believed, "is preeminently a business in which steady employment ought to be an industrial possibility."

Ultimately, despite all the work he put in, nothing came of his efforts. The railroads cleverly refused to assert that they could not afford the raise, thus forestalling any inquiries by the commission into their financial status. The last thing the railroad owners wanted was a public airing of their finances, which would have shown an already-hostile public that, with their very large profits, they could easily afford to meet the workers' demands. Brandeis had prepared to present his brief and testify before the commission, but it refused to hear anything regarding railroad income or to listen to any charges regarding the railroads' possibly illegal ownership of the mines. Disappointed that his work had gone for naught, he philosophically suggested to Lloyd, "Perhaps at some other time and in some other manner we can bring the facts effectively to the attention of the public."

The commission, although not hearing from Brandeis, did hold extensive sessions, and in May 1903 awarded the miners a 10 percent increase in pay, reduced hours from ten per day to nine in most instances and to eight in some jobs, but declined to recognize the union. In addition, to cover the increased labor costs, the commission recommended a 10 percent raise in the price of coal, which the mine owners quickly accepted. Today the strike is remembered primarily for the activism Theodore Roosevelt displayed in threatening to take over the mines, although he had not a shred of constitutional or statutory authority to do so.

BRANDEIS'S SOLUTION to the McElwain difficulties had drawn the attention of local labor advocates, and in 1902 he found himself invited to debate Samuel Gompers, the president of the American Federation of Labor, on the question "Shall Trade Unions Be Incorporated?" The program, under the auspices of the Economic Club of Boston, took place

Samuel Gompers, 1911

in the Tremont Temple on 4 December 1902, just before he left to tour the coalfields in Pennsylvania. It is the first time that Brandeis spoke publicly on his views about trade unions, but over the next few years he gave several addresses on organized labor and the issues confronting it; when he did so, he spoke from growing experience.

Labor unions opposed incorporation, since they would then have been liable to monetary damages in suits; as unincorporated associations of individuals, they stood relatively immune from this danger. Brandeis knew ahead of time, therefore, that an argument for incorporation would give the impression that he opposed unions. He started out trying to assuage this fear, saying that he not only favored unions but believed they had been instrumental in securing better hours, safer conditions, and higher wages for workers and in protecting women and children from "industrial oppression." Moreover, all of society, not just the workers, benefited from these achievements, and although many people did not realize it, employers also gained from union efforts to humanize the workplace. He quoted a "very wise and able" railroad president who said, "I need the labor union to protect me from my own arbitrariness."

Unfortunately, he continued, some in the labor movement acted irrationally and irresponsibly, and this reflected badly on all union members. The struggle to attain great ends "had often been attended by intolerable acts of violence, intimidation and oppression." Nonetheless, the goals of the labor movement, the improvement of the lives and working conditions of millions of men and women, could not be denied, and no greater instance of "enlightened self-sacrifice on so large a scale" could be found than when large numbers of workers voluntarily gave up their employment because their employer refused to recognize a union. "If you search for the heroes of peace," he told the audience, "you will find many among humble workmen who have braved idleness and poverty for principle."

Although the essence of a debate is to win the audience to one's position, Brandeis adopted none of the debater's tricks—no grandiose gestures or phrases, no sly undercutting of the opponent's points. Rather, he seems to have attempted to engage the audience in a conversation, talking to them calmly, almost dispassionately. He stood next to the podium, one arm resting on it and the other hand in his pocket. He and Gompers did not appear as enemies, he seemed to say, but rather all of them, including those who had come to listen, wanted to learn what would be best for unions and their members in the noble search for improving the lot of the nation's workers.

The problem, he explained, is that when strikes involved lawless conduct, the workers forfeited public sympathy. "The American people with their common sense, their desire for fair play and their respect for law, resent such conduct." Brandeis did not defend so much as explain the injunction and its use. Employers could not afford to wait until their property might be damaged or their businesses totally disrupted, especially by lawless acts, because what remedy would they then have? The injunction, moreover, had force behind it: imprisonment for any and all who disobeyed.

The question confronting labor unions, then, was how to neutralize this weapon. While an unincorporated union enjoyed immunity, it tended to make both officers and members reckless, committing lawless acts that alienated the public. Brandeis believed incorporation of unions to be the answer. An incorporated union would be a legal entity, capable of being sued but also of defending itself. While an employer could take a union to court, the union could then fight back, and in doing so expose the employer's guilt. There would be a jury, before which the union could explain why it had acted, and which would surely be more sympathetic than a single judge handing down an injunction at the behest of an employer.

One suspects that Brandeis here spoke more from hope and optimism than from a real grounding in the facts of life as they applied to unions at the turn of the twentieth century. Injunctions could still be issued, whether unions were incorporated or not. The fact that they could seek a jury trial meant little, since factory owners saw as their immediate need the necessity to protect their property and to undermine the unions, attitudes that would not be affected one whit by incorporation. In fact, the issuance of injunctions did not stop until Congress took away the power of federal courts to issue labor injunctions, and the abuse of labor unions continued until the federal government stepped in to back the right of workers to organize and bargain collectively.

Brandeis claimed to speak as a friend of labor, and there is no doubt that he saw himself that way. When it came to matters he considered moral in nature, such as corporate activities that defrauded the public, he could be uncompromisingly rigid and admired the Greek notion of balance, of finding a mean between extremes. He considered unions useful organizations, working to improve the lives of their members, but that did not mean he would unquestioningly accept all they did as legitimate. He also believed employers had rights and that the law should protect private property, but that did not lead him to an unthinking endorsement of injunctions and other anti-union devices. Just as private corporations had to act responsibly and in the public's interest, so, too, did labor unions. That evening, according to the *Boston Post,* a majority of the audience in the Tremont Temple seemed to agree with him.

OVER THE NEXT SEVERAL YEARS Brandeis grew more interested in labor matters, although he did not get involved as he did with the Boston Elevated or the New Haven. He saw savings bank insurance, however, not just as a means of reining in the big companies but also as a way to provide an essential service to working people at an affordable price. In that struggle he successfully brought in labor leaders and unions as part of the Savings Bank Insurance League, and their numbers, if nothing else, helped to sway skeptical lawmakers.

During these years Brandeis came into contact with union leaders such as John Tobin, president of the Boot and Shoe Workers' Union, and nonunion labor activists such as Mary Kenney O'Sullivan of Chicago's Hull House, who had come to Boston to help organize women's trade unions, and he made it clear during some local labor troubles that his sympathies lay with the workers. At the same time he also insisted that unions should act responsibly and, when they did not, took them to task, as he did in the 1904 printers' strike, when he served as counsel to the Boston Typothetae, the association of print shop owners.

In February 1901 the Typothetae and the Boston Typographical Union No. 13 had signed a three-year contract fixing the minimum wage at $16.00 a week for the first year and $16.50 for the next two. Before the contract had expired, the union demanded that the minimum wage be raised in 1904 to $19.00. Management in turn offered $17.00, and the typographers went out on strike. As Brandeis noted, the strike "was shockingly bad business," because if it lasted just three weeks, the workers would have lost the entirety of their dollar-a-week demand. Moreover, the union had no complaints about working conditions, hours, or any of the other issues that unions frequently fought about. Then the union did something that, according to Brandeis, "shocked the conscience."

The International Printing Pressmen and Assistants' Union, which represented non-typographical workers in the shops, had signed a four-year contract with the Typothetae that expressly forbade sympathy strikes. Martin Higgins, the head of the striking Boston Typographical Union, offered strike benefits to the second union that, in many instances, exceeded their wages, to induce pressmen and feeders, who had no grievances, to go out on strike. This, Brandeis declared, "was morally wrong. We believed it to be also illegal." Upon Brandeis's recommendation as their counsel, the Typothetae went into the Supreme Judicial Court of Massachusetts seeking redress, and the court issued an injunction against the strike. Although he believed the injunction to be a poor tool, in the absence of conscientious behavior by the union, he stood ready to utilize it on behalf of his clients.

The injunction marked the beginning of the end, but the real end came in a way far more humiliating to the workers. After the strike had continued five weeks, "and the men had lost twice the paltry sum for which alone they struck," the president and members of the executive committee of the International Typographical Union came to Boston to investigate the situation firsthand. They soon realized that the local leadership had erred grievously, and immediately called off the strike, accepting the $17 figure that the owners had originally offered. It was an ignominious end for Higgins and the local leaders, and for Brandeis an example of how labor unions ought not to act.

The Typothetae's annual banquet that year thus became a victory celebration, and they invited the man who had guided them through the fight to be their speaker. Brandeis knew his audience and believed that his clients, if not in the league of a William McElwain, nonetheless had over the years treated fairly with labor. Although they believed in an open shop, they also recognized the unions as bargaining agents for their workers, and ran their businesses with a concern for safety. So after congratulating them on a well-deserved victory, Brandeis turned to the future and told them what he believed would be necessary to make it an era of peace and prosperity. He laid out what he termed "broad principles which, in my opinion, should govern the relations of employer and employee in all branches of industry."

First, there had to be industrial liberty, which meant that employers could no longer act as masters expecting their workers to be serfs. "Industrial liberty must attend political liberty," and here we have the first statement of an idea that Brandeis was to develop over the next ten years. Political freedom cannot be built upon an economic base in which one group exercises complete domination over another, or in which economic opportunities are denied. The prosperity of the country, the vitality of its industry, would depend on how fairly employer treated employee, and how willing employers would be to give workers a say in the workplace.

Brandeis may well have had in mind the Filene's department store experiment in cooperation between management and labor. The Filene brothers, who also happened to be Brandeis clients, had founded the Filene Cooperative Association in 1901. The store experimented with such then-radical ideas as the employees' power to veto certain management policies, employee representation on the board of directors, and a free medical clinic. As a result, the store had prospered and had been free from labor strife. Brandeis monitored the enterprise, both for professional and for personal reasons, and often spoke to the workers as part of a lecture series they established to learn more about public affairs.

Second, the right of labor to organize ought to be recognized by law as well as by employers. Little possibility existed that optimal working conditions, a necessity for peace and prosperity, could be achieved without the work of the unions, nor could there be industrial democracy without the workers having a venue for their expression. While some employers feared strong unions, Brandeis assured his audience that strong unions acting honorably and responsibly would be the employers' greatest aid in securing the best work from their employees. Therefore, employers should not be reluctant to negotiate with union leaders. With honor and fairness on both sides, employers as well as employees would benefit.

There would, of course, be difficulties, issues on which labor and management would not see eye to eye. Brandeis recalled a story from his law school days, when "a very able man" who taught the law of partnership asked the class, "What shall be done if a controversy arises between partners?" One student after another suggested a legal remedy—a receiver, an injunction, a dissolution. "No," the professor replied, "they should try to agree." In essence, Brandeis told the Typothetae, they and their workers constituted a partnership, and unless both sides could go forward in harmony, their joint business ventures would suffer.

This notion that workers and owners formed a partnership would be refined by Brandeis for the rest of his life. He did not, of course, mean that they stood as actual partners, the way he and Sam Warren had been. He understood that in the sort of business that he represented—small- to middle-sized enterprises like a press shop or a department store or a shoe factory—unless the owners listened to worker complaints, unless they treated workers fairly, unless they allowed their workers to form a union, they would never get the full benefit of their workers' skills and abilities. Over the years his notion of industrial democracy expanded, and he grew more interested in the cooperative movement.

But although he favored the right to organize into unions and to bargain collectively, Brandeis never abandoned the theme he first enunciated in the debate with Samuel Gompers, and he ended his talk to the Typothetae on that note. For the partnership to succeed, for employers to recognize unions and to treat fairly with them, unions in turn had to act honorably and abjure acts of lawlessness and violence. Labor deserved a place at the table, but only if it practiced good table manners.

BRANDEIS EXPANDED ON these ideas, and yet, despite his role in the printers' strike, labor continued to see him as a man who respected labor and whose ideas on the rights of workers did not differ significantly from their own. In January 1906, for example, he spoke to the New England Civic Federation, an association of public-minded businessmen and professionals, on the necessity for shorter hours. He talked about relief from long workdays not in terms of a reduced strain on the workers but rather in terms of the worker's need to have time to enjoy life, to have recreation, and to be able to partake in civic functions. The notion of industrial democracy applied both within the workplace and without.

Brandeis said on many occasions that the highest office a person could aspire to in a democracy was that of citizen. To be a citizen, how-ever, involved not just rights but responsibilities. If one wanted to enjoy the fruits of a free society, then one had to fulfill the civic duties required, such as being abreast of current issues, attending public meetings of school boards or town councils, and, of course, voting. If people worked twelve or fourteen hours a day, how could one expect them to have the energy or the opportunity to fulfill their responsibili-ties, not just as citizens, but as parents and members of their communi-ties? Shorter hours, therefore, went far beyond the matter of the workday and affected the type of society we would have.

The following month, when he addressed the annual meeting of the Boston Central Labor Union, he took his message of support for unions and responsible action directly to the more than nine hundred delegates present. Unions had made many strides in the last few years, he said, and he applauded the greater acceptance that unions now had in the public's mind. But for labor to progress even further, he suggested, it needed to adopt some basic principles.

First, unions should strive to secure a share of all the profits of a com-pany beyond basic payouts, such as cost of materials, overhead such as plant and machinery, operating costs including utilities and taxes, salaries to management, and a fair return on investment. Beyond these fixed costs, workers ought to have a substantial share in the balance, or what we would today call profit sharing. Ironically, those who con-demned Brandeis in 1916 as unfit to sit on the bench because of his alleged radicalism never brought up this speech; in terms of labor pol-icy in 1906 he was indeed making a radical suggestion.

In order for workers to enjoy these fruits, however, unions had to do all they could to make businesses grow and operate more efficiently. There should be as few work stoppages as possible, and if workers came up with ideas as to how to make their labor more productive, these should be shared with the management. Unions should never seek to limit the production of individual workers. If some men or women worked harder or faster than others, they should be rewarded for doing so, and not made to work at the level of the least productive. If workers did this, if they labored diligently and honestly, then there would be no need for industrial espionage, the use of spies by manage-ment to see who shirked and who caused trouble. Trade unions, Bran-deis argued, should teach a worker that it is a disgrace to manhood to require watching.

Finally, but certainly not least, unions should demand steady work.

He repeated his belief that no matter how well paid workers might be, if they could not get steady work, then good wages for irregular work meant nothing. Time and again he would repeat this theme. "For every employee who is steady in his work," he once said, "there shall be steady work. The right to regularity in employment is co-equal with the right to regularity in the payment of rent, in the payment of interest on bonds, in the delivery to customers of the high quality of product contracted for. . . . No business is socially solvent which cannot do so."

The idea of profit sharing never caught on in a large way with American business, and workers did not receive a significantly larger share of industrial revenues until the heyday of unionism after World War II. Then unions, whose legal status had been confirmed by federal law, allowing them to act free from the fear of injunctions, exercised the muscle of their numbers, forcing companies to pay higher wages and to add fringe benefits such as retirement and health plans. While Brandeis would have applauded the fact that workers received better pay, and that most businesses could operate on a year-round basis with few seasonal layoffs, he would have argued that labor had not kept its share of the bargain he had proposed. Unions did not allow for individual workers to excel or to earn more, and in fact tried to keep all workers producing at a common level. Not until the economic crisis of cheaper imports, especially from Japan in the 1980s and 1990s, did more than a few American companies adopt policies seeking worker input in order to increase productivity. The fact that strong unions could act as badly as big companies, however, would not have surprised him.

ONE AREA WHERE Brandeis and labor parted company involved scientific management, which he believed in strongly and labor detested with equal fervor. Whereas Brandeis saw the idea as a means by which workers and management together could achieve the highest productivity with more money for both, labor saw it as a speedup, where they would have to work faster and harder for less reward.

While Brandeis was working on a problem for William McElwain, one of the shoe company's supervisors called his attention to an article by Frederick Winslow Taylor titled "Shop Management" that had appeared in the *Transactions of the American Society of Mechanical Engineers* in 1903. Intrigued by Taylor's ideas for promoting greater efficiency, Brandeis looked for other materials and soon came upon the works of Harrington Emerson, Henry L. Gantt, and Frank Gilbreth, all of whom he would work with in his 1910 call for American railroads to adopt principles of "scientific management," a name that he suggested and that soon gained popular acceptance.

Taylor and others worked out the basic premises of scientific management in the first decade of the twentieth century. Taylor saw that in the modern factory, much of the work was rote and repetitive; machines had replaced craftsmen, and the main job of most factory workers involved feeding materials into and tending the machines. But there still existed a large amount of work involving little more than brute force, the moving around of heavy articles or the casting of pig iron. Taylor believed that if one scientifically analyzed a job involving physical labor by breaking it into its components, then one could rearrange the manner in which the workers did the tasks to make them more efficient. This might involve changing the order of the tasks, the use of different tools, or the number of men on a job. Taylor went into the federal arsenal at Watertown, New York, using a stopwatch to time how long it took to do each chore, and then suggested a plan to restructure the work.

Taylor and followers like Frank Gilbreth (for whom Brandeis wrote the foreword to his *Primer of Scientific Management* in 1914), as well as advocates such as Brandeis, understood that people had different abilities and that the most efficient way for one person to work might not be the same for another. They also understood that the economic interests of labor and management were not identical, so that workers could well resent any plans that increased the profits of the owners at their expense. Taylor and others constantly argued that scientific management could not succeed unless the workers understood that they would share in the profits generated by their increased productivity. While that may have been the ideal, in practice managers who adopted parts of Taylor's ideas essentially tried to make their workers as machinelike as possible, and the greatest success would be found in the assembly line pioneered by Henry Ford. Each worker had one simple task that he or she would do over and over, such as tightening a nut on a wheel or installing a fender. The work became drudge labor, resented by workers as demeaning.

Scientific management fit into a larger movement within progressivism that sought to replace human irrationality with science and efficiency. Brandeis had been caught up as early as law school in this vision, when Langdell and others wanted to make the study of law akin to scientific investigation. In his fight with the New Haven, he insisted that basic rules of accounting, which he treated as a science, could not be ignored, and in *Muller* he presented a brief that invoked the latest scientific findings about women and labor.

Like Taylor, Brandeis saw scientific management not as a discrete process but as part of the larger question of labor-management relations. In his talk to the Central Labor Union, Brandeis had balanced his call for workers to share more in the profits with a demand that they work to their fullest potential to increase the company's earnings. In talking to the Typothetae, he had chastised labor for acting illegally and immorally, but still urged the printers to recognize the unions and to treat with them fairly. So, too, scientific management could not be a one-sided commitment. Owners could not expect to set up a regimen that made their workers more productive without at the same time sharing with them the fruits of their additional labor. "The workman," he explained, "is called upon to do the highest work of which he is capable, and also because in doing this better work he secures appropriate and substantial recognition and reward."

It sounds idealistic, of course, but Brandeis always believed that idealism could have pragmatic benefits. The McElwain factory, by adopting a system that gave the workforce regularity of employment, earned greater profits and enjoyed better relations with its employees. Filene's department store, by instituting a cooperative association, had done away with labor strife almost entirely and had benefited from workers' ideas on how to improve sales. But neither the McElwain company nor Filene's department store compared in size with any of the factories owned by U.S. Steel or International Harvester, and in most plants the owners wanted greater productivity but did not want to pay for it either in increased wages or in profit sharing. The industrial barons who owned and managed these gigantic operations had little use for idealism.

If properly implemented, Brandeis believed, scientific management could also work to increase industrial democracy. If workers had a say in how they worked, if they could see the fruits of their additional labor and ideas, they would also be more fit to carry out their responsibilities as citizens in the political world. Efficiency, he argued, had to be by consent. Even if one accepted the truths of Taylor's arguments, they would be of no value unless implemented, and this could not be done by imposing the process on an unwilling labor force.

Try as he might, Brandeis could never get labor leaders to endorse scientific management. Samuel Gompers opposed it, as did John Mitchell of the United Mine Workers. In an interview Mitchell called

Brandeis "a valued friend of labor" and "a deep thinker," but he thought his friend mistaken in advocating scientific management. Upon reading Mitchell's comments, Brandeis immediately wrote, urging him to rethink his position. "I am convinced that upon a full understanding of what scientific management seeks to accomplish you and other labor leaders would be the strongest supporters that the movement could have." In response to labor charges that Taylorism amounted to little more than speeding up production, Brandeis declared that scientific management removes obstacles to production, thus allowing the worker to "produce results alike beneficial to himself and to management." This proved to be an argument Brandeis could not win.

IN JUNE 1910, Brandeis wrote to his brother that things seemed very quiet. "I am in excellent shape," he told Alfred. "There is not overmuch work awaiting me. If a fellow will only stay away [from the office] long enough, leisure comes easy." He took a long weekend with Alice, Susan, and Elizabeth in Gorham, New Hampshire, and in July the family moved down to South Yarmouth for the summer. While there he received an urgent summons from Lincoln Filene. Could Brandeis come to New York to help settle the great New York garment workers' strike that had broken out on 7 July, a continuation of the three-month "uprising" of twenty thousand mostly female workers in 1909 that had forced about two-thirds of the employers to grant some of their demands? This time the garment makers' unions, backed by the American Federation of Labor, came fully prepared in terms of organization, finance, and public relations, and enjoyed near-universal support among the workers. In a vote taken at the beginning of July, of the 19,586 ballots counted, 18,771 called for a strike.

Unlike industries based in large factories, such as steel, or on a smaller level, shoe manufacturing, the garment business consisted of thousands of small operators. One needed only a few hundred dollars to buy some machinery and materials and rent a loft in which workers could make garments. Few of these "manufacturers" made an entire garment from scratch, but subcontracted with individuals who did buttonholes or zippers or other parts of the process. A man carrying a portable sewing machine on his shoulders was a common sight on New York's Lower East Side, men who would work by the day for any jobber who needed them. In many shops the workers had to pay for their own needles, thread, and even electricity. Indescribably bad and unsafe working conditions plagued the industry, and when 146 mostly young, immigrant women died in the Triangle Shirtwaist Company fire on 25 March 1911, few people expressed surprise, since any of hundreds of other workplaces in the area could just as easily have gone up in flames.

This anarchic situation also operated to thwart any extensive unionization, since it would have been hard to classify many of the men and women who worked there as employees, jobbers, subcontractors, or owners. The International Ladies' Garment Workers' Union (ILGWU) tried to organize the industry but with only partial success; many of the laborers belonged to locals united in the Joint Board of Cloak, Suit, and Skirt Makers of New York, which in turn had a loose affiliation with the ILGWU. The 1909 strike, however, finally convinced many workers and labor leaders that in cooperation there would be strength. Moreover, many of the Jewish laborers from eastern Europe had come with a socialist sensibility that now manifested itself in a militant union movement. There had been no organization for manufacturers either; in a cutthroat business the owners tended to be suspicious of sharing any information. Besides, a person who "owned" a shop on Monday could easily be back carrying his sewing machine on his shoulders by the end of the week.

Now, in the summer of 1910, workers demanded better wages and working conditions and a closed shop; that is, one in which employers could only hire union members. They also wanted an end to the abusive treatment they received at the hands of the shop owners and foremen. The Yiddish phrase *menglekhe bahandlungt*—"humane treatment"— became a common chant at rallies. Although the strike involved bread-and-butter issues, the workers also wanted to be treated decently. Bertha Elkins, a Russian immigrant, said, "I want something more than work and more than money. I want freedom." Had Louis Brandeis heard her, he would have understood exactly what she meant.

The bitterness among workers, the horrible working conditions, and the low wages swept aside any reservations about striking, and before long nearly all of the sixty thousand workers in the garment trades had walked out. Efforts by local officials to mediate failed completely. The employers formed the Cloak, Suit, and Skirt Manufacturers' Protective Association and as long as the strikers demanded a closed shop, would not even talk to the union representatives. Retail distributors, such as the Filene brothers in Boston, faced the prospect of not having any clothes to sell their customers once their current inventory had run out. Brandeis initially refused to go to New York. "I told him that I would

Demonstrators in the 1910 garment workers' strike

have nothing to do with any settlement of the strike involving the closed shop," he later explained. "I did not believe in it, and I thought it was un-American and unfair to both sides." On this issue Brandeis would not budge, then or later. He had no problem with workers electing a union to represent them, but he believed no qualified man should be denied a job because he had chosen not to join a union, nor should an employer have to forgo choosing a qualified worker for the absence of a union card.

Lincoln Filene went to New York and told his brother that he hoped to win over the employers' organization to secure Brandeis to represent it. "If I fail," he said, "it is my intention to get Gompers to secure Brandeis. It does not seem to me to make very much difference which side has him so long as one side gets him." Brandeis, he expected, would understand that both sides had legitimate claims and would insist on acting as counsel to the situation. If that could be arranged, the department store owner believed, Brandeis would also be able to fashion a settlement acceptable to all parties.

(Filene also had firsthand experience, since in 1907 Brandeis had acted as counsel for the Boston clothing manufacturers during a bitter strike. The union had then insisted on a closed shop, and Brandeis had worked long and hard—and ultimately in vain—to get the workers to give up that demand. When efforts at negotiation failed, he had gone to court and gotten an injunction barring picketing, which crushed the strike. Brandeis's efforts to get labor to cooperate and his well-known support for unions made him acceptable to the workers; his toughness and willingness to get an injunction appealed to the manufacturers.)

Both sides agreed to Filene's proposal of inviting Brandeis down to listen to their views. On Saturday, 23 July, Filene wired this "acceptance" to Brandeis, along with assurances that the closed shop would not be on the agenda. Brandeis left South Yarmouth and took the night train to New York. The next day he told Al, "I am trying to bring the parties into conference. It remains to be seen whether my journey will be as futile as that of the French king and his 40,000 men."

Although he had made clear that he would not get involved in negotiations that included a closed-shop provision, he now had to get the General Strike Committee, representing all of the different unions and locals, to agree as well, and apparently he did so that Sunday. He wrote to Julius Henry Cohen, the distinguished New York lawyer representing the protective association, enclosing a full list of the workers' demands. "All of the [union] officers understand fully that under this proposal the closed shop is not a subject which can be discussed at the conference." On Monday the manufacturers formally accepted the list as a basis for discussion, and the two sides agreed to begin the conference the next day. So far Filene's hopes that bringing Brandeis in would at the very least get the two sides to talk seemed to be panning out.

Brandeis's involvement almost ended at this point. On Tuesday morning the *New York Call* carried a victory statement by the protective association that Brandeis had come from Boston to act for the strikers without compensation. He has "acted as attorney in more than a score of strikes, in the majority of instances, acting for the employers." At his behest, the strikers had waived their demand for a closed shop, and it would not be a subject for discussion. The unions reacted furiously. They had not agreed to abandon their claim, but merely to shelve it for the present. They believed that if they could get Brandeis to help negotiate the other items, then they could come back and say that the closed shop still remained one of their demands. The spokesman for the workers, Abraham Rosenberg, accurately denied that Brandeis had been asked to act as their attorney or even offered to do so; he had been invited to see if the two sides could find some basis on which to begin negotiations. Rather than give up the closed shop, the workers would stay out for twenty weeks or more until they won.

At this point not only did the unions and employers stand as far apart as before, but the labor ranks threatened to split between the rad-

Lower East Side sweatshop, 1908

icals demanding the union shop and the moderates who wanted to win on the bread-and-butter issues. Things became so serious that Samuel Gompers came up to New York from Washington to help patch over the differences. Meyer London, the socialist and future congressman, acting as the attorney for the unions, and Julius Cohen, on behalf of the employers, now wired Brandeis inviting him to act as chair of the meeting. Brandeis agreed but could not get away for a few days, a ploy meant to make sure that no other unexpected explosion occurred. Finally, on Thursday, 28 July, the parties sat down for the first time at a conference table, London and Cohen, each with nine members of their parties, representing the two sides.

Edith Wyatt, a writer for the popular magazine *McClure's,* looked around the table and realized the great similarities among all those present—the labor people, the manufacturers, and the negotiators. Nearly all were Jewish. The union side included not only labor activists but intellectuals and socialists. On the management side sat some former union leaders, and nearly all of them had started out as workers in the sweatshops. This commonality of intellect, religion, and experience led many to be overly optimistic about the two sides' quickly reaching an agreement.

Brandeis started with the least contentious issues, delaying the more controversial matters until last. He hoped that reaching accord early on some matters would encourage further agreement down the road. He

Meyer London, attorney for the union, and his office staff, ca. 1908

let the representatives of each side talk as much as they wanted, but when it appeared that they had gotten to the same position, he would intervene to point that out, and move them along. Sometimes, however, no matter how long each side talked, they could not reach a compromise, and then he would propose an arrangement that gave each party something. Above all, by asking questions, by listening, by soothing tempers, he managed, at least for the first few days, to keep matters on an even keel. When Gompers returned to Washington, newspapers reported that an agreement would no doubt soon be forthcoming.

Then, on the third day, 30 July, J. B. Lennon, one of the union representatives, stood up and, before Brandeis could stop him, reiterated the demand for a closed shop. Brandeis immediately tried to avert disaster by pointing out that "Mr. Lennon understands . . . the whole conference proceeds upon the agreement that the closed shop shall not be one of the subjects discussed."

Meyer London responded that he believed that the subject of a closed shop could be brought up under the rubric of "remedies."

Brandeis: "It was my understanding that it could not be discussed at all."

London: "Even under the subject of remedies?"

Brandeis: "Under any circumstances; that it was one of the tabooed subjects, so far as this conference was concerned."

Recognizing a potential bombshell, Brandeis tried to defuse it, suggesting that perhaps, at a later time, one might discuss unions and shop rules. But he reminded the union side that when he had agreed to chair the conference, it had been on their strict assurances to him that the closed shop would not be on the table. Sensing that unless he could come up with a workable alternative the talks would collapse, he then introduced what he called a "preferential shop," an idea he had proposed earlier when he had acted as counsel for manufacturers in a 1907 strike by garment workers in Boston.

He spoke continuously, not stopping to allow either the union or the employer representatives to interrupt him. The "preferential shop," or, as he sometimes termed it, the "union shop," meant that "the manufacturers should, in the employment of labor hereafter, give the preference to union men, where the union men are equal in efficiency to any non-union applicants." Although the manufacturers said they would reluctantly agree, the union representatives backed Lennon and walked out. Brandeis went back to his hotel room to give each side a chance to think things over, but reported to his brother that there would probably be no settlement because of the union demand for a closed shop. Although Julius Cohen tried to keep the negotiations going, and even proposed an arrangement that incorporated a form of the preferential shop, the union representatives rejected it. The *Jewish Daily Forward*, the leading Yiddish newspaper in New York and a strong champion of labor, denounced the preferential shop as "the scab shop with honey and a sugar-coated poison pill," and set about raising a strike fund so the unions could reject Brandeis's plan. Labor leaders seemed caught between the desire to find a useful compromise and the demands of the radicals for all or nothing.

Brandeis washed his hands of the whole matter, and rejoined Alice, Susan, and Elizabeth at South Yarmouth. There he fended off calls on his time, watched with interest as Theodore Roosevelt returned from Africa and stumped around the country, testing the possibilities of a run for the presidency in 1912; and took care of Alice while she suffered through a bad episode of depression, from which she recovered fairly quickly. He said nothing about the garment strike.

While he and his family enjoyed the invigorating breezes of Cape Cod, others labored intensely in New York to end the strike. Moderate union leaders rejected Lennon's all-or-nothing approach and wanted to bring Brandeis back to represent them. The manufacturers went to court to see if they could get an injunction against the unions, although it might not have been very effective given the fragmented nature of the clothing industry. Meyer Bloomfield, a New York lawyer who had worked with Brandeis in setting up the conference, determined that until both sides showed a real willingness to negotiate, Brandeis should remain aloof. Henry Moskowitz, an influential New York social worker heavily involved in labor matters, seconded Bloomfield's strategy. Brandeis "has made a profound impression on both sides," Moskowitz wrote. "He will kill his standing with the workers if the judicial silence is broken."

As the strike dragged on through the hot weeks of August and strike funds ran low, suffering among the workers' families increased, as it did among the small manufacturers who had not received any income for several weeks. Even if the strike ended the next day, it would be a while before they could get their shops back in production and goods flowing to retailers. Edward Filene, still looking to end the strike, along with Moskowitz and Bloomfield appealed to two pillars of the American Jewish community for help—Jacob Schiff, the banker and philanthropist, and Louis Marshall, a leading New York lawyer and future head of the American Jewish Committee. When they asked Meyer London and Julius Cohen to meet, the two could hardly refuse. In the meeting, which Marshall ran, they revived Cohen's earlier draft, which had incorporated many of Brandeis's ideas. With both sides grown weary of the fight, Marshall finessed the language, applied pressure, and secured an agreement. What shall we call it? Cohen and London asked, since any title that seemed to favor one side over the other would immediately be suspect. "Why not call it a 'protocol,' " Marshall suggested. "Neither group will know what that means and it will achieve the result."

Under the settlement, garment workers secured higher wages, improved working conditions, the preferential union shop, and a joint board of sanitary control to hear complaints about safety and health conditions in the shops. Manufacturers gained labor stability since the workers promised not to strike but to take their disputes to a board of grievances and, if the matter could not be resolved there, to a three-member board of arbitration, consisting of one labor member, one manufacturer, and a neutral third party. Both sides agreed—in fact demanded—that Brandeis take the last position. He accepted and would be involved in its operation until he went on the Court in 1916. Similar agreements were signed in the Ladies' Tailors and Dressmakers trade in September 1911, and in the Waist and Dress Makers group in January 1913, and Brandeis accepted their invitations to head those arbitration panels as well. When Chicago clothing workers went on

Demonstrators in 1915 garment industry strike

strike, Jane Addams asked Brandeis to come out and mediate; he could not do so, because of other commitments, but recommended that she contact Lincoln Filene, Henry Moskowitz, or Meyer Bloomfield.

Both sides praised Brandeis for his role, although, as he modestly told Max Meyer, "I think we are all to be congratulated, and it is a satisfaction to know that there are so many who have contributed to the happy result." Although the intervention of Schiff and Marshall had saved the day, in the end the basic components of the protocol had all been outlined by Brandeis before the negotiations broke down, and while recognizing the efforts of others, he could take satisfaction in this. Over the next several years, efforts would be made, some successful and others less so, to replicate the agreement in other places and in other industries.

As always, Brandeis wanted to publicize this new means of settling labor strife. Too busy to write an article himself, he suggested to the editor of the *Outlook* that Henry Moskowitz be called upon for a piece. Brandeis himself later wrote about the protocol, gave interviews to reporters, and followed up with letters to journalists such as Lincoln Steffens and Ray Stannard Baker. "This seems to be the time to commence the campaign of education," he urged Baker. "The preferential union shop seems to be a way out of our present serious difficulty; we must pursue it unless a better way can be found. This could be made into a great human story. Would it not be possible for you to take it up?"

Judgment on the protocol is mixed. For its advocates, the compromise ushered in several years of peace and prosperity hitherto unknown in the garment industry, and the preferential union shop led many workers to join the ILGWU or one of the other unions serving the trade. Brandeis himself saw it as a prime example of democracy in action, and told a reporter that one could never bridge the wide gulf between capital and labor except on a democratic basis. The protocol represented a triumph of moderation and a willingness on both sides to meet halfway, or as he called it, in "the spirit of get-together." Others have been less charitable. One noted labor historian described the era of the protocol as an "armed truce in which unions and employers' associations jockeyed for advantage and ultimate power." This is probably fair, but given the chaotic, indeed anarchic, conditions in the garment trades at the time, it may have been the best that anyone could achieve.

The protocol weakened during the economic recession of 1914–1915. The unions did not become strong enough to maintain discipline over unruly locals—a condition Brandeis had earlier recognized—and sporadic strikes led to an employers' lockout in April 1916. This in turn triggered a large-scale strike, and the arrangement collapsed. Brandeis lamented its demise, but he had never seen it as the end stage of labor-management relations. He praised workers and manufacturers for being open-minded enough to attempt the experiment, for that is what it had been, and not all experiments lead to complete success. He believed that if he or another strong person had been at the head of the arbitration panel, the protocol might have continued, but in a way that would have defeated its purpose. Arbitration had been intended as the last measure when all else failed; if the lower levels of conflict resolution broke down, then the system itself could not survive. As he told Lincoln Filene in relation to the Filene Cooperative Association's board of appeals, "An Arbitration Board is a very good thing to have, but it should be used as little as possible."

NO DOUBT THE SUCCESSFUL conclusion of the garment strike marked the high point of Brandeis's role as a labor mediator, a role he had taken on a handful of times in Boston, usually as counsel to one of his manufacturing clients. The protocol implemented many of the lessons he had been preaching over the past decade—recognition of unions, fair treatment of workers, and union responsibility—but from a personal view, the strike exposed him to a type of Jew new to Brandeis.

Eastern European Jews had, of course, migrated into the Boston area, where they worked for local garment manufacturers and in other trades, but Brandeis had no reason to meet or deal with them directly. His involvement in Boston Jewish affairs had been limited to modest contributions to Jewish charities and occasional consulting with one of the community organizations over policy questions. His Jewish clients belonged to the earlier German migration of the midcentury, people like his own family, and his business with them concerned commercial transactions.

The great mass of Jewish immigration from eastern Europe after 1880 had flooded into New York, and both workers and shop owners in the garment business had gotten off the boats together. Many of the bosses had been workers themselves, and the negotiations amazed Brandeis as workers and manufacturers shouted at each other across the table in Yiddish, which he more or less understood because of his fluency in German. Some of the workers may have complained about the serflike status that they, and especially the women, endured in the shops, but at the conference table Brandeis saw more of what he termed "industrial democracy" than he had ever witnessed before. These workers, many of them literate and articulate, felt no sense of inferiority to their employers and treated them as equals. Certainly in Boston he had never heard a labor man yell at his boss, *"Ihr darft sich shemen! Passt dos far a Idn?"*—"Shame on you! Is this worthy of a Jew?" Workers and shop owners quoted the Bible and the Talmud at each other, and he heard one man shout at his employer in the words of Isaiah, "It is you who have devoured the vineyard, the spoil of the poor is in your house. What do you mean by crushing My people, by grinding the face of the poor?"

Later, when he joined the Zionist movement (see chapter 17) and people asked him how he had come to that decision, he insisted that he had come back to his people through his Americanism, and cited the democracy he saw at work in the garment strike.

CHAPTER ELEVEN

THE PINCHOT-BALLINGER
AFFAIR

On 7 January 1910, Louis Brandeis found himself with a new client, Robert J. Collier. The magazine publisher and his editor, Norman Hapgood, were no strangers either to the Boston attorney or to political controversy. (Brandeis had placed his important savings bank insurance piece with Hapgood.) *Collier's* magazine had run more than a fair share of muckraking articles attacking corruption in both big business and government, but its latest venture into airing the foibles of the powerful had triggered a congressional investigation, and Collier worried that it could expose his magazine to libel charges. Collier chose Brandeis after a conference at which a number of names were proposed. In the end, Norman Hapgood suggested Brandeis for the simple reason that he would be the one most likely to win the case. That argument carried the day. Over the next several months Brandeis practically lived in Washington, returning home on Saturday night and going back the following evening. His investigation of the Taft administration's efforts to cover up a controversial firing added to his reputation and set the stage for six heady years of involvement in national reform and politics, culminating in his appointment to the Supreme Court.

Although the Pinchot-Ballinger affair is often depicted as primarily a fight between protectors of the environment and robber barons who would despoil it, the evidence suggests Brandeis may not have understood the basic issues in the case, insofar as they involved competing philosophies of both conservation and management. He found that Taft had deliberately misdated a letter, and Brandeis focused—one might even say fixated—on that issue to the exclusion of other large and important matters. This does not mean that President Taft acted wisely or correctly in what he did, but rather a debate that should have resulted about conserving the nation's resources never took place.

In part this resulted from the role Brandeis accepted—lawyer for Collier—and he did not try, as he had in other instances, to be counsel to the situation. He had been retained to defend Collier's interests, and the publisher paid him handsomely for his services, $5,000 a month plus expenses. His involvement with conservation issues proved very limited, and it never engaged his interest as did his other reforms.

FIRST THE FACTS, or the facts as Brandeis would have seen them in January 1910.

In the latter part of the nineteenth century, Americans became aware that their march across the frontier and the industrialization of the nation had begun to imperil some of the natural resources they had always taken for granted and believed to exist in infinite supply. In 1872, Congress created the first national park, Yellowstone, covering two million acres in Wyoming, Montana, and Idaho. Although both Benjamin Harrison and Grover Cleveland withdrew federal lands that became national parks and monuments, the conservation movement languished until Theodore Roosevelt took office in late 1901. A young man named Gifford Pinchot, who had studied forestry in France and then almost single-handedly introduced that science into the United States, caught Roosevelt's attention and converted him into a champion of conservation. A major section of Roosevelt's first message to Congress dealt with conservation, and during his administration he established six national parks and sixteen national monuments. In 1901, the government held 45 million acres in government preserves; by the time Roosevelt left office in March 1909, he had added 150 million acres. Roosevelt's conservation program proved to be among his most enduring achievements. Much of that credit belongs to Pinchot, who, as head of the U.S. Forest Service, had created an informal network among several departments to facilitate the withdrawal of lands.

William Howard Taft, Roosevelt's handpicked successor for the White House, promised during the 1908 campaign that he would continue these policies, but many conservationists took alarm when Taft replaced James R. Garfield with Richard A. Ballinger as secretary of the interior. The president, upon Ballinger's advice, also eased out a number of officials in the Interior, Agriculture, and Justice departments who had played key roles in facilitating the removal of public lands to a protected status during the Roosevelt administration. Both Ballinger and the new attorney general, George W. Wickersham, had ties to firms such as the Aluminum Company of America that had long sought open access to public lands to exploit mineral resources and waterpower.

In August 1909, Louis R. Glavis, a field division chief in the General Land Office, informed Ballinger that he had doubts about the legality of the so-called Cunningham claims, in which the Guggenheim mining interests planned to develop Alaskan coalfields that constituted about 15 percent of the Bering River coalfields. These claims had initially been validated by Ballinger himself, back when he served as commissioner of the General Land Office in 1907. A subsequent investigation by federal agents charged that the Cunningham claimants had broken the law by collusive action, and that they planned to sell off some of these lands to a Morgan-Guggenheim syndicate after they had been clear-listed, another violation of federal law. Nonetheless, Ballinger insisted on clear-listing the claims, only to have to reverse himself on the direct orders of Secretary of the Interior Garfield.

Ballinger had left the post of commissioner in 1908, and Glavis, who had been part of the federal team investigating the patents, obtained further evidence that collusion existed; he also found a copy of a contract between the Cunningham group and the Morgan-Guggenheim syndicate. In the meantime, Ballinger accepted a fee to represent the claimants before his old agency, the General Land Office. A short time after Ballinger became secretary of the interior in March 1909, he removed Glavis from the investigation on the grounds that he was moving too slowly. Ballinger apparently believed that an expedited examination would clear the Cunninghams of any allegation of wrongdoing and confirm their claims. At this point Glavis took his story to Pinchot.

Taft had kept Pinchot on as head of the U.S. Forest Service. The "Forester," as everyone called him, took advantage of his direct access to the White House and presented Glavis's charges to Taft, who in turn requested a reply from Ballinger. Ballinger, accompanied by Assistant Attorney General Oscar Lawler, went to see Taft at the president's summer home in Beverly, Massachusetts, with an enormous collection of documentary material. On 13 September, Taft gave the press a lengthy statement in the form of a letter to Ballinger fully exonerating his interior secretary of any charges of wrongdoing and authorizing the dismissal of Glavis from his post. Taft recognized that it could split the party if conservationists saw this as an attack on those policies championed by Roosevelt and Pinchot, so he appealed to the Forester not to let this minor incident mar their good relationship.

This ought to have been the end of a trivial dispute had not both Pinchot and Glavis been so determinedly self-righteous and convinced that Ballinger—and Taft—had undermined the conservation movement. Even as Taft tried to calm the Forester down, Glavis gave his denunciation to *Collier's,* which published it in the 13 November 1909 issue with such striking subtitles as "The Whitewashing of Ballinger." The cover ran a banner asking, "Are the Guggenheims in Charge of the Department of the Interior?" with the head of Richard Ballinger in the crook of the question mark. Glavis, who refused any money for

Secretary of the Interior Richard A. Ballinger, 1911

the article, very carefully avoided any direct charges of criminality. Pinchot kept up his criticism of Ballinger and of the administration's public lands policy, and wrote a letter to Senator Jonathan P. Dolliver (R-Iowa) admitting that the U.S. Forest Service had been supplying anti-Ballinger material to the press, praising Glavis, and indicting the interior secretary as a foe of conservation. Dolliver read it on the floor of the Senate, and Taft now had no choice but to dismiss Pinchot.

The public uproar over the article led to a congressional investigation of the charges. Given the Republican majorities in both houses of Congress, the administration felt confident it could control the hearings. But Collier had Brandeis, and although Pinchot retained the noted Philadelphia lawyer George Wharton Pepper to represent him, he joined with Collier, and Pepper let Brandeis take the lead. Collier secured the services of Joseph Cotton Jr., a top New York lawyer, to represent Glavis, who also agreed to let Brandeis direct the case. With Cotton came one of his associates, George Rublee, a school classmate of Norman Hapgood's who would quickly become Brandeis's right-hand man, both in the Interior Department hearings and later in drafting legislation for the Wilson administration.

Taft also failed to take into account the growing revolt in both chambers by progressive Republicans, led by men such as Robert La Follette in the Senate and George W. Norris in the House. George Rublee believed that the intensity of the Pinchot-Ballinger investigation grew out of this insurgency as much as from conservationists opposed to the Taft-Ballinger policies. Brandeis clearly understood this. He recognized that in order to vindicate his client, he would have to prove Glavis's charges, but from the beginning he appreciated the political nature of the hearings and managed them brilliantly. The Republican members of the committee expected the *Collier's* team to allege fraud, and they believed that such a charge could not be proved. Brandeis adopted a different strategy, one that gave him a great deal more flexibility and also allowed him to bring in issues separate from the Glavis charges. "We're not trying to prove a fraud," he said, "we're just trying to protect the public interest."

THE COMMITTEE MET for the first time on 26 January 1910, chaired by Knute Nelson, the longtime Republican senator from Minnesota. Although some of the conservation forces saw him as an enemy because of his close ties to the Taft administration—Gifford Pinchot later called him "Old Guard to the finger tips"—Nelson's reputation is actually more that of a progressive, albeit not in the same league as Robert La Follette or George Norris. Given the circumstances, Brandeis had little to complain about in regard to Nelson's conduct of the hearings. There would, of course, be disputes over the massive amount of documents that Brandeis wanted from the Interior Department, and Nelson would have no truck with Brandeis's efforts to get documents related to the president. "I had a private tussle with Senator Nelson," he told Alfred, "but won my point & relations are diplomatically friendly."

In his first weeks of studying the case, Brandeis had the benefit of information supplied by both Glavis and Pinchot, in the form of copies of letters and memoranda, as well as notes on specific events and documents. Utilizing this material, on 27 January, Brandeis sent the first of many letters requesting information from the Interior Department, including letters specified by date and correspondent, as well as related material. Number 4 out of a list of twenty-five items read, "Original letter of L. R. Glavis to commissioner, November 12, 1907, and all other papers on file in the General Land Office relating to soldier's additional application No. 69 therein referred to." Number 5 asked for the daily reports and report books for "Special Agent H. K. Love, June 15, 1907, to date of retirement from service." No. 7 referred to "all letters or telegrams received from and copies of letters and telegrams sent bearing date between November 23, 1907, and December 7, 1907, between L. R. Glavis and Fred Dennett, assistant commissioner, or personally, or H. H. Schwartz, chief of field division, or personally in relation to Alaska coal lands." None of the items in these letters referred to the White House, and so did not fall under the rubric of executive privilege. While much of this material involved the internal administrative workings of the Interior Department, none of it would, in modern parlance, be "classified." Brandeis gave enough specifics so that he could not be accused of going on a fishing expedition, but by asking for all materials related to certain documents, events, or persons, he no doubt hoped to uncover evidence supporting Glavis in the secondary material.

Conservationist leader Gifford Pinchot, 1921

Upon receipt of the material Brandeis went over it page by page, making new lists of documents to be submitted to the committee. As Norman Hapgood later wrote, everyone agreed that Brandeis should take the lead because he fully understood the facts. "The business of the Land Office, and of the Interior department generally, is very complicated indeed," Hapgood wrote.

> The only person who was held to understand it in detail was a permanent official named [Edward] Finney; and he was the most important witness in defense of Ballinger. When Brandeis had finished cross-examining him, Finney came impulsively over to where I was sitting in the committee room, and exclaimed, "Mr. Hapgood, I have no respect for you. I think you are doing this to make circulation for your paper. But I want to say you have a wonderful lawyer. He knows the business of the department today as well as I do."

Brandeis led Pinchot, Glavis, and other witnesses through their testimony and appeared very happy with the results. Glavis, he said, "has proved an extraordinary witness. Have never seen his equal. Der junge

Mensch is only 26." He gave Pinchot his head, and in his initial testimony Pinchot made quite clear the points he wanted the committee to understand: Ballinger had become interior secretary determined to undo Theodore Roosevelt's conservation policy; Glavis had been telling the truth about Ballinger and the Cunningham claims all along, and had been ill-treated for his integrity; and the Taft administration had adopted the position of placing the political and legal burden on those who would protect the environment rather than on those who would despoil it. "We had a great day yesterday," Louis told Alfred. "Pinchot's charge was fine & impressive."

Brandeis knew that while the major newspapers all carried stories about the hearings, much of the material would appear complicated to the average reader. So he utilized his contacts with reporters to get them to write stories setting out the charges against Ballinger in plainer language. Norman Hapgood, of course, ran one or more pieces in every issue of *Collier's* magazine, and to ensure accuracy, as well as not to endanger the case, he sent them to Brandeis ahead of time. The Boston attorney made time to read, comment on, and occasionally emend these writings, and also alerted Hapgood as to matters he intended to bring up, so that the editor could start working on those articles.

At the time, the influential New York *Evening Post* and the *Nation*, both owned by Oswald Garrison Villard, had been rather skeptical of the Glavis charges and had been running editorials supportive of the administration. George Rublee knew Villard and with Brandeis's blessing went up to meet with him. Villard agreed that there might be something to the charges and directed his editor to talk with Rublee, who then spent three days going over the testimony point by point. Convinced by this evidence, the paper and the magazine came out with strong editorials favoring Collier, and sent a reporter down to Washington to cover the investigation in person. Rublee believed that once the *Post* came over, the tide turned, and soon other papers that had been hostile, such as the *Springfield Republican,* also changed sides.

Ballinger may have intended to take the stand early to defend himself, but after learning how Brandeis had, on cross-examination, tripped up every witness testifying for the interior secretary into making damning admissions, he decided not to appear until the end of the hearings. Adolph Behrens, for example, had been called by John J. Vertrees, the lawyer representing Ballinger, in order to undermine part of Glavis's testimony. Instead, in his cross-examination of the Seattle real estate speculator, Brandeis discredited Behrens, caught him out in embarrassing lapses of memory about specific events, and then showed his connection to fraudulent Alaskan land claims. "The enemy fell into every trap set," he wrote, and Ballinger's refusal to go on the stand "is better for us than if we had the immediate chance to flay him, which might have resulted in our getting some severe kicks." The rest of the administration witnesses had been nothing but fun, and "Keith's Continuous Vaudeville couldn't compete for a minute." It kept me "laughing 6 hours long & I had to go out to the La Follettes to let off the accumulated merriment."

The hearings, far from being controlled by the administration, turned into a major embarrassment for Taft and his allies. Toward the end of March, Louis ran into his former brother-in-law Charles Nagel, now Taft's secretary of commerce and labor. They met outside the new Willard Hotel on Pennsylvania Avenue, and Nagel seemed uncomfortable. The two men made some small talk—what Louis's old Latin teacher in Dresden called "allotries"—and chatted about Nagel's daughter, Hildegard; Charlie "was pleasant enough; but he looks worn & troubled." The Taft people are "up against it," and the president "can make more mistakes in a week than the rest of them can remedy in a year." In fact, Taft's troubles would soon escalate.

BY MID-FEBRUARY, Brandeis, Collier, and Pinchot could feel fairly certain that regardless of the final committee vote, they had made their case regarding the veracity of Louis Glavis's charges, and that the Interior Department had been less than vigorous in protecting the nation's natural resources. Taft, however, had stood by Ballinger, and many wondered how much longer the secretary would enjoy the president's confidence. Initially, Brandeis suspected Taft of little more than political maladroitness. The president, Louis had told his brother, "is getting into an ever more uncomfortable position & seems ever more foolish in his actions."

Then one night Brandeis called Norman Hapgood and asked him to go out for a walk with him. When Hapgood arrived, he found the Boston lawyer "excited as I have seldom seen him." He swore the editor to secrecy, because he had come up with a theory that seemed "so theatrical" that he did not want anyone else to know until he could prove it. In going over the documents, Brandeis had noticed a number of discrepancies in the dates relating to when the attorney general and the president had gotten certain information, and he had concluded that

Taft could not possibly have studied all of the documents delivered to him. The report had been predated, and Taft had lied about the care he had supposedly given to the matter. The problem would be how to prove it.

Sometime in the third week of February, Brandeis dined with the former interior secretary James R. Garfield and met Frederick M. Kerby, who had been private secretary to Garfield and had then been kept on by Ballinger. Kerby told Brandeis that when Ballinger had gone to see Taft in Beverly the preceding September, he took with him a memorandum prepared by Oscar Lawler, the assistant attorney general who served as the Interior Department's chief counsel. That document fully exonerated Ballinger from Glavis's charges. Taft essentially adopted the Lawler memorandum and a few days later released it over his name. Kerby's story confirmed Brandeis's suspicions: the president had lied and had been a collaborator in Ballinger's efforts to defraud the public. As far as Brandeis was concerned, Taft had committed a sin even greater than those charged against Ballinger; he had violated the public trust and lied to the American people. Had Kerby come forward at that time, it would have been easy enough to prove his allegations, but Kerby had a family to support and could not afford to lose his job. Brandeis would have to prove the charge but with evidence from other sources.

On 21 March, he sent Senator Nelson another request, but not for Interior Department material. This time he wanted documents from Attorney General George Wickersham, "written, dictated or made prior to September 20, 1909 and sent or submitted by him to the President, his private secretary or other assistant or which were received by the Attorney General or any assistant from the President, private secretary, or any other person."

Here Brandeis surely trod on dangerous ground. Ever since the days of Chief Justice John Marshall, the courts had recognized an executive privilege, one in which a president could withhold documents from Congress because they involved discussions with his advisers. The rationale had been that if people speaking or corresponding with the chief executive feared that their advice or their views on events or persons could be made public, they would refuse to be candid, and thus deprive the president of important advice needed to make a decision. Moreover, while Collier, Pinchot, and others always understood that Taft, as president, bore the ultimate responsibility for the actions of his cabinet members, they had never planned on attacking him directly. To show Ballinger up and prove the charges against him would be enough of an assault on the administration.

In fact, the move made Robert Collier a bit nervous, and he asked Brandeis how much longer the hearings would continue. While well-to-do, the publisher did not have unlimited resources, and the monthly fee of $5,000 had been adding up; perhaps a subordinate, someone like George Rublee, could take over the work. However, if Brandeis in his judgment felt he needed to stay with the case, then he should do so. Brandeis assured his client that the investigation

Attorney General George W. Wickersham, 1909

would not "drag along for many months," and he believed it would be over by the end of May. But he would, if possible, hand over some of the work. "Indeed, my Boston interests are so clamorous, that it must be done."

Brandeis in fact had other reasons for ending the work as soon as possible, including loneliness for his wife. In his daily letters he reported about the people he met, the latest political gossip, and doings at the La Follette home. He spent one evening with Justice and Mrs. Holmes, "where we dined aux trios as of old, with most cordial reception." So cordial, he confessed, that "I was led to talk far more than is my wont, or at least, intention. Indeed this Washington Solitude is making me fearfully social." He missed Alice, who, enjoying a period of good health at this time, gladly gave in to her husband's importuning and came down to spend some time with him in Washington. She reported that although Louis "is enjoying the experience, I think he is getting a bit tired of it now and would be glad to be getting home." But with the change in focus from Ballinger to Taft, she figured the prospect of his return "is rather far off."

Indeed, taking on Taft altered the tone of the hearings and also raised the ire of regular Republicans against Brandeis. "I understand Wickersham is very hot against me," he told Al, and he noted that the attorney general had become Taft's chief adviser, leading the attack against reformers within the Republican Party. To Alice he wrote, "I am becoming much hated for the vigor of my attack, & think Ballinger et al. regard me with quite as much disfavor as the New Haven crowd." To some extent he returned the favor, and when he learned that several measures backed by the president had failed to win congressional approval, he noted that the suppression of "Taft measures is a great satisfaction. Like Indians, only dead Taft measures are safe."

When his brother worried that perhaps Louis had for once taken on too powerful an enemy, he replied in what was for him a rare moment of introspection:

> There is nothing for us to do but to follow the trail of evil wherever it extends. Fiat Iustitia! [Let justice be done!] In the fight against special interest we shall receive no quarter and may as well make up our minds to give none. It is a hard fight. The man with the hatchet is the only one who has a chance of winning in the end. This chance is none too good. There is a chance—but a chance merely—that the people will now reverse all history and be able to control. The chance is worth taking, because there is nothing left for the self-respecting man to do. But every attempt to deal mercifully with the special interests during the fight simply results in their taking advantage of the merciful.

There is a note of self-righteousness here, as well as one of despair. The world is not a fair place, and those who have the money and the power will do all they can to get even more. Most people had already given up and made the best bargain they could just to survive in such an environment. But Brandeis could not. He had to fight, he had to try to see justice done, and he could not be merciful in this fight. Several years later when he went on the Court, his wife referred to these years—and to these fights—as his time of knight-errantry. Surely Louis Brandeis never saw himself as a Don Quixote, and did not consider himself a Galahad either. At his death Felix Frankfurter compared him to Bunyan's Mr. Valiant-for-Truth. Brandeis did make all of his reform efforts into moral struggles, and this no doubt gave him the internal strength to carry on against great odds.

TO PROVE KERBY'S ALLEGATION, Brandeis had to show that Taft could not possibly have read the material, digested it, and then written the report exonerating Ballinger. Glavis and Pinchot had seen Taft at Beverly on 18 August 1909. On 6 September, Ballinger and Oscar Lawler went to the president and brought with them the large number of documents that supposedly answered all of Glavis's accusations. The material, which Taft eventually turned over to the committee, ran 661 pages of small type in the hearings report. One week later, on 13 September, the president issued his letter exonerating Ballinger. Brandeis had carefully read all of this material, as well as a "Summary" and a "Separate Report" prepared by Attorney General Wickersham dated 11 September, which filled an additional 87 pages of the report, and it had taken him many hours to do so. Had either Taft or Wickersham done nothing else between Ballinger's visit on 6 September and the issuance of the letter a week later, then possibly they might have done what they had claimed—read the material, prepared a report, and dictated the letter.

As Alpheus Mason wrote, "Brandeis knew only one man who could have done that job in that time, and his name was not Wickersham." Moreover, he knew that during that week the attorney general had been heavily involved in preparing amendments to the Interstate Commerce Act. As for Taft, the daily press always carried a report on what the president of the United States had done, with whom he had met, and when he had played golf, and by examining these reports, one could piece together the president's schedule between 6 and 13 September. Brandeis and Hapgood began collecting news clippings from that period, from which they would painstakingly re-create Taft's daily schedule, as well as those of some of his associates, sometimes down to the minute.

At the same time, in his cross-examination of witnesses, Brandeis began to ask whether a letter had been prepared for Taft, and if so, when? When Edward Finney, the head of the General Land Office and a Ballinger ally, took the stand on 22 April, Brandeis managed to elicit the fact that a report had been written, but that Finney did not know when that had been. "There was a fearful pall on the assembled company when the point was developed," he told Alice. But there had been no denial from either the Justice Department or the White House.

A week later he pressed the committee members to insist on having the attorney general provide the materials he had requested, but they turned him down by a vote of 7–5 along party lines, a vote that Brandeis would continue to run into for the rest of the hearings. "Everything points to our leaving them caught in a trap," he told Alice, and so he would have to seek help from his allies elsewhere. At his request, insurgents introduced a resolution in the House on 2 May echoing the demand for papers that Brandeis had earlier sent to Senator Nelson. This time Wickersham responded in an angry letter, denying any wrongdoing. Even so, he would not comply with the request, since "due regard for the constitutional authority of the Executive forbids that the action of the President and his advisor shall be called into question by a co-ordinate branch of government in any way." Brandeis could not answer the constitutional argument, but he became even more convinced that the administration had engaged in a major deception of the American people.

Finally, on 29 April, Richard Ballinger took the stand and immediately went on the attack, denouncing "lies" and "liars." As Brandeis prepared to cross-examine him, he turned to George Rublee and said, "Hold my hand." Rather than go immediately to the Glavis charges, Brandeis picked up on the interior secretary's insistence that he and all other members of the Taft administration had always been guided by a scrupulous adherence to the law. Why then, Brandeis wanted to know, had he written a letter to a subordinate ordering that all appointments in the Interior Department not filled directly by the president be referred to the postmaster general, Frank Hitchcock, who controlled political patronage? Where, Brandeis wanted to know, did the law state that positions exempted from civil service because of requirements of special knowledge—expertise in coal and minerals—should be filled on the basis of political service, a clear reversal of the policy that had existed under Secretary Garfield? After trying to dismiss the question, Ballinger practically snarled at his foe that such appointments were "a matter of my own concern which I do not propose to state anything further about." In a little over a minute, Brandeis had essentially shown that Ballinger, and by extension the administration, had no respect for the law they had sworn to uphold.

Ballinger from that point on must surely have regretted that he had agreed to appear on the stand. After friendly questioning from Vertrees, in which he had been tossed one softball after another, Ballinger now faced Brandeis, who attacked him on everything he said, forcing him to make corrections, or claim that he had never done something, only to be confronted with the testimony of another witness who said he had done just that. He denied that he had ever acted as counsel to the Cunninghams, only to have Brandeis produce a letter from the former governor of Washington, allied with the Cunninghams, identifying Ballinger as "counsel for our people."

Eventually, Brandeis raised the issue of whether a memorandum had been prepared by Oscar Lawler and delivered to Taft in Beverly on 1 3 September, and after denying that he knew anything about such a memorandum, or what had happened to it, Ballinger reluctantly conceded that Lawler had with him "a sort of résumé of the facts as set forth in the records." Brandeis would not let go, and eventually Ballinger admitted that the report had been prepared at Taft's request and that Ballinger had carefully gone over it. As Brandeis forced one concession after another out of the secretary, Ballinger, who had been on edge since the cross-examination started, would flare up in anger against his accusers. At one point Brandeis cautioned him, "Mr. Secretary, if I may be allowed to suggest, I think the committee is more desirous of light than heat."

In the cross-examination Brandeis showed why opponents feared him as an adversary. Never raising his voice, never engaging in personal attack, he stuck to the points like a bulldog. When Ballinger claimed he could not remember, or misstated events, or refused to make a direct reply, Brandeis simply asked the stenographer to repeat the question. Ballinger's patience, or what little he had left of it, snapped when Brandeis referred to a letter in which the secretary had declared that he intended to "kill some snakes" in the Interior Department.

"When it comes to snake-killing," Ballinger shouted, "I want to say that if I stay at the head of the Department they are going to be killed, and I am going to administer that Department as I consider it should be administered, with loyal support from every man in it, and I want it understood that I am serving notice in that respect."

"Well, now," Brandeis asked, "did it ever occur to you, Mr. Secretary, that this supposed lack of loyalty, or, putting it another way, that the personal loyalty of one in public service to a superior or to an associate might involve disloyalty to 90,000,000 people?"

"I will not argue that question," the secretary responded.

BY NOW BRANDEIS KNEW that there had been a memorandum prepared for Taft, but so long as the committee voted not to demand the documents from Oscar Lawler or George Wickersham, Brandeis could only suggest the possibility, and he understood the credulousness that this suggestion elicited. After all, William Howard Taft was president of the United States, not some robber baron or petty crook! In an era before the likes of Richard Nixon's Watergate or George W. Bush's claim of weapons of mass destruction in Iraq, Americans expected their presidents, if not to tell all of the truth, at least not to lie to them. Brandeis felt more and more exasperated. "The situation is now pretty tense & my disgust for the administration is now unbounded," he told his brother. "If only there were a Democratic Party. What havoc would be wrought!"

Then fate intervened in the form of a young man with a conscience. Frederick M. Kerby had been paying close attention to the hearings, and he realized that without his testimony Brandeis might never be able to prove the truth of the allegations. He had already told the story of taking the dictation for the Lawler memorandum to his former boss, James Garfield, and had repeated it to Brandeis at Garfield's request. He could not afford to be fired, but neither could he keep silent. He asked his wife what to do, and then a newspaper syndicate, piecing out his connection from the Brandeis allegations, contacted him and told him it was his patriotic duty to tell his story. In addition, they offered him a job afterward, thus relieving him of his financial concerns.

On 14 May 1910, Kerby released his statement, and it made the headlines in nearly every afternoon newspaper in the country. In specific detail he told how Oscar Lawler had called him into Ballinger's private office on Friday, 10 September 1909, and there, with Ballinger checking every statement, and with assistance from three of Ballinger's closest aides, Lawler had dictated the statement in the first person, as if he were Taft writing to Ballinger. Kerby had typed it triple-spaced, in case the president wanted to make any corrections. The whole event had been surrounded in secrecy, with Kerby warned against putting any of the early drafts into a wastebasket; every note, every scrap of paper, had been taken into another room and burned. They finished near midnight, and Kerby handed over the original and the carbons, one of which Ballinger put into his confidential file. Lawler took the original and one copy with him to Beverly the following Monday, the "résumé" that Ballinger had vaguely recalled in his testimony.

Ironically, the same William Howard Taft who had been so astute as Roosevelt's secretary of war and would later be so effective as chief justice, proved one of the most politically inept of all American presidents. He had allowed Gifford Pinchot to provoke him into firing the Forester, had managed through his handling of the Glavis charges to make himself appear as an enemy of conservation, and now, in the last scenes of the farce, managed to get caught out in the lie.

As news of the Kerby statement spread, Attorney General Wickersham suddenly contacted Knute Nelson, claiming that he had ordered a further search of Justice Department files and "found a paper which I transmit to you herewith, and is either the original or a copy of the memorandum prepared by Mr. Lawler on September 11, 1909." He had left this with other papers at the president's home in Beverly on 12 September and then received it back, along with other materials about the Glavis matter, about a week later. Since then, they had lain forgotten in the files.

Ballinger, on learning of the Kerby bombshell and unaware of Wickersham's "discovery," went directly to the White House, only to learn that Taft had gone to play golf. The president's secretary managed to get a call through to Taft, and he and Ballinger had a long conversation, after which the interior secretary, acting on Taft's orders, issued the following statement to the press:

> With reference to the published affidavit of Mr. F. M. Kerby, the stenographer in the office of the Secretary of the Interior, to the effect that the President's letter of September 13, 1909, exonerating Secretary Ballinger was substantially prepared for the President's signature by Assistant Attorney-General Lawler, it was said at the White House today that there is absolutely no foundation for any such statement. The President dictated his letter personally as the result of his own investigation of the record and in consideration of documents and papers in his possession at the time and upon the general report to him.

The storm of criticism that greeted this statement when the evidence so convincingly showed just the opposite led to an emergency meeting of Taft's cabinet that night, and then a more forthright statement from the president. In it the White House confirmed Brandeis's assumptions, not only about the 13 September Taft letter to Ballinger, but also that the summary prepared by the attorney general that Taft claimed he had relied upon for that letter had, in fact, not been prepared until several weeks later, following the publication of the Glavis charges, as a post hoc justification for the president's decision.

There would still be a few days of testimony left, in which the Republican members of the committee tried to deflect criticism from Taft. Oscar Lawler appeared on the stand and accused Brandeis, James Garfield, and Gifford Pinchot of having him and other members of the administration "gum-shoed" by professional detectives. When Brandeis denied this, Senator Ollie James (D-Ky.), who had supported Brandeis throughout the investigation, asked him to explain how he had deduced all of the information.

"Every step in regard to the action of the President (and of others) appears by the collation of the Washington and New York newspapers, the Tribune and the Boston papers," Brandeis told the committee. "Now, that is open to anybody. It is a perfectly simple way, but when you put those in sequence, one upon the other, you have what appears to be very extraordinary intimate knowledge."

"Of gum shoeing?" asked Senator William E. Purcell of North Dakota.

"Yes," Brandeis conceded, "of gum shoeing."

Brandeis, who in addition to statistical reports read Arthur Conan Doyle's tales of the Baker Street detective, said that deduction was nothing more than adding two and two, but you had to know which twos to put together. Clearly he and Sherlock Holmes knew how to add.

BRANDEIS AND VERTREES made their closing arguments, the hearings finally adjourned, and Brandeis went back home to Boston and to a much-anticipated vacation with his family on Cape Cod. "Next Saturday I expect to be with you in Dedham 'for keeps,' " he promised Alice, "and not to leave my hearth until we move to South Yarmouth. It will be good to have a united family again." George Rublee prepared the final brief on behalf of Collier, and the committee voted 7–5, as everyone had expected, to exonerate Ballinger of all charges against him. The majority report, signed by seven Republicans, declared, "No ground whatever has been shown justifying the opinion that he is not a faithful and efficient public officer." The four Democrats, on the other hand, derided Ballinger as "an unfit man to hold the office of Secretary of the Interior. . . . He is not sufficiently devoted to the interests of the common people, or sufficiently diligent or resolute in resisting the insidious aggression of special interests." (A second minority report, by Edmond H. Madison, insurgent Republican of Kansas, held the Glavis-Pinchot charges had been proven, and that Ballinger should go.)

In the end, Congress took no action on the reports. Collier and Hapgood had the satisfaction of seeing that the charges in the Glavis article had been vindicated, and that they stood in no danger of a libel suit. Public pressure forced the Interior Department to cancel the Cunningham claims, and as it turned out, the land involved did not have the coal reserves that the Guggenheim syndicate had anticipated. Friends tried to help Glavis and raised the funds for him to have an apple orchard in Oregon, but he abandoned it (losing the investors all of their money) and had a rather checkered career afterward. Ballinger did not lose his job immediately; it would have been too embarrassing to Taft to have fired him, but in March 1911, after a series of political missteps, Ballinger offered his resignation and the president accepted it. Once rid of both the Forester and Ballinger, Taft proved to be a friend of conservation, and actually withdrew more public lands in his four years in office than Roosevelt had in eight. Moreover, where Roosevelt had relied on executive authority, Taft got Congress to pass enabling legislation to provide for an orderly and legitimate means of withdrawal.

The whole affair fed the fires of insurgency, and in the 1910 election the Republicans lost heavily, with Democrats winning control of the House of Representatives for the first time in nearly twenty years. Of the forty-one incumbent Republican congressmen defeated, only one was an insurgent. Three more progressives joined the Senate, the result of insurgent gains in the midwestern and western states. Although the GOP still had a majority of twelve in the upper chamber, Taft could not count on the insurgents to back his plans, nor could he count on a sufficient number of Republicans to sustain a veto.

The fight only enhanced Brandeis as a figure of national importance. When he took on Collier's defense in January, Henry Watterson, the powerful publisher of the *Louisville Courier-Journal,* had to ask a friend about him. By May everyone in the country who read the papers knew his name. He had, of course, become a hero to the insurgents and to the Pinchot-led conservation forces. But his methods, and his embarrassment of the president, had also made him many enemies.

That Republican supporters of Taft would be angry is not surprising. They believed that the president had not done anything terrible and that the real scoundrels were Louis Glavis and Gifford Pinchot, who had taken a minor dispute and magnified it until it ruptured the party. Not only did the quarrel feed midwestern insurgency, but Theodore Roosevelt had come back from lion hunting in Africa and, thanks in part to the Forester's urging, appeared ready to challenge Taft for the Republican presidential nomination in 1912.

Some people, moreover, recoiled in general from the idea of attacking the country's chief executive as Brandeis had done. In 1910 the country could recall only one administration that had been plagued by corruption, that of Ulysses S. Grant after the Civil War, and even then Grant himself had not been personally involved. One believed that the president, no matter how bad his policies or how poorly managed his administration, stood above base dishonesty. In the midst of the hearings, for example, as Brandeis sought to get information on what the president had done, Senator Elihu Root (R-N.Y.) angrily told the Boston attorney, "We are not here to investigate the President of the United States." He charged Brandeis with "endeavoring assiduously and not altogether ingenuously to lead the investigation into a trial of the President." George Sutherland of Utah, later to be Brandeis's colleague on the Court, agreed. To inquire into Brandeis's charges against Taft, Sutherland declared, "is an insult to the President, and I, for one, do not propose to be a party to it."

George Wharton Pepper, the old-line Philadelphia attorney retained to represent Gifford Pinchot, believed that Brandeis had gone too far in attacking Taft and forcing him to admit what, at most, was a common bureaucratic practice. In an interview years later, Pepper said,

I thought what had been done "was not cricket," whereas Brandeis took the view that no public official had any right to have a private file and that as he was to give his whole time to the public, there was nothing beyond the reach of whatever strategy could be invoked to get possession of it. I found myself unable to argue the question effectively with Brandeis. It was a question of original apprehension. He felt thoroughly justified in doing what he did and I had a sporting instinct which condemned it.

Others also shared this view, often to Brandeis's frustration. "New York is in dense ignorance of the subject," he told his brother. Even normally astute persons like his friend Charles C. Burlingham did not understand that the president had, in essence, lied to the people.

Kerby's participation also offended many, since it was expected that a private secretary would respect confidentiality. Theodore Roosevelt held Brandeis responsible for allowing this to happen. "Gifford isn't a lawyer, not that I'm excusing Gifford," Roosevelt told a friend. "But Brandeis is a lawyer, and should have known better than to engage in such business." Brandeis ought to have known better than to use testimony obtained this way. In fact, Kerby had come to Brandeis, and once he knew about the deception, Brandeis figured out how to prove it. In fairness, a number of newspapermen had already begun to suspect that the letter had been written ahead of time, and in the end they came to Kerby and made it possible for him to go public. Brandeis had also questioned the sequence of events, and Kerby did little more than to confirm these suspicions. But the use of a private secretary's information did not seem the "gentlemanly" thing to do.

Brandeis did not take any satisfaction in exposing Taft's and Wickersham's efforts at deception. "Yesterday was a terrible day," he told his wife. "I felt almost like an executioner & was glad to have Norman Hapgood here to share the responsibility. But it was an awful thing for Wickersham to have done & unfortunately the President . . . is as guilty as W." Dishonesty had offended Brandeis even as a boy, and as he grew older, this puritanical strain in him became ever more pronounced. In many of his reforms, such as the fight against the New Haven, he objected less to the goals of big business than to the methods it adopted, which included deceit and fraudulent accounting. In the 1930s, President Franklin D. Roosevelt referred to him as "Isaiah," a reference to the Old Testament prophet's insistence on morality. One should not think of him as a prig, because the practices he objected to had serious consequences, and he believed that if people got away with small dishonesties, these would eventually become larger crimes.

Taft had relied on the Lawler memorandum and also claimed to have utilized the more thorough examination prepared by Attorney General Wickersham. Had he come right out and said that he had engaged in a common administrative practice, to have a subordinate prepare a statement for his signature; that he had spoken with all of the parties involved, and believed Ballinger to have been in the right; that he had then issued a statement to that effect; and in due course the attorney general, who had been heavily engaged in other governmental business at the time, had done a separate investigation whose findings supported his own judgment, then all Taft could have been accused of would have been bad judgment resulting out of loyalty to his cabinet members. If and when it had been proven that the Glavis charges had been true, Taft could then have said he had been deceived, Ballinger would have resigned, and the president would have avoided the stigma of having been shown to have deliberately misled the public. In fact Brandeis had, prior to Kerby's announcement, left Taft a loophole, pointing out that he had been misled, but Taft insisted otherwise. Brandeis would not have been upset by loyalty to subordinates, nor even by simple bad judgment; neither of these traits indicated a moral infirmity. As Brandeis told Hapgood, "It was the lying that did it."

Pepper also hit directly on another aspect of Brandeis's anger. Brandeis knew that people acted unwisely and at times dishonestly, but he drew a line between private acts, which, while regrettable, affected only the actors and those near to them. But deception that affected the public, either by business or by government officials, constituted a greater sin. As he made clear in his fight against the insurance companies and the New Haven, private enterprise, while entitled to a fair return on its investment, also had a duty to the public to provide goods and services at a reasonable rate and in a trustworthy manner. Officials of the government, whether elected or appointed, had an even greater responsibility, and he certainly subscribed to the notion that a public office is a public trust. Taft, Wickersham, Ballinger, and their ilk had violated that trust, not by bad judgment, but by outright dishonesty. That could not be forgiven.

Some people would probably call Brandeis naive, ignorant of the realities of political life, but this would not do justice to the man. He had a very good sense of himself and clearly understood his shortcomings as well as his strengths. He had a brilliant mind, a remarkable memory, and the tenacity to follow evidence trails. His solutions to problems such as savings bank insurance and the preferential shop displayed a creativity all too rare among reformers. His personal standards of honesty and fiscal integrity protected him against charges that he sought to enrich himself through his public efforts. This made him very attractive to reformers who over the years asked him on several occasions to run for political office, but he refused them because he understood that the very traits that made him effective as a reformer would make it impossible for him to be an elective official. He could, when the occasion demanded, negotiate on a solution, but not on principles. He could not have abided a life of constant compromise. The high idealism he cherished all his life would allow concessions to achieve a solution fair to all parties, but he could not tolerate dishonesty, especially by those chosen to guard the public's interests.

OTHER ASPECTS TO THE DEBATE over conservation are worth mentioning, chief of which is the issue of scientific management of national resources. Gifford Pinchot acted as the prophet of this movement, arguing not that the nation's natural treasures should be left in pristine form but that they should be managed and exploited in a manner that would renew the land. Lumbering could and should take place on public lands, but it should be done in a scientific manner. Advocates of progressive conservation included many businessmen, who responded to Pinchot's call for the wise use of resources. "The object of our forest policy," Pinchot declared in 1903, "is not to preserve the forests because they are beautiful . . . or because they are refuges for the wild creatures of the wilderness . . . but . . . the making of prosperous homes. . . . Every other consideration comes as secondary." Today much of the environmental movement aims at the preservation of wilderness areas, and certainly Theodore Roosevelt shared some of that concern. For Pinchot, conservation meant utilization of resources, but in a scientific manner that would not leave forestlands denuded or mineral fields ravaged.

Brandeis himself loved the outdoors, and well into his sixties found time to go hiking and camping with friends and then with his daughters. He, however, would have been attracted to the notion that forests, coalfields, and other natural resources existed for the benefit of the people as a whole. A growing nation needed lumber to build houses, and a means by which forests could be managed to become a perpetual source of wood made eminently good sense. Here as in so many other areas, progressives like Brandeis sought to restore an order they believed had existed earlier in the nation's life. The great sin of the postwar industrialization was that it destroyed the order and the sense of community that accompanied it and left the nation with social as well as economic and political instability.

Although conservationists counted Brandeis as a friend because of his role in clearing Glavis and Pinchot, he did not get involved in the movement to protect the nation's natural resources. When it appeared that the Taft administration had given other lands around Controller Bay to the Morgan-Guggenheim syndicate, Brandeis very reluctantly agreed to look into it at the behest of Congressman James M. Graham (D-Ill.), but happily bowed out of the matter when the new interior secretary, Walter Fisher, resolved it.

In 1911, Senator Robert La Follette asked Brandeis what should be done about Alaska, and his response is interesting less for its practical suggestions than for the sense of idealism that suffuses it. First, adequate public transportation should be built at government expense, because if private capital controlled the railroads, it would also control the land. Lines would only be built to where capitalist enterprises would require them, and not to where the people would need them. Second, there had to be a system in place to prevent large syndicates from gaining control of the land and its resources. Ownership of the land ought to belong only to those who actually lived on and worked the land. "Alaska is the Land of Opportunity," he declared. "Develop it by the People, for the People."

The Brandeis plan is unusual in its emphasis on government ownership and control, unlike anything he ever proposed for domestic reform. It does, however, anticipate the plans for the development of Palestine that he put forward nearly a decade later. For both Alaska and Palestine he advocated a form of social engineering that he knew could not be implemented in the United States, because of the advanced state of industrial society. Alaska and Palestine stood empty (he paid no attention to the native Aleuts of Alaska, or the Arab population of Palestine, a trait common to most of those writing on the two lands at the time), and therefore one could try to create a particular type of society and economy. In the Alaskan proposal Brandeis began to articulate what he believed to be "the good society," reaching back into the early years of the Republic to find his model—the Jeffersonian ideal of a democratic community with small-scale farming and business. There would be no "curse of bigness," because government ownership and regulation would effectively preclude bigness.

Nothing in the plan conflicted with the scientific management of natural resources proposed by Gifford Pinchot and others. Brandeis did not advocate leaving Alaska as a pristine wilderness, and indeed the modern debates over the development of Alaskan oil resources in the Arctic National Wildlife Refuge would have made little sense to him. The question was never "to develop or not to develop," but how it should be done, and how to protect the interests of the people as a whole against the depredations of the magnates. After writing his letter to La Follette, Brandeis said little more about Alaska or conservation, but he had a great deal to say about other things, and by this time his had become an important voice in the progressive movement.

CHAPTER TWELVE
RAILROAD INTERLUDES

Although busy in 1910 with Pinchot-Ballinger, the New York garment strike, and other matters, Brandeis never forgot the New Haven and his defeat at the hands of Charles Sanger Mellen. Railroads became an important part of his life both as a lawyer and as a reformer during these years, working with the Interstate Commerce Commission in several rate cases. The man who had taken on Morgan and Taft captured even more headlines when he announced that railroads could save a million dollars a day by adopting scientific management.

At the beginning of the twenty-first century we tend to forget the central role that railroads played a hundred years ago in the movement of people and goods. Although packet boats plied the coastal waters and some horse-drawn omnibuses traversed narrow and unpaved roads, if people wanted to go from New York to Chicago, or to send goods from St. Louis to Atlanta, they used the railroads. Today, of course, a person driving a car on one of the nation's interstate highways will see uncounted tractor-trailers carrying everything from fresh-cut flowers to industrial machinery. In 1910 cars had yet to become the vehicle of choice for the masses; there were no interstate highways, and no federal routes of any sort, only random and often ill-paved state roads; and neither big nor little trucks played any part in moving goods. The idea of flying between New York and Chicago would have marked a person as a hopeless lunatic.

The fate of railroads and their rate structures mattered, since transportation of raw materials and finished products within the United States went almost entirely by rail. Should a railroad go bankrupt, it could leave towns, factories, and farms without the means either to get their goods to market or to bring in supplies. If railroads raised rates,

"They All Want Mr. Brandeis Now," Boston Post, *1910*

small businesses in one part of the country might be put at a severe competitive disadvantage to competitors nearer to markets. Brandeis knew this from firsthand experience. His family's wholesale grain business depended upon rail transportation, and increased charges of even a few dollars per hundredweight could make a difference between profit and loss.

AFTER THE PASSAGE of the Draper Act in June 1909, the New Haven seemed immune from attack. The attorney general of Massachusetts believed the line had violated the law and thus could have its charter revoked, but he was reluctant to take that step; even the mention of it brought protests from the financial community. In Washington the Taft administration, although vigorously pursuing several major antitrust cases, saw no reason to reopen the New Haven files. At the prodding of members allied with Brandeis and the Anti-merger League, the Massachusetts legislature appointed a special body, known as the Validation Commission, to examine the New Haven's finances, but no one expected that body to turn up damning evidence of wrongdoing.

About this time, however, the New Haven began to suffer financial problems, which were only temporarily relieved when the state made the stock of the Boston Railroad Holding Company—the entity created by the Draper Act and owned by the New Haven that held the Boston & Maine stock—legal investments for savings banks and allowed the Boston & Maine to issue preferred stock. Moreover, when the Validation Commission, as expected, gave the New Haven a clean bill of health, the Boston News Bureau, a firm that put out pro-business releases in the form of news stories, gloated over how wrong Brandeis had been. The Validation Commission had portrayed the New Haven as a picture of "admirable financial and physical integrity," despite the charges made by Brandeis. His pamphlet on the New Haven "is practically forgotten. Even its author might now blush to read it."

Indeed, promerger sentiment seemed to be riding high in early 1911, and included not just business executives but men who took a leading role in Massachusetts reform, such as Charles Sumner Bird (who would head the state's Progressive Party in 1912) and Eugene Foss, who had bolted the Republican Party and as a Democratic governor elected in 1911 oversaw the passage of a number of reform measures. Samuel Bowles, publisher of the *Springfield Republican,* Joseph Walker, a leader in the assembly, and Edward Filene of the Public Franchise League all supported the merger, and all had been and would continue to be close Brandeis allies in other reforms. Brandeis himself recognized that people of goodwill could differ. "I have no objection to those who take the merger side," he said. "There is always room for difference of opinion."

As later historians have noted, the antimerger case had many weaknesses, starting with its attempt to uphold a "status quo" for the Boston & Maine as a Massachusetts-owned railroad. Even before the New Haven had purchased its shares in 1907, the B & M had been controlled by out-of-state investors, especially the American Express Company of New York. By 1908, American Express, for its own reasons, had decided to divest itself of B & M shares and had engaged Lee, Higginson & Company as the broker. State Street bankers could not have been happy at Brandeis's allegations about financial instability as they tried to underwrite a very large sale of B & M stock.

Although Brandeis had believed that the Boston & Maine had been in good financial condition and had been bled by the New Haven, it turned out that the B & M needed a large infusion of money for improvements and had not been able to raise it. In 1906 it had failed to sell $6 million worth of new stock, leading the Massachusetts assembly to liberalize its laws regarding stock issues by public service companies. By then the B & M had found itself trying to sell new shares at the same time that American Express wanted to sell off its very large holdings of the railroad's stock.

Perhaps the weakest part of the antimerger argument was that it could not present an alternative policy to those who saw Massachusetts business interests threatened by external developments. Railroad lines linking New York and Philadelphia to the interior, as well as the diversion of foreign and coastal shipping to those ports, could not be controlled by either the Massachusetts government or its business leaders. Mellen held out a plan—consolidate New England transportation and make it more competitive vis-à-vis the other East Coast regions—that on the face of it seemed to respond to the problem.

Finally, New England shippers worried about the growing powers of the Interstate Commerce Commission. The ICC did not get rate-making power from Congress until the Mann-Elkins Act in 1910, but prior to that the ICC had served as an arbitrator in disputes over rate differentials among trunk lines serving the Atlantic ports and had made several decisions unfavorable to Boston and the merchants involved in its maritime and rail commerce. These fears were not unfounded. In 1909, in defiance of an ICC ruling, the New Haven and other railroads had lowered their rates on goods shipped westward. In 1912, armed with its new powers, the ICC forced the roads to increase their rates to a point higher than they had been in a decade, a step that further weakened the financial status of the Boston & Maine and the New Haven.

In the face of these arguments, merger made sense, and as Congressman Samuel W. McCall noted, New England no longer had the influence it once enjoyed. The growth of the country and migration westward had drained Massachusetts and other northeastern states not just of people but of the political authority they used to wield. Creating a strong and unified transportation system in New England to keep the region's economy strong made very good sense to many people.

Brandeis never really addressed these issues, but rather focused on what he considered unorthodox and illicit financial practices. In the end, as he told Norman Hapgood in late 1911, despite Mellen's broad view that had captured so many people, the rules of arithmetic could not be ignored. By then a careful reading of the balance sheets had shown that the New Haven could barely afford to pay a 4 percent dividend, even though Mellen told stockholders that Mr. Morgan wanted the "New Haven to be recognized as a permanent 8 per cent stock." Even if the road did not earn that much in any given quarter, it would pay the 8 percent to avoid hardship on small investors and prevent any "serious distrust" of the management. By 1911, Brandeis had also become an inveterate foe of monopoly, in part because of the depredations he believed resulted from J. P. Morgan's efforts to control all of New England's transportation through the New Haven. Then Morgan intervened to protect the New Haven and in doing so unleashed a strong attack on the line.

IN 1910, over the objections of the New Haven, Massachusetts had invited the Canadian Grand Trunk Railway to extend its lines to Boston. Construction had started, and even before a single train could run over these tracks, the New Haven's financial condition worsened. On 8 November 1912 the newspapers reported that construction on the Grand Trunk had stopped, and almost immediately Gilson Gardner, a journalist with close ties to Brandeis, wrote an article with the headline "KING MORGAN SLIPS INVADERS $4,000,000 TO STAY OUT." Other newspaper stories followed: Brandeis had gone to Washington to confer with the Pujo Committee, then looking into banking malpractices, to see if the charges against Morgan were true. Attorney General Wickersham had been asked to determine whether the action violated antitrust laws. Brandeis would serve as counsel for a congressional investigation.

In fact, Brandeis had nothing to do with any of these proposals. Sidelined by an eye inflammation for more than a week, he had been confined, as he put it, to dictating interviews for various newspapers on the New Haven, and he felt confident that some of the leading papers in both New York and Boston would this time be with him. He also sent out numerous letters to editors and writers encouraging them to start probing into the New Haven's wicked ways. He told Robert La Follette and Senator Moses Clapp that in view of the Supreme Court's recent ruling holding the purchase by the Union Pacific of 46 percent of Southern Pacific stock to be illegal, perhaps it would be a good time to introduce new and stronger antitrust legislation, and he thought the activities of the New Haven certainly justified such a course.

With his eyes better, Brandeis published his first piece on the New Haven in three years, and in it he attacked the line as "an unregulated monopoly." The article launched a thoroughgoing attack on monopoly that he had clarified in several articles as well as in his role as adviser to Woodrow Wilson in the 1912 presidential race (see chapter 14). Brandeis conceded the necessity of having some local monopolies, especially in public utilities, but those could easily be regulated. Enormous conglomerates like the New Haven, however, could not be. Moreover, like a bloated glutton it suffered from the curse of bigness, which further harmed the public through excessive costs and poor service. To solve the problem, Brandeis demanded that the combination of railroads, steamship lines, and street railways be broken up and competition restored. This could be accomplished either by the federal government instituting a suit under the Sherman Antitrust Act or by Massachusetts exercising its sovereignty to take away the Boston & Maine.

While the actions of Morgan and Mellen could not be excused, the fact is that the simplicity of Brandeis's solution, while reining in some of the excesses, did not address the larger issues. By 1910 railroads in the United States had been overbuilt, and although the great trunk lines that ran across the country did compete, smaller markets did not generate enough business to justify the service of more than one road. The financial shenanigans of Morgan and Mellen affronted Brandeis's moral sensibilities, and rightly so, but he failed to understand that even if he could undo all that had been done over the past decade, serious problems remained to which neither he nor anyone else in the antimerger group had any viable solutions to offer. Mellen may have been right in his vision of a unified transportation system, and he had never tried to hide what he and Morgan wanted to do. Had they done so more honestly, trying to get the legislature to amend the law to accommodate their vision, and then kept honest books, Brandeis might have opposed their plans, but he would have viewed the struggle in far different terms. People could agree or disagree about the wisdom or benefits of the merger, but he could not abide the lying and deceit that had accompanied it.

The New Haven's condition continued to deteriorate so that the end could be delayed but not averted. To continue to pay its regular dividend and service its huge debt—taken on to finance the various acquisitions—the management cut back on critical track and equipment maintenance and reduced its workforce. As a result, the once proud line piled up a horrible record of train wrecks, four in 1911 and seven in 1912, that caused dozens of deaths. Even advocates of the merger began to question the wisdom of Mellen's grand scheme, and Brandeis's attacks now received a far more respectful hearing than they had earlier.

Mellen fought back viciously. He subsidized a Boston publication called *Truth,* edited by George R. Conroy, that attacked Brandeis in an openly anti-Semitic fashion. Brandeis, the publication charged, had for years been an agent of Jacob Schiff of the Jewish banking house of Kuhn, Loeb & Company, which represented the Jewish house of Rothschild in the United States. The Brandeis-Schiff-Rothschild campaign against the New Haven should be seen as part of the "age-long struggle between Jew and Gentile." Schiff, known among his people as a "prince in Israel," had given millions to Jewish charities, "keeping in mind always the Yiddish proverb, 'He who has the money has the authority.'" On 20 December, a week after Brandeis's article appeared in newspapers around the country, Morgan and Mellen issued a joint statement in which they traced every defamatory statement ever made about the New Haven back to Louis D. Brandeis. The accidents, which had also killed "trusted employees," had been exploited by Brandeis and his minions to frighten the public and "to demoralize the transportation and traffic of New England." The public, for its own interest, should call "Halt!" to this irresponsible campaign.

Brandeis, while no doubt appalled by the anti-Semitism of his opponents, chose not to respond. "Mellen continues his fire on me—the root of all offending," he told Alfred, "& I carefully refrain from attacking Mellen personally or answering personalities. The N.Y. papers have been on the job & there is little need for me to hammer now; but I still have some rods in pickle." Brandeis probably had little to do with a federal grand jury indictment of Mellen on antitrust charges, but Mellen no doubt blamed him for it. Initially, Mellen waived immunity, hoping to spare J. P. Morgan additional strain, since the banker now had all he could handle in the Pujo investigations. (Later, when granted immunity, Mellen "almost gloried in the vicious squalor, the total absence of business scruples," and compared railroad competition to "one man cutting the heart out of another.")

In early 1913, Brandeis kept up his search for information about the New Haven and its finances and did play a hand in getting the new attorney general in the Wilson administration, James C. McReynolds, to begin both civil and criminal investigations into the New Haven. Less than a week after Woodrow Wilson took the oath of office, Brandeis went to the White House to meet with him, and also spoke to McReynolds and other officials "pushing along New Haven matters." Less than a month later he went back "mainly on New Haven matters. The Co. & its backers are fighting hard—the inevitable and me—with increasing bitterness. But arithmetic must ultimately prevail, even over false accounting." While in Washington, Brandeis also met with several of the ICC commissioners regarding their plans to investigate the New Haven. After Brandeis had given a speech in early March to the Boston Chamber of Commerce, New Haven stock dropped to a new low, and the company's defenders quickly blamed Brandeis and his rumormongering for the decline. When a reporter asked him about these comments, Brandeis labeled them "nonsense." The trouble, he declared, is due not to the critics but to the New Haven itself. "It's merely a matter of arithmetic, that's all."

Then the bottom dropped out for both Mellen and the New Haven. On 31 March 1913, Mellen's collaborator and greatest defender, J. Pierpont Morgan, died in Rome. In May the Interstate Commerce Commission began hearings on the New Haven, with Brandeis there nominally to represent the Boston Fruit and Produce Exchange, although it quickly became clear that the ICC looked to him as if he were acting as their counsel. (When the New Haven brought pressure on some of the leaders of the exchange, they cut their ties to Brandeis, who then appeared in his capacity as a citizen, one to whom the ICC turned constantly for advice.) With the ICC's subpoena power and investigatory staff, the charges that Brandeis had made for the last seven years suddenly acquired new life. John Billard had made a profit of $2.7 million on the phony transfer of Boston & Maine stock without risking a penny of his own money. An audit of the New Haven's books disclosed an unaccounted amount of $514,000 in general expenses, eight times the amount normally carried by Class A railroads. Instead of earning its dividend, the line actually operated at a loss in 1911 and 1912. Two ships carried on the books as worth $900,000 had recently been sold as junk for $44,000. When the New Haven asked that subsequent hearings be held in private, Commissioner Charles A. Prouty refused. "Sub rosa investigations never achieved anything."

Mellen tried to fight back in his usual manner, accusing Brandeis of all sorts of improprieties dating back two decades, but this time the ploy failed. The *Boston Journal,* which had previously supported the merger, declared that Mellen "does not commend himself to the public by his intemperate and twenty-year belated attack on Mr. Brandeis. We hold no brief for Mr. Brandeis but we are frank to say that Mr. Mellen's twenty-year search for a flaw seems to make a pretty good case for the man he seeks to vilify."

On 12 June a collision between two trains at the Stamford, Connecticut station killed seven passengers and injured dozens more, the worst accident in the New Haven's history, and clearly the result of negligence in maintaining the tracks and equipment.

On 9 July the commission issued its report castigating the New Haven for its financial practices, and took care to point out that many of the charges made by critics of the line (they did not mention Brandeis by name, but surely meant him) had been true. The fault lay not in the critics or their charges but in the New Haven management and its practices. "Had the stockholders of the New Haven, instead of vilifying the Road's critics, given some attention to the charges made, their property would today be of greater value and the problem an easier one." The ICC also recommended that the New Haven be stripped of its trolley and steamship holdings.

Had the older Morgan still been alive, he would have spewed rage and stuck by Mellen. But a new JP now headed the house of Morgan, and Jack had taken his father's seat on the New Haven board. On the same day that the ICC released its report, Jack forced Mellen to resign from the Boston & Maine, and a week later ousted him from the New Haven, overriding the wishes of the rest of the board. ("He who has the money has the authority.") The younger Morgan had no more ideological sympathy with government regulations or bureaucracy than did his father, but he also recognized that the age of the robber barons had passed, and that tactically the house of Morgan had to do something to calm the public uproar generated by the Pujo hearings and the ICC report. The obnoxious Mellen, who by now had few defenders, would be the sacrificial offering.

Brandeis received the news of Mellen's departure from the Boston & Maine with studied indifference. In a statement to the press he called it "a step in the right direction, but it does not go far enough." The public would not be satisfied until the New Haven severed its ties to the Boston & Maine. To his brother, he called Mellen's resignation "interesting," and even more so the fact that several newspaper that had hitherto condemned him and his attacks now echoed his views. The *Boston Herald,* for example, without mentioning Brandeis, endorsed the view that the B & M and the New Haven should be under separate management and ownership, for each line had different problems and each would require the full attention of a capable man.

Mellen's ouster from the New Haven, according to Brandeis, looked "as if the seven year war were drawing to a close." Much remained to be done, including getting a new board of directors, and he doubted that the new president of the New Haven, Howard Elliott, would be much better. In fact Elliott, the former president of the Northern Pacific line, although eschewing Mellen's propensities for monopoly, proved almost as irresponsible and utterly incapable of fixing the situation. In September 1913 a wreck outside New Haven killed twenty-one passengers and trapped forty boys returning from summer camp for hours until they could be rescued. That December the debt-ridden New Haven skipped its dividend for the first time in forty years, making a mockery of the Morgan bank's assertion that the road would always be known as an 8 percent investment. Facing antitrust charges as well as further ICC investigations, the Morgan people, who controlled the New Haven board, finally recognized the depths of their trouble. "Whole situation disgusting," Henry Davison cabled Jack Morgan, "but must recognize that Brandeis et al. have ear of President and Attorney General just now." The younger Morgan wanted to resign from the New Haven board, but stayed on because he recognized that such a step would confirm Brandeis's attacks on banker management.

Although Howard Elliott pleaded for time and cooperation, he got little of either. In July 1914 another ICC report (which Brandeis could have written but did not) detailed the "reckless and profligate" monetary operations of the New Haven. The previous month Attorney General McReynolds had issued an ultimatum to the New Haven—either give up control of the Boston & Maine and divest the trolley and steamship lines or face antitrust proceedings. When the company hesitated, McReynolds, with the full approval of President Wilson, began proceedings under the Sherman Act. On 11 August 1914 the New Haven surrendered, and the seven-year war between Brandeis and the house of Morgan ended, although the tale still had a few sorry chapters to play out. The New Haven would not pay another dividend for fourteen years; it paid $1 per share in 1928 and $5 in 1929 before the Great Depression began, and would never pay another penny to its stockholders. Eventually its passenger services would be incorporated into Amtrak and its freight lines bought out by other roads.

Brandeis believed that the New Haven disaster resulted from immoral business practices. Mellen, despite his great energy and intelligence, could not—nor could any man—take on such enormous and divergent responsibilities as running two railroads and do well by either one. But looming above it all stood the law of arithmetic "by which two and two will always make four, despite reports of presidents and financial advisors who insist on stretching it into five." Brandeis ultimately placed the greatest blame not on Mellen, who had been blinded by his own vision, but on people like Henry Lee Higginson, "the Pillars of Society," who should have known better and did nothing to stop the destruction, not only of the money held by small and large investors alike, but ultimately of a once great railroad. As Brandeis told one correspondent, he hoped that the New Haven debacle "may also bring a renewal of New England's traditional respect for law and for the truth."

IN JUNE 1910, Congress passed the Mann-Elkins Act, enlarging the rate-making powers of the Interstate Commerce Commission. The new law put the burden of proof for any proposed rate increase on the carrier, which had to show the need for and reasonableness of higher charges. A few weeks later, two groups of railroads filed proposed changes that called for a 10 percent rate increase on freight handled east of the Mississippi River and north of the Potomac and Ohio rivers. If the ICC approved, shippers in this area would have to bear millions of dollars in increased transportation costs, and they organized to fight the proposal. In Boston, David O. Ives, the head of the Transportation Committee of the Boston Chamber of Commerce, who had been an ally of Brandeis's in the New Haven merger fight, wanted Brandeis to represent the shippers at the ICC hearing. He went out to South Yarmouth, where Brandeis had gone with his family after the talks in the garment workers' strike had collapsed, and talked him into taking on the shippers as clients.

One week later Brandeis went to New York, where lawyers for both the railroads and the shippers gathered at the Waldorf-Astoria for the preliminary hearings before ICC examiners. Brandeis quickly emerged as the leader of the shippers' attorneys as they attacked the testimony of the railroad witnesses. The railroads had assumed that there would be no difficulty in securing the rate increase, because they had figures to show how much more they had to pay for labor, coal, materials, and other costs. For the most part, relatively minor officials came armed with memoranda detailing these facts, only to have Brandeis, Clifford Thorne, or one of the other attorneys tear apart their testimony on cross-examination. None of the railroad men had evidently had any role in the preparation of the numbers, and the lawyers easily elicited their admissions that they really did not know what the figures had been based on or how they had been arrived at. There had been a wage increase, as everyone knew, but the railroad men seemed unable to explain exactly how that required higher freight rates.

In late September the preliminary hearings ended and resumed in Washington in mid-October before the entire commission, this time with the full attention of the railroad leaders, as the presidents of the Pennsylvania, the Baltimore & Ohio, the Erie, and others all crowded into the hearing room. They had learned from the failure of their underlings that neither the shippers' attorneys nor the ICC commissioners would let them get away with generalities, so they now tried to back up their claim with more facts. The wage increases recently given to their employees would cost the railroads $34 million more in 1910 than they had paid in 1909. In addition, there had been other cost increases. Roads had been extended and service improved—often at the request of the shippers. Newer terminals and equipment provided better and faster freight service, all at a cost, and freight revenues had been dwindling. The railroads had already cut expenses almost to the bone, explained James McCrea, the president of the Pennsylvania, and they needed the rate increase not to pad dividends but so they could continue in business. Representatives of the railway brotherhoods as well as an investors' association also endorsed the rate request.

Brandeis showed no more deference to the presidents and other high officials of the railroads than he had shown to their minions in the preliminary hearings, and gradually a thread emerged in his questioning. He intimated that they really did not need the rate increase, because they had been operating their lines inefficiently. Moreover, the railroad leaders had not yet grasped what the Mann-Elkins Act required; namely, that they justify the need for the rate increase. Brandeis and the other shippers' attorneys knew that they did not have to make a case against the increase; the law required the railroads to prove the need for it. The situation is akin to a criminal trial. The burden of proof is on the prosecution to show that the defendant did in fact commit the crime; the defense does not have to prove that the client is innocent, but only that the prosecution has not proven the case beyond a reasonable doubt. An exchange with Charles F. Daly of the New York Central illustrated this. Brandeis had gotten Daly to concede that the various rates for different articles had been reached not by any systematic process but more by the arbitrary judgment of the railroads as to what they should be.

Daly: We haven't anything from you or from your clients, except your statement which is not in our judgment worth any more than mine, and in this particular instance, I don't think it is worth as much.

Brandeis: I am not undertaking, Mr. Daly, to set up my statement. Fortunately, counsel have only to present the evidence. You
understand, of course, that under this new law the burden rests
upon you . . . to show that the change you propose making is
reasonable?

Daly: Well, in order for you to disprove my statement you must
show to the Commission that what we have done has injured your
industry.

Brandeis: I submit that there is no such obligation resting upon
me or my clients.

As always, Brandeis had made sure to learn everything he could
about the railroads' financial conditions prior to the hearings, and time
and again on cross-examination he confounded the railroad witnesses
by displaying a far better understanding of their revenues and payouts
than they did. In his cross-examination of James McCrea, for example,
Brandeis forced the Pennsylvania Railroad head to concede that he did
not fully understand the actual prosperity of his company. Brandeis had
certainly raised doubts in the minds of the commission about the carriers' need for an increase, but he had another weapon that he had been
preparing.

All through the hearings Brandeis had been meeting with Frederick
W. Taylor, Harrington Emerson, Frank Gilbreth, and other advocates
of scientific management. In a line of questions that had lawyers on
both sides as well as the commissioners a bit confused, Brandeis kept
asking the railroad men about how they managed their business, about
how much it cost to repair certain items, about the costs of running certain operations. He had a purpose, however, which he kept to himself,
but he had set the stage when he dropped his bombshell in early
November.

The railroads did not need a rate increase, he told the commission;
instead, they needed to adopt principles of scientific management. He
proposed to prove to the commission that if the roads implemented scientific management, they could save $1 million a day in operating
expenses, or more than $300 million a year. This estimate, he said, is
"by no means extravagant; and you will see as we develop the science
and develop its application in varied businesses that the estimate is, if
anything, an underestimate instead of an overestimate." Brandeis then

began calling witnesses to testify how scientific management could be applied to railroads. Charles Going, editor of the *Engineering Magazine,* related how Harrington Emerson had reorganized the work in the repair shops of the Atchison, Topeka & Santa Fe Railroad and saved the company over $1 million a year in locomotive repair costs alone. Then Emerson himself took the stand and, under Brandeis's guidance, explained to the commission just what he had done. All told, it appeared that the Atchison alone had saved nearly $6 million a year by running its operations more scientifically.

At first the railroads tended to dismiss the claim. William Ellis, a lawyer for the railroads, argued that the ICC had no right telling his clients how they should run their own business, and certainly not on any strange theories cooked up in "the law library in Boston." Brandeis ignored the sarcasm and won the applause of the audience when he declared that the day had passed when the critics of vested interests could be dismissed as impractical; reformers were nothing if not practical. The new science of management did not come from his law library, but had developed in factories all around the country. The railroads, of course, had not argued that they ran their businesses according to the principles of scientific management, and in fact had admitted they did not. Initially they took a rather bemused view of Brandeis's witnesses, and their cross-examinations, as one paper reported, began "in a spirit of flippancy and ended in a rather awkward silence." What had happened, as the railroad heads began to appreciate, is that Brandeis had completely undermined their credibility. They had failed to understand, and one wonders why their lawyers had not explained it to them, that under the new law they could not just claim they needed a rate increase, they had to prove it. In cross-examination, Brandeis, Thorne, and others had consistently shown that the figures offered by the lines did not make sense and often did not even rely on anything other than arbitrary judgments. With the headline-catching phrase of a million dollars a day, Brandeis had done what any good defense lawyer would do—he had raised a reasonable doubt regarding the railroads' claim. If they could save that much money simply by adopting principles of efficiency, then they certainly did not need a rate increase.

Brandeis did not charge the railroad leaders with incompetence. Rather, there had been a failure "to apply in railroading the new science of management which in a number of competitive businesses has already been applied." Raising rates would not solve this problem, and at some point the railroads would realize that higher rates would in fact lead to diminishing returns. They needed to look at every aspect of their operation, from the laying of tracks to repairs to the scheduling of trains, and examine whether that particular operation, in conjunction with closely related jobs, was being performed in the most efficient and effective manner.

On 23 November, a group of western railroad presidents attempted to discredit Brandeis by calling what they considered his bluff, not realizing with whom they were dealing. They offered to allow Brandeis to set his own salary if only he would point out how these savings could be effected, and closed with the line: "This proposition is made to you in the same spirit in which you rendered your statement to the [Interstate Commerce] Commission." They sent their telegram to him care of the commission, and so he did not respond until it had been forwarded to Boston a few days later. He immediately offered to show them exactly how to save the money, and suggested they call a conference, one that would include the presidents of the eastern lines as well, and there, as a public service, he would do as they had requested. As for money,

> I must decline to accept any salary or other compensation from the railroads for the same reason I have declined compensation from the shipping organizations whom I represent—namely, that the burden of increased rates, while primarily affecting the Eastern manufacturers and merchants, will ultimately be borne in large part by the consumer through increasing the cost of living, mainly of those least able to bear added burdens. I desire that any aid I can render in preventing such added burdens should be unpaid services. Kindly suggest date and place for conference.

The railroad officials never responded.

By this time Brandeis's reputation extended far outside Boston or even Massachusetts. He had, after all, argued before the Supreme Court in defense of protective legislation; he had taken on the house of Morgan over the New Haven, and the Taft administration in the Pinchot-Ballinger hearings; and he had helped resolve the New York garment workers' strike. But none of these brought him the national headlines that accompanied his million-dollar-a-day claim. The *Outlook,* which carried Theodore Roosevelt's articles, noted that Brandeis had been well-known in progressive circles, but nothing had made him a national figure so much as his statement before the ICC. "America is rich in idealists," the editor concluded, "but it is rare to find one whose idealism is, like Mr. Brandeis's, not only aggressive but practical and efficient."

RAY STANNARD BAKER, one of the era's best-known journalists, wrote a firsthand account of Brandeis in these hearings, and it provides a rare portrait of the man physically as well as in action. The hearings had been important, Baker noted, for after all they involved millions of dollars, "but as dull and prosy as ever such a hearing could be." He continued:

> I remember the sudden change in the whole atmosphere, however, the new electricity, when Mr. Brandeis' tall, spare, rugged, slightly stooping figure arose in the middle of the room to dispute the claim of the railroads. Almost from the first sentence—he speaks in a high, rather harsh voice, but with implicit command—one felt a new sense of breadth of grasp, sureness of understanding, aptness of expression, and above all, above that wearisome tinkering with infinitely minute details and musty precedents, a return to constructive principles and vigorous new remedies for ancient evils. . . .
>
> I remember his whole bearing. His large head with the stubborn black hair streaked with iron-gray (he was then 54 years old)—the striking, dark, strong face, the sensitive hands—he has the hand of a musician—gave one singularly an impression of originality and power. His face, indeed, at certain angles, and especially in repose, recalls almost startlingly one of the portraits of Abraham Lincoln. It is more like Lincoln above in the intellectual equipment perhaps, less broadly and commonly Lincoln below, in the wide mouth and chin. There is the same high and broad forehead, prominent cheekbones, strong nose, deep-set, thoughtful, sometimes visionary eyes. The mouth with sharply cut lines above it is emphatically sensitive, rather than so broadly sympathetic as that of Lincoln. It is one of those rare, and indeed scarcely classifiable faces—although Jewish, not typically Jewish, although American, not typically American, in which the qualities of strength of character, side by side with keenness, sensitiveness, depth of vision, and even, at times a kind of sad mysticism, are extraordinarily mingled. Rising in any gathering, stepping forth on any platform, he would instantly command, even from his bitterest enemies, an acknowledgement of force, originality, personality. Here is a man of power!

• • •

WHETHER THE RAILROAD PRESIDENTS appreciated Brandeis as much as Baker did is doubtful, but they had to listen, if for no reason other than the public response to his claim. The *New York Tribune* summed it up in a headlined article on 4 December, "BOMBSHELL WHICH BRANDEIS HURLED INTO CAMP OF THE RAILROADS WAS LABELLED 'EFFICIENCY.' " The story, which ran eighty-four column inches and is typical of newspaper reaction around the country, not only detailed Brandeis's assertions about the potential for savings but carried stories—and details—of shops like the Atchison that had implemented scientific management and how much they had saved.

Ideas of scientific management had, of course, been around for more than a decade, and were well-known in industrial engineering circles, but Brandeis's argument and his parade of expert witnesses, according to one historian, "lifted the Rate Case from inside the daily papers to the front page. It overflowed into the Sunday supplements and was caught up by the weekly magazines." The beauty of the argument is that it did not pit labor against management but, in Brandeis's words, put the interests of the public first, the public that would have to bear the costs of any rate increase. Adopting scientific management would not wound labor, for in a properly run shop good workers would be rewarded. Nor would it harm railroads, whose health everyone understood related closely to the economic well-being of the country.

The Interstate Commerce Commission unanimously rejected the rate request in February 1911, and as Brandeis told Felix Frankfurter, "The Commission did, I think quite as much as they could, and rather more than I thought they would with the efficiency argument. They accepted the fundamental principles that improvements in economy and management were possible, and they must be made before the need [for rate increases] would be recognized." Having no choice, the railroads began to look at scientific management. Daniel Willard, president of the Baltimore & Ohio, told a reporter, "As I see it, there is only one thing for us to do—to put into effect the Brandeis greater efficiency system." Before long, many railroad officials became enthusiasts. By 1916 several officials had claimed large aggregate savings, and in 1919 Ivy Lee of the Pennsylvania Railroad praised Brandeis for making his suggestions, declaring that in the preceding decade the net operating income of the Pennsylvania alone had increased approximately $1 million a day.

The following July, Louis went out to Kentucky to visit his brother and joyously reported to Alice how the cream of Louisville society had come out in ninety-five-degree heat to see him. "The heartiest greeting of all was from the railroad men," he noted. "All the L[ouisville] & N[ashville] chiefs, including W. H. Smith, the President who is over 75, were on hand, & Mr. Egan, the Illinois Central superintendent insisted I must call at his office on my way off this morning. He wanted his 'boys' to see me."

A GREAT DEAL has been written about the relationship of scientific management to the progressive movement, about its potential for elitism and anti-majoritarian rule. It is doubtful if Brandeis gave much thought at the time to the long-term effects or the potential for abuse. He recognized labor's opposition, but did not understand it. To him, in the shop or factory run on the Taylor method, workers would certainly produce more, but their productivity would be rewarded. Labor considered Taylorism nothing more than a speedup, believing that while a few workers might get an occasional bonus, the majority would simply work harder for the same or reduced wages.

Taylorism never really worked as well as its advocates claimed, in part because labor often sabotaged it. After civilian workers struck at the Watertown Arsenal in 1911 over an alleged speedup, Congress held hearings on the system, and investigators concluded that scientific management did not enhance the welfare of the workers. In 1916, Assistant Secretary of the Navy Franklin Roosevelt banned the Taylor system in government arsenals and navy yards.

Brandeis and other progressives saw scientific management as a way to impose some order on an industrial system that had lost its moral bearings. The wastefulness of modern factories relied upon a vast pool of unskilled labor, and big companies could afford to ignore traditional American values such as thrift, hard work, and willpower because unskilled labor cost them so little. Efficiency, progressives believed, would lead to a more humane management and a greater desire by workers to achieve personal satisfaction through a job well done. Personal efficiency would lead to social efficiency. If one could instill pride and self-discipline in the workplace, those values would translate to the greater society and to the political world.

Scientific management required the cooperation of both employer and employee. If one wanted workers to be more productive, the price of lowering costs would be higher wages to the laborer. The selfishness of both groups would balance out, and both would gain, the owner through higher profits and the worker through higher wages. The lessons of the marketplace, cooperation and efficiency, would lead to better government, as well as to a more moral society. How far Brandeis himself took the lessons of scientific management is hard to say, but it is of a piece with his overall philosophy. There is, of course, a large dose of morality here, as there is in all of his reform work: the belief that scientific management could point the way to a better workplace where older virtues could again prevail. Unfortunately, the idealist here failed to pay attention to the realities.

ALTHOUGH SOME RAILROADS began to experiment with scientific management following the 1911 decision, two years later the lines came back to the Interstate Commerce Commission with a request for a 5 percent rate advance, and cited higher wages and taxes, capital charges, and other burdens to justify the request. Brandeis expected the railroads to file the petition, but told his brother that he had not decided whether to get involved. He thought that the request should probably be denied, and he had "inspired some editorials the country over, demanding efficiency & abolishing interlocking directorates first." In the spring of 1913, Brandeis certainly did not need the problem of a major investigatory hearing, with the new Wilson administration and progressive members of Congress calling on him almost daily for advice on policy, appointments, and bill drafting. He had also acquired a new interest, and wrote his brother in early June that he had come down to New York to "spend the day on Zionism" (see chapter 17).

Faced with what they knew would be a complex case, however, the commissioners turned to Brandeis for help. They knew him from the Eastern Rate case and knew that he understood railroad finance as well as anyone in the country. In late June he met with the commission secretary, John Hobart Marble, and, while not taking any formal role, agreed to provide informal advice. On 18 July he sent Marble a list detailing what information the commission should begin to gather in preparation for the hearings. One month later he received a letter from Commissioner James S. Harlan inviting him to serve as special counsel in what would be known as the Advance Rate case. Brandeis accepted, but insisted that the hearings not start before October, "as my vacation was delayed this year and I should be unable to do any work in the case before the middle of September."

In the Eastern Rate hearings, Brandeis, although serving without a fee, had clearly been identified as counsel to the shippers. In the

Advance Rate case he played a different role, one unfamiliar to many of those involved, and which led to numerous attacks by shipping interests and their attorneys, claiming that Brandeis had betrayed their trust. Part of the problem grew out of the ambiguity in Harlan's letter of invitation. Brandeis's task would be "seeing that all sides and angles of the case are presented of record, without advocating any particular theory for its disposition." This did not bother Brandeis, because he saw it as asking him to take on a role he had often performed, counsel to the situation. But another line in Harlan's letter noted, "We are of course aware of the fact that the carriers will not fail fully to present their side of the case and the Commission has felt that every effort should be made in the public interest adequately to present the other side. Would you care to undertake that burden?" On the one hand, Brandeis had been asked to be counsel to the situation, but on the other, the commission apparently wanted him to make sure the shippers' interests received adequate representation.

This led to confusion in some quarters, and bitterness on the part of people like Clifford Thorne who believed that Brandeis had been retained to represent the shippers as he had in the earlier Eastern Rate investigation. Newspapers also assumed that Brandeis had been brought in to oppose the rate hike, and many painted him as an inveterate opponent of the railroads. The *Washington Post,* recalling both the Eastern Rate case and the New Haven fight, labeled him "a consistent foe of the railroads," hiding his prejudices in the "anomalous capacity of 'citizen' in anti-railroad litigation."

The commission, on seeing such comments, tried to make Brandeis's position clear, and the chair, Edward Clark, issued a statement to the fact that Brandeis had been "employed to assist the Commission. . . . We see no reason why anyone should assume that his employment can disadvantageously affect any interest." One of the few people who understood Brandeis's role, Professor Ernst Freund of the University of Chicago Law School, hoped that Brandeis would be able to establish a precedent in administrative law, then a fledgling subject in the nation's law schools. A counsel to the commission, as opposed to a counsel for either side, "represents not one side or the other, but purely the public interest, which is the interest of justice to all concerned." There should not have been any confusion at all whom Brandeis represented. The ICC hired him and paid him nearly $14,000 for his work. Brandeis treated this case as a matter of professional work, with the Interstate Commerce Commission as his client and the public interest his responsibility.

There is no need to go into the details of the hearings. Unlike in the

Eastern Rate case, Brandeis dropped no bombshells, no million-dollar-a-day headline grabbers. People expected him to grill the railroad officials closely, but sparks began to fly when he also started asking shipping representatives discomfiting questions such as about the lower rates enjoyed by the larger shippers. The railroads and the shippers focused their attention on whether existing rates yielded adequate revenues for the lines, but Brandeis and the commission also wanted information on what the carriers ought to do to fix the situation if revenue proved insufficient.

Once again, Brandeis moved down to Washington, spent his days at the hearings, and then retired to his rooms at the Hotel Gordon to study the next batch of documents. By then he had also become involved in the affairs of the Wilson administration, which claimed much of his time. He managed to get in his daily walks, usually early in the morning, and about the only other relaxation he had came from a book he had picked up, Alfred Zimmern's *Greek Commonwealth,* which, as he told the author a few years later, "has given me more pleasure than any other book read within the last ten years except Gilbert Murray's *Bacchae.* During the winter of 1913–1914, when I was absorbed by a Railroad investigation, it was my only recreation. A few pages administered at bedtime provided efficient refreshment." Zimmern's ideas would greatly affect Brandeis's views on the ideal society and his hopes for the type of Zionist commonwealth to be created in Palestine.

Although he initially opposed the rate increase, in the end, and much to the chagrin of the shippers, Brandeis came to the conclusion that in fact some eastern-district rates were too low and should be increased. When the commission issued its report at the end of July 1914, it closely followed Brandeis's recommendations, rejecting most of the railroad requests but allowing some raises in specified areas. It also reflected Brandeis's views that the railroads continued to operate inefficiently, and that additional savings could be secured through better management. Many people suspected that Brandeis had himself written the report, but the evidence suggests that the commission relied upon but did not slavishly follow the arguments he made in his closing brief and argument. Clifford Thorne and other shipping representatives not only saw Brandeis's handwriting in the report but also accused the Boston lawyer of bad faith in backing some of the railroad claims. This returned to haunt Brandeis when nominated to the Court; Thorne was the very first witness against him and one of his most implacable foes during the confirmation hearings.

· · ·

THERE IS A SHORT POSTSCRIPT to the Advanced Rate case. A few days after the commission announced its decision, war broke out in Europe, and reports of the fighting crowded all other news from the front page. The railroads immediately seized upon the disruptions caused by the war to reopen the matter a little over a month after the commission report. On 9 September heads of six large railroads appealed directly to President Wilson, suggesting an era of good feeling in which the roads would cooperate fully with the government in its response to the crisis, and, of course, the railroads would get the rate increase they needed. The commission opened new hearings in mid-October, over the anguished protests of the shippers, and again asked Brandeis to serve as counsel.

Brandeis reluctantly agreed, but feared that reopening the case so soon after the original decision would give the railroads and their bankers the opportunity to undermine the commission's authority. The hearings from his point of view went badly. "The RRs & Bankers did not do themselves much credit," he complained to his brother soon after the hearings reopened. "If they have their way they will utterly break down the Commission & even if they are beaten they will have succeeded in greatly impairing its standing and their own defense against lawlessness and public ownership."

The facts had not changed since the original hearing, he argued, and while the railroads did need additional revenue, they also had to make their operations more efficient before they could justify a rate increase. The commission for its own sake and authority should stick to its initial decision. He suspected, however, that his reasoning would not prevail. On 16 December the commission voted 5–2 to grant the railroads the 5 percent rate increase they had sought. Brandeis predicted the decision would be a "misfortune to both the RRs and the Comm'n & will do much to hasten government ownership."

Although the government did take over the railroads during the war, and in fact ran them efficiently under a unified management, at the end of the conflict the lines returned to private ownership. Brandeis's dire predictions of public anger failed to materialize, at least in part because people understood that the war—even before America's entry in April 1917—caused disruptions of normal economic relationships. What might have angered many before the war now struck them as perhaps undesirable, but explicable.

All told, Brandeis's campaign to explain scientific management to the railroads had not been a failure, certainly when compared with his efforts to get labor to accept it. Some of the more enlightened railroad men, such as Daniel Willard of the Baltimore & Ohio, initially accepted it reluctantly, as the only option available to them after the commission decision in the Eastern Rate case. Once the program began to show the results that Brandeis had predicted, railroads embraced the idea more fully, although not in the manner that Taylor, Brandeis, and others had proposed. Scientific management, as a true partnership between employer and employee, never caught on.

With the successful conclusion of the long struggle against the New Haven and the rather more mixed results of the two rate cases, Louis Brandeis could finally turn away from railroad problems and address other and more pressing interests.

CHAPTER THIRTEEN

THE CURSE OF BIGNESS

P erhaps more than any other reformer of his time, Louis Brandeis stood as the opponent of big business and monopoly. His obser-vations on how to control the depredations of industrialism affected the debate over government control of business in the 1912 election as well as legislation on banking and antitrust passed during the Wilson administration. Whether they agreed with him or not, reformers and business leaders took his views seriously, and his ideas, expressed in articles and testimony, have informed historians ever since about this particular and important aspect of progressive reform. To understand his analysis, however, one has to recognize that it relied far more on principles of morality and political theory than on economics. Brandeis opposed large businesses because he believed that great size, either in government or in the private sector, posed dangers to demo-cratic society and to individual opportunity. Judge Learned Hand, who considered some of Brandeis's ideas "impractical," nonetheless believed that Brandeis's "feeling, his sense, was right" about the impact of big-ness upon the individual. At all times Brandeis maintained his faith in what he saw as the basic American principles of an open competitive society, in which private interests should always yield to the public good.

THE ECONOMIC THEORIES prevalent at the end of the nineteenth century, and the enormous changes that took place in the decades after the Civil War, constitute the milieu in which Brandeis formulated his ideas. If he had studied any economics at all while in school, it would have been what we now term the classical model, emphasizing laissez-faire (lack of government regulation), free competition, and the absence of monopolies. English common law had originally curtailed monopolies for the protection of merchants, but eighteenth-century writers opposed them to protect the consumer. "The price of monopoly," Adam Smith had declared, "is upon every occasion the highest which can be got. . . . The price of free competition, on the contrary, is the lowest which can be taken." In addition to competition, classical economists believed in the self-regulating nature of a free economy, in which the natural laws of economic activity constituted an "invisible hand." Perhaps most important, the classical school posited open access to and exit from the market. High demand would bring in new producers, eventually achieving an equilibrium between supply and demand at the optimum price for the consumer. If supply exceeded demand, then the least efficient producers would leave the market, and balance would automatically be restored.

Americans added a moral ingredient to the mix. The free market served as a testing ground for a man's character and ability. The Protestant ethic, tying labor in a person's calling to individual salvation and a rawboned frontier spirit, produced a curious amalgam of free competition, moral striving, and the pitting of man against nature. Out of this grew a belief that all men deserved an equal opportunity to make the most of their abilities. Americans respected and admired those who succeeded, ignored those who failed, and condemned any efforts to restrict opportunity—either to curb the strong or to help the weak—as immoral and counterproductive. Faith in the open-ended nature of the economy became part of the American ethos in the nineteenth century.

Classical economics and the American creed of opportunity, however, rested on a small-unit economy. Individuals had to be able to start farms or open small businesses with modest amounts of capital. But by the end of the nineteenth century free land for homesteading had begun to dwindle. A flood of immigrants from southern and eastern Europe quickly eliminated what had been a chronic shortage of labor, and more and more men—and women—now worked for other people with little hope of ever owning their own businesses. The manufacturing process grew more complex and required larger and more expensive machinery, restricting access of newcomers. It was one thing to open a dry-goods store with a few hundred dollars of inventory, and quite another to build a steel mill costing hundreds of thousands or even millions. Most ominously, one could discern the consolidation of small and medium-size firms into larger enterprises, many with near-monopolistic control over their particular markets.

In four years alone, from the beginning of 1898 to the end of 1901,

2,274 companies disappeared as a result of mergers, and the capitalization of these new entities totaled $5.4 billion. In the steel industry, new mergers dominated the field: American Tin Plate held 75 percent of the country's capacity in that product; American Steel & Wire, 80 percent; National Tube, 85 percent; and American Bridge, 50 percent. In 1901 all of these firms, plus several more, joined together in the Morgan-sponsored U.S. Steel Corporation. Capitalized at well over $1 billion, U.S. Steel brought under one control 213 different manufacturing plants and transportation companies, 41 mines, 1,000 miles of private railroad, 112 ore vessels, and 78 blast furnaces, as well as the world's largest coke, coal, and ore holdings. It controlled 43.2 percent of the nation's pig-iron capacity, and 60 percent of basic and finished steel products. In oil, John D. Rockefeller put together the Standard Oil Company that ruthlessly drove small, independent operators out of business. The conservative Wall Street publisher John Moody believed this development boded well for the future prosperity of the country and saw it as not only beneficial but inevitable.

Industrialization and the growing concentration of economic power in fewer hands affected how Americans thought about the market and what it meant in terms of both individual and social effects. Defenders of big business essentially married the old classical model to a conservative Darwinism, justifying the emergence of giant corporations as a form of survival of the fittest. To interfere in this process of "natural selection" would only hinder progress and undermine the strength of the American economy. As for the public interest, which Brandeis and others believed to have been at the heart of the older paradigm, industrial leaders offered a new model—let the people learn and profit from hardship. Henry O. Havemeyer, president of the American Sugar Refining Company, put it bluntly: "Let the buyer beware; that covers the whole business. You cannot wet nurse people from the time they are born until the time they die. They have got to wade in and get stuck, and that is the way men are educated and cultivated."

If in the older model success equaled moral uprightness, then even more honor should be paid to Andrew Carnegie, E. H. Harriman, James J. Hill, and other self-made men who had built their empires on skill, good character, and shrewd business sense—indeed, every schoolboy should try to emulate them. The darker side of their business—the shady agreements, the squalid slums spawned by factories, horrendous working conditions—frightened many people, but this only increased the veneration and public homage to the older virtues, the "continuing veneration of individualism, self-reliance, and laissez-faire economics."

At the turn of the century a debate arose within the business community over the benefits of competition. Bold entrepreneurs like Carnegie might welcome an unfettered free competition, confident in their own abilities to succeed. But the advent of gigantic corporations with millions tied up in factories and inventory led to a new emphasis on market stability and cooperation. A new generation of business leaders, including George W. Perkins of the house of Morgan, Elbert H. Gary of U.S. Steel, and John D. Rockefeller Jr., began preaching a system of business that Arthur Jerome Eddy, its chief theorist, called the "New Competition."

Advocates of the new system for the most part opposed any form of government control and proposed that cooperation within an industry be coordinated by the heads of the largest firms. The goal of market stability would ensure that long-term prices would not fluctuate wildly. In prosperous times, prices would rise slightly, while in slack periods they would fall, but again, only slightly. In place of price-cutting and other "unethical" practices, businesses would emphasize the quality of their products and service to customers, and within an industry members would share information and regulate themselves, punishing those who violated the code. In theory, a stable market accompanied by steady prices and improved service would benefit producer, consumer, and investor alike, and harm no one. If nothing else, the "New Competition" faced up to the fact that in many industries, manufacturing and plant costs had risen beyond the point where newcomers could gain easy access to the markets, and those holding large investments in existing plants and equipment could not allow many business failures. It also recognized that in a complex industrial society, employers, employees, and consumers had grown so interdependent that no party could tolerate erratic market fluctuations.

Charles Van Hise, an advocate of industrial concentration, called for "freedom for fair competition, elimination of unfair practices, conservation of natural resources, fair wages, good social conditions, and reasonable prices," and Louis Brandeis, the opponent of concentration, agreed with nearly all of it. Brandeis's view of business as a profession easily accommodated cooperation among producers, the elimination of cutthroat competition, stable pricing, and emphasis on quality and service. In fact, at one time or another he advocated all of these things, albeit in somewhat different form from Arthur Eddy or George Perkins. On the Supreme Court he surprised some of his former reform allies when he dissented in 1921, opposing the application of the antitrust laws to the American Hardwood Manufacturers' Association, a group representing about one-third of the nation's annual hardwood production whose members shared information about costs, sales, and stock.

But while the goals may have been similar, Brandeis and other opponents of bigness questioned whether the alleged benefits of the new industrial age outweighed what they saw as increasingly obvious disadvantages. They believed that big business was inimical to a democratic society and worried over the effect that monopolistic practices would have on government, labor, and the public. Few of them, however, knew exactly what to do about it. While some reformers flirted with socialism, Brandeis opposed government ownership except in the limited case of public utilities. Do not believe, he told Robert Bruère in 1922, "that you can find a universal remedy for evil conditions or immoral practice in effecting a fundamental change in society (as by State Socialism)."

How much grounding Brandeis had in economic theory is hard to say, but given his voracious reading habits, it is safe to say that he was not economically ignorant. The lectures he gave on business law in 1893 show a familiarity with classical theory, especially his arguments on the evils of monopoly. His father ran a successful grain and produce company, and while Frederika may have banned commercial talk from the dinner table, there is no doubt that the family discussed business matters. Moreover, Brandeis's law practice relied on commercial clients, whose affairs and problems he knew intimately.

Brandeis never really questioned the basic rightness of the free enterprise system. He acknowledged that it had defects, and he spent many years trying to correct them. But the achievements of his immigrant father, and his own and his brother's successful careers, imbued him with a sense of the opportunities awaiting the diligent worker. He differed from many of his fellow reformers in Boston when he insisted that risk capital deserved greater returns than money invested in safe measures, although he condemned outright speculation. Despite his involvement in labor matters, Brandeis did not overly concern himself with the weak. It is not that he did not care for people victimized by industrialization, or that he opposed measures to prevent the strong from taking advantage of others. Rather, he approached reform neither as a social worker nor as a leveler to give a leg up to those on the bottom. Life involved risks, and those who competed had to bear the losses as well as enjoy the gains. He always accepted and indeed rejoiced in the competition of life and of the economy, with both the harshness and the rewards. He once told his daughter Susan, when she complained of some difficulty, "My dear, if you will just start with the idea that this is a hard world, it will all be much simpler."

One form of challenge he did not care for involved the stock market, which he viewed as little more than legalized gambling. He made his money from his law practice and then invested it in safe railroad or municipal bonds. "I believe in investing money where it will be so safe," he said, "that I will not have to take time off thinking about it." The idea of making money for its own sake, especially through speculation, repulsed him. In a letter to Alfred in 1904, Louis spelled out his philosophy on the subject:

> I feel very sure that unser eins [people like us] ought not to buy and sell stocks. We don't know much about the business, and beware people who think they do. Prices of stocks are made. They don't grow; and their fluctuations are not due to natural causes. . . . My idea is . . . to treat investments as a necessary evil, indulging in the operation as rarely as possible. Buy only the thing you consider very good, and stick to it unless you have cause to doubt the wisdom of your purchase. And when you buy, buy the thing which you think is safe, and will give you a fair return; but don't try to make your money out of investments. Make it out of your business.

Years later he cautioned his daughter: "Do not invest in any stock, common or preferred. . . . Such investment is mere speculation." The few times he bought stock resulted from the requirements of his law practice; he occasionally had to own a few shares to attend a stockholders' meeting on behalf of a client. Long before he began writing about the curse of bigness and the use by bankers of other people's money, Brandeis distrusted the elaborate and what he considered fraudulent financial edifices created by J. P. Morgan, Jacob Schiff, Henry Lee Higginson, and others.

AT THE TIME BRANDEIS gave the business law lectures at MIT, he spoke primarily about the evils of monopoly and had little to say against bigness; in fact, he even praised some of the larger companies for their market success. But gradually Brandeis and other progressives came to oppose what they saw as the harmful effects of large-scale industrialization on society, labor, the environment, and the political process. In

1906, Brandeis expressed some surprise at the anti-big-corporation attitude held by a federal judge before whom he was trying a case, an attitude that Brandeis at the time did not fully share. By 1911, he had refined his thinking and through articles, interviews, and testimony before congressional hearings had become one of the country's best-known foes of bigness. Unlike Herbert Croly, the intellectual architect of Theodore Roosevelt's New Nationalism, Brandeis did not believe in the inevitability of the large corporation. While certain "natural" monopolies existed—such as municipal gas or water systems—in all other areas there was a limit beyond which a company could only grow through artificial means; namely, the stifling of competition.

Advocates of bigness and monopoly—and the two often went together—decried competition among smaller firms as wasteful; economies of scale made the big company the most efficient producer of goods, and this meant that the consumer would benefit from lower prices. "This argument is essentially unsound," Brandeis declared. "The wastes of competition are negligible. The economies of monopoly are superficial and delusive. The efficiency of monopoly is at best tempo-rary. Undoubtedly competition involves waste. What human activity does not?"

Brandeis believed that the ability and judgment of the person in charge constituted the single most important element of business suc-cess. As firms grew too large, they became unmanageable, because no one person, no matter how talented, could direct them well. Henry Bruère recalled that when the bank he directed celebrated its one hun-dredth anniversary in 1934, Justice Brandeis sent him a telegram read-ing, "BEST WISHES, I HOPE YOU MAY NEVER GROW LARGER." Delegation of authority and responsibility—the keystones of modern management theory—struck Brandeis as exceedingly poor business procedures. He did not insist that all companies be one-man opera-tions. Some people did certain jobs very well, and some could supervise better than others; individual talents differed. He had organized his own law firm on these principles. But, he believed, once a company grew so large that the person in charge operated three or four removes from production, that person did not really know what was happening. "Man's work," he maintained, "often outruns the capacity of the indi-vidual man." Each man, he said, "is a wee thing," and he liked to quote Goethe that "care is taken that the trees do not scrape the skies." Bran-deis's faith in business as in democracy began and ended with what he saw as the natural limits of the individual.

The curse of bigness applied to government as it did to business. Big government could be as bad as big business, because both violated the same rules of efficiency. In limited units, men could function and be on top of their jobs, and the public would be served; if a government agency grew too large, the officers in charge would not be able to control the organization, and everyone would suffer. Big government posed as great a social and political threat as did economic monopoly. "We risk our whole system," Brandeis told the Senate Committee on Interstate Commerce in 1911, "by creating a power which we cannot control."

The obvious answer, at least to Brandeis, was restricting the size of both government and private businesses. He believed that since big firms had grown out of unrestrained, cutthroat competition in which the strongest—albeit not the most moral—had survived, restraints upon unethical business practices had to be enacted. If a company failed as a result of the poor quality of its product or bad management, then the economy and the consumer gained, even if the investors lost. If, on the other hand, a firm used its power illicitly to force out its rivals, then the community suffered.

"There is in every line of business a unit of greatest efficiency," he wrote. "The unit of greatest efficiency is reached when the disadvantages of size counterbalance the advantages. The unit of greatest efficiency is exceeded when the disadvantages of size outweigh the advantages." He understood that this point would vary from industry to industry, company to company, and even from time to time, and hoped that someday it would be possible, through scientific management, to determine with some exactitude the precise point of maximum size.

There are inherent contradictions between wanting to maintain a small-unit or, as some economists describe it, an "atomistic" market structure and the real economies that large-scale firms enjoy. If the government, for whatever political, economic, or social reasons, chose to preserve the small-unit market, then the government itself would have to impose and enforce limitations on competitive behavior, because in an atomistic market competition will almost always lead to the most successful firms crowding out the least efficient.

One of the most incisive critics of Brandeis's views has been Thomas K. McCraw, who has drawn on recent developments in economic theory such as distinguishing "center" from "peripheral" firms and vertical from horizontal integration. McCraw argues that Brandeis's failure to grasp these distinctions "fed his confusion concerning how and why big businesses evolved, which business practices would or would not help consumers, and which types of organizations were or were not efficient." At the heart of this confusion lay Brandeis's stubborn commitment to smallness, an "anti-modern ideology" that would sacrifice the interests of a majority of consumers for the preservation, on political grounds, of inefficient small units threatened by the inexorable march of progress toward concentration. In the end, Brandeis's refusal to separate market facts from morality, his readiness to tailor his economics to his "aesthetic preference for small size," overwhelmed his formidable analytical powers and "doomed to superficiality both his diagnosis and his prescription."

To fault Brandeis on his economic theory, as McCraw does, is to miss the point, because he made these arguments not as an economist but as a moralist and a democrat. "I am no theorist," he candidly admitted, but he knew trusts. "I have had a large experience and know what I am talking about." Big business threatened the economic opportunity of the individual and also posed a danger to a free society. Brandeis did not try to hide these fears behind the façade of the efficiency argument; to him they all went together. The curse of bigness adversely affected everyone and in every way, and therefore had to be fought. "I used to think there were 'good trusts,' " he said in 1912, "that there were big men at the head of some of them and that they worked things out for the benefit of the community. I know better now. There are no good trusts."

"Half a century ago," Brandeis told a congressional hearing in 1912, "nearly every American boy could look forward to becoming independent as a farmer or mechanic, in business or in professional life; and nearly every American girl could expect to become the wife of such a man. Today most American boys have reason to believe, that throughout life they will work in some capacity as employees of others, either in private or public business; and a large percentage of women occupy like positions." The rise of gigantic industries caused this shift, and the consequences would be devastating to the nation. The boy would work, he would produce, he might even do better as an employee than as an independent farmer or mechanic. But where would he be able to test himself? Where would he have an opportunity to wager his future on his own ability? How would he develop the strong and independent character that came from daring and succeeding, or even from daring and failing? Democracy reflected the character of its citizens, and a nation could never have a vibrant democracy without free people, individuals with pride and the strength to take chances.

Time and again Brandeis emphasized that individual opportunity stood at the heart of political freedom. "You cannot have true American citizenship, you cannot preserve political liberty, you cannot secure American standards of living," he informed the Senate, "unless some degree of industrial liberty accompanies it." He understood that not all men would be independent; many would work in factories and for others even on small farms or in small businesses. But if people no longer felt they controlled, at least in some measure, their own economic destiny, then the traditional basis of the political structure would itself be threatened. Jefferson had believed that democracy rested on the shoulders of the yeoman farmer; Brandeis expanded that notion to include small-business men and professionals. Employees dependent upon large corporations could be coerced, and as more and more people worked for these companies with no hope of economic independence, the danger of business influence and control over politics increased. "There cannot be liberty without industrial independence," Brandeis said, "and the greatest danger to the people of the United States today is in becoming, as they are gradually more and more, a class of employees."

He rejected the argument that the growth of large corporations represented an irrevocable law of economic development, nor did he accept the monopolists' claims that by operating more efficiently, they provided the public with better goods at lower prices, so that all Americans could enjoy a higher standard of living. To Brandeis this missed the whole point of what America meant. Yes, he agreed, people should be well housed and well fed and have opportunities for education and recreation. A free nation demanded no less, but "we may have all these things and have a nation of slaves." Material comfort, or at least the basic needs of life, mattered, but freedom, tied to opportunity, mattered more.

Brandeis did not foresee, nor did anyone else, that even in an economy dominated by multibillion-dollar global corporations, there would still be opportunity for those seeking it. Technology in our own time has opened up unlimited possibilities for small and medium-size businesses. While it is true that Microsoft and Apple are gigantic firms, Bill Gates and Steve Jobs started those firms in their garages with limited capital. The service industry as well as computers and other technologies seems to be an infinite source of economic opportunity. An economic scenario that included both gigantic firms and small and successful companies is one that most progressives—including Brandeis—did not envision.

. . .

BRANDEIS HAD HIS FIRST CHANCE to put his ideas into practice when he worked with Robert La Follette in 1911 to draft a measure expanding the 1890 Sherman Antitrust Act. "I want you to give me as many cases as you can of business assassination, attempted and accomplished by the System, cases within your personal knowledge," La Follette wrote, "and with the names of the corporations involved." Because of attorney-client confidentiality, Brandeis could not tell all of his stories, but he did share one that had involved him a great deal, and one that did not show Brandeis at his best.

The story of the United Shoe Machinery Company is tangled and would become part of the attack on Brandeis during the nomination hearings in 1916. His critics charged that Brandeis had helped create United Shoe, defended it and its monopolistic practices, and then turned against the company. While the bare outline is true, the story is complex and revolves around the fact that Brandeis violated his own cardinal rule about investing in a client's company, and lost, at least to some extent, the objectivity he valued so highly in his professional work. While he claimed that he had done no wrong and certainly nothing illegal, the episode shows, at the least, a lapse of judgment on his part.

In 1899, Brandeis represented the Henderson family, which had large holdings in the McKay Shoe Machinery Company. Several of the large firms in the field, including Goodyear and Winslow, had agreed to merge, and invited McKay to join as well. Brandeis later claimed that he had opposed the merger "on ground of general business policy," but this led to a higher offer, and the company decided to join. The Henderson family wanted Brandeis on the board of directors to safeguard their interests, and he agreed, buying five shares of common stock to qualify. But he also invested $10,000 of his own money in preferred stock and later accumulated additional common stock as the company distributed rights to new issues to existing shareholders. He did what many corporation lawyers at the time did, and United Shoe seemed to him and to many others a good investment. It clearly, however, ran in the face of what he had told Alfred about purchasing stock.

Part of the new company's success resulted from so-called tying clauses, which required that a company leasing one machine from United had to rent all of its equipment from United. Since the company held most of the key patents on shoe-manufacturing equipment, and made some machines that no one else did, anyone wanting to make shoes had to take United's entire line. None of the rival companies offered a full line of equipment, so in effect a shoemaker could not lease one or two machines from them and the rest from United. In 1906 these competitors went to the Massachusetts legislature and sought a bill outlawing tying clauses. Sidney Winslow, the president of United, asked Brandeis and James J. Storrow to oppose the measure before the assembly committees.

Several years later Brandeis recalled the circumstances of that request. Due to illness, United's regular counsel, Louis A. Coolidge, could not attend to legislative matters. "I had a great deal of hesitation, and finally decided to go. I say a great deal of hesitation, as I did not like particularly to put myself in the position of testifying on the subject. But I felt the company was being attacked by this bill in the interests of certain shoe machinery manufacturers and not of the public." Although he identified himself at the hearings as a director and stockholder, he nonetheless submitted a brief and received payment as if he had been counsel. Moreover, his argument on behalf of the company seems strange indeed in light of his opposition to monopoly, for that is the only word to describe the United Shoe Machinery Company.

Because United leased equipment to small manufacturers on the same basis as it did to large companies, men with a minimum of capital could enter the shoe-manufacturing business with access to the latest machinery. Brandeis then went on in words that even in 1906 seem strange coming from him:

> What is this so-called monopoly? It is nothing more than that control which to a greater or less extent any successful business acquires by virtue of being successful, and therefore of expanding. If this company has machines which are deemed to be desirable by shoe manufacturers, why should not this company be allowed to increase its own business by refusing to let manufacturers have these machines unless they will purchase also from the same concern other machines which they require? . . . Great corporations have resorted to [the tying clause] from time to time as a means of increasing their already large business.

Not all shoe manufacturers accepted Brandeis's claim that the leases worked to their benefit, and he got some of them, including William H. McElwain, to withdraw their support for the anti-tying-clause measure in return for a promise that United would look into their grievances. In September 1906, however, Brandeis learned of a federal court decision in Wisconsin that held a monopoly resulted, not from the holding of patents, but from the way the holder enforced the patent to eliminate competition. He alerted Sidney Winslow as well as United's general counsel, Elmer Howe, that the ruling, if widely accepted, could adversely affect the company. Winslow insisted that Brandeis again represent the company at the next legislative session, when new attacks upon the tying clause would be introduced. This put Brandeis in a quandary. Despite his earlier defense of monopoly and the tying clause, he considered Judge Seaman, who wrote the Wisconsin opinion, "uncommonly able," and now had doubts as to his earlier position. In December 1906, he resigned as a director of the company, explaining that with United now so well established, the Henderson family no longer needed him as a director to protect their interests, and so he "ought not to continue an exception to my general rule of not holding the office of director in any corporation for which I act as counsel."

Two years later, in 1908, Brandeis told the editor Henry Beach Needham that he had resigned "because I was unable to induce the management to adopt the views which I held from a public standpoint in respect to the operations of the company." He still believed that the past and present operations of United Shoe had been "on the whole beneficial to the trade. The grave objection which I had to it was the principles on which it was operated, and their effect in the future, and to a certain extent incidental methods employed."

Then, in 1912, he told Senator Moses Clapp that he had learned additional information that proved inconsistent with earlier statements made by the company's management. He did not yet know if United's policy was unsound or its methods improper, "but so serious a doubt had been raised in my mind as to the soundness of their general policy, and particularly as to the propriety of some of their methods, that I was unwilling to assume responsibility for the company's actions."

Brandeis was certainly being honest in admitting that during this time he did not complain about the company's monopolistic control over the manufacturing and leasing of shoe-making machinery, but what then did he object to regarding the company's actions? The decision in the Wisconsin case, while surely raising questions about United's policies, did not constitute any sort of definite legal rule on the subject outside Wisconsin. The case never went on appeal to the Supreme Court, and in 1906, and even later, no ruling by the high court would have held the tying clause illegal. Brandeis might have believed that Judge Seaman had gotten it right, but that hardly explains his actions. Moreover, while he had warned Sidney Winslow about the possibilities of legal problems, it is unclear how much he had pushed the company to change those policies he later described as monopolistic. At the 1907 legislative session Brandeis sat in on a few conferences between the company and shoe manufacturers, but he then resigned as counsel to the company, and after that the Brandeis firm apparently had little to do with United Shoe except to finish up a few minor cases. The Massachusetts legislature did, however, enact a measure regulating the sale and lease of shoe-making machinery similar to the measure defeated the year earlier.

Had the story stopped here, Brandeis would have been guilty of little more than bad judgment in violating one of his own rules regarding the separation of his business from investment, and in going onto the board, even for the ostensible purpose of looking after a client's interests (a practice, it should be noted, common to many lawyers of his standing). He had warned the company that there were potential legal problems and, at least according to his later recollections, tried to get Winslow to change those policies, without success. On one occasion, he said, he had spoken to Winslow for five hours "without my making the slightest impression." Brandeis had, as he put it, done all he could and then walked away.

In response to the 1907 law, United Shoe inserted two new clauses into its leases. One said that any section of the lease held to be unlawful would not be deemed part of the lease, and the other gave the company a unilateral right to cancel a lease on thirty days' notice. The first clause meant nothing unless someone tried to take the company to court, which he would not do because of the second proviso. In 1907, United Shoe had no real competition in the making of a full line of shoe machinery, and if it canceled a lease, the shoe manufacturer had no one else to whom he could turn. Cancellation in essence meant ruin.

Then, in 1910, Thomas Plant began to develop an alternative line of shoe machinery independent of United's patents, and he sought to hire Brandeis as counsel. Brandeis refused, carefully abstaining from anything that might bring him into conflict with a former client. Plant did not want to lease his machines, which many considered superior to United's, but to sell them at a small margin of profit. If even one big shoe manufacturer agreed to take Plant's equipment, others would quickly follow. But the shoemakers feared retribution from United, and one of them, Charles Jones of the Commonwealth Shoe & Leather Company, sought advice from his counsel on the legality of United's leases. Brandeis could not deny this request from an existing client, and at his direction William Dunbar drew up an opinion that while the leases may have been legal under Massachusetts law, under the newly re-invigorated Sherman Act the leases probably violated federal law. The memorandum pointed to a recent Supreme Court case that held similar leases invalid. Moreover, Brandeis and Dunbar believed that any effort by United to buy out Plant would also violate the Sherman Antitrust Act.

United, however, figured out a different way to put Plant out of business. In October 1910, Plant had obligations due of $1.5 million. As a matter of course the banks would normally have given him an extension, but United got the First National Bank of Boston to refuse to renew the loan and then used First National's contact with other banks in Boston and New York to refuse Plant credit. Plant had no choice but to sell, and United stepped in to purchase his equipment and patents. Brandeis, who had advised one member of United's executive committee that any man who tried to put Plant out of business "would look jail in the face," learned of the sale in the morning newspapers at the end of September. "I then concluded that the time had come when I could no longer properly remain passive," he told Senator Clapp, and if the opportunity arose, he would "lend aid in any effort that might be made to restore competitive conditions in the industry."

This was the story that Brandeis told to Robert La Follette in 1911. But it was not the end of his involvement with the United Shoe Machinery Company.

IN MAY 1911 officers of the Shoe Manufacturers' Alliance, several of whom counted Brandeis as their lawyer, approached him for help in seeking to restore competition in the shoe-machinery business, and he agreed to do so on one condition. He recognized that the alliance served the commercial interests of shoemakers, so he insisted that they had to pass on to the consumer some of the savings they would realize with the restoration of competition. They agreed to do so, and Brandeis took on their cause. He had already sold off the common stock he owned in United, and now he sold off the preferred, holding on to just one share so he could gain access to the company's annual meeting. Since this would again be a pro bono effort, he charged the alliance a nominal fee of $2,500, which went to his partners, and then he sent the same amount back to the alliance out of his own pocket.

About the same time that Brandeis wrote to La Follette about the sins of the "Shoe Machinery Trust," as he now called it, the federal government brought both antitrust and criminal proceedings against United Shoe for its actions regarding Plant. In mid-July, United's board of directors, belatedly waking up from the failure to heed earlier warnings not only from Brandeis but from other lawyers as well, asked Brandeis to meet with them. Although he could not get them to change their policy, he did manage to make clear to them why he had left the board earlier, and that record stood him in good stead during the confirmation hearings.

Then Governor Eugene Foss of Massachusetts unexpectedly attacked United, and a number of Boston financial men believed Brandeis to be responsible. In fact, Brandeis had met with Foss, who showed him his message just one hour before delivering it to the legislature, but he had, as he told Alfred, done nothing to instigate it. Nonetheless, "my old friends will think I am at the bottom of it—as they do that I am responsible for the government investigation—a belief which is groundless."

When congressional committees began holding hearings on new antitrust proposals as well as on various economic policy matters, Brandeis testified—and at length—before all of them. He now told the story of United in a far different way than he had earlier. He no longer defended the company as a good monopoly, but because of the way in which it had forced Plant out of business, he contended, United stood for the worst aspects of monopolistic industry.

United fought back in an effort to discredit Brandeis, and Sidney Winslow told Senator Clapp that the People's Attorney's allegations regarding United putting Plant out of business had absolutely no foundation in fact. "In his present role of an expounder of public morals, he seeks to hold this company up to public contumely because it opposed a law which he himself denounced publicly as unconstitutional." The company also issued a pamphlet titled *Brandeis and sɪǝpuɐɹᗺ—the Reversible Mind of Louis D. Brandeis, "the People's Lawyer"—As It Stands Revealed in His Public Utterances, Briefs, and Correspondence.* While no one ever claimed responsibility for authorship, it clearly came from either someone within the higher management of United or someone who had access to the company's confidential files. It very cleverly used Brandeis's own words against him, taking passages from letters, testimony, conference memoranda, and briefs, all edited to show that Brandeis spoke out of both sides of his mouth. The company then arranged for all or part of the pamphlet to appear in newspapers and magazines friendly to business. Brandeis, by now accustomed to such attacks, shrugged it off. But in 1916 he would have to expend a great deal of energy during the confirmation fight explaining away United's charges.

Although Brandeis later compared the fight against United with that against the New Haven, even so friendly a biographer as Alpheus Mason found the episode puzzling. For all his antimonopoly talk—and by 1906 he had expressed these sentiments a number of times—he nonetheless agreed to represent United, a company formed through mergers of previously competing companies. He had gone onto the United board to protect the interests of one of his clients, a practice widespread in the legal profession, although one that Brandeis himself had studiously avoided for the simple reason that it might create a conflict between his role as an attorney, representing the Hendersons, and his role as a director, responsible for the company's policies. His clients in the shoe-making business had no problem with the tying clause by itself, but objected to the higher prices that United, as a monopoly, could charge. Had the company lowered its prices, it apparently would have satisfied the shoemakers, who, because of patents, had to use United's equipment. Brandeis had accepted the role of counsel in opposing the 1906 legislation on the understanding that if the bill were defeated, United would renegotiate its leases with more favorable terms to the shoemakers. After the defeat of the measure the company did not renegotiate, and not until Brandeis learned of a case in far-off Wisconsin did he begin to have doubts about the tying clauses. One suspects that he resigned less because of Judge Seaman's opinion than because of his embarrassment that United had not kept its word to McElwain and other shoe manufacturers, a promise that he had helped to elicit.

Yet between 1907 and late 1910, Brandeis said little about either United or the tying clauses. Only after United put Thomas Plant out of business did Brandeis finally begin to talk about the "Shoe Machinery Trust." The company, despite its denials, did change its policies between 1906 and 1910, and it did exploit its monopolistic powers. Long before Brandeis denounced the company to Senator La Follette, it had engaged in the same types of activities that Brandeis had earlier discovered during the New Haven fight. Moreover, United did not try to cloak its actions—with the exception of forcing Plant out of business—and with all of his shoe-making clients, Brandeis certainly would have been kept aware of United's policies and actions. The investigator who had ferreted out William Howard Taft's deceptions in Pinchot-Ballinger ought to have been able to discern United's depredations.

Brandeis's instincts proved wise, and had he followed them, he could have avoided many of the charges made against his alleged ethical flip-flopping. Moreover, he did not have to reenter the fray in 1911. Recognizing his error in going on the United board in the first place, he had maintained a studied neutrality concerning the company after 1906. Perhaps he should have continued to do so.

In the meantime, the federal investigation begun in 1911 led to charges against United, and eventually the U.S. Supreme Court held that tying clauses violated the antitrust laws. Brandeis, by then a member of the high court, recused himself in the case, but the near-unanimous decision against the company must have given him a quiet satisfaction.

WHILE DETAILING THE ABUSES of United to La Follette, Brandeis also helped the senator draft an antitrust measure designed to remedy the weaknesses in the 1890 Sherman Antitrust Act. Going back and forth between Boston and Washington on other business, Brandeis would meet with La Follette when he could, and the two men, along with some other congressional insurgents, discussed various proposals that might be included in the new legislation. Then, in May 1911, the Supreme Court upheld the government's antitrust suit against Rockefeller's Standard Oil, holding that the company had violated the Sherman Act. The decision dismayed progressives, however, for the Court adopted the "rule of reason" to mean that only "unreasonable" restraints of trade violated the federal law. La Follette and others believed that this opened the door to all sorts of special pleading and gave conservative courts the discretionary power to decide what constituted a "reasonable" restraint of trade as opposed to an "unreasonable" one, a change in the Sherman Act that Congress had consistently refused to make.

In response to an emergency telegram from La Follette, Brandeis took the night train from Boston and arrived in the capital on the afternoon of 18 May 1911. He immediately closeted himself with La Follette, Francis J. Heney of California, and Irvine Lenroot of Wisconsin, and the four men worked out the basic provisions of the La Follette–Stanley Antitrust bill introduced into the Senate on 19 August. The bill had a number of sections fine-tuning the Sherman Act and three major substantive provisions. First, it tried to define what constituted a reasonable as opposed to an unreasonable restraint of trade. Second, the bill proposed that when a company is indicted under the antitrust law, the burden of proof would be on the defendant to show the reasonableness of its actions, just as railroads had to prove reasonableness in asking for a rate increase. Finally, to give teeth to the law, the authors wrote that once a company had been found guilty, competitors who had been adversely affected by the illegal practices would only need to prove their harm and receive triple damages in awards.

Brandeis did not expect the La Follette bill to pass, certainly not easily. "The antitrust fight will be a hard one," he predicted to Alice after the meeting, "and our own friends much divided—more or less imbued with the idea of monopoly inevitableness. I think it probable that we shall get some valuable thinking on the subject at any rate. That the country will repeal the Sherman law seems to me almost impossible, but it is highly possible that some changes will be made."

Even before La Follette submitted the bill, the Senate Committee on Interstate Commerce had begun hearings on the growth of big business and what federal policy toward it should be. George W. Perkins and other representatives of big business testified that industries had grown as a result of greater efficiency. Big companies like U.S. Steel, International Harvester, and Standard Oil had given the American public the highest standard of living in the world. The country did not have to fear its great industries, but instead should see them as the inevitable result of market forces.

Brandeis took the stand for three days starting on 14 December 1911 and with one example after another spelled out his message: trusts did not enjoy greater efficiency than smaller firms; they had gained control of the market either by merger or by forcing smaller and weaker competitors out of business; a natural limit existed beyond which no one man or even a small group of men could effectively control a company and exercise good judgment. Big companies that had failed to win control of the market, either through merger or cutthroat competition, had for the most part failed. Moreover, Brandeis began to expand on the theme that behind the drive of companies like U.S. Steel to gain control of the market lay bankers and investment houses, eager to underwrite new stock offerings and gain commissions. In addition to closing off competition in the market, big companies adversely affected the social, political, and economic life of the country. Socialism by itself could make few converts in a country of opportunity, but the actions of the giant trusts did more than anything else to gain converts to that cause. The answer to the problems generated by these monstrous companies could not be simpler. "If we make competition possible, if we create conditions where there would be reasonable competition, these monsters would fall to the ground." He spent five hours on the stand the first day, and as he modestly wrote to Alice, "I am told it was a great speech."

By now the debate over monopoly and bigness had heated up, and Brandeis had become one of its central figures. "The Trust discussion won't let me in peace," he told Alice, as he listed one person after another who had disturbed his quiet in Washington. He thought there would be a "battle royal," and he clearly welcomed it. "I am dead against the middle of the road. No regulated private monopoly of the capitalists. Either competition or State Socialism. Regulate competition, not monopoly, is my slogan. We have trouble enough with vested rights, let us not begin with vested wrongs."

Over the next few months Brandeis would deliver this same message with slight variations to the House Committee on the Judiciary in its hearings on antitrust legislation, the House Committee investigating U.S. Steel, and the House Committee on Patents. He also met with various government officials to discuss antitrust matters, including Commissioner of Corporations Herbert Knox Smith. Although the La Follette–Stanley bill died, Brandeis and other progressives laid the ground for the great debate on monopolies that would be at the center of the 1912 presidential campaign and that would result in the last major revision to the nation's antitrust laws in 1914.

BRANDEIS, LIKE ANY GOOD commercial lawyer, understood the positive role that banks could play in helping business. Many a small entrepreneur had succeeded because some banker, impressed with the person's business idea or personality, had been willing to extend credit and help get the enterprise going. Of this role Brandeis approved. Even a great idea could not be made viable if the person with that idea did not have the resources to begin operations. The banks brought together spare capital, in the form of savings, with investment opportunities, in the form of fledgling companies. Brandeis began to understand, especially in his fight with the New Haven, that the big banks did far more than underwrite new businesses. They issued stock, made fortunes in commissions, controlled the companies through seats on the boards of directors, and scripted the great wave of mergers that resulted in companies like U.S. Steel and International Harvester.

In early 1911, Brandeis started talking about how banks used "other people's money" both for good and for ill. Responsible bankers saw the power they had over people's deposits as a trust (and here he surely had in mind Massachusetts savings bank directors), to be used impartially depending on the degree of an applicant's creditworthiness. But if "they exercise their power regardless of that trust, ignoring the square deal, it amounts practically to their playing the industrial game with loaded dice." This illegitimate use of other people's money, he warned, might ultimately "force the thought of Government control of money in order to insure the square deal."

Later in the year he told a reporter that "the control of capital is, as to business, what the control of water supply is to life. The economic menace of past ages was the dead hand which gradually acquired a large part of all available lands. The greatest economic menace of today is a very live hand—these few able financiers who are gradually acquiring control over our quick capital." It would be one thing if the bankers used their own money; after all, people had a right to refuse to lend their own capital. But bankers held other people's money and therefore had an obligation to manage it in a fair and equitable manner. This they were not doing, he charged, and as a result "the fetters which bind the people are forged from the people's own gold."

A person reading this might have assumed that Brandeis had moved over toward the radical wing of progressivism, those who flirted with socialist ideas and the redistribution of wealth. But Brandeis, like Theodore Roosevelt and Woodrow Wilson, never abandoned his conservatism, his belief that one had to adapt to new conditions in order to preserve the best of the old. There was, however, a growing sense of outrage not so much against the new economic modes (although he did not care for them) as against those who controlled the new industrialism and who he believed had compromised their integrity by catering to the worst aspects of the new order. As early as 1891 he had told his fiancée of his outrage at "the wickedness of people, shielding wrong doers, and passing themselves off (or at least allowing them to pass themselves off) as honest men." The corporation itself had no life, no power to make decisions, no intrinsic good or evil. Rather, in the hands of farsighted leaders like William McElwain and the Filenes, the corporation became a tool to be used to develop a business that benefited not only its owners but its workers and the community. But in the hands of a J. P. Morgan or a John D. Rockefeller, the corporation became an instrument of oppression, stifling individualism and opportunity, and the bankers were the worst of the villains. Brandeis may have sounded like a radical in attacking the so-called captains of industry and the bankers who controlled the economy, but his solution—the restoration of competition and with it individual opportunity—could not have been more conservative.

Beginning in May 1912, a special subcommittee of the House Banking and Currency Committee, chaired by Arsène Pujo of Louisiana, began public hearings on the banking community, during which Samuel Untermyer, the committee counsel, grilled witnesses from the banks and investment houses on the practices of high finance. Although J. P. Morgan and other bankers denied that such a thing as a "money trust" existed, the committee found clear evidence of a concentration of financial power in a handful of men. No sooner had the committee issued its report than the financial community began worrying about what would happen next. A "cold perspiration" gripped bankers, according to one newspaper, "at the thought of an intelligent committee with Louis D. Brandeis as counsel."

Brandeis followed the Pujo hearings closely and had received a copy of the committee report from Untermyer in mid-March 1913. He read it immediately and wrote to Untermyer calling the work "admirable." He agreed with most of the recommendations, but "in some respects it seems to me that the recommendations do not go far enough," and he suspected that in those instances the committee had failed to heed Untermyer's advice. On his next trip to New York he met with Untermyer, and the two men went carefully over the committee's findings. Brandeis then sat down and wrote his most famous nonjudicial work, a series of articles called "Breaking the Money Trust" for *Harper's Weekly,* now edited by his good friend Norman Hapgood, later collected and published as *Other People's Money, and How the Bankers Use It.*

The first installment in the series, titled "Our Financial Oligarchy," appeared in the 22 November 1913 issue of *Harper's,* and the remaining eight articles followed on a weekly basis. The series appeared just as Congress debated reform of the banking system, and Woodrow Wilson received advance copies that he read closely. Wilson had been convinced earlier that a money trust existed and just prior to his inauguration had declared, "The banking system of this country does not need to be indicted. It is convicted." If any one other than bankers doubted that, Brandeis's articles pounded home the message with force and clarity.

In the series, Brandeis repeated many of the arguments he had made before about the inefficiency of big corporations and their threat to democratic institutions. But he went further than in his previous attacks and, according to one scholar, "contributed the first serious challenge to the principal rationale of the consolidation movement." Whatever progressives thought about the social consequences of industrialization, most of them conceded the economic superiority of the large unit. Brandeis laid out what he considered the weaknesses in the arguments of efficiency and inevitability:

Consolidations created companies too big for their managers to manage responsibly, because they could not know what was happening in all of the divisions.

Bankers who promoted the combinations and dominated their management afterward only aggravated the supervisory problem by taking on tasks for which they had no qualifications and that conflicted with their responsibilities as bankers.

Consolidations reduced competition, and in doing so contributed to economic inefficiency by adversely tampering with the market.

Interlocking directorates, in which the same people sat on the boards of companies that should be independent, led to preferential treatment at the expense of the company and of the consumer.

Consolidations that now enjoyed monopolistic status used that power to thwart the entry of new producers and to suppress innovations that jeopardized existing investment.

The concentration of the control of money led to discriminatory credit practices and inflated the cost of money for new capital investments, especially for those attempting to start new businesses. The constricting of competition in banking inevitably led to constriction of competition in all sectors of the economy.

The series presents the quintessential Brandeisian argument against bigness: it is inefficient, it chokes off competition, it stifles opportunity, and it is not inevitable, but only appears so because of the machinations of the bankers.

The core of the argument is moral rather than economic, and almost from the time of its publication economists have noted its weaknesses. They are no doubt right. There is a certain nineteenth-century New England provincialism present, a disregard of market forces and the social as well as economic gains that consolidation often brings. But there is also much to say for morality in the marketplace, as anyone who reads the daily papers in the early twenty-first century can attest. News stories are full of the illegal and arrogant practices of giant corporations, which often see themselves as above the law that applies to everyone else. In this they are no different from J. P. Morgan, who in a meeting with Theodore Roosevelt objected to the application of a federal law to his enterprises. "Just send your man to see my man," Morgan told the president, "and they can work things out."

Hapgood arranged for the articles to be edited for book publication. Both he and the publisher, Frederick Stokes, wanted to call the book *Every Man's Money, and What the Bankers Do with It,* but Brandeis insisted on *Other People's Money,* having used the phrase from Adam Smith's *Wealth of Nations* in previous speeches and articles. The book appeared in 1914, after the passage of the Federal Reserve Act, and has been considered one of the major muckraking works of the progressive era.

In the midst of the Great Depression, following the election of Franklin Roosevelt, Brandeis arranged for a cheap edition of *Other People's Money* to be printed, hoping that as people realized the folly of bankers in the 1920s, they would finish the reforms begun in the Wilson era. But the inner circle surrounding Roosevelt had little use for Brandeis's ideas, finding "his faith in smallness too stark and rigorous." The Glass-Steagall Act and other New Deal measures, however, did much to implement one of Brandeis's main proposals, the separation of investment and banking functions. Although that measure operated well for more than a half century, recent business-oriented administrations gave in to banking demands that they be allowed to reestablish their investment operations. Brandeis would not have approved, and the economic problems generated by poor banking practices would have justified his criticism.

ONE MAN WHO READ the first two articles in *Harper's* took exception to some of the aspersions cast on bankers. Thomas W. Lamont, then forty-three years old, after graduation from Harvard had gone into journalism and business in New York. Through a friendship with Henry Davison of the Morgan company, Lamont had been involved with the founding of the so-called bankers' bank, the Bankers Trust Company, in 1903, and thereafter steadily rose in influence in the financial world. He joined the Morgan firm in 1911, sat as Morgan's representative on a number of banks and manufacturing companies, and in the 1920s became head of J. P. Morgan & Company. It had been La-

J. P. Morgan partner Thomas W. Lamont in the 1920s

mont who had sold *Harper's* to Hapgood, and he contacted the editor to see if a meeting with Brandeis could be arranged. On Tuesday, 2 December 1913, Hapgood, Lamont, Brandeis, Amos Pinchot, and President Wilson's intimate adviser Colonel Edward M. House had lunch at the University Club in New York. Afterward, Lamont and Brandeis retired to one of the private rooms and spoke for three hours.

Lamont objected to Brandeis's charges that bankers exercised the kind of power depicted in the magazine articles, and asked if Brandeis had any firsthand knowledge. The Boston lawyer immediately referred to the New Haven, but Lamont claimed that it had all been Mellen's doing. But what about Morgan, whose firm had financed all of the New Haven's acquisitions? Lamont claimed that Morgan knew little about this. Once the banker had faith in someone, he rarely intervened, and essentially backed Mellen on the railroad head's assurances that the expansion would be a good idea and profitable. While Brandeis listened politely and professed himself interested by this new light on Morgan, he clearly did not accept the portrait of the formidable Morgan (and Lamont admitted that Morgan could indeed be quite formidable) simply acquiescing, without question, in the judgment of an underling on matters involving millions of dollars.

Perhaps the most interesting part of the exchange was as follows:

Lamont: What I cannot understand, Mr. Brandeis, is this fixed impression that you have as to this dangerous power that we have been wielding.

Brandeis: Yes, I do think it is dangerous, highly dangerous. The reason I think it is, is that it hampers the freedom of the individual. The only way we are going to work out our problems in this country is to have the individual free, not free to do unlicensed things, but free to work and to trade without the fear of some gigantic power threatening to engulf him every moment, whether that power be a monopoly in oil or in credit.

Lamont: And you are really convinced, Mr. Brandeis, that our house [Morgan] has this great power that you describe?

Brandeis: I am perfectly convinced of it.

The two men found little that they saw eye to eye on, although Lamont apparently agreed that interlocking directorates did cause conflicts of interests for some board members. Reading the transcript gives the impression of two people talking the same language but meaning far different things. Lamont could not accept Brandeis's basic assumption that a money power existed or that those who controlled it could inflict great harm on the country. Brandeis would not buy Lamont's assertion that the Morgan company did not exercise close control over firms it had helped create or that bankers played no role in the management of those firms. Neither man left the meeting, conducted on the most polite and cordial of terms, convinced one bit by the arguments of the other.

BRANDEIS'S VIEWS on the curse of bigness and banker control of other people's money rested in part on fact—big companies did exist, the house of Morgan and other bankers did control the credit of the country, monopolies did force smaller firms out of the market, often through unfair means of competition, the trusts did buy out new patents to prevent the introduction of more efficient technology. One might believe that the growth of large industries had been inevitable, that a Darwinian survival of the fittest in the end benefited the nation, that bankers exercised their power in a beneficent way, but one could not blink away evidence such as the failed effort of the New Haven, the aggressive tactics of United Shoe, or Rockefeller's ruthless elimination of competitors. Brandeis and many progressives learned one lesson from these stories; advocates of big business and some other progressives took away a different view.

To subject Brandeis's views on the inefficiency of big corporations and his theory of how the market should operate to analysis by economic theory leads, of course, to the conclusion that he had it all wrong. Companies could be efficient; even in a competitive national market, small firms often enjoy monopolistic power in a particular market; only big companies have been able to put aside significant sums of money for research and development; ease of entry is largely a myth, and exists only for a brief period when the market for a new product just opens.

That critique, however, misses the key element of what Brandeis tried to teach; namely, that in a democratic society the existence of large centers of private power is dangerous to the continuing vitality of a free people. This was not simply a question of power corrupting those who wielded it, but rather an assertion that the very existence of such power exerted a chilling effect. Workmen dependent for employment in a large factory could be intimidated regarding their support for "dangerous" political programs or candidates. The fact that a large bank in New York or Boston could exercise influence over its corresponding banks in smaller cities meant that businesses in these cities could be affected by the decisions of New York and Boston bankers. For Brandeis, social institutions, and these included economic organizations, had to be constructed to help individuals develop as responsible citizens, and the existence of large and threatening centers of economic power thwarted this goal.

Brandeis may have been wrong in his economic theory, but not in his cautions about the excesses of big business. The history of firms like Microsoft that built upon original and innovative ideas shows that as they grew bigger, they also began utilizing their power in ways that, if not outright illegal, certainly flouted the spirit of the laws. The failure of savings banks in the 1980s, after decades-old restraints had been removed, emphasizes the wisdom of those policies in the first place. Hardly a week goes by without news of some official of a large corporation going to jail or paying a large fine as a result of arrogance in meeting his or her duties. Brandeis's demand that business be carried on in a moral manner and his insistence that a free and open market benefited democracy—old-fashioned virtues indeed—still ring true.

As Alexander Bickel wrote on the centenary of Brandeis's birth, "Brandeis's achievement is that he gave new content to old ideals, a content immediately and creatively relevant in a society in which, as he himself said, 'the only abiding thing is change.' "

CHAPTER FOURTEEN

NATIONAL POLITICS

I n 1911 and 1912, Brandeis entered a world new to him—national politics. By then he had ceased to have much to do with Boston or Massachusetts affairs, except when the odd progressive such as Eugene Foss or David Walsh came to power. Boston's Irish population, led by James Curley and John "Honey Fitz" Fitzgerald, had taken over city politics, and the state's Republican Party, under the control of Henry Cabot Lodge, while not overtly reactionary, had little sympathy with the type of reform Brandeis and others preached.

He continued to practice law but left more and more of the bread-and-butter business to his partners while he focused on pro bono work and national affairs. Louis guarded what time he could with his family, but calls from the garment industry board in New York, and from the Interstate Commerce Commission and progressive allies in Washington, led him to spend long stretches away from Boston. Although he had often maintained that he did not want elective office but preferred to be "the man behind," he discovered he had a flair for politicking and took to the campaign trail as if he had been doing it all his life. By the end of the 1912 presidential campaign, Louis Brandeis stood in the forefront of national reform politics, and would remain there until named to the Supreme Court in 1916.

BRANDEIS'S ROLE in Pinchot-Ballinger brought him to the attention of many progressives in both the Democratic and the Republican parties, and during his stays in Washington he got to meet many of them. One person made a lasting impression on him, however, and he and Robert La Follette would remain close friends until the latter's death in 1925.

La Follette as much as anyone during this period embodied the progressive spirit. He had started out as a regular Republican, and in the 1880s served three terms in the House of Representatives from Wisconsin. His sponsorship of the McKinley Tariff in 1890, however, led to his defeat in the 1890 Democratic landslide. He returned to Madison to practice law, but after a few years began to argue that the Republican Party had lost its bearings; from the party that had championed anti-slavery, it had become a tool of big business. For the next several years he and like-minded Republicans fought the party regulars, whom the press dubbed "Stalwarts." The reformers unsuccessfully challenged the Stalwarts in the elections of 1896 and 1898, but in 1900 La Follette captured the governor's seat. He served three terms and, by forging a coalition between insurgents and Democrats, managed to force through some of the most progressive reforms in the nation, including a powerful railroad commission, direct primaries, and laws protecting consumers. In 1906 he took his seat as a U.S. senator, the position he would be reelected to three more times. There La Follette aligned himself with other reformers, such as Jonathan Dolliver and Albert Baird Cummins, and soon became the acknowledged leader of the Republican insurgents.

Brandeis first met La Follette in February 1910 and wrote to his wife, "Had a delightful evening at the La Follettes' yesterday. They are quite our kind of people, and if I am here much shall be more apt to loaf with them than anyone else. They received me like an old friend." Of that meeting, Belle La Follette wrote, "Bob was impressed with the personality of Brandeis from the moment he grasped his hand and looked into his keen, thoughtful face. He came to love and admire him and always found him a genial and fascinating companion."

Louis soon had a standing invitation to drop by for dinner with Bob, Belle, and their children—Robert, Philip, and Fola. At first Brandeis felt a little uncomfortable when they discussed important and often sensitive political matters at the dinner table with the children present, but he soon learned that this was part of Bob and Belle's philosophy of educating their offspring. Years later, when Bob junior became a candidate to fill his father's unexpired term in the Senate, some people protested to Brandeis that the thirty-year-old was too young and had no political experience. To this the justice replied, "Bob, Jr., and Phil have had more experience in politics than any boys since the days of the Roman Senators."

The two families got on well. The children soon came to have affection for "Uncle Louis" as well. Belle wrote to Louis that Bob junior had said, "Mother, I believe I like Mr. Brandeis the best of any one we know. . . . Of course, not better than Mr. Steffens but better than almost any one else." With her husband spending more and more time in Washington these years, Alice began making regular trips to the capital, and there she and Belle grew close. Susan and Elizabeth also became frequent visitors and friends of the younger La Follettes. After Elizabeth received her doctorate and began her long teaching career at the University of Wisconsin, she and her husband spent much time with

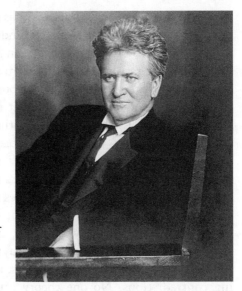

Senator and progressive leader Robert M. La Follette, 1911

Phil La Follette and his family. Years later, after Belle had died midway through her work on a biography of her husband, their daughter, Fola, took up the work, and Louis and Alice made two significant donations to enable her to complete it.

Brandeis and La Follette did not agree on everything, but on the abuses of the financial titans, the curse of bigness, the need for honesty in government, and the desire to serve the public, they saw eye to eye. Each admired the work of the other, and Brandeis especially believed that no one else he met, with the possible exception of Joseph Eastman, stood so ready to sacrifice personal gain for the public good. Both men also shared a pragmatic rather than a theoretical view of government and social problems, and wanted facts to examine before trying to chart a solution. "They never endeavored to solve social and economic problems from the blueprint of Utopian dreams," Belle wrote. "Neither was doctrinaire; but both had a deep conviction that industry, finance and government should be organized to serve the best interests of all the people of the country rather than the special interests of a privileged few." It is little wonder, then, that as La Follette began to think of running for the presidency in 1912, he would turn to his friend for advice and support.

. . .

THE WORD "PROGRESSIVE" has been used frequently, applied both to Brandeis and to La Follette, and the reader may well ask, "What is a progressive?" Historians have been grappling with that question for years, since the record is so full of seeming inconsistencies. Various theories describe progressivism as a response to industrialism or a search for order, and the forces that called it into being have been located in the middle classes, the upper class, the lower class, a displaced elite, and business leaders. There has even been an argument that while there may have been reform during this era, there was no progressive movement because the basic characteristics of a true movement were completely missing. All of these theories have some kernels of truth in them and so cannot be dismissed out of hand, yet all have too many inconsistencies to be fully accepted. In trying to impose a coherent framework on the period, one may lose sight of key factors of progressivism—its internal dynamics, idiosyncrasies, and often confusing contradictions. No one theory can do justice to so variegated a movement.

One of the first efforts to define progressivism came in 1915, when Benjamin De Witt published *The Progressive Movement* and characterized it as the exclusion of privileged interests from political and economic control, the expansion of democracy, and the use of government to benefit the weak and oppressed members of American society. Even if one accepts these as basics, progressivism involved a great deal more—constraints on monopolies, regulation of railroads, protection of consumers, referendum and recall, direct election of U.S. senators, women's suffrage, prohibition, abolition of child labor, wage and hour legislation, workmen's compensation, pure food and drug laws, conservation, and housing, to name but a few. Perhaps most important, not all reformers agreed on all reforms. When both Theodore Roosevelt and Woodrow Wilson, who stood diametrically opposed on trust regulation, can be described as *the* archetypical progressive, it becomes extremely frustrating to delineate a rational framework in which the two can exist in peace and harmony. Even taking certain aspects of progressivism, such as educational reform, the landscape is too crowded with groups and figures, many promoting opposing agendas, to allow simple ordering. Men and women who agreed on the necessity for one reform might then divide over another, such as women's suffrage or prohibition.

There is general agreement that the period of progressive reform, from roughly the late 1890s until the end of World War I, took place during a transitional period in American society, and that the motor force of this change grew out of the rapid expansion and industrialization of the economy, along with the transformation from a primarily rural and agrarian society into an urban and industrial one. These changes touched upon every aspect of American life, and different groups, depending on how they were affected, responded in different ways. One segment, appalled at the waste of natural resources, became conservationists. Another, frightened by the growth of large corporations, turned to antitrust activity. Still others, aggrieved by the terrible toll exacted by factory demands on human life, advocated various protective measures, including wage and hour legislation, factory safety laws, and the abolition of child labor. The list could be expanded still further, to include those who promoted urban planning, good government, prohibition, and so on.

It would be rare for reformers, even those who often fought together, to have agreed on everything. For the most part the factions operated discretely, focusing on their own pet causes. But since they often lacked the votes to secure legislation, they perforce had to form loose coalitions. These alliances came together because of men like Louis Brandeis and women like Jane Addams and Florence Kelley, figures who might properly be called "linchpins of reform." Through their own efforts in particular reforms, and the respect they won from other groups and individuals, they could move easily from one cause to another, helping to create new alliances for different issues. Theodore Roosevelt, Robert La Follette, and Woodrow Wilson all cooperated at one time or another with Brandeis, and each recognized how important an ally he could be. For those committed to their own efforts to improve the world, and unfamiliar with the work of others, a word of support from Brandeis or Addams or Lincoln Steffens carried weight.

In some ways Brandeis could be described as a "reformer's reformer." We can look at the large number of reforms with which he allied himself in the two decades before he went on the Court: good government, care of the mentally ill, traction reform, education, conservation, wage and hour legislation, labor-management relations, scientific management, antitrust, monetary reform—the list seems endless. In another sense, we can refer to the respect he enjoyed among the leaders of these various movements, many of whom he worked with on specific proposals, and here too the list is overwhelming.

By moving among groups and individuals, Brandeis and others like him helped hold together an amorphous mixture of reformers and ideas and uplift we have termed "progressivism." It appears to be less a formal movement with institutional characteristics than the collective result of many individual efforts. While it is true that progressivism may be hard to classify, there is no question that for roughly two decades it defined the public policy debate in the United States.

ALTHOUGH WILLIAM HOWARD TAFT has often been treated as a reactionary, his four years in the presidency (1909–1913) saw the passage of a number of reform measures such as the Mann-Elkins Act, giving the Interstate Commerce Commission real rate-making powers, and the Postal Savings Bank Act. These laws, however, could not have been passed without a coalition of Democrats and insurgent Republicans, and Taft, whose base lay in the conservative wing of the GOP, worried they would gain control of both the party and Congress. He tried to purge some of the rebels in the election of 1910 and failed badly, and when Congress met that December, forty-six insurgents refused to be bound by the decisions of the Republican caucus in the House, while a dozen insurgent senators held the balance of power between the two parties in the upper chamber. Taft could no longer hope to exercise any party leadership in Congress except when he proposed measures acceptable to the insurgents. Worse, the leader of the insurgents appeared ready not only to defy Taft but to challenge him for the 1912 Republican nomination for the presidency.

Robert La Follette traveled around the Midwest that winter calling on reformers to rally to his cause, to take back control of the government from the interests. In speech after speech he spelled out programs that for the most part won Brandeis's endorsement—prohibiting unfair competition, lowering tariff rates, direct primaries, the initiative and referendum, and the development of Alaska by the government. Brandeis disagreed only with the recall of state judges, in which if a certain number of people signed a petition, at the next election there would be a question on the ballot as to whether the judge should be kept in office.

By the time he returned to Washington in January, La Follette had drawn up a declaration of principles and a plan for a National Progressive Republican League that would support reformist legislation at both the state and the national levels. He included the word "Republican" in the title to avoid charges that he wanted to launch a third-party movement. In fact, La Follette hoped to do on the national scale what he had accomplished in Wisconsin: lead an insurgent takeover of the regular Republican Party. After showing his principles to several insurgent colleagues in the Senate, La Follette adopted their suggestions and boiled his declaration down to five policies: popular election of U.S. senators; direct primaries for all state offices; direct election of delegates to national party conventions; adoption of the initiative, referendum, and recall; and a tough federal corrupt practices act. In early January 1911, Louis reported to Alice, "I signed the League, seeming the only chance for congenial political association," and when the league elected La Follette as its head on 21 January, Brandeis sent a congratulatory telegram declaring that "no man in public office today expresses so fully the highest ideals of American democracy."

Brandeis did so with the full realization of what it meant. He had never been a regular party man; by signing on with La Follette, he turned his back on the Democrats and the regular Republicans, and probably felt relieved to do so. In his view the Democrats still seemed wedded to the radical populism of William Jennings Bryan, whom they had run for the third time as their presidential candidate in 1908, while the Republicans had become the party of the interests, big banks, and corporations. Of the many people he met on his trips to Washington, he seemed most comfortable with the insurgents and with other reformers. The league would indeed provide him congenial associates, and on his trips to the capital he spent more and more time with the La Follettes and their allies.

The league grew rapidly, attracting new members in nearly all parts of the country outside the South, and one contemporary later described it as "the culmination of the progressive movement in the Republican Party." The size of the league, and the prominence of many of its members, clearly worried Taft, who had assumed he would have no opposition for the 1912 Republican nomination. He rallied the conservative members of the GOP, and when La Follette demanded that progressives be given membership on Senate committees in proportion to their number—roughly one out of four—the Senate Stalwarts refused. Congress now had three warring parties, and his followers demanded that La Follette seek the Republican nomination. On 30 April leaders of the National Progressive Republican League named La Follette as their candidate for president. After consulting with his family and with close friends, including Brandeis, La Follette announced his candidacy and began a whirlwind tour of the country. Brandeis made some financial contributions, advised La Follette on antitrust and other matters, and went on a speaking tour at the end of January, starting in Chicago and traveling down through the Midwest before returning home.

Brandeis was certainly no stranger to public speaking. As a lawyer he had argued before judges and juries, and as a reformer he had testified before legislative investigations and spoken to various groups seeking their support. But he had never before spoken solely on behalf of a candidate seeking elected office, and he enjoyed the experience. "Two speeches at York yesterday & 2 at Hastings today and another here [Kearney, Nebraska] this evening," he wrote to Alice, "with the thermometer today below zero." He deemed his talk in St. Louis a success and proudly noted that he had outdrawn Taft, although many members of the sponsoring club had not received word of the luncheon until that morning. "Pretty much all the world is progressive here," he told Alice, but privately he doubted that La Follette could succeed.

Even without the benefit of hindsight one could see a number of difficulties attending La Follette's candidacy. Although he sought the Republican nomination, for all practical purposes La Follette ran as a third-party candidate, and faced all the problems associated with such a position, especially the impossibility of putting the political apparatus in place to support a candidacy at the local, state, and national levels in a short time. Supporters of third-party candidates are usually expressing their anger and frustration at existing policies and candidates and have little interest in engaging in the tedious work required to build a political organization. La Follette, because of his blunt language and attacks on big business, struck many people as too radical. Even friends noted his vehemence, narrowness, and lack of a sense of humor. An insurgent distrusted by regular Republicans, he nonetheless still called himself a Republican and thus could not win support from Democrats. While a few states had popular primaries to elect delegates to the national nominating conventions, most states chose their delegates through a party caucus, and over these Taft had total control. Moreover, Taft, whatever his political ineptitude at times, was no fool, and in the fall of 1911 he toured the country, attacking La Follette and bolstering his support among regular Republicans.

Both Taft and La Follette worried about what Theodore Roosevelt would do. The Rough Rider had left office in March 1909 immensely popular with the people and had not been associated with the political foibles of the Taft administration. He kept saying he did not want to run again, but many people did not believe him. As Louis told Alice in November, "The morning papers bring out a rather faint denial by T.R. which is quite aggravating." It would be so easy, Brandeis said, for Roosevelt to give a full and sincere denial and put his "friends" at rest. A number of La Follette supporters hoped that in fact Roosevelt would decide to run in 1912. George Rublee, for one, who knew and liked La Follette, did not believe he could win and prayed that Roosevelt would run. So long as La Follette stayed in the race, Roosevelt knew he would be seen as a spoiler by many progressives if he also declared for the presidency. But by November 1911, many commentators believed La Follette had no chance, and Roosevelt began planning how he might put his name forward.

La Follette's candidacy came to an abrupt end when he spoke at the Periodical Publishers' Association banquet in Philadelphia on 2 February 1912. Common sense should have led him to cancel the engagement. On the following day his daughter, Fola, would undergo a serious operation, and he himself suffered not only from exhaustion but from a stomach virus that induced nausea. He nonetheless insisted on fulfilling his commitment, but instead of making the short political speech that his audience expected and then leaving, he launched into a long, rambling, and often incoherent indictment of the press in general and of the way he had been treated by it. Rumors immediately spread that La Follette had suffered a nervous breakdown, and they gained credence when he went into seclusion for the next few weeks.

Despite their friendship, Brandeis had no illusions about the chances for a La Follette victory. He had tried to interest his brother in organizing a La Follette committee in Kentucky, and in a rare disagreement between them Alfred would have nothing to do with it. Aside from the fact that he did not feel up to getting involved, he believed that the Wisconsin senator had no chance of gaining support in Kentucky, much less winning the nomination. Louis heard about the Philadelphia fiasco while in Nebraska, but not about the seriousness of the collapse. ("No New York paper since last Tuesday," he told Alice, "and only occasional Chicago dailies.") He hoped the trip would be worthwhile, if for nothing else than "giving La Follette some moral support when he was most in need of it." A few days later, when he learned the full extent of La Follette's illness, Louis wrote philosophically that while the news had proved distressing, "if the smash is not a bad one, it may be all for the best to have him completely out of the Presidential race. I was sorry when he concluded to enter it. Personally I shall be glad to have no political obligations."

Whatever his political thoughts, Brandeis worried about his friend and immediately wrote to Belle, urging her to make sure that Bob got the rest he desperately needed. Go overseas, he urged, and "make a pleasure trip out of this necessity. When he comes back we will take up the good fight together again." He asked Alice to go see Bess Evans and have her use her influence with the La Follettes to get them to go abroad. Bob could finish his autobiography, and if necessary, Bess should offer to go with them. "Impress Bess with this & let her hammer Belle."

Although he never formally dropped out of the race, for all practical purposes La Follette's campaign had ended. With the senator on the sidelines, Roosevelt threw his hat into the ring, much to the joy of his followers, and many of the progressives who had backed La Follette now deserted him in unseemly haste. A few felt some regrets, but most rationalized their choice with the argument that only Roosevelt could beat Taft. A number of Brandeis's friends would support Roosevelt in 1912, including some younger ones he had met during his visits to Washington. None would mean as much to him in later years as a young lawyer in the War Department who had been present when Brandeis gave his talk "The Opportunity in the Law" at Harvard— Felix Frankfurter.

BORN IN VIENNA, Felix Frankfurter embodied the American success story. After education in New York City's public schools and at City College, he went to Harvard Law School, where he had one of the highest grade averages since Louis Brandeis. He graduated from the law school in 1906 and, after a few unhappy months in a prestigious New York law firm, took a cut in salary to work for Henry L. Stimson, the U.S. attorney for the Southern District of New York. "I could practice law," he later explained, "without having a client." Brandeis first met Frankfurter while on a trip to New York and then wrote to Alice that he had dined "last evening with Felix Frankfurter & a lot of youngsters at the Harvard Club."

Frankfurter stayed with Stimson in a variety of jobs and went to Washington with him in 1911 to work in the War Department. Between 1911 and 1914, when Brandeis came to Washington on reform business, he often stopped in at the "House of Truth," the bachelors' quarters that Frankfurter and a lively group of young intellectuals, many of them working in government, maintained on Nineteenth Street. Besides Frankfurter, the regular tenants included Winfred Denison, then working in the Justice Department; Loring Christie, a Canadian and one of Denison's friends at Justice; and Lord Eustace Percy from the British embassy staff.

The House of Truth provided a nonstop cauldron of intellectual energy, bubbling over with ideas and political gossip, fueled by good wine, pretty girls, and above all intense conversation. Gutzon Borglum drew his sketches for Mount Rushmore there, much to the delight of Justice Holmes and his wife. Arthur Willert, the Washington correspondent for the London *Times,* contributed to the cosmopolitan flavor of the salon. Learned Hand and the journalist Herbert Croly often came down from New York, and Croly brought with him a younger writer, Walter Lippmann, in the process of writing one of the most memorable books of this period, *Drift and Mastery* (1914). They all welcomed Brandeis, then a hero among progressives for his work endorsing protective legislation and defending Louis Glavis in the Pinchot-Ballinger hearings.

Brandeis and Frankfurter soon established a special relationship that would last for the better part of the next three decades. Frankfurter had those traits that Brandeis greatly appreciated—a fierce intelligence, indefatigable energy ("Do you know what it's like," his wife later exclaimed, "to be married to a man who is never tired?"), and a flair for making friends, especially among people who counted. Felix knew all the gossip, and his gaiety, his talent for flattery, his mastery of detail, made him a marvelous conversationalist. Holmes once said that Frankfurter had "walked deep into my heart." Brandeis might have said the same thing and in fact referred to him as "half brother, half son." Frankfurter, on the other hand, while giving the impression of his wholehearted devotion to Brandeis, nonetheless held him in slightly lower esteem than the other patrons of his career, such as Stimson, Holmes, and above all Franklin Roosevelt. After a lengthy conversation with Brandeis in 1911, Frankfurter wrote in his diary, "Brandeis has depth and an intellectual sweep that are tonical. He has great force; he has Lincoln's fundamental sympathies. I wish he had his patience, his magnanimity, his humor." In later years, even though he claimed to have inherited the mantle of Holmes and Brandeis, he would play down the influence that Brandeis had exercised over him, maintaining that he had gotten his legal philosophy elsewhere. With the election of Wilson, Frankfurter had doubts whether he should stay on in the War Department, but he did so after both Theodore Roosevelt and Brandeis encouraged him to remain. In 1914, Frankfurter accepted an offer to teach at Harvard Law School, an offer prompted in part by Brandeis himself, and, except for brief interludes, taught there until his appointment to the Supreme Court in 1939.

Their age differential—twenty-six years—helped draw them to-

Theodore Roosevelt, ca. 1912

gether. Brandeis throughout his reform career had often attracted young lieutenants and led them into battle, while Frankfurter always found himself drawn to older mentors. The two shared a passionate devotion to the law and looked for the improvement of both legal practice and thought through Harvard Law School. Both treasured facts, and suspected those who did not. Both knew, in varying degrees, the bite of anti-Semitism, and knew what it meant to be an "outsider" in Boston society. Both were relatively indifferent to getting money and disdained those who lived too luxuriously (although Frankfurter seemed to care more than Brandeis did about the amenities of life, such as good food and clothing). Both married high-strung women who suffered from nervous collapses, and each expressed heartfelt sympathies after the other's wife had a "bad week" or a "decline." Both knew a great deal about politics and, despite their frequent denials, loved the game.

Most important, they both had very similar political, economic, and judicial philosophies. Brandeis tended to take the long view and, even in his most impassioned days as a reformer, always remained somewhat aloof, often leading both friend and foe to consider him unfeeling. One cannot imagine Brandeis, for example, throwing everything aside to ride to the rescue of a Tom Mooney or a Bartolomeo Vanzetti. Frankfurter tended to be more excitable in everything from living-room conversations to battles in the Supreme Court, and it is hard to imagine him taking the quiet, laborious steps of building a new system of insurance for Massachusetts workers and then nursing it over several decades. On the whole, however, they agreed on the important things, feared the same evils they saw confronting American society, and shared the same hopes.

In the summer of 1912, however, while the two men enjoyed each other's company and conversation, they disagreed on the great issue facing the country—who would be the next president of the United States. After La Follette's collapse, Brandeis kept his own counsel. He could not, of course, bear "the fat man," as he called Taft. Nor could he support Theodore Roosevelt, whose New Nationalism called for acceptance of big business as a fact of the modern age, with corporate behavior regulated by a powerful government agency. Frankfurter, on the other hand, as well as most of the people at the House of Truth, enthusiastically joined the Rough Rider's parade.

TAFT'S CONTROL of the party machinery denied Roosevelt the Republican nomination, and the Rough Rider decided to launch a crusade to cleanse American politics. "We stand at Armageddon and we battle for the Lord," he told his supporters, and called for a convention of the "National Progressive Party" to meet in Chicago at the beginning of August. The convention appeared to many of the reporters present—as well as to the delegates—as more of a religious revival than a political gathering. When Senator Albert Beveridge concluded his keynote speech, the delegates sang the "Battle Hymn of the Republic," and at another point they marched around the arena singing "Onward, Christian Soldiers." Roosevelt termed his acceptance speech a "confession of faith," and although the party excluded Negro delegates, the platform included just about every major progressive idea put forward in the previous decade.

Roosevelt shaped much of the New Nationalism, as he called his program, on a book written by one of the young progressives, Herbert Croly's *Promise of American Life* (1909). Roosevelt read the book with great approval, met with Croly, and translated Croly's somewhat abstruse language into simple political principles to take on the campaign trail. Croly took a Hamiltonian view toward American history and society, believing that the great concentration of capital and industry had been a natural and inevitable development, but that government, still shackled by Jeffersonian opposition to strong and energetic authority, lagged behind. Property had to be cherished, Croly believed, but it also had to yield to the common good. For Roosevelt this meant acceptance of, indeed rejoicing in, the great American industries, but checking their undesirable actions by a strong government to protect the people. It is little wonder that young progressives like Frankfurter went wild for the charismatic TR.

Roosevelt might have won the election had the Democrats nominated William Jennings Bryan again. Too many people still saw Bryan as a radical, and with Taft firmly ensconced as the conservative candidate, insurgent Republicans and reform-minded Democrats might well have chosen the Rough Rider. Bryan, however, sensed that 1912 could be the year for a Democratic victory, but not with him at the head of the ticket. He dictated most of the party platform and blocked the nomination of the conservative James "Champ" Clark of Missouri, the Speaker of the House. After attacking the money powers, he threw his support to the governor of New Jersey, Thomas Woodrow Wilson.

"The profession I chose was politics," Wilson told his fiancée, but "the profession I entered was law. I entered the one because I thought it would lead to the other." Wilson, however, loathed the law, and soon turned to political science as a vocation. He received one of the first doctorates in the country from Johns Hopkins University in 1885 and then enjoyed a spectacular career as an academic, winning fame as a teacher and writer. He first taught at Bryn Mawr and then returned to his alma mater, Princeton, in 1890. In 1902 he became president of the school and won national renown for his innovations. At the same time he became increasingly identified with the anti-Bryan wing of the Democratic Party, opposing silver, government regulation, and the restrictive practices of labor unions. In 1910, after losing a bitter battle in the university over the direction of the graduate school, he agreed to run for governor of New Jersey. To the surprise of many, he embraced progressivism and won the election by fifty thousand votes. Once in office, he captured national attention by breaking with the party bosses and pushing through the entire reform program he had championed during the campaign—direct primary, corrupt practices legislation, workmen's compensation, and strict control of railroads and public utilities.

Brandeis learned of the Baltimore convention after returning from a yachting trip with Gifford Pinchot, and Bryan's behavior delighted him. Bryan "has certainly handled the Convention in a masterly and masterful way," he told a friend, "and has made an admirable beginning in his effort to purify the Democratic party and drive the money-lenders from the temple." Although he had never met Wilson, "all that I have heard of him and particularly his discussion of economic problems makes me believe that he possesses certain qualities indispensable to the solution of our problems." All progressives, he suggested, who did not feel bound by party affiliation ought to back Wilson.

A few days later Louis told his brother that he would come out for Wilson, even though many of his progressive friends would stand by TR. His decision at least relieved him of one problem. Insurgent Republicans in Massachusetts had wanted him to run for either governor or senator, and coming out for Wilson, as he put it, "ended that agony." In his public statement, Brandeis called Wilson's nomination "one of the most encouraging events in American history." Wilson understood "the dangers incident to the control of a few of our industries and finance. He sees that true democracy and social

Woodrow Wilson, ca. 1913

justice are unattainable unless the power of the few be curbed, and our democracy becomes industrial as well as political." Wilson—and progressivism—could succeed only if reformers rallied to his cause; they would falter if "progressives fail in their duty of giving Wilson their full support."

Many of Brandeis's friends regretted his choice. George Rublee, an ardent Roosevelt supporter, told him, "I grieve that you are not to be in the new party, because I think it needs you more than perhaps any other man." A newspaper report indicated that many progressives had been surprised to learn that Brandeis favored Wilson. He had, after all, supported Taft in 1908 and more recently La Follette, and many of the Wisconsin senator's backers had now gone over to the colonel. After his friend from the New York garment protocol Henry Moskowitz also signed on, Brandeis admitted that "T.R. is pretty nigh irresistible." The Bull Moose Party, as the 1912 Progressive Party came to be known, called upon Americans to recognize the inevitability of big business and monopoly, but also to insist that these industrial giants wield their power responsibly. To ensure this, Roosevelt proposed establishing a strong federal agency, staffed by well-trained experts, to oversee business and to have the authority to force businesses to act within the constraints of the law. In essence, the New Nationalism proposed balancing large economic power with strength elsewhere, such as the government or big labor. While this proposal offended Wilson, at least early in the campaign he had nothing to offer as an alternative.

IN FACT, only a few years earlier Wilson had sounded a lot like Roosevelt. As late as 1908, Wilson condemned any sort of government regulation as socialistic in principle and sure to be followed by government ownership. He praised the trusts for "adding so enormously to the economy and efficiency of the nation's productive work" and blasted the Populist attack on them as socialistic. In a "Credo" written in 1907, he described the trusts as the "most convenient and efficient instrumentalities of modern business," the vast bulk of whose transactions were legitimate. Then a new strain began to appear that was based on Wilson's own stern Protestantism and that tracked very closely the views Brandeis would advocate. Wilson and Brandeis both spoke for a middle class that viewed the economic system not just as a means of production and distribution but also as a moral mechanism to reward desirable character traits. Success recompensed not just energy and ambition but morality as well, and business provided the arena in which such traits could be tested. Wilson and Brandeis both spoke for a middle class being squeezed out by big business; they spoke for young men with no room to rise.

Far more than Brandeis, Wilson personalized the issue and blamed the excesses of big business on individuals. Corporate boardrooms should be open to public scrutiny, because executives would not do wrong if their sins could be exposed. Time and again he emphasized the individual's obligation to control his actions in the light of absolute standards of morality. Wilson's secular concept of sin was selfishness, and his speeches often referred to a dichotomy between action and morality. By the time he won the Democratic nomination, Wilson had no other solution to offer to the trust problem than to enforce morality and the Sherman Act's criminal provisions. This mattered little to most Democrats, who saw the trust issue as one facet of the tariff question, with high tariffs often described as "the mother of trusts." But it did matter to many progressives who thought Wilson's views simplistic at best and useless at worst. If he hoped to win them over, he needed something more specific, something grounded in a theory that rejected the notion of inevitability. Louis Brandeis would provide that, and in doing so would become, in Arthur Link's words, "the architect of the New Freedom."

Brandeis first contacted Wilson directly at the beginning of August 1912, congratulating him on a proposal to reduce tariffs gradually at the rate of 5 percent a year. No other plan, Brandeis declared, is "consistent with the demands of business." Wilson's plan, although simple, impressed Brandeis in that the candidate had not given way to the Bryanite wing of the party that wanted immediate and drastic cuts. Gradualism would allow business to adjust to the change. Wilson responded immediately that Brandeis's letter had given him "a great deal of pleasure" and cheered him with the knowledge of Brandeis's support and approval. "I sincerely hope that the months to come will draw us together and give me the benefit of many conferences with you." Unbeknownst to Brandeis, Wilson had already begun to gather information about the Boston attorney and his views through a mutual friend, Charles R. Crane.

Soon after, Wilson sent word through Crane that he wished to meet with the People's Attorney. On Tuesday, 27 August, Brandeis took the night boat down to New York, breakfasted at the Albemarle Hotel, and then caught a train to Sea Girt, New Jersey, where the governor had a summer cottage. The two men had luncheon and a three-hour talk afterward, during which Brandeis tutored Wilson on the trust issue and hammered out the basic tenets of Wilson's economic platform, the so-called New Freedom.

At a press conference afterward, reporters asked the two men what they had discussed. "Oh, a number of bills," Brandeis responded. "They all had to do with our industries." He would back Wilson because the two men shared "fundamental convictions." As for the Bull Moose Party, it "must fail in all of the important things which it seeks to accomplish because it rests upon a fundamental basis of regulated monopoly. Our whole people have revolted at the idea of monopoly, and have made monopoly illegal, yet the third party proposes to make legal what is illegal. . . . The party is trying to make evil good, and that is a thing that cannot be done."

The meeting left Brandeis "very favorably impressed with Wilson. He is strong, simple, serious, openminded, eager to learn and deliberate." On the way back he also stopped at the Democratic national headquarters in New York, where "a lot of fine fellows . . . very cordially received" him. Two days later he sent in a contribution of $500 to the Wilson campaign, a very sizable donation in those days (nearly $11,000 in current dollars).

Although he had only recently half-jokingly complained that he had to spend some time on his law practice ("real business—a rare occurrence since everybody works but Father"), Brandeis devoted most of the next ten weeks to helping get Woodrow Wilson elected. He gave out press statements, wrote articles endorsing the candidate's position, and took to the campaign trail himself. But the most important thing involved giving Wilson an alternative strategy to counter TR's New Nationalism—instead of regulating the trusts, Wilson and Brandeis proposed the regulation of competition to prevent the abuses by which the trusts had come into being.

In his first speech after seeing Brandeis, Wilson proved an apt pupil. Attacking the Roosevelt plan of regulating monopolies, he asked, "What has created these monopolies? Unregulated competition." The answer lay in remedial legislation to "so restrict the wrong use of competition that the right use of competition will destroy monopoly." A few days later he again attacked monopoly, this time as destructive both of economic and of political freedom. "The alternative to regulating monopoly," he declared, "is to regulate competition."

Although he did not say anything at the time, Brandeis sensed that Wilson had not fully understood his views. For Brandeis the problem was the curse of bigness, not the curse of monopoly. The two clearly intertwined, but a company could be very large and still not be a monopoly (U.S. Steel, for example, the biggest company in the country, never controlled more than half of the nation's steelmaking capacity), while a company could be a monopoly and still not be large (such as a local water or gas company). As he later told Ray Stannard Baker, Wilson probably never understood the distinction and, if he did, chose for political reasons to attack monopoly "because Americans hated monopoly and loved bigness."

It is also apparent that Wilson did not comprehend just what Brandeis meant by the regulation of competition. For Wilson this seemed to imply that the government would pass a few laws establishing basic rules of competition, with criminal penalties for those who violated them, and then leave the market to more or less govern itself. This, of course, fit in perfectly with his desire to have government as little involved in the economy as possible.

When Brandeis spoke about regulation of competition, however, he meant far more; he actually meant the regulation of competition not only by laws but by active policing on the part of regulatory agencies such as the Interstate Commerce Commission. Instead of directly regulating businesses, as Roosevelt suggested, Brandeis wanted to utilize scientific management and cost accounting (then still in its infancy) as means to ensure a competitive market. Once laws prohibited cutthroat competition, intraindustry cooperation would actually work to encourage true competition, and here the government would have a benign oversight role, leaving competitive industries to work out problems and ensuring that no one firm overstepped boundaries. Brandeis had articulated some of these ideas earlier than 1912, but he understood that it would have been too confusing to try to explain these ideas to voters while attacking the New Nationalism for its use of governmental power. When it came time to write legislation during the Wilson administration, Brandeis's ideas played an important role.

If Wilson now argued that monopoly resulted from unrestricted competition, what did that mean in practical terms? If he now understood the causes of the problem, what did he propose as a solution? On this point the candidate's speeches remained embarrassingly vague. In a speech at Boston's Tremont Temple, he added a new note that he had undoubtedly picked up from Brandeis. "There is a point of bigness," he declared, "where you pass the point of efficiency and get to the point of clumsiness and unwieldiness." But here Wilson seemed inconsistent, since he had long maintained that he did not oppose bigness per se, only bigness attained illegally and immorally, as in a monopoly.

To clear up this inconsistency, and also to define his own views more clearly vis-à-vis Roosevelt, Wilson telegraphed Brandeis to "please set forth as explicitly as possible the actual measures by which competition can be effectively regulated. The more explicit we are on this point the more completely will the enemies [*sic*] guns be spiked." Brandeis prepared a lengthy memorandum comparing the New Freedom with the New Nationalism. Although he apologized for its being in draft form, he knew that Wilson would want it before heading out on a campaign swing in the West. In it Brandeis not only listed those points that he and Wilson agreed upon but also explained how they differed from those of Roosevelt:

> The two parties differ fundamentally regarding the economic policy which the country should pursue. The Democratic Party insists that competition can be and should be maintained in every branch of private industry; that competition can be and should be restored in those branches of industry in which it has been suppressed by the trusts; and that, if at any future time monopoly should appear to be desirable in any branch of industry, the

monopoly should be a public one—monopoly owned by the people and not by the capitalists. The New Party, on the other hand, insists that private monopoly may be desirable in some branches of industry, or at all events, is inevitable; and that existing trusts should not be dismembered or forcibly dislodged from those branches of industry in which they have already acquired a monopoly, but should be made "good" by regulation. In other words, the New Party declares that private monopoly in industry is not necessarily evil, but may do evil; and that legislation should be limited to such laws and regulations as should attempt merely to prevent the doing of evil. The New Party does not fear commercial power, however great, if only methods for regulation are provided. We believe that no methods of regulation ever have been or can be devised to remove the menace inherent in private monopoly and overweening commercial power.

Brandeis then went on to list specific proposals so that Wilson could remove some of the ambiguities from his speeches. These included strengthening the Sherman law and removing some of its uncertainties; making it easier to enforce the antitrust law in the courts; and establishing a board or commission to aid in administering the Sherman Act. Although Wilson accepted these ideas, he and Brandeis agreed that it might be best if the candidate did not state them too boldly. William Gibbs McAdoo then suggested that Brandeis work the memorandum into articles; this way the ideas could be circulated without Wilson's incurring any political liability. Brandeis, already under pressure from Norman Hapgood to contribute some articles to *Collier's,* readily agreed. Over the next few weeks several articles appeared over Brandeis's signature, while others manifested themselves as editorials in *Collier's.*

The memorandum and articles argued for a small-unit, highly competitive economy. In the past, such competition had been ruthless, leading to a survival of the fittest. But the most fit in terms of survival may not have been the most fit in terms of moral needs. When the country underwent the pains of economic maturation, many unethical practices prevailed, and the unfair advantages these practices generated led to monopolization in a number of industries. Brandeis and Wilson understood the connection between economic freedom and political independence. "No nation can remain free," Wilson declared in words that echoed his mentor's, "in which a small group determines the industrial development; and by determining the industrial development, determines the political policy."

Nothing could have been more repugnant to Wilson and Brandeis than the idea of accepting the great trusts and then using government to regulate them. To the evil of monopoly would be added the evil of big government controlling the market. The market had to be free so that men could test themselves. "What this country needs above everything else," Wilson declared, "is a body of laws which will look after the men who are on the make rather than the men who are already made." Where Roosevelt argued for the greater efficiency of the big unit, Wilson spoke for the democratic value of the small unit. These smaller entities, as Brandeis recognized, could be inefficient and wasteful at times, but democracy itself is a wasteful system; people cheerfully put up with it because their liberties more than compensate for the wastage. Brandeis and Wilson feared big and ruthlessly efficient government as much as Roosevelt opposed excessive individualism. The former called for greater individual liberty under a simple government, the latter favored a stronger, more efficient social organism, superior to any combination of selfish individuals.

WILLIAM ALLEN WHITE once remarked that "between the New Nationalism and the New Freedom was that fantastic imaginary gulf that always had existed between Tweedledum and Tweedledee," with Roosevelt and Wilson each setting forth, albeit in different phraseology, essentially similar programs. There is more than a little truth in this remark, because, as numerous commentators have suggested, the legislation passed by the New Freedom might well have come from the new party. Certainly the things Wilson and Roosevelt agreed upon were more important than those that divided them. Both urged reform within the traditional political system, both upheld corporate capitalism, both rejected socialism and radical labor groups such as the Industrial Workers of the World, both wanted to strengthen democracy. But for the participants in the election, and for the voters, Roosevelt and Wilson differed from each other not only in style but in substance as well. (There were, of course, two other candidates, the Republican William Howard Taft, whom the reporters ignored, and the socialist Eugene V. Debs.)

It has been argued that Roosevelt and Wilson stood as early-twentieth-century analogues to Hamilton and Jefferson. Roosevelt had been and remained an aristocratic conservative and had originally fashioned his New Nationalism to preserve a dominant Republican Party. If those who enjoyed the country's largesse did not respond to those whom they had disadvantaged, there would be social upheaval. Like Brandeis, Roosevelt believed in Burke's notion that true conservatism rested upon a commitment to traditional values while addressing current social demands. Many of those who followed Roosevelt wanted to go much further than he did in reshaping American society, and he often referred to them as a "lunatic fringe."

Wilson, despite having lived in the North his entire adult life, still identified himself with the hardworking, upwardly striving white people of the South and the West. When he spoke about keeping the American economy open for the young men on the make, he meant people like himself as well as the small-business men and farmers of the South and the West. Bryan's followers had no trouble shifting their allegiance to Wilson because, once the silver issue no longer mattered, the reformers in the Democratic Party wanted pretty much the same things he did—lower tariffs, restraints on big business, reform of the currency—and like them he opposed big government, a trait that had influenced the South since the Revolution. Just as Hamilton and Jefferson had shared much in common, so did Roosevelt and Wilson, and, like their forebears, they believed that a great gulf existed between them, as did their followers.

So, too, did their chief intellectual advisers, Herbert Croly and Louis Brandeis. In addition to advising the candidates, both assumed the task of answering the other side on the question of trusts. The Democrats consistently repeated their position that they stood for the restoration of competition while the new party endorsed both monopoly and big government. This put the Democrats in the long and honorable American political tradition of championing the little man, and their appeal to fairness in the marketplace and equality of opportunity resonated strongly among voters. At the same time Wilson, following Brandeis's lead, worked on maneuvering Roosevelt—who had earned the disdain of big business as a trustbuster during his presidency—into the unpopular position of defending big business.

In mid-September, Judge Learned Hand wrote to Felix Frankfurter from Cornish, New Hampshire. "I am up here for two or three weeks visiting Croly," he reported. "We are each independently trying to say something about the trust plank to meet Brandeis's effort to throw us into the camp of the monopolists. Without in the least meaning to question their good faith, I thoroly believe they are falsifying the actual issue, which is a thoroly good one and upon which we are in our proper position and they in theirs." Frankfurter wrote back congratulating them on the task they had undertaken. "Brandeis, in my opinion, has given, with his wonted power, a very unfair slant to the Progressive position on the issue." (Frankfurter, not at the time as close to Brandeis or his point of view as he later would be, expressed disappointment and occasional anger about him in the fall of 1912.)

Croly, in fact, had tried to tangle with Brandeis's position a year earlier, especially Brandeis's belief that big business could not be efficient, and argued that expert opinion deemed large-scale production to have economic advantages. Whether or not big business could be more efficient did not really matter. The basic issue between the two men, as between Roosevelt and Wilson, involved values. Brandeis and Wilson wanted to maintain economic democracy, a system in which individuals would not be deprived of opportunity by business behemoths. A wide-open competition between individuals, on a level playing field, had contributed greatly to American freedom as well as prosperity. Croly and Roosevelt considered the desire for a small-unit economy naive as well as nostalgic, a scenario that had long since departed from America if it had ever been there at all. Instead of seeing the market as a place where men could test their talents, Croly believed such a scheme to be nothing more than demeaning economic warfare among greedy individuals, far less desirable for the country than a system of efficient large businesses regulated by a government staffed by experts.

A few months after the election, Brandeis explained his opposition to the idea of experts determining the government's policy. In order to succeed, he explained to Felix Frankfurter (who had resented what he took to be Wilson's "sneer against government by experts"), policy had to be developed democratically, and not handed down from on high. Experts had a very important purpose, in that they should maintain an open and critical discussion of legislative proposals, encouraging those with merit and discouraging those that are unsound, but one had to look to the people for the ultimate decision. Brandeis as much as any progressive valued expertise; that had made him a champion of scientific management. But unlike some reformers, he believed in democratic decision making, and the fact that the people could sometimes choose poorly did not trouble him.

Croly may also have had a hand in several editorials that appeared in the *Outlook*, the journal that carried most of Roosevelt's pieces. While expressing high regard for Brandeis personally, the editors took him to task for distorting the new party's program, especially the claim that Roosevelt and his allies embraced monopoly. The "Taft-Wilson" plan involved prosecution after evil had been done, and caused more harm than good; the new party, through regulation of the big companies, would prevent the evil in the first place. In fact, Brandeis, in so many of his speeches, seemed to embrace so much of the new party's platform regarding social issues that they wondered why he did not recognize the fact that he ought to be backing Roosevelt.

Brandeis did, in fact, agree with many of the social justice planks of the new party, but for him bigness in industry constituted the overriding issue in 1912. The concentration of power in industry had grown alarmingly since the turn of the century, when monopolistic groups already accounted for nearly one-third of the annual value added by industry to the gross national product. The concepts of "concentration, combination and control" dominated American industry, and the debate in the 1912 election did involve real questions. Should the country follow Roosevelt and Croly in accepting the facts of large-scale monopolization and subject it to governmental regulation, or should it follow Wilson and Brandeis in their call to reverse this trend, reestablish a basically competitive society, and then regulate that competition?

Had it been only a question of economic policy, it would not have mattered. But the trust "was just as much a psychological creation of the American Progressive mind" as an economic creation of American history. Those who voted for Wilson expressed a choice not only of economic policy (wishful as it may have been) but of moral and psychological imperatives as well. Just as Andrew Jackson a century before had rooted up and destroyed the monstrous Bank of the United States, so they hoped that Wilson, by restoring competition, could root up and destroy the trusts. Wilson and Brandeis may have believed this possible, but it was an exercise in futility. The conditions that had made the big corporations possible also guaranteed their continuance. Even Wilson recognized that the trend toward large businesses could not be stopped. "Nobody can fail to see that modern business is going to be done by corporations," he said. "The old time of individual competition is probably gone by, [and] we will do business, henceforth, when we do it on a great and successful scale." Perhaps, he hoped, competition might be established between the giant corporations.

Driven by the necessities of political expediency to counter Roosevelt's New Nationalism, lured by the hope Brandeis held out, Wilson in fact attempted to do the impossible. He wanted to turn back historical progress, but he was too much the historian not to realize such efforts were likely to end in failure. He wanted to punish those who had succeeded too well, although as the son of a Calvinist minister he appreciated that material reward signified spiritual salvation as well. While he deplored big business and monopoly, as an American he could proudly boast of their achievements. Brandeis, on the other hand, truly believed that the big trusts, if prevented from acting in a predatory and illegal manner, could not compete against efficient smaller businesses. A man whose whole life was devoted to the pursuit of facts to bolster his arguments had examples of inefficiency in big corporations such as railroads. But the facts that held such great importance to Croly and Roosevelt meant little to him. He did not believe in the inevitability of bigness, and he certainly did not believe in the so-called benefits that bigness had brought. Instead, he saw the diminution of opportunity, the stifling of democracy, and the threat that large concentrations of private property posed to liberty. In 1912 he, too, believed that the American people stood at Armageddon, and hoped they would make the right choice.

TO HELP VOTERS make that choice, Brandeis took to the hustings. By now he had become a seasoned campaigner whose name meant a great deal to progressives, and the Democratic National Committee wanted to send him everywhere. In October he took a three-week swing that started in Massachusetts, then went down through New England and out to western New York and the Ohio valley. He worked hard, as he wrote to Alice, but it is also clear that he had a lot of fun. From Cleveland he told Alice, "I am being complimented quite as much upon my youth & fitness as upon my speaking, which is not bad now. Indeed 12 miles a day [on horseback], at a good clip, in the sunshine, & the good sweat & baths, is bringing out my complexion so that a debutante might be proud." At the halfway point he told Alice that he had "been thinking this morning about what I shall say to the students of University of Minnesota whom I am to address next Thursday. I have concluded that such seed so sown is, on the whole, most fruitful." Brandeis finished his tour speaking at the Economic Club in New York, where the speech "apparently went off well." He then went home to Boston to catch up on "the abundance of letters which had accumulated," to cast his own vote, and to await the returns. "It looks pretty certain Wilsonway now," he told his brother, "but I shall feel relieved when the vote is in. The redoubtable Colonel is too formidable an opponent."

On 5 November, the American people went to the polls. Although Woodrow Wilson only received 41.9 percent of the popular vote, he had an easy victory, carrying 40 states and 435 electoral votes. Theodore Roosevelt received 4.1 million votes, or 27.4 percent, and carried

6 states and 88 electoral votes, the best showing of a third party in American history. Taft, as he had expected, finished third, with 23.2 percent of the vote, 3.5 million ballots, and only 2 states—Utah and Vermont—with 8 electoral votes. Eugene Debs received 900,000 votes but carried no states. The combined vote of Roosevelt and Taft (7.6 million) exceeded that of Wilson (6.3 million), and it is possible that had Roosevelt received the Republican nomination, he might have won. Had Roosevelt not run, the election might have been closer, but Wilson would still have carried the day; many of the progressives who supported the Bull Moose ticket would have voted for him.

Once the results became certain, Brandeis sent off a series of telegrams. The first one went to the president-elect. "My dear Governor Wilson: Your great victory, so nobly won, fills me with a deep sense of gratitude, and I feel that every American should be congratulated except possibly yourself. May strength be given to bear the heavy burden." To Bob La Follette, who remained neutral during the race, Brandeis wired: "All true Progressives owe you deep gratitude for yesterday's victory." With much satisfaction Louis wrote to Alfred that what pleased him "most is T.R.'s defeat in the really progressive strongholds—Oregon, California, Iowa, Nebraska, Kansas, Wisconsin, the Dakotas, and our eastern Progressive New Hampshire. Most of the Progressives who went over to T.R.—little Governors and the like—are left without support."

The election left Brandeis exhilarated, and while he had no idea what role he would play in the Wilson administration, he had the president-elect's trust and confidence. He believed that Wilson, as much as any politician he had known, would try to do the right thing, a belief buttressed after he heard Wilson speak at the Southern Society dinner in mid-December. Refreshed from a postelection vacation in Bermuda, Wilson set out to rally progressives, both Democrats and those who had supported Roosevelt, to his side. In a widely quoted phrase, he promised "a gibbet as high as Haman" for any financial oligarchs who tried to oppose reform. "Men have got to stand up and be counted," he said, "and I want to appeal to you, gentlemen, to conceive of yourselves as trustees of those interests of the nation with which your personal interests have nothing to do." It was a noble utterance, Louis told Alfred, "worthy of the man & the cause. A declaration of purpose—not a speech or a sermon. It could leave no man in doubt that he proposes to carry out his promises in letter & spirit, without fear or favor. It was all simple & conversational, almost as if he were talking to his intimates—the people of the United States."

CHAPTER 15

A SNAPSHOT OF MR. BRANDEIS

A few days after the election, Louis Brandeis celebrated his fifty-sixth birthday. If he had felt introspective that day—an unusual sentiment for him—he might have taken a great deal of satisfaction from what he had so far accomplished in life. He had built up one of the most successful law practices in the country, and his large income gave him the freedom he had always wanted to engage in public service. He had revolutionized the way lawyers presented reform legislation to the courts in what would afterward be known as the "Brandeis brief." He had been involved in important reforms at the local, state, and national levels, and savings bank life insurance would remain a testament to him and his vision. He had taken on J. P. Morgan and even the president of the United States. He had been happily married for nearly twenty-two years, and Alice's recurring illness had only deepened the bond between them. His two daughters, Susan in college and Elizabeth about to go, had grown into intelligent and strong-willed young women. And, not incidentally, he had just helped elect Woodrow Wilson to the White House.

Before we embark on a tour of the frenetic three and a half years to follow, let us take a look not at the nationally known reformer but at the man who lived at 6 Otis Place.

DURING THE FIRST DECADE of the twentieth century, even as Louis devoted more of his time to reform work, his law practice thrived. In 1905 he claimed that he had "so devolved my work that I have little to do, save meditate like an East Indian," but three years later he reported to Alfred, "My office is pretty busy now, and even 'Father' must work. This interrupts considerably my Savings Bank Insurance campaign." As much as possible he delegated work to others in his office, but some clients and matters required his personal attention, and so he stayed in touch with his partners and remained available when they needed his advice on difficult cases. In 1911 he jokingly complained to Alice that Ned McClennen had come down to New York to consult with him about a case, and the two of them had been discussing it most of the day, even though "it isn't nearly as interesting as antitrust, or Shoe Machinery, Wage-Earners Insurance or the like." Two days later, still working on the same case, he noted rather proudly that "the old man has been able to show the Junior that there are points not thought of in his philosophy. . . . It is some satisfaction for the arduous labor on private business to find out that there is some use in grubbing up the case."

He utilized the office from time to time for help in his reform work, and in some instances paid out a considerable amount of money to his partners so that they would not lose income from his absence. When he came back to Boston from his increasingly frequent absences, Miss Grady would give him the accumulated mail, and he would go through it with her, answering correspondents, an increasing number of whom wanted him to work on their pet reforms. He remained the senior partner, directing the division of income using a formula that, while never spelled out, always struck his colleagues as fair. The proceeds from his law practice had made him a millionaire by 1907, and he accumulated another million before he went on the Court in 1916.

He saved money because he and Alice lived out the pledge they had made to each other before their wedding—to live well but simply. Although some commentators later described Brandeis as "ascetic," neither he nor his family ever denied themselves what they needed or on occasion wanted. Alice shopped at the better Boston stores, such as Sloan's, S. S. Pierce, and Jordan Marsh. Brandeis spent freely on two of his passions, canoes and equipment for his horses. He did not have an extensive wardrobe, but he bought quality garments in basic styles that would last him for a long time; when a suit wore out, he replaced it with one nearly the same. (In 1913 he paid $100 for a suit, the equivalent of $2,100 in current dollars.) Alice bought more clothes than he did, but not extravagantly, and she, too, bought well. When they rented summer homes, they shipped their piano there, but an examination of the accounts for this period finds many more bills for books than for household furnishings. They kept and used their wedding presents for years, even though they could easily have replaced them. The estate inventory at the time of Brandeis's death listed a painting, two Oriental rugs, one cashmere rug, and assorted silver service, all of which had been given to

Alice Brandeis with Susan, left, and Elizabeth, right,
ca. 1908

the young couple fifty years earlier. The large grandfather clock presented by his client William D. Ellis still works and can be found in his grandson's home in suburban Washington. Ascetics also do not employ servants, and the Brandeises hired a cook when they married, as well as a housemaid, and after the births of the girls added a nurse.

In 1912, Louis did not look fifty-six, and in fact until his eighties always seemed younger than his age. Throughout his life he appeared tall and trim, although slightly stooped, and his regimen of daily walking, riding, or canoeing kept him fit. He had a high brow topped by a thick head of hair, which, despite his best efforts, always seemed a bit unruly. He wore glasses for reading, and a somewhat formal picture taken by Harris & Ewing shows him with a pince-nez perched on his nose. Another picture has him standing on the banks of the Charles next to a canoe, with a paddle in one hand and wearing a straw boater. A newspaper account of the time described him as follows: "His smooth face is square and strong, but irregular, and expresses a lively sense of humor. . . . Brandeis has a large frame, but sparingly filled out. His voice is soft and drawling, but it can snap like a whip on occasion." Many interviewers detected a strong resemblance to Abraham Lincoln. Ray Stannard Baker said that while still, Brandeis "recalls almost startlingly one of the portraits of Abraham Lincoln." He has a "large head with the stubborn black hair streaked with iron-gray," and "sensitive hands—he has the hand of a musician."

In his younger days Brandeis, according to one source, dressed "fastidiously," and certainly appeared in appropriate garb when in court or testifying before a legislative hearing or giving a speech. But in his time off, even though he often wore a tie (as that was the custom in those days), he took little interest in his appearance, often walking around in old pants, a sweater, and worn shoes. He never owned a car, and continued to ride for recreation well into the 1920s, when the growing traffic as well as his own age finally led him to give up his horses. When he traveled, he usually stayed at the Harvard Club in New York and either at the Cosmos Club or at a decent but not expensive hotel, such as the Gordon, in Washington. Louis and Alice spent money on what mattered to them, but that did not include ostentation in any form.

Brandeis nonetheless had a teasing streak, so that he could write to his daughter Susan, "Talking of things sartorial—please note that I wore my gray spring suit [and] had the black suit you love so pressed." To Alice he wrote from Washington that at the suggestion of his friend Walter Child, he had begun a series of chest exercises. "You may be prepared for a real chest development which will overcome even your incredulity. The first two or three days I felt as much exercised as if I had been off on an all day paddle. You shall have an exhibition on my return." Such examples of jest, however, could be found only within the family and with one or two close friends; in his public persona Brandeis almost always appeared stern. His partner George Nutter believed that Brandeis had no sense of humor at all.

The Brandeises donated generously not only to the causes they believed in but to friends and family as well. Brandeis gave away nearly $1.5 million in his lifetime. He helped to support a number of relatives, and in a typical letter he wrote to Alfred, "It occurs to me that Emily's illness may put Aunt Minna into money straights in spite of my $50 a month. If this is so let me know & I will increase her allowance or what perhaps would be wiser, make an extraordinary appropriation." Alfred also shouldered some of this responsibility, but Louis insisted that he be allowed to give more than his brother, since after all Alfred had four daughters to raise while he had only two.

Louis also insisted on making a substantial gift to Alfred on the latter's fifty-second birthday. Alfred had purchased a small farm east of Louisville, initially as a summer house, but eventually he renovated the place and moved in full-time. "I want to have some part in the creation of your farm which you love so much," Louis told him, "and I want therefore to make you a birthday present, either of such part of Walter's [a neighbor's] land as you think you need to give you a scientific frontier, if you can buy it at any price you think reasonable—or to put your house into condition for winter use—or anything else for the place you want." Alfred and his wife, Jennie, lived on the farm, which they called Ladless Hill, until their deaths; it is owned today by the Brown family, which has restored and expanded it beautifully.

Next to Alice and his daughters, Alfred remained the most important person in Louis's life. The two brothers wrote to each other almost daily, talking about what they had done, sending each other books, and recalling their great adventure on the European tour. In the same letter in which Louis offered his gift, he also noted that he had read a

Elizabeth, 1911

book Alfred had sent him and passed it on to a friend, and reminded him that they had "arrived in Trieste 33 years ago today."

Because of Alice's illness, she rarely went to Louisville, but Louis visited regularly. Whenever one of his speaking or court engagements took him anywhere into the Ohio valley, either he would take a day or two and run down to Louisville, or Alfred would take the train up to meet him. He worried about Alfred's health, which, like his, seems to have been affected by periodic spells of exhaustion. On one occasion Louis lectured his brother on working too hard. "I have been thinking over your tired feeling and am convinced that you ought, for a while, to end your day's work at two (2) p.m. and spend the rest of the day in the open—every week day." Alfred should follow his advice, Louis urged, because "I have made a study of mental tire[dness] for a quarter of a century & know more about it than I do of law or insurance." When Alfred suffered a serious illness, such as gallstone attacks, Louis would drop everything and run down to see him.

Alfred and his family often came to the Northeast for their summer vacations, just as Adolph and Frederika had done, and the two families often shared adjoining cottages on Cape Cod or in the mountains. But Brandeis would always love Louisville, and when the girls were older, he would sometimes take one or both of them with him on a trip to visit Uncle Alfred, Aunt Jennie, and their four cousins. From Alfred, in addition to books, also came good Kentucky bourbon, later to be replaced by whole hams, products of Ladless Hill. Louis served the hams to his dinner guests and would send Alfred the names of the people who had enjoyed the feast.

On his visits he and Alfred would sometimes go out to the nearby horse farms that bred some of the nation's finest racing horses. On one of these trips he wrote home almost rhapsodically to Elizabeth about the "wonderful" collection of thoroughbreds and colts they had seen, and how the colts would come right up to them as they walked in the pasture. To Alice he declared that the stallions he saw had been a "revelation" to him, and his visit "revolutionized my ideas of race-horses. I supposed them to be lank, thin, and to the uneducated mind unbeautiful. Quite the contrary is the fact. They are the most beautiful living creatures I have ever seen. The only fit comparison seems to me the marbles of Praxiteles; and for the wonderful Greek marbles I know no fitter comparison than these horses."

The entire Brandeis clan read constantly, but probably no member of the family had such catholic tastes as Louis. He read the classics of Greek, Roman, and German culture, as well as works by English and American authors such as Rudyard Kipling and Richard Henry Dana. Perhaps because they could not travel as much as they would have liked, he and Alice enjoyed travel books. And, perhaps not surprisingly, he liked the Sherlock Holmes stories by Sir Arthur Conan Doyle. In one interview he compared his methods to that of the world's first consulting detective. "I use practically the same method," Louis told a reporter. "It's a matter of having special knowledge and being able to draw the only possible conclusion." He admitted that often he could figure out the solution before finishing the tale, although sometimes the author would conceal important clues so as to surprise the reader. "In the case of Sherlock Holmes he possessed much special knowledge, knowing various cigar ashes, etc. Without that knowledge no one could solve the mystery in advance." In response to a question, he admitted that he had never solved a real crime, but "I think I should like to try to catch a murderer sometime."

BRANDEIS'S REFERENCE TO PRAXITELES indicated a familiarity with the ancient Greeks, their culture, and their philosophy; if

Heine was his favorite German poet, Euripides was his favorite Greek. He could quote whole stanzas of poetry, and one reporter, after listening to Brandeis do so, commented that it seemed Euripides had the last word on virtually anything. During a particularly trying time at the beginning of the New Haven fight, Sam Warren sent him some words from Euripides' *Bacchae,* suggesting he might want to put the passage on his desk to keep up his spirits:

> Thou hast heard men scorn thy city, call her wild
> Of counsel, mad; thou has seen the fire of morn
> Flash from her eyes in answer to their scorn!
> Come toil on toil, 'tis this that makes her grand,
> Peril on peril! And common states that stand
> In caution, twilight cities, dimly wise.
> Ye know them; for no light is in their eyes!
> Go forth, my son, and help.

Louis came to appreciate above all the Greek notion of the golden mean, of maintaining a balance in life. This did not mean that he sought compromise in his reform campaigns—quite the contrary. As he told Alice in regard to monopoly, "I am dead against the middle of the road." Rather, in everyday life one should seek the balance between action and rest, between work and play. In addition, the Greek city-states represented the ideal type of society, small, democratic, and totally lacking the curse of bigness. Although he read many of Gilbert Murray's works on ancient Greece, there is no question that he prized Alfred E. Zimmern's *Greek Commonwealth* above all others.

It is not certain exactly when Louis first picked up this book. He knew Zimmern by reputation, having read through his translation of Guglielmo Ferrero's history of Rome. In July 1914, after a particularly difficult day in Washington, he wrote to Alice that after he got back to his room, he read the *Boston Evening Transcript,* "and to take the taste out of my mouth, some of the *Greek Commonwealth.*" By then Brandeis had already forged much of his philosophy about what an ideal America would look like. He harked back to Jefferson's faith in a small-farm, small-business economy and society serving as the bedrock of a demo-cratic republic. He did not share Jefferson's antipathy to cities and never considered setting up practice in some small town. Zimmern's portrait of ancient Greece fit in perfectly with the Jeffersonian ideals Brandeis espoused.

For Zimmern, Periclean Athens marked the closest mankind had ever come to social perfection in reconciling individual autonomy and communal life. "Politics and Morality," he wrote, "the deepest and strongest forces of national and of individual life, had moved forward hand in hand toward a common ideal, the perfect citizen in the perfect state." The genius of the Athenian city-state lay in its ability to further the common good by, on the one hand, instilling a deep patriotism in its citizens while, on the other, ensuring that individuals used their intellect independently. Adopting a creed of balance, fifth-century Athens promoted the ability of its citizens to cherish a primordial (and irrational) love of family, the seat of morality, and a rational, civil love of community, politics. The true glory of Greece, Zimmern believed, lay not in a static moment but rather in the process. Hellenism, as he saw it, constantly evolved, reinventing itself with each new generation, and this worldview required that citizens always challenge the status quo, always ask how things could be made better, whether in the political or in the cultural sphere. Progressive politics that challenged fixed prejudices constituted a modern manifestation of the Hellenistic spirit.

This attitude with which the Greek citizen approached politics made him both a conservative and a radical. He was a conservative because "he reverenced tradition and recognized the power and value of custom," yet a radical in his readiness "to apply his reason to public affairs without fear or prejudice." The brilliance of classical Greek thought, Zimmern believed, lay in this constant process of evaluation, of applying intellect to problems while at the same time holding fast to traditional values. "How to use the intellect," Zimmern once argued in a lecture, "is what we still have to learn from the Greeks and from the Greeks alone."

Naturally, this would appeal to Brandeis, who had from the time he had been a boy valued ancient Greece and its ideas. He said that his uncle Lewis "reminded one of the Athenians," and would later compare the Framers of the Constitution to the Athenians in his great defense of free speech in *Whitney v. California,* where he paraphrased Pericles' *Funeral Oration.* All of the things that Brandeis treasured in civilized life and that he feared in the modern industrial era had their parallels in the values of fifth-century-B.C. Athens, which he found so eloquently described in *The Greek Commonwealth.* He hoped to re-instill this Hellenistic balance in American life, what Learned Hand called Brandeis's vision of the "Good Life," but recognized that it might be too late. Athenian ideals, however, played a critical role in his efforts to rebuild a Jewish state in Palestine, and when he visited that country in 1919, he took along as one of his two traveling companions Alfred Zimmern.

• • •

DURING THESE YEARS the Brandeis routine at home underwent rather severe dislocations occasioned by Louis's extensive absences, but he tried, with varying success, to continue familiar patterns, weekends at the Dedham house and summers on Cape Cod. "This, dearest," he wrote in the midst of the Pinchot-Ballinger work, "is to establish that I remember (as you desire) that I have a family." Several weeks later, although still in Washington, he suggested that since Susan seemed content with their place in South Yarmouth, they should rent it again for the coming summer. And, of course, as he constantly told Alice, he cherished the time they had together when he was home.

His frequent absences from the city led him to pay less attention than he had previously to Boston matters. When the city debated a new charter in 1911 and Norman Hapgood wrote asking him about it, he confessed, "I know very little about the Boston situation owing to my frequent absences from the Commonwealth during the last fifteen months." Even personal tasks, such as going to a dentist, had to be taken care of while on the road, and he wrote to Alice from Washington, "I am the possessor of several additional teeth purchased at the cost of considerable time & an as yet unknown number of dollars."

When home, he rose early, ate a hearty breakfast, and read the morning papers before walking to his office. When away in New York or Washington, he tried to get in at least one lengthy and brisk walk each day and complained when unable to do so. He also was fond of the dog they had gotten at the children's insistence, and whom they named Frolic. The dog, however, like all members of the Brandeis family, seemed to have a mind of its own, and after taking Frolic for a long walk in Dedham, he told Alice that while the dog had behaved reasonably well, he "has occasional lapses from virtue which convince me he should be muzzled. He does bite sometimes & we shall have claims made against us if we don't act soon."

His growing involvement in national affairs also cut into one of the great joys of his life, travel. Because Alice understood how much he loved to see new places, she had early in their marriage insisted that he go off when he could, often with his friend Herbert White. Occasionally, he would take one of his daughters along on a short business trip, such as when he went to Ohio to argue a case there. "Susan is a good traveler," he reported, and the sixteen-year-old "responds to all suggestions with a smile." Later, after he had gone onto the Court, he would take camping trips with his daughters. But wherever he went, he wrote long, detailed letters to Alice about what he had seen, often expressing the (vain) hope that when she felt better, she would join him. White, an older brother of Louis's frequent ally in Massachusetts reform, had none of his brother Norman's inclination for public service, aside from sitting on numerous boards of various charities. Louis often went sailing with Herbert on board one of his several yachts and, according to his daughter Elizabeth, greatly enjoyed his company, probably as a break from his own austere habits and the pressures of law practice and reform. Moreover, he developed a close friendship with White, who came over to be with him when Louis's mother died.

In the summer of 1899, for example, Louis joined White on board his yacht for a three-week trip and sailed up the coast from Boston toward Nova Scotia and back. Midway through the trip Louis wrote that they had spent the last two days trout fishing, "at which I made very poor success in spite of my new rod bought at North East Maguire. Indeed I am quite over-whelmed by the number of things I can't do and don't know and am filled with admiration for the skill and learning White has acquired in his aquatic and country pursuits. He is ready for every emergency—ever full of resources and knowledge."

Louis and Herbert went on fishing and camping trips to Maine, the Adirondacks, and Canada, and in 1909 took an extended trip across the country to California, on which the two men mixed business and pleasure. Louis had work to do in Chicago for some clients, and wherever he went, he met with reformers, some of whom he knew earlier and some who made it a point to come see him. But his letters to Alice concentrated on descriptions of what he saw. "We are West of Omaha, really West," he told her, and "the broad prairies, well harvested, are stretching out endlessly in their rich colors under beauteous, grateful sunshine and cloudless sky. Before night we should have passed the longitude of Salt Lake City, and then the Rocky Mountains. I feel almost as if it were a trip around the world." The next day "we have been running through Wyoming the last twelve hours or more at an altitude of 6000 to 8000 feet. Glorious air and weather in an equally glorious expanse over endless miles of country. Herbert says it is almost exactly like the Sahara. . . . It is a delight to think that there is still so much out of doors; and in the face of it N.Y. and the eastern cities with their congestion seem the more inexcusable."

He awoke one morning just as the sun rose over the Nevada desert and then watched as the train went through the mountain pass and descended into the fertile valleys of California. "The day is bright and clear and the coloring would do honor to Monet." On the way he met some interesting people, an American mining engineer who had worked for an English firm in Australia, New Zealand, and South Africa, as well as a Berlin judge taking a two-month tour of the United States. "He is obviously not a socialist," Louis noted, "but says the only way for Germany to avoid socialism is to persevere in adopting Socialist measures." Someday, he added wistfully, "I want to introduce you and the children to this other world, so unlike our Eastern fringe." To his brother he also urged travel. "Do arrange to take your family west soon," he told Alfred, "and widen your American horizon." As it turned out, he and Alfred traveled only around Kentucky, while Alice went on just one trip, sailing to England with him for the Zionist conference in the summer of 1920.

ALICE APPARENTLY SUFFERED most from her illness in the first ten to fifteen years after the birth of Susan, and although she would continue to have bouts of debilitating depression into the 1920s, she seemed to have gotten better in the first decade of the new century. In the summer of 1905, however, she entered a sanitarium in Bethel, Maine, and after one weekend visit Louis wrote, "I wish you would tell your esteemed doctor that he must do a hurry-up job, as we don't propose to leave you with him much longer. Indeed I felt quite like carrying you off with us in his absence," a phrase reminiscent of their courting days. Even when Alice was at home, Louis would sometimes take the girls out to Dedham for the weekend to give her some time by herself. When Alfred invited him to come to Louisville in July 1908, Louis had to decline. "It seems to me clear that I ought not to leave Alice this summer. She is gaining steadily but it would be more of a strain than is advisable to leave her alone with the children at So. Yarmouth."

It would be a mistake, however, to think of Alice Brandeis as an invalid, with her only access to the outside world the daily letters of her devoted husband. It is true that had she been more robust, she would have traveled with Louis on many of these trips, and no doubt he would have passed up some jaunts with Herbert White to travel to places that interested her. During these years, especially as the intervals between episodes lengthened, Alice created her own areas of interest, helped along in part by her best friend, Bess Evans. Some of her activities involved local charities and welfare agencies, the type of "do good" work often associated with upper-middle-class women of the time. Then she discovered a cause that would keep her interested and active for over a decade, the fight for women's suffrage.

Her husband had originally not favored the right of women to vote, believing suffrage to be a privilege earned through the types of duties imposed only upon men, such as military service. This, of course, reflected the prevailing masculine mind-set of the late nineteenth century. Brandeis was, at least in some ways, a product of his times, and in almost any area he started out with the assumptions that he would have heard in his parents' household, at law school, or from his clients. Like the Greeks, he valued tradition, but also like them, he stood ready to learn from experience, and there is no question that having an intelligent and articulate wife as well as two bright daughters helped him to change his mind.

Alice met strong independent women through Bess Evans and also had the example of her sister Josephine, who introduced her to women like Florence Kelley at the National Consumers League. Sometime by the spring of 1911, Alice had come to support women's suffrage and, screwing up her courage, began to appear at public meetings urging the right of women to vote. "I am delighted to know of your success as a public speaker," her husband wrote. "As I am about retiring from the platform, there won't be undue rivalry." The cause meant so much to Alice that in early 1913 she broke a long-standing rule about granting interviews and invited John Whitman, a reporter for the *Boston American,* to their house. When he asked why women should have the vote, she said the reason could be given "in a very few words."

"The social philosophy of the past has been a failure; the laissez-faire notion that things will come out all right if not interfered with is nonsense," she said. "Women have been for years the constructive philanthropists, and now that governments are taking up the social side of economics, the women must, as the only logical conclusion, be made a part of the government. When political parties are putting in their platform a program for social and industrial justice, it is certainly true that women can no longer be left out." Giving women the vote would not, as some advocates of the suffrage claimed, bring in the millennium. Just because women voted did not mean that the world would change overnight for the better. Women, just as men, would make mistakes. Alice rejected out of hand the notion of a "straw ballot," in which women would express their preferences but only men's votes would actually count. She and other suffragettes stood ready to fight against a straw ballot with all means available, and she pointedly reminded Whitman that in England the government had to call out a thousand soldiers and a hundred mounted police to control the women protesting in front of Parliament.

By the time Alice took to the platform, Louis had changed his mind as well. He had met women like Jane Addams, Florence Kelley, Mary Kenney O'Sullivan, and of course Bess Evans and his sister-in-law Josephine Goldmark, in whom he recognized strength of character as well as of intellect. In his own office he saw how two women from simple backgrounds, given the opportunity to grow and take on responsibility, had flourished. Alice Grady, his secretary, became his chief assistant on savings bank insurance, and he eventually trusted E. Louise Malloch, who began as an office clerk, to take over not only the bookkeeping responsibilities of the firm but also management of his personal investments. He also recognized that without political power, women would continue to be victimized; while protective legislation would help somewhat, he believed that women needed the power to take care of themselves, and for this the vote was essential.

Alice may well have been on the stage, and certainly in the audience, when Jane Addams came to address the Boston Equal Suffrage Association for Good Government in June 1911, a meeting over which Brandeis himself presided. Although Addams declared that women might have to "throw things" to get what they wanted, Brandeis later told a reporter he did not think that would happen. Common sense dictated that in order to get progress, society needed the efforts of the many, not the few. "We need all the people, women as much as men. The insight women have shown in problems which often men could not understand has convinced me that women not only should have the suffrage, but that we really need women in politics."

If Alice could not go often into the world, the world came to her, and given her keen intellect, she absorbed everything, thought about it, and throughout his life gave her husband advice that he always trusted. Some of this information came from her husband; whenever he went away, he wrote to her every day, and as he grew more involved in progressive politics, he filled his letters with stories of the events he witnessed, the problems he faced, and the people he met. During the Pinchot-Ballinger hearings, for example, Alice could read in the daily papers the reports on which witnesses had been called and what they had said, and the next day a letter would arrive from Louis giving an inside view of why they had asked certain questions, which traps had been set, and, of course, his growing disillusion with and contempt for the "fat man."

Except when she was ill, Alice loved to entertain—not lavish parties, occasions at which both she and Louis would have been uncomfortable—but small dinners with only a few guests, so that people could talk with one another. When interesting people passed through Boston, Louis would often invite them for dinner, sometimes giving Alice only an hour or so to get ready. But since the Brandeises dressed for dinner and had a cook, it meant little in terms of preparation. Lincoln Steffens came, as did Norman Hapgood; Herbert White was always welcome, as was Lincoln Filene. Lawyers, teachers, journalists, politicians, social workers, all came to the Brandeis household, where they learned not only about Alice's graciousness as a host but also about the sharpness of her mind.

Although she loved these gatherings, sometimes even this little bit of extra effort proved too much for her, and during those periods Louis took care not to overburden her. When she felt well, though, her husband's long absences from the hearth distressed her, and she started traveling to New York (where, of course, she still had family) and to Washington, where he would arrange adjoining rooms so she could rest when he had visitors and work to do. Since Louis rarely dined alone when in the capital, she could enjoy the pleasure of small dinner parties without any effort on her part.

Alice understood politics and had no compunction about sharing her views on political matters with Louis. After James J. Storrow lost his bid for Boston's mayoralty, Alice sat down and wrote to Louis, then in New York, that a good part of the problem lay in the fact that although Storrow certainly had the ability to manage, he lacked the common touch that had carried John "Honey Fitz" Fitzgerald into office. Louis told her he thought that absolutely correct, and it should serve as a warning to the better elements of Boston society to stop and think, "if they were capable of the process."

Neither Louis nor Alice had much sympathy for the "better" elements, especially after Louis had taken on the powers of State Street in his fights against the Boston Elevated, the New Haven, and the Morgan interests. How much the Brahmins shunned the Brandeises because of Louis's attacking the powers that be, and how much of it might have been caused by anti-Semitism, is impossible to say. Neither of them identified actively with the Boston Jewish community; they did not belong to a synagogue, nor were they involved in the various charitable and social programs run by the Jewish community. At home they celebrated Christmas as a secular holiday for the children, complete with tree and toys. Louis did have a number of Jewish clients and had actively sought them out as a younger man. He made contributions to various charities, but considering his income, one could describe these donations more as token than as substantial. When asked, he provided legal advice to a few Jewish organizations, but no one in the Jewish community would have considered him "involved." Historians have noted that in Boston and elsewhere, the arrival of the great tide of eastern European immigrants after 1880 triggered a new nativist movement that culminated in the immigration restriction laws of the 1920s as well as quotas for Jews and others at Ivy League schools, gentlemen's clubs, and boardrooms. This prejudice did not bother to distinguish between committed and marginal Jews any more than it could tell the difference between Orthodox, Conservative, or Reform.

Louis and Alice never denied their heritage, and Brandeis himself rarely spoke about being the target of anti-Semitism. He saw the Brahmin attack as growing out of his opposition to the Boston money powers, and since he had little use for either the ethics or the practices of the Lees and Higginsons of the world, he felt no regret at not being invited to socialize with them. He had, of course, enjoyed the cosmopolitanism of Boston when he arrived as the exotic young man from the country, but he and Alice soon decided that they would choose their friends not for wealth or pedigree but for their brains and civic courage.

After he became a Zionist (see chapter 17), Brandeis discussed anti-Semitism both with Horace Meyer Kallen, the progressive era's leading advocate of cultural pluralism, and later with Rabbi Solomon Goldman, and in neither instance did he mention any personal experience. The Brandeises could hardly have been unaware of the existence of prejudice—after all, Louis had not been invited to Sam Warren's wedding—but it did not seem greatly to affect them. Neither Alice nor Louis wanted to belong to the clubs or societies that practiced exclusion; potential law clients who disliked Jews would not have come, and in any event the firm had a large base of loyal clients, Jew and non-Jew alike; the Brandeis children went to private schools where their religion did not constitute a mark against them. That Boston families who had once welcomed them no longer did must have caused some sorrow, but they also recognized that much of the antagonism had grown out of resentment against Louis's reform activities, and for that neither one would apologize.

SUSAN AND ELIZABETH grew up in a household quite different from those of their schoolmates. They did not lack for basic comforts, such as good food, warm clothing, and comfortable shelter; they enjoyed their weekends at Dedham and their summers on Cape Cod. Their mother, however, often went away for weeks at a time, and even when home could fall into bouts of depression, while their father began to spend more and more time in New York or Washington. Moreover, few of their classmates had a father who regularly showed up on the front pages of the local newspapers, praised and damned with equal intensity.

Louis and Alice could do little about either her illness or his fame, but they did give the girls a warm, loving environment, and no matter how busy Louis might be, he always found time to spend with his daughters when home or wrote them letters while on a trip. Unlike his notes to Alice, which included political gossip and news about law cases, the playful letters to the children talked about things he knew would interest them. In an early letter to Elizabeth, then four years old and, along with Alice and Susan, visiting her Goldmark relatives in New York, he wrote, "Do you like New York? And how does your doll like to be with Grandma and all the Aunts and Uncles. I hope she has not cried much. The Christmas tree and Santa Claus are very anxious to see you and Susan again, and want to know whether they shall wait until you come back from New York. Santa Claus would like to come down from the tree and rest in Susan's bed. Do you think I should let him?" Five years later, after Elizabeth wrote reporting on her progress in learning how to swim, her father congratulated her and added that "so great a swimmer will, doubtless, want to become also a great walker," which in fact she did, often accompanying her father on his hikes through the woods. When he visited the Kentucky horse farms in 1906, he wrote to tell the children about what he had seen and how the yearlings and colts came up to them as they walked in the meadows.

The two girls, although both bright and strong willed, differed a great deal in personality. Susan appeared more outgoing as a child, while Elizabeth seemed shier and more reserved. As Alice told Belle La Follette in 1913, Susan's "is a passionate nature, easily roused, capable of deepest affection & also fairly strong hatreds. Her enthusiasm for public service is great." Periodically, Susan would do something that upset her parents, to the point that one time Louis wondered if she were indeed their daughter. Eventually, she outgrew this behavior, but not until after graduation from law school.

In 1911, the eighteen-year-old Susan stood ready to go to college, but first she had to finish all of her high-school exams and was very nervous about them. From New York her father sent her a reassuring note that he had faith in her ability. "Good courage to you," he wrote, "and keep your good wits about you. You will then have what is called 'good luck.' I am sure you know enough." Apparently, she did, for a few days later she reported that the examinations had gone well.

That fall she went off to Bryn Mawr College, much to the joy of her Goldmark aunts who had also attended the school. "I trust the first day at College has been beautiful," her father wrote, "and full of that promise of happiness and usefulness which we wish for you. Take very good care of yourself and be full of courage." When Alice expressed some concern about whether Susan could discipline herself and buckle down to work, Louis assured her that all would be well. "Susan will rise to the responsibility of taking care of herself," he thought. "At all event, she must learn & the conditions are as favorable as it seems possible to create."

Susan had trouble in college with the same subject she had had problems with in high school—English—and with her father's approval arranged to have private tutoring in the subject. In an effort to cheer her up, he confessed that the task of composition "may continue difficult for you, as it has always been for me, but that is no terrible misfortune. The important thing is to have something to say and to learn how to say it, and I have no doubt you will, in good time, have plenty to say, and what you say will be worthwhile, because what you do is high-minded and noble."

The Brandeises believed that Susan's (and later Elizabeth's) collegiate education should include learning how to manage money. Louis sent her a check for $200 (over $4,000 in 2007 currency) when she started school, so she could open her own checking account and pay her bills for tuition, room, board, and books. They also wanted her to support activities and causes. "Remember, we want you to be in a position to contribute your liberal share to all college activities you are interested in." But having money and spending it wisely involved accounting, and Susan apparently did not share her father's passion for keeping accurate records. In the spring of her junior year her father wrote to say how pleased they were in her development and they wanted her to have the financial independence to assume new responsibilities now that she had turned twenty-one. They intended to give her an annual allowance of $1,800, but they expected a better accounting than they had previously received. "We want you to spend the money as seems to you best, but I must ask you to prepare and send to me not later than the 8th of each month an account of the disbursements of the preceding month classified as: 1. College expenses; 2. Dress; 3. Travelling; 4. Amusements; 5. Gifts (to relations or friends); 6. Contributions to public causes; 7. Sundries (& any other subdivisions you may desire)." He also wanted her to show the balance on hand, as well as expenditures for the month and year to date, "as I showed you in the account last summer." Apparently, Susan failed to submit her accounts on time, and there is a constant complaint from Louis to Alice that Susan had not acknowledged receipt of a check or that her monthly statement had not yet arrived.

Susan did well, but not outstandingly, in college. She had to take a foreign language and chose German, which proved difficult, so with her parents' approval she hired a tutor for that subject as well. She really disliked the language, and Louis wrote to Alice, "I hope you can work Susan up to a desire to master her German decently. Whatever she may do with it later she ought to learn to do it because she hates it, & get the 'lust of finishing' instead of skimping. Can Elizabeth help in this?" As her graduation approached, Louis assured Susan that he and Alice did not view her class standing disapprovingly. "You have made good use of your years at college, and have grown most during the past year. I have no doubt but that you will give a good account of yourself after graduation."

Much to Louis's delight, Susan decided to go to law school, but she soon found that her two top choices, Harvard and Columbia, did not admit women at the time. Taking a leaf from her father's history, she wrote what amounted to a brief to the deans of both schools arguing that they should admit women in general and her in particular. Both George W. Kirchwey of Columbia and Roscoe Pound of Harvard knew her father personally and felt they had to explain to him why they could not admit his otherwise well-qualified daughter to their programs. Both men personally believed women should be admitted, but told Brandeis that they did not have the power to do so. The admission of women constituted a major policy decision that could be made only by the whole faculty as well as the governing boards of the schools, and while it would eventually happen, they did not know when.

Disappointed at not getting into the schools of her choice, Susan decided to spend the year after her graduation at home and work on the suffrage cause. Alice initially thought this would be wonderful, and no doubt she and Susan enjoyed laboring for the same goal. But after her relative freedom at school, Susan seemed restless back in Boston and often wound up fighting with her mother. Louis, in Chicago to address the bar association just days before his nomination to the Court, tried to calm Alice: "Of course it is your unappreciated love that hurts in the Susan matter. But remember time and patience are the great remedies," he told her. "She will come clamoring for your love a little later." At the end of the year Susan went off to the University of Chicago Law School, where she managed both to please her parents by her studies and to aggravate them by her personal behavior.*

CONSIDERING HOW BUSY his life had become, Louis could indeed take a great deal of satisfaction not only from his work but from his family as well. As he, Alice, Susan, and Elizabeth enjoyed their Christmas vacation in Dedham in 1912, he no doubt looked forward to what he and other progressives hoped would be a burst of reform energy once Wilson took office in March 1913. He did not know what if any role he would play in the new administration, but could assume that he would remain as busy in reform work in the next few years as he had been in the past. He had no idea how much more hectic his life would soon become.

*Elizabeth Brandeis went to Radcliffe College, where she received her B.A. in 1918, and, after working for a few years, attended the University of Wisconsin, where she earned her doctorate in economics under John R. Commons in 1928. Unfortunately, we have no comparable correspondence between Brandeis and his younger daughter. Susan saved his letters to her, and her children deposited them, along with those to Alice, in the Brandeis library. Elizabeth also saved her letters and provided some of them for *The Brandeis Letters,* but because of her own views on privacy, before her death, she destroyed nearly all of the letters her father had written to her.

CHAPTER SIXTEEN

THE NEW FREEDOM

Within days of the 1912 election rumors abounded that Woodrow Wilson would name Louis Brandeis as a member of his cabinet, to head either the Justice or the Commerce department. Even the thought of Brandeis in a position where he could determine antitrust policy sent a spasm of terror through the business community, and a wave of protests against the Boston lawyer poured in on Wilson headquarters. Henry Lee Higginson, once a friend of the younger Brandeis and now a bitter enemy, had written a virulent letter to Wilson in the middle of October warning him against relying on Brandeis, for whom "no reputable lawyer here has a good word." Higginson did not care to censure Brandeis and would not have done so "if the newspaper reports did not indicate that he is looking for political position, and if he did not continually pose as a friend of the people, a man who helped the underdog, etc."

Immediately after his election Wilson received another salvo from the Brahmins in a letter from the president of Harvard, Abbott Lawrence Lowell. If he were to take a Massachusetts man for the cabinet, it should not be Brandeis, and Lowell wanted Wilson to understand that no one of any standing in Boston trusted Brandeis. Lowell's comments on Brandeis surprised him, Wilson responded, because "I had formed a very high opinion of him, and many of his ideas have made a deep impression on me." But he would certainly examine carefully the credentials of any man he considered for public office.

Both the Brandeis and the Wilson papers are devoid of even the slightest intimation that Brandeis at any time sought political reward from Wilson for his work, and in fact when reporters occasionally asked him what role he saw for himself in a Wilson administration, Brandeis made it clear that he had no ambition for politics. The fact that many of his friends believed he should be in the cabinet may have pleased him, but considering how he valued his independence, it would have been out of character for him in effect to become an aide, even an aide to the president of the United States.

The first evidence of Wilson's considering Brandeis for the cabinet comes from an entry in Colonel Edward M. House's diary for 16 November 1912, when he noted that after a discussion of who should be attorney general, "we practically eliminated Brandeis for this position (because he was not thought to be entirely above suspicion and it would not do to put him in such a place)." Yet less than a week later House had lunch with Brandeis in New York, and the two men seemed impressed by each other. Louis told Alice that House appeared to be "a very good fellow & influential." House in turn reported to Wilson that Brandeis's "mind and mine are in accord concerning most of the questions that are now to the fore." While a large number of reputable people apparently distrusted him, "I doubt whether the distrust is well founded and it would perhaps attach itself to any man who held his advanced views." But although he now said that he "liked him personally," House still advised against putting him in the cabinet, because, among other reasons, Brandeis had been a Republican and had supported Taft in 1908. He began to push Wilson to name James C. McReynolds, the Texas lawyer who had prosecuted the tobacco trust, for the attorney general position.

But if House opposed Brandeis, Wilson found some of his other advisers highly enthusiastic about him. William Jennings Bryan, who still had a large following in the Democratic Party and to whom Wilson owed his nomination, declared that he shared Wilson's high opinion of Brandeis and thought no better man could be found to head the Justice Department. Other favorable reports also came to Wilson, but every time Wilson brought up Brandeis's name, either for attorney general or for solicitor general, House argued against it, claiming that business interests did not trust Brandeis in any position involving legal authority.

Wilson, however, wanted Brandeis in his government and asked Norman Hapgood to look into the charges brought against Brandeis. Hapgood reported back that he had found no basis for any of them. Wilson also recognized that progressive senators and representatives, whose help he would need in passing his program, thought Brandeis should get an appointment. Charles Crane, a friend and client of Brandeis's, wrote Wilson that he had spoken with Senator La Follette, who

Attorney General James C.
McReynolds, 1913

seemed eager to cooperate with Wilson in securing reform legislation. "He is, however, like all other progressives," Crane noted, "most anxious to have Brandeis to work with" as a representative of the administration. La Follette believed that Brandeis more than anyone else would be able to win over insurgent support for a Wilson program. Progressives also urged the president-elect to name him because he had been a Republican, and his appointment would show that Wilson wanted to reach out to all progressives—Democrats, Republicans, and independents. According to Wilson's biographer, "No man mentioned for appointment, not even Bryan, had such wide support from all elements of the progressive movement."

At a lengthy meeting between Wilson and his advisers on 13 February, Wilson declared that he had investigated Brandeis's record and could not bring himself to believe he had done anything to cause the kind of virulent criticism directed against him. House argued that it did not matter if the accusations were true or false, since so many people believed them, and as a result his value to the administration would be diminished. Wilson nonetheless insisted, but gave in to House's urging that Brandeis not be in the Justice Department. At the end of the meeting a tentative cabinet list included Brandeis in the Commerce Department, and he stayed on that list until less than a week before Wilson's inauguration.

Finally, Wilson relented, not because he believed that Brandeis had acted unethically, but because he did not want to disturb the business community. The president-elect faced an uncertain economic situation, with the country experiencing a mild recession. Since much of the legislation he wanted to enact would be perceived by big business as hostile to their interests, it seemed easier to give in to House's argument. Moreover, it would not do for the new administration to face a bruising confirmation battle in the Senate, where Democrats enjoyed only a thin majority. The *Boston American* and many progressives condemned Wilson for giving in to the business interests, which they saw as an abandonment of reform hopes. The paper ran a boxed editorial on the front page that began, "The AMERICAN Congratulates the Corporation Enemies of Mr. Brandeis, Who Have Kept Massachusetts from Representation in the Cabinet." La Follette and others despaired that Wilson had taken "the easy way," while Norman Hapgood lamented that "the interests everywhere . . . and the country will think W[ilson] showed the white feather."

Did anti-Semitism play a part in keeping Louis out of the cabinet? The historian Allon Gal believes that prejudice "in Brahmin circles clearly affected Brandeis's political prospects," and a recent biographer of House's claims that Brandeis thought so as well, relying on his comment to Norman Hapgood that "the Massachusetts opposition to my going into the cabinet was not in its essence political." In looking at Brandeis as a member of his cabinet, Wilson clearly took religion into account, but not in a negative way—Wilson and House wanted a Jew in the cabinet. Jewish voters had traditionally been Republican in national politics. Wilson had made a great effort to reach out to the Jewish community and had been rewarded by the largest percentage of Jewish votes that any Democratic candidate had polled to that time. While the leaders of the German-Jewish community such as Jacob Schiff and Louis Marshall would remain Republican, Wilson hoped to attract the larger number of recent immigrants from eastern Europe who had already attached themselves to local Democratic machines. Just as Theodore Roosevelt had named Oscar Straus to his cabinet to shore up his Jewish supporters, so Wilson hoped naming Brandeis would do the same for him.

House himself, according to Godfrey Hodgson, was not anti-Semitic, although after their first meeting House wrote to Wilson of Brandeis, "There comes to the surface, now and then, one of those curious Hebrew traits of mind that makes one hold something in reserve." The problem, at least from House's point of view, was that the Jews he consulted with about Brandeis had little good to say about him. The banker Jacob Schiff, for example, thought that while not a representative Jew, Brandeis could be considered a representative American, knowing full well that House sought the imprimatur of the community's leaders and refusing to give it. Charles Crane, on the other hand, thought that because Brandeis valued his Americanism so highly, this made him an ideal Jewish candidate. "Brandeis is the only important Jew who is first American and then Jew," Crane told Wilson. "All of the other impor-

tant Jews are first Jews and then Americans and do not hesitate to sacrifice real American interests at any time for what they conceive to be Jewish ones. Brandeis has grown up and developed as an American and, now
that he has become a man of importance, the other Jews are trying hard
to control him but they will not succeed."

Brandeis, of course, knew a great deal about the debate going on
about him, and he resented the idea of being appointed to the cabinet
for no other reason than his religion. Between the election and Wilson's
inauguration, he practically cut off what few ties he had to the Boston
Jewish community and consistently turned down invitations from Jewish and Zionist groups to speak in New York and Chicago. The lawyer
Edward Goulston tried in vain to get Brandeis to address the Elysium
Club, the elite Jewish club in Boston, where he could present himself as
"a representative Jew." Similarly, he turned down an invitation from
Edward Bromberg to speak at the New Century Club in New York.
Brandeis did not accept invitations from Jewish groups until after the
announcement of Wilson's cabinet.

In early 1913, Brandeis in fact would not have been seen as a "representative Jew," although what that meant to Wilson or House is difficult to tell. Perhaps they meant someone connected to the important
Jewish organizations such as the American Jewish Committee and
B'nai B'rith, the leading Jewish men's fraternal organization. But the
committee, led by Jacob Schiff and Louis Marshall, consisted of men
tied to the business establishment who, for the most part, would have
opposed Brandeis as an economic radical, even if he had had strong
Jewish connections. When Brandeis told Norman Hapgood that the
opposition to his going into the cabinet "was not in its essence political," he meant that it grew out of opposition to his reform work and
economic positions, and not from traditional "political" values, such as
party affiliation, work for the party, or patronage connections. After the
announcement of the final list, one banker wrote to Colonel House,
"You little know how much gratification is felt about the 'street' over
the success of eliminating Brandeis from the Cabinet."

During this period Brandeis remained almost completely silent on
the question of a cabinet appointment. He had to go to Chicago in early
January to take care of some matters for Charles Crane and wrote to
Alice, "There is so much Brandeis Cabinet talk that I think it just as
well to be absent." When a reporter and friend wrote to him about the
Commerce position, he replied, "It cannot be necessary to tell an old
newspaper man not to believe all he hears." There is not a written word,

however, to Alice, to Alfred, or to any of his friends that indicates any interest in an appointment, although had the president offered him a cabinet position, it is hard to imagine his saying no.

We do know that he discussed the matter with his wife and brother, because there is a genuine tone of relief in his voice when Wilson announced his cabinet on 2 March. "As you know," he told Alfred, "I had great doubts as for its being desirable for me; so I concluded to literally let nature take its course and do nothing either to get called or to stop the talk, although some of my friends were quite active. State Street, Wall Street and the local Democratic bosses did six months' unremitting work; but seemed not to have prevailed until the last moment." He found it amusing "how much they fear me, attributing to me power and influence which I in no respect possess." To Alice he said, "No office for me. Me for the simple life."

What is clearly missing from this letter is any mention of anti-Semitism, and while Louis might have hidden that consideration from others, he would not have glossed over it in conversations with his wife or brother. Brandeis's religion played a role in the decision, but not anti-Semitism, and Wilson's most thorough biographer has found no evidence of it in the decision process. Wilson, still determined to reward Louis in some way, did offer him the chairmanship of the Commission on Industrial Relations in April, but by then Brandeis knew he would wield considerably more influence by remaining independent.

BRANDEIS HAD NOT BEEN IDLE during these months, and even before the announcement of the cabinet list knew that he would have an important role in the new administration, as well as the president's ear. Between November and March, Brandeis, among other things, worked to help Harvard Law School create a criminal law library and suggested some material to be included in a course on the subject, advised the Senate Commerce Committee on antitrust legislation, caught up with the latest figures showing the New Haven's decline, consulted with the Interstate Commerce Commission on railroad rate increases, and continued his work on the arbitration board for the New York garment industry. Near the top of his agenda, however, stood the problem of helping Norman Hapgood, who had been fired from his position as editor of *Collier's* for backing Wilson.

Brandeis felt personally responsible, and he set about trying not only to make peace with Robert Collier but also to find another outlet for Hapgood. Collier, while insistent that Hapgood had to go, nonetheless wanted to stay on good terms with Brandeis and had wired him that he wanted an opportunity to discuss the matter with him, since he considered it "rather important that we should understand each other." Brandeis met with the publisher, and to show that he had no ill feelings toward his former counsel, Collier invited him to write a piece on Wilson for the magazine. He remained adamant, however, that he would not rehire Hapgood. Brandeis did, however, manage to smooth things over. He got Norman to stop declaring to one and all that he had been stabbed in the back, and Collier agreed to consider the incident with his former editor closed.

With a promise of financial support from Charles Crane, Brandeis and Hapgood began to look around for a journal to purchase. For a while it looked as if *McClure's Magazine* might be available, but aside from other problems it would have had to be converted from a monthly into a weekly. Then Hapgood lunched with Thomas W. Lamont, the Wall Street financier who owned *Harper's Weekly,* and he offered to sell it—essentially the name and goodwill—for $100,000. Brandeis immediately opened negotiations; by late spring Hapgood had become editor of *Harper's,* and Brandeis set about doing everything he could to ensure its success.

He hit upon the idea of providing copies to all the public libraries in New England that did not already subscribe, and paid for the subscriptions himself. He then got other people to pay for the middle Atlantic states, Ohio, Illinois, and the Northwest. He wrote to Alfred in January 1914 that he had tentative sponsors for North Carolina, Georgia, and Florida, and hoped Al would take care of Kentucky, at the very modest cost of $3 per subscription. It then turned out that Kentucky had only twelve libraries that did not take the magazine, and Tennessee eleven, so Louis sent his brother lists of libraries in other southern states.

For the next few years nearly all of the articles he wrote on social and economic issues, including the series that became *Other People's Money,* appeared in *Harper's,* and he refused to accept any money for them. In July 1914 he returned a check for $100 to Hapgood, telling him he did not want to be paid for anything he did for the magazine until it had reached the stage of earning dividends on the common stock. He also turned over to the journal revenue from the publication of *Other People's Money* as a book.

How highly Brandeis valued Hapgood, both as a friend and as a progressive, can be seen from the way he answered an inquiry he received during the publication of the banking series. Professor Joseph Smith considered the articles of such consequence that he thought they should have been published in a journal with a wider circulation, such as *Collier's* or the *Saturday Evening Post.* That might have been true, Brandeis replied, "but I regard Mr. Hapgood as so important a factor in the American advance movement that if I have been of any service in helping *Harper's Weekly,* as his instrument, I shall feel well content with the decision made."

BRANDEIS WENT DOWN to Washington shortly after the inaugural, primarily on Interstate Commerce Commission business, and almost immediately entered the whirlpool that would be his life for the next few years. "Have had a busy day," he wrote to Alice on 8 March. "Saw Jud Welliver, Gilson Gardner, Henry Beach Needham, Senators Clapp, Bourne, James, etc., etc. Had long talk with Prouty and Marble [ICC] . . . and am to have this evening with La Follette." The next day he had a "satisfactory" meeting with Secretary of the Interior Franklin K. Lane and reported, "The way is open to me to help run the Interior [Dept.] and (via Marble) the Interstate Commerce Commission." The following evening he spent over an hour at the White House with Wilson, after conferences during the day with Secretary of State Bryan, Commerce Secretary William C. Redfield, and Attorney General McReynolds. In going to the cabinet members' offices, he noted hordes of office seekers besieging them for jobs and, as he told Alice, thought himself better off for not having to deal with such problems. "Me for the simple life."

Even though he told people he had nothing to do with patronage, Brandeis in fact became a key figure in the administration's distribution of political appointments in Massachusetts, as well as in some of the Washington agencies. As the first Democratic president in sixteen years, Wilson faced a barrage of demands from Democrats for federal jobs, as did his department heads. With the exception of William Jennings Bryan, who saw the State Department as a vehicle for rewarding deserving Democrats, and Postmaster General Albert Burleson, whose department had always been staffed by patronage, the other members of Wilson's cabinet wanted competent people who could be relied upon for their judgment and to do a good job, and they did not want to have the state and city machines sending them hacks. McAdoo, McReynolds, Redfield, and Lane wrote to Brandeis often, either seeking suggestions for particular positions or wanting his evaluation of someone they had under consideration. Over the previous decade Brandeis had gotten to know many people in different reform movements, and he willingly shared this information when requested. On the other hand, he rarely tried to push anyone unless asked; the sole exception seems to have been his determination to get David Ives appointed to the Interstate Commerce Commission. Wilson also consulted him from time to time, although usually when they met rather than through letters, and continued to do so even after Brandeis went on the Court.

Senators, congressmen, government officials, and others also clamored for his advice on the substantive issues facing the Wilson administration, such as antitrust legislation and banking reform. During these weeks and months Louis wrote regularly to Alice, except during those times when she joined him, and of course to Alfred, and one can get a sense of his activity and involvement in the government by sampling a few of those letters:

To Alice, 9 March 1913: At 10:30 I am to see MacFarland. . . . At 1:30 I lunch with the Pinchots & at 7 dine with the Frankfurter contingent. . . . Had a quiet talk a deux with La Follette last evening. He is pretty grim. WW will not be taken on faith by him. Talk with Lane was very satisfactory.

To Alfred, 10 March 1913: I have been engaged largely in promoting the entente cordiale with the Administration. Had a good private talk with the President this evening for an hour—and with Lane, Redfield, Bryan, and McReynolds today . . . & spent this morning at the I.C.C. on New Haven matters. There is no lack of occupation.

To Alice, 10 June 1913: Made good progress yesterday on One price Article campaign, first with Redfield who is thoroughly with me. He made appointment for us to see the President together which we did from 4:30 to 5:15. President was converted from dense ignorance to the light, wants me to make the educational campaign, & to have the Administration come out with a bill in Dec. Redfield & I are to see the Atty Gen'l at 10:45 today to try to get him to be quiescent on prosecution, a harder task. Had long talk with Corporation Com'er Davies who will probably take up the investigation into facts I proposed. On New Haven matters— saw Prouty, Marble & Meyer, & some others at I.C.C. . . . Had satisfactory talk with Gregory who I am to spend hours with today.

Was at La Follettes after dinner. Am to dine there & spend the evening in more serious talk today.

After a while, exciting as the politics may have been, Louis yearned for a little peace and quiet. "Think I shall have to abandon the Cosmos Club soon," he told Alice, "too much 'talkie' at breakfast. It is pretty hard finding a place where reading light is good and man is absent."

WILSON BEGAN HIS ADMINISTRATION by fulfilling a longtime Democratic pledge to reduce the tariff, and he succeeded brilliantly, providing one of the finest examples of presidential leadership since Lincoln. Although Brandeis had first written to Wilson on the tariff and was pleased by the new law, he had nothing to do with passage of the Underwood Tariff Act. But on the other major parts of the New Freedom—banking and currency reform and antitrust—Brandeis played a key role.

Wilson had called the concentration of fiscal power in Wall Street "the most pernicious of all trusts," and between 1910 and 1914 he developed two basic premises. First, a money trust of monopoly proportions existed, and to restore competition, it had to be destroyed. Brandeis's articles on other people's money, which he sent to the president in draft form, confirmed Wilson's belief in a money trust; he read the articles carefully, making notes in the margins. Early in 1913 the president-elect argued, "You must put the credit of this country at the disposal of everybody upon equal terms. Now, I am not entering into an indictment against the banking methods of this country. The banking system of this country does not need to be indicted. It is convicted." Second, Wilson believed banking too important a business to be left to bankers, and reform had to make banks what they should be—the servants and not the masters of business. Not only did one have to destroy the monopoly; but to protect the public interest, some form of government supervision was necessary.

In the spring of 1913, Representative Carter Glass of Virginia and the economist H. Parker Willis, with Wilson's blessing, worked up a plan for a decentralized, privately controlled reserve system of not more than twenty independent reserve banks. Wilson tentatively agreed, but insisted on one additional feature, an "altruistic Federal Reserve Board in Washington to supervise the proposed system," a sort of "capstone" to it. Although Glass did not like the idea, he thought it harmless and acquiesced. In general, the Glass-Willis plan represented the views of the banking and business communities, with control of the system as well as the issuance of currency remaining in private hands.

Once details of the plan became known, it aroused the antagonism of the populist wing of the Democratic Party. William Jennings Bryan and his followers, who carried great weight in the party, had two main objections. First, the Glass proposal allowed banks to elect the members of the Federal Reserve Board, thus ensuring an agency friendly to their interests; second, currency issue remained in bank control. Bryan wanted the board composed solely of government-appointed officials, and money issue to be strictly a government function. Bryan and the progressive wing of the party realized that if the currency power remained in banker control and banker representatives dominated the Federal Reserve Board, then the money trust would not be broken. In fact it would merely be reorganized with more power than ever. Bryan could not support the Glass-Willis bill in its current form, nor could he ask his followers to do so.

By June, with the issue raging in both Congress and the press, Wilson had to decide between the conservative Glass-Willis measure, which had banker support, and the main points of the Bryan wing, endorsed by Samuel Untermyer, counsel to the Pujo Committee, and Secretary of the Treasury William Gibbs McAdoo. He called in one of the few men whose economic views he trusted. Brandeis, however, could hardly be termed a neutral observer. The Boston lawyer distrusted the big banking houses almost to the point of obsession.

Brandeis came down from Boston to the White House on 11 June, and he and the president spent several hours going over the conflicting plans. He convinced Wilson not only of the justness of Bryan's arguments in the light of historic Democratic platform promises but also of their rightness. Even if the backing of the Federal Reserve notes should be commercial paper, currency ought to be an exclusive function of the government. "The American people will not be content to have the discretion necessarily involved vested in a board composed wholly or in part of bankers," he argued, "for their judgment may be biased by private interest or affiliation. The function of the bankers should be limited strictly to that of an advisory council." While public opinion and Congress would accept banker representation on the boards of the regional banks, there would be a public outcry if bankers controlled the issue of currency and the federal board, and there would be no chance at enacting a necessary and long overdue reform.

He also urged Wilson not to take too much stock in the banker arguments that enactment of a proper currency bill, namely, one they controlled, would allay financial disturbances. The effect of the "best conceivable currency bill will be relatively slight," unless the government could also curb the money trust and remove the uneasiness it caused the business community. Nothing would do as much to establish confidence among businessmen "as the assurance that the Government will control the currency issue and the conviction that whatever money is available, will be available for business generally, and not be subject to the control of a favored few." He exhorted Wilson to recognize that a conflict existed between the policies of the administration and the desires of the financiers and of big business, a conflict he deemed "irreconcilable." The president should not be tempted by offers of cooperation; careful consideration should, of course, be given to banker views and their expert knowledge, always keeping in mind that their interests would be hostile to those of reform.

A few days later Wilson called together McAdoo, Glass, Senator Robert L. Owen of Oklahoma, and Bryan to inform them that he had decided on exclusive government control of the reserve system and on making its notes government obligations. An ecstatic Bryan issued a public letter declaring that the new bill was "written from the standpoint of the people rather than from the standpoint of financiers," and that government issue of currency fulfilled Democratic campaign promises. Glass gracefully gave in, and Wilson proposed the new bill to Congress on 23 June. Despite strong attacks from the banking community, he engineered it through Congress and signed it into law before the year ended. It remains the single most constructive piece of legislation enacted by the Wilson administration and one of the most important in the country's history.

Imperfect in many details (it would be revised during the 1930s), it struck a balance between private power and control on the one hand and public supervision on the other, a balance that both Brandeis and Wilson cared greatly about. In a short time it won the support of the banking community, especially the smaller country banks released from the hold of Wall Street. The more radical progressives, however, condemned it. La Follette denounced it as a "big bankers' bill" that legalized the money trust, a charge echoed by Senator Joseph Bristow of Kansas and Representative Charles A. Lindbergh of Minnesota. They failed to understand the nature of Wilsonian reform and, by extension, of Brandeis's views as well.

The New Freedom, basically conservative, did not seek to reform and redo society in a new mode, and neither did Brandeis. He and Wilson hoped to restore an older, more idyllic, and probably semi-mythical past in which there had been a balance among the country's various political and economic groups. Their progressivism lay in their desire to favor popular democracy against wealthy elites, but they wanted to do so with minimal governmental interference and regulation. This explains Wilson's dilemma in 1912 before meeting Brandeis—how to combat big business without resorting to big government. Brandeis proposed and Wilson accepted the notion that one could regulate competition—the market—with less governmental intrusion than if one tried to regulate business. Neither Brandeis nor Wilson wanted the government to go too far; both feared big government as much as big business, and considered both subversive of freedom. The Glass proposal left too much power in the hands of the bankers, while the Bryanites wanted to have a government-owned banking system. Neither plan struck the balance that Brandeis and Wilson sought, and in December 1913, looking over their handiwork, both men could take satisfaction that they had achieved the proper equilibrium. Brandeis recognized that defects existed—such as the lack of a ban on interlocking directorates—but believed these could be remedied in antitrust legislation.

WHEN IT BECAME CLEAR that the banking bill would pass, Wilson turned to the third leg of the New Freedom, antitrust legislation. Several members of the cabinet urged the president to stop and to give the business community a chance to adjust to the tariff and banking measures. Secretary of Agriculture David Houston advised Wilson "to make haste slowly," while Postmaster General Albert Burleson, Secretary of War Lindley Garrison, and Attorney General McReynolds, conservatives all, argued against any new business legislation. Business leaders feared any trust measure drafted by Brandeis, and pleaded with Wilson to do nothing to affect industry and commerce.

William Jennings Bryan, however, urged the president to go forward. Wilson had successfully secured both a lower tariff and currency reform; the time could not be better to fulfill campaign promises. Louis Brandeis also wanted the president to move ahead. Franklin Lane, an old friend from ICC days and now secretary of the interior, had asked Brandeis what he thought the administration should do. In a long letter in mid-December, Brandeis suggested that Wilson remember that the hostility between the banking and big business interests and the forces of reform embodied in the New Freedom could never be resolved.

Most businessmen, in fact, would benefit from a reduced tariff and currency reform, and they would also gain from antitrust legislation, since it would remove the threat of dishonest competition.

To gain their understanding, the administration needed to establish a trade commission that would serve as a resource for business and that would identify anticompetitive practices. The commission should distinguish between monopolistic practices and those arrangements among competitors that were in fact legitimate forms of regulation of competition. The government should also aid business as it did agriculture, establishing industrial experiment stations and bureaus of research, which could disseminate important information such as scientific management. The Sherman law had to be strengthened to include, among other things, a strict prohibition against interlocking directorates and barriers against railroads engaging in any business but transportation.

Brandeis believed enacting such laws to be essential to carrying out the New Freedom but also, and just as important, "politically necessary to satisfy the demands of the very large number of progressive Democrats and near Democrats who are already beginning to express some doubt whether the administration will have the courage . . . to carry out the policy which it has hitherto declared." Talk about a possible business depression meant little, because nothing the administration did or did not do would affect the business cycle. "The fearless course [is] the wise one."

Wilson mulled the issue over during his Christmas vacation, and part of the problem lay in his naïveté. Unlike Brandeis, Wilson had not really thought through the trust problem beyond the fact that he believed monopoly inimical to democracy. Since monopolistic business practices constituted the economic equivalent of sin, men should be punished for their sins and their acts exposed to public condemnation. The simple—and simplistic—answer lay in a stricter enforcement of the Sherman Act's criminal provisions. Wilson had on several occasions stated his belief, very similar to that of Theodore Roosevelt, that big business was here to stay, and yet had also argued "that real dissolution in the case of the trusts is the only thing we can rest satisfied with." Wilson feared big business, and also feared Roosevelt's solution of big government to control the trusts.

Brandeis also saw the trust problem in moral terms, but not those of Wilson's Presbyterian notion of sin. Brandeis feared trusts because they throttled opportunity and deprived men of the chance to prove themselves in the market. Testifying during congressional hearings, Brandeis had maintained that antitrust measures could never effectively be enforced through criminal provisions alone. Exposure and even threat of prosecution would not sear the "alleged consciences" of the monopolists. The proper way to proceed would be to decide on the goals and then frame just laws that reasonable men could follow. Over two decades earlier he had argued that "no regulation can be enforced which is not reasonable."

As Wilson contemplated the problem, it is almost certain that his thoughts returned to the original memorandum Brandeis had prepared for him in 1912. There, and in articles that Brandeis had sent to him from time to time, the People's Attorney had spelled out a specific program: remove the uncertainties and vagaries of the Sherman Act; make enforcement of the law easier in the courts; create a board or commission to aid in administering the law; and allow trade agreements to stand if the commission did not find them in violation of competitive rules. Wilson had some concerns about a regulatory board, since it sounded too much like Roosevelt's notion of a powerful federal agency to control business, and preferred instead to put as much as possible into statutory language.

On 20 January 1914, Wilson went up to Capitol Hill to deliver a special message on the "great question" of trusts and monopolies. Adopting a moderate tone, he suggested that "the antagonism between business and government is over" and the time ripe to proceed with a sensible program, one that represented "the best business judgment in America." He proposed outlawing interlocking directorates, giving the Interstate Commerce Commission power to supervise capital financing and securities issues by the railroads, strengthening penalties for individuals guilty of malpractices, and providing that any facts or judgments decided upon in government suits would not have to be re-proven by private individuals to recover damages for monopolistic practices. He also wanted to create a federal agency to give businessmen "the advice, the definite guidance, and information" they needed to conduct their enterprises properly, but one that did not have the power to "make terms with monopoly or . . . assume control of business."

Reading over Wilson's message, Brandeis thought that the president had somewhat overdone the sweetness in manner, but he admitted that it had its uses and "makes it possible for the big interests to swallow his pills somewhat more easily." To his brother he commented with satisfaction that the president "has paved the way for about all I have asked for and some of the provisions specifically are what I got into his mind at my first interview."

In practical detail the administration proposed three bills. First, a measure drawn up by Henry D. Clayton, chair of the House Judiciary Committee, that would amend the Sherman Act and include particular provisions such as the ban on interlocking directorates. The second bill would create an interstate trade commission to interpret the law and give businessmen guidance and information. Known as the Covington bill, in its original form it did little more than expand the Bureau of Corporations. Finally, the Rayburn bill, which Brandeis helped to draft and which directly reflected his experience with the New Haven, gave the ICC power over railroad securities.

Immediately following the president's message, calls went out from members of the cabinet as well as of Congress for Brandeis to help shape the legislation. Already in Washington for the advance rate case, he found his days and his evenings tied up with meetings with the Interstate Commerce Commission, administration officials, reporters, and congressmen. As he told Alice, there was "no leisure class life" for him amid this turmoil, although whenever possible he tried to find time for a quiet dinner with friends and even managed to go to the theater with the Cranes one evening.

Progressives welcomed the fact that Wilson had decided to go ahead with antitrust legislation, but many felt he had not gone far enough. Brandeis saw Bob La Follette the evening of the president's message, and while the senator approved of Wilson's ideas, he opposed the ICC's passing on railroad securities in any way. Samuel Untermyer complained to Colonel House, called the proposed measures "lamentably weak and ineffective," and begged House to get Brandeis in to redraw the plan. House apparently agreed, and he forwarded Untermyer's letter to Wilson with the suggestion to "put Gregory and Brandeis on this job with the Attorney-General to act as advisor." Wilson acted with alacrity, writing to Congressman William C. Adamson that since Brandeis was already in Washington, he should testify before the House Committee holding hearings on the bills. Brandeis reluctantly agreed; he would have preferred concentrating on the intricate and complicated work of the ICC hearings and, as he told Alfred, "greatly begrudge the time which trust & kindred legislation are taking."

Brandeis himself, while approving the president's message, did not fully approve of the details in the Clayton bill. He had, it will be recalled, already drafted one antitrust measure that incorporated most of his ideas for Senator La Follette, and the Clayton bill seemed far weaker in comparison. McReynolds, urged by Wilson, contacted Brandeis and asked him for ideas as to how to strengthen the bill, and on 22 February, Brandeis sent him a long letter not only detailing general ideas, especially strengthening the ban on interlocking directorates, but also looking at specific clauses and such details as to how one would define a "bank," what sort of information corporations would have to file with the federal agency, the type of legal machinery to be used to enforce the law, how patents could be used, third-party redress, and the like.

Work on the Clayton bill constituted Brandeis's first extensive contact with James C. McReynolds, with whom he would serve on the Supreme Court throughout his twenty-three-year tenure. He had met McReynolds shortly after the new administration came to power, and had on several occasions responded to requests from him or through Assistant Attorney General Thomas W. Gregory for information about lawyers being considered for Justice Department positions. In mid-1913 an attack by a Justice Department lawyer over the way McReynolds had handled a high-profile case led Brandeis to note that the whole incident had been "entirely unnecessary," and he added, "How the fusillade would have poured in on me, had I been there."

Although Brandeis had approved of the way McReynolds had fought against the Taft administration in trying to move forward the Sherman Act suit against the tobacco trust, he realized something that Wilson had missed. A fervent advocate of antitrust laws, McReynolds otherwise was very conservative, even reactionary. "He is a standpatter," Louis told Alice, "without a particle of sympathy with insurgent methods." Brandeis recognized the attorney general's intelligence, and appreciated the way McReynolds understood and tried to utilize Brandeis's suggestions, and tried to explain some of McReynolds's curtness with others as due to overtiredness. This brought a guffaw of laughter from La Follette, who told Louis that his good opinion of McReynolds did little credit to his intelligence. McReynolds's true colors would emerge later, not only as a reactionary, but as a virulent anti-Semite, and possibly the most unpleasant fellow ever to sit on the high court.

On 1 March, Brandeis spent three hours with the attorney general and his advisers going over the Clayton bill and pointing out how it could be strengthened. Two weeks later Clayton agreed to add the stronger wording on interlocking directorates and requested that Brandeis provide the language, which he did. On 5 June a revised Clayton bill, the Rayburn measure on railroad securities, and the Covington bill for a weak trade commission passed the House of Representatives. They faced an uncertain future in the more conservative Senate, where pressure built to amend them based on the belief that the measures were unrealistic, ineffective, and totally unworkable.

The provisions on individual guilt, so dear to Wilson's heart, scared businessmen large and small. After the mad scramble of the Gilded Age, American businessmen had begun looking for methods that would avoid not only the destructive excesses of cutthroat competition but also government regulation. The details for the great trade association activities of the 1920s had just started to take shape, and the Clayton bill threatened to halt this "new cooperation." Conceivably, a zealot in the attorney general's office could interpret any act of cooperation as a restraint of trade, punishable by a fine and/or jail sentence. The long list of proscribed activities also made little sense, especially to reformers, who had no doubts that entrepreneurs could easily invent new ways to get around the prohibitions. Brandeis himself had admitted the near impossibility of trying to define in advance all the illicit means of competition. George Rublee, who was working with Brandeis in early 1914 on this legislation, recalled the fear that in trying to be too specific, the Clayton Act would open the doors to every sort of evasion that could be developed by American ingenuity.

One answer would have the Clayton Act proscribe anticompetitive practices in a broad manner, and then set up a strong trade commission to interpret and apply the broader principles to specific actions, with the power to enforce its decisions. Wilson, upset and confused by the criticism, recognized the validity of the arguments, but hesitated, his old fears against government regulation still strong. At this point Brandeis again acted decisively to change the president's thinking.

ON 10 JUNE, Brandeis went to see Wilson along with Senator Henry Hollis, Congressman Raymond B. Stevens, and George Rublee, a New York lawyer who had worked with Brandeis on Pinchot-Ballinger and had come down to Washington as an unofficial aide on antitrust legislation. At the White House meeting Rublee and Stevens pushed for creation of a strong federal commission with powers to police business behavior. Brandeis seconded the proposal, and Wilson agreed, helping to break the logjam on the antitrust bills in Congress. It is a dramatic story, especially since it would appear that both Wilson and Brandeis turned their backs on their original opposition to just such an agency that Theodore Roosevelt had offered in the 1912 campaign. While the decision did amount to a sort of volte-face by the president, Brandeis reached that position the way he always did, by looking at facts.

Brandeis had never been opposed to a trade commission, and in fact had recommended to Wilson at their first meeting that there be some agency to help administer the Sherman Act. He had in mind, however, the "sunshine" type of commission represented by the Massachusetts Board of Railroad Commissioners. Such a body would collect large amounts of information, especially financial reports, digest them, and then report to the public. Advocates of the sunshine commission believed that by shining light into a company's business practices, it would expose illicit and unethical practices, and the public outcry would force the company to stop its behavior or face legislative action. Other than collecting data, this type of agency had no enforcement powers. It would work in cooperation with the Justice Department so that if it discovered violations of the law, the government could then initiate prosecution, and it stood in marked contrast to the type of regulatory body that Theodore Roosevelt had proposed, and that Wilson and Brandeis had opposed in 1912.

Although the Sherman Act had been on the books since 1890, in its first fifteen years there had been only 24 suits, but this jumped to 180 over the next decade, the result of greater trust-busting by Roosevelt, Taft, and Wilson. Despite the presence of some high-profile cases such as steel, tobacco, and oil, however, most of these cases did not concern the types of monopolies Brandeis condemned. Half of all antitrust suits involved firms Thomas McCraw has termed "peripheral," loose combinations of firms that did not really control their markets. The Justice Department went against these associations of small companies and not the big integrated trusts because it was easier to identify their behavior as fitting the Sherman Act's definition of a combination, contract, or conspiracy in restraint of trade.

Then came the oil and tobacco decisions of 1911, in which the Supreme Court enunciated a "rule of reason" and in effect said that combinations and contracts in restraint of trade would be held illegal only if they "unreasonably" restrained trade. As Brandeis and others immediately recognized, the decisions left "in vast uncertainty the question as to what, in any case, will be deemed a reasonable restraint," and much of the advice he gave La Follette dealt with trying to create a tough law that defined reasonable and unreasonable behavior. Businesses across the spectrum, from small firms to industrial giants, greeted the court decisions with apprehension. In addition to the wording of the Sherman Act, ambiguous at best, the courts would now say what constituted reasonable or unreasonable behavior—and after the fact. If a company wanted to engage in a new pricing scheme, for example, how would it know if the courts would consider it reasonable? Brandeis worried not only that the small companies he represented would now be faced by unpredictability regarding their actions, but that the new rule of reason would make it that much more difficult to prosecute the great monopolies he opposed.

For many businesses, the obvious answer lay in a government agency they could go to ahead of the fact and present their plans. If the body approved them, they would then be immune from antitrust prosecution; if the bureau said no, then they knowingly proceeded at risk. While no one liked the idea of having a governmental body approve or disapprove business decisions, this seemed far preferable to the unpredictable findings of idiosyncratic judges. The National Civic Federation and the U.S. Chamber of Commerce took detailed opinion surveys in 1911 and again in 1914, and the findings showed overwhelming support among all types of businessmen for a new regulatory commission.

Brandeis, who knew his clients and their business practices well, and who had been associated with the National Civic Federation, certainly knew how businessmen felt; the last thing any business owner wants to deal with is uncertainty. But at least until the summer of 1914, when Brandeis spoke of a trade commission, he seemingly had in mind the sunshine model rather than one with real enforcement powers. In his letter to Franklin Lane in December 1913, Brandeis noted, "We have no comprehensive detailed information concerning the character and effect of these trade agreements between competitors; and in the absence of such data we cannot deal with them intelligently." The data had to be obtained and then used, but, at least in this letter, he does not expect anything more than the illumination of business practices. The Covington bill passed by the House followed the sunshine pattern of the Massachusetts model and did little more than expand the fact-finding authority of the older Bureau of Corporations.

Because Wilson preferred to spell out prohibitions in the statute, the draft of the Clayton bill that reached the Senate included many of the proscriptions that Brandeis had first proposed in the La Follette bill and then explained to McReynolds: price-cutting, tying clauses, and the like; and a guilty finding could lead to fine and/or imprisonment for directors as well as managers of the offending company. If the Justice Department decided to vigorously enforce this law, thousands of businessmen, big and small, faced the possibility of jail.

By June the president had recognized the qualms many business leaders had about the discrepancy between the two measures—a strong antitrust law with severe criminal penalties and a weak trade commission that could give business no guidance. Moreover, instead of striking at the great trusts, the two measures seemed more likely to put small businesses in harm's way, and Wilson and his cabinet members were inundated with letters protesting this possibility. Beyond that, in the summer of 1914 a mild recession set in, and Wilson felt increasing pressure not to do anything to upset the business community. Politically, he had already come too far to turn back; he needed an antitrust bill, but one that would win over the support of small and medium-size businesses.

Thomas McCraw, a business historian, charges that Brandeis abdicated his responsibility to the president during these months by failing to push Wilson and Congress toward the type of antitrust legislation he had been advocating for so long. Nobody, according to McCraw, had more influence with Wilson, and one would have expected him to be "working night and day with the congressional committees, shuttling back and forth between the White House and Capitol Hill, taking a major part in drafting and redrafting the bills until they were in exactly the right form." Instead, he was doing "lawyer's work," the ICC case. What might have been the crowning achievement of his career as a reformer, McCraw charges, would be played by a stand-in.

At least one contemporary shared this view of Brandeis as more involved with railroad matters than with antitrust, although without McCraw's condemnation. In April, Norman Hapgood wrote to Wilson:

> Mr. Brandeis has been so tied up with his railroad work that he has given only general thought to the trust question as it has developed in the bills now before Congress, and as it has been affected by recent decisions of the Supreme Court. The most important part of the really hard work done recently by the little group he represents has been carried on by Mr. George Rublee. . . . He is not only in intimate touch with Mr. Brandeis and Senator La Follette, but he has one of the best minds for this sort of thing I ever knew.

This scenario is hardly accurate. From the time Wilson delivered his antitrust message in January, Brandeis had been actively involved; he had met with the president, with cabinet secretaries, and with members of both houses of Congress. He had helped in drafting the Clayton bill and had twice testified before congressional committees. Much of the nitty-gritty work, the markup of drafts, the hashing out of what particular phrases meant—the work that McCraw charges Brandeis with shirking—got done by Brandeis's lieutenant George Rublee, who acted at all times with Brandeis's knowledge and approval.

Perhaps because Brandeis preferred the—to him—far more challenging work of the rate case, Rublee first came to see the need for, and the importance of advocating the idea of, a strong commission. He discussed the plan with Congressman Raymond Stevens of New Hampshire, an old ally of Brandeis's in the New Haven fight. The two of them spent several hours going over what powers such a commission should have and how to structure it. Rublee drafted it, and Stevens then tried to introduce it as a substitute for the Covington bill, only to be told that Wilson supported the Covington plan, the whole thing had been settled, and the committee voted it down.

Rublee and Stevens then decided that if the Senate would not even consider it because the president would accept only the Covington measure, then their only chance would be to talk Wilson into supporting a strong commission. They got Senator Henry Hollis of New Hampshire to make the appointment, and then Rublee went to tell Brandeis what he had done. The Boston attorney questioned him closely, making him defend the change. Rublee may have thought that Brandeis wanted to see if Rublee could convince him; it is just as likely that Brandeis wanted to make sure that Rublee could make a good case to Wilson. After all, the president would have known that Rublee acted as Brandeis's lieutenant and would assume that he was there on Brandeis's behalf. Then Brandeis surprised Rublee by agreeing to go to the White House with him.

The four men originally had a half-hour appointment with Wilson, but he kept them there far longer and, because of the beautiful spring weather, moved the meeting out of the Oval Office onto the White House lawn. Hollis said little. Stevens made the opening remarks, explaining why they had come and why they believed a strong agency necessary. Rublee then went over the proposal in detail, answering Wilson's questions. (Wilson, one can be sure, knew about the Stevens bill and had at least since April, when Hapgood had written to him that Rublee had been the bill's chief author.) Brandeis himself said little, but made it quite clear to Wilson that he supported Rublee's plan. By the end of the meeting Wilson had apparently signed on to the strong-commission proposal, although he still had a few questions. As they left, Brandeis, surprised and pleased by the president's decision, took Rublee's arm and said, "That's the most remarkable interview that I've ever been present at. I've never seen anything like this before."

As it turned out, just as Rublee left, James Covington showed up to see the president, who told him that he had changed his mind and had decided to support a strong regulatory commission. Covington immediately went over to Brandeis's hotel room, where he sat down with Rublee, Stevens, and Brandeis and went over the new measure. That evening Brandeis, Rublee, Hollis, and Stevens dined together at the Tea Cup Inn to prepare answers to the president's queries. Louis told Alice that he felt he had to take a strong hand, not only to help George, but also to ensure that some very bad legislation did not pass.

Within days the Stevens bill, now with Wilson's backing, had been substituted, and the whole tone of the debate shifted. Here again Brandeis did not work the committee rooms, write speeches, or reassure hesitant senators, but his lieutenant did, and everyone Rublee spoke with knew that he carried not only Brandeis's support but Wilson's blessing as well. When necessary, however, Brandeis would step in, as he did when Moses Clapp began fulminating that Wilson, whom he derided as "Morgan in the White House," had given away too much to the interests. Within a short time, Congress created the Federal Trade Commission and, because that agency would, under section 5, be able to issue cease-and-desist orders, deleted some of the more controversial criminal provisions of the Clayton bill. Brandeis later regretted that this had happened, and believed the Clayton Act would have been more effective had the Senate committee not removed some of the provisions he had managed to get into the House draft.

Did Brandeis suddenly abandon the sunshine plan? Did Rublee, on the strength of his argument, suddenly convert Brandeis on that sparkling June day? There is no letter or other document to verify one view as against another, but a reasonable surmise can be made. In a perfect world, Brandeis and Wilson would have both preferred a sunshine agency to one with strong powers, simply because both of them feared big government. Moreover, any mention of strong government invoked Roosevelt's idea of power to control big business. The Federal Trade Commission had far more powers than any sunshine bureau, but while it could issue cease-and-desist orders—a very powerful weapon—it could not regulate business in the way that TR had implied in 1912. The commission, thanks to Brandeis, also had the authority to issue advisory opinions in response to business requests. This fit perfectly with his ideas

on the regulation of competition. Brandeis did not abandon his principles in the revised Covington bill; rather, the bill would, he hoped, lay
the necessary groundwork for a revived and competitive economy.

Brandeis wanted, on the one hand, a proscriptive bill that would
clearly outlaw certain practices, such as interlocking directorates. But
once the worst sins had been identified, businesses would still need
guidance to ensure that they did not act either illegally or in a way that
transgressed the idea of fair competition. Lawyers could advise them on
the overtly illegal, but even the best lawyers could make only a judgment on whether a particular activity would be considered anticompetitive. Businessmen and their lawyers needed more precise information.

Ever since John Jay served as chief justice in the 1790s, federal courts
have refused to give advisory opinions, such as whether a particular
presidential action or a congressional bill would be constitutional or
not. Because the FTC was a federal agency that had quasi-judicial powers, and because the enabling legislation was silent on this point, some
people argued that the FTC should not issue advisory opinions. Brandeis, however, came from a state where the high court did issue advisory opinions in response to questions from the governor or the
assembly. Also, as a commercial lawyer, he thought it made far more
sense to have an agency that could give businessmen and their lawyers
solid information that they could then utilize in formulating business
strategies. When the commission organized in April 1915, it held a
series of hearings on how it could best use its powers and whether it had
certain authority. Brandeis appeared and spent the better part of the
morning convincing the commissioners that they did have the power to
issue advisory opinions.

The FTC, even though hampered by what Brandeis and others
believed to be bad appointments, did take a number of actions that carried out his ideas for regulated competition. In the 1920s the commission worked closely with accounting groups and trade associations to
develop standardized methods of cost accounting, a tool Brandeis
believed essential in providing alternatives to cutthroat competition
based on huge volume sales. The FTC also facilitated the growth of
trade associations and then helped them to draw up codes of fair conduct. In addition, the commission promoted scientific management in
the form of analytical studies that it made available to business.

Wilson and others may have thought that Brandeis's idea of regulated competition meant little more than drawing up a *Robert's Rules of
Order* for the market and then leaving businesses to act accordingly,
relying on an honor system for enforcement and negating the need for

almost any governmental involvement. Brandeis, because of his extensive experience as a commercial attorney, understood that businesses without effective guidance would be at a loss to understand the rules, and because conditions changed continuously, there would always be new questions to be answered. The Federal Trade Commission would be able to do this through advisory opinions. Just as important, the FTC could develop the tools needed to make regulated competition work. Brandeis did not abandon his principles in the revised Covington bill, nor did he find George Rublee's suggestions unfamiliar. He had assumed he would not be able to get anything more than a sunshine agency and jumped at the opportunity to get a commission that he hoped would have the ability to facilitate regulated competition.

BRANDEIS COMPLETELY FAILED in one area, however. He could not get either a price maintenance provision added to the Clayton Act or a separate bill enacted. Long a foe of cutthroat competition, Brandeis believed that manufacturers ought to be able to set the minimum price at which their goods could be sold at retail. He opposed volume discounts, whereby larger purchasers could buy a product at a per-unit cost less than a small retailer would pay. For him, a fixed price worked to the advantage of the small-business man, because he would not be at a disadvantage in competing against bigger stores. Fixing retail prices, he argued, would make it possible for a small retailer, knowing he would not be undersold on a particular item, to offer other items, and thus compete against other stores, even bigger stores, on the basis of service rather than price. "Every dealer, every small stationer, every small druggist, every small hardware man, can be made a purveyor of that article," he argued, "and you have stimulated, through the fixed price, the little man as against the department store, and as against the large unit which may otherwise monopolize that trade."

The only reason department stores could undersell smaller competitors is that they bought in bulk and thus enjoyed quantity discounts. This gave an unfair advantage to larger retailers, Brandeis claimed, and the practice should be prohibited. Alben Barkley, then a first-term congressman from Kentucky, could not believe he had heard Brandeis correctly; after all, quantity discounts had been an accepted business practice for centuries. But Brandeis insisted; he termed such discounts "fraught with a very great evil" and thought they should be outlawed.

Here McCraw's characterization of Brandeis as, if not anticonsumer, then at the least uninterested in the consumer, is surely accurate. Brandeis did not care if a person had to pay a bit more for a specific product, because what he termed fair-trade price maintenance worked to the benefit of small businesses, and they, not consumers who foolishly bought by price, needed protection. In a 1923 letter to the economist George Soule, Brandeis blamed high prices in part on the consumers themselves, who refused to use their heads or their buying power intelligently. "The consumer is servile, self-indulgent, indolent, ignorant. Let the buyer beware." Whether this view can be characterized as the difference between the nineteenth century's producing culture and the twentieth century's consumer culture is open to question, but it is clear that Brandeis had little of the "consumer" in him, and practically no interest in what we now call consumer preference, a bedrock principle of modern economics.

Whatever logic Brandeis marshaled, he never had a chance. To most legislators and businesspeople, quantity discounts made sense, while efforts to fix prices struck many as monopolistic, not much different from tying clauses. Larger retailers of course supported the discounts, and in their campaign labeled price maintenance as a device to get around the antitrust laws. Moreover, the Supreme Court in 1911 had held that patents did not give manufacturers the right to fix retail prices, and termed the practice anticompetitive. That decision would stand for almost a century until overturned in 2007, in a majority opinion by Justice Anthony Kennedy that sounded vaguely Brandeisian.

"ROOSEVELT BIT ME," William Allen White famously remarked, "and I went mad." The same would not be said by Brandeis about Wilson. Although he greatly admired him and advised him on various matters right up to the latter's death in 1924, Brandeis recognized the president's shortcomings. He applauded Wilson's actions to repeal the exemption granted to American coastal vessels traversing the Panama Canal, a clear violation of the 1901 Hay-Paunceforte Treaty, but thought the reasoning behind them pitiable. Wilson needed British backing in the face of potential trouble in Mexico. In essence, Brandeis told Alice, Wilson had gone to the Senate and said, "Gentlemen, if you don't let me bribe the nations of Europe, I don't know how in thunder I shall be able to handle our Mexican situation." The worst of it, Brandeis concluded, was yet to come; after Wilson had paid this bribe, he would still not have any good way to handle Victoriano Huerta and Mexico. Brandeis had been unhappy with Wilson's Latin American policies almost from the beginning.

He also deplored the poor quality of some of Wilson's appointees to the Federal Reserve Board and the Federal Trade Commission. "[Edward N.] Hurley was no good at all," Brandeis told Ray Stannard Baker. "Joe Davies was poor, and Senator [William] Harris small caliber, with no grasp of the real situation. It was a stupid administration." After the Senate would not confirm the appointment of one of the directors of the so-called zinc trust to the Federal Reserve Board, Wilson had to withdraw the appointment and sent an angry letter to the Senate. Alice thought the letter showed poor judgment on the president's part, and Louis agreed. "He isn't a good loser, and that defect will make him less courageous I fear, and perhaps not more careful," he responded. "The general effect will probably be to make him fear progressives more, treating all opposition as cantankerous." Brandeis also believed Wilson failed to comprehend the curse of bigness, focusing on the evils of monopoly rather than on the greater menace of immense size.

With the outbreak of the war in August 1914 and Wilson's sense of needing to placate the business community, Brandeis's influence with the president began to wane, although Wilson continued to hold the Boston attorney in "the highest personal esteem." Years later, Brandeis still spoke approvingly of Wilson during the first few years of his administration, although he made many mistakes, starting in August 1918. With his puritan values, Brandeis appreciated Wilson's stern Presbyterian standards, although he recognized in Wilson a rigidity that often frustrated political negotiations. In all his experience, though, Brandeis had never seen such a purifying influence in Washington as he had in 1913 and 1914. Wilson "changed the atmosphere," he recalled, "and it was the only time in recent American history when rich men had not had an undue influence with an administration."

CHAPTER SEVENTEEN

MEN! MONEY! DISCIPLINE!

In the fall of 1910, an officer of the Savings Bank Insurance League called on Jacob de Haas, the editor of Boston's *Jewish Advocate,* seeking some publicity for the program in the Jewish community. De Haas considered the topic "dry and remote," but thought that if some of the benefits of the program could be made more specific to low-income Jewish households, such as savings for dowry or college tuition, it might attract his readers. De Haas arranged to interview Louis Brandeis, and after spending an hour or so talking about insurance, he asked if the Boston attorney was related to Lewis Dembitz. Brandeis said yes, whereupon de Haas replied that "Dembitz was a noble Jew." Brandeis asked what de Haas meant, and the journalist explained that Dembitz had been one of the first Americans to support Theodor Herzl and his plans to rebuild a Jewish homeland in Palestine.

Four years later—years filled with work on the protocol, political campaigning for La Follette and Wilson, advising on the New Freedom, serving the Interstate Commerce Commission on the advance rate case, writing *Other People's Money,* and, from time to time, looking after his law practice—Brandeis took over the American Zionist movement and turned it from a moribund organization into a powerful political presence. The reasons why Louis Brandeis became a Zionist remain a matter for debate, but the events at the end of August 1914 did not occur without a foundation. Although he had not been active in Zionist or Jewish affairs in these years, neither had he been ignorant of them, and he had gotten to know a number of Jewish leaders and journalists. As had happened so often in his life, Brandeis did not go out seeking a new cause; it came to him.

ALTHOUGH BRANDEIS HAD A NUMBER of Jewish clients and did some legal and advisory work for the Boston Jewish community, he had

Theodor Herzl, founder of the Zionist movement

avoided taking on major responsibilities. His contributions to various Jewish charities had been nominal, well below what a person of his means could have given. As Jacob Schiff told House in 1912, Brandeis could not be considered a "representative" Jew. Nonetheless, when the American Jewish community celebrated the 250th anniversary of the landing of Jews in colonial New Amsterdam, Boston Jewish leaders asked Brandeis to give the keynote talk at the celebration.

The brief remarks he gave at the New Century Club on 28 November 1905 could have been made by any upper-class assimilated Jew. He spoke not at all about religion, but rather addressed the fears of many in his audience—how the great emigration of Jews from eastern Europe would affect the status of Jews already in the United States. The new immigrants had to be taught that loyalty to America required three things. First, they had to abandon all prior loyalties to country or caste or even religion. "There is no place for what President Roosevelt has called hyphenated Americans. There is room here for men of any race, of any creed, of any condition in life, but not for Protestant-Americans, or Catholic-Americans, or Jewish-Americans, not for German-Americans, Irish-Americans, or Russian-Americans."

Second, people had to live their lives according to the ideals embodied in the nation's institutions. "Free government cannot endure, the purposes for which it exists cannot be attained, except among a people honest, courageous, intelligent and just." While America may not discriminate between people of different races or creeds, it was possible to distinguish "between the honest and the dishonest, between the pure and the corrupt, between the just and the unjust, between the man of public spirit and him who is steeped in sordid selfishness."

Third, every citizen had to participate actively in governmental affairs, primarily through the intelligent use of the ballot box. "It is not sufficient that men vote," he declared, "it is essential that they vote right." This meant seeking information on important public issues and deciding between the good and the bad, the genuine and the sham. Here Brandeis enunciated what would later be a central theme of his public philosophy, that in a democracy there is no higher office than that of citizen, and that role requires the intelligent and conscientious effort of each person to live up to democratic ideals.

Financier Jacob Schiff

He had no doubt that Jews, both those who had arrived earlier and those then coming, would be able to live up to these demands. And in what would become the leitmotif of his Zionist philosophy, he declared that these high American values had first been proclaimed by Jews over two thousand years earlier. Jewish ideals and American ideals were in the highest sense the same, and both attempted to inject greater ethical standards into everyday life. This emphasis on the ethical, or prophetic, standards of Judaism fit easily into Brandeis's progressive views on the responsibilities of the citizenry. He totally ignored the ritualistic, or priestly, requirements. This division would be the basis both of his strength in creating an American Zionism and of his weakness in dealing with the European leaders of the movement.

In sending a copy of his talk to his father, Louis said, "I am inclined to think there is more to hope for in the Russian Jews than from the Bavarians & other Germans. The Russians have idealism & reverence." That sense would be reawakened in the summer of 1910 when he went to New York to help establish the Protocol of Peace in the garment industry, and from then on, while still not getting involved in Boston or national Jewish affairs, he started to give more attention to the Jewish community. After his initial meeting with de Haas, he began reading books about Zionism and then discussing them with the journalist. In early 1911 he answered a query from a New York journalist, Bernard

Richards, declaring, "My sympathy with the Zionist movement rests primarily upon the noble idealism which underlies it, and the conviction that a great people, stirred by enthusiasm for such an ideal, must bear an important part in the betterment of the world."

ALTHOUGH THE ANCIENT HEBREWS had been expelled from Palestine by the Romans, they had never given up the dream of someday returning to Zion. Every year at Passover, the holiday marking the exodus from Egypt and signifying the achievement of freedom after slavery, the seder, or ritual meal, ends with the phrase *"L'shanah haba'ah b'Yerushalayim!"*—"Next year in Jerusalem!" For religious Jews redemption would come only in the time of the Messiah and only by God's will. In the latter nineteenth century, however, two factors caused a number of European Jews to start a movement to re-create a Jewish homeland and to do it by the efforts of human rather than divine will. First, rising anti-Semitism, especially in Russia, forced hundreds of thousands of eastern European Jews to flee, many of them coming to America. Second, the forces of nationalism, which redrew the map of Europe and created modern countries such as Germany and Italy, affected Jewish thinkers as well. If Germans or Italians or Spaniards could have a land of their own, why not the Jews?

In 1896 the Austrian journalist Theodor Herzl wrote *Der Judenstaat—The Jewish State*—which became the founding document of the modern Zionist movement. Herzl, a fully assimilated Jew, did not even mention Palestine; he would have accepted any land in which Jews would be the majority and could therefore control their own destiny. Not until the First Zionist Congress in 1897 did Herzl realize that the vast majority of Jews would never accept any place but Palestine as the Jewish homeland. Zionist *chalutzim*—"pioneers"—created small colonies in Palestine, which, with the help of patrons like Baron de Rothschild, grew so that on the eve of World War I, 85,000 Jews lived in Palestine on fifty-nine settlements supported by the World Zionist Organization.

In the United States, Zionism ran headlong into the type of opposition embodied in Brandeis's speech, although at the time he probably did not recognize it, knowing little or nothing about Zionism. The established German-Jewish leadership, people like Jacob Schiff and Louis Marshall, opposed Zionism because they believed it involved "dual loyalties." They took Theodore Roosevelt's opposition to hyphenated Americans to mean that for Jewish immigrants to become fully accepted in America, they could have no other political allegiances. Supporting Zionism, which called for Jews to immigrate to a Jewish homeland, meant one could not be fully devoted to the United States since one had a loyalty to another political entity, the Jewish state, even if it had not yet come into existence.

Schiff and others worried that if the new immigrants from eastern Europe supported Zionism, they would be accused of treachery, and this would in turn jeopardize the status that the earlier, and by now assimilated, German-Jewish immigrants had achieved, as well as fuel the rising nativism they feared. They failed to realize that these immigrants had already chosen their new Jerusalem, and it involved not a return to Palestine but a long and hardship-filled trip to America, which they called *der goldenah medinah*—"the golden land." Those American Jews who joined the Federation of American Zionists (FAZ) did so not because they planned to make aliyah, to "go up" unto the Holy Land, but to help other Jews back in Russia who might not be able to get to the United States and needed a place to escape the pogroms.

The FAZ, despite the great influx of eastern European Jews, remained a marginal group within the Jewish community. At its annual convention in June 1914, the FAZ had a budget of $12,150, which exceeded anticipated revenue by $2,600; no one willing to serve as president (Professor Richard Gottheil of Columbia agreed to continue on as honorary head); and a membership of a little over twelve thousand, out of a Jewish population in the United States of three million. Only a few people at the meeting in Rochester knew that one of those members was the famous Boston attorney Louis Brandeis.

BY 1912, Brandeis's reputation had spread across the country, and Jewish groups wanted to claim him as one of their own. Going out to Chicago to campaign for Wilson that fall, Louis reported to Alfred that rabbis in St. Paul, Omaha, and elsewhere had wanted him to occupy their pulpits, "so you see I am making headway in Judaism." He had also met a number of Jewish editors, interested in him because of both his religion and the role he had played in the New York garment strike.

Brandeis had formally paid the shekel, or membership dues, and joined the FAZ in June 1912, but he resisted any efforts to involve him in Zionist affairs until March 1913, when he agreed to introduce Nahum Sokolow at a Boston rally. Sokolow, a member of the World Zionist Organization's executive committee, had come to the United

States to try to raise both awareness of Zionism among American Jews and money to support the Palestinian settlements. Brandeis told the crowd of twelve hundred in the Plymouth Theatre "that in the message of Judaism, carried by the dispersed race in its wanderings for 2000 years, . . . the world's best hope lies." Zionism provided the means by which the ideal could become real. "The noblest people in every civilized land are striving today for what has been the ideal of the Jew for centuries," he declared—social righteousness, the war against iniquity, relief for the burdens of the oppressed, and the lessening of the toll of the poor.

Sokolow thought he had finally found an American Jew who could lead the movement and raise money, and after the Boston rally he hoped Brandeis would take his rightful place in American Zionism. But in the spring of 1913, Woodrow Wilson had first call on Brandeis's time, and Sokolow wrote rather dejectedly to Brandeis that fall after the Boston attorney had not attended the World Zionist Congress. Sokolow had, after their conversation in Boston, expected him to do so, and "our friends cherished the hope that your presence . . . will be fruitful for the development of this work in America." At Sokolow's urging, the FAZ had elected Louis a member of the national executive committee, but there is no record that Brandeis ever attended any of its meetings.

During this period Brandeis met one other important Zionist, Aaron Aaronsohn. In January 1912 he attended a dinner in Washington in honor of Aaronsohn given by Julius Rosenwald, the Chicago philanthropist, who had funded some of the agricultural experimentation in Palestine. A Romanian-born Jew who had immigrated to Palestine with his family at age five, Aaronsohn had developed a strain of wheat well suited to the arid soil of Palestine. Louis wrote to Alfred, "The talk was the most thrillingly interesting I have ever heard, showing the possibilities of scientific agriculture and utilization of arid or supposedly exhausted land." He urged his brother to send for Aaronsohn's Department of Agriculture publication. Aaronsohn remained a favorite of Brandeis's until his death in a plane crash over the English Channel in 1919. To Brandeis the young Palestinian represented all that he idealized in Zionism—an effort to make an old land fertile again by applying the most modern scientific knowledge, adaptability, and bravery (Aaron and his sister served as spies for the British during the war). As he began to give some speeches on Zionism, Brandeis would constantly cite Aaronsohn as the type of young Jew who would make the Zionist experiment work, and when Aaronsohn came back to

America in 1913, Louis invited him to dinner at 6 Otis Place. For the most part, however, Brandeis resisted efforts to draw him into greater involvement.

THEN, IN EARLY AUGUST 1914, war broke out in Europe. A few weeks later Brandeis received a telegram that the World Zionist Organization, headquartered in Berlin, was in disarray, with its leaders scattered across Europe on both sides of the battle lines. An emergency meeting had been called for 30 August at the Hotel Marseilles in New York. At the urging of Jacob de Haas and Horace Kallen, Brandeis agreed to chair the meeting. Most of those assembled in that hot, crowded room expected little other than some oratory on the seriousness of the situation and the announcement of an emergency fund. For a while the scenario went as expected. After explaining the dangers facing Jews in Europe and Palestine, Brandeis announced the creation of the Provisional Executive Committee for General Zionist Affairs (PEC) to develop a relief program; he contributed $1,000 toward the fund, and then Nathan Straus, the head of Macy's, added another $5,000. Now, according to the script, Brandeis would contact his rich friends for more money while everyone else went home. They were in for a very big surprise.

Pleading his ignorance of the many organizations represented, Brandeis asked the assembly to stay on and meet with him that evening and the following day. He needed to know more about them, their leaders, their memberships, and their administrative arrangements. For the next day and a half, Brandeis sat patiently in a crowded hotel suite, absorbing fact after fact about Zionist and Jewish life in America, occasionally asking a question or repeating a strange-sounding Hebrew or Yiddish name. When he finally adjourned the meeting late on 31 August, his orderly mind might well have been reeling from the realization that nearly all the groups present suffered from poor organization, modest enrollments, minuscule financial resources, and very, very few people to do real work. But the shock to the men and women representing American Zionism was immeasurably greater. Rather than giving them a figurehead, the extraordinary conference had brought them a man who had the ability, determination, and reputation to be their leader, and who intended to be just that. The Hotel Marseilles conference marked a turning point in the fortunes of American Zionism, and also in the life of Louis Brandeis.

Why did Brandeis become a Zionist? There have been many expla-

Professor Horace Meyer Kallen of the University of Wisconsin

nations, but none of them seem quite as perceptive as his own.

The first proposed rationale came from an Israeli political scientist, Yonathan Shapiro, who tied Brandeis's conversion to Zionism to his rejection for a seat in Wilson's cabinet. Brandeis had failed in his "bid for power," Shapiro argues, because he lacked the backing of Jacob Schiff and other influential leaders. According to Shapiro, Brandeis then spent so much time on Zionism and gave great sums of money to Jewish organizations so that when he made his second bid, for the Supreme Court in 1916, the overwhelming support of the Jewish community led to his confirmation. The problem is that in an era of rising nativism, in which each session of Congress saw new attempts to cut back on emigration from eastern Europe, identification as a Jew would do little to bolster one's political prospects. Wilson did, in fact, want a Jew in his administration, but, as we have seen, he decided not to take Brandeis primarily because of opposition from the business community. Moreover, it is hard to describe Brandeis's actions in the winter of 1912–1913 as a "bid for power," and in the confirmation fight the alleged influence of the Jewish community played practically no role.

Ben Halpern believed that despite the claim that Adolph and Frederika raised their children without religion, a certain "elitist, liberal self-consciousness" dating back to Frankist times survived into Louis's generation, and whether he recognized it or not, his devotion to certain principles could be traced back to that heritage. Here the key figure is Lewis Naphtali Dembitz, his beloved uncle. While his parents lived, especially his mother, Louis had to ignore Judaism because of her strong antipathy to religion in general and traditional Judaism in particular. When Lewis Dembitz died in 1907, Louis Brandeis became free from the constraints imposed on him by an earlier generation and adopted the ethnic community exemplified by his uncle. His emergence as a Zionist leader, Halpern claims, "signified no conversion to new beliefs." Rather, it signified a "shift in social attachments and emotional ties to a sharper sense of the American-Jewish terrain and his own place in it and a fatefully deepened personal commitment." In becoming a Zionist leader, Halpern claims, "Brandeis had come home." This psychoanalytic view of the resolution of identity conflict is questionable, but Halpern is close to the mark in noting that the idealism of Zionism appealed to Brandeis, who often said, "Idealism is the most important thing."

Allon Gal, a student of Halpern's, made more than most scholars of the mild anti-Semitism he believed Brandeis faced in Boston, and claimed that Brandeis had begun to feel "the burden of his Jewishness" around 1910. This made him more receptive to a movement that promised to solve the "Jewish problem" and gave him a better understanding of what a homeland for persecuted people could mean. In addition, he looked at Palestine rather naively; both reports of Aaronsohn's wild wheat experiments and claims about the lack of crime in the Jewish colonies led him to see the *yishuv,* the Jewish settlement in Palestine, as a sort of Jeffersonian paradise. The only problem is that no proof exists that Brandeis suffered from anti-Semitism in the years before he became a Zionist, or that he saw it as a reason to join the movement.

It will be more logical if, when we talk about Louis Brandeis as an American Zionist leader, we start with the word "American." It makes no sense to try to define his conversion to Zionism in Jewish terms, either as a political opportunist trying to capitalize on his Jewishness, or as a victim trying to overcompensate, or as a disillusioned visionary seeking to regain his idealism in the new Zion, or as a prodigal returning to his roots. It is true that his uncle Dembitz had inspired him, but not because of his Jewish interests; it had been the abolitionist and the lawyer in his uncle that led Louis David to change his name. He had never been ashamed of being born Jewish, nor had he tried to hide it or that he had little Jewish background. His daughter described Brandeis as "completely non-religious, a non-observant Jew." When a Jewish periodical interviewed him in 1910, the reporter felt he had to confirm that Brandeis was, in fact, Jewish. "There should be no doubt where I stand," Louis said. "Of course, I am a Jew, [but] my early training was not Jewish in a religious sense, nor was it Christian."

Brandeis, however, never allowed himself to be defined by his religion or birth. He understood the notion of communal responsibility and contributed to Jewish charities, but always on a nominal basis; he gave as much or more money to other causes. His success as a lawyer had led Boston Jews to try to enroll him as a leader, an effort he had strongly and successfully resisted. In the fifty-four years before he met Jacob de Haas, things Jewish mattered little to him; on the other hand, things American mattered a great deal. Those ideas of democracy, of opportunity, of challenge that defined American freedom for him had been endangered by industrialization, and while he believed, perhaps wrongly, that controlling competition would ameliorate the worst problems, he also understood that it would be impossible to re-create the America that had existed in the age of Jefferson and Jackson.

Palestine, on the other hand, a country just starting out, could be fashioned into a democratic society, one where there would be no curse of bigness, where the idealism that he believed Jews and Americans shared could be allowed to flower. Unlike those Zionists who wanted to create a nation governed by Jewish religious law, Brandeis envisioned a secular society populated by Jews who lived according to American values that Brandeis conflated with those of the prophets.

Brandeis said on many occasions that he came to Zionism through Americanism, and there is no question that his experiences as an American lawyer and progressive reformer shaped his leadership of the Zionist movement. His approach to the problems of the moribund Federation of American Zionists is identical to his approach in resolving secular problems. Research the matter, devise a workable solution, recruit adherents to the cause, and then educate others to accept the solution. Brandeis and the men and women he attracted to the movement had a firm commitment to American ideals and democratic principles. They objected to anti-Semitism not from personal suffering but because it offended their sense of decency. Zionism reflected progressive ideals, and to some extent became a type of reform, akin to women's suffrage or factory legislation. This outlook on Zionism, as a reform to solve the Jewish problem, provided the strength—and the weakness— of the Brandeis leadership.

The enthusiasm for Aaron Aaronsohn tied in closely to Brandeis's support for scientific management, a trait shared by many progressives. A problem existed—in this case, the need to find a grain that would grow in Palestine's arid soil—and by the application of intelligence and science a solution had been devised, the adaptation of a form of wild wheat that could be cultivated. Brandeis also became involved in a plan proposed by Rabbi Stephen S. Wise of New York, a man who would become one of his closest lieutenants for the next three decades. Wise believed that many possibilities existed in Palestine for development, but no one knew enough about the situation to be able to set priorities or determine areas that needed to be expanded. So in typical progressive fashion, Wise proposed an investigatory commission made up of a team of experts whose report would explain the possibilities of Palestinian development, lay out the problems and proposed solutions, and set a budget for tackling these problems.

The commission members had their bags packed and were ready to depart when one of the sponsors, Jacob Schiff, pulled out because of a controversy over use of the German language at the Haifa Technion. Wise immediately set about finding other sponsors, and in early June, Louis Brandeis agreed to step in with the needed funds, more than $2,000. Here again one has to note the very American progressive nature of the enterprise—the identification of a problem and its examination by experts leading to rational proposals for solutions. Unfortunately, the war broke out in Europe just as the commission was about to sail, thus aborting the project.

There is one difference regarding Zionism that must be noted. While Brandeis cared a great deal about his other reforms, with the exception of savings bank insurance he did not form a lasting and intense relationship to them. He remained, of course, an inveterate foe of bigness, both in business and in government, all his life, but in regard to women's hours legislation, for example, he fought hard, but his great contribution came from his creativity as a lawyer. Not even his sister-in-law claimed that he had been fervent about the *Muller* case. He certainly had been passionate in his fight against the New Haven and in ferreting out the truth in Pinchot-Ballinger, but at the end he walked away, a job done. Within a short time it became clear that he cared a great deal about Zionism, and people who knew him as a Zionist, even his opponents, never doubted his commitment to the cause.

BRANDEIS FACED three great tasks on assuming the Zionist leadership, and his success or failure in handling them would determine whether Zionism would emerge as a potent force in American Jewish life or would continue as a sideshow of little consequence. He had to reorganize Zionist forces into an effective form; he had to identify specific projects that would attract those who shared only a marginal interest in Zionism; and, most important, he had to redefine Zionist assumptions to fit the needs of American as well as Jewish society.

As late as 1910, Louis still held the views he had expressed in his 1905 talk "What Loyalty Demands," and he told a reporter that "habits of living or of thought which tend to keep alive differences of origin or classify men according to the religious beliefs are inconsistent with the American ideal of brotherhood, and are disloyal." In order for Brandeis to overcome the charge of "dual loyalty," he had to come up with some means to make Zionism compatible with the demands of loyalty to America, and here the young philosopher Horace Meyer Kallen played a key role.

Kallen had first met Brandeis while an undergraduate at Harvard. In December 1913, he sent Brandeis a copy of a paper he had written on Zionism and Palestine. Brandeis asked him to work the ideas up more fully, but Kallen, who by then had taken his first teaching position at the University of Wisconsin, did not get a chance to meet with Brandeis and discuss the issue with him until August 1914. They finally held the long-postponed discussion on the overnight boat from Boston to New York on their way to attend the Hotel Marseilles conference.

Kallen would be the chief theorist of a new idea of American society and the role that immigrants played in it, one that he labeled "cultural pluralism." The older notions of assimilation, often labeled loosely as the melting-pot theory, held that when immigrants came to the United States, the shock of adjustment stripped away their Old World characteristics and they emerged as Americans, speaking English (albeit with an occasional accent) and sharing the same attitudes and values as native-born citizens. Kallen believed that in fact immigrants, no matter how hard they might try, never lost the cultural traits of their home countries, and this is what had made America great. Rather than discard their uniqueness, immigrants contributed to a unique American tapestry in which each ethnic group retained some of its own individual flavor while making the whole that much richer. The retention of Old World cultures, Kallen argued, did not lessen one's loyalty to America, but reinforced it.

Kallen would prove to be an important influence in Louis's life, if nothing else, giving him the idea of cultural pluralism. But Kallen also served as a link between Brandeis and Alfred Zimmern. Kallen had met Zimmern in 1912 when the Englishman gave a lecture at the University of Wisconsin, and the two enjoyed a long and intimate correspondence. Kallen kept Zimmern informed of American Zionist developments, and Zimmern, who knew Chaim Weizmann, the head of the English Zionist Federation, passed on information from the Russian-born chemist that could not go through regular mail.

Brandeis quickly grasped how Kallen's ideas could resolve the issue of dual loyalty. Brandeis and other progressives came to understand that diversity need not be detrimental in a democratic society, providing that all groups subscribed to a common set of ethical and social principles. By interpreting Jewish-Zionist idealism as complementary to and supportive of American democracy, Brandeis undercut the claim that Zionism was either inconsistent with or antithetical to American ideals. "America's fundamental law seeks to make real the brotherhood of man. That brotherhood became the Jews' fundamental law more than twenty-five hundred years ago. America's twentieth-century demand is for social justice. That has been the Jews' striving ages-long." Addressing the 1915 Zionist convention in Boston, he proclaimed, "The highest Jewish ideals are essentially American in a very important particular. It is Democracy that Zionism represents. It is Social Justice which Zionism represents, and every bit of that is the American ideals of the twentieth century." Time and again he declared that "Zionism is the Pilgrim inspiration and impulse again." The desire for liberty that had characterized the earliest Americans and had shaped the nation's destiny had been reborn in a movement to allow Jews to live in freedom in a land of their own. How much more American could Zionism be?

(Brandeis, it should be noted, either consciously or unconsciously used "Jewish" and "Zionist" interchangeably. While nearly all Zionists were Jewish, the obverse was far from true. This juxtaposition endowed Zionism with all the traits Louis found so admirable in Jewish culture and ethics and forced anti-Zionist Jews into the awkward position of trying to explain how a Jewish movement was not really Jewish.)

Throughout the rest of 1914 and 1915, Brandeis told numerous audiences that his approach to Zionism had been through Americanism, that the two shared common principles of democracy and social justice. He fully admitted his lack of a Jewish background, but said that since his conversion to Zionism, he had been learning about the Jewish heritage, and proudly declared that "Jews were by reasons of their traditions and their character peculiarly fitted for the attainment of American ideals." This led him to make the ultimate link, not only bridging Zionism and Americanism, but welding the two together: *"To be good Americans, we must be better Jews, and to be better Jews, we must become Zionists!"*

As for the problem of dual loyalties, Brandeis himself had often argued that one could not serve two masters at once. But that assumed that the goals somehow opposed each other, that support of Zionism contradicted support of American values. Such a conflict did not exist, Brandeis explained. "Multiple loyalties are objectionable only if they are inconsistent," he argued, but the American political system clearly proved this need not be the case. "A man is a better citizen of the United States for being also a loyal citizen of his state, and of his city; for being loyal to his family, and to his profession or trade; for being loyal to his college or lodge." An American's true loyalty consisted not of a superficial allegiance to the country's symbols but of a deeper commitment to the principles that the nation represented. One believed in freedom, justice, and democracy not just in one place for one group but everywhere for all people, and in working for these goals, one demonstrated the greatest love of America. "Every Irish-American who contributed toward advancing home rule was a better man and a better American for the sacrifices he made," Brandeis asserted, and the same would be said of Jews. In joining together to build a free and democratic homeland for their brethren in Palestine, they would be giving the best possible proof of their loyalty to the United States.

There remained the problem of aliyah, the bringing into the Jewish homeland of all those who lived in exile. European Zionism had made aliyah a personal requirement, the need to shake off the dust of centuries in exile and return home. Clearly, American Jews had no intention of leaving, neither those whose families had been here for several generations nor those who had gotten off the boat just a few years earlier. Immigrants fleeing from persecution in Europe had already chosen America as their homeland, as their new Zion. This idea had been around since 1841, when Rabbi Gustav Poznanski had dedicated the first Reform Jewish temple in the United States in Charleston, South Carolina: "This country is our Palestine, this city our Jerusalem, this house of God our Temple."

Here again Brandeis proposed a simple and effective solution. Zionism did not require that Jews who lived in countries of freedom, such as the United States and Great Britain, make aliyah. Rather, their obligation lay in political activism and fund-raising to create a Jewish homeland in Palestine to which Jews who lived in lands of oppression, such as Russia, could find haven. While some younger Americans might want to go and be pioneers, no obligation existed for them to do so. American Jewry, however, had the responsibility for making it possible for Jews in distress to make aliyah.

That an established member of the Boston bar, a progressive reformer of national reputation, and a confidant of the U.S. president's said these things gave them a sanction hitherto lacking among Zionist spokesmen. His own personal career, now that he had assumed the mantle of Zionist leadership, confirmed his faith that Zionism and Americanism did not preclude each other. In 1915 he became the first Jew chosen to give the Fourth of July address in Boston's historic Faneuil Hall, an honor by which Boston put its seal of approval on the impeccable character of Brandeis's patriotism. (The choice had been made by the city's Democratic leaders and not by the Brahmins.) And on 28 January 1916, Woodrow Wilson nominated him to the Supreme Court.

*U.S. Circuit Court Judge
Julian W. Mack*

With some satisfaction, Brandeis wrote that "in the opinion of the President there is no conflict between Zionism and loyalty to America."

BRANDEIS'S PERSONAL REPUTATION, as well as the manner in which he articulated an Americanized Zionism, struck a chord among many Jewish progressives who for the most part had had little or no previous contact with either Zionism or Jewish communal life. When the European leader Shmaryahu Levin joyously reported to the Actions Committee in 1915 that a "new Zionism" had developed in the United States, he called the leadership "men of earnestness and of character, who demand logical completeness in the movements with which they affiliate, who devote themselves full-heartedly to the movement of which they are a part." These leaders, many of whom Brandeis personally recruited, shared his view of American ideals and supported Zionism because it reflected that vision.

The most important figure, next to Brandeis himself, was the U.S. circuit court judge Julian W. Mack. Louis had met him in 1911 and had been favorably impressed, describing him to Alice as "quite an up to date Federal judge." Mack, unlike Brandeis, had been heavily involved with Jewish communal life in Chicago, but had made his rep-

Rabbi Stephen S. Wise of the Free Synagogue in New York

utation for pioneering the concept of a juvenile court system. Mack came to Zionism because of his growing convictions on cultural pluralism, and he embraced the cause not for religious reasons but because of what he saw as its inherent justness. At the Paris Peace Conference in 1919 he declared that the Zionists "ask no more for the Jews than we do for anyone else." After Brandeis went on the Court in 1916, Mack became head of the Zionist organization, and although it seemed to some that he still served as no more than Brandeis's lieutenant, in fact he stood on his own feet.

Alongside Brandeis and Mack, the most important voice in the leadership belonged to Stephen S. Wise, the maverick rabbi of the Free Synagogue in New York. Wise had made his reputation as a reformer, first standing up against political corruption in Portland, Oregon, and then founding his own synagogue in New York against the then normal mode of congregational officials' dictating what the rabbi could say in his sermons. Although trained in Hebrew and Talmud, Wise seemed just as at home in the writings of the Transcendentalists and felt a particular kinship with the Protestant reformers of the Social Gospel. He was an unabashed patriot who repeatedly and publicly thanked God for his parents' decision to emigrate from Hungary to America.

Although he eschewed a leadership position, Felix Frankfurter was also a part of the Brandeis coterie. His parents had observed traditional rites, but Frankfurter had little use for Jewish ritual or dogma. "I remember leaving the synagogue in the middle of a service," he recalled, "saying to myself, 'It's a wrong thing for me to be present in a room in a holy service.' . . . I left the service in the middle of it, never to return to this day. By leaving the synagogue I did not, of course, cease to be a Jew." Frankfurter entered the Zionist movement at Brandeis's request, and in 1919 served as legal counsel to the Jewish delegation to the Paris Peace Conference. After the Brandeis group stepped down in 1921, he had little direct connection to Zionism, but continued to serve as an informal adviser to Mack and Wise.

Although Judaism does not canonize, if it did, nearly everyone would demand that Henrietta Szold be made a saint. A gentle woman, she devoted her life to caring for her people, providing medical care in Palestine through the organization she founded, Hadassah, and in the 1930s and 1940s trying to rescue children from the Nazis. She came to Zionism before Brandeis, because, she claimed, it provided an ideal for her. Palestine would be a refuge not just for persecuted Jews but for Judaism itself, a place where the Jewish people could be rehabilitated and regain self-confidence.

Henrietta Szold,
founder of Hadassah

Brandeis admired Miss Szold for her single-mindedness. She had a vision in Hadassah, and she refused to play political games with other Zionist groups. With Brandeis's encouragement, and often with his monetary support, the women's group built hospitals and clinics that ministered to Jew and Arab alike. Hadassah tried to introduce modern sanitary methods and sell clean pasteurized milk to families, again to both Jew and Arab. Brandeis took scrupulous care not to interfere in Hadassah's work, because Szold and her lieutenants had already embraced his philosophy—identify a problem, study it, come up with a solution, and then get the people who can work to make it happen. In nearly every Jewish community in the United States, a Hadassah chapter sprang up, and tens—ultimately hundreds—of thousands of women joined, not out of any religious conviction, but because they had found an area in which they could work for well-defined goals.

Jacob de Haas played a critical, although often shadowy, role in the new leadership. He took the credit for bringing Brandeis into the movement, hailing him as a "second Herzl," and he exploited this relationship to enlarge his own influence. To his credit, de Haas had a clear grasp of Zionist policies and politics and proved an invaluable guide to Brandeis in these years. But his devotion to Brandeis also had a downside. He would brook no criticism of his leader, and when the Brandeisian style of Americanized Zionism began to cause friction with some of the eastern European immigrants, de Haas sheltered him from it, thus leaving Brandeis totally unprepared when the unhappi-

Provisional Executive Committee
Secretary Jacob de Haas

ness broke out into open revolt. Although de Haas irritated many people, Brandeis remained loyal to him until de Haas's death in 1937, always grateful to him as his teacher in Zionism, finding positions for him, and eventually partially supporting him.

This new leadership took an especial interest in recruiting Jewish college students and graduates, a group that the FAZ had ignored. "It is from those still young to whom we must look in Jewish affairs, as in others, for progressive work," Brandeis wrote. The provisional committee agreed to subsidize the work of Henry Hurwitz and the Menorah Society, a Jewish intercollegiate group, and Brandeis and his colleagues personally undertook the sponsorship of the University Zionist Association, a federation of Zionist clubs at different schools. Brandeis himself spoke a number of times to the Harvard group and underwrote the club's expenses in bringing in other speakers. The prestige of Brandeis, Mack, and Frankfurter and their standing as reformers appealed to idealistic college students, and even some papers unfriendly to Zionism conceded that the Brandeis leadership had done a great deal to reclaim Jewish youth alienated from their people.

Brandeis's strategy involved not just attracting college-educated men and women who could provide leadership and funds but also counterbalancing the overwhelmingly eastern European nature of existing Zionist membership. The movement could not afford to be seen as being by and for immigrants who did not understand America and therefore had no loyalty to it. Beyond that, Brandeis realized, perhaps from his experience with the garment workers, that these new immigrants, much as they remained grounded in the religious attitudes of eastern European Jewry, with its commitment to a love of Zion, also saw themselves as greenhorns in America. They wanted to outgrow this status; they wanted to become Americans. In this, of course, they were

Members and staff of the Provisional Executive Committee. Seated from left: Henrietta Szold, Stephen S. Wise, Jacob de Haas, Robert D. Kesselman, Louis Lipsky, Charles Cowen, Shmaryahu Levin, and Meyer Berlin; standing from left: Blanche Jacobson, Adolph Hubbard, and A. H. Fromenson, 1915.

no different from other immigrant groups who submerged their feelings for ethnic nationalism in the desire to Americanize. Given this situation, only a thoroughly assimilated leadership like the Brandeis group could exploit the latent Zionism of eastern European Jewish immigrants while at the same time reassuring them of their acceptance into American culture and society. They all had relatives back in eastern Europe affected by the war, and even those with small means wanted to do something. When Brandeis called upon them to help the Zionists help their European brethren, and then declared Zionism and Americanism compatible, he tapped into deep-seated emotions.

Anti-Semitism also played a role. The new immigrants learned English, shaved off their beards, threw away their skullcaps, and turned their backs on the old ways, just as the German-Americans urged them to do. But one does not become an American overnight, and the newcomers soon ran into prejudice which, while not as pervasive or anywhere near as brutal as in Europe, still reminded them that they were Jews. They found their opportunities restricted and their liberty sometimes not as full as they had hoped it to be. When Brandeis urged them to become Zionists, to be proud of their Jewishness, and said that in so doing, they could stand tall as Americans, they responded wholeheartedly.

Brandeis served as a bridge between two cultures, that of the assimilated American society and that of New York's Yiddish-speaking Lower East Side, even though he had practically no roots among the latter. The man who had, prior to 1914, never set foot inside a synagogue had not forsaken his people, and they saw his return through Zionism, like that of the prodigal son, as a sign. Abe Goldberg, the editor of *Dos Yiddishe Folk,* wrote him a moving note that summed up the thoughts of many recent immigrants. "I am myself mystically and religiously inclined," Goldberg said, "although I usually appear very rationalistic. And believe me, that . . . never yet a day passed that I did not think of you, and I never went to bed without praying for your health."

IN 1914 THE FAZ had a little more than 12,000 members; by 1919 its successor, the Zionist Organization of America, had over 176,000 dues-paying members, with thousands of others associated with Mizrachi (religious Zionists) or various Zionist labor groups affiliated with the ZOA. The huge jump in membership made possible an increased budget to provide war relief to the colonies in Palestine. In all his efforts, Brandeis stood by the motto "Men! Money! Discipline!" He understood that without numbers the Zionists could do nothing, and that while he could attract a few well-known individuals, real growth had to take place at the local level.

Brandeis hammered home the demand for members wherever he went, and until the announcement of his appointment to the Court he traveled all over preaching the message. "Organize! Organize! Organize! Until every Jew in America must stand up and be counted— counted with us—or prove himself, wittingly or unwittingly, of the few who are against their own people." Members provided muscle with which to lobby governments and to spread Zionist propaganda. Members raised money for the Palestinian colonies or, in the case of Hadassah, to provide medical care. Without members, one could do nothing; with members, everything seemed possible.

Brandeis brought to Zionism all the lessons he had learned as a reformer, including how to organize. There had never been any formal method of securing members for the FAZ, so he introduced a multi-tiered system with membership committees at different levels and processes by which follow-ups could be made. Once the local committee got a person's name, it would contact that person again and again until it had secured a new member. Nothing was left to chance, with quotas assigned to different groups for so many new members each month, so much propaganda distributed, so much money raised. Where societies were weak or no Zionist group existed at all, Brandeis co-opted existing Zionists to start new groups. In a typical letter establishing such a committee, Brandeis or the office committee enclosed a set of model bylaws, suggested annual dues, fixed quotas for growth, and explained the form that weekly reports on membership and income should take. Every person who paid the shekel, or who had attended a Zionist meeting, or whose name had been suggested as a potential member or donor, had his or her name entered on a card file kept by Jacob de Haas, which ultimately ran to half a million entries. This list would serve as the basis for a continuous recruiting and fund-raising campaign.

And Brandeis watched over everything. He received daily reports and read them carefully, deluging poor Benjamin Perlstein, the head of the office committee in New York, with long letters of numbered paragraphs and constant demands for detailed information. Why did certain information seem to be missing, why had certain committees not reached their quotas, how could one explain a discrepancy in the accounts? Exceedingly orderly in his own business habits, Brandeis imposed a like regimen on the PEC, formerly the FAZ, staff. He had a time clock installed, a potent symbol that the old days of "slippered ease," as de Haas called them, had ended. Some of the older workers, who had seen their jobs as sinecures requiring little work, suddenly found themselves inundated not only with donations and applications for memberships but with a constant demand for information and more information, all of it accurate, and they left.

Brandeis soon installed Jacob de Haas at PEC headquarters to oversee the general administrative direction for recruiting, although Perlstein remained nominally in charge of the growing office. Perlstein and the staff, however, proved woefully unable to satisfy Brandeis's demand for daily and weekly fiscal reports. As one might expect, nothing irritated Brandeis more than financial mismanagement. Felix Frankfurter recalled that Brandeis wanted the Zionists to handle their money as conservatively as a bank, accounting for every penny collected and expended. Brandeis eventually hired Robert Kesselman, a certified public accountant, and put him in charge of the provisional committee's finances. Kesselman had a tough time getting the old-line workers to accept the need for proper money handling and record keeping. They had always been rather casual about it, collecting when they could, keeping donations in their coat pockets or paper bags, turning the money in whenever they happened to be near the office. Many of them, in fact, never reconciled to the new regime, but by mid-1916 Kesselman could finally send reports that met the chief's demand for accuracy and detail.

In addition to his daily, sometimes hourly, letters to the office, Brandeis wrote directly to local leaders. "Much disappointed by smallness of collection made in Milwaukee," he wired the local chairman. "Feel confident that if you will call on all the members of the Committee that entertained us at dinner, and their friends with whom we spoke after the meeting, you will be able to secure the expected contribution of five thousand dollars from Milwaukee." No detail seemed too small for him to ignore. After a meeting in Connecticut, a tailor came up to Brandeis and gave him $3, saying he wanted to help Jews in Russia. Brandeis wrote out a personal check for the $3 and sent it to the treasurer of the American Jewish Relief Committee with specific details on not only where the money should be directed but how it should be accounted for as well.

We have a portrait of Brandeis as Zionist manager, by Louis Lipsky, one of the leading FAZ officials:

> He would come to the Zionist offices in New York early in the morning and remain for hours, receiving visitors, questioning them and assigning tasks. He presided at the frequent meetings of the committee and won general admiration for the cogency and subtlety of his questions and the sagacity of his conclusions. He was innocent of vanity or conceit and unconventional in his behavior. He had a cordiality that won confidence. He was seldom direct in attack, but with rare subtlety insinuated the trend of his thinking into the discussion. But he could be merciless in judgment too, and his indignation could be devastating. You did not feel that he was forcing his views; he drove them home by logic and dominated the situation with tact and reason. He would take his coat off, loosen his tie, ruffle his hair, use his hands actively and twist his body in the chair as he carried on a hearty discussion with infinite patience.

There is no question that Brandeis micromanaged Zionist affairs in late 1914 and 1915, but he faced a situation different in both quantity and quality from his prior experience. In Boston he had for the most part dealt with educated businessmen and professionals in reforms involving street franchises, gas supply, and the New Haven, men accustomed to running their own affairs the same way he did, with proper accounting, accurate records, and timely reports. One does not find letters to Joseph Eastman of the Public Franchise League that in any way resemble those sent to Perlstein and the PEC staff. These men and women, many of them immigrants, had never been required to manage FAZ affairs with the attention to detail that Brandeis and his peers took for granted. The FAZ had no experience in mounting national drives for membership and money, or setting up the types of records necessary to keep track of people or income, or generating the propaganda needed to educate the wider Jewish community on the immediate and long-term goals of Zionism. There is initially a tone of frustration in Brandeis's letters as he looked for information he expected and could not find. For Zionism to succeed, not only did he need the money and the men to do disciplined work, but he also needed organizational discipline. It frustrated him immensely when people signed up in Boston and their names wound up on lists of other cities. He planned, as he always did, for the long term. Jews not only had to be brought into the Zionist movement but also had to renew their memberships and provide names of others who could be approached; after they gave their initial donation, they had to be asked for more money. This could be done only if the PEC ran its organization on a businesslike basis, something that it had never done before. Moreover, although he did not know it yet, the World Zionist Organization was no better, and its slipshod methods would be one of the causes of the great rupture in 1921.

THE HOTEL MARSEILLES meeting had been about money, primarily to raise funds to help the suffering Jews in the war zones of eastern Europe. Although no one realized it at the time, the war marked a turning point for Zionist finances as well; after 1914, American Jewry provided the bulk of the money for the movement, which meant support of the Palestinian settlements. Considering that the FAZ had never raised more than $12,000 a year before the war, Brandeis's announcement of a $100,000 (between $1.5 million and $2 million today) relief fund struck many of the old-timers as little more than wishful thinking. After all, as Louis Lipsky and others had told the Berlin office just a few weeks before the war, the leading Jewish philanthropists all opposed Zionism and would not give a penny to the *yishuv.* In some ways the doubters were right; not until World War II would the very wealthiest American Jews contribute to Zionism. But in 1914 and 1915, hundreds of thousands could and did donate small amounts, and while it surely would have been easier to get one person to give $10,000, the same amount could be raised by a thousand donations of $10. This is the route the new leadership took.

(Ironically, the American Jewish Committee, whose members included some of the wealthiest Jews in America, found itself paralyzed at the beginning of the war regarding aid to European Jewry. Louis Marshall reported that not only did the AJC not have funds on hand to begin work, but he doubted that it would be able to get the approval of the State Department to transfer funds into the war zone. Only after the Zionists had shown that they could raise money and that the American government would cooperate did the committee establish the American Jewish Joint Distribution Committee.)

It has been said that guilt is the great motive force of charity, and Brandeis laid it out very simply. The Jews in America had been blessed with peace and prosperity, and they now had the duty to help those in Europe who were being devastated by the war. "The Jews in America," he declared, "most fortunately placed, can and must work out the gigantic problem that now confronts our people. And in American Israel—we, the Zionists, must bear the brunt of effort and sacrifice. We are that 'saving remnant' which our traditions tell us have always escaped the holocaust and saved our people." Not since the exile of the Jews from Spain in 1492 had there been such suffering in the Jewish community, and the more fortunate Jews in the United States had to give "quickly and liberally, not from their income merely but from their capital also." Never one to urge others to do what he would not do himself, he pledged $1,000 a month to the general campaign and committed himself for lesser amounts to local Boston funds. He then urged his colleagues to set an example for the rank and file, and form letters poured out of Zionist offices asking every member to give at least $10 a month during the war, with special letters going to those who could afford larger amounts, and allowances for those who could give only $1 or $2 a month. (The Zionists could count on only one very wealthy Jew for support. Nathan Straus of Macy's department store gave the PEC over $50,000 for Palestinian relief and then sold his yacht, with the proceeds going to the PEC. Straus also funded a good part of Hadassah's

work in the Holy Land.) In the nine months following the Hotel Marseilles meeting, the provisional committee brought in $170,000, more
than the FAZ had raised in its entire fifteen years of existence.

In what must be counted a masterstroke, Jacob de Haas proposed
and Brandeis implemented a transfer operation that not only provided
millions of dollars in relief but also won a great deal of favorable publicity for the Zionists. Because of American neutrality between August
1914 and April 1917, both the Allies and the Central Powers allowed
various relief and charitable groups to distribute food, clothing, and
money in the war zones. De Haas suggested that if the belligerent governments would allow it, much more could be sent on an individual
basis. People might give $25 to a general fund, but if they knew they
could send money directly to their relatives, they would give a great
deal more. Utilizing his contacts in the Wilson administration, Brandeis went to the State Department to see if there would be any objections and whether such a program would violate American neutrality.
After receiving approval, the provisional committee established a
transfer department. At first it handled only a few dollars a day, but as
word spread, the volume swelled to thousands, and before American
entry into the war the total sum reached into the millions. The Zionists
had originally planned to aid suffering Jews, but then Christians began
approaching the transfer department to see if they could send funds to
their relatives as well, and the Zionists agreed to handle their donations. The sender paid nothing for the service, and the committee bore
the costs of transmittal and exchange. The State Department utilized
its service to help transfer money and private messages, while large
companies like Standard Oil, which had many overseas branches, facilitated the work. Brandeis also used his good offices with Secretary of
the Navy Josephus Daniels, and the USS *Vulcan* carried sorely needed
foodstuffs and medicines to the Hadassah unit in Palestine.

The hardships of the war made raising money the first priority of the
Zionists. Brandeis recognized that in many ways the emphasis on fund-
raising necessarily diverted Zionists from the prime task of building up
the Jewish settlements in Palestine. But he also understood that American Zionists now had their first opportunity to reach out to the wider
Jewish community. Through fund-raising, Brandeis explained, "we
must unite the Jews and make clear to them also that it is through the
establishment of a publicly recognized, legally secured home for the
Jews in Palestine that our unity must find expression."

The Brandeis leadership has been criticized for diverting the energy of American Jewry from the central goal of Zionism—from Jewish unity built around a Palestinian homeland into mere moneygrubbing— and thus is responsible for the fact that no significant aliyah ever took place from the United States to Palestine/Israel. The exigencies of the situation in 1914 made fund-raising essential and the top priority, but Brandeis never saw it as an end in itself; rather, it provided a means to awaken a Jewish consciousness and a Zionist interest. Money would buy food and clothing and medicine, but the donor had to understand that the situation of the Jews made them suffer more than other victims of the war and that only a homeland would alleviate that condition. "If there can be awakened in America a desire to tackle the problem of the Jew fundamentally and see it through to a successful end," he declared, "we shall have passed on one stage further in our struggle for complete and universal rights." Brandeis said many times that money mattered to him personally only as it made him free; money would be important to the Zionists only if it freed the minds of American Jews to see the ultimate need of a Jewish homeland.

TWO OTHER ISSUES faced the Brandeis leadership: the unification of all American Zionists under one organizational roof, and the role that American Zionism and its leaders would henceforth play in world Zionist affairs. For all practical purposes, the Federation of American

Tipat Halav (Drop of Milk), Hadassah's fresh milk program in Palestine

Zionists ceased to exist after August 1914. Although the skeleton, including the small office staff, remained intact, responsibility for members, money, propaganda, relations with the American government, and correspondence with European Zionists passed into the hands of the Provisional Executive Committee for General Zionist Affairs, and more particularly into those of Louis D. Brandeis.

In the call for members, at least in 1914 and 1915, new Zionists would join a local society, which would then be affiliated to the provisional committee. Those groups with a special Zionist agenda, such as the religious Zionists (Mizrachi) or the various socialist groups (Poale Zion) or Hadassah, remained organizationally independent of the PEC and cooperated with it only insofar as its leaders recognized Brandeis's leadership. The tone of the hundreds of letters Brandeis wrote to local leaders and chapters is conciliatory, urging them to raise more money and get more members, since he had no authority at all to give them directives. Brandeis understood that he would never be able to get the socialists or the Mizrachi to cede all of their authority to one umbrella agency, but he assumed that groups like the Chelsea Zionist Society, and hundreds like it, the so-called general Zionists, would be glad to join a centralized organization that would make both its individual members and its constituent chapters feel more powerful. The Zionists would never have great influence unless they could speak in one voice.

The problem of reorganization stood high on Brandeis's agenda from the moment he assumed the PEC leadership, and by 1915 a plan had developed that ultimately led to the creation of the Zionist Organization of America in 1918 (see chapter 21). The plan involved identifying the PEC as the national spokesman for the American Zionist movement; it would create services for all local societies, and this in turn would attract the interests and loyalties of both chapters and individuals, encouraging them in understanding the need to act together. In typical reform manner, the reorganization could take place only after the educational process; American Jews had to be taught the necessity of becoming Zionists and then the benefits of uniting.

Even such luminaries as Brandeis, Julian Mack, and Stephen Wise could not dictate such a reorganization, but they could focus the attention of all Jews on the PEC. The massive propaganda effort the PEC launched involved not just teaching about the symbiosis between Judaism and Americanism or the importance of a Jewish homeland; it also trumpeted the achievements of the transfer program, the securing of an American naval ship to carry supplies to Palestine, the amount of money raised and distributed. All this would not have happened unless American Zionists acted together, and they needed a better organization to allow them to do so. As Brandeis explained to Nathan Kaplan of the Chicago-based Knights of Zion, by centralizing in the PEC those activities that required national direction, the Knights and other groups would be relieved of an onerous burden and could concentrate on their special interests and responsibilities, the things they did best. Rather than view a central organization as a weakening of the Knights, Brandeis urged Kaplan to see it as a special opportunity to strengthen the group.

To show just how effective unity could be, Brandeis persuaded the ten largest Zionist groups to hold a joint annual meeting in Boston at the end of June 1915. The PEC dominated the gathering, and Brandeis's personal prestige led city officials to prepare a near-royal welcome for the delegates. Special floral arrangements, featuring the Star of David, decorated the Public Gardens; local groups held dozens of receptions for the delegates; and Boston newspapers gave extensive coverage to the convention proceedings. For those who had been in Rochester the year before, the differences between the two gatherings could not have been more striking. In 1914 no one had paid any attention; in 1915 everyone in Boston took notice. The affiliates, whose individual meetings had passed unnoticed, could not help but realize that the simple act of meeting together had made the whole so much more than the sum of its parts. As Brandeis hoped, the Boston meeting provided a marked momentum for the idea of reorganization.

At the same time that Brandeis moved to create a unified American Zionism, he also had to deal with the World Zionist Organization. The international composition of the Actions Committee doomed it to fragmentation at the war's outbreak. The group could no longer meet in Berlin, the WZO headquarters, and many of the members, caught up in war fever, joined governmental bureaus. Those like Shmaryahu Levin and Nahum Sokolow, caught away from the Continent and unable or unwilling to go home, tried to work for the cause through the PEC or the English Zionist Federation. The central committee set up a temporary office in Copenhagen, but in the absence of forceful leadership never exerted any influence. With the WZO institutionally crippled, its sources of revenue closed, and the sudden emergence of the Brandeis faction in America, pressure arose on both sides of the Atlantic to shift the leadership of the world body to the United States.

In calling the Hotel Marseilles meeting, both Levin and Louis Lipsky assumed that the Actions Committee no longer functioned. At the meeting itself, and in the hectic weeks to follow, Brandeis also assumed that the movement had lost whatever central direction it once had. In England, Chaim Weizmann wanted to disassociate Zionism from anything and anybody German and believed the management of Zionist affairs should be entrusted to the PEC. "In view of the tensions now prevailing," he wrote to Brandeis, "I consider the activities of the old Actions Committee impossible and even dangerous for the future of our cause. . . . The American Provisional Committee should be given full power to deal with all Zionist matters until better times come."

Brandeis and his lieutenants were not political naïfs, and well understood the issues. The WZO had been headquartered in Berlin and, even if its executive committee had not disintegrated, would be suspect as under the thumb of one of the combatants. Chaim Weizmann, who would rise to power as head of the WZO after the war, realized that he could not try to claim authority since England had also gone to war. As for Palestine, it formally belonged to Turkey, a member of the Central Powers. In 1914, alone among the great powers, the United States remained neutral. A Zionist movement headquartered there could deal with both sides, without suspicion of favoritism by either.

Jacob de Haas urged Brandeis from the start to push for full and complete autonomy in world Zionist affairs. In October, the PEC informed Weizmann that it stood ready to act "on behalf of the whole Zionist organization at such times when action is necessary." The PEC would send money to Palestine, it would communicate with Zionist bodies in other countries, and it would take political action when necessary, on behalf of the Actions Committee, over all Zionist affairs. By November 1914 a steady stream of telegrams had reached the Copenhagen office urging a full transfer of power to the PEC.

It is doubtful Brandeis wanted to become head of the international Zionist movement, even on a temporary basis. As he had shown at the Hotel Marseilles meeting, he had little knowledge of the American constituents; he had none at all, other than the rough briefings he had gotten from de Haas and Sokolow, on the arcane politics of the WZO, or the complicated problems associated with the Palestinian settlements. As it turned out, within a few weeks of the war's start, enough members of the Actions Committee had made their way back to Berlin to make the office appear at least semi-functional. Sokolow urged the PEC not to push too hard, and Weizmann also retracted his earlier demand that the Americans take over. By the spring of 1915 the Americans had accepted the fact that the Actions Committee had not gone under. This caused little hand-wringing, except from de Haas, since neither Brandeis nor Mack wanted to tackle the international problems. They had their hands full at home.

The PEC did, however, impress upon the Actions Committee that it alone now spoke for American Zionists. It demanded and received full authority to collect moneys and to disburse them as it saw fit, without the approval of the Berlin office. For funds channeled to Palestine, Brandeis insisted on a centralized authority in the Holy Land, in place of the existing patchwork of multiple and semiautonomous recipients, each wanting more money than its neighbors. Arthur Ruppin, the WZO agent in Palestine, had long supported this idea, as well as the introduction of modern business and accounting procedures. Brandeis also urged the WZO to stop sending confidential information to various American Zionist groups; the PEC now stood as the voice of American Zionism, and he demanded that the WZO recognize this and send its information to, and only to, the PEC, which would then determine how to share it. Although the minutes of the PEC meetings went regularly to the Copenhagen office, the flow of information from Europe to America remained sketchy, far more so than could be blamed on the war. Time and again the PEC complained, as had the FAZ before it, that the Europeans demanded more and more money from American Zionists but did not treat them with respect and failed to keep the Americans informed about important matters. It would be an issue that would rise up again and again between the Americans and the WZO for the next thirty years.

AT THE END OF 1915 an American Zionist conversant with the history of the movement would have been well satisfied with recent developments. A new, energized, Americanized leadership had emerged. Membership had increased astronomically, and a highly efficient and effective means had been found to funnel American dollars to European Jews hard-hit by the war. The PEC produced reams of propaganda, and there could hardly have been a Jew in America who had not received at least one piece calling upon him or her to join the Zionists and to make a pledge of money. A haphazard business arrangement had been reorganized, and Brandeis had a level of respect and influence never before enjoyed by a Zionist leader in this country. The slogan of "Men! Money! Discipline!" had wrought a rich harvest in an unbelievably short time.

The success had been due in large measure not just to Brandeis's personal charisma but also to the very American ideas and methods he had employed. This had been the PEC's greatest strength, but in it could be found the seeds of future trouble. An accommodation still had to be reached with the powerful American Jewish Committee regarding who spoke for American Jewry. The increasing prominence of the PEC aroused a great deal of resentment in the European offices of the WZO, and at some point there would have to be a showdown between the Americans and the Europeans over what direction the movement would take. But for now all seemed well.

CHAPTER EIGHTEEN
NOMINATION

On 3 January 1916, Louis Brandeis kept a long-standing commitment to address the Chicago Bar Association; not since his 1905 talk "The Opportunity in the Law" had he spoken so comprehensively about law and the legal profession. Afterward he took the train to Cincinnati for a Zionist meeting and a long visit with Alfred, who came up from Louisville to see him. Once he returned to Boston, he had little time to himself because of the demands of the Provisional Executive Committee and also because he and his colleagues had begun planning for an American Jewish Congress (see chapter 21).

Brandeis certainly knew that Associate Justice Joseph Rucker Lamar had died on 2 January and that rumors had been flying ever since about whom Woodrow Wilson would name in his stead. Charles Sumner Holt, a Chicago lawyer Brandeis had known at Harvard, wrote to tell him that Illinois's governor, Edward Dunne, had been mentioned as a serious possibility and that he considered Dunne a person of "mediocre ability." Brandeis assured Holt that Attorney General Thomas Gregory would carefully screen any recommendations to ensure a qualified appointment, and he promised to take it up with Gregory during a trip to Washington later in the month.

A week later, though, George W. Anderson, a Boston lawyer who had worked with the Public Franchise League, tracked Brandeis down in Bridgeport, Connecticut, where Brandeis had gone to talk about the American Jewish Congress. Anderson had been dispatched by the president and the attorney general to ask Brandeis one question: Would he accept appointment to the Supreme Court? Although Brandeis later said he had some qualms about the offer, he told Anderson he would, and Wilson sent his name up to the Senate shortly after noon on Friday, 28 January 1916. To Alfred he confided, "I am not entirely sure I am to be congratulated, but I am glad the President wanted to make the appointment & I am convinced, all things considered, that I ought to accept."

It is doubtful Brandeis, Wilson, or any of the progressives who applauded the announcement had any idea of the firestorm it would unleash. The next four months would be the most difficult in Brandeis's life, and many times it appeared that he might not be confirmed.

IN "THE LIVING LAW," as he termed his Chicago talk, Brandeis provided the progressive era's clearest and most cited critique of the failure of courts to take into account the facts of the real world.

"Oh, what an associate for such a pure and innocent girl. And we have tried to bring her up so carefully, too!" Cartoon by Nelson Greene in Puck, *February 1916.*

Brandeis began by claiming that in recent years the demand of the people had shifted from the ideal of "a government of laws and not of men" to a call for "democracy and social justice." As democracy had deepened in the United States, people wanted social justice more than legal justice, and their respect for the law had lessened. He attributed this to the swiftly changing economic and social conditions in the country and noted a similar phenomenon in other countries enduring rapid transformations, including ancient Greece, where Euripides had reviled "the trammelings of law which are not of the right." After the French Revolution another period of change led the German writer Goethe to condemn customs and laws from the past that, like a disease, undermined the present health of society.

Brandeis asked whether Goethe's diagnosis might be equally applicable to the United States. "Has not the recent dissatisfaction with our law as administered been due, in large measure, to the fact that it had not kept pace with the rapid development of our political, economic, and social ideals? In other words, is not the challenge of legal justice to conform to our contemporary conceptions of social justice?" The law, however, had not risen to this challenge.

Politics as well as economic and social science noted these revolutionary changes. But legal science—the unwritten or judge-made laws as distinguished from legislation—was largely deaf and blind to them. Courts continued to ignore newly arisen social needs. They applied complacently eighteenth-century conceptions of the liberty of the individual and of the sacredness of private property. Early nineteenth-century scientific half-truths like "The survival of the fittest," which, translated into practice, meant "The devil take the hindmost," were erected by judicial sanction into a moral law.

When state assemblies passed laws that addressed the social and economic needs of the people, such as protective legislation, the courts either declared them unconstitutional or construed them away. Little wonder, then, that people had denounced judges and courts with such anger.

Recently, Brandeis claimed, courts had become more sensitive to social needs, and he pointed as an example to the Illinois Supreme Court, which in 1895 had held an eight-hour law for women unconstitutional and then in 1910 had approved a ten-hour law. The different results had nothing to do with the number of hours involved. Rather, the first court had reasoned from abstract logic, while the second court had taken "notice of those facts of general knowledge embraced in the world's experience." Brandeis pointed to other state courts that had similarly reversed themselves and that now showed a greater awareness of the facts of modern life.

Brandeis rejected notions like judicial recall to correct the problems of judges who failed to heed social changes. He pointed out that legal training remained the best means to fit men not only for judicial training but also for service in the new administrative arms of government, but he noted that that education had to include social, political, and economic studies as well as law. Only when the nation had lawyers who understood the public interest and the changing needs of society would the country have judges who could provide social as well as legal justice.

He ended with the story of Bogigish, a great scholar of the law who had become a professor at the University of Odessa. When Montenegro secured its independence, its prince wanted his country to have a code of laws like all other civilized nations. The prince begged the czar of

Russia to have Bogigish prepare a code for Montenegro; the czar agreed, and Bogigish undertook the task. But instead of relying on law books or his own immense knowledge of the law, he went to Montenegro and for two years lived with its people, studying their customs and their practices. He then embodied in the code he drafted all he had learned from the people, and they respected it, "because it expressed the will of the people."

It is easy to see why progressives responded so favorably to Brandeis's comments. They believed that the reforms they proposed, from factory legislation to protection of natural resources to model housing codes, all reflected what Holmes had called the "felt necessities of the times," and the opposition they had met in courts could be blamed on the lack of knowledge by judges. Once judges understood the social and economic realities, law would no longer be an obstacle to progress, but instead become a source of social as well as legal justice.

Conservatives, however, could not have disagreed more. Talk about social and economic "facts" ignored the plain truth that the law existed to protect property and individual rights and stood as the only barrier between the mob and people of means. The rule of law meant fidelity to ancient precepts, and judges should never forget that they expounded the eternal verities of a law built up over centuries, not some faddish social or economic theory.

How people responded to "The Living Law" provided a good indicator of how they reacted to Wilson's nomination of Brandeis to the high court.

THERE HAS BEEN a minor debate over who first suggested Brandeis to Wilson. William Gibbs McAdoo, Wilson's secretary of the Treasury as well as his son-in-law, claimed that the president asked him about a week after Justice Lamar's death whether he had anyone in mind to replace him. McAdoo immediately put forward Brandeis's name and noted that Wilson seemed surprised but pleased by the idea.

"Do you think the Senate would confirm his appointment?" Wilson asked.

"Yes," McAdoo replied, "he will be confirmed, but it will be a stiff fight."

The credit is also claimed by Wilson's attorney general, Thomas Gregory. After Lamar's death Gregory went to the White House and asked the president whether he had given any thought to Lamar's successor. "No," Wilson replied, "I have been waiting to hear from you."

"I am going to make a suggestion," Gregory said, "and I am going to ask you not to respond for a week. I am going to recommend Louis Brandeis for the Supreme Court. My reason is that he is one of the most progressive men in the United States, and equal to the best in learning and ability." At the end of the week Gregory returned to the White House for his answer. "You are right," Wilson told him. "Send his name in."

Wilson also received letters from leading progressives suggesting Brandeis, but given Wilson's association with the man dating back to that first interview in August 1912, he probably knew Brandeis well enough not to need prodding from anyone to consider him for the Court. Aside from that, however, a number of factors played into the president's decision. For Wilson, not only did the appointment reward a loyal ally and put a man on the Court who embodied ideals that Wilson had once believed unattainable, but it also shored up his chances to be reelected to the White House in 1916. Wilson did not want to repeat the mistake he had made two years earlier when he named the archconservative James Clark McReynolds to the bench.

Wilson had been elected by a plurality in 1912, although he had enjoyed a comfortable margin in the Electoral College. Had Roosevelt not bolted from the Republican Party, it is possible—even likely—that Wilson would have lost to Taft. After all, the country had been at peace and prosperous in 1912, two conditions that usually favored an incumbent. In the 1914 midterm elections, Republicans won back two dozen seats in the House and gained some senators and governors, winning nearly all of these seats from progressives. Theodore Roosevelt believed the reform spirit had faltered and made his peace with the GOP. For Wilson to gain reelection, he had to win over a significant percentage of the more than four million social justice progressives who had cast their ballot for the Bull Moose ticket four years earlier.

The war issue—whether the United States should join the Allies or stay neutral—split both parties, but the Democrats also seemed in disarray on the domestic front. Although the party controlled both houses of Congress, its leaders had been unable to make headway on several modest proposals Wilson had suggested to them. Faced with this scenario, the president came to two crucial conclusions in January 1916. First, in spite of the seeming confusion of views, a majority of the American people favored preparedness in case the United States should have to go to war, but preferred that the country stay neutral. Second, the only hope for victory in the November elections lay in attracting to the Democratic fold the large reform bloc that had supported Roosevelt in 1912.

To do this, Wilson had to abandon the belief that the federal government had no role to play in protecting underprivileged or disadvantaged groups, people whose welfare meant so much to the progressives. Wilson had already started down the road to greater federal involvement in the economy in the Federal Reserve and Federal Trade Commission measures. In the spring of 1916 he abandoned his indecision and helped push through Congress the Hollis-Bulkley Act to provide federal underwriting of a rural farm credits program, the Kern-McGillicuddy bill establishing a model workmen's compensation plan for federal employees, the Keating-Owen child labor bill, a measure giving the Philippines greater autonomy, and the La Follette Seamen's Act to protect merchant sailors. By the fall of 1916, the Democratic Congress under Wilson's leadership had enacted every important plank in the Progressive Party platform of 1912.

More than any other measure, however, the Brandeis nomination won Wilson sustained applause from the independents. The nomination constituted "an open defiance of and a personal affront to the masters of capital as well as to conservative Republicans." Progressives reacted as Wilson hoped they would. Amos Pinchot, a leading Roosevelt supporter in 1912, told Norman Hapgood that it "took courage & sense to make this appointment & I take off my chapeau to the President." Pinchot predicted that the appointment "will pull a strong oar for Wilson in Wis, Minn, S & N Dakota and other Roosevelt strongholds." Judge Learned Hand, one of Roosevelt's strongest supporters in 1912, told Brandeis that "almost Wilson can bring me round after so good a stroke." Robert La Follette, whom Wilson had consulted prior to announcing the appointment, said the American people owed a debt to Wilson. "In appointing Mr. Brandeis to the Supreme Bench President Wilson has rendered a great public service." Wilson had also talked to Samuel Gompers prior to making his announcement, and organized labor spoke with one voice in praising the nomination; whatever quibbles they may have had with Brandeis's support of union incorporation and scientific management, they knew that he had been one of their most effective advocates. The White House received hundreds of letters supporting the nomination.

On a more personal—and admittedly a more speculative—level, Wilson admired Brandeis as the type of lawyer he himself had once yearned to be. Wilson had always wanted to go into politics and early in his life had believed that law would be the road to take him there. But he and the law had been mismatched from the start, and in a letter to his fiancée Wilson had concluded that to earn a sufficient living through the law would preclude his going into politics. "The law is more than ever before a jealous mistress," he told her, and if a man "is to make a living at the bar he must be a lawyer and nothing else. . . . He cannot be both a learned lawyer and a profound and public-spirited statesman, if he must plunge into practice and make the law a means of support." Wilson may have been drawn to Brandeis thirty years later because Brandeis had done what Wilson had deemed impossible— become a learned and successful lawyer as well as an effective political reformer. Surely he had Brandeis in mind when he spoke to the Grid-iron Club about six months after his nominee had taken the oath of office. The old-style judges, those who spun their decisions out of the gossamer of legal theory without reference to worldly realities, "have now gently to be led to a back seat. . . . And men must be put forward whose whole comprehension is that law is subservient to life and not life to law."

IF WILSON'S MOTIVATIONS for naming Brandeis seem straight-forward enough, Brandeis's reasons for accepting are a bit more opaque. He had not looked for any appointment and seemed well content with the advisory role he played in the Wilson administration as well as with his access to the president. He had found a new cause in Zionism, a challenge that tested him every day. He had more than enough money; and the dream he had told Alice about—being financially free to serve the public—had come true. Although almost a year shy of his sixtieth birthday, and still physically and mentally active, he knew that he could not continue the pace he had set in the last two years. He traveled constantly: to New York for the arbitration board; to Washington for the Interstate Commerce Commission; and all over the East Coast and much of the Midwest for Zionism. He spent so much time in Washing-ton he could well have considered his rooms at the Hotel Gordon a sec-ond home. He had had some health problems, and Alice worried that he pushed himself too hard. The Court would not be as physically demanding, yet still offered a chance at service. When the opposition decried the appointment, Louis told his brother, "My feeling is rather—'Go it husband. Go it bear' with myself as 'interested specta-tor.'" This comment must surely be taken with a rather large grain of salt. Although he never lifted a finger to get the nomination, once it was made, he fought hard to ensure his confirmation.

Brandeis saw the appointment as a vindication not only of his belief in the compatibility of Zionism and Americanism, but also of his work as a reformer. A seat on the nation's highest court would give him a forum not only to preach but to practice the message he had been articulating for more than a decade—that the law had to reflect and take into account the realities of modern life. Wilson gave him the opportunity to become the type of judge he said the country needed in his Chicago address; it was an opportunity he could not ignore.

A politically astute man, Brandeis understood that at least in part, Wilson was reaching out to the reformers, and in commenting on the growing opposition, he wrote, "The fight that has come up shows clearly that my instinct that I could not afford to decline was correct. It would have been, in effect, deserting the progressive forces." To Roscoe Pound, he said, "I doubted much whether I ought to accept, but the opposition has removed my doubts." During the long fight reformers from every camp rallied to him, vindicating Wilson's strategy but also giving Brandeis great satisfaction and support.

Shortly after the nomination had been announced, Alice wrote to her brother-in-law that she had some misgivings. "Louis has been such a 'free man' all these years but as you suggested—his days of 'knight-erranting' must have, in the nature of things, been over before long." Her husband would have preferred another five years of "knight-erranting," but the Court, as they both knew, provided a great opportunity for service, "and all our friends here feel that he is the one man to bring to the Court what it greatly needs in the way of strengthening." Some would no doubt call it a political appointment, and she admitted that some of that could not be denied, "but the President himself told Louis that he wanted him in the Court because of his high respect for and confidence in him."

There were, indeed, all of these aspects in the appointment—politics, service, and something Alice did not mention, self-justification on both sides. In late January 1916 the personal and the political came together in a perfect confluence.

FEW EPISODES IN AMERICAN HISTORY shed so much light on their era as the Brandeis nomination, for the lineup of supporters and detractors provided a clear demarcation between progressives and those opposed to the reform movement. Both sides recognized Brandeis as the embodiment of progressive ideas, and as reformers ran into an increasingly hostile political environment, they turned to the courts seeking social progress; no one represented this idea better than Brandeis. His public advocacy, as one historian noted, threw "into high relief the clash between traditional American individualist values and the opposing tendencies of modernization in Western society."

It is not surprising, therefore, that the appointment generated controversy. Brandeis's partner George Nutter noted in his diary, "Brandeis will be opposed because he is supposed to be radical. But he is really not a radical. . . . He is very intense in his beliefs and zealous in forwarding them." He expected there would be a fight, not because Brandeis had done anything wrong, but rather because in his zeal he had occasionally done "foolish things and could have avoided some of the misunderstandings that have arisen." But, Nutter concluded, Brandeis had "always acted with good intentions and from good motives."

Others took a far less charitable view. "If Mr. Wilson has a sense of humor left," a Washington correspondent told former president William Howard Taft, "it must be working overtime today. When Brandeis's nomination came in yesterday, the Senate simply gasped. . . . There wasn't any more excitement at the Capitol when Congress passed the Spanish War Resolution." Brandeis's "notorious reputation" and his ardent progressivism alarmed the financial leadership in Boston and New York and their political spokesmen in Washington. Within twenty-four hours the Senate took the unprecedented step of naming a subcommittee of the Judiciary Committee to investigate the nominee. From the day of Wilson's announcement until the Senate's vote to confirm on 1 June, a battle raged over Brandeis's ethics, his way of practicing law, and, in large measure even if indirectly, reform itself. Both sides saw the struggle as one for the "soul of the Supreme Court."

William Howard Taft (who had long coveted a place on the Court and thought for some reason that Wilson would appoint him) summed up conservative thought in a set of charges that would be seen in almost every facet of the opposition to Brandeis over the next four months:

> It is one of the deepest wounds that I have ever had as an American and a lover of the Constitution and a believer in progressive conservatism, that such a man as Brandeis could be put in the Court, as I believe he is likely to be. He is a muckraker, an emotionalist for his own purposes, a socialist, prompted by jealousy, a hypocrite, a man who has certain high ideals in his imagination, but who is utterly unscrupulous, in method in reaching them, a man of infinite cunning . . . of great tenacity of purpose, and, in my judgment, of much power for evil.

Taft's experience at the hands of Brandeis during the Pinchot-Ballinger affair explains at least some of his hyperbole, but the fact remains that conservatives saw the nation's highest court as a citadel to protect property and individual economic rights, not as a place from which radical ideas of social justice could be spouted. Wilson and Taft both rightly believed that if Brandeis went on the Court, he would bring with him the ideas he had preached about a living law and the need for judges to respond to social change, an idea that pleased one and terrified the other.

Everyone understood that Brandeis came from an entirely different cast from the other members of the Court. Holmes, a unique intellectual loner, actually stood closer to his conservative brethren than to the new men in political life. Charles Evans Hughes had a good mind, and showed promise of being a leader on the bench, but he also fit into the conventional mode. If Brandeis went onto the bench, he would bring with him a new outlook and different experience from the old-school justices, and if his ideas prevailed, they would topple the old bastion of property-oriented classical thought. Both his friends and those opposed to the appointment recognized this, and while his career gave both sides plenty of ammunition to debate the man, in fact the real fight involved the future of the Court.

Response to the nomination in newspapers and magazines reflected this split. Progressive journals like the *New Republic* and *Harper's Weekly* applauded the appointment, while most business-oriented outlets damned it, some of them calling Brandeis "a socialist or a progressive," clearly believing the two meant the same thing. The voice of American capitalism, the *Wall Street Journal,* condemned the appointment and singled out Brandeis as the leader of anti-corporation agitation. "Where others were radical he was rabid; where others were extreme he was super-extreme; where others would trim he would lay the ax to the root of the tree." In a similar vein, the *Los Angeles Times* labeled him a "hypocrite" and a "dangerous demagogue" and said the effort to place him on the high court "is enough to make cold chills run down the spine of every patriot of the nation." The *Boston Evening Transcript,* the voice of State Street and the Brahmins, opposed Brandeis not, according to its editor, because of a lack of ability or questions of honesty but because he had a different code of honor from that espoused by the paper. In an interesting comment, the *Washington Star,* while predicting a "big fight" over the nomination because of Brandeis's reform activities, believed that it would not be "a question about race." Of course, when someone says a matter is "not about race," it often is, and the

question is how much did Brandeis's religion and anti-Semitic prejudice play in the fight over his nomination.

When confronted with the first Jew named to the Supreme Court,
and in a time of growing nativism, clearly those who feared "foreigners"
would oppose the appointment. To the Protestant elite in the country,
the idea of a Jew on the Court—even one born in the United States—
would have seemed proof that an alien invasion had taken over their
country. William F. Fitzgerald ranted that "the fact that a slimy fellow
of this kind by his smoothness and intrigue, together with his Jewish
instinct can [be appointed to the Court] should teach an object lesson"
to true Americans. While some senators may have objected to Brandeis
because he was a Jew, none of them wanted to appear prejudiced, especially as the recent Leo Frank lynching had sensitized people to anti-
Semitism. In fact, according to the *New York Sun,* if Brandeis were not
a Jew and had to go before the Senate only on his merits, he would easily be defeated. "There is, however, danger that the racial issue will
become involved in the struggle, and in that event it would be difficult
to predict how members of the Senate would vote." The journalist Gus
Karger opined that "many Senators who might base their opposition to
him on sound and logical grounds, if he were a Presbyterian, are reluctant to take a stand, lest their opposition be misconstrued." Brandeis
was well aware of these arguments, as well as of the more overt anti-
Semitic attacks on him. At the time, however, he ignored them.

The nomination, of course, played well within the Jewish community, much to Taft's disgust. The Jewish press was ecstatic, and the *Jewish Daily Forward* carried a huge headline announcing the appointment.
Outside Seward Park on the Lower East Side an electric sign, similar to
the news sign in Times Square, blazoned the news in Yiddish: "LOUIS D.
BRANDEIS, THE FIRST JEW NOMINATED BY PRESIDENT WILSON TO THE
SUPREME COURT OF THE UNITED STATES." "God be blest!" one young
Jew declared when he saw the news. "In Russia we dreamed of it. Here
it is a fact." An older man said, "It must be true. Why should they fool
us?" That Friday evening, many rabbis all across the country devoted
all or part of their sermons to the news that had been announced earlier
in the day.

Unlike 1912, when leaders of the Jewish community could tell
Colonel House that they did not consider Brandeis a "representative
Jew," now they had little choice but to laud the nomination. In fact,
one of the first to send a congratulatory telegram had been Jacob Schiff,
who also praised the appointment in a public statement. Taft almost

gloated over their discomfort. "The humor of the situation over Brandeis grows as I think of it," he told his brother. "Speyer, Schiff, Kahn, Louis Marshall all have to praise the appointment and all hate Wilson for making it." Whether they actually hated Wilson, there is no question that the appointment made them uncomfortable. Financiers like Schiff had often felt the barbs of Brandeis's attacks on finance capitalism. Louis Marshall and the American Jewish Committee had worked for years to get new Jewish immigrants to accept their view of what loyalty to the United States meant, only to have Brandeis in less than two years make Zionism a power within the Jewish community and a threat to the hegemony of the committee in speaking for Jews on public issues.

Karger's estimate that if Brandeis had been a Protestant the Senate would easily have defeated the nomination is impossible to verify, for the simple reason that with one exception, Brandeis's religion never came up in the entire hearings. On 2 March, Francis Peabody testified about Brandeis's reputation at the Boston bar. In response to a question from Senator Duncan Fletcher (D-Fla.) about whether Peabody knew any specific cases that would show a lack of ethics on the nominee's part, Peabody responded, "I did not know he was a Jew. I would say that had not been disclosed until a few years ago. That made no difference as far as my opinion of him goes, except so far as it was made prominent and before that had not been known." Fletcher did not ask any follow-up questions, nor did any of the other senators. Peabody had raised an issue none of them wanted to talk about.

By 1916 anti-Semitism had pervaded a good part of Boston society, albeit not the overt Jew hatred found in Europe. In his diary George Nutter, who had been in the Brandeis firm since 1889, noted with disapproval what he considered evidence of anti-Semitism at a meeting of the Boston Bar Association and from attorneys who wondered if Brandeis "understood plain Anglo-Saxon," that is, if he shared Christian values. Yet Nutter himself apparently held some of these same views and, in describing Brandeis, wrote, "He has the ability of his race, and some other racial habits, particularly the zeal for accumulation of wealth. He is very rich, yet he lives a notably simple life and avoids the posturing of the Jews."

Throughout the fight, both Brandeis's allies and his opponents steered clear of his religion, the latter to avoid the appearance of bigotry, and the former to prevent making the matter the central issue. Attorney General Thomas Gregory wanted to play down lobbying by

Jews and Jewish organizations. Any public activity by Jews, he told Ned McClennen, is "not likely to help with the Bourbon Democrats. They know what this support means in coming elections without having it called to their attention." Gregory expected—correctly—that the outcome would be determined by party loyalty. At Brandeis's directions, his allies also worked to keep statements of Jewish support to a minimum, and he quickly scotched an offer to collect signatures of Jewish lawyers on his behalf. Felix Frankfurter, who undertook the coordination of responses to charges made against Brandeis, agreed that the nominee's record and his religion had to be kept separate. "It is terribly important," he told Judge Julian Mack, "that no Jews should make the slightest peep about the race issue. You know as well as I do that the Jew in Brandeis has nothing to do (I except negligible isolated individuals) with the grounds of opposition." Many prominent Jews opposed the nomination, as did prominent Bostonians, "and for about the same reasons."

McClennen later claimed that anti-Semitism constituted the main reason for opposition, especially from southern Democrats. Brandeis himself, at least at one point, believed that people opposed the nomination because he was a radical and a Jew, but he never really explained what he meant. Nearly all of the public opposition to him centered on his allegedly unethical practice of law, and with the exception of the comment from Peabody (which in fuller context related to what Peabody believed to be Brandeis's duplicity in regard to a specific case), the public debate ignored his religion. In the end, while scholars will continue to disagree on how much a role, if any, prejudice played in the fight, people who by all accounts did not care about Brandeis's religion opposed him because of his views on economics, business, and law. As Brandeis himself recognized, his Jewishness, while a complicating factor, had little to do with the extent of the opposition. A Jewish lawyer who worked for a Wall Street bank would not have faced such bitter antagonism. Perhaps the fairest way to treat this question is to note that Brandeis's religion constituted but another marker of his "outsider" status and, as with his alleged radicalism, made him unfit to enter the temple of the law.

THE DAY WILSON ANNOUNCED the nomination found Louis and Alice in Washington to attend a dinner given by Secretary of the Treasury McAdoo for the president prior to Wilson's western trip to drum up support for his preparedness program. Among the guests were Justices

Charles Evans Hughes, Mahlon Pitney, and James Clark McReynolds,
and Wilson personally took Brandeis
over to introduce them to their
newest colleague. Reporters had besieged Louis and Alice as they left
the Hotel Gordon to go to the White
House, but Brandeis would not then,
nor for the next several months, talk
to the press. "I have nothing whatsoever to say," he told them. "I have not
said anything and I will not." When
a reporter for the *New York Sun* asked
about specific charges that might be
made, Brandeis replied, "I have nothing to say about anything, and that
goes for all time and to all newspapers, including the Sun and the
moon."

*The field manager of the
confirmation, Brandeis's law
partner, Edward McClennen*

Brandeis's reticence reflected his
sense of the proprieties a Supreme Court justice, even a nominee,
should follow, namely, insulation from the press. But he also knew that
there would be a fight over confirmation, since approval did not necessarily follow appointment. The Senate in exercising its constitutional
power to advise and consent had at times withheld its approval, going
back to George Washington's failed appointment of John Rutledge as
chief justice. Since then, the Senate had rejected seven other nominees,
while a dozen more had withdrawn in the face of opposition or failure of
the Senate to take up the appointment. Also, at that time nominees did
not appear in person before the Senate Judiciary Committee. Brandeis
apparently gave no thought to breaking this tradition, but he and his
supporters recognized that he would be at a disadvantage in not being
able to defend himself personally. A way would have to be found to
respond to charges brought against him.

The nominee met with George Anderson at the Cosmos Club on
3 February, and after consultation with Attorney General Gregory the
three men agreed that Brandeis would return to Boston. Anderson,
although he had opposed Brandeis in some of the Massachusetts battles, strongly believed the Boston attorney qualified for the Court and
offered to serve as one of his representatives in Washington. But Bran-

deis and his partner Edward McClennen agreed that no one should formally represent the nominee, so Anderson served as counsel to the subcommittee and as a counterweight to Austen Fox, an opponent of the nomination who also offered his services to the senators and then spent several weeks dredging up accusations against Brandeis. Ned McClennen moved down to Washington for the duration, serving as the main conduit for information to and from the nominee. "The Justiceship ist ein bischen langweilig [a little bit boring]," Louis told Alfred, "but I am leaving the fight to others." This was hardly true, and Alfred, who knew his brother well, recognized that the last thing Louis could do was let others fight for him.

Upon his return to Boston, Brandeis adopted a policy of public silence. He did respond to the many letters that came to him, and seemed to take great pleasure when men he had known in law school or had not seen for many years wrote to congratulate him. To Walter Douglas, his friend and roommate at Harvard, he wrote that the nomination had brought messages from a number of their classmates. "I think often of you and of our days at the School; and my interest in Avon Street has been revived through my daughter Elizabeth living at Whitman Hall (Radcliffe College), which is situated but a stone's throw from our old rooms." He stopped going to the Union Club for lunch, made no more public appearances for the Zionists (although he continued to travel to New York for occasional private meetings with the staff), and refused to take any new clients. In some ways, despite the stress of the confirmation fight, Louis and Alice enjoyed more of a "normal" life than they had in a long time, with Louis home for dinner every evening. As winter turned to spring, they moved to the Dedham house to enjoy the nearby woods.

From the beginning of February until the first of June, Brandeis went to the office in the morning, answered his mail, consulted when any of his associates needed an opinion on a problem, and dealt with the charges raised against him. He had an informal war council—Norman Hapgood in New York, Thomas Gregory, George Anderson, and Robert La Follette in Washington, and Felix Frankfurter and George Nutter in Boston. Ned McClennen wrote daily, sometimes several times a day, from Washington, and his letters alerted the office to what charges had been raised and what various allies reported. Brandeis, Nutter, and others, aided by Miss Grady, would then go through the office files researching the old cases, and Brandeis would then dictate long letters for McClennen setting the record straight and explaining why he had acted as he had in particular matters.

Despite his silence, Brandeis served as field marshal of the campaign to get him on the Court. Although Hapgood, the editors of the *New Republic,* La Follette, and Frankfurter all felt free to act on their own, they always reported to him what they had done, to whom they had spoken, and what they had heard. When Senator William E. Chilton (D-W.Va.), head of the subcommittee, suggested that letters from prominent lawyers endorsing the appointment would be helpful, Brandeis contacted George Anderson to begin soliciting Boston attorneys and sent Norman Hapgood a list of attorneys and judges (including Learned Hand and Samuel Seabury) who should be contacted. Unaware that Gregory had decided to play down the Jewish aspect, Brandeis also sent Hapgood a list of prominent Jewish lawyers. He prepared a list of cases he had argued in the U.S. Supreme Court as well as the Supreme Judicial Court of Massachusetts, addresses to bar associations, and law review articles. When friends and professional acquaintances asked him what they could do, he invariably responded that they should write directly to Senator Chilton. He dispatched another partner, George Nutter, to New York and occasionally to Washington to help McClennen when necessary, and directed how supportive letters might best be used. And, from the tone of his early letters, he believed things would go well. "What a rumpus the President has started up," he wrote to one friend, "and all over a peace loving individual."

THINGS, HOWEVER, did not go well, and for a while Brandeis seemed besieged on every side. Wall Street law firms deluged the Senate with hundreds of letters, all suspiciously identical: "Dear Sir: I/we protest against the nomination of Mr. Louis D. Brandeis to be a Justice of the Supreme Court, and urge you to vote against its confirmation." In Boston, Harvard's president, Abbott Lawrence Lowell, a man who made little effort to hide his anti-Semitism (and who in the 1920s would try to restrict the number of Jews attending the university), circulated a petition against Brandeis that carried fifty-five signatures, including some of the oldest Brahmin names in the city, such as Adams, Gardner, and Peabody. J. Butler Studley, a lawyer in the Brandeis office, drew up a chart showing the interconnectedness of all fifty-five signers and how all of their directorships and financial interests overlapped. Behind the scenes Brandeis's longtime foe Henry Lee Higginson stirred up more opposition. Seven of the sixteen living former presidents of the American Bar Association signed a letter to the subcommittee declaring Brandeis unfit to serve on the high court.

George Nutter complained that "we cannot get a petition signed" and that it took forever to get a letter sent, but Brandeis's supporters did take steps to counter the opposition. At Harvard Law School, a third-year student named Shelton Hale, who also served as campus correspondent for the *Boston Post,* asked the eleven members of the law school faculty their view. Nine of the eleven announced their support, one refused to comment, and only one, Edward H. Warren, opposed Brandeis. In praising Brandeis, Roscoe Pound quoted Edmund Burke on the great English jurist Lord Mansfield—that he made the liberality of the law "keep pace with the demands of justice and the actual concerns of the world." In direct response to Lowell's indictment, 713 Harvard University students signed their own petition supporting Brandeis. Newton D. Baker, the mayor of Cleveland and soon to become secretary of war, Frances Perkins, Paul Kellogg, and many others either wrote to the subcommittee or appeared as witnesses.

The Reverend A. A. Berle, a longtime friend of the nominee's whose son had just been hired in Brandeis's law office, suggested to Senator Chilton that the subcommittee not give too much weight to the Lowell petition. The Brahmin community had enjoyed unchallenged control of the Commonwealth for so many years that they had come to believe that anyone who disagreed with them and of whom they did not approve "is ipso facto a person who is either 'dangerous' or lacking in 'judicial temperament.' " They would never give up the idea that only a long New England pedigree made a person worthy of honor.

While conservative newspapers gave play to the charges against Brandeis, his friends kept the periodical press full of rebuttals and articles praising the nominee. Norman Hapgood, as expected, carried on a weekly drumbeat in favor of his friend in *Harper's* and, whenever a new charge arose, quickly answered it, often with information directly from Boston. Brandeis, Hapgood wrote, had never been in the practice of responding to his critics, and now all of the old foes had gone to Washington to resurrect charges, implying that Brandeis's silence constituted an admission of guilt. Nothing could be farther from the truth. In the 1 April edition, Hapgood ran three editorials, one of them noting that much of the criticism had come from cronies of President Taft, whose deceptions had been uncovered by Brandeis in the Pinchot-Ballinger hearings. In response to the Lowell petition, *Harper's* ran letters from Roscoe Pound and the economist William Z. Ripley, both of Harvard, praising Brandeis's work not only in law but also in the railroad hearings.

The editors at the *New Republic,* who had been somewhat estranged from Brandeis because of their support for Theodore Roosevelt's New

Nationalism, now enthusiastically became his champion, and Brandeis jokingly told Learned Hand that the magazine bore at least some of the responsibility for the appointment. During the fight Herbert Croly, Walter Lippmann, and Felix Frankfurter wrote some of the strongest articles in his defense, shredding the attacks made against him. In their first editorial on 5 February, they laid out not only the nominee's qualifications but also why they believed he would be the right man to join the Court. Almost every week afterward they noted the attacks made against Brandeis and then showed up the falsehood of the accusations.

While the support of the *Survey,* a magazine devoted to social justice causes, is not surprising, that of the *Outlook* is. The magazine to which Theodore Roosevelt regularly contributed columns might have looked askance at the man who had helped Woodrow Wilson defeat TR in 1912. The editors, however, spoke for the type of progressive that Wilson hoped to win over in 1916, and they, like many other reformers, praised Wilson for the nomination and urged the Senate to confirm Brandeis to the Court.

Both opponents and proponents of the nomination knew, however, that while all the arguments made in the papers and magazines might influence some public opinion, the only opinions that mattered were those of the men in the Senate, and especially those holding hearings on the nominee's fitness to be a member of the Supreme Court.

THE SUBCOMMITTEE, consisting of three Democrats and two Republicans, began hearings in the ornate Judiciary Committee room on Wednesday, 9 February, to an audience that filled all of the seats and stood jammed in against the windows and wall. Of the three Democrats, William Chilton of West Virginia, Duncan Fletcher of Florida, and Thomas J. Walsh of Montana, the last would become Brandeis's strongest defender during the hearings. The two Republicans were Clarence Clark of Wyoming, who had sat in the upper chamber since 1895, and Albert Baird Cummins of Iowa, certainly the best-known man on the subcommittee. Progressives like La Follette hoped that the insurgent Cummins would endorse Brandeis, but like most other progressive Republicans, Cummins had crawled back into the regular party after their 1912 escapade. A few weeks into the hearings Senator Clark withdrew, and John D. Works of California took his place. Like Cummins, Works had something of an insurgent reputation and had worked closely with La Follette on some proposals. In the end, however, he toed the party line against Brandeis.

Clifford Thorne started off as the first witness, and he immediately tore into Brandeis for betraying his trust in the 1913 Advanced Rate hearings before the Interstate Commerce Commission. Brandeis, Thorne told the senators, "was guilty of infidelity, breach of faith, and unprofessional conduct in connection with one of the greatest cases of this generation." Thorne kept returning to the theme that Brandeis thought a 7.5 percent return on capital stock was inadequate, indeed, using Brandeis's phrase, "niggardly." Thorne's testimony lasted until nearly 10:30 at night, and when he rose, John M. Eshleman, the lieutenant governor of California, immediately took the witness stand to contradict Thorne. Brandeis had acted honorably and had never, despite Thorne's insinuations, suggested that the railroads should get the full 5 percent rate increase. Eshleman said that Brandeis's role had been very clear to everybody; he would not represent either the shippers or the railroads, but would serve as counsel to the ICC in seeking a solution that would be fair to all parties, including the public. He could not fathom why Thorne had ascribed ulterior motives to Brandeis in his testimony. After Eshleman, Joseph Teal, an attorney from Oregon who knew Brandeis personally and had worked with him on the Oregon minimum-wage case, also testified that he could not find any basis for Thorne's testimony. "I was astonished," he told the subcommittee, "not only because I do not believe Mr. Brandeis would betray anybody on earth, much less the public, but with my knowledge of him acquired in the way I stated, I could not believe it possible."

By the time Teal finished and the subcommittee adjourned, the clock read 11:20, much too late for the morning newspapers to carry Eshleman's and Teal's testimony. But they did carry detailed stories on Thorne's testimony. It appeared very damaging to some people, but former president Taft, on reading through it, understood that "if what Thorne had to say against Brandeis is all there is, I should not regard it as a very serious matter." The next day two more witnesses—James Carmalt, the ICC's chief examiner, and Frank Lyon, a Washington attorney who had worked with the commission since its inception—took the stand to rebut Thorne, and the committee began to consider just how it ought to handle the testimony. By the second day it had become clear that Cummins stood opposed to Brandeis and wanted the hearings to proceed as if the nominee were a defendant in the dock, with the witnesses bolstering the prosecution's case that he was unfit for the high court. This did not sit well with his colleagues, especially Walsh, who wanted the witnesses to stick to what they knew personally. Senator Fletcher agreed; witnesses should "not state what Tom,

Dick and Harry have said to them, to make purely hearsay statements, but shall be confined to what they know."

Yet the very next witness, Thomas C. Spelling of New York, launched into a diatribe against Brandeis, who had apparently had the audacity to mark up his brief before the ICC to highlight what Brandeis considered its weaknesses and errors. The committee finally managed to cut off the talkative Spelling, who wanted to read aloud an eight-thousand-word statement he had prepared. Just put it in the record, Senator Fletcher snapped. "We can read, you know!"

And so it went. Clarence Barron called himself a "farmer" but admitted he was "connected with" the *Wall Street Journal* and that he had written some critical editorials about the appointment. "It is not necessary," Barron had written in a piece he read into the record, "to uncover the grave of Patrick Lennox or reopen the Warren settlements to show the moral fiber of Louis D. Brandeis and his unfitness for the Supreme Bench." Barron, of course, did not mention his role as head of the Boston News Bureau in slandering Brandeis at the behest of Charles Sanger Mellen, the president of the New Haven Railroad. The committee did, in fact, hear about the Lennox case and the Warren will and United Shoe, and it also heard, from Ned McClennen, a detailed rebuttal to each and every one of the charges.

Interestingly, Charles Mellen, who people thought would be glad of the opportunity to attack Brandeis for his role in bringing down the New Haven, refused to testify. After the subcommittee issued a subpoena, he wired back that he had "no information of any character" that would be of value in the hearings and asked to be excused. Senator Walsh reported that he had then asked Mellen if he could comment on the truth or falsity of the charge, leveled by Barron, that Brandeis had been employed to "wreck" the New Haven. Walsh read aloud Mellen's response: "I am absolutely without information as to anything that I would be justified to testify under oath. I think it would be a waste of the committee's time and mine for me to go to Washington to testify. I am not at all unfriendly to Brandeis, and I know nothing about his career except hearsay." If any of his colleagues still wanted Mellen, they could insist, but apparently none of them did, and that seemed to take care of the New Haven charge.

Hollis R. Bailey, a Boston lawyer who had known both Brandeis and Sam Warren from their Harvard days (Bailey, in fact, had been one of the students who read to Louis when he had eye trouble), then took the stand to explain the intricacies of the Warren will, another of Brandeis's "sins" that Barron had raised. Bailey testified for more than two hours and conceded that the problem had arisen because Sam's brother Edward, whom Bailey represented, had objected to the trusteeship arrangement Brandeis had drawn that supposedly protected all members of the family. Edward believed that the instrument worked solely for Sam's benefit. Bailey, however, did not accuse Brandeis of unethical conduct, but claimed he should not have tried to represent all members of the family. He ought to have recognized that conflicting interests existed, and recommended that individual members of the family retain independent counsel. When asked about Brandeis's reputation, Bailey called him very able and a man of keen intellect but not entirely trustworthy. Bailey also testified that his client had not complained about the arrangement until a number of years after the trust had been implemented, and that the family had resolved all outstanding issues after Sam's death. Another one of Barron's allegations fell by the wayside.

One person, however, proved highly indignant over Bailey's testimony. Cornelia Warren expressed her anger that the family's affairs had been aired before the committee. She, for one, had full faith in Brandeis and wanted the committee to understand that Edward, and only Edward, had objected. She hoped sincerely that the nomination would be confirmed and that the whole country could benefit from his ability. Brandeis must have taken a great deal of satisfaction from this letter, and said that he regretted that "the attacks on me should be made the occasion to attack" the memory of Sam Warren, a man whom Brandeis called the "soul of honor." Interestingly, Brandeis did not seem to understand Bailey's assertion that conflicting interests within the family should have led Brandeis to advise them to have separate lawyers. He had not been on anyone's side, but "of holding throughout the period of trust, as I had during your father's lifetime, the position of advisor of the family, and during most of the time, of each and every member in their relations to one another, as to outsiders." The only good to come out of the hearings, he believed, was that further investigation would show that all members of the family, including Edward, had for many years lived happily with the original arrangements.

A MORE VIRULENT ATTACK came when Sidney Winslow, president of the United Shoe Machinery Company, took the stand on Tuesday, 15 February, and spent two days accusing Brandeis of "unprofessional conduct and of conduct not becoming an honorable man." Brandeis had helped set up United Shoe, had sat on the board, had gained great knowledge of its business practices, and then, at the instance of a competitor, had turned against the company and unfairly aided government prosecutors in their antitrust suit against the company. Winslow testified for more than five hours and introduced dozens of documents into the record, some from the company's files, some from hearings before congressional committees, and some from other sources. Over and over he charged that Brandeis had betrayed his old client. Buried in this mass of paper was a letter from Brandeis to Senator Moses Clapp explaining his involvement in United Shoe affairs, why he left the company, and his subsequent relations with the firm.

McClennen and Nutter had understood from the beginning that of all the charges leveled against Brandeis, these might be the most damaging. According to Winslow, Brandeis had been a key player in devising the strategy that gave the company its monopolistic power and then he had turned on it, and had used his knowledge of the firm to attack it. Anticipating Winslow's charges, McClennen had prepared a lengthy memorandum tracing Brandeis's involvement with United Shoe up to his letter to Senator Clapp, drawing not only on the office's files but also, at Brandeis's suggestion, on interviews with LaRue Brown, who had prosecuted the antitrust suit during his tenure as U.S. attorney.

All of the charges involving the rate hearings, United Shoe, the Warren will, and other matters could not, as individual episodes, sink the appointment. Together, however, they raised the questions of whether Louis Brandeis could be trusted, whether he had the integrity to take a place on the nation's highest court, and whether his reputation at the Boston bar reflected a flawed character or merely the jealousy of those he had bested in legal combat. A good friend of Brandeis's for many years, Charles C. Burlingham, noted that many lawyers resented Brandeis because he neither asked for nor gave favors in the usual give-and-take of the law. If one lawyer asks for an adjournment, for whatever reason, professional courtesy dictated that the opposing lawyer agree, on the understanding that at some point in the future the tables might be reversed. Brandeis, according to Burlingham, "never gave any favors to anybody. His justification was that he was representing his client." Burlingham thought Brandeis wrong on this, and believed it contributed to the ill feeling against him by the Boston bar. Nutter noted in his diary that "the feeling against Brandeis is so strong that it is difficult to get [favorable] letters from the bar."

Moorfield Storey, a highly respected member of the Boston bar, may have been one of the most damaging witnesses against Brandeis because time and again he returned to the theme that Brandeis had acted unethically and could not be trusted. Storey, then seventy years old, had had a distinguished career as a lawyer, secretary to Senator Charles Sumner, historian, Harvard overseer, and president of the American Bar Association. Moreover, he could not be accused of being just another archconservative; Storey had helped to found and served as first president of the National Association for the Advancement of Colored People. Initially, Storey claimed he did not know why he had been called to Washington, but when told that Clarence Barron had named him as one who could testify as to Brandeis's fitness for the Court, Storey agreed. He then went on to tell the subcommittee that he believed Brandeis had never been honest regarding whom he acted for, and he recounted a proxy fight in 1892 when the New Haven had attempted to take over the old New England Railroad Company. Storey said one could not tell for whom Brandeis had then acted, and he had also been dishonest claiming to represent Louis Glavis in the Pinchot-Ballinger hearings when in fact the real client had been *Collier's*.

When Senator Walsh wanted to know if Storey could back up Barron's claim that Brandeis had tried to wreck the New Haven, Storey said he could not, but immediately went on to tell the subcommittee that he opposed the Brandeis nomination "because of his reputation at our bar as a lawyer." Senator Works then asked, "What is that reputation?" and Storey said, "That of a man who is an able lawyer, very energetic, ruthless in the attainment of his objectives, not scrupulous in the methods he adopts, and not to be trusted."

Senator Works then asked how much contact Storey had had with Brandeis, and Storey conceded that he had been engaged against Brandeis in only three or four matters, and in fact had never had any personal quarrel with him "or any difficulty at all," and their public activities had been in different areas. The two men moved not only in different legal worlds but in different social strata as well. When Works persisted that perhaps many of the rumors against Brandeis had been fomented by agents of the New Haven, Storey denied this and said he had spoken to a number of Boston lawyers and they all had the same view of Brandeis, but he declined to mention any of their names.

Had Storey's testimony stopped then, it could have been extremely damaging, but Senator Walsh and George Anderson kept him on the stand and asked him if he could explain who some of the fifty-five people were who had signed the Lowell petition against the nominee. Storey said he would be glad to do so and then, perhaps unconsciously, showed how they all belonged to very tightly knit social, commercial, and legal circles. Rather than seeing them as a clique, however, Storey lauded the signatories as "representative" of the best men in Boston. He also unwittingly refuted some of Hollis Bailey's testimony regarding the Warren will case, saying, "I should have done perhaps very much as Mr. Brandeis did if I had been in his place."

Anderson wanted to know how, as an overseer at Harvard for many years, Storey could explain the near-unanimous support given to Brandeis at the law school if, in fact, the appointee had such a low reputation at the Boston bar? Well, Storey responded, Roscoe Pound had come to Cambridge only a few years earlier, and Felix Frankfurter was just a young man from New York, so they really did not know much about Boston and its legal culture. Also, Brandeis had always been very "courteous" to the school, had helped it from time to time, so the professors naturally thought well of him.

Before Storey left the stand, Anderson led him through a series of questions which forced Storey to agree that the man who he claimed had such a low reputation at the Boston bar had for many years been a member of the oversight committee of the law school, that Harvard not only had awarded Brandeis a Master of Arts in 1891 but also had admitted him to Phi Beta Kappa the year before. In the end, Storey appeared a somewhat diminished man, the representative of a closed and parochial social group that despised Brandeis for showing up the dishonesty of its financial leaders.

AND SO IT WENT, with witnesses appearing both for and against Brandeis—a total of forty-three in all, with McClennen testifying several times. The subcommittee brought its hearings to an end in late March, although the attacks on Brandeis continued. Sometimes the allegations raised appeared so frivolous that Brandeis could hardly believe that he had to respond to them. In early April both McClennen and Gregory told Brandeis that they had heard comments in the Senate cloakroom that he did not believe in a written constitution, to which another senator had replied that he had heard that Brandeis thought that the nine judges of the Supreme Court should not be restrained from responding to the demands of the people by any constitutional restriction. Both asked Brandeis to search his memory to see if he could identify the source of such comments. McClennen said that to the best of his knowledge, he could not recall his partner's making any reference to the Constitution outside of one or two passages in *Business—a Profession.*

Two months after the hearings had started, Brandeis's self-control began to slip, and he responded to Gregory in a letter that barely contained his anger at these "deliberate lies." No, he had never said any such thing, and as everyone knew, he shared the same views of the Constitution as did Justice Holmes. It had been "sufficiently trying" during the hearings "to have lies and misrepresentations spread in regard to me without the opportunity of being heard by the Committee and the public, but to have these lies circulated privately after the hearings are closed seems to me not in accord with American conceptions of fair play." Gregory took the letter to Senator Thomas Walsh, a Brandeis backer on the Judiciary Committee, who made sure it reached the right people.

By April, Brandeis, despite his close involvement in the struggle, had grown very frustrated. He had never before been engaged in a fight, especially one involving him so intimately, in which he had to remain publicly silent while others bore the burden of defending him. He had wanted to carry the attack to his detractors from the start, but Nutter and others had argued that it would merely serve as an excuse for greater and more virulent assaults on him. Brandeis had years earlier declared that "the man with the hatchet is the only one who has a chance of winning in the end," and he characterized the approach suggested by Nutter and others as "apologetic." His lieutenants in the press, especially Hapgood and the *New Republic* editors, did go on the attack for him, but he wanted to rally the progressives and make it into a fight between the forces of reform and those of reaction. He gave in only because Gregory, speaking for the administration, insisted that the battle had to be won politically. The episode over his alleged disbelief in the Constitution angered him immensely, and he told McClennen that he had strong misgivings that "the course pursued by my friends, and among other things, the delays are not only unwise but perilous." After the battle he indicated that the worst aspect for him had been the absence of strong protests against these character slurs from those who supported him.

ON MONDAY, 3 APRIL, the subcommittee announced that it had approved the nomination 3–2. All three Democrats voted for Brandeis, while the two Republicans voted against. Senators Chilton and

Fletcher signed the majority report, concurred in separately by Senator Walsh, while both Works and Cummins submitted lengthy and strongly worded reports opposing confirmation. Chilton went over the charges against Brandeis and provided the reasons the majority had not found them convincing; Works and Cummins, on the other hand, viewed the charges as credible and the rebuttals inadequate. Senator Walsh, however, put his finger on the heart of the case against Brandeis: "The real crime of which this man is guilty is that he has exposed the inequities of men in high places in our financial system. He has not stood in awe of the majesty of wealth. . . . He has been an iconoclast. He has written about and expressed views on 'social justice.' . . . [He believes] that a man's a man and not a machine." In a direct gibe at the established bar, whose leaders had criticized Brandeis for serving without pay, Walsh declared, "If this is professional misconduct then the bar needs regeneration."

After nearly two months of hearings, a person reading the reports would not know more about Louis Brandeis's fitness to be a justice than when the testimony had begun, and partisans on either side would not have changed their minds. If anything, the nomination had become even more controversial, but the subcommittee vote provided the first sign to Brandeis's supporters that he would be confirmed.

The drama now moved to the full Judiciary Committee, made up of ten Democrats and eight Republicans. The chair of the committee, Charles Culberson, had served in the Senate for three terms, but the once vigorous Texan now suffered from a form of Parkinson's disease; his hands shook almost constantly, and he had trouble speaking. While his mind remained acute, Culberson realized that he would have a heavy fight on his hands, and he doubted whether he had the strength to carry the administration's side. Much to Brandeis's discomfort, nothing seemed to happen for the next month.

Senators on both sides had reason to delay, and on many days so many members of the Judiciary Committee were out of town that there would not have been a quorum to convene. Insurgent Republicans, who might have favored Brandeis from the perspective of their reform inclinations, had no safe haven. The Progressive Party no longer existed, and men like Works and Cummins knew that their future power in the Senate relied on the goodwill of the Republican Party leaders, especially if the GOP should regain control of the upper chamber. Regular Republicans opposed Brandeis, but now with the Seventeenth Amendment in place they could no longer rely on being returned to the Senate by friendly state legislatures. They would have to seek votes, and they understood that Brandeis enjoyed considerable public popularity.*

Rumors flew about who supported the appointment and who opposed it, and as McClennen told Brandeis, "I take the favorable ones for recreation and the unfavorable as the basis for action."

Conservative Democrats who opposed Brandeis faced a different dilemma. Southerners in the then-one-party South did not have to worry about reelection. The party nomination ensured an easy victory in the general election, and Brandeis was far less a hero in the South than in the northern states. But they also understood Wilson's strategy and knew that if they voted against confirmation, the White House might be in Republican hands, and they would once again be in the minority after November.

Republicans and Democrats alike dallied until Gregory advised the president that the time had come for him to act. The attorney general arranged for Senator Culberson to write to Wilson. Normally, Culberson told the president, when a nomination goes to the Senate, the Justice Department provides all papers relating to the person, thus giving the Senate some insight as to why that man had been selected. But apparently the department had no papers in its files relating to Brandeis, and so Culberson would like the president to explain his choice.

Wilson wrote back the same day, praising Louis Brandeis at length. Appointments to the high court constituted one of the most important duties of a president, and he had named Brandeis "because I knew him to be singularly qualified by learning, by gifts, and by character for the

---

*According to Henry Morgenthau, who had just stepped down as American ambassador to Turkey, he and Brandeis met on 1 April 1916 to discuss the question of transferring additional sums to the Palestinian colonies. The two men's schedules had been so tight that the only time and place that gave them some time to talk was while they both changed trains in New London, Connecticut. Morgenthau told Brandeis that he thought the Senate would confirm him, but that immediately after taking his seat, he should declare himself a candidate against Henry Cabot Lodge for the U.S. Senate from Massachusetts. Morgenthau believed that Brandeis could easily defeat Lodge and, in doing so, would help carry the state for Wilson in the fall election.

Brandeis turned Morgenthau's suggestion down. "Brandeis was obviously afraid to act on my recommendation," Morgenthau later wrote. "He said it would be 'undignified' for him to run for office while holding a seat on the Supreme Bench." Morgenthau believed that the Senate would have been a better place for Brandeis to have exercised his great abilities than the "quasi-cloistered obscurity of the Supreme Court."

position." As to the many accusations that had been leveled against Brandeis in the previous months, the report of the subcommittee "has already made it plain to you and to the country at large how unfounded those charges were." Indeed, they threw more light on the character and motives of those who had maligned the nominee than on Brandeis himself. No one who knew Brandeis could believe those allegations, and Wilson knew him.

"I have tested him by seeking his advice upon some of the most difficult and perplexing public questions about which it was necessary for me to form a judgment. I have dealt with him in matters where nice questions of honor and fair play, as well as large questions of justice and the public benefit, were involved." In every test, the president declared, he had received from him "counsel singularly enlightening, singularly clear-sighted and judicial, and, above all, full of moral stimulation." Wilson did not bother answering specific charges, but did take a swipe at Brandeis's attackers by noting that he had consulted men whose integrity he trusted, and that all had endorsed Brandeis's qualifications.

In sum, Wilson told Culberson, he had chosen Brandeis because he knew no one more qualified, no one more committed to the public good, and no one "more imbued to the very heart with our American ideals of justice and equality of opportunity; of his knowledge of modern economic conditions and of the way they bear on the masses of the people. . . . This friend of justice and of men will ornament the high court of which we are all so justly proud."

Culberson immediately released Wilson's letter to the press, and Gregory's strategy, to make this a matter of party discipline, picked up steam. Brandeis's friends inundated members of the Judiciary Committee with letters urging confirmation. And in Boston, George Anderson and William Hitz imposed on Charles W. Eliot, the venerated former president of Harvard, to write a letter, and Eliot said all one could hope for. He had known Brandeis more than forty years, since his law school days, and his professional career had exhibited all the fine qualities of his youth—"a keen intelligence, quick and generous sympathies . . . and a character in which gentleness, courage, and joy in combat were intimately blended." Eliot had never had cause to question Brandeis's honesty, and believed that the Senate's failure to confirm "would be a grave misfortune for the whole legal profession, the court, all American business, and the country." "Next to a letter from God," Ned McClennen told La Follette, "we have got the best."

One by one wavering Democrats fell into line, but it took time and pressure from the White House. In May, Brandeis finally had an opportunity to help his own cause. Two members of the Judiciary Committee, Hoke Smith of Georgia and James Reed of Missouri, both conservative and both reportedly opposed to the nomination, accepted invitations to meet Brandeis at a reception Norman Hapgood gave at his New York apartment on Sunday evening, 14 May. Smith had already told a reporter that he had been "greatly prejudiced against Mr. Brandeis when the appointment was first announced," and if he had had to vote that first day, he would have voted against confirmation. But both Smith and Reed, having seen the alleged devil in the flesh, announced their support.

Although Republicans still tried to derail the nomination, the unified Democrats now stood firm. On 24 May the Judiciary Committee, by a straight party vote of 10–8, approved the appointment in a meeting that lasted less than ten minutes. A week later the Senate went into executive session a little before 5:00 p.m. on 1 June, and a half hour later Vice President Thomas Marshall opened the doors to announce that Louis D. Brandeis had been confirmed to be an associate justice of the Supreme Court by a vote of 47–22. Only one Democrat, Francis Newlands of Nevada, voted against the appointment, while three Republicans, all insurgents, voted for Brandeis—Robert La Follette, George Norris of Nebraska, and Miles Poindexter of Washington. Wilson immediately signed the necessary documents and a few days later told a correspondent, "I never signed any commission with such satisfaction as I signed his."

THE VICTORY CHEERED the progressives as little else had done for several years, and reform journals and the Jewish press carried one article after another praising "Mr. Justice Brandeis." Jacob Schiff predicted that he would become "an adornment" to the bench, and called the confirmation "an honor to our people." The first telegram Brandeis received came from Felix Frankfurter and Harold Laski, a political science professor, "GREETINGS AND WHAT GREETINGS." Mailmen staggered under the weight of congratulatory letters that poured into the Boston office. One letter in particular deserves mention, because while confirmation had surely been a victory, reformers would now have to do battle without one of their strongest champions.

Although he had done all he could in the fight and had earnestly wanted to see Brandeis confirmed, Amos Pinchot told Brandeis, now that the battle had been won, he did not know whether to be sorry or to be glad:

Taking it all together, I don't think it is unfair to say that, for the last ten years, you have been the most vital and disturbing element in our public life. You have worked quietly, doing the unpopular things that reformers have talked or written about. You have made more trouble for injustice than any other man. The passing of your work, both light cavalry and heavy artillery, the knowledge that no longer, when a cause needs a great militant advocate, you will step forward as you have heretofore to fight the exploiters and debauchers of America's men, women and children, makes me feel pretty sad. As long as you were in private life, it seemed to me that, if any monstrous injustice should be attempted upon helpless people, they would not lack protection. You furnished to me personally, and to many people who are making the rather lonely fight against privilege, a kind of confidence that we will sorely miss.

Brandeis understood Pinchot's point because, as he told him, he had those same feelings when Wilson had offered the nomination. He had felt bound to accept, even though he knew the losses a seat on the Court entailed. But "the doubts which I originally felt have been largely removed by the efforts of those who sought to defeat confirmation; and the responses which came from those less favored by fortune. The struggle was certainly worth while. It has defined the issues." And, he added, he hoped he could render service "of real value" while on the bench.

From all reports the calmest man in the country during this time may have been Brandeis himself. The day after the vote he left his home in Dedham at the same time he usually did and caught the 8:15 train into Boston. To fellow passengers, trainmen, and people who stopped him on the way from the station to his office to offer congratulations, he simply said, "Thank you." At the office he found two telegrams that must have touched him greatly. One, from Attorney General Thomas Gregory, urged Brandeis to come to Washington over the weekend so he could be sworn in on Monday morning, a suggestion to which Brandeis responded with alacrity. The other came from his longtime friend and now-colleague, Oliver Wendell Holmes, and had but one word: "WELCOME."

CHAPTER NINETEEN
SETTLING IN

It takes three or four years," Brandeis told Felix Frankfurter, "to find oneself easily in the movements of the Court . . . and it went hard with me." A new justice had to learn to hear and decide cases, write opinions, and also figure out the interpersonal dynamics of the Court; he had to determine when to enter a written dissent and when to simply note disagreement. For Brandeis the hardest thing seems to have been adjusting to a schedule determined by others, "the confinement of work—always have to be there and seven days a week," rather than the freedom he had long enjoyed to make his own schedule. Despite his disclaimer, Brandeis seems to have adjusted quickly to the routine of the Court's work. Within his first few terms on the bench he developed his own style and began to carve out the niche he would occupy for the next twenty-three years—a voice of judicial restraint, deference to legislative policy choices, and a fierce protectiveness of individual rights, especially speech. During this time he also maintained a level of extrajudicial activity that, by current standards of judicial ethics, would be either impermissible or at best questionable in judgment. In his first years on the high court, Louis Brandeis found himself very busy.

AT THE SUGGESTION of both Attorney General Thomas Gregory and Edward McClennen, Brandeis went down to Washington so he could be sworn in on the last day of the Court's term. McClennen had spoken with Chief Justice Edward Douglass White and with Holmes, who both urged this course. White told McClennen that a number of motions had to be considered and the work divided up among the justices before the Court stood down for its summer recess.

The courtroom in the former Senate chamber in the Capitol was

The Supreme Court in 1916. Seated from left: William R. Day, Joseph McKenna, Chief Justice Edward D. White, Oliver Wendell Holmes Jr., Willis Van Devanter; standing from left: Louis D. Brandeis, Mahlon Pitney, James C. McReynolds, John H. Clarke.

jammed with spectators and well-wishers on Monday, 5 June 1916. Alice, Susan, and Elizabeth sat in the reserved seats. Alfred came from Louisville, and Pauline Goldmark from New York. George W. Anderson, who had helped steer the nomination through the subcommittee, sat there, along with a number of other old friends. A little before noon, a visibly nervous Louis Brandeis, Bible in hand, walked across the corridor from the cloaking room to the courtroom, and Chief Justice White administered the oath of office.

Normally, Brandeis would have been the junior justice for at least a term or two, but five days after he took the oath and the Court recessed for the summer, Charles Evans Hughes resigned to seek the Republican nomination for the presidency. To replace him, Wilson named John H. Clarke, a former Ohio railroad lawyer and federal judge known for his progressive views. Brandeis may have known of him, since for many years Clarke's law partner had been William E. Cushing, Brandeis's friend from his Harvard Law days. Clarke, upon his nomination, wrote to Brandeis that he looked forward to working with him because of the "community point of view between us." Moreover, if Brandeis thought half as well of Cushing as Cushing did of him, "there should be a basis for more than formally pleasant relations between you and me." The two men did, indeed, get along well, and Robert La Follette attended a dinner at the Brandeis apartment in December 1916 where he met Clarke for the first time. "He is sincere and modest," he told Belle, "but sure he and Brandeis love each other, and it is a great thing [for Wilson] to have put two such men on the bench." Clarke regularly voted with Brandeis and Holmes, but in 1922 he resigned from the Court to promote American participation in the League of Nations. Had Clarke, who lived until 1945, not left the bench to be replaced with the arch-conservative George Sutherland, the entire constitutional history of the 1920s and 1930s might have been very different.

Over the summer of 1916, Louis and Alice made plans to give up their Boston home and move to Washington. Belle La Follette took it on herself to search for suitable lodgings; the Brandeises wanted a comfortable but not ostentatious building, one in which they could rent two apartments, a larger one in which they would live and a smaller one of two rooms for Louis's office. The justice used the larger and lighter room for his study, while his law clerk had the smaller room. (Until the opening of the current Supreme Court Building in 1935, the justices did not have official offices, but either worked out of their homes or made arrangements for separate space as Brandeis did. Even after the new building opened, Brandeis refused to use the suite of offices assigned to him, considering the edifice far too pretentious for his taste.)

Belle found them just what they needed in Stoneleigh Court, an apartment hotel on Connecticut Avenue; it had the right configuration of rooms, although the dining room had a poor reputation. As compensation, it was little more than a block from where Justice Holmes lived at 1720 I Street, and in good weather the two men would walk together to the Capitol. In addition, the building had some smaller apartments that it rented out by the day or week, and the Brandeises would use them to house visiting family or friends. They immediately left the Stoneleigh in 1926, however, when the management made "improvements" and put in shops on the first floor!

Brandeis moved quickly to make the adjustments he deemed necessary for his new life. The day after his confirmation he dissolved the firm of Brandeis, Dunbar & Nutter, and the new letterhead read "Dunbar, Nutter & McClennen." Brandeis continued to take money out of

Louis and Alice in buggy in Washington, D.C., 1921

the firm, representing payments for work he had earlier done. In 1917 he received more than $27,000, but this quickly tapered off to $2,700 in 1918; he received his last payment from the firm in 1924, $642. He kept a checking account at the Merchants National Bank of Boston, which he used primarily for small expenditures. His gifts and payments to his family continued to be handled by Louise Malloch, who made sure that his taxes were paid on time and that income from bonds got reinvested. She also looked after various mortgages, took care of renting a summer place, and handled his frequent requests for information about his portfolio. For this he paid the firm an annual fee and also made occasional gifts to Miss Malloch. At the time of his appointment his investments totaled more than $2 million, and during his years on the bench his annual income, consisting of his salary as a justice and income from his portfolio, ranged from a low of $108,000 his first year to $144,000 in 1928. In the 1930s, with the country sunk into the worst depression in its history, Brandeis's conservative investment policy paid off handsomely, as his annual income from his portfolio averaged around $120,000.

He resigned from the garment workers' arbitration panels and the numerous reform organizations to which he belonged, but maintained his connection with the Harvard Law School Alumni Association and with the Zionists. Although many people expected that he would take his longtime secretary, Alice Grady, with him, he decided that his only assistant would be a law clerk. Miss Grady eventually left the firm to become deputy commissioner of savings bank life insurance, and Brandeis continued to work closely with her on the program for the rest of her life. For many years he would stop off in Boston on his way between Washington and Cape Cod, and would turn up at the firm's offices to greet old friends and use the conference room to meet his visitors.

Brandeis had invested conservatively, but his portfolio included a large number of railroad bonds, and he worried whether this might disqualify him from hearing the many cases that came to the Court each year involving railroads. He had met with Chief Justice White the morning of his investiture, and the two men had ridden down to the Capitol together. On the ride Brandeis had asked White if he foresaw any problems. White said he did not, but Brandeis wanted some reassurance and on 29 June wrote a long letter to White explaining that he had, over the years, invested "in what were believed to be absolutely safe investments intended to be permanent and yielding a low rate of return." The management of these investments had been given over to the direction of others, and he wanted to continue that practice while on the Court. He had treated his property "like a highly conservative trust estate," and while he did not want to hold anything that might disqualify him from hearing a case, he did not really see how he could change his portfolio to reduce that danger lower than it already was. White wrote back that he fully agreed with Brandeis's view and that he saw no problem with the investments that would affect the work of the Court.

JUSTICE HORACE GRAY hired the first law clerk at the Supreme Court in 1882, a recent graduate of Harvard Law School; Gray had begun the practice when chief judge of the Massachusetts high court, and Louis Brandeis had been one of his clerks. Gray and the other justices who used clerks paid for them out of their own pockets until 1922, when Congress allowed each justice to hire one clerk at an annual salary of $3,600; two years later Congress made law clerk positions at the Court permanent.

Gray relied on his half brother, the Harvard Law professor John Chipman Gray, to choose the clerks for him, and when Oliver Wendell Holmes took Gray's seat on the bench, he continued the arrangement. After John Gray retired, Felix Frankfurter chose the clerks for Holmes, and Brandeis asked Frankfurter to do the same for him. The first man Frankfurter sent down from Harvard, Calvert Magruder, stayed one year; the next two, William A. Sutherland and Dean Acheson, remained for two terms, and the rest of the clerks served one year apiece. It has long been thought that Brandeis, like Holmes, took Frankfurter's students sight unseen. As for choosing the man, "I shall leave your discretion to act untrammeled," he told Frankfurter. "Wealth, ancestry, and marriage, of course, create presumptions; but they may be overcome."

Brandeis used his experience as Gray's assistant as a template for what he expected from his own clerks. They served primarily as research assistants, checking points of

Dean Acheson, Brandeis's law clerk from 1919 to 1921

law and earlier cases but above all providing him with the massive amounts of factual material that he utilized in his opinions, especially his dissents. He did not expect them to write his opinions and would have been appalled at the practice adopted by many later justices of assigning clerks to draft decisions. He assumed, however, that they would be accurate and discreet. When Paul A. Freund met the justice at the start of the 1932 term, the first words Brandeis said to him were: "Here you shall see a good deal and hear a good deal that is highly confidential. There have been no leaks from this office in the past, and I mean that there shall be none in the future." During the term some of the clerks would occasionally get together for dinner, just to trade news and gossip. The most popular clerks at these dinners were from Harlan Fiske Stone's chambers, because Stone loved to tell his clerks stories of what was going on. Brandeis's clerks, on the other hand, could contribute nothing, because he never spoke to them about what occurred in conference. He told Louis Jaffe, his clerk for 1933–1934, that he was never to let anyone know what they were working on, not even the clerks of the other justices. But, he added slyly, "of course you can listen to what they tell you about their Justices."

Above all, Brandeis demanded the highest quality of work from his clerks. Magruder, a scion of southern gentility, had heard stories of

Brandeis's legendary intellect and work habits and, when he met Brandeis for the first time, found all of the stories to be true. "It was a bit disconcerting to see how he eschewed all frivolity," he recalled, "and sought to make every minute count for something worthwhile." When it came time to turn in his first research memo to the justice, Magruder had a minor anxiety attack. "I can't recall ever having been the victim of such terror as L.D.B. caused me at first. The earliest memorandum handed in—well, my hand very nearly shook the words off the paper as I placed it on his desk." The work evidently was satisfactory, and Brandeis told Frankfurter, "Magruder is proving very helpful, and I have added faith in your picking." Although he gave Magruder only qualified praise in a letter of recommendation, he later told Frankfurter, "Among all my law clerks, Magruder was the best critic I had." Graham Claytor said that Brandeis did not feel tied to his opinions and always welcomed suggestions for improvement, and Dean Acheson reportedly had "very heated discussions" with the justice. Just as Gray had expected his clerks to question and thus refine his arguments, Brandeis expected the same of the young men who came to him.

He also expected that in going over his work, they would check for accuracy, especially in the draft that would go out to his fellow justices for comment. After reading it, each of the other justices would send his "return" indicating whether he agreed or disagreed, and any comments on particular points. James Landis, later to be dean of Harvard Law School and chairman of the Securities and Exchange Commission, served as Brandeis's clerk in 1925–1926. He was with Brandeis in his study when Holmes's messenger brought back a return pointing to an obvious proof error. A few minutes later Justice Pierce Butler's return came, with a note regarding an incorrect citation. The justice turned to Landis and asked him if he had ever heard the story of the employee of the Bank of London who when asked by his manager what two and two equaled unhesitatingly said four. The justice then did the same as the bank manager, took out a piece of paper, wrote 2 and 2, drew a line, and then wrote 4.

Brandeis then turned to another opinion that Landis had been working on, and asked whether he had checked to make sure that two statements of fact were indeed correct. Landis had not, assuming that Brandeis would be right. "Sonny, we are in this together," Brandeis said. "You must never assume that I know everything or that I am even correct in what I may say. That is why you are here. Don't let's have it happen again." The worst of it, however, came after Landis went to check out one of the facts and discovered that while it was not entirely wrong, correcting it opened a whole new chain of cases and arguments that he had ignored. He had also made the mistake of supposing that when Brandeis gave him an assignment, it was always a rush order. He now knew that it was never so. The justice wanted accuracy and completeness, and he expected his clerk to take as long as necessary to get it right.

In the prohibition case of *Jacob Ruppert v. Caffey,* the brewer claimed that his beer, which contained 3.4 percent alcohol (well above the Volstead Act limit), was not intoxicating. Neither the lower court nor the Court accepted this contention, and Brandeis decided to dismiss this argument by burying it under pages of footnotes, all of them citing legislation and state court decisions that regulation of intoxicating beverages could not be made effective if it had to depend upon whether or not a particular liquor would cause drunkenness. Dean Acheson had the responsibility for looking up all the statutes and decisions, and he decided to attend Court on the Monday the case was scheduled to come down. While the other justices read their opinions, a page kept bringing Brandeis volume after volume of case reports, and when Chief Justice White nodded at him, Brandeis shook his head, indicating the opinion had to be held over. Acheson realized something "was very wrong" and immediately headed back to the justice's study. When Brandeis came in, he put two volumes of state reports on the desk. "Did you read all of the cases cited in the footnotes?" he asked. Acheson said that he had. "Suppose you read these two again." The cases had no bearing on the argument and had slipped in from digests that Acheson had used to organize the notes. He went in to apologize, and Brandeis dismissed the matter with one sentence: "Please remember that your function is to correct my errors, not to introduce errors of your own." Many of the clerks reported how they had made some error early in their tenures and how Brandeis had never chastised them; one wrote, "I have the best judge in the land to correct my errors, and . . . fortunately for me he is also the gentlest and kindest of men." None of them, apparently, sinned more than once.

Once clerks had proved that they could do the work, the justice showed himself quite receptive to their ideas, and as Landis described it, "He took you in, substantially as a junior partner of his firm." When a clerk raised what Brandeis considered a legitimate argument, he willingly delayed circulating or even handing down an opinion until the two of them came to some settlement. If they could not agree, the clerk understood that the ultimate responsibility lay with the man in the robe. Paul Freund said that the justice would treat a memorandum from his clerk as a working draft of the opinion and subject it to the same treatment as his own early drafts, namely, tear it apart. Occasionally a clerk might recognize a sentence or two from his memo in the final opinion.

Brandeis also expected his clerks to take the initiative when they had an assignment and not just look at the direct cases and facts involved but find whatever might be necessary so that he could write with the assurance that all he needed was at hand. This research took place before the computer age, when a legal researcher can use LexisNexis and Google and instantly have all the citations on the screen. His clerks had to do it the old-fashioned way, going to the law library and using the decennial digests for state and federal case citations, and other tools for statutes. They called government offices to get reports or copies of hearings, kept track of articles appearing in law reviews, and when they spotted a title that might be relevant immediately sent for a copy. Some used typewriters and others wrote by hand, but their research memoranda often ran for dozens of pages. One clerk apologized after he submitted six pages when the justice had asked for a brief memorandum, and promised that in the future he would "try to think more and write less." There is little doubt that Brandeis read all of it. In the *Southwestern Bell* case, in which Brandeis's dissent pointed to a new way of evaluating rate decisions, William F. McCurdy prepared a research memorandum on how different state agencies assessed relevant costs that ran more than two hundred pages, complete with charts.

Until his last few terms, Brandeis did not use his clerks to read the certiorari petitions filed with the Court asking for review of lower-court decisions. Some members of the Court had their clerks go through the hundreds of requests, writing up brief memos on those that seemed to warrant further scrutiny and indicating those that should be dismissed for lack of merit. This practice became more widespread in the 1950s and 1960s, when the number of petitions grew into the thousands. In 1972, Chief Justice Warren Burger began the "cert pool," in which several justices had their clerks divide up the flood of petitions and write one "pool memo." Brandeis read each and every one of the petitions himself, believing that he, and not the clerks, had the responsibility for deciding which cases should go on the Court's docket. He had been appointed to the bench, not they. He did not, however, spend a great deal of time on this chore. Unless the petitioner could make out a clear and convincing case why the Court should accept the case for review, Brandeis tossed it into the "dismissed" pile.

In reading over the memoirs written by some of the clerks, and having spoken to several of them, I am struck by the overwhelming sentiment of enormous respect. Many of them considered Brandeis the greatest man they had ever met, as well as perhaps the greatest justice of his time. James Landis said that his year with Brandeis was the best of his life, a view shared by several others. After their year in Washington many stayed in touch, sent him copies of their writings, and stopped by to see him on the Cape or in Washington. Each of them had his own stories of how hard the justice worked, the high standards he set, and how each felt challenged to meet his demands.

Several of them told a variation of how they worked through the night preparing a research memorandum, how they then would go up to Brandeis's study at five or six in the morning to slide their report under the door, only to feel it being pulled through from the other side. By the time Paul Freund came in 1932, a sort of tradition had grown among the Brandeis clerks, each one of them claiming to have had this experience. Freund said he fell into it as well, although the justice did not care if you worked all night, so long as you did a good job.

His clerks all admired Brandeis and perhaps even felt some affection for him, but he never tried to cultivate the close relations that Holmes, Frankfurter, and later William Brennan enjoyed with their clerks. Holmes looked on his clerks as surrogate sons and used them for all sorts of things besides research, such

Old Supreme Court Library

as pouring drinks and reading to him. Frankfurter's clerks adored him and would not tolerate criticism of him. As one clerk told me, to be with Frankfurter for one year meant being in love with him for life. Walter Gellhorn, who clerked for Stone in 1931, thought Brandeis was "very aloof" from his clerks personally; they had come to work for him, and he was all business. Nathaniel Nathanson, who clerked for Julian Mack before going to Brandeis, found the difference between the two men somewhat jolting. Whereas Mack went out of his way to be cordial and friendly to his clerks, Brandeis "did not immediately clasp his law clerk to his bosom as a member of the family. On the contrary, he seemed to keep personal relations at a minimum."* The Brandeises, however, often invited his clerks to the dinners they gave so that the young men could meet and learn from their guests.

Brandeis expected good work, and when he got it, as Acheson noted, he "was not given to praise in any form." He treated his clerks as adults and left them on their own to do their job; he called them by their last names and was not at all paternal. Robert Page, who clerked for Brandeis in 1926–1927, had gone to a formal party one night in white tie and tails and then, still awake at four in the morning, decided to go to the office to finish an assignment. About 5:30, Brandeis walked in, saw Page in his finery, and said, "Good morning, Page," as if it were the most natural thing in the world. Nathaniel Nathanson, who clerked in 1934–1935, mustered up the courage after several months to ask the justice if he could take a weekend off to go to New York. He received the permission, and when he returned to work on Monday morning, Brandeis greeted him with "Well, sir, have you quite recovered from your debauch?" Nathanson assured him that he had.

The justice had trouble with only one clerk sent down from Harvard—Irving Goldsmith. "It looks at the moment as if Goldsmith would prove himself impossible," Brandeis wrote to Frankfurter, "and that soon. I spoke to him frankly yesterday after the second grave offense." Brandeis had told him to report to work at 9:00 each morning, he had not shown up until noon, and Brandeis had been unable to reach him at his hotel. Goldsmith had apologized, claiming that he had

---

*Brandeis did, however, go out of his way to meet the Holmes clerks, also sent down from Harvard Law by Felix Frankfurter. In part this was a way that Brandeis looked after his friend as Holmes grew older. When Holmes retired from the Court, Brandeis told Frankfurter to keep sending a clerk; now that Fannie Holmes had died, Holmes needed companionship.

food poisoning and that the hotel clerk had failed to wake him; he promised he would buy an alarm clock. Two days later he again failed to show up before Brandeis left for the Saturday afternoon conference, even though the justice had told him that specific work had to be done before that meeting. Brandeis also suspected that Goldsmith had bad habits, "the victim of drink or worse vices."

On receipt a distraught Frankfurter immediately offered to send another man, Harry Shulman, then a research fellow at Harvard, who would, in fact, be Brandeis's clerk the next term. As it happened, Frankfurter's telegram had gone to the Court, and the marshal had called Brandeis's office. Goldsmith had gone down to get it and, seeing the contents, had become very upset, promising Brandeis he would reform and would never be late again, and that all of the work would be done. As Brandeis told Frankfurter, had he seen the telegram first, he would have agreed to take Shulman, but "making the change would be a severe blow to G. and might impair his future success for an appreciable time." So he sat Goldsmith down and made quite clear to him what he expected and the standards involved, and wanted to know if the young man could work at this level. Goldsmith, Brandeis told Frankfurter, "has certainly had the scare of his life and seems determined to make good." But "it is a comfort to think of Shulman as a possible reserve." Goldsmith managed to shape up, and if not the best clerk Brandeis had, the justice sent no more complaints to Frankfurter.

Of all the clerks, only one had reservations about his time with Brandeis. David Riesman went down to Washington and met briefly with Holmes, Brandeis, and Benjamin Nathan Cardozo, and then contacted Frankfurter, telling him that he would much rather clerk for Cardozo than for someone who reminded him of his stern father. Frankfurter insisted that this was precisely the reason that Riesman should take the position with Brandeis. The justice and his new clerk did not hit it off well, when at their first meeting Riesman told Brandeis that he thought Zionism was nothing more than Jewish fascism. After a moment of silence the jurist said he would not discuss the matter because Riesman had no understanding of history. Riesman, who remained critical of Brandeis, later said that he thought he had let the justice down and felt guilty about it. "I always had the impression that Freund and the other clerks had done so much for him, and I didn't feel like I made a real contribution."

When Riesman finished his year, he incurred the justice's displeasure because he chose to go back to Boston and work for a law firm. Whatever their differences, Brandeis recognized Riesman's intellectual talents and wanted him to use them to benefit the less fortunate. "The fact that I had friends in Boston," Riesman told an interviewer, "and season tickets to the Boston Symphony was totally frivolous and unworthy of consideration." Nonetheless, although Riesman thought Brandeis less than responsive to the needs of his clerks, at the end of the year he wrote to Frankfurter that he considered Brandeis the ideal judge, and "I have made his character a test of my own. . . . His severe self limitations will grapple with me throughout life." In the end, Riesman did return to Boston, but not in private practice. He taught at the University of Buffalo Law School and founded a program to place academics fleeing from Hitler in American universities (to which Brandeis donated funds). He became interested in sociology and wrote one of the most influential books about American society after the war, *The Lonely Crowd* (1950). He then returned to Harvard, which created a special chair for him in social sciences. The justice would have been pleased.

In 1936 some of his clerks thought they might arrange a dinner with all his former clerks to mark his twenty years on the Court. They went to Mrs. Brandeis to see what she thought of it, and she immediately squelched the idea. She said the justice would not like it, and would not want them to spend their money that way. He would much prefer it, she said, "if each of us would sit down and write the Justice a letter telling him what we had been doing for the advancement of mankind." As Calvert Magruder noted, "Since most of us couldn't think of anything we had done for mankind, the suggestion fell through!"

That speaks more for modesty on the part of the clerks, since nearly all of them went on to become distinguished lawyers, judges, government officials, and law professors. Dean Acheson held a variety of high-ranking jobs in the government, eventually becoming secretary of state in the Truman administration. James Landis helped to create and then chaired the Securities and Exchange Commission. Calvert Magruder and Henry Friendly became judges on U.S. courts of appeals. Graham Claytor served as secretary of the navy under President Carter and then came out of retirement to head Amtrak.

While Brandeis did not insist that his clerks go into teaching, there is no question that it gave him great satisfaction when they did. Four of them went back to Harvard, including James Landis, who became the youngest dean in the school's history. But Brandeis derived even greater pleasure when they went elsewhere, and his clerks taught at Wisconsin, Yale, Buffalo, Northwestern, and Chicago. Whenever they sought his advice, he suggested they not go to the big cities like New York and Chicago, where a wealth of talent already existed. They should practice or teach in smaller places, which needed them more. When he found out that more than half his clerks had gone into teaching, he remarked with great satisfaction, "Now I have a majority."

One other person played a key role in the smooth operation of Justice Brandeis's chambers: his messenger, Edward Poindexter. In those days every justice had a messenger, and since they worked out of their homes, these men played an important role in bringing mail, briefs, and case files from the clerk's office to the justice, going to the Library of Congress to fetch books, and often assisting in social events. Poindexter became invaluable to Alice once she and the justice began entertaining regularly. Unlike the clerks, Poindexter did not seem to hold Brandeis in awe.

Warner Gardner, who clerked for Harlan Fiske Stone in the 1934 term, recalled that he used to run into Poindexter occasionally at a drugstore, where the elderly black man would take some time for himself. Gardner learned that Brandeis was insistent that his mail be picked up and brought promptly to his home after both the morning and the afternoon deliveries to the Court. Poindexter had decided that nothing terrible would happen to the world or to him if, after picking up the morning mail, he divided it in halves, and delivered one half in the morning and the other in the afternoon.

IN WRITING HIS OPINIONS, Brandeis adopted the same methods he had used as a lawyer. Once he had been assigned a case, he sat down and, using an old-fashioned fountain pen, wrote out in longhand on a yellow legal-size pad the nub of the case, the question posed, the Court's decision, and the rationale. This rarely took more than a page and a half. Because he did not employ a typist, Brandeis sent the handwritten draft to the Court's printer, who would have two typeset proof copies ready the following morning. Edward Poindexter would deliver the drafts and pick up the proofs. The clerk would take one set, go over it for typographical errors, and mark any queries he had for the justice.

Brandeis would then begin revising and expanding the opinion. One of the most tedious parts of this work involved the statement of facts, a task that many justices then and now assigned to their clerks. Brandeis did it himself, because he believed that he could not properly comprehend the legal aspects of a controversy unless he fully understood the facts, a view that had been basic to him since his first years in practice.

He also assumed that if he could convince people who disagreed with him about the correctness of his factual assertions, he would have a better chance of persuading them that he also had the proper legal argument. Once the clerk brought him the results of his research, Brandeis inserted what he needed into the text, often cutting up the research memo and pasting paragraphs in at the appropriate places. One has to admire the printer, not only for being able to read the justice's difficult handwriting, but also for being able to figure out from all the arrows and insertions and emendations just how Brandeis wanted to change the draft. When Brandeis finished with the latest iteration, off it would go to the printer, while the law clerk received a new round of research requests. As one of his clerks said, the old adage that genius is the capacity for taking infinite pains might well have been coined with Brandeis in mind. This process would be repeated through many drafts, in some cases as many as fifteen or twenty, each draft refining an argument, adding proofs, and citing new cases, government reports, and congressional hearings. In a revolutionary step, Brandeis became the first justice to cite a law review article.

Some of the justices found such materials disconcerting, and a few believed them unsuitable for inclusion in Supreme Court opinions, but Brandeis kept using them. Willard Hurst, who clerked for Brandeis in 1936, recalled how they employed law review notes for one opinion and played with the wording so as not to unduly upset the brethren. "Mr. Justice McReynolds," Brandeis remarked with a twinkle, "did not favor Law Review citations." Just as Brandeis had used all sorts of non-case materials in his *Muller* brief, so he utilized them in his Court opinions as well and continued the campaign begun many years earlier, to teach judges—in this case his colleagues on the Supreme Court—the facts of modern industrial life.

Brandeis wrote carefully, organizing his arguments in a logical sequence, buttressing them with facts. As Dean Acheson put it, "Very early in our association I awakened to the fact that the law library did not contain all the tools of our trade." He and all of the clerks spent much of their time at the Library of Congress looking up statistical reports, history books, and other sources. Brandeis instructed his clerks to look with suspicion on every fact until it was proved from the record or other sources, and to look with equal skepticism on every statement of law until they had exhausted all authorities. If his opinions were to provide lessons, they had to be exactly right on both fact and law.

Once satisfied that he had said everything that needed to be said, and

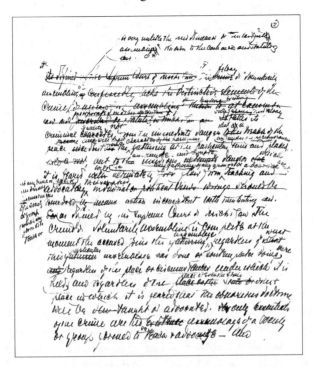

Work sheet for an opinion

in the right manner, he would send out copies to the other justices and await their returns. If he wrote for the majority, most of the time the returns said little more than "Yes" or "Fine" or "I agree." Holmes would be more enthusiastic, with "A sockdoger" or "I am in it with both feet." If one of the justices had a question, or a minor suggestion, Brandeis would make the necessary alteration. Then it would be sent back to the printer and to the clerk of the Court for distribution after the opinion had been announced from the bench.

Over the course of his nearly twenty-three terms, Brandeis wrote 454 opinions speaking for the Court. When he wrote the majority opinion, he recognized that he spoke for at least four others besides himself and so kept the rulings as narrow as possible, a trait that also fit well into his philosophy of judicial restraint. Although only a few of these became landmark decisions, such as his opinion in the *Erie* case, Justice Robert H. Jackson believed that some of Brandeis's lasting work came in these cases where he led the Court in interpreting what Jackson called "the great life-giving clauses of the Constitution," and also in pioneering new fields such as administrative law. Here Brandeis's work as an attorney played a very important role. During his career as a lawyer Brandeis had been "constructive, practical and bold" and honed the skills that would allow him to set up a new interpretation of law, marshal the facts, and set forth an interpretation of the law that commanded the majority.

He felt no such compunction when he wrote in dissent, and in his seventy-four dissents we find all of Brandeis's distinguishing characteristics—attention to the context in which a law had been passed, the factual situation that the legislature had relied on in enacting the law, the necessity for the judiciary to defer to the legislative branch in policy making, the attention to individual liberties, and especially the role that speech played in a democratic society. These lengthy dissents led Harold Laski to suggest to Holmes, "If you could hint to Brandeis that judicial opinions aren't to be written in the form of a brief it would be a great relief to the world." They are, however, legal briefs—Brandeis briefs written to explain to the bench, the bar, and the public why the majority had erred. Brandeis intended them to be convincing, and therefore they needed to be fact laden. But they also had to instruct, and a number of clerks reported a similar story. After justice and clerk had labored over a dozen or more versions of a dissent, Brandeis would then say, "Now I think the opinion is persuasive, but what can we do to make it more instructive."

When it comes to the art of judicial dissent, Brandeis is the acknowledged master. Holmes, perhaps the greatest stylist of the Court, often seemed more concerned with philosophy than with jurisprudence. William O. Douglas, who took Brandeis's seat on the Court in 1939, dissented often, frequently just to register his disagreement with the majority. He did not care if he won other justices over by his arguments, since, as he often put it, "the only soul I have to save is my own." Brandeis wrote to educate. He hoped to teach his brethren, but understood that success with them would be a rare thing. So he kept up collegial relations with them and worked on educating others, especially lawyers and teachers, on the necessity of relying on facts in constitutional interpretation.

This "teaching" is part of a constitutional dialogue, considered by many scholars to be an important function of the Court. Each time the Court is called upon to interpret a constitutional clause, it does so two ways. One is fact specific: What does the clause mean in terms of the case at hand? The other is more general, trying to tease out broader rules for the guidance of lower courts in the future. A dissent may be narrow, in that the justice believes the majority erred in the particular instance, or it may be broad, indicating disagreement with the larger principles. Dissents set up a marker to indicate that there might be something wrong with a decision, and to enunciate what the dissenter believed to be correct. Judges could then respond to that dissent, ignoring it, arguing with it, or adopting it, and they in turn espouse new ideas that may be open to future challenge. Brandeis said that he had great faith in time, and over the more than two decades he sat on the bench, he would see a number of his dissents adopted by the Court; in the years after his retirement and death, the Court came to accept almost all of his views.

Chief Justice John Roberts, in discussing the characteristics of influential justices, suggests that the ones who ranked highest in effectiveness were the "collegial pragmatists," the "secure justices who know who they are," "judges who show personal as well as judicial humility," "those who know when to hold their tongues," and "those who are aware of a case's practical effects." These judges ranked far higher than the self-centered players, the narcissists, the loose cannons, and the ideological purists. Although Roberts did not mention Brandeis by name, certainly he exemplified all of the traits on the first list. He had no need to dominate either the Court or his colleagues, and in many instances shaped the Court's majority to reflect his beliefs in the new jurisprudence that recognized the need to reconcile abstract principles of law with contemporary facts. Because of the heavily conservative makeup of the Court during the time he sat on it, he carefully chose those cases where he could make a statement that would teach, and there are few decisions in the Court's long history that provide as effective lessons as the Brandeis dissents. Modern scholars have consigned many of the conservative decisions of the 1920s and 1930s to footnotes, but they continue to study the Brandeis opinions and hail him as the master of judicial pragmatism.

Although Brandeis—legitimately—is often held up as the model of judicial restraint, this does not mean that he had no judicial philosophy. Judicial restraint, the idea that courts should defer to the legislative branch in policy choices, constituted a key part of his belief, and probably dated back to his law school days and friendship with James B. Thayer, who wrote extensively on the proper role of judges in interpreting the Constitution. Another aspect involved the role of facts in determining law, and Brandeis considered it axiomatic that since facts determined law, the law had to reflect the realities of contemporary life.

There is a great debate between those who subscribe to the notion of a living constitution, in which the meaning of constitutional powers and limits changes to reflect the needs of modern life, and those who advocate the original intent of the Framers as the fixed and unchanging meaning of every constitutional phrase. Champions of this latter view claim they practice judicial restraint, while judges who promote a living constitution are allegedly activists, writing their own ideas into law.

Brandeis would have found this distinction confusing at best and irrelevant at worst. In an early draft of a dissenting opinion in 1922 he wrote: "Our Constitution is not a strait-jacket. It is a living organism. As such it is capable of growth—of expansion and of adaptation to new conditions. Growth implies changes, political, economic and social. Growth which is significant manifests itself rather in intellectual and moral conceptions than in material things. Because our Constitution possesses the capacity for adaptation, it has endured as the fundamental law of an ever developing people." For Brandeis, throughout his career as a lawyer and as a judge, the original intent of the Framers had been to create an instrument that would change as the nation changed, but at all times relying on fixed and immutable moral values. This is, in many ways, a very conservative view.

ON 9 OCTOBER 1916, Brandeis dropped a note to his daughter Susan saying that he had just returned from the opening day of the term. Justice Clarke had been sworn in, many motions had been presented, and the first case had been scheduled for argument the following day. Then, he anticipated, there would be a "steady grind for the next eight months and more. The amount of work piled up is stupendous." He expected that he would be able to keep "Master Magruder fully occupied."

Part of his work that first term would include getting to know the eight men with whom he would sit and deliberate. He had met Chief Justice White before his swearing in, and like most people immediately liked him. A large man, White had a "bulky presence" that, according to one spectator, "broods over the whole courtroom." Originally appointed by Grover Cleveland in 1894 as an associate justice, he was the first person elevated to chief justice from within the Court. A polite and kindly man, he was remembered by Mrs. Joseph Lamar as "quite early Victorian in his courtesies." Brandeis thought he belonged to an even earlier age. White "had the grand manners," Brandeis told

Frankfurter, "and was of the eighteenth century." Brandeis had no illusions, however, about where White stood on the key issues coming before the Court. While not a reactionary, White had a profound respect for property rights and skepticism about reform.

Brandeis knew two of his colleagues fairly well. Oliver Wendell Holmes Jr. had sat on the federal bench since 1902, after two distinguished decades on the Supreme Judicial Court of Massachusetts. The two men had been friends ever since meeting shortly after Brandeis returned to Boston to begin practice with Sam Warren, and during the confirmation fight Brandeis had said that he had the same philosophy of the Constitution as did Justice Holmes. He and Holmes both agreed on the need for judicial restraint, and although the two men would become famous and the darlings of the liberals because of their dissents during the 1920s, in fact they differed significantly in their jurisprudence (see below, chapter 22).

James Clark McReynolds had been attorney general in the Wilson administration, but Brandeis had not realized at the time that McReynolds went so far beyond conservative as to be legitimately called a reactionary. Nor did Brandeis recognize at the time the depth of McReynolds's anti-Semitism. McReynolds detested Brandeis and later Benjamin Cardozo, and there is no official portrait of the Court in 1924 because McReynolds would not sit next to Brandeis as protocol required; when Brandeis retired in 1939, McReynolds refused to sign the traditional letter of farewell. He returned one of Holmes's dissenting opinions with the intimation that Brandeis had made him go wrong and then added a remark that the Lord had tried to make something out of the Hebrews for centuries, but finally gave up and turned them out to prey on mankind "like fleas on the dog." Often during conference McReynolds would ostentatiously get up and leave when Brandeis spoke, standing outside until Brandeis had finished and then returning.

For his part, Brandeis ignored McReynolds's crudity and tried to maintain at least a semblance of civility in the daily workings of the Court. He of course sent drafts of his opinions to McReynolds, who would sometimes send the return with an "OK" or a surly comment that he disagreed but would not bother to dissent. His clerks could remember only one or two times when Brandeis said anything about McReynolds, and then nothing spiteful. Even with Frankfurter he would not denigrate McReynolds, but said that he had an "extraordinary personality," that of a *Naturmensch,* a "child of nature" without cultivation, who could say cruel things to his colleagues, a "lonely person [with] few real friends." Brandeis seemed more upset over the fact that McReynolds did not do his work well, "is lazy, stays away from Court when he doesn't feel like coming," thereby forcing the Court to reschedule oral arguments. Holmes simply called him an irrational savage.

The rest, with the exception of Clarke, could be counted as conservative, but Brandeis enjoyed collegial relations with all of them except McReynolds. He particularly came to admire Willis Van Devanter, whose craftsmanship he greatly respected, a feeling apparently reciprocated. Brandeis compared Van Devanter to a "Jesuit general" in the suppleness of his mind and believed that during much of the 1920s the real leader of the Court was not Chief Justice Taft but Van Devanter, whose advice Taft sought constantly. When the Court divided, Brandeis would say that if he could convince Van Devanter, the opposition would collapse. Brandeis, like Taft, often sent drafts of his opinions to Van Devanter for comment before circulation. Brandeis also thought well of William Rufus Day, an admirer of William McKinley's who would give each justice a carnation on McKinley's birthday. As Brandeis came to know Day better, he realized that the man had intense feelings as well as a good mind, and that on some issues, such as labor unions, he could be a "hot little gent."

BRANDEIS HANDED DOWN his first opinion for the Court on 4 December 1916 in a case involving Iowa and Pennsylvania statutes requiring ice cream to contain a fixed percentage of butterfat. Although some of the conservatives might have grumbled, this case fell squarely into a series of precedents on the police power in which the courts had refused to second-guess the legislature on health matters. The decision—Chief Justice White scribbled on his return, "Yes. E.D.W. Very well done. Indeed fine!"—is a model of how Brandeis would write in the future. First came the statement of the facts of the case, including a definition of commercial ice cream, then a statement of the accepted law on the subject, the practice of the Court to defer to legislative judgments, and then the conclusion that the lower courts had been correct in upholding the laws—all in a little over three pages. During his first term Brandeis delivered the opinion of the Court in twenty-one cases, concurred in or dissented without opinion six times, and wrote two dissents, which, like his opinion in the ice cream case, also set the pattern for the future.

The Court at the time had established "reasonableness" as the criterion for judging the extent of power that Congress enjoyed under the Commerce Clause and the degree to which state laws might impinge on federal authority. But as some commentators pointed out, reasonableness could be a wild card, since its definition depended upon the subjective judgment of five members of the Court. The *Winfield* case showed how wild the card could be.

James Winfield had lost an eye while working for the New York Central in interstate commerce, in a true accident for which no negligence or blame could be ascribed; while tamping down a cross tie, he struck a pebble that bounced into his eye. He could not claim benefits under the Federal Employers' Liability Act, which required that negligence against the railroad had to be proved. So he applied for compensation under New York's workmen's compensation law, which considered railroad work by definition to be hazardous and required employers in hazardous fields to recompense injured workers according to a statutorily defined schedule. To collect under New York law, Winfield did not have to show negligence. The Court had unanimously upheld the New York law against a due process challenge earlier in the term. In the *Winfield* case the Court looked at the question of whether the New York statute could be applied where a federal law also operated but afforded no relief in a particular case.

In a decision marked by near-total disregard for the factual context, Justice Van Devanter, speaking for a 7–2 majority, declared that it had long been settled policy that when Congress acts on any subject, "all state laws covering the same field are necessarily superseded by reason of the supremacy of the national authority." As for Winfield's argument that Congress had not acted in those areas in which no negligence had occurred, Van Devanter admitted that there were conflicting state decisions, but the Court believed that the right rule is that in areas of interstate commerce, only the federal government should determine policy. He then went on to build up a case for the primacy of federal authority, an issue that had never really been in doubt.

Brandeis entered a sixteen-page dissent, nearly three times as long as the majority statement. He carefully filled in the background of the state and federal laws, where they overlapped (in which case federal power would govern), and, more important, the gaps in federal coverage that states had attempted to fill. Conceding that if in fact the federal and state laws intersected, then federal law governed, he set out three rules that the Court had established to make just this determination and then proceeded to show how the majority opinion had either ignored these rules or misconstrued them, all his points undergirded by massive documentation of prior cases as well as the history and purpose of the federal law. He then detailed the evils that the state law had attempted to remedy, and this made clear, he believed, that Congress had not "intended to deny to the states the power to provide for compensation or relief for injuries not covered by it." Rather than claiming the two laws were in conflict, a better argument would be that they stood in a complementary relationship to each other, each with well-defined and limited areas of responsibility.

Brandeis worked on the assumption that unless Congress specifically acted in a way to preclude state action, or indicated its policy to do so, the states should be free to act, and he provided a two-page list of cases in which the Court had adopted that position. Van Devanter's majority view is not intellectually wrong, and is direct—albeit more simplistic—in its assumption that the exercise of federal powers automatically precludes the states from entering the field, even if the law does not apply to the entire field. Brandeis believed that the majority did not understand that in a federal system, the recognition that federal powers exist did not automatically mean the curtailment of state authority. The *Winfield* case, he told Frankfurter, "laid me low." For Brandeis the majority's hairsplitting seemed deliberately ignorant of the fact that Winfield's type of injury had also not been covered.

Given the vagueness that often surrounds the so-called dormant Commerce Clause, and the ongoing debate over when and under what circumstances the exercise of federal power precludes state action, Brandeis's position is logical but, much as he may have thought it self-evident, not necessarily correct. The majority believed that unless Congress specifically created areas of exemption, exercise of a commerce power automatically excluded state action. Brandeis took the other view, that an exemption existed unless Congress definitely stated that it did not. Over the years Congress has on many occasions held that the provisions of a statute did not close the field to the states, but often it has failed to do so, and in such cases the view of the *Winfield* majority has prevailed.

IN HIS OTHER DISSENT of that first term, Brandeis's view would eventually triumph, but until the mid-1930s his remained the rather lonely minority position. Conservatives in the judiciary had, to some extent, accepted that legislatures could pass protective legislation, provided they could show a direct relation between the measure and the health, safety, or welfare of the worker. They had not, however, agreed to minimum-wage legislation, which, in their view, transgressed the limits of the police power and trenched upon the market in a way forbidden to the government. Moreover, maximum hours, abolition of child labor, and factory safety laws for many marked the limits that the government could go to in trying to regulate economic activities. Reformers, on the other hand, argued that in order to protect the citizenry, the state had the power to control any portion of the market that the legislature determined to be in the best interests of the people. *Adams v. Tanner,* announced on the last day of Brandeis's first term, illustrated this divide.

A Washington State law forbade employment agencies from accepting fees from those seeking work. A fee, however, could still be charged to an employer. Joe Adams, the owner of an employment agency, charged that this in effect would put him and all other agencies out of business, since collecting fees from employers would not work. Although the Court had over the years approved a number of state measures regulating various businesses and professions, Justice McReynolds, speaking for a five-man majority, accepted Adams's argument that the law did not regulate but prohibited employment agencies, and this deprived him of his property rights protected by the Fourteenth Amendment. "The statute is one of prohibition, not regulation," McReynolds declared. " 'You take my home when you do take the prop that doth sustain my house; you take my life when you do take the means whereby I live.' " The Court, he noted, had in the previous term agreed that employment agencies could be regulated in order to prevent exploitation of those seeking jobs, but it had never approved an outright ban. "The Fourteenth Amendment protects the citizen in his right to engage in any lawful business," and by denying Adams the right to engage in a calling that surely provided benefits to the community, Washington State had gone too far.

Brandeis, of course, had been defending this type of legislation for years, and he now submitted a Brandeis brief justifying the law and its relation to public welfare in the same way he had defended the Oregon hours law, and with the same purpose—to instruct the Court on the facts of industrial life. Working through draft after draft with Magruder, he amassed mountains of information on what other states had done, the abuses that poor workers suffered at the hands of the agencies, and why the remedy adopted by Washington State made perfectly good sense. Moreover, even if the majority correctly characterized the law as an abolition rather than as a regulation of agencies, the Court had not only in the past approved the prohibitory measures relating to alcohol but less than a year earlier sanctioned the banning of trading stamps. Clearly, the police power could prohibit as well as regulate. Constitutionally, the Court should be asking only whether the legislation could be characterized as arbitrary, unreasonable, or lacking any real and substantial relation to the objective.

To determine this, the Court should not rely on abstract logic, but "the judgment should be based upon a consideration of relevant facts, actual or possible—Ex facto jus oritur [Law must arise from facts]. That ancient rule must prevail in order that we may have a system of living law." The Court, therefore, had to inquire into the evil that the state wanted to mitigate, why this particular remedy had been adopted, and whether the remedy directly affected the problem. What the Court should not do, he pointedly reminded his brethren, is assess the wisdom of the legislation. Courts, unless faced with a clear violation of a constitutional prohibition, should defer to the legislative choice of remedy. Therefore, was the Washington statute, in the light of the relevant facts, so clearly arbitrary or so unreasonable as to violate the Fourteenth Amendment?

One can find this construct in a number of Brandeis's most important dissents over the next two decades. What are the facts the legislature took into account? Did the remedy address the evils? Could a reasonable person find the remedy arbitrary or unreasonable? If not, no matter what individual justices may have thought about the desirability of the legislation, they should defer to the legislative wisdom. Brandeis in his language and cadence thus "projected during this first year of his service the premise and the method of the generation of judges that would succeed him."

Brandeis worked feverishly at the opinion, marshaling his arguments and supporting them in extensive documentation. He cataloged the evils, especially conditions in Washington, looked at the remedy that had been proposed and how it addressed the problem, and showed how courts, including the Supreme Court, had in the past approved similar legislation—and rested it all on massive documentation. He even circulated his "memorandum" before McReynolds had a chance to send his opinion around, in the hope that he might win away a vote or two. He failed in this ploy, but Holmes and Clarke agreed with him enthusiastically. Holmes wrote on the return "Note me as agreeing with you vehemently," while Clarke assured him, "Only the Lord can so harden their heads as well as their hearts as to prevent their confessing their sin of ignorance."

Aside from the cases for which he wrote an opinion, Brandeis participated in the more than 150 decisions handed down by the Court during the term. He provided the fifth vote to sustain the Adamson Act establishing an eight-hour day on the nation's railroads. He joined the majority in upholding the Mann Act prohibiting the transportation of women across state lines for immoral purposes. Although he wrote only two dissents, he disagreed with the majority in a handful of other cases as well, but did not write. Unlike the modern Court, in which a dissent apparently requires an opinion, the Court Brandeis joined often had notations that one or more justices dissented but without an opinion. The justices recognized that at the time the Court's jurisdiction brought it many cases of a nonconstitutional nature, and given the workload of the Court and the fact that no one had more than one clerk, they husbanded their resources. Moreover, Brandeis believed that the Court should decide cases on the narrowest grounds possible, and so if the majority opinion did this, he saw no reason to enter a formal dissent. (After 1925, when Chief Justice Taft secured the Judges' Bill to give the Court greater control over its docket, the minor cases no longer had to be heard, and the Court became what it is today, a forum that hears cases involving the Constitution and questions of federal statutory interpretation.)

Toward the end of the term, the English political scientist Harold Laski, whom Frankfurter had introduced to Brandeis, wrote to congratulate him on his opinions. They seemed to breathe a "refreshing sense of newmindedness" into the Court, a "vivid feeling that it was alert to the readjustment which is characteristic of this age." All told, not a bad note to sum up the first term.

IN HIS SECOND TERM the pattern of the first repeated, although Brandeis disagreed with the majority more. He wrote twenty-two opinions for the Court, concurred once, recused himself in two cases, and dissented eleven times. One case in which he disqualified himself involved a former client whom he had served as counsel in the lower court, and the other involved the United Shoe Machinery Company, which he had attacked prior to his going on the bench. In dissenting, he wrote three opinions, joined in the dissents of others (usually Holmes and Clarke) six times, and disagreed in two cases without opinion.

The cases in which he wrote for the majority covered a wide range of topics, many of them of little importance to anyone except the litigants. They varied from water rights to sheep grazing on federal land, to a contract dispute involving $1,000. Only one of his majority opinions is particularly noteworthy, and that involved a gloss he put on the so-called rule of reason in antitrust cases.

The Chicago Board of Trade, the world's largest grain exchange, had established rules regarding when members could trade in grains already in transit to Chicago from elsewhere in the country. (Members could also deal in grains already in Chicago and in futures, grain still in the ground or to be planted.) The board allowed trading in the "to arrive" category both during the regular session, which ended at one o'clock, and during a special session, the Call, that ran afterward from 1:15 to 2:00. The government attacked the rules regulating the Call as an illegal price-fixing mechanism and won in the trial court, where the judge refused to accept evidence from the board that the rule served the convenience of the members, did not suppress competition, and had been aimed to break up the stranglehold that a handful of warehouses in Chicago had previously had on the "to arrive" grains.

Brandeis, speaking for a unanimous Court (McReynolds as former attorney general recused himself), reversed, and declared that the legality of a commercial agreement cannot be determined by so simple a test as whether or not it restrains competition. Every agreement in some form restrains, because it binds the parties and excludes others. What the courts have to examine is whether a regulation does in fact suppress legitimate competition, or whether, by establishing an orderly market, it actually promotes it. This determination cannot be made other than by looking at the facts specific to the case, including the conditions of the market before and after the imposition of the rule and the actual effects that it had. "The history of the restraint, the evil believed to exist, the reason for adopting the particular remedy, the purpose or end sought to be attained, are all relevant facts," and therefore must be examined by the Court. Good intentions did not determine matters by themselves, but should be taken into account as part of the total set of facts.

After taking all of these considerations into account, Brandeis found the rule to be a reasonable regulation of trade and not a violation of the antitrust laws. "Yes—Simply, clearly and admirably well put," Chief Justice White wrote on the return. But in fact the decision is not all that simple, and indicates that Brandeis's views on competition were never as straightforward as some of his critics as well as supporters thought. When Brandeis called for a "regulation of competition" in 1912, he actually meant regulation, but he wanted it to be self-policing as much as possible. The Board of Trade rule certainly did limit competition in that it wanted to suppress the activities of the warehousemen, which the board (and Brandeis) considered illicit. The Call helped to rationalize the market and to allow a level field for grain traders. This opinion foreshadowed Brandeis's attitude in later cases dealing with trade associations as well as the Court's limited approval of price maintenance agreements, both of which he favored. It would be many years, however, before the Court finally gave its approval to manufacturer price maintenance agreements.

Brandeis's dissents, and not the majority opinions, captured the interest of the legal academy and the reformers, because in the 1917 term the antireform conservatives had their way in three important cases. In the most famous of these, *Hammer v. Dagenhart,* a 5–4 majority struck down the Keating-Owen Child Labor Act of 1916. Solicitor General John W. Davis defended the law and filed a Brandeisian brief laden with references to nonlegal materials addressing the social, economic, and medical aspects of child labor in the country. The members of the Court considered Davis one of the best solicitor generals to practice before them, but he failed to sway a majority of the Court. Taking an extremely narrow view of interstate commerce, Justice Day held that child labor constituted part of the production of goods, separated from actual interstate commerce involving the movement of those goods between one state and another. Manufacturing could be regulated by the states, but not by the federal government. The distinction fully reflected the archaic theory of classical legal thought that Holmes and Brandeis had been attacking for years.

Holmes wrote the dissent in *Dagenhart,* joined by Brandeis, Clarke, and McKenna, and it completely dismembered Day's artificial constructs. The Court had previously approved a variety of regulations, and it had no business voiding one that all sensible people believed necessary. In a powerful call for judicial restraint, Holmes declared that "it is not for this Court to pronounce when prohibition is necessary to regulation if it ever may be necessary—to say that it is permissible as against strong drink but not against the product of ruined lives."

Earlier in the term the Court struck another blow against reformers in general, and labor unions in particular, when it again upheld the notorious yellow-dog contract by which employers made it a condition of employment that workers not join a union. In 1908 the Court had struck down a federal law prohibiting yellow-dog contracts and then in 1915 had told the states they could not proscribe them either. In his dissent in *Hitchman,* Brandeis, joined by Holmes and Clarke, meticulously exposed the anti-union bias of the majority opinion by taking every one of Mahlon Pitney's assertions about the factual situation and showing how they had been distorted. The real case, Brandeis implied, had nothing to do with a yellow-dog contract and everything to do with the majority's hostility toward unions.

Enmity toward unions also lay behind the majority decision in another case, where the Court upheld a sweeping injunction against workers who wanted to organize a glass factory in West Virginia. The federal district court prohibited any of the union officers from organizing, picketing, or in any way attempting to unionize the Eagle Glass Company. The Court, according to Brandeis, should have dismissed the appeal and vacated the injunction, because the record clearly showed that there was no diversity of jurisdiction—that is, all of the parties came from the same state—and the case should never have been entertained in federal court. He later complained that his colleagues did not pay enough attention to jurisdictional issues. Holmes would take any case that had an interesting question, while the conservatives would ignore jurisdictional matters where they did not like the rulings in the lower courts. "Van Devanter knows as much about jurisdiction as anyone—more than anyone," Brandeis told Frankfurter. "But when he wants to decide all his jurisdictional scruples go." For Brandeis jurisdiction constituted part of the checks and balances implicit in the Constitution, a real check against the Court's overreaching its authority.

In both cases Brandeis's style was very low-key, with none of the soaring rhetoric that marked Holmes's opinions and made them so quotable. The Brandeis opinions were nonetheless powerful, primarily because of the force of their logic. His analysis of the facts, whether writing for the majority or in dissent, was clear and compelling. In the few instances when fellow justices dissented from his opinions for the Court, they did so because they disagreed with his law; in no instance did anyone ever dissect Brandeis's statement of the facts and find it wanting or distorted. He liked to remind people that he had been a practicing lawyer for thirty-seven years before going on the Court, and he had learned that the accuracy of his facts could be a more powerful argument than the logic of his law. It is not that his colleagues on the bench did not know how to state the facts of a case, but few could match his ability to marshal the material.

Brandeis did care about style, and in some cases his writing rose to the level of elegance; there are few cases in American constitutional history that can match the powerful rhetoric of his opinion in the *Whitney* case (see chapter 25). One has only to look at how he revised his opinions, draft after draft after draft, to see how he wanted to get just the right word—not for the rhetoric but for the accuracy of his statement. He admired the beauty of Holmes's writing, but also noted that while lawyers quoted Holmes more than anyone else, his flights of language left more loopholes for rehearing petitions than anyone else; Holmes had a tendency to disregard some little fact or fail to spell it out, and this caused problems. No one could accuse Brandeis of that shortcoming.

Brandeis understood the political value of not dissenting every time he disagreed or of filing an opinion when he did. Unless the merits of a case troubled him a great deal, he recognized the futility of writing when the vote would be 8–1. He knew it would be far better to write only when he had something he really wanted people to hear. A judge who files only a few well-reasoned and well-documented dissents will make a greater impact on bench and bar than someone who shoots off an opinion in every other case. Brandeis did not, however, agree with Chief Justice Taft's view that dissents adversely affected the Court or that the Court should speak with one voice. Moreover, even when he decided to write, he would on occasion suppress his dissent. When he said that "the most important thing we do is not doing," he meant it not just for the Court as a whole but for its individual members as well.

AFTER HIS FIRST THREE TERMS Brandeis had acclimated himself to the Court and its work. He set a pattern both for how he and his clerk did their work and for how he would draft his opinions. While his ideas about some matters would change over the next two decades, his methods remained the same. What is not apparent from looking at *United States Reports* and at Brandeis's files is that in addition to doing his full share of the Court's workload, Louis Brandeis carried on a remarkable amount of extrajudicial activity.

CHAPTER TWENTY

EXTRAJUDICIAL ACTIVITIES: I

Though Brandeis claimed that he found the first years on the Court difficult, a thornier problem involved how he would handle his activities off the bench. In the summer of 1916, even as he made preparations to take up his seat, he learned that his new position placed limits on his freedom of action. Brandeis had known this intellectually, but did not grasp how real these constraints would be until after his confirmation. By contemporary standards, some of his activities would be judged inconsistent with the canons of judicial propriety.

THE DELEGATES TO THE HOTEL MARSEILLES meeting in August 1914 had discussed, among other things, convening a conference that would be truly representative of American Jewry. The American Jewish Committee, headed by Jacob Schiff and Louis Marshall, claimed hegemony in Jewish affairs and, despite its highly elitist membership, asserted the right to speak for all American Jews. The Zionists might not have cared, except for the fact that the leaders of the committee opposed Zionism and considered it un-American.

Although Brandeis supported the idea, he did not take a leading role until mid-1915, and then more by default than on purpose. As the momentum picked up for an American Jewish Congress, leaders of Zionist groups and others turned to him for direction. The idea of a democratically elected body appealed to him for several reasons. First, it would embody his ideas of how a community should be organized and respond to issues. Second, because nearly all of the groups endorsing the idea favored Zionism to one degree or another, such an entity would be a great ally in striving for the Zionist goal of legal recognition of a homeland in Palestine. Third, it would be impossible for the

American Jewish Committee to continue to claim that it spoke for American Jewry in the face of a congress elected by a majority of the two million Jews in the United States. Simply in terms of internal Jewish communal politics, the success of the congress movement meant unseating the committee, a body Brandeis and others saw as the major obstacle to the acceptance of Zionism in the United States.

Although Brandeis may have been considered the leader by those who supported the congress, in fact he played a lesser role than many people believed, especially those on the committee. He helped develop strategy and propaganda, he gave speeches on behalf of the congress, but Stephen Wise, Horace Kallen, and a handful of others actually carried the movement. Wise especially believed in communal democracy and had a long record of opposition to the leaders of the committee. By the summer of 1915 the movement could not be stopped, as one Jewish organization after another declared itself in favor of the principle. The leaders of the American Jewish Committee opposed the congress, but realized that they would have to respond in some affirmative manner, especially after three members of its executive body resigned in protest against the committee's refusal to participate.

The momentum, however, also disturbed Brandeis. Although the Zionists had gone to great pains to point out that they were but one part of the movement for a congress, in fact the leadership consisted almost entirely of Zionists, as did the second echelon of people who did the organizing work, sent out mailers, and collected money. This put too great a strain on a small group, and Brandeis worried that it might subvert the work he considered most important, establishing a strong Zionist presence in the United States. At the same time, he recognized the emotional appeal the congress had to eastern European immigrants and the momentum they helped to generate and sustain for both the congress and Zionism. At a rally in Carnegie Hall on 24 January 1916—just four days before his nomination to the Court—Brandeis gave the keynote address, "Jewish Rights and the Congress." In a masterly summation of the main arguments that had fostered the drive for a congress, Brandeis emphasized that only if the Jews of America united in a democratic and representative alliance could they hope to demand and achieve equal rights for their brethren in Europe after the war.

Louis Marshall and Jacob Schiff both pleaded with Brandeis to use his influence to postpone a planning convention scheduled for March. Should the congress be held, Schiff gloomily predicted, "it will not

Louis Marshall, head of the American Jewish Committee

be long before political anti-Semitism will rear its ugly head in the United States." But Brandeis, even if he had wanted to, could not do so. In March 1916, with Brandeis sequestered in Boston during the confirmation fight, 367 delegates from eighty-three cities and twenty-eight states, representing more than one million Jews, met at an organizing convention in Philadelphia, where Stephen Wise spoke on American Israel and democracy.

The committee now tried to compromise, declaring that it would work with the congress but only if the congress did not formally convene until after the war ended. The committee asked for a meeting to reconcile the differences with the congress leadership, so that they could all cooperate to secure Jewish rights after the war. Nearly everyone on the congress side suspected some trick, but since the committee represented a powerful segment of American Jewry, it could not be excluded. When twenty-three other organizations allied with the committee that had not attended the Philadelphia meeting agreed to come as well, Brandeis—in his role as honorary president of the Congress Organizing Committee—and his colleagues believed they had no choice but to attend a meeting at the Hotel Astor in New York on 16 July.

The sticking point appeared to be when the congress would meet, with the committee insisting that it not be until after the war. Brandeis responded that at Philadelphia the congress organizers had decided on an earlier date. At this point several of the committee members present started shouting at Brandeis that this amounted to a dictatorship on his part. A stunned Brandeis retorted that such charges could hardly promote the type of cooperation he had been led to believe the committee wanted. Louis Marshall, chairing the meeting, said nothing until one of the congress delegates objected to the rudeness being shown to Brandeis. Then, and only then, did he suggest that personalities be left out of the discussion. A few minutes later the congress delegation got up and left. As Louis wrote to Alice, "The dove of peace is not likely to light on the Jewish factions."

The next day the *New York Times,* which was closely allied with the committee and rarely printed news stories about Jewish communal happenings, ran a lengthy story with the details of the Hotel Astor meeting, and the day after that carried a sanctimonious editorial praising Brandeis's integrity but lamenting that he had to bear the brunt of the attack against his colleagues. The paper regretted that a justice of the U.S. Supreme Court had been engaged in such a verbal brawl.

What Wise and others had feared now came to pass. They had worried at the time of his confirmation that Brandeis might resign from Zionist and congress activities, and it had been one mark of his dedication to Jewish affairs that he had not even raised the subject then. Now, without consulting any of his colleagues, Brandeis resigned all his offices in the American Jewish Relief Committee, the Jewish Congress Organizing Committee, the American Jewish Joint Distribution Committee, and the Provisional Executive Committee for General Zionist Affairs. "There is at least this compensation," he told Judge Hugo Pam, who had been at the meeting with him as a congress representative. "My enforced withdrawal did not come until after the triumph of the congress movement has been assured, and the desired unity of the Jews of America has been made possible."

Although he downplayed the notion that the attack had been premeditated, the evidence seems fairly strong that the leaders of the committee had intended to provoke Brandeis, and then to use the incident as a means to force the justice to step down from Zionist leadership. Rabbi Judah Magnes, who was to become president of the Hebrew University in Jerusalem, used uncharacteristically provocative language, and Marshall made no effort to quiet him. Immediately after the *Times* editorial appeared, Brandeis received a number of letters criticizing him and told Jacob de Haas that he believed the letters and the editorial had all been planned. Louis Marshall apologized for the behavior of his colleagues, but noted that "when feeling runs high, men too often forget themselves." On reading this, Brandeis could not think of a proper response, and said the matter would have to wait until the two men met. In fact, when they did meet, they began to negotiate, in secret, until they had worked out an arrangement satisfactory to both sides. The committee's demand that the congress be delayed until after the war received a boost when the United States entered the war in April 1917 and the State Department urged that the congress be delayed.

With his ties to Jewish affairs at least nominally severed (Brandeis would, of course, continue to play an important role in American Zionism) and arrangements made for assuming his new role as a justice in the fall, Brandeis and his family went off to Cape Cod to enjoy their vacation, only to have their quiet shattered on 8 August by a call from the White House: Would Brandeis agree to serve as head of the three-man American delegation to meet with a similar group named by the Mexican government to settle differences that had brought the two nations close to war? Brandeis did not know how to respond. He had no international experience other than that gained from his work in Zionism, and that hardly fit him to serve as the nation's negotiator; he knew no more about the issues with Mexico than did anyone else who read the papers. Above all, if he accepted, how would this affect the Court and his service on it? On the other hand, the president had asked him to help; how did one turn down such a request? He dispatched a telegram to the chief justice, and left the following evening to see White at the latter's summer home on Lake Placid.

Members of the high court had in the past accepted extrajudicial assignments, most famously Chief Justice John Jay's negotiating a treaty with Great Britain at President Washington's request. Justice Samuel Nelson had agreed to President Grant's request to represent the United States in arbitrating the Alabama claims with Great Britain in 1871, five justices had served on the commission that had resolved the disputed 1876 election, and several other members of the Court had, on a president's appeal, served on diplomatic missions. White frowned on justices' taking on work that would keep them away from the bench, and easily persuaded Brandeis (who still smarted from the Hotel Astor meeting) to decline. Moreover, he gave the new justice the explanation he needed for Wilson, namely, "the state of the business of the Supreme Court at the present time [is] such that I feel it my duty not to undertake this important additional task." After meeting with White, Brandeis went directly to Washington, where he conferred with Wilson and others and gave them his response.

On the way to Washington, Louis stopped in New York to consult with Felix Frankfurter and Harold Laski about the "painful decision," and wrote to Alice about his reaction to the people at Lake Placid, whom he termed "depressing in the extreme." The only redeeming encounter, other than with the chief justice, had been with a Zionist he met at the train station who had recognized him. "I never felt more the chasm between me & the prosperous gentility," he said, and "it was a wondrous relief to find 'one of my own people.' " Still sensitive after the attacks made on him during the confirmation fight, Brandeis could not have ignored the fact that in Lake Placid, as in many other resort areas, many hotels refused to take Jews as guests.

The Hotel Astor incident as well as the president's offer made Brandeis realize that at the very least, his freedom to act openly had been severely curtailed. He would continue to engage in a number of extrajudicial activities and would resume the de facto leadership of the Zionist movement. But by the time he took his seat on the Court for the October 1916 term, he understood that whatever he chose to do, it would have to be done discreetly.

AS BRANDEIS SETTLED IN at the Court, he maintained his ties with many of the reformers he had known prior to his appointment. He wrote almost daily, sometimes with even greater frequency, to the Zionist office, asking for reports on membership and finances and making suggestions on recruiting new members. In a pattern that began almost as soon as he moved to Washington and would last until after he retired from the Court, people in various levels of government sought him out for advice. Commissioners at the ICC, who believed he knew more about their business than did anyone in the country, came to see him frequently, while the chairman of the Federal Trade Commission, Edward Hurley, wanted his guidance on whether the agency should seek additional powers through new legislation. Senator Hiram Johnson asked for suggestions on a speech he planned to give on railroads, and Huston Thompson visited with him before accepting appointment to the FTC.

His letters to Alice, who sometimes stayed on the Cape to avoid Washington heat in June and September, are reminiscent of the ones he wrote to her when he had traveled so often on Zionist and ICC matters, listing the people he had met, the topics they had discussed, and some of the gossip of the day. He reported that the chief justice had been up most of the night with a sick dog, which he had to take to the veterinary hospital at five in the morning. "Thus are the great affairs of man dependent upon beasts." When alone in Washington, he would often go to the House of Truth to dine with Frankfurter, Harold Laski, and their friends.

Some of his meetings appear very inappropriate in light of current standards for judicial conduct. Today one can hardly imagine the attorney general of the United States stopping by to discuss the business of

Alice, 1924

the Justice Department with a member of the Supreme Court, as Thomas Gregory did with Brandeis. LaRue Brown, the U.S. attorney for Massachusetts, sent Brandeis a long letter detailing negotiations between the Justice Department and United Shoe Machinery, and soliciting the justice's help to forestall any bargain that would let the company off easily.

None of this, however, could compare with his involvement in affairs of the Wilson administration, especially after the United States entered the Great War in April 1917. Not only did he receive constant appeals for help from Wilson and his lieutenants, but many of the men who came to Washington to work in the war programs stopped by to see him and to seek his advice.

Brandeis's initial reaction to the outbreak of the war in August 1914 had been, like that of most Americans, horror. "The war news is terrible," he told Alice after the assassination of the archduke at Sarajevo. "Slowly the proper social conditions have risen for a half century & now comes worse than arrest." In New York the following summer, he went to pay his respects to Jane Addams, then visiting at the Henry Street Settlement. "One felt in her," he reported to Alice, "the terrible horror of war and the sympathy with the suffering." But he did not share Miss Addams's pacifist views, nor did he oppose American entry into the war as did his good friend Robert La Follette. When Mrs. Evans protested against British policies, Louis told her, "You do not know what you are saying, Bess. If the Germans win this war it will put back civilization one hundred years."

In March 1915 he had participated in a symposium before the Economic Club of Boston and told the audience that for there to be a lasting peace, the nations of the world would have to recognize the rise of nationalism among the smaller countries that made up the Austro-Hungarian Empire. Nationalism had been one of the causes of the war; it would not disappear after the hostilities. To ensure peace, some sort of international agency would have to be established to serve as a forum where disagreements between countries could be resolved; democracy had to be fostered; tariff barriers removed; and the nations of the world disarmed. All this, of course, reflected much of liberal thinking in western Europe and the United States at the time and would be at the core of Wilson's Fourteen Points program.

After La Follette failed to block the arming of merchant ships, Brandeis wrote him a note from the bench: "Dear Bob—I think you are wrong, but I love you all the same. Won't you come and dine with me this evening?" Part of Brandeis's support for the administration resulted from his admiration for Wilson, but he had also been reading about the Hapsburg monarchy and came to believe, as he told Alfred, that their father's fear and detestation of the Austrian empire had been justified. In addition, he along with many social justice reformers believed that the war would provide an opportunity to cleanse the nation's soul. A week after the United States entered the war, he responded to a letter from his daughter Susan in which she said she found the situation depressing. To the contrary, he told her. "To me the world seems more full of hope and promise than at any time since the joyous days of '48, when liberalism came with its manifold proposals." In mid-1917 he told Alfred Zimmern that he had "been throughout an optimist on the war. My belief is that the by-products—particularly in Great Britain—will amply repay all the suffering and sorrow." The "social-industrial development," he believed, would help undo decades of economic malfeasance and social irresponsibility.

Brandeis, of course, did not see the war as an unmitigated blessing, and as his letter to Zimmern showed, he recognized the great suffering the conflict would cause. He also worried about the very far different situation in the Far East, which did not hold much promise for the future. The Japanese, he told Alice in mid-1918, "are the Germans of the East, and I never felt so clearly how serious would be the results if we approved of their entry into Siberia. On the other hand the denial to them of Manchurian Expansion is serious also. It is the Anglo-German situation of 1878–84 over again."

DURING THE WAR Brandeis resumed close contact with Wilson and many senior members of the administration. The man who had run in 1912 on a platform opposed to bigness in industry and government now presided over the greatest expansion of federal power in the nation's history. Time and again Wilson had to make decisions about the organization of the war program that ran counter to his ingrained instincts, and he would turn to Brandeis for advice. A matter of especial importance concerned the people Wilson would name to head the various wartime commissions and agencies, men knowledgeable in the area and, if not supportive of progressive principles, at least not opposed to them. Throughout the period of American involvement in the war, Brandeis suggested names to members of the administration and gave his opinion on appointments they were considering.

Shortly after the declaration of war, Secretary of the Treasury William Gibbs McAdoo made the first of many visits to the justice, seeking recommendations not only for expanded Treasury agencies but also for a commission that Wilson planned to send to Russia. Newton D. Baker, the former reform mayor of Cleveland and now secretary of war, had known Brandeis only slightly before the war, but now became a regular caller. He reported to Wilson that he had spent two evenings discussing the labor situation with Brandeis and that the justice, in order to be of whatever help he could, had decided to remain in Washington over the summer of 1917. Brandeis, according to Baker, "has kept himself pretty well informed of the workings of the advisory committees of the Council of National Defense." Baker then told the president that if he "wanted a disinterested view of the whole situation from a man who is thinking hard," he was sure that Brandeis would be willing to come see him at any time. When Baker asked Felix Frankfurter to prepare a memorandum on dealing with strikes in the West called by the radical IWW, Frankfurter submitted the plan with a note that Justice Brandeis had read and approved it. Henry L. Stimson ("really the head of War Intelligence Service, though not such ostensibly"), Bernard Baruch, General Enoch Crowder, and many others all found their way to Stoneleigh Court, some many times.

(Brandeis worked very hard in the heat of the Washington summer that year—his first after going on the Court—and although he tried to get in exercise, nothing could compare with the rest he got either at the Dedham house or on Cape Cod. "My information is that you cut off your vacation at both ends," his former law partner William Dunbar wrote at the end of the summer, "and I heard last week someone who saw you in Washington say that you were not looking rugged. I hope you will be prudent.")

Wilson, perhaps after the rebuff of the Mexican commission, may have felt uneasy about calling Brandeis to the White House, although Brandeis felt no similar qualms and went to see Wilson on Zionist matters more than once. But on a cold Sunday in December 1917, Wilson desperately needed advice about what to do on several matters.

Alice was in the apartment catching up on Boston news with Bess Evans when the phone rang at a little after four o'clock. "Who is there?" she asked the building operator. "The President." When Alice again asked who was calling, the operator said, "President Wilson." Realizing it was no joke, she told the girl, "Call up 809. The Justice is in his office." Within an hour Wilson arrived at Stoneleigh Court and went up to see Brandeis in the small apartment he had rented as a study, while the two Secret Service men who accompanied him waited outside the door.

Alice described the scene to her sister: "You know his study. It is not a very large room & now lined with book shelves on all sides from floor to ceiling. The room was fairly dark with only one strong desk light. He had been working at some opinion, consulting authorities, & law books were lying everywhere about—on his desk, on chairs, even on the floor. . . . Here surely was the scholar, the student at his work." And yet, Alice proudly concluded, "it is as a practical man of affairs, a states-man that Louis' advice is so much sought."

The matter that concerned Wilson that afternoon involved railroads and their seeming inability to move raw materials to plants or desper-ately needed war supplies to Atlantic ports. Wilson had been besieged by people clamoring for the government to take over the rail lines, join them into a unified system, and then give one man the necessary authority to run it. Although the attorney general assured him that such a step would be legal, Wilson had his doubts, both about taking the lines and about setting up such a powerful governmental agency. Brandeis not only reassured him of the legitimacy of the takeover but also urged, as others had done, that he name William Gibbs McAdoo to head the railroads. Wilson, while recognizing McAdoo's energy and tal-ents, needed him at the Treasury to cope with the problems of financing the war. Surprisingly, given his well-known views on the limitations of individuals to run large enterprises, the justice told Wilson that McAdoo could do both jobs and do them well. Less than a week later the president announced that the government would take over opera-tion of the railroads for the duration of the war and named McAdoo as director general. During the year that he oversaw both the Treasury and the railroads, McAdoo more than fulfilled Brandeis's assessment of his abilities, and when an exhausted McAdoo resigned from both posts two weeks after the armistice, Brandeis called his departure from govern-ment service "a measureless misfortune."

Brandeis must surely have anticipated that the president's actions would have constitutional repercussions, and could come before the

Supreme Court eventually. In that case, would Brandeis have to recuse himself, and if so, how would that be explained? Or did he think that the advice he gave Wilson on wartime powers rested on such firm constitutional ground that should the matter reach the high court the justices would overwhelmingly endorse it? While on the Court, Brandeis would act several times in violation of his stated beliefs in strict separation of powers, on the apparent assumption that reliance on his own internal compass would preclude disturbing and potentially embarrassing situations. In this case the seizure of the railroads and their operation during the war did come before the Court, which unanimously upheld the action but in terms so sweeping that Brandeis concurred separately.

Less than a month later Wilson sent Colonel House to ask Brandeis's opinion on the critical question of how American industry should be organized during the war. Congress had created the Council of National Defense in August 1916, a cabinet-level committee with an advisory commission of prominent Americans working without pay. The council had the task of preparing plans for what industry and labor would do should the United States enter the war. The council, however, had no real authority, and its 150 committees often seemed to be working at cross-purposes. By December 1917 the problems of production and distribution had become acute, and various members of the administration blamed one another, with Colonel House scheming to get rid of Secretary of War Baker. Demands came from all corners that a "czar of industry" be established, an idea that appalled Wilson.

Given Brandeis's antipathy to the curse of bigness, he might have been expected to oppose the idea, but instead he pointed out the obvious—the needs of a free society in wartime are different from those of a nation at peace. For the country to win the war, it had to mobilize industry, and because of the interrelated nature of all aspects of the economy, there had to be someone to direct the coordination. It would do no good, for example, to increase coal production when steel mills needed more coal unless the government could ensure that the coal went to the mills. But unlike his recommendation to use McAdoo at both the Treasury and the railroads, Brandeis made it clear that Secretary of War Baker should have no role in managing industry. The secretary of war should be responsible for the raising, training, and outfitting of an army and its dispatch to Europe.

Once again Wilson heeded the justice's advice, and in early March named the Wall Street financier Bernard Baruch to head the reconstituted War Industries Board. Although only eight months remained to the war, Baruch brought order out of chaos, cajoling businessmen to cooperate, bullying them at times, and, if necessary, threatening to take over their plants. The effectiveness of the board served as a model for the early programs of Franklin Roosevelt's New Deal, and during World War II Roosevelt moved immediately to establish government oversight and coordination of industry.

The one area of the war where Wilson did not need to consult with Brandeis involved food production and distribution. Herbert Hoover, a successful mining engineer with an international reputation, had won plaudits for his handling of Belgian relief during the early months of the war. In the summer of 1917, Wilson asked him to take charge of coordinating food production and distribution, and Hoover plunged into sorting out the problems with an energy and efficiency that impressed Brandeis. "The only person who seems to go forward is Hoover," Louis wrote to Alice, "who has no authority in law for anything practically."

Hoover and Brandeis met often during the war, frequently for dinner, and the justice came to believe Hoover extremely capable—"the biggest figure injected into Washington life by the war"—and someone who one day might be president. When Alfred told his brother that he had some ideas on how to improve the movement of grain stuffs, Louis put him in touch with Hoover, and after Alfred had made his suggestions, Hoover asked him to come into the Food Administration as a dollar-a-year man to serve as his special assistant. On one occasion Hoover complained that important legislation that would strengthen the food program had been bottled up by the recalcitrance of Senator James Reed of Missouri. The justice told Hoover that Reed had opposed his nomination, but that after the two men had met, Reed had changed his mind, and suggested that Hoover might well utilize the same tactic. Whether Hoover followed Brandeis's advice is unclear, but Congress ultimately created the position of food administrator with abundant powers in the Lever Food Control Act of August 1917.

Although Wilson recognized that he would not be able to utilize Brandeis's talents in any formal capacity while he remained on the Court, he continued to talk with him on everything from organization to appointments, and every time a new problem came up, people would suggest putting Brandeis in charge. Organized labor demanded that, as a price for war policies that froze wages at the March 1917 level, the government adopt a policy of recognizing unions and labor's right to organize. Brandeis believed that after the war ended, there would be great labor strife unless the government moved to ensure the rights of labor. In April 1918, with signs of labor unrest, Robert Woolley and Matthew Hale suggested that a labor czar be created, akin to positions in food, manufacturing, and railroads, and that Brandeis be named director general of labor. Woolley, without waiting to hear from Wilson, began talking up the idea, and reported that the secretary of labor thought it a wonderful idea, with Brandeis "preeminently the man for the post." This time the president pulled him up short, saying that while he shared a high opinion of Justice Brandeis, it would not be wise to choose a member of the Court "at this juncture." Wilson knew that if he appealed to Brandeis in the name of patriotism, Brandeis would leave the Court and take whatever government position the president offered. But it had been too great a struggle to get Brandeis on the Court, and Wilson had no intention of getting him off. At a meeting with Rabbi Stephen Wise, after Wilson complained about how hard it had been to get someone for an important post, Wise had said, "Why don't you ask Justice Brandeis?" "I need him everywhere," Wilson responded, "but he must stay where he is."

ON 19 NOVEMBER 1916, during his first term on the Court, Brandeis sent a handwritten note to Felix Frankfurter. "My dear Felix," he began. "You have had considerable expense for traveling, telephoning and similar expenses in public matters undertaken at my request or following up my suggestions & will have more in the future no doubt. These expenses should, of course, be borne by me. I am sending check for $250 on this account. Let me know when it is exhausted or if it has already been."

Upon receipt Frankfurter sent the check back, only to receive the following response:

My dear Felix:
Alice and I talked over the matter before I sent the check and considered it again carefully on receipt of your letter. We are clearly of the opinion that you ought to take the check.
    In essence this is nothing different than your taking traveling and incidental expenses from the Consumers League or the New Republic—which I trust you do. You are giving your very valuable time and that is quite enough. It can make no difference that the subject matter in connection with which expense is incurred is more definite in one case than in the other.

I ought to feel free to make suggestions to you, although they involve some incidental expense. And you should feel free to incur expense in the public interest. So I am returning the check.

Several of your friends and mine have expressed to me recently the fear that you were overtaxing your strength. Be very watchful. There is much work for you ahead.

Thus began one of the most fruitful, and later most controversial, relationships of any Supreme Court justice in the nation's history.

Brandeis, from the time he started his law practice, had wanted freedom to act in the public interest. By the time Wilson named him to the Court, he had, for all practical purposes, given up private work for the public. The money he made and invested, however, made this choice possible for him. Felix Frankfurter, like Brandeis, had a passion for public service and less than a year after he graduated Harvard Law School had left a well-paying position with a private law firm to work as an assistant to Henry Stimson, then the U.S. attorney for New York. He did not despise money, did not consider it sordid or disgusting, and it helped maintain his sometimes expensive tastes in food and clothes. But money, he told his future wife, "is wholly irrelevant. I mean this literally." Throughout his life Frankfurter held a series of low-paying government jobs or taught at Harvard Law School at a time of notoriously low academic salaries. Not until he went onto the Supreme Court in 1939 did he have more than a modest income. Unlike Brandeis he had to work, and also unlike Brandeis he did not have the money to subsidize his public work. Frankfurter, for example, could never have offered to reimburse Harvard for the time he spent on the Sacco and Vanzetti case in the 1920s the way Brandeis had paid his firm during the New Haven campaign.

In the fall of 1916, Brandeis knew, after the two episodes that summer, that while he would be able to continue to advise—perhaps at times even to direct—some activities from the bench, he could no longer write muckraking articles attacking the curse of bigness or take on cases for the National Consumers League. Frankfurter had, by then, already stepped in and assumed responsibility for rearguing the Oregon minimum-wage law before the high court. He also served as an unofficial editor of the *New Republic,* had a hand in many editorial decisions, and eventually became the journal's legal affairs correspondent. But he also had a full-time job, and Brandeis, when he had urged Frankfurter to take the Harvard position, had expected Felix to become the type of law professor who would create a living law. This meant not just teaching classes but also doing research and writing, and for none of these would he be richly reimbursed—at least not in dollars. Although not married at the time, Felix had already begun his courtship of Marion Denman; Brandeis assumed they would marry, and then the first call on Frankfurter's income would be to support his family. Frankfurter, whom Brandeis would call the most useful lawyer in America, would never be able to earn his way to freedom for public service, but Brandeis could make at least part of it possible by giving him the resources to underwrite his reform work. Between 1916 and 1939, the year Frankfurter went on the Court, Brandeis put at his disposal at least $50,000, well over $1 million in current value.

Brandeis often made suggestions to Frankfurter, but there is no indication that either man considered them anything other than suggestions, and there is not a single letter in which one could find even a hint of the older man's giving the younger instructions, let alone orders. Frankfurter argued two cases before the Supreme Court, and in both of them Brandeis recused himself, but for reasons other than his closeness to the Harvard professor. In the Oregon minimum-wage case, he absented himself because he had been the attorney for the National Consumers League when the case had first been heard in the Court, and in *Adkins v. Children's Hospital* (1923) because his daughter Elizabeth worked for the District of Columbia commission involved in the case.

Many of Brandeis's proposals involved Frankfurter's getting law school students to write articles about specific Supreme Court decisions or contested doctrinal matters. Brandeis had long believed that the journals put out by the students at the major law schools performed an important critical function, namely, educating the lawyers and judges who read them as to what the law should be. Once Brandeis began citing law review articles in his opinions, their status rose, and readers began looking for comment on contemporary cases. In the 1920s, Frankfurter and James Landis, a former Brandeis law clerk, began a series of articles in the *Harvard Law Review* that became the highly influential book *The Business of the Supreme Court* (1928).

Bruce Allen Murphy's charges that Brandeis paid Frankfurter a substantial annual stipend to engage in partisan political activities are unfounded and can be derived only by misreading what Brandeis actually said. Nonetheless, his book and its allegations made front-page headlines and triggered a storm of accusations and rebuttals. In a critical editorial the *New York Times* declared, "The Brandeis-Frankfurter arrangement was wrong. It serves neither history nor ethics to judge it more kindly. . . . The prolonged, meddlesome Brandeis-Frankfurter arrangement violates ethical standards."

Brandeis's activities were hardly secret, either then or later. Nearly everyone in Washington knew that the justice met regularly with administration officials up to and including presidents, as well as with reformers, reporters, academics, and visiting Palestinians. During the 1930s, his Monday afternoon teas hosted not only senior New Deal members but also, from the justice's viewpoint, the far more important younger men and women just starting out in public service. Neither Woodrow Wilson nor Franklin Roosevelt trumpeted the news that they sometimes sought his advice, but neither did they make any secret of the fact that Brandeis occasionally came to the White House.

Some of the criticism centered on the idea of a Supreme Court justice's having a hired surrogate to take political action that would have been inappropriate for him; that the surrogate was a law school professor appalled some people who believed teachers should be above such sordid activity. Had Frankfurter done anything dishonest, had he acted for Brandeis in a partisan manner, had he funneled Brandeis's money into questionable campaign contributions, then perhaps some of the charges might make sense. (The most controversial of Frankfurter's activities involved his defense of Sacco and Vanzetti; see below, chapter 26.) The arrangement, in fact, was not itself secret, since Frankfurter's colleagues knew that he had a fund provided by Brandeis to cover the costs of his public work. While Frankfurter regarded Brandeis as a mentor and perhaps even as a substitute father, he was never a carbon copy of the justice, and the two men differed on a number of issues, a fact that bothered neither of them. There is not a shred of evidence that Brandeis ever suggested anything to Frankfurter that could be depicted as partisan, secretive, or unethical. The simplest and most supportable explanation is exactly that given by Brandeis himself—namely, he wanted Frankfurter to have the financial freedom to pursue those public causes that mattered to them both. (The only time that Brandeis gave his friend money for personal uses was when Frankfurter's wife was ill and Brandeis, certainly sympathetic, stepped in to help with the medical bills.)

THERE IS, HOWEVER, one extrajudicial activity that Brandeis undertook that deserves condemnation, and that is his involvement in "The Document," a project initiated by Woodrow Wilson after the Republicans' landside victory in the 1920 elections. Wilson had left the White House in March 1921, broken by the stroke he had suffered in 1919 and depressed by the popular rejection of his peace plan. The devoted care of his wife and a small coterie of relatives and friends enabled the ex-president to throw off the outward symptoms of depression, although he remained physically weak. His restless mind and a belief that the American people could and would respond to an idealistic call to service led him to invite a few friends and officials from his administration to join in drafting a statement of progressive principles. Wilson apparently broached the idea first to Brandeis, when the justice went to visit the ex-president at his house on S Street in northwest Washington in the middle of June 1921. Brandeis understood that Wilson hoped the statement would serve as a rallying call and become the platform at the 1924 Democratic convention; what he and the others involved did not know is that Wilson harbored a secret hope that he would be the presidential candidate that year, riding to victory with the progressive forces of the country rallied around him.

Brandeis apparently had no qualms that his judicial status would preclude him from drafting a potential platform for a presidential election, just the type of partisan activity he and Frankfurter avoided in their collaboration. Wilson asked Brandeis to contact Bainbridge Colby and Thomas L. Chadbourne, and before long other members of the Wilson administration, including David Houston, Bernard Baruch, and Newton D. Baker, joined in to comment or to write sections. Brandeis drafted some of the sections, but Wilson also relied upon him to critique and emend materials submitted by others. The former president wrote most of the Document himself, although the final product reflected the contributions of his collaborators.

The very first statement Wilson circulated involved foreign affairs. He bitterly attacked "the most partisan, prejudiced and unpatriotic coterie that has ever misled the Senate of the United States," and called for immediate resumption of America's role in world leadership. By the winter, statements had been roughed out on a number of topics, including foreign policy, development of a merchant marine, agriculture, labor, and the control of big business. The Document eloquently summed up New Freedom progressivism, the ideals that Wilson, Brandeis, and the others had supported for many years, both at home and overseas. The 1912 campaign had been fought on domestic issues, and these appeared in the Document; but now its drafters also believed that the United States had a role to play in world affairs and that it could never again retreat into isolation. "We demand the immediate resumption of our international obligations and leadership."

The lessons of the war regarding the economy could be seen as well. Although they still condemned domination by the great financial interests, they now called for greater cooperation, especially between labor and management. A section Brandeis wrote called for laws allowing retail fair-price agreements, a device he believed would maintain a competitive economy. A whiff of people's socialism can be found in the assertion that all resources ultimately belonged to the people and must, therefore, be administered for their benefit. While the Document reflects the standard progressive belief in the ability of the people to govern themselves intelligently, there is now added a missionary zeal to spread democracy throughout the world. Despite the idealism that permeates the Document, there is also a hard and bitter edge, a combativeness that would have sounded strange in 1912, a partisanship almost as strong as that which it attacked.

The Document never received a wide circulation. Wilson several times tried to devise some means by which the ideas could be aired or presented to the Democratic Party. For a while he played with the idea of having all Democrats up for election in 1922 pledge themselves to support the testament, believing that their victory would then vindicate his own ideas and policies. No one really seemed to know what to do with the Document after it had been written, and Wilson died in early February 1924 before any action could be taken.

It is just as well that the Document then sank into oblivion. Wilson failed to understand that after two decades of idealism and reform, the American people were not in the mood to be rallied; they wanted the "normalcy" that Warren G. Harding and the Republicans promised, and they reaffirmed that demand in the elections of 1924 and 1928. Although a number of people working with Wilson knew of Brandeis's role in the preparation of the Document, had this knowledge become widespread, it would have drawn a great deal of justified criticism. Extrajudicial activities so blatantly political would have been repugnant to most Americans.

Persons appointed to judicial office are named only in part for their judicial capabilities and potential. Men like Holmes and Benjamin Cardozo had been recognized as brilliant jurists before their appointment to the high court, but Brandeis, Felix Frankfurter, George Sutherland, and Harlan Fiske Stone received their seats partially as a reward for political service faithfully rendered. They had the potential to become jurists, but they arrived at the Court because of their political loyalties. Once they were there, it is not surprising that people would want to consult them on matters that they had shown themselves to be knowledgeable about before donning the silk robe. Wilson, Hoover, Franklin Roosevelt, and others trusted the men they named to the Court, and few of them could turn down a request from the chief executive for advice. Brandeis certainly did not. Perhaps it is too much to expect members of the Supreme Court to have an Olympian detachment when it comes to partisan politics, but here Brandeis violated his own concepts of judicial propriety.

IN ADDITION TO HIS NEW DUTIES as a Supreme Court justice, the ongoing demands of the Zionist movement, and the calls for advice by members of the Wilson administration during the war, Brandeis had to deal with domestic tensions. The Brandeises' move to Washington energized Alice, who took on the responsibility for finding an apartment (with the help of Belle La Follette) and then supervising the packing and moving of the household from Boston to Washington. Whatever the Brahmins may have thought of her and her husband, in Washington a Supreme Court justice and his wife stood high on the social ladder. While never a social butterfly, Alice enjoyed dinners at the White House and meeting the interesting people there and those who came to dine at Stoneleigh Court. She became friends with Edith Bolling Wilson, and the two often attended concerts together.

Just as she had in Boston, Alice paid close attention to the guests who came for dinner or simply to pay calls on her and her husband. Since Louis shared just about everything he learned with her, she soon became one of the best-informed women in Washington and, if the information was not confidential, often discussed it in letters to Elizabeth Evans. Alice commented on British politics, her reactions to some of Wilson's speeches (she thought highly of his Fourteen Points address), and analyses of the military situation ("General Crowder and his men were in last evening and all seem to think that the beginning of the end has come"). Although she would have some recurrences of her condition, the episodes became fewer and farther between, and she thrived in Washington. In fact, she seemed to take personal responsibility for Louis's well-being, making sure he took naps and did not work more than two hours at a time. According to one clerk, William Sutherland, she "looked after him like he was a baby."

Louis and Alice, however, had problems with their older daughter. Although Brandeis had praised little Susan for the mature way in which she had handled Alice's frequent absences, Susan could not be described as a "biddable" child. She had a mind of her own, which her parents clearly cherished, but not the self-control that they also valued. Throughout the time she had been in college at Bryn Mawr, there had been issues over her accounts, her apparent carelessness in dress, and her failure to keep her parents informed of things they believed they had a right to know about, such as her grades. As she got older, she seemingly resented her parents'—and especially her mother's—efforts to provide guidance.

It could not have been easy for a high-spirited young woman to have Louis Brandeis as a father. He set what must have seemed impossibly high expectations and imposed strict requirements, such as submitting an accounting of all her expenses. Although we do not have either her letters to her father or her recollections of this period, it is not unreasonable to think that in the company of educated and liberated young women at Bryn Mawr, Susan absorbed some of the restiveness that would mark the young people of the 1920s, and which, of course, had been evident even before the war. Susan's conduct could have been that of many young women her age—rebelliousness, an insistence on independence, the adoption of a different standard for dress—and her parents' reaction of pain and confusion would be duplicated by many other parents who had been under and had never abandoned Victorian standards of propriety. They, too, expressed dismay and alarm at the unorthodox behavior of their offspring.

Louis and Alice rejoiced, however, when Susan informed them that after college she intended to study law. After Susan graduated from Bryn Mawr in 1915, she spent some time working for women's suffrage and looking into law schools. At the time Harvard, Yale, and Columbia did not accept women. Although Brandeis made inquiries at these schools, and learned from the faculty that in the future they expected to admit women, either they were unprepared to do so, or the governing bodies of the schools would not change their policies. So in the fall of 1916, Susan began the study of law at the University of Chicago. "My dearest Susan," her father wrote. "My welcome to the realm of Legal Study. May the next year be filled with happiness and usefulness. . . . You have only to be true to yourself, and in time there will be fine accomplishment."

Over the next few years Brandeis sent a stream of encouraging letters to her, ones full of reminiscences about his own days at law school. "Forty-one years ago I was studying the same subjects with which you are wrestling now," he noted, "and I too found them thrillingly interesting." He gave her his old notes from law school, in the knowledge that

Susan at the University of Chicago Law School, 1916

in many areas of the law little had changed since the 1870s. When she sent him a draft opinion she wrote as an exercise in one class, he praised her for it but called her conclusion "unsound." She had relied on a section of a court opinion in which the judge had expressed his own view rather than a legal ruling, a practice known as obiter dicta (Latin: "something said in passing"). "Beware," he told her, "of obiter dicta."

The year working for suffrage had left her with a desire to do more public service, an idea Brandeis certainly approved, but he urged her to devote her time to her studies while in school. He had provided sufficient money in her allowance so that she would be able to make generous gifts to Hadassah and other causes. "Be liberal with your money, but very economical of your time and vitality." He did, however, endorse her idea to form a Zionist study group, and suggested inviting Judge Mack to speak to it. Apparently, some of her classmates spoke about working in a law office, and Brandeis repeated the same line that he had used for many years when the sons of friends had asked whether they could work in his firm prior to graduation. "There is only one place to study law for the law student," he told her, "and that is at the law school."

Susan did well enough in law school, but did not stand near the top of her class as her father had done in his day. He told her not to worry, since in the long run her ability would determine her success. A high standing would be of help at the beginning of practice when looking for a job, but did not make much difference later. Susan also fretted about the fact that she was no longer the daughter of a Boston attorney, even a famous one, but that her father was now "Mr. Justice Brandeis." She worried that she might not measure up to either his expectations or those of other people, and told him that she believed she had to face the

Rally for women's suffrage in New York, 1915

world as if she were his son. While Brandeis continued to encourage her, he would not be dishonest, and agreed that she would, as far as the world was concerned, be judged as if she were in fact a son. When she told him near the end of her first year that she still enjoyed studying law, he rejoiced. "It is a great field," he told her, "and there is no question but that it will be wide open to women by the time you are fully equipped through study and experience."

Then, in April 1917, shortly after Wilson asked Congress for a declaration of war, Susan attended a peace rally, sent some peace literature home to her mother, and asked what she thought of it. Alice showed these to Louis, who immediately wrote to Susan, "I hope you will refrain from talking or other activity in connection with the Peace Society. It might prove quite embarrassing to me." He did not go into any details, and it is one of the very rare occasions when he asked his family to avoid saying or doing something because it could reflect back on him.

About this time, and perhaps in connection with the peace rally, Susan met a fellow law student at the university, a pacifist and conscientious objector named Magnus Block Rosenberg. She fell in love with him and, much to her parents' chagrin, wanted to get married immediately. Louis and Alice finally prevailed on her to wait six months, and then, if she still felt the same way, they would give their blessing. "Nothing substantial can be lost by that course," Louis wrote, "and it is no more than proper insurance." Although Susan consented, the waiting period did not calm her, and Brandeis on several occasions had to remind her that she had agreed to the plan.

Susan came to Washington at the end of the semester and had a long talk with her father on 23 June. For a man used to questioning clients and getting from them the information he needed, the meeting with Susan, as he told Alice, proved frustrating. At the end, he said, "am not sure that I have added to my knowledge or understanding." Because of the six-month wait, Susan had apparently not told Magnus of her feelings and had stopped him from telling her of his. More than ever, Brandeis felt he did not understand his older daughter. "She has great defects," he wrote to Alice, "and lacks qualities which one might have expected to find in our daughter. Most of all she is lacking in the aesthetics and the graces. Most of her apparent hardness is really that. And she does not belong in our world." Perhaps in the end the young man's qualities, "which appear to be unaggressive," might be what Susan needed.

Louis went down to Louisville to visit Alfred in late June and acceded to Susan's request that he return through Chicago so he could meet Rosenberg. Apparently, the young man made a good impression and, as her father rather tactlessly told Susan, had better posture and dressed more carefully than she did. Brandeis said he wanted to see more of Rosenberg, and to hear more from her about her feelings. He still, however, insisted on her keeping to the six-month plan. Louis copied out his letter to Susan and sent it to Alice, and added his belief that they ought not to do anything more than be firm on the waiting period. He confessed he really did not understand the situation. "This is a realm into which I have no insight. She may be doing just the right thing. And I cannot find fault in her conduct in this respect. There are many defects in her, which are prominent and for which I grieve & the existence of which pains me. I wish they were otherwise but we must accept the situation in this respect & can only be sorry."

Susan had expected more of a reaction from her father, and she complained to him about what she termed his "general calm attitude toward every situation." He responded immediately that this calmness "is a thing I have cultivated these forty years." He recognized that it had at times been annoying to ardent folk such as her, but it did not imply criticism. Rather, he had trained himself to remain calm, believing that only if he kept his emotions under control would he be able to learn. As for his impressions of Magnus, he confessed that at one relatively short meeting he could not go very deep. He wanted to meet the young man again and get to know him better. He did not oppose Rosenberg, but "I want to be sure that you are entirely sure of yourself." The six-month period had been designed for one purpose only, to allow her to be absolutely certain of what she wanted. "Your happiness and worthy development, dearest Susan, is my deep longing." He would do everything he could for her, but realized that in some areas he could do little. The decision would ultimately be hers.

Whether Louis and Alice wanted the six-month wait solely so that Susan could be sure of her mind, or whether they hoped it would lead to her and Magnus separating, we cannot tell. After early July 1917, Rosenberg is no longer a subject in the correspondence. The following summer Susan went to Washington to work at the War Industries Board, and her social life included a number of young men she met in the capital. Apparently, her father still found things to criticize, and in a brief note to Alice told her that "Susan in this AM in good cheer & well dressed which is rare."

Their other daughter, Elizabeth, had entered Radcliffe and did quite well in school. Her second cousin recalled her as "attractive physically and warm. She was a little overwhelming in her intellectual prowess." On her birthday Brandeis wrote that he could wish her "nothing better than that you shall continue to develop as nobly as you have heretofore, and enjoy as much happiness as you are giving us." Then, in July 1918, while Elizabeth was with her mother on Cape Cod, she fell ill, and Alice wrote to her husband, who again had elected to stay in Washington over the summer, asking what to do. He immediately wired her to use her best judgment, and if she agreed with the surgeon that an operation was necessary to go ahead and authorize it. If there is trouble, he told her, "it would seem wise to remove the cause while place and conditions are favorable." The surgeon, however, could not pinpoint the cause of Elizabeth's illness, and after two weeks or so she got better. When Elizabeth went to Washington for a short visit in late October, however, she fell sick again, and Alice became her full-time nurse, not just taking care of her physically but trying to divert her mind by reading to her. On 5 November, Elizabeth had a temperature of 106, and the doctor they called in did not know the cause, but suggested that they treat the symptoms, especially by trying to lower her fever. A week

Elizabeth, ca. 1918

later Louis reported to Susan that they had called in a specialist, who assured them that the worst was over; the temperature had dropped to under 100 as a result of the first doctor's suggestions. Neither doctor recognized that the respiratory disease Elizabeth had was an early manifestation of the great influenza epidemic that swept across much of Europe and the Americas and took the lives of between 20 milliion and 40 million people worldwide, nearly 700,000 in the United States alone.

Fortunately, Elizabeth recovered, and while she did so, the Great War ended. Peace, Brandeis predicted to Susan, would bring a new world, with "problems galore and more difficult than the making of war," but it would also present great opportunities to remake society. In some ways he envied his older daughter, who would soon be finishing her law studies. "You should have a very interesting time the next twenty five years," he told Susan, "taking part in the reshaping. And I am glad that you concluded to study law which will be a great aid in fitting you for the task." She might be interested, he suggested, in reading again his address "The Living Law."

CHAPTER TWENTY-ONE
ZIONISM, 1917–1921

O n 2 April 1917, the justices of the Supreme Court filed in to
the House of Representatives to hear the president of the
United States ask a joint session of Congress to declare war
against Germany. American entry into World War I meant that at some
point Brandeis and the rest of the Court would have to pass on the constitutionality of several measures enacted to further the war program.
For the Zionists the world turned upside down and gave the movement
a chance to secure Theodor Herzl's dream—international sanction of a
Jewish homeland in Palestine. Brandeis played a key role in securing
that charter and, had he wanted, could have become head of the World
Zionist Organization. Instead, within two years of the Zionists' securing their great victory at the Paris Peace Conference, he resigned his
leadership of American Zionism.

AMERICAN NEUTRALITY had made it possible for the Provisional
Executive Committee to raise and transmit hundreds of thousands of
dollars in relief funds, and to send food and medical supplies to Palestine. But Brandeis and his colleagues could not ignore the fact that
Turkey, which controlled Palestine, was a belligerent and that any missteps on their part could doom the colonies. The PEC, therefore,
declared its neutrality and asked the American ambassador Henry Morgenthau to reassure the Turkish government of its desire for the Palestinian colonies to thrive peacefully under Turkish rule. Brandeis tried
to make the committee's position as clear as possible: "Zionism is not a
movement to wrest from the Turks the sovereignty of Palestine. Zionism seeks merely to establish for such Jews as choose to go and remain
there, a legally secured home."

The mass of America's Jews initially sympathized with the Central

*Chaim Weizmann, head of the English
Zionist Federation*

powers, not because they loved Germany, but because they hated czarist Russia, from which so many of them had fled. "The Jews support Germany," ran one editorial in the *Jewish Daily News*, "because Russia bathes in Jewish blood." On the other hand, Brandeis and many of the leaders of the PEC, such as Wise and Mack, had always privately favored the Allies. The situation changed dramatically when in February 1917 the Kerensky revolution in Russia overthrew the czarist regime and replaced it with a government pledged to democracy, and less than two months later the United States entered the war on the Allied side. American Zionist leaders received an added impetus to support the Allied cause after they learned that in England, Chaim Weizmann had been secretly negotiating with His Majesty's Government to declare Palestine a Jewish homeland once the British army had conquered the land.

Weizmann, of course, had not been under the constraints of neutrality as had Brandeis and the Americans, but aware of the American need to maintain neutrality, he had chosen not to inform them of his work. Initially, Weizmann had run up against a wall of indifference, but by early 1916 the idea of establishing a Jewish homeland in Palestine had begun appealing to the British for a variety of reasons, not the least of which would be their greater influence in the Middle East. After the United States entered the war, however, any British statement on the future of Palestine would have to be acceptable to its new ally.

Brandeis had received intimations about Weizmann's work as early as December 1915, when he met Alfred Zimmern, then a visiting professor at the University of Wisconsin, who also participated in conversations between the British Zionists and His Majesty's Government. Not until January 1917, however, did American leaders first begin to discuss a British declaration with Colonel Edward M. House, and this set a pattern for future contacts with the administration. Wilson considered the creation of foreign policy a presidential prerogative, with the secretary of state and his department responsible for gathering information and implementing his decisions. This attitude, of course, upset the professionals in the State Department, especially those on the Middle Eastern desks, nearly all of whom were pro-Arabic and anti-Zionist, if not outrightly anti-Semitic.

Less than a week after the United States entered the war, Weizmann wrote to Brandeis on the status of the proposed declaration, stating, "An expression of an opinion coming from yourself and perhaps from other gentlemen connected with the government in favor of a Jewish Palestine under a British protectorate would greatly strengthen our hands." Weizmann put the Americans in an awkward position. It was one thing to talk to House or even Wilson, and in fact even as Weizmann's letter crossed the Atlantic, Stephen Wise reported that House believed the Jews would get Palestine after the war. Brandeis, however, could not publicly approve the activities of a foreign country, even an ally, since such a statement would embarrass not only the American government but the Zionists as well. Moreover, Weizmann wanted him to endorse not only a Jewish Palestine but one under a British protectorate, and Brandeis, well aware of Anglo-French tensions in the Middle East, had no intention of stepping into that quagmire.

To cement relations with their new ally, the British sent a high-level delegation to the United States a few weeks after Congress approved the war declaration. The foreign secretary, Arthur James Balfour, sought out Brandeis almost immediately upon his arrival in Washington, and the two men took an immediate liking to each other. At a White House reception on 23 April, and in several private interviews, they explored the problems of a declaration, the need for an American endorsement of it, and the intricacies of Anglo-French rivalry. When Balfour suggested that perhaps the United States would assume a protectorate over the Holy Land, Brandeis quickly told him that it was out of the question. The justice knew that the Wilson administration had no interest in expansion on the other side of the globe; American Zionists wanted British control. Balfour had been hoping to hear this, since a British protectorate over Palestine would make England the dominant colonial power in the region, and he urged the justice to secure American approval of a declaration. At about the same time the Foreign Office encouraged Weizmann and Baron James de Rothschild, the head of British Jewry, to press Brandeis for a speedy American endorsement.

Brandeis held off responding until he had a copy of the draft declaration in hand, and then on 6 May went to the White House and spent nearly an hour with Wilson discussing Anglo-French friction in the Middle East and the desire of the Jews to reestablish a homeland in Palestine. The president gave his approval not only to a British protectorate over the Holy Land but also to the British formula of "a publicly assured, legally secured homeland for the Jewish people in Palestine." Wilson, however, could not publicly affirm his backing until he could calm the French. That same day Brandeis cabled Weizmann: "We approve your program and will do all we can to advance it. Not prudent for me to say anything for publication now. Keep us advised." Over the next few weeks the justice met with Balfour again and sent encouraging notes to the British Zionists. By 20 May, Weizmann felt so confident that he openly informed the English Zionist Federation that a British decision on Palestine would soon be announced.

There has been criticism of American Zionists in general and of Brandeis in particular for failing to take a more aggressive role at this point, for not speaking out and forcing the Wilson administration to endorse what has become known as the Balfour Declaration. Much of this censure assumes that Brandeis, despite his position on the Court, could act as a free agent. It also implies that the reason for the delay in announcing the Balfour Declaration rested on British perceptions that neither American Zionists nor the Wilson administration cared.

In fact, this friction arose from the same set of differences that would drive a wedge through the Zionist movement in 1921. Whatever their passports read, people like Chaim Weizmann and Nahum Sokolow saw themselves as citizens of a future Jewish state, a sort of Zionist government in exile, and ready to act as such no matter their private or professional positions. Moreover, Weizmann could wheedle and cajole His Majesty's Government not because Prime Minister David Lloyd George personally favored Zionism but because Zionism benefited imperial designs. Had the British not wanted Palestine for their own purposes, all of Weizmann's efforts would have been in vain.

The United States, however, had no territorial ambitions in the Middle East, a fact Brandeis understood; had American Zionists employed the same tactics as Weizmann, it would have done no good at all. Wilson had given Brandeis all the assurances he could; he sympathized with Zionist aims, but his responsibilities required him to serve American interests first. The United States had never declared war on the Ottoman Empire, and although the Turks had severed diplomatic relations, Wilson and House for a long time hoped that Turkey might be wooed away from the Central Powers to negotiate a separate peace with the Allies. For the United States to openly approve a plan to dismember Turkey would have doomed any chance of such an arrangement. Brandeis understood the man and the situation—Wilson had made a promise, and he would keep it in due time. Brandeis's well-known ties to Wilson, as well as his position on the Court, precluded him from saying anything, since Turkish officials might interpret his views as those of the president. Given this situation, Brandeis left Weizmann to pressure the British, while he urged American Zionists to build up organization and resources so that at the proper time they could back their colleagues overseas.

The British government hoped to secure American endorsement through private contacts such as Balfour's conversations with Brandeis. The State Department did not even see a draft copy of the declaration until June 1917, submitted not by the Foreign Office but by Justice Brandeis. Only in September, after the British government had thrashed out a number of internal issues, did Whitehall submit a proposed declaration to Wilson. Secretary of State Robert Lansing immediately objected, noting that the United States had not gone to war against Turkey. Even though he had promised to act when necessary, Wilson for the moment acceded to Lansing's request that he do and say nothing. Then, when the British did ask for his views, Wilson sent a message through Colonel House that he considered the timing inopportune, throwing both the British government and the English Zionists into confusion. Two weeks later, Brandeis cabled Weizmann to inform him of a complete reversal of the administration's view.

From the sequence of messages, it is possible to reconstruct what happened. Wilson, preoccupied with problems of faltering war production, did not realize from the almost casual tone of Lord Robert Cecil's inquiry that the British considered the American president's response critical to their going forward. Certainly Wilson did not discuss the matter with either Brandeis or Stephen Wise, and there is some evidence that House may have made Wilson's message seem more negative than the president had intended. Upon receiving panic-stricken cables from Weizmann, Brandeis arranged to see Colonel House on 23 September and at the meeting convinced him that the American government should endorse the proposal. Soon after, he sent a wire to

Weizmann: "From talks I have had with President and from expressions of opinion given to closest advisers I feel I can answer you that [Wilson] is in entire sympathy with declaration."

Balfour now sent a formal request for approval along with a final draft of the declaration through the State Department. The president passed it on to Brandeis, who, after consulting with Stephen Wise, suggested a minor change in wording. Wilson informed the British of his consent, and with the dam now broken, Balfour sent his famous letter to Lord Rothschild on 2 November 1917: "His Majesty's Government view with favor the establishment in Palestine of a national home for the Jewish people, and will use their best efforts to facilitate the achievement of this object."

The Balfour Declaration lacked one thing to make Jewish delirium complete—actual possession of the Holy Land. As Jacob de Haas noted amid the great outpouring of Jewish emotion, at least some people felt that "the bear's skin was being divided before the bear was caught." Then, just a few weeks later, General Edmund Allenby captured Jerusalem and occupied all of Palestine. Regina Goldmark, Brandeis's mother-in-law, sent him a note to congratulate him on these great happenings, and in a rare moment of introspection he responded, "The work for Zionism has seemed to me, on the whole, the most worthwhile of all I have attempted, and it is a great satisfaction to see the world gradually acquiescing in its realization." To his immediate associates, he was far less sentimental. "I note your telegram, fall of Jerusalem creating 'Big Sensation,' " he wrote to Jacob de Haas. "Is it creating big 'Money & Members'?"

Brandeis understood the Balfour Declaration, and even the capture of Palestine, to be no more than promissory notes. Wilson, under pressure from Lansing and House, did not announce his endorsement of the declaration until September 1918, and Brandeis had to fight off Weizmann's repeated demands that the American government proclaim its support publicly. Brandeis also understood that Wilson's Fourteen Points speech, delivered in January 1918, complicated matters further by its renunciation of imperial designs when it came time to redraw the maps of Europe and the Middle East. The Zionists would have to wait until after the war and then see if in fact the victorious Allies would redeem their promises at the peace conference.

AS ALLENBY'S FORCES swept into the Holy Land, they found a country exhausted by war, with both Arab and Jewish settlements facing dire poverty. Weizmann, taking the British declaration at face value, offered to form a Zionism commission to go to Palestine, assess the problems, and begin the rebuilding with Zionist funds, most of which would come from the United States. He wanted strong American representation, either Felix Frankfurter or Brandeis himself. Here once again Weizmann failed to understand the American government, its policies, and how Louis Brandeis saw himself. The justice recognized that the State Department would not give its approval, because to do so would give tacit endorsement to Britain's postwar aspirations in the region and might involve the United States in some joint occupation with the English. Brandeis had turned down Wilson's request to serve on the Mexican commission; how could he now accept a position on the Zionist delegation? Instead, Brandeis urged the PEC to raise more money and, without seeking explicit State Department permission, dispatched the New York lawyer Walter Meyer to accompany Weizmann.

Brandeis's response to Weizmann is the first time that he shared his hopes for the development of Palestine with the British leader. It not only rebuts later charges made against him that he wanted the country developed with private capital but also perfectly expresses his idealism. "The utmost vigilance should be exercised to prevent the acquisition by private persons of land, water rights, or other natural resources or any concessions for public utilities." Such resources, he declared, "must be secured for the whole Jewish people. In other ways, as well as this, the possibility of capitalistic exploitation must be guarded against." While room existed for growth in many areas, "our pursuit must be primarily agriculture in all its branches. The industries and commerce must be incidental merely, and such as may be required to ensure independence and national development."

Brandeis hoped that Palestine might develop as a primarily agricultural country with minimal industry. No large cities then existed, nor evidence of large mineral deposits that could serve as an industrial base. Brandeis might later be described as a prophet, but he most certainly could not see into a future in which a small Jewish state would have to fight for its survival against its Arab neighbors, or that Israelis would prove quite adept at creating large industries based on electronics. In 1918 he and most Zionists assumed that Palestine would remain a British protectorate for decades to come and, by focusing all of its energies inward, would be able to develop the just and humane society that Herzl had depicted. As for the Arabs in Palestine, practically none of the Zionist leaders paid any attention to them. In the Zionist slogan, Palestine was a land without people for the people without a land.

Weizmann and his commission did not expect the levels of destruction and poverty they witnessed upon their arrival. Daunted by the magnitude of the problems facing them, they again appealed to the Americans not just for money but for immediate participation in the work, and pleaded in vain for Brandeis to get the American government to change its mind. Given the devastation of Jewish communities in Europe, Weizmann said that for the foreseeable future, "We shall all turn to you and to your great country for help, advice and guidance—help in men and money." At the annual meeting of the American Zionists later that year, the delegates heard a letter from Weizmann asking for, at the very least, a loan of several million dollars. A frustrated Weizmann sent Aaron Aaronsohn to the United States to explain in person to the justice the full dimensions of the dangers facing the Zionists in Palestine and the need for American participation.

Aaronsohn left Palestine with instructions to determine why Brandeis remained impassive in the face of the great problems confronting Zionists. He explained Weizmann's difficulties to the Americans, and they educated him on the political realities that limited their options. The American government had different policy objectives from the British, and as American citizens they could not go any faster than the Wilson administration did. For the Zionists to try to pressure the American government as Weizmann had lobbied Great Britain would be counterproductive. Weizmann should stay in Palestine, Brandeis told Aaronsohn, and American Zionists would do everything they could, within the limits imposed on them, to supply the commission with additional technical and financial resources.

The young Palestinian, whom Brandeis greatly admired, easily healed this minor rift between the two Zionist leaders, but the incident presaged the friction between the two men, and between European and American Zionists. Weizmann had seen it as his duty to go to Palestine, to start work immediately on the Jewish homeland that would be ratified after the war. He felt abandoned by the Americans, who refused to join him in the task or to provide the large amounts of money he deemed necessary for the commission's work. Brandeis, on the other hand, much as he believed his Zionist work important, saw himself as an American whose primary responsibility involved his role as a justice of the Supreme Court. He distrusted Weizmann's unceasing demands for money without any specific plans for how the money should be spent.

In addition, people like Stephen Wise, Louis Lipsky, and Jacob de

Haas, who had been active in American Zionism before the war, remembered all too well how they had been shut out of leadership in the movement and treated as nothing more than fund-raisers who never brought in the amounts the Europeans expected from rich American Jews. Only the American Jewish community had escaped harm during the war; it now had an effective and respected leadership; and American Jewish leaders resented the Europeans who continued to see the Americans as good for little more than money. They urged Brandeis to assert American primacy in the movement, but while he did not want to become head of the world movement, neither did he want the WZO officials to tell Americans what to do.

BRANDEIS RECOGNIZED that when the war ended, American Jewry would be the primary source of financial support for the *yishuv.* The old slogan of "Men! Money! Discipline!" mattered more than ever, but American Zionism could not thrive as simply a large membership organization devoted to raising funds. There had to be a common vision of what Zionism meant, one that transcended party factions and reflected American ideals. Brandeis had already explained how one could be a good American by being a good Jew and a Zionist, because Zionist ideals of democracy and social justice reflected the same values in American life. But what exactly did this mean? How did democracy manifest itself in Zionist life, and where in the enterprise did one find social justice?

The pragmatism that initially attracted the eastern European Jews to the Brandeis leadership also confused them. They were shaken by the war's great devastation of their homelands, and the demand for action served as a tonic. They could do something, and the great respect accorded to Brandeis transformed Zionism from a marginal activity into one of influence and recognition. But they chafed at the lack of ideology and at the failure to pay attention to the importance of the cultural revival centered on the rebirth of the Hebrew language. Even though many of them had wandered away from the orthodoxy of their youth, they still expected some nod toward religion. Activism was all well and good, but at the 1915 Zionist convention in Boston some grumblings could already be heard that too little time had been devoted to theoretical review and the formulation of policy. The leadership's uninterest in doctrinal discussion especially upset the editors of the Yiddish press, who saw it as a sign of the gulf between the immigrant membership and the Americanized leaders.

Europeans in general had always been more interested in theory than

Americans, and European Zionists gloried in ideological debate. Perhaps because the movement had so little to show in terms of actual accomplishment, there had been solace in discussing how a Jewish homeland might theoretically be crafted. Brandeis and his lieutenants had little time and no patience for ideology. "We are now facing the critical period of Zionist history," said de Haas, clearly speaking for Brandeis. "We shall be judged not by our abilities to formulate theories . . . but by the judgments we employ in meeting the practical features of the Zionist program." The time for sterile ideological debate had passed; Zionists now had work to do. While always an idealist, Brandeis believed principles had to be translated into action; they had to have practical results.

Friction also developed over Brandeis's alleged dictatorial posture; he commanded, and the troops were supposed to follow without question. Brandeis had shown himself a firm organizational disciplinarian in his earlier reforms, but a great gulf existed between the work of the Public Franchise League or the Savings Bank Insurance League and that of the Zionists. Brandeis had crafted the reform lobbies out of whole cloth; they existed for a specific practical purpose, and the members followed Brandeis because he articulated exactly what had to be done to achieve those goals. One cannot imagine a meeting of the Boston groups devoted to theoretical discussions of the role of subways in urban life or the psychology of insurance programs in labor-intensive enterprises. In Boston, Brandeis's coolness, his aloofness, and his self-discipline did not offend his colleagues; they saw such qualities as typically Brahmin.

Many Zionists wanted a *mensch,* a man of the people, one who could walk and talk with them in terms familiar to their way of life, a man who had a Jewish soul, or *yiddishkeit.* Whatever else he may have been, Brandeis was never a man of the people. His partner George Nutter wrote that Brandeis's "interest lies in Man and not in men. He is singularly lacking in sympathetic touch with men and never understands them." Although Brandeis could when necessary talk to workingmen as well as merchant princes, he recognized his limits. He had refused to run for public office not just because he believed it would restrict his opportunities but because he understood quite well that he did not have the temperament for electoral politics.

By 1918, Brandeis had recognized that two things had to be done for American Zionists to act effectively after the war. First, there had to be a total reorganization of the movement so that all Zionist groups came under one umbrella, and, second, there had to be a platform upon which all American Zionists could stand.

THE FEDERATION OF AMERICAN ZIONISTS had been a loose coalition of literally dozens of groups, many of them small neighborhood clubs or local fraternal organizations, with little in common other than a general desire to rebuild a Jewish homeland. Some of these groups, such as the socialists and the religious Zionists, had commitments to specific ideological programs; others, like the Knights of Zion, were essentially social or insurance associations. The war crisis and Brandeis's leadership had allowed them to work together in the short-term task of raising relief money, but as early as 1915 Brandeis realized that a better-developed and more hierarchical organization had to be established. He understood that these groups would never give up their independence until they could be convinced of the necessity of a unified national Zionist organization. Factional infighting at the 1917 Baltimore convention convinced some of the local chieftains of the necessity for reorganization. Then the Balfour Declaration and the capture of Jerusalem made it clear that unless the Zionists acted, they would lose their chance to influence events after the war.

In the spring of 1918, Brandeis presented a five-point plan to the PEC. First, there would be a single national organization to which every Zionist in the country would belong directly, not through membership in an affiliated society. Second, this new entity would have a new name, the Zionist Organization of America (ZOA), to distinguish it from other groups. Third, members would belong to local chapters that would be subservient to the national ZOA, and these districts, in the fourth point, would be grouped by regions. Finally, existing clubs and societies would retain the independence to work out their own goals and ideas, but the ZOA would hold full responsibility and authority for Zionist policy in the United States. Centering national work on the ZOA would allow Zionist groups such as Hadassah to put additional energy into their local or specialized projects.

Brandeis, it should be noted, never saw organization as anything more than a tool, a means of managing and utilizing resources more efficiently and effectively. "Organization," he said, "is never a substitute for initiative and judgment." But without good organization, the best initiative and judgment could go to naught.

Although the plan demonstrated Brandeis's awareness of and sensitivity to the needs of the small local societies, they saw it as an attack on their independence and the enlargement of power in the hands of a few people who, unlike them, did not share the culture of the immigrant Jewish community. In Europe every ideological group, no matter how small its constituency or narrow its base, had its own party within the World Zionist Organization, a condition that satisfied local Zionists but hamstrung the WZO. In the United States political parties have traditionally sought to blur ideological lines in order to appeal to a wider constituency, basing their power on broad consensus rather than on narrow principle. The plan Brandeis presented reflected progressive American thought on popular organization and assumed general agreement on important policies. To those who already complained that the Brandeis group dismissed ideological considerations, the plan seemed like little more than a power grab.

At the 1918 convention in Pittsburgh, one group after another got up to denounce the plan in whole or in part and tried to introduce amendments that would have exempted them from subordination to the new national body. Rather than address the individual complaints, the Brandeis group hammered away at the benefits of the new organization and reminded the delegates that if they wanted to have a say in the postwar planning, American Zionists had to speak with one voice. One after another, first Hadassah, then the Knights of Zion, and then others agreed, and when the final vote came, the proposal carried easily, although many who voted "yes" did so resentfully and with misgivings.

As the clerk read the results, one of the delegates on the convention floor spied Louis Brandeis sitting alone in the gallery and, jumping to his feet, began to cheer and wave frantically in his direction. Soon the entire convention joined in the spontaneous demonstration, with delegates standing on their chairs shouting, *"Hadad! Hadad!"* They may not have liked his plan, but American Zionists still revered their leader.

A more muted resentment greeted the statement of principles proposed in response to those who wanted a clarification of exactly what the American Zionist movement stood for. While raising money had been and would remain a priority, for what purposes did they raise these funds? What should Zionists do other than write checks? The Pittsburgh meeting marked the first gathering of Zionists after the Balfour Declaration and the capture of Jerusalem, and Brandeis believed it important to set forth a policy statement that would not only guide

American Zionists but also represent their views in the debates that would take place over the development of Palestine. Although he consulted with his colleagues, Brandeis essentially wrote the "Pittsburgh Platform" by himself, and it reveals, as do few other documents, how he hoped to merge the progressive goal of social justice into Zionism. On 25 June 1918, the convention unanimously approved a resolution that, after acknowledging Herzl's dream and how recent events had brought it closer to fruition, declared:

> Therefore, we desire to affirm anew the principles which have guided the Zionist Movement since its inception and which were the foundation of the ancient Jewish State and of the living Jewish law embodied in the traditions of two thousand years of exile.
>
> First, We declare for political and civil equality irrespective of race, sex or faith of all the inhabitants of the land.
>
> Second, To insure in the Jewish national home in Palestine equality of opportunity, we favor a policy which, with due regard to existing rights, shall tend to establish the ownership and control by the whole people of the land, of all natural resources and of all public utilities.
>
> Third, All land, owned or controlled by the whole people, should be leased on such conditions as will ensure the fullest opportunity for development and continuity of possession.
>
> Fourth, The co-operative principle should be applied so far as feasible in the organization of agriculture, industrial, commercial and financial undertakings.
>
> Fifth, The system of free public instruction, which is to be established, should embrace all grades and departments of education.
>
> Sixth, Hebrew, the national language of the Jewish people, shall be the medium of public instruction.

Although nearly all the tenets of the Pittsburgh Platform eventually became accepted policy in Palestinian development, it is clear they reflected the social concerns of the American leadership. The Mizrachi, the religious Zionists, felt religion had been ignored, while the Hebraicists believed the last item failed to emphasize sufficiently the importance of the Hebrew language in a cultural renascence. The masses of immigrant Jews could not understand it and could not find reference to ideas familiar to them, such as the mysticism associated with nationalist redemption. Only the moderate socialist Poale Zion embraced it warmly, while old-line socialists condemned it as vapid. The Yiddish press ignored it.

Emanuel Neuman, then a delegate and a future ZOA president, concluded that despite the bitterness at the beginning, "there has hardly been a convention that adjourned with such a feeling of solidarity, with such unanimity, and with such a common, all-embracing enthusiasm as this one." By bringing out some of the tensions over organization and purpose, Brandeis succeeded in calming the waters for a while. It is doubtful he understood the depth of feeling in the immigrant community, which reluctantly swallowed the reorganization plan and statement of principles. Brandeis remained their leader, and they took much of what he proposed on faith. But just as he failed to discern the extent of nationalist feeling among rank-and-file Zionists, they could not understand his failure to give them what they sought in Zionism—a feeling for Jewishness and national rebirth.

BY THE TIME THE PEACEMAKERS met in Paris in 1919, the United States, France, Italy, China, and Japan had endorsed the Balfour Declaration, and from their comments it seems clear that David Lloyd George, Arthur Balfour, and other top British officials all interpreted it to mean that there would be a future Jewish state in Palestine. Career officers in the army and in the Foreign Office, however, studiously ignored the statement, and when Weizmann arrived in Palestine he had quickly discovered the rampant anti-Semitism among Allenby's officers. In Whitehall the career Arabists promoted a Pan-Arab union under British sponsorship that would exclude both the French and the Zionists from the Middle East. Only if the Paris conference endorsed the Balfour Declaration and gave the mandate over Palestine to Great Britain would there be a chance for the Zionist dream to come true. Before going overseas, Woodrow Wilson had told Stephen Wise that the Zionists could count on his full support, and after returning from his first trip abroad met with the delegation from the American Jewish Congress. As the meeting broke up, the president called Wise to a corner, reaffirmed his support, and, as they shook hands, said: "Don't worry, Dr. Wise, Palestine is yours."

Wilson, however, had the whole world to save, and despite his best intentions Palestine occupied only a small corner of it. The American commissioners quickly agreed with the experts from the State Department and the Foreign Office that the Balfour Declaration had been a bad idea and should be ignored. Anti-Zionists as well as Christian missionary groups in the United States and Great Britain inundated the delegates with petitions against creating a Jewish homeland. Wilson's Fourteen Points also worked against Zionist aspirations; if self-determination were to be taken seriously in deciding what to do in Palestine, then Arab interests should prevail. It would take months of difficult negotiations until the peace conference endorsed the Balfour Declaration, and the mandate over Palestine would not be awarded to Great Britain until the San Remo Conference in 1920. Throughout these trying months the Zionists kept up their pressure on different governments.

In February 1920, when the commissioners seemed to be wavering about Palestine, Brandeis contacted Wilson directly, reminding him that the United States had endorsed the Balfour Declaration. Wilson, who more and more had come to see it as his Christian duty to ensure the return of Jews to Palestine, sent a copy of the letter to Secretary of State Lansing, directing him to instruct the American representatives in Paris that under no circumstances could the Balfour promise be abandoned. "All the great powers are committed to the Balfour declaration," said the president, "and I agree with Mr. Justice Brandeis regarding it as a solemn promise which we can in no circumstances afford to break or alter."

DURING THIS PERIOD Brandeis could do only so much, relying on Felix Frankfurter in Paris to keep him abreast of the situation. In the spring of 1919, however, he decided that he would personally go to Paris and Palestine. He had been under constant pressure from Weizmann and the European Zionists to attend the peace conference, although no one seemed sure exactly what he would do there. Then, after the State Department dispatched the King-Crane Commission to Palestine, Frankfurter began insisting to Brandeis that he had to go to Palestine and contain the danger. Brandeis agreed, since he also wanted to see the problems and opportunities in Palestine personally and to get a better sense of what the Zionists should do.

Brandeis sailed on board the RMS *Mauretania* with a small party that included Jacob de Haas and his wife and Susan Brandeis, who apparently had mixed feelings about the trip, acting, as her father put it, "comme il faut." They arrived in London on 20 June, and as soon as he set foot on the ground, all of his old Anglophilic sentiments rose to the fore. "London is civilization," he told Alice, and "it would be worth millions of men's lives to preserve it. Our American cities are business machines; London is living. All the horrors of bigness are absent." He also plunged into a series of meetings with Zionist leaders, caught up on what he needed to know about the peace conference from Felix Frankfurter, and concluded, "My coming was very much needed." He and Chaim Weizmann finally met in person, and as Louis told Alice, "Weizmann is neither as great nor as objectionable as he was painted; but he is very much of a man & much bigger than most of his fellows." As a diversion from Zionist business, he, Susan, and Frankfurter enjoyed a long talk with Graham Wallas, one of the early Fabians and a founder of the London School of Economics.

The party then went on for a very short stay in Paris. In the evening the justice walked along the Champs-Élysées and the Seine, "a new world for me of beauty." Brandeis then met with members of the American delegation and with Louis Marshall and the Congress mission. No one, he discovered, had much good to say about the pending peace treaty, and while Zionist "problems are sufficiently serious, one bears them with becoming lightness in the world of gloom." Brandeis and Frankfurter also had a private discussion with Balfour and Lord Eustace Percy, and Balfour assured Brandeis that the British intended to fulfill their pledge. Brandeis, in turn, reiterated that the United States wanted England to have the mandate.

Alfred Zimmern, at Brandeis's request, now joined them, and along with de Haas they took an uncomfortable train to Marseilles, where they boarded the Pacific & Orient ship *Malwa* to Port Said. While at sea Brandeis read a satchelful of reports and also looked into the small library that the party carried with them that included a Hebrew phrase book, a Baedeker's guide to Palestine, and several books on the history and geography of the Holy Land. After the usual delays in port, they took a train to Cairo, where a twenty-three-member Jewish band of Maccabees and Boy Scouts greeted him by playing "Hatikvah," the Zionist hymn that would become the Israeli national anthem. The Jews "bore their heads high and the backs were straight and they bore the blue and white [flag] like a free and independent people."

Because he needed to speak with General Allenby before going on to Palestine, Brandeis spent nearly a week in Cairo waiting for the general's delayed return from Syria, comfortably ensconced in one of the "luxurious" apartments of the famed Shepheard's Hotel. Each day he went out and reported faithfully to Alice and Elizabeth back home what he saw and the people he met. Although he complained about the dreariness, he found the locals superior in "moral, mental and physical cleanliness. But why our lack of beauty and joyousness which life here is full of? And why should western women have made such a lamentable failure in utilizing the colors and flowing gowns with which man here makes every moment interesting and every scene a picture?" He found these long gowns so graceful "that I am almost reconciled to the habit of priests and acolytes, which used to fill me with unspeakable horror, and which a peep into the Roman Catholic Church (with Zimmern) has served to revive. If only dress makers and milliners and their fashions could be exterminated there would be hope." He hoped that Susan, who waited for him in London, had grown "as enthusiastically pro-British as I am," and felt sure she would if she saw all the "fine clean looking young officers and Tommies" that he found in Cairo.

Allenby finally returned and Brandeis dined with him and his senior officers on 5 July, doing his best to correct some of the ideas Allenby had about Zionism. The next day the party traveled to Alexandria, and arrived in Jerusalem on 8 July, and it is not too much to say that Louis Brandeis fell in love with the country immediately. He stayed at a house in which several Zionists lived, including Dr. Harry Friedenwald and Henrietta Szold, and "I am taken care of much in the manner of a Swiss landlady. Living conditions couldn't be better." There were

Brandeis and Jonas Friedenwald in Palestine, 1919

indeed problems—serious and numerous—that would have to be resolved. "The way is long, the path difficult and uncertain; but the struggle is worthwhile. It is indeed a Holy Land."

Altogether the Brandeis party spent seventeen days in Palestine. Dressed in a lightweight summer suit, bow tie, and pith helmet, he visited all of the cities and twenty-three of the forty-three Jewish settlements, asking questions at every stop about crops, schooling, health, and other matters. He made no speeches. As he told Alice, "The most I said on any one occasion did not exceed a few short sentences. There were few such occasions & when I spoke I said mainly sweet nothings." Although he tried to travel as unostentatiously as possible, the colonists of the *yishuv* insisted on showing their gratitude to the man they believed had made their survival during the war possible. Every place he went, Jews turned out to greet him, and while the youngsters danced and sang for him, the proud settlers served him the fruits of their own fields and vineyards. Exploring the cactus-covered Temple area by moonlight moved him deeply, as did his visit to Rachel's tomb on the Bethlehem road. There, watching the sun set over the Judaean Hills, he turned to his traveling companions and said, "I know now why all the world wanted this land and why all peoples loved it." For the rest of his life he would refer to this trip as setting the final seal on his commitment to Zion. The trip gave Brandeis an essential experience that had been missing from his Zionism, a quality he could not get from books and reports—a love for the land and an understanding of what Palestine meant to the Jewish people.

Brandeis had not come to Palestine as a tourist, however, and while he took great pride in the accomplishments of the settlers, he also saw hundreds of adults and children suffering from the lingering effects of malaria, an illness he knew well from his youth in Kentucky. Hadassah nurses told Brandeis of a settlement near Tiberias where seventy-eight out of eighty workers fell victim to the disease in one summer, each person suffering an average of two episodes. Before the *yishuv* could prosper, before hundreds of thousands of immigrants could come to build the land, this danger to its health would have to be eradicated— a practical problem that practical people could solve.

Prior to leaving Palestine, Brandeis penned a letter to General Allenby: "What I have seen and heard strengthen greatly my conviction that Palestine can and must become the Jewish Homeland as promised in the Balfour declaration. The problems and the difficulties are serious and numerous, even more so than I had anticipated, but there is none which will not be solved & overcome by the indomitable spirit of the Jews here and elsewhere."

HAVING SPENT TIME in Palestine, Brandeis felt more confident about the practical work facing the Zionists. He sailed back to France and spent "busy and profitable" days in Paris, happily discovering that American and British officials now felt certain that the treaty would recognize the Balfour promise and that the proposed League of Nations would award the mandate to Great Britain. "On the whole," he told Alice, "I think Zionist affairs about the most hopeful of all the world's problems."

Brandeis the idealist had seen the Palestine that he and many of the settlers believed it would become—democratic, egalitarian, and Jewish, the latter in terms of the ethical teachings of the prophets and not the ritualistic prescriptions of the rabbis. Brandeis the pragmatist saw specific problems to be solved, chief among them the eradication of malaria by draining the great Huleh swamp in the Galilee. He now had to convince the World Zionist Organization that it, too, must abandon its old policies, its fixations on ideological debate, its obsession with still more political assurances. The British had promised Palestine to the Jews, the peacemakers in Paris had ratified that pledge, and all signs pointed to the award of the mandate to England. The time had come to make the land habitable, to pour money not into the Zionist Organization but into bricks and mortar, roads and trees, schools and hospitals. The time, in short, had come to stop talking and to start doing.

This is the message Brandeis tried to drive home both in Paris and at the Actions Committee meeting in London in early August. The man who had said so little in Palestine now found himself talking nonstop, and in German. "I have labored hard," he told Alice, "and at length. It is a wearing performance to me & doubtless to the others although I have recovered a bit of my fluency." The message he brought and worked so hard to deliver did not, however, sit well with the European Zionist leadership. Brandeis advocated the abolition of the Zionist Commission and its replacement by moving all Zionist offices to Palestine. Funds would have to be raised, of course, and in this the Americans would do all they could. That money, however, had to be spent efficiently and effectively, and too many layers of Zionist bureaucracy stood between the donors and the recipients.

Brandeis found the Europeans fixated on political issues, and he could not get them to look at the practical problems in Palestine, such as the need to fight malaria, which they dismissed as irrelevant. The Europeans opposed dismantling the Zionist Commission, which they wanted to strengthen and put in direct charge of all work in Palestine. They even attacked the highly successful Hadassah Medical Unit for its failure to conduct its business in Hebrew or to commit to living in Palestine permanently. Dr. Isaac Max Rubinow, a noted physician and social worker, headed the unit, and he had come to Palestine to treat sickness and establish health facilities, not to make aliyah or play politics. Brandeis was appalled to learn that all of the official reports written by Rubinow to the London office had to be translated into Hebrew in Jerusalem and then translated again back into English when they arrived in London.

The two groups also fought over the question of the Jewish agency that the mandate called for to assist in Palestinian development. Everyone agreed that membership should be open to non-Zionist Jewish groups, such as the American Jewish Committee. But Weizmann and the Europeans wanted to bring in representatives of the "National Councils" that had sprung up after the war in eastern Europe to protect Jewish rights. The WZO planned to work with these councils to develop Jewish and Hebrew culture in the Diaspora. The Americans strongly opposed such an approach since it encouraged "Diaspora nationalism," the idea that all Jews, wherever they might be, owed political and national loyalty to a Jewish peoplehood. If the National Councils wanted to work for Palestine, let them pay the shekel and join the Zionist organization. Brandeis won a temporary victory on this point, but Weizmann remained bitter over it and accused the Americans of "lacking in historic understanding of Jewish life and wanting in Jewish soul."

Brandeis returned to the United States rapturous about what he had seen in Palestine, and greatly disturbed over his first extended contact with the European Zionist leadership. The demand for money and more money, without proper accounting practices, and too much of it diverted to support what he considered a bloated Zionist bureaucracy, upset him greatly. The failure of the Actions Committee to consider dealing with malaria led him to direct that for the immediate future, all ZOA funds should go directly to the Hadassah Medical Unit and be controlled by Dr. Rubinow. Brandeis also made a personal donation of $10,000 to Hadassah for a pilot project in the Galilee that proved remarkably successful. The same settlement near Tiberias that reported

*Brandeis on ship with Nathan Straus, Stephen Wise,
and James Waterman Wise, 1920*

seventy-eight people ill from malaria in the summer of 1919 had only two cases the following year, and the surrounding area, with a population of over one thousand, had only five cases. Swamp drainage and the planting of eucalyptus trees proved extremely effective. The diversion of funds to Hadassah meant a corresponding sharp drop in American support of other programs and less money to the Zionist organization, a fact that increased friction between the two groups. When Brandeis sent Robert Kesselman to Palestine to help develop better administrative and accounting practices, the Europeans fought him every step of the way.

TO STRENGTHEN THEIR POSITION, the Europeans wanted to call a *Jahreskonferenz* in London in early 1920, a meeting of important Zionist officials but a lesser gathering than a full-fledged congress. Brandeis said he would not be able to attend until after the Court recessed for the summer, but he also wanted to replenish ZOA coffers so he would be in a better bargaining position. The severe postwar depression that afflicted the United States led not only to a sharp drop in donations but also to a decline in membership. From a high of 180,000 in the summer of 1919, Zionist rolls fell off in the next eighteen months to a little more than 25,000. At the very time that Brandeis needed more men and money, he had little of either.

Yet when Brandeis went off, accompanied by Alice, to the 1920 meeting, he actually stood in higher regard with the WZO than before. Although many of the European leaders disagreed with his emphasis on practical work, they recognized that no Jew in the world enjoyed greater prestige than he did—a justice of the U.S. Supreme Court, a confidant of President Wilson's, and a man who could converse as an equal with the heads of other countries. Some American Zionists wanted Brandeis

Louis Lipsky, American Zionist official

to take over the leadership of the WZO, and had he been willing to do so, the Europeans would gladly have given him the office.

On board the *Lapland* on the way to London, Brandeis apparently gave the idea some thought. De Haas and Louis Lipsky urged him to do so, but Felix Frankfurter vehemently argued that he had a higher obligation to stay on the bench. Brandeis was torn between the opportunities he saw to create an ideal society in Palestine and the view he had argued for six years that one could be both a good Zionist and a good American. To leave the court that he called "the highest tribunal in the world" would give the lie to all that he had said; it would prove that Zionists pledged their primary allegiance not to the United States but to the movement.

Brandeis reached his final decision after a meeting with Bernard Rosenblatt, a young American lawyer whom Brandeis liked and had sent on a fact-finding mission to Palestine. At breakfast on 4 July, Rosenblatt told the justice (a man thirty years his senior whom he revered) that he doubted if Brandeis had the temperament to lead the movement. "As the first Jewish member of the United States Supreme Court you can be a very important figure for us," Rosenblatt declared. "If you become the leader of Zionism, you'll have to go to Palestine; you'll have to meet opposition, difficulties, disputes with Ussischkin, and I don't know whether it wouldn't be a means of breaking you." The Zionist methods that Rosenblatt had seen while in Palestine made no sense to the efficiency and rationality of American business and administrative practices and would prove too frustrating to Brandeis. The justice had more than a taste of that frustration at the *Jahreskonferenz*.

Brandeis accepted the chairmanship of the meeting at its opening on 7 July and in his speech enthused over the possibilities of Palestine and the great responsibility that now rested on the Zionists. Theodor Herzl had sought an international charter, and the great nations of the world had provided that through the Balfour Declaration and the mandate. "The rest lies with us. The task before us is the Jewish settlement of Palestine. It is the task of reconstruction. We must approve the plans on which the reconstruction shall proceed. We must create the executive and administrative machinery adapted to the work before us. We must select men of the training, the experience and the character fitted to conduct that work. And finally, we must devise ways and means to raise the huge sums which the undertaking demands."

The following week must surely have been one of the most frustrating of Brandeis's life. He saw problems waiting to be solved, and assumed that the Zionist leaders would settle down to figure out the proper solutions. That people might disagree over whether one particular plan would be more efficacious than another would not have upset him. Nor would he have objected to a debate over priorities; with limited funds, some projects would have to be delayed. Given some study, rational choices could be made. But instead of clear thought and calm rhetoric, he found a babel of voices in London, all yelling and shouting and haggling not only over minor matters but also over ones totally irrelevant to the important work at hand. He had come to London to build a Jewish homeland and wound up presiding over a "talkfest."

For their part, the Europeans resented his insistence on parliamentary order, his emphasis on economic matters, and his lack of *yiddishkeit*. He unknowingly insulted them when he declared that dues money should not be used to pay the salaries of old-line Zionists (who saw their positions as rewards for service), or called veterans of the movement like Yehial Tschlenow and Leo Motzkin "pensioners." Weizmann failed to keep promises, and even some of the British chemist's friends charged him with not dealing honestly with the Americans. Above all the Europeans objected when Brandeis told them that the time for propaganda had ended and that for real work had begun. Propaganda, they believed, was real work and, no matter what the American said, would always be needed. Although the Europeans wanted to elect Brandeis and one other American to the Actions Committee, Brandeis refused. He recognized that he would always be outvoted, and the American presence would be interpreted as condoning a bad policy. "Things will go on in London of which I may not be aware," he told Julius Simon. "How can I assume responsibility?" The executive, indeed the whole organization, had to be revamped.

The issue that upset Brandeis most grew out of Weizmann's plan to launch a brand-new fund, the Keren Hayesod, which would solicit both donation and investment funds. Brandeis had no problem with a new donation fund to which contributors gave money as a gift to be used at the discretion of the WZO. Nor did he have problems with people investing in Palestinian enterprises. While he had no desire for the *yishuv* to become a capitalist enclave, he accepted the idea that some projects might better be conducted through private ventures. But the two types of moneys should never be intermingled. The very idea of mixing gifts and investments, with little or no auditing oversight, appalled him; the two moneys had to be handled differently and audited in different ways, and there had to be accountability for each. When Weizmann broached the idea, Brandeis lost all confidence in him and thereafter considered him little more than a trickster.

BRANDEIS LEFT THE LONDON CONFERENCE in far weaker position than when he arrived, vis-à-vis both the Europeans and his own American followers. The Americans did not object to Brandeis's economic plans nor to his charges of inefficiency in the WZO, which were all too true; they did balk at his abdication of power and responsibility, and those with a deep commitment to cultural work resented his seeming denigration of that part of Zionist work. From this point on, Weizmann would insist that Brandeis had no right to criticize the work of the executive since he had refused to assume responsibility. The Englishman claimed he would be willing to give up his own policies and give all power to the Brandeis group, if only it would assume the work that went with it. Brandeis, he charged, had for too long been the "silent leader" of the ZOA, hidden in Washington and sending out directives through lieutenants. World Zionism did not need silent leaders; it needed people who would openly accept their responsibilities.

On the way home aboard the *Zeeland,* Brandeis drafted a memorandum summarizing all of his objections to the current WZO policy and what he believed should be the movement's objectives. Above all else, there had to be immigration to Palestine, and to facilitate that, money had to be raised for economic development and health improvement. The political stage of Zionism had ended, and now the Zionists must make a reality of the opportunity at hand. From the time Brandeis landed in New York in late August, he and his followers stood on this platform—the reorganization of the movement, the phasing out of political work, an emphasis on practical projects to make Palestine fit for development, and fiscal responsibility in Zionist affairs. If these issues had been somewhat blurred at the London conference, they were crystal clear when the ZOA met in Cleveland in June 1921.

By early in the year Weizmann and his followers had gained the upper hand. The very traits that had made Brandeis such an attractive figure during the war—his decisiveness, his American values, his ability to delegate and to set a clear vision for his followers—now came back as charges of autocracy, a lack of *yiddishkeit,* a hidden leadership too far removed from the masses. Louis Lipsky, for decades a workhorse of American Zionism, told the National Executive Committee that he had loyally followed the Brandeis group even if he did not always agree with its policies. But Brandeis, at least, had led them; he had been out in front; he had given them the message and the inspiration. In London, however, the justice had abdicated; he had been offered full authority to direct the movement and had refused. Now he wanted to call the tune without the responsibility; he declined to lead yet refused to follow.

Lipsky's speech cut close to the bone. Brandeis had in fact fallen victim to the delusion that he could lead in absentia. A man of reason, he naively assumed his ideas and not his personality had been the unifying force in the American Zionist movement. The masses of Jews had followed him more than they had followed his ideas, and they demanded only that those ideas point toward re-creating a Jewish homeland. Ideas did matter, but not as much as the visible participation of a charismatic leader. Brandeis failed to understand that his program to rejuvenate American Zionism could not be executed without him. If at any time before the Cleveland convention he had put the mantle of leadership back on, protests against his policies would have been immediately muted. No matter how much the immigrant Jewish community adored him—he had once been called "the greatest Jew since Jesus"— they would not accept a program handed down from Washington.

Brandeis recognized "that my so-called leadership is an anomaly, seemingly inconsistent with doctrinaire democracy." He would not resent it, he claimed, if the Zionists "like Plato 'declined with thanks.'" But he also resented the criticism. Part of his effectiveness lay in the fact that he did hold high government office, and to give it up would change both who he was and what he represented. The Zionists, he told de Haas, "have brains enough to understand the necessary limitations."

Weizmann decided to push ahead with his plans for the Keren Hayesod, although Brandeis believed that they had agreed the matter

Weizmann party, with Albert Einstein, arrives in America, 1921

would not be brought up until the following summer. The Englishman
landed in New York to a great welcome in early April 1921, accompanied by none other than Albert Einstein, who came to help raise funds
for the new Hebrew University in Jerusalem. Julian Mack, Stephen
Wise, Felix Frankfurter, and others met with him in an effort to heal
the widening breach, but the minute Weizmann showed any sign of
compromising, the zealots who had come in his party, notably
Shmaryahu Levin and Menachem Ussischkin, threatened to return to
London and break him politically. So Weizmann toured the country,
supposedly raising money for the Keren Hayesod but spending much of
the time denouncing Brandeis for his lack of *yiddishkeit*. There could be
no peace, he declared, between Pinsk and Washington.

Brandeis's suspicions of Weizmann's duplicity had now been confirmed. At London the justice had negotiated in good faith with the
chemist, only to see him break his word almost immediately; the same
thing had happened again. Brandeis, a puritan as much as a Zionist,
believed the whole matter no longer represented one man's opinion of
policy against another but involved fundamental questions of principle. "Our aim is the kingdom of heaven," he told his lieutenants, paraphrasing Cromwell. "We take Palestine by the way. But we must take
it with clean hands; we must take it in such a way as to ennoble the
whole Jewish people. Otherwise it will not be worth having."

• • •

BY THE TIME THE ZIONISTS met in Cleveland on 5 June, the momentum had clearly gone over to those forces led by Louis Lipsky and committed to Chaim Weizmann. On the crucial motion to establish the Keren Hayesod in the United States, the Brandeis group lost by a lopsided vote of 153–71. At 1:30 in the morning a weary Julian Mack rose to speak. He thanked the delegates for the great honor that American Zionism had bestowed upon him by electing him president of the ZOA. He had worked faithfully, he said, to carry out the policies adopted by previous conventions, policies he fully endorsed. On principle, however, he could not go along with the decision to establish a major funding agency without proper safeguards, a move he interpreted as a repudiation of all that he and his colleagues believed.

He then submitted his resignation as president of the ZOA, as a member of the executive committee, and as a member of the Greater Actions Committee of the WZO. He reached into his jacket pocket, and pulled out a letter from Brandeis, and read it to the now-hushed throng:

> With the principles and policies adopted by the National Executive Committee under your leadership I am in complete agreement. Strict adherence to those principles is demanded by the high Zionist ideals. Steadfast pursuit of those policies is essential to early and worthy development of Palestine as the Jewish Homeland. We who believe in those principles and policies cannot properly take part in any administration of Zionist affairs which repudiates them.
>
> Upon the delegates in convention assembled rests the responsibility of deciding whether those principles and policies shall prevail in the immediate future. If their decision is adverse, you will, I assume, resign, and in that event present also my resignation as Honorary President. Our place will then be as humble soldiers in the ranks to hasten by our struggle and policies, which we believe will be recognized as the only ones through which our great ends may be achieved.

Amid stunned silence Mack went on to submit the resignations of thirty-six other members of the National Executive Committee, including Stephen Wise, Nathan Straus, Felix Frankfurter, and Horace Kallen, as well as three members of the administrative staff. The sounds of weeping could be heard in the hall as Mack concluded: "No action which you have taken, no action that you can take will ever drive me or any of the other gentlemen whose names I have mentioned from the ranks of membership . . . and will never lessen by the slightest degree the intensity of their Zionism, their devotion to Palestine, and their continuous zealous work."

At a little after two in the morning the Brandeis era of American Zionism came to a close.

ALMOST FROM THE TIME that Mack read the resignations to the convention, people have been trying to explain the schism at Cleveland and how Brandeis, normally so astute, could have so badly misjudged the mood of the rank-and-file Zionists. Weizmann's backers picked up on the theme of "Washington versus Pinsk" and saw it as a fight between an Americanized leadership and immigrants who still valued *yiddishkeit,* the Jewish soul. The journalist Shmuel Melamed accused Brandeis of having departed too far from his Jewish roots. "His entire conception of Zionism was *goyish* [gentile] and not Jewish, and this *goyish* conception of Zionism he wanted to impose upon American Zionism."

Such criticism is only partially right. Brandeis indeed had no Jewish background, and he did see Zionism as an extension of the ideals he found most worthwhile in the American tradition. But if he and immigrant American Jews shared this ideal, they parted on his methods. Brandeis, contrary to some of their charges, never wanted to run Zionism as a business, nor did he want to have Palestine develop solely through private enterprise. The idealist, however, believed in more than just talking about dreams; he insisted on trying to achieve them. Herzl had dreamed, and his dream had incited a people. Brandeis also dreamed, but he saw the achievement made possible through such projects as the eradication of malaria, a proposal that could not compare to Herzl's vision in rousing passion.

Where Weizmann and his followers saw Brandeis ignoring the greater dream for mere accounting principles, he saw the mundane as making possible the grandiose. The idea of a mixed fund struck many of the Europeans as questionable, but they accepted it because the money would support the things that did matter to them, such as the revival of Hebrew and cultural development. Brandeis wanted to change the movement since he believed the era of politics had come to an end; Zionists now had to focus on the hard practical work of building the homeland. He failed to realize the importance that many Zionists gave to cultural work, and had he understood this, it would have been so easy for him to say that practical work included not only draining swamps but reviving Hebrew; not only building roads but building schools; not only training farmers and engineers but training teachers.

Brandeis did not grow up in an atmosphere where a divide existed between the secular and the holy, and where embracing the holy could be dangerous. For Jews who still recalled the persecutions they faced in eastern Europe, the notion of a Jewish homeland meant, above all else, the freedom to be Jewish without fear. Few Americans understood how the cultural work—the idea of people living openly as Jews, conversing in Hebrew, attending schools where all subjects would be taught in Hebrew—could mean so much. For Brandeis, the cultural work mattered little, not because it was unimportant, but because he assumed others would take that burden upon themselves. He and those Zionists he led had to do the practical work, and after that others would do the cultural. But they had to do that work, as he said, with clean hands, or they would not be worthy of Palestine.

In the end, the practical policies that Brandeis championed prevailed, since he correctly analyzed the economic and fiscal needs of the movement. Within a very short time Weizmann began to downplay political work, and instead emphasized practical efforts needed to rebuild Palestine. The Palestine Development Council handled funds earmarked for investment, while the Keren Hayesod took in donations. Simple necessity required sanitary work to precede immigration. As Weizmann grew more familiar with the United States and its Jewish community, he stopped talking about Jewish nationalism and started preaching the gospel of Palestinian work. But he never understood what Brandeis had contributed to the movement.

Brandeis made Zionism acceptable to American Jewry, not only for those who had already acculturated, but for those who hoped to do so. He calmed the unwarranted fears of so-called dual loyalty and legitimized the movement in non-Jewish eyes. His emphasis on practical work gave American Jews a concrete task they needed, the only way they could transform the abstractions of Zionism into a relevant movement. He could not, however, give them that Jewish soul they so craved; Weizmann could. Neither man understood that most American Jews did not want Washington or Pinsk. They wanted both.

At the convention Brandeis had told the delegates that he and his associates would be retiring from offices in the ZOA but not from Zionism itself. Within days of the Pittsburgh meeting the Brandeis group met in New York, established the Palestine Endowment Funds to funnel money to projects in the Holy Land, and began their wait for what they recognized as their inevitable return to power.

CHAPTER TWENTY-TWO

WAR AND SPEECH—
AND HOLMES

A s Brandeis labored in the Washington heat in the summer of
1918, neither the Wilson administration's demands for advice
nor the needs of Zionism prevented him from paying attention
to his responsibilities on the Supreme Court. He wrote to Alice, then
on Cape Cod, that he was at work revising an opinion, had "started
Sutherland on further investigation," and had another case far enough
along to send a draft to the printer. "So you see that the law is not
entirely silent amidst arms."

During World War I, the powers of the federal government expanded
enormously, and the irony is that big government came in the administration of Woodrow Wilson, a man who feared strong federal authority.
Many wartime measures faced constitutional challenges, but during the
conflict the judiciary heard only those cases in which the government
needed a quick decision. The Court delayed other matters until after
hostilities had ended. If at that time the measure proved constitutional,
then its validation simply showed the administration had acted legitimately; if not, its demise would no longer affect the war program.

The administration also wanted to clamp down on dissent. Brandeis
initially, albeit doubtfully, went along in approving these laws, but
then he and Holmes changed their minds and emerged as champions of
free expression. Holmes penned memorable lines, but it would be
Brandeis who put together the bases for modern First Amendment
jurisprudence. In the process, the names of the two men became in-
extricably and forever linked.

THE UNITED STATES was ill equipped to go to war in April 1917.
Despite the preparedness legislation of 1916, the federal bureaucracy

remained small, the army and navy stood on peacetime footings, and cooperation between the government and the private sector was minimal. When Congress declared war, it began enacting legislation that not only strengthened the national government but also impinged on the lives of individuals. All of these laws wound up in court, but the judiciary expedited only one case, that involving military conscription. Both the administration and opponents to the law wanted a swift resolution; men should not be allowed to die should the law be unconstitutional, nor should the government's mobilization be derailed if it were valid. (The Court unanimously upheld the law.)

Brandeis recognized that fighting a modern war required centralized authority, and in challenges to the draft and other war legislation he voted with the majority of the Court in almost every instance. He spoke for the Court upholding the Wartime Prohibition Act as well as the Volstead Act implementing the Eighteenth Amendment.

During the war the Food Administration had controlled how much grain could go to distillers, but one week after the 11 November 1918 armistice, Wilson signed the Wartime Prohibition Act, which made it illegal to sell alcoholic beverages in the domestic market. The Kentucky Distilleries Company could not market whiskey it had in its warehouses and went to court arguing that since the war had ended, Congress could no longer exercise its war powers. The law, it claimed, was an unconstitutional use of federal police power in violation of the Tenth Amendment.

A unanimous Court upheld the law. As Brandeis explained, although the Tenth Amendment normally conveyed the power to regulate alcohol to the states, Congress had a legitimate interest in maintaining wartime mobilization even though the fighting had ended. Just because hostilities had ceased did not mean that they could not break out again; Congress had the responsibility for ensuring that the country would be prepared if that occurred.

In January 1919 the thirty-sixth state ratified the Eighteenth Amendment, giving both Congress and the states concurrent powers to enforce the prohibition of the manufacture, sale, and transportation of intoxicating beverages. That October, Congress, over Wilson's veto, passed the Volstead Act, defining an intoxicating beverage as one with 0.5 percent or more alcohol by volume.

The Jacob Ruppert Company, which distilled liquor and beer, claimed that despite the Eighteenth Amendment the Volstead Act was an unconstitutional use of federal power. Moreover, while the Wartime

Prohibition Act would remain valid only during wartime, a vague but finite span, the Volstead Act would be in effect indefinitely. It therefore was not a war measure but an invasion of states' rights. Although four members of the Court—William Rufus Day, Willis Van Devanter, James C. McReynolds, and John H. Clarke—showed themselves more sympathetic to this argument than in the prior case, a majority upheld the law. Under the new amendment, Brandeis explained, Congress needed to establish some definitive standard. He dismissed the company's claims that 0.5 percent was not intoxicating as irrelevant. That issue did not concern the Court; Congress had made a policy decision, and the judiciary would not second-guess the legislature.

Brandeis's voting record, however, was not a blanket endorsement of the administration's program. In the summer of 1916, Congress, as part of its preparedness legislation, had authorized the president to take over the railroads in wartime, and in late December 1917 Wilson, after consulting with Brandeis, did so. Under the terms of the takeover, the government would run the railroads, finance the purchase of new equipment, and compensate the owners for the use of their property. The act did not suspend "the lawful police regulations of the several states," and allowed the states to continue to tax the railroads.

Director General McAdoo established a rate system that covered intrastate as well as interstate service and, despite the statutory language, had no intention of submitting intrastate schedules to state regulatory agencies. The North Dakota Utilities Commission filed suit to block the action and won a victory in state court, which ruled that the federal government had exceeded its authority under the Commerce Clause. McAdoo appealed, and thirty-seven states joined the suit on behalf of North Dakota.

The Supreme Court unanimously reversed, with Chief Justice White writing a sweeping opinion upholding the authority of the president. In taking over the roads, the chief executive had not been bound by the limits of the Commerce Clause, but operated under the war powers of the United States, which, according to White, reached as far as necessary. The United States had promised to compensate the owners of the railroads, so it had not violated the Takings Clause. Once it assumed operational authority, it also acquired the accompanying power to set rates.

That same day, the Court, this time by an 8–1 vote, upheld the government's takeover of telegraph, telephone, radio, and marine cable communications systems. The president had put Postmaster General

Albert Burleson in charge, and like McAdoo, Burleson established both intrastate and interstate rates. In a series of cases argued together with the North Dakota railroad question, the Supreme Court, again speaking through the chief justice, upheld a broad interpretation of presidential authority.

Brandeis, who a year and a half earlier had advised Woodrow Wilson that he had the power to take over the railroads, did not recuse himself. There would have been no purpose, since his individual vote in these cases did not matter, but he concurred without opinion in the railroad case. In the telephone case, Brandeis dissented, again without an opinion.

The only distinction between the two congressional statutes is that the railroad law explicitly provided the power to set rates, while the communications act, which in most provisions tracked the railroad bill word for word, failed to include rate-making authority. Lacking an explanation from him, we must assume that Brandeis objected not to the government's takeover of the railroads (which he believed constitutional) but rather to White's overbroad interpretation of the war powers. In the telephone and telegraph case he would have again found the definition of the war powers too expansive, but also that without explicit rate-making authority, the federal government could set only interstate rates. The distinction, which can be inferred only from the cases, is one that most commentators have found to be meaningless. Congress appeared to have omitted the rate-making power by accident, and if the federal government were to run the telephones as a unified system as it did the railroads, then clearly it required the authority to set intrastate as well as interstate rates. This is how the majority saw it, and White judicially read the rate-making authority into the statute. As one sympathetic study noted, the opinion-less concurrence and dissent were "entirely characteristic" of Brandeis, reflecting his refusal to take shortcuts in order "to get things done."

IRONICALLY, the war "to make the world safe for democracy" triggered one of the worst invasions of civil liberties in the nation's history. The government admittedly had to protect itself from subversion, but the laws seemed aimed more at suppressing leftist criticism of administration policy than at ferreting out spies. The Selective Service Act authorized the jailing of people who obstructed the draft. The Espionage Act of 1917, aimed primarily at treason, also punished anyone making or conveying false reports for the benefit of the enemy, seeking to cause disobedience in the armed services, or obstructing recruitment or enlistment in the armed forces. The Trading with the Enemy Act gave the postmaster general power to ban foreign-language and other publications from the mails. The 1918 Sedition Act struck out at a variety of "undesirable" activities and forbade "uttering, printing, writing, or publishing any disloyal, profane, scurrilous, or abusive language." Finally, the Immigration Act of 1918 expanded the government's authority to deport alien anarchists or those who believed in the use of force to overthrow the government.

All of these laws severely restricted free speech, and there would be court challenges, but those hoping to utilize the First Amendment faced a difficult road. There had been very little jurisprudence about the Speech Clause, and the few cases on record followed Blackstone's view that free speech meant little more than the absence of prior restraint. While the government could not stop someone from saying or publishing something, it could punish that person afterward, especially if the courts found that the speech had a "bad tendency," that is, it fostered undesirable actions or behavior. Between the Civil War and World War I, both state and federal courts rejected free-speech claims or ignored them, and no court seemed more unsympathetic than the U.S. Supreme Court.

Holmes had written the leading opinion on speech in *Patterson v. Colorado* (1907), a case in which the Democratic senator and newspaper publisher Thomas Patterson had been convicted of contempt for a series of editorials, stories, and cartoons ridiculing the Republican-dominated state supreme court. Under state law, Patterson could not even offer the truth of his accusations as a defense, because any criticism of the court amounted to an obstruction of justice. He appealed to the Supreme Court, claiming that the state courts had restricted his constitutional right to free expression by denying him the opportunity to prove the truthfulness of his allegations.

Speaking for a seven-man majority, Holmes upheld the conviction, relying primarily on Blackstone's view that the truth or falsity of the statement had nothing to do with criminal libel—"the provocation [that is, the bad tendency] and not the falsity is the thing to be punished criminally." Holmes broke no new ground here and did little more than reiterate that states had the power to punish bad tendencies in speech. This violated no federal rule, and so he dismissed the case. In 1915, Holmes again spoke for the Court in sustaining the constitutionality of a law punishing speech that had a tendency to encourage the commission of a crime, but he made no effort to see if there had been any actual consequences of the speaker's words. These rules constituted the Court's position when it began to hear cases arising from the wartime laws.

The first case to reach the high court involved the conviction of Charles Schenck, general secretary of the Socialist Party, for printing and distributing a leaflet attacking the draft. He mailed the article to men eligible for conscription, urging them to assert their constitutional rights by refusing to go into the army. Its "impassioned language," wrote Holmes for a unanimous Court, "intimated that conscription was despotism in its worst form and a monstrous wrong against humanity in the interest of Wall Street's chosen few."

But what about the First Amendment and its protection of speech? Holmes went on to draw what many people considered a commonsense conclusion, namely, that while this activity might have been legal in peacetime, war changed everything. "The character of every act depends upon the circumstances in which it is done, and when a nation is at war many things that might be said in time of peace are such a hindrance to its effort that their utterance will not be endured so long as men fight and that no Court could regard them as protected by any constitutional right."

In order for courts to evaluate the speech, Holmes set forth the "clear and present danger" test: "The question in every case is whether the words are used in such circumstances and are of such a nature as to create a clear and present danger that they will bring about the substantive evils that Congress has a right to prevent. It is a question of proximity and degree." The clear-and-present-danger test quickly became the established standard by which courts would judge free-speech tests for the next half century, and immediately raised objections from free-speech advocates who recognized its subjectivity. In the hands of conservatives almost anything that even questioned the established order or criticized the free enterprise system could be considered clearly and presently dangerous. Holmes thought the statement so obvious that he never defined what he meant by "clear" or "present" or "danger." Nonetheless, the Court applied this test in two other cases that term, *Frohwerk v. United States* and *Debs v. United States.* Brandeis joined the Court's opinion in each case, although he would have been happier if *Debs* had been decided on war powers rather than on clear-and-present danger, since that could have restricted the espionage legislation to wartime. He also wrote for a unanimous Court in a companion case, *Sugarman v. United States,* decided the same day as *Schenck,* dismissing a challenge to the Espionage Act for lack of jurisdiction. Brandeis paid no attention to the First Amendment issues; the case had not raised any substantial constitutional issues at the trial level, and therefore the high court had no authority to review.

"I have never been quite happy about my concurrence," he later told Felix Frankfurter. "I had not then thought the issues of freedom of speech out—I thought at the subject, not through it." "Thinking at" the issue would have meant relying on the state of First Amendment jurisprudence in 1919, a far cry from what it later became, thanks in very large measure to Brandeis himself.

Brandeis had written his first speech opinion a year earlier in *International News Service v. Associated Press,* which raised the question of whether a property right existed in news. The AP ran a wire service to subscribing newspapers providing news stories from around the country and from many foreign capitals, an essential service to the vast majority of papers that could not afford to maintain correspondents far from home. The INS, which did not have as extensive a system of reporters, pirated the stories from the AP and sold them to its subscribers at a lower price. Since news cannot be copyrighted, the AP claimed that its stories constituted a property right and sought an injunction to stop what it labeled an unfair trade practice.

Justice Mahlon Pitney, speaking for the Court, ignored any First Amendment questions or whether the public had any rights in the news, accepted the AP argument, and treated news as a property interest. "The right to acquire property by honest labor or the conduct of a lawful business," he declared, "is as much entitled to protection as the right to guard property already acquired."

Holmes apparently would have gone along with Pitney until he read a circulation of Brandeis's dissent, and the approaches the two men took reflected the differences between them. Holmes, joined by Joseph McKenna, entered a special opinion that in effect dissented from the majority view. He had difficulty in finding a property right in news, but recognized that the INS had acted badly, and would have solved the problem by sending the case back to the trial court with instructions to determine a number of hours during which the INS would not be allowed to circulate the stories originally carried by the AP. In the absence of specific legislation, both the majority and Holmes favored a judicial resolution; they stood ready to act.

Brandeis dissented by himself. The majority rule making news property "would effect an important extension of property rights and a corresponding curtailment of the free use of knowledge and of ideas." His opinion, however, centered not on the public's right to know but rather on the fact that the courts should defer to the legislative branch in making policy. "Courts are ill-equipped to make the investigations which should precede a determination" of what should be included in this new property right, and are also "powerless to prescribe the detailed regulations essential to the full enjoyment for enforcement of such regulations." A remedy was certainly necessary, but Congress and not the Court should provide the solution.

Initially, Pitney's opinion, one of his best, received widespread approval, and some commentators described it as a fine example of progressivism in the law, reflecting the Court's adaptability in meeting new conditions—exactly what Brandeis had been calling for courts to do. But whereas the majority and Holmes focused on the problem of unlawful appropriation, Brandeis looked at the broader issue—one that would concern him the entire time he sat on the bench—of federal courts creating common law. He saw courts limited in their powers by the Constitution, in the same way the document also restricted the powers of the executive and legislative branches. Over time, the law moved in the direction Brandeis had pointed, and while Pitney's notion of fairness remained attractive, the majority opinion lost its force and judges looked to the dissent for guidance.

THE COURT DECIDED *Schenck* and its companion cases in the spring of 1919, and that fall handed down a decision in *Abrams v. United States.* Jacob Abrams and his anarchist colleagues had been convicted for publishing leaflets in English and Yiddish calling for a general strike in protest against what they called the American attempt to destroy the Russian Revolution. Writing for a seven-man majority in a poorly reasoned opinion, Justice John Clarke dismissed the free-speech claim as taken care of by *Schenck,* applied the clear-and-present-danger test, and upheld the conviction. Holmes dissented, joined by Brandeis.

It remains one of Holmes's most famous dissents and still resonates as a call for intellectual freedom. It is a typical Holmes opinion, running just twelve paragraphs. The first ten recount the various charges and conclude that none of the actions complained of posed any threat to society or the state. He had no use for the ideas that Abrams and others put forth, but they posed no danger, and their beliefs—as opposed to their actions, of which there had been none—should never be taken into consideration.

The First Amendment sup-
ported the free exchange of ideas,
not their suppression. "When men
have realized that time has upset
many fighting faiths, they may
come to believe . . . that the ultimate good desired is better reached
by free trade in ideas—that the
best test of truth is the power of
the thought to get itself accepted
in the competition of the market;
and that truth is the only ground
upon which their wishes may be
safely carried out. That, at any rate,
is the theory of our Constitution. It
is an experiment, as all life is an
experiment." On the return Brandeis wrote, "I join you heartily &
gratefully. This is fine—very."

*Jacob Abrams and his wife, Mary,
just before he entered prison in 1919*

What had changed their minds?
Scholars have offered several reasons, although it appears that no
single factor led to the about-face. Holmes met Learned Hand on a
train, and the two men began a correspondence debating the meaning of the First Amendment. Hand had earlier delivered a far more
speech-protective decision in the *Masses* case that libertarians had
applauded. Progressive magazines like the *Nation* and the *New Republic* carried articles criticizing the initial decisions. In June 1919 the
Harvard Law Review published Zechariah Chafee's "Freedom of Speech
in Wartime," the first part of what would be his classic treatise on free
speech in the United States. Holmes read that article, and so did Brandeis, who would cite it in a 1920 dissent. Harold Laski arranged a
meeting between Holmes and Chafee, and the justice, who had been
stung by the unexpected criticism of his *Schenck* decision, listened
carefully.

Brandeis also learned about the suppression of speech through dozens
of letters he received from correspondents. Felix Frankfurter wrote to
him from Bisbee, Arizona, to describe how mine owners violated the
civil rights of striking workers under the guise of patriotism. Amos Pinchot wanted Brandeis to intervene with the Justice Department to stop
the prosecution of the editors of the *Masses*. A former neighbor and a lec-

Judge Learned Hand, 1924

turer at Harvard, Samuel Eliot Morison, told Brandeis he had been charged with disloyalty and wanted help in securing an investigation to clear his name. Two of the very few federal judges not to be carried away by the mass hysteria wrote to tell him of the evils of Espionage Act prosecutions. Brandeis also kept an extensive clippings file of items from both the general and the trade presses, which detailed the attacks on labor leaders and pacifists. Even without Chafee's intercession, Brandeis knew about the Wilson administration's violations of civil liberties.

Since he was not about to admit that he had been wrong only a few months earlier, Holmes went out of his way to explain that the clear-and-present-danger test meant "immediate danger" or "a clear and imminent danger," and he began to pay more attention to the ideas implicit in the First Amendment. He undoubtedly consulted with Brandeis, who alone of all the members of the Court joined his dissent. In the remaining two speech cases of the term, Brandeis wrote the opinions, joined by Holmes, and in doing so moved well beyond his colleague in terms of speech protectiveness.

DURING THIS TIME the hysteria generated by the so-called First Red Scare appalled both men. Beginning in the late nineteenth century, socialist and anarchist groups had protested, sometimes violently, against the evils of the industrial system and the way it treated working people. During the war a number of these groups objected to American entry into what they described as a battle of, by, and for the capitalists against the people. Then came the Russian Revolution and the victory of the communists. In the United States the chaotic demobilization after the armistice and the ensuing recession led some four million workers to go out on strike in 1919. More than sixty thousand heeded a call for a general strike in Seattle, which Mayor Ole Hanson denounced as a Bolshevik plot. The four-month strike in the steel mills certainly had its share of radicals among the strike leaders, and in early September most of Boston's police force walked off the job. In April the Justice Department uncovered a plot to mail thirty-six bombs to prominent Americans, including J. P. Morgan Jr., John D. Rockefeller, and, for some strange reason, Oliver Wendell Holmes Jr. On 2 June, bombs did in fact explode in eight different cities within the same hour.

These events triggered an unparalleled wave of antiradical and anti-immigrant hysteria. Attorney General A. Mitchell Palmer (who had replaced Thomas Gregory) initiated what came to be known as the Palmer Raids, a series of mass arrests and deportations of immigrants suspected of radicalism. Over a two-year period the government, under the direction of the young J. Edgar Hoover, arrested between four thousand and ten thousand individuals, held them without access to lawyers, and deported many of them without even a minimal façade of due process. The *Washington Post* praised the raids and proclaimed, "There is no time to waste on hairsplitting over infringement of liberty."

Eventually, calmer heads prevailed, and as the tensions lessened, Palmer, who hoped to capture the 1920 Democratic presidential nomination, warned of a new wave of bombings that would take place on May Day. The day came and went without incident, Palmer was widely ridiculed, and the Red Scare collapsed. Brandeis, writing to his sister-in-law, compared events to the Spanish Inquisition. "The intensity of the frenzy is the most hopeful feature of this disgraceful exhibition—of hysterical, unintelligent fear—which is quite foreign to the generous American nature. It will pass like the Know-nothing days, but the sense of shame and sin should endure." When his law clerk asked him whether the police harassment of labor activists and socialists lessened his hopes for democracy in America, the justice said he was not discouraged, but "simply deeply humiliated and filled with a sense of sin that we with the greatest possibilities of any people should waste ourselves on these age-old methods of oppression."

One incident of the Red Scare touched Brandeis in particular, the attack on Zechariah Chafee, his young friend at Harvard Law. The scion of a wealthy Rhode Island industrial family, Chafee had written a series of articles in the *Harvard Law Review* attacking the Court's decisions in the speech cases and applauding Holmes's dissent in *Abrams.* In addition, he had joined with Felix Frankfurter in criticizing Palmer and asking President Wilson for clemency for Abrams and others convicted under the sedition and espionage laws.

Because Frankfurter and other faculty supported the rights of labor and free speech, conservatives began assailing the law school, much to Brandeis's chagrin. When Dean Roscoe Pound wrote to him about these attacks and said that he was considering resigning, Brandeis urged him to stay and asked him not to make any decisions until they had a chance to talk. "To lose you as a teacher of law and of lawyers would be a calamity." They are "gunning hard for Felix," Louis wrote to Alice. "Old Boston is unregenerate. . . . F.F. is evidently considered by the elect as 'dangerous' as I was." After further harassment of Pound, Brandeis wrote again. He and Holmes believed the assault on the law school "the saddest thing" they had heard in a long while, and they applauded Pound's decision to fight back.

When the attack on Pound failed, conservative alumni decided to move against Chafee. Austen Fox, who had been one of the leading opponents of Brandeis in 1916, and twenty other alumni asked the Harvard Board of Overseers to investigate Chafee's "fitness to teach," on the grounds that his articles included "deliberate falsehoods" and "reckless indifference to the truth." The overseers, instead of dismissing the ludicrous charges outright, appointed a special committee. At the hearings Chafee acquitted himself brilliantly and, when reminded that he came from the capitalist class, said that was true, but that he wanted his side to fight fairly. The committee absolved Chafee of all charges, but by a bare 6–5 vote.

A thoroughly dispirited Chafee thought about resigning, but Holmes and Brandeis reassured him that the fight had been worthwhile. "Word comes of the attack on you for daring to be free," Brandeis wrote to Chafee. "You did a man's job. The persecution will make it more productive. By such follies is liberty made to grow; for the love of it is re-awakened. Of course there are growing pains; but with these come also the joys of the struggle and of creation." The incident "illustrates the value of a law school professorship—as a fulcrum in efforts to improve the law and through it society." The justice expressed his certainty that Chafee could be of infinitely more use in the law school than in private practice.

IT IS AGAINST THIS BACKGROUND that Brandeis had been "thinking through" the basic ideas of free speech. Holmes's marketplace of ideas, while attractive to the idealist as a theory, did not satisfy him from a pragmatic stance. If clear-and-present danger allowed too much subjectivity on the part of judges and juries, the marketplace analogy gave lower courts no guidance in establishing parameters of

First Amendment protection. Brandeis began working on that problem in the series of dissents he wrote in the 1920s, culminating in the great concurring opinion in *Whitney v. California* in 1927. He did so the same way he had argued economic cases, by grounding his position in facts. "I made up my mind I would put it all out," he told Frankfurter, and "let the future know what we weren't allowed to say in the days of the war and following." A person might disagree with him about the scope of free speech, but no one would be able to say that he got his facts wrong. And as in all his opinions, he believed if the facts were right, it would be difficult to go against his conclusions. "Knowledge is essential for understanding," he wrote in a 1924 dissent, "and understanding should precede judging." Of course, facts could always be found to support either side of an issue; once Brandeis made up his mind, he would utilize every fact that would support his position. He knew that "facts" were rarely as objective as he sometimes claimed.

Peter Schaefer and his co-defendants edited small German-language newspapers in Philadelphia, for which they reprinted or rewrote articles that appeared elsewhere. They had been prosecuted under the falsity provision of the Espionage Act, but the government had never proved that anything they published had been false, only that certain of the articles they printed differed in some respect from their original form. The government had secured a conviction on these grounds, and the Court, speaking through Justice McKenna, upheld the verdict.

Brandeis analyzed four of the reprinted articles, and in his usual thorough way went and read both the original German pieces and those published by Schaefer. He discovered that one charge of falsity resulted from an error by the government translator of the original German piece; other charges rested on the omission of a single sentence in the reprint and the mistranslation of "breadlines" as "breadriots." In the Espionage Act, he contended, Congress had meant to punish only those false statements that might "interfere with the operation or success of the military or naval forces of the United States or to promote the success of its enemies."

The articles published by the defendants were not false, and the mistranslation of one word in a long passage could not possibly have interfered with the war. Brandeis categorized the other articles as "likewise impotent to produce the evil against which the statute aimed." One of the articles from a Berlin newspaper resembled those circulated by patriotic societies in the United States to arouse "American fighting spirit," and its "coarse and heavy humor" could in no way be considered an obstruction to recruitment. Suppressing publications on such flimsy grounds, Brandeis concluded, "would subject to new perils the constitutional liberty of the press."

In *Schaefer,* Brandeis maintained that the government's grounds for prosecution had been so fragile that they could not support a conviction, and certainly did not present a clear-and-present danger to anything. In the second 1920 case, *Pierce v. United States,* Brandeis moved closer to a modern understanding of the meaning of the Press Clause and free speech.

Clinton Pierce circulated a four-page leaflet, "The Price We Pay," written by a prominent Episcopalian clergyman who charged the war had been started by the capitalists. He and the other defendants received the leaflet from Socialist Party headquarters, but did not distribute it until a Maryland judge ordered an acquittal in a case involving the same pamphlet. Pierce, like Schaefer, was convicted under the falsity provisions of the Espionage Act. Justice Pitney rejected the defendants' claim that the pamphlet's sole purpose had been to recruit members for the Socialist Party, and found the jury could have determined that the document had been intended to interfere with the war.

Brandeis argued that to punish a person for a false statement, the government had to prove the passage to be false in fact and that the defendant had known its falsity at the time of publication or utterance. But an expression of opinion can never be proved false, because the accuracy of an opinion is indeterminate. No matter how "grossly unfair as an interpretation of facts or even wholly unfounded in fact," an opinion represented what a person believed, and that could not be criminalized.

Brandeis and his clerk found the one precedent that supported this distinction, in which the Court had held that claims by Christian Scientists are "mere matters of opinion upon subjects which are not capable of proof as to their falsity." The roots of a war can rarely be identified in a specific manner, Brandeis asserted, and even historians, with all the benefits of training and hindsight, could not agree on either the identity or the importance of specific events in causing a war; laymen, discussing a contemporary war, could hardly be expected to do better than historians. Moreover, at the time Woodrow Wilson had asked for a declaration of war, a number of senators and congressmen disagreed with the president's justification and expressed many of the views for which the defendants had been prosecuted. If such statements were indeed criminally false, Brandeis implied, then a number of high-ranking government officials ought to be in the dock alongside Pierce.

The intent of the leaflet had clearly been to promote socialism. It did contain "lurid and perhaps exaggerated" descriptions of war's horrors, and one could characterize its arguments as "shallow and grossly unfair." Nothing in the leaflet, however, could in any way be construed as criminal incitement to disobey the law. The fact that judges might have interpreted the pamphlet as "mistaken in its assumptions, unsound in reasoning or intemperate in language" did not make it a violation of the law. To show this, and to counter the majority's claim that it was a dangerous document, Brandeis published the whole of the pamphlet at the end of his dissent.

In *Schaefer* and *Pierce,* Brandeis wanted to extend the protection of the First Amendment and yet avoid rejecting Holmes's clear-and-present-danger test. Holmes had gone out of his way in *Abrams* to "clarify" what he meant in such a way as to protect speech, but had been unable to say that he had been wrong in *Schenck.* Because Holmes was his natural ally on the Court as well as his friend, Brandeis would have to play that game as well. In his *Schaefer* dissent he described clear-and-present danger, adopted by a "unanimous court" in *Schenck,* as a "rule of reason" that required judges to apply it in "calmness" and using "good judgment." He then added two other qualifications, immediacy and gravity.

The danger could not be theoretical or remote or merely possible, but it had to be about to happen, and for this he cited not a case but Zechariah Chafee's article in the *Harvard Law Review.* He also tightened the test by utilizing Judge Learned Hand's notion of direct incitement. The speech complained about had to pose an immediate danger and also constitute the proximate cause of that danger. Speech that merely discussed violence but did not call for it in a specific circumstance could not be deemed a danger. Finally, Brandeis added the rule of gravity; the feared action could not be trivial, and even potential destruction of property or trespass did not qualify. The danger had to be the "probability of serious injury to the State."

One function of the Supreme Court is to provide guidance to lower courts, and Brandeis tried to do what he had always done as an advocate and would continue to do on the high court—instruct the judiciary. While external evidence—such as the existence of a conspiracy—may be necessary to create a context, the judge had to read the material itself. What are "the nature of the words used and the circumstances under which they were used"? Perhaps most important, the words had to be evaluated calmly. By these standards, freedom of speech would be

Letter applauding Chafee's defense of free speech,
May 1921

the rule, and restrictions based on clear-and-present danger would be the exception.

IN THE THIRD SPEECH case of 1920, Brandeis dissented alone and showed how far he had moved past Holmes, who some commentators believed never really advanced beyond his *Abrams* opinion. Joseph Gilbert, a leader of the Minnesota Nonpartisan League, had been arrested and convicted under a state statute that prohibited interference with military recruiting. He had given a speech charging that the average person knew nothing about why the country had declared war or why there had to be a draft. In a true democracy, he claimed, the people would have voted on whether to go to war and if there should be conscription.

In the Supreme Court, Gilbert's attorneys made two points: the state law violated freedom of speech and also trespassed unconstitutionally on grounds preempted by the federal government. Justice McKenna made short shrift of both arguments. Nothing the federal government did precluded states from acting to preserve public order; as for the speech itself, he cited the three 1919 cases establishing the clear-and-present-danger test. Chief Justice White briefly dissented from the war powers conclusion, while Holmes silently joined the majority. Only Brandeis dissented.

McKenna had made war powers the crux of his opinion, believing that the Court had no jurisdiction over state measures that restricted speech. Brandeis quickly dismissed this argument; if a measure related to war, then only the federal government and not the states could act. He spent the bulk of his dissent on speech. Unlike the federal Espionage Act, the Minnesota statute applied in peacetime as well as during war, and was designed to "prevent teaching that the abolition of war is possible." Repeating an earlier warning from *Schaefer,* Brandeis contended that allowing suppression of speech in wartime only made it easier to restrict free expression afterward. The law made the teaching of pacifism itself illegal and therefore "Father and mother may not follow the promptings of religious belief, of conscience or of conviction, and teach son and daughter the doctrine of pacifism."

Despite the "judicial" language he used, there is no doubt of Brandeis's anger in this case, an anger that led him to invoke the Fourteenth Amendment's Due Process Clause as justification for protecting the right of a parent to teach a child and of a free man to speak his mind. Referring to the many times that the Due Process Clause had been used to strike down economic regulations, he vehemently declared:

> I have difficulty in believing that the liberty guaranteed by the Constitution, which has been held to protect the right of an employer to discriminate against a workman because he is a member of a trade union, the right of a businessman to conduct a private employment agency, or to contract outside the state for insurance of his property, although the Legislature deems it inimical to the public welfare, does not include liberty to teach, either in the privacy of the home or publicly, the doctrine of pacifism. . . . I cannot believe that the liberty guaranteed by the Fourteenth Amendment includes only liberty to acquire and enjoy property.

Brandeis, of course, had never believed that the Court should have used the Due Process Clause to strike down the other laws, and he later regretted that he had tried to utilize it as a basis for free expression here.

Holmes and Brandeis, early 1920s

He would much prefer, he told Frankfurter, to repeal the clause altogether. But if his more conservative brethren intended to use the clause to protect property rights, then they ought to be willing to use it to protect other rights as well, and he included such basic rights as speech, education, choice of profession, and travel.

The *Gilbert* dissent, however, is an important milestone in the history of modern jurisprudence. Brandeis's suggestion that the Fourteenth Amendment could be used to protect other rights soon found an unlikely champion in James Clark McReynolds, who used exactly this argument in two important rights cases just a few years later. More important, the opinion led to the doctrine of incorporation, which would be at the very heart of the rights revolution in the 1950s and 1960s. Ever since the 1833 case *Barron v. Baltimore,* the Bill of Rights had been held applicable only to the federal government ("Congress shall make no law . . .") and not to the states. The Fourteenth Amendment, and especially its Due Process and Equal Protection clauses, had been intended to rein in state power following the Civil War, and from time to time the argument had been raised that the Due Process Clause "incorporated" the Bill of Rights and applied it to the states. Brandeis's claim that it did so would start bearing fruit in only a few years.

Beyond that, Brandeis took an important step in *Gilbert* toward identifying an intellectual rationale for free speech in a democracy. In *Schaefer* and *Pierce* he had shown himself sensitive to protecting free expression, but had not explained the importance of doing so. A free marketplace of ideas is very well for a philosopher, but how, if at all, did it apply to the daily life of a citizen?

A citizen, he explained, cannot participate in the affairs of a democratic society without the right of free speech, and he has a corresponding duty to speak out on matters of importance, "to endeavor to make his own opinion concerning laws existing or contemplated prevail, and to this end, to teach the truth as he sees it." Therefore, the exercise of the right of free speech is also a citizen's duty, "for its exercise is more important to the nation than to himself. . . . In frank expression of conflicting opinion lies the greatest promise of wisdom in governmental action; and in suppression lies ordinarily the greatest peril." This theme would reach its full elaboration seven years later in *Whitney v. California.*

Holmes in this case could not go along with Brandeis (on the return he wrote, "I think you go too far"), even though, as he wrote to Sir Frederick Pollock, he "heartily disagreed with the reasoning of the majority." Brandeis had only one ground "worthy of serious consideration and the others I thought all wrong." The one ground may have been the preemption of state action by the national government, and Brandeis did cite a recent Holmes decision that states could not act regarding limitation of postal service because of federal primacy. Holmes may have objected to the new—and radical—idea that the Fourteenth Amendment limited state action, a step that the full Court would not take for another five years.

Zechariah Chafee, however, read the *Gilbert* dissent with great approval. The Harvard Law professor had expanded his original articles into a book, *Freedom of Speech,* and sent proofs of the early chapters to Brandeis, who clearly had studied them closely. After the opinion came out, Brandeis sent a copy to Frankfurter, asking him to "tell me frankly whether you or Chaffee [*sic*] see any flaw in the reasoning in the dissent." To Chafee must go some of the credit in helping Brandeis down the jurisprudential road.

IN *PIERCE,* Brandeis had criticized postal authorities for going beyond their authorized power in curtailing speech. He returned to this issue in the *Milwaukee Leader* case in 1921.

Among the members of Wilson's original cabinet, two stood out for their archconservative views, Attorney General James Clark McReynolds and Postmaster General Albert Sidney Burleson. The full extent of McReynolds's conservatism would emerge after he went onto the high court, that of Burleson during the war. Described by Colonel House as the most "belligerent member" of the cabinet, Burleson used his authority to block mailings of any publication he deemed subversive. When asked about his standards for allowable comment, he replied that it was impermissible to say "that this Government got in the war wrong, that it is in for the wrong purposes, or anything that will impugn the motives of the Government for going into the war," or that "the Government is controlled by Wall Street or munitions manufacturers," or even to criticize the Allies "improperly." When the *Milwaukee Leader* did raise such questions, Burleson revoked its second-class mailing privileges.

The paper went to court, but to no avail, and on appeal the Supreme Court upheld Burleson's actions in an intemperate opinion by Justice Clarke. Brandeis dissented, and once again raised the due process argument he had used in *Gilbert*—which led Holmes, "after fasting and prayer," to enter a short dissent of his own rather than joining—but also raised another issue that should have won support from other members of the Court. Even if the postmaster general had the power under the Espionage Act to ban particular issues of a journal because of allegedly subversive articles, he did not have the power to ban future numbers. Yet that is exactly what happened when Burleson revoked the mailing privilege, and this amounted to prior restraint, a clear violation of the Blackstonean view on speech that the Court had endorsed in the past. Moreover, in the *Associated Press* case the Court had held news to be a property interest, and Brandeis reminded them that a law that arbitrarily denied publishers the low second-class rates deprived them of their property without due process of law. Even though the fighting had stopped more than two years before the Court heard this case, the hysteria generated by the war continued, even among the justices.

That fall Dean Acheson joined the Brandeises for Thanksgiving dinner, and, as he told Frankfurter, "himself" was in excellent form. After the justice had expounded on the evils that were going to overtake the press in the wake of the *Milwaukee Leader* case, Acheson suggested that perhaps liberals were rather "unsympathetic with people justifiably scared to death," only to earn a lecture on the evils of sympathizing with fear. (That evening Brandeis also had little use for the French, then trying to renegotiate terms of their wartime loans, and the justice condemned them as "a wretched greedy lot at best." Acheson said he was somewhat tempted to discuss French contributions to civilization at the end of the eighteenth century, "but I knew he would floor me by quoting their export statistics for the same years, so I gave it up.")

IN FEBRUARY 1928, Oliver Wendell Holmes wrote to his friend the English legal scholar Sir Frederick Pollock, noting that Brandeis had dissented from one of his opinions. "We are so apt to agree that I

am glad that he dissents. . . . It will indicate that there is no preestablished harmony between us." Holmes took pains to point this out
because he recognized that many people believed that Brandeis had a
great sway over him. Chief Justice William Howard Taft, for example,
complained to Henry Stimson that Holmes was "so completely under
the control of Brother Brandeis that it gives to Brandeis two votes
instead of one." Holmes knew of these views, and at times they irked
him. He told an old friend, Nina Gray, that some thought him "under
the influence of the Heb. I am comfortably confident that I am under
no influence except that of thoughts and insights. Sometimes my
brother B. seems to me to see deeper than some of the others—and we
often agree." He went on to argue that in many areas, especially free
speech, he had reached his conclusions independently. "In two or three
cases he has perhaps turned the scale on the question whether I should
write—but in each of those I was and am more than glad that I did."

Brandeis did have an impact on Holmes, just as Holmes had for so
many years affected his thought. The two men differed on many issues,
most importantly on how they faced life and law, but they also had
a deep affection for each other, and in the sixteen years they served
together, their ideas and philosophies proved complementary. Although liberals rejoiced when they saw "Holmes and Brandeis dissenting," very few recognized that Holmes's soaring rhetoric and Brandeis's
inexorable fact-laden logic arose from different worldviews.

The two men had known each other from the time Brandeis came to
Boston to join Sam Warren, who introduced them. Brandeis sat in the
audience at the Lowell Institute when Holmes delivered his lectures on
the common law. When Brandeis came to Washington, he would often
visit Holmes, and during the nomination fight said that he shared
Holmes's view of the Constitution. Holmes, who so valued the mind,
regarded Brandeis as far superior in intellectual power and ability to
any of the other men he served with.

Affection was there from the start. Once Holmes, beset by a cold,
did not attend the weekly conference, and Brandeis reported that it
"seemed dreary without him." Brandeis told Harold Laski that he considered Holmes's companionship "the crown of his life." "I have had
one or two good talks with Brandeis," Holmes told Frankfurter. "They
always rejoice me." The two men often walked home together after
work and would then go through a routine. Brandeis would insist on
taking Holmes to his door, and then Holmes would worry whether
Brandeis would find his way back across the street. Even with the Court

in recess Brandeis made it a point to see Holmes often. "Brandeis has delighted me by an occasional call during the adjournment," Holmes reported. "I am richer after a talk with him." On their birthdays the two men would exchange brief notes. In 1930, for example, Brandeis passed a note down the bench calling 8 March "a red white & blue letter day for U.S.A. and L.D.B." On Brandeis's seventieth birthday Holmes told a friend that Brandeis "has done great work and I believe with high motives." When Holmes wrote an introduction to a book of essays celebrating Brandeis's seventy-fifth birthday, it touched him greatly and, according to Alice, was "the crowning point of it all."

As the years went on, Brandeis took greater efforts to keep an eye on the aging Holmes, whose mind remained sharp despite growing physical infirmity. "There can't be too much apprehension about evil effects of old age," Brandeis told Frankfurter in 1922, and said that John Marshall and Joseph Story both outlived their usefulness because of a failure to grow. This could not be said of Holmes, whose mind seemed to improve with the years. Eventually, of course, age did begin to tell on Holmes, especially when his wife of sixty years fell ill. Ten days before the death of Fanny Holmes, Brandeis wrote to Frankfurter that Holmes's current secretary should plan to stay with him over the summer at Beverly Farms. "He is needed," Brandeis said, "as no secretary ever has been."

After Holmes retired from the bench, Brandeis visited him at least once a week. Holmes's housekeeper, Mary Donnellan, recalled that when she would tell Holmes that Brandeis was on his way, "he would get awfully excited. I would take Justice Brandeis up in the elevator to the library where Justice Holmes was seated in his big chair. He was awfully weak and frail by this point. But when Justice Brandeis walked in the room, Justice Holmes would lift himself up, and he would smile broadly and say, 'My dear friend,' and the two of them would embrace."

BECAUSE THEY AGREED on so many things, their differences received little attention at the time. In cases that mattered to liberals, only Holmes and Brandeis could be counted upon to vote for reforms and rights. Both men believed in judicial restraint, but Holmes voted as he did out of skepticism, not believing in the reforms or, other than as an intellectual matter, in the rights either. Brandeis, even when he disagreed with a policy, believed fervently that the people should make policy through their elected representatives, and he valued rights, especially speech, as essential components of a free society. Above all, Brandeis cherished facts, while Holmes hated them.

"Brandeis the other day drove a harpoon into my midriff with reference to my summer occupations," Holmes complained to Sir Frederick Pollock. "He said you talk about improving your mind, you only exercise it on the subjects with which you are familiar. Why don't you try something new, study some domain of fact." Brandeis wanted Holmes to study factory reports and then take a trip to the Lawrence mills to get a sense of what these facts meant in terms of human lives. Although Holmes dutifully carried a few volumes with him to his summer home in 1919, he could not really get into them, and resented the time taken away from his Greek poets. The next summer he gratefully confessed, "In consideration of my age and moral infirmities, [Brandeis] absolved me from facts for the vacation and allowed me my customary sport with ideas."

Holmes preferred the abstract and never made any pretext otherwise, but admired Brandeis and understood his need for details. He "is the most thorough of men. If I wanted to be epigrammatic I should say that he always desires to know all that can be known about a case whereas I am afraid that I wish to know as little as I can safely go on. He loves facts and I hate them except as the necessary peg to hang generalizations on. Think not that I don't appreciate the power his knowledge gives him."

Holmes never completely reconciled himself to Brandeis's heavily annotated opinions, or the use of nonjudicial materials as sources. "I can't think it good form to treat an opinion as an essay and put in footnotes" from so many sources, he complained. (Holmes once circulated an opinion that included a quotation from Byron—to "pain the boys," as he put it—and the first objection came in Brandeis's return. Law reviews were one thing, English poets quite another!) "I don't believe in long opinions," he told a friend. He thought a judge should "state the case shortly and the ground of decision as concisely and as delicately as you can." He took as part of his charge the necessity to write his opinions quickly and, if at all possible, deliver them the following week.

To some extent the difference between the two came out of their far different backgrounds. The Brahmin Holmes, after his experience in the Civil War, had devoted himself to ideas, and seven decades after his death is still considered one of the greatest philosophers in American law. Although his vanity led him to care deeply about what people thought about him, he believed that lasting fame, if any came to him, would be because of the impact of his ideas. If we look at those ideas, we find in them a far different moral universe from that of Louis Brandeis.

Holmes's reputation has over the years seesawed from near idolization to near dismissal, as later generations of scholars have assessed his writings with the hindsight of history. His marvelously quotable opinions turned out to be more worthwhile as literary gems than as guides for future jurisprudence, something that Brandeis recognized at the time. "Holmes is more often quoted by lawyers," Brandeis told Felix Frankfurter in 1922, "but also leaves more loopholes for rehearing petitions than anyone else; he disregards some little fact or doesn't spell it out." Despite the justifiable literary fame of the *Abrams* dissent, it speaks primarily from the viewpoint of the theorist, the thinker who values the marketplace of ideas far above whatever practicalities may result from new thought. Holmes, Brandeis said, did not "sufficiently consider the needs of others to understand."

Part of the greatness of Holmes's lectures on the common law is that he dislodged morality as the guiding star in civil law. Early law writers condemned breach of contract as a moral transgression; Holmes argued that in terms of business a breach sometimes made sense. Moreover, the other party should only be made whole again, that is, put back in the position he would have been had the contract been fulfilled; he could not sue for nor should he receive punitive damages. Holmes's view of the rights of man, despite the high-flown rhetoric of some of his opinions, never developed beyond "what the crowd would fight for." His own morality consisted of what he called his "can't helps," those things that he intuitively followed.

Brandeis, in contrast, saw law as a surrogate for religion in establishing and preserving morality. An incident recounted by Dean Acheson illuminates this point perfectly.

Brandeis always welcomed visits from Harvard Law faculty whenever they happened to be in Washington, and on one occasion Manley O. Hudson came to see him. As he usually did, the justice asked his visitor about his current project, and Hudson started to talk about his work with the League of Nations. In international law, Hudson declared, even more so than in domestic matters, "moral principles were no more than generalizations from the mores or accepted notions of a particular time or place." There followed a "spectacular" eruption as Brandeis began, in Acheson's words, to "prophesy." Morality was truth, he declared, and "truth had been revealed to men in an unbroken, continuous, and consistent flow by the great prophets and poets of all times." Truth was absolute, not relative, a fact that Hudson should never forget, and after he finally escaped from the apartment, the Harvard professor stood "shaking with emotion on the street." After watching this "impressive, almost frightening, glimpse of an elemental force," Acheson concluded, so much for the idea of Brandeis as the morally neutral scientist of the law. One cannot imagine this response from Holmes, who did believe in moral relativism and would probably have entered into conversation with Hudson comparing how moral values could change and quoting a variety of esoteric sources in the process.

Although Holmes would allow legislatures to experiment with different social approaches, he did so without much caring about them. In his fatalistic view, none of them would affect the world one way or the other. He did not share Brandeis's enthusiasm for reform. "Generally speaking I agree with you in liking to see social experiments tried," he told his colleague, "but I do so without enthusiasm because I believe that is merely shifting the pressure and that so long as we have free propagation Malthus is right in his general view." He said that every "sensible man in the country knows that the Sherman law is a damned nonsense, but if my country wants to go to hell, I'm here to help."

As a result, he was often as ready to approve repressive legislation as he was social reform. Brandeis the political and social activist did think that reforms could make a difference. He did not assume that all legislative acts would be wise, but because of his faith in democracy he wanted to give them a chance at success. Late in his life he told his niece, "I always went on the principle of 'Do what you can and hope for the best'—I worked on the problem at hand." He knew from personal experience that while some proposals, like savings bank insurance, succeeded, others, like the sliding scale, had failed. The great feature of a federal system, he declared, was that it allowed states to serve as laboratories of reform.

The two men, of course, did not differ on everything. Like Brandeis, Holmes valued ideals—"without ideals what is life worth?" Rather, they came to similar conclusions from different perspectives. They both believed in judicial restraint, but Brandeis saw legislative policy making as a positive good in a democratic society, while Holmes believed that in the end it would do no good. Whereas Brandeis followed closely the great social movements of his time, Holmes ignored them, and did not even read newspapers. Both men believed that legislative majorities could infringe upon individual rights. "Above all rights," Brandeis declared, "rises duty to the community." Holmes saw this as a matter of course, but when individual liberties were concerned, Brandeis had to be persuaded of at least the logic of the legislative action, if not its rightness.

Brandeis understood where he and Holmes differed, and at times these differences found them on opposite sides of a decision; there never was a "preestablished harmony." They generally agreed on important matters, and beyond that enjoyed a great friendship.

CHAPTER TWENTY-THREE
BRANDEIS AND TAFT

One month after the armistice, Louis excitedly wrote to Alice that the previous day he had an experience

which I did not expect to encounter in this life. As I was walking toward the Stoneleigh about 1 p.m. [William Howard] Taft & I met. There was a moment's hesitation, & when he'd almost passed, he stopped & said in a charming manner: "Isn't this Justice Brandeis? I don't think we have ever met." I answered: "Yes, we met at Harvard after your return from the Philippines." He at once began to talk about my views on regularity of employment. After a moment I asked him to come in with me. He spent a half hour in 809, talking about labor & War Labor Board experiences. Was most confidential—at one point put his hand on my knee. I told him of the great service he had rendered the country by his action on the Labor Board, & we parted with his saying in effect— He hoped we would meet often.

That hope came true in June 1921, when Warren Harding nominated the former president to be chief justice of the United States. The man who had been so politically inept while in the White House proved to be an exceptionally fine administrator of the nation's judiciary, and while Louis Brandeis often disagreed with the jurisprudence that Taft and a majority of the Court embraced, he nonetheless respected the man and his abilities. The years of the Taft Court produced nearly all of Brandeis's most influential dissents, opinions that would eventually be accepted by the Court as correct.

• • •

The Supreme Court in 1925. Seated from left: James C. McReynolds, Oliver Wendell Holmes Jr., Chief Justice William Howard Taft, Willis Van Devanter, Louis D. Brandeis; standing from left: Edward T. Sanford, George Sutherland, Pierce Butler, Harlan Fiske Stone.

IN APRIL 1922, Felix Frankfurter recorded the first conversation he had had with Brandeis since William Howard Taft had become chief justice. Admitting that Taft had been very "gentlemanly" and "cultivated," he nonetheless was "the Taft we thought he was. He has all the defects but also the advantages of the aristocratic order." That summer, however, while walking with Frankfurter near his Chatham home on Cape Cod, Brandeis put his arm through Frankfurter's and in a soft voice asked, "Felix, do you still think Taft was as bad a president as we thought he was?"

This question took the Harvard professor by surprise, and he responded that he still considered Taft's record in the White House a poor one. "Why do you raise the question? Why are you ready to reconsider that judgment?"

Because, Brandeis explained, "it's difficult for me to understand why a man who is so good as Chief Justice, in his function as presiding officer, could have been so bad as a President. How do you explain that?"

"The explanation is simple," said Frankfurter. "He loathed being President and being Chief Justice [is] all happiness for him."

There is much truth in Frankfurter's response. William Howard Taft had never really wanted the White House and had always yearned for a seat on the high court. "I love judges and I love courts," he once said. "They are my ideals, that typify on earth what we shall meet hereafter in heaven under a just God." Now he had his heart's desire, and Brandeis viewed with approval the changes that Taft initiated. The chief justice had "admirable qualities, a great improvement on the late C.J. [White]; he smoothes out difficulties instead of making them. It's astonishing that he should have been such a horribly bad President, for he has considerable executive ability. . . . He has an excellent memory and makes quick decisions on questions of administration that arise." Brandeis, however, found him lacking in one important area. "He is," he told Frankfurter, "a first-rate second-rate mind." That second-rate mind, however, had the virtue of often being open to argument.

One might have expected relations between Brandeis and Taft to have been strained at best. The Boston lawyer had humiliated the president during the Pinchot-Ballinger investigation, and Taft had vigorously opposed Brandeis's confirmation to the Court in 1916. Taft, however, had held out an olive branch to Brandeis when they met on the street, and the new chief justice went out of his way—and successfully—to cultivate camaraderie among the brethren. On taking office, Taft sent Brandeis a long letter stating that he hoped they would be able to work well together on the bench. The two men met soon afterward, and Taft happily reported to his brother, "Brandeis and I are on most excellent terms. . . . He can not be any more cordial to me, than I am to him, so that honors are easy." Later, when Brandeis began dissenting more, Taft found him less charming.

Thanks in large measure to Taft, the deep jurisprudential divisions on the Court never became personal. The atmosphere on the Court, he said, "is very friendly. When we differ, we agree to differ, without any ill feeling. It's all very friendly." Brandeis found Taft to be the only man other than Holmes "with whom it is a pleasure to talk—you feel you talk with a cultivated man. He knows a lot, he reads, he has wide contacts." On the chief justice's seventieth birthday Brandeis sent him a note that went well beyond the requirements of formal politeness. "To you of Eternal Youth," he wrote, "it must be permissible to tell that Mrs. Brandeis and I send best wishes for the birthday on which we congratulate ourselves."

Brandeis enjoyed good relations with the other members of the Taft Court with the exception of McReynolds, and even McReynolds acted civilly in the business of the Court. He returned Brandeis's drafts, noting either concurrence or disagreement and occasionally adding a few words of explanation. In 1923, Brandeis wrote to his wife, "My friendly relations with my 'brothers' took a new advance yesterday when I asked McReynolds to write the dissent in a case in which we two are unable to concur with the majority. He seemed greatly pleased at being asked." Brandeis never commented on how McReynolds acted toward him, but the fact that McReynolds did the work of the Court in a sloppy manner, even missing sessions when he did not feel like attending, offended him. Taft deemed McReynolds's opinions "simply dreadful," and while he wanted conservatives on the Court, he considered McReynolds a reactionary.

(There is, however, another side to McReynolds, one never seen by the public and rarely seen by his colleagues. Every year when the circus came to town, McReynolds organized and paid for a trip for the Court's pages. During World War II he adopted thirty-three British war orphans, corresponding with them and providing financial support. On his death, he bequeathed significant sums to various charities.)

Although Mahlon Pitney is remembered primarily for several opinions restricting the rights of labor unions, Brandeis thought well of him. He had real character, he told Frankfurter, welcomed correction and discussion, and listened carefully to Brandeis's comments on his drafts. He worked hard, and Brandeis believed he had "intellectual honesty that sometimes brought him out against his prejudices and first judgment."

Brandeis was closest to Holmes of course, both in thought and in affection, and although he got along well with John H. Clarke, he had nothing more than thinly disguised contempt for him when Clarke resigned from the Court to devote his attention to the League of Nations rather than to "unimportant cases."

George Sutherland replaced Clarke in the fall of 1922 and quickly became the intellectual leader of the conservative bloc. Brandeis, however, did not hold Sutherland's mental abilities in the highest esteem: "I am much disappointed in Sutherland. He is a mediocre Taft." He liked the man, however, even though as a senator Sutherland had voted against Brandeis's confirmation. But as Sutherland's biographer noted, "These affairs seem to have reflected only the differences of opinion between two honest men." Brandeis had invited Sutherland to dinner in his apartment even before his nomination to the Court, and his guest ate, as Brandeis approvingly noted, "like an expert." In the years they served together on the Court, they were often in disagreement, but that did not affect their cordial personal relationship.

Brandeis and Pierce Butler, a former railroad lawyer, seem to have coexisted peacefully; moreover, they were the only two members of the Court to understand the complexities of rate regulation. A die-hard conservative, Butler valued principle above all else, a position that might have appealed to Brandeis except for Butler's dedication to a rigid jurisprudence out of touch with modern life. He opposed any form of government involvement in the economy or in the lives of individuals, and he alone dissented from Holmes's opinion upholding involuntary sterilization.

If Taft provided political direction for the Court conservatives, and Sutherland the intellectual heft, Willis Van Devanter acted as the coordinator and strategist. One of the least productive members of the Taft Court in terms of output, he wrote few controversial opinions, and his colleagues seemed happy for him to take on the often tedious cases involving public land law, admiralty, and corporation law. Even if Van Devanter wrote no opinions, Taft declared, "we could hardly get along without him." Brandeis admired him for his skill and knowledge in procedural and jurisdictional cases, being one of the few men on the high court besides himself to think those matters important, and like Taft, Brandeis often sent his draft opinions to Van Devanter before circulating them to the rest of the Court. Van Devanter "worked" the Court on behalf of Taft, who called him his "chancellor," checking with the different justices, sometimes trying to persuade them to change their votes. Brandeis saw how this would be useful to Taft: "Ein treuer Diener seines Herrn"—"He is the true servant of his master." On one occasion Brandeis said that Van Devanter would make an ideal cardinal, and on another described him as a "Jesuit general," the man who really runs the Court. Despite their jurisprudential differences, the two men apparently enjoyed warm and respectful personal relations.

Although Brandeis admired these skills, he recognized that he could never work that way. In his first terms on the bench, Brandeis claimed, "I could have had my views prevail in cases of public importance if I had been willing to play politics. But I made up my mind I wouldn't— I would have had to sin against my light, and I would have hated myself. And I decided that the price was too large for the doubtful gain to the country's welfare." But, he added, one should not underestimate the "large part played by personal considerations." There is a certain sanctimony here, a belief that "politicking" would somehow soil the sanctity of the Court. Personal relations did matter, and since he had no hesitation in pushing Holmes to act at times, one wonders exactly what sin he would have committed by talking to other members of the Court, trying to persuade them to support a particular position. It is possible, although he does not say so explicitly, that the price of support for his views in some cases would have meant his vote in others, and on matters that meant a great deal to him.

Brandeis considered Joseph McKenna the one completely incompetent member of the Court. Although he had had a distinguished political career, he was a poor lawyer and knew it, and in twenty-seven years on the bench never developed a consistent judicial philosophy. His last coherent opinion came in the speech case *Gilbert v. Minnesota* (1920), but he stayed on the Court even though he no longer could understand the issues. "The only way of dealing with him is to appoint guardians," Brandeis told Frankfurter. Taft, Van Devanter, and to a lesser degree McReynolds tried to manage his outbursts with varying degrees of success. McKenna knew "he doesn't count, he sends up a balloon just to show that he is there. He breaks loose occasionally." Although Taft on several occasions tried to get him to resign, McKenna refused, and so the others joined together to minimize any damage he might do. The chief justice assigned him only the simplest cases and then suppressed his opinions, holding them up until McKenna got mad and threw away the cases so they could be reassigned. The other justices, at Taft's suggestion, agreed not to make any decisions in which his vote would be the deciding one. After his wife's death in late 1924, McKenna finally resigned.

To replace McKenna, Calvin Coolidge appointed his college classmate Harlan Fiske Stone, the former Wall Street lawyer and dean of Columbia Law School who had become attorney general to clean up the mess of the Harding scandals. Within a few years Stone would become a close ally of Brandeis's, but relations between the two did not start off well, even though Brandeis wrote encouragingly on his return of Stone's first circulation, "Uncommonly good." Stone did not like Brandeis's highly documented opinions, which he considered ostentatious, although before long he, too, began citing law review articles in his opinions—and to similar disapproval from his conservative colleagues. In one of the first cases Stone heard, he thought that Brandeis used "bad economics to support bad law." In a case assigned to him that the new justice believed had been decided unanimously, he worked long and hard on the opinion, and then in what he considered an unsportsman-

Justices Stone, Holmes, and Brandeis, ca. 1927

like move, Brandeis entered a well-reasoned dissent that the case should be dismissed for want of jurisdiction, an issue that had not been discussed at the conference. Stone's annoyance did not abate when, after long hours of further research, it became clear that Brandeis was right. Brandeis, for his part, initially thought Stone too academic, wanting to discuss endlessly the pros and cons of each case. "I think it's wrong, but. I think it's right, but. Doesn't know and doesn't take trouble to find out." Although the two eventually agreed on nearly all major jurisprudential issues, they never developed the warmth that marked the Holmes and Brandeis relationship, or even the guarded affection of Brandeis for Sutherland or Van Devanter.

Although learned in law, Stone felt unsure of himself in his first months on the Court, and since Chief Justice Taft frowned on dissents, Stone decided not to oppose the majority unless he felt very strongly on the subject. He dissented only four times in his first year on the Court, leading the *New Republic* to lament that "he aligns himself with the majority without reservation." When Harold Laski complained about Stone's vote, Holmes responded, "Don't make a mistake about Stone. He is a mighty sound and liberal-minded thinker." Starting in 1926, liberal fears abated as more and more cases came down tagged "Holmes, Brandeis, and Stone dissenting," and Taft complained to his brother that insofar as maintaining the proper conservative jurisprudence, "Brandeis is of course hopeless, as Holmes is, and as Stone is."

The three men did not agree on everything, but they did share a belief in what Brandeis had called a "living law," one attuned to changes taking place in the broader economy and society. They thought that judges should practice judicial restraint and not impose their policy views in place of the legislative act. They also realized that judicial outcomes might not always be the best solution to particular problems; in a democracy, however, the process of airing a dispute would be worthwhile.

The three had different approaches as well. Holmes had the best writing style, but he loved to play with generalizations, so that he often failed to meet the majority on its own ground. "This is a pretty good opinion on the point he decides," Stone once commented, "but the old man leaves out all the troublesome facts and ignores all the tough points." Brandeis, on the other hand, often seemed to delight in taking the fight to the majority, confirming what Holmes had said early after Brandeis joined the Court: "I told him long ago that he really was an advocate rather than a judge. He is affected by his interest in a cause." Stone, more dispassionate than Brandeis and less philosophical than Holmes, had the academic's interest in developing jurisprudential theory, and this bothered Taft a great deal. "He is a learned lawyer in many ways," Taft said, "but his judgments I do not altogether consider safe." Taft worried that Stone would develop theories to overthrow the legal classicism that the chief justice and his conservative allies so treasured.

TAFT MADE SUCH A GOOD IMPRESSION on Brandeis in 1921 because the former president brought much-needed administrative ability to the Court, a skill that Chief Justice White had sorely lacked. The Court had an enormous backlog of undecided cases—343 cases had been carried over from the 1920 term—and the average time for an appeal to be heard after filing ran more than eighteen months. Within a few years the backlog had been all but eliminated, and the average time from filing to oral argument reduced to six months. Some of this improvement came simply from having a better and harder-working administrator in the center chair. Before a heart attack slowed him down in 1925, Taft routinely took on 50 percent more cases than did the associate justices, writing an average of thirty opinions per term compared with twenty for his colleagues. But Taft also believed in "massing the Court" and having it speak with a single voice. During the eight full terms that Taft presided over the Court (he suffered a stroke and resigned in the middle of the 1929 term), it handed down 1,554 full opinions, of which 84 percent were unanimous. By contrast, during the 1990s only 27 percent of the opinions had the support of all the justices.

Brandeis, despite his reputation as a great dissenter, had from the time he joined the Court believed that justices should refrain from dissenting except when necessary, but he did not share Taft and Butler's general opposition to all dissents. "I don't approve of dissents generally," Taft wrote, "for I think that in many cases, where I differ from the majority, it is more important to stand by the Court and give its judgment weight." Most dissents, he thought, "are a form of egotism. They don't do any good, and only weaken the prestige of the Court." Pierce Butler also saw dissents as an expression of vanity and would just as soon have done away with them. As chief justice, Taft worked hard to build consensus and stood ready to modify his own opinions to gain support from the others. Over his eight and a half years on the Court, Taft dissented only seventeen times, wrote only three dissenting opinions, and suppressed nearly two hundred of his own dissenting votes.

Brandeis drew a distinction between cases involving constitutional questions and those involving common legal matters. "In ordinary cases there is a good deal to be said for not having dissents. You want certainty & definiteness & it doesn't matter terribly how you decide, so long as it is settled." It is usually more important, he declared, "that a rule of law be settled than that it be settled right."

One also had to weigh the effect of dissents on the relations with the other justices. "There is a limit to the frequency with which you can [dissent], without exasperating men." Silence did not mean concurrence, Brandeis told Frankfurter. But one had to husband resources, and dissenting too often would weaken the force of a dissent when it became important to write. So "I sometimes endorse an opinion with which I do not agree, 'I acquiesce'; as Holmes puts it 'I'll shut up.' " A dissenting justice has to be careful not to "vent feelings or raise a rumpus." "You may have a very important case of your own as to which you do not want to antagonize [other justices] on a less important case." In a return of a Stone opinion, Brandeis wrote, "I think this is woefully wrong, but do not expect to dissent." On a Holmes opinion he remarked, "I think the question was one for a jury—but the case is of a class in which one may properly 'shut up.' "

Just as Brandeis acquiesced in the opinions of others, they concurred with him even when they had doubts. Holmes wrote back on one return, "I am unconvinced. I think the other interpretation more reasonable." In the same case, McReynolds also disagreed, but said, "I shall not object." Pierce Butler noted that he "inclined the other way," but Brandeis had made a strong case, so "I am content—& concur." In another opinion, McReynolds wrote on his return, "Sorry but I cannot agree," and still did not dissent.

Brandeis, like all justices, showed a willingness to change particular words or even sections to satisfy criticism and keep another justice on board. He proved particularly receptive to suggestions made by Willis Van Devanter, knowing that if "the Cardinal" agreed, he would bring along other members of the Court. Brandeis occasionally went further, actually drafting a dissent and then withdrawing it once his point had been made. In the *Coronado* labor case (see next chapter), he got Chief Justice Taft to modify the majority opinion in a way that did less harm to the union position.

In the circulation of one dissent he wrote, "Our Constitution is not a strait-jacket. It is a living organism. As such it is capable of growth. . . . Because [it] possesses the capacity of adaptation, it has endured as the fundamental law of an ever developing people." Taft refused to join the dissent unless Brandeis deleted these sentences, which he did. Brandeis told the chief justice that while he believed strongly in what he had written, "they are not necessary and I am perfectly willing to omit them." While the sentiment may have been incidental to this particular case, it marked the limits to which Brandeis would go in acquiescing for the sake of unanimity. When the idea of a "living Constitution" really mattered in cases involving rights or where Brandeis could not accept the majority's legal classicism, he would dissent, and nothing Taft said had any effect.

On occasion Brandeis changed his mind and brought his colleagues around from their original position. In *McCarthy v. Arndstein* (1924), for example, the conference originally voted that a lower court had been wrong in holding that the Fifth Amendment right against self-incrimination applied to the financial papers of a petitioner in bankruptcy, and Taft had assigned the opinion to Brandeis. After studying the case, however, Brandeis concluded that the lower court had been right, and drafted an opinion to this effect. Chief Justice Taft responded, "I am inclined to go with you because I don't know where else to go." Van Devanter, Butler, and Edward Sanford all suggested changes, which Brandeis accepted, and he handed down the decision for a unanimous Court. In at least two other cases draft opinion by Brandeis led to the Court's unanimously reversing itself from an earlier decision.

In the middle of the decade, pressure grew even stronger on the Court to suppress dissent in order to fend off political attacks. In 1919 the American Federation of Labor began a campaign against judicial review to protest what it saw as a wave of anti-union decisions by the high court. Then, in 1922, Senator Robert La Follette introduced a constitutional amendment giving Congress the power to overturn Supreme Court decisions that declared a federal law unconstitutional. The following year Senator William Borah proposed a bill that would require at least seven votes to void an act of Congress, and in 1924 La Follette included his proposed amendment as part of the Progressive Party platform.

Critics seized upon dissents to claim that the majority had not made the right decision, and in place of law had substituted their own views. Had the law been as clear as the majority opinions had claimed, there would have been no need for dissents. Taft followed the attacks on the Court closely, and to one friend he claimed that La Follette was no doubt discovering "a good deal of material in Brandeis's dissenting opinions." Taft found Brandeis's dissents ever more exasperating, not only giving aid to enemies such as La Follette but also undermining the need of the Court to speak with one voice. Brandeis's ultimate purpose, he told Willis Van Devanter, "is to break down the prestige of the Court."

Whatever their political differences, all of the justices rejected the notion of Congress's limiting the Court's decision-making authority. Taft stepped up pressure on the brethren to speak with one voice, and it worked. Brandeis told Frankfurter the political attack on the Court had tended to reduce dissents. "The whole policy is to suppress dissents, that is one positive result of Borah 7 to 2 business, to suppress dissent so as not to make it 7 to 2," he said. "You may look for fewer dissents. That's Van Devanter's particularly strong lobbying with the members individually, to have them suppress their dissents. . . . The prudential arguments of Van D. as to what is 'good—or bad—for the Court' are weighty with him & with all of them."

BRANDEIS DREW AN IMPORTANT DISTINCTION between constitutional and nonconstitutional cases, and he, perhaps more than anyone on the Court at that time, cared deeply about jurisdictional limits. It is somewhat surprising, therefore, that he alone of all the justices opposed Taft's efforts to give the Court greater control over its docket and to make it into a true constitutional tribunal.

A court's jurisdiction is the area over which it has authority, and one has to go into the proper court when conducting legal business. A person with a traffic ticket would not go into a small-claims court, while someone seeking a divorce cannot file in a criminal court. In the federal system, district courts will hear trials involving a federal crime, or suits between citizens of different states. For federal appellate tribunals, those that hear appeals from trial courts and lower appeals courts, the types of cases they may hear are determined by the Constitution and by legislation. The Constitution provides that the Supreme Court has original jurisdiction—that is, it will hear a case as the trial court—in suits involving ambassadors of foreign countries and those in which a state is a party. It may hear any case involving matters arising under the Constitution, federal laws, and treaties, as well as maritime and admiralty appeals. Beyond that, the Court's jurisdiction is defined by federal law and by the interplay of the federal system. Federal courts do not hear suits arising under state law unless there is diversity of citizenship

Old Court Chamber

(the parties come from different states) or a constitutional right is asserted. State court systems have similar jurisdictional definitions.

Brandeis believed that jurisdictional limitations should be strictly enforced, and voted against taking any case that he believed did not meet the Court's requirements. His law clerk Paul Freund asserted that "Brandeis was prepared to reject the claims, almost literally, of a workman, a widow and an orphan in pursuance of what seemed to him a more harmonious federalism." In conference Brandeis would "pound on jurisdictional observance." Some of the cases most criticized by reformers should never have been heard by the Court, he argued, and if the justices would just pay more attention to jurisdiction, the Court could avoid a great deal of censure. Throughout the 1920s he constantly urged Frankfurter to have his students write and publish articles on the Court's jurisdictional limits, in the hope that if bench and bar read them, it would do a great deal to eliminate needless filings. "The most important thing we do," he declared, "is not doing."

Brandeis may have been a bit unfair in his characterization of Taft, whom he charged with ignoring jurisdictional limits because he liked to decide issues. The chief justice had, after talking with Brandeis, changed his mind and adopted his argument on jurisdictional limits in an important labor case. Moreover, Taft, even before becoming chief justice, had worried about the Court's caseload and the almost total lack of administrative coherence within the federal judiciary. His work in addressing these issues remains one of his great legacies as chief justice.

As early as 1908, Taft had called for reform of the judiciary and, after leaving the White House, had used his platform as professor at Yale Law School to promote judicial reorganization. When he became chief justice, he had a clear idea of what he wanted to do. He achieved his first victory in 1922, when Congress at his request established a conference of each circuit's senior judges, who would meet on a regular basis with the chief justice to identify problems in the system, and empowered the chief justice to reassign district court judges on a temporary basis to reduce backlogs. In promoting the measure, Taft became the first chief justice to testify before a congressional committee. The law also required an annual report on the judiciary, analogous to the president's State of the Union. Most important, the act treated the federal courts as a single administrative unit; it made Taft and his successors not only the chief justice of the Supreme Court but, as the Constitution had envisaged, the chief justice of the United States and head of the entire judicial system.

Three years later Congress gave Taft the second tool he needed in the Judiciary Act of 1925, also known as the Judges' Bill. A committee of Sutherland, McReynolds, and Van Devanter had drawn up the measure, after Brandeis declined to be a member. The Judges' Bill gave the Supreme Court control over its docket. Ever since the first Judiciary Act in 1789, Congress had defined the Court's jurisdiction, but in doing so had never given the Court the power to say it would not hear certain types of cases. It could dismiss appeals for lack of standing, for frivolity, and for other causes, but all sorts of minor matters could be appealed by writ of error to the high court. There was more than a grain of truth in Justice Clarke's complaint when he resigned that more than half of the cases heard by the tribunal "are of no considerable importance whether considered from the point of view of the principles or of the property involved." Not only did many of these cases have nothing to do with constitutional questions; they did not even involve federal law.

Taft believed that the Supreme Court should primarily be a constitutional court, with its chief function of interpreting the Constitution "so as to furnish precedents for the inferior courts in future litigation and for the executive officers in the construction of statutes and the performance of their legal duties." The Judges' Bill reduced the mandatory jurisdiction of the Court—those cases it had to accept under a writ of error—and gave it the power to pick and choose the cases it would hear through the discretionary writ of certiorari. The law implemented Taft's belief that the main business of the Supreme Court should be the development of federal constitutional law.

Brandeis initially opposed Taft's proposal. He believed that changes to jurisdiction in a 1916 act had already enlarged the Court's discretionary powers and simply expanding them further would be neither the safest nor the most effective manner to limit the Court's docket. He recognized, however, that the 1916 act contained a number of inconsistencies; all the other justices supported Taft's proposal, and from an institutional perspective Brandeis agreed that the chief justice had a mandate from the Court. "I am willing," he told Taft, "that you should say that the Court approves the bill—without stating whether or not individual members approve it. For, in relation to proposed legislation directly affecting the Court, the Chief Justice, when supported by a clear majority, should be permitted to speak for it as a unit; and the difference of view among its members should not be made a matter of public discussion."

As the bill moved through final reading toward passage in early 1925, Brandeis wrote the following to Felix Frankfurter:

> U.S.S.C—venerated throughout the land. Despite the growth of population, wealth and governmental functions, & development particularly of federal activities, the duties of the Court have, by successive acts passed from time to time throughout a generation, been kept within such narrow limits that the nine men, each with one helper, can do the work as well as can be done by men of their caliber, i.e., the official coat has been cut according to the human cloth.
>
>   Congress, Executive Depts., Commissions & lower federal courts.—All subject to criticism or execration. Regardless of human limitations, increasing work has been piled upon them at nearly every session. The high incumbents, in many cases, perform in name only. They are administrators, without time to know what they are doing or to think how to do it. They are human machines.

Brandeis had been concerned about the workload of the Court for a long time and was not sure that the changes Taft had recommended would in fact cut down on congestion in the Court's docket. Throughout his tenure he took pride that nine men, each with a single clerk, did all the work of the nation's highest court efficiently and effectively, while the other branches of government swelled with hundreds and thousands of employees, each one, in his opinion, making that particular agency or office less efficient and more removed from the people. Nowhere else, Brandeis thought, had the ideal of small government proved so successful as in the Supreme Court. Within a few years, however, he recognized that Taft had been right, as the Court gained control over its docket and eliminated the backlog of cases. When his former law clerk James Landis and Frankfurter wrote approvingly of the Judges' Bill, Brandeis concurred in their judgment.

Brandeis also opposed Taft when he wanted to streamline the bankruptcy procedures in New York. A majority of the district and circuit judges approved, but Brandeis did not, believing that such changes should be uniform throughout the federal system, and therefore that Congress should implement these changes. Taft lashed out at Brandeis in a letter to his nephew, charging that the justice "always finds some reason for interfering with the course necessary to accomplish real reform." Then, in a disgusting display of anti-Semitism, Taft said that the real reason for Brandeis's opposition was that he did not want to interfere with "the young Russian Jews" who composed the bulk of the bankruptcy petitioners.

As part of his campaign to overhaul the federal court system, Taft also wanted to simplify the rules that governed procedure of cases in federal courts. The chief justice believed not only that out-of-date regulations hampered the effective administration of justice but also that inordinate complexity led to unnecessary delays in bringing cases to trial. In May 1926 the Senate Judiciary Committee unanimously reported a procedures bill drafted by Senator Albert Cummins and supported by Taft. Then the bill stalled, with rumors that Holmes, McReynolds, and Brandeis had all communicated their doubts about the measure to Senator Thomas Walsh. Taft and Van Devanter worked on Holmes and McReynolds and got them to agree not to communicate with the Senate committee. Brandeis would make no such promise, and this worried Taft considerably. Unwilling to confront Brandeis directly, Taft asked the chairman of the American Bar Association's Committee on Uniform Judicial Procedure, T. W. Shelton, to see Brandeis and to press him not to send a letter. Brandeis, however, remained noncommittal, and there is no record to indicate whether he wrote or even spoke to Walsh, who single-handedly stopped the bill dead in its tracks. Eventually, Congress in 1934 authorized the establishment of the uniform Federal Rules of Civil Procedure, which went into effect in 1938. By then, however, Taft had passed from the scene.

Brandeis, despite his refusal to join Taft in pushing for the Judges' Bill, nonetheless did his bit when Taft asked him and Holmes to join him before the House Appropriations Committee. The entire judicial system at the time was inadequately financed, and the U.S. Court of Appeals for the First Circuit lacked not only a law library but the funds necessary to purchase one. Taft recognized that Holmes and Brandeis would be the "big guns" to appeal to progressives on the committee, and he was right. They successfully made the case for a deficiency allotment to enable the First Circuit to secure a law library.

The final part of Taft's plans involved finding the Supreme Court more dignified quarters. Since 1860 the Court had met in the Old Senate Chamber in the Capitol. The justices had no privacy (after robing in one room, they paraded down a corridor to the courtroom), no separate chambers, a small room for conferences, and cramped library space. Taft lobbied for and Congress approved the construction of a large and magisterial building, one befitting a co-equal branch of government, on a site across from the Capitol and next to the Library of Congress. Taft, however, did not live to see completion of the building in 1935. Brandeis, who thought the old courtroom not only adequate but symbolic of small government, opposed the new Court building and, while he joined the other justices in hearing cases in what came to be called the Marble Palace, refused to occupy the large set of offices reserved for him. Instead, the Court used those rooms as an exhibition suite for visitors, and Mrs. Brandeis went down one day to take a tour of the new building. When she came back home, she declared, "They showed me the running ice water and the shower bath, two things my husband never uses."

IN IMPORTANT CASES involving property rights and labor legislation, Taft knew that despite his best efforts, he would not be able to silence Brandeis's dissents, but he never expected disagreement in the case that may have been the nearest to Taft's heart during this time, one explicating the powers of the presidency.

In order to prevent President Andrew Johnson from removing any government official appointed by Abraham Lincoln, Congress passed the Tenure of Office Act in 1867, requiring the president to get the Senate's approval to dismiss certain appointed officials, including postmasters. In 1920, Woodrow Wilson removed Frank S. Myers as postmaster of Oregon without the consent of the Senate. Myers died a little while later, and his wife, as executor of his estate, sued for damages and lost wages, claiming that Wilson needed the Senate's approval before firing Myers. She lost in the U.S. Court of Claims and then appealed to the Supreme Court. The Court heard oral argument on 5 December 1924 but, unable to reach agreement, restored the case to the docket and had it reargued on 13 and 14 April 1925. The Court did not hand down its decision until 25 October 1926, when by a 6–3 majority it found in favor of the president's power. The delay resulted at least in part from the time it took Taft to write a seventy-one-page majority opinion, McReynolds a sixty-two-page dissent, and Brandeis a fifty-five-page dissent. (Holmes said he agreed with everything McReynolds and Brandeis wrote and then added a mere two paragraphs of his own.)

Taft, as well as McReynolds and Brandeis, relied heavily on history, each going back to the Constitutional Convention of 1787, Taft to prove the Framers' intent to develop a strong executive power that, at least in the area of appointments, Congress could not limit, the other two to prove just the opposite. All three embraced what we today call "original intent," and their opinions illustrate how history can "prove" arguments on both sides of a dispute.

As president, Taft had believed that the Constitution strictly limited the power of the chief executive. In *Myers,* however, he put forth one of the broadest expressions of presidential power heard until that point. Although Congress clearly had the power to create a postal system, establish post offices, and provide for the hiring and pay of postal workers, Taft found the Tenure of Office Act an unconstitutional invasion of presidential authority. His reading of history led to the conclusion that the Framers had intended the chief magistrate to have an unrestricted power to remove any officials he appointed. Since the Constitution made the president responsible for the faithful execution of the laws, he had to have complete discretion in removing those officers who, in his judgment, did not carry out that duty. For Taft, the question involved separation of powers between the executive and the legislative, and the requirement for the Senate's advice and consent should be interpreted as narrowly as possible so as not to diminish presidential authority. Except for judges, who under Article III are appointed for life, the president ought to have complete discretion over removal of government officers. To allow Congress any intrusion on this authority would prevent the president from carrying out his duties. "I never wrote an opinion that I felt to be so important in its effect," Taft said.

The dissenters tore his argument apart. McReynolds ridiculed the idea of any inherent presidential power to remove government employees. The Constitution gave Congress the power to place the appointment of lesser officials in hands other than the president's and to provide the means by which they could be removed. Because Congress gave the president authority to appoint certain officials did not deprive Congress of the power to place limits on their removal. Had Taft not stretched his opinion to include the commissioners of the regulatory commissions, perhaps Brandeis's dissent would not have been so forceful. But the justice believed that if Taft's ruling were fully implemented, it would undermine the independent agencies.

Brandeis's first draft ran a mere page and a half, and he then assigned his law clerk for the term, James Landis, to investigate the history of the presidential appointment power and what lower courts had said. Landis went to the Library of Congress and spent months there. As Landis later noted, "I paged, literally paged every one of the Senate journals from the time of the passage of the Tenure of Office Act just in order to determine what the practice was." Brandeis had taught him that "practice is the important thing in determining constitutional law." As he turned in his notes, Brandeis's opinion grew and grew, until eventually it ran fifty-five pages in *United States Reports,* much of it devoted to the eighty-seven footnotes that contained Landis's research.

Whereas Taft had framed the question broadly—"whether under the Constitution the President has the exclusive power of removing executive officers of the United States whom he has appointed"—Brandeis structured his argument far more narrowly: "May the President, having acted under the statute in so far as it creates the office and authorizes the appointment, ignore, while the Senate is in session, the provision which prescribes the condition under which a removal may take place?" He then carefully examined the Framers' writings on the removal power, the experience of the early Republic, the conditions under which Congress had enacted the Tenure of Office Act, other statutes restricting presidential removal authority, and how succeeding presidents had fully obeyed their provisions.

Brandeis dismissed Taft's separation of powers argument and argued instead that the checks and balances among the three branches constituted the most important principle involved. That is why the Framers had refused to give the president an unlimited removal power. "The conviction prevailed then that the people must look to representative assemblies for protection of their liberties," he wrote. "And protection of the individual, even if he be an official, from arbitrary or capricious exercise of power was then believed to be an essential of free government." Separation of powers had been established "not to promote efficiency but to preclude the exercise of arbitrary power. The purpose was not to avoid friction, but, by means of the inevitable friction incident to the distribution of the governmental powers among three departments, to save the people from autocracy." To Brandeis, Congress, in protecting government employees from arbitrary dismissal, was also protecting free government.

Taft saw the *Myers* case as a test of loyalty to the American system of government, and Brandeis's dissent infuriated him. "He is opposed to a strong Executive," he fumed.

He loves the veto of the group upon effective legislation or effective administration. He loves the kicker, and is therefore in sympathy with the power of the Senate to prevent the Executive from removing obnoxious persons, because he always sympathizes with the obnoxious person. His ideals do not include effective and uniform administration unless he is the head. That of course is the attitude of the socialists till he and his fellow socialists of small number acquire absolute power, and then he believes in a unit administration with a vengeance.

A year later the chief justice still fumed at Brandeis and McReynolds. "They have no loyalty to the court and sacrifice almost everything to the gratification of their own publicity and wish to stir up dissatisfaction with the decision of the Court, if they don't happen to agree with it."

Taft had claimed far too much in his opinion. At a time when Congress had created administrative agencies such as the Federal Trade Commission designed to be independent of presidential authority, Taft's assertion of an unlimited right of removal undermined congressional policy-making powers. The decision made the front pages of the newspapers and met a barrage of criticism ranging over the political spectrum from the liberal Robert La Follette Jr. to the conservative senator George Wharton Pepper. The law journals almost unanimously sided with the dissenters, and Senator Hiram Johnson scoffed that the only people who supported the Taft opinion were those who believed the country needed a Mussolini.

Although Brandeis did not live to see all of his dissents become accepted by the Court, in this case he did, and he did not have to wait long. Nine years later a unanimous Court overturned *Myers* and held that when Congress created positions, especially in the quasi-independent administrative agencies, it could also protect the members of those agencies from presidential removal. (The president, of course, retains the power to remove officials performing strictly executive functions.)

BY THE TIME of the *Myers* case, Taft's initial praise of Brandeis had evaporated, as Brandeis, Holmes, and soon Stone stopped being, at least in Taft's eyes, "team players." Although he understood and supported Taft's desire to improve the administration of the judicial system, Brandeis did not share the chief justice's views on how those reforms should be implemented. Brandeis considered this a difference in opinion, one that could be discussed among the brethren, and when he saw that a majority of the justices supported Taft, he went along. Taft, on the other hand, saw anything less than full endorsement as a betrayal not only of himself but of the Court. Brandeis shared Taft's views that dissents ought to be infrequent, and on many occasions he suppressed his disagreement. Taft, however, wanted near-constant unanimity, and this Brandeis would not and could not give him. Perhaps worst of all, Taft understood that Brandeis's dissents posed a great danger to the legal classicism that the chief justice believed to be the heart of constitutional jurisprudence. In cases involving property rights, labor, and civil liberties, Brandeis did in fact undermine legal classicism, setting up its ultimate demise in the 1930s.

CHAPTER TWENTY-FOUR

THE TAFT COURT AND
LEGAL CLASSICISM

There is a curious dichotomy marking the Court's jurisprudence during the Taft years, one best understood by seeing the Court in a transitional stage, a condition that reflected the country as well. In the decades following the Civil War, the United States had begun the great transformation from a primarily agrarian society to an urban industrialized nation with large corporations dominating the economy. The changes sped up after World War I and did not sit well with many people. Scholars see the 1920s as a battleground between traditionalists fearful of the new ways and modernists eager to shed the shackles of older ideas and practices. The high points of this battle in secular society—the *Scopes* evolution trial, the struggle over prohibition, and the Sacco and Vanzetti case—played out in the battle within the Court over those struggling to maintain the older jurisprudence and those wanting the Court to promote a law reflective of newer ideas and conditions. Although Louis Brandeis found much to dislike in the modern temper, he nonetheless believed in and fought for what he had called "a living law."

THE YEARS OF THE TAFT COURT marked the high point of legal classicism, a jurisprudential theory that arose in the latter part of the nineteenth century and that ultimately fell apart during the constitutional crisis of the 1930s. Legal thinkers developed a jurisprudence reflecting the predilections of the Gilded Age—protection of property rights, fear of government intervention in the market, and disdain for labor and minority rights. It rested on two pillars: freedom of contract, interpreted so as to prevent the government from interfering with the labor market; and substantive due process, derived from the Fourteenth Amendment and used to protect property rights from the state. Classicism also elevated formal logic above any consideration of the real world around it. The innovations introduced by Christopher Langdell at Harvard in the 1870s, which Brandeis prized so greatly, replaced the older learning by rote and emphasized the evolution of legal rules through cases. Langdell wanted to make law into a science, and within a short time casebooks stopped using names and referred to litigants as "A" and "B" or "buyer" and "seller." The flexibility of the common law in meeting new factual situations vanished, to be replaced by a set of formal rules that paid little attention to the realities of the economy or the society. If the facts in some cases did not quite fit the rule, then judges ignored them.

Brandeis on his way to the Court, mid-1920s

Today most people who think seriously about the law see it as a social development reflecting the changing needs of an evolving society. The post–Civil War generation believed, as had Blackstone a century earlier, that law rested on universal principles that did not alter with the times, but stood as an unyielding arbiter of right and wrong. Because law embodied morality, judges had to administer it impartially to all, rich or poor, great or humble, but to do so, they had to "discover" the right rule and then administer it neutrally. When judges ruled against protective legislation or restrictions on property rights, they claimed that they were not making policy or law but merely applying the proper rule. Abstract reasoning, deliberate ignorance of the facts of industrial society, a limited role for the state, and a belief in immutable law combined with an emphasis on individualism to make up classical legal thought.

Brandeis, despite his fond memories of Harvard Law and his belief in absolute rules of morality, had long since gone a different way. Like Holmes and Roscoe Pound, he advocated a "sociological jurisprudence" that took facts into account and demanded that law respond to changing social and economic conditions. His brief in *Muller v. Oregon* remains the great practical embodiment of that view, and once on the bench Brandeis tried to educate his brethren about the real world.

A majority of the Court, however, clung to classical legal thought, and its clearest expression came in Justice Sutherland's opinion in *Adkins v. Children's Hospital* (1923). The federal government had enacted a minimum-wage statute covering women workers in the District of Columbia. The hospital brought suit against the Minimum Wage Board created to administer and enforce the law, and because Brandeis's younger daughter, Elizabeth, worked for the board, he recused himself from the case. Felix Frankfurter, who had taken over as counsel for the National Consumers League, presented a fact-laden "Brandeis brief" to explain why Congress considered the law necessary. Although the Court had never upheld a minimum-wage law, the rationale of *Muller*—facts to prove the need for the law under the police power and judicial restraint in leaving policy judgments to the legislature—would have encouraged the belief that the justices would sustain the law. Instead, by a 5–3 vote the Court struck it down, and in the minds of many turned the jurisprudential clock back twenty years to *Lochner.*

Sutherland, after piously noting that the decision to declare an act of Congress unconstitutional is "one of great gravity and delicacy," and noting that the courts did not review policy decisions of the legislature, then went on to do just that. The statute in question involved one of the most cherished of all rights, freedom to make a contract. "That the right to contract about one's affairs is a part of the liberty of the individual protected by [the Fifth Amendment] is settled by the decisions of this court, and is no longer open to question." While conceding that "there is, of course, no such thing as absolute freedom of contract," he stated that it is nevertheless "the general rule and restraint the exception." To abridge it, therefore, required the existence of exceptional circumstances.

The work that Frankfurter and the National Consumers League had put into their brief might as well have not existed, for the majority opinion dismissed it as irrelevant. Sutherland could not, however, ignore the many cases where the Court had approved restrictions on contracts, such as those involving labor on public works, methods of payment, and hours of labor. The last category by 1923 encompassed a variety of laws affecting men as well as women, but Sutherland denied that any general rule existed that automatically permitted regulation of hours; rather, in every case there had been special circumstances. As for the most famous of these cases, *Muller v. Oregon,* the passage of the Nineteenth Amendment giving women the vote had done much to eliminate "the ancient inequality of the sexes," and he intimated that such laws would no longer be either needed or deemed valid.

Even though special circumstances had been found in prior cases to limit contract, the minimum-wage act struck at the very heart of a labor contract—how much would the worker receive in exchange for his or her labor? None of the prior exceptions for hours laws applied here, and the law impinged on what the Constitution expressly protected, "two parties having lawful capacity to freely contract with one another in respect to the price for which one shall render service to the other in a purely private employment where both are willing, perhaps anxious, to agree." There could be no special circumstances to justify any interference with this right. The law exacted an arbitrary payment—the minimum wage—without any reference to the type of work or the manner in which it would be performed. It interfered with the right of two free people to reach a lawful agreement, and nothing more important could be done to protect the public welfare than to ensure individual liberties against arbitrary restraints.

Van Devanter, McReynolds, and Butler joined Sutherland's opinion, and thus formed the conservative bloc that would oppose reform legislation by both the states and the federal government for the next fourteen years, the group that would be known as the "Four Horsemen," a reference to the four riders of the Apocalypse. McKenna—who in the past had written several opinions upholding the use of the police power—signed on as well, although whether he understood the case by this time is questionable.

The decision proved too much even for Chief Justice Taft. In words that Holmes or Brandeis could have written, he conceded that people could differ over the wisdom or efficacy of minimum-wage legislation but said that "it is not the function of the Court to hold congressional acts invalid simply because they are passed to carry out economic views which the Court believes to be unwise or unsound." Holmes, aware that Brandeis could not write, made sure to speak for him. Alone of all the opinions, his took notice of the material Frankfurter had entered. He thought that such questions about the right of the state to protect workers in the marketplace had long been settled, and that "*Lochner* would be allowed a deserved repose." As for Sutherland's claim that the Nineteenth Amendment had eliminated the differences between men and women, Holmes declared it would take far more than that "to convince me that there are no differences between men and women, or that legislation cannot take these differences into account." Holmes also dismissed Sutherland's elaborate explanation that all the judges did was apply law here, noting that the only real criterion applied was whether the majority considered the law a good thing; it did not, and so the law—one reasonable people could support—had been declared unconstitutional. The merit of the law was not a question that he as a judge should decide, and neither should the majority.

Sutherland's opinion had all the hallmarks of classical legal thought: a complete disregard for the real world in which a minimum-wage law had been deemed necessary; an assumption that courts were better equipped to judge the wisdom of policy than legislatures; a formalism that elevated rules, especially those relating to freedom to contract, to a sacrosanct position; and an unrelenting opposition to government intervention in the market.

Brandeis, throughout his tenure on the bench, regularly dissented from legal classicism, joined first by Holmes and then also by Stone. During the Taft years no opinion better captures Brandeis's efforts to educate the Court than his dissent in *Jay Burns Baking Co. v. Bryan* (1924).

In 1921, Nebraska enacted a law establishing standard weights for loaves of bread sold at retail. The state wanted to make it easier for customers to understand the sizes and prices of bread and to prevent "short weights" (bread sold as a loaf that weighed less because of air), and to protect honest bakers from unfair competition. Violation of the law could lead to fines and/or imprisonment. The Burns Baking Company challenged the law as an unconstitutional infringement on its property as the law limited its right to operate its business free from government interference.

Speaking for the 7–2 majority, Pierce Butler agreed, holding that the police power of the state did not extend to unreasonable regulations, and he condemned the law as setting arbitrary requirements that most bakers could not attain. The only way that bakers could prevent shrinkage by evaporation after baking was to wrap the loaves, and most people preferred to buy unwrapped bread. In essence, the market should not be tampered with by the government. Bakers should be free to put out loaves of any size, and then consumers should be free to purchase them or, if unhappy with the size and quality, take their business elsewhere. Like Sutherland in *Adkins,* Butler opposed government regulation of the market in any form and substituted the majority's evidence for that of the legislature.

Brandeis entered an elaborate dissent that ran more than twice as long as the majority opinion and, to make sure that the brethren understood why the legislature had enacted the law, gave them a lesson in bread making. "Unless we know the facts on which the legislature may have acted, we cannot properly decide whether they were (or whether their measures are) unreasonable, arbitrary, or capricious. Knowledge is essential to understanding; and understanding should precede judging. Sometimes, if we would guide by the light of reason, we must let our minds be bold." What did the Court need to know in order to understand? "Merely to acquaint ourselves with the art of bread making and the usages of the trade; with the devices by which buyers of bread are imposed upon and honest bakers or dealers are subjected by their dishonest fellows to unfair competition; with the problems which have confronted public officials charged with the enforcement of the laws prohibiting short weights; and with their experience in administering those laws." Because the State of Nebraska had not filed a "Brandeis brief" in support of the law, the justice had to develop one of his own.

Brandeis then proceeded to tell the brethren more than they ever wanted to know about bread making. He documented his argument with materials from state legislative as well as congressional hearings, articles in trade journals, publications from state and federal bureaus of weights and measures, reports from the wartime Food Administration, dozens of examples of states establishing standard sizes and weights for food, and testimony on the effectiveness of similar legislation and how such measures did not harm the business of honest bakers. His law clerk that term, Samuel Maslon, collected everything he could find on bread making and regulation, composed a nineteen-page memorandum, and got copies of dozens of state laws. When Representative Charles Brand heard about the case, he wrote directly to Brandeis to tell him about his experience in the Ohio legislature, where he had sponsored a similar law, and sent him a copy of hearings before the U.S. House Agriculture Committee on a so-called Bread Bill. "Full weight bread," Brand declared, "is extremely important to the consumers of the country."

Brandeis's wealth of facts upset the already-confused McKenna, who noted that "disturbing doubts have come to me," although in the end he stayed with the majority. "A1. A Sockologgo. I agree of course," wrote Holmes on the return, and he told Frederick Pollock that Brandeis had written a good dissent, "showing profound study of the art of bread making."

None of this, of course, should have been necessary. The only question should have been whether the states, under the police power, could establish a system of standard weights, something states had been doing for decades. Absent any constitutional provision specifically enjoining the states from this task, the whole matter involved a policy judgment by the state legislature, a decision that the courts had no business reviewing. Because the majority had insisted on doing so and declaring the law arbitrary, Brandeis went to great lengths to expose the fallacy of that claim. The Court, he said in conclusion, had no authority to act as a super-legislature, a power that went far beyond the limits of acceptable judicial review.

THE BAKERY CASE displayed another aspect of the conservative mind-set that prevailed on the Taft Court. When the justices believed that an activity clearly and historically belonged in the public domain, laws regulating that activity could meet constitutional muster. When, on the other hand, the actions were private in nature, the Due Process Clause of the Fourteenth Amendment protected them from governmental interference. The war had led to governmental regulation of many hitherto private relationships, and conservatives looked to the courts to, as much as possible, reestablish the boundaries that had existed earlier. Just as Warren Harding wanted to lead the country back to "normalcy," so the conservatives on the Taft Court felt the need to reestablish the normal peacetime constitutional order. Butler's opinion in *Burns Baking* cries out in protest at the idea that the government should interfere in the essentially private business of a consumer purchasing a loaf of bread. As law professor Robert Post noted, Butler's opinion was neither as formalistic nor as arbitrary as Brandeis painted it, but rather it attempted to preserve certain areas of experience once thought to be totally private—such as the choice of what kind of bread to buy—from governmental regulation.

In this dichotomy it would be unfair to say that Brandeis favored extensive government regulation as opposed to letting individuals make certain decisions. Rather, he believed that courts should not sit in judgment of policy decisions. The Court's second-guessing of legislative facts represented the "exercise of the powers of a super-legislature—not the performance of the constitutional function of judicial review." Brandeis the democrat and the judge believed that the people, through their elective bodies, should determine policy. If facts showed Congress or a state legislature had reasonable grounds to enact a particular regulation, and if no specific constitutional bar existed, then judicial restraint required that courts allow the law to stand, whether the judges agreed with it or not. The Brandeis dissents in the 1920s, with their lengthy historical and factual expositions, all carry the same message: there is enough justification for the legislature to have enacted this law; there is no constitutional barrier to it; it is not the Court's business to pass on its wisdom.

The majority, however, with its narrow view of what constituted an activity affected with a public interest, struck down 140 state laws between 1920 and 1930, a large majority on the grounds that not being affected with a public interest, they invaded the sphere of the private and thus violated the Due Process Clause. For example,

• A Pennsylvania health statute prohibited the use of shoddy (reclaimed wool) in bedding materials; the Court ruled the measure arbitrary and unreasonable and so violated due process.

• New York forbade brokers from selling theater tickets at a price more than fifty cents above the box-office price; the Court held theaters to be essentially private undertakings and therefore immune from state regulation of their tickets.

• New Jersey set maximum fees for an employment agency, and a majority ruled that employment agencies were private undertakings and therefore beyond the reach of state interference.

Brandeis, along with Holmes and Stone, nearly always dissented.

IN ONE OF THE MOST FAMOUS of these cases, *Pennsylvania Coal Company v. Mahon* (1922), Brandeis entered a lone dissent against a majority opinion written by none other than Holmes. The Kohler Act prohibited mining coal within the limits of a city so as to prevent the subsidence—or collapse—of any building. The coal company had sold land in Pittston, Pennsylvania, for development purposes, but had retained mineral rights under that land, a common reservation at the time. It now wanted to exercise that right, but could not do so, because the mining threatened the Mahon home at 7 Prospect Place, and thus violated the Kohler Act.

In his opinion, Holmes noted that property always stood subject to government regulation, but in this case the regulation went too far. "The natural tendency of human nature is to extend the qualification more and more until at last private property disappears. But that cannot be accomplished in this way under the Constitution of the United States." The company had from the beginning reserved the right to coal in the ground, and that right could be realized only through actually mining it. To prohibit mining destroyed the value of the coal in a constitutionally impermissible way. In essence, the Kohler Act took away private property in the form of minable coal deposits without compensation.

Brandeis in his dissent noted that all property is subject to constraint when the public welfare is involved, and the fact that the company had reserved rights to the coal did not place that particular property beyond the reach of the police power. That the value of that land had been diminished was irrelevant. "Restriction upon use does not become inappropriate as a means, merely because it deprives the owner of the only use to which the property can be profitably put." The only questions the courts need ask were whether the legislature had a valid reason for enacting the law and whether the law reasonably protected the public interest. If so, the restriction on property had to be maintained. In essence, Brandeis would effectively have nullified the Takings Clause except where the government took full title to the land.

The following summer on Cape Cod, Felix Frankfurter asked Brandeis about the case, since Holmes's opinion seemed so out of character for him. Brandeis thought about the question, and said that growing old had led Holmes to an increased respect for property and a fear that he might outlive his own resources. Intellectually, Brandeis thought, Holmes knew better, but emotionally he was vulnerable. Taft and the conservatives had caught Holmes at a weak moment, right after his prostate operation, and "played him to go whole hog."

Although the case drew relatively little notice at the time, it has gained in interest over the years. Holmes's champions downplayed the opinion, treating it as an aberration from his typical respect for judicial restraint, and even the normally fulsome Frankfurter avoided comment after Holmes sent him a copy. In an unsigned editorial Dean Acheson claimed that Holmes had reached the "wrong" results and praised Brandeis's dissent as more "statesmanlike." Moreover, Acheson termed the case "an outstanding illustration of the way in which fundamental constitutional decisions depend at bottom not upon ascertainable rules of law but upon personal judgment," and cited as the source of this wisdom Holmes himself.

Yet although Brandeis's view of property and the Takings Clause has gained dominance over the years, the majority holding in *Mahon* has never been overruled. Modern commentators praise both Holmes and Brandeis for the cogency of their arguments, and the case is often used in Property classes as a means of balancing differing views of property rights and state regulation. In takings cases before the courts, Holmes's opinion is cited when the judges believe that a state has gone "too far," while the Brandeis opinion becomes the authority if a majority believes that the state had valid public interest reasons for its action. In many ways the two opinions also mirror the two warring jurisprudential theories—that of Holmes reflecting the older legal classicism and that of Brandeis, the newer.

THE TAFT COURT seems to have had a particular animus against labor and showed little sympathy for union rights to organize or strike. Brandeis, while far more favorable to organized labor than his colleagues, could never be described as an all-out champion of unions or their methods. "Neither the common law, nor the Fourteenth Amendment," he wrote, "confers the absolute right to strike."

The Taft Court's first major labor case illustrated the various themes that played throughout the decade—the desire to retreat from the extensive powers given to government during wartime and the rigid distinction between those areas affected with a public interest and those considered wholly private in nature. In an experiment that summed up a great deal of progressive thought about the role of government, Kansas had enacted the so-called Allen Bill. Governor Henry Allen had returned from Europe after the war to confront a serious emergency caused by a midwinter coal strike. A Bull Moose Republican, he acted as he believed his hero Theodore Roosevelt would have done, breaking the strike by calling up a volunteer army, mostly men recently discharged from war service, to mine the coal. He resolved that the public should never again suffer because of private labor conflict. His proposal went far beyond the "voluntary" agreements between labor and management during the war, and required compulsory arbitration in labor disputes. To provide this arbitration, the state legislature created the Kansas Court of Industrial Relations.

The Kansas court perfectly reflected progressive ideas about factual information and the ability to resolve—to "master"—problems through knowledge. Both organized labor and capital opposed the plan, the former because it took away the strike and the latter because it forced management not only to defend its labor policies and wages in court but to accede to a third-party determination. Several members of the Supreme Court, including Taft and Sutherland, believed strongly that in most labor disputes the public interest received little or no attention. During the war Taft had worked hard to resolve labor differences in light of the greater need of the nation—the public—to pursue the war effort. Allen believed that the impetus that had forced wartime cooperation could be exercised by the state in peacetime. Not all progressives, of course, supported the Kansas experiment; Felix Frankfurter and the editors of the *New Republic* condemned it, and there is reason to believe that Brandeis did as well, probably due to the compulsory nature of the Allen Bill.

The conservatives on the Court disliked it because it smacked too much of the big government that had existed during the war. In *Wolff Packing Co. v. Court of Industrial Relations* (1923), Chief Justice Taft spoke for a unanimous Court in declaring the Allen Bill unconstitutional. While a meatpacking house could certainly be subjected to state-imposed health regulations, it did not constitute that sort of business affected with a public interest to permit the state to fix wages for its employees. A butcher was but one of the common callings, an ordinary way for a person to earn a living, and therefore beyond the reach of such extensive regulation. To allow meat processing to be tagged as clothed with a public interest through a legislative declaration would be revolutionary in its implications. As for wartime regulations, that time had come and gone; the type of control that the Court had been willing to permit during the war would no longer be entertained. The power of the industrial court to fix wages in a business not affected with a public interest intruded into the realm of the private and violated the company's rights of liberty and property without due process of law.

Brandeis and Holmes went along, and there is no indication that they disagreed with the result. In all probability Brandeis shared the views expressed by Felix Frankfurter, a relief that the Court of Industrial Relations no longer existed, because he did not believe in compulsory arbitration to settle labor disputes. But the method of its demise concerned the Harvard professor. "Thus fails another social experiment, not because it has been tried and found wanting, but because it has been tried and found unconstitutional. . . . It was for the legislature of Kansas, and not for the Supreme Court, to kill it." Brandeis also believed that experiments in social legislation, unless specifically barred by the Constitution, should be subject to public criticism, and if found wanting, then the legislature, and not the courts, should act.

Organized labor did not care for the Kansas scheme, but it cared greatly about section 6 of the Clayton Antitrust Act, which had explicitly declared that labor did not constitute a commodity or an article of commerce and that consequently the antitrust laws should not be interpreted to forbid unions from seeking their legitimate objectives. Section 20 went even further and prohibited federal courts from issuing injunctions or restraining orders in labor disputes, "unless necessary to prevent irreparable injury to property, or to a property right." The same section also forbade injunctions against peaceful picketing or primary boycotts. At the time of its passage, labor leaders had hailed the Clayton Act as a Magna Carta and believed that the wording of the law made perfectly clear that federal courts should no longer be involved in labor disputes.

The Supreme Court did not rule on these sections until 1921, in *Duplex Printing Press Co. v. Deering.* Unions had boycotted a manufacturer's products in New York to enforce a strike in Michigan. Justice Pitney's opinion for the majority held that the Clayton Act had never legitimized secondary boycotts, nor had section 6 provided a blanket exemption from the antitrust laws; rather, it protected labor only when engaged in legitimate activities. Since a secondary boycott was unlawful, neither section 6 nor section 20 applied. Moreover, despite the wording of the latter section, Pitney interpreted the Clayton Act not only to allow injunctions against the immediate parties—the employer and the striking workers—but also to restrain another union from supporting the strikers.

Later in the year the Court handed down its decision in *Truax v. Corrigan,* invalidating a state anti-injunction law. An Arizona restaurant owner sought an order in state court against peaceful pickets, claiming that the law deprived him of property rights without due process of law. Chief Justice Taft agreed and declared the law unconstitutional as an arbitrary and capricious exercise of power. Taft drew property rights and their constitutional protection in the broadest strokes and then concluded that "the Constitution was intended—its very purpose was—to prevent experimentation with the fundamental rights of the individual." Even Mahlon Pitney, who had written the *Duplex* opinion, found this too much and argued in dissent that states had considerable latitude to determine "each for itself, their respective conditions of law and order, and what kind of civilization they shall have as a result." Holmes dissented separately, denouncing the probusiness activism of Taft's opinion. Business activity in and of itself did not invoke any "sacred" property right, and a state had the power to respond to abuses of property as well as to attacks upon it. Both Pitney and Holmes believed that Arizona had the right to ban labor injunctions, and the Supreme Court had no business second-guessing the legislature.

Brandeis dissented in both cases. In *Truax* he differed from Holmes, even though they reached the same result. The skeptical Holmes had no faith in reform legislation and thought much of it useless and mis-guided, but such judgments did not concern the courts. If the elected branches wanted to do something foolish and the Constitution did not forbid it, then let them do it. Brandeis, on the other hand, saw the anti-injunction statute as a positive good and, as he often did in his dissents, explored the economic and social conditions that had led the legislature to adopt the law. His dissent shredded the chief justice's reasoning, especially his assumption that property rights stood beyond legislative reach. Brandeis delved into labor conditions in the United States and changes that had taken place earlier in England in response to that nation's Industrial Revolution. He cited not only English cases but those from other countries, such as Australia, as well as from numerous American states, writing in effect a history of peaceful picketing and the changing laws that eventually approved and protected such practices.

In every change of law, there had been voices raised to claim that property rights would be destroyed, that anarchy and lawlessness would prevail. What the Arizona legislature had recognized was that business owners sought injunctions not to protect property, or even to protect the owners in its use, but to give them sovereignty over their workers. Many disinterested men, he declared, "solicitous only for the public welfare, believed that the law of property was not appropriate for dealing with the forces beneath social unrest; that in this vast struggle it was unwise to throw the power of the state on one side or the other; . . . that pending the ascertainment of new principles to govern industry, it was wiser for the state not to interfere in industrial strug-gles by the issuance of an injunction." Reasonable men could and did decide to limit injunctions, and the Court had no business passing on that decision.

In *Duplex* at least two members of the Court had firsthand knowl-edge of what Congress had wanted to do; Justices McReynolds and Brandeis had both played important roles in drafting the legislation. McReynolds, however, voted with the majority to negate congressional intent, while Brandeis argued that Congress had meant what it said in sections 6 and 20. In hearings on the Clayton bill Congress had determined that abuses of the injunction had gone too far in limiting labor's legitimate activities, and had then established a standard it considered fair to both sides. Judges did not have the prerogative to undo congressional policy because they happened to disagree with it or because their own economic views ran counter to those of the legislative branch.

The two decisions created a zone in which neither the states nor the federal government could act to prevent the abuses of labor injunctions. Whenever unions threatened to strike, employers would go to court and get an injunction barring them from doing so. Throughout the 1920s, liberals condemned the excessive use of the injunction, but not until the Depression undermined the dominance of business interests did reformers finally succeed. Congress passed the Norris–La Guardia Anti-injunction Act in March 1932 with language that made it impossible for federal courts to ignore its provisions, and a number of states soon followed with similar measures reining in the excesses of state courts.

THE EROSION OF LABOR RIGHTS during the 1920s might have been even worse save for Brandeis, Holmes, and Stone. In some instances, such as *Duplex* and *Truax,* Brandeis's efforts took the form of powerful dissents. When he could, however, he tried to convince his brethren that labor, too, had rights that needed protection. In a decision that came down shortly before *Truax,* Taft had allowed that a local union, if it acted peacefully, might engage in reasonable "persuasion" to make a strike effective. In that case, Brandeis did not dissent, despite the generally hostile tone toward labor of the chief justice's opinion, but rather concurred "in substance in the opinion and the judgment of the court." In another case, Brandeis went so far as to write a dissent and then withdraw it when Taft agreed to modify his opinion.

The Coronado Coal Company, located in the mountains of western Arkansas, had decided to break its contract with the United Mine Workers. It closed one of its mines and then reopened it with nonunion laborers, a pattern it announced it would follow in all its other mines. The local UMW chapter retaliated by deliberately destroying mining equipment and other company property. In coalfields that had a long history of violence, the workers armed themselves, attacked security guards and nonunion employees, and used dynamite to blow up coal shipments, all clearly designed to prevent Coronado from shipping its coal. The violence escalated until the workers and their supporters had destroyed all of the company's mines. Coronado then sued both the local union and the national UMW for treble damages, claiming the action had been a conspiracy in restraint of interstate trade as prohibited by the Sherman Act. During the trial the jury seemed unable to agree, so the judge practically ordered the twelve men to find for the company.

The case came to the Supreme Court in October 1920, when Edward White still presided as chief justice, and the union secured the services of the former justice Charles Evans Hughes. "Since I've been on the Bench," Brandeis later told Frankfurter, "only one labor case [was] well argued, Hughes' argument on first hearing of *Coronado* case." Despite Hughes's efforts, at conference the vote went against the union and upheld the award. Brandeis prepared a dissent, in which he clearly described the lawlessness of the violence in the coalfields and argued that unions, just as corporations, should be suable, a position he had argued against Samuel Gompers nearly two decades earlier. Whatever else might be said about the destruction and the actions of the workers, however, they could not be deemed a conspiracy in restraint of interstate commerce. He then quoted from *Hammer v. Dagenhart,* where over his and Holmes's dissent the Court had ruled that Congress could not control child labor because manufacturing was a local activity and not part of interstate commerce. If manufacturing in the earlier case did not constitute interstate commerce, then neither could coal mining be considered as such. Even if the United Mine Workers had been successful and had organized every miner in the country, it still would not violate the Sherman Act, because mining remained a local activity. Interstate trade would be affected only if the union attempted to monopolize the production, distribution, and price of coal sold in interstate commerce, and that had been neither claimed nor shown in this case.

Brandeis finished his revision at the end of March 1921 and waited for Chief Justice White to circulate the majority opinion. But on 19 May, White died, leaving the case to be held over and reargued in March 1922, with William Howard Taft now in the center chair. Week after week passed with no sign of a decision. Then at one Saturday conference Taft reported that he believed that the union, although an unincorporated association, could be sued; that the evidence supported the charge that the union had intended to restrain commerce in violation of the antitrust laws; and that the union was liable for the damages imposed at the jury trial. Taft had not yet written his opinion when Brandeis showed him his proposed dissent, and at first it did not seem to affect the chief justice's views. But as Taft tried to write he found

Brandeis's arguments unassailable, and in conversations with the chief Brandeis strongly argued his view that any liability existed at common law and not under a federal statute, that there had been no evidence of a conspiracy, and that by the Court's own definition there had been no interstate commerce. "The wrongs committed were violations of the law of Arkansas," Brandeis emphasized, "not of any federal law." In the final opinion for a unanimous Court, Taft held the union not liable because the actions did not constitute a conspiracy in restraint of trade. Brandeis took particular satisfaction in the last paragraph of Taft's opinion, since, as he told Frankfurter, "I pounded on jurisdictional observance & glad to get Taft to say what he did." "The circumstances are such as to awaken regret," Taft wrote, "that, in our view of the Federal jurisdiction, we cannot affirm the judgment. But it is of far higher importance that we should preserve inviolate the fundamental limitations in respect to federal jurisdiction." Brandeis knew that Taft shared his views on jurisdiction, and appealed to him not on prolabor grounds but rather on the "higher" ideal of sustaining jurisdictional standards. The brethren would accept this argument from Taft, Brandeis told Frankfurter without rancor, but not from him. "If good enough for Taft good enough for us, they say, and a natural sentiment."

BRANDEIS'S LAST MAJOR DISSENT in a labor case came in 1927, when the conservative majority found a way to get around the jurisdictional and logical barriers that Taft, at Brandeis's urgings, had created in *Coronado.* The Bedford Cut Stone Company for many years had a contract with the Journeymen Stone Cutters' Association, but in the antilabor agitation following World War I had decided to terminate the agreement and to hire nonunion workers. In conformity with their union's constitution, journeymen stonecutters employed by other firms refused to "finish" stone from the Bedford company, in effect setting up a secondary boycott. The company sought an injunction that the lower court granted on the Sherman Act's restriction of secondary boycott, but based on the high court's prior rulings, both the district court and the court of appeals refused to issue a restraining order. The Supreme Court did.

The definitions of commerce in the two child labor cases and in *Coronado* had been very narrow, and certainly if manufacturing and mining were, as the Court had insisted, local exercises, then surely the output of a stone quarry would be as well. But Sutherland's majority opinion in *Bedford Cut Stone Co. v. Journeymen Stone Cutters' Association* practically obliterated any distinction between local and national commerce. The real question, Sutherland declared, was whether the union had attempted to prevent the shipment of the stone in interstate commerce. He found that it had, and therefore had violated the Sherman Act. Observers could hardly fail to note that while conservatives on the Court would ignore reasonable restrictions on trade caused by industry under a rule of reason, they would ignore this same rule when asked to apply it to a clearly reasonable act of labor.

The logic of the decision insofar as it blurs distinctions between local and interstate commerce is not by itself wrong; later courts would use it to justify national intervention in the economy. But the ruling in effect told lower federal court judges to issue as many injunctions against unions as they wanted, because the labor provision of the Clayton Act meant nothing. In those rare instances when the high court would overturn an injunction, so much time had passed from the initial issuance that the restraining order had served its purpose and no real relief would be had. Many conservatives believed the Court had gone too far, and one wrote that after reading the high court's labor opinions, "one is apt to arrive at the conclusion that the activities of labor are lawful so long as they are confined to means which are ineffective for achieving perfectly legitimate purposes."

Brandeis, joined by Holmes, dissented, pointing up the inconsistency of the majority opinion with prior holdings of the Court. The actions taken by the journeymen had been peaceful and certainly reasonable by the principles of common law. The lower courts had quite properly refused to issue injunctions, because nothing in state or federal law required them to do so. Even under the rules of *Duplex,* "the propriety of the union's conduct can hardly be doubted by one who believes in the organization of labor." Brandeis went on to show that the company was not some small firm threatened by a national union; quite the opposite, Bedford and the companies that had joined it in the suit shipped 70 percent of all cut stone in the country. The labor union had 150 locals, with an average membership of thirty-three workers.

There had been no bloodshed; the journeymen "were innocent alike of trespass and of breach of contract. They did not picket. They refrained from violence, intimidation, fraud and threats. They refrained from obstructing otherwise either the plaintiffs or their customers." Taking the Court's position to a logical extreme, Brandeis argued that the majority opinion turned the Sherman and Clayton acts into instruments "for imposing restraints upon labor which reminds of involuntary servitude." It would be strange, he concluded, if Congress had intended "to deny to members of a small craft of workingmen the right to cooperate in simply refraining from work, when that course was the only means of self-protection against a combination of militant and powerful employers. I cannot believe that Congress did so."

As soon as the Court adjourned, Brandeis sent a copy of the opinion to Felix Frankfurter, with a note saying, "If anything can awaken Trade Unionists from their lethargy, this should." While the decision infuriated organized labor, the justice was perhaps somewhat unrealistic in what the unions could or should do. With Calvin Coolidge in the White House, Republicans controlling both houses of Congress and most state legislatures, and the courts following the lead of the Taft majority, labor could actually do very little. Not until the Depression broke the power of both business and the Republican Party, and the New Deal passed prolabor legislation, would unions come into their own.

The dissents did establish Brandeis as a champion of labor, although not in the sense that later liberals viewed unions. Brandeis had always believed in the right of workers to organize; labor needed to cooperate to resist the demands of employers and to secure decent wages and working conditions. But he had also believed that unions should be incorporated and that they should be answerable for their actions. The *Coronado* decision for the first time held that unions could be sued, a position that appalled many labor leaders but one that Brandeis firmly endorsed. While he recognized that in the battle between labor and management union strength provided balance, he never saw unions as weapons against capitalism. He wanted them to be strong but also responsible, and when they abused their power, they should pay the price, the same as corporations should.

The Taft Court's labor decisions would be repudiated both by Congress in the 1930s and by subsequent courts. What strikes one looking at the Brandeis record is how often the arguments made in dissent would become the accepted jurisprudence of the Court. In some instances it happened while the justice still sat on the bench; other times his position would not be adopted until decades had passed. He saw his dissents as part of a constitutional discourse, a view that other judges recognized. He did not feel the need to win so much as to start the dialogue, one that would be picked up in the law journals, where arguments could be dissected and refined. "You and Holmes set the pace," Benjamin Cardozo wrote to him in gratitude. "The rest of us are merely imitators who try to keep in line." If judges like Cardozo, Julian

*Henry J. Friendly, law clerk
in the 1927 term*

Mack, and the Hands recognized and joined in this effort, then his faith, as he said so often, was great in time, and by all measures time has justified that faith.

A SOLICITOR GENERAL once told the lawyer George Farnum that "when Mr. Justice Brandeis writes an opinion dealing with a question of federal practice, the law is settled for fifty years to come." While this may be somewhat exaggerated, Brandeis did have a great impact not only on jurisdictional matters but on commercial law, antitrust, administrative law, utility regulation, federalism, and individual liberties, and while not every one of his views has been accepted, many have been.

The most influential antitrust scholar of the twentieth century, Milton Handler, believed that no one on the Court affected this field of law more than Brandeis. Of course Brandeis went on the Court with fairly well-defined views on big business and monopoly; he had written extensively on the subject, testified before congressional hearings, advised Wilson, and helped draft the Clayton Act. His views on bigness as a curse and monopoly as inefficient were well known by the time he went onto the bench. During his tenure the Court heard thirteen merger cases, and he wrote in none. He disqualified himself in five cases, and voted in six cases for dissolution and in two against. The nearest he came to expressing these views can be found in his dissent in *Liggett Co. v. Lee,* in which he supported the constitutionality of a Florida tax on chain drugstores. Brandeis's contribution to antitrust law, however, came not in his opposition to bigness but in his sophisticated development of the "rule of reason," first enunciated by Chief Justice Edward White in the 1911 *Standard Oil* case. A combination by itself, or even actions that restrained trade, would not be considered illegal if reasonable. The courts then had to deal with what constituted a "reasonable" combination or action in restraint of trade.

The first cases in which Brandeis wrote on antitrust amazed some of his reform colleagues. He spoke for a unanimous Court in holding that the Chicago Board of Trade's rules on futures trading, which essentially locked out a group of warehousemen, did not violate the antitrust law.

Then Brandeis dissented when his colleagues held that an association of hardwood manufacturers violated the antitrust law, arguing that the group had legitimate reasons for sharing pricing and other information and that their cooperation fostered rather than limited competition. As one might expect, Brandeis wanted the courts to examine the facts. Courts must "consider the facts peculiar to the business to which the restraint is applied; its condition before and after the restraint was imposed; the nature of the restraint; and its effect, actual or probable. The history of the restraint, the evil believed to exist, the reason for adopting the particular remedy, the purpose of or end sought to be attained, are all relevant facts."

Thirteen years later, in the so-called Cracking Oil case Brandeis presented a highly sophisticated analysis of competition that still governs antitrust jurisprudence. He developed what Professor Handler called the "concentric circle rule of reason." The fact that a combination eliminated competition among a small group of companies (the inner circle) did not matter if the quality of competition in the market as a whole (the outer circle) remained unimpaired. In the case Brandeis spoke for the Court in reversing a government conviction of four major gasoline producers using a new "cracking," or refining, technology. The companies had established a horizontal price agreement on royalties for pooled patent sublicenses, which the government claimed violated the antitrust law. Brandeis looked at various dimensions of competition in the industry and determined that while the merger effectively ended competition among the four producers, it did not have a negative effect on competition in the larger gasoline market. The companies had done what many companies in changing markets did, join together to take advantage of and to share new technology. The companies did not prevent other firms from utilizing the new cracking methods, but established a rational and fair system by which their patents could be licensed.

Although Brandeis emphasized the finding of facts relating to various layers of the market and the actions of the companies, the facts by themselves did not tell the Court enough. It then had to evaluate these facts in light of the total market; per se rules would not do. In the early twenty-first century this type of multidimensional analysis is the beginning of all antitrust law.

AT THE TIME, a large number of utility rate cases came to the Supreme Court, the result of earlier decisions by a Court hostile to the new administrative agencies at both the state and the federal levels that had been given authority to set rates for public utilities and common carriers. The courts distrusted these creations, since they had not been envisioned by the Framers and because they had a mix of legislative, executive, and judicial powers. *Smyth v. Ames* (1898) may have been one of the worst mistakes the high court ever made, because by appropriating to the judiciary the power to review rates after they had been set by an administrative agency, it plunged the courts into the business of second-guessing both agencies and legislatures on the complex issue of establishing fair rates, a job for which very few of the judges were qualified.

Taft hated these cases. "I dislike them extremely and don't feel competent in them," he told his son. "We have some experts on our Court. One is Pierce Butler, the other is Brandeis." Taft relied on the two men in this area, and their competence relieved him of much anxiety. In October 1922, Brandeis worked on several complicated cases from North Carolina, and Taft wrote to him, "I have tried to be gentle with you on account of them." When he saw the work, he wrote on the return, "Admirable, compact, forcible, and clear. It relieves me greatly to get rid of such a case so satisfactorily."

Brandeis and Butler, of course, came at the problem of evaluating a just return from completely different perspectives. The key question involved the actual value of the railroads' properties, because rates were supposed to bring a fair return on that investment. Butler, a former railroad lawyer, agreed with the lines that the property ought to be assessed at the cost of replacement, which, in times of rising prices, meant higher rates. Brandeis did not oppose a fair return on investment, as he had shown in the sliding-scale fight; but he believed that a better way existed to determine the real value of the property. He recognized that most of the brethren, with the exception of Butler, had no grasp of the issues involved. The chief justice, despite his vast experience, "hasn't the slightest grasp of fiscal or utility aspects of these cases." So Brandeis tried, albeit unsuccessfully, to educate them.

As he had noted in his dissent in the *Associated Press* case, courts had no expertise to valuate property. Therefore it made little sense to lay upon the courts the burden of reviewing rates determined by those who had the knowledge and the facts needed. The replacement theory of *Smyth v. Ames* also struck him as wrong and impractical; railroads and other utilities should get a fair return based on the actual value of their property. The rate of return on that investment, he believed, should be the same as that earned by a prudent investor. No magic formula existed to determine either valuation or rates, and the courts would be better off leaving that task where it belonged, in the hands of the appropriate administrative agencies, which could adjust formulas to take into account inflation and other factors. (Most economists believe the prudent investment theory a better basis for rate determination than reproduction costs.)

Brandeis's opportunity came when the Southwestern Bell Telephone Company alleged that in setting telephone rates, the Public Service Commission of Missouri had not allowed for a sufficient return on its investment because it had undervalued its property; the commission had used original costs rather than replacement value in its calculations. At the conference a majority of the justices voted to reverse the commission and require it to allow the company a higher rate. There had, however, been a lot of discussion among the brethren, since they had recently heard several other rate cases, and in one of them Brandeis, speaking for all save McKenna, managed to work in the idea that reproduction costs, while important, were but one of numerous factors involved in rate setting. Believing that the justices might be willing to jettison *Smyth v. Ames,* Brandeis decided to see if Taft would be amenable to changing his mind. If he did, that would bring over a majority of the other justices. He went to see Taft and explained to him what he saw as the problems in the current system. Although Taft did not see eye to eye with Brandeis, and certainly did not understand the issue well, he agreed that Brandeis should present the matter to the conference and put aside a whole day to discuss the issue.

Brandeis set to work and over the next few months prepared a sixty-two-page memorandum dissecting all of the flaws in the current system and suggesting why the prudent investment basis would be better. McReynolds objected, since he had already written what he assumed would be the majority opinion in the case, but Taft and Van Devanter insisted. "It was a thorough discussion," Brandeis reported. "Some didn't grasp the facts & hadn't thoroughly mastered the memorandum, but it was a new method in consideration of issues." In the end, the justices voted 7–2 to stay with the old formula, and McReynolds delivered the opinion directing the commission to reopen the rate hearings. Brandeis utilized his memorandum as he thought he would, in the form of a dissent.

The case demonstrated how a determined public utility could eviscerate state rate-making agencies through constant appeals to sympathetic courts, claiming that the state had failed to establish a fair base for rates. Brandeis cared less about which method to use than that the courts should get out of the business of rate review completely. If the state agency had followed all of the rules of fair procedure, utilities would have a proper opportunity to present all of the necessary data regarding property, investment, and expenses, and then the agency's determination would be final unless negligence could be proved. But conservatives, who disliked the rate-making agencies to begin with, had no desire to see the courts leave the field. Not until business dominance collapsed in the Depression did Brandeis's arguments prevail, and the judiciary began to withdraw from reviewing rates, a process finally completed in 1944. Although some state agencies adopted the prudential investment theory, over the years the process of property valuation and rate making have grown exceedingly complex, requiring that public service commissions take into account more and more data that need to be assessed by experts in various ways. Brandeis would have been pleased.

IN ONE ADDITIONAL AREA Brandeis helped to transform American law. According to one scholar, "The contributions of one man, Justice Louis D. Brandeis, reoriented the focus of administrative law toward the appropriate allocation of functions and power between courts and agencies." Courts had been leery of federal administrative agencies ever since the creation of the Interstate Commerce Commission in 1887. The ICC seemed to violate one of the cardinal tenets of the Constitution, the separation of powers, because it exercised executive, legislative, and judicial functions. Initially, the Supreme Court hamstrung the ICC through a series of decisions that either took a very narrow view of its delegated authority or permitted extensive judicial review of its findings. Then, in *Smyth v. Ames* (1898), it reserved to the courts the power to review rates set by public service commissions. Not until the progressive era, when Congress significantly strengthened the ICC and lawyers became more comfortable with administrative regulation, did the Supreme Court begin to allow the agency leeway to operate. In one of his first administrative law decisions, Brandeis upheld the doctrine of primary jurisdiction, in which federal rate making took precedence over state judicial scrutiny.

In 1923, Brandeis entered a dissent in *Pennsylvania v. West Virginia,* a suit by Pennsylvania and Ohio to enjoin West Virginia from enforcing a state law designed to divert or retain, for the benefit of its own citizens, natural gas in an interstate pipeline passing through the state that would otherwise have gone to neighboring states. West Virginia created a public service commission that had the power to limit the amount of gas going through the state and to divert it to West Virginia consumers. A majority of the Court held the statute unconstitutional as interference with interstate commerce.

In his dissent Brandeis maintained that the determination of an equitable allotment of natural gas required an investigation into production, demand, reserves, and the business practices of the various companies, all requiring expert knowledge and experience and beyond the abilities of the courts. The situation would change regularly, thus requiring constant adjustment and fact-finding, duties properly exercised by an administrative agency. To determine what the responsibilities of an agency should be and what the courts should do, Brandeis developed four criteria: Did the problem's complexity require expert knowledge? Was the question one that could be conclusively resolved in one sitting (a court case) or that required continued involvement over time by the regulatory body? Were the problems presented, by their very nature, "administrative" in scope? Were the particular issues ones of "fact" or of "law"? Responses to the first two provided the criteria to answer the third; only in the fourth area, where questions of law arose, should the courts get involved. These standards became the primary criteria for allocating power between courts and administrative agencies in modern America, and came into full flower with the great explosion of administrative agencies during the New Deal, World War II, and postwar America.

A majority of the Taft Court, however, had no desire to turn over what they considered a judicial function to administrative agencies, even though it was becoming increasingly clear that judges lacked the expertise to establish rates, much less review complex administrative findings. In addition, conservative justices disliked the idea of a federal agency's regulating business practices. Although the Taft Court tended to support national power vis-à-vis the states, it had no love for the Federal Trade Commission, and the FTC had no worse enemy than Justice McReynolds, who had helped draft the measure creating it.

In *FTC v. Gratz* (1920) McReynolds spoke for the majority in denying the commission the power to determine "unfair methods of competition," because the statute had not defined what this phrase meant. Three years later McReynolds again delivered an opinion overturning a cease-and-desist order after extensive investigation and held that the courts had the power to look at the evidence de novo. If a judge agreed with the agency's findings, then they would be considered conclusive; if not, the court could make its own determination. Brandeis dissented in *Gratz,* and in several more cases during the decade, trying to get the Court to recognize administrative agencies not only as legitimate but also as entrusted with particular duties requiring expert knowledge that the courts lacked.

While willing to give administrative agencies broad discretion in matters of economic regulation, Brandeis held them to a higher standard when individual rights came into play. Although the *Milwaukee Leader* is normally discussed as a speech case, it was also a case testing the power of the postmaster general to award and retract valuable mailing privileges, a decision often considered administrative in nature. When agency decisions affected individual liberties, Brandeis could be just as insistent as his colleagues on judicial review. In *Ng Fung Ho v. White* (1922), two Chinese immigrants had been summarily deported by an immigration official, and they challenged his action, claiming they were American citizens. Writing for a unanimous Court, Brandeis held that their claim of citizenship was entitled to judicial review, since the immigration agency's power to deport a person depended solely on the fact of that person's being an alien. To refuse to review a claim of citizenship would be a denial of due process.

Brandeis's concern with delineating the powers of administrative agencies led Felix Frankfurter to offer one of the first courses in administrative law at Harvard, and when Frankfurter decided to edit a book of cases for use as a text, Brandeis put additional moneys at his disposal to hire a student and also to get out a book on the related subject of federal jurisdiction.

During the New Deal, Brandeis's dissents began to bear fruit, and following the 1937 Court fight open resistance to the idea of administrative agencies collapsed. In 1939, just a few months after he stepped down, Brandeis learned that the Court, after several hearings, had finally decided *United States v. Morgan,* a case that had been going back and forth between the high court and a Missouri district court for three years, involving the administrative power of the secretary of agriculture to dispose of moneys held in escrow following a controversy over stockyard fees. The Court said that while there had been procedural irregularities, the secretary could correct his own missteps without further judicial scrutiny. In his opinion, Justice Stone essentially followed the criteria that Brandeis had set up fifteen years earlier.

· · ·

DURING THE TAFT YEARS Brandeis, Holmes, and Stone, but especially Brandeis, fought the rigidity of the conservative majority's attachment to legal classicism, with its emphasis on unyielding rules that ignored social and economic facts. Brandeis from the time he had been in law school believed that law divorced from factual reality could only be sterile, and the more separated it became, the greater a threat to society. At times his dissents seemed too concerned with facts, as in the bread case, but he had a reason, to drive home the sins of the majority in refusing to recognize that law had to fit the conditions of society.

The factual underpinnings of his jurisprudence fit in well with his idea of judicial restraint. Policy making should be a function of the legislative branch. If Congress or a state assembly identified a problem, analyzed the facts, and then came up with a plan, then judges should not interpose their views on the correctness of those choices. The relevance of facts shaped his belief in a living law, and as facts changed, judges had to take into account what impact this had on the law, even on constitutional law. Although he was seemingly a voice in the wilderness in the 1920s, in the end his faith in time, as he put it, led to the acceptance of his views. The decisions of the majority, with their rigidity and formalism, have been overturned. Brandeis's dissents pointed the way to the future.

CHAPTER TWENTY-FIVE

A NEW AGENDA: THE COURT AND CIVIL LIBERTIES

The speech cases following World War I ushered in a new era in Supreme Court history. From John Marshall to the Civil War the Court had been concerned with defining governmental powers and allocating those powers between the states and the federal government. After 1865, the justices had focused on the protection of property rights and the extent of state police powers in regulating the industrial market and workplace. The Court still accepted these types of cases for another two decades, but starting in the 1920s more and more of the docket involved issues of individual rights and liberties, and especially the question of "incorporation," whether the protections embodied in the Bill of Rights applied to the states as well as to the federal government.

Brandeis wrote many of his most important opinions in the 1920s, pointing the way to an expansion of civil liberties, establishing a constitutional basis for privacy, and supplying an enduring rationale for why free speech is essential to a democratic society. He did not, of course, always prove to be a prophet, and not all of his jurisprudence has been greeted with applause by liberals. Yet if he had never written anything other than the *Olmstead* and *Whitney* opinions, his impact on American constitutional law would still have been great.

THE FRAMERS INTENDED the Bill of Rights to apply only to the national government and not to the states, a position affirmed by the Supreme Court in *Barron v. Baltimore* (1833). Scholars now believe that the Fourteenth Amendment, with its call for due process and equal protection of law, was intended to extend the protection of the Bill of Rights to the states. Brandeis took this position in his dissent in *Gilbert v. Minnesota* in 1920. In rebutting the majority opinion that the abridgment of speech had been done by a state and therefore outside the protection of the Constitution, he declared that such an infringement on basic rights "is not one merely of state concern. The state law affects . . . rights, privileges, and immunities of one who is a citizen of the United States; and it deprives him of an important part of his liberty. These are rights which are guaranteed protection by the Federal Constitution." He could not believe, he famously concluded, "that the liberty guaranteed by the Fourteenth Amendment includes only liberty to acquire and to enjoy property." Within a few years the first fruits of Brandeis's dissent appeared in, of all places, an opinion by Justice McReynolds.

After the war, Nebraska banned the teaching of foreign languages in elementary schools, and a jury convicted Robert Meyer for teaching German in a parochial school. Justice McReynolds utilized the due process argument of *Lochner* to rule that the Fourteenth Amendment did protect liberty, "not merely freedom from bodily restraint but also the right of the individual to contract, to engage in any of the common occupations of life, to acquire useful knowledge, to marry, to establish a home and bring up children, to worship God according to the dictates of his own conscience, and generally to enjoy those privileges long recognized at common law as essential to the orderly pursuit of happiness by free men." McReynolds framed much of his argument in terms of property rights—the Nebraska law interfered with the callings of modern language teachers—but he also found violation of free speech. While the legislature's goal of fostering patriotism had been understandable during the war, "peace and tranquility" now reigned, and no adequate justification for the law now existed. Without using the exact words, McReynolds had applied the clear-and-present-danger test and found the statute lacking.

Although Holmes dissented, Brandeis joined the McReynolds opinion and did not disagree with its reasoning. As he often said, he would have preferred if the Fourteenth Amendment's Due Process Clause had never been passed, but unless repealed, it had to be applied and to protect what he considered fundamental rights—speech, education, choice of profession, and the right to travel—none of which should be restricted except on a showing of clear-and-present-danger.

That same term the federal courts for the first time overturned a state criminal decision. In 1920 an all-white jury convicted six black men to death and dozens of others to long prison terms for the death of a white person during the 1919 Arkansas race riots. Black witnesses at the trial were whipped until they agreed to say that the accused were guilty, and a mob outside the courtroom threatened violence and death if the jury did not convict all of the defendants. The defense lawyer appointed by the court called no witnesses and did not ask for a change of venue to a safer place. The trial took less than an hour, and the jury brought back guilty verdicts in only five minutes.

Appalled by this clear travesty of justice—Brandeis called the Arkansas reports too horrendous to ignore—the Supreme Court granted the National Association for the Advancement of Colored People's petition for writs of habeas corpus, reversed the convictions, and ordered new trials. The threat of mob violence had permeated the trial, Holmes declared, and the trial itself had been little more than a judicially sanctioned lynching. When state courts could not provide minimal procedural fairness, the federal courts had a clear duty "to secure to the petitioners their constitutional rights." The decision marked a departure for the Court, which had previously avoided taking an oversight role over state criminal courts. Holmes's opinion, however, did not apply the Sixth Amendment's right of a fair trial to the states; rather, he utilized the Due Process Clause of the Fourteenth Amendment.

Two years later Brandeis joined in another McReynolds opinion extending the reach of constitutional protection into the states. The Ku Klux Klan had pushed through a law in Oregon requiring children to attend public schools, with the clear intent of driving Catholic parochial schools out of business. Again McReynolds used the clear-and-present-danger test to find no justification for the law, as well as a property right in the parochial schools. But the law also interfered with personal rights. "The child is not the mere creature of the State," he wrote, "those who nurture him and direct his destiny have the right, coupled with the high duty, to prepare him for additional obligations."

McReynolds's two school decisions and Holmes's trial opinion all rested on the Due Process Clause, and the authors did not claim that the clause applied the Bill of Rights to the states. All three opinions, however, took a very broad view of what due process encompassed, and quite explicitly said that it included rights other than those of property. This Brandeis had said in 1920; it would be only a matter of time before some enterprising lawyer would ask the Court to overturn *Barron v. Baltimore.* In the meantime, the Court had to deal with an avalanche of cases generated by prohibition.

. . .

Prohibition officers raiding a Washington, D.C., lunchroom, 1923

PROHIBITION SENTIMENT had been growing for decades, and proponents, including a large number of progressives, shepherded the Eighteenth Amendment through Congress during the war; three-fourths of the states ratified by the end of January 1919. Advocates believed that it would usher in a new golden age for America, protecting families against the abuses of drunken husbands and increasing production as men came to work regularly instead of missing their shifts while in a stupor. Underneath the reformist rhetoric could be found a deep distrust of the city and its immigrant masses, for whom the saloon served as a social center.

Brandeis had liked his beer and an occasional whiskey, and as his brief for the liquor dealers in Boston indicated, he preferred policies that would foster temperance, not prohibition. Prior to the war Alfred regularly sent his brother good Kentucky bourbon, which Louis apparently enjoyed and served to his guests. Even if he had opposed prohibition personally, his views on democratic governance led him to support it after ratification. In a democracy the people governed, and if occasionally they made the wrong choice, then the country would have to live with it until a majority chose another path. The people had spoken, whether wisely or not.

Brandeis had spoken for the Court in upholding the Wartime Prohibition Act and joined the majority in approving the Volstead Act implementing the Eighteenth Amendment. During the 1920s a clear majority of the Court supported the great experiment. Butler, Sutherland, and McReynolds detested prohibition because they opposed the expansion of the national administrative state and believed that positive law—that is, statutory enactments—should not overthrow received social values. Taft reported to his brother, "Holmes, Van Devanter, Brandeis, Sanford and I are still steady in the boat." Holmes and Brandeis bowed to the will of the people, although Holmes thought that this did not mean he could not continue to enjoy his drink and receive bottles from his friends. Taft and Van Devanter saw opposition to dryness as resistance to the legal order itself. But everyone on the Court understood that the Eighteenth Amendment had opened a Pandora's box of constitutional problems, not the least of which involved the nature of the federal system itself.

There had been state prohibition laws since the late nineteenth century, and at the time of American entry into the war twenty-six states, more than half of the Union, were legally dry; in addition, a number of so-called wet states permitted local option that allowed some rural areas to ban liquor. Enforcement of these laws had been the responsibility of the states, and while effectiveness varied, there had been no reports of massive criminality or widespread public flouting of the laws. The National Commission on Law Observance and Enforcement later called state enforcement effective, and another study termed local laws "fairly well obeyed and respected." In contrast, federal enforcement of prohibition quickly turned into a "nation-wide scandal" that in President Harding's words was "the most demoralizing factor in our public life."

At the heart of the problem lay the impossible task demanded of the Eighteenth Amendment, the moral reform of a nation that had been drinking since colonial times. Prohibition stands as the preeminent example of law's inability to change the personal behavior of people who do not want to change. Beyond that, the amendment's division of responsibilities left it unclear who had the primary responsibility for enforcement, the states or the national government. Section 2 read, "The Congress and the several States shall have concurrent power to enforce this article by appropriate legislation." Did that mean that Congress could set up police functions inside the states? What if a state did not pass the necessary enforcement law or, as New York did in

1923, repealed its statute? Could states set up barricades to prevent alcohol's coming in from other states or from Canada? Who had the responsibility to patrol the shores to prevent smuggling? Did the federal government have the authority to conscript state law enforcement officers? The federalism that had been so essential a part of the American constitutional scheme for more than 130 years reeled from the onslaught of issues never imagined by the Framers.

Brandeis had a strong and commonsensical approach from which he never wavered, but which also showed how far he misjudged the deep opposition to prohibition. When Woodrow Wilson began putting together the Document, he asked Brandeis to draft the section on prohibition enforcement, and it reflected his deep commitment to traditional notions of federalism. The idea of "concurrent power" in section 2 indicated that the American people "recognized fully that the law could not be enforced without the co-operation of the States within the Nation." Both the states and the national government "should perform that part of the task for which it was peculiarly fitted." The federal government should act "against illegal importation of liquor from foreign countries and to protect each state from the illegal introduction into it of liquor from another State."

Brandeis—a great opponent of large government—admitted that to enforce prohibition effectively, the government of the United States "requires centralized, unified action and the employment of the large federal powers and resources." The states for their part had to police illegal sales of illegally manufactured liquor within their borders. Such a task, he believed, states could do far better than the national government, because it involved "diversified governmental action and adaptation to the widely varying conditions in, and the habits and sentiments of the people of, the several States. It is a task for which the Federal Government is not fitted." When their good friend Emory Buckner became U.S. attorney for the Southern District of New York, Brandeis told Frankfurter to urge Buckner to divide up all cases coming to his office between those involving smuggling from abroad or bringing in alcohol from other states and those wholly intrastate. He would find that the first class would occupy all of his time and resources, and he should ignore the second group completely.

Brandeis assumed that because prohibition had been adopted as the law of the land, it would be enforced, and therefore all one had to do was determine how the states and the national government should share in the enforcement. It made perfectly good sense to assign

Washington the problems of interstate and foreign shipments, and have the states police their own people. In many ways this is the solution that the Framers could have agreed upon, since it treated the federal system as one in which the states and the national government shared powers and responsibilities. Brandeis did not expect the widescale flouting of the law, or that some states would refuse to enforce prohibition, although he should have.

In his brief for the Massachusetts Protective Liquor Dealers' Association thirty years earlier, Brandeis had written, "Liquor drinking is not a wrong; but excessive drinking is. Liquor will be sold; hence the sale should be licensed. Liquor is dangerous; hence the business should be regulated. No regulation can be enforced which is not reasonable." He had urged the legislature to try to imagine a community in which men cannot drink because the state says they may not do so. "No law can be effective which does not take into consideration the conditions of the community for which it is designed; no law can be a good law—every law must be a bad law—that remains unenforced."

Throughout the 1920s the problems of prohibition enforcement exploded astronomically. Federal courts found their dockets overloaded with cases that should have been heard in a municipal night court. In the big cities, a stranger could stop a policeman on the street and be courteously informed of the location of the nearest speakeasy as well as the phrase—"Joe sent me"—needed to enter. And to supply bootleg liquor or illegally imported alcohol, crime flourished as it never had before in the United States. Even Brandeis could not ignore the relation of illegal drink and crime.

ONE MIGHT HAVE EXPECTED a conservative Court to have embraced Brandeis's assumptions about the proper roles of state and federal responsibility and power; instead, the majority consistently took an expansive, indeed almost unlimited, nationalistic tone when it came to enforcement. In one case Justice Sanford, speaking for a unanimous bench, said that since prohibition "is within the authority delegated to Congress by the Eighteenth Amendment, its validity is not impaired by reason of any power reserved to the States." In the enforcement of prohibition, the Tenth Amendment meant nothing, since the Eighteenth gave Congress all necessary powers. Fear of overweening national authority, a bedrock of conservative as well as federalist thought since the founding of the Republic, vanished in the Taft Court's enthusiasm for the great experiment. Brandeis, who had shared Wilson's aversion to big government, went along with nary a murmur.

Alpheus Mason, in his biography of the justice, termed the section on prohibition "The Prophet Stumbles," noting that Brandeis showed little sympathy for those adversely affected by the Eighteenth Amendment and was "less alert to the invasion of liberty." Another biographer, Philippa Strum, agreed. Brandeis "did not merely uphold the Prohibition laws as a regrettable but legitimate government experiment, but permitted enforcement even when it violated civil liberties." Brandeis wrote the Court's opinion allowing the government to close distilleries and breweries without compensation to the owners, and also spoke for the Court in ruling that the ban against double jeopardy did not apply when a person had been convicted of one crime for possessing alcohol and then convicted for selling that same liquor. He wrote the majority opinion that sustained the federal government's confiscation of an automobile that carried illegal alcohol, as well as that upholding the congressional ban against the then common prescription of wine and liquor for medicinal purposes.

Brandeis fully supported prohibition, not only as a member of the Court but also as an individual. Unlike Holmes, who had no personal liking for the regime, Brandeis and his wife came to believe that the abolition of strong drink could be in the national interest. In 1917 Brandeis encouraged the editor of the *Survey,* Arthur Kellogg, to look into the social and industrial effects of wartime prohibition, indicating that he expected them to be positive. In 1920 he told Kellogg's brother that "we shall soon have had a year of freedom from what has been regarded as the main causes of misery—unemployment, low wages, and drink," and he urged him to investigate just what effect prohibition had had on America. With frequent recourse to the justice for advice, the *Survey* began an intensive study of Grand Rapids, Michigan, and came out with a special prohibition number in November 1920, reporting that drunkenness had disappeared, families spent more time together, the saloon was no longer the visitor's entry to the city, and the number of arrests had dropped so much that the police force had been reduced— all a result of prohibition. The article drew an enthusiastic response from Brandeis, who suggested that Grand Rapids could serve as a model for what could be done on a local level by right-minded citizens.

As Brandeis grew older, the ascetic streak in him strengthened, and he and Alice had no problem eliminating beer, wine, and whiskey from their household. While historians have concentrated on what might be called the darker side of prohibition—nativism, fear of cities, and resentment of the new—many Americans who had none of these traits believed that the elimination of intoxicating beverages would be a boon for society, and it should be no surprise that Brandeis belonged to this group. Unfortunately, in this as in so many other areas of his life, we can see a shift in views but have little from the man himself to explain it.

AS FOR THE CASES that Mason and Strum see as a failure to support civil liberties, a closer examination of these decisions indicates a somewhat different story. To begin with, the incorporation of the Bill of Rights, which Brandeis helped to begin in the 1920s, did not reach fruition until well after World War II. What we today consider normative interpretations of the Bill of Rights did not exist in the 1920s, and it is ahistorical to demand that Brandeis—or any member of the Taft Court—abide by standards that would not be in place for another three to four decades. The Court did not even agree on the idea of incorporation until 1937, when Justice Benjamin Cardozo, speaking for an eight-man majority that included Brandeis, set out the notion of selective incorporation. The Fourteenth Amendment did not automatically subsume the entire Bill of Rights. It did, of course, include the First Amendment, because freedom of speech and thought "is the matrix, the indispensable condition, of nearly every other form of [freedom]." But for the other amendments, the Court should apply only those that are "of the very essence of a scheme of ordered liberty" and "so rooted in the traditions and conscience of our people as to be ranked as fundamental." Brandeis, of course, began this process, and before he left the bench in 1939 had helped to lay the foundation for what became the postwar rights revolution.

Not all of these decisions, even if they strike a modern civil libertarian as perverse, are necessarily wrong. The so-called dual-federalism double jeopardy, that prosecutions could be launched under separate state and federal laws for the same act and not be considered a violation of the Fifth Amendment ban on double jeopardy, remains valid law to this day. Brandeis also joined in Taft's opinion in *Carroll v. United States* (1925), holding that police could, under probable circumstances, search a car without a warrant. Taft argued that whenever possible a warrant should be secured, but said that without any legal means to hold the car, it and any evidence it contained would be gone before the warrant would arrive. Although the *Carroll* doctrine has over the years been the subject of much criticism, it remains valid constitutional law. And, it should be noted, Brandeis wrote the opinion in *Gambino v. United States* (1927) that reinforced the exclusionary rule that is at the heart of the Fourth Amendment, holding that evidence illegally seized in a warrantless search cannot be used in federal court.

To describe Brandeis as an unquestioning supporter of prohibition in any and all forms misses the fact that while he supported the idea—perhaps even wrongheadedly and against his better judgment—he grew increasingly upset by the methods employed, especially the use of paid informants, or spies, by the federal government. The main source of the abuses could be found in the Federal Bureau of Investigation, headed by the notorious William J. Burns, former chief of a private detective agency. Under the sponsorship of Attorney General Harry M. Daugherty, the bureau had become a private snooping agency for all the corrupt forces within the Harding administration, and its agents collected or created evidence against critics of the administration. Calvin Coolidge fired Daugherty and asked his old friend from college Harlan Fiske Stone to become attorney general and clean up the mess. Stone found, as he later recalled, a "Bureau filled with men of bad records, and many of them had been convicted of crime. The organization was lawless, maintaining many activities which were without any authority in federal statutes, and engaging in many practices which were brutal and tyrannical in the extreme." Brandeis spoke with Stone in October 1924, a few months after the latter had taken over at the Justice Department, and learned that while he had corrected many of the problems, much remained to do; agents could still be found working as spies and informants. Brandeis urged him to do more.

Brandeis also objected to industrial espionage, employers hiring spies to get information about union activists among their workers. If the spy system survived, he warned, "our ideals cannot survive. If I were dictator, I should abolish the system today without reserve." He urged Herbert Croly to have the *New Republic* look into the abuses, and he wanted Frankfurter to put a student to work to find out what the Founding Fathers had thought about the use of secret political operatives. Thanks to his efforts, the Scripps-Howard newspapers put a reporter to work on the subject and published an eleven-part series in 1927. When Senator Burton Wheeler announced that he would investigate the espionage system, Brandeis suggested that for the moment Wheeler ignore private industry and focus on the abuses in the government, especially those tied to the enforcement of prohibition, as his prime concern. The justice considered it a major triumph when Congress finally struck out the appropriations that had been supporting informants for the enforcement of prohibition.

Brandeis had one opportunity on the Court to protest against the use of informants. Thomas J. Casey, a lawyer, had been convicted under the 1914 narcotics act, and while he was in prison, the warden suspected him of peddling morphine to his fellow prisoners. The warden set a trap, sold some drugs to Casey, and then filed additional charges against him. Casey protested that in being sold the drugs, he had not only been entrapped, but by government agents violating the law themselves.

Holmes, speaking for a 5–4 majority, dismissed the case and said the Court could not accept Casey's view that the government had induced the crime; sufficient other evidence existed to make it likely that he had been selling drugs. McReynolds, Butler, Sanford, and Brandeis dissented. McReynolds denounced the government's actions as conflicting "with those constitutional guaranties heretofore supposed to protect all against arbitrary conviction and punishment."

Brandeis went even further and declared that the entire prosecution "must fail because officers of the government instigated the commission of the alleged crime." He then detailed how Casey had been entrapped—details left out of Holmes's majority opinion—and denounced the government for its base role, noting that even "a desirable end cannot justify foul means." Brandeis well understood that government often used informants to trap criminals and, while he may not have personally condoned the method, saw no legal objection. But for the informants—the spies—to have been government agents who, in order to capture Casey, had committed crimes themselves went beyond the pale. It enraged him, and his reasons can be found in the powerful dissent he wrote in still another prohibition case, *Olmstead v. United States*.

IN ORDER TO SERVE THEIR CLIENTS, bootleggers availed themselves of the latest technology, the automobile and the telephone. The mastermind of one operation, a Seattle policeman named Roy Olmstead, set up an elaborate telephone bank so purchasers could call in their orders and then arrange for delivery. Federal agents responded with a new technology of their own—wiretapping—essentially adding an extra phone set to the wires outside Olmstead's office and listening in on his conversations. With this evidence they arrested and convicted Olmstead and his colleagues, who appealed on the basis that the evidence should not have been admitted because the police had failed to secure a warrant, thus violating the Fourth Amendment. The Court had already held that government agents could not search an office without a warrant, but the government responded that its men had

never entered the premises. Since they gath‑
side, they did not need a warrant.

Chief Justice Taft agreed with this argu‑
wrote a formalistic decision that practic‑
intent behind the Fourth Amendment.
he declared, only the use of an enhance‑
much attention to "nice ethical cond‑
make society suffer and give crimin‑
known heretofore."

The Taft opinion elicited dissents from ‑
deis, with Stone signing on to each of them. In a w‑
cal analysis, the generally conservative Butler repudiated ‑
interpretation of what the Fourth Amendment meant. Holmes,
comment that soon caught the liberal imagination, condemned wiretapping as a "dirty business." Holmes had not intended to write at all,
since, as he said, "My brother Brandeis has given this case so exhaustive
an examination," but he did so for two reasons. First, Brandeis asked
him to do so, and, second, he did not completely agree with all that
Brandeis said.

Brandeis used his dissent to drive home several points. His general
abhorrence of the methods used by prohibition agents is clear, and the
reason for his antipathy is one that should be read every day by government officials, including presidents:

> Decency, security and liberty alike demand that government offi-
> cials shall be subjected to the same rules of conduct that are com-
> mands to the citizen. In a government of laws, existence of the
> government will be imperilled if it fails to observe the law scrupu-
> lously. Our Government is the potent, the omnipresent teacher.
> For good or for ill, it teaches the whole people by its example.
> Crime is contagious. If the Government becomes a lawbreaker, it
> breeds contempt for law; it invites every man to become a law
> unto himself; it invites anarchy. To declare that in the administra-
> tion of the criminal law the end justifies the means—to declare
> that the Government may commit crimes in order to secure the
> conviction of a private criminal—would bring terrible retribu-
> tion. Against that pernicious doctrine this Court should res-
> olutely set its face.

But Brandeis had another argument to make, one that he had been
advocating for nearly four decades—the right to privacy. In his earlier

n Warren, Brandeis had relied on private action and tort
alleged violators of privacy had been the press and com-
ors. Now, because the government had been involved, he
personal privacy as a matter of constitutional law, and mar-
earlier notion of the right to be let alone with the Fourth
dment's ban on unreasonable search and seizure and the Fifth
endment's protection against self-incrimination. To justify reading
rivacy into these amendments, he assigned his law clerk that term,
Henry Friendly, to researching the circumstances surrounding the
drafting of the Fourth Amendment. The case also shows how Brandeis
expected his clerks to argue with him, and when they did make a convincing argument, he would listen. At first the justice wanted to base
his dissent on the violation of a state statute, but Friendly convinced
him that it must rest on a constitutional basis. The result is one of the
landmark dissents in constitutional history.

Taft had emphasized that the Framers had nothing more in mind
than the general warrants used by the British in the 1760s and 1770s,
and the Fourth Amendment applied to little else. Brandeis cited Chief
Justice Marshall's reminder: "We must never forget that it is a constitution we are expounding." Times had changed since 1791, and Brandeis
cited case after case to show that the Court had constantly read constitutional provisions to take into account conditions never envisioned by
the Framers. The technical nature of the entry did not matter as much
as the intent of the amendment to protect people in their homes and
businesses. "Time works changes, brings into existence new conditions
and purposes. Subtle and more far-reaching means of invading privacy
have become available to the Government. Discovery and invention
have made it possible for the Government, by means far more effective
than stretching upon the rack, to obtain disclosure in court of what is
whispered in the closet." (At this point Brandeis wanted to refer to a
new device recently developed by the General Electric Company called
television, but removed the note in deference to Friendly's skepticism.)

He then went on to write one of the most eloquent—and most
quoted—passages in American law:

> The makers of our Constitution undertook to secure conditions
> favorable to the pursuit of happiness. They recognized the signifi-
> cance of man's spiritual nature, of his feelings and of his intellect.
> They knew that only a part of the pain, pleasure and satisfactions
> of life are to be found in material things. They sought to protect

Americans in their beliefs, their thoughts, their emotions and their sensations. They conferred, as against the Government, the right to be let alone—the most comprehensive of rights and the right most valued by civilized men. To protect that right, every unjustifiable intrusion by the Government upon the privacy of the individual, whatever the means employed, must be deemed a violation of the Fourth Amendment.

Brandeis dismissed Taft's mechanistic view that no intrusion had occurred, since it did not matter where the actual physical connection with the telephone wires took place.

And it is also immaterial that the intrusion was in aid of law enforcement. Experience should teach us to be most on our guard to protect liberty when the Government's purposes are beneficent. Men born to freedom are naturally alert to repel invasion of their liberty by evil-minded rulers. The greatest dangers to liberty lurk in insidious encroachment by men of zeal, well-meaning but without understanding.

In the *Olmstead* dissent Brandeis reinvented Fourth Amendment jurisprudence. Taft's majority opinion, as well as prior search-and-seizure cases, had been grounded in conceptions of property, whether or not police had actually entered the home or business. Brandeis shifted the emphasis from where the alleged wrong took place to how it affected the individual. While Brandeis disliked the "dirty business" of wiretapping as much as Holmes, for him the more important issues were the conduct of the police and the individual's right to be let alone. If the police had probable cause to suspect a person of wrongdoing, the Constitution required that a warrant be secured. Warrantless searches, except in very special circumstances, could not be allowed.

The chief justice reacted furiously to the dissents. "If they think we are going to be frightened in our effort to stand by the law and give the public a chance to punish criminals," he told his brother, "they are mistaken, even though we are condemned for lack of high ideals." He believed that Brandeis had originally agreed to limit the discussion and had then gone off on ethical issues, and he termed Brandeis "the lawless member of the Court" for doing so. Holmes had written "the nastiest opinion," and Taft claimed that Holmes had voted the other way "till Brandeis got after him and induced him to change." But, he told Justice Sutherland, "I hope that ultimately it will be seen that we in the majority were right."

Taft's prediction proved wrong, although it took many years before Brandeis's dissent became established as a constitutional right in *Griswold v. Connecticut* (1965). Brandeis did, however, live to see Congress prohibit wiretapping evidence in federal courts in the federal Communications Act of 1934 and the Court to partially reverse *Olmstead* in 1937. In 1967 the Supreme Court fully adopted Brandeis's position and overturned *Olmstead* completely, bringing wiretapping within the ambit of Fourth Amendment protection. That same year, Justice Potter Stewart explained the Court's new philosophy in words that grew directly out of Brandeis's dissent: "The Fourth Amendment protects people, not places." In a more recent case, Justice Antonin Scalia used the logic of Brandeis's dissent to hold that federal agents could not use a new technology, thermal imaging, to look through the walls of Danny Lee Kyllo's house to determine if the occupant was raising marijuana. Even though the agents used the machine outside the premises, they had secured information about the inside and could not use that evidence without a warrant.

Brandeis understood the role that dissent played in constitutional discourse, and in *Olmstead* he wanted the justices to talk not only about privacy and respect for the law but also about how the Due Process Clause of the Fourteenth Amendment should be interpreted. If nothing else, he told Frankfurter, reviewers of the opinion would see that "in favor of property the Constitution is liberally construed—in favor of liberty, strictly." He especially wanted to advance the idea that the Fourteenth Amendment incorporated the Bill of Rights and applied it to the states, a position that made Holmes uncomfortable, at least in regard to the Fourth and Fifth amendments. Brandeis had first planted this seed in *Gilbert v. Minnesota* (1920), and then, wittingly or not, McReynolds had advanced the cause in his two school opinions. Attorneys for the American Civil Liberties Union picked up on these cues and decided to challenge the traditional doctrine that the First Amendment did not apply to the states. Their opportunity came in *Gitlow v. New York* (1925).

BENJAMIN GITLOW, a leading figure in the American Communist Party, had been convicted under New York's 1902 Criminal Anarchy Act for publishing a radical newspaper and other allegedly subversive materials. In a now familiar scenario, seven members of the Court sustained the conviction while Holmes and Brandeis dissented. What is interesting, however, is that Justice Sanford, without elaboration, announced, "For present purposes we may and do assume that freedom of speech and of the press—which are protected by the First Amendment from abridgment by Congress—are among the fundamental personal rights and 'liberties' protected by the due process clause of the Fourteenth Amendment from impairment by the States." With this bare-bones statement, the Supreme Court for the first time put forward, as the majority view, what came to be known as the doctrine of incorporation, by which the Due Process Clause of the Fourteenth Amendment applied the liberties protected in the Bill of Rights to the states. This doctrine, begun in Brandeis's *Gilbert* dissent, would be at the heart of the constitutional revolution that transformed American law after World War II.

Sanford's opinion in *Gitlow* is not a knee-jerk reaction to radical ideas, such as McKenna's was in *Gilbert.* It is a workmanlike product, and while we may no longer subscribe to its jurisprudence, he took the time to examine what Gitlow had said in the documents, and did not dismiss the American Civil Liberties Union argument about the First Amendment's applying to the states; in fact he agreed with it. But ironically, he practiced what Brandeis and Holmes had called for in property and labor cases—deference to the legislative judgment. The New York legislature had determined that this type of speech fomented rebellion and violence. Sanford explored different types of speech and concluded that when a statute proscribed a class of speech that contained general advocacy of violence, the boundaries of free speech had been reached. Holmes in his dissent dismissed the speech as having no chance of inciting anything, and Sanford responded to it. He agreed that the state had presented no evidence that Gitlow's speech would incite anyone, but that did not matter. The state had the power to define categories of expression that might provoke violence. The bad tendency of such speech justified the state's restriction.

Like Sanford, Holmes utilized clear-and-present danger, but came to the conclusion that no danger existed. "It is said that this manifesto was more than a theory, it was an incitement. Every idea is an incitement [and] eloquence may set fire to reason. But whatever may be thought of the redundant discourse before us it had no chance of starting a present conflagration." As he told Frankfurter, "I gave an expiring kick (Brandeis was with me) in favor of the right to drool on the part of believers in the proletarian dictatorship."

Holmes, however, did not deal with a critical question, namely, whether the Court should simply accept a legislative judgment that some types of speech were dangerous and could therefore be proscribed. There is no indication in his very brief dissent that the New York statute might be unconstitutional. He also did not address Sanford's notion that the courts should accept legislative determination, a position Holmes and Brandeis had long held in economic cases. If a case concerned civil liberties, did that put it into a different category or give judges greater responsibilities? These questions would concern Brandeis in the next speech case to come to the Court.

IN THE MID-1920S two speech cases began making their way toward the Supreme Court. In both the petitioners had been accused and convicted of violating state laws restricting allegedly radical speech. Charles Ruthenberg was the son of immigrants, a lifelong radical arrested time and again for street demonstrations, and a national executive of the Communist Party. A Michigan court, acting under a state law that clearly met then-existing First Amendment guidelines, found Ruthenberg guilty of conspiring to "teach and advocate the doctrines of criminal syndicalism." The Michigan Supreme Court upheld the verdict, and in January 1925 Ruthenberg began a term of between three and ten years. He had served only three weeks when Justice Brandeis granted his attorneys a writ of error allowing them to seek review of the conviction. Brandeis ordered that the writ would also operate as a supersedeas (an order delaying execution of the imprisonment pending review), allowing Ruthenberg to go free on a bail of $7,500. He got out in time to address the first annual Lenin memorial at Madison Square Garden in New York.

After oral argument in *Ruthenberg v. Michigan,* the justices met and decided the case. The facts, for all practical purposes, tracked those in *Gitlow,* and the lineup appeared to be identical, with Sanford utilizing the same bad-tendency test he had in the earlier case. Holmes and Brandeis would dissent, but this time Brandeis would write, and he planned to go much further than Holmes, not only in meeting Sanford's argument, but also in establishing a jurisprudential framework for deciding First Amendment cases.

The justice and his law clerk, James Landis, worked for weeks on the dissent, and then on 3 March 1927 they opened the morning newspaper to discover that Ruthenberg had died the day before in a Chicago hospital of acute peritonitis. Within days the writ of error had been dismissed, and Brandeis consigned his draft to the files. Soon after he pulled it out, as the case of Charlotte Anita Whitney returned to the high court.

A niece of former justice Stephen J. Field, Miss Whitney at the time of her arrest was described as a woman nearing sixty, a Wellesley graduate long known for her philanthropic work. She had been convicted under the California Criminal Syndicalism Act of 1919 for helping to organize the Communist Labor Party in the state. The law made it a felony to organize or to knowingly become a member of an organization founded to advocate the commis-

Socialist activist Charlotte Anita Whitney, ca. 1928

sion of crimes, sabotage, or acts of violence. Whitney denied that the communist group had ever intended to become an instrument of crime or violence, and the state offered no evidence at her trial that the party had ever engaged in violent acts. Nonetheless, the trial court found her guilty, and on appeal Justice Sanford, utilizing the bad-tendency test of *Gitlow,* upheld the conviction. The 1919 act clearly lay within the purview of the state legislature in its efforts to prevent the violent overthrow of society. The Due Process Clause did not protect one's liberty to destroy the social and political order.

Because of technical issues, Brandeis chose to concur rather than dissent. He noted that the Court in this case lacked "the power occasionally exercised on review of judgments of lower federal courts to correct in criminal cases vital errors, although the objection was not taken in the trial court." Because free-speech issues had not been raised at the trial, and since Whitney presented only due process and equal protection claims in her appeal, the Supreme Court could not reach the First Amendment grounds. But since the Court had not yet fixed a standard by which to determine when a danger shall be deemed as clear, Brandeis found it necessary to discuss the issue. His opinion, joined by Holmes, has never been seen as anything other than a protest against the Court's restrictive interpretation of free speech.

Since he had first joined Holmes in the wartime cases eight years earlier, Brandeis had given a great deal of thought to speech and the necessity of protecting it in a free society. Holmes's "marketplace of ideas" struck Brandeis as not going far enough to protect speech in a positive manner; surely the Framers had more in mind than simply letting people engage in rancorous debate. His thought, which has been described as republican "civic virtue" or "civic courage," summed up his ideas not only on speech but also on the nature of democratic society, and in it he achieved an eloquence rarely matched in the annals of the Court.

> Those who won our independence believed that the final end of the State was to make men free to develop their faculties; and that in its government the deliberative forces should prevail over the arbitrary. They valued liberty both as an end and as a means. They believed liberty to be the secret of happiness and courage to be the secret of liberty. They believed that freedom to think as you will and to speak as you think are means indispensable to the discovery and spread of political truth; that without free speech and assembly discussion would be futile; that with them, discussion affords ordinarily adequate protection against the dissemination of noxious doctrine; that the greatest menace to freedom is an inert people; that public discussion is a political duty; and that this should be a fundamental principle of the American government. . . .
>
> Fear of serious injury cannot alone justify suppression of free speech and assembly. Men feared witches and burnt women. It is the function of speech to free men from the bondage of irrational fears. . . . Those who won our independence by revolution were not cowards. They did not fear political change. They did not exalt order at the cost of liberty. To courageous, self-reliant men, with confidence in the power of free and fearless reasoning applied through the processes of popular government, no danger flowing from speech can be deemed clear and present, unless the incidence of the evil apprehended is so imminent that it may befall before there is opportunity for full discussion. If there be time to expose through discussion the falsehood and fallacies, to avert the evil by the processes of education, the remedy to be applied is more speech, not enforced silence. Only an emergency can justify repression. Such must be the rule if authority is to be reconciled with freedom. Such, in my opinion, is the command of the Constitution. It is therefore always open to Americans to challenge a law

abridging free speech and assembly by showing that there was no
emergency justifying it.

Although Brandeis paid lip service to the older clear-and-present-
danger test, he in essence abandoned it in *Whitney*. Even the destruction
of property, the bugaboo of conservatives, did not justify restricting
speech; speech could be shut off only in the case where the social and
political order itself faced imminent danger and no time existed to reason or debate. Otherwise, the cure for "bad" speech must be "good"
speech.

But why should society put up with ideas it found offensive? For
Brandeis the most important position in a democratic society belonged
not to any elected or appointed official but to the individual citizen.
Citizenship in a democracy conferred privileges but also carried responsibilities, especially the need to participate in debate over public policy.
From the time he had been a local reformer, Brandeis had believed that
no reform could succeed unless the people understood it and supported
it. But citizens could not make informed judgments unless they understood all sides of an issue, and this meant that opposing speakers had to
have the right to lay out their ideas, while the citizenry had the right to
hear conflicting views. This included not just questions of whether a
street railway should get a franchise or whether a state should establish
savings bank life insurance but more fundamental questions about the
nature of government and the economy. Brandeis never subscribed to
any of the doctrines brought to the Court in the speech cases starting in
1919, but he thought that their merits or lack of merits had to be
decided by people who could hear both sides of the question.

How did this differ from Holmes's marketplace analogy? For
Holmes the entire question was an abstraction, a means of philosophical inquiry; all his life he remained aloof from the political process, not
even reading newspapers. For Brandeis, who devoured not only the
daily news but also dry corporate and governmental reports, free speech
and an informed citizenry had practical purposes. After the debate, the
people could, through their elected representatives, translate these
ideas into specific policies. Citizens had the civic duty to participate
in politics, to deliberate important questions. Only in that way could
the state provide conditions of freedom which were "the secret of
happiness."

Implicit in the opinion is a notion of civic virtue that derives from
classical Greek theory, and in *Whitney* one can easily discern Brandeis's

long fascination with ancient Greece. The sentence "They believed liberty to be the secret of happiness and courage to be the secret of liberty" comes almost directly from Pericles, and much of the paragraph is fashioned after the *Funeral Oration*. There is a great idealism in this passage, a belief that if men and women can learn and make informed decisions, they can create a better society. However, it is not just idealism here but pragmatism as well. Political liberty is at best a fragile construct, and it will fail if citizens become inert.

Brandeis, like his colleagues, wanted to maintain public order. But whereas Sanford would allow the government to clamp down on any speech that had a "bad tendency," Brandeis believed this policy would be counterproductive. "Those who won our independence," he declared, "knew that order cannot be secured merely through fear of punishment." It is not simply a "safety valve" that Brandeis talks about, the idea that if the state allows dissidents to let off steam they will do little harm. Rather, he wanted the debate, he wanted people with radical ideas to challenge the mainstream, to make people think about the values they cherished and not be complacent about them.

Throughout his life Brandeis always balanced his idealism with a sense of realism, and it would be wrong to think of him as naive. He did not assume that truth will always win out. He had spent years battling special interests and knew how successful demagogues could be. Rather, he chose to rely on reason as an alternative to the state's silencing those with unpopular opinions. His innate faith in democracy demanded that one had to trust the people; they could make mistakes, but that was part of the price of freedom. Like Thomas Jefferson, whom he quoted in a footnote, he thought it would be better to trust the good judgment of the people than the consciences of judges.

Perhaps more than any other of his opinions, Brandeis's *Whitney* concurrence has shaped American constitutional law, and its influence can be seen in the powerful First Amendment opinions later penned by Justices Hugo Black, William O. Douglas, William Brennan, and John Marshall Harlan II. Gradually, the Court abandoned Sanford's bad-tendency standard and also moved away from Holmes's clear-and-present-danger test until it adopted Brandeis's notion of free speech in 1969. Debate about the reach of the First Amendment continues, such as whether it embraces only political discourse, or if it takes in other forms of expression such as commercial and artistic speech. But *Whitney* continues to be the touchstone, not only for the rationale it provides for the First Amendment, but also for the unusual eloquence of a man known for his detached, fact-laden, and lawyerly opinions.

• • •

THE GREATEST CRITICISM of Brandeis's jurisprudence of the 1920s, by early-twenty-first-century standards, is his "remarkable indifference" to matters of race. While Brandeis did not author a single opinion dealing with racial issues in his twenty-three terms, he voted with the majority in every one of those cases, and according to one critic "Brandeis's curious complacency on racial issues stands in dramatic contrast with the healthy enthusiasm and sense of perseverance he brought to bear on other causes he chose to champion." It would be easy to condemn Brandeis as someone who never abandoned the southern prejudices against black people, while pointing to other southerners who spoke out for racial equality in the first half of the twentieth century. The record, however, is a bit more complex.

In the first major race case to be decided after his confirmation, Brandeis joined the unanimous opinion in *Buchanan v. Warley* (1917) striking down residential segregation ordinances in his home city of Louisville. A decade later, in another unanimous opinion, the Court struck down the Texas white primary law, but a few years later Brandeis was in the 5–4 majority voiding a state law delegating to the Democratic Party the power to exclude blacks from a state-run primary. He was in the majority in both *Scottsboro* cases that nullified convictions of black defendants secured in trials that could best be described as perversions of justice, as well as in *Brown v. Mississippi* (1936), which overturned murder convictions of black tenant farmers secured by torture. In 1938 he joined in Justice Stone's opinion in *United States v. Carolene Products Co.,* with its famous footnote 4 that laid the basis for the Court to begin a closer scrutiny of laws aimed at "discrete and insular minorities." The Court decided its first modern civil rights case the following term when, with Brandeis again in the majority, it ordered the University of Missouri to admit an African-American to its law school. Two months later Brandeis resigned from the bench. All told, in nearly all the major cases involving African-Americans in which he took part, Brandeis and a majority of the Court upheld the black petitioners.

Asians fared poorly at the hands of the Taft Court, which ruled in several cases that Congress under the Constitution had plenary power over immigration and therefore could decide which immigrant groups it chose to grant or to deny citizenship. Brandeis agreed with this view (as did all the members of the Court), but he and they drew the line when an Asian claimed to be an American citizen. He spoke for a unanimous Court in 1922, ruling that immigration officers could not arbitrarily deport an Asian who claimed American citizenship, and had to provide an administrative hearing to determine the truth of that claim. Shortly after the Court accepted two cases involving Chinese merchants denied admission to the United States, Brandeis told Frankfurter that these matters should be taken up by the American Civil Liberties Union and that the Chinese consular officials should help their countrymen get better legal assistance in American courts.

For all that people called him a prophet, and for all that his ideas pointed the way in many areas of reform and law, Brandeis was a man of his times. That he did not always escape the restraints of those times may be regrettable to some, but it certainly does not prove bigotry. Surely there is some trace of his abolitionist background in his encouragement of Felix Frankfurter to work with the National Association for the Advancement of Colored People, and in his indirect aid to one of Frankfurter's students, Nathan Margold, who in 1931 sketched out the litigation strategy that eventually led to the overthrow of legal segregation in *Brown v. Board of Education* (1954). Brandeis knew of this, and to some degree his subsidy to the Harvard Law professor helped underwrite Margold's work.

Few black lawyers appeared before the Court during Brandeis's tenure, and at the time most law schools did not accept black students. (There were a few, very few, at Harvard, and he wanted Frankfurter to encourage them to take cases for the NAACP.) Brandeis told Mordecai Johnson, the incoming president of Howard University in the late 1920s, "I can tell most of the time when I am reading a brief by a Negro attorney. You've got to get yourself a real faculty out there or you're always going to have a fifth-rate law school. And it's got to be a full-time and a day school." Brandeis believed Howard could be a good law school, but only if they put energy and resources into it.

It is regrettable that he did not go further, that he did not become an ardent opponent of racial segregation, but he lived in a particular time and place in which such a stance would have been totally out of character with his views of how the Court should act. Perhaps the harshest indictment might be that he shared the attitude of most other progressive reformers, whose agenda did not include racial equality.

LOOKING BACK at Brandeis's opinions, it is fair to say that no justice of the twentieth century had a greater impact on American constitutional jurisprudence. Historians now believe that the Reconstruction Congress intended the Fourteenth Amendment to apply the Bill of Rights to the states, but in 1920 neither scholars nor judges shared that view. Brandeis's assertion that the Due Process Clause implicated rights other than property is the starting point for the idea of incorporation, by which the states became bound by the same standards for individual liberties as the national government. While the Court applied the Speech and Press Clauses to the states during Brandeis's tenure on the bench, the great "rights revolution" of the 1950s and 1960s also grew out of the seed he had planted.

Although a few scholars and judges continue to argue against the idea of a constitutional right to privacy, the vast majority of Americans agree with Brandeis's assertion that the Framers intended to protect the right to be let alone. Brandeis's warnings resonate powerfully as modern technology threatens to make public information that many people consider private. The dispute today is not whether a right to privacy exists but what its parameters are. Brandeis might not have agreed with the limits that some people propose, but he would certainly have approved of the debate.

Incorporation and privacy raised the level of rights that individuals enjoy, but his lasting contribution to democracy itself is the towering opinion he wrote in *Whitney*. Not only has it informed all discussions of free speech since, but it is also Brandeis's view not only of how democracy works but, more important, of the role of the citizen in the polis. Democracy, he taught, is not easy, and for it to work, for it to continue to support a climate of freedom, individuals have to do the hard labor of learning, of debating, and of making informed decisions. That lesson, as he well understood, has to be taught anew in each generation.

CHAPTER TWENTY-SIX
EXTRAJUDICIAL ACTIVITIES: II

In the spring of 1925 a delighted Oliver Wendell Holmes wrote to Felix Frankfurter, asking him if he had seen the "report that I was to resign in the spring and that Brandeis had just returned from a sanitarium—one as true as the other." The article in the *Washington Post* claimed that Brandeis had been a patient at the Hinsdale Sanitarium outside of Chicago for a week. Attendants at the institution said that Brandeis "displayed great recuperative power and in eight days built himself up to normal conditions from a state of exhaustion." What do you think? Brandeis wrote to Holmes. "It looks as if the game of imagining the king's death were in full play."

As he entered his eighth decade, Louis Brandeis seemed indefatigable. Aside from his work at the Supreme Court, he kept up extrajudicial activities that one might easily have mistaken for full-time employment. At times Alice probably wondered why in 1916 she thought that her husband's days of knight-errantry were over.

THROUGHOUT THE 1920S Brandeis stayed in touch with many of his former colleagues in the progressive movement, some directly and some through intermediaries such as Felix Frankfurter. The subsidy that the justice provided allowed the Harvard Law professor to use his considerable talents in support of a variety of reforms, just as Brandeis hoped he would. During these years Brandeis called Frankfurter "the most useful lawyer in the United States." In Frankfurter he found the one person he could talk to about the law and the business of the Supreme Court, knowing that the Harvard professor would be discreet.

Brandeis watched over Frankfurter like a proud parent, and indeed once told him that he considered the younger man "half brother, half son." After Frankfurter married Marion Denman in December 1919, an amused Brandeis wrote to Alice, "Felix is not at the Law School as much . . . and has not as much hold on the individual students as formerly. Thus does matrimony mar!!" When he thought that Frankfurter had taken on too many courses, he urged him to concentrate in areas such as state and federal jurisdictions where much work had to be done. In 1932, Governor Joseph Ely offered Frankfurter a seat on the Supreme Judicial Court of Massachusetts, but Brandeis counseled Frankfurter not to accept; he could do far more important work at the law school. "If ever the time comes when you should be asked to go on the Supreme Court," Frankfurter recalled his saying, "talk to me about it, and if you're then old enough, there might be some reason to leave the law school." And, of course, when Marion Frankfurter began to suffer psychological problems in the mid-1920s, Brandeis not only understood his protégé's suffering but also sent him money to help defray the medical expenses.

Frankfurter played a central role in one of the most notorious incidents of the 1920s, the effort to gain a new trial for Nicola Sacco and Bartolomeo Vanzetti, convicted of a payroll robbery and murder. Their 1920 trial had drawn little attention, but as information about the conduct of the proceedings, the apparent bigotry of the presiding judge, and allegations about the prosecution's manipulation of evidence became known, a groundswell of liberal opinion coalesced into seven years of effort to have the verdict overturned and the men either tried again or pardoned. All efforts failed, and Massachusetts put the two to death shortly after midnight on 23 August 1927.

As a judge, and especially as a judge on a court that conceivably might hear an appeal, Brandeis could not make any public statements, but he clearly believed the two men had not had a fair trial. Frankfurter kept him apprised of his work, and Brandeis encouraged him in his efforts. In the summer of 1927, Brandeis offered to add more money to the special account to cover "heavy demands for incidental expenses" relating to the case. In addition, both Alice and Elizabeth had become involved in the defense effort at the behest of Auntie B., and Alice made financial contributions to the defense fund that her husband could not. Certainly Louis must have known—and approved—when Alice gave Mrs. Evans permission to save Rosina Sacco and her children from the press and hide them in a house Brandeis owned in Dedham.

As the execution date approached, desperate defense lawyers went to Holmes's summer place in Beverly and appealed for a stay. He told them he sympathized, but he refused to act. The two men had been

*Professor Felix Frankfurter of the
Harvard Law School*

accused of committing a crime in Massachusetts; they had been tried and convicted in a state court; and the verdict had been reviewed by the state's appellate courts. In the 1920s, before the incorporation of the Bill of Rights, the Supreme Court as a rule did not review state criminal decisions. While Holmes believed that if he stretched, he might find some grounds for issuing a stay, he did not believe that his brethren on the Court would accept the case and reverse the judgment. He told them to try Brandeis.

Arthur Hill jumped into his car and drove out to Chatham, but Brandeis would not even let the lawyer into his house. Rosina Sacco had stayed at his house (a fact not generally known but one that could prove embarrassing should he grant a stay), two of his closest friends—Mrs. Evans and Frankfurter—had been leaders of the protest, and his wife and daughter had been supporters. As Hill later reported, Justice Brandeis "stated that because of his personal relations to some of the people who had been interested in the case he felt that he must decline to act on any matter connected with it." The next evening the two men went to their deaths.

Frankfurter, grief stricken as he was, understood why both Holmes and Brandeis had declined to act. He had tried to explain the situation to his distraught wife, but to no avail, and when Gardner Jackson questioned Brandeis's actions, Frankfurter exploded. "Don't talk to me about that because I have had to listen to my wife all day. I can shut you up but not her. Gardner, it is terribly important not to have the fight go over into unclean hands." Frankfurter may have understood, but others did not. Vanzetti, in one of his last letters, lamented that both Holmes and Brandeis, "the symbols of liberalism in the Federal Supreme Court turned us their shoulders." The *Worker,* a leftist New York paper, put up a poster in its window titled "Brandeis, Pontius Pilate," describing the justice as washing his hands of innocent blood. Later writers who know the law, as well as Brandeis's concern for propriety and jurisdictional limits, have understood his actions. Others have chastised both him and Holmes for failing to act. Judicial proprieties are all well and good, but they cut too fine a line in a case involving life and death.

Shortly after the two men had died, Brandeis wrote to Frankfurter, "To the end, you have done all that was possible for you. And that all was more than would have [been] possible for any other person I know. But the end of S.V. is only the beginning." No doubt Frankfurter took some balm from that letter, but the bitterness of the case and its aftermath stayed with him his whole career.

FRANKFURTER ALSO WAS Brandeis's chief connection to Harvard Law School, to which he remained a devoted alumnus. During the Red Scare the justice wrote encouraging letters to faculty under attack, especially Zechariah Chafee. Aside from taking a graduate each year as his law clerk, Brandeis supported fellowships and new programs presented to him by Frankfurter and the school's dean, Roscoe Pound. Frankfurter wanted to create a research fellowship, in part to get the assistance of a bright young man in his own work, and Brandeis willingly helped fund it. The first year's incumbent, Thomas Corcoran, would later be a law clerk to Holmes and a major political influence during the New Deal. Brandeis occasionally put prospective donors in touch with the school, and when some of the justice's friends wanted to honor him on his seventieth birthday, they raised money to endow a research fund for the law school.

Brandeis also kept up with law school affairs through the other faculty, since anyone coming down to Washington or going to Cape Cod had a standing invitation to stop in and visit with the justice. Charles Warren, Zechariah Chafee, Manley Hudson, Thomas Reed Powell, and Roscoe Pound were regular visitors, as well as those Brandeis clerks who returned to teach in Cambridge, such as James Landis. Brandeis expected—and received—copies of their books and articles, which he read closely, and he felt no hesitation in suggesting new lines of inquiry to them. After Charles Warren sent Brandeis a copy of his three-volume *The Supreme Court in United States History* (1922), Brandeis praised the book fulsomely, declaring, "Since I joined the Court no book has given me so much instruction or more pleasure." But, "much having makes me hunger more," and he advised Warren to now turn his sights to the lower federal courts, although the work need not be as large.

Not everything about the law school in the 1920s pleased him, and he and Frankfurter broke with Roscoe Pound over the future direction of the school. Brandeis and Frankfurter essentially wanted to keep Harvard as it had been, a small school with extensive contacts between students and faculty with high standards for both. Ideally, professors would teach a small number of very bright students, and if the regular faculty could not teach every course, then visiting scholars would fill in, both enriching their own experience and providing new ideas.

Pound did not oppose the elitism, but considered Harvard designed for an early-nineteenth-century agrarian society and ill suited to provide the type of legal education needed in twentieth-century America. The school now had to teach more aspects of the law and bring in economics, sociology, and philosophy to inform the curriculum. The separation of law from other social sciences had created "a gulf between legal thought and popular thought on matters of social reform," resulting in a bench and bar out of touch with the real world. Brandeis agreed completely with these ideas. He had argued for a sociological jurisprudence for years, and he greatly admired Pound's writings on the law. He and Frankfurter, however, objected to Pound's plan to enlarge the law school—the physical facilities, the faculty, and the student body. Above all, they feared that once expansion began, it would be impossible to stop and would go on "forever like an industrial plant."

Pound wrote to Brandeis in early October 1924 about his plans and received a curt and rather negative reply: "Thank you for letting me know about the plans under consideration. Do let me talk with you when you are next here. I have grave apprehensions and want to suggest an alternative." The alternative proposal damned the whole idea of having a student body larger than a thousand and 350-seat lecture halls as "irreconcilable with H.L.S. traditions and aims." The next suggestion certainly reflected Brandeis's fear of bigness and his growing belief that real progress would come not from the large cities like New York, Chicago, and Boston but from the heartland and smaller places like Madison and Louisville. While perhaps idealistic, it lacked that attribute which had made Brandeis so effective a lawyer and reformer—pragmatism. He wanted Harvard to limit its own growth and place its resources at the disposal of smaller schools in the form of exchange professorships. Both the Harvard faculty and those brought in for a year would benefit from the experience, especially the latter, who would have a year in which to learn. The result, instead of a big Harvard Law School, would be twenty properly sized Harvard clones around the country. He admitted that there would be difficulties in this scheme, but it would, he declared, be "constructive—not destructive." He also went and spoke to the other Harvard graduates on the bench, Holmes and Edward Sanford, as well as to Stone, who had been dean at Columbia, and reported to Frankfurter that they all opposed Pound's plans. The dean, with the blessing of the overseers and President Abbott Lawrence Lowell, determined to expand the law school. Brandeis could, of course, do nothing about it; he continued to give money, not to Pound's drive, but to finance Frankfurter's smaller and more discrete projects. Whether the expansion had anything to do with his decision is impossible to say, but he refused to sit for a portrait to be hung in the law school. No doubt disgust with Pound's plan led him to turn his attention toward Louisville and its fledgling university.

IN THE 1920S, Brandeis began to expound the theme that the future progress of the country and a concomitant development of high ideals would occur not in the large cities but in smaller urban areas. "I think the advice to be given serious-minded public-spirited men for the immediate future is to devote themselves to State, City, municipal and non-political affairs. If we are to attain our national ideals, it must be via the states." Always delighted when his clerks chose to enter teaching, he was even happier when they went to smaller law schools like those at Buffalo and the University of Wisconsin in Madison. When President James B. Conant offered the deanship of Harvard Law School to the thirty-seven-year-old James Landis in the mid-1930s, Landis immediately went to see the man he had clerked for a decade earlier. Landis told him about the offer.

"You mean the Harvard Law School?" Brandeis asked.

"Yes," Landis replied.

"Why do you want to take that?"

"Well," Landis stumbled, "it's a great position."

"Anybody can be a good Dean of the Harvard Law School," Brandeis told him. "Why not take some smaller school and do something with it?"

By then Brandeis no doubt was thinking of his own efforts to build up a smaller school, efforts that began in the fall of 1924. He entered this project with the same energy and enthusiasm he had earlier brought to reforms, and the same attention to detail. But because of his judicial duties and his distance from the scene, he had to work through surrogates—members of Alfred's family and especially Alfred's daughter Fannie.

Brandeis began by donating portions of his sizable personal library to the University of Louisville, along with sufficient funds to hire a librarian to catalog these and other materials to come and to shelve them in a proper manner. As he made additional donations of books and documents, he began to earmark some of them as "for the Economics library" or "for the History library." He also secured a copy of the university catalog, and as he told his niece Maidie, while it would take a long time to build up all of the programs, it was not too early to start planning what would be needed and then to secure people to help make it happen. One piece fell into place almost immediately when his old friend from elementary school Hattie Bishop Speed donated her art collection to the university and a building to house it in memory of her late husband, James Speed. Louis and Alice, upon learning of this, sent a piece of old Japanese lacquer that had been given to them early in their marriage, as well as other artworks, to add to the collection, but warned Fannie not to let the Brandeis name creep in—even though Aunt Hattie, as Alfred's children called her, wanted to give Louis credit. His name, Brandeis warned, could be used for publicity and as a lever to move other donors, but neither he nor Alice wanted to be seen as the prime movers.

As he told his nephew Frederick Wehle, "I assumed that the University is poor in possessions—including the instructors. What I aim to do is to make them rich in ideals and eager in the desire to attain them. I want the authorities to dream of the University as it should be; and I hope to encourage this dreaming by making possible the first steps toward realization." Brandeis did not plan to give a huge gift to the university, although over the years the value of his contributions of books, documents, artwork, and the moneys to process them added up to many thousands of dollars. He did not urge the university to start a large endowment campaign. He wanted the people of Louisville to support the school, and small gifts should be welcomed because they would indicate community support. If an occasional wealthy donor stepped up, such as Aunt Hattie, and contributed a building or endowed a professorship, all to the good. But Louisville was a small university in a small city, and Brandeis hoped to make it a model of the type of practical idealism and accomplishment he believed could take place outside the big metropolitan areas.

On 18 February 1925, Louis wrote to his brother that the development of the university

is a task befitting the Adolph Brandeis family, which for nearly three-quarters of a century has stood in Louisville for culture and, at least in Uncle Lewis [Dembitz], for learning. For the undertaking conditions seem favorable now. It would be fine if all the grandchildren could take an active part. But six of them are disqualified, for the present, by non-residence. . . . So the task devolves upon your family—yourself, Jennie, the girls and the sons-in-law—and upon Alice and me. If we elders have ten years to work in, the preliminary work will have been done. The rest can be left wholly to your descendants and the Centuries.

Money alone cannot build a worthy university. Too much money, or too quick money, may mar one; particularly if it is foreign money. To become great, a university must express the people whom it serves, and must express the people and the community at their best. The aim must be high and the vision broad; the goal seemingly attainable but beyond the immediate reach. . . . History teaches, I believe, that the present tendency toward centralization must be arrested, if we are to attain the American ideals, and that for it must be substituted intense development of life through activities in the several states and localities. The problem is a very difficult one; but the local university is the most hopeful instrument for any attempt at solution.

Brandeis asked family members to assume particular responsibilities. Alfred took on Kentuckiana; his daughter Adele had the Department of Economics and Sociology, and her sister Fannie bore the responsibility for archaeology, art, and music. Using his own holdings, as well as Zionist and government offices, Brandeis helped to establish a number of departmental libraries and arranged to name them in memory of prominent Kentuckians. Bookplates in the Palestine-Judaica Library bore the name of Lewis Dembitz, and those in music of Brandeis's own music teacher from many years before, Louis H. Hast. After Alfred died, the economics and sociology, war library and government publications, and the classical literature and history collections bore his name. Brandeis used his own contacts in government and elsewhere to secure ongoing publications of groups like the Carnegie Endowment for International Peace and the League of Nations.

When the university president, Arthur Y. Ford, began talking about an endowment drive, Brandeis immediately protested. "I am particularly desirous of preventing Louisville from taking foreign money, notably not from 'foundations.' If we are to have a worthy Kentucky institution, it should be through Kentucky support. The other is the 'easier way'—but like most 'easier ways'—apt to defeat the best development." The university would become great only if "it is essentially Kentuckian, an institution for Kentuckians developed by Kentuckians."

When Alfred expressed discouragement at the slow pace of their work, and the seeming inability of university officials to understand, the justice urged him to have faith. "The future has many good things in store for those who can wait, have patience, and exercise good judgment." Some things would work well and others would not, and the only thing they could count on was that there would be surprises both in progress and in setbacks. "My faith is great in time," he told his brother, "and that which shapes it to its perfect end."

It took several years before the board of trustees began to appreciate the Brandeis plan of slow and steady growth. In the heyday of the 1920s, many thought a drive to corral large sums of money would be the way to put up new buildings and expand the faculty—the same mind-set the justice had opposed at Harvard. Eventually, Ford left, to be replaced by Raymond A. Kent, who understood and backed the Brandeis family in its work.

Given his concern over the direction taken by Harvard Law, Brandeis paid special attention to the University of Louisville Law School. He wanted the students to be primarily local, from Louisville and Kentucky, since he believed most of them would return there to practice. The school could develop only if the quality of education impressed those at the head of the local bench and bar—lawyers, judges, and public officials. Aside from occasional monetary gifts, Brandeis arranged for the law library to receive a complete set of Supreme Court case briefs and records starting in 1924, a practice that has continued to this day. To honor those Kentuckians who had previously served on the Court, he gave funds so the library could obtain a complete set of *United States Reports*. Similarly, he arranged to secure a complete set of *Federal Reports* in memory of those from the state who had rendered distinguished service as federal judges, and a complete set of *Attorney General Opinions* to mark Kentuckians who had served in that office.

Brandeis personally intervened to bring in the distinguished local lawyer Robert Neville Miller as dean in 1930, and that same year the American Bar Association put Louisville on its approved list of law schools. Miller raised money, primarily from local donors, to erect a new building, and the cornerstone was laid on 6 June 1938, with Justice Stanley Reed, another Kentuckian, as the main speaker. Miller said that he could not imagine the development of the law school without

Brandeis's aid. "He always kept in the background, seeking no word of appreciation for himself or for what he had done. It was his vision of the Law School as an active force in the community, rather than just another school turning out lawyers, which really decided me to give up the practice of law and become Dean. He always anticipated our wishes."

Brandeis's dreams for the law school came to fruition, although it took many years, a fact that would not have bothered him. The school is still small by the standards of Harvard or Michigan, and it is ranked as a second-tier school. Renamed the Louis D. Brandeis School of Law in 1998, it remains regional, with two-thirds of the students coming from Louisville and Kentucky, and most of these stay to practice in the state. The faculty is heavily engaged in policy research, and each year distinguished visiting professors come in to work on issues relating to the economic and social conditions of the region. The school was one of the first five in the country to incorporate a mandatory public service requirement, and currently each student must do thirty hours of public service, generally by representing poor clients. Rather than a deterrent, the public service aspect has become a major reason students choose the school, and alumni report that they have continued pro bono work once in practice.

Here in many ways is the quintessential Brandeis—opponent of bigness, champion of the small institution, be it a business or a university, idealism tempered by pragmatism, a belief that only if the people "owned" the solution would they throw themselves into making the experiment succeed, realism about the difficulties involved, attention to details, extraordinary patience, and a commitment to the education necessary for success. All the elements that made Brandeis a successful lawyer and reformer can be seen here, as well as a mature philosophy regarding bigness. It may have been too late to save Washington and the big cities, but hope existed in small-city and small-state America.

LIVING IN WASHINGTON for much of the year permitted Brandeis to watch closely the political doings in the 1920s, although he found little to cheer him. The two decades of progressivism had led to the enactment of numerous laws, but in that period of time, he asked, had the country "gained or lost ground—in civilization—[and] in that which America is supposed to stand for—in liberty and tolerance; in security to life and property; in morality; in culture"? His tone indicated that he doubted much improvement had been made.

The nomination of Warren Harding as the Republican standard-bearer in 1920 instead of Herbert Hoover constituted a "sad story of American political responsibility." Hoover had impressed Brandeis during the war, and had he announced as a Democrat could have had that party's nomination. Hoover's declaration as a Republican struck the justice as "a terrible blunder." After Hoover landed in the cabinet, Brandeis's opinion of him went down, and within a few months he wrote to his brother, "I am sorry to say, your impression as to Hoover is shared by many here who have been watching affairs this summer. They speak of his 'insatiable and absurd graspingness' and 'insane longing for publicity'; and it is said that this is common talk among newspapermen."

He had little use for Harding or his successor. At a dinner party, he, in Dean Acheson's words, "assumed a prophetic role and denounced our rulers for promising the people what they knew they could not fulfill." After attending Calvin Coolidge's Washington birthday speech in 1927, he told Frankfurter, "You cannot conceive how painful, distressful & depressing it was. . . . When I tried to recall the next most depressing & distressful experience of a lifetime, I had to go back to 1894, when in preparing for the Public Institutions Hearings, I went to Long Island (Boston Harbor) Poor-House hospital & passed through the syphilitic ward. I had a like sense of uncleanness."

During these years a handful of the old progressives tended the flame. In 1924, Robert La Follette decided to run for president as a third-party candidate, and rumors abounded that the senator would choose Louis Brandeis as his running mate. When Chief Justice Taft heard of this, he accurately predicted, "I know enough about Brandeis to know that [the vice presidency] is the last position which he would accept, but his sympathies may be with La Follette." Actually, by the time Taft wrote this, Brandeis had already declined the offer.

La Follette from the beginning realized that Brandeis would not leave the Court, but he had such a high regard for his friend that he wanted to offer him the opportunity. In late July he dispatched the journalist Gilson Gardner, an old friend of the justice's, to see him on Cape Cod. As Alice told her daughter, "You will understand the situation—politics in the air—it seemed quite like old times." Gardner made a strong plea, but Brandeis refused and said he thought he could do more for the public good on the Court than anywhere else. The next day Alice wrote to Belle, "My great—indeed only regret is that Louis should not be standing shoulder to shoulder with Bob in the fight. But he will help, I feel sure in his own way when the opportunity offers."

Belle in turn wrote to Bess Evans, "The optimism and the widespread appeal to have Louis' name on the ballot seemed to justify at least putting the matter before him. It would have been a great adventure but it could hardly be expected that Louis would make it. With Bob it is the logic of his life. With Louis it would be stepping into a new field." Later in the campaign Alice Brandeis came out and worked for La Follette, even writing an article supporting his record.

The campaign proved to be La Follette's last hurrah. He did not do badly for a third-party candidate, winning one out of every six votes, but in the all-important Electoral College he carried only the thirteen votes of his home state of Wisconsin. The La Follettes came to dine at the Brandeis apartment in March 1925, and the justice told his brother that the senator "is in good form, but does not bear his years as well as you do." Ten weeks later, on 18 June, La Follette died, worn out by his three decades of battling for reform. "He had put all there was in him into the great fight," Brandeis said, "never sparing himself. And he knew not fear."

There were few other moments of hope for progressives in the 1920s. Brandeis took heart when his old friend the Massachusetts senator David Walsh easily won reelection in 1926 over Republican William Morgan Butler, a close friend of Calvin Coolidge's. The GOP had poured both men and money into the campaign, sending in heavyweights such as Hoover and Charles Evans Hughes to campaign for Butler. And, surprisingly, Brandeis enthusiastically favored the candidacy of Alfred E. Smith in 1928 and thought he would win.

In 1927, Brandeis had ventured the idea that "after timid, safe and sane Cal" the country might fly to a courageous man. Reports from Susan about the four-time governor of New York and his support among the people led Brandeis to take a closer look. After Smith won the Democratic nomination, Brandeis excitedly wrote to his brother, who also favored Smith, that all of the "family and friends" had better get on the bandwagon soon, before there would be no room to stand. When Smith asked Susan about meeting with her father, Brandeis said it would be "inadvisable for me to see him during the campaign except under conditions which would preclude publicity." But he hoped to see much of him in Washington after his inauguration. A week before the election he told his daughter that "political news is certainly exciting now." All the people he knew in Boston told him that they had never seen such an outpouring as the popular sentiment for Smith.

On 6 November, Smith suffered a smashing defeat at the hands of

La Follette for president, 1924

Herbert Hoover. The Democrat received only 40 percent of the vote and carried eight states—six in the old South, Massachusetts, and Connecticut. Brandeis had completely underestimated the factors that doomed Smith's candidacy—his religion, his opposition to prohibition, his identification with the new urban America, and the prosperity of the 1920s, for which the Republicans claimed full credit. "I feel almost as if an 'Earth Shaker' had been at work on us Smithites during the past week," he told Elizabeth, but "the experience adds to my militancy. There is an opportunity ahead for great fighting." He wrote a bit more forlornly to the Kansas editor William Allen White: "Shall we have soon another 'Great Rebellion'?" White feared not, for one thing the election showed was that the "old order holds fast."

There was one bright spot in the election returns. Even though Smith had lost his home state of New York, the Democratic gubernatorial candidate had won. Brandeis sent word through Felix Frankfurter that if Franklin Roosevelt would care to stop by the next time he was in Washington, the justice had a few ideas he wanted to discuss with him.

TWO OTHER EFFORTS occupied Brandeis's extrajudicial time in the 1920s: savings bank life insurance and Zionism.

Of all his reform efforts, savings bank insurance remained to him the most important and the most satisfactory. From the time he went on the Court until his death a quarter century later, he followed the program's progress, read its annual reports carefully, sent a stream of letters offering advice and encouragement to its officials, and took near-parental pride every time another bank joined the network or the system achieved another milestone in coverage. He also had an able lieutenant on the spot who kept him informed of both the trials and the triumphs of the system.

Brandeis's secretary at the law firm, Alice Harriet Grady, had been interested in savings bank insurance from the time that her boss had started work on the project. In 1920 she left the firm and became deputy director of the state agency that administered and oversaw the plan. From that time until her death in 1934, she and Brandeis corresponded frequently, at least weekly and sometimes more often when a problem arose.

The chief danger came from the private insurance companies that never reconciled themselves to savings bank insurance. Each year they would offer one or more proposals aimed at limiting the amount of insurance that could be written or changing the conditions that made savings bank insurance attractive as well as affordable to working people. Miss Grady, however, had learned from the master, and during her tenure put into practice those lessons. She maintained close touch with legislators, especially those friendly to savings bank insurance, who would alert her at the first sign of another attack. She also cultivated relations with important local businessmen and professionals who sat on the boards of the savings banks and had influence with the legislators from their districts. When an occasional attack threatened to become dangerous, Judd Dewey, Miss Grady's boss, might arrange for Brandeis to talk to the governor.

Brandeis never doubted Miss Grady's ability, but understood that she needed constant encouragement, which he provided in abundance. "You remind of Antaeus," he wrote in 1923, "only they never throw you to the ground; & Hercules would have had a hard time throttling you on high." "I know you are a 'bonnie fighter,' " he told her on another occasion, "and with the right, for which you always battle, on your side." After one victory he told his son-in-law, "I have just had word from Boston that Miss Grady has won a very nobly contested legislative fight on Savings Bank Insurance. I am a strong believer in Amazons." Whenever he came through Boston on his way to or from the Cape, he would stay overnight, and Miss Grady would arrange appointments for him with people he wanted to see or with some whom she wanted him to meet regarding insurance.

Clyde Casady, later to be the executive vice president of the Savings Bank Life Insurance Council, recalled how he had met the justice in September 1932. He had just joined the agency, and Miss Grady invited him to go to the train station and see Brandeis off. "I expected merely to sit in a corner of the stateroom," he said, "and listen to conversation between the Justice and his intimate friends. You can imagine my surprise when he met me at the door, excused himself and took me into the next compartment, and spent practically the entire twenty minutes talking about the need and means of promoting savings-bank insurance."

IMMEDIATELY AFTER the members of the Brandeis group resigned from leadership of American Zionism at the 1921 Cleveland convention, they met in New York and heard from their leader. They had not resigned from Zionism, Brandeis reminded them, and they still believed in the goal of a Jewish homeland in Palestine. "We are from now on to free ourselves from all entanglements in order that we may the sooner accomplish that end with the least possible embarrassment." They would, of course, remain members of the Zionist Organization of America, but so long as the new administration led by Louis Lipsky pursued policies they deemed wrong, they could not share in the work. They would for the moment go their separate ways.

So they watched as membership in the ZOA eroded during the 1920s and as the World Zionist Organization was forced to adopt, one after another, many of the steps that Brandeis had proposed. The Brandeis group set up several funds to support economic development in the Holy Land. The Palestine Endowment Funds (PEF), organized under Julian Mack's direction in 1922, utilized charitable contributions for a variety of purposes. One of its first—and largest—donations went to support the new Hebrew University in Jerusalem. In 1935, at David Ben-Gurion's request, the PEF helped purchase land near Aqaba on the Red Sea, now the site of the important Israeli port and resort city of Eilat. During these years Brandeis personally donated more than $750,000 to the funds.

A more ambitious scheme led to the establishment of the Palestine Development Council (PDC), the investment counterpart to the donation-fed PEF (and an illustration of Brandeis's demand that investment and charitable funds be kept separate). In creating the PDC, the Brandeis group tried to blend social idealism with economic realism, reflecting the progressive view of enlightened business. The PDC never really got off the ground, not because it could not find businesses with a social orientation, but rather because, when it did, the Brandeis group lacked the resources to fund it. Pinhas Rutenberg came up with a practical plan to generate hydroelectric power, but it required far more investment money than the PDC could command.

Throughout the 1920s, Brandeis met constantly with individual Zionists from both the American and the world organizations and with Palestinians who came to the United States, whom he grilled on the yield of their crops or the size of their orchards. To say that he led a government in exile might be too strong, but his extensive correspondence with Julian Mack, Stephen Wise, Felix Frankfurter, and others on Zionist matters shows that they followed ZOA developments closely and believed that at some time they would regain power. When a group within the ZOA disillusioned with Lipsky plotted to overthrow him, Brandeis met with the leaders, but refused to be drawn into the scheming. When the Lipsky administration collapsed early in the Depression and the Brandeis group returned to power, its members stepped into positions of authority and responsibility with little need for acclimation.

Brandeis, however, played a personal role in two major developments in American Zionism during the decade. First, he kept Hadassah strong and focused. The women's group nearly split apart in 1921, because its leaders had husbands on both sides of the controversy. Henrietta Szold, the founder of Hadassah, had moved to Palestine to supervise its work there (supported by a fund that Brandeis, Julian Mack, and others had anonymously established). She worried how to keep Hadassah alive after the Cleveland debacle and thought she would need to return to America. Brandeis, when he learned of this, immediately declared that Miss Szold had to remain in Palestine, which desperately needed her leadership. He called in Rose Jacobs and told her that she would have to assume part of the burden, and by this step guaranteed the future of Hadassah. By insisting that new women come forward and new talent be developed, he prevented Hadassah from becoming the lengthened shadow of one person. Henrietta Szold would be given another quarter century to serve the cause, but in those years she could rely on a strong organization that admired her and supported her work but that no longer needed her daily presence.

Brandeis also encouraged Hadassah to remain independent of the Zionist Organization of America, and alone in the 1920s it did not suffer the reversals in fortune that plagued the ZOA. Hadassah had a mission—health care in Palestine—and so long as it focused on that mission, it remained strong. After the World Zionist Organization refused to fund his plan for eradication of malaria in the Huleh valley, Brandeis arranged for gifts to Hadassah, which successfully did the work. When the women's organization needed funds to expand its medical work and its children's services and keep them available to Jew and Arab alike, Brandeis talked to Nathan Straus, one of the early supporters of Miss Szold, and he provided funds. He funneled some donations to Hadassah through Susan and let the Hadassah leaders know they could also turn to Alice for help.

The other major Zionist development in the 1920s involved the so-called pact of glory creating the Jewish Agency for Palestine. The League of Nations mandate to Britain required that a governing body be established with representatives not only from the Jewish settlements in Palestine and from the World Zionist Organization but from non-Zionist groups as well. Chaim Weizmann realized that if he wanted to raise large sums of money for Palestine, it would have to come from non-Zionist groups such as the American Jewish Committee and from wealthy Jews who did not subscribe to Zionism. He began a long courtship of Louis Marshall, the head of the committee, who had already been quietly talking with Brandeis and Julian Mack. Marshall never subscribed to Jewish nationalism, but he accepted Brandeis's argument that all Jews had to play a role in developing Palestine, whether they chose to live there or not. By the time Weizmann came to America in early 1924, the groundwork had been laid, but everyone recognized that if the Brandeis group refused to cooperate, there would be little chance of success.

Although invited to the conference in New York on 17 February, neither Brandeis nor Mack attended, but they both sent letters of support and promised to work for Palestine. The justice reiterated his belief that the Jews of America had a special role to play, but he also pointed out that no progress could be made without careful study of the facts, efficient use of available funds, and above all effective leadership. Given all this, "we may hope for great advance in the economic, social and cultural development of the country." Beyond offering encouragement, however, Brandeis would wait and see. He still did not trust Chaim Weizmann.

HIS ONLY JOY in an otherwise depressing political and economic era came from his family. With the exception of a few setbacks, Alice seemed to have outgrown the problems that had plagued her in Boston.

Whenever weather permitted, she and Louis went for a stroll along the C & O canal towpath or for an occasional paddle. She kept in touch with old friends such as Bess Evans, who came often to visit, and made new friends, with whom she would go to concerts, museums, or even luncheons of the Democratic Women's Club. The explosion of automobile traffic made continued use of the horse and buggy not only impractical but also dangerous, so the Brandeises made an arrangement with a chauffeur to have him and his black Pierce-Arrow available when they needed it, and by the end of the decade the car would pick him up in the morning to take him to the Court and then bring him home in the afternoon.

Alice and Louis entertained more than they had in Boston, since without his need to travel for reform and Zionist work, he would be home every evening. When they first arrived in Washington, they went often to dinner parties but eventually stopped. Apparently, Louis made this decision, since he felt more comfortable in his own place, with a guest list that he and Alice had chosen. The Brandeises continued to like small gatherings where conversation would flow. In addition to a maid and cook named Susan, Alice pressed into service the justice's messenger, Edward Poindexter, and the various Harvard men her husband employed as clerks to help her either at the dinners or at the weekly teas where the justice met—and questioned—not only old friends but also newcomers to Washington. The clerks apparently enjoyed these responsibilities because of the interesting and occasionally famous people they met. At dinner they had the chore of making sure that all of the guests had left by ten o'clock so that the justice could go to bed. At the Monday afternoon gatherings, aside from helping Alice serve, they were to make sure that no one monopolized the justice's time and would bring over a new person for him to talk to, a sign that time had expired for his current guest. The courtly Brandeis would not sit if a woman was standing, and Thomas Austern recalled running around the apartment making sure there were enough chairs and having the female guests seated.

With the exception of the war years, when he stayed in Washington over the summer, the Brandeises left the capital almost as soon as the Court term ended and headed for Cape Cod, with a stop of a day or two in Boston to take care of business and see friends. In late September they would reverse the trek, arriving in time to get ready for the Court's convening on the first Monday in October. For years the Brandeises rented houses on Cape Cod, eventually coming to prefer a place in Chatham.

Alice, ca. 1930

Then, in 1924, their landlord announced that he wanted to get rid of the property, and Louis and Alice decided to buy. The location suited them well, a plain, even austere house on a bluff a mile and a half outside of Chatham overlooking Stage Harbor with a few nearby buildings that could be rented by family and friends. There in the summers Louis and Alice would canoe, walk, pick wild blueberries, and entertain friends, albeit without the help of either Poindexter or the clerks.

And he would catch up on his reading, including Zionist literature and the state and federal government reports that he alone of all the members of the Court so enjoyed. He does not seem to have read any modern fiction; there is no reference to Hemingway, Fitzgerald, or any contemporary European authors. He continued to study ancient Greece and Rome, revisited some of the classics that he had read as a young man, and looked forward to new books by Walter Lippmann and Harold Laski, as well as works on the law by Roscoe Pound and others.

The one major change in their routine came in the fall of 1926. The Stoneleigh on Connecticut Avenue, where they had lived since his appointment to the Court, had decided to "modernize" by converting ground-floor space into shops for the "convenience" of its residents. The Brandeises found a similar and quieter residence hotel at Florence Court at 2205 California Street, where they again rented two apartments, No. 503 for their living quarters and No. 601 for his study. Sadie Nicholson, who had worked for them in Boston and occasionally on the Cape, came down to Washington in August to oversee the transfer of furniture from the Stoneleigh, while Louis's messenger, Edward Poindexter, supervised moving the justice's office. (A Miss Turner rented but did not live in a small furnished apartment in the building that she often sublet to a Brandeis clerk.)

Aside from an occasional trip to New York, where Alice still had family, the Brandeises rarely varied their routine. Susan and Elizabeth would occasionally go camping with Louis, but those trips ended after the girls married. So the justice was somewhat surprised when, in September 1927, Alice arranged for them to spend a weekend in Charlottesville to visit Monticello, the home of the Founding Father Louis most admired, Thomas Jefferson. "I have just been rambling about the town," he wrote to Alfred, "with its old houses like, or a little better than Louisville's near-best of a half-century ago." They stayed in a hotel near the court buildings, and "it is good to see the old time law offices from which even the omnipresent typewriter cannot remove the inherent calm." The next day he walked around Charlottesville some more, basking in how much it reminded him of Louisville. After visiting Monticello and the University of Virginia (which Jefferson founded), he returned home, he said, with the "deepest conviction of [Jefferson's] greatness. He was a civilized man." In a note to Alice Grady, Brandeis told her he thought Jefferson "would have no difficulty in appreciating S.B.I."

NOTHING GAVE BRANDEIS more joy, however, than his daughters, Susan and Elizabeth, whose personal development and professional experience more than lived up to his expectations. All the tensions that had existed between Susan and her parents seem to have disappeared after she finished law school and entered practice. On a two-week camping trip the two took in Canada in July and August 1921, Brandeis wrote in an almost blissful tone about how he had enjoyed Susan's company. Susan "has been quite charming & interesting—eager to see & most reasonable." She has "exhibited capacity for silence as well as speech" and is "always good company." "She has passed far beyond the period of grievances for treatment of the family," he told Alice, "and is rather inclined to overestimate what she has gained from us or has been permitted to enjoy."

Susan began her practice renting some space in the office of Louis Posner, a New York attorney, and almost immediately began securing business. Posner recommended her to David L. Podell, a well-respected New York trial lawyer who had just become assistant U.S. attorney for the Southern District of New York in charge of antitrust, and he hired Susan to work on cases involving the building trades. Although Susan never asked her father for help in getting clients, some of Brandeis's friends decided to lend a hand. Julian Mack and Learned Hand heard a number of bankruptcy cases in their courts and began assigning receivership work to Susan. After she had proved her ability in this area, it became a reliable source of income as she built up her practice and reputation. Above all, her father delighted that she loved the practice of law as much as he had. Susan "is having a joyous time with an endless succession of professional thrills." After receiving a bubbling letter from her that reported getting new clients, he responded, "I always found so much of romance and adventure in securing a new client and in their confidence that the ordinary essays of the imagination presented by all but the best novels or stories seemed pretty poor by comparison."

As a practicing attorney, Susan also began appreciating some of the advice her father gave her, advice that had not made a great impression on her in law school. He suggested that she learn more about the law of evidence, "a branch which one must have at the fingertips." She decided to take an accounting course, and he approved, since "accounting is the language of business." She also had a greater sensitivity to her father's position, and on a number of occasions wrote to ask him whether if she took a particular case or client it would embarrass him. In nearly every instance he told her she could go ahead, and said that if a conflict should arise—such as a case coming to his court—he would recuse. He also arranged to be transferred from oversight of the Second Circuit (which included New York and New Jersey, where Susan practiced) so that neither would be embarrassed if a case needed to be appealed.

He made little effort to hide his pride. When Susan received a sizable fee from one of her cases, she sent it to her father and asked him how to invest it. He sent it to Miss Malloch at his old law firm for deposit in his account, "so they may see my lawyer daughter's check." At a dinner for the circuit court judges in the fall of 1924, several members came up to the justice to tell him how well Susan was doing, a fact that he promptly shared with her. After Susan appeared before the high court, with her father of course absent, some of his colleagues came over to tell him that she had done well in presenting her case.

Susan, of course, was not the first woman to argue before the Supreme Court, and by the 1920s the presence of a female attorney no longer seemed such an oddity. But while Brandeis had no problems with women lawyers—unlike Justice McReynolds, who thought they should not be admitted in the courtroom—he did insist on standards, and he wrote to his daughter that a Rose Rothenberg, whom Susan knew, had been admitted to practice before the Supreme Court and had shown up quite inappropriately dressed. "Her next friend ought to have supplied her own lack of the sense of propriety in coming into Court, with 2/3 short sleeves, & décolleté and a long necklace!!" Brandeis never reconciled himself to the new fashions.

In February 1925, Susan informed her parents of a tentative engagement to Jacob "Jack" Gilbert, a lawyer she had met when they had been on opposite sides of a minor litigation. This time her parents did not question her judgment. "There is nothing which we could wish more for you than a husband worthy of you whom you deeply love," her father wrote. "And we have confidence in your mature judgment." Susan took her time, and not until October did she tell her parents that she and Jack had definitely decided to marry. Brandeis told her that a wise man had said to him many years ago: "Take all the time necessary for deliberation; but when you have decided, act thereon for life without doubting." On 29 December, Felix Adler, the bride's uncle and the same person who had presided over her parents' wedding, performed the ceremony in New York.

AFTER GRADUATING FROM RADCLIFFE, Elizabeth Brandeis worked for a few years as secretary of the District of Columbia Minimum Wage Board until the Court declared the law creating the board unconstitutional. She decided to go to law school and also to study economics, a plan of which her father strongly approved, especially after she chose to go to the University of Wisconsin. "It will be particularly satisfying to live in an atmosphere which breathes La Follette's air." She moved to Madison in the late summer of 1923 and before long had abandoned law to study under the great labor economist John R. Commons. After she completed her dissertation in 1927, Commons invited her to contribute the section on labor legislation to the monumental four-volume history of labor in the United States that he edited.

EB, as she was called throughout her adult life, finished her course work in 1924 and began looking for a job, but not one in a big city. She had an offer to teach part-time at Smith College, an offer her father recommended she take. John Commons, however, wanted her to stay at Wisconsin and arranged for her to teach there while she completed her dissertation. One of the attractions in Madison was Paul Raushenbush, a fellow student in the Economics Department and the son of the noted Social Gospel minister Walter Rauschenbusch. They married at the end of June 1925 at a small ceremony in Chicago, with none of her family present. This seems to have been a preference of both hers and Paul's, and not a sign of estrangement; the Brandeises liked Paul a great deal, and soon after the ceremony the newlyweds came to Chatham before spending time in the Canadian woods.

The Raushenbushes faced a problem common to many couples in academia: how to get jobs at the same colleges or at ones in the same

Paul, Walter, and Elizabeth
Raushenbush, at Chatham
in the 1930s

city. Swarthmore offered Paul a full-time position to start in the fall of 1927 and agreed to hire EB at the same rate of pay per course, but only on a part-time basis. The two did not know what to do, and so returned to Madison to seek the advice of Commons and their other professors. This time the faculty insisted that they both stay, and Paul and EB taught at Wisconsin until their retirement.

ON 4 NOVEMBER 1926, Susan gave birth to the Brandeises' first grandchild, Louis Brandeis Gilbert. The justice wrote to Felix Frankfurter, "I suppose you and Marion have heard from Auntie B. that Susan's son is a strapping fellow & that all goes well with them." The austere justice became a doting grandfather, referring to his namesake as "the Crown Prince," or "C.P.," and was always eager to hear news about his latest exploits. In December 1926, when he had to make a trip to New York on Zionist business, he told Susan that the "rest of time is to be devoted to the contemplation of C.P.—and of the Eternal Verities." Louis and Alice liked to have the boy around in the summer at Chatham. The Gilberts at first took a small house down the hill and later built a summer home on an adjacent parcel they purchased. Over the next few years Louis had a sister, Alice (born 14 May 1928 and called Adee), and a brother, Frank (3 December 1930). Elizabeth and Paul also had a child, Walter, born on 13 June 1928. At the house in Chatham, Brandeis would measure the children every summer when they arrived, and make a mark on the kitchen wall with the name and date showing their growth.

The success and maturity of their daughters, as well as their growing families, led Louis and Alice to begin giving them large sums of money later in the decade, which served several purposes. Louis and Alice had far more money than they used, and even with his significant gifts to Zionist enterprises his fortune kept growing. He understood that neither Jack nor Susan would ever have the type of practice that he had enjoyed, or the income that came with it. Elizabeth and Paul would be academics all of their lives, and professorships would not make them rich. Both the daughters and their husbands had interests in public service, and Brandeis wanted them to have some of the freedom that he so prized. Elizabeth and Paul had serious qualms about accepting these gifts, but her father insisted. "Our purpose," he told her, "was to impose upon you responsibility for the care of property, which would, in any event, naturally go to you someday."

He also understood that growing families entailed costs, and in 1928 learned that Susan and Jack had gone into debt because their expenses outran their income. He immediately arranged to cover

Brandeis in a canoe at Chatham

their outstanding obligations, but did not want them to have to come to him whenever they were short; it would be better to give them money and to let them do with it as they wanted. He put no strings on his gifts and left "wholly to you two the disposition to be made of the income."

BRANDEIS SUFFERED a grievous personal loss when his best friend and brother, Alfred, died on 8 August 1928. The two had corresponded almost daily their entire adult lives, and whenever business brought Louis to the Midwest, he would somehow find a way to detour to Louisville. Later, their families had vacationed together, and Susan and Elizabeth spent a great deal of time with their Louisville cousins. When Alfred came to Washington for a visit in the spring of 1925, Louis remarked that "he seemed finer than ever. A man who has developed steadily throughout his life."

Alfred and his family in Louisville had enthusiastically joined Louis's project to build up the University of Louisville, but in May 1927 Louis heard that Al had been having health problems. He tried to get his

Susan, Elizabeth, and their children, Chatham in the 1930s

brother to take it easy, since he and Alice did not want to lose their managing partner. "It's just 50 years since my eyes gave out," he told Alfred. "Since then, there has never been a time that I haven't had to bear in mind physical limitations of some sort. The walls curbing activity were always in sight; and I had to adjust my efforts. Your superb constitution relieved you from that necessity. But age is a fact that may not be ignored . . . and there is not a day when I am not reminded of it. Your constitution has been better than mine. But you are nearly three years older. Remember that—and Act Accordingly."

News of Alfred's death came to Louis and Alice in Chatham, and they spent a long time remembering him and all he had meant in their lives. He had, Louis wrote to Alfred's widow, Jennie, a "beautiful, gladsome life." He brought happiness to his family and help to individuals in need and had been a good citizen of his community and country; in return he had received love, friendship, and appreciation. Louis dug out old files with Alfred's letters and read again about their boyhood adventures, the great family trip to Europe, and the problems Alfred overcame to rebuild A. Brandeis & Son. Alfred had a "radiant, generous nature," and Louis would miss him for the rest of his life.

IN NOVEMBER 1926, Louis Brandeis celebrated his seventieth birthday, and he spent several days responding to greetings from well-wishers all over the country. Julian Mack wrote to tell him that his friends had raised the money to endow a research fellowship in his name at Harvard Law School. From Holmes came a note full of appreciation for his friend. "You turn the third corner tomorrow," Holmes wrote. "You have done big things with high motives—have swept over great hedges and across wide ditches, always with the same courage, the same keen eye, the same steady hand. As you take the home stretch the onlookers begin to realize how you have ridden and what you have achieved. I am glad that I am still here to say: Nobly done."

Louis and Alfred at Chatham, ca. 1926

To honor Brandeis, the faculty at Yale Law School proposed giving him an honorary degree. According to Thurman Arnold, President James Rowland Angell turned down the recommendation. The following year the faculty again nominated the justice, Angell agreed, but the trustees said no. The third year the faculty sent in Brandeis's name, Angell approved, the trustees agreed, but the Yale Corporation turned it down. Finally, in the fourth year the faculty said yes, Angell said yes, the trustees said yes, and the corporation also approved. Justice Brandeis, however, said no, having imposed upon himself a rule against such honors, and on that decision there could be no appeal.

One birthday letter in particular must have given Brandeis satisfaction in knowing that lessons he had taught years earlier had taken hold. His old friend Edward Filene wrote to explain to the justice an incident that had taken place at the management committee meeting of Filene's department store. Lincoln Filene had read a letter from Judge Mack soliciting money for the gift to Harvard, and everyone on the committee had been enthusiastic about Filene's making a donation of $10,000—everyone except Edward. He wanted Brandeis to understand that he did not object to the fund, but did not think that the store ought to be using corporate money, since this would raise the price of goods to its customers. He would make a private gift, but did not want store moneys involved. "I have a very strong feeling," he told Brandeis, "that judging by what you have said to me about the inexcusable high cost of doing business, you would like me to take the stand which I adopted." Brandeis told him not to worry. "I understand fully."

CHAPTER TWENTY-SEVEN

DEPRESSION

On 27 October 1929, Louis Brandeis wrote to his son-in-law Jack Gilbert, "There has been a very severe engagement on Wall St. It will be months before the direct casualties are ascertained or disclosed, and . . . its effect upon general business becomes apparent." There had indeed been a "severe engagement" four days earlier, when the New York Stock Exchange saw six million shares change hands, erasing more than $4 billion in paper value, but this paled when the following day nearly thirteen million shares traded and losses exceeded $9 billion. Then, on Tuesday, 29 October, the bottom fell out of the great bull market of the 1920s, with stock prices in free fall and no buyers to be found. By mid-November, American stocks had depreciated by $26 billion, nearly a third of their value just a few months earlier, and Brandeis wrote to his daughter Elizabeth that he thought a general depression had begun.

The stock market crash did not cause the Great Depression that followed, but it did serve as a vivid opening act. It took some time before Americans realized that the most severe economic downturn in the nation's history had been under way since earlier that summer. President Herbert Hoover, trying to reassure worried investors, announced on 25 October that "the fundamental business of the country, that is, production and distribution of commodities, is on a sound and prosperous basis," and most businessmen and economic analysts agreed with him. By the time Franklin D. Roosevelt took the oath of office on 4 March 1933, however, four in ten Americans had lost their jobs, factories worked at minimal production or had closed, the nation's banking system had failed, and farmers could not sell their crops.

The Great Depression affected Louis Brandeis in many ways, but not in terms of his personal finances. He had invested in safe bonds, and his income suffered only a minor diminution; his gross income in 1929 had been $137,372, and never dropped below $134,000 over the next decade. He increased his gifts to relatives and friends and also maintained his level of giving to Zionism, savings bank insurance, and the Harvard and Louisville law schools.

The Depression bore out Brandeis's prophecies that Republican prosperity rested on a foundation of sand and that gambling—which is how he saw the stock market—would eventually lead to great losses. But even though he did not anticipate how great those losses would be or how severe the economic disaster, he saw hope in having the bubble burst. Perhaps saner heads would now prevail and put in place the remedies that would allow the country to flourish without the distortions and the bigness that had marked the prior decade.

The Depression also challenged the Court, as first states and then the federal government enacted measures to ameliorate the hardships. William Howard Taft left the Court in 1930, but his replacement, Charles Evans Hughes, presided over a bench in which four hard-line conservatives still opposed every effort by government to interfere with the market, and the Four Horsemen could usually pick up a fifth vote. Brandeis's pleas for judicial restraint fell on deaf ears.

WHATEVER ONE THINKS of Brandeis and his views on bigness, even a cursory reading of his letters in the 1920s shows his economic sophistication. He recognized and called attention to nearly every problem of production and finance later identified as causes of the Depression. "I wish to record my utter inability to understand why a lot of folks don't go broke," he declared in 1926. He knew there would be a reckoning, but did not foresee when that would come, how severe it would be, or how long it would last. But he was certain that "the blood-letting will doubtless be as good for the body politic as cupping and leeching was supposed to be for humans half a century ago."

As early as 1922, Brandeis recognized that the so-called boom had very weak underpinnings. In the nineteenth century, innovations in production and transportation had led to cost reductions that had been passed on in the form of lower prices to the consumer. Since 1900, quite the opposite development had taken place, with production costs and consumer prices rising, not for lack of invention, but because large companies increased their profit margins. Distribution had become the job of middlemen, whose costs added to the final price of every product. Consumers paid more, but workers did not see an equivalent rise in their wages. As a result, a small percentage of the population realized great wealth, while the majority of Americans paid more for their costs of living on wages that failed to increase. As the decade wore on, the discrepancy in income distribution grew worse.

The following year Brandeis complained about the tax policies of the Harding administration and Secretary of the Treasury Andrew W. Mellon, which benefited large corporations and railroads at the expense of the middle class. If bigger companies were as efficient as they claimed to be, they could easily afford to pay higher taxes and should consider it a sort of excess profits tax.

Analysts and economic historians have seen agriculture as the weakest part of the 1920s economy, and the depression in agricultural prices began well before the 1920 stock crash. Brandeis, aside from his passion for government reports, had direct links to the farm sector through his brother, Alfred, and visitors from the Midwest. He understood that farmers faced a terrible squeeze between costs related to the overpriced value of their land and the prices they received for their goods.

The Federal Reserve System had been intended to free smaller banks from the tyranny of the large Wall Street firms, by allowing them to discount their loans directly to the Fed without having to go through Wall Street. This, however, had the unintended consequence of freeing up billions of dollars in credit, which banks lent for all sorts of speculative purposes, including buying stocks on margin and investing in European ventures. Instead of putting money into productive uses, Americans now had more funds with which to gamble. Brandeis also thought the new mode of consumers buying on credit contributed to this problem, and considered it a form of speculation.

Brandeis understood that despite the promises of Republican politicians, the country had not reached a "permanent plateau of prosperity." In February 1933, Bruce Barton, one of the most influential advertising men of the twentieth century, said that the only person who had foreseen events clearly had been Louis Brandeis. In a 1922 rate case, a Texas electric company had complained of the rate set by the city's utility commission, claiming that a plateau of prices at least 70 percent above the 1914 level should be accepted as the proper basis for rate setting. Brandeis spoke for a unanimous Court in upholding a special master's finding that such a level did not exist. The following year he pointed to the history of the past century and noted that the one thing anyone could say with certainty about prices is that they went up and they also came down; there was no permanent plateau. "Who else in 1923," asked Barton, "would have had the temerity to believe that prices could again drop below the 1914 lows?"

Brandeis read government reports and in March 1928 declared that the Labor Department numbers grossly misled the public regarding unemployment. The actual jobless rates far surpassed those announced by the secretary of labor, and he began to drum up support for his old battle against irregularity in employment. He told Paul Kellogg that the *Survey* should "take up vigorously and persistently the musts of Regularity in Employment." The recent rise in unemployment should be the occasion to assert a worker's right to regularity in his or her job—"a moral right, in a civilized community, superior to the right to dividends and equal, at least, to the right to regularity in the receipt of income from rents and interest."

When Kellogg and Robert Bruère asked the justice to define what he meant, he wrote out a paragraph that they could use. According to his daughter, while Brandeis had certainly argued for employment regularity, he had never before defined it that cogently, and when the two editors wanted to identify Brandeis as the author, he agreed on the condition that they attribute it to his earlier writings. It appeared on the front page of the April 1929 issue of *Survey Graphic:*

> For the Commonwealther who is "steady in his work," there shall be steady work. The right to regularity in employment is co-equal with the right to regularity in the payment of rent, in the payment of interest on bonds, in the delivery to customers of the high quality of product contracted for. No business is conducted successfully which does not perform fully the obligations incident to each of these rights. Each of these obligations is equally a fixed charge. No dividend should be paid unless each of these fixed charges has been met. The reserve to ensure regularity of employment is as imperative as the reserve for depreciation; and it is equally a part of the fixed charges to make the annual contribution to that reserve. No business is socially solvent which cannot do so.

Although the statement did not receive much attention in 1928, by the early 1930s reformers seeking to change the labor market referred to it constantly.

In February 1932, Brandeis declared that "the widespread suffering, the economic helplessness and the general dejection are appalling; and most painful the absence of any sense of shame on the part of those primarily responsible for existing conditions. But the process of debunking continues; and if the depression is long continued—which seems likely—America will gain much from her sad experience." He did not believe there would be a violent revolution, but he did not know how or when the country would recover. The hardships would contribute to a revival of liberalism after too many years of Harding-Coolidge-Hoover cynicism and materialism.

The justice himself played a critical role at one point in preventing violence. In the spring and summer of 1932 thousands of war veterans converged on Washington. Calling themselves the Bonus Expeditionary Force, they lobbied for the early payment of the war service "bonus" passed by Congress in 1920 and payable in 1945. When the Senate refused to pass the bill, a majority of the bonus marchers returned home. But several thousand of them—many of them homeless and with their families in tow—stayed in the buildings they had occupied on Pennsylvania Avenue and on Anacostia Flats. At Hoover's urging, the District of Columbia police tried to evict them on 28 July 1932, and an ugly riot ensued in which two of the veterans were shot.

Bonus marchers' camp on Anacostia Flats, Washington, D.C., 1932

The police chief, Pelham D. Glassford, known to everyone as Happy Glassford, had tried to avoid this violence as much as possible; a former officer in the army, Glassford had no desire to fight the veterans. The newspaperman Gardner Jackson took him to see Brandeis several times while the bonus marchers were in town, and the justice counseled the chief that he should do everything possible to avoid violence. For Brandeis, whatever other issues might be involved, the veterans had done no more than to invoke a basic constitutional right—the right of the people to petition their government. After the 28 July debacle, Glassford refused to use his police force to evict the marchers, and President Hoover, fearful of revolution, sent in the army under General Douglas MacArthur. The ultraconservative MacArthur used bayonets and tear gas to disperse the veterans, and the "Battle of Anacostia Flats" marked the low point of the Hoover administration.

INITIALLY, NEITHER THE FEDERAL nor the state governments reacted to the Depression. It had never been assumed by most Americans that government had any obligation to act in such circumstances. While reformers wanted to level the playing field between labor and management and to impose fair working conditions, neither Democrats nor Republicans believed that government should go any further. When the Great Depression proved to be more than a "minor correction," government slowly began to respond with a variety of relief measures. These measures would be challenged in the courts, and given the judiciary's previously hostile attitude to any effort of the state to interfere with business, they faced an uncertain future. Moreover, the Court that would hear these cases had changed.

In the fall of 1929, with his health failing, Taft began to worry about the future of the Court. He did not trust Herbert Hoover to make the right kinds of appointments, suspecting the president of being "a Progressive just as Stone is, and just as Brandeis is and just as Holmes is." To Pierce Butler he wrote that his most fervent hope was for "continued life of enough of our present membership . . . to prevent disastrous reversals of our present attitudes. With Van [Devanter] and McReynolds and Sutherland and you and Sanford, there will be five to steady the boat." In December Taft fell fatally ill and did not sit with the Court after 6 January 1930; he retired on 3 February and died a little over a month later.

When Taft stepped down, Hoover sent in the name of Charles Evans Hughes to take his place. Taft must have been pleased. He had, after all, named Hughes to the bench as an associate justice in 1910 and had considered Hughes to have the stature to head the Court. As far as Taft could tell, Hughes shared his basic judicial philosophy and would keep the Court on its proper course. Although progressives attacked Hughes as a tool of big business, the former secretary of state and Wall Street lawyer was no Taft clone. Far more than Taft, he understood the dangers of a judiciary blindly defending property and ignoring the general welfare.

When Brandeis heard of Hughes's nomination, he declared that "confirmation ought to be made at once and ought to be unanimous." Brandeis had first met Hughes when the latter had just started out in practice, and had thought well of him during the insurance investigations and as a progressive governor of New York. Above all, Hughes had a passion for data almost as great as that of Brandeis. The new chief trusted facts, looked to them to guide his thinking, and once said that he "believed in God but believed equally that God was on the side of the facts." When Brandeis had joined the bench in 1916, Hughes had welcomed him warmly.

Brandeis valued how well Hughes managed the conference, which in Taft's later years had often run on for hours and hours. Hughes had a simple, direct manner. He would summarize the facts of the case, and while the justices had time to discuss the merits, the chief moved things along briskly, so that Brandeis and others could now plan on the Saturday conference ending at 4:30. When on a few occasions the meeting ran later, Brandeis picked up the old-fashioned green bag he used to carry his papers (perhaps even the same one he had used at Harvard) and announced to Hughes: "Your jurisdiction has expired and that of Mrs. Brandeis has begun. I am leaving my vote." Although some of the justices growled at the chief's hyper-efficiency, Brandeis welcomed it. He told a friend that Hughes was the greatest executive genius he had ever encountered in law, in business, or in government.

On the very same day that Taft died, so, too, did Edward Terry Sanford, one of the men he had counted on to keep the conservative boat stable. To replace him, Hoover nominated Owen Josephus Roberts, a Philadelphia lawyer who had won renown as one of the two special U.S. attorneys assigned to investigate the Teapot Dome scandals. Roberts had then returned to private practice, and had not sought a judicial appointment; in fact, he had no clear judicial philosophy and lacked the temperament to be a member of the high court. He tended to side with liberals in civil liberties cases but wavered on economic questions. Roberts ignored the dynamic aspects of law and assumed that both law and society remained static.

The greatest change, and the one that affected Brandeis most, involved Holmes. Throughout the 1920s, Brandeis had kept a careful watch over his friend. Holmes had been ill several times and hospitalized for surgery once, and each time had recovered, much to Brandeis's joy. In 1925, Brandeis reported how finely Holmes had "borne himself in the struggle against Father Time. There is no impairment of his working powers; and he retains equally his keen senses for the enjoyment of things worthwhile." During the interregnum following Taft's last illness, Holmes as senior justice presided over the Court. "He is indeed 'to the manner born,' " Brandeis told Frankfurter. "He is presiding with great firmness, alertness and joy. A marked rejuvenescence has been effected." Following one meeting, Brandeis reported that Harlan Stone had said it was the best conference he had attended since coming on the Court.

By the start of the October 1931 term, however, age and illness had sapped Holmes's ability to work. In his autobiography, Hughes wrote that "it appeared that [Holmes] was slipping. While he was still able to write clearly, it became evident in the conferences of the Justices that he could no longer do his full share." Three months passed before his colleagues decided that something had to be done. Hughes then consulted privately with Brandeis, and on a Sunday morning, 10 January 1932, went to see Holmes. The old soldier understood what had to be done, asked his clerk to get the proper volume of statutes, and wrote out his resignation. As soon as Hughes left, Brandeis arrived, clearly by a prior arrangement with Hughes, and spent an hour with his old friend. Later that day, Brandeis dropped him a note: "O.W.H. Dec. 8, 1902–Jan. 12, 1932. 'Ich habe gelebt und geliebt.' [I have lived and loved]." For the next three years Brandeis went to see Holmes two or three times a week until his death in March 1935.

Hoover faced a great deal of pressure in choosing Holmes's successor; no ordinary appointee would do to replace the Magnificent Yankee. Many people wanted the president to name the chief judge of the New York State Court of Appeals, Benjamin Nathan Cardozo, but Hoover hesitated. Cardozo was a Democrat, a Jew, and a New Yorker, and there was already one Jew (Brandeis) and two New Yorkers (Stone and Hughes) on the high court. In the end he gave in to the pressure and named Cardozo, which may have been the most popular act of his beleaguered presidency.

Cardozo had a reputation as a judge's judge, and next to Holmes was perhaps the greatest common-law jurist of the century. Scholars credit him with transforming major sections of the law, and his 1921 Storrs

Lectures at Yale, published as *The Nature of the Judicial Process,* constituted a key building block of Legal Realism. Cardozo believed that
legal rules had to be measured by their social utility and their contributions to the overall good of society. Brandeis had enormous respect for
Cardozo, and once wrote in amazement to Frankfurter after the
Supreme Court reversed a Cardozo opinion *per curiam.* A judge of Cardozo's stature deserved better than Brandeis's brethren had given him.

Cardozo never became a great Supreme Court justice, although he
wrote several important opinions. A shy, retiring man, he was used to
the civility of the New York courts, and he did not like Washington or
the nastiness of McReynolds's behavior toward him. He had a frail constitution, and Brandeis tried to look after him. Louis and Alice regularly asked the bachelor to dinner on Thanksgiving and before
Christmas and also to the Monday afternoon teas. Cardozo did not like
to go too often, because he found the Brandeis apartment overheated.
He and Brandeis also disagreed on just how certain a judge must be
before deciding a case. Cardozo liked to be completely sure of his decision, and Brandeis once commented to one of Cardozo's law clerks,
"The trouble with your Judge is that he thinks he has to be one hundred percent right. He doesn't realize that it is enough to be fifty-one
percent right." Cardozo had the intellectual ability to become a great
justice, but in 1938 he fell ill and died after only five terms on the
bench.

What would these changes mean as the Depression deepened? No
one had any idea what sort of judge Roberts would be. Cardozo in
Holmes's seat would make little difference, and while Hughes appeared
to be more liberal in some areas than Taft, in economic matters he probably stood fairly close to the old chief. Hughes and Roberts defied
simple characterization, but in general they eschewed ideological ab-
solutes, believed in fidelity to precedent, and tried to decide each case
on its own facts. When a high-school student asked Hughes to catego-
rize himself as a liberal or a conservative, he replied that he had no use
for either label. "Such characterizations," he explained to a meeting of
Fourth Circuit judges, "serve as a very poor substitute for intelligent
criticism. A judge who does his work in an objective spirit, as a judge
should, will address himself conscientiously to each case, and will not
trouble himself about labels." The first signs, however, gave liberals
hope.

In a free-speech case, Hughes spoke for a 7–2 majority in striking
down a California law prohibiting the flying of a red flag in a public

place. In an opinion happily joined by Brandeis, Hughes made clear that he considered free speech and expression so important that they should not be cramped within narrow brackets. The following week Hughes dissented, joined by Holmes, Brandeis, and Stone, in *United States v. Macintosh.* The United States had denied American citizenship to the Canadian-born chaplain at the Yale Graduate School solely on the grounds that, as a pacifist, he could not swear to take up arms in defense of the United States. Hughes wrote a moving dissent that echoed much of what Holmes had written two years earlier in the *Schwimmer* case, that the government ought not to punish people for holding unpopular ideas.

The most important case grew out of a Minnesota law authorizing the suppression of any "malicious, scandalous and defamatory newspaper or other periodical" as a public nuisance. The statute had been enacted specifically to silence the *Saturday Press,* a tabloid that had the annoying habit of exposing corruption in Minneapolis. The case had been argued after Taft had fallen ill, but not decided until Hughes came onto the bench. Given the speech decisions of the prior decade, it is likely that had Taft voted, he would have joined the Four Horsemen to uphold the law, and there is evidence that if that occurred, Brandeis stood ready to prepare a dissent. But a five-man majority, consisting of the chief justice, Holmes, Brandeis, Stone, and Roberts struck the law down as a violation of the First Amendment protection of the press, and in doing so extended the Press Clause to the states.

But would this majority hold together when it came to economic regulations?

ONE OF THE EARLIEST Depression cases to come before the Court involved an Oklahoma statute that treated the manufacture of ice as a public utility and required a certificate of convenience for entering the business. The legislature had reasoned that during the Depression stabilizing the market mattered more than promoting an unfettered competition that could deprive some parts of the state of ice. In practical terms, however, it shut out new enterprises and gave existing companies a monopoly. When Ernest Liebmann opened an ice business without a state certificate, New State Ice, which had a license, sued to stop him. The previous term Brandeis had written a 5–4 opinion sustaining a New Jersey law regulating insurance companies, and both Hughes and Roberts had been with him. Now the two joined the conservative bloc to strike down the Oklahoma statute. Speaking through Justice Sutherland, the majority denied that ice could be considered affected with a public interest and concluded that it could not be legitimately regulated by the state. In addition, the law fostered monopoly. Perhaps most galling to reformers, Sutherland dismissed the idea that economic difficulties confronting the states allowed them to ignore the Due Process Clause. New conditions did not justify experimentation with eternal verities.

One might have expected Brandeis, with his well-known antipathy to monopoly, to have voted against the regulation; instead, he entered a powerful dissent (joined by Stone) that would be a rallying point for judicial liberals in the next five years. His opinion encapsulated all the arguments that opponents of substantive due process had been making ever since Holmes's dissent in *Lochner.* "Whether the local conditions are such as to justify converting a private business into a public one is a matter primarily for the determination of the state legislature," he declared. "Whether the grievances are real or fancied, whether the remedies are wise or foolish, are not matters about which the Court may concern itself." Brandeis anticipated the stance that the Court would adopt within a few years, namely, that no arbitrary distinction existed between private property and that affected with a public interest, because all depended upon the facts of the situation. This determination, he insisted, had to be left to the legislature, and the "action of the State must be held valid unless clearly arbitrary, capricious or unreasonable."

To determine that, the Court had to understand the facts behind the legislative decision, and with characteristic thoroughness he lectured the Court on the complexities of the ice business and the conditions in Oklahoma that led the legislature to make its decision. Ice had "come to be regarded as a household necessity, indispensable to the preservation of food and so to economical household management and the maintenance of health," especially in a state like Oklahoma, where the warm climate made it impossible to rely on natural ice and where mechanical household refrigerators were still a rarity. Examining the highly competitive character of the industry, he concluded that the legislature could reasonably have determined that the ice industry lent itself to monopoly, and thus could be regulated as a public utility. The legislature had studied the problem of ice making and its regulation for seventeen years; the courts had no business second-guessing its conclusion. While conceding that courts had the power to strike down legislation, he warned that "in the exercise of this high power, we must be ever on our guard, lest we erect our prejudices into legal principles. If we would guide by the light of reason, we must let our minds be bold."

Finally, Brandeis called upon a principle that most constitutional conservatives held dear—federalism. Although "man is weak and his judgment is at best fallible," the conditions of the Depression cried out for experimentation. "I cannot believe that the framers of the Fourteenth Amendment, or the States which ratified it, intended to deprive us of the power to correct the evils of technological unemployment and excess productive capacity." But although the Depression affected the entire nation, the country as a whole did not have to undertake untried programs. "It is one of the happy incidents of the federal system that a single courageous State may, if its citizens choose, serve as a laboratory; and try novel social and economic experiments without risk to the rest of the country."

Although reformers saw the majority decision as a setback, many predicted—or at least hoped—that Brandeis's dissent would exert a powerful influence on legislators and courts to become more flexible, and that in time it would be accepted as the majority view in the high court. This, of course, did happen, and the distinction between public and private, as a constitutional matter in economic policy, all but disappeared. But Brandeis's opinion had an even greater influence on modern notions of federalism. Instead of looking at the states and the federal government as antagonists, each fighting to protect its powers, Brandeis suggested a new paradigm in which the states and the national government held sovereignty over clearly defined areas, a notion he had earlier advanced regarding prohibition enforcement. The Court has recognized that the federal power not only is supreme in many instances but in modern times must be. The economy of the late twentieth and early twenty-first century not only is national in scope but is rapidly becoming global. One cannot have Massachusetts or New Jersey negotiating commercial treaties (a fact recognized by the Framers), and one cannot have states establishing regulations that impact far outside their borders.

What Brandeis suggested has been called "experimental federalism," and looks to the states as laboratories of democracy. Throughout his life Brandeis believed that the greatest opportunities for establishing good government responsive to popular needs existed at the state level, and not in Washington (which would be the reason he distrusted much of the New Deal). Adaptation to changing times required knowledge of local conditions, which varied enormously across the country. A one-size-fits-all solution, the only kind that Congress could enact, did not take into account local differences. This the states could do, and if a solution to a novel problem worked in Oklahoma or California, then other states—without risk to themselves—could discuss whether the plan might succeed for them. Brandeis may or may not have supported the notion of physician-assisted suicide, but it is likely that he would have backed the right of Oregon to enact such a plan. In the Supreme Court case challenging laws against assisted suicide, the justices cited Brandeis's *New State Ice* dissent as the proper way to go forward with such a radical idea.

Two years after *New State Ice,* the conservatives voided another law, one that struck a responsive chord with Brandeis. A 1931 Florida law imposed a 25–50 percent higher tax per store on owners who had outlets in different counties, a measure clearly aimed at chain stores. The conservative majority, utilizing the Equal Protection Clause, declared that the state could not discriminate solely on the basis that an owner had several stores in different counties. Roberts distinguished the case from an earlier decision in which the Court had upheld an Indiana tax on chain stores. That tax had been justified because chain stores did business in a substantially different manner from individual enter-prises; Florida's discriminatory tax, based on nothing more than location, could not be deemed reasonable.

Brandeis, who personally opposed chain stores, entered a long dissent, and here there is no question that he strongly supported the legislation under attack. The distinction that Roberts drew between a valid Indiana chain store tax and the Florida statute made no sense, since the Florida legislature had clearly intended the tax to apply to chain stores. Each of the twelve petitioners in the suit was a corporation—not an individual—and each operated a series of chain stores of varying sizes. Then, in the typical Brandeis manner, he went into the facts that the Florida legislature had taken into account, the problem it tried to solve, and the reasonableness of its solution, about which the courts had no business second-guessing.

Many people believed, he claimed, that part of the current unemployment problem resulted in the "gross inequality in the distribution of wealth and income which giant corporations have fostered." The Florida legislature could reasonably have concluded that encouraging individual initiative would help restore prosperity and protect liberty. If a state believed that adequate protection against the abuse of corporate privilege can be secured through discriminatory taxes rather than revoking the corporate charters, "I know nothing in the Fourteenth Amendment to prevent it from making the experiment." He then reviewed the history of the different ways in which various states had attempted to manage corporations and prevent them from abusing their powers. The Florida tax, therefore, was not a simple revenue measure, but had social and economic goals, namely, to rein in the menace of chain stores and to foster competition by individual stores. To Brandeis this seemed a very reasonable thing to do, and he marshaled his facts to back his assertion.

Even though he called for judicial restraint, in this case Brandeis the jurist strongly approved of what Florida had tried to do, and Brandeis the reformer explained why. In doing so, he went so far that Stone could not join him. "I think you are too much an advocate of this particular legislation," Stone told him, "I have little enthusiasm for it, although I think it constitutional. In any case I think our dissents are more effective if we take the attitude that we are concerned with power and not with the merits of its exercise." Paul Freund, Brandeis's clerk that term, agreed that Brandeis really cared about this case; he may have had some reservation about the Oklahoma ice law, but not about the Florida tax. Brandeis adapted the long written opinion to a shorter version for oral delivery, something he rarely did in dissent. He spoke with great feeling, leaning forward on the bench and saying almost colloquially, "You know, we all know, why states pass these laws," and the judgment of Florida ought to be confirmed.

THE COURT SEEMED TO RESPOND to Brandeis's plea for judicial restraint and allowing the states greater leeway in meeting the challenge of the Depression when it reviewed the Minnesota Mortgage Moratorium Act in 1933. Farmers, because of collapsed markets, had no money to pay their mortgages and were losing their homesteads. The statute, clearly an emergency measure, permitted local courts to extend the period of redemption between foreclosure and sale to give farmers additional time to raise money. The statute did not permit an indefinite extension, nor did it cancel the debt; it merely adjusted the remedy available to the creditor.

Brandeis, Stone, Roberts, and Cardozo joined the chief justice's opinion sustaining the law. While "an emergency does not create power," Hughes declared, it could be the occasion for the exercise of latent power. He then recited a long list of measures adopted by the states and approved by the courts under the police power to protect the health and safety of the citizens. Responding to Sutherland's dissent that the Framers had intended the Contract Clause to be inviolate under any and all circumstances, Hughes quoted John Marshall's famous dictum:

"We must never forget that it is a constitution we are expounding, a constitution intended for ages to come, and, consequently, to be adopted to the various crises of human affairs." Hughes found the crisis of the Depression sufficiently serious to allow Minnesota to act as it had. The majority had upheld the law primarily because it had been limited and did not prevent foreclosures; when Arkansas tried to go further and permanently exempt payments for life insurance from garnishment, Hughes spoke for a unanimous Court in striking it down.

Then in another state Depression law, a 5–4 majority upheld the New York State Milk Act of 1933, and Justice Roberts's opinion echoed Brandeis's dissent in *New State Ice* insofar as it dismissed any distinction between public and private. In the face of declining milk prices for dairy farmers, the state established a control board to regulate the entire milk industry, with power to set minimum wholesale and retail prices. The law aimed to stabilize markets and eliminate cutthroat competition. Leo Nebbia, a Rochester grocer, had been convicted of selling milk below the price set by the board. He claimed that the law unduly restricted his property, and beyond that, the milk business could not be considered as affected with a public interest, so any state control unconstitutionally interfered with the market. Had this case been heard with Taft and Sanford on the Court, it is likely that the law would have been struck down.

But Roberts apparently adopted Brandeis's argument that the public need overrode traditional property rights. The state had recognized a problem and had taken reasonable steps to try to mitigate the difficulties; the wisdom of these steps did not concern the Court. Roberts asked if any constitutional prohibition existed to prevent a state from attempting to alleviate problems caused by an aberrant market. In words that chilled the conservatives, he declared, "We think there is no such principle." The relation of any business to the public interest depended on current conditions, and any business might legitimately be deemed affected with a public interest and subject to regulation. Only a showing that the regulations had been unreasonable, arbitrary, or discriminatory would justify judicial intervention. Roberts's definition of the public interest took away any distinction between public and private property, leading McReynolds to declare that *Nebbia,* taken together with *Blaisdell,* "marked the end of the constitution as you and I regarded it. An alien influence has prevailed."

Certainly liberal commentators believed that the Brandeis point of view had prevailed and that the Court would now routinely approve

The Supreme Court in 1932. Seated from left: Louis D. Brandeis, Willis Van Devanter, Chief Justice Charles Evans Hughes, James C. McReynolds, George Sutherland; standing from left: Owen J. Roberts, Pierce Butler, Harlan Fiske Stone, Benjamin N. Cardozo.

state and federal anti-Depression measures. The *New Republic,* for example, predicted that it would be difficult for conservatives to recapture the lost ground, because the likelihood of continued economic turmoil would demand new measures. Liberals, however, had miscalculated where Hughes and Roberts would wind up. Roberts apparently paced the floor of his home for hours in indecision before casting his vote in *Nebbia,* and he would be won over by the conservatives in a series of important cases involving both federal and state legislation. While Hughes had sounded liberal in *Blaisdell,* he had also had important institutional concerns. When it became apparent that the conservatives could count on Roberts, he often joined them to avoid 5–4 decisions.

Those who thought the Court had abandoned the last vestiges of substantive due process and freedom of contract learned differently in June 1936. Roberts joined the conservatives to invalidate a 1933 New York minimum-wage law for women and children. Sutherland's opinion for the Four Horsemen and Roberts relied entirely on *Adkins v. Children's Hospital* (1923) and resurrected *Lochner* in full strength. Even normally conservative newspapers termed the ruling "regrettable," and the Republican candidate for president, Alfred M. Landon, carefully distanced himself from the Court's conservative bloc. The Republican Party platform that year specifically approved of state regulation of wages and hours for women and children.

Brandeis joined the dissents of both Stone and Hughes. Stone called for the Court to be consistent and follow the precedent of *Nebbia,* leaving the wisdom of solving problems to the legislative branch. Hughes found the majority opinion incomprehensible and declared that he found nothing in the Constitution "which denies to the State the power to protect women from being exploited." The slim majorities in upholding state legislation, and the lack of clear statements from Hughes and especially Roberts, raised the very real specter that when the statutes passed by the federal government came before the Court, the conservatives would have enough votes to invalidate them.

THE GREAT DEPRESSION not only touched Brandeis's work on the Court; it also affected at least one aspect of his extrajudicial activity. Brandeis, Julian Mack, Stephen Wise, and the other members of the Brandeis faction in American Zionism had believed from the time they resigned from leadership in 1921 that the policies of Chaim Weizmann and his lieutenant Louis Lipsky would lead to disaster for the Zionist Organization of America. The ZOA struggled throughout the 1920s, and when Weizmann went to set up the Jewish Agency for Palestine, he all but ignored Lipsky. The Depression did not sink the Lipsky leadership—it was already in serious trouble—but it hastened the end.

By 1929 many of the people who had supported Weizmann at Cleveland were speaking of the need for private investment and the development of small business in Palestine. In lobbying Louis Marshall and the American Jewish Committee, Weizmann abandoned his earlier program and, although he did not mention Brandeis by name, adopted all of his main arguments. Shortly after the establishment of the Jewish Agency, Horace Kallen and others issued a statement that the Brandeis plan now stood triumphant. With the growing acceptance of Brandeis's ideas came a demand for the return of the old leadership.

Brandeis understood when a few members of his group tried to make peace with Louis Lipsky and his backers and served on the United Palestine Appeal or other ZOA committees, but he insisted there could be no compromise with "Lipsky or any of his ilk." Brandeis's antipathy to Lipsky went far beyond resentment over the loss of power; indeed, in no other area of his voluminous correspondence can we find such hostility toward an individual. Zionism had appealed to him because of what he saw as its nobility and idealism, and part of the synthesis of Zionism and Americanism had been the emphasis on moral uplift and on sacrifice. While he did not trust Weizmann or believe in his policies, Brandeis met with the WZO leader several times in the 1920s and on occasion sent written approval of some particular action. He did this because, no matter how wrongheaded he thought Weizmann was, he recognized his deep commitment to Zionism, and he saw Weizmann devoting his entire life to the cause and at great personal sacrifice.

In New York he saw nothing but men drawing salaries while they ran the ZOA into the ground, mismanaged its finances, allowed its membership to dwindle, and incurred a debt of over $140,000. When Charles Cowen visited the justice for advice on some Zionist matters, he got more than he had bargained for. "For five minutes," Brandeis wrote, "I spoke to him impressively and torrentially of the shame to the Jewish people which had come from this self-seeking, incompetent and dishonest administration, which had prostituted a great cause; which, enjoying fat salaries in New York, had let school teachers in Palestine starve with six months of salaries in arrears; which had defied the teachings of the prophets that had sustained and maintained the Jewish People throughout the centuries." When Cowen feebly asked what should be done, Brandeis, who had begun to look like an Old Testament prophet himself, answered: "Only the teachings of the prophets; return to truth, put an end to the lying. Turn out those who have obtained money under false pretenses and misappropriated that which they secured."

As dissatisfaction with Lipsky grew, and as the ZOA's troubles deepened, Jacob de Haas, Stephen Wise, and others began holding meetings to see what could be done to recapture the organization. Lipsky, no political naïf himself, managed to stay in power, but he saw his base of support dwindling. Then, on 23 August 1929, Arab mobs rioted in Palestine, leaving 125 Jews dead. Jews all over the world protested, and prominent non-Zionists like Herbert Lehman and Adolph Ochs publicly proclaimed their support of the *yishuv* and contributed generously to an emergency fund that raised $2.1 million to aid the victims. Jews called on Britain to live up to its obligations, but Chaim Weizmann could not influence his British friends at all, and eventually the British government issued a white paper temporarily stopping all immigration into Palestine. Felix Warburg, the chairman of the Jewish Agency, resigned, and this non-Zionist became the symbol of Jewish protest.

Lipsky, like Weizmann, appeared impotent; he carried no influence in the American government or with his alleged non-Zionist colleagues, and very little within the movement. By the fall of 1929, American Zionism was falling apart, and its leadership seemed totally incapable of leading.

Without a base in the Zionist movement, Brandeis and his followers felt helpless in responding to the crises both in Palestine and in the ZOA. They would not work with Lipsky, so they decided to feel out Warburg and the non-Zionists. Bernard Flexner approached the banker on the justice's behalf, and Warburg jumped at the chance. It was indicative of the changed circumstances in American Jewry that Warburg suggested that Brandeis leave the bench and assume direction not only of the Zionist movement but of the American Jewish Committee as well. This, of course, Brandeis would not do, but he agreed to participate in a conference on economic aid for Palestine and deemed the occasion so grave that he agreed to give a talk there, his first public pronouncement on Zionism in over eight years, and one of the very few he made while on the bench.

The meeting sealed the rapprochement between the Brandeis Zionists and the German Jews who had opposed them. No one spoke of the old wounds, but only of Palestine and the future. Brandeis publicly declared his faith that Jewish intelligence and fortitude would triumph in Palestine, and he reaffirmed his belief in the inevitability of a strong Jewish homeland there. "The road is economic," he said, "and the opportunity is open." (The conference established a committee to raise funds for economic development, but the plan had to be scrapped once the full extent of the Depression became known.) The main import of the conference, of course, lay in the apparent return of Brandeis to an active role in Zionism. Rabbi Louis I. Newman wrote a rhapsodic article titled "The Return of the Pilot." The *Jewish Tribune* declared that the conference had brought back "a great leader to public participation in the tasks of rebuilding a Jewish homeland." Even the ZOA organ printed his speech in full.

Although, as he told Felix Frankfurter, "the severe limitations which judicial office and my small vitality impose" would make active leadership impossible, Brandeis began directing the recapture of the ZOA with all the energy and hardheadedness that had marked his earlier reform efforts. To Jacob de Haas, Julian Mack, Stephen Wise, Frankfurter, and others went a stream of letters directing them to speak to particular people, make sure news stories were released, arrange for support of Hadassah, and to take other steps. When the ZOA met in Cleveland in June 1930, the atmosphere was tense. Representatives of the Brandeis-Mack faction met secretly with the Lipsky group to try to work out a compromise and avoid bloodletting that could only weaken the ZOA even further, but these negotiations proved difficult and protracted. From time to time someone would appear in the hall to announce that no agreement had yet been hammered out. During one of these moments, Robert Szold, a New York lawyer and cousin of Henrietta Szold's, took the podium and read the following letter from Brandeis to the delegates:

> I appreciate the generous suggestion which many of you have made that I should again assume the official responsibility of leadership in the Z.O.A. When eighteen years ago I first gave serious thought to the problems of Jewry and began to search for the means of preserving the spiritual legacies of Israel as an active force in the world, I became a Zionist and a follower of Herzl. My visit to Palestine in 1919 rendered more powerful the appeal; removed any lingering doubts as to the practicability of the undertaking; and convinced me that in carrying out the principles of the Balfour declaration the welfare of both Jews and Arabs would be advanced. The events since have deepened these convictions.
>
> Added years make it impossible for me to assume now the official responsibilities of leadership as I did prior to 1921, but I am ready now as then to serve the cause. Necessarily the service to be rendered must be limited in scope to advising from time to time when requested on questions of major policy. Such service I am now rendering through Mr. Warburg to the Jewish Agency. Such service I can render also to the Z.O.A. In my opinion it will be far more effective if rendered to an administration formed on the general lines of the memorandum of May 22nd, 1930.
>
> My warm greetings and best wishes.

Actually, this letter marked a softening of tone from the earlier memorandum, which had demanded a totally new Zionist Organization of America—new in organization, new in leadership, new in efficiency, and with all of its efforts directed toward the economic rebuilding of Palestine. In the weeks between the release of the memorandum and the convention, Brandeis insisted that no one should attempt to interpret it. The thing that the members had to do, he declared, "is to find themselves. That involves thinking." The memorandum had caused an uproar since among other things it demanded that all officers of the ZOA serve without salary, and the Lipsky forces decided they would not go down without a fight. Szold, however, softened the tone of this memorandum when, after reading Brandeis's letter, he informed the delegates that the justice would advise whether or not the convention accepted the memorandum. Brandeis had been under great pressure from his lieutenants, many of whom had come to Chatham to plead with him to withdraw the demands.

In the end the two groups worked out a compromise that provided for an eighteen-member "neutral committee," six members of which would be appointed by the Lipsky faction and twelve by the Brandeis-Mack group. This committee would then have eighteen months to try to reenergize the ZOA. For all practical purposes, the Brandeis-Mack group had regained control of American Zionism.

Although Brandeis did not take a formal leadership role, informally he resumed the same flow of letters with their recommendations, demands for information, comments on finances, and other details that had marked his Zionist correspondence from 1914 to 1921. The people who had urged his return should be contacted immediately and asked for money: "Let no guilty man escape." There ought to be a complete audit of the books to determine the true financial situation of the ZOA. He needed information on the Hedera settlement and had questions on some reports regarding the cooperative movement in Palestine. He approved of some steps Hadassah had taken in transferring some of its medical work to local communities. Each response led to new queries, new requests for information.

But even while he amassed this information, asked questions, and gave advice, he left the day-to-day operations of the ZOA in the hands of Bob Szold, whom he trusted implicitly. The constraints of office and his age did make it impossible for him to be the type of leader he had been earlier. It made little difference to the rank-and-file Zionists, for, as far as they were concerned, the "pilot," in Louis Newman's phrase, had returned.

The victory, however, proved somewhat hollow. The Brandeisians had assumed that everything wrong with the ZOA could be fixed by throwing out Lipsky and his ilk, but they soon learned differently. The return to power came at a time when the Depression made it almost impossible to secure men or money. Many Jews just did not have the cash either to pay the Zionist dues or to donate to a fund; they had all they could handle in trying to find work and keep their families together. The wealthier Jews gave their moneys to Palestine through the Jewish Agency, but even they felt the pinch of the Depression, and the agency never realized Weizmann's hopes for it.

Beyond that, in the 1930s Great Britain seemed determined to appease the Arab world and slowly but surely reneged on its commitment in the Balfour Declaration. Weizmann had little authority with His Majesty's Government, and Brandeis, while he had some contacts in London, lacked the influence in Washington he had when Woodrow Wilson had been president. The British cut off immigration to Palestine at the same time that Adolf Hitler came to power in Germany, a time when European Jews more than ever needed a safe haven. The 1930s would be difficult years for American Zionism, but the Brandeis group did lay a foundation for its rebirth at the end of the decade.

IN NOVEMBER 1931, Louis Brandeis celebrated his seventy-fifth birthday, and congratulations poured in from everywhere. The *New York Times,* which had once doubted his fitness to sit on the bench, now declared that "the country, and not he, is to be congratulated. . . . Year by year his stature as a Judge has increased." The Harvard, Yale, and Columbia law reviews dedicated their issues to him. Felix Frankfurter collected some of the articles and published them as *Mr. Justice Brandeis,* and asked Oliver Wendell Holmes to write the introduction. Holmes happily obliged, and spoke of their long friendship over the years. "Whenever he left my house I was likely to say to my wife, 'There goes a really good man.' I think that the world would now agree with me in adding what the years have proved—'and a great Judge.' "

By this time Brandeis had assumed an iconic role for reformers. Aside from his career defending progressive measures before he went onto the bench, Brandeis's espousal of judicial restraint endeared him to those who believed that the states had the constitutional authority to respond to a crisis as great as war or the Depression. As questions of civil liberties rose to the fore, the justice's strong stand on freedom of expression appealed to those whose liberal—and in many cases radical—ideas aroused the wrath of the conservative establishment. When Franklin D. Roosevelt proposed his New Deal, they fully expected Brandeis to be a champion of those measures.

CHAPTER TWENTY-EIGHT

THE NEW DEAL

I n the spring of 1934, Rexford Guy Tugwell, a former Columbia University economist and an original member of Franklin Roosevelt's brain trust, scribbled in his diary that Louis Brandeis "was declaring war" against the New Deal. The problem was simple: Brandeis stood against the enlargement of government functions.

Tugwell and other proponents of the early New Deal measures saw the aging justice as the champion of an outmoded atomistic individualism, but Brandeis had mixed feelings about Roosevelt's programs. On the bench, his credo of judicial restraint led him to support most congressional attempts to ameliorate the Great Depression, and he strongly approved of some of the experiments of the 1930s. But when Roosevelt, frustrated by the conservative bloc on the Court invalidating one New Deal law after another, tried to pack the Court with friendlier judges, a furious Brandeis took an active and highly effective role in helping to defeat the plan.

Roosevelt once said, "Brandeis is one thousand percent right on principle," and then added, "But in certain fields there must be a guiding or restraining hand of Government because of the very nature of the specific field." The justice might have agreed with that sentiment, but not with the way the New Deal implemented it.

BRANDEIS HAD KNOWN about Franklin Roosevelt ever since the young man served as assistant secretary of the navy in the Wilson administration and had run as the vice presidential candidate on the Democratic ticket in 1920. During the following decade Felix Frankfurter and Roosevelt, who had met during the war, became friends, and after the 1928 defeat of Al Smith for the presidency Frankfurter saw Roosevelt as the likely Democratic nominee in 1932. A few weeks after

Franklin D. Roosevelt, 1933

the election the justice met with the president-elect and reported, "He has learned much; and realizes, I think, the difficulties of the task."

Although Frankfurter turned down—partly at Brandeis's insistence—the position of solicitor general, the Harvard professor remained an important adviser to the president, and became a one-man employment agency as he directed dozens of his former students to Washington to work in New Deal agencies. Some of these young men had been clerks to Brandeis or Holmes, and kept the justice informed on the latest developments in their work. Frankfurter also served as the conduit by which Brandeis sent bits of advice to the White House. Occasionally, the president asked Brandeis to come to the White House, and after one visit declared, "I had a most satisfactory talk with Justice Brandeis before he left [for Chatham]. He has and is a 'great soul.' "

Brandeis and his ideas had such a powerful influence because the Depression laid bare many of the problems that had been hidden by Republican prosperity, and that Brandeis had been arguing about for more than two decades: manipulation of stocks and securities, the overweening power of big banks, irregular employment, and, of course, the curse of bigness. While the men gathered in the original brain trust, such as Tugwell, Adolf A. Berle Jr., and Raymond Moley, preached government regulation of business and protection of labor—both ideas requiring the expansion of government power—many of the young men who came to Washington in the 1930s found the Brandeis view more attractive, and people such as Thomas Corcoran, Benjamin Cohen, William O. Douglas, Jerome Frank, and David E. Lilienthal gravitated toward Brandeis. With his shock of white hair, the aging justice looked more and more like an Old Testament prophet, and the president and others in the administration began referring to him as "Isaiah."

Hosts of young New Dealers came to see the justice at the Monday afternoon teas, where he would grill them on their work and the accomplishments of their agencies, and he basked in their company. To a cousin he wrote, "Life in Washington now is striving, intellectually far more so than I have ever known it. There is much noble thinking and high endeavor," although he noted also a great deal of impatience. Occasionally, Brandeis could offer solutions to particular difficulties. Hallie

Paul Freund, clerk for the 1932 term

Flanagan, the director of the Federal Theatre Project, had a problem, and she talked about it with James Landis, a former Brandeis clerk who had roomed with her husband at Harvard. The law creating the project prohibited the payment of royalties to authors, which Flanagan considered decidedly unfair to the playwrights. Landis took her to see Brandeis, who after a moment came up with a perfect way out: instead of paying royalties, they should rent the plays on a weekly basis.

Because of his extensive connections, New Dealers from the president down asked the justice if he knew someone for a particular slot, or for his opinion of a potential nominee. For only one position did Brandeis go directly to Roosevelt. In late November 1932, Alice Brandeis called Paul Freund, the justice's clerk that term, and told him to arrange a car for the next day to take her husband to the Mayflower Hotel, where the president-elect had set up his headquarters. Then, she said, you must call Roosevelt's people and tell them that all the windows must be closed because the justice cannot tolerate drafts. Freund decided to go down to the Mayflower that afternoon to scout the area, determine where the meeting would take place, and locate the elevators. He rather diffidently conveyed Mrs. Brandeis's instructions, only to be told not to worry; Roosevelt did not like drafts either.

The next day Freund accompanied the justice to the hotel, went up in the elevator with him, and then waited outside the door while Brandeis and Roosevelt spent about a half hour together. On the way back in the car the jurist told his clerk that he had had only one mission that day, to recommend Frances Perkins as secretary of labor. Roosevelt, of course, knew Madam Perkins well from his days in New York politics, and already had her under consideration. When Roosevelt announced his cabinet—including Perkins—in late February, Brandeis heartily approved. In Perkins, he declared, "we have the best the U.S. affords, and besides it is a distinct advance to have selected a woman for the Cabinet."

Although influential, Brandeis did not have the power that critics attributed to him. A recrudescent anti-Semitism in the 1930s charged that Cardozo, Frankfurter and his "happy little hot dogs" (all Jewish of course), Herbert Lehman, and the president (whose real name was Rosenfelt) worked under the direction of the chief Jew, Brandeis, in the "Jew Deal." The house of Morgan blamed many of its troubles on Brandeis, and believed that the recent reissue of *Other People's Money* had led to the Glass-Steagall Act and its prohibition against banks selling stocks. Russell Leffingwell told Thomas Lamont that he had no doubt that Brandeis had been directly responsible for the law, perhaps even had drafted it. "The Jews do not forget. They are relentless," he claimed. "I believe we are confronted with the profound politico-economic philosophy, matured in the wood for twenty years, of the finest brain and the most powerful personality in the Democratic party, who happens to be a Justice of the Supreme Court."

Scholars disagree on whether there have been one, two, or three New Deals, but there is a consensus that the laws passed in 1933 differed significantly from those passed later. The so-called First New Deal reflected the ideas of Theodore Roosevelt's New Nationalism, as well as ideas of cooperation between business and government gleaned from the war. The Second New Deal had as its antecedent the New Freedom as expounded by Wilson and Brandeis, as well as a strong aversion to monopoly and Wall Street. But during the alleged New Nationalistic phase Congress passed a decidedly Brandeisian measure in the 1934 Securities Exchange Act, while some of the post-1935 laws could hardly be described as "Brandeisian."

Because of the severity of the Depression, Roosevelt and his advisers had insufficient time to plan a coherent policy and instead attacked particular problems piecemeal, trying to satisfy as many constituencies as they could. Roosevelt compared the Depression to a crisis as grave as war itself, and the New Deal in its various measures called upon powers never exercised by the government in peacetime. No one doubted that nearly every one of them would be challenged in the courts.

BY ROOSEVELT'S INAUGURATION on 4 March 1933, thirty-eight states had closed their banks, and night seemed to have fallen when the governors of New York and Illinois suspended banking operations in the nation's two leading financial centers. That same day the New York Stock Exchange closed, as did all the regional commodity and stock exchanges. When Roosevelt took the oath of office, he exclaimed with as much literal as figurative truth that "the money changers have fled from their high seats in the temple of our civilization." When Brandeis heard of the Michigan closings, he termed it "a striking manifestation of the Curse of Bigness," an example of how great corporations, with huge amounts of cash at their disposal, can ruin not only a bank but the individual depositors by transferring their balances. Until they could get honest bankers, however, no remedy would fix the system.

The morning after he took office, the president called Congress into special session, to start on 9 March, and then, acting under the rather doubtful authority of the old 1917 Trading with the Enemy Act, issued a proclamation halting all transactions in gold and declaring a national bank holiday. Roosevelt understood that most of the banks were sound but lacked the liquidity to survive a sustained run on deposits. He went on the radio and told the American people that government examiners were auditing the banks and that after the weekend, if a bank opened, then depositors could be sure their money would be safe. In fact the government lacked the personnel for more than a cursory examination of the banks' books, but psychologically the ploy worked. Although in some ways little more than showmanship, the bank holiday gave the appearance of action—something that had been sorely missing in the Hoover years. On the following Monday people lined up well before the banks opened, but this time to put money into their accounts.

The Congress that convened on 9 March waited for word from the White House as an army awaits orders from a commanding general, and one after another Roosevelt sent bills up to the Capitol—bills on banking, relief, agriculture, public works, labor, conservation—and the Democratic Congress passed them, at times without copies available for all the members to read.

On 21 March, Roosevelt asked Congress to approve a relief measure to put some 250,000 people to work and to send large amounts of money to the states for relief programs. The men would be put to work on conservation, flood control, and other public works projects. The proposal "was just what I should have wished him to say," Brandeis explained, "except that it asks for only a trial order. I want 10 times as much. Perhaps he does also, and this is merely his trial balloon. He certainly has the most extraordinary political sagacity." In fact Roosevelt did want more, and in the Public Works Administration, the Civilian Conservation Corps, and the Works Progress Administration the government would give jobs to millions of unemployed men and women.

Then, on 12 April, at the president's request, Brandeis went to the White House and "had a satisfactory hour with FDR." They discussed where Dean Acheson would best fit into the administration, reform and expansion of postal savings as an alternative to banks, the need to protect the common person's savings account, and the demand for greater public works programs. Roosevelt mentioned that Myron Taylor, the president of U.S. Steel, had recently been in, and as the justice told Frankfurter, this gave him the opportunity "for a few words on Bigness and Overcapacity." Roosevelt wanted Brandeis to look at some papers that Taylor had left, and since he could not find them immediately sent them over later by courier. The one thing Brandeis and Roosevelt did not get a chance to discuss involved the growing plight of German Jews at the hands of the Hitler regime, a problem that would concern Brandeis for the rest of the decade.

One facet of the president's leadership that caused dismay among conservatives did not bother Brandeis all that much—the willingness to experiment. During the campaign, when critics tried to pin him down on what specifics his New Deal would include, Roosevelt would not tell them (primarily because he did not yet know) but instead said that if they tried one program and it did not work, then they would try something else until they found the right answer. "F.D.'s readiness to experiment is fine," Brandeis said, although he had doubts about the financial manipulations involved with going off the gold standard. "I wish he would experiment instead with banishing the bankers . . . and putting on heavier estate taxes." When he learned the full implications of the abandonment of the gold standard, the justice was horrified.

ON 19 APRIL, Roosevelt announced that he had taken the United States off the gold standard. He did so in part to forestall more radical measures that proinflationists had introduced into Congress, and also to counter the severe deflation in wages and prices then gripping the country. Gold would no longer be used for the satisfaction of either public or private obligations, although all government bonds and nearly all private contracts specifically called for payment in gold as a hedge against devaluation of paper currency. While the action appalled some conservatives, others recognized it as a stroke of near genius. Russell Leffingwell of the house of Morgan wrote to the president that the action "saved the country from complete collapse. It was vitally necessary and the most important of all helpful things you have done."

Brandeis expressed himself in far less complimentary terms. The action "is terrifying in its implications." A declaration of bankruptcy, he charged, "is honorable if warranted by existing conditions. But the deliberate repudiation by the Government of its own obligations, entered into freely in contemplation of the contingency which has arisen and for the purpose of dealing with it, involves an alarming application. If the Government wished to extricate itself from the assumed emergency, taxation would have afforded an honorable way out."

The Court heard three challenges to the gold policy in January 1935, and seven of the justices considered the government repudiation of the gold clause in its own obligations unconstitutional, while a narrow 5–4 majority upheld the government's right to alter the terms of private and corporate contracts. In fact a majority would have liked to strike down the nullification of the gold clause in private contracts, but Hughes and four other members of the Court, including Brandeis, understood that for the past two years the business of the country had been on a paper currency basis, and to require debtors to pay back their borrowings in gold would have driven many small firms out of business. To allow the holder of a government bond to collect $16,931.25 on a $10,000 bond would be unjust enrichment. Moreover, even if the government had acted unconstitutionally, John Perry had not shown, or even tried to show, that as a government bondholder he had sustained any loss whatsoever. Not since *Marbury v. Madison* had a chief justice come up with such an ingenious way out of a political thicket.

But Hughes would not let the government off the hook so easily, and Brandeis approved of the tongue-lashing the chief justice administered the government. Hughes scolded the government, according to one witness in the courtroom that day, "in a voice that sounded like that of a Secretary of State rebuking Latin American banana republics for their repudiations." As to the Roosevelt administration's claim "that the Congress can disregard the obligations of the Government at its discretion and that, when the Government borrows money, the credit of the

United States is an illusory pledge," he replied, "We do not so read the Constitution." Hughes's denunciation of the government may have been the only thing that kept Roberts from joining the Four Horsemen, who, speaking through McReynolds, objected in all of the gold clause cases. In his dissent McReynolds declared that "loss of reputation for honorable dealing will bring us unending humiliation," but he brushed aside his written opinion and in a rage declared, "This is Nero at his worst. The Constitution is gone. Shame and humiliation are upon us."

When Felix Frankfurter came down to Washington the following week, he asked Brandeis why he had not asked any questions at oral argument. The justice replied that he already knew where he stood, and he was completely out of sympathy with what the government had done, so "I thought it best to say nothing." He was glad that Hughes had not asked him to write the decision, since he completely abhorred the morality of the repudiation.

A jittery president received news of the decision with a sigh of relief, and he rather smugly told Joseph Kennedy that the Court had finally "put human values ahead of the 'pound of flesh' called for by the contract." The administration had been prepared to shut down the New York Stock Exchange to avoid what it anticipated would be the financial chaos resulting from an adverse ruling. Roosevelt had also prepared a radio address to calm the nation, and he could now put it away. Raymond Moley drily suggested that Roosevelt keep the speech in a drawer nearby for the time when the National Industrial Recovery Act, or NIRA, would be declared unconstitutional.

NO PART OF THE NEW DEAL went so much against Louis Brandeis's beliefs as did the NIRA, nor did any other law so personally discomfit him. The heart of the NIRA revolved around Roosevelt's belief that the crisis of the Depression could revive the spirit of cooperation that he believed marked business-government relations during the Great War. Business and labor leaders had come to Washington ready to work together to do what the country needed to produce war material and get it to the men at the front. Everyone had realized that the normal rules, such as antitrust laws, made no sense in wartime, and that to secure the full contribution of workers, concessions had to be made to their legitimate demands. To Roosevelt, fighting the Depression would give Americans the chance to show their better side by working together for a common goal—recovery.

The basic idea involved getting all of the firms in a single industry to work together in hammering out a code of fair conduct that would have the force of law. Everybody got something. Business received permission to draft code agreements free from the antitrust laws, although another section declared that nothing in the bill would suspend the Sherman and Clayton acts. The long-standing proposal for federal incorporation of interstate business emerged in a new form, with federal licensing through approval of the codes. Section 7(a), patterned after the policies of the National War Labor Board, guaranteed the rights of workers to join unions and to bargain collectively with management. The fair labor provisions set out both maximum hours and minimum wages. The National Recovery Administration would oversee all of these provisions (with the exception of the massive $3.3 billion public works program), enforce the codes, and, when an industry could not reach agreement, had the power to impose a code. All codes approved by the president would have the force of law. The preamble to the act read like a lawyer's brief, justifying the measure as a legitimate response by Congress to removing burdens on interstate commerce. Some of the drafters believed the law would not withstand a constitutional challenge, and many in Congress voted for it in the belief it would be in effect only two years, and thus could possibly evade review by the Supreme Court.

Even if there had been no conservative bloc on the Supreme Court, the sloppy legislative draftsmanship of most of the early New Deal measures, as well as the poor quality of the lawyers in the attorney general's office who defended these cases before the Court, would inevitably have caused the administration trouble with the judiciary. The cavalier attitude of many New Dealers toward constitutional considerations bothered all the members of the Court. Brandeis, while sympathetic to some of the Roosevelt program, commented caustically on what he called the president's *kunststücke,* or "clever tricks," by which he tried to sneak things through. Even while they adhered to their stance of judicial restraint and gave the administration the benefit of the doubt, Brandeis, Stone, and Cardozo found some of the New Deal measures personally distasteful.

The first case involving the NIRA, *Panama Refining Co. v. Ryan* (1935), displayed many of the problems New Deal laws would face, and would be a harbinger of those to follow. To maintain stable oil prices, several states had imposed maximum production limits on wells within their borders. Section g(c) of the NIRA, the so-called hot oil clause, gave the president power to bar interstate shipment of oil produced in excess of state limits, a policy akin to the earlier Webb-Kenyon Act of 1913, where federal power had been used to enforce state prohibition statutes.

The justices listened in amazement as counsel for the oil producers told how they had been unable to secure copies of the regulations and of the slapdash way in which these rules, which had the force of law, had been promulgated. At one point Brandeis asked Assistant Attorney General Harold Stephens, "Is there any way by which to find out what is in these executive orders when they are issued?" An embarrassed Stephens confessed that no general government publication carried the orders and that they would be "rather difficult" to obtain, although he believed that certified copies could be gotten from the NRA.

By a vote of 8–1 the Court held section g(c) unconstitutional. Although Congress could certainly delegate power to the president to regulate aspects of interstate commerce, in this instance the legislature had failed to provide the executive with sufficient guidelines. Chief Justice Hughes considered the delegation so sweeping that approving the law would wipe out any "limitations upon the power of Congress to delegate its law-making functions." Only Justice Cardozo dissented, arguing that the statute had been designed to preserve natural resources and that Congress had not abused its authority. But even he condemned the administration for its slipshod practices.

(Later in 1935 the House Judiciary Committee deplored the "utter chaos" involved in promulgating NRA rules, and Congress created the *Federal Register* in which all administrative rules having the force of law and proposals for changing them must be published. The proposal for such a publication had been made earlier by Erwin Griswold of Harvard Law School, who sent the article to Brandeis, who no doubt had it in mind when he grilled Stephens. Griswold now wrote to commiserate with Stephens, and got his cooperation in pushing the measure at the same time that other members of the administration recognized the need for it.)

UNLIKE THE GOLD CLAUSE CASES, in which Brandeis had for the most part remained silent, he was quite active in the "hot oil" case. He not only vigorously questioned the government attorney but also had prompted his "brethren on either side to ask some of their questions." After the conference the chief justice asked Brandeis if he would care to write the opinion in light of an extremely unfortunate episode involving General Hugh Johnson. Brandeis thought about it, but believed it would be better if the chief wrote it. He wanted to call no more attention to what had been a painful matter.

Roosevelt had named Johnson to head the National Recovery Administration. The general had helped organize the draft in the war, and Roosevelt had known him as the army liaison to the War Industries Board. A bombastic man, he flung himself into the work, helping industries write codes and drumming up support for the program. The NRA adopted a symbol, a blue eagle, with the legend "We Do Our Part." Johnson led a parade of a quarter-million people down New York's Fifth Avenue, and the NRA eagle appeared everywhere, in shop-windows, on newspaper mastheads, and even on chorus girls.

Shortly after his appointment Johnson had called Brandeis, then at Chatham, to ask his advice. Brandeis had met Johnson during the war, when he had been an aide to General Enoch Crowder, who occasionally came to the justice to discuss problems of war production. Brandeis told Johnson that labor unions had to have real protection and that unless the government could secure regularity of employment, there would be no hope for recovery. He promised that he would meet with Johnson when he returned to Washington at the end of September. When they did get together, Brandeis laid out his concerns about the NRA, namely, the impossibility of enforcement, the dangers to small businesses, and the innate inefficiency of the big unit. He said that he thought Johnson as capable a man as any, but that he had an impossible job.

By the spring of 1934 the initial public enthusiasm for the NRA had faded, and criticism poured in from every side. Brandeis told his daughter Elizabeth that he thought the NRA was "going from bad to worse." In March, Roosevelt created the National Recovery Review Board and named Clarence Darrow to head it. After a brief study, the Darrow group reported that giant corporations dominated the NRA code-making practices and squeezed small business, labor, and the public. A furious Johnson began to drink even more heavily than usual. In May he came to see the justice, who described him as "a crushed man." Brandeis again told him that the job was impossible, and the best thing that could be done was to liquidate the NRA as soon as possible. To Frankfurter he said he thought Johnson "had showed manliness in coming to me who had predicted failure, instead of avoiding me as most men would have done. I am sure he felt I was his friend."

Then, in a radio address on 14 September, in which Johnson criticized labor in general and textile union leaders in particular, he suddenly blurted out: "During this whole intense experience, I have been in constant touch with that old counselor, Judge Louis Brandeis." The next few weeks saw Brandeis pilloried in some newspapers; the *Chicago Tribune* called it a departure from American custom and from judicial ethics which "is as truly revolutionary as any project in the program of the New Deal." Several newspapers demanded that Brandeis recuse himself from cases involving the NRA.

Brandeis could not understand Johnson's actions and noted that "the General seems to be worse. One from the Labor Dept. spoke of him as a 'maniac.' " It must have been more than liquor, he concluded, because it was not only an indiscretion but also a lie. From the very beginning he had told Johnson that he "was ag'in the Experiment." He warned Frankfurter that if Roosevelt did not shut Johnson up or remove him, the president would also be embarrassed. Frankfurter contacted the White House, but Roosevelt already knew he had to rid himself of Johnson. Within a few days Johnson had offered his resignation, which Roosevelt immediately accepted.

The president thought about having Johnson apologize publicly to Brandeis, and through their common friend Julian Mack asked the justice what to do. Mack called the Brandeis apartment to set a time when he could talk to the justice. Mrs. Brandeis immediately called Paul Freund, then in the solicitor general's office, and had him come to California Street to handle the conversation. Mack explained to Freund what the president offered; Freund relayed the message, and Brandeis responded, "Tell the General to say nothing." Freund told Mack what Brandeis had said, and Mack exploded. "Did you tell him what I said?" "Yes," Freund answered. "Tell him again!" Freund did, and Brandeis repeated his answer, adding that he would explain the facts to the chief justice. Brandeis understood that the incident should be allowed to die as quickly as possible, and the erratic Johnson might well add fuel to the flames in his "apology."

The idea of having to recuse in the upcoming NRA case was "not agreeable to contemplate," but Brandeis did not want to do anything that would jeopardize the Court or the legitimacy of the ruling. The justices were then filing back into Washington in advance of the opening of the October 1934 term, and he went to see each of them personally to explain the facts. None of them thought he should recuse. Neither did he answer Johnson, but wrapped the judicial robe around himself and kept silent, correctly anticipating that before long the whole episode would be forgotten. The incident, he said, "must be regarded as a casualty, like that of being run into by a drunken autoist, or shot by a lunatic."

Neither Brandeis, the press, nor most of the men and women he spoke with during the 1930s considered his advice a breach of judicial ethics. One syndicated news story carried the headline "BRANDEIS'S VIEWS VITAL FORCE WITH NEW DEAL," and noted that Washington insiders could not recall any justice in their memory who would not discuss social and economic questions "with at least a select few." Brandeis during the 1930s, however, spoke with more than just a "few." As one of his clerks noted, he did not tell them anything new, but rather repeated the ideas he had been developing all of his life. Nor did the unpleasantness of the episode stop him from continuing to meet with New Dealers seeking his counsel.

NEW DEALERS WORRIED about the conservatism of the Court saw their fears justified on 27 May 1935—Black Monday—when in three cases a unanimous Court not only struck down the NIRA but also called into question the extent of presidential and congressional power to fight the Depression.

The Court handed down its decisions that day in the new building that William Howard Taft had planned, and which one of the justices called the Temple of Karnak. Justice Brandeis began the morning by invalidating the 1934 Frazier-Lemke Act. Faced with the growing number of farm foreclosures, Congress changed the bankruptcy law to allow a farmer to buy back his farm and then make deferred payments on the debt. If the bank refused to enter into such an agreement, the farmer could then make payments to a court that would disperse the money to the bank. A Louisville bank had foreclosed on William Radford Sr. and taken possession of his farm. When he tried to make an arrangement under the new law, the bank refused, and the two parties went to court, with the bank arguing the unconstitutionality of the Frazier-Lemke Act.

A unanimous Court agreed. Although Brandeis conceded that the government had the power to change the terms of federal bankruptcy law, it could not out and out transfer property to a debtor that now belonged to the creditor. If Congress changed the law, it could apply only to future mortgage arrangements. The Louisville bank owned the former Radford farm, and the government could not force it to give it back. The law, Brandeis held, violated the Fifth Amendment prohibition against taking private property without just compensation. As for the Court's holding in *Blaisdell* a year earlier, Brandeis noted that the state mortgage moratorium had done no more than change the time and manner for debtors to pay their loans and avoid foreclosure. Here the debtor no longer had a property interest in the farm.

Brandeis then sat back and, while he kept his face impassive as always, listened with deep satisfaction as Justice Sutherland read the Court's opinion in *Humphrey's Executor v. United States.* Brandeis had entered a strong dissent in *Myers v. United States* less than a decade earlier, protesting Taft's opinion that the president had authority to remove any executive branch officer without senatorial approval. In that dissent Brandeis had pointed out that separation of powers had been adopted by the Framers "not to promote efficiency but to preclude the exercise of arbitrary power."

Roosevelt had consulted with James Landis, who had been Brandeis's clerk at the time of *Myers* and who, although sympathetic to his judge's dissent, had assured Roosevelt of his authority to fire William Humphrey, a conservative advocate of big business, from the Federal Trade Commission. The president had dismissed Humphrey because he feared the adamant conservative would sabotage New Deal programs.

The reasons for the firing mattered not to the Court. In *Myers* the president had fired a postmaster, a position that had traditionally been part of the federal patronage system. While Sutherland, Van Devanter, and Butler had joined *Myers* out of deference to Taft, they clearly had not agreed entirely with his broad assertions of presidential power. Sutherland noted that Congress, in setting up the independent commissions, had intended them to be just that—independent—and therefore protected from political firings. Unlike the post office, the FTC "cannot in any proper sense be characterized as an arm or an eye of the executive."

The most important case that day, the one that everyone had been waiting for, involved the National Industrial Recovery Act, *Schechter Poultry Corp. v. United States.* The Court had heard arguments over two days on 2 and 3 May, and the decision came down only three weeks later. Although the Court as a matter of jurisdictional practice tries to decide cases on the narrowest basis possible, Chief Justice Hughes posed three major questions: Did the economic crisis create extraordinary government powers? Had Congress lawfully delegated power to the president? Did the act exceed the government's authority under the Commerce Clause? This radical departure from the traditional procedures convinced many observers that not only Hughes but the entire bench wanted to kill off the NRA and then make sure it stayed dead.

In *Blaisdell,* Hughes had agreed that emergencies could call forth latent powers not explicitly spelled out in the Constitution, but in *Schechter* he reversed himself completely, declaring that "extraordinary conditions do not create or enlarge constitutional power." Hughes dispatched the second question by reiterating the Court's objections in *Panama Refining.* Congress had the power to delegate, but the NIRA gave "a sweeping delegation of legislative power," a blank check by which private parties could write codes that would then be enforced as the law of the land. (Justice Cardozo, in his concurrence, described the problem as "delegation running riot.")

In answering the third question, Hughes took an exceptionally restrictive view of commerce. He revived the old—and what many thought had been abandoned—distinction between the direct and the indirect effects of local activity on interstate commerce. Only those activities that directly affected interstate commerce fell within the reaches of federal power. The kosher chicken market run by the Schechter brothers in Brooklyn had no direct effect, and very little indirect effect, on interstate commerce, and thus could not be regulated by Congress.

Roosevelt received the news in shock and could not believe that all three decisions had been unanimous.

"Well, what about old Isaiah?"

"With the majority," replied one of his legal advisers.

"Where was Cardozo? Where was Stone?"

"They too were with the majority."

Why Roosevelt should have expected "old Isaiah" to support the NRA is puzzling. Throughout 1933 and 1934, Brandeis had made clear to a number of top New Dealers and to the president himself that he considered the program wrongheaded as well as impossible to administer. He and his followers had reiterated their opposition to government centralization and the curse of bigness, and had called for vigorous enforcement of the antitrust laws. Brandeis believed that "our Court did much good for the country," and he asked Ben Cohen to deliver a message to Felix Frankfurter. "You must see that Felix understands the situation and explains it to the President. You must explain it to the men Felix brought into the Government. They must understand that these three decisions change everything. The President has been living in a fool's paradise." When Hughes had wondered whether three such defeats should be inflicted on the administration the same day, Brandeis declared that he saw no problem. He wanted to jolt the president and his advisers awake.

• • •

ALTHOUGH ROOSEVELT DECLARED that the *Schechter* decision relegated the country to the horse-and-buggy definition of interstate commerce, many in the New Deal breathed a sigh of relief. Other than its public works components, the NRA had never worked, and even the president had become aware of its flaws. Other New Deal programs, however, had worked, and with one exception the Court attacked them as well, only this time with Brandeis, Stone, and Cardozo in the minority.

Brandeis had never liked the Agricultural Adjustment Act. The law imposed crop quotas and gave government price guaranties to those who participated, paid for by a tax on processors, and had proved successful in raising farm income. Although concerned about the plight of the rural poor, Brandeis worried about the growing size of government agencies, and he expressed his doubts to Tugwell, Henry Wallace, and Gardner Jackson, who served in the AAA as legal counselor of consumer affairs. Instead of reducing output through government-imposed quotas, the government, he thought, should buy up land and then lease it to farmers who would work it in smallholdings. The program paid no attention to sharecroppers, tenants, and migrant workers. Brandeis warned that the AAA would speed up the trend toward fewer farmers owning larger and larger spreads, thus increasing monopoly and absentee ownership. The New Dealers would not listen. Although there were reports that Brandeis had threatened to vote against the AAA, when a group of agriculture officials went to see him on Cape Cod in the summer of 1934, supposedly to discuss problems of monopoly, they came away with a sense that when push came to shove, old Isaiah would support the program.

The AAA came before the Court in *United States v. Butler,* and by a 6–3 majority the justices declared it unconstitutional. Officials of the Hoosac Mills Corporation had attacked the processing tax that underwrote the costs of the program as an unconstitutional means of doing what the government could not do directly, namely, control agricultural production. Although the Court had previously ruled that taxpayers had no standing to challenge in court how the government spent tax revenues, Justice Roberts brushed this concern aside, since the tax was no more than "a mere incident of such regulation."

The Roberts opinion is one of the most tortured and confusing of all the New Deal decisions. The tax, he wrote, could not be considered a true tax, since the proceeds went not into the general coffers but rather into a special fund; agriculture constituted a local activity, and therefore could not be regulated under the commerce power; even if the sum of many local conditions had created a national problem, Congress could not ignore constitutional limitations. Denying that the decision reflected the personal economic views of the majority, Roberts offered a wooden and mechanistic definition of what the Court did, the so-called T-square rule: "When an act of Congress is appropriately challenged in the courts as not conforming to the constitutional mandate the judicial branch of the Government has only one duty—to lay the article of the Constitution which is invoked beside the statute which is challenged and to decide whether the latter squares with the former." The only positive aspect of the opinion is that Roberts, and supposedly the other five justices who voted with him, affirmed that the taxing power, as Hamilton had argued, could be used to promote the general welfare.

Justice Stone, joined by Brandeis and Cardozo, lacerated the Roberts opinion, showing up its manifest contradictions with past rulings as well as the logical inconsistencies of the argument. How could one say that "there is a power to spend for the national welfare while rejecting any power to impose conditions reasonably adapted to the attainment of the end which alone would justify the expenditure"?

The attack on New Deal legislation continued. In *Jones v. Securities and Exchange Commission,* the Court seriously curtailed the power of the Securities and Exchange Commission to monitor proposed stock issues; Cardozo, joined by Brandeis and Stone, dissented. Then, in *Carter v. Carter Coal Co.,* the Court struck down the Guffey-Snyder Act of 1935, passed in the wake of the *Schechter* decision. The NRA code had brought a desperately needed stabilization to the coal industry, which had been especially hard-hit by the Depression. The law essentially replicated the NRA code, with protection of labor and price agreements, but through statute. Congress also declared coal production affected with a public interest. The Four Horsemen and Roberts held the entire statute unconstitutional based on *Schechter*'s definition of commerce, holding coal mining a local activity beyond the reach of federal control. Cardozo dissented, joined by Brandeis and Stone, and Hughes dissented in part.

ASIDE FROM PUBLIC WORKS, the one major New Deal initiative to escape wholly unharmed was perhaps the most radical measure, the Tennessee Valley Authority. The ambitious experiment covered a seven-state area for the nominal purpose of erecting dams for flood control. But the TVA, under the direction of a confirmed Brandeisian, David Lilienthal, also set out to reclaim land, build parks, and raise the standard of living in one of the poorest parts of the country. The dams also produced electricity, and the TVA sold this power to distribution companies, not to the general public. Roosevelt and Senator George W. Norris wanted to use the TVA's hydroelectric production as a yardstick to determine what the proper cost of electricity should be to the public, an idea vehemently opposed by the electricity interests.

Hughes, no doubt aware of the growing concern about the Court's anti–New Deal decisions, persuaded all of the four conservatives except McReynolds to go along with a very narrow decision on whether the government had the authority to enter into a contract selling electricity. Congress clearly could build dams for national defense and to facilitate interstate commerce; the electricity produced by these dams was a mere by-product, and its sale could be justified under Article IV, Section 3, which allows the government to sell property it owns.

Before he could get this agreement, however, Hughes had to deal with an important technicality: Did minority shareholders in this case have standing to sue? Brandeis, Stone, Cardozo, and Roberts said they did not, and Brandeis felt so strongly that he prepared a partial dissent on this point. Courts, he declared, should not interfere in the internal policies of corporations at the behest of a minority. Without a proper cause of action, they wanted to dismiss, but the four conservatives wanted some assurance that the plaintiffs would not be thrown out of a court on a technicality, and Hughes agreed, so the Court accepted jurisdiction and kept the decision centered on the single question of selling power.

Brandeis entered a concurrence in *Ashwander v. TVA,* joined by Stone, Roberts, and Cardozo. Though he had no quarrels with the chief justice's opinion on the merits, he believed the case should have been dismissed, and he detailed the reasons why. From the time he had come on the Court two decades earlier, Brandeis had been concerned about maintaining strict jurisdictional standards. He had also warned his colleagues time and again not to decide more than necessary to determine the matter. Often he had declared that "the most important thing we do is not doing," and now he set out his mature philosophy in seven points that have since become the definitive statement of what types of cases the Court should take, and how justices should decide matters before the bench:

Refuse jurisdiction of collusive suits. The Court should not pass upon the constitutionality of legislation in a friendly, non-adversarial suit.

Do not anticipate constitutional questions, but ʼ
  when legitimately in front of the Court.
Do not formulate constitutional rules broaꞈ
  the precise facts in the case.
Do not decide a case on constitutional groꞈ
  ent a nonconstitutional argument that can ꞁ
Do not pass upon the validity of a statute unless tꞁ
  party can show that he is injured by its operation.
Do not pass upon the constitutionality of a law at the requꞈ
  one who has benefited from it.
Whenever possible, a statute should be construed in a way to
  avoid constitutional issues.

Brandeis also argued what many consider an eighth point. Reciting a string of authorities, he then quoted Chief Justice John Marshall: "In no doubtful case, would [the Court] pronounce a legislative act to be contrary to the Constitution." Although the conservatives on the bench in the 1930s refused to pay heed, later courts affirmed the wisdom of Brandeis's rules.

THE TVA was one of the very few early New Deal proposals of which Brandeis approved, but by the time the Court decided *Ashwander,* the Roosevelt administration had taken a sharp turn to the left, and began enacting legislation more to the justice's liking. Some of the so-called Second New Deal measures had been on the president's agenda since his election, but had taken a backseat to relief measures. The Banking Act of 1935 strengthened the Federal Reserve Board and fulfilled Roosevelt's plan to bring all banking and currency under government control. The National Labor Relations Act, or Wagner Act, finally secured labor's right to organize and bargain collectively and established the National Labor Relations Board to enforce that policy. In Social Security the government took the first steps to providing a safety net for the elderly and the infirm. The bête noire of the 1920s, the gigantic public utilities holding companies, were broken up by statute, and the Wealth Tax Act for the first time imposed significant taxes on the richest segment of society. The Emergency Relief Appropriation Act gave birth to one of the most remarkable programs in American history, the Works Progress Administration, which not only funded large-scale public works but also provided meaningful labor in their own fields to unemployed artists, writers, playwrights, and historians, and did much to enrich the cultural life of the country.

.oughout this time Brandeis maintained good relations with most
.e high-ranking members of the administration, including
.klin Roosevelt. When the president did something of which the
.stice approved, such as moving all fifteen thousand postmasters into
civil service categories, Brandeis called it "superb." He supported the
decision to seek tighter regulation of the stock market and to lower tariffs in order to stimulate foreign trade. As business attacks on Roosevelt
increased, Brandeis hoped the president would recognize the real enemies of reform, and he applauded when Roosevelt began striking out at
big business and authorized the Justice Department to step up
antitrust activities. "F.D. is making a gallant fight," he told Norman
Hapgood, "and seems to appreciate fully the evils of bigness."

Brandeis, of course, had his own ideas of what should be done to end
the Depression, and although he never set them down in any formal or
organized document, we can piece them together from various sources:

Limit the power of bankers by expanding the postal savings bank
    system and giving it the authority to provide checking ac-
    counts and to underwrite corporate debentures.
Increase sharply the income tax at the upper ends of the spectrum
    both on corporations and on individuals.
First borrow and then appropriate revenue from federal taxes to
    finance major public works programs and put people to work
    on projects of social utility, such as dams, parks, irrigation, and
    schools.
Break up the banking system into separate commercial, savings,
    and investment units to avoid the evils of a concentrated money
    power.
Use federal excise taxes in such a way as to limit the size of corpo-
    rations.
Impose a steep federal inheritance tax to limit the amount that
    any one person could pass down to the next generation to
    $1 million.
Create a system of unemployment insurance that put responsibil-
    ity upon individual companies to guarantee regularity of
    employment and maintain the purchasing power of laid-off
    workers.

One of his former clerks, Harry Shulman, thought that his critics
would say that Brandeis wanted to turn back the clock. Why not? The

justice responded. Why not turn back the clock after the failed policies of the present? People had repudiated other failed programs, such as prohibition. "We must determine what is desirable to do and then we can find ways and means to do it." But the federal government could become too big, and this had to be avoided. He warned his daughter to remember that "if the Lord had intended things to be big, he would have made man bigger—in brains and character."

Many but not all of his proposals wound up in New Deal legislation in one form or another, although not always as he would have preferred it; taxes were increased, but never to the near-confiscatory levels he wanted, and despite increased antitrust prosecutions the government did nothing to break up big business. Brandeis, however, heartily approved of the unemployment insurance plan and took a great deal of satisfaction from the key roles that his daughter Elizabeth and her husband, Paul, played in drafting the plan and then seeing it through to acceptance.

Brandeis had for years preached the importance of regularity of employment, but he understood that during the Depression even the most willing employer could not afford to keep workers on if no market existed for the plant's goods. His daughters had heard his sermon on this many times, and Elizabeth, a labor economist at the University of Wisconsin, saw a chance in 1931 to start putting it into effect. She and Paul helped draft the Groves Employment Act, which set up a state-administered insurance fund. Employers would pay into the fund, and their contribution would be determined by the number of workers in their business and also by the stability of their workforce. Those firms that managed to keep their people working regularly would pay a lower premium than ones who had high turnover.

When Elizabeth reported this accomplishment to her delighted father, he pronounced it consonant with the "one true faith." Even with the Depression distorting the usual labor market, the plan rewarded those employers who tried to ensure regular employment for their workers, penalized those who did not, and provided unemployed workers with at least some money for subsistence until they could get other jobs. Best of all, a state, and not the federal government, had adopted it; Wisconsin, by leading the way, served as a laboratory for democracy.

Brandeis worried that state experimentation would be stopped if Congress passed a national unemployment insurance law, which he opposed. In September 1933 he wrote to Elizabeth that he had thought of a way to finesse the problem. Providing unemployment insurance to workers should be left wholly to the states, but the federal government should serve as a "discourager of hesitancy" by laying a tax on every employer who had not joined some program under state law. This tax should go into a general fund and not into an unemployment compensation account, "lest by so doing we start national provision." The president had asked him to come to the White House, and the justice planned to talk about irregularity of employment. He asked Elizabeth and Paul to send him their views and if possible a rough suggestion for a bill. After that he began to talk up what he called the "Wisconsin idea" so that by the time Roosevelt was ready to act, the idea had wide circulation in Washington.

Brandeis had to fight what he called the "social worker error," whereby there would be a single unified program for the whole country administered by Washington. The justice talked about the Wisconsin plan to Secretary of Labor Frances Perkins, who promised to try to curb some of the nationalists. Elizabeth attended a dinner in Washington in January 1934, where Lincoln Filene introduced her to Senator Robert F. Wagner of New York, and she took the opportunity to explain the Wisconsin plan to him. Wagner and Representative David J. Lewis of Maryland introduced a bill in April 1934. The heart of the plan was an ingenious tax scheme devised by Brandeis and modeled on the Wisconsin idea, a payroll tax on employers with the provision that in those states where employers were already contributing to state funds, the amounts paid to the state would be deducted from the federal tax. This way states could establish new programs without new costs to handicap industries involved in interstate commerce. The Wagner-Lewis bill set minimum standards, but allowed the states much leeway. The proposal picked up support in Congress, much to the annoyance of some of Roosevelt's nationalistic advisers, who pressured him to stop the bill.

Roosevelt prepared a message adopting the nationalist view, when Tom Corcoran and Ben Cohen reminded him that Brandeis had discussed this subject with him soon after the inauguration. The president invited old Isaiah to the White House on the afternoon of 7 June and started to read the message he had prepared on proposals to deal with several issues, including "social insurance." Brandeis immediately stopped him and told Roosevelt he had it all wrong; he then spent forty-five minutes explaining to him why the Wisconsin plan would be better than the federal government proposal. The president said that the message had already been sent up to the Capitol, but that he would make sure that the right steps were taken. Brandeis immediately contacted friends both in Congress and in government agencies and, as he put it, set them "to work for the true faith during the summer."

By then sentiment had grown in Congress not only for unemployment insurance but also for some sort of old-age assistance. The Wisconsin plan had many champions, but others criticized it on the grounds that it did not provide a big enough pool, and that in any event unemployment insurance should be national. Roosevelt tentatively endorsed the Wagner-Lewis bill but asked Congress to delay further action until the fall,

Labor Secretary Frances Perkins, 1945

and then to combine unemployment compensation with a sweeping program to provide for "the security of the men, women, and children of the nation." He proposed that unemployment insurance be national in scope and standards, but that management be left to the states with the federal government investing and safeguarding the reserves. The Wagner-Lewis bill failed, but the final program, although more nationalistic in scope than Brandeis would have liked, preserved enough of the Wisconsin plan and a large enough role for the states to satisfy him.

DURING THE 1936 CAMPAIGN Roosevelt barely mentioned the Court, and in November he won the most lopsided victory in American history, carrying every state except Maine and Vermont. He rightly interpreted the election results as a popular mandate, but worried not only about how the Court would deal with measures Congress had passed in 1935 and 1936 but also about other proposals he had in mind for his second term. The president and a small group of advisers had been mulling over the Court problem for two years. Given the age of most justices, there should have been a retirement or death to give him a vacancy. Beyond that, the most reliable member of the Court was Louis Brandeis, who was also the oldest; the Four Horsemen, all in their seventies, seemed indestructible. A constitutional amendment, either

Supporting the National Recovery Administration —
"We Do Our Part"

limiting the Court's jurisdiction or requiring six or seven votes to declare a congressional law unconstitutional, would take time and could be blocked by only thirteen states refusing to ratify. Then Homer Cummings brought him a plan he found in the old files of the Justice Department prepared, ironically, by one of his predecessors as attorney general, none other than the current Justice James Clark McReynolds. Roosevelt loved it.

Had Roosevelt been open and aboveboard, had he said to the American people that their political mandate, that the measures they and their elected representatives had approved, that all chances of economic recovery, and that democratic government itself were being thwarted by five men, and that he needed to change that if the country were ever to regain its economic vitality, he would have had a fight on his hands, but it would have been straightforward. Instead, in what Brandeis had called his *kunststücke,* he tried to justify his plan by claiming that the elderly members of the high court had fallen seriously behind in their work, with a huge backlog of unresolved cases. To remedy that situation, he asked for the authority to add one new member to the Court for every current justice over seventy, to a maximum of six new appointments. No one was the least bit fooled; Roosevelt wanted to pack the Court with men who would approve New Deal measures.

Roosevelt quietly prepared a special message to Congress, but just before he sent it to the Hill on 5 February 1937, Tommy Corcoran said,

"What about Isaiah?" The president agreed that the justice should be given the courtesy of an advance warning, and sent Corcoran over to the Supreme Court. The justices were in their robing room, preparing to go onto the bench, when Corcoran came in, and as they walked to the Court chamber, he quietly told Brandeis about the president's proposal. The justice thanked Corcoran for coming over, and asked him to thank the president for letting him know, but said that he thought the plan was absolutely terrible and that the president had made a very great mistake.

At a little after one o'clock, as the Court listened to oral argument in a minor case, the clerk of the Court stepped through the velvet curtains and handed Chief Justice Hughes a sheaf of mimeographed papers. Shortly after that, a page came through the curtains and put a copy of the document before each justice. When the page handed Brandeis his set, he turned on the antique desk lamp he had brought over from the old courtroom, and the spectators could see only his shock of white hair as he bent over to read. When he finished, he looked over to Van Devanter, who waved his arm as if in dismissal.

That evening Brandeis wrote to Felix Frankfurter asking, "Whom did F.D. rely on for his Judiciary Message and bill? Has he consulted you on any of his matters of late?" In fact, Roosevelt, knowing of Frankfurter's close ties to Brandeis, had deliberately not informed him, but had written on 15 January, "Very confidentially, I may give you an awful shock in about two weeks."

Judicial propriety prevented the justices from openly attacking either Roosevelt or his plan, but quietly they let it be known how much they opposed it. Moreover, all of them deeply resented the rationale he had used, and this estranged those members of the Court who had been at least partially supportive of New Deal measures and who had themselves criticized the conservative bloc for its activism. The scheme particularly alienated eighty-year-old Louis Brandeis, by then an icon of the liberals and considered by many of them the original New Dealer.

Opponents of the scheme knew they faced an uphill battle. Roosevelt's victory in 1936 had given the Democrats a four-to-one majority in the House of Representatives, while in the Senate Republicans held only sixteen of the ninety-six seats. Critics of the president's plan needed the Court's help and approached Hughes and several other justices, asking them to testify; all refused. With hearings scheduled to open before the Senate Judiciary Committee on Monday morning, 22 March, there seemed little hope of derailing the Court-packing plan.

Then, on Saturday, 20 March, Alice Brandeis drove down to Alexandria, Virginia, bringing a gift to the new baby born to Elizabeth Colman, the daughter of Senator Burton Wheeler of Montana. Although a Democrat, Wheeler had had a falling-out with Roosevelt, and he now opposed the Court bill. As Alice Brandeis left the Colmans, she turned to Elizabeth and said, "Tell your father I think he's right." Closing the door, Elizabeth immediately called her father. A veteran of Washington politics, he correctly read the message Mrs. Brandeis had sent: Contact the justice! Wheeler telephoned the Brandeis apartment, where the justice, awaiting the call, invited Wheeler over immediately.

Brandeis confirmed that he would not testify, but told him to call the chief justice, who would give him a letter. Wheeler, who had opposed Hughes's appointment, responded that he did not know him. "Well, the Chief Justice knows you," Brandeis responded, "and knows what you are doing." Brandeis, despite his well-known aversion to the telephone, then went over and called Hughes, who told Wheeler to come right over. Wheeler went to the chief justice's apartment, Hughes agreed to write a letter, and the next day, after consulting with Brandeis and Van Devanter, the chief justice summoned Wheeler back, handed him the letter, and with a big grin on his face declared, "The baby is born."

It's a good story, but actually a little more complex than Wheeler's recollection. Mrs. Brandeis did go to Alexandria, Wheeler did come to the Brandeis apartment and then went over to see Hughes, but at least two days earlier the Montana senator had spoken with Hughes on the phone. The chief justice had told Senator William H. King, a conservative Democrat from Utah who also opposed the bill, that while neither he nor any of the other justices would testify, if the Judiciary Committee wanted specific information and wrote to the Court, he would of course be glad to give the Senate the facts. Hughes then called Wheeler and repeated this information, so even before he went to see Brandeis, Wheeler knew that Hughes would provide a letter.

Although the documentary evidence is sparse, the following scenario seems to have occurred. King had gone to see Hughes to ask him to testify about the facts of the Court's work, and the chief had been amenable, but only if another justice accompanied him, and he thought the best choice would be Brandeis because of his standing as a Democrat and a liberal. When Hughes spoke to Brandeis, he found him strongly opposed to having any member of the Court testify. The two men agreed that a letter would be appropriate, and Hughes so informed

King and Wheeler. The critical factor was time. By the time the Judiciary Committee met and framed a letter to Hughes, the huge Democratic majorities in both houses could already have steamrolled the bill through. Hughes, an experienced politician himself, understood this and, after consulting with Brandeis and Van Devanter, decided to push the schedule up; he would prepare a letter, but needed the cover of having been asked to do so. Mrs. Brandeis (who vehemently opposed the plan because of the aspersions it cast on the older judges, especially her husband) went to Alexandria, Wheeler was guided from the Brandeis apartment to that of Hughes, and he got the letter to take with him on Monday morning to the Judiciary Committee meeting. Beyond that, in a city where secrets usually cannot be kept, no one in the White House had any inkling about this.

Wheeler began his testimony in a sort of rambling manner and then suddenly expressed shock at the allegations by Attorney General Homer Cummings that the Court had fallen behind in its work. He just could not believe that and knew that only one man could really provide the facts to rebut that accusation. Wheeler now had the full attention of the committee and of the spectators as he reached into his pocket and announced, "I have here now a letter by the Chief Justice of the United States . . . written by him and approved by Mr. Justice Brandeis and Mr. Justice Van Devanter."

"The Supreme Court is fully abreast of its work," Hughes declared. "There is no congestion of cases upon our calendar, and this gratifying condition has obtained for several years." In fact, before rising for their recess on 15 March, the Court had heard argument in all cases for which certiorari had been granted only four weeks earlier on 15 February. There were indeed large numbers of petitions for review, but most of them had little merit, and the members of the current Court, with their years of experience, could easily winnow out the chaff from the wheat. Brandeis had earlier admired Hughes for his command of the facts in the insurance investigation, and like Brandeis, Hughes believed in marshaling facts and letting them make the case. He presented data from the time he had become chief justice to show that the Court had not shirked its work, and in fact the solicitor general's report for 1936 showed no backlog of any sort. The proposal to put more judges on the bench would not improve efficiency but have just the opposite effect— "more judges to hear, more judges to confer, more judges to discuss, more judges to be convinced and to decide."

The letter proved to be the beginning of the end, as opposition swelled to the president's plan, not only among conservatives but among many liberals as well. Roosevelt tried to rally the troops, but to no avail, and finally, after 169 days, he conceded defeat and accepted a substitute bill that embodied some procedural reforms and provided better terms for judicial retirement.

During this fight Henry Friendly, one of Brandeis's former clerks, had been scheduled to debate Charles Clark at Yale Law School, but with the announcement of the Court plan the sponsors asked if Friendly would mind if they changed the debate to the merits of the scheme. Friendly agreed, provided he could speak against it. The next morning he was horrified to see a newspaper headline, "BRANDEIS LAW CLERK ATTACKS COURT PLAN." Knowing how the justice felt, Friendly immediately wrote to him explaining what had happened, and Brandeis wrote back, "Don't let the incident give you concern. I have only heard of it from you, and cannot believe anything you may have said will do any harm."

Brandeis, although he remained on amiable terms with Roosevelt, never forgave him for this *Kunststück,* nor did he forgive Felix Frankfurter for backing the proposal. Relations between the justice and the professor cooled considerably after 1937, as they did with some of Frankfurter's acolytes who also backed the plan, such as Tommy Corcoran, who had served as the administration's hatchet man during the fight. In turn Corcoran and other New Dealers, such as Harold Ickes, thought Brandeis had let them down by signing onto the Hughes letter. "He did not shoot straight with us," Corcoran fumed, and refused to see Brandeis again. Corcoran and Ickes both thought that Brandeis ought to have stepped down from the Court, so that Roosevelt could have named Frankfurter to his seat. When Brandeis heard about this, he tartly remarked that "he was not sure that Frankfurter could not do more by teaching the younger generation."

IRONICALLY, HAD ROOSEVELT WAITED only a little longer, he could have had victory without paying such a heavy political price. On 29 March, exactly one week after Wheeler presented Hughes's letter, the Court handed down a 5–4 decision upholding the constitutionality of a Washington State minimum-wage law indistinguishable from the New York statute it had struck down the previous June. Speaking for the Court, Chief Justice Hughes specifically rejected *Adkins v. Children's Hospital* (1923), declaring it to have been wrongly decided. Sutherland, dissenting for the Four Horsemen, lashed out against what

"You gave me the authority to pick my kind of umpire last November!"
C. K. Berryman, Washington Star, *June 1937*

he saw as the theory that the Constitution's meaning changed depending on current economic conditions. A pleased justice Brandeis dropped a note to Frankfurter, the man who had argued the 1923 case. "Overruling Adkins' Case must give you some satisfaction."

That same day the Court approved three other federal statutes. Brandeis spoke for a unanimous Court in *Wright v. Vinton Branch,* upholding the revised Frazier-Lemke bankruptcy law for farm debtor relief, now cured of the defects that had led to invalidation of the first act in *Louisville Bank v. Radford* two years earlier. In two other unanimous cases, the Court upheld the constitutionality of the regulatory firearms tax and an amendment to the Railway Labor Act permitting collective bargaining. The way was now clear for the Court to approve the National Labor Relations Act, which it did two weeks later.

A few days before the Court handed down two decisions on 24 May upholding provisions of the Social Security Act, Justice Willis Van Devanter announced his retirement after twenty-seven years on the bench. Then, in January 1938, George Sutherland stepped down. With

Hughes and Roberts seemingly ensconced in the liberal camp, Roosevelt appointees could presumably ensure safe majorities in cases testing New Deal legislation. Despite their differences of opinion, Brandeis expressed regret at the departure of the two conservatives. He had always gotten along well with Van Devanter, and in 1934 and then again in 1935, when he thought that Van Devanter had considered resigning, he implored him to remain on the Court. In the spring of 1935, Brandeis wrote, "Dear Van, I am sorry to learn that you have not been feeling well. Take the best care of yourself. The Court never needed you more." He told his son-in-law that Sutherland's resignation would be regretted by the entire Court despite their disagreements. "He is a man of unusually high character and of true patriotism, as he considers the public welfare."

Roosevelt later commented that he had lost the battle but won the war, although it would be more accurate to say he lost the battle, won the campaign, and then lost a war. Opposition to the Court-packing plan rejuvenated the Republican Party, which had been left for dead after the 1936 election. It also energized southern conservatives who disagreed with much of the New Deal program and whom Roosevelt unsuccessfully tried to purge from the party in 1938. Although he managed to get a few more measures through, the New Deal ended with recovery still not achieved.

Roosevelt would eventually get to make more appointments to the Supreme Court than any president since George Washington, and after 1937 the Court rarely struck down economic regulations. But the Court emerged as institutionally stronger, with liberals like Brandeis and Stone and conservatives like Van Devanter and Sutherland uniting to oppose the Court-packing scheme. Brandeis took little satisfaction from the victory, angry at how Roosevelt had subjected the Court to unwarranted attack. Now eighty years old, he had other challenges confronting him in the 1930s.

CHAPTER TWENTY-NINE

EXTRAJUDICIAL ACTIVITIES: III

I n the midst of the Court-packing fight, Drew Pearson and Robert Allen published *Nine Old Men at the Crossroads,* an attack on the Court for being out of touch with the reality of Depression-era America. A friend of Brandeis's asked whether he had read the book, and he replied, "Oh, no, there are some things in it that Mrs. Brandeis tells me I should not know." In fact, little that happened in Washington in the 1930s escaped Brandeis's notice, and neither did the worsening international conditions, especially as they affected Palestine and the Jews of Germany.

BRANDEIS LEARNED MUCH about politics and the workings of the government from his contacts with people like Felix Frankfurter and cabinet secretaries and from his access to the president. He perhaps learned even more from the Monday teas he and Alice hosted in their California Street apartment and from the dinners they gave. Hundreds of people came to talk to him, to discuss their problems, and to hear his advice. At the teas a visitor could find Supreme Court justices, members of regulatory commissions, such as William O. Douglas of the SEC and James Landis of the FTC, congressmen and senators, young lawyers whom Frankfurter had sent down to work in the New Deal, visitors from Palestine, and old friends. The Danish ambassador came often. Brandeis, a great admirer of Denmark's social democracy, would tell people, "Why visit Russia when you can go to Denmark?"

People in town for just a few days would call, and if the justice was free, he would invite them over to talk, especially the young law professors from Harvard. Sheldon Glueck, who became one of the nation's leading criminologists, often dropped in, but one time he had to write a note apologizing for his twelve-year-old daughter, Joyce, who had been visiting relatives in Washington. The girl had heard so much from her father about Brandeis that she insisted her aunt call up his office so she could go over to see him. When Brandeis's law clerk answered and said the justice was busy, Joyce "strongly insisted upon her inalienable right" to see him. "Justice Brandeis ought never to be too busy to see a nice little girl!" Unfortunately, we do not know if she succeeded in her quest.

Charles E. Wyzanski Jr., a Harvard Law graduate and clerk to Learned Hand, had come to Washington as the solicitor for the Department of Labor. Because of the interest Brandeis had in his work, Wyzanski was a frequent visitor both in Washington and in Chatham, and left this portrait:

> Were you to see the Justice in his home, there you would find no display of wealth or elegance. He himself would probably be wearing the dark blue serge suit that annually he bought by mail from Filene's Boston store. If he were in his apartment at Florence Court, the furniture would be typified by a green sofa with a long stiff back which perhaps began its career in a shipment from a Victorian store to Otis Place in Boston. On the wall was a photographic reproduction of the statue of Venus de Milo. If you were allowed to go to a floor above, to his crowded study, the surrounding books were law reports from the federal and Massachusetts courts, and a collection of albums filled with clippings. . . .
>
> You might be invited to the Justice's summer cottage at Chatham for an hour's visit strictly clocked by Mrs. Brandeis. If possible, there were even fewer signs of luxury there than on California Street in Washington. Some books were placed not on shelves but in packing cases. And on the wall were framed not famous etchings or impressionist paintings but something far more revealing: a legal instrument—a contract executed several decades before in which Mr. Brandeis agreed to pay to each of his daughters an allowance of five cents each week and they in turn agreed to polish his shoes, all on the understanding that "there are no catchwords in this contract."

The stories of the teas and dinners are legion and appear to have left an indelible memory with those who attended. At tea, Alice, assisted by Poindexter and that year's clerk, would make sure that no one person took up too much of her husband's time. One, of course, did not come to the Brandeis home to eat; Mrs. Brandeis served tea and gingersnaps, and nothing else. According to a number of people, the man with the great white shock of hair whom many considered a legend had the knack of putting people at ease within a few minutes. He would be glad to answer their questions, but always prefaced his comments with "Assuming there are no constitutional or other legal questions. . . ."

One time a young woman commented on a case in a lower federal court that had been in the newspapers that morning and, unaware of the proprieties, asked Brandeis if he thought the case had been decided correctly. Everyone present suddenly went silent, and as one person put it, the only question was whether she would be hanged or boiled alive. Instead, Brandeis smiled tolerantly and replied, "Madam, I think you should refer your question to a good lawyer." Immediately the tension dissipated. Brandeis had turned the joke on himself by implying that a "good lawyer" could give a better opinion than he could, and yet informed the lady of her indiscretion.

The Brandeises valued conversation, and their Monday afternoons may have been the best political salon in America during the 1920s and 1930s. Stanley Reed, later to be a colleague on the Supreme Court, had come to Washington as general counsel to the Reconstruction Finance Corporation, an agency mandated to loan money to private business. The invitation to visit Brandeis never meant a "Hello, glad to see you, good-bye," but rather a chance to sit for an hour or two talking to fifteen or twenty other people, learning from them, and, of course, getting advice from the justice. If a particular agency had been in the news recently, the commissioner as well as the general counsel often wound up on California Street the following Monday. There might be a librarian from the Labor Department who had been helpful in some research or some young people from the Brookings Institution. If a congressman or senator made a speech with which Brandeis agreed, he would be invited, in his clerk's phrase, as a "tacit laying on of hands." All of the justices except McReynolds and Butler came over, but no one discussed Court business.

Each year Brandeis would invite over Andrew Furuseth, the grand old man of the seamen's union, and then ask him to tell his clerk and the other young people there why he had gone to sea. "Well," Furuseth would answer in his accented English, "I had this great delusion that I could be a free man." Brandeis would then sit back while Furuseth told harrowing tales of the treatment accorded to seamen prior to the passage of the La Follette Act.

Above all, Brandeis wanted to talk with young people, to learn their ideals, why they had come to Washington, and what they hoped to do with the rest of their lives. Walter Gellhorn, a Columbia Law graduate clerking with Justice Stone, went to see Brandeis one afternoon and discovered that the Brandeis family of Louisville had long known the Gellhorns in St. Louis. During the year, Gellhorn returned frequently, often as a guest for dinner. Brandeis knew that Gellhorn shared an apartment with his own clerk, Henry Hart, and asked Hart one day if he knew what Gellhorn planned at the end of the year. Hart told him that Gellhorn had an offer from the big New York law firm of Sullivan & Cromwell. "Tell him to come see me as soon as he can get free." Hart called Gellhorn, relayed the message and its sense of urgency, and Gellhorn came over later that day.

Why, Brandeis wanted to know, did Gellhorn want to go to Sullivan & Cromwell? Well, he replied, he wanted to be independent, and he believed that meant he had to be economically independent. "Walter, a man is not independent according to what he makes," the justice said. "He's independent according to what he spends." He then told the young man a story about when he had been leading some reform campaigns in Boston, and in the middle of the night men came to him who were the heads of large corporations, some making $100,000 or more, and they gave him large sums of cash to be used in his fight against the New Haven or for savings bank insurance but under a pledge of secrecy, because if it became known that they supported Brandeis, they might lose their positions. "These men couldn't afford to lose their positions," Brandeis explained, "because they were spending close to what they were making and any loss of income for them would have meant destruction. Mrs. Brandeis and I talked this over and we decided that I could always be sure of making at least a moderate income, and so we would live moderately, no matter what income I happened to be making. And so we did." The young man thought about this and decided not to go with the New York law firm; he joined the faculty of Columbia University and became a noted scholar in administrative law as well as a champion of civil rights.

Dinners at the Brandeises' lasted longer than the teas and had fewer people, but the emphasis remained on ideas, stimulating conversation, and idealistic encouragement to younger people. There was not a great deal of food. When you went to dinner at the Brandeis home, Alger Hiss recalled, "you seldom got enough to eat. What you were served was tasty but sparing portions because he himself ate sparingly. . . . It wasn't a matter of parsimony. It was just a matter of Spartan tastes." At ten o'clock the justice would rise, a sign to everyone that the evening had ended. Poindexter and the clerk would have the job of making sure that no one lingered to talk; Brandeis needed his sleep before rising to work at five o'clock.

Brandeis also urged the young men to leave Washington after their stint in government and, instead of going to New York, to go back home. He wanted Walter Gellhorn to go back to St. Louis, and in fact Roger Baldwin, later the founder of the American Civil Liberties Union, had started his career in the Midwest because of Brandeis's advice. When Willard Hurst considered leaving Wisconsin for Yale, Brandeis dissuaded him from doing so. To some extent he believed that the young men who had worked in Washington owed it to their home-towns to go back there, settle in, and work for the betterment of the community. He feared that the brilliant young law graduates who came down from Harvard, Columbia, and elsewhere would get in a rut, stay in the nation's capital, and die there. They might have successful careers, but they would have missed the opportunity to take their Washington experience and use it for the benefit of smaller communi-ties in the Midwest and elsewhere. While he never disparaged Susan for choosing to practice law in New York (because it would have been dif-ficult indeed for her to have gone back to Boston), he rejoiced that Paul and Elizabeth had chosen Madison, and in the work they did there.

Brandeis did not always appreciate that smaller communities did not have all of the resources available that bright young people might need in their work. His law clerk David Riesman took to heart the justice's suggestion that he go to a smaller law school and accepted a position at the University of Buffalo. There he started work on the law of libel, but, as he told Brandeis, "I am particularly hampered by the [poor] library situation here—one of the factors, incidentally, which militates against your repeated wish to see bright young men go out to the small communities."

BRANDEIS MAINTAINED many of the activities and interests he had cultivated throughout his life. Although he eschewed modern fiction, he continued to read widely and would often return to some book or author that he had enjoyed years earlier, especially Goethe. "Whenever one returns to Goethe," he told his sister-in-law, "there are new revela-tions." His interest in the ancient Greeks remained unabated, although unlike Holmes he did not read them in the original. Through his niece

Alice, Louis, and their grandchildren, late 1930s

Fannie, he kept his eye on developments at the University of Louisville, sending checks to cover particular outlays such as indexing or binding and urging the administration to build up the law school.

He continued to provide $3,500 a year to underwrite Felix Frankfurter's public service and kept up suggestions for articles by Frankfurter's students. He also corresponded with historians and helped promote work in early American legal history, a subject in which he had long been interested and which he would occasionally use in his opinions. Frankfurter continued to send a bright young Harvard man down each fall; in 1934, however, Brandeis told his cousin, somewhat in amazement, that he had taken a Yale graduate for his clerk, although Nathaniel Nathanson, the editor of the *Yale Law Review,* by then had a year of seasoning as a research fellow at Harvard and another year as Judge Mack's secretary.

In 1936 the occasion of his eightieth birthday led to a torrent of congratulatory messages. "You have built your ideals into the hearts of your countrymen," William Allen White declared, and your work will be "an inspiration to youth and a comfort to all who love freedom institutionalized into law." Because even at age eighty Brandeis believed that he should answer his mail personally, he wrote dozens, perhaps hundreds, of short notes, and complained to his son-in-law that it would be well into 1937 before he caught up. "It is fortunate that one reaches 80 only once." He wondered what all the fuss was about, since a man of eighty in public life "might indifferently be made the courting stock for all to practice on."

Although Alice declared that her husband "moves along each day as you have known him to do these many years," Brandeis no doubt became aware of his own mortality as people very near to him died during the decade. In April 1934 his former secretary and longtime ally in the fight for savings bank insurance, Alice Harriet Grady, passed away. As always aware of his sense of privacy, she left instructions that her correspondence with the justice should be destroyed, but before carrying out that wish, her brother Talmage Grady thought it best to have Brandeis look through the files. While destroying all that he considered confidential, he kept any documents he thought might be worthwhile to have for the records and sent them over to the Savings Bank Insurance League.

The death of Holmes came in March 1935, ending a friendship of nearly sixty years, and then, at the end of March 1937, his "teacher in Zionism" Jacob de Haas died. Although de Haas had managed to alienate many people in the Zionist movement, he never lost Brandeis's confidence. Throughout the 1920s and 1930s, Brandeis arranged for de Haas to have work, often providing the funds himself, and when de Haas came down with his terminal illness, Brandeis paid the hospital bills. To the end Brandeis remained loyal to de Haas, declaring that "he served the Jewish People throughout long years, to the best of his ability."

The following month Norman Hapgood died, and later that year Elizabeth Evans, after a long illness, passed away, much to the sorrow of both Alice and Louis. Auntie B. had been Alice's closest friend, and just as her husband could talk confidentially with Felix Frankfurter, so Alice could unburden herself to Bess Evans, who had been like a sister to her from the day they met. Hers was "a great life," he told Frankfurter, but when the Harvard professor asked for some message to read at her funeral, Brandeis could not do it. She was so much a member of the family, he said, it would be better that "what is to be said of her should be said by others."

WHATEVER OTHER PROBLEMS afflicted the country or mankind, Louis and Alice reveled in their roles as grandparents. In December 1930, Susan gave birth to her third child, Frank, and Alice, after having had two daughters, especially enjoyed the idea of three grandsons. Although they occasionally saw them during the Court term, the grandchildren now played a major role during the months at Chatham. Susan and Jack bought some property adjacent to her parents' home and built a house there. During the summer Jack worked in the city, coming up for weekends and an occasional longer vacation. Susan tended to take more time off from work, and her children ran freely between their home and that of their grandparents. Both houses had guest rooms for when Elizabeth, Paul, and Walter came.

Louis and Alice brought the children into their pastimes, canoeing, hiking, looking for wildflowers, and picking berries. When they had a question about anything, Louis would repeat the same ritual he had practiced when Susan and Elizabeth were young—send them to the encyclopedia or dictionary to look up the answers. Susan introduced them to tennis, and one summer bought a small boat to teach her children how to sail. Louis would occasionally write to his son-in-law reporting on the family and its doings. "Your family was on full exhibit yesterday and never in better form," he said. The older children had accompanied Alice on a visit to a neighbor, Mrs. Butler, and their behavior had been "exemplary." Then young Louis came over to entertain his grandfather for a while.

Brandeis fussed over the children when they caught colds, and recommended to Elizabeth and Paul as well as to Susan and Jack that they adopt a tried-and-true formula he had used for years—avoid drafts, wear rubbers, and apply a patent medicine called "V.E.M." morning and evening. "It's cheap at the price." As the grandchildren learned to write, he exchanged letters with them, and in much the same way he had written to his own girls four decades earlier. "Dear Walter: I was very glad to get your letter written in ink. I hope your bird-house is finished. Do you like this one? I hope the cat won't eat the bird." Bess Evans, a frequent houseguest in Chatham, became Auntie B. to another generation of Brandeis children, who wrote to her when they returned home. "I get the most adorable letters from your little grands," she told Alice. "Walter writes me that the longest word he can write is thanksgiving."

Much of the enjoyment in their grandchildren resulted, at least in part, from the fact that during the 1930s Alice and Louis enjoyed relatively good health. There were no more bouts of deep depression, and Louis described his wife as "energetic and joyous—quite her old self." Alice was not, however, immune to aging, and occasionally suffered the physical distress that accompanied it. "My legs have been troublesome," she told Mrs. Evans. "Bodies are such stupid and uninteresting things; I try not to notice mine." Louis in turn, although seeming frailer, continued to canoe and hike and to work at a steady pace.

They transferred additional wealth to their children on a regular basis, wanting them to be able to do as they had done, support causes they believed in strongly, and in February 1932 they set up a school fund for their grandchildren. They also helped out substantially when Susan and Jack ran into financial troubles in the middle of the decade. The Gilberts had high household expenses that included hired help and a nanny, since Susan continued to work. But the Depression reduced their legal business significantly, and, thinking that the loss of business would just be temporary, they borrowed some money to tide them over. Business did not pick up, and when Brandeis learned of this, he insisted on sending them money both to pay expenses and to satisfy their loans. He was more than happy to do this, he told them, "for I think it very unwise for either of you to borrow a penny from anyone."

There was never a word of reproach, save for one letter to his son-in-law, who apparently complained that he had been unable to secure the big break that would make his practice successful, as his father-in-law had done years earlier. Brandeis chided him on this philosophy, saying that his own practice ought not to be a model for anyone. "I hope nothing I have ever said indicated a desire that you and Susan should adopt in either your professional or personal lives, views or standards on which I act now or acted when of your age," he said. "No one is a stronger believer in the sanctity of each individual's choice."

He had always believed in Jack's legal ability, character, and willingness to work hard, which, when applied to his practice, should give him "a reasonable net income adequate to keep you from financial worry." Success could be achieved not by "adventurous strokes, but by the humdrum life—remaining at one's post and keeping down fixed charges." That is how one built up a law business, and he said this based on six decades as an observer of the lives of practicing lawyers.

But even if they had business problems, Brandeis approved of what his children and their spouses were doing with their lives. Susan and Jack became interested in Zionism, and Susan began a long tenure as a member of the New York Board of Regents, the body charged with oversight of all public education in the state. In Wisconsin both Elizabeth and Paul not only taught at the university but also were active in helping the state develop its social insurance programs, and Paul became a frequent visitor to Washington to work with the Social Security Administration. Much to the Brandeises' amusement and satisfaction, they heard Elizabeth described as "a real rabble-rouser" for speeches she gave on the state's social insurance plan. "Isn't that a grand name?" Alice asked Bess.

UNFORTUNATELY, aside from his grandchildren, little in the 1930s pleased Brandeis, especially news relating to Jewish affairs. Hope that the Brandeis faction would reinvigorate the ZOA soon withered in the realization that the Depression made it impossible either to raise funds or to launch new programs. In October 1930 the Passfield White Paper marked the beginning of a wholesale repudiation of the Balfour pledge, and despite strong Zionist objections Great Britain practically closed the doors of Palestine to further Jewish immigration in 1939. The betrayal of the terms of the mandate would have been a severe blow to Zionist hopes at any time, but the rise of Adolf Hitler in Germany and his plans to cleanse Germany and ultimately Europe of Jews meant that hundreds of thousands of Jews who might have found a haven in Palestine met their deaths in the gas chambers of Auschwitz and the other death camps. Ironically, the growing threat of Nazism led American Jews to return to Zionism in droves toward the end of the decade.

Brandeis kept in close touch with Robert Szold, Stephen Wise, and the other men who took over the ZOA administration, but even he realized the difficulty of the task without men, money, or discipline. They inherited an organization with $8 in its treasury and then had to borrow $20,000 just to pay overhead expenses during their first three months in office. Of the $100,000 pledged at the convention to help pay debts, less than one-third actually materialized. At the end of two years, membership had dropped to 8,800, despite a 50 percent dues reduction. (In 1933, $6 could easily feed a family of four for a week.) The *New Palestine* disappeared, replaced by an occasional newsletter. Even Hadassah lost membership, from 35,000 to 20,500, but remained in far better shape than the ZOA. About the only positive note Szold could point to was a $20,000 reduction in debt, a not insignificant feat considering the times.

Had the Brandeis group been concerned only with American Zionist affairs, the condition of the ZOA would have been sad but not serious, in that one could expect the organization to rebound as the country came out of the Depression. But the ZOA, and indeed the World Zionist Organization, stood ill prepared to confront the shift in British policy in the Middle East and the rise of fascism in Germany.

Great Britain found the realities of the Middle East far more com-

Nazi rally in Nuremburg, 1934

plex than it had anticipated. The sheer number of Arabs in the region compared with Jews, as well as the great oil reserves in Arab land, led to a reorientation of British policy around the concept of an Arab-dominated region under English tutelage. This idea had been pushed by Foreign Office careerists who considered the wartime pledges a mistake and who found the Jews irksome. Norman Bentwich, the attorney general of Palestine during this period, commented that the Jewish settlers and British colonial officers seemed to speak different languages. The Jews did not behave like the native Arabs; instead of obeying the orders of British officials, the Jews argued.

With very few exceptions, Zionists did not understand Arab nationalism and severely underestimated its strength. Brandeis had the same blind spot as did Weizmann, Lipsky, and other Zionist leaders. Following the 1929 riots, which left 125 dead, he wrote: "As against the Bedouins, our pioneers are in a position not unlike the American settlers against the Indians. I saw myself the need of their self-defense in 1919 in Poreah, with our Shomer [watchman] mounted on the hill top, and the blacktented Bedouins who had peaceably but with ever robber purpose, crossed the Jordan. As to other Arabs, the position is not different in essence, of course. Most Arabs will have guns, or at least knives, concealed, if possession is prohibited." Brandeis saw neither Indians nor Arabs as native people with prior attachments to and rights in the land.

He did not understand why Arabs did not welcome Jews, since they, too, would benefit from the economic growth and progress that the Jews would bring. At a meeting in November 1929 to review what should be done, Brandeis predicted:

> When the recent disorders shall have been overcome the work which has been done by the Jews for Arabs will be appreciated. Through our medical organizations, through the elimination of malaria and other diseases, we have done, the amelioration of the condition of the Arabs, an extraordinary amount, considering the shortness of time. Arabs, unlike some other peoples, have no inherent dislike of the Jews—certainly they did not have it. Jews lived among them in perfect amity before and during the war. I have confidence they will again do so.

In this area at least, the prophet erred badly.

Brandeis, even though out of power at this time, did what he could in the battle against the white paper. With his encouragement, Stephen Wise and Jacob de Haas compiled a list of statements of government documents issued by prior British administrations, proving that the Balfour Declaration and the mandate specifically promised Palestine to the Jews. Felix Frankfurter, who had more or less dropped out of Zionist affairs in the 1920s, came back and contributed an article on Albion's perfidy in the influential journal *Foreign Affairs.*

The justice and Frankfurter also contacted their common friend the English political theorist Harold Laski, pressing him to get information about England's intentions. Then suddenly, in late November 1930, Brandeis had an entrée to His Majesty's Government. Prime Minister Ramsay MacDonald had come under increasing attack for the Passfield White Paper, and he called in Laski to see if some sort of agreement could be worked out between the government and the Zionists. Laski thought that the two sides could each compromise, but Brandeis refused to do so and insisted that the British live up to their word. "Our rights legal and moral, seem clear," he told Bernard Flexner, then in London and serving as a conduit to Laski. "We shall

Louis, Alice, and Zionist leaders at Chatham, ca. 1940

succeed, provided we make sure that no part of our rights is frittered away by concession."

This obstinacy, along with the public outcry, gave Weizmann the leverage he needed in his talks with the government and forced Mac-Donald to back down from the severe strictures of the white paper. On 13 February 1931 the prime minister issued a letter that would "remove certain misconceptions and misunderstandings" with regard to British policy in Palestine. In essence, he repudiated the anti-Zionist passages of the Passfield statement and praised the Jewish work to rebuild Palestine. Immigration would be encouraged, limited only by the ability of the land to absorb people.

The victory, however, proved only temporary. The spirit behind the white paper, the desire of the British government to appease both Nazis and Arabs, and the anti-Zionism and anti-Semitism rampant in the Foreign Office would triumph before the decade ended.

FEW PEOPLE at first took seriously the rise of Adolf Hitler and Nazism. After all, the man must be crazy, and only the most rabid Jew hater could applaud his demagoguery. Even Charlie Chaplin's later caricature of him in *The Great Dictator* could not convey the sense of burlesque that he himself generated. A study of editorial attitudes in America's most influential newspapers found a range of response from concern to disbelief that anyone would pay this lunatic any attention at all. Jewish journals, of course, could not ignore any anti-Semitism, but they, too, vacillated in their response. German Jews also failed to show much concern at this time. Very few of them emigrated from Germany in the early years of the Hitler regime, and in fact German refugees did not use up that country's annual quota for entry into the United States until 1938. Martin Rosenblüth, a German Zionist who tried to warn Jew and non-Jew alike of the Nazi menace, found that no one would listen to him.

In 1931, before Hitler came to power, Felix Frankfurter received papers about Nazi ventures in Bavaria and the riots caused by the Brown Shirts. He sent them on to Stephen Wise, who from that time on kept an eye on German affairs and became the first, and for a long time the lone, American Jewish leader to warn against fascism. He kept Brandeis informed, and the justice, who also took German matters seriously, received a great deal of information about affairs in Nazi Germany from a variety of sources, including the State Department.

One day his clerk picked up the phone, and Raymond Moley told him that he understood the justice wanted to see Secretary of State Cordell Hull, and the secretary would be happy to call on him at Brandeis's convenience. Paul Freund said he would check and call Moley back. "No, that's wrong," Brandeis said, "it's not I who want to see Secretary Hull, it is he who wants to see me." Protocol had no role here. Rather, from an institutional standpoint, it would not do for a member of the judiciary to involve himself in foreign affairs. "I will see the Secretary at his convenience here in my apartment." Freund called back and conveyed the message to Moley, who immediately understood Brandeis's point. "Of course, of course," Moley said, laughing, "it's Secretary Hull who wants to see the Justice." At the appointed time Hull called, and Brandeis told him what he knew about events in Germany. Hull responded that if this were indeed the case, the United States would not be able to stand by idly.

At the beginning of 1933 a wave of anti-Semitic riots spread across Germany just as Hitler took power; in March the Nazis instigated riots in Berlin and other cities and called for a boycott of all Jewish stores and businesses. Finally the leaders of American Jewry paid attention, and the American Jewish Committee and B'nai B'rith invited Wise, as head of the American Jewish Congress, to meet with them. The conference fell apart at once over the same strategy that had plagued Jewish responses during World War I; the committee and B'nai B'rith opposed Wise's plans for rallies to protest German policy. When he persisted, they brought immense pressure on him to call off a mass meeting at Madison Square Garden in New York, warning him that a public outcry would only bring further harm to German Jews.

Not knowing what to do, Wise sought advice from the one man whom he trusted implicitly—Louis Brandeis. On 13 March 1933, Wise went to Washington and spent over two hours in the justice's study, telling him about what he had learned, the dangers he foresaw, the fearfulness of other American Jewish leaders in speaking out, and what he saw as the moral need for American Jews to protest. Brandeis listened carefully, asked questions, and at the end told Wise, "Go ahead and make the protest good as you can." On 27 March more than 22,000 people jammed Madison Square Garden, an additional 30,000 listened to speeches over loudspeakers set up outside, and untold numbers listened in on the radio, including Bess Evans.

Shortly after the rally Wise went to Washington again to lobby congressmen to protest German actions, and he went over to see Brandeis. The justice met him at the door and told him, "You have done a mighty fine job." Then, in a rare display of emotion, Brandeis took Wise's hands in his own and said, "You must go on and lead. No one could have done a finer piece of work." Reinforcing Wise's own beliefs, Brandeis said there could be no compromise, no negotiations with what he called the "supercautious" establishment Jews; the protest had to continue. A few weeks later, after another attack from the American Jewish Committee, Wise opened his mail to find a one-line message scribbled on Supreme Court notepaper: "Merely to say you are doing 'splendid.' " Later, Brandeis believed that the Roosevelt administration, then itself new to office, might have been prevailed upon to speak out had it not been for Jews like Max Warburg telling Roosevelt that nothing could be done.

Wise also reported that when he first told Brandeis about German policies in March 1933, a little over a week after Hitler had taken office, the jurist had said, "The Jews must leave Germany!" Wise protested that a half-million Jews could not leave. "It is an impossibility." Brandeis repeated, "They must leave Germany, and they will. The day must come when Germany shall be Judenfrei and Germany shall see for itself how to live without its Jewish population." Brandeis did not assent to Hitler's policy; rather, he believed that no self-respecting Jew could remain within the so-called Third Reich. When Gardner Jackson and his wife went to Europe in the mid-1930s, Brandeis pleaded with them not to visit Germany, because any American dollars spent there supported Hitler's work.

It must have been difficult for Brandeis to say this, raised as he had been to venerate German culture, to speak its language as a child, to have been sent to school there. There is of course an element of un-reality here, the notion that an entire population could just turn its back on its home, and in doing so teach its tormentors how much German Jewry meant to the nation's culture and prosperity. In fact, between 1933 and 1939 over 300,000 Jews did emigrate from Germany and from the territory it took over before the war, the Czech Sudetenland and Austria, and more than 62,000 of them came to the United States.

(Among these were Betty and Louise Brandeis, second cousins who lived in Vienna. Brandeis swore out an affidavit in May 1938 that he had ample resources and would be willing to sponsor them in the United States so they would not become public charges. The two women arrived in New York in July, where officials of the Hebrew Immigrant Aid Society met them and secured temporary lodgings for them. Brandeis also made contributions to a group organized by his former law clerk David Riesman to rescue academics and find them positions in American universities.)

Brandeis had another destination in mind—Palestine. If even a quarter-million people went to the *yishuv*, its future would be guaranteed. He had no doubt that hardworking emigrants, people like his father and uncles, would be able to prosper in a new country, and in turn would ensure the success of the Zionist experiment. In fact, some 55,000 German Jews did manage to get to Palestine, and in the early years many of them were able to take at least some of their resources with them to start life anew.

Other persecuted Jews, however, would never get a chance to make aliyah. Even as Nazi persecution increased, Great Britain, despite MacDonald's letter, moved relentlessly toward a policy of restricting immigration. Ironically, as these two threats to the Jewish future grew, the fortunes of the ZOA improved. The American Jewish Committee and the other established German-American groups still clung to what Wise called their "sh-sh" policy, preferring to work quietly behind the scenes, even after it became clear that such tactics did not work. Only the ZOA and the American Jewish Congress spoke out openly, and in the 1930s Zionist membership swelled. It became increasingly difficult for American Jewry to remain silent either to the plight of German refugees or to the needs of Palestine.

The Zionists did not have a problem of entrée to the White House. Felix Frankfurter and Julian Mack, a friend of the president's from Harvard affairs, both sent Roosevelt information on Nazi depredations.

Both men kept Brandeis informed, and Isaiah himself spoke to Roosevelt about the worsening situation. Also, at their request, Roosevelt directed the State Department to provide Zionist leaders with information received about Palestine. What Brandeis, Wise, and the other leaders of the ZOA failed to understand is that the United States at this time could do very little. The American people, or at least those who paid attention to foreign affairs, might express revulsion at Hitler, but the only political issue they cared about was revival of the American economy. Even if Franklin Roosevelt had wanted to have an active foreign policy, he enjoyed little support for it either from Congress or from the American people, both of which grew increasingly isolationist in the early 1930s. And although polite people did not talk about it, anti-Semitism grew significantly in the United States during this time, especially with the prominence of so many Jews in the Roosevelt administration. Fear of adding to this problem led Brandeis to decline an honorary degree from the Hebrew University in 1936, an honor that he had been inclined to accept to highlight the importance of the school in building Palestine. "We must run no risk of raising another groundless ground for Anti-Semitism."

Both because of his role on the Court and his age, Brandeis in the 1930s became what he had promised when his followers regained leadership of the ZOA—an adviser. He nonetheless followed Jewish affairs closely, received and read reports from the ZOA, and made specific suggestions on particular problems. When Stephen Wise proposed a boycott of German goods after Hitler took power, the justice asked his law clerk if he could get some information on the use of the boycott in America in colonial times. After Roosevelt named Robert Bingham, the owner of Louisville's *Courier-Journal* and an old friend of the Brandeis family's, as ambassador to Great Britain, Bingham asked the justice if, being a Kentuckian, he could have the honor of having Brandeis swear him into office. Brandeis replied that he would be delighted to do so, but after the ceremony spent some forty-five minutes talking to the new ambassador on Palestine and British obligations there.

His interest in Palestine did not falter; if anything, it increased. Visiting Palestinians made their way to Florence Court, where the elderly jurist eagerly listened to their stories and quizzed them on minute details of life on a kibbutz or in the new towns. Brandeis had given $50,000 to help establish a kibbutz that would be populated primarily by Americans. When Shmuel Ben-Zvi, an American who made aliyah and lived on that kibbutz (which had been named Ein Hashofet— "Well of the Judge"—in honor of Brandeis), returned to the United

States for a visit, he went to Washington to talk to Brandeis. Brandeis quickly put the younger man at ease, and, Ben-Zvi recalled, "I found myself talking and telling him all kinds of details and stories. I told him about our work, about the members we lost in attacks, relations with the Arabs, cultural life . . . and the blankets we make out of our own wool."

Ben-Zvi later expressed amazement at how much Brandeis knew about Palestine in general, and about life on a kibbutz in particular; when Mrs. Brandeis came into the room, Louis asked Ben-Zvi to repeat some of the stories for her. He, of course, wanted to know specific figures about their crops and what percentage of their food and clothing they produced for themselves, and Ben-Zvi promised to send the information to him. When he did, Brandeis wrote back, "Congratulations that you keep such an accurate accountancy." Ben-Zvi, of course, was an avatar of the type of Jew who Brandeis hoped would make Palestine into the ideal society he envisioned: a university-educated person whose idealism had led him to leave home and settle in a new and challenging place in which one could live simply but in fulfillment of one's hopes. He derived great satisfaction when two of his cousins on the Dembitz side moved their families to Palestine in 1935, and he exchanged letters with them on the political situation over the next few years, always confident that in the end "our righteous cause must prevail."

Brandeis also continued to contribute significant amounts of money to Zionist work in Palestine. In 1935, for example, he gave $20,000 toward a project to buy land in the Aqaba region, after the importance of the site had been explained to him by David Ben-Gurion. In Ben-Gurion and in his associate Moshe Shertok, Brandeis correctly saw the future of Zionism, young, smart Palestinians who had already begun supplanting Weizmann's group. He had great confidence in them, and after Ben-Gurion founded the Haganah, Brandeis secretly provided at least $45,000 to purchase arms so that the settlers could defend themselves against Arab attacks. As early as 1929, Brandeis had declared that Jews in Palestine should not be denied the chance to defend themselves, and when new riots broke out in 1937, he sent an additional $10,000 "to Palestine for disposition as Ben-Gurion may direct, as with earlier remittances." Once the terrorists were soundly beaten, he believed, arrangements could be made to get along with the other Arabs.

A touchstone of both European and American Zionism had been that Palestine would be the haven to which persecuted Jews could flee, and Brandeis like many Zionists wanted to believe that Great Britain would keep the promise it had made in the Balfour Declaration and validated in accepting the mandate. Between 1933 and 1935, some 134,000 people legally entered Palestine, far beyond what the Colonial Office considered the country's capacity, yet with their coming the *yishuv* flourished. Like an oasis amid the worldwide Depression, Palestine prospered—exports and imports rose 50 percent in just two years, the Jewish population grew to 400,000, and 160 agricultural settlements dotted the countryside. Immigration would probably have increased even more had the Colonial Office not imposed restrictions or denied the Jewish Agency for Palestine the number of visas it requested.

Although the Arab population benefited from this prosperity, resentment against the newcomers increased, and in April 1936 isolated attacks on individual Jews escalated into wide-scale rioting. The Arab Higher Committee, led by the mufti of Jerusalem, called for a general strike and encouraged guerrilla bands to attack Jewish settlements. Most ominously, neighboring Arab countries supported the attacks, and the Nazis, recognizing the importance of the Middle East in any future war, established links with the mufti, inviting him to visit Berlin. The British government reacted more firmly than it had in 1929, brought in more troops, and quickly suppressed the riots. His Majesty's Government also decided to halt further immigration and appointed still another royal commission to study the Palestine problem.

Wise, in London at the time on his way back from Palestine, joined Weizmann, Ben-Gurion, and Shertok in trying to negotiate with the Crown. He conveyed the futility of this effort in a letter to Brandeis, believing that nothing could now avert suspension of immigration. When Wise arrived back in the United States, he requested and received an interview with Franklin Roosevelt, who much to Wise's surprise seemed well informed on Palestine. At Wise's request, the president had Secretary of State Cordell Hull inform the British that the United States "would regard suspension of immigration as a breach of the Mandate." The prime minister, Stanley Baldwin, decided that by a small gesture he could placate both the Zionists and the American president, and announced that until the royal commission finished its work, there would be no change in Palestinian immigration policy.

"You have performed a marvelous feat," Brandeis told Wise, "nothing more important for us has happened since the Mandate, perhaps nothing so important as to make clear to Great Britain America's deep interest. . . . It will show that F.D.'s administration 'means business'; and will be a record for the future." It meant no such thing, and Brandeis should have known better. American rights in the Holy Land had been defined and circumscribed in the Anglo-American Convention of 1924, and aside from some commercial interests the United States had little to say about the government of Palestine or its immigration policy. In an election year Roosevelt had nothing to lose by this piece of theater. If His Majesty's Government had said no, then he had tried; by granting a delay, the British had sacrificed nothing, and gave Roosevelt another card to play in his bid for reelection.

The Peel Commission, by all reports the most able of all the royal inquiries, finished its work in July 1937 and, recognizing the intractable problems, recommended the partition of Palestine into Jewish and Arab territories and the severe restriction of further Jewish immigration. Brandeis was furious, and he urged the Zionists to oppose partition with all their might. American Jewish leaders pleaded with Roosevelt to act, and the justice went to the White House himself in October 1938 for the first time since the Court-packing plan had failed. He urged Roosevelt to pressure the British into doing the right thing, and he reported that he had found the president sympathetic. Following the bloody Kristallnacht riots in Germany on 9 and 10 November 1938, it became clear that only Palestine could be a haven for Hitler's victims, and Brandeis again pleaded with Roosevelt to act.

This time His Majesty's Government stood determined, and Zionists learned that a white paper essentially closing Palestine to all but a handful of immigrants would be forthcoming. Brandeis appealed to Roosevelt at least four times between 6 March and 10 May 1939 for the United States to stop Britain from shutting the doors to the one place that could take the growing tide of refugees. The campaign that the ZOA mounted led Roosevelt, who believed that a major shift in policy would be a mistake for the British, to have the State Department inform the Foreign Office that the United States hoped that no drastic changes would be implemented in Palestinian immigration. All to no avail. On 17 May 1939 the Crown issued a white paper declaring that an independent Jewish state would be created in ten years, and that immigration to Palestine would be limited to a total of 75,000 people over the next five years; after March 1944 there would be no further Jewish immigration without Arab permission, and Jewish settlements would be limited to restricted areas. The anguish felt by millions of Jews in Europe and elsewhere found expression in Louis Brandeis's simple question: "Where will a poor Jew go now?"

CHAPTER THIRTY

THE PASSING OF ISAIAH

During the Court-packing fight, rumors had abounded that Brandeis would step down, thus giving Roosevelt an appointment and ending the jarring battle. Roosevelt, according to one story, wanted to appoint Felix Frankfurter to Brandeis's seat. The justice, however, would not be budged. To resign in the midst of the struggle would harm the Court, and as for Frankfurter, the Harvard professor had lost some of his sheen by backing Roosevelt's plan.

Brandeis knew, and those close to him recognized, that age had begun taking an increasing toll on his strength since his eightieth birthday. His mental capacity remained unimpaired, but he now wrote fewer than half the number of opinions he had written in his first two decades on the bench. Where he used to greet his guests at the door, they now found him seated at the Monday afternoon teas. He and Mrs. Brandeis continued to have people in for dinner, though the occasions were fewer, and Alice moved the departure time to nine o'clock. But he still had work to do, and in some ways his last terms on the Court gave him a great deal of satisfaction.

FOR ALL PRACTICAL PURPOSES, the decision in *West Coast Hotel* ended the fight between the Court and the New Deal, and although there would still be some 5–4 decisions, the Court did not strike down any more New Deal measures. With the retirement of Willis Van Devanter in June 1937 and of George Sutherland in January 1938, Roosevelt's two appointees to replace them, Hugo Black and Stanley Reed, gave the Court a clear majority backing New Deal economic measures. Although Black would go on to become one of the great justices of the twentieth century, Brandeis at first mistrusted him and believed he did not have either the legal or the intellectual ability to sit on the nation's highest bench. Within a short time Brandeis's opinion of the Alabaman shot up. He approved of Black's first opinion, and after his retirement told a visitor that Black was a hard worker and diligent. On the other hand, "the Court will welcome Stanley Reed," he told Frankfurter. The justices knew Reed from his appearances as solicitor general, and the Kentuckian had been a frequent visitor to tea or dinner at the Brandeis apartment. Then in early 1938, Benjamin Cardozo became gravely ill, and died on 9 July. To replace him, Roosevelt, after teasing his friend unmercifully, named Felix Frankfurter to the Court, and he took his seat at the end of January 1939.

During these years Brandeis saw some of his dissents adopted by the Court. A series of cases first upheld the Norris–La Guardia Act prohibiting injunctions in labor disputes and then gave labor the protection that it had sought from prosecution under the antitrust laws, thus repudiating the *Duplex* decision. In *Nardone v. United States* (1937), the Court sustained a congressional statute outlawing wiretapping by federal agents, validating Brandeis's dissent in *Olmstead*. Chief Justice Hughes spoke for the Court upholding the National Labor Relations Act and validating Brandeis's argument that the state had the power to protect the liberty of workingmen by enforcing the right of collective bargaining.

In the last of the 5–4 labor cases decided in the 1930s, Brandeis spoke for the Court and took another step in expanding freedom of speech and also in validating the power of the states to bar injunctions in strikes. In *Senn v. Tile Layers Protective Union,* Brandeis brought picketing as a means of communication under the aegis of the First Amendment. "Members of a union might, without special statutory authorization by a State, make known the facts of a labor dispute," he wrote, "for freedom of speech is guaranteed by the federal Constitution." While a state could regulate the manner in which picketing took place so as to preserve order, it could not bar peaceful picketing, which had the intention of communicating to the public and to other workers the nature of the labor grievance.

Had this case arisen before the Taft Court, it would have undoubtedly been decided the other way. Paul Senn, an independent tile contractor, did half of the actual tile laying himself, with the help of one or two assistants. He could not join the union, because he had never served an apprenticeship under union sponsorship. The union demanded that he run a closed shop, which meant he would not be able to lay tile himself, in effect putting him out of business. He refused, and the union picketed his job site. Senn's position represented a pure example of an individual seeking to pursue an occupation, a right that the Court had on numerous occasions held as fundamental. Brandeis's description of picketing as the equivalent of commercial advertising ignored the fact that this "advertising" aimed to cut off a man's livelihood. The conservatives of the Taft Court would have fastened on that; Brandeis's credo of self-restraint led him to look for a rational legislative reason. Finding that, he ignored the practical results.

LOUIS BRANDEIS'S LAST GREAT CASE involved a cause to which he had been committed ever since going onto the bench, keeping federal jurisdiction within its constitutional bounds. A key element in his jurisprudence was the belief that the Constitution limited the power of federal courts, just as it did the executive and legislative branches. In *Erie Railroad Co. v. Tompkins* (1938), Brandeis not only overturned a century of precedent, but did so in a most unusual manner.

In 1812, the Marshall Court held that no federal common-law jurisdiction existed in the new nation; that is, federal judges were bound by the jurisdictional and statutory rules of the states in which the federal courts were located. In the next three decades, however, the nation's economy grew far more rapidly than local laws could accommodate, and companies that did business in more than one jurisdiction began demanding consistency across state lines. Then Justice Joseph Story in *Swift v. Tyson* (1842) interpreted section 34 of the Judiciary Act of 1789 to mean that federal courts did not have to follow the decisional rules of the state courts, but only state statutory law. Since the decisional rules were often part of the state's common law, this meant that federal courts were now free to create a separate federal common law when hearing commercial questions.

The importance of this decision to the new commercial interests cannot be overestimated. As firms grew larger and operated in more than one state, they could "forum shop" to find a federal court whose rules would be most receptive to their claims. Despite the barriers that the Constitution had supposedly erected to limit federal court jurisdiction, it did not prove hard to find a judge sympathetic to commercial interests who could stretch the meaning of such terms as "diversity of citizenship," a constitutional rule barring citizens of the same state from going into federal courts. By the end of the nineteenth century there were practically no jurisdictional limits on the federal courts. They had achieved primacy not only over state courts and legislatures but to some extent even over Congress.

One of the most notorious abuses of this practice came in 1928 when a Kentucky taxicab company went across the state line, reincorporated

Work sheet for Erie v. Tompkins, *1938*

in Tennessee, and then went into federal court to secure an injunction against a Kentucky competitor that had followed Kentucky law. The Supreme Court upheld the lower court, leading Holmes, joined by Brandeis, to enter a vigorous dissent in which he termed the *Swift* decision "an unconstitutional assumption of powers by courts of the United States which no lapse of time or respectable array of opinions should make us hesitate to correct."

Brandeis had recognized this problem well before the taxicab case. The use of the injunction against labor, as well as opposition to state progressive legislation, led many reformers to call for restrictions on federal jurisdiction. Not only populists and progressives joined the fight; proponents of states' rights opposed what they saw as augmentation of federal authority at the expense of the states. In the academy liberal law professors like Felix Frankfurter supported the case for restricting federal courts, and throughout the progressive era and again in the 1920s reformers introduced bills in Congress to that end. They met strong resistance from powerful business interests that did not want to lose their access to sympathetic federal judges.

The first break came in 1932, when Congress passed the Norris–La Guardia Act restricting the power of federal courts to issue injunctions in labor disputes. Public faith in business and the legislative influence of corporations waned during the Depression. But average people had no idea what diversity of jurisdiction meant, nor did they care; one can work up public enthusiasm for a social security act or the electrification of rural America, but not for a bill dealing with a technical aspect of the law. Moreover, conservative members of Congress saw the federal courts as a bulwark not just for business but also against wild-eyed reformers. If change were to come, it had to come from within the high court itself. That chance grew out of a railroad accident.

Harry Tompkins was walking along the right-of-way of the Erie Railroad, a New York corporation, in Hughestown, Pennsylvania, late one night. A train with an object protruding from it struck Tompkins, knocking him under the wheels of the train. He was found unconscious, his right arm severed. After recovering from the accident, he filed suit against the railroad. According to Pennsylvania law, Tompkins would have been considered a trespasser, weakening his case for a judgment against the Erie. His lawyer, therefore, filed suit in federal court in New York, which viewed Tompkins as a "licensee" permitted to walk on the right-of-way. Tompkins won his suit, and the railroad appealed. Neither party, it should be noted, wanted to overrule *Swift,* and the railroad argued only that the lower federal court had misinterpreted the law. At conference the justices voted to reverse, and Hughes, knowing Brandeis's interest in jurisdiction, assigned the case to him, not expecting the length to which he would go.

Had Brandeis followed the criteria he had set out in *Ashwander,* he could not have mounted his assault on *Swift,* since the constitutional argument had not been made either in the lower court, in the appeals briefs, or in oral arguments. The case, however, gave him the first opportunity since the taxicab case ten years earlier to deal with federal jurisdiction head-on, and he took the opportunity. Two members of the Old Guard—Van Devanter and Sutherland—had left the Court, and their replacements sympathized with reform efforts to limit jurisdiction. Moreover, Justice Cardozo's absence due to illness also worked to Brandeis's advantage. Had he been there, Cardozo would undoubtedly have argued for a narrowing of *Swift* rather than its outright reversal. Brandeis had to reach out well beyond the original borders of the case to attack the *Swift* doctrine, and despite the effort to sound dispassionate, Brandeis in this opinion is writing his personal view into law just as he had criticized the Four Horsemen for doing.

Ever the teacher, he spent half of the opinion detailing the mischievous results of *Swift*. Whereas Holmes in the taxicab dissent had objected primarily on intellectual grounds to the notions of a general common law, Brandeis the reformer pinpointed the abuses that flowed from Story's doctrine. He also attacked Story's interpretation of the 1789 Judiciary Act as historically wrong. The heart of his opinion, however, lay in its constitutional architecture, something that befuddled many people who, even if they agreed with the result, found the argument confusing. Because the decision required federal courts to follow state decisional rules and did away with forum shopping, most commentators have focused on the choice of law issues and ignored the constitutional argument. They did not understand what Brandeis meant when he termed *Swift* an unconstitutional decision. Many law professors and judges—even Felix Frankfurter—have ignored Brandeis's constitutional argument because they did not appreciate it.

To Brandeis, the Constitution set up not only a separation of powers but a balance of powers as well, and he considered it clear (as do most modern scholars) that the Framers intended Congress to be the prime agency of the national government. This meant not that Congress overshadowed or could dominate the other two branches but that, in the delegation of powers, the Framers intended Congress to have the lion's share as well as the initiative in setting policy. While in some areas the Court's authority correlated to that of the other two branches, and while it ruled supreme within its designated domain, it could never assume primacy within the government ahead of Congress. The Court had done just that; it had extended its power to make itself the prime branch of government, against the intentions of the Framers and the clear wording of the Constitution itself.

The breathtaking scope of the opinion left some of the brethren unhappy. Stanley Reed, who had just joined the Court, wound up concurring in part because he could not go along with the constitutionality argument. The same reason upset Stone, who nonetheless agreed to go along after meeting with Brandeis, and he even suggested strengthening the constitutional basis. Stone may also have been more sympathetic because Brandeis had signed on to his opinion in the *Carolene Products* case handed down that same day, with its revolutionary argument that courts would apply strict scrutiny to laws affecting discrete minorities.

Although it initially appeared that Brandeis had done away with all federal law, that would have been impossible. Federal courts also had to deal with matters arising on land owned by the national government, as well as interstate matters where the laws of a state did not apply. Brandeis made this abundantly clear in a companion case, *Hinderlider v. La Plata River & Cherry Creek Ditch Co.* A Colorado state engineer stopped the company from siphoning water from the La Plata River in violation of a congressionally approved compact between Colorado and New Mexico over how the river's waters would be divided. The company, relying on state law, claimed he had no authority. Speaking for a unanimous Court, Brandeis held there is a federal common law when interstate boundary and water disputes are involved, as well as in matters affecting federal lands.

Erie has had a troubled history. In part this is due to what is for Brandeis an uncharacteristically obtuse opinion, one in which he violated several of the rules he had set down as guides to the Court in the *Ashwander* case. Later in the year Congress approved the Federal Rules of Civil Procedure (FRCP), which set up independent decisional rules for federal courts, although they are still required to follow state statutory law. Brandeis had wanted the courts to follow state decisional rules as well as statutory law, but the FRCP gave federal courts more leeway in which to fashion a federal common law. In addition, the growth of uniform codes, especially the Uniform Commercial Code, led to an increasing congruence of commercial law among the states and between the states and the federal courts. Some commentators believe that most private law cases heard in federal courts would be decided the same way under *Swift* as under *Erie.* Story's opinion served its purpose at a time when American commercial law had been a patchwork of different state laws, and by 1938 had outlived its usefulness.

But *Erie* also has to be seen as the private law counterpart to the abandonment of substantive due process after the 1937 fracas. Federal courts had used substantive due process to control the legislature in its efforts to regulate the economy and the labor market, and had used the *Swift* doctrine to essentially control state legislatures in terms of private law. The demise of both these doctrines marked a fitting end to Brandeis's tenure on the Court.

IN THE FALL OF 1938, Brandeis's law clerk, Adrian Fisher, working in the justice's study at Florence Court, received a phone call from a clearly upset Alice Brandeis. The elevator in the building was out of commission, the justice was on his way home from Court, and he could not be allowed to climb five steep flights of stairs. What would Fisher do about it? Fisher immediately went downstairs and found a straight-backed wooden chair; he then sought the help of the janitor, a big man who Fisher thought ought to have been playing professional football. When the eighty-two-year-old Brandeis entered, Fisher explained that the elevator was not working and asked him to sit down; then the two men carried him in the chair up the stairs to his apartment. "I will never forget that," Fisher later recalled. "Brandeis in his overcoat and derby, serene as could be, taking it all in stride as though there was not the slightest problem." In the meantime, Alice had run downstairs to supervise, and since she also had a weak heart, Fisher and the janitor came down and then carried her up as well.

Shortly after the new year, Fisher received another call, this one from Graham Claytor, who had been Brandeis's clerk the preceding term. The justice had become ill while on the bench, and Fisher should arrange for a doctor to be at the apartment. Brandeis had a bout of flu (or grippe as they then called it) and probably suffered a minor heart attack as well. It took him a while to recover, and he uncharacteristically missed a month of work.

Brandeis had always been concerned about the effects of age on performance; Marshall and Story, he thought, had stayed too long, past the point where they stopped growing intellectually. Particularly since Holmes's resignation, the justice had been concerned that he might not recognize when he should leave, and because he trusted Chief Justice Hughes, he had gone to him at the end of the term in 1937 and asked if he should retire. Hughes had responded that he saw no justification in doing so. Brandeis went again the following year, and this time the chief laid out what he thought were cogent reasons for Brandeis to stay. On 4 February, after returning to the Court, Brandeis again sought out Hughes, and again the chief saw no reason for him to retire.

The next day Brandeis had a long conversation with the newest member of the Court and told Frankfurter that he would resign the following week. While he believed that his judgment was as good as ever, he no longer had the physical stamina that the job demanded. He had not carried his share of the workload, and he did not want to continue unless he could do the job thoroughly; he did not know how to do it any other way. He would continue sitting so as not to give advance notice, and then on the chosen day he would send a note to the president. Frankfurter had started to express his regret at great length when Brandeis cut him off. "That's not why I called you here. What are we going to do with Adrian?" Frankfurter agreed to use Fisher himself, although the young man continued to help out Brandeis on nonjudicial tasks.

A little over a week later, a courier delivered the following note to the White House: "Dear Mr. President: Pursuant to the Act of March, 1937, I retire this day from regular active service on the bench. Cordially, Louis D. Brandeis." That day he joined the other justices, and a reporter in the chamber noted that no ceremony marked the occasion. Brandeis walked with a firm step that gave no indication either of his age or of his recent illness. He listened carefully as Justice Stone read the sole opinion of the day, but he asked no questions in oral argument in a case where the government wanted to deport Joseph Strecker, a former communist, knowing he would take no part in the decision.

Upon news of his leaving, newspapers all over the country lauded his service, and letters flowed in from hundreds of people. Roosevelt's secretary called the president, who was in Hyde Park, to read him the letter, and Roosevelt immediately responded. Although "one must perforce accept the inevitable," he had come to think of the justice as a "very permanent part of the Court," one who in fact would still be there long after Roosevelt left Washington. He would, of course, accede, but hoped their long association would continue, with "the hope that you will be spared for many long years to come to render additional services to mankind."

From his brethren on the Court came the traditional farewell letter, signed by all of the justices save McReynolds, who continued his anti-Semitic stance to the end. The letter said, in part, "It has always been gratifying to observe that the intensity of your labors has never been permitted to disturb your serenity of spirit. . . . We trust that, relieved of the pressing burden of regular court work, you may be able to conserve the strength which has been so lavishly used in the public service, and that you may enjoy many years of continued vigor." Brandeis replied briefly that the justices were "very generous," and their past friendship would ensure that they would remain companions in the years to come.

Newspapers that had once condemned him as a "radical" now praised him as a great jurist. Solicitor General Robert H. Jackson (who Brandeis had said should hold that position for life) wrote a moving essay recalling Brandeis's lifelong fight against industrial injustice, and noting that in the lobby of the Justice Department building there was a large mural bearing an inscription from a Brandeis opinion, "If we would guide by the light of reason, we must let our minds be bold." In Congress, David Walsh, an old Brandeis ally, rose to laud him in the

Senate, while columnists as varied as David Lawrence, Walter Lippmann, and Max Lerner praised him, albeit for differing reasons.

The letter that no doubt touched him most came from his daughter Elizabeth. It had been hard to write, she confessed, and she did not want to sound mawkish. She understood that there should be no grieving; everything had to have an end. She did not fully comprehend all that he had done, but each year she came to have a greater appreciation, and expected that others would as well. "If the lessons you have taught do not seem to be learned very well yet, that is not for any lack on your part. Measuring my words, I do not see how any person could have done more than you have done." Nonetheless, endings are always sad, but she promised that she and Paul would try, as would countless others, to carry on his work. "We shall all know how inadequate we are and how far we fall short of the standards you set. But I know you will be generous in your judgment of us."

Despite the outpouring of praise, life in Washington went on, and speculation soon reached a fever pitch as to whom Roosevelt would appoint to take Brandeis's place. Western senators wanted a man from their region, and liberals inside the administration persuaded the president to appoint the controversial head of the Securities and Exchange Commission, William O. Douglas, who originally came from the state of Washington. Douglas then and later considered himself a Brandeis disciple. During the 1930s he had been a regular visitor to Florence Court, and sent Brandeis SEC reports that echoed the indictment Brandeis had made years earlier of the New Haven's finances. Both men had a strong aversion to the curse of bigness. Once, when Douglas left the apartment, Brandeis turned to his clerk and said with a smile, "He's quite a fellah."

Roosevelt sent in Douglas's nomination on 20 March 1939, and that day Brandeis received an emotion-filled letter from Douglas. He was overwhelmed with humility, Douglas wrote, aware of the enormous task ahead of him, and mindful of the "great responsibility of one who is asked to wear your robe. The honor of the position is a great one. But the honor of following in your footsteps is even greater." Years later Douglas claimed that before his retirement Brandeis had recommended him to the president as his successor, but no one has ever found evidence to back this up, and Douglas's memoirs are full of exaggerations, misrepresentations, and out-and-out falsehoods. Brandeis did in fact approve of Douglas as his successor, and would certainly have approved of Douglas's strong defense of freedom of speech and the right to privacy. Many other aspects of Douglas's long tenure on the high court, however, would have filled him with dismay.

DURING HIS RETIREMENT Brandeis followed pretty much the same routine he had adopted nearly a quarter century earlier. As soon as the weather became warm, he and Alice went up to Chatham, staying there until late September. He continued to receive visitors both on the Cape and at Florence Court, although Mrs. Brandeis watched over him to make sure he did not tire. These callers brought him news of government and of Zionism, both of which he continued to watch closely. Members of the Court, particularly Stone, Frankfurter, and Douglas, stopped by and sent him their opinions, which he almost invariably praised.

Alice and Louis at Chatham, 1941

After the Court upheld the 1938 Fair Labor Standards Act, Brandeis dropped Stone a note calling his opinion "powerful and persuasive," and saying "it must be a satisfaction to have buried *Hammer v. Dagenhart.*"

When Charles Evans Hughes retired at the end of the term in 1941, Roosevelt named Stone to chief justice, a move that won universal plaudits. Brandeis immediately wrote to Stone, "To have the office go to the most deserving must encourage the whole country." To a visitor Brandeis inquired, "Aren't you delighted with what the President has done? No other President has performed such a signal service." When his caller reminded Brandeis that President Taft, a Republican, had elevated White, a Democrat, to head the Court, the elderly jurist dismissed it. "White cannot be compared to Stone." To Roosevelt, Brandeis wrote, "For the Court and for our Country the nomination for Chief Justice is the best conceivable."

He continued to spend a great deal of time on Zionism, advising Robert Szold and the ZOA, providing generous gifts for projects, and, as the British marched headlong toward closing Palestinian immigration, trying unsuccessfully to devise a strategy to keep immigration open. Now that he had stepped down from the Court, he felt less reluctance to urge Roosevelt to act, although the justice understood, as did everyone else, that the outbreak of war in September 1939 changed everything. In April and May 1941 he sent notes to the president warning that the Jewish community in Palestine faced annihilation should the German armies sweep across Africa, and he wanted Roosevelt to pressure the British to arm the settlers for self-defense. Roosevelt, trying to help the British and aware that the United States would soon become involved, had the State Department forward the request. The Colonial Office, however, feared that arming the Jews could take place only if they also armed the much larger Arab population, a development no one wanted. Brandeis, although greatly disappointed by the actions of His Majesty's Government, nonetheless remained confident that "the great work in Palestine will go forward."

IN JUNE 1940, Alice wrote to an old friend, "I am glad to say Louis is as usual—serene and helpful whenever he can be." He enjoyed his family, took pleasure in writing letters to his growing grandchildren, and, at the request of a young political scientist from Princeton, agreed to cooperate on a biography, although he went to great pains to make sure that everyone understood it was not an "official" work. Alpheus Thomas Mason had come to Brandeis's attention for the works he had written in the 1930s: *Brandeis: Lawyer and Judge in the Modern State* (1933) and *The Brandeis Way* (1938), a study of savings bank insurance. Although Felix Frankfurter disapproved of Mason and wanted to choose the Brandeis biographer himself, the justice liked the young man and not only gave him full access to the papers he had earlier deposited at the University of Louisville but also agreed to interviews. Mason spent ten days at Chatham in July 1940 while the justice reminisced about his career, the people he had known, and his reform fights. Mason did not get to see the Court papers at Harvard, however, because Brandeis, at Frankfurter's urging, had closed them.

Brandeis's health slowly deteriorated, and while continuing his routine he found himself tiring more easily. He told his niece Fannie, "All I can do now is let people talk to me and imagine I can help. I don't, but . . ." and his voice trailed off. In the summer of 1941 while at Chatham, he suffered a bout of pneumonia and came back to Washington without the sense of rest and well-being that the Cape had usually given him. A spell of unusually hot weather in Washington incapacitated him. Alice told their nephew that "he is going it slowly but serene as ever," and she hoped that perhaps the worst was over.

In late September, Frankfurter came over for one of his periodic visits, which seemed to cheer the older man, and they talked about many things. The greatest mistakes men made, Brandeis said, derive from two weaknesses—the inability to say no and the unwillingness to take a vacation when they should, so that they make important decisions when tired. He also lauded Roosevelt, calling him a "noble figure" and, at least according to Frankfurter's recollection, "greater than Jefferson and almost as great as Lincoln." As Frankfurter left, he said he would be back soon for another talk.

On Wednesday morning, 1 October, Louis and Alice drove out to Rock Creek Park, where he lounged under a tree while she read to him. They returned home, and after lunch he suffered a heart attack; an ambulance rushed him to a hospital, where his condition deteriorated, and on Saturday evening he fell into a coma. Late afternoon on Sunday, 5 October, Louis Brandeis died.

The next morning close friends received telephone calls that Mrs. Brandeis would like them to attend a private service in the apartment on California Street on Tuesday afternoon at 3:30. About fifty people gathered in the living room, including the family, members of the Supreme Court and their wives, former chief justice Hughes, Mrs. Wilson, some leaders from savings bank insurance and Zionism, and several former law clerks. A string quartet played Beethoven.

Brandeis's former law clerk Dean Acheson, now assistant secretary of state, delivered the eulogy. Of all his clerks, Acheson had remained closest to Brandeis, and he spoke on behalf of all the men who had "the great joy and the great fortune of serving him so intimately as his secretaries." But what he meant to them, Acheson added, was not that different from what he had meant to hundreds of other young men and women who came to him for guidance and imbibed his ideas. "Throughout these years we have brought him all of our problems and all our troubles, and he had time for all of us. A question, a comment, and the difficulties began to disappear."

Our generation, living between the two wars, often cried out, "What is truth?" and "saw in his action his burning faith that the verities to which men had clung through the ages were verities; that evil never could be good; that falsehood was not truth." "Truth was less than truth," Acheson concluded, "unless it was expounded so that the people could understand and believe. During these years of retreat from reason, his faith in the human mind and in the will and capacity of people to understand and grasp the truth never wavered or tired. . . . He handed on the great tradition of faith in the mind and spirit of man which is the faith of the prophets and poets, of Socrates, of Lincoln."

The justice's longtime friend and colleague Felix Frankfurter also spoke briefly, and recited a passage from Bunyan's *Pilgrim's Progress* that would be read at his own memorial service a quarter century later, the section on the death of Mr. Valiant-for-Truth: "My sword I give to him that shall succeed me in my pilgrimage, and my courage and skill to him that can get it. My marks and scars I carry with me, to be a witness for me that I have fought his battles who now will be my rewarder."

The family had the justice's body cremated, and on the anniversary of his death placed the urn containing his remains beneath the portico of the University of Louisville Law School. When Alice died in 1945, her ashes were placed next to his.

His estate amounted to more than $3 million, the bulk of it in bonds ($2.875 million) and nearly $300,000 in cash, and even after the heavy estate tax and executor fees tallied $1.9 million. Of this he left three-eighths to Alice ($712,500), and three-sixteenths each to Susan and Elizabeth ($356,250). The residual estate, after gifts to family members and associates such as Louise Malloch, went to Survey Associates, the University of Louisville, Hadassah, and the Palestine Endowment Funds.

A GREAT PERSON ACHIEVES that stature in part because of the times in which he or she lives. It is difficult, for example, to imagine Thomas Jefferson out of the historical context of America in the Revolutionary era and early Republic. But while the times may provide opportunity, the chance must be seized. Jefferson's ideas transcend the period in which he wrote and still evoke our admiration, and his words in the Declaration of Independence continue to stir men and women to action. The eras of the Civil War, the Great Depression, and World War II were critical in American history; Abraham Lincoln and Franklin Roosevelt are considered great presidents because they met those challenges and led the nation to safety.

So, too, with Louis Brandeis. He had the good fortune to live in an age when the causes that mattered to him could be shaped by a man with a powerful vision and the intellect and personality to transform ideas into action. He entered law practice at a time when an industrializing economy demanded that lawyers take on new roles and provide new skills to their clients, and his success reflected his ability to understand his clients' needs and advise them accordingly.

Legal classicism reached the peak of its power during this era, with bench and bar united in an effort to defend the status quo and private property while ignoring major social and economic changes in the country. Holmes, Pound, and others preached a "sociological jurisprudence," one that took the realities of everyday life into account; Brandeis turned that theory into practice.

His reform efforts succeeded in part because of his exceptional organizing ability, and his understanding that in politics no single voice could secure legislative action unless backed by some group, citizens whose numbers—and votes—politicians could count. But to look just at his talent to organize would miss his capacity to rally his troops with ideas and moral fervor, at a time when morality in public affairs meant much more than it does today.

Brandeis's role as a Zionist remains confusing to many people, since it lacked the religious fervor often associated with that movement. In the early part of the twentieth century, however, Zionism in the United States faced ideological problems unknown in the Old World, where Jews labored under severe political, social, and economic restrictions. The millions of Jews who immigrated to the United States beginning in 1880 saw this country and not Palestine as their promised land. They retained a fervor for Zion, but it could be awakened only by a plan that did not call into question their commitment to their new homeland. Only someone who shared the idealism of Zion without the religious components could have devised that plan, and only in that time.

Brandeis's nearly twenty-three years on the bench epitomized what he had been preaching for much of his adult life—a living law, a Constitution responsive to the country's needs, judges sensitive to changes going on around them. As much as anyone, he helped dismantle the old legal classicism and, at the same time, usher in a new concern for individual rights and liberties.

To say that Brandeis was a man of his time, however, is to ignore his unique intellectual and physical abilities. Other men and women lived in that same time and took part in reform, yet their names are almost lost to history. Louis Brandeis brought to his battles not only the courage to fight powerful foes and to face the resulting social ostracism but also an unbounded energy, a determination never to lose a struggle because he tired of fighting it. The traits were unique to him, and allowed him not only to grasp the opportunities his times offered to him but to succeed as well.

Nor can one say that Brandeis is only a figure from history. His ideas on lawyers as public servants, the use of the law in support of reform, and his sense that reform could not succeed without education and wide popular support are still relevant. Neither are his writings on privacy, freedom of expression, and other constitutional matters time-bound; they continue to instruct and shape modern jurisprudence. While historical events have greatly changed both the American Jewish community and the Jewish settlement that became Israel, the idealism he preached in his Zionist career still echoes, albeit faintly at times, in relations between American Jewry and Israel.

He became Isaiah, however, not because of his accomplishments as a lawyer, a reformer, or even a judge, but for the high moral standards he demanded of those in public life. In an era of continuous scandals involving public officials, when the highest offices in the land are tainted by unethical and at times illegal activity, it is perhaps hard for us to recall a time when standards of honesty, truthfulness, and respect for the law meant so much, and when they could inspire young people to devote their lives to public service. Ever an idealist, Brandeis was also a realist, and expected to be disappointed by the actions of his fellow men, who, as he constantly said, were wee beings. Yet he always had hope that in the long run right ideas and moral behavior would triumph. "My faith in time is great."

ACKNOWLEDGMENTS

If it takes a village to raise a child, it certainly takes an academic village to bring a book into existence, and my debts to various teachers, fellow scholars, members of the Brandeis family, former law clerks, librarians, research assistants, and funding agencies extend over four decades.

My greatest debt is to David W. Levy, now emeritus professor at the University of Oklahoma. Many years ago David and I ventured forth on a project to edit the Louis Brandeis Letters, and we have remained friends and colleagues for more than four decades. I would not think of publishing anything on Brandeis without David's looking at it, and his meticulous reading and unerring eye not only saved me from error, but helped me to refine my ideas.

Jill Norgren of the City University of New York also read the entire manuscript, and her acute questions assisted me in making parts clearer both to myself and, I hope, to the readers as well. Robert Post of the Yale Law School, William Wiecek of Syracuse Law, Jonathan Lurie of Rutgers, and Nancy Woloch of Barnard College all read various chapters, and I am grateful for their comments.

Several members of the Brandeis family patiently answered questions, and I want to thank Alice Brandeis Popkin, Frank Brandeis Gilbert, and Walter Raushenbush, the Justice's surviving grandchildren, as well as two members of Alfred's family, Charles Tachau and David Tachau. And although they are gone, David's parents, Eric and Mary K. Tachau, were dear friends and a great help to David Levy and me when we were working on the Letters.

My two sons, Philip and Robert, served as research assistants at various stages of the Letters, and their labors proved equally valuable for this volume. In addition, Arielle Kristan, Jessica Milling, Joshua Perelman, and Bonnie Speck worked on different chores.

Lewis J. Paper and Philippa Strum have written extensively on Brandeis, and although they did not read this manuscript I owe them a great deal. Lew graciously opened his papers, now at the Harvard Law School, so I could use his interviews with former Brandeis law clerks. Philippa and I over the years spent many hours discussing Brandeis, and I have profited greatly from her ideas. Barbara Sicherman came to my rescue with information on women's health in the nineteenth century in order to understand Alice Brandeis's illness, while Jonathan Sarna of Brandeis University answered questions on American Jewish history. Tanya Harvey of the Washington office of Bryan Cave, LLP, went over Brandeis's will with me and helped clear up some long-standing misconceptions about its provisions.

This work utilized materials from literally dozens of libraries and hundreds of manuscript collections, and I could not have done that work without the help of the dedicated librarians and archivists who not only guard and preserve their treasures but make them available to researchers. At the Library of Congress, which is truly one of the world's great scholarly repositories, the staffs of the Manuscript Division, the Law Library, and the Prints and Photographs Division made my time there not only productive but pleasant. Scott Campbell and Kurt X. Metzmeier at the Brandeis Law School Library of the University of Louisville, Gary Zola of the American Jewish Archives, and David Warrington of the Harvard Law School Library are all old friends, and they went out of their way to make my time at their institutions a joy.

In addition, the following helped me locate books, documents, pictures, and all the other items one needs for research and writing: Karen Abramson and Sarah Shoemaker of Special Collections at Brandeis University; Melinda Spitzer Johnson and Margaret Peachy of the Harvard Law School Library; Robin L. Wallace of the Filson Club in Louisville; Susan Woodland of the Hadassah Archives; Erika Gottfried of the Tamiment Institute; Barbara Ward Grubb of the Bryn Mawr Library; Lyn Slome of the American Jewish Historical Society; Mary Marshall Clark, the director of the Columbia University Oral History Research Office; and a special thanks to Steve Petteway, the curator of the photograph collection at the U.S. Supreme Court, and his assistant, Lauren Morrell. Much of the research material I collected for the Letters has been deposited in the Special Collections Department of the State University of New York at Albany, and its head, Brian Keough, made it possible for me to use this material at home, a luxury for which I am very grateful.

I have been very fortunate in the generous financial support given to this project. Ambassador John L. Loeb Jr. made three separate foundation grants to cover research expenses, and I am grateful not only for the funds but for his encouragement and friendship. The National Endowment for the Humanities was the primary funder for the Brandeis Letters, and I greatly appreciate their awarding me a Senior Research Fellowship under the "We the People" initiative. Additional funding came from Virginia Commonwealth University, and I want to thank the former dean of the College of Humanities and Sciences, Robert D. Holsworth, for his support of this project. David Pride and Kathleen Shurtleff of the Supreme Court Historical Society oversaw the administration of grant funds and also helped me in numerous other ways.

The Rockefeller Foundation awarded me a fellowship to spend a month at the study center it operates in Bellagio, Italy. I and all the other fellows consider the Villa Serbelloni to be what heaven must be like for scholars. There I had a chance to work on revising the manuscript and benefiting from the views of the other scholars and artists in residence. The wonderful atmosphere and support is due to Pilar Palaciá, the managing director, and Elena Ongania, the residents' assistant, who kept us fed well and made sure the Xerox and the computers worked.

My agent and friend, Loretta Barrett, encouraged this project from the start and hooked me up with one of the smartest editors I have known, Vicky Wilson. She and her staff at Pantheon—Carmen Johnson, Iris Weinstein, and Jonathan Sainsbury—transformed an unwieldy manuscript into the book you hold in your hand. Other writers will understand when I say that I would gladly have Ingrid Sterner copyedit any future books I write.

While all these people have given me great assistance, any errors and defects remaining in this book are, I am afraid, mine alone.

Finally, this book is dedicated to my wife, who has endured having Louis Brandeis live with us for so many years. My love and gratitude for her putting up with me (and with Louis) all these decades are boundless.

NOTES

LDB-UL	Louis Dembitz Brandeis Papers, Brandeis Law School, University of Louisville, Louisville, Ky. All letters, unless otherwise cited, come from this main depository of his papers. Throughout the notes, Brandeis is referred to as LDB.
LDB-BU	Louis Dembitz Brandeis Papers, Robert D. Farber University Archives and Special Collections Department, Brandeis University, Waltham, Mass. This collection consists primarily of the letters and documents found after the death of Susan Brandeis Gilbert. All letters to and from Alice Goldmark Brandeis, unless otherwise cited, are from this collection. Throughout the notes, Alice is referred to as AGB after her marriage to Brandeis.
LDB-HLS	Louis Dembitz Brandeis Papers, Harvard Law School Library, Cambridge, Mass.
LDB-SC	Louis Dembitz Brandeis Papers, Supreme Court Files, Harvard Law School Library, Cambridge, Mass.
Aaronsohn MSS	Aaron Aaronsohn Papers, Central Zionist Archives, Jerusalem, Israel
Baker MSS	Ray Stannard Baker Papers, Manuscript Division, Library of Congress, Washington, D.C.
Berlin Office	Records of the Central Zionist Office, Berlin (Zionistisches Zentralbüro), Central Zionist Archives, Jerusalem, Israel
Billikopf MSS	Jacob Billikopf Papers, American Jewish Archives, Hebrew Union College–Jewish Institute of Religion, Cincinnati
Bliss MSS	Tasker Howard Bliss Papers, Manuscript Division, Library of Congress, Washington, D.C.
Breslau MSS	Isadore Breslau Papers, American Jewish Historical Society, New York
Brodie MSS	Israel Benjamin Brodie Papers, Central Zionist Archives, Jerusalem, Israel
Burlingham MSS	Charles Culp Burlingham Papers, Harvard Law School Library, Cambridge, Mass.

Chafee MSS	Zechariah Chafee Jr. Papers, Harvard Law School Library, Cambridge, Mass.
Copenhagen Office	Records of the Provisional Zionist Office at Copenhagen, Central Zionist Archives, Jerusalem, Israel
de Haas MSS	Jacob de Haas Papers, Central Zionist Archives, Jerusalem, Israel
Dewson MSS	Mary Dewson Papers, Arthur and Elizabeth Schlesinger Library on the History of Women in America, Harvard University, Cambridge, Mass.
Douglas MSS	Douglas Family Papers, Missouri Historical Society, St. Louis
EBR	Letters provided by the late Elizabeth Brandeis Raushenbush, Madison, Wis., now University of Louisville collection
Eliot MSS	Charles William Eliot Papers, Harvard University Archives, Cambridge, Mass.
Evans MSS	Elizabeth Glendower Evans Papers, Arthur and Elizabeth Schlesinger Library on the History of Women in America, Harvard University, Cambridge, Mass.
FF-HLS	Felix Frankfurter Papers, Harvard Law School Library, Cambridge, Mass.
FF-LC	Felix Frankfurter Papers, Manuscript Division, Library of Congress, Washington, D.C.
Filene MSS	Edward Albert Filene Papers, Bergengren Memorial Museum Library, World Council of Credit Unions, Inc., Madison, Wis.
Foreign Office Records	Records of Her Majesty's Government Foreign Office, National Archives, Kew, U.K.
Freund MSS	Paul Abraham Freund Papers, Harvard Law School Library, Cambridge, Mass.
Glueck MSS	Sheldon Glueck Papers, Harvard Law School Library, Cambridge, Mass.
Goldberg MSS	Israel Goldberg Papers, American Jewish Historical Society, New York
Goldsmith MSS	William Goldsmith Papers, Robert D. Farber University Archives and Special Collections Department, Brandeis University, Waltham, Mass.
Gottheil MSS	Richard James Horatio Gottheil Papers, Central Zionist Archives, Jerusalem, Israel
Grady MSS	Alice Harriet Grady Papers, Robert D. Farber University Archives and Special Collections Department, Brandeis University, Waltham, Mass.
Greene MSS	Evarts Boutell Greene Papers, Special Collections, Columbia University Library, New York

Gregory MSS	Thomas Watt Gregory Papers, Manuscript Division, Library of Congress, Washington, D.C.
Hand MSS	Billings Learned Hand Papers, Harvard Law School Library, Cambridge, Mass.
Hilburn MSS	Walter Hilburn Papers, American Jewish Archives, Hebrew Union College–Jewish Institute for Religion, Cincinnati
Holmes MSS	Oliver Wendell Holmes Jr. Papers, Harvard Law School Library, Cambridge, Mass.
House MSS	Edward Mandell House Papers, Sterling Library, Yale University, New Haven, Conn.
H. Szold MSS	Henrietta Szold Private Papers, Central Zionist Archives, Jerusalem, Israel
Hudson MSS	Manley Hudson Papers, Harvard Law School Library, Cambridge, Mass.
Kallen MSS	Horace Meyer Kallen Papers, American Jewish Archives, Hebrew Union College–Jewish Institute of Religion, Cincinnati
Kellogg MSS	Paul Underwood Kellogg Papers, Robert D. Farber University Archives and Special Collections Department, Brandeis University, Waltham, Mass.
La Follette MSS	Robert Marion La Follette Papers, Manuscript Division, Library of Congress, Washington, D.C.
Laski MSS	Harold Joseph Laski Papers, Yale University Law Library, New Haven, Conn.
Lloyd MSS	Henry Demarest Lloyd Papers, State Historical Society of Wisconsin, Madison
London Office	Records of the London Office of the World Zionist Organization/Jewish Agency for Palestine, Central Zionist Archives, Jerusalem, Israel
Mack MSS	Julian William Mack Papers, Central Zionist Archives, Jerusalem, Israel
Magnes MSS	Judah Leon Magnes Papers, Central Archives for the History of the Jewish People, Hebrew University, Jerusalem, Israel
Marshall MSS	Louis Marshall Papers, American Jewish Archives, Hebrew Union College–Jewish Institute of Religion, Cincinnati
McAdoo MSS	William Gibbs McAdoo Papers, Manuscript Division, Library of Congress, Washington, D.C.
McCarthy MSS	Charles McCarthy Papers, State Historical Society of Wisconsin, Madison
McReynolds MSS	James Clark McReynolds Papers, Alderman Library, University of Virginia, Charlottesville
Morgenthau MSS	Henry Morgenthau Sr. Papers, Manuscript Division, Library of Congress, Washington, D.C.
Nagel MSS	Hildegard Nagel Papers, Schlesinger Library, Harvard University, Cambridge, Mass.

Nutter Diaries	George Read Nutter Diaries, Massachusetts Historical Society, Boston
OHRO	Oral History Research Office, Butler Library, Columbia University, New York
Paper MSS	Lewis Paper Papers, relating to his biography of Brandeis, Harvard Law School Library, Cambridge, Mass.
Pinchot MSS	Amos Pinchot Papers, Manuscript Division, Library of Congress, Washington, D.C.
Popkin MSS	Letters from Louis Brandeis to Alice Goldmark, courtesy of Alice Brandeis Popkin, Chatham, Mass.
Pound MSS	Roscoe Pound Papers, Harvard Law School Library, Cambridge, Mass.
Powell MSS	Thomas Reed Powell Papers, Harvard Law School Library, Cambridge, Mass.
Rauch MSS	Joseph Rauch Papers, Filson Club, Louisville, Ky.
Richards MSS	Bernard Gerson Richards Papers, Central Zionist Archives, Jerusalem, Israel
Roosevelt MSS	Franklin Delano Roosevelt Papers, Roosevelt Library, Hyde Park, N.Y.
R. Szold MSS	Robert Szold Papers, Central Zionist Archives, Jerusalem, Israel
SBLI	Division of Savings Bank Life Insurance Archives, Boston
Schiff MSS	Jacob Henry Schiff Papers, American Jewish Archives, Hebrew Union College–Jewish Institute of Religion, Cincinnati
Speed MSS	Hattie Bishop Speed Papers, Speed Art Museum, University of Louisville, Louisville, Ky.
State Department Records	Records of the U.S. Department of State, National Archives, Washington, D.C.
Steffens MSS	Lincoln Steffens Papers, Special Collections, Columbia University Library, New York
Stone MSS	Harlan Fiske Stone Papers, Manuscript Division, Library of Congress, Washington, D.C.
Swope MSS	Gerard Swope Papers, Institute Archives and Special Collections, Massachusetts Institute of Technology, Cambridge
Taft MSS	William Howard Taft Papers, Manuscript Division, Library of Congress, Washington, D.C.
Tannenbaum MSS	Frank Tannenbaum Papers, Special Collections, Columbia University Library, New York
Thayer MSS	James Bradley Thayer Papers, Harvard Law School Library, Cambridge, Mass.
Thompson MSS	Samuel Huston Thompson Papers, Manuscript Division, Library of Congress, Washington, D.C.
Tugwell MSS	Rexford Guy Tugwell Papers, Franklin D. Roosevelt Library, Hyde Park, N.Y.

Vanderlip MSS	Frank Vanderlip Papers, Special Collections, Columbia University Library, New York
Van Devanter MSS	Willis Van Devanter Papers, Manuscript Division, Library of Congress, Washington, D.C.
Walsh MSS	David Ignatius Walsh Papers, Manuscript Division, Library of Congress, Washington, D.C.
Warren MSS	Charles Warren Papers, Harvard Law School Library, Cambridge, Mass.
Watterson MSS	Henry Watterson Papers, Filson Club, Louisville, Ky.
W. Douglas MSS	William O. Douglas Papers, Manuscript Division, Library of Congress, Washington, D.C.
Wehle MSS	Louis Brandeis Wehle Papers, Franklin Delano Roosevelt Library, Hyde Park, N.Y.
Weizmann MSS	Chaim Weizmann Papers, Library of Yad Chaim Weizmann, Rehovot, Israel
White MSS	William Allen White Papers, Manuscript Division, Library of Congress, Washington, D.C.
Wilson MSS	Woodrow Wilson Papers, Manuscript Division, Library of Congress, Washington, D.C.
Wingate MSS	Charles Wingate Papers, Autograph Collection, Houghton Library, Harvard University, Cambridge, Mass.
Wise MSS	Stephen Samuel Wise Papers, American Jewish Historical Society, New York
Woolley MSS	Robert W. Woolley Papers, Manuscript Division, Library of Congress, Washington, D.C.
Zimmern MSS	Alfred Eckhard Zimmern Papers, Bodleian Library, Oxford University, Oxford, U.K.

CHAPTER 1: LOUISVILLE ROOTS

3 **"the Washington end"**: LDB to Alfred Brandeis, 25 August 1925.

3 **from his family:** See, for example, Alfred Brandeis to LDB, 2 August 1909, LDB-BU.

4 **private tutors:** At LDB's request, Frederika, between 1880 and 1886, wrote a memoir of her family and of her life before coming to the United States. The original German was translated by LDB's wife, Alice, after his death, and privately printed for distribution to her children, grandchildren, and other members of the family. *Reminiscences of Frederika Dembitz Brandeis* (1943). Material on the early life of LDB's parents is drawn from the memoir, as well as from Josephine Goldmark, *Pilgrims of '48* (New Haven, Conn., 1930).

4 **Jacob Frank:** According to the noted scholar Gershon Scholem, Prague was one of the centers of nineteenth-century Frankism, led by members of two distinguished families, Bondi and Wehle; Frederika's mother was a Wehle. See Scholem, "Jacob Frank and the Frankists," *Encyclopedia Judaica* 7 (1972), 55–71.

5 **"So provide yourself":** Goldmark, *Pilgrims,* 209.

6 "I feel my patriotism": *Id.,* 202.

6 "common beast of burden": *Id.,* 207.

7 "only at a sacrifice": *Id.,* 207–8.

7 "hotbed of commercial capitalism": Amy Shevitz, *Jewish Communities on the Ohio River: A History* (Lexington, Ky., 2007), 54. Between 1830 and 1850, a period Shevitz describes as Madison's "golden years," the population quintupled from eighteen hundred to nine thousand.

8 too diffident to use it: Excerpts from diary of John Lyle King, enclosed in Joseph M. Cravens to LDB, 19 November 1938, Wehle MSS.

8 The families started: Dr. Dembitz had chosen to stay in Cincinnati and practice there; Adolph's brother Samuel set up a medical practice in Madison, while one of the Wehles opened a cigar store. Gottfried Wehle took an active role in Jewish affairs and has been described as the head of the often fractious Jewish community before he left for New York. Shevitz, *Jewish Communities,* 55.

9–10 Brandeis and his new partner: Very little is known about Crawford, a native New Yorker who settled in Louisville in the 1840s. His partnership with Brandeis made him "a business man of high standing" in the community. E. Polk Johnson, *History of Kentucky and Kentuckians,* 3 vols. (Chicago and New York, 1912), 3:309.

10 campaigns in the upper South: Carol Ely, *Jewish Louisville: Portrait of a Community* (Louisville, Ky., 2003), 47.

10 On one of those occasions: Ernest Poole, "Brandeis," in LDB, *Business—a Profession* (Boston, 1914), xi; Alice Harriet Grady to Brenda Ueland, 14 July 1916.

11 never received a caning: C. B. Robinson to Alice Grady, 2 June 1916, LDB-BU.

11 spared the ordeal: The following section is based on Alice Harriet Grady, "Notes on Trip to Louisville," 20 May 1916, Brandeis MSS-BU.

12 love of good music: LDB to Fannie Brandeis (niece), 11 June 1926; LDB to Hattie Bishop Speed, 11 March 1933.

12 "fun-loving American BOY": Bert Ford, "Boyhood of Brandeis: An Early View of the Man," *Boston Sunday American,* 4 June 1916.

12 scars went away: Alfred Brandeis to LDB, 20 June 1906, LDB-BU.

13 family left for Europe: Around 1910, Alfred read in the newspapers that Durastus had died and, thinking the family might need aid, called at the home and offered to pay the funeral expenses. The widow was appreciative of the thought, but explained that Durastus had carried sufficient life insurance to cover burial costs, that they owned their own home, and that their daughter was now a teacher in the Louisville public school for colored children and earned a good salary.

14 The water often enough: Grady, "Notes."

14 taught at home: See, for example, Abraham Flexner, *I Remember* (New York, 1940), for a portrait of Louisville's intellectual life in this period.

14 "I know will make many mistakes": Frederika Brandeis to Fannie and Amy Brandeis, 11 August 1865; see also Adolph Brandeis to the girls, 15 August 1865, where he started the letter in German and then recollected that he had promised to write to them in English. The other letters written on that trip mix sections of German with sections of English. Letters courtesy of Charles Tachau.

14 **in the original:** For a sample of Brandeis's vacation readings, see LDB to Amy Brandeis Wehle, 9 July 1891.

14 **German author in translation:** LDB to Alfred Brandeis, 20 March 1888. But, as he explained, the German edition of Karl Franzos, *For the Right* (1888), had not been available.

15 **"sagacity and integrity":** Johnson, *History of Kentucky,* 2:972.

15 **at the dinner table:** According to William Hard, LDB credited his father with this rule; *Philadelphia Public Ledger,* 12 May 1916.

15 **"have more children":** LDB to Frederika Brandeis, 12 November 1888 (fragment), quoted in Alpheus T. Mason, *Brandeis: A Free Man's Life* (New York, 1946), 94. Frederika told LDB that "in you, my youngest child, everything is present that should make a mother proud and happy, that all my dreams of high ideals and of purity are united in you." *Reminiscences,* 22.

16 **When the children went out:** Grady to Brenda Ueland, 14 July 1916.

16 **"It seems to me":** Frederika Brandeis, *Reminiscences,* 20.

17 **loyalties and support:** See below, chap. 26.

17 **for a good cause:** Charles Nagel to Jennie Brandeis, 12 August 1928, courtesy of Fannie Brandeis (Alfred's daughter).

17 **"beautiful, gladsome life":** LDB to Jennie Brandeis, 8 August 1928, courtesy of Fannie Brandeis.

17 **in King's office:** King Diary, 14 April 1849.

18 **"reminded one of the Athenians":** LDB to Stella and Emily Dembitz, 22 April 1926.

18 **"Dembitz in bed":** Ely, *Jewish Louisville,* 41.

18 **thriving Jewish community:** Adolph, of course, did business with other Jewish merchants, and the city served as a hub for Jewish peddlers traveling throughout the Ohio valley. Frederika knew some of the women through her activities, and the children, because they went to the same schools, knew other Jewish children. LDB would enjoy lifelong friendships with the Flexner brothers.

18 **"secular Christianity":** Philippa Strum, *Louis D. Brandeis: Justice for the People* (Cambridge, Mass., 1984), 9.

19 **"than for individuals":** Frederika Brandeis, *Reminiscences,* 33–34. LDB's younger daughter, Elizabeth, would marry the son of a noted Christian theologian. LDB described him as a "rare find" and expressed great pleasure at her choice.

19 **"broader aspects of humanity":** *American Hebrew,* 2 December 1910.

19 **Day of Atonement:** Grady, "Notes."

19 **"foretaste of heaven":** Solomon Goldman, *The Words of Justice Brandeis* (New York, 1953), 160. Why alone of that large family Lewis Dembitz chose to be observant is unknown, and if he ever explained it to his nephew, LDB did not retell it in any of his speeches or letters. Unfortunately, no Dembitz papers survived, nor copies of letters that LDB undoubtedly wrote to his uncle.

20 **A scholar of religion:** Moshe Davis, *The Emergence of Conservative Judaism* (Philadelphia, 1963), 333–35.

20 **Zionist leadership:** See below, chap. 17.

21 **"as agreeable as possible":** Quoted in Mason, *Brandeis,* 28–29.

21 **"every damned river in Europe":** Grady, "Notes."

22 **"remember the thrill":** LDB to Alfred Brandeis, 20 August 1927, 20 Octo-

ber 1908. LDB kept the ticket stub from a German production of *Hamlet* that he saw in Dresden on 22 September 1874, starring Richard Turschmann, LDB-BU.

22 **so impressed Herr Job:** Grady, "Notes." Apparently, the rector told LDB he would have to take an examination but, because of the unusual circumstances, would give him three weeks in which he could be tutored. LDB took advantage of the time to study, but at the end of the time Herr Job allowed him to matriculate without an examination.

22 **received a grade:** His school notes, written in German in an old marbleized-cover copybook, include subjects such as "Projektion," "Trigonometric," "Geom. Examples," and "Physik." LDB-BU.

23 **"a new discovery for him":** Mason, *Brandeis,* 31.

23 **"believed in taking pains":** Felix Frankfurter, "Mr. Justice Brandeis," 55 *Harvard Law Review* 181, 183 (1942).

23 **"This made me homesick":** Poole, "Brandeis."

CHAPTER 2: HARVARD, ST. LOUIS, AND BACK

25 **practicing attorney's office:** Nearly all states then barred women from the practice of law. Justice Joseph Bradley, in a case supporting this view, declared that God had ordained women to be the protectors of the hearth, and thus unfitted them for the rough realities of a law practice. *Bradwell v. Illinois,* 16 Wallace (83 U.S.) 130 (1873).

26 **"discourage real students":** Holmes, "Harvard Law School," 5 *American Law Review* 177 (1870), quoted in G. Edward White, *Justice Oliver Wendell Holmes: Law and the Inner Self* (New York, 1993), 91.

26 **transformation in the law school:** This section is based on material from Arthur E. Sutherland, *The Law at Harvard: A History of Ideas and Men, 1817–1967* (Cambridge, Mass., 1967), chap. 6; Charles Warren, *History of the Harvard Law School, and of Early Legal Conditions in America,* 2 vols. (New York, 1908), chap. 43; and Robert Stevens, *Law School: Legal Education in America from the 1850s to the 1980s* (Chapel Hill, N.C., 1983), chaps. 2–4.

27 **"earnest student of law":** Christopher Columbus Langdell, preface to his *A Selection of Cases on the Law of Contracts* (Boston, 1871), vi.

27 **Socratic dialogue:** Langdell wrote the first casebook on contracts in 1871, and then one on sales. James Barr Ames put together a massive tome on bills and notes in 1881, and by then both men included doctrinal readings as well as cases.

28 **"the drama of life":** LDB, "The Harvard Law School," 1 *Green Bag* 18–21 (1889).

28 **to reason deductively:** He took careful notes in his courses, written in full sentences. He later gave them to his daughter Susan when she entered law school some four decades later. They are now in LDB-BU.

29 **that first year in law school:** LDB to Wehle, 12 March 1876. LDB remained a lifelong enthusiast of both the law school and the Langdellian method. See his "Harvard Law School."

29 **the rest of his life:** See, for example, LDB to Zechariah Chafee Jr., 5 June 1921, Chafee MSS.

29 **" 'morally right' ":** LDB to Wehle, 12 November 1876. Bradley, according to Sutherland, only stayed for three years and resigned in 1879, and "was

perhaps the last Harvard Law professor entirely unaffected by Langdell's method of teaching." *Law at Harvard,* 179n.21.

29 **"great majority of the Judges":** LDB described Ames as "a man of the most eminent abilities as instructor, possessing an infallibly logical mind and a thorough knowledge of the Common Law." LDB to Wehle, 12 November 1876.

29 **an insurance company:** *Insurance Company v. Mosley,* 75 U.S. (8 Wall.) 397 (1869).

29 **"most dreadful punishment":** LDB to Wehle, 12 November 1876.

30 **"he knows the facts":** Alpheus T. Mason, *Brandeis: A Free Man's Life* (New York, 1946), 248–49.

30 **to factual conditions:** Some critics have accused Langdell of being a formalist, that is, one whose law is grounded in abstract theory, but in fact Langdell anticipated much of the so-called sociological jurisprudence and its emphasis on facts. Bruce A. Kimball, "Langdell on Contracts and Legal Reasoning: Correcting the Holmesian Caricature," 25 *Law and History Review* 345 (2007).

30 **"habits of industry":** Franklin G. Fessenden, "The Rebirth of the Harvard Law School," 33 *Harvard Law Review* 493, 505 (1920).

30 **Langdell's new method:** LDB kept up with other members of the club and with its doings after he left the law school. A file in LDB-BU marked "Pow-Wow" runs to 1937.

30 **"his attractive personality":** *Boston American,* 4 June 1916; Alice Harriet Grady, "Notes of Trip to Louisville," 20 May 1916, LDB-BU.

31 **"it is generally correct":** William E. Cushing to Mrs. B. M. Cushing, 17 March 1878, in Mason, *Brandeis,* 3.

31 **in his lifetime:** Or perhaps since. According to Arthur Sutherland, the grading system at Harvard Law had changed over the years, so that one could not convert LDB's grades into a modern scale. Nonetheless, "the astonishingly high quality of Brandeis's work is still entirely evident." *Law at Harvard,* 198n.44.

31 **resolving the issue:** Grady, "Notes."

32 **"terribly distressing":** Adolph Brandeis to LDB, 7 October 1877, quoted in Mason, *Brandeis,* 45.

32 **turned in their weapons:** For the national railroad strikes, see Philip S. Foner, *The Great Labor Uprising of 1877* (New York, 1977). For Louisville, see Bill L. Weaver, "Louisville's Labor Disturbance, July 1877," *Filson Club Historical Quarterly* 48 (April 1974), 177–86. In comparison to labor disturbances in other cities, the detective Allan Pinkerton dismissed the Louisville riot as "a tempest in a teapot." LDB's recollection was in an interview with Alpheus Mason, in *Brandeis,* 48.

32 **Louis borrowed money:** Allon Gal, *Brandeis of Boston* (Cambridge, Mass., 1980), 16, claims that the wealthy Boston Jewish merchant Jacob Hecht put up surety for LDB's tuition at law school, and cites as sources oral traditions in both families. Surety might have been necessary if LDB owed Harvard money, but since LDB had enough money, first from his brother and then from tutoring, to pay his tuition, it is unclear what role Hecht played. Moreover, queries of Frank Gilbert, LDB's grandson, elicited no recollection of his ever having known about Hecht. The assertion by Gal that "Brandeis's career at Harvard was first supported by Jacob H. Hecht" (34) appears to be totally

without substantiation. LDB as a Jewish student at Harvard probably attended the Hechts' open houses, but while these might have been pleasant socially, they did not, as Gal suggests, increase his sense of Jewishness.

33 **he kept long afterward:** LDB to Alfred Brandeis, 28 June and 5 July 1878.

33 **problems with his eyesight:** Mason is the only source for the suggestion that LDB was a sickly youth whose parents always worried about him. This hardly squares with stories of him ice-skating, fighting over a girl, or hiking through the Alps.

34 **of judgment as well:** Entry for 17 October 1946, in Joseph Lash, ed., *From the Diaries of Felix Frankfurter* (New York, 1975), 271.

34 **these included Shakespeare:** LDB to Otto Wehle, 12 November 1876.

34 **"of one or more persons":** Sutherland, *Law at Harvard,* 194.

34 **until he recovered:** LDB to Otto Wehle, 31 August 1876.

34 **Dr. Knapp found nothing:** Grady, "Notes."

35 **His friend Philippe Marcou:** LDB to Walter Bond Douglas, 31 January 1878, Douglas MSS.

35 **"I am not doing":** *Id.*

35 **large and legible hand:** LDB to Alfred Brandeis, 28 June 1878.

35 **"Cambridge is beautiful":** *Id.*

36 **"surely bore me":** LDB to Amy Brandeis Wehle, 2 December 1877, Wehle MSS.

36 **"most girls here":** LDB to Amy Brandeis Wehle, 5 April 1877, Wehle MSS; LDB to Alfred Brandeis, 28 June 1878.

36 **After several evenings:** LDB to Amy Brandeis Wehle, 5 April 1877, Wehle MSS.

37 **Emerson lecture:** Thayer also proved to be one of his most influential teachers in terms of constitutional theory. See LDB to Thayer, n.d. 1889.

37 **"descendants of the Romans":** LDB to Alfred Brandeis, 28 June and 5 July 1878, EBR.

37 **"for the first time":** James Burchard Howard to LDB, 2 March 1916; LDB to Howard, 7 March 1916.

37 **excelled in the art of living:** "He is one of the men who, opportunities and obstacles considered, made the most of life. He overcame the inherited appetite for drink. He bore & lived down the terrible misfortune inherent in his wife, and he functioned in business despite his lack of business ability. His happiness he earned through pursuit of art & the history which went with it; and the pursuit of orchids & the science which attended it; and took perhaps equal pleasure in the cultivation of a few worthy friends." LDB to Alfred Brandeis, 19 June 1927.

38 **"the world's center":** Ernest Poole, "Brandeis," in LDB, *Business—a Profession* (Boston, 1914), xii.

38 **He also played ball:** LDB to Alfred Brandeis, 11 August 1878.

38 **"humbly beg your pardon":** LDB to Frederika Brandeis, 2 August 1878, in Mason, *Brandeis,* 50.

39 **"without your permission":** Fannie Nagel to LDB, 4 October 1877, Nagel MSS.

39 **number of attorneys:** Much of this section is based on Burton C. Bernard, "Brandeis in St. Louis," 11 *St. Louis Bar Journal* 1 (1964).

39 **to live there as well:** Charles Nagel to LDB, 23 March 1878, LDB-BU.

39 **The larger firms:** Nagel to LDB, 10 July 1878, LDB-BU.

40 **recuperating in Louisville:** Taussig kept the position open for him and told him "to take all the time necessary for a radical [complete] cure." James Taussig to LDB, 22 September 1878.

40 **admitted to practice:** He kept the certificate and nearly fifty years later gave it to his daughter Susan. LDB to Susan Brandeis Gilbert, 7 June 1926, LDB-BU.

40 **"interesting & instructive":** For LDB's practice, see Bernard, "Brandeis in St. Louis."

40 **"onto my shoulders":** LDB to Amy Brandeis Wehle, late January 1879.

40 **"as right and justice demands":** LDB to Otto Wehle, 1 April 1879.

40 **"abstract of Record":** *Buford v. Keokuk Northern Line Packet Co.,* 69 Mo. 611 (1879).

40 **" 'bad cases' hereafter":** LDB to Otto Wehle, 10 February 1879.

41 **"under lock & key":** LDB to Otto Wehle, 1 April 1879.

41 **pronounced it "excellent":** Holmes to LDB, 7 July 1881, Holmes MSS; LDB, "Liability of Trust-Estates on Contracts Made for Their Benefit," 15 *American Law Review* 449 (1881).

41 **"A hash of old cases":** LDB to Otto Wehle, 1 April 1879.

41 **"Do you know the law":** LDB to Otto Wehle, 10 February 1879.

41 **off family incomes:** Thomas W. Thrash, "Apprenticeship at the Bar: The Atlanta Law Practice of Woodrow Wilson," 28 *Georgia State Bar Journal* 147 (1992); Warren to LDB, 31 March 1879, FF-HLS.

41 **" 'lots' of nice people":** LDB to Amy Brandeis Wehle, 1 February 1879, quoted in Mason, *Brandeis,* 54.

42 **Warren had been second:** For Sam Warren and the Warren family, see Martin Green, *The Mount Vernon Street Warrens: A Boston Story, 1860–1910* (New York, 1989).

42 **"civilized man can exist":** Warren to LDB, 9 November 1878, in *Nutter, McClennen & Fish: The First Century* (Boston, 1979).

42 **"much in common with me":** Warren to LDB, n.d. [1879], FF-HLS.

42 **"a more gallant fight":** Warren to LDB, 5 May 1879 and 9 November 1878, in Green, *Mount Vernon Street Warrens,* 67.

43 **"social and financial position":** LDB to Warren, 30 May 1879, in *id.*

44 **a lucrative practice:** Warren to LDB, 31 March and 4 June 1879, in *id.*

44 **"birds worth chasing":** LDB to Douglas, 6 July 1879, Douglas MSS.

44 **"nothing in St. Louis":** Nagel to LDB, 5 July 1879.

45 **Taussig also wrote:** LDB to Nagel, 12 July 1879; Taussig to LDB, 15 July 1879.

45 **"offer a sacrifice":** LDB to Frederika Brandeis, 20 July 1879.

CHAPTER 3: WARREN & BRANDEIS

46 **the right decision:** LDB to Nagel, 12 July 1879; LDB to Frederika Brandeis, 20 July 1879, in Alpheus T. Mason, *Brandeis: A Freeman's Life* (New York, 1946), 59–61.

46 **"I will stand it":** LDB to Alfred Brandeis, 31 July 1879, EBR.

46 **later in Washington:** For how Gray utilized his clerks, see Todd C. Peppers, "Birth of an Institution: Horace Gray and the Lost Law Clerks," 32 *Journal of Supreme Court History* 229 (2007).

47 **"even contradiction":** LDB to Nagel, 12 July 1879.

47 **"I shall learn very much"**: *Id.* A few weeks later he told Alfred that his work with Gray "is as pleasant and interesting as ever, and I feel very much its instructiveness."

48 **career at the bar**: This aspect of LDB's law practice has been well discussed in David W. Levy, "The Lawyer as Judge: Brandeis' View of the Legal Profession," 22 *Oklahoma Law Review* 374 (1969).

48 **to save rent**: Warren to LDB, 29 May 1879, FF-HLS.

48 **Sam's mother**: Martin Green, *The Mount Vernon Street Warrens: A Boston Story, 1860–1910* (New York, 1989), 63. Many years later LDB told his son-in-law that during his practice "I had practically no experience in drawing wills. Many were drawn in our office, but my partner [Sam] did all that work in his days. Even for my personal clients; and I relied wholly on his skill in that branch." LDB to Jack Gilbert, 16 November 1933, LDB-BU. This is no doubt true for the practice, but a young man who spent so much time at the Warrens' could hardly say no to his partner's mother.

49 **"principles and precedent"**: LDB to Alfred Brandeis, 31 July 1879, EBR.

49 **in his ability**: *Id.*

49 **Sam had worked**: Warren had written to Brandeis, "The office in which I have been has not afforded me all the opportunities for learning procedure that I could have wished, but on the other hand it has given me the acquaintance & I think the friendship of Mr. O. W. Holmes, Jr. He is a fellow after my own heart in his way of looking at the law." Warren to LDB, n.d. [probably April 1879].

50 **trespass and negligence**: LDB to Amy Brandeis Wehle, 4 December 1879, Wehle MSS. The reference is to a German proverb, "*Was versteht der Bauer von Gurkensalat?*" ("What does a peasant know about cucumber salad?")—that is, it is quite above his head. However, whist appears to have been played, if not well, fairly frequently in the Brandeis family. Amy reported to her brother that "Otto, Al, Pa and I are playing whist. O, if you knew how horribly poor Uncle L[ewis] plays and still the dear man enjoys a game immensely." Amy Brandeis Wehle to LDB, 23 November 1880, Wehle MSS.

50 **for generations**: *Nutter, McClennen & Fish: The First Century, 1879–1979* (Boston, 1979), 3.

50 **"you among my tutors"**: LDB to John F. Warren, 3 August 1914.

51 **lawyers and businessmen**: *Allen v. Woonsocket*, 13 R.I. 146 (1880); LDB to Amy Brandeis Wehle, 6 April 1880.

51 **"most promising law firms"**: Gray told this to one of LDB's relatives, and it was passed along in Amy Brandeis Wehle to LDB, 23 November 1880, Wehle MSS.

51 **the best lawyer in Boston**: Arthur B. Lisle, memorandum, 9 January 1943, LDB-BU. Perry did employ LDB in a complicated case involving securities issues, for which LDB devised a creative solution.

51 **"and he generally wins"**: *National Monthly*, December 1911.

52 **company's legal business**: LDB to Alfred Brandeis, 11 September 1880, EBR.

52 **"our opponent for a client"**: LDB to Amy Brandeis Wehle, 2 January 1881. The quotation is from Shakespeare, *Macbeth*.

52 **"success of W&B is assured"**: LDB to Alfred Brandeis, 30 July 1881, EBR.

52 **go buy candy**: Interview with William Sutherland, Paper MSS. Sutherland

said he met the man on a plane, and while they were chatting, the man learned that Sutherland had clerked for LDB and related this story.

52 **did he broadcast them:** See, for example, Edward Martin's comment that LDB "is a Jew, but I knew him for years in Boston without being aware of it." Martin to Henry Watterson, 9 February 1910, Watterson MSS. There is no implication in Martin's letter that LDB was trying to hide anything, but rather that his religion mattered little to him in terms of his public persona.

53 **majority of its clients:** Allon Gal, *Brandeis of Boston* (Cambridge, Mass., 1980), 72ff.

53 **in his reform work:** *Id.,* 44; LDB to Amy Brandeis Wehle, 2 January 1881. A Turnverein was a German-American social and athletic club.

53 **three decades later:** Associated Charities of Boston to LDB, 12 January 1895, LDB-BU. According to Barbara Solomon, LDB, especially as he became better known through both his reform and his legal work, would occasionally take part in ceremonial functions, such as the dedication of the new quarters of Mount Sinai Hospital in 1903. *Pioneers in Service: The History of the Association of Jewish Philanthropies of Boston* (Boston, 1956), 59.

54 **and other aliens:** E. Digby Baltzell, Allen Glicksman, and Jacquelyn Litt, "The Jewish Communities of Philadelphia and Boston: A Tale of Two Cities," in Murray Friedman, ed., *Jewish Life in Philadelphia, 1830–1940* (Philadelphia, 1983), 290–313.

54 **business and financial community:** George Nutter, who became one of his law partners, did not note any evidence of anti-Semitism against LDB until late November 1905, when a nominee for the Massachusetts Supreme Judicial Court, angry at LDB's position in a municipal dispute, attacked him as a Jew ashamed of his race. This comment, according to Nutter, "disgusted all decent people." Nutter Diaries, 11 November 1905. I am indebted to William E. Leuchtenburg for calling this material to my attention.

54 **closed to Jews:** See, for example, LDB to Alfred Brandeis, 10 October 1914.

54 **city's social elite:** Leonard Dinnerstein, *Antisemitism in America* (New York, 1994), 52.

54 **"twenty-five following":** LDB to Alfred Brandeis, 30 July 1881, EBR.

54 **log of cases had reached:** LDB to Edward F. McClennen, 9 March 1916.

55 **"my first lieutenant":** The firm took a few Jewish associates, but most of the lawyers were Christian. Warren & Brandeis, and its successors, never acquired the reputation of a "Jewish firm," a place where bright Jewish law school graduates could gain employment when shut out by the white-shoe Protestant offices.

55 **"Mr. Warren's room":** "We must have rooms in the same building as S. D. Warren & Co. in order that I may see something of Sam." LDB to Alfred Brandeis, 20 March 1889, EBR.

56 **Harvard Law School:** Dunbar to LDB, 17 August 1896, in Mason, *Brandeis,* 82–83.

56 **real partnership they sought:** LDB to Dunbar, 2 November 1896, in *Nutter, McClennen & Fish,* 11–12.

56 **flooded through the doors:** "With me work is plenty, at present. Indeed I feel as to myself now as when I see water running over a dam—sad that I cannot reservoir it against the coming draught." LDB to Alfred Brandeis, 23 March 1889, EBR. The drought, of course, never came.

57 **advised the great author:** James M. Landis, "Memorandum Detailing Conversation with LDB at a Dinner at the Hotel Bellevue," 2 June 1932, FF-LC.

57 **resumed the next morning:** Elizabeth Evans to Ethel Unwin, 26 April 1934, Evans MSS. The letter, written on news of Grady's death, also mentioned that the very religious Miss Grady feared that it would be a terrible thing if this brilliantly endowed Jew should use his talents for his own gain, and would pray for him as she took dictation.

57 **adopt that rule:** Samuel Williston, *Life and Law: An Autobiography* (Boston, 1940), 112.

57 **reform work he did:** Adolf A. Berle Jr. Memoir, OHRO.

58 **"Common Sense of the people":** LDB to Amy Brandeis Wehle, 1 February 1895, Wehle MSS.

58 **He argued, successfully:** *Wisconsin Rail Road v. Price County*, 133 U.S. 496 (1889).

58 **"do himself credit":** LDB to AGB, 25 June 1914.

58 **best lawyer he ever knew:** Charles Wyzanski Memoir, 296, OHRO. Judge Wyzanski, before whom McClennen often appeared, had a far lower opinion of him.

59 **eastern and southern Europe:** Figures on economic growth and other indexes of change can be found in Susan B. Carter et al., eds., *Historical Statistics of the United States: Earliest Times to the Present*, 5 vols. (New York, 2006).

59 **"the rush of an express":** Quoted in Levy, "Lawyer as Judge," 374.

59 **problems of industrial change:** The conservatism of the bar, and LDB's reaction to it, are discussed in chap. 18 below.

60 **"out of litigation":** James Willard Hurst, *The Growth of American Law: The Law Makers* (Boston, 1950), 345; Kermit Hall, *The Magic Mirror: Law in American History* (New York, 1989), 212.

60 **"the wisdom of conciliation":** Filene to LDB, 11 November 1935, Filene MSS.

60 **"master of economics":** Oliver Wendell Holmes Jr., "The Path of the Law," in *Collected Legal Papers* (New York, 1920), 187.

61 **throughout the country:** Wayne K. Hobson, "Symbol of the New Profession: Emergence of the Large Law Firm, 1870–1915," in Gerard W. Gawalt, *The New High Priests: Lawyers in Post–Civil War America* (Westport, Conn., 1984), 3–27; Robert T. Swaine, *The Cravath Firm* (New York, 1946), chap. 1. The Cravath firm is the predecessor of the current Cravath, Swaine & Moore, which, compared with some other firms, is considered small, with 390 lawyers and offices only in New York and London.

61 **"any other occupation":** Felix Frankfurter with Harlan B. Phillips, *Felix Frankfurter Reminisces* (New York, 1960), 128; Levy, "Lawyer as Judge," 377–78.

61–62 **"or anything else":** Nutter to Frankfurter, 19 March 1929, quoted in Hobson, "Symbol of the New Profession," 21.

62 **they had previously enjoyed:** The classic statement of this is Richard Hofstadter, *The Age of Reform: From Bryan to F.D.R.* (New York, 1955). chap. 4. See below, chap. 9.

62 **great New York law firms:** LDB to Dunbar, 19 August 1896, in Edward F. McClennen, "Louis D. Brandeis as a Lawyer," 33 *Massachusetts Law Quarterly* 1, 19 (1948).

62 **"bed of Procustes":** LDB to Dunbar, 2 February 1893, FF-HLS.

63 **"most profitable preparation"**: LDB to Jacob Meyer Rudy, 14 April 1913.

63 **"facts and law that surround"**: Memorandum, "What the Practice of Law Includes," n.d.

63 **"in the Commonwealth"**: Brandeis to Alfred Brandeis, 12 January 1908, courtesy of Fannie Brandeis.

64 **"not a good way to live"**: "An Unusual Man of Law," *New York Times Annalist,* 27 January 1913.

65 **regular wages**: See Edward Filene, "Louis D. Brandeis as We Know Him," *Boston Post,* 4 March 1916; LDB, "Business—a Profession," speech at Brown University, 1912 commencement, in LDB, *Business—a Profession* (Boston, 1914), 5–9.

65 **given such a task**: William Hard, "Brandeis the Adjuster and Private-Life Judge," *Philadelphia Public Ledger,* 14 May 1916. Another time one of his clients, a successful businessman, suddenly decided that he wanted to go into the ministry and sought LDB's advice. The answer: the work of God might better be done by an experienced merchant running his shop on a humanitarian basis than by a novice cleric. The man took the advice. McClennen, "Brandeis as Lawyer," 26.

66 **Lennox into bankruptcy**: The Lennox story is examined in U.S. Senate, *Hearings Before the Subcommittee of the Committee on the Judiciary . . . on the Nomination of Louis D. Brandeis to Be an Associate Justice of the Supreme Court of the United States,* 64th Cong., 1st sess., 2 vols. in 1 (Washington, D.C., 1916), 787ff. (hereafter cited as *Hearings on Nomination*); Mason, *Brandeis,* 232–37; Morris Weisman, "Brandeis and the Lennox Case," *Commercial Law Journal* (February 1942), 36–41; and especially Clyde Spillenger, "Elusive Advocate: Reconsidering Brandeis as People's Lawyer," 105 *Yale Law Journal* 1445, 1502–11 (1996).

67 **"interests of everyone"**: *Hearings on Nomination,* 287.

67 **profession had abandoned**: This is the conclusion or, as some would say, the rationalization for LDB's action. See John P. Frank, "The Legal Ethics of Louis D. Brandeis," 17 *Stanford Law Review* 683, 698–703 (1965), a piece which concludes that LDB's ethical stance should be copied by more members of the legal profession.

67 **"render to anyone"**: Geoffrey C. Hazard, *Ethics in the Practice of Law* (New Haven, Conn., 1978), 65.

68 **or with guidance**: Milner Ball, "Lawyers in Context: Moses, Brandeis, and the A.B.A.," 14 *Notre Dame Journal of Law, Ethics, and Public Policy* 321, 333–34 (2000).

68 **conflicts of interest**: See Edward F. McClennen to Felix Frankfurter, 1 February 1916, and to William Dunbar, 30 March 1916; Mason, *Brandeis,* 238–40; Richard W. Painter, "Contracting Around Conflicts in a Family Representation: Louis Brandeis and the Warren Trust," 8 *University of Chicago Law School Roundtable* 353 (2001); and Green, *Mount Vernon Street Warrens,* 81–85.

69 **number of years**: Sam Warren to Edward Warren, 4 May 1889; see also the testimony of Ned's attorney, William S. Youngman, in *Hearings on Nomination,* 461–519, and exhibits, 519–607.

69 **passion for art**: Ned detested Boston, in part because its puritanical culture frowned on his homosexuality, and as soon as he graduated Harvard went to live abroad.

70 "intentional fraud": *Hearings on Nomination,* 278, 283–84.
70 "our right impulses": Sam Warren to LDB, 7 September 1901, in Green, *Mount Vernon Street Warrens,* 64–65.
70 leveled against Louis: Edward McClennen to Felix Frankfurter, 1 February 1916.
71 Warren's full consent: Mason, *Brandeis,* 239–40.
71 "skirmishes cannot afford": LDB to Alfred Brandeis, 21 March 1887.
71 worked in these areas: McClennen, "Brandeis as Lawyer," 22–23.
72 another railroad baron: See below, chap. 8.
73 "raised that question": *Hearings on Nomination,* 336–44.
74 leaving an estate: Hall, *Magic Mirror,* 213; Hurst, *Growth,* 311–12. Mason, *Brandeis,* 691, has a chart of LDB's income and finances from 1915 until his death, as well as some figures for 1901–1915.

CHAPTER 4: FIRST STEPS

75 "fixed for the evening": LDB to Amy Brandeis Wehle, 25 November 1880, Wehle MSS.
76 lecture by Holmes: For *The Common Law,* see the introduction to the 1963 reprint by Mark DeWolfe Howe, as well as G. Edward White, *Justice Oliver Wendell Holmes: Law and the Inner Self* (New York, 1993), chap. 5.
76 "end of Solomon Grundy": LDB to Alfred Brandeis, 11 September 1880; Union Boat Club, certificate of election of LDB as a member, 3 May 1880; LDB to Brandeis family, n.d. [winter 1880–1881].
76 "her grip on me": LDB to Amy Brandeis Wehle, 2 January 1881.
77 rest of her life: LDB to Alfred Brandeis, 21 March 1887.
78 "a broader growth": Evans to Alfred Lief, 27 March 1934, Evans MSS. In that letter she noted that not only did LDB keep an eye on her, but there was a mentally retarded young girl, Edith May, the niece of a mutual friend, and LDB would visit her, year after year, even after the aunt herself was declared insane, until he went on the Court. He had, she told Lief, an "extraordinary loyalty."
78 "like one of my own family": See memoir about LDB, n.d., in Evans MSS, which served as a draft for Elizabeth Glendower Evans, "Mr. Justice Brandeis: The People's Tribune," *Survey,* 1 November 1931; LDB to Evans, 3 March 1889, Evans to LDB, 1 December 1908, Evans MSS; Evans to LDB, 11 November 1926, LDB-BU. See also Mary Dewson, "Mrs. Glendower Evans," 28 January 1938, Dewson MSS.
78 and the school: Although he gave generously at all times, in the early years he did not have the financial resources he enjoyed later. A typical gesture can be seen in 1916, when he told the dean of the school that he would give $1,000 a year for five years to help establish a legislative law program. LDB to Roscoe Pound, 27 March 1916, Pound MSS.
78 "his first crusade": James M. Landis, "Mr. Justice Brandeis and the Harvard Law School," 55 *Harvard Law Review* 184, 186 (1941).
79 the entire amount: For further details, see White, *Holmes,* 200–201.
79 "I congratulate you": Alpheus T. Mason, *Brandeis: A Free Man's Life* (New York, 1946), 65; White, *Holmes,* 198–205; LDB to Holmes, 9 December 1882, Holmes MSS. Mason writes that Weld insisted on anonymity, but in fact the chair has been called the Weld professorship almost from the start.

Despite LDB's tutoring, Weld had failed to complete one course at the law school and contemplated going back to take it and finish his degree. He had concerns that should this donation be known, it would make completing the degree awkward both for him and for the faculty. Weld completed the work, and Harvard awarded him the degree, dating it back to the year of his class, 1879.

80 "indulge in now extensively": Mason, *Brandeis,* 66; LDB to Alfred Brandeis, 11 September 1880, EBR. "I am rather disgusted with myself physically," he told his father in May 1883. "I have taken good care of myself—worked moderately, and still find myself below par; that is, I am easily exhausted and worn out, without good reason."

80 an assistant professorship: Winthrop Wade took a full set of notes in that class, and either the contents or the notes themselves proved so good that Oliver Wendell Holmes borrowed, and eventually kept, them. LDB's own notes for the course, written in hand on all sorts and sizes of paper, are in LDB-BU.

81 gesture to the law school: LDB to Christopher Columbus Langdell, 30 December 1889.

81 Law School Association: LDB to Winthrop Wade, 9 June 1886; LDB and others to alumni of the Harvard Law School, 9 August 1886, Harvard Law School Association, *Report of Organization and of the First General Meeting at Cambridge, November 5, 1886* (Boston, 1887).

82 to recruit applicants: Landis, "Brandeis and the Law School," 186–87.

82 "learned from text-books": LDB, "The Harvard Law School," 1 *Green Bag* 10, 21–22 (1889). LDB maintained this view throughout his life.

82 reports of important cases: Within a short period of time "making law review" became one of the credentials for the best students and a factor in their employment by the top law firms.

82 means to finance it: McKelvey went on to a successful legal career in New York; Mack became a federal circuit court judge and a close friend and ally of LDB's in the Zionist movement; and Beale enjoyed a long and distinguished career as a teacher at the law school.

83 for the *Review:* Warren and LDB, "The Watuppa Pond Cases," 2 *Harvard Law Review* 195 (1888), and "The Law of Ponds," 3 *Harvard Law Review* 1 (1889). The third article, on privacy, is discussed below. For a discussion of the riparian articles, see Stephen W. Baskerville, *Of Laws and Limitations: An Intellectual Portrait of Louis Dembitz Brandeis* (Rutherford, N.J., 1994), 79–82.

83 first in the country: Langdell to LDB, 2 February 1891.

83 proposals he made: Landis, "Brandeis and the Law School," 188; for the University of Louisville, see below, chap. 26.

84 "bring about justice": LDB to Frederika Brandeis, 12 November 1888; Edward F. McClennen, "Louis D. Brandeis as a Lawyer," 33 *Massachusetts Law Quarterly* 17 (1948).

84 "Democratic rule yet": LDB to Alfred Brandeis, 11 September 1880, EBR.

85 "It is not pleasant": Nagel to LDB, 17 June 1884, LDB-BU.

85 he met Woodrow Wilson: See chaps. 14, 16.

85 effective administration: The literature on mugwumps is quite extensive. See especially John G. Sproat, *The Best Men: Liberal Reformers in the Gilded Age* (New York, 1968); Gerald W. McFarland, *Mugwumps, Morals, and Politics,*

1884–1920 (Amherst, Mass., 1975); and David M. Tucker, *Mugwumps: Political Moralists of the Gilded Age* (Columbia, Mo., 1998).

85 **drop the "investigation"**: Alice Harriet Grady, "Boyhood of Brandeis," *Boston American,* 4 June 1916.

85 **"Am well & busy"**: LDB to Alfred Brandeis, 30 January 1884, EBR.

86 **to the male sex**: Women had been eligible to serve on school boards in Massachusetts since the late 1860s and got the right to vote in school board elections in 1879. They did not receive the general suffrage until after the ratification of the Nineteenth Amendment in 1920.

86 **against his client**: *Train v. Boston Disinfecting Co.,* 144 Mass. 523 (1887).

87 **"will not be forgotten"**: LDB to Bacon, 6 August 1890, in Alfred Lief, ed., *The Brandeis Guide to the Modern World* (Boston, 1941), 200–201; see also LDB to Charles Frederick Wingate (editor of the *Springfield Republican*), 23 September 1886, Wingate MSS.

87 **"that we must fear"**: LDB to Alfred Brandeis, 20 March 1886, EBR.

87 **for various offices**: LDB to Alice Goldmark, 10 and 17 October 1890, Popkin MSS.

88 **political scene for decades**: Richard M. Abrams, *Conservatism in a Progressive Era: Massachusetts Politics, 1900–1912* (Cambridge, Mass., 1964), 3–4.

88 **"fool for a client"**: Geoffrey Blodgett, *The Gentle Reformers: Massachusetts Democrats in the Cleveland Era* (Cambridge, Mass., 1966), 107.

89 **number of years**: Argument before Joint Committee on Liquor Law of the Massachusetts Legislature, copy in Brandeis MSS, Scrapbook 1; *Boston Evening Transcript,* 9 February 1891; LDB to Alice Goldmark, 9 February 1891, Popkin MSS.

89 **pro bono basis**: Lewis J. Paper, *Brandeis* (Englewood Cliffs, N.J., 1983), 38.

90 **"sense of uncleanness"**: LDB to Felix Frankfurter, 26 February 1927, FF-HLS. He compared this experience to having to sit through Calvin Coolidge's Washington birthday speech.

90 **more effective advocate**: LDB to Elizabeth Glendower Evans, 14 November 189[4], Evans MSS.

91 **"Did you think"**: *Boston Herald,* 29 December 1894.

91 **gave to charity**: Paper, *Brandeis,* 39–40.

91 **recommend paying clients**: LDB to Jack Gilbert, 8 November 1928, LDB-BU.

92 **"let him run down"**: *Boston Herald,* 12 January 1897; *Springfield Republican,* 13 January 1897.

92 **"save American civilization"**: Quoted in Allon Gal, *Brandeis of Boston* (Cambridge, Mass., 1980), 24.

93 **fallacy of free silver**: LDB to AGB, 13 July 1896, Gilbert MSS; LDB to Elizabeth Evans, 6 August 1896, Evans MSS.

93 **support from, the party**: Blodgett, *Gentle Reformers,* 272–73.

94 **"cost of the service rendered"**: The notes for the lectures, running to 361 pages, are in LDB-UL.

95 **unions as outlaw groups**: The debate with Gompers is reported in the *Boston Herald,* 5 December 1902; see also LDB, "The Incorporation of Labor Unions," originally published in 15 *Green Bag* 11 (January 1903), and reprinted in LDB, *Business—a Profession* (Boston, 1914), 88–98.

95 ***Treatise on the Constitutional Limitations***: There is, unfortunately, no good study of Cooley, who has often been accused, unjustly, of fostering the

worst aspects of classical legal formalism. See, however, Alan Jones, "Thomas M. Cooley and 'Laissez-Faire Constitutionalism': A Reconsideration," *Journal of American History* 53 (1967), 759.

96 **events at Homestead:** Paul Krause, *The Battle for Homestead, 1890–1892: Politics, Culture, and Steel* (Pittsburgh, 1992).

96 **"in my own career":** Livy S. Richard, "Up from Aristocracy," *Independent,* 27 July 1914, 130–32.

97 **are quite negative:** Gerard Swope, student notes, "Business Law Fall 1893," Swope MSS; see also Baskerville, *Of Laws and Limitations,* 107–12.

97 **triggered that change:** Brandeis had originally agreed to give the course every other year, and he apparently gave it again in 1895–1896, but not afterward.

97 **"sort of social education":** Martin Green, *The Mount Vernon Street Warrens: A Boston Story, 1860–1910* (New York, 1989), 104.

98 **one of the most celebrated articles:** LDB and Samuel Warren, "The Right to Privacy," 4 *Harvard Law Review* 193 (1890). There has been a great deal of speculation as to what actually triggered Sam Warren's anger. Alpheus Mason wrote that "the *Saturday Evening Gazette,* which specialized in 'blue blood items,' naturally reported [the Warrens' entertainments] in lurid detail." Mason, *Brandeis,* 70. Dean William Prosser, the twentieth century's foremost authority on torts, claimed that news reports of his daughter's wedding aroused Warren's ire. Prosser, "Privacy," 48 *California Law Review* 383, 423 (1960). Harry Kalven Jr., one of the leading scholars of free speech, thought the article's argument erroneous, but also claimed that "it is now well known that the impetus for the article came from Warren's irritation over the way the press covered the wedding of his daughter in 1890." Kalven, "Privacy in Tort Law—Were Warren and Brandeis Wrong?" 16 *Law & Contemporary Problems* 326, 329n.22 (1966). Other sources suggest that reporters infiltrated the Warren household as members of the catering staff, and that one even smuggled in a camera, which Sam saw and knocked out of his hand. Still others claim that Warren resented political attacks on his father-in-law that depicted the former senator in a less-than-wholesome manner. James H. Barron, "Warren and Brandeis, . . . Demystifying a Landmark Citation," 13 *Suffolk University Law Review* 85 (1970).

The problem is that none of this is true. Sam and Mabel Warren had six children, but their oldest daughter was only six years old in 1890. Given the state of photographic art at the time, one could hardly have smuggled a large camera, tripod, film plates, and a powder flash into a private home. The *Saturday Evening Gazette,* it turns out, was not a scandal sheet but a weekly paper that devoted most of its column space to news, political analysis, and art and literary reviews, and even the newspaper's competitors in Boston recognized it as a first-class operation. The *Herald,* for example, called the *Gazette* the "queen of society newspapers. It is printed for a special class of patrons, is admirably edited, [and is] almost indispensable to every household."

While some of the penny press did report on the social doings of the elite, the details, especially when compared with today's tabloids, could only be considered tame: "Miss Grant . . . popped corn and ate baked apples with the second Comptroller and Congressman Ned Burnett the other afternoon in their bachelor quarters." According to Lewis Paper, Sam Warren's name only appeared twice in the *Gazette,* once in 1883, when he, Brandeis, and others announced they were bolting the Republican Party, and then in June 1890, when a Katherine H. Clarke married, and the paper reported that "Mr. and Mrs. Samuel D. Warren, the former a cousin of the bride, gave a breakfast for the bridal party" (Paper, *Brandeis,* 34–35). As for attacks on Senator Bayard, no politician—then or now—could afford to have a thin skin.

Fifteen years later Brandeis wrote that the inspiration for the article had been Sam Warren's "deep-seated abhorrence of the invasions of social privacy." LDB to Warren, 8 April 1905.

98 **enunciated it in 1965:** *Griswold v. Connecticut,* 381 U.S. 419 (1965).

98 **unpublished authors and articles:** I am much indebted in this section to Robert C. Post, "Rereading Warren and Brandeis: Privacy, Property, and Appropriation," 41 *Case Western Reserve Law Review* 647 (1991).

98 **right "to be let alone":** *Olmstead v. United States,* 277 U.S. 438, 471, 478 (1928) (Brandeis dissenting).

98 **work on torts:** Thomas M. Cooley, *A Treatise on the Law of Torts . . . ,* 2nd ed. (Chicago, 1888), 29. The two men also read, and cited, an article that had appeared earlier in the year by E. L. Godkin, "The Rights of the Citizen: IV. To His Own Reputation," *Scribner's Magazine,* July 1890, 58–67, who also used the phrase "to be let alone." Several years later someone asked Brandeis if he and Warren had gotten the idea for doing the law review article from Godkin, and both men said that there had been other issues, without explaining them. LDB to Warren, 8 April 1905.

100 **sense of private space:** Prosser, "Privacy," 389. His distinctions were later incorporated into *Restatement of the Law Second: Torts,* §652A (1976); Kalven, "Privacy in Tort Law"; Barron, "Warren and Brandeis," 907; Ruth Gavison, "Privacy and the Limits of Law," 89 *Yale Law Journal* 421, 428 (1980).

100 **and regimented society:** Baskerville talks of "the wider intellectual relevance of the issue," *Of Laws and Limitations,* 87, and he points out that the article relies very heavily on the notion that the common law remained sufficiently elastic to respond to all new conditions, at a time when the legal system in the country was already moving away from a common-law-centered jurisprudence toward one based on statutory and constitutional interpretation.

100 **would be undermined:** Post, "Rereading Warren and Brandeis," 651–52, and citing Roscoe Pound, "Interests of Personality," 28 *Harvard Law Review* 343, 363 (1915). For further elaborations on this notion, see also Sheldon W. Halpern, "The 'Inviolate Personality,' " 10 *Northern Illinois University Law Review* 387 (1990); Edward J. Bloustein, "Privacy as an Aspect of Human Dignity," 39 *New York University Law Review* 962, 1000ff. (1964); and Rochelle Gurstein, *The Repeal of Reticence* (New York, 1996), 149ff.

100 **numbing of the senses:** For a discussion of privacy in the twenty-first century, see Erwin Chemerinsky, "Rediscovering Brandeis' Right to Privacy," 45 *Brandeis Law Journal* 643 (2007).

101 **invited may enter:** For an interesting contrarian view, see Jessica Bulman, "Edith Wharton, Privacy, and Publicity," 16 *Yale Journal of Law and Feminism* 41, 81 (2004). "While Warren and Brandeis argue that the individual's independent personality must be protected through being let alone, Wharton insists that personalities are necessarily interdependent and that privacy is always bound up in publicity. For her, the female personality in particular relies on other people."

101 **no individual boundaries:** For a good overview of current privacy concerns, including informational privacy, see Philippa Strum, *Privacy, the Debate in the United States Since 1954* (Fort Worth, Tex., 1998).

101 **most thoroughly disapproved:** LDB to Alice Goldmark, 28 December 1890, Popkin MSS.

101 **ignored the request:** Warren to LDB, 10 April 1905. That same year LDB wrote to the editor of the *Harvard Law Review,* calling his attention to the case of *Pavesich v. New England Life Insurance Co., 50 S.E. 68* (1905), sustaining "the right to privacy, for which we contended," and suggesting the subject still a "lively" one that deserved further attention. LDB to Edward H. Letchworth, 20 April 1905.

101 **"literature of the law":** Elbridge L. Adams, "The Right of Privacy and Its Relation to the Law of Libel," 39 *American Law Review* 37 (1905).

101 **"new field of jurisprudence":** Wilbur Larremore, "The Law of Privacy," 12 *Columbia Law Review* 693 (1912).

101 **the article's premises:** Fred R. Shapiro, "The Most-Cited Law Review Articles," 73 *California Law Review* 1540, 1545 (1985); for early cases on privacy, see Morris L. Ernst and Alan U. Schwartz, *The Right to Be Let Alone* (New York, 1952), chap. 4.

CHAPTER 5: ALICE

103 **"if not enlarge it":** Nagel to LDB, 18 March 1885.

103 **in a serious way:** Once, when LDB returned to visit the Nagels in St. Louis, Fannie wrote to her sister, Amy, "What do you think of Lutz this morning. Else Meier is here almost constantly."

104 **for its extravagance:** LDB to Otto Wehle, 13 July 1878; LDB to Amy and Otto Wehle, 16 September 1880. Otto had written, "Amy hopes in this wise to get some of your brains into the boy. . . . If you want to protest against the abuse of your name you had better be in a hurry before the deed is done." Amy Wehle to LDB, 26 September 1880, Wehle MSS.

104 **had the best mind:** Alpheus T. Mason, *Brandeis: A Free Man's Life* (New York, 1946), 71.

104 **"so much is a bore":** Fannie Nagel to LDB, 4 October 1877, Nagel MSS. Unfortunately, Fannie did not keep the letters from her brother. LDB, however, kept the ones Fannie sent to him, and years later gave them to her daughter, Hildegard.

104 **a very good father:** Fannie Nagel to LDB, 21 October 1877, Nagel MSS. The sentiment of concern, indeed almost fear, in not hearing from LDB for more than a few days is repeated in a number of letters.

104 **woods and meadows:** Fannie Nagel to LDB, 28 December 1877, 18 January [n.d.], Nagel MSS.

104 **"world had forsaken me":** Fannie Nagel to Amy Wehle, 11 October 1884 and n.d.

105 **"the one sane wish":** LDB to Adolph Brandeis, 16 December 1889.

105 **killed herself:** Most biographers of LDB have merely said that Fannie died (Mason, *Brandeis,* 71; Philippa Strum, *Louis D. Brandeis: Justice for the People* [Cambridge, Mass., 1984], 44), but conversations with the family, as well as with Bertram Bernard, who wrote about LDB and St. Louis, all indicate that she committed suicide, and Charles Tachau (Alfred's grandson) confirmed

this via telephone on 10 April 2007. Lewis Paper (*Brandeis* [Englewood Cliffs, N.J., 1983], 43) says she fell into a postpartum depression following the birth of her daughter, Hildegard, in 1889, but Hildegard had been born in 1886, and in the contacts that I have had with members of the family over the years, no one has ever suggested that there had been another child.

106 **national labor laws:** The best source on the Goldmark family is Josephine Goldmark, *Pilgrims of '48* (New Haven, Conn., 1930). Although there is no biography of Josephine, her book on her colleague Florence Kelley, *Impatient Crusader* (Urbana, Ill., 1953), contains a great deal of information about herself.

107 **democracy and education in Denmark:** Karl Goldmark, *Notes from the Life of a Viennese Composer* (New York, 1927); *Democracy in Denmark* (Washington, D.C., 1936).

107 **stopped traveling:** AGB showed the letters LDB had written to her during their courtship to Alpheus Mason, who used them in his biography, and before her death gave them to their daughter Elizabeth Brandeis Raushenbush, who in turn passed them on to her niece, Alice Popkin. Ms. Popkin provided David Levy and me with copies for our edition of the Brandeis family letters, where they are reprinted almost in their entirety. Urofsky and Levy, *The Family Letters of Louis D. Brandeis* (Norman, Okla., 2002), 34–72. Letters written to AGB after their marriage came into the possession of Susan Brandeis Gilbert, and after her death her children deposited them, as well as a host of other family materials, in the Goldfarb Library at Brandeis University.

107 **"we have found each other":** AGB's diary, which she showed to Mason, is no longer available. The quotations are from Mason, *Brandeis*, 72.

108 **"and felt with us":** In 1895, Nagel married Anne Shepley, and in late 1894 he wrote to LDB to inform him of the engagement. Perhaps he expected LDB to feel that Nagel had betrayed Fannie's memory, because he begged him "to be as considerate as a brother's love can make you." LDB, of course, did not oppose the remarriage, and the two men saw each other from time to time over the years. Whenever possible, Nagel also arranged for his daughter, Hildegard, to visit her cousins in Louisville and Boston.

108 **not like smoking:** LDB to Alice Goldmark, 6 and 7 September 1890, Popkin MSS.

108 **"they will interest you":** LDB to Alice Goldmark, 9 September 1890, *id.*

108 **"has come to me":** Alice Goldmark to Elizabeth Evans, 8 December 1890, Evans MSS.

108 **of the troth:** LDB to Alfred Brandeis, 8 September 1890; LDB to Alice Goldmark, 9, 12, and 29 September, 1 October 1890, Popkin MSS; LDB to Alice Goldmark (fragment), 15 September 1890, in Mason, *Brandeis*, 72; LDB to Walter Bond Douglas, 1 October 1890, Douglas MSS.

108 **make another arrangement:** LDB to Alice Goldmark, 13 September 1890, Popkin MSS. In the same letter he wrote of James H. Young, a partner in Hutchins & Wheeler: "We have lived together now six years with uninterrupted harmony and a broad sympathy. I cannot remember that in all those years one irritable or irritating word was spoken by one of us to the other, or that either appeared without the other being glad."

109 **"we have in common":** Sam Warren to Alice Goldmark, September 1890, in Mason, *Brandeis*, 73.

109 **"without reserve"**: LDB to Alice Goldmark, 2 and 27 October 1890, Popkin MSS. Professor Strum discounts the first letter as "indicating nothing more than that he was finally in love" (Strum, *Brandeis,* 45), but I think it reflected more than that, and indicated how much that love meant to him.

110 **make their lives good ones:** LDB to Alice Goldmark, 20 October 1890, Popkin MSS.

110 **striving counted:** LDB's notion of a life of service is well captured in Learned Hand, "Justice Louis D. Brandeis and the Good Life," 4 *Journal of Social Philosophy* 144 (1939), a radio address Hand had delivered to mark LDB's eighty-second birthday in November 1938.

110 **"being and becoming"**: The exact quote from Arnold's *Culture and Anarchy* (1889) is "Not a having and a resting, but a growing and a becoming."

110 **"is to be admired"**: LDB to Alice Goldmark, 27 October 1890, Popkin MSS.

110 **worthwhile that matters:** *Id.*

111 **"particularly the right"**: LDB to Alice Goldmark, 9 and 28 December 1890, Popkin MSS.

111 **"carry you off"**: LDB to Alice Goldmark, 29 September, 1 and 24 December 1890, 13 and 15 March 1891, Popkin MSS.

112 **and the like:** The clock came from William D. Ellis, with whom LDB had worked on liquor legislation, and whom LDB described to Alice as a "client-bringing client." LDB to Alice Goldmark, 17 January 1891. The clock, still working, is now in the possession of LDB's grandson Frank Brandeis Gilbert in suburban Washington, D.C. Among the other wedding presents was a Japanese gold-lacquer box, given to them by Percival Lowell, the famous astronomer. LDB's art critic friend Denman Ross called it one of the best pieces of old gold lacquer in the country, and at the time gold lacquer was no longer being made. That piece is now in the Speed Art Museum in Louisville, Kentucky. See "Addendum of Art Objects to be Presented . . . by Mr. Justice and Mrs. Brandeis," in LDB to Hattie Speed, 9 October 1927, Speed MSS.

113 **afflict him less often:** LDB told Alice of his tiredness and said it did not result from his working too hard. Indeed he felt tired even after a day's recreation on vacation, and suggested that it might not be physical fatigue so much as loneliness. This is the only time he makes this suggestion. LDB to Alice Goldmark, 11 October 1890,

113 **wear the latest style:** In 1952, Elizabeth Brandeis Raushenbush asked her aunt Pauline Goldmark to tell her about some of the family history, which included the wedding of her parents. "Alice spent an intolerably long time getting ready her trousseau, a very important matter in those days. Underwear was bought, a dozen of each, and table linens. A home dressmaker named Dora came with an assistant every Thursday and worked in our basement; Alice or Chris [Christine Goldmark] had to be there all the time, and Milly had to take trips to nearby stores for 'notions,' i.e., hooks and eyes, linings, etc." Pauline Goldmark to Elizabeth Brandeis Raushenbush, memorandum, n.d., 1952. The original came to Professor Levy from Walter Raushenbush after his mother's death, and is now in the Brandeis Papers in Louisville.

114 **"speak the truth"**: LDB to Alice Goldmark, 21 October 1890 and 7 February 1891, Popkin MSS.

114 **"disgust of the carriers"**: Pauline Goldmark, memorandum; Josephine Goldmark to LDB and AGB, 21 March 1941, LDB-BU.

115 **"cumbersome furniture"**: *Boston Sunday American,* 2 July 1916.

115 **"from inner conviction"**: *La Follette's Magazine,* June 1916; Elizabeth Evans, "People I Have Known: Alice Goldmark Brandeis," *Progressive,* 26 July 1930.

115 **possible without Alice**: Remarks by Felix Frankfurter at memorial service for AGB, 15 October 1945, Rauch MSS.

116 **bring back to her**: Evans, "Alice Goldmark Brandeis."

117 **"strength to go on"**: Mason, *Brandeis,* 76; LDB to AGB, 28 December 1903; Evans, "People I Have Known."

117 **happiest in their lives**: See, for example, Charles Nagel to LDB, 18 May 1891, LDB-BU. Nagel was visiting in Louisville, and wrote LDB on the many reports he had of how happily he and Alice had settled in to their new home.

117 **"happiness was possible"**: AGB to Elizabeth Evans, 27 March 1891, Evans MSS.

117 **the house for dinner**: The following is typical of dozens of such notes: "Will you dine with us tomorrow (Monday) at seven o'clock, entirely informally?" LDB to Philip S. Abbott, 11 December 1892, Abbott MSS.

118 **"will be your very best"**: Elizabeth Evans, "Interesting People I Have Known—Margaret Deland, Wife and Author," *Springfield* (Mass.) *Sunday Union & Republican,* 19 March 1933.

118 **"above things worldly"**: LDB to Elizabeth Evans, 3 and 27 March 1893, Evans MSS; see also LDB to Amy Brandeis Wehle, 5 April 1893, LDB-BU.

118 **regained her strength**: AGB to Elizabeth Evans, 3 May and 31 August 1893, Evans MSS.

118 **preparation for the day**: Everyone knew about his early rising, and once, when LDB suggested that Emory Buckner meet him for breakfast, Buckner demurred. "I seldom rise earlier than six," he wrote, and since he lived eight miles from where LDB proposed they meet, he would not be able to get there until around eight. "I realize that by this late hour your usual working day is well advanced." Buckner to LDB, 26 May 1916.

118–119 **knowledge casually handed**: Conversations with Alice Popkin, Frank Gilbert, and Walter Raushenbush, Louisville, Ky., 12 November 2006.

119 **"inhabitants are called 'suckers' "**: LDB to AGB, 8 April 1897.

120 **chocolates and candied fruits**: Paper, *Brandeis,* 46.

120 **to bed by ten**: *Id.,* 45, based on a 1980 interview with Elizabeth Brandeis Raushenbush; Elizabeth Evans, "Justice Brandeis in the Intimacy of His Home," *Jewish Advocate,* 14 November 1931. During the time that Professor Levy and I worked on the first five volumes of the Brandeis letters, we had several opportunities to talk with Mrs. Raushenbush, and she told us some of these same stories.

121 **"Shall we do it soon"**: AGB to Elizabeth Evans, 13 July 1892, Evans MSS; LDB to AGB, 27 November 1899.

121 **the sights he saw**: See *Family Letters,* 126–32.

121 **on Zionist business**: See chap. 21.

121 **"the art can be compassed"**: LDB to AGB, 11 August 1899. His daughter Elizabeth said that while her father could sail, "he wasn't very good at it." Paper MSS.

122 **"trouble the spirit"**: Remarks by Fola La Follette, memorial service for AGB, 15 October 1945, Rauch MSS.

122 **these "dark" days**: "Life is strange & very, very difficult. Some day perhaps I shall understand what now seems very dark." AGB to Elizabeth Evans, n.d., Evans MSS.

123 **"happiness is granted"**: LDB to AGB, 31 January and [n.d.] September 1900.

123 **"very carefully"**: LDB to AGB, 28 December 1900.

123 **"anything but cheerful"**: AGB to Elizabeth Evans, 18 January 1900, Evans MSS.

123 **"advantage over short stories"**: LDB to AGB, 11, 21, and 31 January 1901.

123 **" 'read aloud to Sister' "**: LDB to AGB, 26 and 28 January 1900.

124 **their sweet ways**: LDB to AGB, 2 February 1901.

124 **"carrying you off with us"**: LDB to AGB, 17 February 1907, 23 November 1906, 7 July 1905.

124 **specific to women**: Strum, *Brandeis,* 45.

124 **other possibilities**: The pioneering work in this field is Phyllis Chesler, *Women and Madness* (New York, 1972), which showed that women were more likely to be labeled mentally ill and institutionalized than were men for comparable symptoms. A good overview of the literature, on which I have relied in this section, is Nancy Tomes, "Historical Perspectives on Women and Mental Illness," in Rima D. Apple, ed., *Women, Health, and Medicine in America: A Historical Handbook* (New York, 1990), 143–72. I am very indebted to Professor Barbara Sicherman for pointing me toward this material.

125 **fashionable disease**: Ann Douglas Wood, "The Fashionable Diseases," *Journal of Interdisciplinary History* 4 (1973), 25–52. For a classic example of how men viewed women with nervous conditions in the late nineteenth century, see the biting portrait of the husband in Charlotte Perkins Gilman, *The Yellow Wallpaper* (Boston, 1899).

125 **pressures confronting them**: Neurasthenia did not afflict just married women; Jane Addams suffered a severe bout of it in her younger days, before she found her calling at Hull House. See Louise W. Knight, *Citizen: Jane Addams and the Struggle for Democracy* (Chicago, 2005), chap. 5.

125 **what might they have been**: Some scholars have also suggested sexual pressure, and there are accounts of Harriet Beecher Stowe and other nineteenth-century women going to the hot baths to escape their husbands and avoid pregnancy. In this instance, we have absolutely no evidence that negative sexual tension existed between LDB and his wife. Moreover, as Peter Gay has shown, the Victorians were far more sexually enlightened and active than many people believed. See *Education of the Senses* (New York, 1984) and *The Tender Passion* (New York, 1986).

125 **these assaults began**: My colleague David W. Levy has suggested that Alice, who considered herself a person of intelligence and ability, with a contribution to make to society, looked around and saw people like Bess Evans, her sister Josephine, Jane Addams, and Florence Kelley actually out in the world, doing good work, accomplishing things, and felt not only jealous of the exciting lives they led but also demeaned and inferior. This is certainly a possibility, but one for which proof of its truth or falsity does not exist.

126 **"shall be later"**: LDB to AGB, 7 and 13 August 1901.

127 **eventual shipment back home:** LDB to AGB, 11, 21, and 22 August 1901.

127 **"I could not well spare":** Adolph Brandeis to LDB, 26 July 1904.

128 **"of those about him":** LDB to AGB, 10, 15, and 21 August 1905.

128 **"better come at once":** Alfred Brandeis to LDB, 27 and 29 December 1905; LDB to AGB, 29 December 1905.

128 **Amy passed away:** Otto Wehle to LDB, 8 January 1906, LDB-BU, informing him of the seriousness of Amy's illness; *Louisville Courier-Journal,* 18 February 1906.

CHAPTER 6: TRACTION AND UTILITIES

130 **their own studies:** Author's conversation with Elizabeth Brandeis Raushenbush.

132 **the legislative hearings:** LDB to Edward McClennen, 17 February 1916.

132 **the commission's approval:** Massachusetts Board of Railroad Commissioners, *29th Annual Report* (1898), cited in Richard M. Abrams, *Conservatism in a Progressive Era: Massachusetts Politics, 1900–1912* (Cambridge, Mass., 1964), 64–65.

133 **greedy speculators:** Abrams, *Conservatism,* 65–66.

133 **figure was unjustified:** LDB to Board of Railroad Commissioners, 21 October 1897.

133 **"demand like privileges":** LDB to *Boston Evening Transcript,* 30 April 1897; the letter appeared in the paper the following day. For an analysis of this letter as indicative of LDB's social ethics, see James F. Smurl, "Allocating Public Burdens: The Social Ethics Implied in Brandeis of Boston," 1 *Journal of Law and Religion* 59, 63–65 (1983).

134 **"are in close connection":** LDB to Bancroft, 20 May 1897; see also LDB to Albert Enoch Pillsbury, 20 May 1897.

135 **financial integrity:** Abrams, *Conservatism,* 54n.1.

136 **"any man I have ever known":** Claude Moore Fuess, *Joseph B. Eastman: Servant of the People* (New York, 1952), 81. Fuess shows that LDB's influence on Eastman was "decisive and continuous over many years." As he became more prominent in national affairs, LDB recommended Eastman for several positions, and Eastman held a number of important jobs in Washington, especially on the Interstate Commerce Commission, from the Wilson administration into that of Franklin Roosevelt.

137 **"what to expect":** LDB to Edward McClennen, 28 February 1916; LDB to Crane, 7 and 20 June 1901; *Boston Post,* 19 June 1901. Crane had warned the legislature a few days before meeting with LDB that he would veto the bill if it omitted a referendum. Ignoring this warning, the Senate approved the House measure, which lacked a referendum, and thus the governor was already primed to be persuaded by LDB.

138 **support the league measure:** LDB to James R. Carter, to Laurence Minot, to George B. Upham, and to Edward R. Warren, all on 24 February 1902; LDB to Edward Filene, 11 April 1902.

138 **"master of the public":** LDB's comments of 14 April 1902 were transcribed and included in a pamphlet issued by the league and the Board of Trade, "Shall the Boston Elevated Railway Co. Be the Servant or Master of the People?"

139 **analysis as "sophistries":** LDB to Pillsbury, 30 April 1902; Pillsbury to LDB, 30 April 1902.

139 **Commonwealth's traditional pattern:** Alpheus T. Mason, *Brandeis: A Free Man's Life* (New York, 1946), 116.

140 **large industrial concerns:** Abrams, *Conservatism,* 73.

140 **fares they charged:** LDB, "The Experience of Massachusetts in Street Railways," *Municipal Affairs* 6 (1902–1903), 721–29; a few years later LDB expanded on this theme in a speech at the Cooper Union, "The Massachusetts System of Dealing with Public Franchises," 24 February 1905, typescript. About this time, Charles Evans Hughes, then beginning his reform career in New York, also advocated strong regulatory commissions with overarching mandates of authority from the state. Merlo J. Pusey, *Charles Evans Hughes,* 2 vols. (New York, 1951), 1:201.

141 **"the people's standpoint":** Comment on LDB paper, *Municipal Affairs,* 809, 811.

141 **asked for his help:** LDB to Mrs. Roland Lincoln, 30 June 1903, 6 May 1904.

141 **Good Government Association:** Copies of speeches before Good Government Association, 11 December 1903, and Brighton School Association, 2 December 1904; *Boston Journal,* 9 April 1903.

141 **of interest to him:** See, for example, the large blaring headlines "BRANDEIS FOR MAYOR?" *Boston Traveler,* 14 April 1903, and "THREE MEN NOW IN THE FIGHT," 15 September 1904, suggesting LDB was one of the three fighting for the Democratic gubernatorial nomination.

141 **"attend to law business":** LDB to Adolph Brandeis, 1 August 1905.

141 **might be founded:** Warren to LDB, 30 April 1904.

142 **pipelines were laid down:** I am indebted to Professor David Marks of the Massachusetts Institute of Technology for information on coal gasification at the turn of the twentieth century.

142 **$7 million in profit:** In the 1960s, Brandeis University established a commission (of which I was a member) to look into the possibility of publishing LDB's public papers. As an example of how this might be done, Professor William Goldsmith, a member of the political science department at Brandeis, produced a memorandum on the sliding scale, utilizing various LDB documents and letters as well as other sources, and including a history of the gas companies in Boston in the 1880s and 1890s. "Memorandum to Brandeis Commission, March 1968," Goldsmith MSS.

142 **into his snares:** Thomas W. Lawson, *Frenzied Finance,* 2 vols. (New York, 1905), 1:69–70.

143 **became law in May 1903:** *Boston Evening Transcript,* 8 May 1903.

143 **"new men you have in mind":** LDB to Warren, 2 May 1904.

144 **current price of a dollar:** *Boston Evening Transcript,* 7 March 1905.

145 **bill already presented by the board:** LDB had drafted the measure and had sent a copy to Governor William Lewis Douglas two days earlier; LDB to Douglas, 7 March 1905.

145 **historic and successful traditions:** "Consolidation of Gas Companies and Electric Light Companies: Argument of Louis D. Brandeis, March 9, 1905," Goldsmith MSS.

145 **unsuccessfully tried to calm:** See, for example, LDB to Warren, 16 March and 5 May 1905, and especially the sharp exchange in Warren to LDB, 10

March 1905 (following LDB's testimony), and LDB's response, 13 March 1905.

146 **"gods to sacrificial feasts"**: LDB to Edward McClennen, 14 March 1916; LDB, *Index,* quoted in Mason, *Brandeis,* 133. He had once told Bess Evans, "Remember, to succeed you must: First: Sleep and keep well. Second: Not appear fanatical." LDB to Evans, 14 November [1894].

146 **Warren failed to heed**: See, for example, LDB to Thomas M. Babson (Boston corporate counsel), 31 March 1905: "You will of course understand that in what I have stated as to sliding scale, I do not represent the State Board of Trade . . . nor do I write as representing the Public Franchise League."

146 **story on the plan**: *Boston Evening Transcript,* 2 June 1905; the news story closely tracked the memorandum.

147 **mislead the public**: *Outlook,* 3 June 1905, 254–55; see also LDB to Bowles, 8 May 1905.

148 **confirmation to the Court**: LDB to Edward Filene, 24 May 1905; testimony of Edward R. Warren, U.S. Senate, *Hearings Before the Subcommittee of the Committee on the Judiciary . . . on the Nomination of Louis D. Brandeis to Be an Associate Justice of the Supreme Court of the United States,* 64th Cong., 1st sess., 2 vols. in 1 (Washington, D.C., 1916), 1612. George Anderson also objected to the compromise measure and said that since LDB had done all of the work, he and he alone should get the credit for it. Anderson to LDB, 6 May 1905. But after the sliding scale came into existence and worked, Anderson, alone of the opponents to the measure in the league, handsomely apologized to LDB.

148 **urging its adoption**: Report of the Special Committee, copy in Goldsmith MSS; LDB to Hall, 25 January 1906 (suggesting changes in the minority report), and to Edward McClennen, 14 March 1916 (admitting the major role he played in drafting that report).

148 **necessity of life**: Supporters of municipal ownership, such as the Hearst newspapers, opposed the sliding scale. See Editorial, *Boston Evening Transcript,* 2 April 1906.

149 **Curtis Guild signed**: *Boston Evening Transcript,* 26 May 1906. Even though the league sponsored the bill, Warren and others made known their opposition to it, and the local Hearst paper, opposed to the measure, ran a story with a large headline, "FRANCHISE LEAGUE SPLIT ON GAS SCALE," *Boston American,* 14 May 1906. A few days later it ran another headlined—and rather misleading—story claiming that eighty-cent gas had been demanded in the House, when in fact, as noted in the body of the story, only one representative had "demanded" that rate. *Boston Evening Transcript,* 18 May 1906.

149 **"out of politics"**: LDB to Alfred Brandeis, 27 May 1906.

149 **a number of times**: See, for example, LDB to Clinton Rogers Woodruff, 13 June 1906.

150 **treated the consumer honestly**: The Hearst newspapers attacked the sliding scale during the hearings precisely on the ground that it would deter the coming of municipal ownership. See editorial criticizing the Hearst papers in *Boston Evening Transcript,* 2 April 1906.

150 **details of the scheme**: See, for example, *New York Evening Post,* 29 May 1906.

150 **"a private corporation"**: LDB, "How Boston Solved the Gas Problem,"

American Review of Reviews, November 1907, 594–98, reprinted in LDB, *Business—a Profession* (Boston, 1914), 99–114. See also James L. Richards, "The Boston Consolidated Gas Company: Its Relation to the Public, Its Employees, and Investors," *Annals of the American Academy of Political and Social Science* 31 (January–June 1908), 593–99, a piece that LDB could have written and whose premises echoed his own.

151 " 'the man behind' ": LDB to Alfred Brandeis, 27 May 1906.

153 **a much lonelier place:** Livy S. Richard, "Up from Aristocracy," *Independent,* 27 July 1914, 131. There is some evidence that this social ostracism initially bothered Alice, but that LDB did not take much notice. Philippa Strum, *Louis D. Brandeis: Justice for the People* (Cambridge, Mass., 1984), 63.

153 **"you can get my assent":** LDB to Charles Palen Hall, 13 July 1906.

153 **"fully half his time":** Edward Filene, "Louis D. Brandeis as We Know Him," *Boston Post,* 14 July 1915.

154 **"I want to be free":** *Current Literature* (March 1911), cited in Alfred Lief, ed., *The Brandeis Guide to the Modern World* (Boston, 1941), 38.

CHAPTER 7: A PERFECT REFORM

155 **"Story of Life Insurance":** Louis Filler, *The Muckrakers,* enl. ed. (University Park, Pa., 1976), 190–91, 97.

156 **"love of the golden rule":** Quoted in Michael McGerr, *A Fierce Discontent: The Rise and Fall of the Progressive Movement in America, 1870–1914* (New York, 2003), 170.

156 **demands for reform:** For the overall response to the insurance scandals, see H. Roger Grant, *Insurance Reform: Consumer Action in the Progressive Era* (Ames, Iowa, 1979); for savings bank insurance, see Alpheus T. Mason, *The Brandeis Way: A Case Study in the Workings of Democracy* (Princeton, N.J., 1938).

157 **serve without compensation:** Alpheus T. Mason, *Brandeis: A Free Man's Life* (New York, 1946), 153.

157 **in the system itself:** LDB to Policy-Holders' Protective Committee, 19 May 1905.

157 **to mend their ways:** *New York Insurance Journal,* 10 July 1905.

158 **thus paid in more:** *Moody's Magazine,* May 1906.

160 **which included profit:** Filler, *Muckrakers,* 195–96; see Merlo J. Pusey, *Charles Evans Hughes,* 2 vols. (New York, 1951), chap. 15.

160 **"an insignificant investment":** *Report of the Joint Committee . . . ,* Assembly Document 41 (1906), quoted in Mason, *Brandeis Way,* 110.

160 **next several years:** LDB, *Life Insurance: The Abuses and the Remedies,* published as a pamphlet in 1905 by the Policy-Holders' Protective Committee, and reprinted in *Business—a Profession* (Boston, 1914), 115–59.

163 **"our political evils":** John Graham Brooks, "Moralized Insurance," *Collier's Weekly,* 15 June 1907.

164 **matter of interstate commerce:** *Paul v. Virginia,* 8 Wall. 168 (1869). That case would not be overturned until *United States v. South-Eastern Underwriters Association,* 322 U.S. 533 (1944), and even then Congress declined to institute national regulation, leaving control of the insurance industry in the states.

165 **received wide circulation:** See, for example, LDB to Ralph Montgomery Easley, 28 October 1905, to Samuel Bowles, 31 October 1905, to John Combe Pegram, 1 November 1905, and to Samuel D. Warren, 1 November 1905.

166 **nonsalaried trustees:** Richard M. Abrams, *Conservatism in a Progressive Era: Massachusetts Politics, 1900–1912* (Cambridge, Mass., 1964), 141–42.

167 **those of the banks:** LDB to Wright, 24 November 1905. To get this information, LDB agreed to pay Wright $100 for the work, a sum he paid for out of his own pocket.

167 **"their present function":** Wright to LDB, 13 December 1905; LDB to Wright, 29 December 1905.

168 **east of Louisville:** See Melvin I. Urofsky and David W. Levy, eds., *Letters of Louis D. Brandeis,* 5 vols. (Albany, N.Y., 1971–1978), 1:395–444.

168 **"office and Legislature":** LDB to Alfred Brandeis, 2 March 1906, EBR.

168 **"injustice in the process":** LDB to Alfred Brandeis, 22 February 1906, EBR.

169 **"to help themselves":** LDB to Hughes, 13 June 1906; Hughes to LDB, 6 July 1906; LDB to Herrick, 27 June 1906; Herrick to LDB, 5 July 1906.

169 **with Norman Hapgood:** LDB, "Wage Earners' Life Insurance," *Collier's Weekly,* 15 September 1906, 16ff., reprinted as "Savings Bank Insurance" in *Business—a Profession,* 154–81.

169 **Pinchot-Ballinger hearings:** For Hapgood's relations with LDB, see his "Americans We Like: Justice Brandeis, Apostle of Freedom," *Nation,* October 1927, 330–31, and chap. 13 of his autobiography, *The Changing Years* (New York, 1930).

170 **"the Boston theorist":** *Insurance Press,* 19 September 1906 and 30 January 1907; *Insurance Post,* 2 February 1907.

171 **"lose their foundation":** LDB to Henry Morgenthau Sr., 5 December 1906, SBLI.

171 **rest of the community:** LDB, "Savings Banks' Life Insurance," *American Federationist,* October 1907, 777, 779.

171 **"success of the plan":** LDB to Henry Morgenthau Sr., 20 November 1906, SBLI.

173 **become an actor:** LDB to Charles F. F. Campbell, 11 February 1916; Mason, *Brandeis Way,* 243–44. The short film was shown widely throughout Massachusetts.

173 **"a grand life":** Beulah Amidon, "Other People's Insurance," *Survey Graphic,* November 1936, 600; LDB to Felix Frankfurter, 16 May 1934, Frankfurter MSS-LC. See also Elizabeth Glendower Evans, "Interesting People I Have Known: Mr. Justice Brandeis and Alice H. Grady," draft of an article following Miss Grady's death, 1934, Evans MSS.

174 **as the situation demanded:** For the full story of LDB's leadership of the campaign, see Mason, *Brandeis Way,* or a shorter version of it in Mason, *Brandeis,* chap. 11.

175 **White should contact him:** LDB to White, 30 November 1906, SBLI.

175 **make a convert:** For a detailed account of LDB's legislative campaign, see Mason, *Brandeis Way,* chap. 7, and letters between April 1906 and June 1907 in Urofsky and Levy, *Letters of Brandeis,* vol. 1.

176 **legislators would ignore it:** Reed to LDB, 23 March 1907.

176 **"the coming campaign":** LDB to White, 17 April 1907; for LDB's activi-

ties on behalf of the bill, see letters in March and April 1907 in Urofsky and Levy, *Letters of Brandeis.*

177 **"personal missionary work":** LDB to White, 8 December 1906, SBLI.

177 **"for anything new":** Jones to LDB, 18 March 1907.

177 **governor's consideration:** LDB to Guild, 25 June 1907, SBLI.

177 **"step nearer vacation":** LDB to Alfred Brandeis, 10 July 1907.

177 **plan would die aborning:** *Boston Evening Transcript,* 14 May 1908.

178 **"going amazingly well":** LDB to Steffens, 10 December 1909, Steffens MSS; LDB to Charles Goldmark, 19 September 1941, EBR.

178 **$1 million a year:** Ernest Poole, "Brandeis," *American Magazine,* February 1911, 486.

178 **"vice pays to virtue":** LDB to Warren A. Reed, 15 October 1907.

178 **performance of private companies:** For a portrait of savings bank life insurance a few years after its establishment, see Shelby M. Harrison, "The Massachusetts Scheme of Savings Bank Insurance," *Survey,* 7 May 1910, 237–49.

CHAPTER 8: TAKING ON MORGAN

181 **asked his partner:** LDB to Dunbar, 12 June 1907.

181 **anything but simple:** The only full-length study of the New Haven fight is Henry Lee Staples and Alpheus T. Mason, *The Fall of a Railroad Empire: Brandeis and the New Haven Merger* (Syracuse, N.Y., 1947), which expands upon chaps. 12 and 13 in Alpheus T. Mason, *Brandeis: A Free Man's Life* (New York, 1946), and unabashedly backs the Brandeis view. Richard M. Abrams, "Brandeis and the New Haven–Boston & Maine Merger Battle Revisited," *Business History Review* 36 (Winter 1962), 408–30, looks more dispassionately at the economic issues posed by the plan. Albro Martin, *Enterprise Denied: Origins of the Decline of American Railroads, 1897–1917* (New York, 1971), blames the economic simplemindedness of LDB and other reformers for causing the decline and collapse of what had once been the world's greatest railroad system.

182 **" 'mother of safety' ":** LDB to Norman Hapgood, 25 September 1911. LDB had copied this quotation into a notebook years earlier; it comes from Victor Cherbuliez's novel *Samuel Brohl and Partner* (New York, 1883).

182 **Boston's leading businessmen:** For two contemporary and highly favorable views of Mellen (1851–1927), see E. P. Lyle, "Master of Traffic," *World's Work,* May 1905, 6147–51; and Frederick W. Coburn, "Railroad Lord of New England," *World Today,* August 1907, 829–32. Apparently, once Morgan trusted a person, he rarely interfered directly in how that man ran the business. Mellen would not have attempted the monopolization of New England transportation without Morgan's blessing, but neither would Mellen be looking over his shoulder to see if Morgan approved of each step. Paul B. Abrahams, "Brandeis and Lamont on Finance Capitalism," *Business History Review* 47 (1973), 72, 77.

182 **"maintaining standards":** Quoted in Philippa Strum, *Brandeis: Beyond Progressivism* (Lawrence, Kans., 1993), 139.

183 **profitable commuter traffic:** Abrams, "Battle Revisited," 411–12.

184 **name of efficiency:** Thomas K. McCraw, *Prophets of Regulation: Charles Francis Adams, Louis D. Brandeis, James M. Landis, Alfred E. Kahn* (Cambridge, Mass., 1984), 32–33.

184 to have succeeded: See, for example, "Why Business Men Favor the Merger," *Boston American,* 16 April 1908.

184 "we have the power": *Boston Herald,* 7 March 1907, cited in Abrams, "Battle Revisited," 409.

185 "street railway companies": *Boston Herald,* 27 June 1906.

186 colleagues in the league: Eastman, "Annual Report of 1907."

186 "inspiration of her ideals": *Boston Globe,* 23 June 1906.

186 "being much attacked": LDB to Alfred Brandeis, 26 June 1907.

186 commercial law practice: See, for example, LDB to C. B. Fillebrown, 3 November 1906.

187 "foreign to our tradition": LDB to Edward Filene, 29 June 1907, Filene MSS.

188 "became a great system": LDB, *Other People's Money, and How the Bankers Use It* (Boston, 1914; Abrams ed., Boston, 1995), 119–20. Forbes had indeed been a great entrepreneur, but as Richard Abrams pointed out, Brandeis's encomium to him reflected more of his provincial Boston bias than the actual facts. The man who built the Chicago, Burlington & Quincy Railroad had been primarily a financier, not a manager. He did have a reputation for being scrupulously honest, but much of this reputation derived from "a stubborn Boston conservatism" that led him to suspect and reject newer forms of finance. While Brandeis equated this with simplicity and integrity, business historians of the era have considered him "unprogressive" and not very innovative. Brandeis's lament is likewise a rejection of the new financial system, and for a business ethic that had, by then, almost died out. *Id.,* 119n.12.

189 "for services on account": LDB to Malloch, 4 November 1907.

189 reimbursed them appropriately: Edward McClennen, "Louis D. Brandeis as a Lawyer," 33 *Massachusetts Law Quarterly* 24 (September 1948).

190 "as to what it means": Memo of LDB interview with Mark Sullivan, 4 January 1908.

191 " 'properly safeguard it' ": *Boston American,* 10 June 1907.

191 "if you please": *Boston Morning Herald,* 12 June 1907; *Boston Evening Transcript,* 12 June 1907; Mason, *Brandeis,* 180–81.

191 "cross-examining him": Memo of LDB interview with Mark Sullivan, 4 January 1908.

192 weakened it even more: LDB, "The New England Transportation Monopoly," in *Business—a Profession* (Boston, 1914), 255–78. This message he emphasized in all of his talks against the merger; see, for example, *Medford Mercury,* 14 February 1908, and *Boston Evening Transcript,* 9 March 1908.

193 "gone into dividends": LDB to Alfred Brandeis, 19 October 1907.

193 " 'available' candidate": *Id.*

193 disagree on that point: Elizabeth Glendower Evans, "Mr. Justice Brandeis: The People's Tribune," *Survey,* 1 November 1931, 138–41, at 139.

194 Higginson never replied: LDB to Higginson, 6 June 1902.

194 "they have vanished": Irving Katz, "Henry Lee Higginson vs. Louis Dembitz Brandeis: A Collision Between Tradition and Reform," *New England Quarterly* 41 (March 1968), 75. Katz, I think, is mistaken in ascribing a "traditional" stance to Higginson and a "reform" posture to Brandeis. In many ways, Brandeis subscribed far more than did Higginson to traditional Boston views on investment and banking.

195 **Interstate Commerce Commission:** See, for example, letters in fall 1907, in Melvin I. Urofsky and David W. Levy, eds., *Letters of Louis D. Brandeis,* 5 vols. (Albany, N.Y., 1971–1978), vol. 2.

195 **bondholders of the two lines:** *Boston Journal,* 8 January 1908.

195 **"only incidental":** LDB to Louis F. Buff, 3 February 1908.

195 **technical financial reports:** See, for example, *Wall Street Journal,* 14 January 1908.

196 **"my previous fights together":** Reaction in the press can be found in Mason, *Brandeis,* 184–86; *Boston Evening Transcript,* 7 January 1908; LDB to Alfred Brandeis, 2 January 1908.

196 **Savings Bank Insurance League:** LDB to George L. Barnes, 13 February 1908.

196 **man in the cause:** LDB to George L. Barnes, 7 April 1908.

196 **interests against Morgan:** George R. Nutter to Sullivan & Cromwell, 22 May 1908; LDB to Robert L. O'Brien, 22 May 1908.

197 **against the New Haven:** In a typical week, LDB spoke in Winter Hill, Gardner, Worcester, and three times in Boston; Alice Harriet Grady to George L. Barnes, 22 April 1908.

197 **"progress with the public":** LDB to Alfred Brandeis, 3 May 1908.

197 **the necessary legislation:** *Gardner News,* 12 April 1908.

197 **for possible editorials:** LDB to Edwin A. Grozier, 18 May 1908.

198 **that much longer:** LDB to Alfred Brandeis, 14 June 1908.

198 **"to pound the enemy":** LDB to Alfred Brandeis, 5 June 1908.

198 **"the present management":** *Boston Journal,* 11 July and 15 October 1908; Abrams, "Battle Revisited," 423–24; LDB to Alfred Brandeis, 13 July 1908.

198 **appeared wrong to him:** LDB to Board of Railroad Commissioners, 23 February 1909.

198 **at the current session:** LDB to William E. Chandler, 8 April 1908, Chandler MSS.

199 **but to no avail:** LDB to Alfred Brandeis, 22 May 1909; LDB to E. J. Bliss, 22 May 1909.

199 **"the fight made":** LDB to Edward Filene, 24 May 1909; LDB to Alfred Brandeis, 6 and 15 June 1909.

200 **"habit of lying":** Abrams, "Battle Revisited," 424n.59.

200 **at the polls:** *Id.,* 425.

200 **financial ruin could be avoided:** Asa French, the U.S. attorney, later said that he hated to do it, since he had spent some two years working up the case, but he had his orders from the attorney general. In light of the Draper Act, no reason existed to go forward with the suit. It is very likely that the two Republican senators from Massachusetts, who both favored the merger, interceded on the New Haven's behalf.

200 **"their lawyer minions supply":** LDB to Alfred Brandeis, 19 August 1909, in Mason, *Brandeis,* 198.

CHAPTER 9: AN ATTORNEY FOR THE PEOPLE

202 **"any other occupation":** George F. Shelton, "Law as Business," 10 *Yale Law Journal* 275 (1900); see also David W. Levy, "The Lawyer as Judge: Brandeis' View of the Legal Profession," 22 *Oklahoma Law Review* 374, 377–80 (1969);

Robert Treat Platt, "The Decadence of Law . . . ," 12 *Yale Law Journal* 441 (1903); and John Randolph Dos Passos, *The American Lawyer as He Was—as He Is—as He Can Be* (New York, 1907).

202   **"more or less on trial":** Cited in Levy, "Lawyer as Judge," 379–80.

202   **"The Opportunity in the Law":** 39 *American Law Review* 555 (1905), reprinted in LDB, *Business—a Profession* (Boston, 1914), 313–27.

203   **they are advocates:** Alexis de Tocqueville, *Democracy in America,* edited by Sanford Kessler, translated by Stephen D. Grant (Indianapolis, 2000), 121.

203   **"even fifty years ago":** Richard Hofstadter, in his classic work *The Age of Reform: From Bryan to F.D.R.* (New York, 1955), chap. 4, relied a great deal on this section of LDB's talk and argued that this loss of status not just in the law but in other professions as well constituted a root cause of progressivism.

205   **"their point of view":** LDB to AGB, 18 October 1912.

206   **lose your soul:** See William H. Simon, "Babbitt v. Brandeis: The Decline of the Professional Ideal," 37 *Stanford Law Review* 565 (1985).

207   **sanctity of private property:** For the changing jurisprudential philosophy, see Kermit L. Hall, *The Magic Mirror: Law in American History* (New York, 1989), and especially William M. Wiecek, *The Lost World of Classical Legal Thought: Law and Ideology in America, 1886–1937* (New York, 1998).

207   **by constant change:** See especially Morton J. Horwitz, *The Transformation of American Law, 1780–1860* (Cambridge, Mass., 1977); Lawrence M. Friedman, *A History of American Law,* 2nd ed. (New York, 1985); and the older but still useful J. Willard Hurst, *Law and the Conditions of Freedom in the Nineteenth-Century United States* (Madison, Wis., 1956).

209   **"the social state":** Sidney Fine, *Laissez-Faire and the General Welfare State* (Ann Arbor, Mich., 1956), 139; Arnold M. Paul, *Conservative Crisis and the Rule of Law: Attitudes of Bar and Bench, 1887–1895* (Ithaca, N.Y., 1960), 164, 65.

209   **"tradition of the common law":** Statement to Massachusetts Joint Legislative Committee, 27 February 1891; statement to House Committee on Patents, 15 May 1912, cited in Alfred Lief, ed., *The Brandeis Guide to the Modern World* (Boston, 1941), 165; Paul Freund, "Mr. Justice Brandeis," in Allison Dunham and Philip Kurland, eds., *Mr. Justice* (Chicago, 1956), 102.

209   **"logic of realities":** LDB to Norman Hapgood, 30 July 1912; *DeSanto v. Pennsylvania,* 273 U.S. 34, 37, 43 (1927) (LDB dissenting).

209   **"fifty years back":** Poole, "Brandeis," in LDB, *Business—a Profession,* liv.

210   **"to the public welfare":** Christopher G. Tiedeman, *A Treatise on the Limitations of Police Power in the United States* (St. Louis, 1886); *Noble State Bank v. Haskell,* 219 U.S. 104, 111 (1911).

210   **unanimous approval:** *Sturges & Burns Manufacturing Co. v. Beauchamp,* 231 U.S. 325 (1913); for child labor laws in this period, see Stephen B. Wood, *Constitutional Politics in the Progressive Era: Child Labor and the Law* (Chicago, 1970).

210   **hazardous to their health:** *Holden v. Hardy,* 169 U.S. 366 (1898).

211   **type of statute:** Melvin I. Urofsky, "State Courts and Protective Legislation in the Progressive Era: A Re-evaluation," *Journal of American History* 72 (1985), 63–91.

211   **in tenement basements:** See Paul Kens, *Judicial Power and Reform Politics* (Lawrence, Kans., 1990).

211 **"rights of the individual":** *Lochner v. New York,* 198 U.S. 45, 56 (1905).

212 **on its wisdom:** *Id.* at 75 (Holmes dissenting); Harlan's dissent is at *id.,* 65.

212 **future protective legislation:** For a sampling of response to the decision, see Paul Kens, "Lochner v. New York," in Melvin I. Urofsky, ed., *The Public Debate over Controversial Supreme Court Decisions* (Washington, D.C., 2006), 95–103.

212 **and the conviction:** *State v. Muller,* 8 Oregon 252 (1906).

212 **freedom of contract:** The most balanced treatment of the case is the introduction in Nancy Woloch, *Muller v. Oregon: A Brief History with Documents* (Boston, 1996).

213 **would take the case:** For a description of the league, its members, and its activities, see Florence Kelley, "Twenty-five Years of the Consumers' League Movement," *Survey,* 27 November 1915, 212–14.

213 **"more than ten hours a day":** Josephine Goldmark, *Impatient Crusader: Florence Kelley's Life Story* (Urbana, Ill., 1953), 154; Kelley, letter to the editor, *Survey,* 13 May 1916. According to Goldmark, Florence Kelley never wanted Choate, but her board insisted that she approach a recognized leader of the New York bar, since that would be a coup for the league.

214 **"social workers":** Goldmark, *Impatient Crusader,* 154, 155.

214 **police power argument:** *Ritchie v. People,* 155 Ill. 98 (1895). There had also been three earlier state cases upholding such legislation: *Commonwealth v. Beatty,* 15 Super. Ct. (Pa.) 5 (1890); *Wenham v. State,* 65 Neb. 394 (1902); and *State v. Buchanan,* 29 Wash. 602 (1902).

215 **how it should be:** See "A Hearing Without Being Heard," *Washington Post,* 20 February 2007, A3. Lilly Ledbetter, who had instituted a pay discrimination case, had come to the Supreme Court to hear her case argued, and the only time she heard her name was when Chief Justice John Roberts called the case name (*Ledbetter v. Goodyear Tire and Rubber Co.*) to begin oral argument. The story also cites the common belief of both Justice Stephen Breyer (considered a liberal on the Roberts Court) and Justice Antonin Scalia, a conservative, that in the Supreme Court the most important thing is not doing justice in a particular case but establishing a clear rule of law.

216 **devoted to the law:** *Muller v. Oregon,* 208 U.S. 412 (1908); the National Consumers League published the brief as *Women in Industry* (1908) and, at LDB's insistence, listed Josephine Goldmark as coauthor.

217 **"ten hours a day":** Brief, 113. The reader may also wonder at the rather strange grammatical construction of this sentence. See Clyde Spillenger, "Revenge of the Triple Negative: A Note on the Brandeis Brief in *Muller v. Oregon,*" 22 *Constitutional Commentary* 5 (2005).

217 **itself to change:** Some of these issues are discussed in Miriam Theresa Rooney, "Law as an Instrument of Social Policy: The Brandeis Theory," *New Scholasticism* 22 (1948), 34–88.

217 **evils of industrial transition:** For LDB's conservatism, which will be explored in different areas in this volume, see Melvin I. Urofsky, "The Conservatism of Mr. Justice Brandeis," *Modern Age* 23 (1979), 39–48.

218 **"as in a bakery":** The brief for Muller can be found in Philip B. Kurland and Gerhard Casper, eds., *Landmark Briefs and Arguments of the Supreme Court of the United States* (Arlington, Va., 1975), vol. 16. The State of Oregon filed a separate brief that can also be found here.

218 **interruptions for questions:** Josephine Goldmark to Alpheus Mason, memorandum, 6 November 1944, cited in Alpheus T. Mason, *Brandeis: A Free Man's Life* (New York, 1946), 250.

219 **the statute and health:** See Nancy Woloch, "Muller v. Oregon," in Urofsky, *Public Debate,* 105–7, for press response.

219 **"spread over the country":** Goldmark, *Impatient Crusader,* 159. The *Louisville Herald,* 1 June 1908, ran a feature on LDB's "fight for the people's rights" and identified him as "brother of Alfred Brandeis, who was born and raised in this city."

220 **Michigan Law School:** *Brown v. Board of Education,* 337 U.S. 483 (1954); *Grutter v. Bollinger,* 539 U.S. 306 (2003).

220 **"such a question":** Edward F. McClennen, "Louis D. Brandeis as a Lawyer," 33 *Massachusetts Law Quarterly* 16–19 (1948); Roscoe Pound to Senator William E. Chilton, 8 February 1916, U.S. Senate, *Hearings Before the Subcommittee of the Committee on the Judiciary . . . on the Nomination of Louis D. Brandeis to Be an Associate Justice of the Supreme Court of the United States,* 64th Cong., 1st sess., 2 vols. in 1 (Washington, D.C., 1916).

221 **"validity of the law":** See, for example, Ellie Margolis, "Beyond Brandeis: Exploring the Uses of Non-legal Materials in Appellate Briefs," 34 *University of San Francisco Law Review* 197 (1999); Paul Freund, *On Understanding the Supreme Court* (Boston, 1950), 87.

221 **"the law must stand":** From oral argument in *Stettler v. O'Hara,* printed in *Survey,* February 1915, 521, and reprinted as "The Constitution and the Minimum Wage," in LDB, *The Curse of Bigness* (New York, 1934), 65–66.

222 **"would have us believe":** This issue is explored in David P. Bryden, "Brandeis's Facts," 1 *Constitutional Commentary* 281 (1984).

222 **the authorities cited:** Judith A. Baer, *The Chains of Protection* (Westport, Conn., 1978), 57–61.

222 **uphold the Oregon law:** Woloch, *Muller v. Oregon,* 32; Dean Acheson, *Morning and Noon* (Boston, 1965), 53; Bryden, "Brandeis's Facts," 294–95.

222 **needed special protection:** One, of course, need not be "inferior" to need protection, but merely "different" in the light of specific obligations or circumstances. The statute books in both the United States and Europe are filled with protective measures for many people that do not imply inferiority.

223 **little better than children:** Baer, *Chains of Protection,* is perhaps the most vociferous advocate of this position, but she is not alone. See Nancy S. Erickson, "Muller v. Oregon Reconsidered: The Origins of a Sex-Based Doctrine of Liberty of Contract," *Labor History* 30 (1989), 228–50; Susan Lehrer, *Origins of Protective Labor Legislation for Women, 1905–1925* (Albany, N.Y., 1987); and Joan Hoff, *Law, Gender, and Injustice* (New York, 1991), among others.

223 **wives and mothers:** *Bradwell v. Illinois,* 83 U.S. 130 (1873).

223 **retreating from *Lochner:*** Owen M. Fiss, *Troubled Beginnings of the Modern State, 1888–1910* (New York, 1993), 177–78.

223 **meet in the courts:** Deborah L. Rhode believed reformers should have attacked *Lochner* directly, but does not take into account what LDB and others believed at the time. *Justice and Gender: Sex Discrimination and the Law* (Cambridge, Mass., 1989), 40.

223 **in the 1920s:** *Adkins v. Children's Hospital,* 261 U.S. 525 (1923); see Howard Gillman, *The Constitution Besieged: The Rise and Demise of Lochner Era Police Powers Jurisprudence* (Durham, N.C., 1993).

223 **"taxation without representation":** Alice Stone Blackwell, "An Important Decision," *Woman's Journal,* 29 February 1908, cited in Woloch, "Muller," 108.

224 **for women to make:** *United Auto Workers v. Johnson Controls,* 499 U.S. 197 (1991). The company made batteries that required large-scale usage of and exposure to lead. This situation apparently did not affect male reproductive organs, but studies showed that it did affect women and could cause birth defects. As a result, the company refused to hire women for good-paying jobs in the battery plant. The Court said the company could not make this decision, but had to open all jobs to women and let them decide what to do. See Cynthia R. Daniels, *At Women's Expense: State Power and the Politics of Fetal Rights* (Cambridge, Mass., 1993).

225 *Ritchie v. Wayman:* LDB to AGB, 11 February 1910; *Ritchie v. Wayman,* 244 Ill. 509 (1910).

225 **pages of factual material:** Woloch, *Muller v. Oregon,* 41–43; *People v. Charles Schweinler Press,* 214 N.Y. 395 (1915); *Ex parte Anna Hawley,* 85 Ohio 495 (1911). When a second attack was launched against the Illinois law, LDB once again successfully defended it in *People v. Eldering,* 254 Ill. 579 (1912).

225 *Fatigue and Efficiency:* Wilson named LDB to the Court before oral argument in *Bunting v. Oregon,* 243 U.S. 426 (1917), and Felix Frankfurter took over as counsel for the National Consumers League. The Court heard oral argument on 18 April 1916, before LDB had been confirmed, and then rescheduled it for 12 June 1916. Because of the role he had played, LDB recused himself, but the Court, by a 5–3 vote, upheld the law.

225 **to cover only women:** Not too much earlier LDB had expressed reservations about the constitutionality of minimum-wage legislation. LDB to Mary McDowell, 8 July 1912 and 8 April 1913.

226 **" 'into the Supreme Court' ":** Hitz to Frankfurter, 17 December 1914. Frankfurter sent it on to LDB with a notation: "I envy Hitz. I wish I had heard it."

226 **by a chief justice:** "A Brandeis Argument," in Babbitt's Column, *Boston Herald,* 3 January 1915; Warren to Frankfurter, 6 April 1939, Warren MSS.

227 **upheld the law:** *Bosley v. McLaughlin,* 236 U.S. 385 (1915).

227 **Oregon court decision:** LDB to Alfred Brandeis, 27 February 1915; *Stettler v. O'Hara,* 243 U.S. 629 (1917).

227 **Goldmark had produced:** LDB to R. F. Mitchell, 22 March 1916.

CHAPTER 10: DEMOCRACY IN THE WORKPLACE

228 **with that view:** *Commonwealth v. Hunt,* 45 Mass. 111 (1842).

229 **involve interstate commerce:** *In re Debs,* 158 U.S. 564 (1895). Two years earlier in *Pettibone v. United States,* 148 U.S. 197 (1893), the Court unanimously reversed a federal conviction for conspiracy to obstruct justice in a labor dispute, ruling that federal courts did not have jurisdiction, directly or indirectly, over a state's criminal law process. Since the *Debs* case involved a labor dispute totally within Illinois borders, it should have remained a matter for state courts and beyond the jurisdiction of federal courts.

230 **cite it frequently:** LDB to Edwin Doak Mead, 9 November 1895, Lloyd MSS.

230 **condemned the owners:** See Joseph M. Gowaskie, "John Mitchell and the

Anthracite Coal Strike of 1902: A Century Later," in Robert A. Janosov, ed., *The Great Strike: Perspectives on the 1902 Anthracite Coal Strike* (Easton, Pa., 2002), 123–38.

231 **counsel to the Union:** The story is pieced together from several sources, but primarily from the exchange of letters between Lloyd and LDB, and Darrow and LDB, between 24 November 1902 and 2 February 1903, in Melvin I. Urofsky and David W. Levy, eds., *Letters of Louis D. Brandeis,* 5 vols. (Albany, N.Y., 1971–1978), 1:208–23. See also Clarence S. Darrow, *The Story of My Life* (New York, 1960), 112–17; Janosov, *Great Strike;* Perry K. Blatz, *Democratic Miners: Work and Labor Relations in the Anthracite Coal Industry, 1875–1925* (Albany, N.Y., 1994); and "The Anthracite Coal Strike," www.eHistory.osu.edu.

231 **"any disbursements":** Darrow to LDB, 28 November 1902; LDB to Darrow, 2 December 1902.

232 **might be illegal:** LDB to Darrow, 13 December 1902.

232 **"an industrial possibility":** LDB to Darrow, 12 December 1902.

232 **"attention of the public":** Lloyd to LDB, 26 January 1902; LDB to Lloyd, 2 February 1902.

233 **owners quickly accepted:** *The Anthracite Coal Commission Proceedings* (Washington, D.C., 1903) ran fifty-six volumes and is a treasure trove of information about the coal industry and labor conditions in the mines.

233 **"Unions Be Incorporated":** LDB, "The Incorporation of Trade Unions," 15 *Green Bag* 11–14 (January 1903), reprinted in *Business—a Profession* (Boston, 1914), 82–92. A few weeks later LDB talked again on this subject to the American Social Science Association at the behest of John Graham Brooks. See LDB to Brooks, 8 April 1903.

233 **from growing experience:** In *Business—a Profession,* published in 1914, six of the eighteen articles dealt directly with labor, and labor matters figured in others as well.

235 **to agree with him:** *Boston Post,* 5 December 1902; a description of LDB's demeanor is from the *Boston Herald,* 5 December 1902.

235 **lay with the workers:** LDB to Philip Cabot, 19 September 1904, commenting on a strike at the textile plants in Fall River, Massachusetts.

236 **print shop owners:** The account of the strike can be found in "The Employer and the Trade Unions," a talk LDB gave before the Typothetae on 21 April 1904, and is reprinted in *Business—a Profession,* 13–27; see also LDB to John Tobin, 25 April 1904.

237 **about public affairs:** See LDB to Edward Filene, 25 June 1906. An examination of the Filene experiment is Mary La Dame, *The Filene Store: A Study of Employees' Relation to Management in a Retail Store* (New York, 1930). It is unclear how great a role LDB actually played in creating the association, although there is little doubt that he approved and that, as the Filenes' lawyer, he would have been involved in drafting the necessary legal papers.

239 **society we would have:** LDB, "Hours of Labor," address to New England Civic Federation, 11 January 1906, in *Business—a Profession,* 28–36; see also LDB's concurrence in *Whitney v. California,* 274 U.S. 357 (1927).

239 **to require watching:** *Iron Age,* 30 March 1905.

240 **irregular work meant nothing:** "Lawyer Brandeis Advises Labor Unions," *Boston Post,* 6 February 1905; a fuller version appeared as LDB, "An Eco-

nomic Exhortation to Organized Labor," *Civic Federation Review,* March 1905.

240 **"which cannot do so":** This quotation appeared in a number of places at different times, all with approximately the same wording. See *Philadelphia Tribune,* 13 February 1930.

240 **for less reward:** LDB set out some of his views on scientific management and tried to rebut some of labor's objections in a speech to the Boston Central Labor Union, 2 April 1911, published as "Organized Labor and Efficiency," *Survey,* 22 April 1911, 148–51, and reprinted in *Business—a Profession,* 37–50.

241 **gained popular acceptance:** Oskar Kraines, "Brandeis and Scientific Management," *Publications of the American Jewish Historical Society* 41 (1951), 43. For the origin of the term, see LDB to Horace Bookwalter Drury, 31 January 1914. For railroads, see chap. 12.

241 **science and efficiency:** For this, see the classic work by Samuel Haber, *Efficiency and Uplift: Scientific Management in the Progressive Era, 1890–1920* (Chicago, 1964).

242 **"recognition and reward":** LDB, foreword to *Primer of Scientific Management,* by Frank B. Gilbreth, 2nd ed. (New York, 1914), vii.

242 **unwilling labor force:** Kraines, "Brandeis and Scientific Management," 51.

243 **"leisure comes easy":** LDB to Alfred Brandeis, 14 June 1910.

243 **some of their demands:** Steven J. Diner, *A Very Different Age: Americans of the Progressive Era* (New York, 1998), 64–65; Leon Stein, ed., *Out of the Sweatshop: The Struggle for Industrial Democracy* (New York, 1974), pt. 4.

243 **called for a strike:** Richard A. Greenwald, *The Triangle Fire, the Protocols of Peace, and Industrial Democracy in Progressive Era New York* (Philadelphia, 2005). Some older narratives are still useful, including Alpheus T. Mason, *Brandeis: A Free Man's Life* (New York, 1946), chap. 19; Louis Levine, *The Women's Garment Workers* (New York, 1924); and Julius Henry Cohen, *Law and Order in Industry* (New York, 1916).

244 **gone up in flames:** Leon Stein, *The Triangle Fire* (Philadelphia, 1962).

245 **"unfair to both sides":** *Echo,* 19 March 1913.

245 **"one side gets him":** Lincoln Filene to Edward Filene, 18 and 23 July 1910, Filene MSS.

246 **appealed to the manufacturers:** Greenwald, *Triangle Fire,* 59.

246 **"his 40,000 men":** LDB to Alfred Brandeis, 24 July 1910. The reference is to the nursery rhyme: "The King of France went up the hill / With forty thousand men / The King of France came down the hill / And ne'er went up again."

246 **"at the conference":** LDB to Cohen, 24 July 1910.

247 **reaching an agreement:** *McClure's Magazine,* November 1910, 710–11.

248 **soon be forthcoming:** *New York Times,* 29 July 1910; *New York Globe,* 28 July 1910.

249 **and walked out:** "Minutes of Joint Conference . . . ," 294–98.

249 **for a closed shop:** LDB to Alfred Brandeis, 31 July 1910.

249 **representatives rejected it:** Cohen to LDB, 1 August 1910; LDB to Cohen, 1 August 1910, suggesting some minor modifications in Cohen's draft, which the New York lawyer accepted.

249 **all or nothing:** Stein, *Out of the Sweatshop,* 111–14.

249 **recovered fairly quickly:** LDB to Alfred Brandeis, 21 August 1910, and to Amos Pinchot, 1 September 1910.

250 **the clothing industry:** Judge John W. Goff did, in fact, issue an injunction on 27 August 1910, but it had no effect, as the strike ended only a few days later.

250 **"silence is broken":** Max Meyer to LDB, 3 August 1910; Moskowitz to Bloomfield, n.d. [August 1910].

250 **"achieve the result":** Mason, *Brandeis,* 300, citing a letter from Julius Cohen to Max Meyer, 18 December 1941. Marshall later seemed miffed that LDB had gotten all of the credit for the protocol while his own contributions had been ignored. See Marshall to Gertrude Barnum, 29 November 1912, in Charles Reznikoff, ed., *Louis Marshall: Champion of Liberty,* 2 vols. (Philadelphia, 1957), 2:1127–28, correcting a reporter regarding an article she had written on the protocol.

251 **or Meyer Bloomfield:** Julius Cohen to LDB, 6 October 1911; LDB to Cohen, 7 October 1911; Addams to LDB, 21 November 1910; LDB to Addams, 26 November 1910. During part of the time LDB headed the arbitration panels, he worked with a young economist named Walter Weyl, who would later be a co-founder of the *New Republic* and would, as a result, bring LDB into that particular group of reformers.

251 **"the happy result":** LDB to Meyer, 6 September 1910.

252 **"to take it up":** LDB to Baker, 26 February 1912; LDB, "The Spirit of Get-Together," *American Cloak and Suit Review,* September 1911. See also interviews with LDB in this journal, January and March 1911, reprinted in LDB, *The Curse of Bigness* (New York, 1934), 191, 266. For some of the journalistic response, see Greenwald, *Triangle Fire,* 75ff.

252 **"spirit of get-together":** LDB, "Purpose of the Protocol," from a decision handed down by the Board of Arbitration, 21 January 1915, in Stein, *Out of the Sweatshop,* 121–23; LDB, "Trade Unionism's Next Step," *Boston Common,* 2 March 1912; Henry Moskowitz, "An Army of Striking Cloakmakers: Reminiscences, 1910–1916," *Jewish Frontier,* November 1936, 14–16; *Strauss Magazine Theatre Program,* 31 March 1913.

252 **"advantage and ultimate power":** Melvyn Dubofsky, *When Workers Organize: New York City in the Progressive Era* (Amherst, Mass., 1968), 86.

252 **"as little as possible":** La Dame, *Filene Store,* 217. At the time Filene said he thought the arbitration panel had been used too often for trivial cases.

253 **"face of the poor":** Isaiah 3:14–15; Milton R. Konvitz, "Louis D. Brandeis," in Simon Noveck, ed., *Great Jewish Personalities in Modern Times* (Washington, D.C., 1960), 300.

CHAPTER 11: THE PINCHOT-BALLINGER AFFAIR

254 **carried the day:** Present at the conference were Henry L. Stimson, Gifford and Amos Pinchot, George Wharton Pepper, James R. Garfield, and Norman Hapgood. Norman Hapgood, *The Changing Years* (New York, 1930), 185–86.

255 **First the facts:** The original story of the Pinchot-Ballinger affair, portraying Taft and Ballinger as the villains and Gifford Pinchot as the hero, has been found in the memoirs of progressives like Hapgood, *Changing Years,* and in many popular history textbooks, such as Samuel Eliot Morison and Henry

Steele Commager, *The Growth of the American Republic* (New York, 1930). Then, in 1940, Secretary of the Interior Harold Ickes, who had reviewed some of the department's documents, published "Not Guilty! Richard A. Ballinger," *Saturday Evening Post,* 25 May 1940, and an expanded version, *Not Guilty! An Official Inquiry into the Charges Made by Glavis and Pinchot Against Richard A. Ballinger, Secretary of the Interior, 1909–1911* (Washington, D.C., 1940), which portrayed Ballinger as a victim of baseless accusations. This brought forth a heated rebuttal (very likely at LDB's urging) from Alpheus T. Mason, *Bureaucracy Convicts Itself: The Ballinger-Pinchot Controversy of 1910* (New York, 1941), which is condensed in his *Brandeis: A Free Man's Life* (New York, 1946), chap. 17. When Gifford Pinchot published his autobiography, *Breaking New Ground* (New York, 1947), he of course pictured himself in the most favorable light. Two books that are invaluable in understanding the broader aspects of conservation as well as the managerial philosophies involved are Samuel P. Hays, *Conservation and the Gospel of Efficiency* (Cambridge, Mass., 1959); and James L. Penick Jr., *Progressive Politics and Conservation: The Ballinger-Pinchot Affair* (Chicago, 1968). There is a gold mine of materials in the hearings themselves. U.S. Senate Document 719, *Investigation of the Department of the Interior and of the Bureau of Forestry,* 61st Cong., 3rd sess., 13 vols. (Washington, D.C., 1910) (hereafter cited as *Investigation of Interior and Forestry*).

255 **champion of conservation:** For Pinchot, see his autobiography, *Breaking New Ground,* as well as M. Nelson McGeary, *Gifford Pinchot, Forester-Politician* (Princeton, N.J., 1960), and Char Miller, *Gifford Pinchot and the Making of Modern Environmentalism* (Washington, D.C., 2001). The chapters on conservation in Theodore Roosevelt, *Autobiography* (New York, 1913), appear to have been written by Pinchot and James R. Garfield, Roosevelt's secretary of the interior.

256 **Bering River coalfields:** The filing of these claims by Clarence Cunningham seems to have been done in the most haphazard manner; see Penick, *Progressive Politics and Conservation,* 80–82.

257 **but to dismiss Pinchot:** George E. Mowry, *The Era of Theodore Roosevelt* (New York, 1958), 252–55; Hays, *Conservation and Efficiency,* 165–69; Penick, *Progressive Politics and Conservation,* chap. 5; Paolo E. Coletta, *The Presidency of William Howard Taft* (Lawrence, Kans., 1973), 84ff. Even before Collier hired him, LDB thought Taft had acted badly in firing Pinchot, and "owned to a feeling of disappointment in Taft," whom he had voted for in 1908. Nutter Diaries, 30 December 1908.

257 **take the lead:** Pinchot wound up being frustrated by Pepper's inability to understand that the Forester did not want to be defended, but that he wanted to utilize the hearings to make the case for conservation. Pinchot eventually hired another lawyer to assist Pepper. See *Breaking New Ground,* 470–73.

257 **for the Wilson administration:** See Marc Eric McClure, *Earnest Endeavors: The Life and Public Work of George Rublee* (Westport, Conn., 2003).

258 **"protect the public interest":** George Rublee Memoir, 56–57, OHRO.

258 **conduct of the hearings:** For example, when LDB had to go to Springfield to argue the Illinois ten-hour law, *Ritchie v. Wayman,* he asked for and Nelson granted him a recess in the hearings. LDB to Nelson, 7 February 1910. As he wrote to his brother, "The Ballinger Com'tee treated me better than the

papers reported. They were entirely willing to adjourn to let me go to Illinois." LDB to Alfred Brandeis, 9 February 1910.

258 **"diplomatically friendly":** *Id.*

258 **events and documents:** The issue of Glavis having these documents came up during the hearings, and LDB called William H. Barr, a Seattle lumberman and friend of Glavis's, to testify that Glavis had not been conspiring against his superiors.

259 **"Alaska coal lands":** LDB to Knute Nelson, 27 January 1910, in *Investigation of Interior and Forestry,* 3:328–29.

259 **the secondary material:** The Interior Department, as might be expected, proved slow and very reluctant in producing these materials, and LDB had to repeat his requests to Nelson often, to bring congressional pressure on the department. See, for example, LDB to Nelson, 21 March 1910, in *id.,* 5:2110.

259 **" 'as well as I do' ":** Hapgood, *Changing Years,* 186–87.

259–260 **"Der junge Mensch":** LDB to Alfred Brandeis, 31 January 1910.

260 **"fine & impressive":** *Investigation of Interior and Forestry,* 4:1143ff.; LDB to Alfred Brandeis, 27 February 1910. To Norman Hapgood, he wrote that Pinchot's presentation "made a profound impression and was just what we needed." LDB to Hapgood, 27 February 1910.

260 **on those articles:** See, for example, LDB to Hapgood, 27 February 1910, commenting on an editorial Hapgood wrote, "Veracity, etc.," *Collier's,* 12 March 1910, 7–8, dealing with the conflicting stories of who had lied to the president, and concluding that Ballinger had consistently misled Taft. See also LDB to Henry Watterson, 25 May 1910, and to Mark Sullivan, 2 June 1910.

260 **also changed sides:** Rublee Memoir, 64.

260 **Glavis's testimony:** LDB had little regard for Vertrees as a lawyer, and wrote that "Taft's marvelous capacity for blundering" had led to his choosing Vertrees, when far abler lawyers working for the Interior Department could have defended Ballinger more capably. LDB to AGB, 11 February 1910.

261 **Alaskan land claims:** *Investigation of Interior and Forestry,* 5:2393–410.

261 **"the accumulated merriment":** LDB to Alfred Brandeis, 27 March 1910; LDB to AGB, 27 March 1910.

261 **"can remedy in a year":** LDB to AGB, 25 and 27 March 1910.

261 **"foolish in his actions":** LDB to Alfred Brandeis, 28 February 1910.

262 **how to prove it:** Hapgood, *Changing Years,* 187–89.

262 **"or any other person":** *Investigation of Interior and Forestry,* 5:2110.

263 **the La Follette home:** LDB to AHG, 5 and 13 February 1910.

263 **"making me fearfully social":** LDB to AHG, 5 March 1910.

263 **"is rather far off":** Robert Collier to LDB, 6 April 1910; LDB to Collier, 7 April 1910; AGB to Alfred Brandeis, 11 April 1910.

264 **"the New Haven crowd":** LDB to Alfred Brandeis, 7 April 1910; LDB to AGB, 9 April 1910.

264 **"dead Taft measures":** LDB to AGB, 4 March 1910.

264 **"advantage of the merciful":** LDB to Alfred Brandeis, 1 May 1910.

265 **Interstate Commerce Act:** Mason, *Brandeis,* 261–62.

265 **down to the minute:** Scrapbook 1, "Insurgency: Pinchot-Ballinger," has a day-by-day account of what Taft, Lawler, and other members of the administration did, many with LDB's comments attached.

265 **when that had been:** *Investigation of Interior and Forestry,* 6:3198.

265 **the White House:** LDB to AGB, 23 April 1910.

266 **his allies elsewhere:** LDB to AGB, 26 April 1910. In this same letter he applauded Taft's appointment of Charles Evans Hughes to the Supreme Court. "He is quite conservative," LDB noted, "but well equipped & progressive as compared with most of the mossbacks."

266 **"co-ordinate branch of government":** Wickersham to Richard Wayne Parker (chairman of the House Judiciary Committee), 9 May 1910, in *Investigation of Interior and Forestry,* 7:4139.

266 **"Hold my hand":** Mason interview with Rublee, in *Brandeis,* 266.

266 **"anything further about":** *Investigation of Interior and Forestry,* 7:3787–88.

267 **carefully gone over it:** *Id.,* 7:3865–68.

267 **"of light than heat":** *Id.,* 7:3881.

267 **the secretary responded:** *Id.,* 7:3978.

269 **forgotten in the files:** *Id.,* 7:4364; see also *New York Sun,* 13 May 1910.

269 **general report to him:** *Philadelphia North American,* 15 May 1910.

269 **the president's decision:** For the chronology, see LDB to Henry Watterson, 25 May 1910. LDB told George Nutter that the "Administration people are filled with fear at the situation." Nutter Diaries, 17 May 1910.

270 **"Of gum shoeing":** *Investigation of Interior and Forestry,* 8:4495.

270 **knew how to add:** *Boston Traveler,* 10 June 1910. The story, which reported LDB's interest in the Holmes stories, ran under this headline: "BRANDEIS, SHERLOCK HOLMES' RIVAL: DEDUCTIVE POWERS AMAZE ENEMIES."

270 **"united family again":** LDB to AGB, 22 May 1910.

270 **"efficient public officer":** *Investigation of Interior and Forestry,* 1:90–91.

270 **"aggression of special interests":** *Id.,* 1:94.

270 **syndicate had anticipated:** Rublee Memoir, 65–66.

270 **checkered career:** *Id.,* 66; for Glavis's later career, see James L. Penick Jr., "Louis Russell Glavis: A Postscript to the Ballinger-Pinchot Controversy," *Pacific Northwest Quarterly* 55 (April 1964), 67–75. In the 1930s, Secretary of the Interior Harold Ickes brought Glavis back to the department, but he proved as annoying to his superiors then as he had been earlier.

271 **president accepted it:** Penick, *Progressive Politics and Conservation,* 175–80. Attorney General Wickersham kept his position, albeit with his reputation tarnished. Harvard had planned to bestow an honorary degree on the attorney general in 1910, but the uproar led President Lowell to ask Wickersham to withdraw. He eventually got the honor in 1921. Paul Buck, "An Honor Deferred: The Doctorate of Laws That Waited 11 Years," *Harvard Alumni Bulletin,* 65, 16 March 1963, 468–73.

271 **means of withdrawal:** Altogether Taft withdrew 71.5 million acres of coal land in the continental United States, and another 770,000 in Alaska. He also withdrew 8.5 million acres of waterpower, phosphate, and petroleum lands, an area equal to that of the states of New York, Pennsylvania, and South Carolina. Coletta, *Presidency of Taft,* 98. As a number of historians have pointed out, Roosevelt and Taft did not stand that far apart during their tenures in the White House. The dynamic Teddy seemed more progressive, but in many aspects was as conservative as any of the Old Guard Republicans. The stodgy Taft seemed conservative, and his real accomplishments for reform are often obscured by his political maladroitness.

271 **sustain a veto:** *Id.,* chap. 5.

271 **a friend about him:** Edward S. Martin to Watterson, 9 February 1910, Watterson MSS.

271 **Republican presidential nomination:** In fact, Pinchot had complained to Roosevelt, still in Africa, about Taft and Ballinger at the end of 1909. In March, after TR had arrived in Europe, he asked Pinchot if he could meet him before his return to the United States. Pinchot immediately left for Italy, where on 11 April 1911 he and the former president spent an entire day discussing the Taft administration's policies. The next day TR wrote to Henry Cabot Lodge that Taft had "completely twisted around the policies I advocated." Pinchot, *Breaking New Ground,* 497–504; McGeary, *Pinchot,* 174–78.

272 **"which condemned it":** Mason, *Brandeis,* 276.

272 **lied to the people:** LDB to Alfred Brandeis, 23 May 1910.

272 **obtained this way:** James T. Williams Jr. Memoir, OHRO.

273 **"as guilty as W":** LDB to AGB, 23 April 1910.

273 **become larger crimes:** See "Belligerent Mr. Brandeis," *Harper's Weekly,* 21 May 1910. The editorial noted that LDB had waged an often bitter fight and wondered if it had been necessary. In the end, the piece concluded, it might have been necessary, and if nothing else LDB had ensured a thorough investigation.

273 **loyalty to his cabinet:** See "Mr. Taft's Explanation," *Nation,* 19 May 1910, holding that if Taft had just told the truth in the beginning, a truth he owed to the American people, he could have avoided all this unpleasantness.

273 **Taft insisted otherwise:** LDB to Regina Wehle Goldmark, 2 March 1910.

273 **"lying that did it":** Hapgood, *Changing Years,* 190.

275 **"comes as secondary":** Hays, *Conservation and the Gospel of Efficiency,* 41–42.

275 **political instability:** On this, see especially Robert H. Wiebe, *The Search for Order, 1877–1920* (New York, 1967).

275 **Fisher, resolved it:** For the Controller Bay debate, see Melvin I. Urofsky and David W. Levy, eds., *Letters of Louis D. Brandeis,* 5 vols. (Albany, N.Y., 1971–1978), 2:460–516.

275 **"for the People":** LDB to La Follette, 29 and 31 July 1911. The senator offered the proposal embodying LDB's ideas, calling for extensive government ownership of Alaskan land, but although the entire Senate debated the matter, it eventually was tabled. *Congressional Record,* 62nd Cong., 1st sess. (1911), 5:4197, 4262–305.

CHAPTER 12: RAILROAD INTERLUDES

279 **issue preferred stock:** Richard M. Abrams, "Brandeis and the New Haven–Boston & Maine Merger Battle Revisited," *Business History Review* 36 (1962), 425.

279 **"blush to read it":** Reprinted in the *Manchester Union,* 16 February 1911.

279 **"difference of opinion":** Elizabeth Glendower Evans, "Mr. Justice Brandeis: The People's Tribune," *Survey,* 1 November 1931, 140.

280 **maritime and rail commerce:** Abrams, "Battle Revisited," 426–28.

280 **could not be ignored:** LDB to Hapgood, 25 September 1911.

281 **of the management:** LDB to Frank Basil Tracy, 6 December 1911; *Boston Advertiser,* 7 September 1911.

281 **"KING MORGAN SLIPS INVADERS":** The article is dated 23 November 1912 and was syndicated by the Newspaper Enterprise Association.

281 **congressional investigation:** *Boston Evening Transcript,* 9 December 1912.

281 **New Haven's wicked ways:** LDB to Alfred Brandeis, 8 December 1912; LDB to Treadwell Cleveland Jr., 29 November 1912; and to Gilson Gardner and Walter Hines Page, 2 December 1912.

281 **justified such a course:** LDB to Clapp, 26 November 1912; LDB to La Follette, 3 December 1912. The Supreme Court ruling is *United States v. Union Pacific Railroad Company,* 226 U.S. 61 (1912).

281 **"unregulated monopoly":** LDB, "The New Haven—an Unregulated Monopoly," *Boston Journal,* 13 December 1912, reprinted in *Business—a Profession* (Boston, 1914), 279–305.

282 **dozens of deaths:** See, for example, *Boston Evening Transcript,* 29 August 1911, reporting on an accident near Middletown, Connecticut. New Haven officials claimed that the mishap had been caused by vandals tampering with switches, but the local police chief said that the rails, which had not been well maintained, had buckled in the August heat under the weight of the locomotive.

282 **more respectful hearing:** LDB's law partner George R. Nutter may have been privately sympathetic to the philosophy behind the merger, but he now wrote in his diary, "I believe in common with many others that we are being slowly tied up in this monopoly." Nutter Diaries, 2 December 1912.

283 **irresponsible campaign:** Ron Chernow, *The House of Morgan: An American Banking Dynasty and the Rise of Modern Finance* (New York, 1990), 176–77; *Boston Record,* 20 December 1912.

283 **"some rods in pickle":** LDB to Alfred Brandeis, 20 December 1912.

283 **"heart out of another":** Chernow, *House of Morgan,* 176.

283 **civil and criminal investigations:** LDB to Charles A. Lutz, 23 January 1913; LDB to Franklin K. Lane, 1 February 1913; LDB to McReynolds, 5 March 1913.

284 **"over false accounting":** LDB to Alfred Brandeis, 10 March and 9 April 1913.

284 **investigate the New Haven:** LDB to James L. Richards, 20 March 1913.

284 **"a matter of arithmetic":** *Boston Evening Transcript,* 14 March 1913.

284 **"Sub rosa investigations":** Alpheus T. Mason, *Brandeis: A Free Man's Life,* 205–8.

284 **"seeks to villify":** *Boston Journal,* 25 April 1913.

285 **sacrificial offering:** Chernow, *House of Morgan,* 177.

285 **require the full attention:** LDB to Alfred Brandeis, 9 July 1913, and to Norman Hapgood, 9 July 1913; *Boston Herald,* 9 July 1913.

285 **Howard Elliott, would:** LDB to Alfred Brandeis, 19 and 28 July 1913; LDB to Livy S. Richard, 28 July 1913.

286 **attacks on banker management:** Chernow, *House of Morgan,* 178.

286 **"stretching it into five":** *Business America,* August 1913.

287 **"for the truth":** LDB to Joel Goldthwait, 18 July 1913.

287 **shippers as clients:** LDB to Alfred Brandeis, 21 August 1910.

287 **higher freight rates:** Mason, *Brandeis,* 316; *New York Evening Post,* 8 September 1910.

288 **continue in business:** *Evidence Taken by the Interstate Commerce Commission in the Matter of Proposed Advances in Freight Rates by Carriers, 1910–1911,* 61st Cong., 3rd sess., Senate Document 725 (1911), 4:2328.

289 **"or my clients":** *Id.,* 4:2033–34.

289 "of an overestimate": *Id.,* 4:2620.

290 more scientifically: *Id.,* 4:2822, 2846–47.

290 new science of management: *Id.,* 4:3723–24.

290 "awkward silence": *New York Evening Post,* 26 November 1910.

291 efficient and effective manner: LDB to Rudolph Gaar Leeds, 9 November 1910, Pinchot MSS.

291 officials never responded: LDB to O. L. Dickinson (president of the Chicago, Burlington & Quincy Railroad), telegram, 29 November 1910, *New York Times,* 30 November 1910.

292 "practical and efficient": "An Attorney for the People," *Outlook,* 24 December 1910, 919–20.

292 "a man of power": Ray Stannard Baker, "Short Article on Brandeis," prepared sometime in 1916, possibly at the time of the confirmation hearings, but not marked as published. Baker MSS.

293 "the weekly magazines": Samuel Haber, *Efficiency and Uplift: Scientific Management in the Progressive Era, 1890–1920* (Chicago, 1964), 53. After LDB's testimony, Ray Stannard Baker arranged for Taylor's *Principles of Scientific Management* to be serialized in the *American Magazine.*

293 "would be recognized": LDB to Frankfurter, 27 February 1911, FF-LC. Commissioner James S. Harlan later said that although LDB's arguments about scientific management played a role in the ICC's decision, they had not and could not have been the sole factor. U.S. Senate, *Hearings Before the Subcommittee of the Committee on the Judiciary . . . on the Nomination of Louis D. Brandeis to Be an Associate Justice of the Supreme Court of the United States,* 64th Cong., 1st sess., 2 vols. in 1 (Washington, D.C., 1916), 2:160 (hereafter cited as *Hearings on Nomination*).

293 $1 million a day: *New York Times,* 24 February 1911; LDB to Norman Hapgood, 17 November 1916; Oscar Kraines, "Brandeis and Scientific Management," *Publications of the American Jewish Historical Society* 41 (1951), 50.

294 "his 'boys' to see me": LDB to AGB, 3 July 1911.

294 anti-majoritarian rule: See, for example, Nancy Cohen, *The Rise of American Liberalism, 1865–1914* (Chapel Hill, N.C., 2002), 233–35; and especially Haber, *Efficiency and Uplift.*

294 did not understand it: Philippa Strum, *Louis D. Brandeis: Justice for the People* (Cambridge, Mass., 1984), 165–70.

294 arsenals and navy yards: Steven J. Diner, *A Very Different Age: Americans of the Progressive Era* (New York, 1998), 36–37.

295 more moral society: Haber, *Efficiency and Uplift,* 59.

295 "abolishing interlocking directorates": LDB to Alfred Brandeis, 12 May 1913.

295 "the day on Zionism": LDB to Alfred Brandeis, 8 June 1913.

295 "middle of September": Harlan to LDB, 15 August 1913; LDB to Harlan, 21 August 1913.

296 "anti-railroad litigation": *Washington Post,* 11 October 1913.

296 "justice to all concerned": *New York Times,* 27 November 1913; Freund to LDB, 27 October 1913.

297 headline grabbers: For details of the hearings, see U.S. Senate Document 466, *Five Per Cent Case (1913–1914),* 63rd Cong., 2nd sess. (1914); and Mason, *Brandeis,* chap. 21.

297 **"efficient refreshment"**: Alfred Zimmern, *The Greek Commonwealth: Politics and Economics in Fifth-Century Athens* (Oxford, 1911); LDB to Zimmern, 21 July 1917, Zimmern MSS.

297 **opposed the rate increase**: LDB to B. W. Porter, 17 October 1913.

297 **confirmation hearings**: For Thorne's testimony, see *Hearings on Nomination,* 1:5–62, and for other witnesses on the same issue, *id.,* 62–103.

298 **increase they needed**: *New York Evening Post,* 10 September 1914.

298 **"public ownership"**: LDB to Alfred Brandeis, 24 October 1914.

298 **"hasten government ownership"**: LDB to Alfred Brandeis, 23 December 1914.

CHAPTER 13: THE CURSE OF BIGNESS

300 **upon the individual**: Learned Hand Memoir, 122, OHRO.

301 **automatically be restored**: For a survey of classical economic thought, see Samuel Hollander, *Classical Economics* (Oxford, 1987).

302 **John D. Rockefeller**: For statistics on consolidation, see Naomi R. Lamoreaux, *The Great Merger Movement in American Business, 1895–1904* (New York, 1985); House of Representatives, Committee on the Judiciary, *Hearings . . . on Study of Monopoly Power,* 81st Cong., 1st sess. (1949), 103; Abraham Berglund, *The United States Steel Corporation* (New York, 1907), 78; Henry Demarest Lloyd, *Wealth Against Commonwealth* (New York, 1894). See also Ron Chernow, *Titan: The Life of John D. Rockefeller, Sr.* (New York, 1998).

302 **beneficial but inevitable**: John Moody, *The Truth About the Trusts* (New York, 1904).

302 **"educated and cultivated"**: Sidney Fine, *Laissez-Faire and the General Welfare State* (Ann Arbor, Mich., 1956), 111.

302 **to emulate them**: Not all of these men had risen from rags to riches, but a sufficient number had. Andrew Carnegie constituted the greatest success story, an immigrant bobbin boy who single-handedly created the American steel industry. See Irvin G. Wyllie, *The Self-Made Man in America* (New Brunswick, N.J., 1954).

302 **"laissez-faire economics"**: John A. Garraty, *The New Commonwealth, 1877–1890* (New York, 1968), 31.

303 **"New Competition"**: Arthur Jerome Eddy, *The New Competition* (New York, 1912); see also Charles R. Van Hise, *Concentration and Control* (New York, 1912); and Herbert Croly, *The Promise of American Life* (New York, 1909).

303 **nearly all of it**: Quoted in Robert Wiebe, *The Search for Order, 1877–1920* (New York, 1967), 218.

303 **George Perkins**: See, for example, "Business—a Profession," in LDB, *Business—a Profession* (Boston, 1914), 1–12; "Cutthroat Prices: The Competition That Kills," *Harper's Weekly,* 15 November 1913, 10–12, reprinted in *id.,* 236–54; "On Maintaining Makers' Prices," *Harper's Weekly,* 14 June 1913, 6, reprinted in *The Curse of Bigness* (New York, 1934), 125–28; and "Co-operation vs. Cut-Throat Competition," *Harper's Weekly,* 12 June 1915, 573–74, reprinted in *id.,* 195–201.

304 **costs, sales, and stock**: *American Column and Lumber Co. v. United States,* 257 U.S. 377, 413 (1921) (LDB dissenting).

304 **obvious disadvantages**: For the diversity of thought about bigness as it

appeared in popular magazines, see Maxwell H. Bloomfield, *Alarms and Diversions: The American Mind Through American Magazines, 1900–1914* (The Hague, 1967), chap. 1.

304 **"State Socialism":** LDB to Bruère, 25 February 1922; years earlier LDB had been intrigued by the utopian views of Henry George. LDB to Adolph Brandeis, 21 November 1889.

304 **economically ignorant:** Albro Martin, who blames much of the decline of the American railroad system on LDB, has a different view. He sees "a certain intellectual coarseness in Brandeis' grasp of the workings of the capitalistic economy" and charges that LDB was devoted "to a set of economic and social doctrines which were at best rather old fashioned, and at worst distinctly inimical to the interests of the very people whom he claimed to represent." *Enterprise Denied: Origins of the Decline of American Railroads, 1897–1917* (New York, 1971), 217.

304 **evils of monopoly:** Notes for lecture of 11 November 1893, Swope MSS.

305 **"all be much simpler":** Alpheus T. Mason, *Brandeis: A Free Man's Life* (New York, 1946), 642.

305 **"thinking about it":** Conversation with Alfred Lief, 15 April 1934, in Alfred Lief, ed., *The Brandeis Guide to the Modern World* (Boston, 1941), 116. LDB did, of course, pay attention to his investments, but he did not have to worry about fluctuations in the prices of stocks.

305 **"mere speculation":** LDB to Alfred Brandeis, 28 July 1904; LDB to Elizabeth Brandeis Raushenbush, 20 November 1933, EBR.

305 **market success:** Lecture notes, Swope MSS.

306 **did not fully share:** LDB to Alfred Brandeis, 22 February 1906, EBR.

306 **foes of bigness:** To get some idea of LDB's activities in this area, see "Testimony in Hearings, Arguments, and Briefs," and "Articles, Addresses, Interviews and Letters," in Roy M. Mersky, *Louis Dembitz Brandeis, 1856–1941: A Bibliography* (New Haven, Conn., 1958), 14–18, 19–28.

306 **believe in the inevitability:** See David W. Levy, *Herbert Croly of the "New Republic": The Life and Thought of an American Progressive* (Princeton, N.J., 1985), esp. chaps. 4–6.

306 **"competition involves waste":** LDB, "Shall We Abandon the Policy of Competition?" *Case and Comment* 18 (1912), 494, reprinted in *Curse of Bigness,* 105.

306 **"NEVER GROW LARGER":** Henry Bruère Memoir, OHRO.

306 **"scrape the skies":** LDB, "Trusts, Efficiency, and the New Party," *Collier's Weekly,* 14 September 1912, 14; LDB to Harold Laski, 21 September 1921, Laski MSS. The Goethe quotation is cited in Paul Freund, "Mr. Justice Brandeis," in Allison Dunham and Philip B. Kurland, eds., *Mr. Justice* (Chicago, 1956), 178.

307 **"we cannot control":** LDB, "Shall We Abandon Competition?" 494.

307 **the community suffered:** LDB intimated that even if the company did not use its power, the threat by itself would restrict competition. Cf. Justice Harold Hitz Burton: "The material consideration in determining whether a monopoly exists is not that prices are raised and that competition actually is excluded but that power exists to raise prices or to exclude competition when it is desired to do so." *American Tobacco Co. v. United States,* 328 U.S. 781, 811 (1946).

307 **"outweigh the advantages":** LDB, "The New England Transportation

Monopoly," in *Business—a Profession,* 275–76. The sentiment is expressed elsewhere as well; see interview in *Boston Journal,* 13 December 1912, and *Collier's Weekly,* 14 September 1912, 14.

307 **point of maximum size:** LDB to Harold Laski, 21 September 1921, Laski MSS.

307 **the least efficient:** Stephen A. Weiner, "Comment: Mr. Justice Brandeis, Competition, and Smallness: A Dilemma Re-examined," 66 *Yale Law Journal* 69, 71 (1956).

308 **"his diagnosis and his prescription":** Thomas K. McCraw, "Rethinking the Trust Question," in McCraw, ed., *Regulation in Perspective: Historical Essays* (Cambridge, Mass., 1981), 36–46, 54. See also McCraw, "Louis D. Brandeis Reappraised," *American Scholar* 54 (1985), 525–36; and his Pulitzer Prize–winning *Prophets of Regulation: Charles Francis Adams, Louis D. Brandeis, James M. Landis, Alfred E. Kahn* (Cambridge, Mass., 1984).

308 **"I am talking about":** *Hastings* (Neb.) *Daily Republican,* 3 February 1912.

308 **a free society:** LDB is not the only person to have seen morality at the center of capitalism. See George Gilder, *Wealth and Poverty* (New York, 1980); and Nelson Dawson's explication of the two men's views, "Louis D. Brandeis, George Gilder, and the Nature of Capitalism," *Historian* 47 (November 1984), 72–85. See also Benjamin M. Friedman, *The Moral Consequences of Economic Growth* (New York, 2005), in which the author believes that economic growth in a fair market is essential to social progress.

308 **"There are no good trusts":** *Hastings* (Neb.) *Daily Republican,* 3 February 1912; 1893 lecture notes, Swope MSS.

308 **"occupy like positions":** Testimony before Stanley Committee in January 1912, revised as "Our New Peonage: Discretionary Pension," *Independent,* 25 July 1912, 187, reprinted in *Business—a Profession,* 65–81.

309 **"a class of employees":** Lief, *Brandeis Guide,* 124.

309 **higher standard of living:** Richard P. Adelstein, " 'Islands of Conscious Power': Louis D. Brandeis and the Modern Corporation," *Business History Review* 63 (1989), 614–56, accepts LDB's basic arguments and suggests there is good economic theory to support them.

309 **"a nation of slaves":** Testimony before U.S. Commission on Industrial Relations, in LDB, *Curse of Bigness,* 81.

310 **"the corporations involved":** La Follette to LDB, 17 February 1911.

310 **Brandeis at his best:** LDB to La Follette, 24 February 1911.

310 **nomination hearings:** The story is pieced together primarily from the charges made in the hearings, and LDB's answers to them in the form of letters to Edward F. McClennen.

310 **company decided to join:** LDB did not in the 1890s oppose trusts per se, and in his lectures on business law portrayed the trust device as a useful tool, although noting that its chief purpose was to limit competition. Notes for 7 and 21 October 1893, Swope MSS.

310 **five shares of common stock:** LDB to Edward McClennen, 16 February 1916.

311 **"not of the public":** U.S. Senate, *Hearings Before the Subcommittee of the Committee on the Judiciary . . . on the Nomination of Louis D. Brandeis to Be an Associate Justice of the Supreme Court of the United States,* 64th Cong., 1st sess., 2 vols. in 1 (Washington, D.C., 1916), 221 (hereafter cited as *Hearings on Nomination*).

311 **"already large business":** LDB, memo on House Bill 472, 28 March 1906, in *id.*, 257.

311 **into their grievances:** McElwain to LDB, 21 May 1906, enclosed in LDB to Moses Clapp, 24 February 1912, Woolley MSS.

312 **enforced the patent:** *Indiana Manufacturing Co. v. J. I. Case Threshing Machine Co.*, 148 F. 21 (E.D. Wis. 1906).

312 **"I act as counsel":** LDB to Sidney Winslow, 6 December 1906, U.S. Senate, Committee on Interstate Commerce, *Hearings on Control of Corporations, Persons, and Firms Engaged in Interstate Commerce*, 62nd Cong., 2nd sess., 3 vols. (Washington, D.C., 1912), 3:2653.

312 **"incidental methods employed":** LDB to Needham, 18 March 1908.

312 **"the company's actions":** LDB to Clapp, 24 February 1912, Woolley MSS.

313 **then walked away:** *Hearings on Nomination*, 222.

314 **similar leases invalid:** *Continental Wall Paper Co. v. Louis Voight and Sons Co.*, 212 U.S. 227 (1909).

314 **end of September:** *Boston Herald*, 28 September 1910.

314 **"conditions in the industry":** LDB to Clapp, 24 February 1912, Woolley MSS.

314 **the story that Brandeis told:** LDB detailed the financial means by which United had forced Plant out of business in a letter to La Follette, 5 May 1911.

314 **out of his own pocket:** *Hearings on Nomination*, 737.

315 **confirmation hearings:** *Id.*, 221–24.

315 **"which is groundless":** LDB to Alfred Brandeis, 18 July 1911.

315 **"denounced publicly as unconstitutional":** Winslow to Clapp, 19 January 1912, *Hearings on Nomination*, 957–58.

315 ***"Briefs and Correspondence":*** The pamphlet is printed in its entirety in *id.*, 936ff.

317 **the antitrust laws:** *United Shoe Machinery Corporation v. United States*, 258 U.S. 451 (1922).

317 **Rockefeller's Standard Oil:** *Standard Oil Company v. United States*, 221 U.S. 1 (1911).

317 **La Follette–Stanley Antitrust bill:** La Follette to LDB, 17 May 1911; LDB to La Follette, 23 and 26 May, 13 June 1911. Augustus O. Stanley, a congressman from and future governor of Kentucky, sponsored the measure in the House.

318 **"changes will be made":** LDB to AGB, 14 November 1911.

319 **"fall to the ground":** *New York Times*, 14 December 1911; *Philadelphia North American*, 15 December 1911; U.S. Senate Committee on Interstate Commerce, *Hearings on Control of Corporations, Persons, and Firms Engaged in Interstate Commerce*, 1171. LDB's testimony runs from 1146 to 1291.

319 **"a great speech":** LDB to AGB, 14 December 1911.

319 **"vested wrongs":** LDB to AGB, 15 November 1911.

319 **Committee on Patents:** House Committee on the Judiciary, *Hearings on Trust Legislation*, 62nd Cong., 2nd sess. (1912), 13–54 (26–27 January 1912); Special House Committee on Investigation of the United States Steel Corporation, *Hearings*, 62nd Cong., 2nd sess. (1912), 2835–72 (29–30 January 1912); House Committee on Patents, *Hearings . . .*, 62nd Cong., 2nd sess. (1912), 1–25 (15 May 1912).

319 **Commissioner of Corporations:** Smith to LDB, 8 December 1911; see also

Felix Frankfurter to LDB, 21 November 1911, reporting on conversation with Herbert Stimson on antitrust.

320 **"insure the square deal"**: LDB to Norman Hapgood, 27 February 1911.

320 **"our quick capital"**: *Boston American,* 14 December 1911.

320 **"people's own gold"**: LDB, *Other People's Money, and How the Bankers Use It* (New York, 1914), 19.

320 **best of the old**: See Louis Hartz, *The Liberal Tradition in America* (New York, 1955); John Morton Blum, *The Republican Roosevelt* (Cambridge, Mass., 1954), 121–22; and Melvin I. Urofsky, "The Conservatism of Mr. Justice Brandeis," *Modern Age* 23 (1979), 39–48.

320 **"as honest men"**: LDB to AGB, 2 February 1891, quoted in Richard M. Abrams, introduction to *Other People's Money,* by LDB (New York, 1967), xxi.

321 **"Brandeis as counsel"**: *Chicago Journal,* 4 January 1913.

321 **Untermyer's advice**: LDB to Untermyer, 18 March 1913. The committee report is U.S. House of Representatives, *Report of Committee Appointed Pursuant to H.R. 429 and 594 . . . ,* 62nd Cong., 3rd sess. (1913). Despite his interest in this area, LDB did not testify before the committee, probably because of his involvement with the Wilson campaign. (See chap. 14.)

321 **"It is convicted"**: Woodrow Wilson, "Speech to Commercial Club of Chicago, 11 January 1913," in Arthur S. Link et al., eds., *The Papers of Woodrow Wilson,* 69 vols. (Princeton, N.J., 1966–1984), 27:33.

322 **"the principal rationale"**: Abrams, introduction, xxxi.

322 **its weaknesses**: See, for example, Lawrence Chamberlain, representing the Investment Bankers Association of America, "A Reply to Mr. Brandeis," *Harper's Weekly,* 4 April 1914, 22. For a modern critique, see Richard A. Posner, "Brandeis and Holmes, Business and Economics, Then and Now," *Review of Law and Economics* (2005), www.bepress.com/rle/vol1/iss1/art1/.

323 **"faith in smallness"**: Arthur M. Schlesinger Jr., *The Politics of Upheaval* (Boston, 1960), 387; see also Max Lerner, "Brandeis and the Curse of Bigness" (1935), in *Ideas Are Weapons: The History and Uses of Ideas* (New York, 1939), 105–8.

323 **Morgan & Company**: See Thomas W. Lamont, *Across World Frontiers* (New York, 1951).

324 **spoke for three hours**: This account is based on a memorandum, probably by Lamont, and from its fairly precise nature no doubt written shortly after the meeting. The memorandum has been transcribed by Paul P. Abrahams, "Brandeis and Lamont on Finance Capitalism," *Business History Review* 47 (Spring 1973), 72–94. Abrahams suggests that one reason for the meeting is that the house of Morgan wanted to get a sense of what the Wilson administration planned for antitrust legislation. Lamont, however, who had a wide-ranging curiosity, may simply have wanted to understand how and why he and his colleagues had been painted as such monsters.

326 **centers of economic power**: L. S. Zacharias, "Repaving the Brandeis Way: The Decline of Developmental Property," 82 *Northwestern University Law Review* 596, 597 (1988).

326 **spirit of the laws**: See the 5 June 2005 issue of the *New York Times Magazine,* with articles like Joseph Nocera, "The Quantitative Data-Based, Risk-Massaging Road to Riches," and Gretchen Morgenson, "What Are Mergers Good For?"

326 **a result of arrogance:** For just one example, see the *Washington Post,* 30 April 2003, reporting that ten Wall Street firms had paid fines totaling $1.4 billion, and had agreed to change their practices of giving biased stock ratings to lure investment banking business. Among the firms were Citigroup, Merrill Lynch, and J. P. Morgan.

326 **"new content to old ideals":** Alexander M. Bickel, "Passion and Patience: Centennial-Year Thoughts on 'the Brandeis Way,' " *New Republic,* 12 November 1956, 16.

CHAPTER 14: NATIONAL POLITICS

328 **the Republican insurgents:** See Robert M. La Follette, *La Follette's Autobiography* (Madison, Wis., 1913); Belle Case La Follette and Fola La Follette, *Robert M. La Follette,* 2 vols. (New York, 1953); David P. Thelen, *Robert M. La Follette and the Insurgent Spirit* (Boston, 1976); and Bernard A. Weisberger, *The La Follettes of Wisconsin* (Madison, Wis., 1994).

328 **"an old friend":** LDB to AGB, 5 February 1910; see also chap. 26 of La Follette and La Follette, *La Follette,* titled "Brandeis Becomes Our Friend."

328 **"fascinating companion":** Lucy Freeman, Sherry La Follette, and George A. Zabriskie, *Belle: The Biography of Belle Case La Follette* (New York, 1986), 100.

328 **"the Roman Senators":** La Follette and La Follette, *La Follette,* 1:295. Bob junior would be reelected to the Senate three times in his own right, until defeated by Joseph McCarthy in 1946.

329 **"almost any one else":** Alpheus T. Mason, *Brandeis: A Free Man's Life* (New York, 1946), 368.

329 **"a privileged few":** Freeman et al., *Belle,* 100.

330 **Various theories:** See, among others, Samuel P. Hays, *The Response to Industrialism, 1885–1914* (Chicago, 1957); Robert Wiebe, *The Search for Order, 1877–1920* (New York, 1967); Richard Hofstadter, *The Age of Reform: From Bryan to F.D.R.* (New York, 1955); Irwin Yellowitz, *Labor and the Progressive Movement in New York State, 1897–1916* (Ithaca, N.Y., 1965); Russel B. Nye, *Midwestern Progressive Politics: A Historical Study of Its Origins and Development, 1870–1958* (East Lansing, Mich., 1959); and Gabriel Kolko, *The Triumph of American Conservatism: A Reinterpretation of American History, 1900–1916* (New York, 1963). Newer works that also differ on what progressivism meant and where its motive forces originated include Steven J. Diner, *A Very Different Age: Americans of the Progressive Era* (New York, 1998); Robert Sherman La Forte, *Leaders of Reform: Progressive Republicans in Kansas, 1900–1916* (Lawrence, Kans., 1974); Michael McGerr, *A Fierce Discontent: The Rise and Fall of the Progressive Movement in America, 1870–1920* (New York, 2003); David Sarasohn, *The Party of Reform: Democrats in the Progressive Era* (Jackson, Miss., 1989); Bob Pepperman Taylor, *Citizenship and Democratic Doubt: The Legacy of Progressive Thought* (Lawrence, Kans., 2004); and Shelton Stromquist, *Reinventing "The People": The Progressive Movement, the Class Problem, and the Origins of Modern Liberalism* (Urbana, Ill., 2005).

330 **completely missing:** Peter G. Filene, "An Obituary for 'The Progressive Movement,' " *American Quarterly* 22 (Spring 1970), 20–34.

330 **oppressed members:** Benjamin Parke De Witt, *The Progressive Movement: A Non-partisan Comprehensive Discussion of Current Tendencies in American Politics* (New York, 1915), 4–5.

330 **allow simple ordering:** Lawrence A. Cremin, *The Transformation of the School* (New York, 1961), pt. 1.

331 **list is overwhelming:** See letters from LDB to these and to many other reformers in Melvin I. Urofsky and David W. Levy, eds., *Letters of Louis D. Brandeis,* 5 vols. (Albany, N.Y., 1971–1978), vols. 2 and 3.

332 **in the upper chamber:** See LDB to La Follette, 9 November 1910, La Follette MSS, congratulating him on the election results. Among other things that Taft had done to upset the reformers had been his blatant use of patronage to try to punish the insurgent Republicans. See *St. Louis Post-Dispatch,* 16 September 1910.

333 **corrupt practices act:** "Declaration of Principles," enclosed in La Follette to LDB, 30 December 1910.

333 **"ideals of American democracy":** LDB to AGB, 5 January 1911; LDB to Charles R. Crane, telegram, 21 January 1911. Crane had been elected as treasurer of the league.

333 **the radical populism:** David Sarasohn, however, makes the argument that although Bryan nominally headed the party between 1896 and 1912, in fact control had been taken not by the populists but by mainstream reformers akin to the insurgents in the Republican ranks. See *Party of Reform.*

333 **big banks, and corporations:** In the summer of 1910, LDB ran into his former brother-in-law Charles Nagel, Taft's secretary of commerce and labor, and reported, "Charlie N's growing disgust of the Republican Party is interesting." LDB to Alfred Brandeis, 26 July 1910, EBR.

333 **seemed most comfortable:** LDB had taken part in an attempt to plan a national progressive meeting that failed because of the inability to coordinate dozens of schedules; in goals and membership, however, it anticipated La Follette's league by more than a year. See LDB to Lincoln Steffens, 9 November and 8 December 1909, to Frederic C. Howe, 7 February 1911, and to Gifford Pinchot, 27 February 1911.

333 **"culmination of the progressive movement":** Benjamin Parke De Witt, quoted in Paolo E. Coletta, *The Presidency of William Howard Taft* (Lawrence, Kans., 1973), 220.

333 **began a whirlwind tour:** LDB had gone to Washington to, among other things, discuss pending antitrust legislation, and wrote to Alice that he had spent the evening at the La Follettes' with Gifford Pinchot and Francis Heney, but instead of discussing antitrust had wound up talking about La Follette's candidacy. LDB to AGB, 19 May 1911.

333 **before returning home:** LDB to La Follette, 23 and 26 May, 13 June, 29 and 31 July 1911.

334 **privately he doubted:** LDB to AGB, 3, 4, and 7 February 1912.

334 **among regular Republicans:** Coletta, *Presidency of Taft,* 220–22. Archie Butt, Taft's friend and confidant, noted that Taft was "really out after La Follette. He hated the Wisconsin man with a consuming hatred." Archie Butt to Clara Butt, 20 July 1911, in Archibald W. Butt, *Taft and Roosevelt: The Intimate Letters of Archie Butt,* 2 vols. (Garden City, N.Y., 1930), 2:700–701.

334 **full and sincere denial:** LDB to AGB, 25 November 1911.

335 **prayed that Roosevelt would run:** George Rublee Memoir, 79–80, OHRO.

335 **went into seclusion:** La Follette and La Follette, *La Follette,* 1:399–409.

335 **much less winning:** Alfred Brandeis to LDB, n.d. [early 1912].

335 "some moral support": LDB to AGB, 3 February 1912.

335 "no political obligations": LDB to Alfred Brandeis, 7 February 1912.

336 "let her hammer Belle": LDB to Belle La Follette, 7 February 1912, La Follette MSS; LDB to AGB, 9 February 1912.

336 "without having a client": For Frankfurter's early life and career, see Michael E. Parrish, *Felix Frankfurter and His Times: The Reform Years* (New York, 1982), chaps. 1–3; Liva Baker, *Felix Frankfurter* (New York, 1969), 1–141; and the interesting although not always reliable Felix Frankfurter with Harlan B. Phillips, *Felix Frankfurter Reminisces* (New York, 1960), a distillation of Frankfurter's oral history memoir at Columbia University.

336 "youngsters at the Harvard Club": LDB to AGB, 13 September 1910.

337 defending Louis Glavis: Parrish, *Frankfurter*, 52.

337 next three decades: See Melvin I. Urofsky and David W. Levy, eds., *"Half Brother, Half Son": The Letters of Louis D. Brandeis to Felix Frankfurter* (Norman, Okla., 1991). This section relies on the introduction to that volume.

337 "deep into my heart": For the relationship between the two men, see Robert H. Mennel and Christine L. Compston, eds., *Holmes and Frankfurter: Their Correspondence, 1912–1934* (Hanover, N.H., 1996).

337 "his magnanimity": Diary entry for 20 October 1911, in Joseph P. Lash, ed., *From the Diaries of Felix Frankfurter* (New York, 1975), 104.

337 encouraged him to remain: Frankfurter to Emory Buckner, 4 March 1912, cited in Martin Mayer, *Emory Buckner: A Biography* (New York, 1968), 67.

337 appointment to the Supreme Court: LDB to Roscoe Pound, 12 July 1913, Pound MSS.

338 drawn to older mentors: For this trait, see the discussion in H. N. Hirsch, *The Enigma of Felix Frankfurter* (New York, 1981), 27–32.

339 as he called Taft: See, for example, LDB to AGB, 4 February 1912.

339 to protect the people: For Croly's thought, and his influence on Roosevelt, see David W. Levy, *Herbert Croly of the "New Republic": The Life and Thought of an American Progressive* (Princeton, N.J., 1985), chaps. 4 and 5.

340 governor of New Jersey: See Arthur S. Link, *Wilson: The Road to the White House* (Princeton, N.J., 1947), chap. 13.

340 "lead to the other": Wilson to Ellen Axson, 30 October 1883, in Arthur S. Link et al., eds., *The Papers of Woodrow Wilson*, 69 vols. (Princeton, N.J., 1966–1984), 2:500.

340 strict control of railroads: See Henry W. Bragdon, *Woodrow Wilson: The Academic Years* (Cambridge, Mass., 1967); John W. Mulder, *Woodrow Wilson: The Years of Preparation* (Princeton, N.J., 1978); and David W. Hirst, *Woodrow Wilson, Reform Governor: A Documentary Narrative* (Princeton, N.J., 1965).

340 "purify the Democratic party": LDB to Charles F. Amidon, 3 July 1912.

340 bound by party affiliation: LDB to Norman Hapgood and LDB to Robert M. La Follette, both 3 July 1912.

341 "ended that agony": LDB to Alfred Brandeis, 10 July 1912.

341 "their full support": *Boston American*, 10 July 1912.

341 "it needs you more": Rublee to LDB, 18 July 1912.

341 over to the colonel: In June, LDB paid a visit to the La Follettes and reported that the senator had been in "rollicking humor," even joking about his defeats. But he "is as bitter as ever, and more so about T.R. It is difficult to see how that breach can heal." LDB to AGB, 8 June 1912.

341 **"pretty nigh irresistible"**: *Boston Evening Transcript,* 1 September 1912; LDB to Alfred Brandeis, 28 July 1912.

342 **transactions were legitimate**: Woodrow Wilson, *A History of the American People,* 5 vols. (New York, 1902), 5:167; William Diamond, *The Economic Thought of Woodrow Wilson* (Baltimore, 1943), 21–22.

342 **no room to rise**: Hofstadter, *Age of Reform,* 22–23; see also his essay on Wilson in *The American Political Tradition* (New York, 1958 ed.). A similar sentiment is in Thomas W. Gregory to Josephus Daniels, 19 February 1924, Gregory MSS.

342 **"mother of trusts"**: Sarasohn, *Party of Reform,* 144.

342 **"architect of the New Freedom"**: Link, *Wilson: Road to White House,* 489; Arthur S. Link, *Wilson: The New Freedom* (Princeton, N.J., 1956), 95. Most commentators then and later believe LDB to have been a potent influence on Wilson's thinking; only John Milton Cooper Jr. disagrees. See *The Warrior and the Priest* (Cambridge, Mass., 1983), 194.

343 **reduce tariffs gradually**: Four years earlier LDB had told his brother, "I am dead against any tariff revision except a horizontal scaling down in annual instalments, and maximum and minimum tariffs." LDB to Alfred Brandeis, 20 June 1908.

343 **"give me the benefit"**: LDB to Wilson, 1 August 1912; Wilson to LDB, 7 August 1912, Wilson MSS.

343 **a mutual friend**: Charles McCarthy to Wilson, 15 July 1912, McCarthy MSS, reporting on Crane's very favorable views of LDB.

343 **"that cannot be done"**: *New York Times,* 29 August 1912; *Boston Evening Transcript,* 1 September 1912.

343 **in current dollars**: LDB to Alfred Brandeis, 29 August 1912; certificate receipt for donation of $500 to Democratic National Committee, 31 August 1912. LDB made similar comments about Wilson to Josephus Daniels, 4 September 1912.

344 **"everybody works but Father"**: LDB to Alfred Brandeis, 14 July 1912.

344 **"to regulate competition"**: John Wells Davidson, *A Crossroads of Freedom: The 1912 Campaign Speeches of Woodrow Wilson* (New Haven, Conn., 1956), 79, 113, 171.

344 **"Americans hated monopoly"**: LDB to Baker, 5 July 1931, and notes of interview with Justice Brandeis, 23 March 1929, Baker MSS.

345 **"guns be spiked"**: Wilson to LDB, 28 September 1912, Wilson MSS.

346 **"overweening commercial power"**: LDB to Wilson, 30 September 1912, along with memorandum, "Suggestions for Letter of Governor Wilson on Trusts," Wilson MSS.

346 **others manifested themselves**: LDB to Ray Stannard Baker, 27 September 1926, Baker MSS; "Memorandum of Conversations," 2–3 October 1912; Hapgood to LDB, 12 September 1912; LDB, "Trusts, Efficiency, and the New Party," *Collier's Weekly,* 14 September 1912, 14–15, and "Trusts, the Export Trade, and the New Party," *Collier's Weekly,* 21 September 1912, 10–11, both reprinted in *Business—a Profession* (Boston, 1914).

347 **"determines the political policy"**: Davidson, *Crossroads of Freedom,* 393.

347 **controlling the market**: For a good statement of Roosevelt's philosophy, see his article "The Trusts, the People, and the Square Deal," *Outlook,* 18 November 1911, 649.

347 **"men who are already made":** Woodrow Wilson, "The Old Order Changeth," the first part of Wilson, *The New Freedom,* edited by William E. Leuchtenburg (Englewood Cliffs, N.J., 1961), 25.

347 **"Tweedledum and Tweedledee":** William Allen White, *Woodrow Wilson* (Boston, 1924), 264.

347 **Eugene V. Debs:** There are many studies of the 1912 campaign. See, for example, James Chace, *1912: Wilson, Roosevelt, Taft & Debs—the Election That Changed the Country* (New York, 2004); and Lewis L. Gould, *Four Hats in the Ring: The 1912 Election and the Birth of Modern American Politics* (Lawrence, Kans., 2008).

348 **a great gulf existed:** Cooper, *The Warrior and the Priest,* 217–18.

348 **resonated strongly among voters:** Years later, the Supreme Court justice Robert H. Jackson recalled the 1912 election, when he had been a young man, and said, "I was a believer in the Wilsonian philosophy of maintaining competition and in the Louis Brandeis philosophy of the curse of bigness. I didn't like business getting too darn big." Robert Jackson Memoir, 99, OHRO.

349 **"a very unfair slant":** Levy, *Croly,* 155–56. Hand's devotion to TR led him to accept the Progressive Party nomination for the New York Court of Appeals, which earned LDB's condemnation. Hand wrote to Croly, "I was a little surprised to learn that Brandeis had told both George [Rublee] and Norman [Hapgood] that he thought I ought not to have done it. His theory was that a judge ought never to run for any elective office." Hand did not long hold this criticism against LDB, and supported him during the confirmation fight in 1916. Taft, however, never forgave Hand, and during the 1920s blocked his appointment to the Supreme Court. Gerald Gunther, *Learned Hand: The Man and the Judge* (New York, 1994), 238–39.

349 **"government staffed by experts":** Levy, *Croly,* 157–58; see also Taylor, *Citizenship and Democratic Doubt.*

349 **handed down from on high:** Parrish, *Frankfurter,* 56.

349 **the ultimate decision:** LDB to Frankfurter, 28 January 1913, FF-LC.

350 **backing Roosevelt:** "Mr. Brandeis on Trusts" and "The Outlook on Mr. Brandeis," *Outlook,* 28 September 1912, 146–47; "Mr. Brandeis on Labor and the Trusts," *Outlook,* 2 November 1912 469–70.

350 **an economic creation:** Louis Hartz, *The Liberal Tradition in America* (New York, 1955), 232.

350 **the giant corporations:** Link et al., *Papers of Wilson,* 2:410–11, 347.

351 **the Ohio valley:** LDB to Homer Cummings, 14 September 1912.

351 **"such seed so sown":** LDB to AGB, 17 and 18 October 1912.

351 **"the redoubtable Colonel":** LDB to AGB, 4 November 1912; LDB to Alfred Brandeis, 2 November 1912.

352 **the best showing:** In 1856 the Republicans appeared for the first time on the ballot, but they in essence replaced the Whigs, who had disappeared from the scene.

352 **he might have won:** Taft in 1908 had received more votes than he and Roosevelt combined in 1912, while Wilson received fewer votes than William Jennings Bryan had in 1908.

352 **"All true Progressives":** LDB to Wilson and to La Follette, 6 November 1912. Although LDB had urged La Follette to support Wilson, the Wisconsin senator was still nominally a Republican. He would not support either Taft or Roosevelt, and sent word to Wilson that although he could not sup-

port the Democrat outright, he hoped that Wilson would not say or do anything to force La Follette to oppose him. As the campaign progressed, La Follette's support, although still nonpublic, increased, and Wilson praised La Follette in his speeches.

352 **"left without support"**: LDB to Alfred Brandeis, 7 November 1912. In fact, California and South Dakota eventually wound up in the Roosevelt column.

352 **"people of the United States"**: "Speech to Southern Society of New York, 17 December 1912," in Link et al., *Papers of Wilson*, 25:593–603; LDB to Alfred Brandeis, 18 December 1912; see also LDB to AGB, 18 December 1912.

CHAPTER 15: A SNAPSHOT OF MR. BRANDEIS

353 **"This interrupts considerably"**: LDB to AGB, 2 June 1905; LDB to Alfred Brandeis, 20 September 1908. Although the savings bank insurance bill had been enacted, LDB continued to campaign for individual banks to join the new system.

354 **"grubbing up the case"**: LDB to AGB, 2 and 4 June 1911.

354 **from his absence**: See LDB to E. Louise Malloch, 4 November 1907.

354 **on the Court in 1916**: See Account Books, LDB-BU. LDB invested primarily in bonds, but he also bought and sold properties, on which he would often take back a mortgage.

355 **"hand of a musician"**: See pictures of LDB at this time, and some shots of him when younger, in Ernest Poole, "Brandeis," *American Magazine,* February 1911, 481–93; *Louisville Herald,* 8 February 1910; *Literary Digest,* 1 July 1916.

356 **ostentation in any form**: Philippa Strum, *Louis D. Brandeis: Justice for the People* (Cambridge, Mass., 1984), 47–48.

356 **"on my return"**: LDB to Susan Brandeis, 24 March 1910; LDB to AGB, 18 November 1911.

356 **no sense of humor**: Nutter Diaries, 12 November 1911.

356 **in his lifetime**: Alpheus T. Mason, *Brandeis: A Free Man's Life* (New York, 1946), 692.

356 **"extraordinary appropriation"**: LDB to Alfred Brandeis, 27 May 1906. Aunt Minna was Wilhelmina Dembitz, the widow of LDB's beloved uncle Lewis, and Emily was their daughter.

357 **"the place you want"**: LDB to Alfred Brandeis, 21 March 1906.

357 **"law or insurance"**: LDB to Alfred Brandeis, 29 May 1906.

358 **good Kentucky bourbon**: LDB to Alfred Brandeis, 4 December 1909. "It is a great comfort to know that so good a supply is near."

358 **"than these horses"**: LDB to Elizabeth Brandeis, 11 August 1906, and to AGB, 13 August 1906.

358 **"catch a murderer"**: Strum, *Brandeis,* 51.

359 **"Go forth, my son"**: Warren to LDB, 13 September 1907.

359 **"middle of the road"**: LDB to AGB, 15 November 1911.

359 **history of Rome**: Guglielmo Ferrero, *The Greatness and Decline of Rome,* 5 vols., translated by Alfred Zimmern and H. J. Chaytor (New York, 1907–1909). "In the Roman survey . . . Ferrero [Zimmern's translation] was my entrée." LDB to Felix Frankfurter, 1 September 1925, FF-LC.

359 **"the *Greek Commonwealth*"**: LDB to AGB, 11 July 1914. Zimmern (1879–1957), an English Jew born to German immigrants, had excelled as a

student and by twenty-five had become a fellow and tutor at New College, Oxford. Unlike his friend Gilbert Murray, Zimmern had a peripatetic academic as well as political career, teaching at Oxford, the London School of Economics, the University College of Wales, Trinity College in Connecticut, and Cornell. He worked with British intelligence during World War I on plans for the League of Nations, received a knighthood in 1936, and then worked with the Foreign Office again during World War II. For information on Zimmern, see Jeanne Morefield, *Covenants Without Swords: Idealist Liberalism and the Spirit of Empire* (Princeton, N.J., 2005).

360 **the Hellenistic spirit:** Alfred Zimmern, *The Greek Commonwealth: Politics and Economics in Fifth-Century Athens,* 7th ed. (Oxford, 1961), 70, 72, 482. Neither Zimmern nor Murray paid any attention to the centrality of the slave economy in Athens.

360 **"the Greeks alone":** Alfred Zimmern, "Political Thought," in R. W. Livingston, ed., *The Legacy of Greece* (Oxford, 1921), and lecture, "The Greeks and Their Civilization" (20 June 1905), both cited in Morefield, *Covenants Without Swords,* 72, 75.

360 **Pericles' *Funeral Oration: Whitney v. California,* 274 U.S. 357 (1927); see below, pp. 643–47. For a fuller analysis of LDB's identification with ancient Greek ideals and Zimmern's writing, see Strum, *Brandeis,* 237–42.

360 **might be too late:** Learned Hand, "Mr. Justice Brandeis," 317 U.S. xii (1942), part of the memorial for LDB that Hand delivered before the U.S. Supreme Court.

361 **when he was home:** LDB to AGB, 15 January and 11 March 1910, 26 December 1913.

361 **"unknown number of dollars":** LDB to Hapgood, 29 March 1911; LDB to AGB, 8 July 1914.

361 **"we don't act soon":** LDB to AGB, 7 September 1909.

361 **"suggestions with a smile":** LDB to AGB, 26 June 1909.

362 **"resources and knowledge":** LDB to AGB, 5 August 1899.

362 **"the more inexcusable":** LDB to AGB, 21 and 22 October 1909.

363 **"our Eastern fringe":** LDB to AGB, 23, n.d. [probably 24], and 27 October 1909.

363 **"your American horizon":** LDB to Alfred Brandeis, 5 November 1909.

363 **summer of 1920:** See below, pp. 543ff.

363 **their courting days:** LDB to AGB, 7 July 1905.

363 **"to leave her alone":** LDB to Alfred Brandeis, 17 July 1908. The girls were then teenagers, but apparently a Miss Parker who had served as a governess had left the Brandeis employ.

364 **"undue rivalry":** LDB to AGB, 25 March 1911.

364 **front of Parliament:** John P. Whitman, "Mrs. Brandeis Talks on Suffrage," *Boston American,* 2 February 1913.

365 **"women in politics":** *Boston Herald,* 14 June 1911. See also his recollection of experiences with women workers in Alfred Lief, *Brandeis: The Personal History of an American Ideal* (New York, 1936), 256.

365 **contempt for the "fat man":** See letters from LDB to AGB in Melvin I. Urofsky and David W. Levy, eds., *The Family Letters of Louis D. Brandeis* (Norman, Okla., 2002), 12 January 1910 et seq.

366 **"capable of the process":** LDB to AGB, 12 January 1910.

367 **Conservative, or Reform:** The classic work on this subject remains John

Higham, *Strangers in the Land: Patterns of American Nativism, 1860–1925* (New Brunswick, N.J., 1955).

367 **any personal experience:** Strum, *Brandeis,* 229.

368 **walked in the meadows:** LDB to Elizabeth Brandeis, 29 December 1900, 19 August 1905, and 11 August 1906.

368 **"public service is great":** AGB to Belle Case La Follette, 30 January 1913, La Follette MSS.

369 **examinations had gone well:** LDB to Susan Brandeis, 2 June 1911, and to AGB, 4 June 1911.

369 **"full of courage":** Alice and Elizabeth accompanied Susan to school; LDB to Susan Brandeis, 3 October 1911, and to AGB, 17 October 1911.

369 **"possible to create":** LDB to AGB, 26 October 1911.

369 **"high-minded and noble":** LDB to Susan Brandeis, 24 April 1913.

370 **"account last summer":** *Id.* and 26 February 1914.

370 **not yet arrived:** LDB to AGB, 6 March and 19 May 1914.

370 **"after graduation":** LDB to AGB, 20 July 1914; LDB to Susan Brandeis, 23 March 1915.

370 **did not know when:** LDB to Susan Brandeis, 24 February 1915, and to AGB, 19 July 1915.

371 **"a little later":** LDB to AGB, 2 January 1916.

CHAPTER 16: THE NEW FREEDOM

372 **"the underdog, etc.":** Higginson to Wilson, 11 October 1912, in Arthur S. Link et al., eds., *The Papers of Woodrow Wilson,* 69 vols. (Princeton, N.J., 1966–1984), 25:414–15. Wilson ignored the letter, directing his press secretary to send a routine acknowledgment of its receipt. Joseph Tumulty to Higginson, 16 October 1912, in *id.,* 423.

372 **for public office:** Lowell to Wilson, 9 November 1912, Wilson to Lowell, 12 November 1912, in *id.,* 535, 541.

373 **"in such a place":** House Diary, *id.,* 550.

373 **"good fellow & influential":** LDB to AGB, 21 November 1912.

373 **"his advanced views":** House to Wilson, 22 November 1912, in Link et al., *Papers of Wilson,* 25:558.

373 **attorney general position:** House Diary, 18 December 1912, in *id.,* 610.

373 **involving legal authority:** William Jennings Bryan to Wilson, 25 December 1912, in *id.,* 622. See, for example, an unsolicited letter from James M. Head (a former mayor of Nashville and a classmate of LDB's at the Harvard Law School) to Wilson, 22 January 1913, in *id.,* 27:67–68. House Diary, 17 and 24 January 1913, in *id.,* 62, 71.

373 **for any of them:** Hapgood to Ray Stannard Baker, 23 July 1928, Baker MSS.

374 **Republicans, and independents:** Crane to Wilson, 10 February 1913, in Link et al., *Papers of Wilson,* 27:107–8.

374 **"all elements of the progressive movement":** Arthur S. Link, *Wilson: The New Freedom* (Princeton, N.J., 1956), 11n.36.

374 **before Wilson's inauguration:** House Diary, 13 and 14 February 1913, Link et al., *Papers of Wilson,* 27:110, 112.

374 **the business community:** William Gibbs McAdoo, *Crowded Years: The Reminiscences of William G. McAdoo* (Boston, 1931), 182–83.

375 "showed the white feather": *Boston American,* 7 March 1913; LDB to AGB, 9 March 1913; Belle Case La Follette and Fola La Follette, *Robert M. La Follette,* 2 vols. (New York, 1953), 2:463; Hapgood to LDB, 4 March 1913.

375 "its essence political": Allon Gal, *Brandeis of Boston* (Cambridge, Mass., 1980), 195; Godfrey Hodgson, *Woodrow Wilson's Right Hand: The Life of Colonel Edward M. House* (New Haven, Conn., 2006), 73.

375 the same for him: Lawrence H. Fuchs, *The Political Behavior of American Jews* (Glencoe, Ill., 1956), 60. In the Wilson Papers there is a list of Jewish appointments, marked "Jews File."

375 "something in reserve": House to Wilson, 22 November 1912, in Link et al., *Papers of Wilson,* 25:558.

376 "will not succeed": Schiff to Max Mitchell, 17 February 1913, cited in Yonathan Shapiro, *Leadership of the American Zionist Organization, 1897–1930* (Urbana, Ill., 1971), 64; Crane to Wilson, 10 February 1913, in Link et al., *Papers of Wilson,* 27:108. Crane, who had extensive business interests in Russia, may well have been thinking of the success of Schiff and the American Jewish Committee in having the Russo-American Trade Treaty nullified during the Taft administration in protest against Russian pograms.

376 after the announcement: Gal, *Brandeis of Boston,* 189–90.

376 strong Jewish connections: For the committee, see Naomi W. Cohen, *Not Free to Desist: The American Jewish Committee, 1906–1966* (Philadelphia, 1972).

376 "from the Cabinet": William A. Tucker to House, 4 March 1913, cited in Link, *Wilson: The New Freedom,* 15.

376 "to be absent": LDB to AGB, 9 and 10 January 1913, LDB to Maurice Leon, 28 February 1913.

376 "believe all he hears": LDB to Harry Bullock, 25 February 1913.

377 "for the simple life": LDB to Alfred Brandeis, 2 March 1913; LDB to AGB, 9 March 1913.

377 the decision process: Link, *Wilson: The New Freedom,* 11–15.

377 by remaining independent: Wilson to LDB, 24 April 1913, LDB to Wilson, 19 May 1913, in Link et al., *Papers of Wilson,* 27:353, 456.

378 not rehire Hapgood: Collier to LDB, 28 October 1912; LDB to Collier, 31 October and 3 November 1912.

378 consider the incident: Hapgood to LDB, 18, 30, and 31 October 1912; LDB to Collier, 7 November 1912; LDB to Hapgood, 14 November 1912.

378 monthly into a weekly: LDB to Thomas D. Jones, 27 February 1913. The McClure organization, however, took over the management of subscriptions as well as the financial operations for *Harper's.*

378 other southern states: LDB to Alfred Brandeis, 3 and 11 January 1914.

378 as a book: LDB to Hapgood, 15 July 1913, LDB to E. F. Chase, 6 July 1914.

379 "I shall feel well content": LDB to Smith, 2 February 1914. Unfortunately, the magazine became a victim of the economic difficulties caused by the war, and in May 1916 merged with the *Independent.* Hapgood then worked as a freelance journalist.

379 "Me for the simple life": LDB to AGB, 8, 9, and 10 March 1913. See also LDB to Alfred Brandeis, 10 March 1913.

379 **sending them hacks:** LDB to Norman Hapgood, 12 March 1913; LDB to AGB, 7 June 1914.

380 **information when requested:** See, for example, J. Butler Studley to LDB, 11 August 1913; LDB to McReynolds, 28 March and 13 September 1913; LDB to McAdoo, 14 April and 12 May 1913, McAdoo MSS; Thomas W. Gregory to LDB, 23 December 1913; LDB to Charles McCarthy, 19 October 1914; and LDB to Louis F. Post, 9 June 1915.

380 **David Ives appointed:** LDB to Senator Henry F. Hollis, 20 October 1913, and to J. Russel Marble, 17 November 1913.

380 **on the Court:** Wilson to George W. Anderson, August [1917 or 1918]. "I shall seek Justice Brandeis's opinion [regarding an appointment to the ICC] just as soon as he gets here."

380 **a few of those letters:** I am indebted to David Levy for these choices; see his "Brandeis, the Reformer," 45 *Brandeis Law Journal* 711, 729–30 (2007).

380 **"thoroughly with me":** LDB had long believed that some cutthroat competition could be eliminated if manufacturers were allowed to set the retail prices for their products, and enforce this price against dealers who would sell at a discount.

381 **"and man is absent":** LDB to AGB, 9 December 1913.

381 **leadership since Lincoln:** Link, *Wilson: The New Freedom,* chap. 6.

381 **"It is convicted":** "Speech to Commercial Club of Chicago, 11 January 1913," in Link et al., *Papers of Wilson,* 27:33.

382 **in private hands:** Link, *Wilson: The New Freedom,* 203–4.

382 **his followers to do so:** William J. Bryan and Mary B. Bryan, *The Memoirs of William Jennings Bryan* (Philadelphia, 1925), 370; Joseph P. Tumulty, *Woodrow Wilson as I Know Him* (Garden City, N.Y., 1921), 205.

382 **point of obsession:** Alfred Lief, ed., *The Brandeis Guide to the Modern World* (Boston, 1941), 205.

383 **those of reform:** LDB to Wilson, 14 June 1913.

383 **hold of Wall Street:** In less than three months 7,571 banks joined the system; only 18 national banks remained aloof.

383 **Charles A. Lindbergh:** La Follette and La Follette, *La Follette,* 2:486–87; "Legalizing the 'Money Power,' " *La Follette's Weekly,* 27 December 1913, 1.

384 **antitrust legislation:** LDB to Samuel Untermyer, 2 October 1913.

384 **affect industry and commerce:** David Houston, *Eight Years with Wilson's Cabinet,* 2 vols. (Garden City, N.Y., 1926), 1:85–86; House Diary, 16 January 1914; J. J. Wilbur to Frank Trumbull, 16 December 1913, Vanderlip MSS.

385 **anticompetitive practices:** LDB had suggested such a commission in "The Solution of the Trust Problem," *Harper's Weekly,* 8 November 1913, 18–19.

385 **any business but transportation:** See LDB, "The Endless Chain" (pt. 3 of "Breaking the Money Trust"), *Harper's Weekly,* 6 December 1913, 13–17, and "Serve One Master Only" (pt. 4 of "Breaking the Money Trust"), *Harper's Weekly,* 13 December 1913, 10–12.

385 **"The fearless course":** LDB to Franklin K. Lane, 12 December 1913, McReynolds MSS.

385 **"can rest satisfied with":** Ray Stannard Baker, *Woodrow Wilson: Life and Letters,* 8 vols. (Garden City, N.Y., 1927–1939), 4:365–66.

386 **"is not reasonable":** House Committee on the Judiciary, *Hearings on Trust Legislation,* 62nd Cong., 2nd sess. (Washington, D.C., 1912), 22; Senate Com-

mittee on Interstate Commerce, *Hearings . . . on Control of Corporations,* 62nd Cong., 2nd sess. (Washington, D.C., 1911), 4:1291; Statement before Joint Committee of Massachusetts Legislature on Liquor Law, 27 February 1891.

386 **violation of competitive rules:** LDB to Wilson, 30 September 1912; LDB had most recently expressed these views in "Solution of the Trust Problem," 8–19.

386 **"assume control of business":** Link et al., *Papers of Wilson,* 29:153–58.

387 **"my first interview":** LDB to AGB, 21 January 1914, EBR; LDB to Alfred Brandeis, 23 January 1914.

387 **over railroad securities:** Link, *Wilson: The New Freedom,* 426.

387 **to go to the theater:** LDB to AGB, 14 January, 5 February, and 28 March 1914.

387 **"trust & kindred legislation":** LDB to AGB, 21 January 1914, EBR; Untermyer to House, 25 January 1913; House to Wilson, 27 January 1914, Wilson MSS; Adamson to LDB, 29 January 1914; *Hearings . . . on Trust Legislation,* 63rd Cong., 2nd sess. (Washington, D.C., 1914), serial 7, pt. 22; LDB to Alfred Brandeis, 22 February 1914.

388 **third-party redress, and the like:** Franklin Lane also urged McReynolds to get in touch with LDB, and forwarded him LDB's earlier letter with suggestions. Lane to McReynolds, 30 January 1914, McReynolds MSS; LDB to McReynolds, 22 February 1914. The letter runs twelve typeset pages in Melvin I. Urofsky and David W. Levy, eds., *Letters of Louis D. Brandeis,* 5 vols. (Albany, N.Y., 1971–1978), 2:246–58, when it breaks off suddenly, and it is impossible to know how much more might have been in it.

388 **"had I been there":** John McNab, a U.S. attorney, had charged McReynolds with dragging his feet in the Diggs-Caminetti sex case because of connections the men's families had in the Democratic Party. *New York Times,* 22 June 1913; LDB to AGB, 24 June 1913. See also David J. Langum, *Crossing over the Line: Legislating Morality and the Mann Act* (Chicago, 1994), chap. 5.

388 **credit to his intelligence:** LDB to AGB, 1 March and 23 May 1914.

388 **provide the language:** George Rublee to LDB, 13 March 1914.

389 **by American ingenuity:** LDB, memorandum on La Follette bill, 8 November 1911; George Rublee, "The Original Plan and Early History of the Federal Trade Commission," *Proceedings of the Academy of Political Science* 11 (January 1926), 115.

389 **as an unofficial aide:** For Rublee's life, see Marc Eric McClure, *Earnest Endeavors: The Life and Public Work of George Rublee* (Westport, Conn., 2003).

390 **by looking at facts:** The following section draws on Thomas K. McCraw, *Prophets of Regulation: Charles Francis Adams, Louis D. Brandeis, James M. Landis, Alfred E. Kahn* (Cambridge, Mass., 1984), chap. 3.

390 **"unreasonably" restrained trade:** *Standard Oil Co. v. United States,* 221 U.S. 1 (1911); and *United States v. American Tobacco Co.,* 221 U.S. 106 (1911).

390 **reasonable and unreasonable behavior:** LDB to Robert La Follette, 13 June 1911, to Moses Clapp, 22 June 1911, and to Edward Atkins Grozier, 19 September 1911.

391 **new regulatory commission:** McCraw, *Prophets of Regulation,* 116.

391 **illumination of business practices:** LDB to Lane, 12 December 1913, McReynolds MSS.

392 **played by a stand-in:** McCraw, *Prophets of Regulation,* 122.

392 **"he has one of the best"**: Hapgood to Wilson, 21 April 1914, in Link et al., *Papers of Wilson,* 29:481–82.

394 **"most remarkable interview"**: George Rublee Memoir, 102–14, OHRO.

394 **some very bad legislation**: LDB to AGB, 10 June 1914.

394 **into the House draft**: LDB to Ray Stannard Baker, 5 July 1931, Baker MSS. On 24 July 1914, LDB wrote to Alice that the Clayton bill was "in very bad shape."

395 **issue advisory opinions**: Heinrich Kronstein and Joachim Volhard, "Brandeis Before the FTC in 1915: Should Advisory Opinions Be Given?" 24 *Federal Bar Journal* 609 (1964). McCraw, *Prophets of Regulation,* 131–32, says that LDB opposed advance advice, but this is certainly not the case. LDB's testimony before the FTC, dated 30 April 1915, and quoted at length in the Kronstein and Volhard article, clearly demonstrates his support for advisory opinions.

395 **available to business**: For a more extended analysis, see Gerald Berk, *Louis D. Brandeis and the Making of Regulated Competition, 1900–1932* (New York, 2009), pt. I.

396 **"monopolize that trade"**: House Committee on Patents, *Oldfield Revision and Codification of the Patent Statutes,* 62nd Cong., 2nd sess. (Washington, D.C., 1912), 4. See also LDB, "On Maintaining Makers' Prices," *Harper's Weekly,* 14 June 1913, 6, reprinted in *The Curse of Bigness* (New York, 1934), 125–28; and LDB, "Cutthroat Prices: The Competition That Kills," *Harper's Weekly,* 15 November 1913, 10–12, reprinted in *Business—a Profession* (Boston, 1914), 243–61.

396 **should be outlawed**: House Committee on Interstate and Foreign Commerce, *Hearings on Regulation of Prices,* 64th Cong., 1st sess. (Washington, D.C., 1915), 49–54.

397 **a bedrock principle**: McCraw, *Prophets of Regulation,* 105–8; LDB to George Soule, 22 April 1923.

397 **around the antitrust laws**: George Rublee, while working on the bill at LDB's behest, did not share LDB's passion for it and put his energies into other parts of the antitrust program. Rublee Memoir, 144–45.

397 **sounded vaguely Brandeisian**: *Dr. Miles Medical Company v. John D. Parks & Sons Company,* 220 U.S. 373 (1911), overturned in *Leegin Creative Leather Products, Inc. v. PSKS, Inc.,* 127 S.Ct. 2705 (2007).

397 **"and I went mad"**: *Emporia Gazette,* 25 May 1916, cited in David Sarasohn, *The Party of Reform: Democrats in the Progressive Era* (Jackson, Miss., 1989), 198.

397 **from the beginning**: LDB to AGB, 6 March 1914 and 8 December 1913. AGB also thought poorly of Wilson's Mexican strategy. See AGB to Elizabeth Evans, 21 July 1914, Evans MSS.

398 **"a stupid administration"**: Ray Stannard Baker, memo of interview with LDB, 23 March 1929, Baker MSS.

398 **"opposition as cantankerous"**: LDB to AGB, 24 and 27 July 1914.

398 **"highest personal esteem"**: Wilson to Admissions Committee, Cosmos Club, 1 February 1915, in Link et al., *Papers of Wilson,* 32:167. LDB had occasionally stayed at the Cosmos while in Washington, probably because of reciprocity for his membership in the Harvard Club in New York. In 1914, William Hitz, a Washington lawyer and later a federal judge, nominated

him for membership, and apparently some of the more conservative members had held up action. "Because of the injustice done Mr. Brandeis by these covert attacks to which he cannot reply," Hitz hoped that Wilson, as a member of the club, would write a word to the Admissions Committee. Wilson did so promptly, and LDB was immediately admitted to membership.

398 **"when rich men":** Baker, memo of interview with LDB, 23 March 1929, Baker MSS.

CHAPTER 17: MEN! MONEY! DISCIPLINE!

399 **Jewish homeland in Palestine:** Jacob de Haas, *Louis D. Brandeis: A Biographical Sketch* (New York, 1929), 51–52. According to Alpheus T. Mason, *Brandeis: A Free Man's Life* (New York, 1946), 443, LDB in 1940 recalled this meeting as having taken place in August 1912, and indeed there is a letter from LDB to Alfred, 14 August 1912, about de Haas's coming out to South Yarmouth. The evidence, however, suggests 1910 as the proper date, because by August 1912 LDB had already expressed support for Zionism and had joined the movement.

399 **powerful political presence:** This story is told in detail in Melvin I. Urofsky, *American Zionism from Herzl to the Holocaust* (Garden City, N.Y., 1975), chap. 4.

401 **greater ethical standards:** LDB, "What Loyalty Demands," ms. 28 November 1905.

401 **"idealism & reverence":** LDB to Adolph Brandeis, 29 November 1905, EBR.

402 **"betterment of the world":** LDB to Richards, 2 February 1911, Richards MSS.

402 **knowing little or nothing:** There is a story that at the Hotel Fusta in Milwaukee in 1897, LDB, reading a newspaper story about the Zionist Congress, supposedly said to AGB, "Now there is something to which I could give myself." Mason, *Brandeis,* 442, citing a memorandum from Stephen Wise to Julian Mack, 29 November 1937. Although I have heard this story several times, it strikes me as apocryphal, nor does Mason appear to believe it.

403 **of three million:** *Maccabean,* July 1914, 17–38.

403 **"headway in Judaism":** LDB to Alfred Brandeis, 25 October 1912.

403 **New York garment strike:** Bernard G. Richards Memoir, 37–38, OHRO.

403 **joined the FAZ:** *Boston Jewish Advocate,* 7 March 1913. This is disputed, for reasons that are not clear, by Sarah Schmidt, *Horace M. Kallen: Prophet of American Zionism* (Brooklyn, 1995), 55. Since LDB knew de Haas, it is unlikely that the *Advocate* would have published that story unless it were true. A shekel was one of the coins of ancient Judaea.

404 **toll of the poor:** *Boston Journal,* 31 March 1913; *Boston Jewish Advocate,* 4 April 1913. The headline in the 7 March 1913 issue of the *Jewish Advocate* read, "FIRST OCCASION THAT HE [LDB] WILL APPEAR ON ZIONIST PLATFORM."

404 **Brandeis ever attended:** Sokolow to LDB, 15 September 1913; Louis Lipsky to LDB, 26 October 1913. LDB had in fact been elected by the FAZ as a delegate to the Congress but declined.

404 **Agriculture publication:** LDB to Alfred Brandeis, 7 January 1912; Aaron

Aaronsohn, *Agricultural and Botanical Explorations in Palestine,* U.S. Department of Agriculture Bulletin 180 (Washington, D.C., 1910).

405 **invited him to dinner:** See LDB's speech to the Chelsea, Massachusetts, Young Men's Hebrew Association, 18 May 1913, in Solomon Goldman, ed., *Brandeis on Zionism* (New York, 1942), 39–42; LDB to Aaronsohn, 21 April 1913, Aaronsohn MSS.

405 **at the Hotel Marseilles:** Shmaryahu Levin and Louis Lipsky to LDB, telegram, 20 August 1914.

405 **fortunes of American Zionism:** Urofsky, *American Zionism,* 118–21.

406 **to his confirmation:** Yonathan Shapiro, "American Jews in Politics: The Case of Louis D. Brandeis," *American Jewish Historical Quarterly* 55 (December 1965), 199–211, expanded in Shapiro, *Leadership of the American Zionist Organization, 1897–1930* (Urbana, Ill., 1971). Shapiro displayed the then almost universal Israeli scholarly antagonism to American Zionism. For a more extensive critique of Shapiro's book, see the essay review by Stuart M. Geller, "Why Did Louis D. Brandeis Choose Zionism?" *American Jewish Historical Quarterly* 62 (January 1973), 383–400.

406 **practically no role:** As for the donation of money to Jewish causes, Shapiro cited a letter from LDB to Alfred in which he wrote, "I have so much more [money] to donate to Boston Y.M.H.A. and Zionism," but he took the quotation out of context. Louis and Alfred had been making donations for a number of years to the Louisville YMHA, and then something happened that led the two men not to renew that subscription. The full quotation is "Guess we may as well omit the gift to the Louisville Y.M.H.A. I shall have so much more [that is, what had gone to Louisville] to donate to Boston Y.M.H.A. and Zionism." LDB to Alfred Brandeis, 12 May 1913.

407 **"Brandeis had come home":** Ben Halpern, "Brandeis' Way to Zionism," *Midstream* 17 (October 1971), 5, 13, and *A Clash of Heroes: Brandeis, Weizmann, and American Zionism* (New York, 1987), 94.

407 **Jeffersonian paradise:** Allon Gal, *Brandeis of Boston* (Cambridge, Mass., 1980). In an earlier article Gal extends some of Halpern's views on LDB, redefining his experiences to make them more amenable to the idealism and high morality he found in Zionism. In 1915, LDB declared that "in the Jewish colonies of Palestine there are no Jewish criminals; because everyone old and young alike, is led to feel the glory of his people and his obligations to carry forward its ideals." Quoted in Mark A. Raider, *The Emergence of American Zionism* (New York, 1998), 79.

407 **"a non-observant Jew":** "We did not observe any Jewish holidays such as Yom Kippur or Chanuka. We did have a Christmas tree, but it had no religious connotations." Elizabeth Brandeis Raushenbush to Lewis Paper, 7 June 1980, Paper MSS.

407 **"nor was it Christian":** *American Hebrew,* 2 December 1910.

408 **those of the prophets:** Simon Noveck, *Great Jewish Personalities in Modern Times* (Washington, D.C., 1960), 312–13.

408 **shaped his leadership:** See, for example, LDB, "The Rebirth of the Jewish Nation," *Boston American,* 4 October 1914, a speech LDB gave in Symphony Hall, Boston, a few days earlier.

409 **the Haifa Technion:** Instruction had always been in German, for the institute had been founded by Germans and supported by German and German-

American Jews. By 1914, however, Zionist settlers were insisting that instruction be given in Hebrew, which would be the language of the new Jewish homeland. Schiff, who opposed Zionism, withdrew his support. See Schiff to Stephen Wise, 27 January, 18 and 25 June 1914, Schiff MSS.

409 **aborting the project:** LDB to Wise, 3 June 1914, and memorandum of announcement, 10 June 1914, Wise MSS.

409 **commitment to the cause:** Many years ago I was fortunate enough to interview a number of people, such as Emanuel Neuman, Bernard G. Richards, and Israel Goldstein, who had worked with LDB, and all of them commented that even if they at times disagreed with his policies, they never doubted his intense commitment to the Zionist movement. See also Halpern, "Brandeis' Way to Zionism," 3.

410 **"American ideal of brotherhood":** *Boston Jewish Advocate,* 9 December 1910. Interestingly enough, LDB's reiteration of his 1905 statement appeared in the context of an interview headlined as supporting Zionism.

410 **played a key role:** For Kallen's life, see Schmidt, *Kallen.*

410 **but reinforced it:** Kallen expressed these ideas in a number of works. See, among others, "Democracy Versus the Melting Pot," *Nation,* 18 February 1915, 190–94, 217–20; "Zionism and the Struggle Towards Democracy," *Nation,* 23 September 1915, 379–80; *Culture and Democracy in the United States* (New York, 1924); and *Cultural Pluralism and the American Idea* (Philadelphia, 1956). For Kallen's role in tutoring LDB, see Schmidt, *Kallen,* chap. 4.

410 **go through regular mail:** For Kallen on LDB, see his "Philosopher of Americanism," *Jewish Frontier* (November 1936), 12–13; Harry Barnard, *The Forging of an American Jew: The Life and Times of Judge Julian W. Mack* (New York, 1974), 181; Zimmern to Kallen, December 1915, Kallen MSS.

411 **"the Pilgrim inspiration":** LDB, "A Call to the Educated Jew," *Menorah Journal* 1 (January 1915), 4; *Maccabean,* July 1915, 34; and "True Americanism," *Boston American,* 4 July 1915.

411 **"we must become Zionists":** *Baltimore American,* 16 September 1914.

412 **loyalty to the United States:** LDB, *The Jewish Problem, and How to Solve It* (New York, 1915), 12. This pamphlet, originally a speech to Reform rabbis, represents the best single presentation of LDB's Zionist philosophy and, with the exception of some of Mordecai Kaplan's writings, the most developed ideological statement of American Zionism. LDB originally wanted to call it "The Jewish Problem and the Organization of American Israel," but Louis Lipsky persuaded him to change the name. Lipsky to LDB, 2 June 1915.

412 **"this house of God our Temple":** Cited in Henry L. Feingold, *Zion in America* (New York, 1974), 99.

413 **"loyalty to America":** The speech, "True Americanism," is in Goldman, *Brandeis on Zionism,* 3–11; LDB to Jacob H. Kaplan, 10 February 1916.

413 **"which they are a part":** Levin to Actions Committee, 6 October 1915.

413 **"up to date Federal judge":** LDB had already met him, albeit briefly, in the 1890s when Mack was one of the three student founders of the *Harvard Law Review.*

414 **juvenile court system:** See Barnard, *Forging of an American Jew.*

414 **stood on his own feet:** LDB to AGB, 29 August 1911; Barnard, *Forging of an American Jew;* Moses Rischin, "The Early Attitude of the American Jewish

Committee to Zionism (1906–1922)," *Publications of the American Jewish Historical Society* 49 (1959), 192.

414 **from Hungary to America:** Melvin I. Urofsky, *A Voice That Spoke for Justice: The Life and Times of Stephen S. Wise* (Albany, N.Y., 1982); Stephen S. Wise, *Challenging Years* (New York, 1949).

414 **to Mack and Wise:** Felix Frankfurter with Harlan B. Phillips, *Felix Frankfurter Reminisces* (New York, 1960), 290; Michael E. Parrish, *Felix Frankfurter and His Times: The Reform Years* (New York, 1982).

415 **well-defined goals:** Joan Dash, *Summoned to Jerusalem: The Life of Henrietta Szold* (New York, 1979); Marlin Levin, *It Takes a Dream: The Story of Hadassah* (Jerusalem and Hewlitt, 1997). LDB and Mack both contributed secretly to a fund to support Miss Szold so that she could devote all of her time and energy to Hadassah's work. See Ida S. Danziger to LDB, 7 April 1915.

416 **partially supporting him:** There is no biography of de Haas, but much information can be gleaned from his *Brandeis* and from Frankfurter with Phillips, *Felix Frankfurter Reminisces,* 181–82.

416 **"for progressive work":** Brandeis to Morris Lazaron, 17 November 1915.

416 **bringing in other speakers:** See LDB to Richard Gottheil, 22 June 1915, and to Office Committee, 21 February 1916, Gottheil MSS; Horace Kallen to LDB, 11 March 1915, Kallen MSS; LDB to Israel Friedlander, 3 March 1916.

416 **from their people:** See, for example, *Jewish Monitor,* 1 July 1915. Looking even more to the future, the PEC also supported the Young Judaea movement, aimed at high-school students. Brandeis called Young Judaea "the apprenticeship school of the Zionist movement, from which the younger generation is to graduate into active membership in our various organizations."

418 **"praying for your health":** Goldberg to LDB, 31 March 1916, cited in Shapiro, *Leadership,* 155.

418 **everything seemed possible:** LDB, *Jewish Problem,* 16; see also LDB to Louis Lipsky, 31 December 1914, and to Horace Kallen, 23 February 1915.

419 **so much money raised:** See Urofsky, *American Zionism,* 134–40.

419 **half a million entries:** LDB to Jews of Chelsea, Massachusetts, 22 June 1915; LDB to Abraham Alpert, 19 March 1915.

419 **discrepancy in the accounts:** See letters to Perlstein in Melvin I. Urofsky and David W. Levy, eds., *Letters of Louis D. Brandeis,* 5 vols. (Albany, N.Y., 1971–1978), 3:295ff.

419 **all of it accurate:** De Haas, *Brandeis,* 62–63.

420 **for accuracy and detail:** Kesselman to LDB, 29 March 1916.

420 **"dollars from Milwaukee":** LDB to Joseph Saffro, 28 November 1914; a similar telegram went to Israel J. Biskind in Cleveland.

420 **accounted for as well:** LDB to Abraham Koshland, 7 September 1915.

420 **"with infinite patience":** Louis Lipsky, *A Gallery of Zionist Profiles* (New York, 1956), 157–58. One should note that Lipsky was one of the first to break with LDB's leadership of Zionism after the war and became Chaim Weizmann's chief lieutenant in America during the 1920s.

422 **a penny to the *yishuv*:** Lipsky to Zionistisches Zentralbüro, 23 July 1914, Berlin office; speech by Henrietta Szold to Actions Committee, 15 October 1941, Szold MSS.

422 **Joint Distribution Committee:** Jacob Schiff to Marshall, 18 September

1914; Marshall to Schiff, 22 September 1914, Schiff MSS; Oscar Handlin, *A Continuing Task: The American Jewish Joint Distribution Committee, 1914–1964* (New York, 1964).

422 **"their capital also"**: *Boston Herald,* 28 June 1915; *Philadelphia Public Ledger,* 15 September 1914; LDB to Bernie F. Green, 28 January 1915, and to Abraham B. Cohen, 13 February 1915.

423 **fifteen years of existence**: Louis Kirstein to Henry Morgenthau Jr., 26 November 1917, Magnes MSS; LDB to Alfred Brandeis, 27 November 1914; LDB and Louis Lipsky to Zionists, 1 June 1915.

423 **Hadassah unit in Palestine**: LDB to Julius Rosenwald, 4 February 1915, and to Judah L. Magnes, 13 March 1915.

424 **need of a Jewish homeland**: LDB to Edward Bromberg, 19 March 1915; *Baltimore Jewish Comment,* 24 September 1915.

426 **strengthen the group**: LDB to Kaplan, 6 December 1915.

427 **whatever central direction**: Levin and Lipsky to LDB, 20 August 1914; minutes of Provisional Executive Committee, 27 March 1915, Magnes MSS.

427 **"until better times come"**: Weizmann to LDB and Levin, 18 October 1914, quoted in *Trial and Error: The Autobiography of Chaim Weizmann* (New York, 1949), 165.

427 **transfer of power to the PEC**: De Haas to LDB, 6 October 1914; Judah Magnes to Weizmann, 4 October 1914, Berlin Office; PEC to Zionistisches Zentralbüro, 2 November 1914, Berlin Office; Levin, Straus, and Magnes to Zionistisches Zentralbüro, 28 November 1914, Berlin Office; Leo Motzkin to Copenhagen Office, 28 November 1914, Copenhagen Office.

427 **Americans take over**: Sokolow to PEC, 17 November 1914, Berlin Office; Weizmann to Horace Kallen, 24 January 1915, de Haas MSS.

428 **determine how to share it**: See, for example, the printed letter from the Zionist Actions Committee to Fellow Zionists, 9 July 1915, translated from the German and distributed to American Zionists by the PEC, 23 August 1915.

428 **about important matters**: Brandeis to Arthur Hantke, 19 March 1915, Berlin Office; Benjamin Perlstein to Copenhagen Office, 22 June 1915, Copenhagen Office; LDB to Henry Morgenthau, 22 October 1914, Morgenthau MSS; LDB to Actions Committee, 15 September 1915, Berlin Office, and 23 January 1916, Copenhagen Office.

CHAPTER 18: NOMINATION

430 **later in the month**: Holt to LDB, 15 January 1916; LDB to Holt, 19 January 1916.

431 **"ought to accept"**: LDB to Alfred Brandeis, 28 January 1916.

431 **facts of the real world**: LDB, "The Living Law," 10 *Illinois Law Review* 461 (1916), reprinted in *The Curse of Bigness* (New York, 1934), 316–26. See also David W. Levy, "The Lawyer as Judge: Brandeis's View of the Legal Profession," 22 *Oklahoma Law Review* 374 (1969).

432 **with such anger**: LDB was not alone, of course, in his criticism of the courts for failing to take into account economic and social realities; this idea lay at the heart of so-called sociological jurisprudence. Roscoe Pound had charged that "courts are less and less competent to formulate rules for new relations which require regulation. They have the experience of the past. But they do

not have the facts of the present." "Common Law and Legislation," 21 *Harvard Law Review* 383, 403–7 (1908).

432 **ten-hour law:** *Ritchie v. People,* 40 N.E. 454 (1895); *Ritchie v. Wageman,* 91 N.E. 695 (1910). LDB had argued the second case.

433 **"a stiff fight":** William Gibbs McAdoo, *Crowded Years: The Reminiscences of William G. McAdoo* (Boston, 1931), 342–43.

434 **"Send his name in":** Ray Stannard Baker, "Interview with Thomas W. Gregory, 14 and 15 March 1927," Baker MSS. Apparently, the president's personal physician, Admiral Cary T. Grayson, also suggested LDB.

434 **consider him for the Court:** See, for example, William Kent to Wilson, 27 January 1916, Amos Pinchot to Wilson, 27 January 1916, and Norman Hapgood to Joseph Tumulty, 28 January 1916, all in Arthur S. Link et al., eds., *The Papers of Woodrow Wilson,* 69 vols. (Princeton, N.J., 1966–1984), 36:19–20, 22–23, 25–26.

434 **McReynolds to the bench:** Some people have suggested that McReynolds's sour disposition and his inability to get along with any other members of the cabinet led Wilson to get rid of him by naming him to the Court.

434 **suggested to them:** Arthur S. Link, *Wilson: Confusions and Crises, 1915–1916* (Princeton, N.J., 1964), 321. This view has been disputed by David Sarasohn, *The Party of Reform: Democrats in the Progressive Era* (Jackson, Miss., 1989), 184ff.

435 **"conservative Republicans":** Arthur S. Link, *Woodrow Wilson and the Progressive Era, 1910–1917* (New York, 1954), 225.

435 **"Roosevelt strongholds":** Pinchot to Hapgood, 29 January 1916, enclosed in Hapgood to Joseph Tumulty, 1 February 1916 in Link et al., *Papers of Wilson,* 36:86.

435 **"so good a stroke":** Hand to LDB, 28 January 1916, Hand MSS.

435 **"great public service":** Robert M. La Follette, "Brandeis," *La Follette's Magazine,* February 1916, 1–2. Philip La Follette wrote to "Uncle Louis" that the nomination "is going to draw us nearer to the administration more than anything the President could have done."

435 **supporting the nomination:** Wilson MSS, file 6, box 522.

436 **"means of support":** Wilson to Ellen Axson, 30 October 1883, in Link et al., *Papers of Wilson,* 2:501. For Wilson's law practice, see Thomas W. Thrash, "Apprenticeship at the Bar: The Atlanta Law Practice of Woodrow Wilson," 28 *Georgia State Bar Journal* 147 (1992); and Melvin I. Urofsky, "Woodrow Wilson: Reluctant Lawyer," in Norman Gross, ed., *America's Lawyer-Presidents* (Evanston, Ill., 2004), 230–39.

436 **"not life to law":** Address to Gridiron Club, 9 December 1916, quoted in Link, *Wilson: Confusions and Crises,* 324.

436 **grain of salt:** LDB to Alfred Brandeis, 12 February 1916.

437 **work as a reformer:** "The nomination should at least serve to convince our Cincinnati friends that in the opinion of the President there is no conflict between Zionism and loyalty to America." LDB to Jacob H. Kaplan, 10 February 1916.

437 **"progressive forces":** LDB to Alfred Brandeis, 12 February 1916.

437 **"removed my doubts":** LDB to Pound, 24 February 1916, Pound MSS.

437 **"confidence in him":** AGB to Alfred Brandeis, 31 January 1916. LDB's partner George Nutter also expressed surprise that LDB had been willing to accept, because he had always been free. Nutter Diaries, 28 January 1916.

437 **justification on both sides:** Because LDB stayed in Boston throughout the confirmation fight, there are no letters from him to Alice, nor any indications of her response. Bess Evans was also in Boston, so Alice did not need to write to her either. As a result, we know very little about what Alice felt or thought during the confirmation fight.

438 **"in Western society":** Thomas K. McCraw, "Louis D. Brandeis Reappraised," *American Scholar* 54 (1985), 527.

438 **"from good motives":** Nutter Diaries, 28 January and 2 February 1916.

438 **"Spanish War Resolution":** George W. "Gus" Karger to Taft, 29 January 1916, quoted in Link, *Wilson: Confusions and Crises,* 325.

438 **"soul of the Supreme Court":** Trevor Parry-Giles uses that phrase in his study of the nomination fight, *The Character of Justice: Rhetoric, Law, and Politics in the Supreme Court Confirmation Process* (East Lansing, Mich., 2006), chap. 2.

438 **"much power for evil":** Taft to Karger, 31 January 1916, in Link, *Wilson: Confusions and Crises,* 325.

439 **"a socialist or a progressive":** The *Washington Post,* 29 January 1916, carried a digest of press response from around the country. The "a socialist or a progressive" comment came from the *Detroit Free Press.*

439 **"root of the tree":** Quoted in Lewis J. Paper, *Brandeis* (Englewood Cliffs, N.J., 1983), 213.

439 **"spine of every patriot":** Quoted in *Current Opinion,* March 1916, 158.

439 **espoused by the paper:** James T. Williams Jr. Memoir, OHRO.

439 **"a question about race":** *Washington Star,* 29 January 1916, quoted in Parry-Giles, *Character of Justice,* 27.

440 **oppose the appointment:** An offer had supposedly been made by President Millard Fillmore to name Judah P. Benjamin, who was Jewish, to the Court in early 1853, but Benjamin, recently elected as a senator from Louisiana, declined and took his seat in the Senate.

440 **to true Americans:** Fitzgerald to Thomas Walsh, 29 January 1916, quoted in Link, *Wilson: Confusions and Crises,* 325. A conservative Boston Democrat, Fitzgerald had locked horns with LDB over municipal matters.

440 **"Senate would vote":** *New York Sun,* 29 January 1916.

440 **"opposition be misconstrued":** Karger to Taft, 29 January 1916; this part of the letter is cited in A. L. Todd, *Justice on Trial: The Case of Louis D. Brandeis* (New York, 1964), 77.

440 **he ignored them:** Two years later, on 11 October 1918, he wrote to Philip La Follette, who had reported prejudice toward immigrants, some of whom were Jewish, in the army: "I am of the opinion that the best thing for the Service and for you and the officers named is to ignore it. It is one of those intangible things which cannot well be met by protest. . . . I know how you feel because in years past I have experienced in other connections similar indignities." La Follette MSS.

440 **to Taft's disgust:** "I believe the whole business and intelligent part of the community to be thoroughly aroused against Wilson," the former president wrote in October 1916, "except maybe the Jews and the college professors." Taft to George W. Wickersham, 15 October 1916, cited in Arthur S. Link, *Wilson: Campaigns for Progressivism and Peace* (Princeton, N.J., 1965), 140. For Jewish political response, see Lawrence H. Fuchs, *The Political Behavior of American Jews* (Glencoe, Ill., 1956), 60.

440 **earlier in the day:** *Literary Digest,* 26 February 1916. The papers also quoted one man who claimed to be a friend of LDB's and who said that for years LDB had "devoted his personal attention to the poor of Boston, to the relief of Jews the world over."

440 **a public statement:** Schiff to LDB, 31 January 1916, Schiff MSS; *New York Times,* 1 February 1916. Schiff also invited LDB to dine with him when he came to New York next so they could discuss Jewish affairs, and Brandeis accepted. LDB to Schiff, 7 February 1916, Schiff MSS.

441 **"all hate Wilson":** Todd, *Justice on Trial,* 80.

441 **the entire hearings:** LDB's religion was mentioned in some articles, usually those praising the nomination, for example, "Let the Senate not hesitate to confirm the appointment of this able and great-hearted Jew." *Independent,* 7 February 1916, 175.

441 **"had not been known":** U.S. Senate, *Hearings Before the Subcommittee of the Committee on the Judiciary . . . on the Nomination of Louis D. Brandeis to Be an Associate Justice of the Supreme Court of the United States,* 64th Cong., 1st sess., 2 vols. in 1 (Washington, D.C., 1916), 754 (hereafter cited as *Hearings on Nomination*).

441 **"posturing of the Jews":** Nutter Diaries, 12 and 23 February, 6 April, and 17 June 1916.

442 **by party loyalty:** McClennen to LDB, 3 February 1916.

442 **on his behalf:** LDB to Samuel R. Stern, 10 February 1916.

442 **"about the same reasons":** Frankfurter to Mack, 31 January 1916, quoted in Leonard Baker, *Brandeis and Frankfurter: A Dual Biography* (New York, 1984), 99.

442 **from southern Democrats:** *Id.,* 102. McClennen, however, also told LDB that some southerners believed his "liberality in the interest of all humanity" would lead him to declare segregation unconstitutional. McClennen to LDB, 3 May 1916.

442 **what he meant:** Stenographic transcript of conference between LDB and McClennen, 22 March 1916. However, in a letter to Judge Charles Amidon after he had been confirmed, 27 June 1916, LDB did not even mention anti-Semitism.

442 **such bitter antagonism:** Allon Gal, who argued that LDB's Jewishness played such a large role in shaping his career, devotes a scant two pages to the confirmation fight, and merely repeats that by 1912 Brandeis had faced anti-Semitism in Boston; he introduces no new evidence that prejudice played a significant role in 1916. Gal, *Brandeis of Boston* (Cambridge, Mass., 1980), 195–96. Alpheus Mason, Philippa Strum, and Lewis Paper all play down the role anti-Semitism played in the fight, as does A. L. Todd. Richard Friedman maintains that anti-Semitism played "a subsidiary role in the dispute," while Ronald Rotunda claims that the opposition "laced its rejection of his social activism with extensive anti-Semitic rhetoric," both quoted in Parry-Giles, *Character of Justice,* 42.

443 **"the Sun and the moon":** *New York Sun,* 31 January 1916.

443 **insulation from the press:** "I am sorry I cannot assent to your suggestion of an interview. It would hardly be proper for me to speak on any subject at the moment." LDB to Charles A. Seldon, a reporter for the *New York Times,* 8 February 1916.

443 **nominees did not appear:** Although the Judiciary Committee had been

established in 1816 as one of the Senate's original eleven standing committees, it did not begin to examine the qualifications of judicial appointees
until 1868; before then the entire Senate had sat as a committee of the whole
to consider nominations. No appointee testified personally before the committee until Harlan Fiske Stone appeared in 1925 to answer questions about
how he had discharged his duties as attorney general. Next, Felix Frankfurter addressed the committee in 1939 to respond to slanderous accusations
made following his nomination. There would not be another appearance
until John Marshall Harlan II in 1955, and since then all appointees to the
high court have testified before the committee.

444 **"the fight to others"**: LDB to Alfred Brandeis, 12 February 1916.

444 **"from our old rooms"**: LDB to Douglas, 11 February 1916, Douglas MSS.

444 **Nutter in Boston:** Several times during the hearings, Nutter scribbled in
his diary that no law work had been done at the office that day. See, for example, Nutter Diaries, 2 and 16 February 1916.

444 **in particular matters:** These letters constitute the nearest LDB ever came
to writing an autobiography, and they do much to shed light on not only his
law practice in general but also his creative approach to problems brought to
him by clients. See Melvin I. Urofsky and David W. Levy, eds., *Letters of Louis
D. Brandeis,* 5 vols. (Albany, N.Y., 1971–1978), 4:27–182.

445 **prominent Jewish lawyers:** LDB to Hapgood, 1 February 1916, two letters.

445 **law review articles:** LDB to Edward McClennen, 7 February 1916.

445 **might best be used:** See, for example, LDB to Norman Hapgood, 28 April
1916. Nutter's role during these months can be found in his diaries, along
with comments about some of the people who opposed the nomination.
Nutter Diaries.

445 **"peace loving individual":** LDB to Harrington Emerson, 17 March 1916,
and to Charles E. Russell, 10 February 1916.

445 **"against its confirmation":** Todd, *Justice on Trial,* 94–95.

445 **financial interests overlapped:** The chart can be found in Alpheus T.
Mason, *Brandeis: A Free Man's Life* (New York, 1946), 485.

445 **stirred up more opposition:** See, for example, Higginson to Woodrow
Wilson, 4 March 1916, in Link et al., *Papers of Wilson,* 36:250.

446 **counter the opposition:** Mason, *Brandeis,* 473.

446 **petition supporting Brandeis:** Apparently, Lowell's prominent voice in
the anti-LDB campaign generated a great deal of protest from some Harvard
alumni, and he tried to explain his position in a letter to the alumni bulletin,
which had voiced concerns over his action. Nutter Diaries, 18 March 1916.

446 **person worthy of honor:** Berle to Chilton, 18 February 1916.

446 **farther from the truth:** "The Rumpus over Brandeis," *Harper's Weekly,*
19 February 1916, 169.

446 **Pinchot-Ballinger hearings:** "Truth," "Lest We Forget," and "The Committee's Method," *Harper's Weekly,* 1 April 1916, 324–25.

446 **the railroad hearings:** "From the Brandeis Records," *Harper's Weekly,*
29 April 1916, 455–56.

447 **for the appointment:** LDB to Hand, 9 February 1916, Hand MSS.

447 **to join the Court:** "Brandeis," *New Republic,* 5 February 1916, 4–6.

447 **falsehood of the accusations:** The journal did not always give its editorials
titles, but rather ran a series of comments divided by spacing. However, see

"Brandeis and the Shoe Machinery Case," 4 March 1916, 117–19; and "The Case Against Brandeis," 25 March 1916, 202–4.

447 **support of the *Survey*:** Editorial, *Survey,* 4 March 1916, 681. LDB at his death left one-fourth of his residual estate to Survey Associates, "for the maintenance of civil liberty and the promotion of workers' education in the United States."

447 **confirm Brandeis to the Court:** See, for example, "The President and Mr. Brandeis," *Outlook,* 17 May 1916, 109–10; and the highly admiring word portrait, "Brandeis," by William Hard, *Outlook,* 31 May 1916, 271–77.

448 **using Brandeis's phrase, "niggardly":** *Hearings on Nomination,* 8; Thorne's testimony is on 5–62.

448 **in his testimony:** *Id.,* 63.

448 **"not believe it possible":** *Id.,* 68.

448 **"a very serious matter":** Todd, *Justice on Trial,* 101.

448 **to handle the testimony:** *Hearings on Nomination,* 75–93.

449 **"We can read, you know":** *Id.,* 93–116.

449 **"unfitness for the Supreme Bench":** *Id.,* 123–24; Barron's testimony is on 116–34.

450 **after Sam's death:** *Id.,* 153; the full testimony is on 137–59.

450 **the original arrangements:** Cornelia Warren to LDB, 16 February 1916; LDB to Warren, 17 February 1916.

451 **relations with the firm:** *Hearings on Nomination,* 159–261; the LDB letter to Clapp, 24 February 1912, is at 217–21.

451 **the most damaging:** Nutter Diaries, 2 February 1916.

451 **his tenure as U.S. attorney:** LDB to McClennen, 7 and 16 February 1916.

451 **by the Boston bar:** Charles C. Burlingham Memoir, OHRO. Mason and others noted that LDB's attitude often annoyed other lawyers even when they agreed with his position. See, for example, a letter from a Boston attorney on 5 October 1896 in which he apologized for the fact that he had gotten mad at LDB, and did not know why LDB's attitude so often angered him, even when they agreed. Mason, *Brandeis,* 507n.

451 **"letters from the bar":** Nutter Diaries, 19 February 1916.

452 **real client had been *Collier's*:** *Hearings on Nomination,* 264–80.

452 **"not to be trusted":** *Id.,* 271. Nearly a half century after the appointment, John P. Frank did an exhaustive analysis of all the charges brought up against LDB in terms of the prevailing ethics of the legal profession. He found that at times LDB had engaged in new and creative practices, such as acting as counsel for the situation, but had done nothing that could be labeled ethically wrong or irresponsible. Frank, "The Legal Ethics of Louis D. Brandeis," 17 *Stanford Law Review* 683 (1965).

452 **any of their names:** *Hearings on Nomination,* 272.

453 **"in his place":** *Id.,* 278.

453 **thought well of him:** *Id.,* 280.

453 **its financial leaders:** McClennen worried more about the damage that the reputational charges could do than about specific allegations that could be rebutted. LDB acknowledged his awareness of the charges regarding "my alleged reputation at the Boston bar," but noted that since 1893 he had had a diminishing contact with other lawyers, and in recent years had been more engaged in reform matters. About the only contact he had with other

lawyers was when they joined or opposed him on matters of public concern. In the 1890s, however, he had done a fair amount of work involving other Boston attorneys, and had often been called in by them for advice. LDB to McClennen, 17 February 1916.

453 **attacks on Brandeis continued:** For day-to-day narratives of the hearings, see Mason, *Brandeis,* chaps. 30 and 31; and Todd, *Justice on Trial.*

454 *Business—a Profession:* McClennen to LDB, 11 April 1916; Gregory to LDB, 12 April 1916.

454 **"deliberate lies":** "For the first time Brandeis seemed stirred up. I could not blame him." Nutter Diaries, 10 March 1916.

454 **reached the right people:** LDB to Gregory, 14 April 1914; Gregory to Walsh, 17 April 1916, both in Walsh MSS.

454 **others as "apologetic":** Alpheus Mason to Charles Burlingham, 16 June 1914, Burlingham MSS.

454 **"unwise but perilous":** LDB to McClennen, 14 April 1916.

454 **who supported him:** LDB to Charles F. Amidon, 27 June 1916.

455 **"the bar needs regeneration":** *Reports from the Subcommittee . . . on the Nomination of Louis D. Brandeis . . . ,* 64th Cong., 1st sess. (1916), 59. Several years later Walsh told a correspondent that he considered his championship of LDB in the subcommittee one of the most important things he had done in the Senate, and one that gave him the greatest satisfaction. Walsh to John Temple Graves, 20 August 1919, Walsh MSS; see Miles Dunnington, "Senator Thomas J. Walsh and the Vindication of Louis D. Brandeis," typescript, 1943.

455 **he would be confirmed:** McClennen, aware of what the vote would be, predicted to his partner George Nutter that "the certainties of confirmation appear to increase." McClennen to Nutter, 30 March 1916; Nutter Diaries, 29 March 1916.

456 **"the basis for action":** McClennen to LDB, 2 May 1916.

456 **"obscurity of the Supreme Court":** Henry Morgenthau, "All in a Lifetime: The Campaign of 1916," *World's Work,* December 1921, 138–45. Morgenthau repeated his suggestion to Colonel House, who passed it on to the president; Wilson did not like the idea at all. House Diary, 6 April 1916, in Link et al., *Papers of Wilson,* 36:425. Morgenthau, incidentally, did not include the story when he published his reminiscences in book form in 1922.

456 **come for him to act:** McClennen reported to LDB on 2 May that there had been a strategy session involving the president, but he had no details of what had been decided.

457 **"we are all so justly proud":** Culberson to Wilson, 5 May 1916; Wilson to Culberson, 5 May 1916, *Hearings on Nomination,* Senate Committee Print, 1–4. According to the editors of the *Papers of Wilson* (where this letter is also found at 36:609–11), Wilson drew heavily on a draft prepared by Attorney General Gregory, who in turn had been supplied with material by George Anderson. Gregory, of course, orchestrated the request from Culberson and Wilson's ability to respond the same day.

457 **"we have got the best":** Eliot to Culberson, 17 May 1916; Mason, *Brandeis,* 501; John Lord O'Brian Memoir, OHRO.

458 **pressure from the White House:** Todd, *Justice on Trial,* chap. 8.

458 **voted against confirmation:** *Boston Herald,* 11 April 1916.

458 **announced their support:** Nutter Diaries, 13 May 1916; Mason, *Brandeis,* 503–4.

458 **"satisfaction as I signed his"**: Wilson to Henry Morgenthau, 5 June 1916, in Link et al., *Papers of Wilson*, 37:163.

458 **"an honor to our people"**: *American Hebrew*, 9 June 1916; along with Schiff's comments, the journal carried statements by Simon Wolf and Samuel Untermyer.

458 **"WHAT GREETINGS"**: Frankfurter and Laski to LDB, 1 June 1916.

459 **"we will sorely miss"**: Pinchot to LDB, 6 June 1916. A similar comment had come earlier from Henry L. Levenson, a Boston attorney, who feared the loss of LDB from Jewish and Zionist activities. Levenson to LDB, 28 January 1916.

459 **while on the bench**: LDB to Pinchot, 27 June 1916.

459 **responded with alacrity**: Gregory to LDB, 2 June 1916; LDB to Gregory, 2 June 1916.

459 **"WELCOME"**: Holmes to LDB, 2 June 1916.

CHAPTER 19: SETTLING IN

460 **"it went hard with me"**: Notes of 3 July 1923, Brandeis-Frankfurter Conversations, LDB-HLS. After LDB went on the Court, Felix Frankfurter would visit with him in Washington or, during the summers, on Cape Cod. Frankfurter kept notes of their conversations in blue exam books and on loose-leaf pages. Since Frankfurter destroyed some of the letters and other papers exchanged between himself and LDB after the latter's death, we have no idea how extensive the original papers were. The remaining notes range primarily from 17 April 1922 to 17 June 1926, with a few in the 1930s. The originals have been transcribed and annotated in Melvin I. Urofsky, "The Brandeis-Frankfurter Conversations," 1985 *Supreme Court Review* 299.

460 **his own schedule**: *Id.*, 26 June 1922.

460 **its summer recess**: Gregory to LDB, 2 June 1916; McClennen to LDB, 2 June 1916.

461 **oath of office**: *Boston Globe*, 6 June 1916.

462 **"between you and me"**: Clarke to LDB, 18 August 1916.

462 **"two such men on the bench"**: Belle Case La Follette and Fola La Follette, *Robert M. La Follette*, 2 vols. (New York, 1953), 1:586–87. Although LDB had nothing against Clarke, he indicated that he hoped Wilson would appoint Attorney General Gregory to the bench.

462 **been very different**: The only biography is Hoyt Landon Warner, *The Life of Mr. Justice Clarke* (Cleveland, 1959).

462 **poor reputation**: AGB to Belle La Follette, 8 July 1916, La Follette MSS.

462 **walk together to the Capitol**: Holmes did not use the phone, a habit Brandeis quickly adopted, and so if the two men wanted to communicate, they would send their law clerks over with a message; as a result, LDB and Holmes got to know each other's clerks (all of whom had come from Harvard per Felix Frankfurter) fairly well. Dean Acheson, *Morning and Noon* (Boston, 1965), 63.

462 **family or friends**: See, for example, LDB to Frankfurter, 20 October 1924, FF-LC.

462 **the new letterhead**: Apparently, the initial proposal would have made Studley a named partner as well, but Nutter said he objected to a four-name law firm. Nutter Diaries, 16 June 1916.

463 **gifts to Miss Malloch:** See the several folders of letters from Malloch to LDB, LDB-BU. He also left her a bequest at his death.

463 **$2 million:** Malloch to LDB, statement of accounts, 20 January 1916, LDB-BU.

463 **around $120,000:** Alpheus T. Mason, *Brandeis: A Free Man's Life* (New York, 1946), 691. In 1915, LDB received $47,694, and in 1916 $37,919 from the firm. His salary from the Supreme Court reached $20,000 a year in the 1930s.

464 **work of the Court:** LDB to White, 29 June 1916; White to LDB, 17 July 1916.

465 **served one year apiece:** There is a complete list of LDB's clerks in Mason, *Brandeis,* 690. Other justices took their clerks from different schools, and had varying practices on how long each would stay. Pierce Butler, for example, kept the same clerk from 1923 until his retirement in 1939, while Owen Roberts had the same clerk during his entire fifteen-year tenure on the Court. During LDB's tenure, all justices could have one clerk, with the exception of the chief justice, who in the 1930s had two. Since then, as the Court's workload has increased, that number has grown to four per justice.

465 **"they may be overcome":** LDB to Frankfurter, 23 October 1922, FF-HLS. Henry Friendly may have been the only one to have a job interview. Henry J. Friendly to author and to David W. Levy, 14 June 1967. For Friendly's year with LDB, see his *Benchmarks* (Chicago, 1967), 291–307. Most clerks interviewed by Lewis Paper in the 1980s recalled that the first time they met LDB was when they showed up for work at his apartment. Paper MSS.

465 **"none in the future":** Paul Freund, "The Supreme Court: A Tale of Two Terms," 26 *Ohio State Law Journal* 225 (1965). Freund notes that when Drew Pearson and Robert S. Allen published their book *The Nine Old Men* (Garden City, N.Y., 1936), purportedly using "inside" information about the Court, a friend asked LDB whether he had read it. "Oh, no," he replied, "there are some things in it that Mrs. Brandeis tells me I should not know."

465 **occurred in conference:** Paul Freund Memoir, 65, New York Times Oral History Program. However, the clerks did know how the votes went thanks to their access to LDB's docket book, in which he, like the other justices, kept track of who voted and how, and occasionally LDB added comments on the discussion. They, of course, never spoke of this to others. One time, when Louis Jaffe saw that LDB was going to affirm a case with which the clerk disagreed, he tried to argue LDB out of it. "Never again did the sheet bearing his votes on the agenda of the Saturday conference appear on my desk."

465 **"about their Justices":** *Harvard Law School Bulletin,* April 1957, 11.

466 **"placed it on his desk":** George Dargo, "Calvert Magruder of the First Circuit: The Law Professor as Judge," 74 *Massachusetts Law Review* 239 (1989); Philippa Strum, *Louis D. Brandeis: Justice for the People* (Cambridge, Mass., 1984), 357.

466 **"faith in your picking":** LDB to Frankfurter, 1 December 1916, FF-LC.

466 **"best critic I had":** Magruder "has a good legal mind and good working habits—and is a right-minded Southern Gentleman. He is not of extraordinary ability or brilliant or of unusual scholarship, but he has stability." LDB to Thomas Nelson Perkins, 25 March 1920; Felix Frankfurter, "Calvert Magruder," 72 *Harvard Law Review* 1201 (1959). After leaving LDB,

Magruder served in the army during the war and in 1920 became a professor at Harvard Law School, specializing in torts. In 1939, Roosevelt named him to the U.S. Court of Appeals for the First Circuit.

466 **"very heated discussions"**: Graham Claytor interview, Paper MSS; James M. Landis Memoir, 38, OHRO.

467 **to get it right**: Landis to Felix Frankfurter, 1 November 1925, FF-LC; James M. Landis, "Mr. Justice Brandeis: A Law Clerk's View," *Publications of the American Jewish Historical Society* 46 (1957), 468. "He believed in taking pains, and the corollary of taking pains is taking time." Felix Frankfurter, "Mr. Justice Brandeis," 55 *Harvard Law Review* 181, 183 (1941).

467 **was not intoxicating**: *Jacob Ruppert v. Caffey,* 251 U.S. 264 (1920).

467 **"of your own"**: Acheson, *Morning and Noon,* 79–80. Chapter 5 of this memoir, "Working with Brandeis," is one of the most charming reminiscences by any clerk.

467 **"kindest of men"**: Paul Freund to Felix Frankfurter, 15 November 1932, FF-LC; see also William Sutherland interview, Paper MSS.

468 **in the robe**: Landis Memoir, 37–38.

468 **tear it apart**: Freund Memoir, 54–55; Friendly interview, Paper MSS.

468 **for a copy**: "Capt. Oliver of the Office of the Chief of Engineers telephoned to say . . . ,": Dean Acheson to LDB, 7 April 1920, LDB-SC; "Mr. Justice: I have just learned that the Virginia Law Review's current issue contains an article by Jerome Frank. . . . I think the article is worth waiting for, and I have sent for a copy." Paul Freund to LDB, 10 May 1933, Freund MSS.

468 **read all of it**: Thomas H. Austern to LDB, 13 November 1930, in relation to a patent case, LDB-SC.

468 **complete with charts**: *Southwestern Bell Telephone Company v. Public Service Commission of Missouri,* 262 U.S. 276 (1923); the memo is in the case file, LDB-SC.

468 **bench, not they**: Freund Memoir, 52. During LDB's tenure Justices McReynolds and Stone turned over review of petitions to their clerks. Dennis Hutchinson and David Garrow, eds., *The Forgotten Memoir of John Knox: A Year in the Life of a Supreme Court Clerk in FDR's Washington* (Chicago, 2002), 56–57; Walter Gellhorn Memoir, 171, OHRO. Knox and Gellhorn were clerks to McReynolds and Stone, respectively. Adrian Fisher, LDB's last clerk, says that during his time the justice did ask him to type up memoranda on the cert petitions. Fisher interview, Paper MSS.

469 **the "dismissed" pile**: Paul Freund, "Mr. Justice Brandeis," in Allison Dunham and Philip B. Kurland, eds., *Mr. Justice* (Chicago, 1956), 189.

470 **was all business**: Gellhorn Memoir, 17.

470 **"at a minimum"**: Nathaniel L. Nathanson, "Mr. Justice Brandeis: A Law Clerk's Recollections of the October Term, 1934," *American Jewish Archives* 15 (1963), 9.

470 **learn from their guests**: AGB to Paul Freund, n.d. "Will you please dine with us on Wednesday at 7 o'clock. . . . Andrew Furuseth, the grand old man of Labor is to be here." Freund MSS.

470 **in the world**: Freund Memoir, 68–69.

470 **that he had**: Walter Raushenbush, "Brandeis as Jurist: Craftsmanship with Inspiration," Brandeis Lecture at the University of Louisville, 26 January 1965.

470 **Holmes needed companionship:** Alger Hiss Memoir, 217–18, OHRO. "Rose [Holmes's clerk] was in this A.M. and I gave him some directions," LDB to Frankfurter, 2 October 1931, FF-LC.

471 **"or worse vices":** LDB to Frankfurter, 7 October 1928, FF-HLS.

471 **complaints to Frankfurter:** LDB to Frankfurter, 12 and 15 October 1928, FF-HLS.

471 **critical of Brandeis:** See, for example, "Notes for an Essay on Justice Brandeis," Riesman to Frankfurter, 22 May 1936, FF-LC. Riesman noted that some people considered LDB intellectually dishonest, since his purported disinterestedness really masked a passionate interest in reform, which he furthered on the Court when he could.

472 **"unworthy of consideration":** Riesman interview, Paper MSS.

472 **"throughout life":** Riesman, "Notes for an Essay."

472 **"suggestion fell through":** Philip Elman Memoir, 139–40, OHRO.

473 **needed them more:** See, for example, Dean Acheson to Frankfurter, 11 December 1920, FF-LC, in which Acheson, trying to decide where to practice, reports LDB's strong advice against New York, and Paul Freund to LDB, 17 June 1933, FF-LC, explaining why he had chosen to stay in Washington rather than take a teaching job at Northwestern.

473 **"I have a majority":** Francis Biddle, "The Friendship of Holmes and Brandeis," *Atlantic Monthly,* December 1965, 89. James Landis said that LDB was very proud of the men who went into teaching, and he kept in contact with them, more so than with his clerks who went into practice. Landis Memoir, 71.

473 **other in the afternoon:** Warner W. Gardner, "Pebbles from the Paths Behind," 8 *Green Bag 2nd* 189, 191n.7 (2005).

473 **the following morning:** LDB seems to have been the only justice to make use of the printer this way. Each justice had an allowance to cover the costs of a messenger, a clerk, and a secretary. The others would have their secretaries type up the various drafts and not use the printer until an opinion was ready for circulation. Some of the clerks speculated that LDB made an arrangement to use the printer in lieu of the secretary and to have the allowance diverted for that purpose.

474 **proper legal argument:** "The logic of words should yield to the logic of realities." *DiSanto v. Pennsylvania,* 272 U.S. 34, 43 (1927) (LDB dissenting).

474 **Brandeis in mind:** Dean Acheson to Felix Frankfurter, 15 March and 6 April 1920, FF-LC.

474 **law review article:** *Adams v. Tanner,* 244 U.S. 590, 613n.21 (1917).

474 **"did not favor Law Review":** Strum, *Brandeis,* 364.

474 **both fact and law:** Acheson, *Morning and Noon,* 80–83. He also had to make sure that the opinion hid any doubts he might have had. He once told Robert H. Jackson that "the difficulty with this place is that if you're only fifty-five percent convinced of a proposition, you have to act and vote as if you were one hundred percent convinced. . . . You've got to decide the case one way or the other. Therefore the result oftentimes doesn't reflect the residue of doubt that remains in the minds of the men who've decided it." Robert H. Jackson Memoir, 1104, OHRO.

475 **such as administrative law:** *Erie Railroad v. Tompkins,* 304 U.S. 164 (1938); see below, chap. 30.

476 **commanded the majority:** Robert H. Jackson, "Mr. Justice Brandeis:

'Microscope and Telescope,' " in Alan F. Westin, ed., *An Autobiography of the Supreme Court* (New York, 1963), 235–36. The original article appeared in 9 *Vital Speeches* 664 (1943).

476 **"great relief to the world":** Harold Laski to Oliver Wendell Holmes Jr., 13 January 1918, in Mark DeWolfe Howe, ed., *Holmes-Laski Letters,* 2 vols. (Cambridge, Mass., 1953), 1:27.

476 **"make it more instructive":** Paul Freund, "Justice Brandeis: A Law Clerk's Remembrance," *American Jewish Archives* 68 (1977), 11.

476 **"save is my own":** James F. Simon, *Independent Journey: The Life of William O. Douglas* (New York, 1980), 250.

477 **ideological purists:** Jeffrey Rosen, "Roberts's Rules," *Atlantic Monthly,* January/February 2007, 113.

477 **judicial pragmatism:** See, for example, Daniel A. Farber, "Reinventing Brandeis: Legal Pragmatism for the Twenty-first Century," 1995 *Illinois Law Review* 163.

477 **interpreting the Constitution:** Thayer had taught LDB, the two became friends, and when Thayer went on leave in 1882, LDB, at Thayer's request, taught his course on evidence. Thayer published the first casebook on constitutional law in 1895, two years after his classic essay on American constitutional law in 7 *Harvard Law Review* 129 (1893). For Thayer's influence on LDB, see Wallace Mendelson, "The Influence of James B. Thayer upon the Work of Holmes, Brandeis, and Frankfurter," 31 *Vanderbilt Law Review* 71 (1978); and LDB to Thayer, 24 November 1889, Thayer MSS.

478 **"an ever developing people":** Draft of dissent in *United States v. Moreland,* 258 U.S. 433, 441 (1922). The majority found that a sentence to hard labor for failure to make child support payments amounted to cruel and unusual punishment, since hard labor had been reserved for more serious crimes. LDB traced changes in penal ideas and concluded that in modern times a sentence at hard labor could be justified by Congress.

478 **a very conservative view:** Louis Jaffe, one of his law clerks, argues that LDB could not, by contemporary standards, be called an activist and that he believed not only in judicial restraint but wherever possible in judicial abstention. "Was Brandeis an Activist? The Search for Intermediate Premises," 80 *Harvard Law Review* 986 (1967).

478 **"Magruder fully occupied":** LDB to Susan Brandeis, 9 October 1916.

479 **skepticism about reform:** Alexander M. Bickel and Benno C. Schmidt Jr., *The Judiciary and Responsible Government, 1910–1921* (New York, 1984), 39; Brandeis-Frankfurter Conversations, 3 August 1924. The only biography of White is Robert B. Highsaw, *Edward Douglass White: Defender of the Conservative Faith* (Baton Rouge, La., 1981).

479 **and then returning:** Bickel and Schmidt, *Judiciary and Responsible Government,* 354, 516.

480 **"few real friends":** Brandeis-Frankfurter Conversations, 3 July 1923.

480 **irrational savage:** *Id.,* 3 July 1924.

480 **Taft sought constantly:** *Id.,* 30 November 1922.

480 **"hot little gent":** *Id.,* n.d. July 1922. Brandeis apparently thought well of Mahlon Pitney; see Dean Acheson to Felix Frankfurter, 22 April 1921, FF-LC.

480 **percentage of butterfat:** *Hutchinson Ice Cream Co. v. Iowa,* argued together with *Crowl v. Pennsylvania,* 242 U.S. 153 (1916).

480 **pattern for the future:** In his first six terms LDB wrote 146 majority opinions, an average of 24 per term, but he also wrote 33 dissents. This gave him a comparable output to Justice Day, who in a similar period wrote 180 opinions for the Court.

481 **five members of the Court:** Bickel and Schmidt, *Judiciary and Responsible Government,* 553.

481 **earlier in the term:** *New York Central Rail Road Co. v. White,* 243 U.S. 188 (1917).

481 **should determine policy:** *New York Central Rail Road Co. v. Winfield,* 244 U.S. 147, 148–49 (1917).

482 **"injuries not covered by it":** *Id.,* at 163 (LDB dissenting). See the discussion of the case in Bickel and Schmidt, *Judiciary and Responsible Government,* 553–58.

482 **"laid me low":** Brandeis-Frankfurter Conversations, 10 August 1923.

483 **illustrated this divide:** *Adams v. Tanner,* 244 U.S. 590 (1917).

483 **those seeking jobs:** *Brazee v. Washington,* 241 U.S. 340 (1916). In this case McReynolds spoke for the majority.

484 **banning of trading stamps:** *Rast v. Van Deman & Lewis Co.,* 240 U.S. 342 (1916).

484 **"system of living law":** *Adams,* 244 U.S. at 600 (LDB dissenting).

484 **the legislative wisdom:** See, for example, the dissents in *Jay Burns Baking Co. v. Bryan,* 264 U.S. 504 (1924); *New State Ice Co. v. Liebmann,* 285 U.S. 262 (1932); and *Liggett Co. v. Lee,* 288 U.S. 517 (1933), all discussed in subsequent chapters.

484 **"that would succeed him":** Bickel and Schmidt, *Judiciary and Responsible Government,* 607–8.

485 **"sin of ignorance":** Case file, LDB-SC. Justice Joseph McKenna did not join LDB's opinion, but dissented separately in one sentence: "Under the decisions of this court—some of them so late as to require no citation or review—the law in question is a valid exercise of the police power of the state, directed against a demonstrated evil."

485 **the nation's railroads:** *Wilson v. New,* 243 U.S. 332 (1917). Chief Justice White spoke for the majority that expanded federal powers under the Commerce Clause in an emergency, while the four dissenters—Day, Pitney, McReynolds, and Van Devanter—argued that the clause gave the federal government supremacy over the states, but not over individuals or private companies.

485 **for immoral purposes:** *Caminetti v. United States,* 242 U.S. 470 (1917).

485 **but did not write:** See, for example, *Clyde Steamship Co. v. Walker,* 244 U.S. 255 (1917); and *Green v. Louisville & Interurban Railroad Co.,* 244 U.S. 499 (1917).

485 **"characteristic of this age":** Laski to LDB, 8 April 1917.

485 **going on the bench:** *William Filene's Sons Co. v. Weed,* 245 U.S. 597 (1918); and *United States v. United Shoe Machinery Co.,* 247 U.S. 32 (1918).

486 **dispute involving $1,000:** *Sears v. Akron,* 246 U.S. 242 (1918); *Omaechevarria v. Idaho,* 246 U.S. 343 (1918); and *Egan v. McDonald,* 246 U.S. 227 (1918).

486 **total set of facts:** *Chicago Board of Trade v. United States,* 246 U.S. 231, 238 (1918).

487 **which he favored:** See *American Column & Lumber Co. v. United States,* 257

U.S. 377, 413 (1921) (LDB dissenting); and *Maple Flooring Manufacturers Association v. United States,* 268 U.S. 563 (1925). See also LDB, "Competition That Kills," in *Business—a Profession* (Boston, 1914), 236–54. In the 1917 term LDB also filed a concurrence in *Boston Store v. American Graphophone Co.,* 246 U.S. 8, 27 (1918), in which he concurred with a decision holding a price agreement illegal under the Sherman Act. Although he disagreed with the policy, the Court's precedents required that finding, and relief would have to be found through legislative change of the antitrust laws.

487 **price maintenance agreements:** *Leegin Creative Leather Products v. PSKS,* 127 S.Ct. 2705 (2007), overturning the nearly century-old precedent of *Dr. Miles Medical Co. v. John Park & Sons,* 220 U.S. 373 (1911), a decision of which LDB disapproved because it condemned such agreements as violating the antitrust law.

487 **Child Labor Act of 1916:** *Hammer v. Dagenhart,* 247 U.S. 251 (1918). See Stephen B. Wood, *Constitutional Politics in the Progressive Era: Child Labor and the Law* (Chicago, 1958).

487 **by the federal government:** The Court had, in fact, unanimously approved state laws regulating child labor in *Sturges & Burns Manufacturing Co. v. Beauchamp,* 231 U.S. 325 (1913).

487 **"product of ruined lives":** *Hammer,* 247 U.S. at 280 (Holmes dissenting).

488 **workers not join a union:** *Hitchman Coal & Coke Co. v. Mitchell,* 245 U.S. 229 (1917).

488 **could not proscribe them:** *Adair v. United States,* 208 U.S. 161 (1908); and *Coppage v. Kansas,* 236 U.S. 1 (1915).

488 **hostility toward unions:** LDB's dissent is in *Hitchman Coal,* 245 U.S. at 263.

488 **entertained in federal court:** *Eagle Glass & Manufacturing Co. v. Rowe,* 245 U.S. 275, 284 (1917); Holmes and Clarke joined LDB's dissent.

488 **"jurisdictional scruples go":** Brandeis-Frankfurter Conversations, 28 June 1923.

489 **this caused problems:** *Id.,* 1 July 1922.

489 **speak with one voice:** *Id.,* 20 July 1922. Nor did he agree with the view that dissents "merely afford play to the vanity of the dissenting justice." Letter from Frederick S. Tyler, *American Bar Association Journal* 398 (1923).

489 **individual members as well:** Brandeis-Frankfurter Conversations, 28 June 1923. LDB related to Frankfurter that he had said this to Holmes, in protest against Holmes's ignoring a jurisdictional objection.

CHAPTER 20: EXTRAJUDICIAL ACTIVITIES: I

491 **Zionism in the United States:** For the fight over the congress, see Melvin I. Urofsky, *American Zionism from Herzl to the Holocaust* (Garden City, N.Y., 1975), chap. 5.

491 **leaders of the committee:** Wise had been invited to become rabbi of the prestigious Temple Emanu-El in New York, but had publicly turned down the offer when Louis Marshall and Jacob Schiff insisted that the trustees of the synagogue have the power to review the content of the rabbi's sermons. In protest he had founded the Free Synagogue. See Melvin I. Urofsky, *A Voice That Spoke for Justice: The Life and Times of Stephen S. Wise* (Albany, N.Y., 1982), chap. 4.

491 **after the war:** The speech is in Jacob de Haas, *Louis D. Brandeis: A Bio-graphical Sketch* (New York, 1929), 218–31.

492 **"ugly head in the United States":** Marshall to LDB, 14 February 1916, Marshall MSS; Schiff to LDB, 29 February 1916, Schiff MSS; *American Hebrew*, 3 March 1916.

492 **American Israel and democracy:** Urofsky, *Voice That Spoke for Justice,* 129ff.

492 **delegation got up and left:** A verbatim transcript of the meeting is in the *American Hebrew,* 21 July 1916; and most of the details are in the *New York Times,* 17 July 1916.

493 **"on the Jewish factions":** LDB to AGB, 16 July 1916.

493 **a verbal brawl:** Editorial, "Out of Place," *New York Times,* 18 July 1916.

493 **"has been made possible":** LDB to Pam, 21 July 1916. Jacob Schiff had earlier suggested to LDB that after his confirmation he ought to resign from his Zionist positions, believing that the resignation would be a great incentive to Jewish unity. Schiff to LDB, 29 February 1916, Schiff MSS.

493 **step down from Zionist leadership:** Yonathan Shapiro notes that while it may not be possible to "find direct evidence to prove that what occurred at the meeting was shrewdly prearranged, the indirect evidence is impressive." *Leadership of the American Zionist Organization, 1897–1930* (Urbana, Ill., 1971), 95.

493 **had all been planned:** De Haas to Louis Lipsky, 21 July 1916, de Haas MSS.

493 **until the two men met:** Marshall to LDB, 24 July 1916, Marshall MSS; LDB to Marshall, 8 September 1916.

493 **congress be delayed:** See Urofsky, *Voice That Spoke for Justice,* 153ff.

494 **two nations close to war:** *Boston Globe,* 9 August 1916; for the problems with Mexico, see Arthur S. Link, *Wilson: Confusions and Crises, 1915–1916* (Princeton, N.J., 1964), chap. 10. Apparently, Attorney General Gregory had suggested that Wilson tap LDB.

494 **home on Lake Placid:** LDB to Franklin Lane, to Robert Lansing, and to Edward White, telegrams, all 9 August 1916.

494 **on diplomatic missions:** Chief Justice Melville Fuller and Justice David Brewer served as boundary arbitrators between Great Britain and Venezuela in 1897, and John Harlan I was on the Fur Seal arbitration. Stephen Field, a former California judge, served on the commission that revised that state's laws. In 1930, Hoover named Justice Day to the American-German claims commission, while Willis Van Devanter was the American arbitrator in a dispute with Great Britain over the seizure of a ship. Alpheus T. Mason, *Harlan Fiske Stone: Pillar of the Law* (New York, 1956), 704n. Justice Owen J. Roberts would head the commission that investigated the Japanese attack on Pearl Harbor, and earlier served on a Mexican claims commission. Robert H. Jackson would be the chief American prosecutor at the trial of Nazi leaders at Nuremberg, and Chief Justice Earl Warren would lead the inquiry into the assassination of John Kennedy.

494 **"important additional task":** LDB to Wilson, 14 August 1916; LDB to White, 14 August 1916.

494 **gave them his response:** LDB to Frank Walsh, 23 August 1916, LDB-HLS.

495 " 'one of my own people' ": LDB to AGB, 13 August 1916.

495 **recruiting new members:** See, for example, LDB to Harry Friedenwald, 15 September 1916.

495 **through new legislation:** LDB to AGB, 29 June 1916.

495 **appointment to the FTC:** Johnson to LDB, 8 March 1918; LDB to Thompson, 12 December 1918, Thompson MSS.

495 **Laski, and their friends:** LDB to AGB, 9 March 1917, EBR; LDB to AGB, 20 July and 2 September 1917. Judge Learned Hand often came down to Washington and, when he did, would try to meet with LDB. After one meeting he wrote: "I never had so much pleasure in my meetings with you as yesterday. I have not yet straightened out what I think about it. When I do, you may hear from me." Hand to LDB, 18 November 1918, Hand MSS.

496 **Gregory did with Brandeis:** LDB to AGB, 10 July 1917.

496 **let the company off easily:** Brown to LDB, 11 July 1917.

496 **"sympathy with the suffering":** LDB to AGB, 31 July 1914 and 21 July 1915.

496 **"one hundred years":** Evans to AGB, 4 April 1935, Evans MSS.

497 **the world disarmed:** LDB, "An Essential of Lasting Peace," *National Economic League Quarterly* 1 (May 1915), 24–26; the piece also appeared in *Harper's Weekly,* 13 March 1915, 250, and *The Curse of Bigness* (New York, 1934), 267–69.

497 **"dine with me this evening":** Belle Case La Follette and Fola La Follette, *Robert M. La Follette,* 2 vols. (New York, 1953), 1:633.

497 **had been justified:** LDB to Alfred Brandeis, 14 October 1917; LDB had read Henry Wickham Steed's *Hapsburg Monarchy* (New York, 1913), as well as some writings by Tomáš Masaryk, the intellectual and patriot who would become the first president of the new Czech Republic in 1918.

497 **the nation's soul:** See, for example, Alan Dawley, *Changing the World: American Progressives in War and Revolution* (Princeton, N.J., 2003); and David W. Levy, *Herbert Croly of the "New Republic": The Life and Thought of an American Progressive* (Princeton, N.J., 1985), chap. 8. The philosopher John Dewey initially supported the war as a spur to higher social goals, but later changed his mind. See the critique of Dewey and other pro-war reformers in Randolph Bourne, *War and the Intellectuals: Essays, 1915–1919* (New York, 1964). Bourne compared so-called pragmatists who wanted to use the war for certain ends and guide its course to a child riding on an elephant.

497 **"manifold proposals":** LDB to Susan Brandeis, 15 April 1917, LDB-BU.

497 **social irresponsibility:** LDB to Zimmern, 21 July 1917, Zimmern MSS.

497 **Anglo-German situation:** LDB to AGB, 19 June 1918.

498 **to send to Russia:** McAdoo to Wilson, 17 April 1917, in Arthur S. Link et al., eds., *The Papers of Woodrow Wilson,* 69 vols. (Princeton, N.J., 1966–1984), 42:80–81. LDB recommended Eugene Meyer, but Edward House, who himself on several occasions came to seek LDB's opinion, worked to undercut the recommendation. House to Wilson, 2 May 1917, in *id.,* 42:194–95. In the end Meyer received the appointment only to have it withdrawn. Robert Lansing to Wilson, 3 May 1917, in *id.,* 42:204.

498 **at any time:** Baker to Wilson, 18 June 1917, in *id.,* 42:533. LDB even gave Baker some advice on a military campaign, and the secretary said he would take it to his strategists. LDB to AGB, 24 July 1918.

498 **read and approved it:** Baker to Wilson, 7 September 1917, enclosing Frankfurter to Baker, 4 September 1917, in Link et al., *Papers of Wilson,* 44:161–64.

498 **to Stoneleigh Court:** See the letters from LDB to AGB during 1917 and 1918 in Melvin I. Urofsky and David W. Levy, eds., *The Family Letters of Louis D. Brandeis* (Norman, Okla., 2002). LDB also met from time to time with Edward Hurley, named to coordinate U.S. shipping, and with Winthrop Daniels, whom Wilson had asked to look into the matter of providing public utilities with rate relief from the problem of soaring fuel costs. See Hurley to Wilson, 12 March 1918, in Link et al., *Papers of Wilson,* 46:610; and Daniels to Wilson, 2 September 1918, in *id.,* 49:420–22.

498 **"you will be prudent":** Dunbar to LDB, 15 October 1917, LDB-BU.

499 **"is so much sought":** AGB to Susan Goldmark, 20 April 1918.

499 **powerful government agency:** Wilson's changing views on his constitutional authority are explored in Daniel D. Stid, *The President as Statesman: Woodrow Wilson and the Constitution* (Lawrence, Kans., 1998).

499 **"measureless misfortune":** LDB to McAdoo, 23 November 1918, McAdoo MSS.

500 **concurred separately:** *Northern Pacific Railway v. North Dakota,* 250 U.S. 135 (1919); see below, pp. 555–56.

500 **dispatch to Europe:** LDB to Edward M. House, 9 January 1918. Ironically, House, who had been sent to seek LDB's advice, seems to have resented the fact that after their meeting LDB followed up with other suggestions on organization of the War Department. House Diary, 23 February 1918, in Link et al., *Papers of Wilson,* 46:429–30. Moreover, just a few weeks later House once again approached Brandeis seeking his evaluation of a plan by General George Washington Goethals. LDB to House, 3 March 1918, House MSS.

501 **coordination of industry:** For the WIB, see Robert D. Cuff, *The War Industries Board* (Baltimore, 1973), esp. chap. 5. The model of the WIB for the New Deal is articulated in William E. Leuchtenburg, "The New Deal and the Analogue of War," in John Braeman et al., eds., *Change and Continuity in Twentieth Century America* (Columbus, Ohio, 1965), 81–144.

501 **early months of the war:** It is rather strange to find LDB saying a decade later and rather offhandedly, "Perhaps you had in mind my introducing Hoover to the Wilson administration." LDB to Felix Frankfurter, 13 February 1929, FF-LC. There is no contemporary record of his doing this.

501 **"for anything practically":** LDB to AGB, 10 July 1918.

501 **might be president:** "Hoover came in at 9 p.m. to advise with me on a matter of international importance which occupied much time." LDB to AGB, 21 June 1918. Hoover frequently sent over his secretary, Lewis L. Strauss, to get LDB's opinion on particular matters.

501 **Lever Food Control Act:** LDB to Norman Hapgood, 21 July 1917, in Alpheus T. Mason, *Brandeis: A Free Man's Life* (New York, 1946), 520. LDB told Mason of the meeting with Hoover and his suggestion that he talk to Reed. Mason also credits Brandeis with bringing Hoover to the attention of Wilson, although many people in Washington knew of Hoover's success in Belgium.

501 **from organization to appointments:** "Was with President half hour on I.C.C. nominations." LDB to AGB, 30 August 1917.

502 **the rights of labor:** Robert W. Woolley to Wilson, reporting on conversations with LDB, 30 March 1918, in Link et al., *Papers of Wilson,* 47:210.

502 **director general of labor:** Woolley and Hale to Wilson, 19 April 1918, in *id.,* 47:376–78.

502 **"at this juncture":** Woolley to Wilson, 25 April 1918, and Wilson to Woolley, 27 April 1918, in *id.,* 47:425, 449.

502 **of getting him off:** Woolley, who seemed fixated on the idea, then wrote back with a harebrained proposal: The Court would soon end its term and go on summer recess, not meeting again until the first Monday in October. LDB could be "drafted" for the post of labor czar from June through September, by which time he would have organized the post and gotten everything under control, and then rejoin the Court. Woolley to Wilson, 29 April 1918, in *id.,* 47:467.

502 **"stay where he is":** Wise, "Justice Brandeis," sermon delivered following LDB's death, Wise MSS.

502 **"if it has already been":** LDB to Frankfurter, 19 November 1916, FF-LC.

503 **"work for you ahead":** LDB to Frankfurter, 25 November 1916, FF-LC.

503 **"I mean this literally":** Michael E. Parrish, *Felix Frankfurter and His Times: The Reform Years* (New York, 1982), 28. Parrish's book is the single best source for Frankfurter's pre-Court career.

503 **legal affairs correspondent:** During this time LDB's relations with the editors of the journal had reached the point where he frequently sent Herbert Croly suggestions for editorials and news stories. See Levy, *Croly,* 203; Croly to LDB, 21 September 1918 and 29 January 1919.

504 **in current value:** See David W. Levy and Bruce Allen Murphy, "Preserving the Progressive Spirit in a Conservative Time: The Joint Reform Efforts of Justice Brandeis and Professor Felix Frankfurter, 1916–1933," 78 *Michigan Law Review* 1252 (1980), which is a well-balanced appraisal of the relationship; and Bruce Allen Murphy, *The Brandeis/Frankfurter Connection: The Secret Political Activities of Two Supreme Court Justices* (New York, 1982), a highly sensationalistic work.

504 **heard in the Court:** *Stettler v. O'Hara,* 243 U.S. 629 (1917).

504 **Brandeis actually said:** One could follow Murphy's charges in *The Brandeis/Frankfurter Connection,* and read the actual letters in Melvin I. Urofsky and David W. Levy, eds., *"Half Brother, Half Son": The Letters of Louis D. Brandeis to Felix Frankfurter* (Norman, Okla., 1991), to see how distorted the charges appear.

504 **accusations and rebuttals:** See, for example, *New York Times,* 14 February 1982, 1. A complete list of law review and non-law articles about the Murphy book can be found in Gene Teitelbaum, *Justice Louis D. Brandeis: A Bibliography of Writings and Other Materials on the Justice* (Littleton, Colo., 1988), chaps. 2 and 5.

505 **"violates ethical standards":** Editorial, *New York Times,* 18 February 1982. Murphy's book also detailed Frankfurter's more overt political activities while on the bench. He, of course, did not have a Frankfurter of his own to act for him. In addition, LDB's near-saintly status made his alleged sins far greater in the eyes of people who claimed to have been betrayed.

505 **costs of his public work:** Robert Cover, "The Framing of Justice Brandeis," *New Republic,* 5 May 1982, 20.

505 **bothered neither of them:** Parrish, *Frankfurter,* 210.

505 **mattered to them both:** Murphy makes a number of accusations, most of which prove to be unsustainable on closer examination. For example, he takes the story of LDB's meeting with Hoover and suggesting that he meet with Reed as the reason that the Lever Act passed. There is no evidence of whether Hoover actually met with Reed, and certainly none that by making this suggestion, LDB caused the Lever Act to come into existence. Murphy then chastises LDB for sitting on a case involving a challenge to the law, *United States v. Cohen Grocery,* 255 U.S. 81 (1921), in which one section was held unconstitutional. LDB also approved the idea of the government's taking over the railroads and then took part in *Northern Pacific Railway v. North Dakota ex rel. Langer,* 250 U.S. 135 (1919), which sustained the takeover. Throughout the book Murphy ascribes enormous power to LDB; if the justice approved of an idea, then he must be held responsible should others implement that idea.

One of the most balanced reviews of the Murphy book is by a former student of Frankfurter's and a Brandeis law clerk, Nathaniel L. Nathanson, "The Extra-judicial Activities of Supreme Court Justices: Where Should the Line Be Drawn?" 78 *Northwestern Law Review* 494 (1983). See also David J. Danelski, "The Propriety of Brandeis's Extrajudicial Conduct," in Nelson L. Dawson, ed., *Brandeis and America* (Lexington, Ky., 1989), 11–37, which explores changing standards of judicial conduct.

506 **rallied around him:** The evolution of the Document can be followed in Link et al., *Papers of Wilson,* starting with a note from Wilson to LDB, 20 June 1921, at 67:319–20, and concluding with the final draft, 20 January 1924, at 68:535–43.

506 **to write sections:** Colby had been a Republican, but in 1916 rallied former Roosevelt supporters to Wilson's cause; he served as Wilson's last secretary of state, and he and Wilson opened a short-lived law practice after Wilson left the White House. Chadbourne, a New York attorney, had been prominent in Democratic circles and a confidant of Wilson's. Houston had served in both Wilson terms as secretary of agriculture. Bernard Baruch, a Wall Street financier, had been an early backer of Wilson's and headed the War Industries Board. Baker had been Wilson's secretary of war during the preparedness campaign and during the war.

506 **world leadership:** Enclosed in Wilson to LDB, 20 June 1921.

507 **ideas and policies:** Wilson to LDB, 7 January 1922; Wilson to Colby, 11 April 1922, Wilson MSS.

508 **judicial propriety:** There is nothing in the Brandeis Papers to suggest that he had any qualms about undertaking such an assignment, possibly because he did not know Wilson's plans for using it.

508 **"the end has come":** AGB to Elizabeth Evans, 26 February 1917, others n.d., but in 1917 and 1918, Evans MSS.

508 **"like he was a baby":** William Sutherland interview, Paper MSS.

509 **of their offspring:** Pauline Fass, *The Damned and the Beautiful: American Youth in the 1920s* (New York, 1977). I am greatly indebted to David Levy for this suggestion. However, Charles Tachau, a grandson of Alfred's, described her when she was a married woman as seemingly "very unconcerned with her appearance." Tachau interview, Paper MSS.

509 **"fine accomplishment":** LDB to Susan Brandeis, 29 September 1916,

LDB-BU. LDB did, however, caution her that while a woman could practice law, she would be shut out of the profitable work involving important business transactions. LDB to Susan Brandeis, 10 November 1914, LDB-BU.

510 **since the 1870s:** These notes are available in LDB-BU.

510 **"of obiter dicta":** LDB to Susan Brandeis, 16 May 1917, LDB-BU.

510 **"at the law school":** LDB to Susan Brandeis, 15 November 1916 and 14 May 1917, LDB-BU; cf. LDB to Thomas F. Bayard Sr., 17 May 1890, Bayard MSS.

510 **much difference later:** LDB to Susan Brandeis, 11 April 1917, LDB-BU. Although Susan saved many of the letters her father wrote to her, he did not save hers or, what is more likely, destroyed them in his last years when he burned a number of family letters. One must infer some of what Susan told him from his response, and fortunately it was his habit to repeat an incoming statement before responding to it.

511 **in fact a son:** LDB to Susan Brandeis, 15 April 1917, LDB-BU.

511 **"study and experience":** LDB to Susan Brandeis, 14 May 1917, LDB-BU.

511 **what she thought of it:** Susan claimed to have been converted to pacifism after meeting with Rosika Schwimmer in 1914. Susan Gilbert to Oliver Wendell Holmes, 3 June 1929, LDB-BU. The occasion of the letter was Holmes's eloquent dissent in *United States v. Schwimmer,* 279 U.S. 644 (1929), a dissent in which her father joined.

511 **reflect back on him:** LDB to Susan Brandeis, 11 April 1917, LDB-BU.

511 **Magnus Block Rosenberg:** Little is known about Rosenberg. He received an undergraduate degree from the University of Chicago in 1915 and completed his law degree in 1917. It is possible that he then entered law practice in Chicago with his brother Harry, who had finished law school two years earlier. Kristi L. Ovist (University of Chicago reference librarian) to author, 24 February 1999.

512 **agreed to the plan:** LDB to Susan Brandeis, 16 and 31 May 1917, LDB-BU.

512 **be what Susan needed:** LDB to AGB, 24 June 1917.

512 **"can only be sorry":** LDB to Susan Brandeis, 5 July 1917; LDB to AGB, 9 July 1917, LDB-BU.

513 **ultimately be hers:** LDB to Susan Brandeis, 9 July 1917, LDB-BU.

513 **"which is rare":** LDB to AGB, 25 July 1918.

513 **"intellectual prowess":** Tachau interview, Paper MSS.

513 **"as you are giving us":** LDB to Elizabeth Brandeis, 23 April 1918, LDB-BU.

514 **nearly 700,000:** LDB to Susan Brandeis, 5 and 14 November 1918, LDB-BU. For the devastation caused by the disease, see Alfred Crosby, *America's Forgotten Pandemic: The Influenza of 1918* (Cambridge, U.K., 1989).

514 **"The Living Law":** LDB to Susan Brandeis, 14 November 1918, LDB-BU.

CHAPTER 21: ZIONISM, 1917–1921

515 **"a legally secured home":** Stephen Wise to Morgenthau, 26 October 1914, Morgenthau MSS. Similar statements from other American Jewish leaders can be found in Joseph Rappaport, "Jewish Immigrants and World War I: A Study of American Yiddish Press Reactions" (Ph.D. diss., Columbia University, 1951), 132–34.

516 **"bathes in Jewish blood":** *Jewish Daily News,* 12 August 1914; Rappaport, "Jewish Immigrants and World War I," 75, 98.

516 **the Middle East:** Assimilated English Jews like Edwin Montagu opposed the idea and held up a draft declaration for several months. See Montagu, "The Anti-Semitism of the Present Government," 23 August 1917, and "Zionism," 9 October 1917, Foreign Office Records. There was also a strong strand of Christian Zionism among high-ranking members of the government; see R. H. S. Crossman, "Gentile Zionism and the Balfour Declaration," *Commentary* 33 (June 1962), 487–94. The standard work on the British decision remains Leonard Stein, *The Balfour Declaration* (New York, 1961), but see also Isaiah Friedman, *The Question of Palestine: British-Jewish-Arab Relations, 1914–1918,* 2nd expanded ed. (New Brunswick, N.J., 1992), and Evyatar Friesel, *The Balfour Declaration in Historical Perspective* (Rondebosch, South Africa, 1988).

517 **with the administration:** LDB to Weizmann, 8 December 1915, Weizmann MSS; Stephen Wise to House, 29 January 1917, Wise MSS.

517 **outrightly anti-Semitic:** The most explicit statement of this view is Selig Adler, "The Palestine Question in the Wilson Era," *Jewish Social Studies* 10 (1948), 303–34.

517 **after the war:** Weizmann to LDB, 8 April 1917, Weizmann MSS; Wise to Jacob de Haas, 9 April 1917, de Haas MSS.

517 **Zionists as well:** Weizmann did not understand the American form of government in which the judiciary stood independent of the administration. In England the government included the lord chief justice, who at times would undertake special assignments for the prime minister.

517 **into that quagmire:** Neither LDB nor Weizmann knew that in January 1916 the British and the French had signed the Sykes-Picot Agreement, carving up the Ottoman Empire after the war, with much of Palestine in a special international zone. Under Weizmann's prodding the British began rethinking that arrangement.

517 **to each other:** Balfour later told his niece Blanche Dugdale that LDB "was the most remarkable man I met in the United States."

517 **wanted British control:** LDB repeated this view to Sir Eric Drummond, who reported it to Balfour on 24 April 1917, Foreign Office Records.

518 **American endorsement:** Ronald Graham to Lord Hardinge, 23 April 1917, Foreign Office Records; Rothschild to LDB, cable, 25 April 1917; Weizmann, Rothschild, and Joseph Cowen to PEC, 30 April 1917; Stein, *Balfour Declaration,* 426.

518 **calm the French:** LDB, memorandum of meeting with Wilson, 6 May 1917, de Haas MSS.

518 **soon be announced:** LDB to Weizmann, 6 May 1917, and to Norman Hapgood, 14 May 1917, Weizmann MSS; LDB to James de Rothschild, 17 May 1917, London Office.

518 **Wilson administration cared:** See, among others, Jacob A. Rubin, *Partners in State Building: American Jewry and Israel* (New York, 1969), 56; Herbert Parzen, "Brandeis and the Balfour Declaration," *Herzl Year Book* 5 (1963), 328; Ben Halpern, "Brandeis and the Origins of the Balfour Declaration," manuscript. Some of this criticism echoes the charges that American Jewry failed the Jewish people during the Holocaust.

518 **have been in vain:** Although one should not dismiss British idealism, the

most exhaustive study of British policy at this time makes it quite clear that above all else, His Majesty's Government acted out of self-interest. Friedman, *Question of Palestine.*

519 **peace with the Allies:** This hope lay behind the bizarre Morgenthau mission of 1917, in which the former ambassador believed he could persuade the sultan to come to terms with the United States. Morgenthau never got beyond Paris when the whole fiasco petered out. For details, see *Trial and Error: The Autobiography of Chaim Weizmann* (New York, 1949), 196–99; Felix Frankfurter with Harlan B. Phillips, *Felix Frankfurter Reminisces* (New York, 1960), 151 (LDB sent Frankfurter along to make sure that Morgenthau did nothing to harm Zionist interests in Palestine); and William Yale, "Ambassador Morgenthau's Special Mission of 1917," *World Politics* 1 (April 1948), 308–20. Morgenthau came to believe that Zionist interference had thwarted his mission, and he became an avowed anti-Zionist.

519 **do and say nothing:** LDB to Lansing, 2 June 1917, State Department Records. Wilson had previously reasserted his support for a Jewish homeland to Rabbi Stephen Wise; see Wise, *Challenging Years* (New York, 1949), 189. In his memoirs, Secretary of the Navy Josephus Daniels recalled that Wilson had a real commitment to the Balfour Declaration, and saw it as not only the rebirth of the Jewish people but (and here the wording is positively Brandeisian) "the birth also of our new ideals, of new ethical values, of new conceptions of social justice which shall spring as a blessing for all mankind from that land and that people." Daniels, *The Wilson Era: Years of War and After, 1917–1923* (Chapel Hill, N.C., 1946), 219–20.

519 **Zionists into confusion:** Minutes of War Cabinet meeting, 3 September 1917, and House to Sir Eric Drummond, for Lord Robert Cecil, 10 September 1917, Foreign Office Records.

520 **"sympathy with declaration":** It is impossible to tell from the evidence whether LDB saw Wilson again at this time, or whether House, convinced by the justice, checked with Wilson and secured his approval of the LDB cable to Weizmann, 24 September 1917, Weizmann MSS.

520 **minor change in wording:** Weizmann to Harry Sachar, 18 September 1917, LDB to Weizmann, 26 September 1917, and Weizmann to LDB, 7 and 10 October 1917, all in Weizmann MSS; Weizmann to LDB, two cables, 19 September 1917; Weizmann to Jacob de Haas and E. W. Lewin-Epstein, 20 September 1917, and LDB to de Haas, 17 October 1917, de Haas MSS; LDB to House, 24 September 1917, House MSS; Balfour to House, 6 October 1917, Foreign Office Records.

520 **"achievement of this object":** The letter went on to state: "It being clearly understood that nothing shall be done which may prejudice the civil and religious rights of existing non-Jewish communities in Palestine or the rights and political status enjoyed by Jews in any other country."

520 **"the bear was caught":** De Haas to Weizmann, 13 December 1917, Weizmann MSS. For reaction in the Jewish press, see Charles Israel Goldblatt, "The Impact of the Balfour Declaration in America," *American Jewish Historical Quarterly* 57 (1968), 476–80. Non-Zionists received the news more with anger than with joy; see Melvin I. Urofsky, *American Zionism from Herzl to the Holocaust* (Garden City, N.Y., 1975), 200–204.

520 **" 'Money & Members'?":** LDB to Regina Goldmark, 20 December 1917, EBR; LDB to de Haas, [20] December 1917.

520 **proclaim its support publicly:** Wilson to Stephen Wise, 31 August 1918, *New York Times,* 5 September 1918.

521 **to accompany Weizmann:** Nahum Sokolow, Weizmann, and Yehial Tschlenow to LDB, 10 January 1918, Foreign Office Records; Jacob de Haas to Copenhagen Bureau, 3 February 1918, Copenhagen Office. There are indications that LDB consulted with Colonel House, who strongly advised not only against American participation on the commission but even against an advisory conference to meet in London prior to the commission's departure to Palestine.

521 **"for public utilities":** These ideas are similar to those he proposed for the development of Alaska; see LDB to Robert La Follette, 29 July 1911.

521 **"national development":** LDB to Weizmann, 13 January 1918, Weizmann MSS.

522 **upon their arrival:** Despite the devastation, Weizmann boldly laid the cornerstone for a new Hebrew University on Mount Scopus in Jerusalem, a step that fired the imagination of many. Felix Frankfurter, then in England, seized upon the university as the ideal opportunity to increase American influence in Palestine, but the key would be, as he told de Haas, "money, money, money. With that all other things will come to us." Michael E. Parrish, *Felix Frankfurter and His Times: The Reform Years* (New York, 1982), 140.

522 **to change its mind:** LDB promptly replied, "International situation definitely renders American membership on Commission impossible." LDB to Weizmann, 5 April 1918.

522 **several million dollars:** Nahum Sokolow to Sir Mark Sykes, 13 June 1918, Weizmann to LDB, 25 April 1918, Foreign Office Records; Weizmann to LDB, 17 June 1918, Weizmann MSS; Weizmann to LDB, 31 October 1918, London Office.

522 **technical and financial resources:** Aaronsohn to Weizmann, 25 September 1918, Weizmann MSS. By the time Weizmann received this letter, Wilson had already announced his support of the Balfour Declaration.

523 **tell Americans what to do:** See, for example, Lipsky to LDB, 30 December 1914.

523 **Americanized leaders:** See, for example, *Jewish Morning Journal,* 2 July 1918, quoted in Yonathan Shapiro, *Leadership of the American Zionist Organization, 1897–1930* (Urbana, Ill., 1971), 105.

524 **now had work to do:** *Maccabean,* July 1916, 161.

524 **"never understands them":** Nutter Diaries, 17 June 1916.

525 **events after the war:** LDB to Nathan D. Kaplan, 29 November 1915; *Maccabean,* August 1917, 311.

525 **specialized projects:** Minutes of meeting, PEC, 25 May 1918, de Haas MSS. For Hadassah, which eventually proved to be the most Brandeisian and the most successful Zionist organization in the United States, see Marlin Levin, *It Takes a Dream: The Story of Hadassah* (Jerusalem, 1997); and Hazel Krantz, *Daughter of My People: Henrietta Szold and Hadassah* (New York, 1987).

528 **Yiddish press ignored it:** The text of the ZOA constitution can be found in the *Maccabean,* August 1918, 258–60. For comments on the convention, see Meyer Berlin, "The Week in Pittsburgh," and Nachman Syrkin, "The Triumph of Social Democracy," *id.,* 124–28, 248–50.

528 **"as this one":** *Maccabean,* August 1918, 251–52.

528 **"Palestine is yours"**: Stein, *Balfour Declaration,* 595; Wilson statement, 3 March 1919, State Department Records; Bernard G. Richards Memoir, 89, OHRO. After the collapse of talks at the Hotel Astor meeting in July 1916, LDB and Marshall had worked out an arrangement that the congress would not meet until after hostilities ended (a condition reinforced by a State Department request after the United States entered the war), and that it would function only to the end of the peace conference. The American Jewish Committee and its allies thereupon joined the congress, and in fact the body elected Marshall as one of the commissioners to argue in Paris for Jewish rights.

529 **a Jewish homeland**: Morris Jastrow, *Zionism and the Future of Palestine: The Fallacies and Dangers of Political Zionism* (New York, 1919); "Appeal to the Representatives of the United States," January 1919, Bliss MSS; *New York Times,* 5 March 1919; Joseph L. Graybill, *Protestant Diplomacy and the Near East: Missionary Influence on American Foreign Policy, 1810–1927* (Minneapolis, 1971). For Zionism at the peace conference, see Urofsky, *American Zionism,* 214ff.

529 **on different governments**: See, for example, Stephen Wise and Julian Mack to Woodrow Wilson, 27 October 1920, State Department Records; LDB to Zionist Organization, 7 April 1920, London Office; Chaim Weizmann to Arthur Balfour, 2 July 1920, and LDB to Balfour, 28 October 1920, Foreign Office Records.

529 **"to break or alter"**: LDB to Wilson, 3 February 1920; Wilson to Lansing, 4 February 1920, in Arthur S. Link et al., eds., *The Papers of Woodrow Wilson,* 69 vols. (Princeton, N.J., 1966–1984), 64:358, 361.

529 **abreast of the situation**: See, for example, Frankfurter to LDB, 25 May 1919, FF-LC.

529 **contain the danger**: Wilson agreed to the King-Crane Commission in part because he had promised Arab leaders that no Middle East settlement would be made without consulting them. The commission visited thirty-six major towns, heard delegations from many more, and received almost nineteen hundred petitions, most opposing Zionist plans. Harry N. Howard, "An American Experiment in Peace Making: The King-Crane Commission," *Moslem World* 32 (1942), 124, 130.

529 **Zionists should do**: LDB to Frankfurter, 19 May and 5 June 1919, FF-LC; Frankfurter to LDB, two cables, 6 June 1919, and LDB to Frankfurter, 9 June 1919, Wise MSS.

529 **"comme il faut"**: "Ladylike and proper," LDB to AGB, 18 June 1919, EBR. Two days later Louis reported that Susan, who had planned on returning early, was now rethinking her plans. She "is not yet joyous, but the interest seems to be taking hold."

530 **London School of Economics**: LDB to AGB, 22 June 1919, LDB-UL. Weizmann's initial response to LDB was also positive, and the American struck him as messianic. For Weizmann's later recollections, colored by the bitter strife between the two men, see *Trial and Error,* 248.

530 **"world of gloom"**: LDB to AGB, 24 and 25 June 1919, LDB-UL.

530 **to have the mandate**: Memorandum of interview, dictated by Frankfurter, 24 June 1919, London Office.

530 **of the Holy Land**: Jacob de Haas, *Louis D. Brandeis: A Biographical Sketch* (New York, 1929), 114.

530 **usual delays in port:** "We are moving on as planned, with no greater annoyance than the passport and permit regulations which survived the war intact. They are enough to make a pacifist or internationalist out of the most belligerent of mortals, but the East and the heat make man patient and a fatalist." LDB to Susan Brandeis, 3 July 1919, LDB-BU.

531 **"there would be hope":** LDB to AGB, 1 July 1919, LDB-UL. See letters to Alice, Susan, Elizabeth, and Alfred in Melvin I. Urofsky and David W. Levy, eds., *The Family Letters of Louis D. Brandeis* (Norman, Okla., 2002), 336–52.

531 **found in Cairo:** LDB to Susan Brandeis, 3 July 1919, LDB-BU.

532 **"indeed a Holy Land":** LDB to AGB, 10 July 1919, LDB-UL.

532 **and other matters:** See William E. Smythe, "Justice Brandeis in Palestine," *American Review of Reviews,* December 1919, 609–16.

532 **"mainly sweet nothings":** LDB to AGB, 8 August 1919, LDB-UL.

532 **commitment to Zion:** LDB to Chaim Weizmann, 20 July 1919, Weizmann MSS; de Haas, *Brandeis,* 116; *Boston Post,* 25 June 1923; Robert Szold, *77 Great Russell Street* (privately printed, 1967), 9.

532 **the Jewish people:** There is no record that LDB visited any Arab or Bedouin communities or spoke with any Arabs. He had, of course, gone to Palestine to see the Jewish community and, like most other Zionists of this time, ignored the Arabs in Palestine. In addition, the Arab community in Palestine had always been seen as an adjunct to larger political entities who claimed governance of it, and there were few if any local "leaders" who could have spoken out for the wishes of the Arab residents. Arab nationalism was certainly germinating at this time, but it would have taken someone very familiar with the area and its people to have discerned it, knowledge that LDB did not have.

532 **two episodes:** ZOA press release, translating report of Dr. Auerbach, 12 September 1919, Berlin Office; Henrietta Szold to her family, 14 September 1920, in Marvin Lowenthal, *Henrietta Szold: Life and Letters* (Westport, Conn., 1975), 146–47.

533 **"Jews here and elsewhere":** Quoted in LDB to AGB, 1 August 1919, LDB-UL.

533 **"bit of my fluency":** LDB to AGB, 8 August 1919, LDB-UL.

534 **"in Jewish soul":** De Haas, *Brandeis,* 119–20.

535 **proved extremely effective:** The Zionists also secured an additional $200,000 for the Hadassah mission from the American Jewish Joint Distribution Committee.

535 **every step of the way:** LDB to Kesselman, 15 December 1919, de Haas MSS.

536 **frustrating to Brandeis:** Bernard Rosenblatt interview, Hebrew University Oral History Collection; Julius Simon to Benjamin I. Brodie, 14 November 1964, and Brodie to Simon, 8 December 1964, Brodie MSS. Menachem Ussischkin was the official representative of the Actions Committee in Jerusalem, and thus technically in charge of all Zionist programs there. LDB also rejected a proposal that he go onto a restructured WZO executive of seven men.

537 **"the undertaking demands":** "The Upbuilding of Palestine," in de Haas, *Brandeis,* 233–34.

537 **over a "talkfest":** See the sympathetic treatment by Julius Simon, *Certain Days: Zionist Memoirs and Selected Papers* (Jerusalem, 1971), chap. 13.

537 **Brandeis refused:** Although there had been some grumbling about LDB's leadership before, many in the American delegation almost broke away at this decision, and only LDB's personal intervention forced the delegates to yield to his motion that no American accept any position other than the honorary presidency, since that carried no responsibility. Alexander Sachs to Julian Mack, 22 July 1920, de Haas MSS.

537 **had to be revamped:** Interview with Emanuel Neuman; Louis Lipsky, *A Gallery of Zionist Profiles* (New York, 1956), 162; Bernard G. Richards Memoir, Hebrew University Oral History Collection; Felix Frankfurter to Weizmann, 15 July 1920, Weizmann MSS; Simon, *Certain Days,* 103; Statement of Justice Brandeis to American Delegation, 14 July 1920.

538 **opportunity at hand:** "The Zeeland Memorandum," in de Haas, *Brandeis,* 260–72.

539 **refused to follow:** Minutes of National Executive Committee, 29 August 1920, de Haas MSS.

539 **handed down from Washington:** For details of the growing schism, see Urofsky, *American Zionism,* 261–72.

539 **"necessary limitations":** LDB to de Haas, 16 September 1920; and to de Haas, 25 September 1920, de Haas MSS.

540 **break him politically:** Memorandum, "Negotiations Between Dr. Weizmann and the Zionist Organization of America," giving the chronology of meetings in April and May 1921, London Office.

540 **between Pinsk and Washington:** Weizmann to Mack, 24 April 1921, and reply, 25 April 1921, Weizmann MSS; memorandum of telephone conversation, LDB and Mack, 15 April 1921. LDB later met with Einstein and gave him information on Zionist affairs, but to no avail. Weizmann remained his leader. LDB to Einstein, 29 April 1921, Mack MSS.

540 **"not be worth having":** Stephen Wise to Felix Frankfurter, 18 April 1921, Wise MSS.

542 **"continuous zealous work":** *Report of the Proceedings of the 24th Annual Convention of the Zionist Organization of America* (New York, 1921), 119–21. On 19 June, LDB also resigned as honorary president of the WZO. See Harry Barnard, *The Forging of an American Jew: The Life and Times of Judge Julian Mack* (New York, 1974), chap. 33.

542 **"impose upon American Zionism":** S. M. Melamed, "L. D. Brandeis and Chaim Weizmann," *Reflex,* May 1928, 6; along this same line, see Lipsky, *Gallery of Profiles,* 153.

CHAPTER 22: WAR AND SPEECH — AND HOLMES

545 **"silent amidst arms":** LDB to AGB, 5 July 1918. The reference is to the Latin phrase *"inter arma silent leges,"* "during war laws are silent." William Sutherland was LDB's clerk for that term.

545 **affect the war program:** In the Lever Food Control Act of 1917, for example, the government authorized the food administrator to set maximum prices for certain foodstuffs and imposed fines for those who sold over that price. The Court struck down this provision for vagueness in *United States v. Cohen Grocery Store,* 255 U.S. 81 (1921). However, the Court narrowly upheld a wartime statute imposing rent control in the District of Columbia, *Block v. Hirsch,* 256 U.S. 135 (1921).

546 **upheld the law:** *Selective Draft Law Cases,* 245 U.S. 366 (1918).

546 **the Eighteenth Amendment:** For an overview of these laws and the Court's responses, see Melvin I. Urofsky and Paul Finkelman, *A March of Liberty,* 2nd ed. (New York, 2001), chap. 27.

546 **if that occurred:** *Hamilton v. Kentucky Distilleries & Warehouse Co.* (also known as the Wartime Prohibition Cases), 251 U.S. 146 (1919).

546 **more alcohol by volume:** For Prohibition, see Richard F. Hamm, *Shaping the Eighteenth Amendment: Temperance Reform, Legal Culture, and the Polity, 1880–1920* (Chapel Hill, N.C., 1995). For Prohibition, the Court, and LDB, see chap. 25.

547 **second-guess the legislature:** *Jacob Ruppert v. Caffey,* 251 U.S. 264 (1920).

547 **power to set rates:** *Northern Pacific Railway v. North Dakota,* 250 U.S. 135 (1919).

548 **presidential authority:** The lead case was *Dakota Central Telephone Co. v. South Dakota,* 250 U.S. 163 (1919).

548 **"to get things done":** Alexander M. Bickel and Benno C. Schmidt Jr., *The Judiciary and Responsible Government, 1910–1921* (New York, 1984), 517–18.

549 **overthrow the government:** A good overview of this remains Harry N. Scheiber, *The Wilson Administration and Civil Liberties* (Ithaca, N.Y., 1960). See also Paul L. Murphy, *World War I and the Origins of Civil Liberties in the United States* (New York, 1979).

549 **seemed more unsympathetic:** See David M. Rabban, *Free Speech in Its Forgotten Years* (New York, 1997).

549 **dismissed the case:** *Patterson v. Colorado,* 205 U.S. 454 (1907). Justice John Marshall Harlan wrote an impassioned dissent that contained a vigorous but undeveloped view of free speech under the First Amendment. See Rabban, *Free Speech,* 132–34.

550 **the speaker's words:** *Fox v. Washington,* 236 U.S. 273 (1915).

550 **"Wall Street's chosen few":** *Schenck v. United States,* 294 U.S. 47, 51 (1919).

550 ***Frohwerk v. United States*:** 249 U.S. 204 (1919). Frohwerk and others had been convicted of violating the Espionage Act by writing a series of articles in a Missouri German-language newspaper questioning the legality of the draft. Holmes admitted in his opinion that the material used to convict the men seemed scanty, but on the other hand there did not appear to be sufficient evidence to exonerate them either.

   Debs v. United States, 249 U.S. 211 (1919). The American Socialist Party leader Eugene V. Debs had been sentenced to ten years in prison for attempting to obstruct the conduct of the war by describing it as caused by capitalists, and he praised others who had been convicted of helping young men evade the draft.

550 **legislation to wartime:** Melvin I. Urofsky, "The Brandeis-Frankfurter Conversations," 1985 *Supreme Court Review* 299, 324.

551 **no authority to review:** *Sugarman v. United States,* 249 U.S. 182 (1919). The trial court judge had refused to submit the defendant's request for jury instructions regarding free speech in the exact form that the defendant had requested, and LDB held that this did not represent the type of substantial constitutional question required for review on a writ of error.

551 **"not through it":** Urofsky, "Brandeis-Frankfurter Conversations," 323–24. David Rabban finds this explanation less than satisfactory, claiming that

LDB still approved of the convictions and only questioned the legal theory supporting the conclusions. While it is true that in these conversations Frankfurter does not report LDB's saying the convictions should have been overturned, his later dissents on speech make it clear he would not support conviction on the grounds submitted in the initial decisions. Rabban, *Free Speech,* 363.

551 **existed in news:** *International News Service v. Associated Press,* 248 U.S. 215 (1918).

552 **provide the solution:** LDB had made a similar argument earlier that year in *Boston Store v. American Graphophone Co.,* 246 U.S. 8, 27–28 (LDB concurring).

552 **courts to do:** Bickel and Schmidt, *Judiciary and Responsible Government,* 701n.198.

552 **dissent for guidance:** See Learned Hand in *Cheney Bros. v. Doris Silk Corp.,* 35 F.2d 279 (2nd Cir. 1929). Bickel and Schmidt believe that although the dissent is not cited, the various majority opinions in the Pentagon Papers case, *New York Times Co. v. United States,* 403 U.S. 713 (1971), follow LDB's logic in the *International News Service* case. *Judiciary and Responsible Government,* 702.

552 *Abrams v. United States*: 250 U.S. 616 (1919).

552 **Russian Revolution:** For the case, see Richard Polenberg, *Fighting Faiths: The Abrams Case, the Supreme Court, and Free Speech* (New York, 1987).

553 **"This is fine—very":** *Id.,* 236.

553 **libertarians had applauded:** *Masses Publishing Co. v. Patten,* 244 Fed. 535 (S.D.N.Y. 1917); Gerald Gunther, *Learned Hand: The Man and the Judge* (New York, 1994), 161–67. In the appendix to "Learned Hand and the Origins of Modern First Amendment Doctrine," 27 *Stanford Law Review* 719 (1975), Gunther provides the texts of all the letters between Hand and Holmes, and between Hand and Zechariah Chafee, regarding free speech during the war era.

553 **initial decisions:** See, for example, the article by Ernst Freund, the University of Chicago law professor whom both LDB and Holmes greatly respected, "The Debs Case and Freedom of Speech," *New Republic,* 3 May 1919, reprinted in 40 *University of Chicago Law Review* 239 (1973).

553 **free speech in the United States:** Zechariah Chafee, "Freedom of Speech in Wartime," 32 *Harvard Law Review* 932 (1919).

553 **a 1920 dissent:** *Schaefer v. United States,* 251 U.S. 466, 482, 486 (1920) (LDB dissenting).

553 **listened carefully:** The meeting and how it came about are discussed in Fred D. Ragan, "Justice Oliver Wendell Holmes, Jr., Zechariah Chafee, Jr., and the Clear and Present Danger Test for Free Speech: The First Year, 1919," *Journal of American History* 58 (1971), 24–45.

553 **guise of patriotism:** Frankfurter to LDB, 20 October 1917. The fact that most of the workers belonged to the radical Industrial Workers of the World (IWW) further complicated matters.

553 **editors of the *Masses:*** Pinchot to LDB, 24 May 1918, enclosing his own letter of protest to President Wilson.

554 **clear his name:** Morison to LDB, 1 September 1918.

554 **Espionage Act prosecutions:** Charles F. Amidon to LDB, 5 August 1918; and George W. Anderson to LDB, 7 December 1918.

554 **violations of civil liberties:** For other examples, see David M. Rabban,

"The Emergence of Modern First Amendment Doctrine," 50 *University of Chicago Law Review* 1205, 1326–27 (1983).

555 **within the same hour:** The best account remains Robert K. Murray, *Red Scare* (Minneapolis, 1955), but see also William Preston, *Aliens and Dissenters: Federal Suppression of Radicals, 1903–1933,* 2nd ed. (Urbana, Ill., 1994); and Geoffrey R. Stone, *Perilous Times: Free Speech in Wartime* (New York, 2004), 220–26.

555 **"shame and sin should endure":** LDB to Susan Goldmark, 7 December 1919, EBR.

555 **"methods of oppresion":** Dean Acheson, *Morning and Noon* (Boston, 1965), 100.

555 **friend at Harvard Law:** For Chafee, see Donald L. Smith, *Zechariah Chafee, Jr.: Defender of Liberty and Law* (Cambridge, Mass., 1986).

556 **"would be a calamity":** LDB to Pound, 25 May 1919, Pound MSS.

556 **"as 'dangerous' as I was":** LDB to AGB, 13 and 14 June 1919, EBR. See also Felix Frankfurter with Harlan B. Phillips, *Felix Frankfurter Reminisces* (New York, 1960), 169–70.

556 **to fight back:** LDB to Pound, 26 April and 15 May 1920, Pound MSS.

556 **a bare 6–5 vote:** Arthur E. Sutherland, *The Law at Harvard: A History of Ideas and Men, 1817–1867* (Cambridge, Mass., 1967), 251–59; Michael E. Parrish, *Felix Frankfurter and His Times: The Reform Years* (New York, 1982), 126–27; Jerold S. Auerbach, "The Patrician as Civil Libertarian: Zechariah Chafee, Jr., and Freedom of Speech," *New England Quarterly* 42 (1969), 511.

556 **"struggle and of creation":** LDB to Chafee, 19 May 1921, Chafee MSS.

556 **in private practice:** LDB to Chafee, 5 June 1921, Chafee MSS.

556 **a pragmatic stance:** For one analysis of LDB's thought, as well as a review of his stance in cases involving speech, see Rabban, "Emergence of Modern First Amendment Doctrine," 1320–45.

557 **"war and following":** Urofsky, "Brandeis-Frankfurter Conversations," 324.

557 **"should precede judging":** *Jay Burns Baking Co. v. Bryan,* 264 U.S. 504, 520 (1924) (LDB dissenting).

557 **upheld the verdict:** *Schaefer v. United States,* 251 U.S. 466 (1920). Holmes joined LDB's dissent, while Justice Clarke dissented on separate grounds. He would have sent the case back to the trial court for rehearing.

558 **and free speech:** *Pierce v. United States,* 252 U.S. 239 (1920).

558 **"to their falsity":** *American School of Magnetic Healing v. McAnnuity,* 187 U.S. 94, 104 (1902).

560 **be the exception:** LDB: "The right to your education and to utter speech is fundamental *except* clear and present danger." Urofsky, "Brandeis-Frankfurter Conversations," 320.

560 **his *Abrams* opinion:** See, for example, Bradley Bobertz, "The Brandeis Gambit: The Making of America's 'First Freedom,' " 40 *William and Mary Law Review* 557, 632 (1999).

561 **clear-and-present-danger test:** *Gilbert v. Minnesota,* 254 U.S. 325 (1920). McKenna sent LDB a polite note stating, "We are in conflict," and LDB's arguments did not convince him any more than they had in *Schaefer.* McKenna to LDB, 27 November 1920, LDB-SC.

561 **during war:** This point failed to move Holmes at all. The statute was a "war

statute—it was passed and applied in time of war. It was none of the defendant's business whether it would or would not be applied in time of peace, or would or would not be repealed then." Oliver Wendell Holmes Jr. to Felix Frankfurter, 22 December 1920, in Robert H. Mennel and Christine Compston, eds., *Holmes and Frankfurter: Their Correspondence, 1912–1934* (Hanover, N.H., 1996), 99.

561 **"and enjoy property":** *Gilbert,* 254 at 343 (LDB dissenting).

562 **profession, and travel:** Urofsky, "Brandeis-Frankfurter Conversations," 320.

562 **a few years later:** *Meyer v. Nebraska,* 262 U.S. 390 (1923); and *Pierce v. Society of Sisters,* 268 U.S. 510 (1925); see chap. 25.

562 **not to the states:** *Barron v. Baltimore,* 32 U.S. 243 (1833).

562 **applied it to the states:** On this issue, see William E. Nelson, *The Fourteenth Amendment: From Political Principle to Judicial Doctrine* (Cambridge, Mass., 1988); and Akhil Reed Amar, *The Bill of Rights: Creation and Reconstruction* (New Haven, Conn., 1998).

563 **"I thought all wrong":** Holmes to Brandeis, n.d. (on Gilbert return), LDB-SC; Mark DeWolfe Howe, ed., *Holmes-Pollock Letters,* 2 vols. (Cambridge, Mass., 1941), 2:61.

563 **federal primacy:** *Johnson v. Maryland,* 254 U.S. 51 (1920).

563 **the jurisprudential road:** Chafee to Dean Acheson (then LDB's law clerk), 20 November 1920, LDB-SC; LDB to Frankfurter, 6 December 1920, FF-HLS; Rabban, "Emergence of Modern First Amendment Doctrine," 1343–44.

563 ***Milwaukee Leader* case:** *United States ex rel. Milwaukee Social Democratic Publishing Co. v. Burleson,* 255 U.S. 407 (1921).

563 **he deemed subversive:** Ronald Schaffer, *America in the Great War: The Rise of the Welfare State* (New York, 1991), 14.

564 **the Allies "improperly":** *New York Times,* 10 October 1917, cited in Philippa Strum, "Brandeis: The Public Activist and Freedom of Speech," 45 *Brandeis Law Review* 659, 691 (2007).

564 **"after fasting and prayer":** Holmes to LDB, 21 February 1921, LDB-SC; see also G. Edward White, *Justice Oliver Wendell Holmes: Law and the Inner Self* (New York, 1993), 437–38.

564 **"I gave it up":** Acheson to Frankfurter, 26 November 1921, FF-LC.

565 **"harmony between us":** Holmes to Pollock, 17 February 1928, in Howe, *Holmes-Pollock Letters,* 2:215. The case was *Casey v. United States,* 276 U.S. 413 (1928).

565 **"two votes instead of one":** Alpheus T. Mason, *William Howard Taft: Chief Justice* (New York, 1964), 220. In 1926, Taft wrote to one of his sons that Holmes "is not a great constitutional lawyer . . . but that is due to his training and point of view and influence which Brandeis has had on him." White, *Holmes,* 321.

565 **"glad that I did":** Holmes to Gray, 5 March 1921, quoted in White, *Holmes,* 319. On 5 November 1923 he wrote to Pollock, "I have interrupted myself at this point to consider a case in which Brandeis wants me to be ready with a dissent." Howe, *Holmes-Pollock Letters,* 2:124.

565 **affected his thought:** There is one social science analysis of Court votes that concludes that LDB led Holmes to a more "liberal" position while at the

same time reinforcing McReynolds's conservatism. Donald C. Leavitt, "Attitude Change on the Supreme Court, 1910–1920," *Michigan Academician* 4 (Summer 1971), 55–59.

565   "crown of his life": Laski to Holmes, 19 April 1924 and 28 May 1928, in Mark DeWolfe Howe, ed., *Holmes-Laski Letters,* 2 vols. (Cambridge, Mass., 1953), 2:812, 1060.

565   "They always rejoice me": Holmes to Frankfurter, 21 May 1921, in Mennel and Compston, *Holmes and Frankfurter Correspondence,* 116.

565   across the street: LDB to Frankfurter, 8 April 1922, FF-LC; Holmes to Frankfurter, 26 January 1924, in Mennel and Compston, *Holmes and Frankfurter Correspondence,* 168.

566   "after a talk with him": Holmes to Frankfurter, 15 February 1929, in Mennel and Compston, *Holmes and Frankfurter Correspondence,* 236. On another occasion he told Harold Laski, "Brandeis has always left me feeling happier about the world." Holmes to Laski, 8 May 1918, in Howe, *Holmes-Laski Letters,* 1:153.

566   "for U.S.A. and L.D.B.": LDB to Holmes, 8 March 1930, Holmes MSS.

566   "crowning point of it all": Holmes to Pollock, 31 October 1926, in Howe, *Holmes-Pollock Letters,* 2:191; Frankfurter to Holmes, 21 March and 23 May 1932, in Mennel and Compston, *Holmes and Frankfurter Correspondence,* 269, 271. The volume is Felix Frankfurter, ed., *Mr. Justice Brandeis* (New Haven, Conn., 1932).

566   improve with the years: Urofsky, "Brandeis-Frankfurter Conversations," 305–6.

566   "secretary ever has been": LDB to Frankfurter, 21 April 1929, FF-LC. Cf., however, "I made my adieux to Judge Holmes yesterday. It was sad to see him—with the work of the term over he relaxed and grew old overnight. A disillusionment like seeing the prima donna the next day in bright daylight with curlpins in dishabille." LDB to AGB, 15 June 1918.

566   "two of them would embrace": Mary Donnellan interview, Paper MSS.

566   of a free society: Pnina Lahav examines the roots of the two men's thoughts on speech, and concludes that Holmes essentially came at it from a negative or pessimistic viewpoint, while the optimistic Brandeis saw speech as a positive good. "Holmes and Brandeis: Libertarian and Republican Justifications for Free Speech," 4 *Journal of Law & Politics* 451 (1988).

567   his Greek poets: Holmes to Pollock, 26 May 1919, in Howe, *Holmes-Pollock Letters,* 2:13.

567   "sport with ideas": Holmes to Laski, 11 June 1920, in Howe, *Holmes-Laski Letters,* 1:268. Brandeis, who had admired Oriental art since his Harvard days, could never get Holmes interested in it. See, for example, Holmes to Pollock, 24 January 1919, in Howe, *Holmes-Pollock Letters,* 2:3. He did, however, occasionally give books to the older justice that he knew Holmes would like. "No Keynes for me just now," Holmes told Felix Frankfurter. "Brandeis has put me on to a book about Crete and I am absorbed." Holmes to Frankfurter, 20 February 1922, in Mennel and Compston, *Holmes and Frankfurter Correspondence,* 136.

567   "knowledge gives him": Holmes to Felix Frankfurter, 3 December 1925, in Mennel and Compston, *Holmes and Frankfurter Correspondence,* 194. "Brandeis has an insatiable appetite for facts and . . . I admire the gift and wish I had a barn in which I could store them for use at need. I hope they manure

my soil but they disappear in specie as soon as taken." Holmes to Harold Laski, 27 December 1925, in Howe, *Holmes-Laski Letters,* 2:810.

567 **he complained:** Paul Freund, "Mr. Justice Brandeis," in Allison Dunham and Philip Kurland, eds., *Mr. Justice* (Chicago, 1956), 186; Holmes to Harold Laski, 16 January 1918, in Howe, *Holmes-Laski Letters,* 1:128.

567 **English poets quite another:** Francis Biddle, "The Friendship of Holmes and Brandeis," *Atlantic Monthly,* December 1965, 87.

567 **the following week:** White, *Holmes,* 312. See Holmes's complaint when two of his opinions were held up. Holmes to Frederick Pollock, 26 November 1922, in Howe, *Holmes-Pollock Letters,* 2:106.

568 **hindsight of history:** G. Edward White, "The Canonization of Holmes and Brandeis: Epistemology and Judicial Reputations," 70 *New York University Law Review* 576 (1995); the "canonization" of LDB is treated at 596–616. The beloved Yankee from Olympus, Grant Gilmore charged, "was a myth concocted principally by Harold Laski and Felix Frankfurter. . . . The real Holmes was savage, harsh and cruel, a bitter and life-long pessimist who saw in the courts of human life nothing but a continuous struggle in which the rich and powerful impose their will on the poor and weak." *The Ages of American Law* (New Haven, Conn., 1977), 48–49.

568 **"of others to understand":** Urofsky, "Brandeis-Frankfurter Conversations," 306; see also John Lord O'Brian Memoir, 349, OHRO, reporting his conversations with several justices.

568 **he intuitively followed:** G. Edward White, *The American Judicial Tradition* (New York, 1976), 169. The most scathing attack on Holmes and his alleged lack of morals is Albert W. Alschuler, *Law Without Values: The Life, Work, and Legacy of Justice Holmes* (Chicago, 2000).

569 **scientist of the law:** Acheson, *Morning and Noon,* 96.

569 **"in his general view":** Quoted in Samuel Konefsky, *The Legacy of Holmes and Brandeis: A Study in the Influence of Ideas* (New York, 1956), 9.

569 **"I'm here to help":** Quoted in Mark Silverstein, *Constitutional Faiths: Felix Frankfurter, Hugo Black, and the Process of Judicial Decision Making* (Ithaca, N.Y., 1984), 44.

569 **"the problem at hand":** Quoted in Nelson L. Dawson, *Louis D. Brandeis, Felix Frankfurter, and the New Deal* (Hamden, Conn., 1980), 11–12.

569 **laboratories of reform:** "It is one of the happy incidents of the federal system that a single courageous state may, if its citizens choose, serve as a laboratory; and try novel social and economic experiments without risk to the rest of the country." *New State Ice Co. v. Liebmann,* 285 U.S. 262, 280, 311 (1932) (LDB dissenting). See below, text pp. 686–89.

569 **"what is life worth":** White, *Judicial Tradition,* 158.

569 **it would do no good:** LDB understood this, and later told John Lord O'Brian that Holmes believed in the end only power would rule. O'Brian Memoir, 350.

569 **"duty to the community":** *Duplex Printing Press Co. v. Deering,* 254 U.S. 443, 479, 488 (1921) (LDB dissenting).

CHAPTER 23: BRANDEIS AND TAFT

571 **"we would meet often":** LDB to AGB, 4 December 1918, EBR. During the war Taft had headed the War Labor Board, charged with settling labor

disputes that might affect war production, and had won plaudits from both labor and management for his fairness and his willingness to work with both sides to compromise. In that position he might well have learned about LDB's views on regularity of employment. The Taft visit is confirmed in William Sutherland interview, Paper MSS.

572 "aristocratic order": Melvin I. Urofsky, "The Brandeis-Frankfurter Conversations," 1985 *Supreme Court Review* 302–3.

572 "all happiness for him": Felix Frankfurter with Harlan B. Phillips, *Felix Frankfurter Reminisces* (New York, 1960), 85. Frankfurter had written an unsigned editorial that reaffirmed liberal belief not only that Taft had been a bad president but that he had few qualifications to sit upon the Supreme Court. All one could expect, he lamented, was that there would be one more conservative, antilabor vote on the high court. "Mr. Chief Justice Taft," *New Republic*, 27 July 1921, 230–31.

573 "under a just God": Quoted in Robert C. Post, "William Howard Taft," in Melvin I. Urofsky, ed., *Biographical Encyclopedia of the Supreme Court* (Washington, D.C., 2006), 525.

573 open to argument: Urofsky, "Brandeis-Frankfurter Conversations," 313, 320.

573 together on the bench: Taft also consulted LDB on the action he had taken to replace the deputy clerk before all of the justices met, since he believed the office could not be left without someone formally in charge. Taft to LDB, 19 August 1921.

573 "honors are easy": Taft to Horace Taft, 6 July 1921, in Alpheus T. Mason, *William Howard Taft: Chief Justice* (New York, 1964), 200.

573 "he has wide contacts": Urofsky, "Brandeis-Frankfurter Conversations," 311, 307.

573 "we congratulate ourselves": LDB to Taft, 13 September 1927, in Henry F. Pringle, *The Life and Times of William Howard Taft: A Biography*, 2 vols. (New York, 1939), 2:1074.

574 few words of explanation: See, for example, the return in *Galveston Electric Co. v. Galveston*, 258 U.S. 388 (1922): "I am in harmony with your result but would like to see the modification suggested on p. 7. It seems to me undesirable to express the idea that no allowance can be made for franchise rates. There may be times when it should be." LDB made the adjustment, and McReynolds signed on to the opinion. LDB-SC.

574 "pleased at being asked": LDB to AGB, 8 May 1923, EBR. The only case after this date in which LDB and McReynolds dissented is *Pennsylvania v. West Virginia*, 262 U.S. 553 (1923). Holmes also dissented, and all three in separate opinions indicated that they did not believe a true case or controversy existed and therefore the Court had no jurisdiction. But where McReynolds said this in less than two pages (262 U.S. at 603–5), LDB wrote eighteen pages (262 U.S. at 605–23).

574 a reactionary: Mason, *Taft*, 164. On another occasion LDB told Frankfurter, "McReynolds is one of the most interesting men on the present Court. He would have given Balzac great joy. I watch his face closely & at times, with his good features, he has a look of manly beauty, of intellectual beauty & at other times he looks like a moron and an infantile moron. I've seen him struggle to think & to express himself & just can't do it coherently." Urofsky, "Brandeis-Frankfurter Conversations," 333.

574 **various charities:** Michael Allan Woolf, "James Clark McReynolds," in Urofsky, *Biographical Dictionary,* 356. A good view of daily life with the cantankerous justice can be found in Dennis J. Hutchinson and David J. Garrow, eds., *The Forgotten Memoir of John Knox: A Year in the Life of a Supreme Court Clerk in FDR's Washington* (Chicago, 2002). McReynolds could also be quite charming; see Dean Acheson, *Morning and Noon* (Boston, 1965), 75.

574 **"and first judgment":** Urofsky, "Brandeis-Frankfurter Conversations," 322, 328–29; Holmes to Frankfurter, 9 December 1924, reporting LDB's views, in Robert H. Mennel and Christine L. Compston, eds., *Holmes and Frankfurter: Their Correspondence, 1912–1934* (Hanover, N.H., 1996), 177.

574 **the conservative bloc:** Joel Francis Paschal, *Mr. Justice Sutherland: A Man Against the State* (Princeton, N.J., 1951), is a fine study of the justice's life and thought, and is far better than the more recent and highly ideological Hadley Arkes, *The Return of George Sutherland* (Princeton, N.J., 1994).

575 **cordial personal relationship:** Urofsky, "Brandeis-Frankfurter Conversations," 310; Paschal, *Sutherland,* 116–17.

575 **rate regulation:** David J. Danelski, *A Supreme Court Justice Is Appointed* (New York, 1964), has some biographical information. See also Barry Cushman, "The Secret Lives of the Four Horsemen," 83 *Virginia Law Review* 559 (1997).

575 **involuntary sterilization:** *Buck v. Bell,* 274 U.S. 200 (1927).

575 **"along without him":** Mason, *Taft,* 221.

575 **really runs the Court:** Urofsky, "Brandeis-Frankfurter Conversations," 310, 322; there is, unfortunately, no biography of Van Devanter.

575 **personal relations:** See, for example, LDB to Van Devanter, 25 December 1926, Van Devanter MSS.

575 **"by personal considerations":** Urofsky, "Brandeis-Frankfurter Conversations," 315.

576 **understand the issues:** *Gilbert v. Minnesota,* 254 U.S. 325 (1920).

576 **McKenna finally resigned:** Holmes refused to join in pushing for the retirement because he was two years older than McKenna and thought that Taft would come after him next. This led LDB to refrain as well. Mason, *Taft,* 214–15; Urofsky, "Brandeis-Frankfurter Conversations," 327.

576 **of the Harding scandals:** Alpheus T. Mason, *Harlan Fiske Stone: Pillar of the Law* (New York, 1956). For his stint in the Justice Department, see chap. 10.

576 **his conservative colleagues:** In fact, although LDB was the first to cite a law review article, he tended to refer to them only in his dissents, aware that several of his colleagues objected to them. Stone, however, started the practice of using them in his regular opinions as well.

577 **Brandeis was right:** Mason, *Stone,* 219, based on the recollections of Stone's law clerk, Alfred McCormack. However, McCormack cites the case as *Louisville & Nashville Railroad v. Sloss-Sheffield Steel & Iron Co.,* 269 U.S. 217 (1925), but in that case LDB wrote the opinion for an 8–1 majority in which the Court affirmed the decision of the lower court on merits, with Stone entering a one-paragraph dissent.

577 **"take trouble to find out":** Urofsky, "Brandeis-Frankfurter Conversations," 336. While Stone would contribute a great deal to constitutional law during his time as an associate justice, his tenure as chief justice (1941–1946) was marked by constant bickering among the brethren, due in no small part to

Stone's tendency to run the conferences as academic seminars where every point would be discussed endlessly, a situation that Felix Frankfurter shamelessly exploited.

577 **"liberal-minded thinker"**: *New Republic,* 4 November 1925, cited in Mason, *Stone,* 252; Holmes to Laski, 29 November 1925, in Mark DeWolfe Howe, ed., *Holmes-Laski Letters,* 2 vols. (Cambridge, Mass., 1953), 1:800.

578 **"and as Stone is"**: Taft to Horace Taft, 1 December 1929, in Mason, *Stone,* 275.

578 **allies so treasured**: Alpheus T. Mason, *The Supreme Court from Taft to Warren* (Baton Rouge, La., 1968), 141–44; see also the very perceptive eulogy to Stone in Herbert Wechsler, "Stone and the Constitution," 46 *Columbia Law Review* 771 (1946). See below, chap. 24.

578 **reduced to six months**: Robert Post, "The Supreme Court Opinion as Institutional Practice: Dissent, Legal Scholarship, and Decisionmaking in the Taft Court," 85 *Minnesota Law Review* 1267, 1276–77 (2001). Post's article has a wondrous amount of detail and analysis on the internal processes of the Court in the 1920s.

579 **of all the justices**: *Id.,* 1383. "Many cases C.J. takes for himself because important, others because points are interesting, others because some of the justices don't like to take a case. Taft does about two men's work—with his added administrative tasks, extra work on certiorari, etc." Urofsky, "Brandeis-Frankfurter Conversations," 321.

579 **"prestige of the Court"**: Taft to John H. Clarke, 10 February 1922; Post, "Supreme Court Opinion," 1311; Taft to Willis Van Devanter, 26 December 1921, Van Devanter MSS. In 1927, Taft said, "I would not think of opposing the views of my brethren if there was a majority against my own." Pringle, *Taft,* 2:1049.

579 **done away with them**: Urofsky, "Brandeis-Frankfurter Conversations," 314. The most extreme view was that of the lawyer Frederick S. Tyler, who said that not even the votes of the Court should be announced, only the results. *American Bar Journal* 398 (1923).

579 **own dissenting votes**: When Taft had been a U.S. Court of Appeals judge in the 1890s, he wrote two hundred opinions for the court and entered only one dissent. Jonathan Lurie, "Chief Justice Taft and Dissents: Down with the Brandeis Briefs!" 32 *Journal of Supreme Court History* 178, 181 (2007).

579 **"it be settled right"**: Urofsky, "Brandeis-Frankfurter Conversations," 314, 328; *De Santo v. Pennsylvania,* 273 U.S. 34, 42 (1927) (LDB dissenting); *Burnet v. Coronado Oil & Gas Co.,* 285 U.S. 393, 406 (1932) (LDB dissenting). In another case LDB suppressed a dissent because "after all, it's merely a question of statutory construction," and at LDB's suggestion the chief justice had removed the worst things. *Railroad Commission of California v. Southern Pacific Co.,* 264 U.S. 331 (1924).

579 **"less important case"**: Urofsky, "Brandeis-Frankfurter Conversations," 317.

579 **"properly 'shut up'"**: Post, "Supreme Court Opinion," 1341. Post includes examples from nearly all the justices, indicating that they shared this view of not dissenting except when it could not be helped.

580 **"I am content—& concur"**: The first case was *Taubel-Scott-Kitzmiller v. Fox,* 264 U.S. 426 (1924), and the second was *Davis v. Cornwall,* 264 U.S. 560 (1924), LDB-SC.

580 **the union position:** Alexander M. Bickel gives several examples of this in *The Unpublished Opinions of Mr. Justice Brandeis: The Supreme Court at Work* (Cambridge, Mass., 1957).

580 **"willing to omit them":** Draft of dissent in *United States v. Morehead,* 258 U.S. 433 (1922), LDB-SC. Taft to LDB, 30 March 1922, and LDB to Taft, 31 March 1922, Taft Papers, cited in Post, "Supreme Court Opinion," 1352–53.

581 **a unanimous Court:** *McCarthy v. Arndstein,* 266 U.S. 34 (1924); comments on returns are in LDB-SC.

581 **an earlier decision:** *St. Louis Southwestern Railroad Co. v. United States,* 262 U.S. 70 (1923); and *Sprout v. South Bend,* 277 U.S. 163 (1928). See Post, "Supreme Court Opinion," 1302–3.

581 **Progressive Party platform:** William G. Ross, *A Muted Fury: Populists, Progressives, and Labor Unions Confront the Court, 1890–1937* (Princeton, N.J., 1994), 170–232.

581 **"Brandeis's dissenting opinions":** Taft to Gus Karger, 30 August 1924, cited in Post, "Supreme Court Opinion," 1317.

581 **"is to break down the prestige":** Taft to Van Devanter, 26 December 1921, Van Devanter MSS.

581 **"with all of them":** Urofsky, "Brandeis-Frankfurter Conversations," 228, 230.

583 **"more harmonious federalism":** Paul Freund, *On Understanding the Supreme Court* (Boston, 1950), 67. The cases he referred to were *Bradley Electric Light Co. v. Clapper,* 284 U.S. 221 (1931); *John Hancock Mutual Life Insurance Co. v. Yates,* 299 U.S. 178 (1936); and *Yarborough v. Yarborough,* 290 U.S. 202 (1933).

583 **great deal of censure:** Urofsky, "Brandeis-Frankfurter Conversations," 305, 309.

583 **"is not doing":** See, for example, LDB to Frankfurter, 17 December 1924, FF-HLS; Urofsky, "Brandeis-Frankfurter Conversations," 313.

583 **important labor case:** In the *Coronado* case, Taft had written: "The circumstances are such as to awaken regret that, in our view of federal jurisdiction, we can not affirm the judgment. But it is of far higher importance that we should preserve inviolate the fundamental limitations in respect to the federal jurisdiction." *United Mine Workers v. Coronado Coal Co.,* 259 U.S. 344, 413 (1922).

583 **as chief justice:** The following section is based on Robert Post, "Judicial Management and Judicial Disinterest: The Achievements and Perils of Chief Justice William Howard Taft," *Journal of Supreme Court History* (1998), 50–78; Melvin I. Urofsky, "The Taft Court, 1921–1930: Groping for Modernity," in Christopher Tomlins, ed., *The United States Supreme Court* (Boston, 2005), 199–202; and Mason, *Taft,* 105ff.

583 **entire judicial system:** For an analysis of the importance of the 1922 law, see Post, "Judicial Management," 54–57; and Felix Frankfurter and James M. Landis, *The Business of the Supreme Court of the United States* (New York, 1927), chap. 6.

584 **"the property involved":** Clarke to Woodrow Wilson, 9 September 1922, in Mason, *Taft,* 165.

584 **federal constitutional law:** See Taft, "The Jurisdiction of the Supreme Court Under the Act of February 13, 1925," 35 *Yale Law Journal* 1 (1925);

H. W. Perry Jr., *Deciding to Decide: Agenda Setting in the United States Supreme Court* (Cambridge, Mass., 1991); and Edward A. Harnett, "Questioning Certiorari: Some Reflections Seventy-five Years After the Judges' Bill," 100 *Columbia Law Review* 1643 (2000).

584 **the Court's docket:** "Congress determined in 1916 that even cases involving constitutional questions should be reviewed here only when the public interest appeared to demand it." *Dahnke-Walker Co. v. Bondurant,* 257 U.S. 282, 294 (1921) (LDB dissenting). See also Frankfurter and Landis, *Business of the Supreme Court,* 210–15.

584 **"matter of public discussion":** LDB to Taft, 30 November 1924, Taft MSS.

585 **"They are human machines":** LDB to Frankfurter, 6 February 1925, FF-HLS. These lines were incorporated into a *New Republic* editorial, 25 February 1925, 3–4.

585 **in fact cut down:** LDB to Frankfurter, 14 February 1925, FF-LC.

585 **in their judgment:** LDB to Frankfurter, 23 November 1928, commenting on Frankfurter and Landis, "The Supreme Court and the Judiciary Act of 1925," 42 *Harvard Law Review* 1 (1928).

586 **bankruptcy petitioners:** Taft to Charles P. Taft II, 3 November 1929, in Mason, *Taft,* 219. A comment such as this brings into question A. L. Todd's assertion that Taft lacked any prejudice against Jews. *Justice on Trial: The Case of Louis D. Brandeis* (New York, 1964), 216–17.

586 **secure a law library:** Taft also concerned himself with small things. When an unknown lawyer from South Dakota wrote complaining that under federal law a defendant cannot get a copy of the indictment against him except after paying a fee, Taft followed through, and Congress passed enabling legislation in 1927 to provide copies of charges to all federal defendants without fee.

587 **"my husband never uses":** Paul Freund Memoir, 84, New York Times Oral History Program.

587 **two paragraphs of his own:** *Myers v. United States,* 272 U.S. 52 (1926). The Holmes dissent is at 177, that of McReynolds at 178, and that of Brandeis at 240.

588 **both sides of a dispute:** On this, see Theodore Y. Blumoff, "The Third Best Choice: An Essay of Law and History," 41 *Hastings Law Journal* 537 (1990); and the older but still useful Charles A. Miller, *The Supreme Court and the Uses of History* (Cambridge, Mass., 1969), chap. 4.

588 **"I never wrote an opinion":** Taft thought the opinion one of the most important he had written and worked on it for the better part of two years. He recognized that his initial draft rambled far too much, and he asked the newest member of the Court, Harlan Fiske Stone, to edit it down. Stone voted with Taft and as attorney general had prepared a memorandum on the president's removal authority that also took a broad view of that power. Nine years later Stone, along with the other remaining members of Taft's majority, voted to overturn the decision. The previous year Taft had written another decision upholding the presidential pardoning power, but in that case had a unanimous Court. *Ex parte Grossman,* 267 U.S. 86 (1925). Mason, *Taft,* 253.

588 **the independent agencies:** Apparently, even some of the justices who voted with Taft were unhappy over the breadth of the opinion. LDB to Frankfurter, 28 October 1926, FF-HLS.

589 **contained Landis's research:** James M. Landis Memoir, 39, OHRO; LDB told Frankfurter that Landis had done "notable work" on the case. LDB to Frankfurter, 9 November 1926, FF-HLS.

589 **obeyed their provisions:** LDB had been through this process before, in a case involving the discharge of a landscape architect, George Burnap, who had been appointed by the secretary of war but discharged by a military officer. In that case, LDB for a unanimous Court held that even though the original appointment may have been faulty, the law did not require that the secretary of war personally remove from office those people he had appointed. *Burnap v. United States,* 252 U.S. 512 (1920).

590 **"to agree with it":** Mason, *Taft,* 226.

590 **needed a Mussolini:** William E. Leuchtenburg, "The Case of the Contentious Commissioner," in John A. Garraty, ed., *Quarrels That Shaped the Constitution,* rev. ed. (New York, 1987), 67.

590 **strictly executive functions:** *Humphrey's Executor v. United States,* 295 U.S. 602 (1935). In this case, Sutherland, who had supported Taft in *Myers,* wrote for the Court. For a full discussion of the case in the context of presidential-legislative history, see Louis Fisher, *Constitutional Conflicts Between Congress and the President,* 5th ed. (Lawrence, Kans., 2007), 59–61.

CHAPTER 24: THE TAFT COURT AND LEGAL CLASSICISM

592 **older ideas and practices:** Good introductions to America in the 1920s are William E. Leuchtenburg, *The Perils of Prosperity, 1914–1932* (Chicago, 1958); Lyn Dumenil, *Modern Temper: American Culture and Society in the 1920s* (New York, 1995); and the older but still charming Frederick Lewis Allen, *Only Yesterday* (New York, 1931), all of which explore the themes of change.

592 **crisis of the 1930s:** The following section relies on William M. Wiecek, *The Lost World of Classical Legal Thought: Law and Ideology in America, 1886–1937* (New York, 1998). See also Morton Horwitz, *The Transformation of American Law, 1870–1960: The Crisis of Legal Orthodoxy* (New York, 1992); and Herbert Hovenkamp, *Enterprise and American Law, 1836–1937* (Cambridge, Mass., 1991).

594 *Adkins v. Children's Hospital:* 261 U.S. 525 (1923).

594 **sustain the law:** In *Stettler v. O'Hara,* 243 U.S. 629 (1917), a divided Court, with LDB recusing, left a lower-court decision upholding an Oregon minimum-wage law in place, but that decision had no value as precedent.

594 **dismissed it as irrelevant:** Regarding the materials in the league's brief, Sutherland noted, "We have found [them] interesting but only mildly persuasive." While proper for consideration by a legislative body, they cast no light on the validity of a law, and that is the question the Court had to decide. *Adkins,* 261 U.S. at 559–60.

595 **use of the police power:** See, for example, *Hoke v. United States,* 227 U.S. 308 (1913); and *Bunting v. Oregon,* 243 U.S. 426 (1917).

595 **"unwise or unsound":** *Adkins,* 261 U.S. at 562 (Taft dissenting). Justice Edward Sanford joined Taft's dissent.

596 **neither should the majority:** *Id.* at 567 (Holmes dissenting). For response to the decision, see Vivian Hart, "Adkins v. Children's Hospital," in Melvin I. Urofsky, ed., *The Public Debate over Controversial Supreme Court Decisions* (Washington, D.C., 2006), 121–31.

596 *Jay Burns Baking Co. v. Bryan*: 264 U.S. 504 (1924).

596 **fines and/or imprisonment**: The law established standard sizes at one-half pound, one pound, one and a half pounds, or multiples of one pound for larger sizes. The variance could not be more than two ounces per pound, determined by the average weight of test lots of not fewer than twenty-five loaves.

597 **lesson in bread making**: *Jay Burns Baking,* 264 U.S. at 517 (LDB dissenting); the dissent ran seventeen pages, and the footnotes cited hundreds of sources.

597 **"let our minds be bold"**: LDB repeated this line in his dissent in *New State Ice Co. v. Liebmann,* 285 U.S. 262, 280, 311 (1932) (LDB dissenting), which is often given as its source, but he said it first several years earlier in this case.

597 **"consumers of the country"**: Brand to LDB, 25 March 1924, LDB-SC. LDB used material from the hearings as well as the Ohio law in his dissent.

598 **stayed with the majority**: McKenna to Brandeis, 4 April 1924, LDB-SC.

598 **"art of bread making"**: Holmes to Brandeis, [n.d.] April 1924, LDB-SC; Holmes to Pollock, 11 May 1924, in Mark DeWolfe Howe, ed., *Holmes-Pollock Letters,* 2 vols. (Cambridge, Mass., 1941), 2:136–37.

598 **governmental interference**: This notion of public versus private is most clearly set out in Robert Post, "Defending the Lifeworld: Substantive Due Process in the Taft Court Era," 78 *Boston University Law Review* 1489 (1998). It is also the basis for the argument Barry Cushman makes in *Rethinking the New Deal Court: The Structure of a Constitutional Revolution* (New York, 1998).

598 **from governmental regulation**: Post, "Lifeworld," 1504.

599 **"function of judicial review"**: *Jay Burns Baking,* 264 U.S. at 534.

599 **violated the Due Process**: *Weaver v. Palmer Brothers Company,* 270 U.S. 402 (1926). LDB and Stone joined Holmes's dissent.

599 **regulation of their tickets**: *Tyson & Brother v. Banton,* 273 U.S. 418 (1927). Holmes dissented, joined by LDB; Stone dissented, joined by Holmes and LDB; Sanford also dissented.

599 **reach of state interference**: *Ribnik v. McBride,* 277 U.S. 350 (1928). Holmes and LDB joined Stone's dissent.

599 **none other than Holmes**: *Pennsylvania Coal Co. v. Mahon,* 260 U.S. 393 (1922). The case is only one of five in which LDB entered a written dissent to a majority opinion by Holmes.

600 **"of the United States"**: *Id.* at 415.

600 **"can be profitably put"**: *Id.* at 418 (LDB dissenting).

600 **"to go whole hog"**: Melvin I. Urofsky, "The Brandeis-Frankfurter Conversations," 1985 *Supreme Court Review* 321.

600 **over the years**: David Bryden, "But Cf. . . . ," 1 *Constitutional Commentary* 183 (1984).

600 **sent him a copy**: G. Edward White, *Justice Oliver Wendell Holmes: Law and the Inner Self* (New York, 1993), 403.

600 **Holmes himself**: *New Republic,* 3 January 1923, 136–37.

601 **and state regulation**: See, for example, the discussion of the case in Evan B. Brandes, "Legal Theory and Property Jurisprudence of Oliver Wendell Holmes, Jr., and Louis D. Brandeis: An Analysis of *Pennsylvania Coal Company v. Mahon,*" 38 *Creighton Law Review* 1179 (2005).

601 **reasons for its action**: Professor Michael Wolf to author, 28 January 2008. See Charles M. Haar and Michael Allan Wolf, "*Euclid* Lives: The Survival of

Progressive Jurisprudence," 113 *Harvard Law Review* 1889 (2002), for a discussion of the two major takings cases of the 1920s, *Mahon* and *Village of Euclid v. Ambler Realty Co.*, 272 U.S. 365 (1926). The latter, with both Holmes and LDB in the majority, upheld a zoning scheme despite the landowner's claims that the regulation reduced the market value of its property by at least 75 percent.

601 **of Brandeis, the newer:** The following term LDB dropped a note to Frankfurter: "I was sorry that I had to dissent on Holmes J. today. But there was another incident à la Scranton" (24 April 1924). Holmes had written the opinion upholding the District of Columbia's wartime rent-control act in 1921, but in 1924 Taft, following up on the *Mahon* case, convinced Holmes that since the wartime emergency had ended, the act could no longer be considered valid. *Chastleton Corp. v. Sinclair*, 264 U.S. 543 (1924). LDB's opinion, a partial dissent, is at 549.

601 **"absolute right to strike":** *Dorchy v. Kansas*, 272 U.S. 306, 311 (1927). The case involved the conviction of August Dorchy for conspiring to lead men out on strike in violation of an injunction entered under a legitimate state law. LDB spoke for a unanimous Court.

602 **little or no attention:** Post, "Lifeworld," 1514n.128 cites statements on this issue.

602 **due process of law:** *Wolff Packing Co. v. Court of Industrial Relations*, 262 U.S. 522 (1923). Justice Van Devanter, who reviewed Taft's opinion, believed that even if one could describe the packinghouse as a business affected with a public interest, the state still did not have the power to fix wages.

602 **"to kill it":** Unsigned editorial, "Exit the Kansas Court," *New Republic*, 27 June 1923, 112–13.

603 **involved in labor disputes:** Stanley I. Kutler, "Labor, the Clayton Act, and the Supreme Court," 3 *Labor History* 19 (1962).

603 **supporting the strikers:** *Duplex Printing Press Co. v. Deering*, 254 U.S. 443 (1921). The case came down in the last months of Chief Justice White's tenure.

603 **"rights of the individual":** *Truax v. Corrigan*, 257 U.S. 312, 338 (1921).

603 **"have as a result":** *Id.* at 344, 349 (Pitney dissenting).

604 **protected such practices:** See memoranda by Dean Acheson (LDB's law clerk) on the laws of various countries and states in *Truax* files, LDB-SC.

604 **"issuance of an injunction":** *Truax*, 257 U.S. at 354, 368 (LDB dissenting).

605 **the legislative branch:** *Duplex Printing Press*, 254 U.S. at 479 (LDB dissenting). LDB's clerk, Dean Acheson, told Frankfurter, "I was more responsible for the Duplex case than I have been for any yet—particularly for the Clayton Act part." Acheson to Frankfurter, 17 January 1921, FF-LC.

605 **excesses of state courts:** Felix Frankfurter and Nathan Greene, *The Labor Injunction* (New York, 1930).

605 **"judgment of the court":** *American Steel Foundries v. Tri-city Central Trades Council*, 257 U.S. 184 (1921).

606 **"of *Coronado* case":** Urofsky, "Brandeis-Frankfurter Conversations," 306.

606 **not part of interstate commerce:** *Hammer v. Dagenhart*, 247 U.S. 251 (1918).

606 **shown in this case:** The dissent is in LDB-SC, and is reprinted in Alexander M. Bickel, *The Unpublished Opinions of Mr. Justice Brandeis: The Supreme*

Court at Work (Chicago, 1967), 84–91. For the drafting of the dissent, see Dean Acheson's recollection on p. 92.

607 **no interstate commerce:** Urofsky, "Brandeis-Frankfurter Conversations," 305.

607 **"not of any federal law":** Draft dissent, LDB-SC.

607 **"respect to federal jurisdiction":** *United Mine Workers v. Coronado Coal Co.,* 259 U.S. 344, 413 (1922). See also Felix Frankfurter, "The Coronado Case," *New Republic,* 16 August 1922, 328, which in LDB's eyes missed some of the importance of the decision; see LDB to Frankfurter, 31 August 1922, FF-LC. LDB expressed himself better pleased with a note on the case in 32 *Yale Law Journal* 59 (1922), which called the decision "an excellent example of judicial courage." The case was returned to the lower court for a rehearing, and once again a jury assessed damages against the national union, this time holding it liable for the actions of its local chapter. In the second *Coronado* case, a unanimous Court held that absent specific evidence of collusion, the national union could not be held responsible for local lawlessness. *Coronado Coal Co. v. United Mine Workers,* 268 U.S. 295 (1925).

607 **"a natural sentiment":** Urofsky, "Brandeis-Frankfurter Conversations," 307.

607 **quarry would be as well:** The two child labor cases were *Hammer v. Dagenhart,* 247 U.S. 251 (1918); and *Bailey v. Drexel Furniture Co.,* 259 U.S. 20 (1922). LDB had dissented in the first case, which struck down a federal child labor law based on the commerce power, but had voted with the majority in invalidating a second effort that relied on the taxing power. See LDB to Felix Frankfurter, 16 May 1922, FF-LC.

608 **local and national commerce:** *Bedford Cut Stone Co. v. Journeymen Stone Cutters' Association,* 274 U.S. 37 (1927). Stone entered a short concurrence that said he thought the majority opinion wrong in its logic, but that he felt bound on the authority of the *Duplex Printing* case. *Id.* at 55.

608 **reasonable act of labor:** For a more sympathetic portrayal of Sutherland's views, see Joel Francis Paschal, *Mr. Justice Sutherland: A Man Against the State* (Princeton, N.J., 1951), 146–48.

608 **in the economy:** See, for example, *Wickard v. Filburn,* 317 U.S. 11 (1942), holding that even grain grown for a farmer's own consumption could have an impact on interstate commerce.

608 **no real relief:** To cite but one example, the Court overturned an injunction in *United Leather Workers v. Herkert & Meisel et al.,* 265 U.S. 457 (1924), four years after the order had been issued by the lower court.

608 **"legitimate purposes":** Arthur Sutherland, quoted in Morton Keller, *Regulating a New Economy: Public Policy and Economic Change in America, 1900–1933* (Cambridge, Mass., 1990), 145.

609 **"Congress did so":** *Bedford Cut Stone,* 274 U.S. at 56, 65 (LDB dissenting).

609 **"from their lethargy":** LDB to Frankfurter, 11 April 1927, FF-LC. Frankfurter wrote an article, "Reminds of Involuntary Servitude," *New Republic,* 27 April 1927, 262, taking the title from the line in LDB's dissent. Referring to that dissent, he declared that "the only consolation about the . . . case is that the moral judgment upon the decision has already been authoritatively uttered as part of the decision."

609 **"who try to keep in line":** Cardozo to LDB, 17 October 1926, LDB-SC.

610 **"fifty years to come":** George R. Farnum, *Some Men of the Law: Selected Stud-*

ies ([Brooklyn?], 1941), 28. Note also a memorandum from Harlan Stone on an LDB circulation: "Your disposition of the jurisdictional matter is very convincing." Stone to LDB, 10 February 1928, Stone MSS.

610 **many have been:** On commercial law, see, for example, Edward J. Janger, "Brandeis, Progressivism, and Commercial Law: Rethinking *Benedict v. Ratner,*" 37 *Brandeis Law Journal* 63 (1998), arguing that although LDB's views on the need for certain creditors to keep closer watch over so-called floating liens were rejected by drafters of the Uniform Commercial Code, his views on the need for creditor awareness are gaining new acceptance. For individual liberties, see next chapter; jurisdiction is discussed in the *Erie* case in chap. 30.

610 **draft the Clayton Act:** See above, chaps. 13, 16.

610 **and in two against:** Milton Handler, "The Judicial Architects of the Rule of Reason," in *Twenty-five Years of Antitrust* (New York, 1973), 28. Handler, who had clerked for Justice Stone, taught for many years at Columbia Law School and was considered the dean of the antitrust bar.

610 **tax on chain drugstores:** *Liggett Co. v. Lee,* 288 U.S. 517, 541 (1933) (LB dissenting).

610 **illegal if reasonable:** *Standard Oil Co. v. United States,* 221 U.S. 1 (1911); Holmes had first suggested such a rule in his dissent in *Northern Securities Co. v. United States,* 193 U.S. 197, 400 (1903).

610 **violate the antitrust law:** *Chicago Board of Trade v. United States,* 246 U.S. 231 (1918).

611 **than limited competition:** *American Column & Lumber Co. et al. v. United States,* 257 U.S. 377, 413 (1921). He told Frankfurter that he had been "waiting for a chance to say some of those things." LDB to Frankfurter, 31 December 1921, FF-LC.

611 **"are all relevant facts":** *Chicago Board of Trade,* 246 U.S. at 238.

611 **antitrust jurisprudence:** *Standard Oil Co. (Indiana) v. United States,* 283 U.S. 163 (1931).

611 **patents could be licensed:** Charles D. Weller, "A 'New' Rule of Reason from Justice Brandeis's 'Concentric Circles' and Other Changes in Law," 44 *Antitrust Bulletin* 881, 919–25 (1999).

612 **judges were qualified:** *Smyth v. Ames,* 169 U.S. 466 (1898).

612 **"the other is Brandeis":** Taft to Robert A. Taft, 21 October 1928, cited in Henry F. Pringle, *The Life and Times of William Howard Taft: A Biography,* 2 vols. (New York, 1939), 2:1066.

612 **"a case so satisfactorily":** The several cases were all decided with *Southern Railway Co. v. Watts,* 260 U.S. 519 (1923); Taft to LDB, 23 December 1922, LDB-SC.

612 **real value of the property:** See the discussion of the components of rate setting in Alpheus T. Mason, *Brandeis: A Free Man's Life* (New York, 1946), 547–53.

612 **"aspects of these cases":** Urofsky, "Brandeis-Frankfurter Conversations," 312.

612 **to valuate property:** *International News Service v. Associated Press,* 248 U.S. 215 (1918).

613 **involved in rate setting:** *Georgia Railway & Power Co. v. Railroad Commission of Georgia,* 262 U.S. 625 (1923). Urofsky, "Brandeis-Frankfurter Conversations," 314.

613 **would be better:** His law clerk for the term, William McCurdy, gathered an immense amount of data, as well as numerous law review articles all criticizing *Smyth* as well as the reproduction value theory. LDB-SC.

613 **"consideration of issues":** Urofsky, "Brandeis-Frankfurter Conversations," 316.

613 **form of a dissent:** *Southwestern Bell Telephone Co. v. Public Service Commission of Missouri,* 262 U.S. 276 (1923); LDB's dissent is at 289.

614 **finally completed in 1944:** The *Smyth* doctrines were finally buried in *Federal Power Commission v. Hope Natural Gas Co.,* 320 U.S. 591 (1944).

614 **"between courts and agencies":** G. Edward White, "Allocating Power Between Agencies and Courts: The Legacy of Justice Brandeis," 1974 *Duke Law Journal* 195, 196–97.

614 **review of its findings:** See, for example, *Cincinnati, New Orleans, and Texas Pacific Railway v. ICC,* 162 U.S. 184 (1896); *ICC v. Cincinnati, New Orleans, and Texas Pacific Railway,* 167 U.S. 479 (1897); and *ICC v. Alabama Midland Railway Co.,* 168 U.S. 144 (1897).

614 **over state judicial scrutiny:** *Northern Pacific Railway Co. v. Solum,* 247 U.S. 477 (1918). The question was whether a Minnesota state court, in the absence of initial consideration by the ICC, could investigate the reasonableness of rate-setting practices of railroads operating in interstate commerce passing through Minnesota. LDB held that the railway's decision to follow the practices of the ICC trumped state claims.

615 **with interstate commerce:** *Pennsylvania v. West Virginia,* 262 U.S. 553 (1923).

615 **the courts get involved:** *Id.* at 605 (LDB dissenting).

615 **postwar America:** White, "Allocating Power," 214.

615 **what this phrase meant:** *FTC v. Gratz,* 253 U.S. 421 (1920).

616 **its own determination:** *Federal Trade Commission v. Curtis Publishing Co.,* 260 U.S. 568 (1923).

616 **that the courts lacked:** See, for example, his dissents in *Ohio Valley Water Co. v. Ben Avon Borough,* 253 U.S. 287, 292 (1920); and *Crowell v. Benson,* 285 U.S. 22, 65 (1932).

616 **administrative in nature:** *United States ex rel. Milwaukee Social Democratic Publishing Co. v. Burleson,* 255 U.S. 407 (1921); see pp. 571–72.

616 **denial of due process:** *Ng Fung Ho v. White,* 259 U.S. 276 (1922). The opinion substantially modified an earlier opinion by Holmes in *United States v. Ju Toy,* 198 U.S. 253 (1905).

616 **of federal jurisdiction:** LDB to Frankfurter, 6 March 1929 and 17 May 1931, FF-LC. The books are Felix Frankfurter and Wilber G. Katz, *Cases and Other Authorities on Federal Jurisdiction and Procedure* (Chicago, 1931); and Felix Frankfurter and J. Forrester Davison, *Cases and Other Materials on Administrative Law* (New York, 1932).

616 **fifteen years earlier:** *United States v. Morgan,* 307 U.S. 183, 191 (1939).

CHAPTER 25: A NEW AGENDA:
THE COURT AND CIVIL LIBERTIES

618 ***Barron v. Baltimore:*** 32 U.S. (7 Pet.) 243 (1833). The literature on the Bill of Rights is extensive, but all sources agree that it was designed to protect the citizenry from the national government; the states were at the time seen

as the protectors of individual liberties. See, among many others, Leonard W. Levy, *Origins of the Bill of Rights* (New Haven, Conn., 1999); Ronald Hoffman and Peter J. Albert, eds., *The Bill of Rights: Government Proscribed* (Charlottesville, Va., 1997); and the older but still useful Robert A. Rutland, *The Birth of the Bill of Rights, 1776–1791* (Chapel Hill, N.C., 1955).

618 **to the states:** For this argument, as well as the change in attitude after the Civil War, see Akhil Reed Amar, *The Bill of Rights: Creation and Reconstruction* (New Haven, Conn., 1998); and the dueling histories offered by Justices Black and Frankfurter in *Adamson v. California,* 332 U.S. 46 (1947).

619 **"and to enjoy property":** *Gilbert v. Minnesota,* 254 U.S. 325, 334, 336, 343 (1920) (LDB dissenting). Two years later, in *Prudential Insurance Co. v. Cheek,* 259 U.S. 530 (1922), the Court reiterated that the Bill of Rights did not apply to the states.

619 **the statute lacking:** *Meyer v. Nebraska,* 262 U.S. 390, 399 (1923). See also William G. Ross, *Forging New Freedoms: Nativism, Education, and the Constitution, 1917–1927* (Lincoln, Neb., 1994), chap. 6.

619 **with its reasoning:** Holmes and Sutherland dissented without opinion in *Meyer,* but in a companion case Holmes entered a dissent based on judicial restraint. He saw nothing wrong with the ideal that all American citizens should speak a common language, and therefore the Nebraska and Iowa requirements were reasonable. *Bartels v. Iowa,* 262 U.S. 404, 412 (1923) (Holmes dissenting).

619 **of clear-and-present danger:** Melvin I. Urofsky, "Brandeis-Frankfurter Conversations," 1985 *Supreme Court Review* 320. According to the eminent constitutional scholar Gerald Gunther, *Meyer* "was a watershed; in every threat to civil liberties for the rest of the decade, the *Meyer* precedent prompted liberals to look to the courts for the protection of personal rights they cherished." Although there had been rights cases earlier, *Meyer* served as a major impetus in moving the Court's docket away from property and business matters to questions of civil rights and liberties. Gunther, *Learned Hand: The Man and the Judge* (New York, 1994), 377.

620 **in only five minutes:** Robert Whitaker, *On the Laps of Gods* (New York, 2008).

620 **"their constitutional rights":** *Moore v. Dempsey,* 261 U.S. 86 (1923). McReynolds filed a dissent, joined by Sutherland. LDB termed Holmes's opinion "a satisfaction." LDB to Felix Frankfurter, 19 February 1923, FFLC. The opinion vindicated Holmes, who in 1915 had entered a powerful dissent when the majority refused to review the Atlanta trial of Leo Frank, in which a lynch mob had intimidated the jury. *Frank v. Mangum,* 271 U.S. 3089 (1915).

620 **"for additional obligations":** *Pierce v. Society of Sisters,* 268 U.S. 510 (1925).

620 **generated by prohibition:** See especially two articles by Robert Post, "Federalism in the Taft Court Era: Can It Be 'Revived'?" 51 *Duke Law Journal* 1513 (2002); and "Federalism, Positive Law, and the Emergence of the American Administrative State: Prohibition in the Taft Court Era," 48 *William and Mary Law Review* 1 (2006) (hereafter cited as Post, "Prohibition").

621 **as a social center:** For prohibition, see Thomas R. Pegram, *Battling Demon Rum: The Struggle for a Dry America, 1800–1933* (Chicago, 1998); James H. Timberlake, *Prohibition and the Progressive Movement, 1900–1920* (Cam-

bridge, Mass., 1963); and Richard F. Hamm, *Shaping the Eighteenth Amendment: Temperance Reform, Legal Culture, and the Polity, 1880–1920* (Chapel Hill, N.C., 1995). John C. Burnham was one of the first historians to identify prohibition as a progressive reform, in "New Perspectives on the Prohibition 'Experiment' of the 1920s," *Journal of Social History* 51 (1968). The classic charge connecting prohibition to nativism is Richard Hofstadter, *The Age of Reform: From Bryan to F.D.R.* (New York, 1955), 287–93.

621 **temperance, not prohibition:** The Anti-saloon League had opposed LDB's nomination to the high court because of his earlier representation of the Massachusetts liquor dealers and his stand for temperance as opposed to prohibition.

622 **the Eighteenth Amendment:** *Hamilton v. Kentucky Distilleries & Warehouse Co.*, also known as the Wartime Prohibition Cases, 251 U.S. 146 (1919); *Jacob Ruppert v. Caffey*, 251 U.S. 264 (1920); and the *National Prohibition Cases*, 253 U.S. 350 (1920). See pp. 554–55.

622 **received social values:** Post, "Prohibition," 9.

622 **"steady in the boat":** Taft to Horace Taft, 12 December 1927, cited in *id.*, 8.

622 **from his friends:** Holmes personally had little use for prohibition, and let this show up occasionally in his judicial opinions. "Wine has been thought good for man from the time of the Apostles until recent years." *Tyson v. Banton*, 273 U.S. 418, 446 (1927) (Holmes dissenting).

622 **legal order itself:** Taft could not figure out where to count Harlan Stone, who "wobbles a good deal on the subject, and I don't quite see where he stands, and I am not quite sure that he does." Taft to Horace Taft, 12 December 1927, cited in Post, "Prohibition," 8.

622 **"in our public life":** State of the Union message, 8 December 1922, cited in Post, "Prohibition," 11.

623 **"is not fitted":** Enclosed in LDB to Wilson to Frank I. Cobb, 15 April 1923, in Arthur S. Link et al., eds., *The Papers of Woodrow Wilson*, 69 vols. (Princeton, N.J., 1966–1984), 68:335–36.

623 **second group completely:** LDB to Frankfurter, 7 February 1925, FF-LC.

624 **"that remains unenforced":** Argument before Joint Committee on Liquor Law of the Massachusetts Legislature (1891).

624 **illegal drink and crime:** LDB to Frankfurter, 2 September 1928, FF-LC.

624 **all necessary powers:** *James Everard's Breweries v. Day*, 265 U.S. 545, 558 (1924), supporting a congressional ban on the medicinal use of beer.

625 **"violated civil liberties":** Alpheus T. Mason, *Brandeis: A Free Man's Life* (New York, 1946), 566–67; and Philippa Strum, *Louis D. Brandeis: Justice for the People* (Cambridge, Mass., 1984), 330. Natalie Wexler has tried to rebut some of these charges by claiming that the more important cases LDB wrote for the Court involved property rather than civil liberties, but this ignores all of the cases in which he voted with the majority. Wexler, " 'The Prophet Stumbles': Brandeis, the Bill of Rights, and Prohibition," 13 *Cardozo Law Review* 1355, 1358 (1991).

625 **compensation to the owners:** *Jacob Ruppert v. Caffey*, 251 U.S. 264 (1920).

625 **that same liquor:** *Albrecht v. United States*, 273 U.S. 1 (1927), speaking for a unanimous Court. The justices had already upheld multiple convictions for different uses of the same item. In *United States v. Lanza*, 260 U.S. 377 (1922), Chief Justice Taft, also for a unanimous Court, upheld separate convictions in state and then federal courts for manufacturing liquor, transport-

ing it, possessing it, and having a still to manufacture it, reaffirmed unanimously in *Hebert v. Louisiana,* 272 U.S. 312 (1926).

625 **carried illegal alcohol:** *United States v. One Ford Coupe Automobile,* 272 U.S. 321 (1926). Justice Butler dissented, joined by McReynolds and Sutherland. Stone concurred with the results after failing to get LDB to modify some of his assertions. Stone to LDB, 10 November 1926, Stone MSS. Mason incorrectly describes this case as the confiscation of an innocent owner's car simply because a guest-passenger had a small flask of whiskey on his person. In fact the car belonged to the Garth Motor Company, and it was used by one Killian to transport contraband liquor. The Court had to deal with the question of whether the car could be seized for evasion of taxes, and when it agreed with the government, the Garth Motor Company lost the car and Killian went free.

625 **for medicinal purposes:** *Lambert v. Yellowley,* 272 U.S. 581 (1926). Sutherland wrote a strong dissent, joined by McReynolds, Butler, and Stone. He claimed the federal government had gone too far and had invaded an area, the regulation of medicine, reserved to the states under the Tenth Amendment. *Id.* at 597.

625 **to be positive:** LDB to Arthur Kellogg, 22 October 1917, Kellogg MSS.

625 **had on America:** LDB to Paul Underwood Kellogg, 25 April 1920.

625 **right-minded citizens:** *Survey,* 13 November 1920, 183–228; LDB to Paul Underwood Kellogg, 7 November 1923, which the editors used as a preface to the articles.

626 **"ranked as fundamental":** *Palko v. Connecticut,* 302 U.S. 319, 325, 327 (1937).

626 **valid law to this day:** LDB supported this view in *Lanza* and in *Hebert.* The Court reaffirmed the rule as recently as *United States v. Lara,* 541 U.S. 193 (2004).

626 **warrant would arrive:** *Carroll v. United States,* 267 U.S. 132 (1925).

627 **used in federal court:** *Gambino v. United States,* 275 U.S. 310 (1927). The case also had significant federalism importance; see Post, "Prohibition," 34–35.

627 **"tyrannical in the extreme":** Alpheus T. Mason, *Harlan Fiske Stone: Pillar of the Law* (New York, 1956), 149.

627 **to do more:** LDB to Frankfurter, 3 October 1924, FF-LC. Only after Stone named the young J. Edgar Hoover to head the FBI did real reforms come in the form of stricter hiring standards, better training, and an emphasis on legitimate police work. In his later years, however, Hoover himself collected files on people in the government he suspected of "disloyalty," including LDB.

627 **"abolish the system today":** LDB to Frankfurter, 15 March 1924, FF-LC.

627 **eleven-part series:** LDB to Frankfurter, 21 May 1927, FF-LC.

627 **enforcement of prohibition:** LDB to Frankfurter, 12 August 1925, 28 January, 23 June, and 30 December 1926, FF-LC; *Christian Century,* 28 January 1926, 101.

628 **"conviction and punishment":** *Casey v. United States,* 276 U.S. 413, 420 (1928) (McReynolds dissenting).

628 **beyond the pale:** *Id.* at 421 (LDB dissenting). On this case, see John Wiltbye, "Jesuits, Crooks, and the Police," *America,* 21 April 1928.

628 *Olmstead v. United States:* 277 U.S. 438 (1928).

628 **without a warrant:** *Weeks v. United States,* 232 U.S. 383 (1914); *Silverthorne Lumber Co. v. United States,* 251 U.S. 385 (1920).

629 **"been known heretofore":** *Olmstead,* 277 U.S. at 468.

629 **Fourth Amendment meant:** *Id.* at 485 (Butler dissenting).

629 **a "dirty business":** *Id.* at 469, 470 (Holmes dissenting).

629 **all that Brandeis said:** Holmes to Frederick Pollock, 20 June 1928, in Mark DeWolfe Howe, ed., *Holmes-Pollock Letters,* 2 vols. (Cambridge, Mass., 1941), 222.

629 **"resolutely set its face":** *Olmstead,* 277 U.S. at 471, 485 (LDB dissenting).

630 **on a constitutional basis:** Henry Friendly interview, Paper MSS.

630 **"whispered in the closet":** *Olmstead,* 277 U.S. at 473.

630 **Friendly's skepticism:** A Schenectady, New York, paper, dated 28 January 1928, refers to the new device, LDB-SC. For more details on the development of the *Olmstead* dissent, see Paul Freund, "The Evolution of a Brandeis Dissent," *Manuscripts* 10 (Spring 1958), 18–25, 34; and Friendly interview, Paper MSS.

631 **"without understanding":** *Olmstead,* 277 U.S. at 478.

632 **"the majority were right":** Alpheus T. Mason, *William Howard Taft: Chief Justice* (New York, 1964), 227, 259; Henry F. Pringle, *The Life and Times of William Howard Taft: A Biography,* 2 vols. (New York, 1939), 991. Interestingly, Taft claimed that the argument LDB used was that Washington State forbade wiretapping.

632 ***Griswold v. Connecticut:*** 381 U.S. 479 (1965); see Wayne V. McIntosh and Cynthia L. Cates, *Judicial Entrepreneurship: The Role of the Judge in the Marketplace of Ideas* (Westport, Conn., 1997), 25ff., for this development.

632 **partially reverse *Olmstead*:** *Nardone v. United States,* 302 U.S. 379 (1937). The Court, with LDB in the 7–2 majority, held that the federal Communications Act did apply to the federal government, that wiretapping in general was illegal, and that no wiretapping evidence secured without a warrant could be admitted in federal courts.

632 **"protects people not places":** *Berger v. New York,* 388 U.S. 41 (1967); *Katz v. United States,* 389 U.S. 347 (1967).

632 **without a warrant:** *Kyllo v. United States,* 533 U.S. 27 (2001). Justice John Paul Stevens, normally considered a moderate liberal, wrote a dissent joined by Justices William Rehnquist, Sandra Day O'Connor, and Anthony Kennedy that echoed Taft's opinion in insisting that no penetration of the house had taken place, and therefore a warrant was unnecessary.

632 **"in favor of liberty, strictly":** LDB to Frankfurter, 15 June 1928, FF-LC. In fact, the opinion received scant attention at the time. Newspapers covered the Court in a desultory fashion, and while law reviews noted it, they did not recognize it as an important case at the time, and certainly not a landmark decision. Only a note by Henry Hasley in the *Notre Dame Lawyer* praised LDB's dissent and strongly criticized the majority opinion. Alan Barth, *Prophets with Honor: Great Dissents and Great Dissenters in the Supreme Court* (New York, 1974), 69.

632 **and Fifth amendments:** "While I do not deny it, I am not prepared to say that the penumbra of the 4th and 5th amendments cover the defendant, although I fully agree that Courts are apt to err by sticking too closely to the words of a law where those words import a policy that goes beyond them." *Olmstead,* 277 U.S. 469 (Holmes dissenting).

632   *Gitlow v. New York:* 268 U.S. 652 (1925).

633   "impairment by the States": *Id.* at 666.

633   the state's restriction: See the analysis of Sanford's opinion in Harry Kalven Jr., *A Worthy Tradition: Freedom of Speech in America* (New York, 1988), chap. 11, where it is juxtaposed with LDB's *Whitney* opinion.

633   "a present conflagration": *Gitlow,* 268 U.S. at 672 (Holmes dissenting).

633   "proletarian dictatorship": Holmes to Frankfurter, 14 June 1925, in Robert H. Mennel and Christine L. Compston, eds., *Holmes and Frankfurter: Their Correspondence, 1912–1934* (Hanover, N.H., 1996), 184.

634   **Madison Square Garden:** Ronald K. L. Collins and David M. Skover, "Curious Concurrence: Justice Brandeis's Vote in Whitney v. California," 2005 *Supreme Court Review* 333 (2006), has extensive information about Ruthenberg and his case.

635   **returned to the high court:** *Whitney v. California,* 274 U.S. 357 (1927). The case reached the high court in a curious manner. Following her trial, the California intermediate appeals court sustained the conviction. The state supreme court denied review, and the case went to the Supreme Court on a writ of error allowed by the presiding judge of the intermediate appeals court. The Court heard oral argument in October 1925, but dismissed the case two weeks later for lack of federal jurisdiction. On the dismissal, see Landis to Felix Frankfurter, 5 November 1925, FF-LC. Apparently, in her appeal, Whitney's lawyers asserted claims regarding evidence, prosecutorial misconduct, and lack of knowledge of wrongdoing, all matters of state law. The state court of appeal then entered an order, with both parties agreeing to it, that the court had in fact "considered and passed upon" federal due process and equal protection claims. With this new order added to the record, the Supreme Court set aside its dismissal and granted the petition for rehearing. Bradley C. Bobertz, "The Brandeis Gambit: The Making of America's 'First Freedom,' " 40 *William and Mary Law Review* 557, 641–42 (1999).

635   **philanthropic work:** For Whitney, see Lisa Rubens, "The Patrician Radical: Charlotte Anita Whitney," *California History* 65 (1986), 158ff.

635   **found her guilty:** The circumstances of her trial, by modern standards, would have certainly led to a mistrial. The judge refused to grant a continuance when her lead attorney first fell ill and then died, and then the prosecution turned the trial into a denunciation of the Industrial Workers of the World, an organization with which Whitney had no direct ties. The judge's instructions left the jury little choice but to find the defendant guilty. Collins and Skover, "Curious Concurrence," 346–49. The verdict aroused nationwide condemnation, and even the sponsor of the California act expressed dismay that it should have been applied to Whitney, stating that "the law was never intended to halt free speech nor to punish persons for their thoughts." Assemblyman William J. Locke, quoted in "The Jailing of Anita Whitney," *Literary Digest,* 14 November 1925, 14–15, cited in Vincent Blasi, "The First Amendment and the Ideal of Civic Courage: The Brandeis Opinion in *Whitney v. California,*" 29 *William and Mary Law Review* 653 (1988).

635   **to discuss the issue:** Apparently, LDB first drafted a two-paragraph dissent contesting the majority's assumption of jurisdiction on the grounds that no federal issues had been raised. At some point he decided to adopt the

Ruthenberg draft. Collins and Skover, "Curious Concurrence," 372. The two authors believe that LDB should have dissented, and thus forced the First Amendment issue. Since he had on so many occasions criticized his colleagues for reaching out to take cases, it is highly unlikely that he would do that. The concurrence allowed him to note the jurisdictional issue and then address the First Amendment.

636 **annals of the Court:** For "civic virtue," see Pnina Lahav, "Holmes and Brandeis: Libertarian and Republican Justifications for Free Speech," 4 *Journal of Law & Politics* 451, 458 (1988). For "civic courage," see Blasi, "First Amendment and Civic Courage."

637 **"emergency justifying it":** *Whitney,* 274 U.S. 357, 372, 375 (LDB concurring).

638 *Funeral Oration:* Lahav, "Holmes and Brandeis," 462.

638 **will always win out:** As Blasi notes, there is no echo in *Whitney,* as there is in Holmes's opinions, of John Milton's famous rhetorical question, "Who ever knew truth put to the worse, in a free and open encounter?" "First Amendment and Civic Courage," 676–77.

638 **consciences of judges:** In addition to Jefferson and the work of Charles Beard on American history, LDB cited Zechariah Chafee. He sent Chafee a copy of the opinion with a note: "You will see how much I have borrowed from you." LDB to Chafee, 21 May 1927, Chafee MSS.

638 **free speech in 1969:** *Brandenburg v. Ohio,* 395 U.S. 444 (1969).

638 **and lawyerly opinions:** See, among many others, Kalven, *Worthy Tradition,* chap. 11; Lillian R. BeVier, "The First Amendment and Political Speech," 30 *Stanford Law Review* 299 (1978); Ashutah A. Bhagwat, "The Story of Whitney v. California: The Power of Ideas," in Michael C. Dorf, ed., *Constitutional Law Stories* (New York, 2004), chap. 12; Helen Garfield, "Twentieth Century Jeffersonian: Brandeis, Freedom of Speech, and the Republican Revival," 69 *Oregon Law Review* 527 (1990). The only scholar I found who argued that Sanford's position is the better is Robert H. Bork, "Neutral Principles and Some First Amendment Problems," 47 *Indiana Law Journal* 1 (1971). The best analysis remains that of Blasi in "First Amendment and Civic Courage."

639 **matters of race:** Christopher A. Bracey, "Louis D. Brandeis and the Race Question," 52 *Alabama Law Review* 859, 863 (2001). LDB also joined Holmes's opinion in what is now considered the notorious opinion of *Buck v. Bell,* 274 U.S. 200 (1927), approving a state involuntary sterilization law.

639 **"he chose to champion":** Bracey, "Race Question," 863. LDB did speak for a unanimous Court in *Ziang Sun Wan v. United States,* 266 U.S. 1 (1924), reversing the conviction of a Chinese man for murder after he had been subjected to a ten-day third degree that left him in such shape that he would have confessed to anything. Although the petitioner was an Asian, the case did not concern race directly, but only the abuse by police.

639 **city of Louisville:** *Buchanan v. Warley,* 245 U.S. 60 (1917).

639 **state-run primary:** *Nixon v. Herndon,* 273 U.S. 536 (1927), and *Nixon v. Condon,* 286 U.S. 73 (1932). After these decisions southern states declared the Democratic Party to be a private organization and therefore immune from constitutional limitations on who could vote in its primaries. The Court unanimously upheld this arrangement in *Grovey v. Townsend,* 295 U.S.

45 (1935). Not until *Smith v. Allwright,* 321 U.S. 649 (1944), did the Court outlaw white primaries altogether.

639 **secured by torture:** *Powell v. Alabama,* 287 U.S. 45 (1932); *Norris v. Alabama,* 294 U.S. 587 (1935); *Brown v. Mississippi,* 297 U.S. 278 (1936).

639 **"insular minorities":** *United States v. Carolene Products Co.,* 304 U.S. 144 (1938).

639 **to its law school:** *Missouri ex rel. Gaines v. Canada,* 305 U.S. 337 (1938).

639 **to deny citizenship:** See, for example, *Ozawa v. United States,* 260 U.S. 178 (1922), and *United States v. Bhagat Singh Thind,* 261 U.S. 204 (1923); see also Lucy S. Salyer, *Laws Harsh as Tigers: Chinese Immigrants and the Shaping of Modern Immigration Law* (Chapel Hill, N.C., 1995).

639 **be an American citizen:** Although an Asian immigrant could not become a citizen, if that immigrant had a child born in the United States, under the Fourteenth Amendment that child would be a citizen.

640 **the truth of that claim:** *Ng Fung Ho v. White,* 259 U.S. 276 (1922).

640 **assistance in American courts:** LDB to Frankfurter, 26 September 1927, FF-HLS; the two cases were *Nagle v. Loi Hoa,* argued and decided with *Nagle v. Lam Young,* 275 U.S. 475 (1927).

640 **underwrite Margold's work:** For the Margold strategy, see Mark V. Tushnet, *The NAACP's Legal Strategy Against Segregated Education, 1925–1950* (Chapel Hill, N.C., 1987), 25–26. For LDB's interest in Margold, see LDB to Frankfurter, 11 and 29 February and 29 March 1928, FF-HLS.

640 **energy and resources into it:** Richard Kluger, *Simple Justice: The History of Brown v. Board of Education and Black America's Struggle for Equality* (New York, 1975), 125; Strum, *Brandeis,* 333. Ultimately, Johnson named Charles Houston as dean of the law school. Houston had been a disciple of Frankfurter's at Harvard and argued several cases before the Supreme Court employing Brandeis-style briefs.

640 **the Court should act:** The most complete analysis of LDB's vote in race-related cases, including Asian as well as African-American, is Larry M. Roth, "The Many Lives of Louis Brandeis: Progressive Reformer, Supreme Court Justice, Avowed Zionist, and a Racist?" 34 *Southern University Law Review* 123, 151–63 (2007). Roth also concludes that while it would have been nice had LDB taken on the fight, it would not have made sense given the time in which he lived and the Court on which he served.

CHAPTER 26: EXTRAJUDICIAL ACTIVITIES: II

642 **"as true as the other":** Holmes to Frankfurter, 22 May 1925, in Robert H. Mennel and Christine L. Compston, eds., *Holmes and Frankfurter: Their Correspondence, 1912–1934* (Hanover, N.H., 1996), 183.

642 **"were in full play":** *Washington Post,* 19 May 1925. LDB to Holmes, 19 May 1925, Holmes MSS. Holmes replied, "If anything should happen to you the Court and I both would lose an eye."

642 **"the most useful lawyer":** LDB to Harold Laski, 29 November 1928. Frankfurter's work during these years is well described in Michael E. Parrish, *Felix Frankfurter and His Times: The Reform Years* (New York, 1982).

642 **"half brother, half son":** LDB to Frankfurter, 24 September 1925, FF-LC.

643 **"does matrimony mar":** LDB to AGB, 20 April 1920.

643   **work had to be done:** LDB to Frankfurter, 6 April 1923, FF-HLS; Parrish, *Frankfurter,* 152.

643   **"leave the law school":** Felix Frankfurter with Harlan B. Phillips, *Felix Frankfurter Reminisces* (New York, 1960), 232. Frankfurter's own inclination was to decline, but there were also political reasons involved in his refusal; see Parrish, *Frankfurter,* 210–11.

643   **defray the medical expenses:** LDB to Frankfurter, 24 September 1925, FF-LC.

643   **put the two to death:** For Frankfurter's involvement, see Parrish, *Frankfurter,* chap. 10. The literature on Sacco and Vanzetti is immense, and after eight decades there is still debate about whether the men were innocent or not. Frankfurter wrote a book that emphasized the procedural irregularities: *The Case of Sacco and Vanzetti: A Critical Analysis for Lawyers and Laymen* (Boston, 1927). Marion Frankfurter and Gardner Jackson edited *The Letters of Sacco and Vanzetti* (New York, 1928). See, among many others, Francis Russell, *Tragedy in Dedham* (New York, 1962), which suggests that Sacco but not Vanzetti was involved in the crime, a position shared by some other writers; Roberta Strauss Feuerlicht, *Justice Crucified: The Story of Sacco and Vanzetti* (New York, 1977); and Bruce Watson, *Sacco and Vanzetti: The Men, the Murders, and the Judgment of Mankind* (New York, 2007).

643   **encouraged him in his efforts:** See letters from LDB to Frankfurter starting on 20 November 1924 in Melvin I. Urofsky and David W. Levy, eds., *"Half Brother, Half Son": The Letters of Louis D. Brandeis to Felix Frankfurter* (Norman, Okla., 1991).

643   **relating to the case:** LDB to Frankfurter, 2 June 1927, FF-LC.

643   **owned in Dedham:** Roger Nash Baldwin Memoir, 235, COHC; Watson, *Sacco and Vanzetti,* 227.

644   **"matter connected with it":** *New York World,* 22 August 1927, cited in Feuerlicht, *Justice Crucified,* 399.

644   **"into unclean hands":** Parrish, *Frankfurter,* 195.

645   **of innocent blood:** Vanzetti to Harry Dana, 22 August 1927, printed in *Nation,* October 1927; Holmes to Laski, 1 September 1927, in Mark DeWolfe Howe, ed., *Holmes-Laski Letters,* 2 vols. (Cambridge, Mass., 1953), 976.

645   **involving life and death:** Feuerlicht, *Justice Crucified,* 399.

645   **his whole career:** LDB to Frankfurter, 24 August 1927, FF-LC; Parrish, *Frankfurter,* 176–77.

645   **during the New Deal:** Frankfurter to LDB, 28 September 1926 and 12 November 1928.

645   **endow a research fund:** LDB to Frankfurter, 6 January 1924, reporting on a conversation with Victor S. Morawitz about contributing to the law school, FF-LC; Julian Mack to LDB, 10 November 1926. The Brandeis Research Fellowship was established in 1926 by gifts from LDB's former law clerks, former law partners, and friends, and is still in operation. David Warrington to author, 12 February 2008.

645   **lines of inquiry to them:** See the numerous letters from Brandeis in the Chafee, Hudson, Pound, and Powell papers in the Harvard Law School.

645   **not be as large:** LDB to Warren, 23 June 1922, Warren MSS.

646   **with the real world:** David Wigdor, *Roscoe Pound: Philosopher of Law* (Westport, Conn., 1974), 192.

646   "like an industrial plant": Parrish, *Frankfurter,* 152–53.

646   around the country: LDB to Frankfurter, 1 January 1925, FF-HLS.

647   opposed Pound's plans: LDB to Frankfurter, 9 and 25 October 1924, FF-LC.

647   expand the law school: Arthur Sutherland, *The Law at Harvard: A History of Ideas and Men, 1817–1967* (Cambridge, Mass., 1967), 262–70.

647   more discrete projects: This included funding for research assistants for Frankfurter's casebooks on federal jurisdiction and administrative law, as well as the work he did with James Landis leading to *The Business of the Supreme Court* (New York, 1927).

647   hung in the law school: Harvard managed to secure a portrait that had been painted earlier by an artist named Tompkins but for which LDB had not sat. Mrs. Evans purchased it at an auction of Tompkins's estate and then at Frankfurter's urging donated it to the law school. LDB to Alfred Brandeis, 12 February 1927, courtesy of Fannie Brandeis.

647   "via the states": LDB to Frankfurter, 8 November 1920, FF-HLS.

647   "do something with it": Donald A. Ritchie, *James M. Landis: Dean of the Regulators* (Cambridge, Mass., 1980), 82.

647   University of Louisville: At the time the university was a semi-private, semi-municipal school; it became part of the Kentucky state system in 1970. The full story and documents of LDB's efforts can be found in Bernard Flexner, *Mr. Justice Brandeis and the University of Louisville* (Louisville, Ky., 1938); and *Brandeis at 150: The Louisville Perspective* (Louisville, Ky., 2006). The Flexner brothers, who all knew Louis and Alfred as boys, played a major role in the work.

648   in a proper manner: LDB to Adele "Maidie" Brandeis, 24 September 1924. A few days later he wrote to Maidie that a fourth crate had been shipped, but before turning its contents over to the university, she should look for some six or seven books on ancient Greece that "the faithful Poindexter mistakenly" packed. LDB to Adele Brandeis, 29 September 1924.

648   to give Louis credit: The artworks included a painting by a Kentucky artist that the Speeds had given to LDB and AGB, and also a fourteenth-century Japanese sword. LDB to Hattie Bishop Speed, 9 October 1927, Speed MSS, includes a listing of the items. In 1935, LDB sent some additional drawings. LDB to Speed, 27 February 1935, Speed MSS.

648   as the prime movers: LDB to Fannie Brandeis, 20 October 1924 and 14 February 1925, and to Frederick Wehle, 28 October 1924.

648   "first steps toward realization": LDB to Wehle, 19 November 1924.

649   League of Nations: LDB to Charles Tachau (Alfred's son-in-law), 2 November 1925; LDB to Manley Hudson, 30 December 1927, and Hudson to LDB, 3 January 1928, Hudson MSS.

650   "defeat the best development": LDB to Alfred Brandeis, 9 March 1925.

650   "developed by Kentuckians": LDB to Alfred Brandeis, 18 February 1925.

650   "to its perfect end": LDB to Alfred Brandeis, 29 November 1927.

650   judges, and public officials: Robert N. Miller, relying on notes and conversations with LDB, conveyed this sentiment to the board of trustees. Flexner, *Brandeis and Louisville.*

650   continued to this day: In 1927, Brandeis, in a talk with university officials, offered to donate $10,000 a year for ten years to the law school, providing twice that sum was raised by subscription from members of the Kentucky

bar. It is unclear whether this plan worked out. LDB to Robert N. Miller, 18 January 1927.

650 **served in that office:** LDB to Robert N. Miller, 10 August 1926.

651 **"anticipated our wishes":** Flexner, *Brandeis and Louisville,* 63. Miller continued to set a model for public service. In 1933 he was elected Louisville's mayor, the first Democrat in fifteen years, and led the city through the crises of the Depression. He gained national fame in 1937 when the Ohio River flooded and Miller took to the new invention of radio to warn citizens, direct volunteers, and appeal for donations to help the victims.

651 **once in practice:** Former dean Laura Rothstein to author, 13 February 2008.

651 **"in morality; in culture":** LDB to Frankfurter, 27 March 1921, FF-LC.

652 **"a terrible blunder":** LDB to Alfred Brandeis, 20 June 1920; LDB to Frankfurter, 4 December 1920, FF-HLS. Hoover, however, had grown up in a small Iowa town where the only Democrat had been the town drunkard. Although he had never announced any political affiliation, it would have been inconceivable for him to choose the Democrats.

652 **"talk among newspapermen":** LDB to Alfred Brandeis, 6 September 1921.

652 **"they could not fulfill":** Acheson to Frankfurter, 9 September 1921, FF-LC.

652 **"sense of uncleanness":** LDB to Frankfurter, 26 February 1927, FF-LC.

652 **"sympathies may be with La Follette":** Taft to Max Pam, 12 September 1924, quoted in Alpheus T. Mason, *William Howard Taft: Chief Justice* (New York, 1964), 218. Taft doubted, however, that LDB would go along with La Follette's proposal to abolish the Court's power of judicial review.

652 **than anywhere else:** AGB to Elizabeth Brandeis, 16 July 1924, EBR.

652 **"when the opportunity offers":** AGB to Belle Case La Follette, 16 July 1924, La Follette MSS.

653 **supporting his record:** Belle Case La Follette and Fola La Follette, *Robert M. La Follette,* 2 vols. (New York, 1953), 2:1116.

653 **state of Wisconsin:** See David Waterhouse, *The Progressive Movement of 1924 and the Development of Interest Group Liberalism* (New York, 1991).

653 **"And he knew not fear":** LDB to Alfred Brandeis, 26 March 1925; LDB to Frankfurter, 20 June 1925, FF-LC. To Norman Hapgood he wrote on 30 June 1925, "In the last fortnight our thought has been much of La Follette, of what he has been to the country, and what next." Hapgood MSS.

653 **campaign for Butler:** LDB to Frankfurter, 28 October 1926, FF-HLS.

653 **sentiment for Smith:** LDB to Alfred Brandeis, 2 July 1928; LDB to Susan Brandeis Gilbert, 2 September and 28 October 1928, LDB-BU.

654 **claimed full credit:** See Edmund A. Moore, *A Catholic Runs for President: The Campaign of 1928* (New York, 1956); and Christopher M. Finan, *Alfred E. Smith: The Happy Warrior* (New York, 2002).

654 **"old order holds fast":** LDB to Elizabeth Brandeis Raushenbush, 13 November 1928, EBR, and a similar sentiment to Susan Brandeis Gilbert, 7 November 1928, LDB-BU; LDB to White, 29 December 1928, and White to LDB, 12 January 1929, White MSS.

654 **to discuss with him:** Frankfurter to Roosevelt, 21 November 1928, in Max Freedman, ed., *Roosevelt and Frankfurter: Their Correspondence, 1928–1945* (Boston, 1967), 39.

655 **"battle, on your side":** LDB to Grady, 1 April 1923 and 16 March 1928,

Grady MSS. The collection is full of notes providing reassurance and encouragement and longer letters asking for details, suggesting people to see, wanting to know why something had happened.

655 **"strong believer in Amazons":** LDB to Jack Gilbert, 20 March 1928, LDB-BU.

656 **"promoting savings-bank insurance":** Casady to Alpheus Mason, 11 December 1941, quoted in Alpheus T. Mason, *Brandeis: A Free Man's Life* (New York, 1946), 583.

656 **their separate ways:** Minutes of meeting on 10 June 1921, in Jacob de Haas, *Louis D. Brandeis: A Biographical Sketch* (New York, 1929), 273.

656 **Brandeis had proposed:** Details are explored in Melvin I. Urofsky, *American Zionism from Herzl to the Holocaust* (Garden City, N.Y., 1975), chaps. 8 and 9.

656 **$750,000 to the funds:** Robert Szold, *77 Great Russell Street* (privately printed, 1967), 8.

657 **the PDC could command:** The plan also got caught up in intra-Zionist politicking, and even if the Brandeis group had had the resources, it is unlikely that progress could have been made. See Urofsky, *American Zionism,* 316–17.

657 **they would regain power:** He even agreed to meet with Chaim Weizmann when the latter came to the United States. LDB to Frankfurter, 2 December 1926, FF-HLS.

657 **drawn into the scheming:** See, for example, memo of meeting at LDB's apartment, 1 June 1927, Goldberg MSS.

657 **anonymously established:** LDB paid in $1,000 annually to the fund; LDB to Mack, 6 November 1925, R. Szold MSS.

657 **future of Hadassah:** Rose Jacobs, "Justice Brandeis and Hadassah," *New Palestine,* 14 November 1941, 17–19.

658 **Alice for help:** LDB to Susan Brandeis Gilbert, 4 May 1928, LDB-BU.

658 **Jewish Agency for Palestine:** See Urofsky, *American Zionism,* chap. 8.

658 **"development of the country":** LDB to Jacob de Haas (who attended the meeting as LDB's representative), 14 February 1924, Weizmann MSS.

658 **did not trust Chaim Weizmann:** LDB to Frankfurter, 1 January 1927, FF-HLS.

658 **plagued her in Boston:** There seems to have been only two serious episodes, one in the spring of 1923 and a recurrence, or continuation of it, in the fall, and these can be traced in letters to Susan Brandeis. "Mother had a bad collapse (nervous) yesterday afternoon which sent her to bed under Dr. Parker's care" (5 March); "Monday night was ghastly. . . . You should not be near her or communicate with her until she spontaneously ask you to come" (11 April); "Mother's condition is now so perplexing, and she is so far below the usual level" (4 October); "She seems to be overcoming her deep depression and is surely struggling gallantly to control herself and to look hopefully toward the future" (14 October); "After three good nights of sleep Mother has recovered her cheerfulness and is about where she was when the slump overcame her" (18 November).

659 **an occasional paddle:** LDB to Susan Brandeis Gilbert, 8 February 1927, LDB-BU ("Mother & I had 40 minutes on the towpath"), and to Elizabeth Brandeis Raushenbush, 22 April 1929, EBR ("yesterday we had a joyous paddle on the Canal").

659 **female guests seated:** Thomas Austern interview, Paper MSS.

660 **the justice's office:** LDB to Alfred Brandeis, 11 September 1926. Poindexter, whom the early clerks recalled as old when they arrived, finally retired, to be replaced by a man called Smallwood in the 1930s.

660 **a Brandeis clerk:** Adrian Fisher interview, Paper MSS. Fisher, the last of LDB's clerks, said that "you were expected to sublease" Miss Turner's apartment; he did not elaborate on why Miss Turner had the apartment or why she did not live there.

661 **"He was a civilized man":** LDB to Alfred Brandeis, 20 and 22 September 1927. To Frankfurter he wrote of his visit: "It is a strong confirmation that T.J. was greatly civilized. Washington, Jefferson, Franklin, Hamilton were indeed a Big Four." LDB to Frankfurter, 22 September 1927, FF-LC. It is interesting that LDB omitted John Adams from this pantheon, since in many ways he shared many of his fellow Massachusetts man's characteristics.

661 **"appreciating S.B.I.":** LDB to Grady, 22 September 1927, Grady MSS.

661 **"permitted to enjoy":** LDB to AGB, 24 and 27 July, 2 August 1921; LDB to Alfred Brandeis, 9 August 1921.

662 **"succession of professional thrills":** LDB to Frankfurter, 3 November 1921, FF-LC. "I am glad to know from your yesterday's letter that you have had some further court experience and that you are enjoying it so much." LDB to Susan Brandeis, 21 June 1921, LDB-BU.

662 **"poor by comparison":** LDB to Susan Brandeis, 17 January 1925, LDB-BU.

662 **"the language of business":** LDB to Susan Brandeis, 21 June and 9 October 1921, LDB-BU.

662 **it would embarass him:** "Is it all right with you if I volunteer legal services for Bob Dunn in Passaic?" Susan Brandeis Gilbert to LDB, telegram, 13 April 1926. LDB replied, "All right so far as I am concerned. Thank you." Passaic was the scene of a bloody textile strike, and sympathetic lawyers like Susan and Justine Wise became involved trying to help the strikers.

662 **needed to be appealed:** LDB to Susan Brandeis, 14 October 1921, 20 March 1925, LDB-BU.

662 **presenting her case:** The case was *Margolin v. United States,* 269 U.S. 93 (1925), in which Susan and her partner Benjamin Kirsch argued unsuccessfully on behalf of a lawyer who had been convicted for charging a veteran more than the permissible amount for a filing fee. LDB to Susan Brandeis, 6 July 1921, 4 October 1924, and 6 October 1925, LDB-BU. Only a minor criticism came from Justice Sanford, who said that she occasionally let her voice fall so that it was hard to hear her at the end of the bench.

662 **"and a long necklace":** LDB to Susan Brandeis, 18 March 1924, LDB-BU. "Next friend" is a legal term for a person acting for the benefit of another, usually minors or those legally incapable of speaking for themselves.

663 **"your mature judgment":** LDB to Susan Brandeis, 6 February 1925, LDB-BU. Gilbert came down to Washington to meet Susan's parents in April and received, according to his recollection, a warm reception. See his memo "Some Items and Observations of LDB," n.d., LDB-BU.

663 **"life without doubting":** LDB to Susan Brandeis, 23 October 1925, LDB-BU. To Frankfurter, LDB wrote, "Susan is making an unambitious marriage upon which we look hopefully." LDB to Frankfurter, 11 December 1925, FF-HLS.

663 **"breathes La Follette's air":** LDB to Elizabeth Brandeis, 7 August 1923, EBR.

663 **that he edited:** The dissertation was titled "The Wage Earner and the Common Rule: A Study of the Employer-Employee Relation." Her work makes up half of volume 3 in John R. Commons et al., *History of Labour in the United States,* 4 vols. (New York, 1921–1935).

663 **recommended she take:** LDB to Elizabeth Brandeis, 8 February 1924, EBR.

663 **none of her family present:** As LDB told Susan, EB objected to the word "wedding." Some historians have suggested that "marriage" implied a joining of two equals, whereas "wedding" had the old Blackstone notion of one male giving a female, his daughter, to another male to own as a wife. The two would then be merged into one, the one, of course, being the male. Elizabeth expected that she and Paul would retain their own professional identities. Jill Norgren to author, 10 February 2008; Ellen Chesler to author, 12 February 2008; and Nancy Cott to author, 12 February 2008.

663 **in the Canadian woods:** LDB to Susan Brandeis, 12 April 1925, LDB-BU.

664 **until their retirement:** LDB to Susan Brandeis Gilbert, 27 March, 10 and 17 April 1927, LDB-BU; LDB to Elizabeth Brandeis Raushenbush, 24 April 1927, EBR.

664 **"goes well with them":** LDB to Frankfurter, 4 November 1926, FF-LC.

664 **the summer at Chatham:** LDB to Susan Brandeis Gilbert, 31 May 1928, LDB-BU, insisting that he and Alice would pay all of their expenses in Chatham. "You and your family are to be as much our guests as if you were in our own house."

664 **fortune kept growing:** E. Louise Malloch, who supervised LDB's investments, reported that at the end of the decade the market value of his investments was $2,554,338.35, a shrinkage of about 3 percent from the cost, an almost insignificant amount considering that the stock market had crashed two months earlier. Malloch to LDB, 17 January 1930, LDB-BU.

665 **freedom that he so prized:** "Mother and I are glad that you propose devoting much more of your working time to unpaid professional services." In the summer of 1929 LDB gave to each of his daughters $11,000, and in the fall gave them an additional gift of $10,000 in cash and $19,000 in registered bonds. LDB to Susan Brandeis Gilbert, 31 July and 31 August 1929, LDB-BU.

665 **"go to you someday:** LDB to Elizabeth Brandeis Raushenbush, 28 November 1929; see also Elizabeth to LDB, 9 June 1931, EBR.

665 **as they wanted:** LDB to Susan Brandeis Gilbert, 29 December 1928, LDB-BU, informing her that Miss Malloch would send a check for $9,650.20 to pay off debts, and that he would send a monthly check of $125, and a like amount to Elizabeth.

665 **"made of the income":** LDB to Susan Brandeis Gilbert, 8 November 1929, LDB-BU. At this time LDB informed his daughters that the monthly allowance would stop, as they had understood, after he had transferred a specific amount of money. With this letter he informed them that he had directed Miss Malloch to transfer an additional $30,000 in bonds to each of them.

665 **"throughout his life":** LDB to Susan Brandeis, 10 May 1925, LDB-BU.

666 **"and Act Accordingly":** LDB to Alfred Brandeis, 26 May 1927.

666 **the rest of his life:** LDB to Jennie Brandeis, 8 and 14 August 1928, courtesy of Fannie Brandeis.

667 **"Nobly done":** Holmes to Brandeis, 12 November 1926, Holmes MSS.

667 **there could be no appeal:** Joseph Alsop and Robert Kintner, "The Capital Parade," *Milwaukee Journal,* 8 May 1938; the actual refusal is LDB to Charles E. Clark, then dean of the Yale Law School, 12 March 1930. The Alsop column reported that Harvard wanted to award LDB an honorary degree, and predicted that he would say no. It recalled that in 1916 Abbott Lowell had joined the pack protesting LDB's nomination to the Court.

668 **"I understand fully":** Edward Filene to LDB, 27 October 1926; LDB to Filene, 23 November 1926, Filene MSS.

CHAPTER 27: DEPRESSION

669 **"business becomes apparent":** LDB to Gilbert, 27 October 1929, LDB-BU.

669 **depression had begun:** LDB to Elizabeth Brandeis Raushenbush, 13 November 1929, EBR. Lively accounts of the crash can be found in John Kenneth Galbraith, *The Great Crash* (Boston, 1955); and Frederick Lewis Allen, *Only Yesterday* (New York, 1931). A more scholarly analysis is Robert Sobel, *Panic on Wall Street* (New York, 1968).

669 **economic analysts agreed:** David M. Kennedy, *Freedom from Fear: The American People in Depression and War, 1929–1945* (New York, 1999), 39.

670 **Louisville law schools:** Alpheus T. Mason, *Brandeis: A Free Man's Life* (New York, 1946), 691, 692.

670 **"a century ago":** *Id.,* 598.

671 **failed to increase:** LDB to Frankfurter, 30 September 1922, FF-HLS. The memo had been written at Frankfurter's request, but was really for the benefit of Herbert Croly, who had asked what matters LDB thought the *New Republic* should explore.

671 **excess profits tax:** LDB to Frankfurter, 4 January and 20 November 1923, FF-LC.

671 **received for their goods:** LDB to George Soule, 22 April 1923; LDB to Frankfurter, 24 January 1926, FF-HLS.

671 **with which to gamble:** LDB to Harlan Fiske Stone, 20 July 1930, Stone MSS; LDB to Alfred Brandeis, 2 June 1923.

671 **form of speculation:** LDB to Frankfurter, 5 December 1926, FF-HLS.

671 **level did not exist:** *Galveston Electric Co. v. Galveston,* 258 U.S. 388 (1922).

672 **"below the 1914 lows":** Bruce Barton, "There Is No 'Normal,' " *New York Herald-Tribune Magazine,* 19 February 1933. The case is *Southwestern Bell Telephone Co. v. Public Service Commission of Missouri,* 262 U.S. 276, 289, 303n.16 (1923) (LDB concurring).

672 **"rents and interest":** LDB to Kellogg, 11 and 15 March 1928, Kellogg MSS. For the government report by Secretary of Labor James J. Davis that so incensed LDB, see *New York Times,* 27 March 1928.

672 **his earlier writings:** Elizabeth and Paul Raushenbush Memoir, 130, OHRO.

673 **cynicism and materialism:** LDB to Harold Laski, 28 February 1932, Laski MSS; LDB to Frank Tannenbaum, 29 May 1931, Tannenbaum MSS; LDB to Elizabeth Evans, 30 October 1929, Evans MSS.

674 **Hoover administration:** Gardner Jackson Memoir, 370, OHRO; Kennedy, *Freedom from Fear,* 92; Paul Dickson and Thomas B. Allen, *The Bonus Army: An American Epic* (New York, 2004).

674 **"steady the boat":** Alpheus T. Mason, *William Howard Taft: Chief Justice* (New York, 1964), 295; and Henry F. Pringle, *The Life and Times of William Howard Taft: A Biography,* 2 vols. (New York, 1939), 2:1044.

675 **the general welfare:** There is, unfortunately, no good biography of Hughes. Merlo J. Pusey, *Charles Evans Hughes,* 2 vols. (New York, 1952), is very much an "official" work. David J. Danelski and Joseph S. Tulchin have edited *The Autobiographical Notes of Charles Evans Hughes* (Cambridge, Mass., 1973). See also Paul Freund, "Charles Evans Hughes as Chief Justice," 81 *Harvard Law Review* 4 (1967).

675 **"ought to be unanimous":** Pusey, *Hughes,* 2:694; James Landis Memoir, 89, OHRO. The Brandeis law firm had been a correspondent in Boston to Hughes's firm in New York.

675 **welcomed him warmly:** Pusey, *Hughes,* 2:692.

675 **or in government:** *Id.,* 2:673.

675 **society remained static:** There is little written on Roberts, but Charles A. Leonard, *A Search for a Judicial Philosophy: Mr. Justice Roberts and the Constitutional Revolution of 1937* (Port Washington, N.Y., 1971), is useful.

676 **"of things worthwhile":** LDB to Harold Laski, 3 August 1925, Laski MSS.

676 **coming on the Court:** LDB to Frankfurter, 9 and 11 January 1930, FF-LC.

676 **"his full share":** Danelski and Tulchin, *Autobiographical Notes,* 299.

676 **"lived and loved":** G. Edward White, *Justice Oliver Wendell Holmes: Law and the Inner Self* (New York, 1993), 466–67. LDB to Holmes, 12 January 1932, Holmes MSS. The quotation is from the German poet Schiller's "Thekla's Song," and the dates those of Holmes's service on the Supreme Court. Hughes held the retirement letter for a day so that Holmes could deliver his finished opinions the next morning.

677 **brethren had given him:** *State Industrial Board of the State of New York v. Terry & Tench Co. and United States Fidelity & Guaranty Co.,* 273 U.S. 639 (1926). Frankfurter picked up on the suggestion, and an unsigned note in 40 *Harvard Law Review* 485 (1926–1927) condemned the Court for its treatment of an opinion by so distinguished a jurist.

677 **behavior toward him:** Charles C. Burlingame Memoir, 12, OHRO; Andrew I. Kaufman, *Cardozo* (Cambridge, Mass., 1998), 477. When Cardozo was nominated, McReynolds commented that to become a justice one only had to be a Jew and have a father who was a crook, and at the swearing-in ceremony ostentatiously buried himself behind a newspaper. Richard Polenberg, *The World of Benjamin Cardozo: Personal Values and the Judicial Process* (Cambridge, Mass., 1997), 171.

677 **"fifty-one percent right":** Cardozo did not disagree with LDB that a judge was often left with doubts, but he told the clerk, "The trouble with that is that when you think you are fifty-one percent right, it may really only be forty-nine percent." Kaufman, *Cardozo,* 212.

677 **"trouble himself about labels":** William G. Ross, *The Chief Justiceship of Charles Evans Hughes, 1930–1941* (Columbia, S.C., 2007), 35.

678 **within narrow brackets:** *Stromberg v. California,* 283 U.S. 359 (1931).

678 **holding unpopular ideas:** *United States v. Macintosh,* 283 U.S. 605 (1931); *United States v. Schwimmer,* 279 U.S. 644 (1929). See Ronald B. Flowers, "The

Naturalization of Douglas Clyde Macintosh, Alien Theologian," 25 *Journal of Supreme Court History* 243 (2000).

678 **to prepare a dissent:** LDB to Thomas Austern (his clerk for 1930–1931), 14 October 1930, LDB-SC.

678 **extended the Press Clause:** *Near v. Minnesota,* 283 U.S. 697 (1931). For the case, see Fred W. Friendly, *Minnesota Rag* (New York, 1981). The dissenting opinion by Butler expressed an uncharacteristic devotion to judicial restraint, but agreed with the majority that the Press Clause applied to the states.

678 **had been with him:** *O'Gorman and Young v. Hartford Fire Insurance Co.,* 282 U.S. 251 (1931). Hughes and Roberts apparently considered regulation as less intrusive on the market than barriers to entry. Ross, *Chief Justiceship of Hughes,* 37.

679 **with eternal verities:** *New State Ice Co. v. Liebmann,* 285 U.S. 262 (1932). Justice Cardozo did not take part in this case. For a defense of Sutherland's position and an attack on LDB, see Hadley Arkes, *The Return of George Sutherland* (Princeton, N.J., 1994), 54ff. Joel Paschal notes that for Sutherland, the Constitution did not trim rights because some people thought new ways were needed; the Fourteenth Amendment in his mind did not allow experimentation. *Mr. Justice Sutherland: A Man Against the State* (Princeton, N.J., 1951), 163.

679 **"capricious or unreasonable":** *New State Ice,* 285 U.S. at 280, 284–85 (LDB dissenting).

679 **"our minds be bold":** *Id.* at 287, 294, 311.

680 **"rest of the country":** *Id.* at 310, 311.

680 **all but disappeared:** *Wickard v. Filburn,* 317 U.S. 111 (1942).

680 **laboratories of democracy:** See E. E. Steiner, "A Progressive Creed: The Experimental Federalism of Justice Brandeis," 2 *Yale Law & Policy Review* 1 (1983), which includes a number of cases citing the LDB statement.

681 **such a radical idea:** See *Washington v. Glucksberg,* 521 U.S. 702 (1997), decided along with *Vacco v. Quill,* 521 U.S. 793 (1997).

681 **in different counties:** *Liggett Co. v. Lee,* 288 U.S. 517 (1933).

681 **tax on chain stores:** *State Board of Tax Commissioners of Indiana v. Jackson,* 283 U.S. 527 (1931). LDB joined Roberts in this decision, while Sutherland, Butler, Van Devanter, and McReynolds dissented.

681 **no business second-guessing:** *Liggett,* 288 U.S. at 541 (LDB dissenting).

682 **"merits of its exercise":** Alpheus T. Mason, *Harlan Fiske Stone: Pillar of the Law* (New York, 1956), 350. Stone joined Cardozo's dissent that avoided some of the implications of LDB's opinion, and was unusual in that it treated LDB's dissent almost as critically as the majority opinion. *Liggett,* 288 U.S. at 580 (Cardozo dissenting). When LDB saw Cardozo's circulation, he told Paul Freund, "Well, it's probably better this way. I can speak for myself."

682 **to be confirmed:** Paul Freund interview, Paper MSS.

683 **to act as it had:** *Home Building & Loan Association v. Blaisdell,* 290 U.S. 398 (1934). The quotation is from Marshall's opinion in *McCulloch v. Maryland,* 17 U.S. (4 Wheat.) 316 (1819). See Samuel R. Olken, "Charles Evans Hughes and the Blaisdell Decision: A Historical Study of Contract Clause Jurisprudence," 72 *Oregon Law Review* 513 (1993).

683 **striking it down:** *W. B. Worthen Co. v. Thomas,* 292 U.S. 426 (1934). The

dissenters in *Blaisdell* concurred in *Worthen,* but said they saw no difference between the two laws insofar as both violated the Contract Clause.

683 **judicial intervention:** *Nebbia v. New York,* 291 U.S. 502 (1934).

684 **demand new measures:** "The Supreme Court Eats Crow," *New Republic,* 21 March 1934, cited in Ross, *Chief Justiceship of Hughes,* 52–53; see there similar comments from other journals.

684 **in full strength:** *Morehead v. New York ex rel. Tipaldo,* 298 U.S. 587 (1936).

685 **now stood triumphant:** *New Palestine,* 25 January 1929, 53. The great historian of Zionism, Adolf Böhm, concurred in this assessment.

685 **"or any of his ilk":** LDB to Jacob de Haas, 5 June 1927, de Haas MSS.

686 **"which they secured":** LDB to Jacob de Haas, 24 December 1927, Mack MSS.

686 **support dwindling:** For details, see Melvin I. Urofsky, *American Zionism from Herzl to the Holocaust* (Garden City, N.Y., 1975), 35off.

687 **while on the bench:** Minutes of meeting among Justice Brandeis, Felix Warburg, and Bernard Flexner, 9 September 1929, FF-HLS. LDB later said, "I made the single departure from my rule in 1929 and attended the Warburg meeting because I deemed it very important—as if it were a war measure—to let the British know that, despite retirement of our group from the Z.O.A. management, I was still active in Zionist affairs. There was [also] necessity of telling Americans of my active interest." LDB to Julian Mack, 26 November 1931.

687 **"opportunity is open":** *New York Times,* 25 November 1929; *Jewish Tribune,* 29 November 1929.

687 **his speech in full:** *Jewish Tribune,* 20 December 1929; *Jewish Guardian,* 21 November 1929; LDB, "The Will to a Jewish Palestine," *New Palestine,* 29 November 1929.

688 **and to take other steps:** See letters in Melvin I. Urofsky and David W. Levy, eds., *Letters of Louis D. Brandeis,* 5 vols. (Albany, N.Y., 1971–1978), 5:388ff.

688 **"and best wishes":** LDB to Delegates to ZOA Convention, 28 June 1930, R. Szold MSS.

688 **economic rebuilding of Palestine:** The memorandum, signed by LDB, Robert Szold, Julian Mack, and Jacob de Haas, appeared in the *New Palestine* of 30 May 1930 under the caption "Brandeis Defines the Terms."

689 **"That involves thinking":** LDB to Julian Mack, 12 June 1930, Mack MSS.

689 **new requests for information:** See material in Urofsky and Levy, *Letters of Brandeis,* 5:43off.

690 **" 'a great Judge' ":** *New York Times,* 9 November 1931. Among the essayists was the journalist Max Lerner, who had first met LDB in 1924. Periodically, the justice would invite a group of students over to his apartment on Sunday afternoons and talk informally to them about Zionism and comparing the ancient Greek city-state to America in the age of Jefferson. Lerner interview, Paper MSS.

CHAPTER 28: THE NEW DEAL

691 **of government functions:** Rexford Guy Tugwell Diary, 26 April 1934, Tugwell MSS. My thanks to Professor John Q. Barrett for calling this item to my attention.

691 **"the specific field"**: Roosevelt to Norman Hapgood, 24 February 1936, Roosevelt MSS.

691 **Democratic nominee in 1932**: For relations between Frankfurter and Roosevelt, see Max Freedman, ed., *Roosevelt and Frankfurter: Their Correspondence, 1928–1945* (Boston, 1967); and Michael E. Parrish, *Felix Frankfurter and His Times: The Reform Years* (New York, 1982), chap. 11.

692 **"difficulties of the task"**: LDB to Elizabeth Evans, 27 November 1932, Evans MSS.

692 **of solicitor general**: Frankfurter, memorandum of 8 March 1933, in Freedman, *Roosevelt and Frankfurter,* 114.

692 **New Deal agencies**: G. Edward White, "Felix Frankfurter, the Old Boy Network, and the New Deal: The Placement of Elite Lawyers in Public Service in the 1930s," 39 *Arkansas Law Review* 631 (1986).

692 **" 'a great soul' "**: Frankfurter to Roosevelt, 12 November 1932, Roosevelt to Frankfurter, 11 June 1934, in Freedman, *Roosevelt and Frankfurter,* 94, 222.

692 **curse of bigness**: The Depression revived interest in LDB's 1913 attack on the banks, and in 1933 the National Home Library Foundation published an inexpensive edition of *Other People's Money*. See LDB to Louis Wehle, 19 January 1932, Wehle MSS, and to Sherman F. Mittell, 25 August 1933 (saying he would pay the necessary permission fee to the original publisher). The new edition did well, and Mrs. Brandeis commented to a visitor, "We are a best seller." Alpheus T. Mason, *Brandeis: A Free Man's Life* (New York, 1946), 605.

692 **gravitated toward Brandeis**: See, for example, William O. Douglas, *Go East, Young Man* (New York, 1974), 441–49. For Lilienthal, whom one scholar has called "more Brandeisian than most New Deal Lawyers," see Jordan A. Schwarz, *The New Dealers: Power Politics in the Age of Roosevelt* (New York, 1993), chap. 10.

693 **great deal of impatience**: LDB to Alice Park Goldmark, 11 January 1934, EBR.

693 **on a weekly basis**: Donald A. Ritchie, *James M. Landis: Dean of the Regulators* (Cambridge, Mass., 1980), 233n.5. Landis was then in Washington as a member of the Securities and Exchange Commission.

693 **a potential nominee**: See, for example, Harold Ickes to LDB, 15 June 1933; LDB to Ickes, 14 June 1933, recommending Philip La Follette; Frankfurter to LDB, 13 September 1935; LDB to Frankfurter, 14 September 1935 ("I think highly of Fahey").

694 **"woman for the Cabinet"**: Paul Freund Memoir, 78, New York Times Oral History Program; LDB to Frankfurter, 23 February 1933, FF-LC.

694 **attributed to him**: "Don't believe all you read or hear . . . of my influence." LDB to Jack Gilbert, 13 December 1933, LDB-BU.

694 **the "Jew Deal"**: *National Jewish Ledger,* 29 October 1937; William E. Leuchtenburg, *Franklin D. Roosevelt and the New Deal, 1932–1940* (New York, 1963), 276–77.

694 **"of the Supreme Court"**: Ron Chernow, *The House of Morgan: An American Banking Dynasty and the Rise of Modern Finance* (New York, 1990), 378–79. Chernow adds that the main players who helped chase the money changers from the temple included Irish, Italians, and Jews—the groups that had been excluded from WASP Wall Street in the 1920s.

694 **monopoly and Wall Street:** See, for example, Arthur M. Schlesinger Jr., *The Politics of Upheaval* (Boston, 1960).

694 **described as "Brandeisian":** Michael E. Parrish, *Securities Regulation and the New Deal* (New Haven, Conn., 1970); William E. Leuchtenburg Memoir, 28, OHRO.

695 **fix the system:** LDB to Frankfurter, 15 February and 3 March 1933, FF-LC.

695 **money into their accounts:** For the failure of the system and Roosevelt's response, see Susan Estabrook Kennedy, *The Banking Crisis of 1933* (Lexington, Ky., 1973).

695 **the members to read:** Leuchtenburg, *New Deal,* 43.

696 **"political sagacity":** LDB to Frankfurter, 22 March 1933, FF-LC.

696 **rest of the decade:** LDB to Frankfurter, 12 April 1933, FF-LC. For the problem of European Jewry, see next chapter.

696 **the justice was horrified:** LDB to Frankfurter, 14 May and 13 June 1933, FF-LC.

697 **"things you have done":** Leffingwell to Roosevelt, 2 October 1933, quoted in Leuchtenburg, *New Deal,* 51.

697 **"honorable way out":** LDB to Frankfurter, 13 June 1933, FF-LC.

698 **"so read the Constitution":** Paul Freund, quoted in William E. Leuchtenburg, "Charles Evans Hughes: The Center Holds," 83 *North Carolina Law Review* 1187, 1191 (2005); *Perry v. United States,* 294 U.S. 330, 350 (1935), decided with *Nortz v. United States,* 294 U.S. 317 (1935). See also Merlo J. Pusey, *Charles Evans Hughes,* 2 vols. (New York, 1952), 1:736–37.

698 **gold clause cases:** The other two, involving private obligations, were *Norman v. Baltimore & Ohio Railroad Co.,* decided together with *United States v. Bankers' Trust Co.,* 294 U.S. 240 (1935).

698 **"Shame and humiliation":** William G. Ross, *The Chief Justiceship of Charles Evans Hughes* (Columbia, S.C., 2007), 63.

698 **morality of the repudiation:** Melvin I. Urofsky, "Brandeis-Frankfurter Conversations," 1985 *Supreme Court Review* 337.

698 **be declared unconstitutional:** Marian McKenna, *Franklin Roosevelt and the Great Constitutional War: The Court-Packing Crisis of 1937* (New York, 2002), 62–63.

698 **common goal—recovery:** See William E. Leuchtenburg, "The New Deal and the Analogue of War," in John Braeman et al., eds., *Change and Continuity in Twentieth Century America* (Columbus, Ohio, 1965).

699 **review by the Supreme Court:** For the NRA, see Ellis Wayne Hawley, *The New Deal and the Problem of Monopoly* (Princeton, N.J., 1966); Robert F. Himmelberg, *The Origins of the National Recovery Act* (New York, 1976); and Bernard Bellush, *The Failure of the NRA* (New York, 1977).

699 **trouble with the judiciary:** Despite the hundreds of lawyers who had descended on Washington, Roosevelt had pitifully inadequate legal talent defending his programs. Attorney General Homer Cummings spent most of his time aggrandizing the Justice Department and refused to allow the better-trained and more capable lawyers in the various agencies and departments to litigate challenges to the laws. The solicitor general, J. Crawford Biggs, lost ten of the first seventeen cases he handled, and one of the justices referred to him as "Serjeant Buzfuz" after a character in Charles Dickens's *Pickwick Papers.* "Our Court," LDB complained, "will apparently be con-

fronted, in time of greatest need of help, with a Department of Justice as incompetent as was that of Mitchell Palmer." LDB to Frankfurter, 13 June 1933. At the end of the October 1933 term, the justices conveyed word to the president that Biggs should be kept from arguing in their court if the government hoped to win any cases. See Peter H. Irons, *The New Deal Lawyers* (Princeton, N.J., 1982).

699 **harbinger of those to follow:** *Panama Refining Co. v. Ryan,* 293 U.S. 388 (1935).

700 **be gotten from the NRA:** Pusey, *Hughes,* 2:734.

700 **"law-making functions":** *Panama Refining,* 293 U.S. at 430. On the circulation LDB wrote, "Yes, Sir, complete and even the layman can understand."

700 **slipshod practices:** *Id.* at 433 (Cardozo dissenting).

700 **need for it:** Erwin Griswold, "Government in Ignorance of the Law: A Plea for Better Publication of Executive Legislation," 48 *Harvard Law Review* 198 (1933–34); Jerome Frank Memoir, 84–85, OHRO.

701 **a painful matter:** Urofsky, "Brandeis-Frankfurter Conversations," 337.

701 **on chorus girls:** Leuchtenburg, *New Deal,* 65–66.

701 **the end of September:** LDB to Frankfurter, 14 August 1933, FF-LC.

701 **an impossible job:** LDB to Frankfurter, 22 September 1934, FF-LC.

701 **"from bad to worse":** LDB to Elizabeth Brandeis Raushenbush, 22 April 1934, EBR.

701 **labor, and the public:** The Darrow report is generally considered biased, with Darrow suggesting socialized ownership of industry as the only remedy.

701 **"I was his friend":** LDB to Frankfurter, 22 September 1934, FF-LC.

702 **involving the NRA:** Bruce Allen Murphy, *The Brandeis/Frankfurter Connection: The Secret Political Activities of Two Supreme Court Justices* (New York, 1982), 146.

702 **rid himself of Johnson:** LDB to Frankfurter, 19 and 29 September 1934, FF-LC; Frankfurter to Roosevelt, 20 September 1934, in Freedman, *Roosevelt and Frankfurter,* 233.

702 **fuel to the flames:** Paul Freund interview, Paper MSS.

703 **"shot by a lunatic":** LDB to Frankfurter, 25 and 29 September 1934, FF-LC; Frankfurter to Alfred E. Cohn, 30 October 1925, recalling the episode, in Freedman, *Roosevelt and Frankfurter,* 288–91.

703 **more than just a "few":** "Brandeis's Views Vital Force with New Deal," *Albany (N.Y.) Evening News,* 11 October 1934.

703 **all of his life:** Freund interview, Paper MSS.

703 **fight the Depression:** Three weeks earlier the Court buttressed these fears when by a 5–4 vote it struck down the 1933 Railroad Retirement Act in *Railroad Retirement Board v. Alton Railroad,* 295 U.S. 330 (1935). Justice Roberts's opinion followed the conservative line of denying that the government had any role to play in social welfare, that the Due Process Clause protected property, and that the Court reserved the right to pass on the wisdom of the legislation. LDB, along with Stone and Cardozo, joined the chief justice in his dissent.

703 **Frazier-Lemke Act:** *Louisville Joint Stock Land Bank v. Radford,* 295 U.S. 555 (1935).

704 **interest in the farm:** LDB's opinion drew rave reviews from his fellow justices. On the return Hughes wrote, "I agree. A most thorough and admirable

opinion." Sutherland: "Am glad to agree. A sound opinion." Stone: "Yes sir. A very strong opinion." Van Devanter and Roberts also praised it, although Van Devanter picked up some typographical errors, a discovery that LDB's law clerk no doubt heard about. LDB-SC.

704 *Humphrey's Executor v. United States*: 295 U.S. 602 (1935). Justice McReynolds concurred without opinion.

704 **Federal Trade Commission**: James Landis Memoir, 39–41, OHRO.

704 **New Deal programs**: William E. Leuchtenburg, *The Supreme Court Reborn* (New York, 1995), 76.

704 **"eye of the executive"**: *Humphrey's Executor*, 295 U.S. at 629, 628. Unlike other decisions striking down New Deal legislation, nearly all of which have been reversed, the basic principle of *Humphrey's Executor* remains intact, and was later reaffirmed by the Court in *Wiener v. United States*, 357 U.S. 349 (1958).

704 *Schechter Poultry Corp. v. United States*: 295 U.S. 495 (1935). Cardozo entered a concurring opinion joined by Stone.

705 **"with the majority"**: Pusey, *Hughes*, 2:742.

705 **"in a fool's paradise"**: Parrish, *Frankfurter*, 261–62; Benjamin Cohen interview, Paper MSS. That summer LDB spoke to some reporters at Chatham and said that the three decisions "compelled a return to human limitations. . . . The curse of bigness has prevented proper thinking." Mason, *Brandeis*, 620.

705 **he saw no problem**: Pusey, *Hughes*, 2:742.

706 **and migrant workers**: Frankfurter to Roosevelt, 15 November 1933, in Freedman, *Roosevelt and Frankfurter*, 294; LDB to Frankfurter, 24 and 27 February 1935, FF-LC.

706 **support the program**: Gardner Jackson Memoir, 490–94, OHRO; Murphy, *Brandeis/Frankfurter Connection*, 139–42; McKenna, *Great Constitutional War*, 128–30.

706 **declared it unconstitutional**: *United States v. Butler*, 297 U.S. 1 (1936), also known as the Hoosac Mills case. By all rights, the case should not have been accepted by the courts, since it originated as a collusive and fraudulent suit rather than as a true case or controversy.

706 **spent tax revenues**: *Frothingham v. Mellon*, 262 U.S. 447 (1923).

707 **"squares with the former"**: *Butler*, 297 U.S. at 62.

707 **"justify the expenditure"**: *Id.* at 78, 85 (Stone dissenting). See also "Memorandum re No. 401," 4 February 1936, Stone MSS.

707 **and Stone, dissented**: *Jones v. Securities and Exchange Commission*, 298 U.S. 1 (1936).

707 **Hughes dissented in part**: *Carter v. Carter Coal Co.*, 298 U.S. 238 (1936). There is a memorandum in LDB's Court files on this case, the type that he would then expand into a dissent, but in this case did not.

708 **the electricity interests**: For the background and history of the TVA, see Preston J. Hubbard, *Origins of the TVA: The Muscle Shoals Controversy, 1920–1932* (Nashville, 1961); Steven M. Neuse, *David E. Lilienthal: The Journey of an American Liberal* (Knoxville, Tenn., 1996); and Edward W. Chester and James S. Fralish, eds., *Land Between the Lakes* (Clarksville, Tenn., 2002).

708 **question of selling power**: McKenna, *Great Constitutional War*, 188–89.

708 **the reasons why**: *Ashwander v. Tennessee Valley Authority*, 297 U.S. 288, 341 (1936) (LDB concurring).

709 "avoid constitutional issues": *Id.* at 346–48.

709 "contrary to the Constitution": *Id.* at 354, citing *Dartmouth College v. Woodward,* 17 U.S. (4 Wheat.) 518, 625 (1819). See also William M. Wiecek, *The Lost World of Classical Legal Thought: Law and Ideology in America, 1886–1937* (New York, 1998), 221–22; and the section on *Ashwander* and the adoption of its norms in "The Debut of Modern Constitutional Procedure," 26 *Review of Litigation* 641, 651ff. (2007).

709 wisdom of Brandeis's rules: See, for example, *Rescue Army v. Municipal Court of Los Angeles,* 331 U.S. 549, 568 (1947).

709 broken up by statute: "If F.D. carries through the Holding Company bill we shall have achieved considerable toward curbing Bigness." LDB to Norman Hapgood, 15 June 1935, Roosevelt MSS.

710 stimulate foreign trade: LDB to Frankfurter, 14 July 1933, 11 February and 4 March 1934, FF-LC.

710 "evils of bigness": LDB to Hapgood, 1 August 1935, Roosevelt MSS.

710 laid-off workers: See especially LDB to Elizabeth Brandeis Raushenbush, 19 November 1933, EBR; Harry Shulman, "Memorandum of a Talk with Louis D. Brandeis," 8 December 1933, FF-HLS; and LDB to Frankfurter, 3 August 1934, FF-LC.

711 "brains and character": LDB to Elizabeth Brandeis Raushenbush, 19 November 1933, EBR.

711 break up big business: When Roosevelt announced his income tax proposal in 1935, Frankfurter wrote to him: "I wish you could have seen Brandeis's face light up when I gave him your message about tax policy. . . . His eyes became glowing coals of fire, and shone with warm satisfaction." Frankfurter to Roosevelt, 16 May 1935, in Freedman, *Roosevelt and Frankfurter,* 271.

711 through to acceptance: The key document is Paul A. Raushenbush and Elizabeth Brandeis Raushenbush, *Our "U.C." Story, 1930–1967* (Madison, Wis., 1979), which is an expansion of the oral history interviews, OHRO. See also Wilbur J. Cohen, "The Development of the Social Security Act of 1935: Reflections Some Fifty Years Later," 68 *Minnesota Law Review* 379 (1983).

711 laboratory for democracy: Raushenbush and Raushenbush, *Our "U.C." Story,* chap. 6; Elizabeth Brandeis Raushenbush to Frankfurter, 21 September 1931, FF-LC; LDB to Harold Laski, 28 February 1932, Laski MSS.

712 suggestion for a bill: LDB to Elizabeth Brandeis Raushenbush, 16 September 1933, EBR.

712 circulation in Washington: LDB to Elizabeth Brandeis Raushenbush, 17 November 1933, EBR. He also circulated copies of articles EB had written.

712 Wisconsin plan to him: Elizabeth Brandeis Raushenbush to author, 7 February 1976.

713 "during the summer": LDB to Elizabeth Brandeis Raushenbush, 8 June 1934, EBR.

713 to satisfy him: *New York Times,* 9 June 1934; Arthur M. Schlesinger Jr., *The Coming of the New Deal* (Boston, 1958), 301–7; Raushenbush and Raushenbush, *Our "U.C." Story,* chaps. 9–11; LDB to Paul Raushenbush, 2 December 1935, EBR.

714 Roosevelt loved it: Leuchtenburg, *Supreme Court Reborn,* chap. 4.

714 approve New Deal measures: There has been an enormous amount writ-

ten about the Court fight; a good narrative account is McKenna, *Great Constitutional War.*

715 **a very great mistake:** Thomas Corcoran interview, Paper MSS.

715 **as if in dismissal:** William E. Leuchtenburg, "The Nine Justices Respond to the 1937 Crisis," *Journal of Supreme Court History* (1997), 55–56.

715 **"matters of late":** LDB to Frankfurter, 5 February 1937, FF-LC.

715 **"an awful shock":** Roosevelt to Frankfurter, 15 January 1937, in Freedman, *Roosevelt and Frankfurter,* 377. For Frankfurter's response, and his support of the plan, see pp. 380ff.

715 **they opposed it:** Leuchtenburg, "Nine Justices," 57–62.

715 **original New Dealer:** Robert H. Jackson, *The Struggle for Judicial Supremacy* (New York, 1941), 190.

716 **"The baby is born":** Burton K. Wheeler, *Yankee from the West* (Garden City, N.Y., 1962), 327–29; Alpheus T. Mason, *Harlan Fiske Stone: Pillar of the Law* (New York, 1956), 450; Pusey, *Hughes,* 2:755.

716 **Hughes would provide a letter:** Leuchtenburg, "Nine Justices," 63.

717 **"obtained for several years":** Hughes's letter implied that all of the justices had approved its contents, but in fact it is unclear how many other members of the Court he spoke to besides LDB and Van Devanter. It is possible that he spoke to none of them, believing that if one or more raised objections, he would not be able to give Wheeler a letter or he might have to give him a different type of message, one that would be less useful. See Mason, *Stone,* 451–52.

717 **"to be convinced and to decide":** The full letter can be found in "Reorganization of the Federal Judiciary: Hearings Before the Senate Judiciary Committee," 75th Cong., 1st sess. (1937), 491–92. For another view of the letter, see Richard D. Friedman, "Chief Justice Hughes' Letter on Court-Packing," *Journal of Supreme Court History* (1997), 76–86. There remains controversy over whether Hughes should have written the letter at all, but no one denies its effectiveness.

718 **"will do any harm":** LDB to Friendly, 1 April 1937, courtesy of Henry Friendly; Friendly to author, 14 June 1967; Henry Friendly interview, Paper MSS.

718 **backing the proposal:** Frankfurter, in turn, believed LDB should never have signed on to the Hughes letter, which he also condemned. See Frankfurter to Roosevelt, 30 March 1937, in Freedman, *Roosevelt and Frankfurter,* 392.

718 **to see Brandeis again:** More than forty years later Corcoran still fumed at what he considered LDB's backstabbing in the Court fight, and blamed LDB for preventing Van Devanter from retiring earlier. Corcoran interview, Paper MSS.

718 **"the younger generation":** Parrish, *Frankfurter,* 275. At one point during the Court fight former president Hoover suggested that LDB resign in protest against the president's plan, and that Justice McReynolds be the one to present this idea to LDB.

718 **the previous June:** *West Coast Hotel Co. v. Parrish,* 300 U.S. 379 (1937). For the scene in the courtroom that day, see Dennis Hutchinson and David Garrow, eds., *The Forgotten Memoir of John Knox: A Year in the Life of a Supreme Court Clerk in FDR's Washington* (Chicago, 2002), 200–201.

719 **current economic conditions:** *West Coast Hotel,* 300 U.S. at 400 (Sutherland dissenting).

719 **"give you some satisfaction"**: LDB to Frankfurter, 29 March 1937, FF-LC.

719 **two years earlier:** *Wright v. Vinton Branch of the Mountain Trust Bank of Roanoke,* 300 U.S. 440 (1937).

719 **permitting collective bargaining:** The first case was *Sonzinsky v. United States,* 300 U.S. 506 (1937); the majority reaffirmed the use of taxation for regulatory purposes, the direct opposite of Roberts's conclusion in *Butler.* The second case was *Virginia Railway Co. v. System Federation No. 40,* 300 U.S. 515 (1937).

719 **two weeks later:** *National Labor Relations Board v. Jones & Laughlin Steel Company,* 301 U.S. 1 (1937), was the lead case in five NLRB cases decided on 12 April.

719 **twenty-seven years on the bench:** Apparently, Van Devanter had considered retiring sooner. Once Roosevelt announced his plan, both Hughes and LDB persuaded him to stay on, since if he left during the furor over the plan, it would appear that Roosevelt had scared him off the Court. Benjamin Cohen, who lacked the rancor of Thomas Corcoran, believed that LDB and Hughes had thus been unfair to Roosevelt. Cohen interview, Paper MSS.

720 **"never needed you more":** Joseph Lash, ed., *From the Diaries of Felix Frankfurter* (New York, 1975), 60; Paul Freund, "The Supreme Court: A Tale of Two Terms," 26 *Ohio State Law Journal* 225, 227 (1965); see also LDB to Van Devanter, 17 April 1929, Van Devanter MSS.

720 **"the public welfare":** LDB to Jack Gilbert, 5 January 1938, LDB-BU.

CHAPTER 29: EXTRAJUDICIAL ACTIVITIES: III

721 **"I should not know":** Paul Freund, "The Supreme Court: A Tale of Two Terms," 26 *Ohio State Law Journal* 225 (1965). Had LDB looked into the book (and he may well have), he would have discovered an exceedingly flattering portrait of himself, thanks to the efforts of James Landis, his former clerk then in Washington at the Securities and Exchange Commission. Landis had gotten to know Pearson and secretly helped him with the book, making sure that the reporter looked at "his justice" positively.

721 **"go to Denmark":** LDB had the Library of Congress prepare an annual updated bibliography on Denmark, and AGB translated from the German a book on Bishop Gruntvig's program of adult education in the folk high schools, under the title *Democracy in Denmark* (Washington, D.C., 1936). LDB also sent clippings about Denmark to his sister-in-law Josephine Goldmark. Paul Freund thought that LDB's ideal for Palestine would be a Jewish Denmark. Freund Memoir, 75, New York Times Oral History Program.

722 **succeeded in her quest:** Sheldon Glueck to LDB, 6 June 1937, Glueck MSS.

722 **"'in this contract'":** Charles E. Wyzanski Jr., "Brandeis," *Atlantic Monthly,* November 1956, 66.

722 **those who attended:** In the 1960s, when David Levy and I first began work on the *Brandeis Letters,* Mrs. Raushenbush suggested that next time in Washington, I stop in to see Mary Switzer, an old friend of hers who had come to work in the New Deal. Ms. Switzer, after more than three decades, still vividly recalled the Monday teas.

722 **her husband's time:** Poindexter took this work very seriously, and reminded one of the clerks of the butler Mr. Hudson on *Upstairs, Downstairs.*

723 **of her indiscretion:** Samuel Pettengill, "Justice Brandeis," 28 February 1939. Pettengill was a reporter who had a syndicated weekly column.

723 **the following Monday:** Stanley Reed Memoir, 101–2, OHRO. See also Marquis Childs Memoir, 66–67, OHRO; and William O. Douglas, *Go East, Young Man* (New York, 1974), 442.

723 **discussed Court business:** Freund Memoir, 59; Reed Memoir, 183.

723 **La Follette Act:** Dean Acheson, *Morning and Noon* (Boston, 1965), 110.

724 **champion of civil rights:** Walter Gellhorn Memoir, 201–7, OHRO; see also Thomas I. Emerson Memoir, 150, OHRO.

725 **"of Spartan tastes":** Alger Hiss Memoir, 219, OHRO. Hiss goes on to tell how at one dinner their hosts served new asparagus, and Hiss, having grown up on a farm, helped himself to a farmer's portion. The other guests, more familiar with the regimen, each took only a spear or two, but even so, by the time the serving plate reached the other end of the table, there was no asparagus for the last guest. Apparently, Mrs. Brandeis forgave him, for they did invite him back. *Id.*, 219–21.

725 **to work at five o'clock:** The elderly Poindexter could be quite intimidating. One time Erwin Griswold and his wife, Harriet, came to dinner, and were standing waiting for Justice and Mrs. Brandeis to sit, unaware that the host would not sit down until all of the ladies had been seated. Poindexter shoved Mrs. Griswold's chair forward and said, "Sit down." She sat. Griswold, *Ould Fields, New Corne* (St. Paul, 1992), 103–4.

725 **because of Brandeis's advice:** Roger N. Baldwin, "Affirmation of Democracy," *Jewish Frontier*, November 1936, 10.

725 **dissuaded him from doing so:** LDB to Frankfurter, 17 January 1938. Hurst would stay in Madison for the rest of his career and become the nation's leading legal historian.

725 **Midwest and elsewhere:** John Lord O'Brian Memoir, 359, OHRO.

725 **"the small communities":** Riesman to LDB, 14 November 1940, LDB-BU. Riesman eventually returned to Harvard. See also Riesman to LDB, 3 December 1940, noting that he had just published a book review, since "reviewing books is of course one way, though a slow one, to build up a personal library."

725 **"there are new revelations":** LDB to Susan Goldmark, 7 October 1934, EBR.

726 **build up the law school:** LDB to Fannie Brandeis, 6 and 14 January 1930; LDB to Robert Kent, 17 January 1930; LDB to Neville Miller, 18 January 1930.

726 **in his opinions:** See Evarts Boutell Greene to LDB, 6 September 1929, Greene MSS. Greene had written at the suggestion of Arthur Meier Schlesinger Sr., who knew of LDB's interest. With the justice's encouragement, Greene helped start the publication of American Legal Records, with the assistance of a young historian who would become the dean of American colonial legal history, Richard B. Morris. The first book in the series, *Proceedings of the Maryland Court of Appeals, 1695–1729*, appeared in 1933.

726 **Judge Mack's secretary:** LDB to Alice Park Goldmark, 30 September 1934, EBR.

726 **"all who love freedom":** White to LDB, 12 October 1936, White MSS.

726 **"reaches 80 only once":** LDB to Jack Gilbert, 14 November 1936, LDB-BU.

727   **"all to practice on"**: LDB to Jack Gilbert, 1 October 1936, LDB-BU; the quotation is from Ben Jonson, "Love" (1616).

727   **"moves along each day"**: AGB to Elizabeth Evans, 15 January 1935, Evans MSS.

727   **Alice Harriet Grady, passed away**: Bess Evans attended the funeral and wrote that it was "something perfectly lovely. She lay in an awful coffin, but one that suited her like her clothes, but she looked grand as she lay there almost buried in flowers." Evans to LDB and AGB, 23 April 1934, Evans MSS.

727   **Savings Bank Insurance League**: LDB to Leila E. Colburn, 22 August 1934, SBLI. It is impossible to tell how many LDB destroyed, but there are literally hundreds of letters and memoranda that survive either in SBLI or in LDB-BU.

727   **"best of his ability"**: LDB to Robert Szold, 11 March 1937, R. Szold MSS; LDB to Jack Gilbert, 24 March 1937, LDB-BU. When de Haas had considered moving his family to Palestine prior to his illness, LDB had said that if he chose to do so, he would contribute "liberally" to a fund to permit them to live there modestly. LDB to Julian Mack, [December 1924], Wise MSS.

727   **"be said by others"**: LDB to Frankfurter, 15 December 1937 and 5 January 1938, FF-LC.

727   **three grandsons**: LDB to Susan Brandeis Gilbert, 4 December 1930, LDB-BU.

728   **of their grandparents**: Telephone conversation with Frank Gilbert, 15 February 2008.

728   **look up the answers**: Conversations with Alice Popkin, Frank Gilbert, and Walter Raushenbush in Louisville, Ky., 12 November 2006.

728   **entertain his grandfather**: LDB to Jack Gilbert, 30 July 1934, LDB-BU.

728   **"cheap at the price"**: LDB to Jack Gilbert, 8 January 1930, LDB-BU.

728   **"the longest word"**: LDB to Walter Raushenbush, 25 November 1932, EBR; Evans to AGB, 13 January 1936, Evans MSS.

729   **at a steady pace**: "I have had a good winter," AGB to Evans, 13 April 1936, Evans MSS; LDB to Elizabeth Brandeis Raushenbush, 20 September 1937, EBR; undated letter in 1930s files, Evans MSS.

729   **for their grandchildren**: See, for example, LDB to Susan Brandeis Gilbert, 3 June 1931, LDB-BU, and to Elizabeth Brandeis Raushenbush, 3 June 1931, EBR, noting the transfer of $10,000 in coupon bonds to each; another distribution had been made in December 1930. LDB to Susan Brandeis Gilbert, 26 February 1932, LDB-BU, transferring $10,000 for a school fund.

729   **"to borrow a penny"**: LDB to Susan and Jack Gilbert, 27 February 1935, LDB-BU. From conversations with Alice Popkin and Frank Gilbert, it would appear that the Gilbert family lived comfortably but not extravagantly. The employment of servants would not have struck either LDB or AGB as a "luxury," and certainly if Susan continued to work, someone had to be there to watch the children. Elizabeth and Paul Raushenbush also had household help. Since LDB tried to be scrupulously fair in distributing funds to his children, one can assume that he sent Elizabeth an equal amount.

729   **lives of practicing lawyers**: LDB to Jack Gilbert, 27 September 1936, LDB-BU.

730 "a grand name": AGB to Evans, n.d. [1937], Evans MSS.

730 other death camps: For a fuller exposition of Zionist policies and challenges in the 1930s, see Melvin I. Urofsky, *American Zionism from Herzl to the Holocaust* (Garden City, N.Y., 1975), chap. 10.

731 the Jews argued: Norman Bentwich and Helen Bentwich, *Mandate Memories, 1918–1948* (London, 1965), 91.

731 same blind spot: The chief exception was Judah Magnes, the president of the Hebrew University, who throughout this period was a lone voice calling for a binational state; see William Brinner and Moses Rischin, eds., *Like All the Nations? The Life and Legacy of Judah L. Magnes* (Albany, N.Y., 1987). The classic work on early Arab nationalism is George Antonius, *The Arab Awakening* (London, 1938).

732 "if possession is prohibited": LDB to Frankfurter, 20 September 1929, FF-HLS.

732 "will again do so": LDB, "Jews and Arabs," address before emergency Palestine economic conference in Washington, 24 November 1929, in Solomon Goldman, ed., *Brandeis on Zionism* (Washington, D.C., 1942), 152.

732 influential journal: Stephen Wise and Jacob de Haas, *The Great Betrayal* (New York, 1930); Felix Frankfurter, "The Palestine Situation Revisited," *Foreign Affairs* 9 (April 1931), 409–34.

732 live up to their word: There does not appear to have been direct correspondence between LDB and Laski, but word came through Frankfurter or Bernard Flexner. We get Laski's side from his letters to Oliver Wendell Holmes Jr., 15 June, 22 and 30 November, and 27 December 1930, in Mark DeWolfe Howe, ed., *Holmes-Laski Letters,* 2 vols. (Cambridge, Mass., 1953), 2:1261, 1296, 1298–99, 1301–2.

733 "frittered away by concession": LDB to Flexner, 22 November 1930.

734 in their response: Margaret K. Norden, "American Editorial Response to the Rise of Adolf Hitler: A Preliminary Consideration," *American Jewish Historical Quarterly* 59 (March 1970), 290–301.

734 no one would listen: Urofsky, *American Zionism,* 365.

734 warn against fascism: Melvin I. Urofsky, *A Voice That Spoke for Justice: The Life and Times of Stephen S. Wise* (Albany, N.Y., 1982), chap. 18.

734 to stand by idly: Freund Memoir, 70–71.

735 including Bess Evans: Stephen Wise, "Louis D. Brandeis," sermon delivered at the Free Synagogue, 12 October 1941, Wise MSS; Wise to LDB, 23 March 1933, in Carl Hermann Voss, ed., *Stephen S. Wise: Servant of the People* (Philadelphia, 1969), 180–81; Evans to Ethel Unwin, 29 March 1933, Evans MSS.

735 "you are doing 'splendid'": Justine Wise Polier and James Waterman Wise, *The Personal Letters of Stephen Wise* (Boston, 1956), 220; Wise to Albert Einstein, 9 May 1933, and LDB to Wise, 28 April 1933, Wise MSS. Throughout the decade LDB would periodically drop Wise a note praising and encouraging him; see LDB to Wise, 9 August 1934, Wise MSS.

735 nothing could be done: Wise to John Haynes Holmes, 12 February 1936, Wise MSS. There has been both a scholarly and a popular debate over whether Roosevelt could have done anything even if he had wanted to, and whether the president harbored anti-Semitic feelings.

735 so-called Third Reich: Wise, "Brandeis."

735 supported Hitler's work: Gardner Jackson Memoir, 653, OHRO.

736 **secured temporary lodgings:** The two women were grandchildren of Carl Brandeis, a cousin of LDB's father, and LDB had met him when they were in Europe in the 1870s. Affidavit of LDB, 11 May 1938; Isidore Hershfield (counsel to HIAS) to LDB, 27 July 1938; Albert Hirst (a lawyer and friend of the Goldmark family's) to LDB, 27 July 1938, all in LDB-BU.

736 **American universities:** Riesman to LDB, 14 November and 3 December 1940, LDB-BU.

736 **on Nazi depradations:** Frankfurter to Roosevelt, 17 October and 20 November 1933, in Max Freedman, ed., *Roosevelt and Frankfurter: Their Correspondence, 1928–1945* (Boston, 1967), 173–74, 211–13; Mack to Roosevelt, 30 January 1935, and Roosevelt to Mack, 12 February 1935, Roosevelt MSS.

737 **Jews in the Roosevelt administration:** Arthur M. Schlesinger Jr., *The Politics of Upheaval* (Boston, 1960), 78–82. There has been an intense scholarly and popular debate over whether American Jewry did all that it could have done to save European Jewry from the Holocaust. The literature on that subject is immense, but I tend to agree with Henry L. Feingold that in the 1930s American Jewry lacked the political influence it had during the three decades following World War II. See Feingold, *Bearing Witness: How America and Its Jews Responded to the Holocaust* (Syracuse, N.Y., 1995).

737 **"ground for Anti-Semitism":** LDB to Wise, 19 January 1936, Wise MSS. Frankfurter had also urged him to decline, not on these grounds, but because it would be insulting to all of the American schools that had wanted to give the justice a degree. LDB to Frankfurter, 18 January 1936, FF-LC.

737 **on particular problems:** See, for example, the detailed letters he sent to ZOA officials in the 1930s in vol. 5 of Melvin I. Urofsky and David W. Levy, eds., *Letters of Louis D. Brandeis,* 5 vols. (Albany, N.Y.).

737 **use of the boycott:** Paul Freund, "Justice Brandeis: A Law Clerk's Remembrance," *American Jewish History* 68 (1977), 17.

737 **British obligations there:** LDB to Wise, 24 March 1933, Wise MSS. LDB suggested to Bingham that he meet with Wise before sailing to take up his new post.

738 **"an accurate accountancy":** LDB to Frankfurter, 5 April 1937, FF-LC; Shmuel Ben-Zvi, "The Kind of Israel Brandeis Wanted to See," *Israel Horizons* 10 (December 1962), 17–18.

738 **"cause must prevail":** LDB to Miriam and Arthur Dembitz, 13 July and 9 September 1936, 11 October 1937, 30 June 1938, 18 October 1939.

738 **importance of the site:** LDB to Robert Szold, 23 June and 10 October 1935, Wise MSS.

738 **against Arab attacks:** Apparently, Ben-Gurion first convinced Wise, who then helped to convince LDB. The complicated transactions can be traced in Stephen Wise to LDB, 5 May 1935; Wise to Julian Mack, 7 May 1936; Ben-Gurion to Wise, 20 August 1936; Eliezer Kaplan to Wise, 17 December 1936, all in Wise MSS. Wise to Ben-Gurion, 24 May 1937, Mack MSS; LDB to Robert Szold, 10 October 1935, R. Szold MSS, sending an initial check for $25,000; Wise to Kaplan, 15 October and 9 November 1936, transferring funds, Wise MSS.

738 **with the other Arabs:** LDB to Frankfurter, 20 September 1929, FF-HLS; LDB to Robert Szold, 4 March 1937 and 11 November 1938, R. Szold MSS.

739 **suspension of immigration:** Wise to LDB, 24 July 1936, in Voss, *Servant of the People*, 213.

740 **"record for the future":** LDB to Wise, 4 September 1936, R. Szold MSS.

740 **the president sympathetic:** LDB to Frankfurter, 16 October 1938, FF-LC.

740 **Roosevelt to act:** LDB to Roosevelt, 28 December 1938, Roosevelt MSS.

740 **tide of refugees:** LDB to Roosevelt, 16 March, 17 April, and 4 May 1939; Henry Montor to LDB, 8 May 1939; Sumner Welles to Roosevelt, 11 May 1939, all in Roosevelt MSS.

CHAPTER 30: THE PASSING OF ISAIAH

741 **the jarring battle:** See, for example, *Boston Herald*, 29 May 1937.

741 **moved the departure time:** Alpheus T. Mason, *Brandeis: A Free Man's Life* (New York, 1946), 633.

741 **nation's highest bench:** William O. Douglas said that during the fifteen months that Black served on the Court with LDB, something unpleasant happened between the two men, but Black would never talk about it. Douglas, *Go East, Young Man* (New York, 1974), 449. Black certainly had a difficult time adjusting to the Court, and his unorthodox ideas—such as dissenting from a per curiam—offended some of the brethren. Stone wrote to Frankfurter, suggesting he might help Black acclimate to the work on the bench. Then Stone leaked to Marquis Childs that Black's first term was proving difficult for him and the Court. See Alpheus T. Mason, *Harlan Fiske Stone: Pillar of the Law* (New York, 1956), 468–72.

742 **hard worker and diligent:** *Johnson v. Zerbst*, 304 U.S. 458 (1938). Black held that the Sixth Amendment right to counsel applied in all felony cases tried in federal courts, and constituted the first step in Black's eventually successful crusade to extend the right to counsel to the states as well. Jacob Billikopf to Mrs. Max Sloss, 28 October 1939, Billikopf MSS.

742 **"welcome Stanley Reed":** LDB to Frankfurter, 17 January 1938.

742 **Cardozo became gravely ill:** "It is encouraging that the country had appreciated Cardozo during his lifetime," LDB wrote. "At no time could his service on our Court have been of greater value than during the years allotted." LDB to Harlan Stone, 28 July 1938, Stone MSS.

742 **he took his seat:** For the appointment, as well as Frankfurter's politicking to get it, see Michael E. Parrish, *Felix Frankfurter and His Times: The Reform Years* (New York, 1982), 273–79.

742 **repudiating the *Duplex* decision:** *Lauf v. E. F. Skinner & Co.*, 308 U.S. 323 (1938); *Apex Hosiery Co. v. Leader*, 310 U.S. 434 (1940).

742 **validating Brandeis's dissent:** *Nardone v. United States*, 302 U.S. 379 (1937).

742 **right of collective bargaining:** The cases are grouped with the lead case, *National Labor Relations Board v. Jones & Laughlin Steel Corporation*, 301 U.S. 1 (1937).

742 **of the labor grievance:** *Senn v. Tile Layers Protective Union*, 301 U.S. 468, 478 (1937).

743 **the practical results:** William M. Wiecek, *The Birth of the Modern Constitution* (New York, 2006), 171.

743 **most unusual manner:** *Erie Railroad Co. v. Tompkins*, 304 U.S. 64 (1938).

In the following section I am greatly indebted to Edward A. Purcell Jr., *Brandeis and the Progressive Constitution* (New Haven, Conn., 2000).

743 **federal courts were located:** *United States v. Hudson and Goodwin,* 11 U.S. (7 Cr.) 32 (1812), holding no federal common law of crimes; and *Wheaton v. Peters,* 33 U.S. (8 Pet.) 591 (1834), holding no federal civil common law.

743 **commercial questions:** *Swift v. Tyson,* 41 U.S. (16 Pet.) 1 (1842). For the idea of a federal common law, see Martha A. Field, "Sources of Law: The Scope of Federal Common Law," 99 *Harvard Law Review* 883 (1986).

743 **even over Congress:** Purcell, *Brandeis and the Progressive Constitution,* chap. 2. Purcell points to the case of *Ex parte Young,* 209 U.S. 123 (1908), in which the Supreme Court upheld a lower federal court injunction against the attorney general of Minnesota to prevent him from enforcing a state's rate regulations against a railroad, without ever passing on the merits of the law.

744 **"hesitate to correct":** *Black & White Taxicab Co. v. Brown & Yellow Taxicab Co.,* 276 U.S. 518, 408 (1928) (Holmes dissenting).

744 **introduced bills in Congress:** LDB to Frankfurter, 11 February 1928, FF-HLS.

745 **misinterpreted the law:** *Erie Railroad,* 304 U.S. 64 (1938).

746 **historically wrong:** In his opinion LDB cited Charles Warren, "New Light on the History of the Judiciary Act of 1789," 37 *Harvard Law Review* 49 (1923), to support his argument that Story had misinterpreted section 34, and that Congress had never intended to allow federal courts to adopt decisional rules different from those of the states in which the courts were located. *Erie Railroad,* 304 U.S. at 73 n.5. Warren's research has since been challenged, as has LDB's use of history.

746 **the argument confusing:** See the discussion of this point in Henry Friendly, "In Praise of *Erie*—and of the New Federal Common Law," 39 *New York University Law Review* 383, 384ff. (1964).

746 **did not appreciate it:** Purcell, *Brandeis and the Progressive Constitution,* pt. 3.

746 **constitutionality argument:** Reed to LDB, 21 March 1938, and LDB's effort to calm him, 24 March 1938, LDB-SC.

746 **strengthening the constitutional basis:** Stone to LDB, 23 and 25 March 1938, Stone MSS; Purcell, *Brandeis and the Progressive Constitution,* 108–11.

746 **affecting discrete minorities:** *United States v. Carolene Products Co.,* 304 U.S. 144, 153n.4 (1938).

747 **affecting federal lands:** *Hinderlider v. La Plata River & Cherry Creek Ditch Co.,* 304 U.S. 92 (1938).

747 **state statutory law:** LDB had opposed the Rules, just as he had opposed the 1934 Declaratory Judgment Act. He nonetheless did not argue that Congress lacked power to enact such laws.

747 **outlived its usefulness:** For the problems generated by *Erie* and efforts to impose some consistency on federal decisional rules, see Purcell, *Brandeis and the Progressive Constitution,* pt. 3; Tony Freyer, *Harmony and Dissonance: The Swift and Erie Cases in American Federalism* (New York, 1981); and William M. Wiecek, "The Debut of Modern Procedure," 26 *Review of Litigation* 641, 671ff. (2007).

748 **carried her up as well:** Lewis J. Paper, *Brandeis* (Englewood Cliffs, N.J., 1983), 390.

748 **growing intellectually:** Melvin I. Urofsky, "Brandeis-Frankfurter Conversations," 1985 *Supreme Court Review* 305–6.

748 **cogent reasons:** Although LDB did not spell these out, it is most likely that with two new men on the Court who were still far from acclimated, it would not be good for the Court to get a third. Then, of course, Cardozo fell ill.

748 **a note to the president:** Urofsky, "Brandeis-Frankfurter Conversations," 338–39.

749 **nonjudicial tasks:** Adrian Fisher interview, Paper MSS.

749 **"I retire this day":** LDB to Roosevelt, 13 February 1939, Roosevelt MSS. A wealthy man, Brandeis could have just resigned and forgone the pension the 1937 law provided. He recognized, however, that other judges might take his example as a rule to follow. Those without independent means would be tempted to stay on the bench since they could not afford to give up their salaries. When Hughes stepped down in 1941, he followed LDB's example, although he, too, had ample means of support. Merlo J. Pusey, *Charles Evans Hughes*, 2 vols. (New York, 1951), 2:787.

749 **his recent illness:** In a letter to Jennie Brandeis on 13 February 1939, LDB tried to reassure her that he had not retired because of ill health. "Mine seems to be as good as heretofore." But he could no longer do the work as well as a young man would. Mason, *Brandeis*, 634.

749 **he would take no part:** *Boston Globe*, 14 February 1939.

749 **"services to mankind":** Roosevelt to LDB, 13 February 1939, Roosevelt MSS.

749 **the years to come:** Court to LDB, 17 February 1939; LDB to Charles Evans Hughes, 18 February 1939.

749 **a great jurist:** For a sampling of press opinion, see Irving Dilliard, ed., *Mr. Justice Brandeis: Great American* (St. Louis, 1941).

749 **"our minds be bold":** *Washington Star*, 19 February 1939.

750 **for differing reasons:** *Congressional Record*, 16 February 1939 (Senate); David Lawrence, "Today in Washington," *Boston Globe*, 14 February 1939; Walter Lippmann, "Louis D. Brandeis," 16 February 1939, in *Public Persons* (New York, 1976), 139–42; Max Lerner, "Homage to Louis D. Brandeis" (February 1939), in *Ideas Are Weapons: The History and Uses of Ideas* (New York, 1939), 108–12.

750 **"judgment of us":** Elizabeth Brandeis Raushenbush to LDB, 14 February 1939, in Mason, *Brandeis*, 634–35.

750 **"in your footsteps":** Douglas to LDB, 20 March 1939, W. Douglas MSS.

750 **full of exaggerations:** Douglas, *Go East, Young Man*, 449. The only Brandeis scholar to believe this happened is Lewis Paper, and he admits that all he has is circumstantial evidence. Paper agrees that LDB would not have made the recommendation prior to his own departure nor would he have used a telephone for this type of message, but believes that when LDB went to the White House on 9 March to discuss Palestine and the British white paper, he had the opportunity to praise Douglas. There is, however, no proof that he actually did so. Paper, *Brandeis*, 391, 432n.12. Adrian Fisher, LDB's last clerk, recalled that at a tea after LDB's retirement he met Douglas, and LDB introduced him by saying, "This is the man I recommended to take my seat on the Court." Fisher interview, Paper MSS.

750–751 **right to privacy:** "The appointment of Douglas has given him a great deal of satisfaction." Jacob Billikopf to Mrs. Max Sloss, 28 October 1939, Billikopf MSS, reporting on interview with LDB that day.

751 **him with dismay:** Bruce Allen Murphy, *Wild Bill: The Legend and Life of William O. Douglas* (New York, 2003).

751 **he did not tire:** Apparently, rumors reached the Federal Bureau of Investigation that LDB was giving advice to a known subversive, and it assigned Agent J. F. Elich to investigate. LDB's FBI file, heavily blacked out, has only a few lines legible, but they indicate that LDB "had no dealings with Subject." Copy in LDB-BU.

751 **"it must be a satisfaction":** *United States v. Darby Lumber Co.,* 312 U.S. 100 (1941), overturned the earlier ruling in *Hammer v. Dagenhart,* 247 U.S. 251 (1918), in which LDB had joined Holmes's dissent against the Court's narrow view of interstate commerce. LDB to Stone, 16 February 1941, Stone MSS. On another opinion Stone sent over, LDB replied, "Your No. 343 is A.1." LDB to Stone, 2 January 1940.

751 **"the best conceivable":** Mason, *Stone,* 570; LDB to Roosevelt, 13 June 1941, Roosevelt MSS; see also LDB to Charles Warren, 23 June 1941, Warren MSS. Unfortunately, although Stone had an outstanding career as an associate justice, his years as chief proved very unhappy, as he contended with such prima donnas as Frankfurter, Black, Douglas, and Jackson.

751 **time on Zionism:** The Robert Szold Papers for this period show LDB writing to him at least weekly and usually more than that.

752 **keep immigration open:** See, for example, memorandum of 26 February 1940 by Isadore Breslau, head of the Washington bureau established by the ZOA, following a meeting with LDB, Breslau MSS.

752 **development no one wanted:** LDB to Roosevelt, 26 April and 5 May 1941; Sumner Welles to Roosevelt, 2 May 1941; Roosevelt to LDB, 5 May 1941, all in Roosevelt MSS.

752 **"great work in Palestine":** LDB to Jack Gilbert, 21 May 1939, LDB-BU.

752 **"whenever he can be":** AGB to Charles C. Burlingham, 19 June 1940, Burlingham MSS. The New York lawyer had known LDB and AGB from the days when they vacationed in the Adirondacks.

752 **had closed them:** See E. Louise Malloch to LDB, 17 August 1938, confirming details of shipping of personal papers from firm archives to Louisville; LDB to Bernard Flexner, 7 August 1940, Flexner MSS, insisting that the book not be called "official"; LDB to Frankfurter, 21 February 1940, FF-LC, "I have a much better opinion of [Mason] than you have," but agreeing that the Court papers should be closed. Frankfurter allowed his former clerk, Alexander Bickel, access to do *The Unpublished Opinions of Mr. Justice Brandeis* (1957), but other scholars would not see the papers until well after Frankfurter's death in 1965. The difference that access to the Court papers would have meant is clearly seen by comparing Mason's biography of LDB with that of Stone, where he had full access.

752 **voice trailed off:** Fannie Brandeis, "Conversation with LDB," 19 May 1940.

753 **worst was over:** AGB to Louis Wehle, 27 September 1941, Wehle MSS.

753 **"as great as Lincoln":** Joseph P. Lash, ed., *From the Diaries of Felix Frankfurter* (New York, 1975), 271; Max Freedman, ed., *Roosevelt and Frankfurter: Their Correspondence, 1928–1945* (Boston, 1967), 618.

753 **A string quartet:** Mason, *Brandeis,* 637.

754 **"will be my rewarder"**: Acheson's remarks are in 55 *Harvard Law Review* 191 (1941), Frankfurter's at *id.,* 181.

754 **placed next to his:** Copies of the remarks made by Fola La Follette and others at her memorial ceremony are in the Rauch MSS.

754 **The residual estate:** LDB will and codicils, plus notes made by Edward McClennen, one of the executors. Alice, Susan, and Elizabeth were also named executors, and thus shared in the 4 percent fee charged to the estate. Mason misread the will, stating that Alice received $400,000 and Susan and Elizabeth $200,000 apiece. The will read for Alice three-eighths or $400,000, whichever shall be larger, and for his daughters three-sixteenths or $200,000, whichever shall be larger. In both cases the fraction was far larger. Mason's reading that the bulk of the estate went to the four charities is also wrong, with each one getting about $60,000. Mason, *Brandeis,* 638–39. I am indebted to Ms. Tanya A. Harvey of Bryan Cave, LLP, for helping to sort out the provisions of LDB's will.

INDEX

Page numbers in *italics* refer to illustrations.

ILLUSTRATION CREDITS

A NOTE ON THE TYPE

The text of this book was set in Garamond No. 3. It is not a true copy
of any of the designs of Claude Garamond (ca. 1480–1561), but an
adaptation of his types, which set the European standard for two centuries. It probably owes as much to the designs of Jean Jannon, a
Protestant printer working in Sedan in the early seventeenth century,
who had worked with Garamond's romans earlier, in Paris, but who was
denied their use because of Catholic censorship. Jannon's matrices came
into the possession of the Imprimerie nationale, where they were
thought to be by Garamond himself, and were so described when the
Imprimerie revived the type in 1900. This particular version
is based on an adaptation by Morris Fuller Benton.

COMPOSED BY
North Market Street Graphics, Lancaster, Pennsylvania

PRINTED AND BOUND BY
Berryville Graphics, Berryville, Virginia

DESIGNED BY
Iris Weinstein